The SIS Football Rookie Handbook 2021

Comprehensive Scouting and Analytics Guide

Sports Info Solutions

Edited by Matt Manocherian

with

Nathan Cooper   John Todd

Alex Vigderman

The SIS Football Rookie Handbook 2021
Comprehensive Scouting and Analytics Guide
Sports Info Solutions
Edited by Matt Manocherian

Cover Design by Tom A. Wright and Corey March

First Edition: February 2021

Published by:
ACTA Sports, a division of ACTA Publications
4848 North Clark Street
Chicago, IL 60640
(800) 397-2282
www.actasports.com www.actapublications.com

ISBN (book) 978-0-87946-692-3
ISBN (e-book) 978-0-87946-967-2

Printed in the United States of America by McNaughton & Gunn

Dedication

This book is dedicated to anyone who has ever charted a football game at Sports Info Solutions.

From the original five in 2015 to "G3" to all of those who persevered through the pandemic, without you none of what we do would be possible. You are the reason that the SIS football operation lives, and thrives.

Thank you.

Table of Contents

Introduction

Now that we are in our third year of producing the *SIS Football Rookie Handbook*, instead of using this space to explain how our operation works, new features, or the purity of a February draft board, it's time for a crash course on our "role-based" final grading system for scouting and how it relates to the "horizontal" draft board.

If you've read our books before, you're probably familiar with how our final (overall scouting) grades work. The final grades are related to but different from the individual trait grades (explained in the "Sports Info Solutions Grading Scale" section) in that they contain decimal places and describe the overall outlook for the player, as opposed to an individual trait. At the beginning of each position, there is a rankings page with all of the players and how they stack up. Each player has their final grade listed, and the final grade definitions are explained at the top of the page.

These definitions are very important, as they relate to the philosophy of role-based final grading that SIS and many NFL teams use. The idea is that instead of esoteric round-based grading—which assumes that scouts are calibrated in how they value players (does anybody agree on the value of RBs?) and have a mystical ability to orient themselves to how good all the players that they haven't seen in the draft are—we tie our final grades to something that is stable and meaningful: what role does this player project to fill on a Super Bowl-level team by the beginning of his second season?

Some scouts hate the shackles of a role-based system, but these final grades give us the ability to rank each position in a meaningful way that translates from season to season. This gives us what we call our vertical stack at each position. The vertical stack is exactly what it sounds like: it puts all of the players in a given position in order from top to bottom. But one vertical draft board for each position isn't enough. This is where the horizontal draft board comes into play.

The horizontal draft board is the answer for how we integrate our vertical positional stacks so that we can more effectively compare players across positions. As you will see on the next pages, it simply consists of creating a matrix so that in addition to the final grades going from top to bottom, we can lay out each position from left to right. This is the horizontal aspect of it.

Inherent to this scale is that we have predetermined what the value of each role is (as defined by the final grade). Each offseason we revisit and recalibrate the value of each role to keep up with the modern NFL, but it mostly doesn't change much from year to year. By having a clear definition of what the roles are and how valuable each of them is before the season begins, our sprawling scouting department can put its best foot forward in terms of staying on the same page.

Now that I have evangelized the benefits of role-based final grading and the horizontal draft board, I want to be clear that this system, like any, comes with its limitations. For one, the scale is rigid and difficult for many scouts to adapt to, especially if they are more familiar with a different system. Some players don't fit perfectly into any individual role based on the letter of the law. The most important thing for you to keep in mind is that the scale isn't meant to make draft decisions for you; it is simply a system for organizing the massive amount of information that you have collected.

If you don't like that Kadarius Toney is just a 6.4 final grade, you're not alone. But, here's the good news: you're the GM! These grades aren't meant to be identical to who you should draft in any given situation; they are meant to give you the context to make that decision. So, just because our grading system dictates that starting-level slot receivers who aren't well-suited to play out wide must be either above 7.0 or stuck in the 6.4 crowd doesn't mean that we wouldn't advise drafting Toney before a 6.6 tight end...it just means that doing so would entail believing that he could benefit your team more than a player who typically fills his role would (by the way, our scouting directors Nathan Cooper and John Todd have been lobbying for an additional receiver grade level for years, and they may get their wish soon to help account for players like Toney and D'Wayne Eskridge).

The one position that the grading system is sort of powerless to fully account for is quarterback. QBs are so valuable and volatile that it's difficult to calibrate them to other positions. Suffice it to say that unless you already have a Patrick Mahomes, if you have a choice between a quarterback who is a 7.0 and a player at another position with the same grade, you don't really have a choice. This is part of what explains Trevor Lawrence being the most valuable player pre-draft in Football Rookie Handbook history without having the highest final grade.

In general, you can think of the final grade levels across positions as:

- 7.0 and above: blue-chip players who the opponent must center their gameplan around
- 6.7-6.9: strong starters who are part of the reason why you win
- 6.2-6.6: situational starters and role players
- 6.0-6.1: developmental prospects who need extra time but have starting-level upside
- 5.7-5.9: backups
- 5.5-5.6: practice squad players
- 5.4: training camp players

Remember, when we define these levels, we are referring to those on a Super Bowl-level team. The idea is to build a Super Bowl team, so a 6.7 doesn't just mean that the player is projected to become a starter. They are projected to become a strong starter on a Super Bowl-level team. It's also worth noting that the final grades reflect what we expect these players to become by the beginning of their second seasons.

Got all that?

Then without further ado, we present to you our *horizontal* February draft board.

Matt Manocherian
Remotely connected via VPN to Coplay, PA
February 11, 2021

	QB	RB	FB	WR	TE	OT	OG	OC
9.0-7.0	High-End 3-down Starter	High-End 3-down Starter		High-End 3-down Starter(SWR - 7.0 Elite only)	High-End 3-down Starter	High-End 3-down Starter	High-End 3-down Starter	High-End 3-down Starter
6.9-6.7	Solid Starting QB	Solid Starter (ALL 3 downs)		Solid Starter (ALL 3 downs)	Solid Starter (Y & H ability)	Solid Starter (w/ 2 position flex)	Solid Starter (w/ 2 position flex)	Solid Starter (w/ 2 position flex)
6.6-6.5	Lower-End Starting QB	Lower-End Starter (1st & 2nd down)			Lower-End Starter (Y or H ability)	Lower-End Starter (1 position)	Lower-End Starter (Backup 2 position flex)	Lower-End Starter (w/ Backup OG ability)
6.4	Starter traits with limited opportunity		Starting FB	Role-Playing Starter 3rd down (True #3)			Limited Starter (OG only)	Limited Starter (OC only)
6.3	Circumstantial Starter	Role-Playing Starter (3rd down)				Backup - #3 OT (Swing)		
6.2	Good Quality Backup	Backup All 3 downs (Backup - COP)				Multi-position Backup	Multi-position Backup	Multi-position Backup
6.1-6.0	Developmental Player	Developmental Player	Developmental Player	Developmental Player	Developmental Player	Developmental Player	Developmental Player	Developmental Player
5.9	Career #2			Backup - #4 (w/ SPT ability)	Backup - #2 (Y & H ability)	Backup LT (1 position)		
5.8	Eventual #2			Backup - #5 (w/ SPT ability)	Backup - #2 (Y or H ability)	Backup RT (1 position)		
5.7	#3 QB				#3 TE	#4 OT	Backup OG (1 position)	Backup OC (1 position)
5.6-5.5		Backup 1st & 2nd down Backup 3rd down	Backup FB	Backup - #4 (w/o SPT) Backup - #5 (w/o SPT)		Developmental OT (Practice Squad)	Developmental OG (Practice Squad)	Developmental OC (Practice Squad)
5.4	Priority FA - Solid Camp	Priority FA - Solid Camp	Priority FA - Solid Camp	Priority FA - Solid Camp	Priority FA - Solid Camp	Priority FA - Solid Camp	Priority FA - Solid Camp	Priority FA - Solid Camp

	NT	DT/5T	EDGE	MIKE	WILL	DC	DS
9.0-7.0	High-End 3-down Starter	High-End 3-down Starter	High-End 3-down Starter	High-End 3-down Starter	High-End 3-down Starter	High-End 3-down Starter	High-End 3-down Starter
6.9-6.7	Solid Starter (ALL 3 downs)	Solid Starter (ALL 3 downs)	Solid Starter (ALL 3 downs)	Solid Starter (ALL 3 downs)	Solid Starter (ALL 3 downs)	Solid Starter (ALL 3 downs)	Solid Starter (ALL 3 downs)
6.6-6.5		Lower-End Starter (1st & 2nd OR 3rd)	Lower-End Starter (1st & 2nd OR High-End 3rd)	Lower-End Starter (ALL 3 downs)	Lower-End Starter (ALL 3 downs)	Role-Playing Starter (#3 DC - I/O flex)	
6.4						Role-Playing Starter (#3 DC - lacks I/O flex)	Role-Playing Starter (#3 DS - 3rd down)
6.3	Starter (1st & 2nd down)						
6.2	Backup (w/ TRUE position flex)	Backup (w/ TRUE position flex)	Backup (w/ TRUE positional flex)	Backup (w/ TRUE IB/OB flex)	Backup (w/ TRUE IB/OB flex)	Backup (w/ position flex - DC/DS)	Backup (w/ position flex - DS/DC)
6.1-6.0	Developmental Player	Developmental Player	Developmental Player	Developmental Player	Developmental Player	Developmental Player	Developmental Player
5.9	Backup NT (1 position)	Backup (ALL 3 downs)	Top Backup (ALL 3 downs - w/ SPT)	Top Backup (ALL 3 downs - w/ SPT)	Top Backup (ALL 3 downs - w/ SPT)	Backup - #4 CB (quality SPT player)	Top Backup (1st & 2nd down)
5.8	Middle of the road Backup (1 position)	Role Backup (Base or Sub)	Backup - #4 EDGE (w/ SPT)	Backup - Coverage LB (w/ SPT)	Backup - Coverage LB (w/ SPT)	Backup - #4 CB (w/o SPT) Backup - #5 CB (w/ SPT)	Backup - #4 DS (w/ SPT)
5.7	Lower-End Depth Backup (1st & 2nd down only)	Lower-End Depth Backup	Lower-End Depth Backup	Lower-End Depth Backup (w/ SPT)	Lower-End Depth Backup (w/ SPT)	#6 CB	Backup - #5 DS (w/ SPT)
5.6-5.5	Practice Squad 5.6 high / 5.5 low	Practice Squad 5.6 high / 5.5 low	Practice Squad 5.6 high / 5.5 low	Practice Squad 5.6 high / 5.5 low	Practice Squad 5.6 high / 5.5 low	Practice Squad 5.6 high / 5.5 low	Practice Squad 5.6 high / 5.5 low
5.4	Priority FA - Solid Camp	Priority FA - Solid Camp	Priority FA - Solid Camp	Priority FA - Solid Camp	Priority FA - Solid Camp	Priority FA - Solid Camp	Priority FA - Solid Camp

Evaluating Quarterback Accuracy

John Shirley

The evaluation of quarterback accuracy has drastically improved in recent years, as it has transitioned away from using simple completion percentages. Completion percentage had its usefulness in the past as it was the best measure of accuracy available. But with advancements in charting, tracking, and publicly available data, more advanced measures of quarterback accuracy have been created with different levels of complexity. At SIS, our measures of accuracy range from the relatively straightforward Catchable% and On-Target%, to our more advanced model-based measures, which include Predicted Completion% (pComp) and Expected On-Target% (xOn-Target).

Catchable% and On-Target%

SIS Video Scouts chart the accuracy of every throw on two main levels beyond whether the pass was completed or not:

- Whether the pass was Catchable
- Whether the pass was On-Target (off-target throws are classified as overthrown, underthrown, in-front, or behind the receiver, but that's a discussion for another day)

A catchable pass is fairly straightforward in that it is put in a spot where the receiver has an opportunity to catch it, whether a significant adjustment is needed or not. An on-target pass, on the other hand, is the highest level of accuracy we chart. An "on-target" pass is one in which the receiver is able to make the catch with minimal to no adjustment. While they measure a similar concept, by having multiple levels of accuracy, we are better able to understand what truly happened on a given play.

These levels of accuracy allow us to differentiate between throws that appear the same under completion percentage, but potentially have very different context behind them. A few examples of this include:

- An overthrown uncatchable incompletion versus a pass that is thrown well enough but the receiver couldn't reel in.
- An off-target throw that is completed only because the receiver made a highlight reel catch versus an on-target throw that hits the receiver in stride.

A look at the leaders in On-Target% among current draft eligible quarterbacks over the past two seasons shows two quarterbacks above the rest and that some higher profile prospects rank lower than you might expect.

On-Target% Leaderboard (2019-2020) for 2021 Draft Class

Player	Team	Attempts	Catchable%	On-Target%
Mac Jones	Alabama	543	89.1%	82.5%
Feleipe Franks	Arkansas	309	88.0%	81.8%
Kyle Trask	Florida	791	87.8%	79.5%
Trevor Lawrence	Clemson	741	86.4%	79.2%
Peyton Ramsey	Northwestern	581	85.9%	77.6%
Davis Mills	Stanford	436	85.6%	77.5%
Trey Lance	North Dakota State	317	84.5%	76.6%
Shane Buechele	SMU	861	82.9%	76.1%
Zach Wilson	BYU	653	85.7%	75.1%
Ian Book	Notre Dame	752	84.0%	74.6%
Sam Ehlinger	Texas	776	80.8%	74.5%
Kellen Mond	Texas A&M	716	83.4%	74.5%
Justin Fields	Ohio State	579	85.2%	73.7%
Brady White	Memphis	841	81.6%	72.2%
Jamie Newman	Wake Forest / Georgia	360	79.4%	65.4%

The fact that Alabama's Mac Jones ranks highest among the draft class in On-Target% over the past two seasons is somewhat unsurprising. Although he filled in due to injury for part of 2019, most of his career attempts came this past season when he broke the NCAA completion percentage record. He also is tied for the highest Accuracy grade given by our scouting staff within this year's *Football Rookie Handbook.*

Feleipe Franks joins Jones as the only two quarterbacks in the class to top an 80% On-Target%. Franks enjoyed a solid senior season at Arkansas after transferring from Florida. Comparing his 2019 and 2020 numbers gives a prime example for why Completion% can be misleading:

2019:   71 Atts, 76.1 Comp%, 80.1 On-Target%

2020:   238 Atts, 68.5 Comp%, 82.1 On-Target%

Even though it was on only 71 attempts, his 2019 Completion% shows a quarterback with top-tier accuracy who had a drastic drop-off in 2020. But, his On-Target% shows a quarterback with consistent raw accuracy numbers who actually improved in 2020. The biggest reasons for the discrepancy in his Completion% were an increase in dropped passes (his receivers dropped a single pass in 2019 and 12 in 2020) and a decrease in his receivers' ability to haul in off-target but still catchable throws (they caught 18% of these throws in 2019, but only 8% in 2020).

Justin Fields' low ranking in On-Target% is a bit surprising considering that he is a highly rated prospect—he is the second ranked quarterback by our scouting staff. Fields' low ranking is representative of a problem with raw accuracy metrics that even measuring On-Target% instead of Completion% does not account for: the difficulty of each throw.

When comparing the average depth of target (ADoT) of each quarterback, it becomes apparent that Fields was asked to make more difficult throws than most of the players listed, including Jones and Franks. Fields' ADoT of 10.8 was much higher than Franks' 7.0 and Jones' 8.2. To account for this, we can adjust Completion% and On-Target% by the difficulty of each throw and measure accuracy on a more level playing field.

pComp and xOn-Target

Over the past few seasons there has been an increase in the use of more advanced measures of quarterback accuracy than using just raw numbers. These are led by expected completion percentage models, which attempt to account for the context surrounding each throw. SIS's model, Predicted Completion Percentage (pComp), factors in charting data to account for route type, coverage scheme, distance of throw, and pressure on the quarterback to determine how likely each pass was to be completed.

We can use pComp and each player's actual Completion% to calculate pComp +/-, or how much better or worse a player's actual completion percentage was than what was predicted. This is a similar metric to the NFL's NextGen Stats based Completion Percentage Over Expectation (CPOE). In fact our NFL version of pComp +/- has a correlation of 0.9 to CPOE, without needing the tracking data. This comes in handy when applying the metric to the college game.

pComp +/- helps add context that raw numbers are unable to show. It is also useful as a way to compare not only quarterbacks, but receivers and defensive backs as well. However, it falls prey to the same limitation as Completion% when attempting to solely evaluate quarterback accuracy. Since it uses completions as its basis, pComp-and other expected completion models such as the NFL's NextGen CPOE-attributes the entire outcome of the pass to a single player.

In an attempt to more accurately measure only a quarterback's contribution, SIS created an Expected On-Target% Model (xOn-Target). This model uses our on-target accuracy classification as described above as the basis, instead of completions.

As with expected completion models, throw depth is a main component of Expected On-Target Rate. While throw depth can explain a large part of a throw's difficulty, it is only one of many inputs into our model. Inputs also include the throw's horizontal location, whether the quarterback was pressured, whether the quarterback was moving, the throw's trajectory, route type, coverage type, stadium roof type, and other factors SIS collects.

Also similar to pComp, we can use each quarterback's xOn-Target% and his actual On-Target% to calculate how far above or below expected he performed or xOn-Target +/-.

Now let's take a closer look at how SIS's pComp and xOn-Target models affect the accuracy leaderboards for the 2021 Draft Class.

pComp +/- Leaderboard (2019-2020) for 2021 Draft Class

Player	Team	pComp	Comp%	pComp +/-
Mac Jones	Alabama	65.5%	75.1%	9.7%
Justin Fields	Ohio State	59.3%	68.4%	9.1%
Zach Wilson	BYU	60.6%	67.7%	7.3%
Kyle Trask	Florida	61.0%	68.0%	7.1%
Feleipe Franks	Arkansas	63.7%	70.2%	6.5%
Peyton Ramsey	Northwestern	59.8%	64.7%	4.9%
Trevor Lawrence	Clemson	62.8%	67.3%	4.5%
Trey Lance	North Dakota State	62.1%	65.3%	3.2%
Kellen Mond	Texas A&M	59.9%	62.3%	2.4%
Jamie Newman	Wake Forest / Georgia	58.8%	61.1%	2.3%
Shane Buechele	SMU	61.7%	63.9%	2.2%
Ian Book	Notre Dame	60.1%	62.2%	2.1%
Davis Mills	Stanford	63.8%	65.8%	2.1%
Brady White	Memphis	61.5%	62.3%	0.8%
Sam Ehlinger	Texas	62.8%	63.1%	0.4%

Mac Jones once again leads the way, with a pComp +/- of 9.7% over the past two seasons. If we only look at his 2020 season, his pComp +/- increases to 11.7%, which ranks as the second best season in the past three years only behind Joe Burrow's pComp +/- of 16.1% in 2019.

pComp +/- has a much more favorable view of Justin Fields than the previous measures, as he now ranks second among his peers. He got a boost mainly due to his aforementioned high ADoT, which increased the difficulty of his throws.

Altogether, the entire 2021 class ranks as above expectation in pComp. This should be unsurprising, as they are NFL prospects being compared to an expectation based on all FBS quarterbacks. However, we also have to remember that pComp is based on completions and therefore includes factors outside the quarterback's control. The final leaderboard, xOn-Target +/-, will show how the class performed when evaluating only their accuracy and not the throw's final outcome.

On-Target +/- Leaderboard (2019-2020) for 2021 Draft Class

Player	Team	xOn-Tgt%	On-Tgt	On-Tgt +/-
Kyle Trask	Florida	72.9%	79.5%	6.6%
Mac Jones	Alabama	76.3%	82.5%	6.2%
Feleipe Franks	Arkansas	76.6%	81.8%	5.2%
Trevor Lawrence	Clemson	74.1%	79.2%	5.1%
Peyton Ramsey	Northwestern	73.4%	77.6%	4.1%
Davis Mills	Stanford	74.9%	77.5%	2.6%
Zach Wilson	BYU	72.4%	74.8%	2.6%
Justin Fields	Ohio State	71.6%	73.7%	2.1%
Trey Lance	North Dakota State	74.7%	76.6%	2.0%
Shane Buechele	SMU	74.2%	76.0%	1.9%
Ian Book	Notre Dame	73.1%	74.6%	1.5%
Kellen Mond	Texas A&M	73.0%	74.5%	1.5%
Sam Ehlinger	Texas	73.3%	74.5%	1.2%
Brady White	Memphis	72.6%	72.2%	-0.4%
Jamie Newman	Wake Forest / Georgia	72.4%	65.4%	-7.0%

For the first time, we see someone other than Mac Jones at the top of the leaderboard. Over the past two seasons, Kyle Trask ranked only third in On-Target%. But once we adjust for the difficulty of throw, he actually rates as the most accurate quarterback in the class. Jones and Franks don't drop too far though, as they rank 2nd and 3rd respectively, with top prospect Trevor Lawrence coming in 4th.

Fields ranks higher here than raw On-Target%, but not as high as his pComp +/- ranking would suggest. This is due to the fact that while he completed a lot of difficult throws, his receivers helped him out quite a bit. They were able to reel in 23% of his off-target throws over the past two years, which is the third-highest rate among the quarterbacks listed above.

Jamie Newman—who opted out of 2020 after playing at Wake Forest in 2019—was the quarterback whose receivers bailed him out the most over the past two years, by catching 26% of his off-target throws. This resulted in Newman being above expectation in pComp, but well below expectation with an On-Target +/- of -7%.

Accuracy is one of the most important factors in quarterback evaluation. But, as shown above there are many ways to actually measure it and most come with critical flaws. The days of using simple completion percentages should be well behind us. Using better data that reflects the quarterback's accuracy and not the outcome of the throw is a step in the right direction. Another step is to use advanced models to account for the difficulty of each throw—such as our pComp +/- model metric, which unlike NFL's NextGen's CPOE has the added benefit of being able to be applied to the college game. Combining the two into a new metric such as xOn-Target +/- can provide a more in-depth understanding of quarterback accuracy.

Which Splits Translate from College to the NFL?

Alex Vigderman

In this book, we want to give detailed analysis of what NFL prospects did during their college years, and we also want to give a sense for what they might do when they get to the NFL.

Last year, we investigated the question, "Which stats are most consistent between college and the NFL?" We learned that certain trait-oriented stats, like Scramble Rate for quarterbacks or Average Depth of Target for receivers, are really sticky, and a few others are a step below that.

In that piece, we looked at several passing, rushing, and receiving stats and compared players' results in their college years to their NFL output. This year, we'll go through a similar analysis, but this time the focus is not on the kind of stat that translates to the NFL, but instead the different situations that translate well to the pro level.

Two UNC running backs are top prospects this year (Javonte Williams and Michael Carter). They obviously ran behind the same offensive line, but have opposite splits in terms of their effectiveness in zone versus gap blocking. Is that something we can trust heading into their NFL careers?

As a data company, we have lots of different angles from which to analyze a player. We can look at performance by coverage, by blocking scheme, with different play designs, and the list goes on. All of these situational factors are interesting when reviewing what a player has seen and done in his college career, But if performance in a given situation can be treated as more of a trait of the player than a statistical quirk, we can feel more confident in our projection of that player into the NFL, at least in that respect.

Two points before we get started:

1) In a complex system like football, a correlation above even 0.30 is pretty good. Anything below 0.20 is probably safe to consider as not predictive. As we'll see, certain positions are just more statistically consistent than others, and that's something else to keep in mind.

2) While we like harping on sample size in the stats world, when you're looking at a particular slice of situations, you can get away with smaller samples because the set of plays is more homogeneous. That said, keep in mind that we're still talking about relatively small samples.

Passing

Last year's article concluded that Scramble Rate and Average Throw Depth were the most consistent stats between college and the pros. And that isn't surprising, because they're more indicative of the style of the player as opposed to his ability to perform. So while I'll remind you to consider those stats as the most relevant in assessing how a player will translate to the NFL, we'll use the next-best option, Catchable Throw Percentage.

The table below shows how a sample of recent rookies' Catchable% in their last two college seasons relates to their Catchable% in their first two NFL seasons. For comparison, we've also included the NFL two-year-to-two-year correlations over the last four years. Players must have at least 50 qualifying attempts in both time periods in the given split to be considered.

The "Under Center", "Play Action", "On Short Drops", "On Intermediate Drops", "On Deep Drops", and "Throws 15 Yards or More" splits were excluded due to small samples.

Catchable Percentage Correlations, Consecutive Two-Year Periods (n >= 20)

Split	NFL 17-18 to 19-20	Last 2 College to First 2 NFL
Shotgun	0.08	0.40
No Play Action	0.36	0.38
Under Pressure	0.25	0.33
Throws <15 Yards	0.12	0.32
In Pocket	0.12	0.31
No Pressure	0.46	0.16
vs. Man Cov	0.37	0.15
vs. Zone Cov	0.41	-0.01

This table typifies the change in thought process we need to engage in when evaluating the transition from college to the NFL.

Several different splits have correlations between 0.30 and 0.40, which for this purpose we can consider similarly valuable. The first on the list is Catchable% from Shotgun, which is surprisingly inconsistent among NFL passers. There is a possibility that there's a selection effect here, where poor shotgun performers are weeded out in their early years and so there's less to learn from shotgun performance among veterans. But this isn't definitive evidence of that.

The next thing to note is that performance against different coverages, while relatively consistent among NFL QBs, isn't something that college performance can help with. The talent level and scheme complexity ramps up dramatically in the NFL, so your ability to process common situations in college is only so helpful as a pro.

On the other hand, while performance under pressure is much less consistent in the NFL than performance without pressure, the opposite relationship holds for the transition from college to the NFL. This might be a counterintuitive but real phenomenon. While "pressure is pressure" to some extent regardless of the level of competition, a clean pocket in college isn't quite the same as a clean pocket in the NFL. There is a lot less consistency in what college pockets look like because of the variability in the caliber of athletes a team boasts along the offensive line.

Rushing

Last year, we found that by far the most valuable statistic in projecting a running back was Broken Tackle Rate. Of course, like Scramble Percentage and Average Throw Depth for quarterbacks, that reflects a characteristic of the style of player more than other stats we might consider. None of the other rushing stats was particularly predictive, but the best option it makes sense to consider is Positive%, or the percent of runs where the offense improved its Expected Points.

To be considered in the table below, a player must have accumulated 30 carries in the given split across each paired two-year period under consideration, and a split must have at least 20 such qualified players. And in the interest of apples-to-apples comparisons, quarterbacks were excluded from this analysis.

The "With Lead Blocker" split was left out due to insufficient sample.

Rushing Positive Percentage Correlations, Consecutive Two-Year Periods (n >= 20)

Split	NFL 17-18 to 19-20	Last 2 College to First 2 NFL
No Lead Blocker	0.13	0.25
Under Center	0.16	0.22
Inside	0.20	0.21
Outside	0.20	0.21
Off-Tackle	-0.01	0.17
Hit at the Line	0.12	0.15
Shotgun	0.23	0.15
Gap Blocking	0.12	0.14
Zone Blocking	0.27	0.12
Not Hit at the Line	0.12	0.12
1 TE Personnel	0.18	0.10
2 TE Personnel	0.27	-0.10

If you were paying attention earlier, you might notice that none of these college-to-pro correlations are worth writing home about. This is as much about the lower year-to-year consistency of the position in general as anything. Among the more useful splits is performance without a lead blocker, which makes sense because it depends less on the talent level of other players.

Many of the other rushing splits are similarly interesting-but-not-projectable, with performance in certain personnel being the least useful for projection to the NFL. One point of interest would be the different run direction splits, because performance is more consistent on inside and outside runs than it is on off-tackle runs for both veterans and incoming rookies. This is intuitive from the perspective that the ability to break tackles is always relevant on inside runs, and speed and agility are always relevant on outside runs, so players who either excel or lack in those talents are going to be (relatively) consistent in that regard.

Receiving

Now, on to receivers…

The most consistent metric that we found last year was Average Depth of Target, which again is logical but not really a measure of how good a player is. The next-best options are sort of complementary metrics, so we'll consider both of them: Yards After Catch per Reception, and Catch Rate.

With receiving, there are distinct but relevant groups based on position. Running backs are increasingly relevant in the passing game, but they're asked to do very different things than tight ends and wide receivers. So for the purposes of this analysis we considered them separately.

As you might suspect, the samples here are even smaller than for running backs. Here we consider consecutive two-year periods either within the NFL or from college to the NFL, and players with at least 20 receptions in the given split in both timeframes are included. Only splits for which at least 20 players qualify are listed.

The "On Throws of 15 Yards or More" and "From Tight End" splits were left out because the sample wasn't big enough. That's a shame because, at the NFL level at least, the deep throws split is the most consistent in terms of Catch Rate, and the tight end split is the most consistent in terms of Yards After Catch per Reception.

Yards After Catch per Reception Correlations, Consecutive Two-Year Periods (n >= 20)

Split	NFL 17-18 to 19-20	Last 2 College to First 2 NFL
On Throws < 15 Yards	0.49	0.40
From the Slot	0.31	0.34
vs. Zone Cov	0.38	0.33
From Out Wide	0.37	0.20
RB - On Throws < 15 Yards	0.33	0.15
vs. Man Cov	0.44	0.07
RB - From Backfield	0.25	-0.05

After-catch ability is pretty consistent across the board at the NFL level, but the ability to make plays after the catch hasn't shown the same consistency for running backs entering the NFL. The ability to exploit zone coverage appears more transferable to the NFL than making plays against man coverage, which is consistent with the notion that coverage schemes are more consistent from college to the NFL than defensive talent level is.

Catch Percentage Correlations, Consecutive Two-Year Periods (n >= 20)

Split	NFL 17-18 to 19-20	Last 2 College to First 2 NFL
vs. Zone Cov	0.28	0.33
From Out Wide	0.07	0.31
On Throws < 15 Yards	0.17	0.30
vs. Man Cov	0.29	0.25
RB - On Throws < 15 Yards	0.23	0.07
From the Slot	0.29	0.02
RB - From Backfield	0.10	-0.03

Catch Rate is less consistent in general than after-catch ability, although the story is generally similar. Running backs don't bring their Catch Rate with them to the NFL (for better or worse), while receivers and tight ends show some consistency in this regard. There's also more consistency against zone coverage than against man coverage, but the difference is pretty small in this case. One result that's a bit bewildering is that a player's hands are much more consistent from the slot than out wide in the NFL, but the opposite is true for players transitioning into the NFL.

We'll be re-examining these research directions as we accumulate more seasons of data (and more and more compelling stats and splits). Check out our work at the Sports Info Solutions Blog and Sharp Football Analysis to see what else we come up with. In the meantime, it's illuminating that because of the differences between pro and college football, the kinds of metrics we believe are valuable at one level of play aren't necessarily the ones we would use to evaluate players entering that level.

Total Points Overview

Alex Vigderman

In this book and in scouting in general, we evaluate each position differently based on the requirements of the position and the traits we look for in effective players. On the stats side, we have similar stats for different positions (after all, a reception is a reception regardless of what position you are), but it's not clear how we should evaluate a player based just on a collection of statistics.

Which stats are the most important? How do we evaluate players who don't accumulate many statistics? How do we evaluate players who might perform similarly in different contexts?

To answer these kinds of questions, SIS has created a system that we call Total Points, which appears all over this book because we believe it's the best way to evaluate a player's performance in its entirety.

What does Total Points do?

Total Points takes nearly everything that SIS measures about a play and uses it to evaluate each player on a scale that allows you to compare them more easily.

It's always useful to be able to understand the different ways in which players can be valuable. Does he break a lot of tackles? Does he get a lot of yards after the catch? Does he make the best out of a poor offensive line? Total Points offers the opportunity to take all of those elements and get a quick picture of how well a player is performing overall.

What does the number mean?

All of Total Points uses the Expected Points Added (EPA) framework. EPA works by taking any given situation and finding the odds that each different scoring possibility comes next. For example, if the next scoring play is a field goal by the current defensive team two drives from now, you count that as a -3. Average those values across all instances of the same situation and you get its Expected Points. Take the change in Expected Points on any given play and you get its EPA.

Roughly, you can think of a 0 EPA play as one that "stays on schedule", an EPA of 1 or more as a big play for the offense, and an EPA of negative-1 or less as a big play for the defense.

Total Points starts by evaluating each player on that scale, where 0 is average. That's what we call Points Above Average. Then to both reward players who play full seasons and keep the sum of Total Points around what we'd expect a team to score or allow, we scale the results to the league scoring average (around 22 points per game). So when you see a player's Total Points value, you should be able to judge it as roughly the number of points he was responsible for creating or saving while he was on the field.

How does it work?

We won't go into complete detail here, but let's run down the different data elements we consider, how they are evaluated in terms of EPA, and how they get bundled together.

Total Points works on each of the passing game and running game as a whole, so we'll walk through them that way.

Any changes from previous years will be highlighted using asterisks, like this.

Pass Plays

Blocking

Everything starts up front. We start with identifying who was rushing the passer and who was blocking. Then, we estimate how likely each person was to either blow a block (offense) or force a blown block (defense). On each play, credit is assigned to each player based on how they performed compared to that expectation, and the resulting blown block plus-minus value is multiplied by the average EPA of a blown block.

Players are additionally credited or debited if they were involved in a batted pass, deflection, or pressure, based on the average EPA of those events.

Pass Attempts

Each pass attempt gets split into four portions: the throw, the catch, yards after catch before contact, and yards after contact. For any throw, we take the value of the route at the intended depth in terms of its completion rate and interception rate and give the quarterback a big chunk of that value. A similar basis is used to estimate how much of the two YAC components we expect, and we give the receiver credit based on the difference in EPA between what he achieved and what was expected. The receiver and quarterback split the value of the throw, air yards, and yards after catch before contact, while the receiver gets the after-contact value on his own. Beyond that, we ensure off-target throws don't hurt the receiver and drops don't hurt the quarterback.

The defense at large takes responsibility for the throw itself because many factors contribute to the throw that's selected, but the primary defender in coverage is responsible for the catch and yards after catch. Any broken or missed tackles are evaluated according to their average EPA impact. If the pass is intercepted, the quarterback and defender are equally debited and credited based on where the ball was caught. The defender then gets extra credit for the change in field position from his return.

All players running routes or defending in coverage have an expected target rate based on the coverage scheme, number of routes being run, route type, and alignment. Each player is assigned a value according to how many targets above expectation they had, scaled according to the EPA value of the potential target.

Pressure, Sacks, and Fumbles

Quarterbacks are given full responsibility for the sacks they incur (less the value of any blown blocks by the offensive line). They are given neither credit nor blame for pressure unrelated to blown blocks, with the idea that their throws are made more difficult but they also had some part in the pressure in the first place.

Sacks or evaded sacks are measured using the EPA of the sack (or potential sack). The sacker(s) get full credit, unless it was deemed a coverage sack, in which case the coverage unit splits the credit.

Pass rushers are given credit for how well they generate pressures relative to the average of players lined up at the same position. Any pressure-related events that might have been debited from the line are given back to the receivers (and quarterback in the case of blown blocks), owing to their having a harder job as a result of the pressure.

All fumbles, recovered or lost, are evaluated similarly, because putting the ball on the ground is a big problem even if you're fortunate to have most of them recovered. The value of the potential turnover from that spot on the field is multiplied by the odds that possession will be lost based on whether it was in the backfield or not. The person who recovers the fumble gets the inverse of the value that would be lost if the offense recovers, or the "rest" of the fumble value if the defense recovers (i.e. the value of the turnover multiplied by the odds that it is recovered).

Run Plays

Blocking

Like with passing, the first step is to identify the blockers and box defenders. In addition, we use the intended ***and eventual*** run direction to identify the key blockers and defenders on the play ***(based on data elements like defensive techniques)***.

From there, we calculate the play's expected yards before and after contact based on the number of box defenders, the blocking scheme, the run direction, the spot on the field, etc. The blockers are evaluated based on the play's performance above that expectation, with most of the credit or blame going to the key blockers identified earlier (unless the runner cut the run back or bounced outside, in which case things are more balanced among blockers).

The earlier the back is contacted on the play, the more responsibility the offensive line takes for the result of the play. That ranges from taking on 90% of the responsibility for plays that are blown up to 25% of the yards before contact beyond the first 15.

The same value is distributed among the box defenders, again focusing on the defenders at the intended gap. Blown blocks are evaluated similarly to what's done in the passing game.

On plays where the back bounces or cuts the run back, the linemen initially run behind are evaluated differently from those who the back eventually runs behind. The extent of the difference depends on the direction and magnitude of the back's movement. For example, cutbacks of 3 or more gaps are the most valuable bounce or cutback, so the value lost by the initial linemen is small because the cost of the cutback is small.

Rushing

The runner is evaluated against the offensive line's expected performance calculated above. The rusher is given some credit for yards before contact because elusive runners can generate their own space, but most of his value will come after contact. ***The back's responsibility for yards before contact increases the more yards he gains before contact, as it's more likely he had a role in that result.***

On any play where a broken tackle was charted, we ignore the yards after contact portion and instead give the back a standard EPA amount based on the average value of a broken tackle. Fumbles are treated like they are on pass plays.

Tackling

Given each defender's initial alignment, the heaviness of the box, and the run direction, we estimate the ***probability that each player would make the tackle and the*** EPA that would be expected if each of the possible defenders made the tackle.

A plus-minus system is used to combine the expected tackle rate and tackle value for each player and measure that against whether the player actually recorded a tackle. That system is also modified to ensure that making a tackle is always better than not making one, regardless of the value of said tackle compared to expectation.

Broken or missed tackles are taken independent of where they are on the field, so each one is considered worth the value of an average broken or missed tackle in terms of EPA.

Additional Adjustments

Play Selection

At this point it's common knowledge that run plays are less valuable on average than pass plays. At a basic level we can see this because the average yards per attempt on passes is much higher than it is on runs. At a more granular level, coaches can make inefficient decisions by electing to, for example, run from heavy personnel on second-and-10.

In order to more accurately evaluate the players on a play as opposed to the coaches or situations, we implemented a Play Selection Adjustment, which applies to each player on each play. We take the expected value of the play given the run/pass decision and some personnel and game state information, compare it to an average play, take the difference, and distribute that value among the players involved. That way, a back being run into a heavy box time and again isn't punished simply for being on the field in a sub-par situation for him.

This adjustment generally moves a player a handful of points one way or the other depending on how often he was involved in pass or run plays.

Season Scoring

As mentioned above, after all of the initial calculations are done, we re-scale everything so that the league total is in line with the league's scoring average, or just over 22 points per team per game. Because the quarterback represents the most obviously critical position, he's given 1/3 of this adjustment for the offense, and the rest is split among the other offensive players.

The Gist

Let's say that you read all this stuff and already kind of forget what you read at the beginning. Here's a quick-and-dirty version:

- We take Expected Points Added and give individual value to every player on every scrimmage play, starting in 2018
- You can find it on the player pages and leaderboards in this book.
- Pass Offense: Quarterbacks and receivers split value for the throw, the catch, after-catch yards, and after-contact yards. There are additional considerations for offensive line performance, uncatchable passes, and drops.
- Pass Defense: Defensive backs are measured on how often they are targeted above expectation, and much of the value that the receivers or QB get on a completion is correspondingly taken away from the defender. Pass rushers are credited for forcing blown blocks and disruptions at the point of attack.
- Rush Offense: The offensive line and running back both take responsibility for yards before contact (weighted towards the O-line), while yards after contact beyond what's expected are totally owned by the back. Broken tackles hold a lot of value.
- Rush Defense: Preventing yards before contact is the name of the game for the defensive line, while linebackers and defensive backs get value from making tackles that limit yardage compared to expectation ***and not missing out on easy tackle opportunities***.
- In general, there's a lot of value to be gained and lost from turnovers (or turnover-worthy plays) and plays in key spots (e.g. just outside field goal range, third down).

What do we do with it?

Now that you're familiar with what goes into Total Points, what do you do with it?

The first thing you might do is find players whose traditional stats or reputation don't line up with their rank in Total Points. In those situations, it'll often be some of the key aspects that make this system unique that will be the reason for it.

Sometimes it'll be a quarterback who fumbled a few too many times or who makes too many uncatchable throws. Sometimes the offensive line will be particularly good or bad in front of a running back. A receiver who makes most of his bones after the catch or who is targeted much more often than expected could surprise you.

Nose tackles are finally getting credit for their ability to force runners to bounce outside. An edge rusher who gets to the quarterback but doesn't quite finish the deal will get his due. So will linebackers and safeties who impact the run game by making tackles close to the line of scrimmage The deterrent value of a shutdown corner is a great example of the system's ability to evaluate players who don't accumulate typical statistics.

Total Points gives us the opportunity to more critically engage with the stats players compile and consider the context in which they compiled them. And as SIS continues to add more data points to its operation, our assessment of those things will only get better.

Differences at the College Level

In college specifically, because the spread of talent across different conferences can be pretty wide, there is also an adjustment for the quality of opponent. To address this concern within Total Points, a team quality estimate is calculated for both sides of the ball, and then each play is modified using a multiplier that is based on the quality of the unit on the other side of the field.

This adjustment (done similarly for both offense and defense) is calculated over a rolling 12- week window for each team with adjustments based on the Expected Points Added per game of their opponents and their opponents' opponents. Those combine to form a measure of how much that team affects the EPA of their opponents. The adjustment will range from about a 25% downgrade when facing a bottom-of-the-barrel outfit to about a 25% upgrade when facing a top-shelf opponent. Over the course of a full season, because teams face a variety of opponents, the effect is most often within 5% either way.

FBS Total Points Leaders

Below are the leaders in Total Points at the college level this season. This isn't limited to players in this book, so you'll see some names to watch for future years as well!

Quarterbacks

Player	Pos	School	Total Points
Mac Jones	QB	Alabama	194
Sam Howell	QB	North Carolina	171
Kyle Trask	QB	Florida	159
Matt Corral	QB	Ole Miss	147
Zach Wilson	QB	BYU	139

Non-Quarterback Offense

Player	Pos	School	Total Points
Javonte Williams	RB	North Carolina	74
Najee Harris	RB	Alabama	69
DeVonta Smith	WR	Alabama	61
Michael Carter	RB	North Carolina	57
Khalil Herbert	RB	Virginia Tech	51
Breece Hall	RB	Iowa State	50
Javian Hawkins	RB	Louisville	48
Elijah Moore	WR	Ole Miss	44
Jaret Patterson	RB	Buffalo	41
Tank Bigsby	RB	Auburn	40

Defense

Player	Pos	School	Total Points
Derrick Canteen	CB	Georgia Southern	58
Will Anderson Jr.	EDGE	Alabama	56
Josh Jobe	CB	Alabama	54
Jabril Cox	LB	LSU	54
Jalen Catalon	CB	Arkansas	52
Tarron Jackson	EDGE	Coastal Carolina	52
Mike Rose	LB	Iowa State	51
Jon Rhattigan	LB	Army	50
DeMarvin Leal	EDGE	Texas A&M	50

Example Use Cases for Total Points at the College Level

Total Points is incredibly useful as a quick way to measure players against each other because it distills player value into a single number. This is especially true for defensive players, because it's not clear how one should compare a tackle in the run game to a sack or a pass defensed, for example. Total Points allows us to discuss players with different roles and statistical profiles apples-to-apples.

With the strength-of-schedule adjustment added on top of the existing Total Points methodology we can quickly evaluate a player compared to the full swath of college football players, which can help point scouting staffs in the direction of players whose raw statistics don't tell the full story (for better or for worse).

For example, Derrick Canteen had a fantastic freshman season at corner for Georgia Southern, with 11 passes defensed and an FBS-leading 6 interceptions. That shoots him to the top of the leaderboard, and by a decent margin. But his opponents were unsurprisingly a few percentage points below average. Pair that with a leaderboard full of Big Ten and SEC defenders whose opponents tend to be above average and you get a tighter leaderboard than just a comparison of stat lines would suggest. And Total Points allows us to have a conversation about defensive backs and linebackers alike among defensive standouts.

Introducing Total Points Rating

One thing you might note about the leaderboards we show above is that volume is a big factor in whether a player appears toward the top of the list. You can make these leaderboards by being "merely" very good with a lot of playing time.

In 2020, though, the schedules of different conferences varied so wildly that we can't make the usual assumption that most teams played a roughly similar number of games. So just looking at total stats tells us as much about which conference you were in as how good you were.

Enter Total Points Rating. This stat starts with Total Points and puts it on a per-play basis, meaning that we can show how good a player was on whatever snaps he played, regardless of how often he made it onto the field. You'll find this on every player page and leaderboard alongside the standard Total Points data.

Instead of just dividing Total Points by a play count and calling it a day, we wanted to represent the number as something that was easy to judge at a glance. To that end, Total Points Rating is on a 50-99 scale, which puts it in the same neighborhood as number grades in school or player ratings in video games. So instead of showing that a quarterback had an excellent 0.21 Total Points per dropback, we might instead say he was a 92.

How do we calculate this rating? We take a player's Total Points per play in a given component (say, his Receiving Total Points per route run) and compare that to the average rate in that season. That is turned into a percentile (which normally runs from 1 to 99) and then compressed to the more familiar 50-99 scale.

We do that using a Z-score, which is the number of standard deviations away from the average that person is. If you're familiar with traditional statistics, you've probably seen them before. And if you're not, just know that it is a way to compare values to their average when the populations aren't the same. So we can say that a passer who's one standard deviation above the average is roughly as good relative to his peers as a pass-catcher who's one standard deviation above the average pass-catcher.

Z-scores also correspond to a distribution of percentiles, although not like the traditional definition of percentiles. A Z score of 0 is right at the average, which is considered 50th percentile. A player who's at least a standard deviation above the average will be at least in the 84th percentile, and a player who's at least a standard deviation below the average will be at most in the 16th percentile. You can see that a large portion of the population will sit in the middle, with a few getting out to the extremes.

This is a little different from traditional percentiles, which we can illustrate with an example. Say there are 100 players at a given position, and 50 of them are basically average. Statistically, they have some slight differences, but we're talking hundredths of a Total Point per play.

A traditional percentile has to rank these players in order, so two players who are negligibly different might end up in the 30th or 60th percentile, which look very different. The percentile used in Total Points Rating treats everyone with a similar Z-score similarly, so they all end up at roughly the 50th percentile. This does a much better job in characterizing the players who sit around the average.

Each individual component (e.g. passing, run blocking, run defense) is calculated separately, but if you want a total picture of a player you'll also find a Total Points Rating across all plays for a player. That's tabulated by taking a weighted average of the player's ratings in the different components based on how often he did each of those things.

Total Points Rating helps give the appropriate context for players who either played much more or much less than their peers. Top QB prospect Justin Fields, for example, doesn't appear on the leaderboard above (he accumulated 107 Total Points) thanks to Ohio State's shortened schedule. In terms of Total Points Rating, he rates a 97. Similarly, Michigan edge rusher Kwity Paye played only four games but was terrific in that short sample, earning a 99 Total Points Rating on pass rushes.

On the flip side, Alabama defensive backs played as much as anyone in the country this season, so Josh Jobe cracks the Total Points leaderboard despite an 84 Total Points Rating. His highly-regarded teammate Patrick Surtain II allowed some bigger plays as a defender which left him off the Total Points leaderboard, but he had a similarly unexciting Total Points Rating in his final season in Tuscaloosa.

How to Explore Total Points

You can find Total Points and Total Points Rating in the Deep Dive section of the player pages as well as the leaderboards for each position. Not every component of Total Points will be listed separately for each position, so keep in mind that a player's Total Points might include components you don't see listed separately (e.g. pass blocking for running backs).

Each position's glossary will give a little bit of information about Total Points as it relates to that position. If you want to learn more about the system in detail, you can check out the Total Points Primer on the Sports Info Solutions blog located at sportsinfosolutionsblog.com or through this convenient QR code:

A Look at Press Coverage in the NFL and NCAA

John Shirley

Analyzing cornerback play is a difficult task. Looking at their overall metrics is a good start. Breaking down their play by coverage type and alignment is even better, as man vs zone schemes and slot vs wide alignment are all fundamentally different. Going a step further, here at SIS we break down their play by Press Type. This allows us to separate off coverage from tight bump-and-run coverage, which again are fundamentally different techniques and situations.

Press Coverage—defined as a corner lining up within two yards of the receiver and attempting to make contact at the snap—data is tracked on every play for both man and zone coverage, but for this analysis the focus will be on press-man compared to off-man coverage plays.

Usage and Performance at the NFL Level

Since the start of the 2019 season, NFL corners have used press coverage on 42% of their man coverage snaps. Corners have generally been more successful while in press coverage, as they allow a lower completion percentage, yards per target, and EPA per target, and average a higher Total Points Per 60 Snaps (which is good for defenders). However, when a reception was allowed while in press coverage, receivers averaged around two more Yards Per Reception.

Off-Man vs Press-Man in the NFL (2019-2020)

Man Coverage Type	Usage%	Comp%	Yds/Trgt	Yds/Rec	EPA/Tgt	Total Points / 60 Snaps
Off-Man	58%	59.9%	7.6	12.7	0.21	2.4
Press-Man	42%	50.4%	7.4	14.7	0.12	2.9

Corners in press coverage were also able to get their hand on the ball (HOB%)—including interceptions, dropped interceptions, and passes defensed—at a higher rate (15%) than corners playing off coverage (12%). However, they were called for pass interference at a higher rate: 5% of targets in press compared to 2% while playing off of receivers.

Usage and Performance at the NCAA Level

Corners at the college level have similar results to those in the NFL when comparing their performance between press-man coverage and off-man coverage. They also allow a lower completion percentage, fewer yards per target, lower EPA per target, and average a higher Total Points Per 60 Snaps while in press-man. The main difference between levels is the rate at which teams employ press coverage. At the NFL level, press-man usage is only slightly below off-man usage. At the college level, the national average use is much lower.

Off-Man vs Press-Man in the NCAA (2019-2020)

Man Coverage Type	Usage%	Comp%	Yds/Trgt	Yds/Rec	EPA/Trgt	Total Points / 60 Snaps
Off-Man	72%	52.7%	7.5	14.2	0.14	2.3
Press-Man	28%	40.1%	6.8	16.9	0.00	2.5

Similar to corners in the NFL, NCAA corners also allowed a higher yards per reception and were flagged for pass interference at a higher rate while in press-man. Although the overall usage of press-man was relatively low, 14 schools used it on at least 40% of their individual man coverage snaps over the past two years, led by Oklahoma at 57%.

The Difference Between Levels

When comparing the NFL and NCAA average performances, we see similar results. So, then why don't college defenses employ press-man coverage more often?

The answer to that question is actually fairly simple. It is much harder to find elite cornerbacks at the collegiate level and there is an immense talent disparity between both teams and conferences. The talent disparity really shows itself when we compare the press-man coverage performance of the Power 5 (P5) conferences to the Group of 5 (G5) conferences.

NCAA Press-Man Performance (2019-2020) Separated by Conference Groupings

Conference Group	Usage% When in Man Coverage	EPA/Trgt	Total Points / 60 Snaps
Power 5*	31%	-0.05	3.1
Group of 5	26%	0.05	1.8

Also includes Notre Dame

As the table highlights, P5 teams have been more willing to employ press-man coverage, likely due to having the talent to do so. When in press-man, P5 teams performed much better in both EPA/Target Allowed and Total Points Per 60 Snaps than their G5 counterparts. This discrepancy in conference usage and performance is even more stark when we compare the level of offense faced.

NCAA Press-Man Performance (2019-2020)
Separated by Conference Grouping and Conference Grouping of Offense Faced

Conference Group	Usage% When in Man Coverage	EPA/Trgt	Total Points/ 60 Snaps
P5* Defense vs G5 Offense	32%	-0.10	3.7
P5 Defense vs P5 Offense	30%	-0.05	2.9
G5 Defense vs G5 Offense	26%	0.03	1.9
G5 Defense vs P5 Offense	25%	0.18	0.2

Also includes Notre Dame

Once again, it is evident how the talent disparity between conferences affects both usage and performance of press-man coverage. The overall results are unsurprising, as it should be expected that within any split P5 players would perform better when facing G5 competition and vice versa. But, what should be noted is that even when the level of competition is held relatively even (P5 vs P5 and G5 vs G5), P5 teams are more willing and able to employ press-man.

One possible explanation for this is that press-man success is highly dependent on the talent of the corner, regardless of competition faced. The theory being that it is easier for an elite corner to perform well in press-man even against an elite receiver than it is for an average corner to perform well in press-man against an average receiver.

Top NCAA Press-Man Corners in the 2021 Draft Class

In regard to elite corners in press-man coverage, the 2021 draft class is well represented. There are eight cornerbacks who our scouting staff has graded as having very good press-man ability. Our metrics also back this up, especially with our top two ranked corners Patrick Surtain II from Alabama and Jaycee Horn from South Carolina.

Among all FBS corners who played at least 100 man coverage snaps in 2020, Horn and Surtain ranked 2nd and 4th in press-man usage, respectively. Horn pressed on 75% of his man coverage snaps, while Surtain pressed on 73%. Along with their high usage, they performed at an elite level as well.

Performance in Press-Man Coverage (2020)

Player	Tgts	Comp%	EPA/Trgt	HOB%	Total Points / 60 Snaps
Jaycee Horn	11	18.2%	-0.69	55%	8.6
Patrick Surtain II	14	50.0%	0.06	21%	3.9

Horn was one of the best corners in the nation this past season, and he was especially effective in press-man. Surtain was also no slouch in press-man, performing at an above-average level in Total Points Per 60 Snaps. Their performances in 2020 were especially impressive as they both only played an SEC schedule, along with a playoff and national championship game in Surtain's case.

Last Word

SIS's press coverage data allows for a deeper analysis of corner play in the NFL and at the FBS NCAA level. Overall it shows a trend that press-man is generally more successful than off-man coverage. However, it is worth noting that there is definite selection bias when considering press-man statistics because generally teams are more likely to play press-man if they believe they have the personnel to do so. This analysis does show how effective press-man coverage can be when used properly and that if a team has an elite-level corner, it might be a good idea to use it more often.

Notable On-Off Splits Among Draft Prospects

Mark Simon

One of the most important things that Sports Info Solutions' Video Scouts do is chart player participation for every play of every game. This requires a painstaking look at game film to identify every player on their screen.

The payoff for this is in being able to evaluate how teams fare with different players and different combinations of players in and out of games. Doing so requires interpretation beyond just looking at the numbers. On-off splits give additional perspective.

Keep in mind that context matters. A player who missed entire games due to injury will have different on-off splits than someone whose only absence from the field came when the second and third-string players were in during garbage time.

Here are some players whose splits we found interesting in evaluating their draft value:

Kyle Pitts, TE, Florida

Kyle Pitts, a two-time All-SEC First Team selection, played in eight of the Gators' 12 games in 2020, missing time with a concussion and foregoing the team's 55-20 loss to Oklahoma in the Cotton Bowl to prepare for the Draft.

Pitts' value can be articulated in his receptions, yardage, and touchdowns, but if you want to see the difference-maker impact, his on-off splits make it clear. Florida's offense ran much more efficiently with Pitts on the field and had a much easier time throwing its way into the end zone.

Kyle Pitts – On/Off Splits – Team Stats

	On Field	Off Field
EPA per 60 plays	15.7	3.4
Comp Pct	70%	66%
TD-Int	29-3	17-7
Pass Attempts	241	232

Kadarius Toney, WR, Florida

Similar to Pitts, Florida was a different team when Kadarius Toney was off the field. Most notably, Gators quarterbacks threw four interceptions on 349 attempts when he was on the field, but six interceptions on the 124 attempts when he was off the field.

Kadarius Toney – On/Off Splits – Team Stats

	On Field	Off Field
EPA per 60 plays	11.9	2.6
Comp Pct	70%	63%
TD-Int	40-4	6-6
Pass Attempts	349	124

The absences of Toney and Pitts make it difficult to project Florida quarterback Kyle Trask, who dominated when both played, but struggled significantly when both were off the field.

Kyle Trask, 2020 Season with Pitts & Toney

	Attempts	Comp Pct	TD-Int
Both on Field	210	70%	26-2
Neither on Field	68	62%	1-4
Only Pitts On Field	27	74%	3-0
Only Toney on Field	132	70%	13-2

Kwity Paye, Edge, Michigan

A lower-body injury and a shortened schedule due to the pandemic limited Kwity Paye, a senior, to four games in 2020, and the Wolverines were considerably worse for his absence. Paye had shown in his junior year that when he was on the field he could cause trouble and rack up tackles for loss. Likewise, opposing offensive lines had much more to concern themselves with when Paye played than when he didn't, as his on-off numbers show.

Kwity Paye – On/Off Splits – Team Stats

	On Field	Off Field
EPA Allowed per 60 plays	2.0	9.4
Pressure%	39%	33%
Opp Yds Per Rush	3.9	5.2
Opp Blown Block %	11%	5%

Chris Rumph II, Edge, Duke

Chris Rumph was on the field for close to 70% of Duke's snaps this season, earning second-team All-ACC honors on a 2-9 squad.

Duke's defense was much better when Rumph was on the field. He had a team-high 8.5 sacks and was part of a unit that limited opposing quarterbacks to a 56% completion percentage when he was on the field.

A good way to consider Rumph's performance is to look at the boom-bust ratio on pass plays for Duke's defense. A "boom" is any play that gains at least one Expected Point for the offense (EPA ≥ 1), while a "bust" is any play that loses at least one Expected Point (EPA ≤ -1). The big pass plays against Duke were more frequent when he was out of the game.

Chris Rumph II – On/Off Splits – Team Stats

	On Field	Off Field
Opp Comp Pct	56%	62%
Opp Pass TD-INT	14-7	8-1
Opp Boom Pct - Pass Plays	22%	29%
Opp Bust Pct- Pass Plays	18%	16%

Teven Jenkins, OL, Oklahoma State

Sometimes the stats tell you something unexpected, like in the case of Teven Jenkins, a first-team All-Big 12 selection who opted out of the college football season at the end of November. As such, there's about an equal number of snaps taken with and without him.

The EPA splits for Oklahoma State when Jenkins was on-and-off the field necessitated a double take: The Cowboys were 3.1 points per 60 plays worse when Jenkins was on the field compared to when he was off. The issues were in the number of interceptions thrown and the number of sacks taken with Jenkins in the game. On/off splits are notoriously susceptible to teammate effects, so this is not to say that Jenkins is doomed. But at the very least, any time the numbers and the reputation don't seem to match, the player warrants further examination.

Teven Jenkins – On/Off Splits – Team Stats

	On Field	Off Field
EPA per 60 plays	-4.2	-1.1
Sack Pct	9.7%	3.4%
INT	6	4
Pass Attempts	161	175

Examining College Football Injuries in 2020

John Verros

Every player within *The SIS Football Rookie Handbook* has had their injury history examined. Each player profile has a space to indicate two types of injury designations: long-term injury risk or currently injured. Long-term injury risk denotes when players have had an extensive injury history or suffered injuries which historically have a high rate of recurrence. Injuries such as shoulder or hip labral tears, multiple knee sprains, nerve injuries and numerous concussions are likely to prompt the long-term injury risk tag.

As an example, Tua Tagovailoa was flagged as a long-term injury risk in last year's book after his dislocated and fractured hip during college. The currently injured tag is used for players dealing with an injury that will limit their participation in the draft process, but will not necessarily have lasting effects during their career.

Most Injured Teams of 2020

In this section, there are multiple tables displaying aggregated 2020 injury information collected here at Sports Info Solutions. The injury data is accumulated via our Video Scouts recording every injury event that occurred in the FBS. Every tagged injury is video-audited by our injury department and updated using media reports until the player has healed.

Along with tagging the injured players during a play, scouts will also record the initial injury severity, using a scale from 1 to 5 with objective definitions.

- Severity 1 equates to an apparent injury with no visible reaction by a player. These are particularly difficult to notice, like when a lineman gets rolled up on from behind but shows no signs of pain after the play.
- Severity 2 occurs when a player physically shows pain, but stays on the field for at least one more play.
- Severity 3 takes place when an injury forces a player to remove himself from a play.
- Severity 4 happens when the player requires a timeout on the field prior to receiving assistance leaving the field.
- Severity 5 injury is reserved for an extreme situation when a player requires a cart or stretcher to be removed from the field.

On the next page are the most-injured teams in the FBS during the 2020 season. The table breaks down each teams' injuries by severity (in-game injuries only) and then adds injuries that were reported in practice or away from football. The teams are sorted by the total number of games missed due to these injuries and listed in descending order.

Most Injured Teams of 2020

Team	Severity 1	Severity 2	Severity 3	Severity 4	Severity 5	Total Injuries	Games Missed
Florida State	1	5	8	26	1	51	79
BYU	3	2	7	7	0	28	78
NC State	1	4	14	41	2	66	66
Clemson	0	10	15	15	0	54	62
Alabama	3	11	15	8	1	41	62
Oklahoma	3	9	12	14	0	53	58
Louisiana Lafayette	0	1	6	10	0	27	56
Texas State	1	5	13	24	1	46	55
South Carolina	0	0	5	22	0	34	54
Texas A&M	0	5	4	18	1	32	50
Texas	2	9	12	32	1	62	49
Indiana	0	1	7	12	1	27	48
LSU	4	10	9	19	0	48	44
Boston College	0	2	7	14	0	30	44
Virginia	0	3	9	19	0	36	43
Tennessee	1	4	4	17	0	30	42
TCU	2	5	6	12	0	31	42
Georgia Southern	1	2	15	21	1	43	41
Syracuse	4	3	10	33	0	55	40
Wake Forest	0	3	2	18	0	27	40
Pittsburgh	0	3	13	20	0	41	39
Missouri	0	3	12	29	0	51	37
Duke	1	4	16	27	0	50	37
Arkansas	1	3	14	11	0	32	36
North Carolina	2	4	10	13	0	31	36

Injuries by Position

When looking at injuries that occur during a game, it's particularly interesting to break down the data by position. In the positional table below, the 'Severe' and 'Severe%' columns denote injuries that were charted as Severity 4 or 5. The 'Injuries/1,000' and 'Severe/1000' look at how many injuries occurred per 1000 snaps, which accounts for the discrepancy in snap counts across positions. The 2020 data indicates the defensive line (interior and edge) as the most dangerous positions in football based on both the percentage of their total injuries that were deemed severe, and the overall likelihood of suffering a severe injury on a per snap basis. This was also the case in

2019. In general, players on the defensive side of the ball are suffering seemingly severe injuries on a per-play basis more often than players on offense. Also of note is that quarterbacks and running backs suffer a high amount of severe injuries on a per-play basis despite a small percentage of their total injuries being severe. This is not entirely surprising given that they have the potential to face higher impact hits on a high percentage of a team's plays.

Injuries by Position in 2020

Position	Total Injuries	Severe	Severe%	Injuries/1000	Severe/1000
DL	490	373	76%	1.2	0.9
LB	445	295	66%	1.2	0.8
DB	639	446	70%	1.1	0.8
RB	372	98	26%	2.6	0.7
QB	346	72	21%	2.8	0.6
TE	151	53	35%	1.1	0.4
WR	466	150	32%	1.4	0.4
OL	304	213	70%	0.5	0.3

Injuries by Body Part

In 2020, defensive backs endured the most injury events involving the head which required a timeout (78). That accounts for 36% of all severe head injuries across all positions this past season. This doesn't mean there were 78 diagnosed concussions to DBs, only that there was at least a stoppage of play necessitating the medical staff to come onto the field. This can also include any eye injuries, nose injuries, players who will clear concussion protocol, etc.

Overall, the body parts with the most injury events this season were knee and ankle. Knee injuries were most prevalent among offensive and defensive linemen (combining for 283 injury events), and of those injury events, 82% were charted as severe. This is a dramatic increase of Severe% when compared to only 58% across all other positions with knee injuries. When looking into ankle injuries, running backs were the position group with the highest total (127). These ankle injuries had a dramatically lower percentage deemed severe (24%) in comparison to all other positions (56%). Offensive linemen (knee) and running backs (ankle) have noticeable differences in Severe% when compared to other positions and it could be a trend to keep an eye on going forward.

The following image illustrates the five body parts with the most recorded injury events in 2020. These events can range from something as simple as a bruise, all the way up to a fracture or tear.

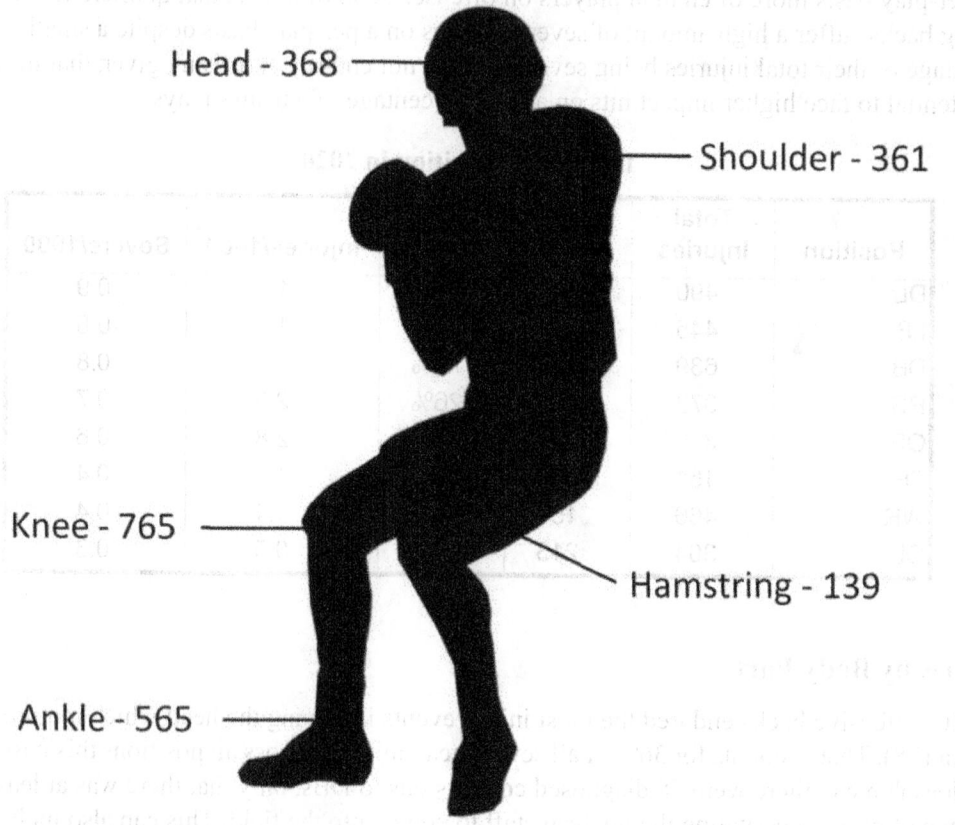

Head - 368

Shoulder - 361

Knee - 765

Hamstring - 139

Ankle - 565

Injuries by Diagnosis

Finally, we can look at the most granular level of our injury data and break down the most severe injuries in terms of games missed by diagnosis. Not surprisingly, torn Achilles, fractured ankle and Anterior Cruciate Ligament (ACL) sprains ranging from grade 1 to grade 3 come in as the most severe injuries.

The Season Ending % for ACL sprains was 97%. The ACL sprain number was 97% and not 100% because Alabama's Landon Dickerson played the final couple of snaps in the National Championship Game shortly after his ACL reconstruction.

Due to the nature of a shortened season, most teams saw a higher likelihood of concussions and ankle sprains resulting in a player's season ending when compared to previous years.

Injuries by Diagnosis in 2020

Region	Diagnosis	Avg Games Missed	Season Ending %
Achilles Tendon	Tear	7.9	100%
Knee	ACL Sprain	6.7	97%
Fibula	Fracture	4.6	100%
Ankle	Fracture	4.0	100%
Ankle	Sprain	2.7	25%
Foot	Fracture	2.2	60%
Hamstring	Strain	2.1	29%
Neurological	Concussion	1.3	47%

Injury Designations

The player injury designation table summarizes only the players within *The SIS Football Rookie Handbook* who have been identified in their player profile as having at least one of the two designations.

Player Injury Designations

Player	School	Position	Long-Term Risk	Currently Injured
Trevor Lawrence	Clemson	QB		X
Zach Wilson	BYU	QB	X	
Sam Ehlinger	Texas	QB	X	
Shane Simpson	Virginia	RB	X	
Elijah Mitchell	Louisiana	RB	X	
Rakeem Boyd	Arkansas	RB	X	
Jaylen Waddle	Alabama	WR		X
Amari Rodgers	Clemson	WR	X	
Tylan Wallace	Oklahoma State	WR	X	
Marquez Stevenson	Houston	WR	X	
Bailey Gaither	San Jose State	WR	X	
Damonte Coxie	Memphis	WR	X	
Tamorrion Terry	Florida State	WR	X	
Matt Bushman	BYU	TE	X	X
Pat Freiermuth	Penn State	TE		X
Dylan Soehner	Iowa State	TE	X	
Briley Moore	Kansas State	TE	X	
Liam Eichenberg	Notre Dame	OT	X	
Teven Jenkins	Oklahoma State	OG		X

Player Injury Designations

Player	School	Position	Long-Term Risk	Currently Injured
Donavaughn Campbell	Louisiana Tech	OG	X	
Trey Hill	Tennessee	OC	X	X
Landon Dickerson	Alabama	OC	X	X
Malik Herring	Georgia	DT	X	X
Dayo Odeyingbo	Vanderbilt	DT	X	X
Charles Snowden	Virginia	EDGE		X
Azeez Ojulari	Georgia	EDGE	X	
Daelin Hayes	Notre Dame	EDGE	X	
Jaelan Phillips	Miami FL	EDGE	X	
Monty Rice	Georgia	MLB		X
Jabril Cox	LSU	WLB	X	
Chazz Surratt	North Carolina	WLB	X	
Justin Hilliard	Ohio State	WLB	X	
Caleb Farley	Virginia Tech	CB	X	
Marco Wilson	Florida	CB	X	
Olaijah Griffin	USC	CB	X	
Andre Cisco	Syracuse	S		X
Richard LeCounte	Georgia	S		X
Talanoa Hufanga	USC	S	X	

John Verros worked for Indiana University Hospital as a Rehabilitation Specialist following his graduation from the University of Michigan. He graduated in 2015 with an M.S. in the field of Kinesiology with an emphasis in Biomechanics. Specializing in the diagnosis of injury using video, John is the Injury Coordinator at Sports Info Solutions.

COVID-19 Effects in the NFL

Dan Foehrenbach & Sarah Thompson

Sports Info Solutions keeps track of in-depth injury data throughout the season and in the offseason for both College Football and the NFL, including on-field and off-field injuries and illnesses. According to our injury database, there were 86 NFL players who were publicly confirmed to have been diagnosed with COVID-19 in 2020. This subset of players does not include any player who was added to the COVID list due to contract tracing.

Of the 86 players, 60 of them played in at least one 2020 regular season or postseason game before and after their coronavirus diagnosis. Thirty-four of that group played in at least 100 snaps both before and after missing time. To help gauge performance of these players, pre- and post- COVID, an analysis was performed exploring Total Points performance from games played before and after contracting the virus. There are notable differences before and after COVID for many players, but there was almost no evidence that the coronavirus had a measurable effect on player performance in the aggregate.

Overall

For the 60 players who played in at least one game in 2020 before and after coming down with COVID, the average change in Total Points per game is virtually non-existent (and slightly positive) from before the diagnosis to after with an average increase of just under 0.05 Total Points per game. The median change in Total Points per game is a slightly more intuitive but equally miniscule decrease of just under -0.09 Total Points per game. 58 percent of players' performance declined in Total Points per game, but 42 percent of players saw their performance increase. On a per-game basis, it is hard to find evidence that COVID has an overall effect on player performance.

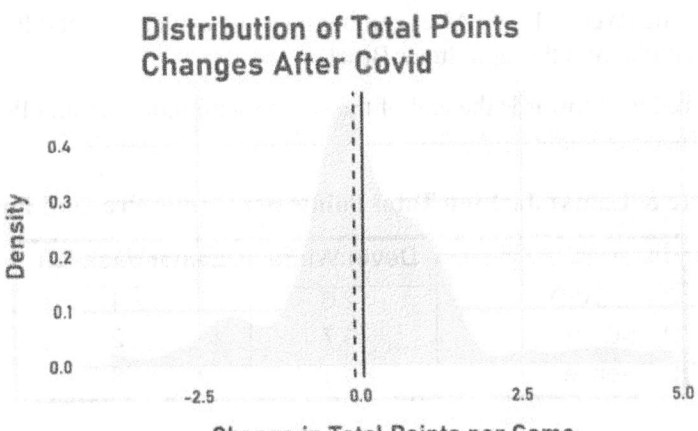

Distribution of Total Points Changes After Covid

If we cut the sample to the 34 players who played at least 100 snaps before and after contracting the virus and look at things on a per-snap basis, the results look similar. The average change from pre- to post-virus was very slightly positive and the median was slightly negative, but both were close to zero. Here we will scale the per-snap rate stats to 60 snaps to approximate the number of non-special teams snaps in a game:

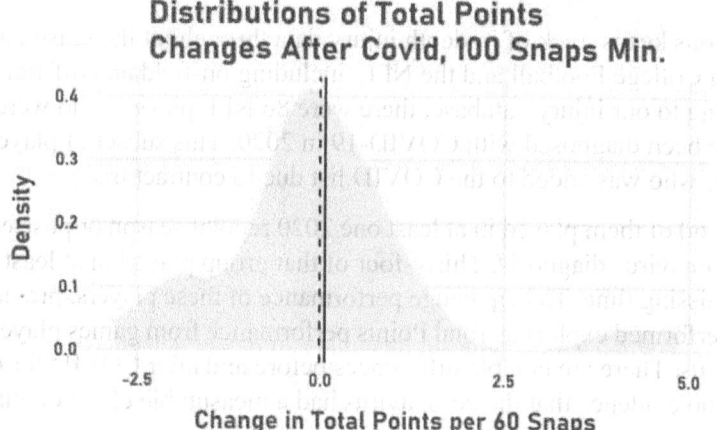

Outliers

While 27 of these 34 players moved by fewer than two Total Points per 60 snaps, there were two players included in the dataset who may have swayed the average. Devin White, who missed Week 17 and Wild-Card weekend, and Lamar Jackson, who missed Week 12, each saw their performance increase by over four Total Points per Game after resuming their seasons.

White, the Tampa Bay Buccaneers linebacker, played extremely well in the postseason, leading his team to the Super Bowl. He was exceptional in pass coverage. He accrued 0.3 Pass Coverage Points Saved per Game before COVID, but since then he was worth a whopping 5.6 Pass Coverage Points Saved per Game. Likewise, before going out he earned 39 Total Points overall, averaging 2.6 per game (Weeks 1-16). After coming back, he earned 20 Total Points, averaging 6.7 per game (Divisional Playoffs through Super Bowl).

Lamar Jackson played well towards the end of the season with more Passing Points Earned and Rushing Points Earned per game.

Devin White & Lamar Jackson Total Points per Game: Pre- and Post-COVID

	Devin White	Lamar Jackson
Pre-COVID	2.6	2.4
Post-COVID	6.7	7.2
Difference	+4.1	+4.8

Quarterbacks

There were two prominent quarterbacks who were diagnosed with the coronavirus during the 2020 season: Cam Newton in October, causing him to miss Week 4, and Lamar Jackson in November, causing him to miss Week 12. In the games prior to testing positive, Cam Newton earned 17 Total Points, averaging 5.5 per game. When he returned, Newton earned 41 Total Points, averaging 3.4 per game. In the games prior to his illness, Lamar Jackson earned 24 Total Points, averaging 2.4 per game, but after he returned Jackson earned 51 Total Points, averaging 7.2 per game.

Newton and Jackson are both dual-threat quarterbacks. Looking at the passing data from before and after, Cam Newton had a negative change in Completion Percentage, On-Target Percentage, Passing Yards per Game and Passing Points Earned per Game. However, Lamar Jackson had a positive change in Completion Percentage and Passing Points Earned per Game, but a negative change in On-Target Percentage and Passing Yards per Game.

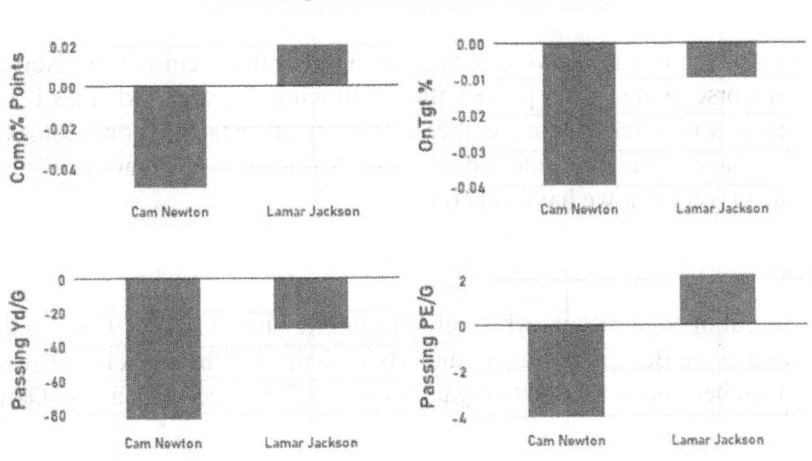

QB Passing Performance Changes Post-Covid

Because these two quarterbacks tend to run the ball effectively, rushing data was also evaluated.

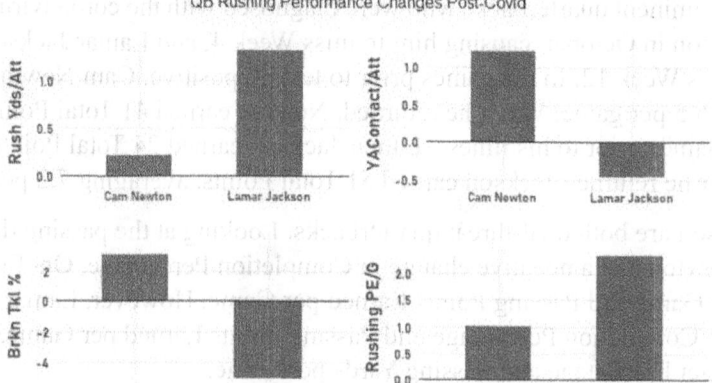

QB Rushing Performance Changes Post-Covid

Both quarterbacks were more effective running the ball after their return. Cam Newton's overall performance was worse in the games played after contracting the virus, whereas Lamar Jackson's overall performance was better. Of course, there are many other factors going into why their performances may have changed besides coronavirus. Suffice it to say that there is no evidence of a pattern from the players that we have data on.

Edge Rushers

There were a handful of edge rushers who were diagnosed with COVID-19 during the 2020 season. Matt Judon of the Baltimore Ravens and Myles Garrett of the Cleveland Browns were both diagnosed in November. Judon missed two games (Week 12 & Week 13), as did Garrett (Week 11 & Week 12).

Before contracting the virus, Matt Judon earned 19 Total Points, averaging 1.9 per game, but after coming back he earned 15 Total Points, averaging 2.5 per game. On the other hand, before he got sick, Myles Garrett earned 30 Total Points, averaging 3.3 per game, but after returning, Garrett earned just 9 Total Points, averaging only 1.3 per game.

Judon, who will be entering free agency this off-season, led the Ravens in 2020 with six sacks and 40 QB pressures. Garrett led the Browns with 12 sacks and 47 QB pressures. Both players were important playmakers on their defensive units. Looking at the data from games played pre- and post-COVID, Judon played fewer snaps, had a lower Rush Percentage and Pressure Percentage, but had a slight increase in Total Points Saved per Game in the games he played after the virus. Garrett, who was revealing in talking about the lingering effects from COVID-19, played more Snaps per Game, had a lower Rush Percentage and Pressure Percentage and a clear negative impact in Pass Rush Points Saved per Game and Run Defense Points Saved per Game after coming back.

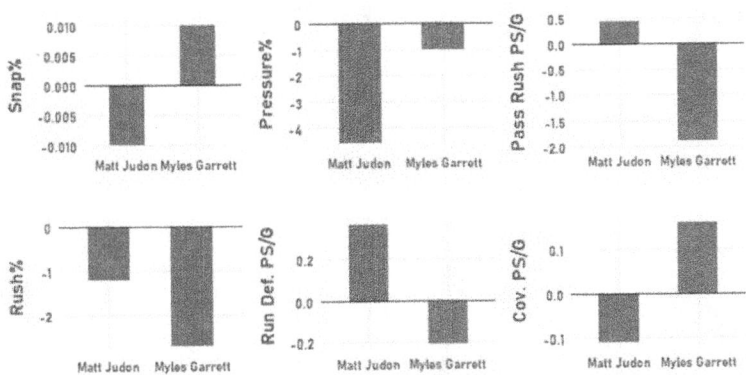

Edge Rusher Performance Changes after Covid

Conclusion

There are still a lot of unknowns about the effects of the coronavirus, especially how the virus impacts players differently. As mentioned earlier, Sports Info Solutions recorded 86 NFL players who were publicly confirmed to have been diagnosed with COVID-19 in 2020. Some players showed a decline in performance and some players showed an increase in performance. So far, no pattern has emerged that leads us to believe that aside from missing playing time, the virus has a measurable on-field effect. We wish everybody dealing with the effects of COVID a healthy and speedy recovery through these unprecedented times.

Conclusion

The Effects of Turf on Injuries in the NFL

Matt Manocherian

Most people who have played football on turf will generally agree that—well—it hurts! Even as technology has improved and artificial surfaces have gotten better, NFLPA President JC Tretter made the case as recently as 2020 that the NFL should move away from turf fields for both practices and games because of the impact that they can have on players' bodies.[1] He cited injury data from the NFL that showed elevated injury risk on turf relative to grass to back up his point. Specifically, he pointed to non-contact lower extremity injuries as the main culprit.

Previous research jibes with Tretter's argument to varying degrees. Our friend, Dr. Zach Binney, wrote for Football Outsiders in 2017 about how certain turf types performed slightly more poorly in terms of injury risk when compared to grass, but he stopped short of making any definitive conclusions.[2] Additionally, Loughran et al. wrote about knee injury incidence on turf versus grass in college football in the American Journal of Sports Medicine in 2019, finding that artificial turf was a significant risk factor for certain knee ligament injuries.[3]

Since we have the most comprehensive football injury database in existence, we decided to take a look to see what we could find.

Are NFL injury rates higher on turf or grass?

In the NFL over the last four years, there have been both more total injuries and more injuries forcing players to leave the game on games played on turf relative to grass.

NFL Injuries by Field Type (2017-2020, Regular Season only)

Field Type	Games	Injuries Per Game	Left the Field Per Game
Grass	587	5.0	4.1
Turf	437	5.4	4.5
Percent Change		+7.8%	+9.2%

This indicates that about 48 extra injuries that cause players to leave the field are occurring each regular season needlessly because almost half of NFL teams play their home games on turf.

---

1. JC Tretter, "Only Natural Grass Can Level The NFL's Playing Field," NFLPA.com, https://nflpa.com/posts/only-natural-grass-can-level-the-nfls-playing-field.
2. Zachary Binney, "Turf Type and NFL Injuries Part I," FootballOutsiders.com, 2017, https://www.footballoutsiders.com/stat-analysis/2017/turf-type-and-nfl-injuries-part-i.
3. Galvin J Loughran, Christian T Vulpis, Jordan P Murphy, David A Weiner, Steven J Svoboda, Richard Y Hinton, Dave P Milzman, "Incidence of Knee Injuries on Artificial Turf Versus Natural Grass in National Collegiate Athletic Association American Football: 2004-2005 Through 2013-2014 Seasons," American Journal of Sports Medicine, May 2019, https://pubmed.ncbi.nlm.nih.gov/30995074/.

To be fair, these numbers could be biased by the teams that play in the stadiums. In other words, any team-level factor from the players to the training staff to the cafeteria could be a confounding factor that is actually responsible for the injury rates. To account for this, we can look at just away players to help control for the fact that the home team's players make up about half of all snaps played in any given stadium.

NFL Injuries by Field Type (Away Players only)

Field Type	Games	Injuries Per Game	Left the Field Per Game
Grass	587	2.5	2.1
Turf	437	2.8	2.3
Percent Change		8.8%	7.7%

The effect appears to be about as large for the road teams, indicating that our initial finding isn't a result of home teams biasing the study. For the rest of the article, we will generally use the totals across home and away players for the sake of sample size, but we will indicate if/where there are any differences of note.

As an aside, if you notice that away players are generally slightly more likely to be injured and leave the game than home players, that is an astute observation by you. This result is consistent from season to season, but it's not the subject of this article.

Which body parts are most affected by turf?

Previous research suggests that lower extremity injuries, specifically, are more likely to see an increase on turf. We found this to be true in the case of ankle/foot injuries, but not so for the rest of the legs, including knees.

NFL Injuries Per Game by Field Type and Body Part

Body Part	Grass	Turf	Percent Change
Head	0.76	0.90	+18%
Shoulder	0.39	0.42	+9%
Arm/Hand	0.42	0.43	+1%
Core	0.34	0.37	+9%
Upper Legs / Hips	0.46	0.46	-1%
Lower Legs / Knee	1.25	1.23	-2%
Ankle/Foot	0.96	1.05	+10%

It's worth noting that these results are generally very consistent when we split the sample to look at away players only, injuries that forced the player to leave the field only, and both.

One thing that sticks out is that shoulder, core, and to an even larger extent head injuries are occurring considerably more often. While it's not clear why this is happening, when we consider that each team hosts eight regular season games per year, the increase of 0.14 head injuries per game represents an additional 1.12 head injuries per team that chooses to play on turf per season. Another way to think of that is that each year that each turf team continues to play on their surface, they are adding more than one unnecessary head injury every time.

Still, the most surprising finding was that lower leg and knee injuries decreased on turf fields when compared to grass fields. While the difference was small and inconsistent from year to year, previous research had indicated that these were precisely the injuries that turf seemed to induce, so the finding that there is no real difference in this sample is notable.

One potential explanation for this is that the makers of the artificial turf that the NFL teams have been using have been able to focus their technological improvements on this previously identified weakness. If that is the case and not a four-year anomaly, then hopefully head, shoulder, core, and ankle/foot injuries can see a positive change as well.

What types of injuries are occurring more (or less) on turf?

The specific injury diagnoses that had been found by previous research to increase on turf included knee and ankle sprains. To be clear, sprains include what people colloquially describe as tears. Anytime a ligament is sprained, that just means that there is some level of tearing going on.

Percent Difference in NFL Injury Diagnoses Per Game on Turf Compared to Grass

Diagnosis	All Players	Away Players Only
Knee Sprain	-3%	-6%
Ankle Sprain	+4%	+6%

The numbers mostly match up with what we saw when breaking things down by body part. In this sample, knee sprains are slightly down on turf and ankle sprains are slightly up, but neither change by significant amounts. The magnitude of these changes were much smaller than what was observed by previous research, which in some cases found double-digit increases on turf.

How do contact vs non-contact injuries factor into this?

NFL Injuries per Game by Field and Contact Type (2017-2020)

Field Type	Non-Contact	Contact with Ground	Contact with Player
Grass	0.82	0.80	3.39
Turf	0.80	0.85	3.76
Percent Change	-3%	+6%	+11%

Once again, our findings are at odds with previous research. We're again seeing a slight decrease in injury rates on turf relative to grass where we expected to see an increase, this time in the form of non-contact injuries. Still, injuries involving contact between two players are much more common, and the magnitude of increase in those sorts of injuries on turf compared to grass offsets the decrease in non-contact injuries several times over.

The effects are consistent whether we look at all players, only away players, only injuries that cause players to leave the field, or away players whose injuries cause them to leave the field.

Percent Difference in NFL Injuries Per Game By Contact Type on Turf Compared to Grass

Contact Type	All Injuries	Injuries to Away Players Only	Significant Injuries (Left The Field)	Away Players & Left The Field
Non-Contact	-3%	-14%	+1%	-13%
Contact with Ground	+6%	+8%	+10%	+8%
Contact with Player	+11%	+15%	+11%	+13%

What about non-contact lower body injuries?

JC Tretter mentioned three specific data points when he called on the NFL teams to adopt grass practice and playing surfaces in September of 2020:

> "Specifically, players have a 28% higher rate of non-contact lower extremity injuries when playing on artificial turf. Of those non-contact injuries, players have a 32% higher rate of non-contact knee injuries on turf and a staggering 69% higher rate of non-contact foot/ankle injuries on turf compared to grass."

While he was citing the NFL's own injury data, which is both from different seasons (2012 to 2018) than our dataset covers and seems to mix data from practices and games, these results were not at all consistent with our findings.

Percent Difference in NFL Non-Contact Injuries Per Game By Body Part on Turf Compared to Grass

Body Part	All Injuries	Injuries to Away Players Only	Significant Injuries (Left The Field)	Away Players & Left The Field
Lower Extremity	-12%	-17%	-11%	-15%
Knee	-18%	-30%	-16%	-23%
Ankle/Foot	-3%	+6%	-2%	0%

Just about any way we sliced it, non-contact lower extremity injuries were reduced, not increased, on turf relative to grass. It was "Contact with Player" injuries, which are much more common to begin with, that drove the overall increase in injury rates on turf.

Last Word

The SIS Injury Database matched previous research on the topic of grass versus turf in that we have observed a clear increase in injuries per game in stadiums with turf in NFL games over the last four years. However, our findings do not match prior research in that we did not find an increase in non-contact and/or knee injuries. Instead, we found that injuries occurring because of contact between players were overwhelmingly what accounted for the increase in injuries.

Somewhat concerningly, we saw an increase in head injuries on turf, so we will keep a close eye on how these trends continue to develop in the years to come.

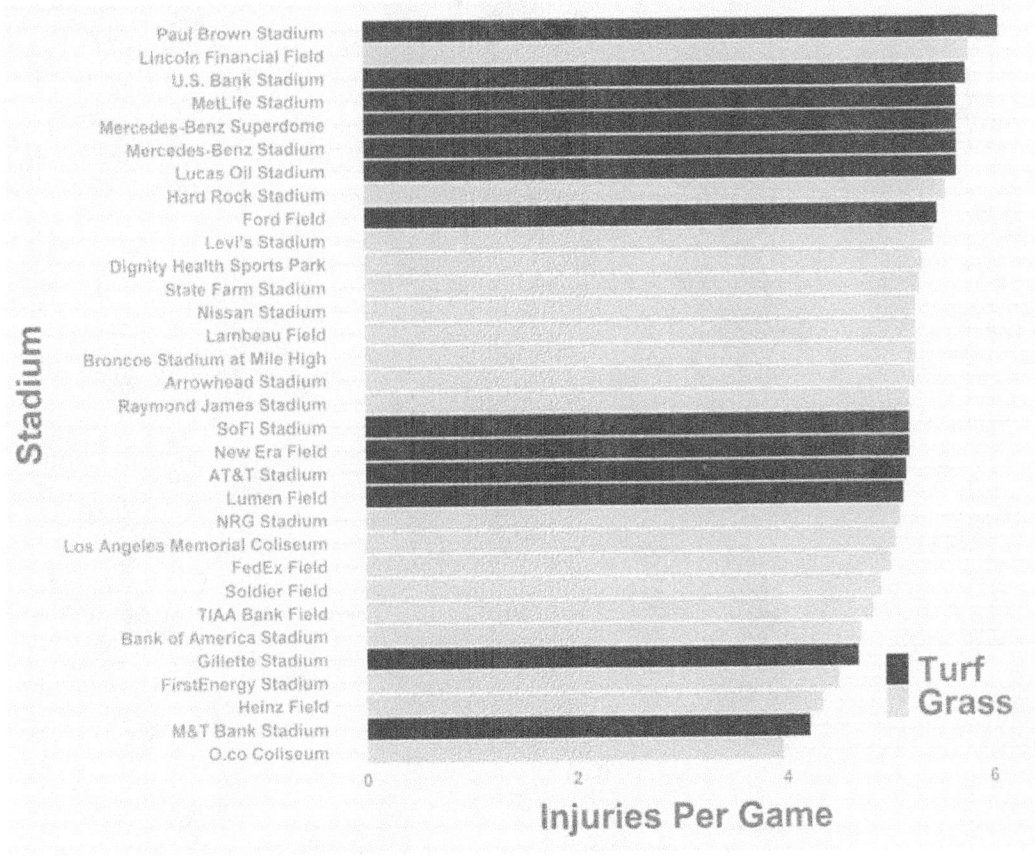

NFL Injuries Per Game by Stadium and Field Type (2017–2020)

Projecting Injury Risk in the NFL

John Shirley

Unfortunately, injuries are a fact of life in the NFL. Every year there are multiple star players whose seasons are derailed and teams whose championship aspirations are dashed due to injury. Last season we saw this play out in Dallas, when quarterback Dak Prescott's season-ending ankle injury effectively marked the end of the Cowboys' playoff hopes. We also saw it in San Francisco, where injuries plagued the defending NFC champions and resulted in a disappointing 6-10 record.

Due to their impact on shaping how each season plays out, understanding injuries is an important part of football research. Previous sections of this book have highlighted the extensive data that SIS collects on every NFL and NCAA injury, as well as a look at how it can be used to show the effects field surface type has on injuries. In this section we will discuss SIS's next step in injury research: projecting injury risk.

It should be noted that any attempt at predicting injuries, as with any projection system, will never be an exact science. We do not have access to players' medical records or biometric data. Injuries are also relatively rare events, and some are the result of truly random events on the field. Even with that knowledge, we can still do our best to attempt to model a relationship between what we know about each player's relevant metrics and his risk of being injured during a given season.

This past fall in the 2021 *Bill James Handbook*, SIS released a first glimpse at injury risk projections for MLB players. Over the past few months, we have worked on applying a similar projection system to the NFL. This system covers all position groups, but for the purposes of this article we will only be discussing it in terms of offensive skill position players.

These NFL injury risk projections were built using a machine learning model to calculate the probability of each player sustaining a relevant injury during the rest of the season. For the purposes of this research, a relevant injury is defined as any injury that results in the player being expected to miss at least 10 days.

Our models separate players by position groups to better capture unique aspects of what each player is asked to do on the field. Offensive skill players are grouped together, but within the grouping we include specific positional and playing-time metrics that allow the models to get a complete picture of each player's true role.

Other inputs into our models include metrics that measure each player's age, body type, injury history, and playing style. These models were trained on a random selection of player seasons from 2017-2020 and then tested on an out-of-sample portion of player seasons from the same time period. A look at how well our model performed on our out-of-sample dataset is shown below:

Predicted Injury Probability	Number of Cases in Out-Of-Sample Dataset	Relevant Injuries	Percentage Injured
30% and Up	87	23	26%
20-29%	317	66	21%
10-19%	1052	172	16%
0-9%	2378	144	6%

The results of looking at the models during the offseason provide us with some insight into which inputs known before the season have the most impact on injuries (the model updates to incorporate up-to-date information during the season). Some of the most critical inputs within our model for skill position players included speed and agility measures, alignment usage, how often the player was asked to block, broken tackles per touch, yards gained after contact, and of course injury history metrics.

Our injury risk projection models are a first step towards more accurately predicting injury risk. Over the offseason, and in the years to come, we will be continuing this research and more like it. For now though, we offer our readers a glimpse at our initial 2021 NFL injury risk projections.

Before we show some examples of our 2021 projections, we want to point out that these are very early initial projections of the likelihood each player is to sustain a relevant injury during next season. A lot can change over the course of the next few months before the start of the season. Obviously there will be a lot of roster movement over this time, and therefore players' roles will change. There will also be injuries along the way. These and other factors will impact our projections as we gain new information and get closer to the season.

With that said, here are the top players at each skill position with the highest injury risk projection for the 2021 season:

Top QB's by 2021 Injury Risk Projection (Min 300 Snaps in 2020)

Player	2021 Injury Risk Projection
Mitchell Trubisky	19%
Gardner Minshew	19%
Alex Smith	16%
Dak Prescott	16%
Drew Lock	15%

By looking at the quarterbacks with the highest injury risk projection, you should be able to immediately see why we warned that these are initial projections. Per our model, Mitchell Trubisky and Gardner Minshew both project as having a relatively high injury risk. But, what the model is unable to know at this moment in time, is that both are more than likely going to be backups by the start of next season. This would of course decrease their projections as playing time is a part of the model.

The next quarterback on the list is probably more in tune with your expectations. Alex Smith sustained a career threatening injury two years ago and, despite making a recovery, was still dealing with some of the effects in 2020. Other quarterbacks who just missed this list include Lamar Jackson, Kyler Murray, Joe Burrow, and Cam Newton.

Top RB's by 2021 Injury Risk Projection (Min 200 Snaps in 2020)

Player	2021 Injury Risk Projection
Rex Burkhead	59%
Darrell Henderson Jr.	49%
Raheem Mostert	34%
Le'Veon Bell	33%
Zack Moss	33%

Running backs as a group had the highest average injury risk, which makes sense due to the high number of hits they are asked to take. Rex Burkhead has the distinction of having the highest projected injury risk of any skill player entering 2021. This is due to his dual role as a running back and core special teamer, along with his long injury history, which most recently includes a torn ACL suffered in November.

Similar to Burkhead, Darrell Henderson Jr. and Raheem Mostert also ended 2020 on IR, which impacts their projections. Henderson Jr. suffered a high ankle sprain in December, while Mostert suffered multiple injuries in 2020, including a MCL sprain, concussion, and multiple high ankle sprains.

In what might be a surprise to some, Titans running back Derrick Henry was nowhere near the top of our projections. Despite leading the NFL in carries in both of the last two years, Henry has a remarkably clean bill of health. Our model does factor in usage and playing time, but Henry still has an injury risk projection of only 12% entering 2021.

Top WR's by 2021 Injury Risk Projection (Min 200 Snaps in 2020)

Player	2021 Injury Risk Projection
Marvin Jones	28%
Mike Evans	28%
Sammy Watkins	25%
Randall Cobb	24%
Odell Beckham	24%
Will Fuller V	23%

The top of the wide receiver list probably has the fewest surprises of any of these leaderboards. Watkins, Cobb, and Beckham all suffered relevant injuries within the past year, while Fuller has one of the longest injury histories at the position. Evans also has a long injury history, though his are mostly minor in-game injury events charted by our video scouts. Marvin Jones having the highest projection is the one surprise at the position after having a clean bill of health in 2020, though he did end 2018 and 2019 on IR.

Top TE's by 2021 Injury Risk Projection (Min 200 Snaps in 2020)

Player	2021 Injury Risk Projection
Darren Waller	36%
Noah Fant	32%
Jordan Reed	21%
Logan Thomas	20%
Evan Engram	18%

Darren Waller having the highest injury risk projection among tight ends is a little surprising. He does not have the type of injury history that would normally be a red flag, but rather has been a high-volume player who has similar relevant metrics as past players who have sustained injuries.

Jordan Reed having the third highest injury risk projection among tight ends is also a little surprising, but in the opposite direction as Waller. Reed has the significant injury history of a player who we would normally expect to have a higher risk. But, at this point in his career he is a backup who played sparingly in 2020, which the model is aware of and takes into account. Just missing the list is Zach Ertz, another player with a long injury history.

As mentioned, these are only the initial 2021 projections and we have a long way to go until the season starts. As we get closer to the start of the season our projections will update with new information. This is also just the first of our steps into both projecting injury risk and creating more advanced injury related metrics. Our research efforts into injuries will continue in the future and we hope to offer updates along the way.

NFL Team Pages

Before we get into the prospects heading into the league this year, we want to give you a look at the league they're entering. The goal of the team pages is to provide detailed information about each NFL team as constructed at the end of the season, prior to free agency. Whether it be determining which positions a team may be looking to draft early or which players in later rounds may fit best based on scheme, the team pages provide a broad look at the most important information to know entering draft season.

The high-level summary for each team includes Pythagorean Wins, SIS WAR-xWins, and Decision Score Rank. Pythagorean Wins and SIS-WAR xWins each calculate how many games a team would have been expected to win based on their performance. Pythagorean Wins uses score differential to make this estimate, while SIS-WAR xWins uses SIS's proprietary WAR metric, which is otherwise only available to NFL teams. Comparing each to a team's actual wins can be a good barometer for whether a team underperformed or overperformed in a given season. A team's raw Decision Score is calculated based on how often a team's decision on fourth down was in line with what would have been recommended by SIS's win probability model. Their Decision Score Rank represents how they compare to the league, with '1/32' being the best, and '32/32' being the worst.

Each team page also includes a comprehensive positional breakdown using SIS's proprietary player-value metric, Total Points, as well as a breakdown of a team's personnel usage, key rookies from this past season, and performance splits on both offense and defense.

Top Personnel Groupings looks at the team's three most commonly used personnel packages from the 2020 season.

Key 2020 rookies were determined based on player performance in 2020, as well as their expected contribution in 2021.

Man and zone splits for both offense and defense exclude prevent defense, combo, screens, and spikes.

Arizona Cardinals

3rd NFC West

SIS-WAR xWins	Pythagorean Wins	Actual Wins	Decision Score Rank
8.3	9.3	8	4 / 32

Position Strengths

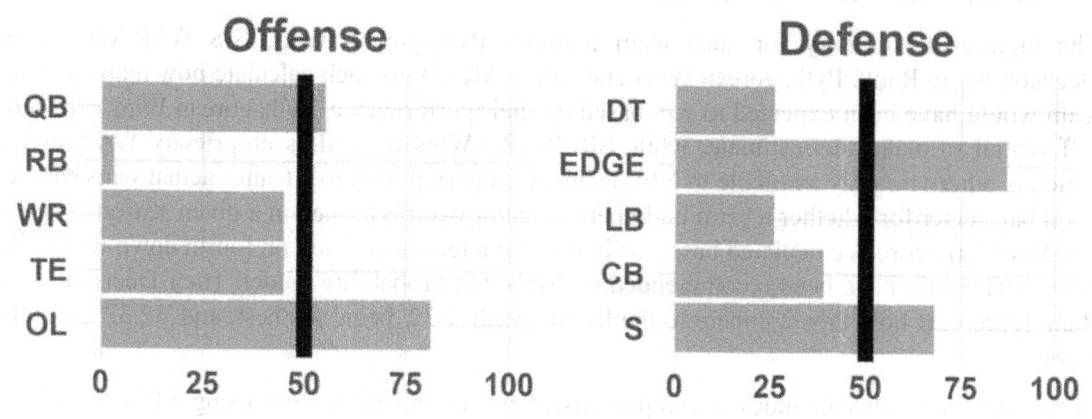

Percentile rank of Total Points for each team by position

Top Personnel Groupings

Group	Pct	Rank	EPA/P	Rank
11	46%	28	0.00	19
12	28%	7	0.02	15
10	21%	1	0.05	10

Key 2020 Rookies

Rd	Player	Pos	Total Points
1	I. Simmons	LB	15
4	L. Fotu	DT	4
3	J. Jones	T	1

Offensive Identity

Split	Pct	Rank	EPA/P	Rank
Shotgun	91%	2	0.01	18
Under Center	9%	31	0.07	4
Motion	21%	32	0.13	4
No Motion	79%	1	-0.01	17
Gap Run	32%	13	-0.08	19
Zone Run	68%	20	0.00	2
Play Action	30%	8	0.16	12
Dropback	70%	25	-0.01	20
vs. Man	20%	32	-0.03	19
vs. Zone	64%	2	0.05	19
vs. Blitz	20%	31	0.05	17
Under Pres	24%	30	-0.61	26

Defensive Identity

Split	Pct	Rank	EPA/P	Rank
Base	31%	8	0.05	27
Nickel	53%	23	-0.05	7
Dime+	1%	26	-0.02	16
Gap Run	30%	17	-0.05	10
Zone Run	70%	16	-0.08	21
Man	44%	2	-0.03	15
Zone	46%	31	0.06	14
3 Rushers	4%	23	0.12	16
4 Rushers	56%	26	0.00	12
5 Rushers	27%	4	0.07	20
6+ Rushers	12%	2	0.00	15
Pressure	34%	11	-0.44	8

Atlanta Falcons

4th NFC South

SIS-WAR xWins	Pythagorean Wins	Actual Wins	Decision Score Rank
7.7	7.5	4	8 / 32

Position Strengths

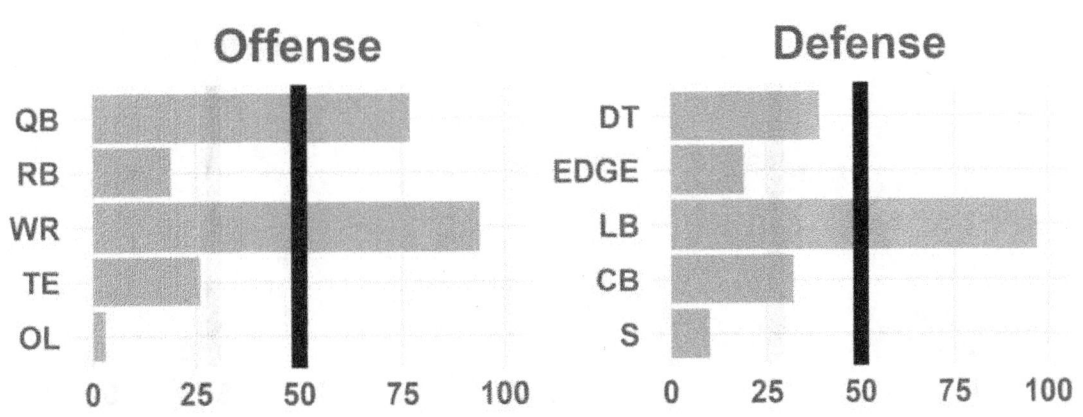

Percentile rank of Total Points for each team by position

Top Personnel Groupings

Group	Pct	Rank	EPA/P	Rank
11	62%	16	0.05	11
12	14%	24	0.03	10
21	12%	8	-0.08	22

Key 2020 Rookies

Rd	Player	Pos	Total Points
1	A. Terrell	CB	15
4	M. Walker	LB	12
2	M. Davidson	DT	1

Offensive Identity

Split	Pct	Rank	EPA/P	Rank
Shotgun	54%	26	0.03	14
Under Center	46%	7	-0.03	15
Motion	45%	14	-0.03	21
No Motion	55%	19	0.02	11
Gap Run	32%	12	-0.16	26
Zone Run	68%	21	-0.12	22
Play Action	26%	17	0.21	6
Dropback	74%	16	0.02	17
vs. Man	33%	13	-0.11	24
vs. Zone	60%	9	0.20	4
vs. Blitz	26%	16	0.10	11
Under Pres	36%	7	-0.27	8

Defensive Identity

Split	Pct	Rank	EPA/P	Rank
Base	23%	16	-0.16	4
Nickel	75%	4	0.09	25
Dime+	0%	32	1.42	32
Gap Run	26%	23	-0.14	5
Zone Run	74%	10	-0.14	8
Man	36%	12	0.16	27
Zone	49%	24	0.12	23
3 Rushers	9%	11	0.49	31
4 Rushers	61%	20	0.10	23
5 Rushers	25%	7	0.03	17
6+ Rushers	4%	21	0.15	23
Pressure	32%	18	-0.26	21

Baltimore Ravens

2nd AFC North

SIS-WAR xWins	Pythagorean Wins	Actual Wins	Decision Score Rank
10.4	12.6	11	6 / 32

Position Strengths

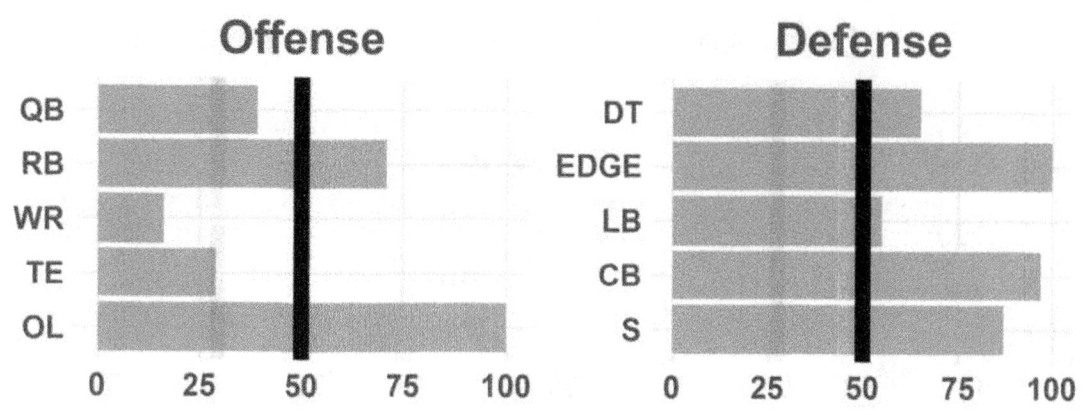

Percentile rank of Total Points for each team by position

Top Personnel Groupings

Group	Pct	Rank	EPA/P	Rank
11	53%	26	0.09	7
22	15%	1	0.04	5
21	13%	6	0.13	9

Key 2020 Rookies

Rd	Player	Pos	Total Points
1	P. Queen	LB	34
3	T. Phillips	G	15
2	J. Dobbins	RB	10

Offensive Identity

Split	Pct	Rank	EPA/P	Rank
Shotgun	95%	1	0.07	6
Under Center	5%	32	-0.14	26
Motion	68%	2	0.12	6
No Motion	32%	31	-0.07	24
Gap Run	54%	1	0.24	1
Zone Run	46%	32	-0.11	19
Play Action	31%	6	0.08	19
Dropback	69%	27	0.04	14
vs. Man	23%	31	0.02	18
vs. Zone	69%	1	0.09	14
vs. Blitz	23%	22	-0.07	25
Under Pres	32%	16	-0.37	16

Defensive Identity

Split	Pct	Rank	EPA/P	Rank
Base	20%	22	-0.06	17
Nickel	61%	15	-0.10	4
Dime+	16%	13	-0.03	15
Gap Run	25%	25	-0.24	2
Zone Run	75%	8	-0.09	20
Man	37%	9	-0.15	5
Zone	49%	25	-0.02	7
3 Rushers	6%	18	-0.57	1
4 Rushers	54%	30	-0.08	6
5 Rushers	32%	1	0.08	23
6+ Rushers	7%	10	-0.09	11
Pressure	36%	7	-0.43	9

Buffalo Bills

1st AFC East

SIS-WAR xWins	Pythagorean Wins	Actual Wins	Decision Score Rank
13.7	11.3	13	T1 / 32

Position Strengths

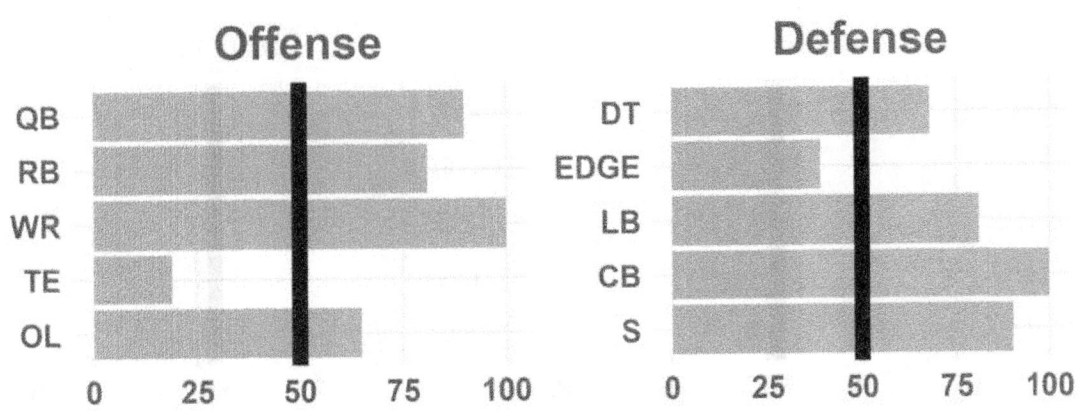

Percentile rank of Total Points for each team by position

Top Personnel Groupings

Group	Pct	Rank	EPA/P	Rank
11	73%	4	0.12	4
10	15%	2	0.20	5
12	8%	31	0.11	6

Key 2020 Rookies

Rd	Player	Pos	Total Points
3	Z. Moss	RB	11
4	G. Davis	WR	10
2	A. Epenesa	DE	5

Offensive Identity

Split	Pct	Rank	EPA/P	Rank
Shotgun	69%	12	0.16	2
Under Center	31%	21	-0.04	16
Motion	41%	21	0.05	11
No Motion	59%	12	0.14	1
Gap Run	27%	17	-0.22	31
Zone Run	73%	16	-0.11	17
Play Action	33%	2	0.22	4
Dropback	67%	31	0.22	2
vs. Man	36%	5	0.32	1
vs. Zone	52%	29	0.15	8
vs. Blitz	33%	2	0.24	2
Under Pres	35%	9	-0.09	2

Defensive Identity

Split	Pct	Rank	EPA/P	Rank
Base	6%	30	0.17	31
Nickel	91%	1	-0.04	11
Dime+	1%	27	0.59	31
Gap Run	28%	19	0.08	27
Zone Run	72%	14	-0.06	23
Man	27%	22	-0.08	10
Zone	61%	12	0.01	9
3 Rushers	1%	31	-0.31	3
4 Rushers	67%	12	0.01	13
5 Rushers	23%	10	-0.07	8
6+ Rushers	8%	8	-0.06	13
Pressure	32%	20	-0.35	16

Carolina Panthers

3rd NFC South

SIS-WAR xWins	Pythagorean Wins	Actual Wins	Decision Score Rank
6.9	6.4	5	19 / 32

Position Strengths

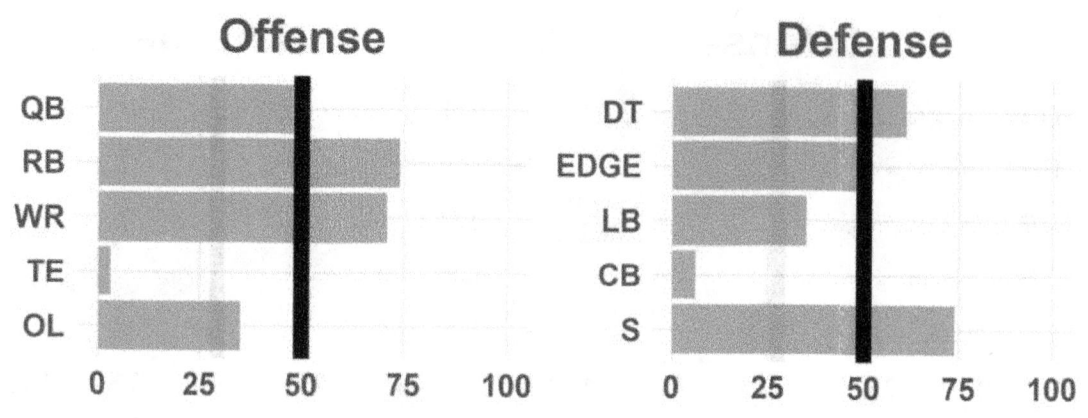

Percentile rank of Total Points for each team by position

Top Personnel Groupings

Group	Pct	Rank	EPA/P	Rank
11	56%	21	0.02	14
12	18%	19	-0.06	25
21	8%	12	0.00	20

Key 2020 Rookies

Rd	Player	Pos	Total Points
2	J. Chinn	S	29
1	D. Brown	DT	21
2	Y. Gross-Matos	DE	13

Offensive Identity

Split	Pct	Rank	EPA/P	Rank
Shotgun	61%	20	-0.01	21
Under Center	39%	13	-0.05	18
Motion	51%	8	0.01	13
No Motion	49%	25	-0.05	21
Gap Run	34%	8	0.09	7
Zone Run	66%	25	-0.17	29
Play Action	20%	28	-0.08	27
Dropback	80%	5	0.03	16
vs. Man	29%	24	0.07	14
vs. Zone	59%	10	0.00	23
vs. Blitz	26%	14	-0.06	24
Under Pres	31%	18	-0.39	19

Defensive Identity

Split	Pct	Rank	EPA/P	Rank
Base	5%	31	-0.11	12
Nickel	52%	24	-0.02	14
Dime+	41%	3	0.08	21
Gap Run	34%	8	0.02	18
Zone Run	66%	25	-0.10	17
Man	17%	32	0.13	25
Zone	69%	2	0.09	21
3 Rushers	20%	2	0.08	14
4 Rushers	60%	23	0.02	14
5 Rushers	15%	27	0.16	26
6+ Rushers	4%	22	0.17	24
Pressure	32%	22	-0.32	17

Chicago Bears

2nd NFC North

SIS-WAR xWins	Pythagorean Wins	Actual Wins	Decision Score Rank
6.0	8.1	8	22 / 32

Position Strengths

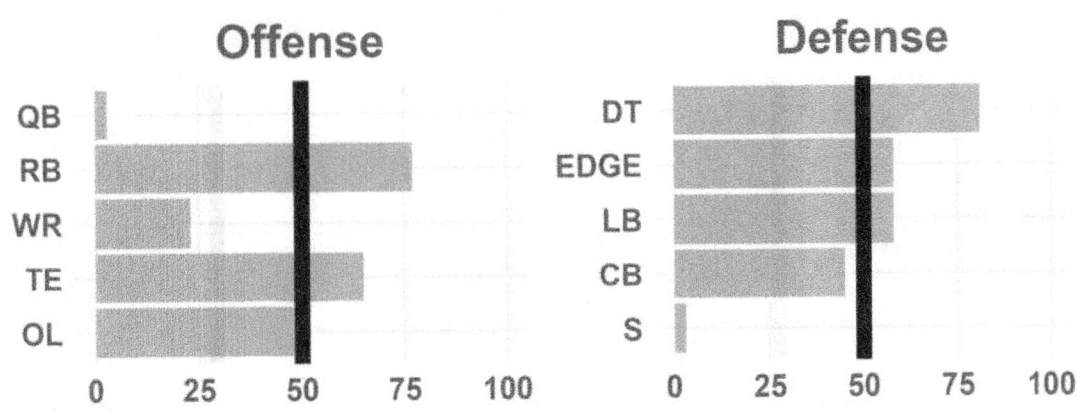

Percentile rank of Total Points for each team by position

Top Personnel Groupings

Group	Pct	Rank	EPA/P	Rank
11	55%	22	-0.08	26
12	19%	16	0.02	12
01	8%	1	-0.13	18

Key 2020 Rookies

Rd	Player	Pos	Total Points
2	J. Johnson	CB	32
5	D. Mooney	WR	17
2	C. Kmet	TE	10

Offensive Identity

Split	Pct	Rank	EPA/P	Rank
Shotgun	64%	18	-0.09	28
Under Center	36%	15	0.01	9
Motion	37%	26	-0.01	18
No Motion	63%	7	-0.08	26
Gap Run	16%	31	-0.22	30
Zone Run	84%	2	-0.04	7
Play Action	28%	10	0.16	13
Dropback	71%	23	-0.13	27
vs. Man	31%	19	-0.04	21
vs. Zone	60%	7	-0.02	25
vs. Blitz	22%	27	-0.05	22
Under Pres	30%	22	-0.31	12

Defensive Identity

Split	Pct	Rank	EPA/P	Rank
Base	33%	6	-0.14	6
Nickel	52%	25	0.08	24
Dime+	13%	15	-0.14	6
Gap Run	23%	29	0.05	24
Zone Run	77%	4	-0.18	1
Man	28%	20	-0.09	8
Zone	62%	10	0.15	25
3 Rushers	5%	19	0.13	18
4 Rushers	74%	5	0.06	20
5 Rushers	18%	21	0.02	13
6+ Rushers	2%	30	-0.14	8
Pressure	32%	23	-0.25	22

Cincinnati Bengals

4th AFC North

SIS-WAR xWins	Pythagorean Wins	Actual Wins	Decision Score Rank
2.7	4.5	4	9 / 32

Position Strengths

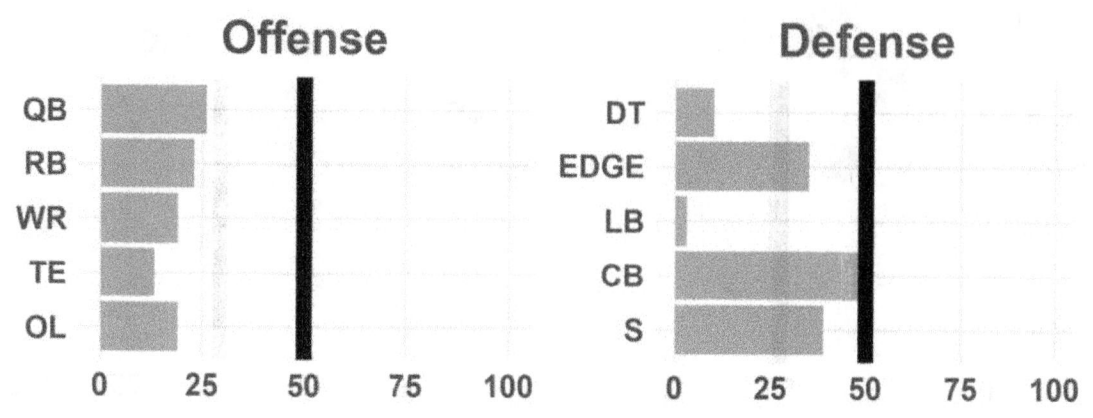

Percentile rank of Total Points for each team by position

Top Personnel Groupings

Group	Pct	Rank	EPA/P	Rank
11	76%	2	-0.08	25
12	15%	23	-0.03	22
10	4%	4	-0.33	16

Key 2020 Rookies

Rd	Player	Pos	Total Points
1	J. Burrow	QB	49
2	T. Higgins	WR	24
3	L. Wilson	LB	11

Offensive Identity

Split	Pct	Rank	EPA/P	Rank
Shotgun	76%	9	-0.09	26
Under Center	24%	24	-0.06	20
Motion	40%	23	-0.06	24
No Motion	60%	10	-0.09	27
Gap Run	25%	21	-0.32	32
Zone Run	75%	12	-0.03	4
Play Action	22%	25	-0.01	22
Dropback	78%	8	-0.09	25
vs. Man	32%	17	-0.12	25
vs. Zone	58%	17	-0.05	27
vs. Blitz	23%	21	0.06	15
Under Pres	32%	17	-0.61	27

Defensive Identity

Split	Pct	Rank	EPA/P	Rank
Base	21%	21	-0.04	18
Nickel	62%	13	0.10	27
Dime+	13%	16	-0.01	17
Gap Run	43%	1	0.09	28
Zone Run	57%	32	-0.10	16
Man	41%	5	0.10	22
Zone	49%	27	0.20	28
3 Rushers	7%	12	-0.02	12
4 Rushers	64%	19	0.17	28
5 Rushers	20%	17	0.02	14
6+ Rushers	9%	4	0.02	16
Pressure	27%	31	-0.24	23

Cleveland Browns

3rd AFC North

SIS-WAR xWins	Pythagorean Wins	Actual Wins	Decision Score Rank
8.3	7.7	11	3 / 32

Position Strengths

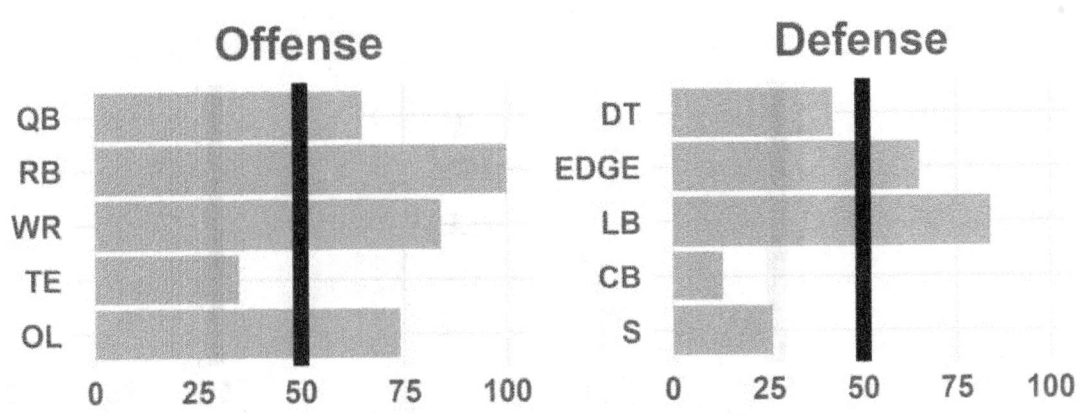

Percentile rank of Total Points for each team by position

Top Personnel Groupings

Group	Pct	Rank	EPA/P	Rank
11	41%	30	0.13	2
12	28%	6	0.05	8
13	14%	1	-0.05	15

Key 2020 Rookies

Rd	Player	Pos	Total Points
1	J. Wills	T	21
6	D. Peoples-Jones	WR	6
2	G. Delpit	S	–

Offensive Identity

Split	Pct	Rank	EPA/P	Rank
Shotgun	42%	31	0.06	10
Under Center	58%	2	0.01	8
Motion	48%	11	0.04	12
No Motion	52%	22	0.02	12
Gap Run	41%	6	0.06	9
Zone Run	59%	27	-0.12	23
Play Action	29%	9	0.23	3
Dropback	71%	24	0.05	13
vs. Man	27%	27	0.03	15
vs. Zone	63%	3	0.16	7
vs. Blitz	31%	5	0.10	12
Under Pres	27%	27	-0.42	20

Defensive Identity

Split	Pct	Rank	EPA/P	Rank
Base	26%	12	0.03	26
Nickel	68%	7	0.01	16
Dime+	3%	22	0.45	30
Gap Run	35%	7	0.03	21
Zone Run	65%	26	-0.10	18
Man	21%	27	0.16	28
Zone	67%	5	0.09	19
3 Rushers	4%	25	-0.05	9
4 Rushers	78%	4	0.06	21
5 Rushers	14%	28	0.19	27
6+ Rushers	3%	26	0.39	30
Pressure	30%	26	-0.46	6

Dallas Cowboys

2nd NFC East

SIS-WAR xWins	Pythagorean Wins	Actual Wins	Decision Score Rank
4.9	5.9	6	7 / 32

Position Strengths

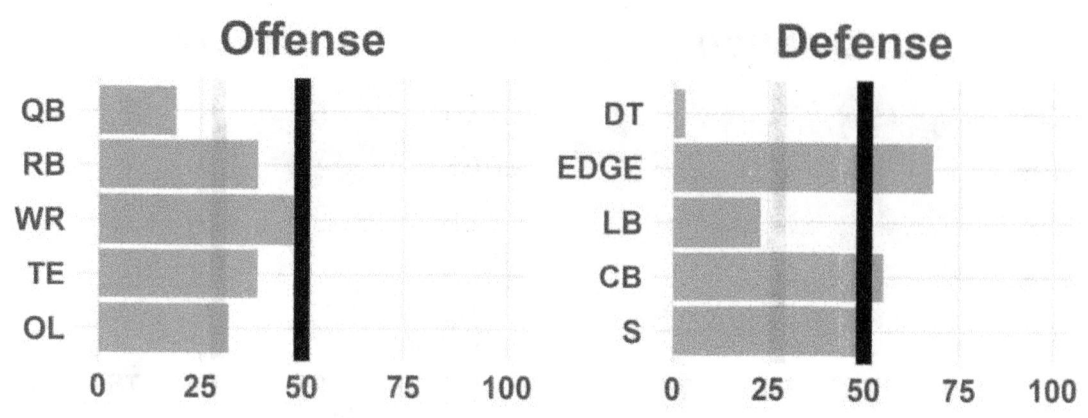

Percentile rank of Total Points for each team by position

Top Personnel Groupings

Group	Pct	Rank	EPA/P	Rank
11	72%	6	0.00	18
12	21%	13	-0.12	29
10	2%	7	0.01	12

Key 2020 Rookies

Rd	Player	Pos	Total Points
2	T. Diggs	CB	21
3	N. Gallimore	DT	10
1	C. Lamb	WR	6

Offensive Identity

Split	Pct	Rank	EPA/P	Rank
Shotgun	65%	15	-0.02	22
Under Center	35%	18	-0.07	21
Motion	46%	12	-0.08	26
No Motion	54%	21	0.00	15
Gap Run	20%	26	0.03	11
Zone Run	80%	7	-0.08	14
Play Action	21%	27	-0.01	23
Dropback	79%	6	-0.03	22
vs. Man	29%	23	-0.05	23
vs. Zone	59%	12	0.02	21
vs. Blitz	27%	13	-0.06	23
Under Pres	31%	19	-0.56	25

Defensive Identity

Split	Pct	Rank	EPA/P	Rank
Base	18%	26	0.19	32
Nickel	70%	5	0.00	15
Dime+	9%	19	0.03	19
Gap Run	37%	4	-0.01	15
Zone Run	63%	29	0.01	29
Man	29%	19	-0.05	13
Zone	61%	13	0.06	13
3 Rushers	11%	9	0.16	19
4 Rushers	67%	10	0.04	19
5 Rushers	17%	23	-0.04	10
6+ Rushers	2%	29	-0.08	12
Pressure	32%	19	-0.41	10

Denver Broncos

4th AFC West

SIS-WAR xWins	Pythagorean Wins	Actual Wins	Decision Score Rank
5.6	4.4	5	32 / 32

Position Strengths

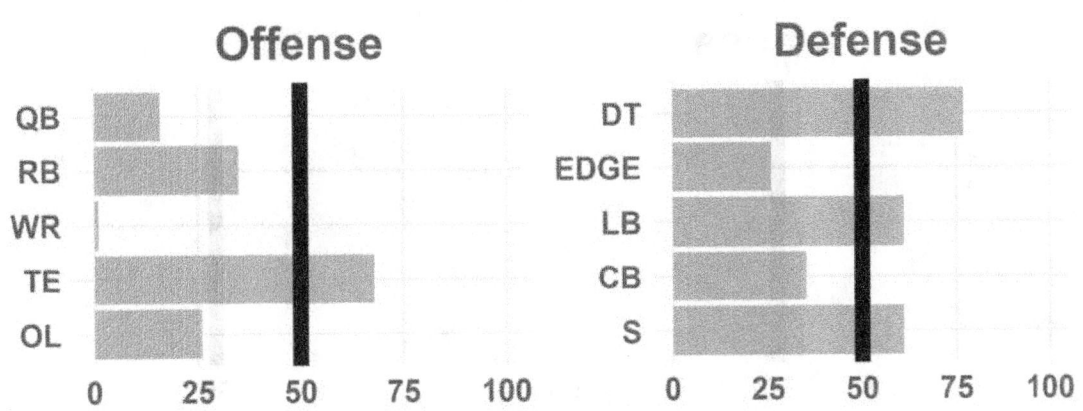

Percentile rank of Total Points for each team by position

Top Personnel Groupings

Group	Pct	Rank	EPA/P	Rank
11	67%	12	-0.10	28
12	21%	14	-0.12	28
22	5%	10	-0.33	18

Key 2020 Rookies

Rd	Player	Pos	Total Points
3	M. Ojemudia	CB	25
3	L. Cushenberry	C	14
1	J. Jeudy	WR	6

Offensive Identity

Split	Pct	Rank	EPA/P	Rank
Shotgun	67%	14	-0.13	30
Under Center	33%	19	-0.14	27
Motion	38%	24	-0.10	28
No Motion	62%	9	-0.15	32
Gap Run	43%	5	-0.05	18
Zone Run	57%	28	-0.18	31
Play Action	23%	21	-0.01	24
Dropback	77%	12	-0.17	30
vs. Man	33%	11	-0.21	29
vs. Zone	59%	11	-0.06	29
vs. Blitz	30%	6	-0.34	32
Under Pres	36%	5	-0.62	28

Defensive Identity

Split	Pct	Rank	EPA/P	Rank
Base	25%	13	-0.01	22
Nickel	65%	10	0.02	18
Dime+	9%	18	-0.08	10
Gap Run	27%	21	0.11	30
Zone Run	73%	12	-0.09	19
Man	37%	10	-0.09	9
Zone	51%	20	0.15	26
3 Rushers	6%	17	-0.07	7
4 Rushers	66%	15	0.10	25
5 Rushers	21%	15	-0.08	7
6+ Rushers	6%	13	-0.14	9
Pressure	34%	13	-0.16	31

Detroit Lions

4th NFC North

SIS-WAR xWins	Pythagorean Wins	Actual Wins	Decision Score Rank
5.7	4.4	5	28 / 32

Position Strengths

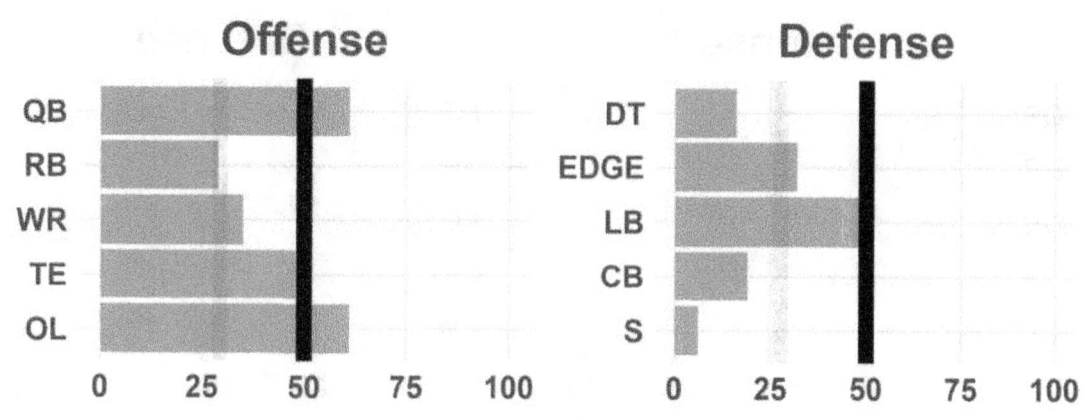

Percentile rank of Total Points for each team by position

Top Personnel Groupings

Group	Pct	Rank	EPA/P	Rank
11	68%	10	0.01	17
12	15%	21	-0.03	21
21	7%	13	-0.16	23

Key 2020 Rookies

Rd	Player	Pos	Total Points
3	J. Jackson	G	24
1	J. Okudah	CB	10
2	D. Swift	RB	5

Offensive Identity

Split	Pct	Rank	EPA/P	Rank
Shotgun	62%	19	0.01	16
Under Center	38%	14	-0.07	22
Motion	43%	17	-0.03	22
No Motion	57%	16	-0.01	16
Gap Run	34%	9	-0.12	24
Zone Run	66%	24	-0.16	28
Play Action	23%	23	0.22	5
Dropback	77%	10	0.01	19
vs. Man	28%	26	0.07	13
vs. Zone	59%	13	0.07	16
vs. Blitz	26%	15	-0.18	29
Under Pres	28%	24	-0.28	10

Defensive Identity

Split	Pct	Rank	EPA/P	Rank
Base	19%	25	0.08	29
Nickel	60%	16	0.17	32
Dime+	19%	12	0.02	18
Gap Run	24%	26	0.13	31
Zone Run	76%	7	-0.05	24
Man	42%	4	0.23	32
Zone	50%	22	0.24	32
3 Rushers	12%	7	0.00	13
4 Rushers	66%	17	0.24	31
5 Rushers	16%	25	0.31	32
6+ Rushers	5%	17	0.37	29
Pressure	27%	30	-0.19	29

Green Bay Packers

1st NFC North

SIS-WAR xWins	Pythagorean Wins	Actual Wins	Decision Score Rank
12.4	11.6	13	T1 / 32

Position Strengths

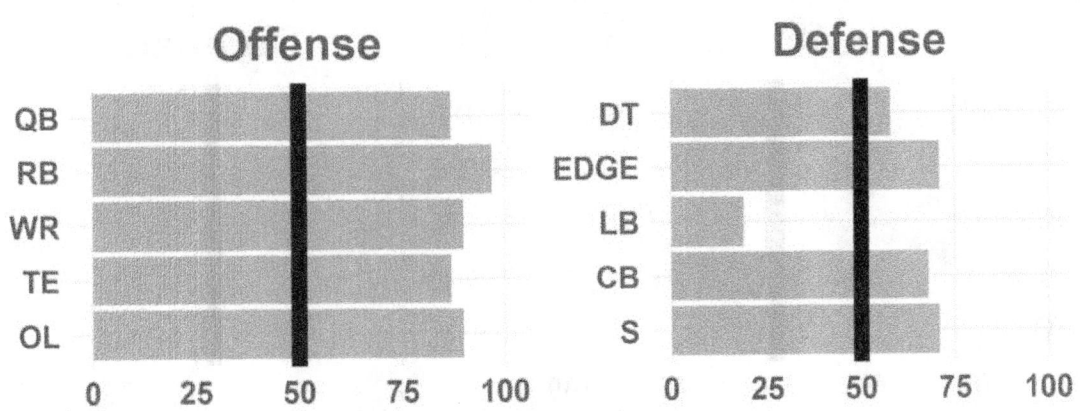

Percentile rank of Total Points for each team by position

Top Personnel Groupings

Group	Pct	Rank	EPA/P	Rank
11	54%	25	0.20	1
12	22%	11	0.11	5
21	17%	4	0.07	12

Key 2020 Rookies

Rd	Player	Pos	Total Points
2	A. Dillon	RB	10
UD	K. Barnes	LB	8
5	K. Martin	LB	4

Offensive Identity

Split	Pct	Rank	EPA/P	Rank
Shotgun	57%	23	0.21	1
Under Center	43%	10	0.05	7
Motion	54%	5	0.16	2
No Motion	46%	28	0.12	2
Gap Run	16%	32	0.17	2
Zone Run	84%	1	-0.04	6
Play Action	30%	7	0.39	1
Dropback	70%	26	0.18	3
vs. Man	33%	12	0.32	2
vs. Zone	51%	31	0.27	2
vs. Blitz	25%	17	0.20	4
Under Pres	24%	31	-0.28	9

Defensive Identity

Split	Pct	Rank	EPA/P	Rank
Base	20%	23	0.00	24
Nickel	27%	32	0.02	17
Dime+	50%	1	-0.04	13
Gap Run	24%	28	0.05	25
Zone Run	76%	5	-0.05	27
Man	20%	30	-0.13	7
Zone	68%	4	0.05	12
3 Rushers	7%	13	0.19	20
4 Rushers	70%	9	0.00	10
5 Rushers	19%	19	0.09	24
6+ Rushers	2%	31	-0.80	1
Pressure	28%	27	-0.54	3

Houston Texans

3rd AFC South

SIS-WAR xWins	Pythagorean Wins	Actual Wins	Decision Score Rank
5.3	5.8	4	24 / 32

Position Strengths

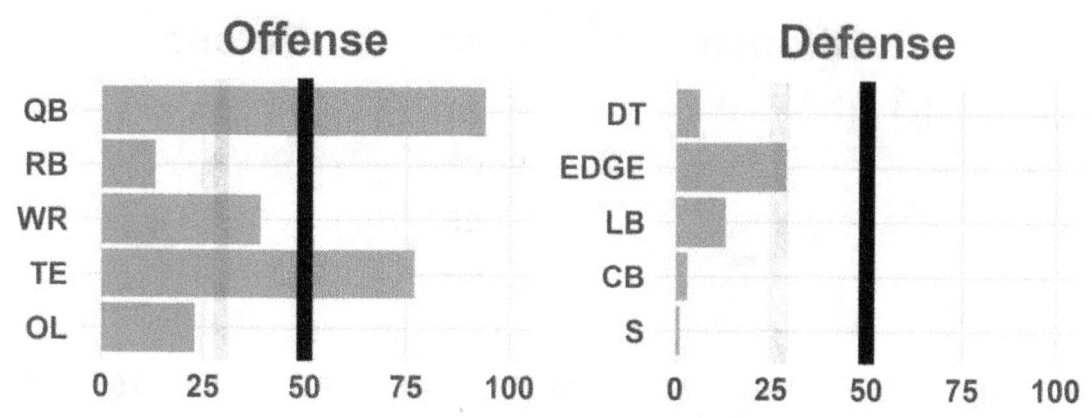

Percentile rank of Total Points for each team by position

Top Personnel Groupings

Group	Pct	Rank	EPA/P	Rank
11	63%	15	0.08	8
12	29%	5	0.04	9
21	2%	19	0.31	4

Key 2020 Rookies

Rd	Player	Pos	Total Points
3	J. Greenard	LB	2
4	J. Reid	CB	2
2	R. Blacklock	DT	0

Offensive Identity

Split	Pct	Rank	EPA/P	Rank
Shotgun	82%	3	0.11	5
Under Center	18%	30	-0.15	29
Motion	37%	25	-0.02	19
No Motion	63%	8	0.12	3
Gap Run	22%	23	-0.18	28
Zone Run	78%	10	-0.18	30
Play Action	20%	29	0.18	9
Dropback	80%	4	0.17	4
vs. Man	34%	9	0.11	8
vs. Zone	56%	20	0.23	3
vs. Blitz	24%	20	0.15	7
Under Pres	32%	15	-0.32	13

Defensive Identity

Split	Pct	Rank	EPA/P	Rank
Base	35%	4	0.07	28
Nickel	41%	29	0.16	31
Dime+	20%	10	0.18	26
Gap Run	26%	22	0.02	19
Zone Run	74%	11	0.03	31
Man	33%	14	0.15	26
Zone	55%	19	0.20	29
3 Rushers	14%	5	0.21	21
4 Rushers	53%	31	0.26	32
5 Rushers	26%	6	0.07	19
6+ Rushers	5%	18	0.21	25
Pressure	31%	24	-0.20	28

Indianapolis Colts

2nd AFC South

SIS-WAR xWins	Pythagorean Wins	Actual Wins	Decision Score Rank
10.9	10.5	11	23 / 32

Position Strengths

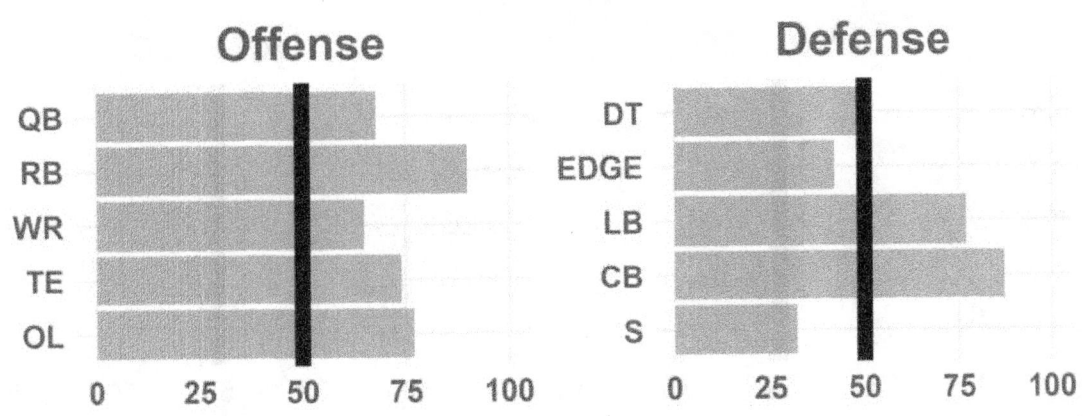

Percentile rank of Total Points for each team by position

Top Personnel Groupings

Group	Pct	Rank	EPA/P	Rank
11	69%	9	0.10	5
12	20%	15	-0.04	23
13	8%	5	-0.04	11

Key 2020 Rookies

Rd	Player	Pos	Total Points
2	J. Taylor	RB	37
2	M. Pittman Jr.	WR	11
3	J. Blackmon	S	9

Offensive Identity

Split	Pct	Rank	EPA/P	Rank
Shotgun	73%	10	0.07	8
Under Center	27%	23	-0.02	12
Motion	37%	27	0.00	14
No Motion	63%	6	0.07	6
Gap Run	25%	20	0.04	10
Zone Run	75%	13	-0.06	9
Play Action	23%	22	-0.05	26
Dropback	77%	11	0.16	5
vs. Man	32%	16	0.21	5
vs. Zone	53%	24	0.05	18
vs. Blitz	20%	30	0.19	5
Under Pres	25%	28	-0.17	5

Defensive Identity

Split	Pct	Rank	EPA/P	Rank
Base	21%	18	-0.10	14
Nickel	78%	3	-0.05	8
Dime+	1%	31	0.36	28
Gap Run	29%	18	-0.01	16
Zone Run	71%	15	-0.14	9
Man	21%	29	-0.02	16
Zone	69%	1	-0.01	8
3 Rushers	2%	30	0.08	15
4 Rushers	82%	2	-0.04	7
5 Rushers	11%	30	0.07	18
6+ Rushers	4%	23	-0.01	14
Pressure	31%	25	-0.37	13

Jacksonville Jaguars

4th AFC South

SIS-WAR xWins	Pythagorean Wins	Actual Wins	Decision Score Rank
3.0	3.1	1	20 / 32

Position Strengths

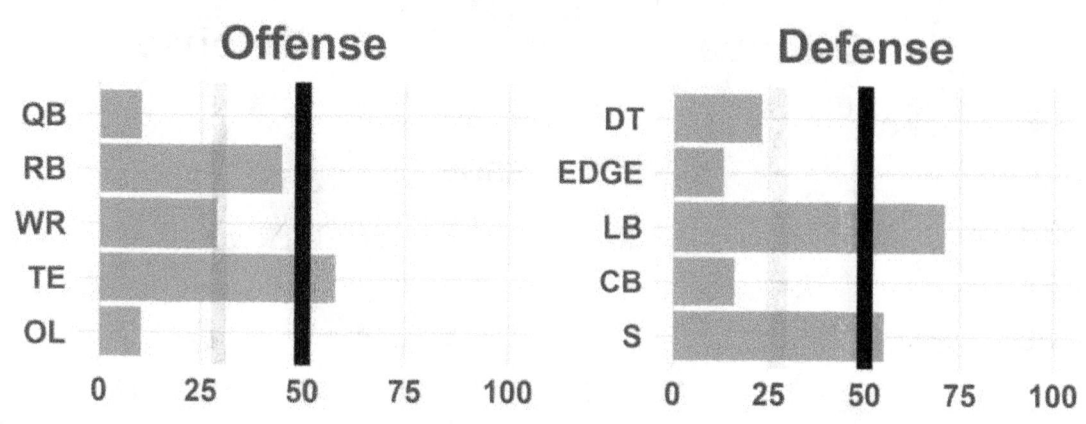

Percentile rank of Total Points for each team by position

Top Personnel Groupings

Group	Pct	Rank	EPA/P	Rank
11	73%	3	-0.07	23
12	11%	28	-0.07	26
13	6%	7	-0.24	18

Key 2020 Rookies

Rd	Player	Pos	Total Points
1	C. Henderson	CB	14
2	L. Shenault	WR	12
UD	J. Robinson	RB	6

Offensive Identity

Split	Pct	Rank	EPA/P	Rank
Shotgun	69%	11	-0.09	27
Under Center	31%	22	-0.08	23
Motion	35%	30	-0.11	29
No Motion	65%	3	-0.07	25
Gap Run	25%	19	-0.17	27
Zone Run	75%	14	-0.06	11
Play Action	18%	31	0.10	18
Dropback	82%	2	-0.13	28
vs. Man	32%	15	-0.15	26
vs. Zone	57%	19	-0.03	26
vs. Blitz	22%	28	-0.01	20
Under Pres	32%	14	-0.63	29

Defensive Identity

Split	Pct	Rank	EPA/P	Rank
Base	40%	1	-0.01	23
Nickel	55%	19	0.15	30
Dime+	3%	23	-0.13	7
Gap Run	20%	31	0.05	23
Zone Run	80%	2	-0.05	25
Man	41%	6	0.21	29
Zone	47%	30	0.11	22
3 Rushers	4%	28	0.35	27
4 Rushers	67%	13	0.11	26
5 Rushers	23%	9	0.23	30
6+ Rushers	6%	12	0.40	31
Pressure	26%	32	-0.15	32

Kansas City Chiefs

1st AFC West

SIS-WAR xWins	Pythagorean Wins	Actual Wins	Decision Score Rank
11.3	11.0	14	5 / 32

Position Strengths

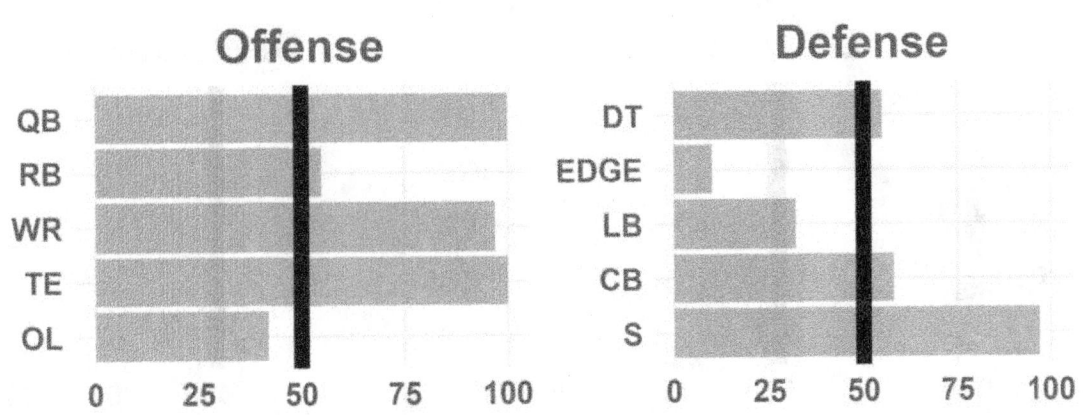

Percentile rank of Total Points for each team by position

Top Personnel Groupings

Group	Pct	Rank	EPA/P	Rank
11	72%	5	0.12	3
12	19%	17	0.15	1
13	3%	15	-0.04	10

Key 2020 Rookies

Rd	Player	Pos	Total Points
4	L. Sneed	CB	16
2	W. Gay	LB	15
1	C. Edwards-Helaire	RB	13

Offensive Identity

Split	Pct	Rank	EPA/P	Rank
Shotgun	80%	7	0.14	3
Under Center	20%	26	-0.03	13
Motion	60%	3	0.13	5
No Motion	40%	30	0.08	5
Gap Run	22%	24	-0.12	23
Zone Run	78%	9	-0.07	13
Play Action	33%	3	0.14	15
Dropback	67%	30	0.25	1
vs. Man	30%	22	0.27	3
vs. Zone	59%	14	0.19	5
vs. Blitz	18%	32	0.39	1
Under Pres	32%	13	-0.15	4

Defensive Identity

Split	Pct	Rank	EPA/P	Rank
Base	22%	17	-0.04	19
Nickel	41%	30	-0.03	12
Dime+	35%	4	0.07	20
Gap Run	37%	3	0.15	32
Zone Run	63%	30	-0.05	26
Man	40%	8	-0.07	11
Zone	48%	29	0.09	18
3 Rushers	4%	24	0.26	23
4 Rushers	61%	21	0.03	18
5 Rushers	20%	18	-0.03	11
6+ Rushers	14%	1	-0.10	10
Pressure	38%	6	-0.29	20

Las Vegas Raiders

2nd AFC West

SIS-WAR xWins	Pythagorean Wins	Actual Wins	Decision Score Rank
6.8	6.9	8	21 / 32

Position Strengths

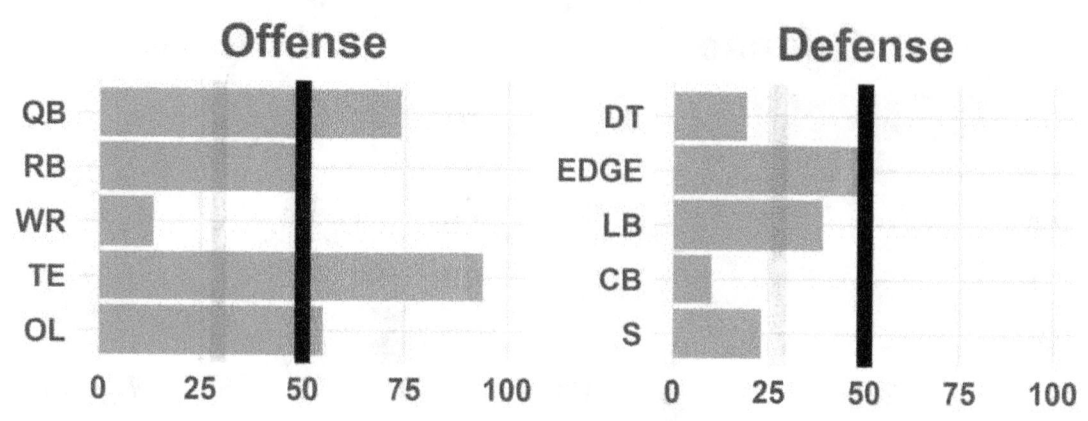

Percentile rank of Total Points for each team by position

Top Personnel Groupings

Group	Pct	Rank	EPA/P	Rank
11	50%	27	0.05	10
12	19%	18	0.02	13
22	13%	2	-0.17	11

Key 2020 Rookies

Rd	Player	Pos	Total Points
4	J. Simpson	G	8
1	D. Arnette	CB	-1
1	H. Ruggs	WR	-3

Offensive Identity

Split	Pct	Rank	EPA/P	Rank
Shotgun	57%	24	0.07	7
Under Center	43%	9	-0.03	14
Motion	52%	7	0.05	10
No Motion	48%	26	0.00	14
Gap Run	28%	16	0.08	8
Zone Run	73%	17	-0.11	18
Play Action	24%	20	0.03	21
Dropback	76%	13	0.10	8
vs. Man	33%	14	0.03	16
vs. Zone	58%	18	0.13	9
vs. Blitz	25%	18	0.14	8
Under Pres	27%	26	-0.38	18

Defensive Identity

Split	Pct	Rank	EPA/P	Rank
Base	23%	15	-0.13	7
Nickel	69%	6	0.15	29
Dime+	5%	21	0.45	29
Gap Run	32%	11	0.02	17
Zone Run	68%	22	0.03	30
Man	31%	16	0.22	30
Zone	56%	17	0.14	24
3 Rushers	6%	15	-0.08	6
4 Rushers	72%	6	0.20	30
5 Rushers	17%	24	-0.09	6
6+ Rushers	3%	25	0.63	32
Pressure	34%	12	-0.18	30

Los Angeles Chargers

3rd AFC West

SIS-WAR xWins	Pythagorean Wins	Actual Wins	Decision Score Rank
7.4	6.8	7	12 / 32

Position Strengths

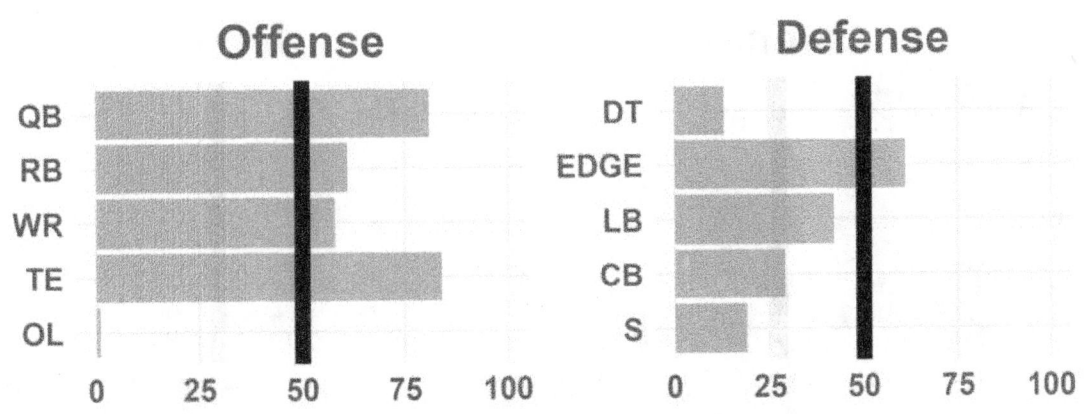

Percentile rank of Total Points for each team by position

Top Personnel Groupings

Group	Pct	Rank	EPA/P	Rank
11	72%	7	0.05	12
12	12%	27	-0.01	17
21	9%	10	-0.07	21

Key 2020 Rookies

Rd	Player	Pos	Total Points
1	J. Herbert	QB	116
1	K. Murray	LB	9
7	K. Hill	WR	-2

Offensive Identity

Split	Pct	Rank	EPA/P	Rank
Shotgun	65%	17	0.04	13
Under Center	35%	16	0.00	10
Motion	37%	28	-0.01	16
No Motion	63%	5	0.05	8
Gap Run	24%	22	-0.11	22
Zone Run	76%	11	-0.13	26
Play Action	27%	13	0.16	11
Dropback	73%	21	0.10	7
vs. Man	34%	8	0.10	10
vs. Zone	54%	23	0.12	12
vs. Blitz	23%	23	0.07	13
Under Pres	36%	8	-0.08	1

Defensive Identity

Split	Pct	Rank	EPA/P	Rank
Base	21%	19	-0.19	3
Nickel	65%	9	0.03	19
Dime+	13%	17	0.13	25
Gap Run	27%	20	-0.20	3
Zone Run	73%	13	-0.08	22
Man	26%	23	0.06	19
Zone	61%	11	0.09	20
3 Rushers	4%	27	0.38	28
4 Rushers	82%	3	0.02	15
5 Rushers	11%	31	0.23	31
6+ Rushers	3%	27	0.08	20
Pressure	32%	21	-0.30	19

Los Angeles Rams

2nd NFC West

SIS-WAR xWins	Pythagorean Wins	Actual Wins	Decision Score Rank
11.3	10.6	10	10 / 32

Position Strengths

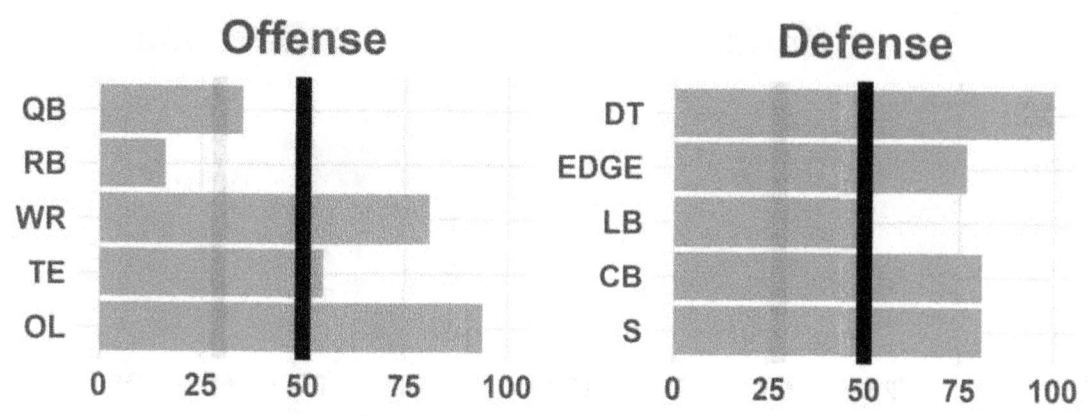

Percentile rank of Total Points for each team by position

Top Personnel Groupings

Group	Pct	Rank	EPA/P	Rank
11	64%	13	0.01	15
12	30%	3	-0.06	24
13	5%	8	-0.35	23

Key 2020 Rookies

Rd	Player	Pos	Total Points
6	J. Fuller	S	25
2	V. Jefferson	WR	3
2	C. Akers	RB	-6

Offensive Identity

Split	Pct	Rank	EPA/P	Rank
Shotgun	42%	29	-0.01	20
Under Center	58%	4	-0.05	17
Motion	49%	10	-0.04	23
No Motion	51%	23	-0.02	18
Gap Run	17%	29	-0.03	16
Zone Run	83%	4	-0.08	15
Play Action	32%	4	0.05	20
Dropback	68%	29	-0.02	21
vs. Man	28%	25	-0.04	22
vs. Zone	58%	16	0.04	20
vs. Blitz	28%	10	0.13	9
Under Pres	35%	10	-0.51	22

Defensive Identity

Split	Pct	Rank	EPA/P	Rank
Base	16%	27	-0.25	2
Nickel	59%	18	-0.09	5
Dime+	25%	8	-0.32	4
Gap Run	25%	24	-0.18	4
Zone Run	75%	9	-0.15	7
Man	21%	28	-0.23	4
Zone	66%	8	-0.16	1
3 Rushers	4%	26	-0.03	10
4 Rushers	70%	7	-0.20	1
5 Rushers	22%	11	-0.13	4
6+ Rushers	2%	28	0.14	22
Pressure	35%	10	-0.62	2

Miami Dolphins

2nd AFC East

SIS-WAR xWins	Pythagorean Wins	Actual Wins	Decision Score Rank
8.4	10.1	10	29 / 32

Position Strengths

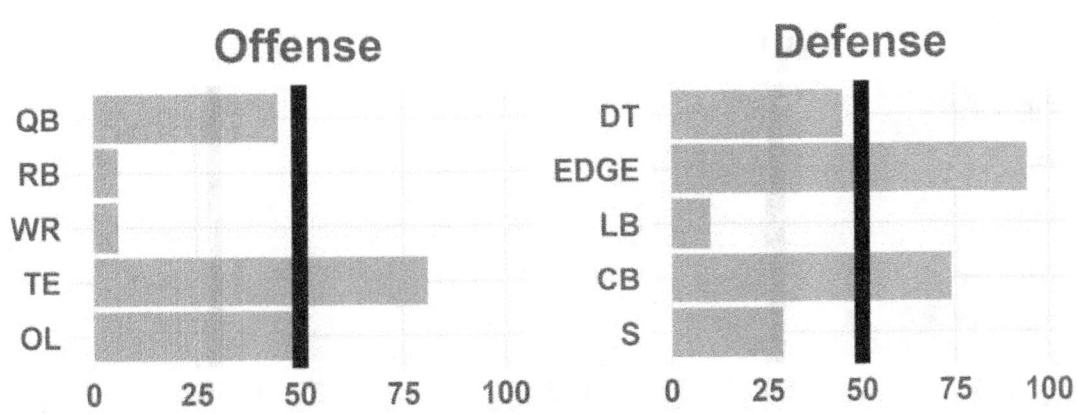

Percentile rank of Total Points for each team by position

Top Personnel Groupings

Group	Pct	Rank	EPA/P	Rank
11	58%	20	-0.02	20
12	27%	8	0.00	16
21	4%	17	0.01	17

Key 2020 Rookies

Rd	Player	Pos	Total Points
1	T. Tagovailoa	QB	25
2	R. Hunt	T	21
4	S. Kindley	G	19

Offensive Identity

Split	Pct	Rank	EPA/P	Rank
Shotgun	80%	6	0.01	17
Under Center	20%	27	-0.15	28
Motion	42%	19	-0.01	17
No Motion	58%	14	-0.03	19
Gap Run	29%	15	-0.19	29
Zone Run	71%	18	-0.11	20
Play Action	25%	19	0.11	17
Dropback	75%	14	0.02	18
vs. Man	38%	1	-0.03	20
vs. Zone	50%	32	0.11	13
vs. Blitz	31%	4	0.00	19
Under Pres	31%	20	-0.15	3

Defensive Identity

Split	Pct	Rank	EPA/P	Rank
Base	27%	10	-0.02	20
Nickel	47%	28	-0.03	13
Dime+	24%	9	-0.24	5
Gap Run	34%	9	0.06	26
Zone Run	66%	24	-0.11	15
Man	42%	3	-0.13	6
Zone	49%	26	-0.10	3
3 Rushers	17%	3	-0.20	4
4 Rushers	52%	32	-0.11	3
5 Rushers	20%	16	0.08	22
6+ Rushers	8%	7	-0.31	5
Pressure	40%	4	-0.54	4

Minnesota Vikings

3rd NFC North

SIS-WAR xWins	Pythagorean Wins	Actual Wins	Decision Score Rank
7.2	6.8	7	17 / 32

Position Strengths

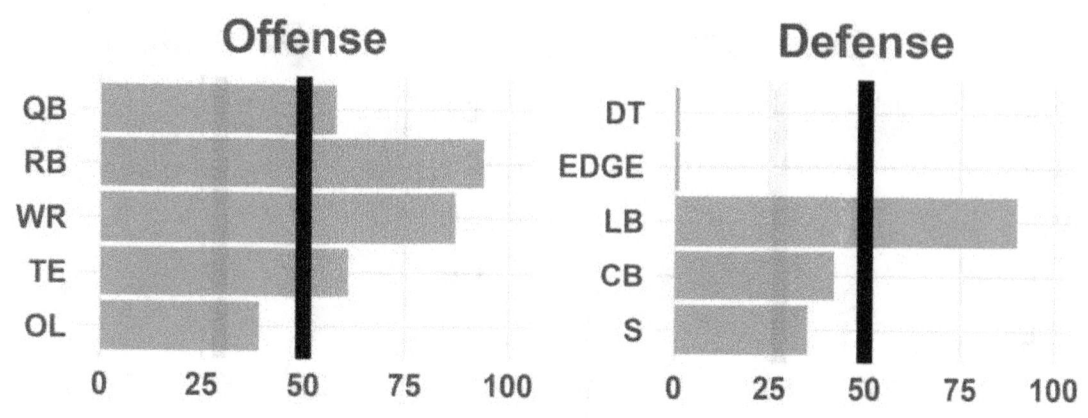

Percentile rank of Total Points for each team by position

Top Personnel Groupings

Group	Pct	Rank	EPA/P	Rank
11	28%	32	-0.05	22
21	27%	3	0.11	10
12	22%	10	0.02	11

Key 2020 Rookies

Rd	Player	Pos	Total Points
1	J. Jefferson	WR	45
3	C. Dantzler	CB	43
2	E. Cleveland	G	15

Offensive Identity

Split	Pct	Rank	EPA/P	Rank
Shotgun	37%	32	0.05	12
Under Center	63%	1	0.06	5
Motion	43%	16	0.09	7
No Motion	57%	17	0.03	10
Gap Run	18%	28	0.15	3
Zone Run	82%	5	-0.04	5
Play Action	27%	11	0.16	10
Dropback	72%	22	0.09	10
vs. Man	31%	20	0.26	4
vs. Zone	58%	15	0.05	17
vs. Blitz	28%	12	0.03	18
Under Pres	38%	1	-0.24	6

Defensive Identity

Split	Pct	Rank	EPA/P	Rank
Base	35%	3	0.13	30
Nickel	62%	14	0.05	21
Dime+	1%	28	-0.43	3
Gap Run	19%	32	0.04	22
Zone Run	81%	1	0.05	32
Man	31%	17	-0.06	12
Zone	56%	18	0.23	31
3 Rushers	5%	22	0.34	26
4 Rushers	70%	8	0.10	24
5 Rushers	19%	20	0.08	21
6+ Rushers	5%	20	0.05	18
Pressure	27%	28	-0.23	24

New England Patriots

3rd AFC East

SIS-WAR xWins	Pythagorean Wins	Actual Wins	Decision Score Rank
6.7	7.1	7	27 / 32

Position Strengths

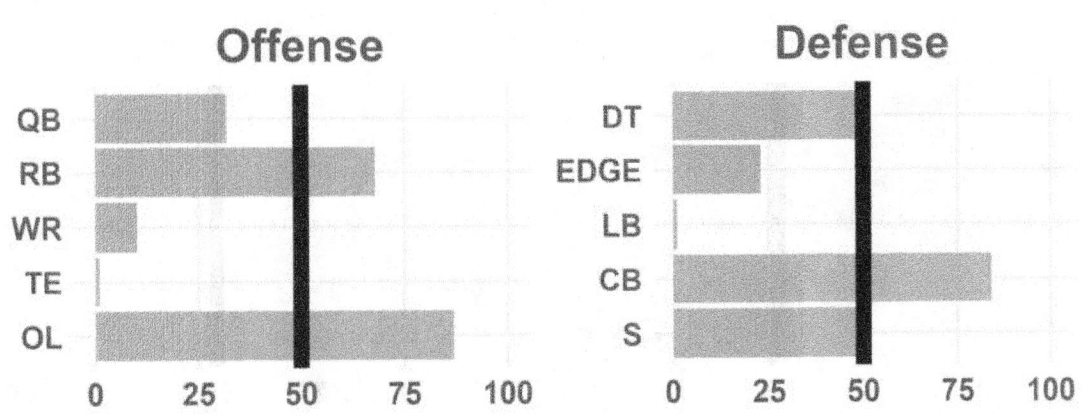

Percentile rank of Total Points for each team by position

Top Personnel Groupings

Group	Pct	Rank	EPA/P	Rank
11	55%	24	-0.07	24
21	38%	1	0.03	15
20	4%	2	-0.09	12

Key 2020 Rookies

Rd	Player	Pos	Total Points
6	M. Onwenu	G	29
2	K. Dugger	S	14
2	J. Uche	DE	7

Offensive Identity

Split	Pct	Rank	EPA/P	Rank
Shotgun	53%	28	-0.06	24
Under Center	47%	5	0.00	11
Motion	46%	13	-0.01	15
No Motion	54%	20	-0.06	22
Gap Run	46%	4	0.12	4
Zone Run	54%	29	-0.04	8
Play Action	31%	5	-0.12	31
Dropback	69%	28	-0.08	24
vs. Man	33%	10	-0.38	32
vs. Zone	52%	27	0.08	15
vs. Blitz	41%	1	-0.30	31
Under Pres	32%	12	-0.65	32

Defensive Identity

Split	Pct	Rank	EPA/P	Rank
Base	4%	32	-0.29	1
Nickel	47%	27	0.09	26
Dime+	47%	2	-0.05	12
Gap Run	21%	30	-0.05	12
Zone Run	79%	3	0.00	28
Man	40%	7	0.02	18
Zone	50%	23	0.02	11
3 Rushers	22%	1	0.13	17
4 Rushers	56%	28	-0.03	9
5 Rushers	15%	26	0.22	29
6+ Rushers	6%	16	-0.15	7
Pressure	36%	8	-0.23	25

New Orleans Saints

1st NFC South

SIS-WAR xWins	Pythagorean Wins	Actual Wins	Decision Score Rank
12.3	11.9	12	16 / 32

Position Strengths

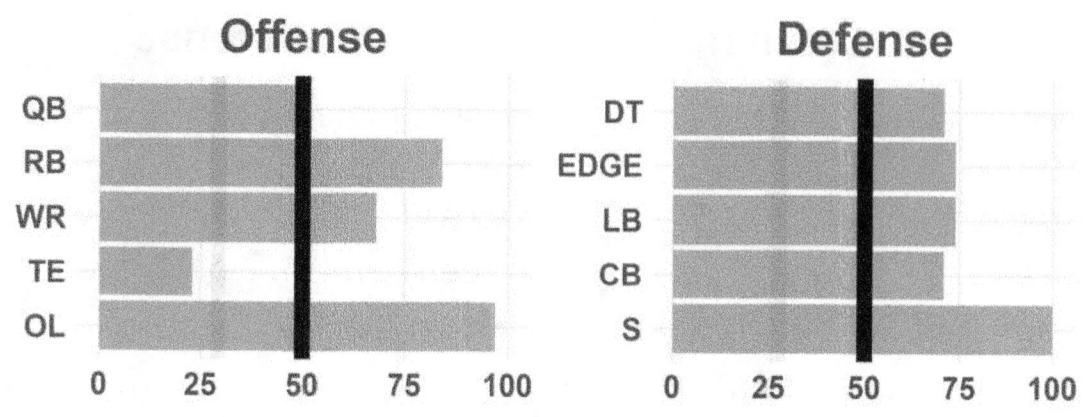

Percentile rank of Total Points for each team by position

Top Personnel Groupings

Group	Pct	Rank	EPA/P	Rank
11	58%	19	0.06	9
12	13%	25	0.14	3
21	13%	5	0.23	6

Key 2020 Rookies

Rd	Player	Pos	Total Points
1	C. Ruiz	G	25
UD	M. Callaway	WR	8
3	A. Trautman	TE	5

Offensive Identity

Split	Pct	Rank	EPA/P	Rank
Shotgun	53%	27	0.05	11
Under Center	47%	6	0.07	2
Motion	43%	18	0.05	9
No Motion	57%	15	0.07	7
Gap Run	32%	11	0.02	12
Zone Run	68%	22	0.00	3
Play Action	21%	26	0.18	8
Dropback	79%	7	0.09	9
vs. Man	26%	30	0.10	9
vs. Zone	60%	8	0.18	6
vs. Blitz	22%	25	0.16	6
Under Pres	28%	25	-0.35	14

Defensive Identity

Split	Pct	Rank	EPA/P	Rank
Base	10%	29	-0.16	5
Nickel	60%	17	-0.07	6
Dime+	28%	5	-0.12	8
Gap Run	31%	15	-0.09	9
Zone Run	69%	18	-0.17	4
Man	47%	1	0.07	20
Zone	44%	32	-0.14	2
3 Rushers	11%	8	0.44	30
4 Rushers	60%	22	-0.09	5
5 Rushers	21%	14	-0.28	1
6+ Rushers	6%	11	0.12	21
Pressure	41%	2	-0.39	11

New York Giants

2nd NFC East

SIS-WAR xWins	Pythagorean Wins	Actual Wins	Decision Score Rank
4.8	5.2	6	26 / 32

Position Strengths

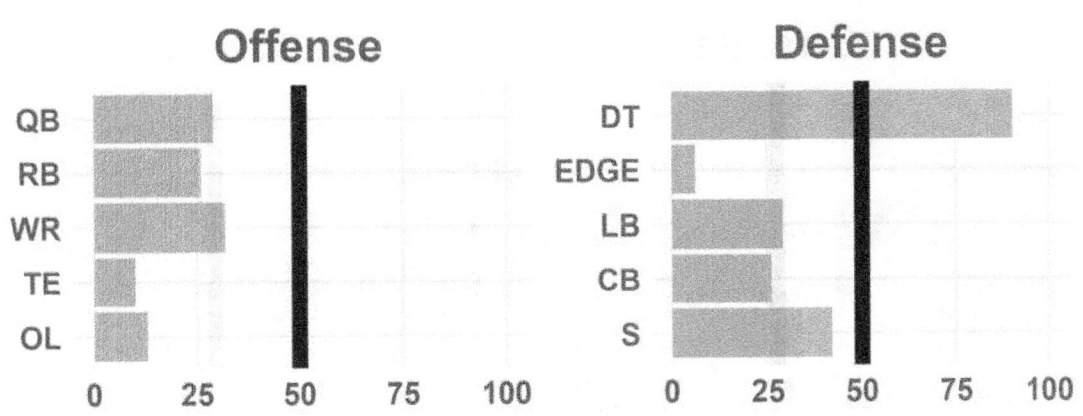

Percentile rank of Total Points for each team by position

Top Personnel Groupings

Group	Pct	Rank	EPA/P	Rank
11	55%	23	-0.08	27
12	27%	9	-0.03	18
13	11%	2	-0.30	19

Key 2020 Rookies

Rd	Player	Pos	Total Points
1	A. Thomas	T	17
4	D. Holmes	CB	17
2	X. McKinney	S	2

Offensive Identity

Split	Pct	Rank	EPA/P	Rank
Shotgun	65%	16	-0.07	25
Under Center	35%	17	-0.18	31
Motion	30%	31	-0.07	25
No Motion	70%	2	-0.12	29
Gap Run	53%	2	-0.15	25
Zone Run	47%	31	-0.09	16
Play Action	26%	16	-0.12	30
Dropback	74%	17	-0.09	26
vs. Man	35%	6	-0.20	28
vs. Zone	55%	21	0.00	24
vs. Blitz	32%	3	-0.27	30
Under Pres	38%	2	-0.49	21

Defensive Identity

Split	Pct	Rank	EPA/P	Rank
Base	19%	24	-0.11	11
Nickel	54%	21	0.07	23
Dime+	26%	7	-0.08	9
Gap Run	39%	2	0.03	20
Zone Run	61%	31	-0.13	12
Man	23%	26	-0.01	17
Zone	66%	6	0.07	15
3 Rushers	17%	4	0.21	22
4 Rushers	66%	14	-0.04	8
5 Rushers	14%	29	0.19	28
6+ Rushers	2%	32	0.03	17
Pressure	33%	14	-0.36	14

New York Jets

4th AFC East

SIS-WAR xWins	Pythagorean Wins	Actual Wins	Decision Score Rank
3.0	2.1	2	15 / 32

Position Strengths

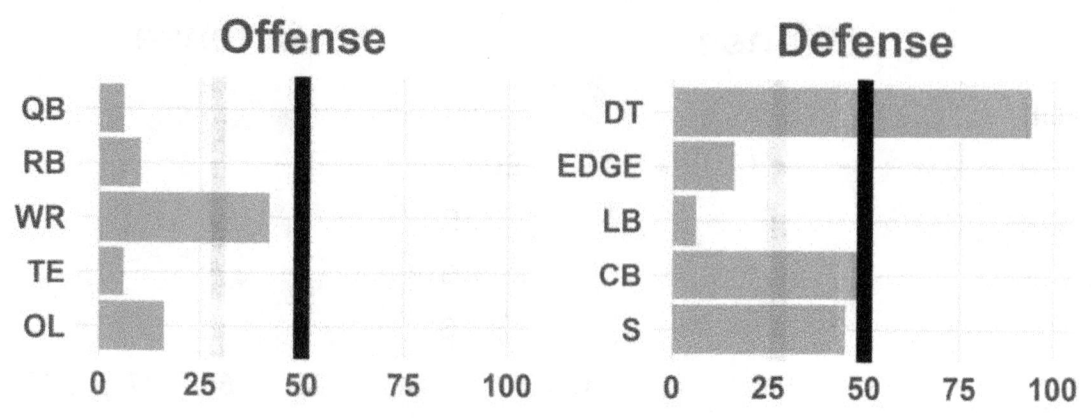

Percentile rank of Total Points for each team by position

Top Personnel Groupings

Group	Pct	Rank	EPA/P	Rank
11	71%	8	-0.14	32
12	16%	20	-0.12	27
13	4%	10	-0.49	27

Key 2020 Rookies

Rd	Player	Pos	Total Points
1	M. Becton	T	21
5	B. Hall	CB	18
2	D. Mims	WR	9

Offensive Identity

Split	Pct	Rank	EPA/P	Rank
Shotgun	60%	21	-0.17	32
Under Center	40%	12	-0.13	25
Motion	41%	22	-0.17	31
No Motion	59%	11	-0.14	30
Gap Run	19%	27	-0.08	20
Zone Run	81%	6	-0.15	27
Play Action	23%	24	-0.10	29
Dropback	77%	9	-0.18	32
vs. Man	37%	2	-0.29	31
vs. Zone	52%	30	-0.14	31
vs. Blitz	29%	9	-0.14	27
Under Pres	37%	3	-0.54	24

Defensive Identity

Split	Pct	Rank	EPA/P	Rank
Base	16%	28	-0.08	16
Nickel	82%	2	0.05	20
Dime+	1%	29	-0.03	14
Gap Run	31%	14	-0.10	8
Zone Run	69%	19	-0.17	3
Man	29%	18	0.09	21
Zone	60%	14	0.22	30
3 Rushers	7%	14	0.26	24
4 Rushers	60%	24	0.18	29
5 Rushers	27%	5	0.02	15
6+ Rushers	6%	14	0.31	27
Pressure	32%	16	-0.22	26

Philadelphia Eagles

4th NFC East

SIS-WAR xWins	Pythagorean Wins	Actual Wins	Decision Score Rank
6.0	5.4	4	11 / 32

Position Strengths

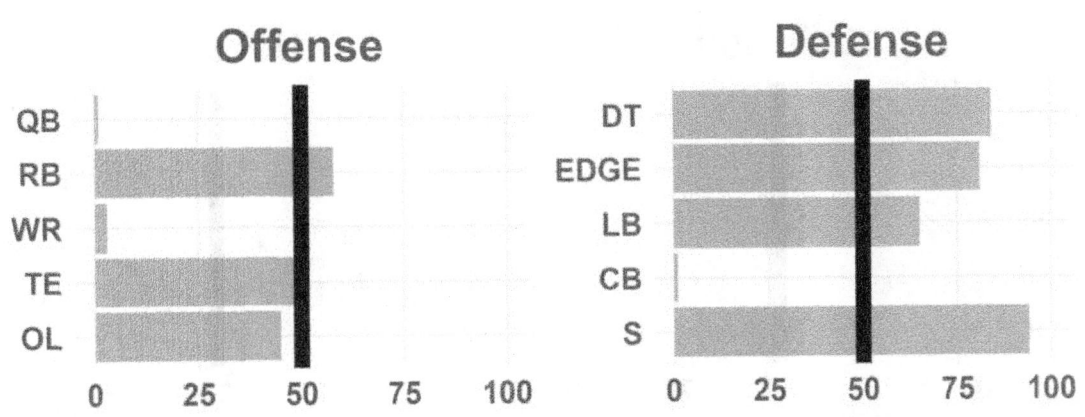

Percentile rank of Total Points for each team by position

Top Personnel Groupings

Group	Pct	Rank	EPA/P	Rank
11	59%	18	-0.12	31
12	34%	1	-0.14	30
21	2%	21	-0.68	29

Key 2020 Rookies

Rd	Player	Pos	Total Points
4	J. Driscoll	T	9
1	J. Reagor	WR	8
2	J. Hurts	QB	2

Offensive Identity

Split	Pct	Rank	EPA/P	Rank
Shotgun	81%	4	-0.13	31
Under Center	19%	29	-0.13	24
Motion	35%	29	-0.25	32
No Motion	65%	4	-0.07	23
Gap Run	30%	14	-0.02	15
Zone Run	70%	19	-0.13	25
Play Action	26%	15	-0.19	32
Dropback	74%	18	-0.14	29
vs. Man	36%	4	-0.26	30
vs. Zone	53%	25	-0.06	28
vs. Blitz	24%	19	-0.16	28
Under Pres	37%	4	-0.64	30

Defensive Identity

Split	Pct	Rank	EPA/P	Rank
Base	24%	14	-0.10	13
Nickel	53%	22	-0.05	9
Dime+	15%	14	0.11	24
Gap Run	36%	5	-0.12	6
Zone Run	64%	28	-0.13	13
Man	37%	11	0.11	23
Zone	48%	28	-0.03	6
3 Rushers	1%	32	0.43	29
4 Rushers	84%	1	0.03	17
5 Rushers	9%	32	-0.11	5
6+ Rushers	6%	15	0.06	19
Pressure	40%	3	-0.45	7

Pittsburgh Steelers

1st AFC North

SIS-WAR xWins	Pythagorean Wins	Actual Wins	Decision Score Rank
9.5	11.2	12	25 / 32

Position Strengths

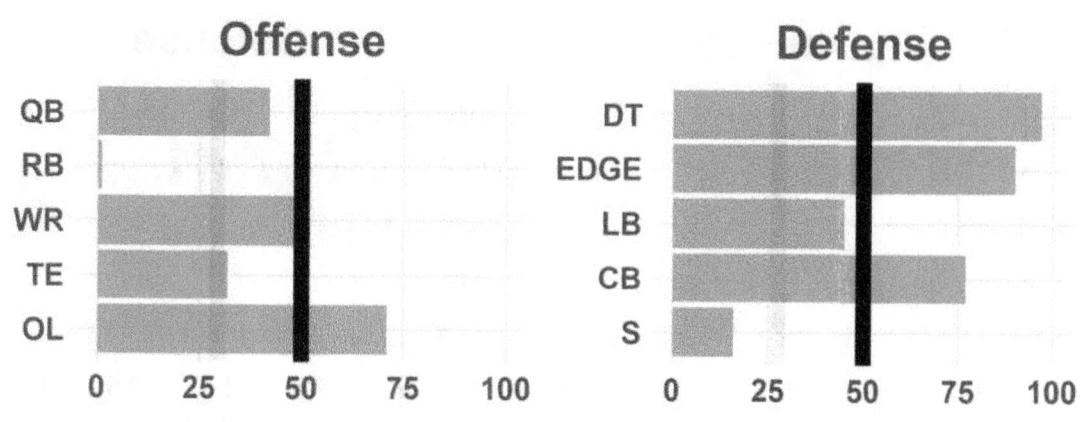

Percentile rank of Total Points for each team by position

Top Personnel Groupings

Group	Pct	Rank	EPA/P	Rank
11	78%	1	-0.03	21
12	9%	30	-0.03	20
01	6%	2	0.28	11

Key 2020 Rookies

Rd	Player	Pos	Total Points
3	A. Highsmith	LB	23
2	C. Claypool	WR	21
4	K. Dotson	G	10

Offensive Identity

Split	Pct	Rank	EPA/P	Rank
Shotgun	81%	5	0.00	19
Under Center	19%	28	-0.21	32
Motion	42%	20	-0.14	30
No Motion	58%	13	0.03	9
Gap Run	46%	3	-0.09	21
Zone Run	54%	30	-0.25	32
Play Action	11%	32	-0.05	25
Dropback	89%	1	0.04	15
vs. Man	31%	18	0.14	7
vs. Zone	53%	26	0.02	22
vs. Blitz	22%	26	0.12	10
Under Pres	21%	32	-0.25	7

Defensive Identity

Split	Pct	Rank	EPA/P	Rank
Base	35%	5	-0.12	8
Nickel	39%	31	-0.20	1
Dime+	20%	11	-0.06	11
Gap Run	32%	12	-0.04	13
Zone Run	68%	20	-0.11	14
Man	32%	15	-0.31	2
Zone	60%	15	-0.09	5
3 Rushers	5%	20	0.50	32
4 Rushers	56%	27	-0.19	2
5 Rushers	30%	2	-0.25	2
6+ Rushers	8%	5	-0.32	4
Pressure	44%	1	-0.53	5

San Francisco 49ers

4th NFC West

SIS-WAR xWins	Pythagorean Wins	Actual Wins	Decision Score Rank
9.6	7.6	6	13 / 32

Position Strengths

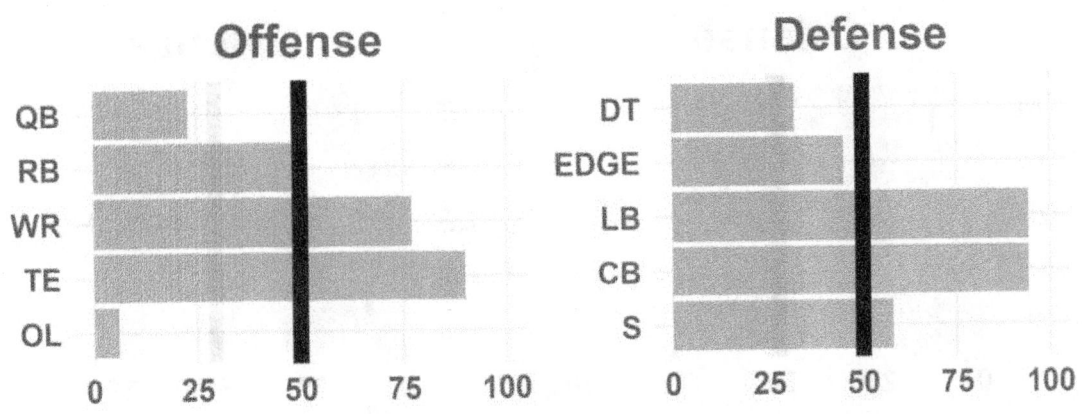

Percentile rank of Total Points for each team by position

Top Personnel Groupings

Group	Pct	Rank	EPA/P	Rank
11	44%	29	-0.11	30
21	33%	2	0.01	18
12	12%	26	0.02	14

Key 2020 Rookies

Rd	Player	Pos	Total Points
1	B. Aiyuk	WR	23
1	J. Kinlaw	DT	16
UD	J. Hasty	RB	-1

Offensive Identity

Split	Pct	Rank	EPA/P	Rank
Shotgun	58%	22	-0.04	23
Under Center	42%	11	-0.05	19
Motion	73%	1	-0.02	20
No Motion	27%	32	-0.11	28
Gap Run	26%	18	0.00	13
Zone Run	74%	15	-0.12	21
Play Action	27%	12	0.14	14
Dropback	73%	20	-0.07	23
vs. Man	27%	28	0.08	11
vs. Zone	60%	6	-0.08	30
vs. Blitz	28%	11	0.05	16
Under Pres	36%	6	-0.51	23

Defensive Identity

Split	Pct	Rank	EPA/P	Rank
Base	31%	9	-0.09	15
Nickel	66%	8	-0.04	10
Dime+	2%	25	-0.66	1
Gap Run	32%	12	-0.05	11
Zone Run	68%	20	-0.15	6
Man	27%	21	-0.31	1
Zone	59%	16	0.08	17
3 Rushers	2%	29	-0.45	2
4 Rushers	64%	18	0.00	11
5 Rushers	23%	8	0.03	16
6+ Rushers	9%	3	-0.24	6
Pressure	32%	17	-0.31	18

Seattle Seahawks

1st NFC West

SIS-WAR xWins	Pythagorean Wins	Actual Wins	Decision Score Rank
9.9	10.5	12	18 / 32

Position Strengths

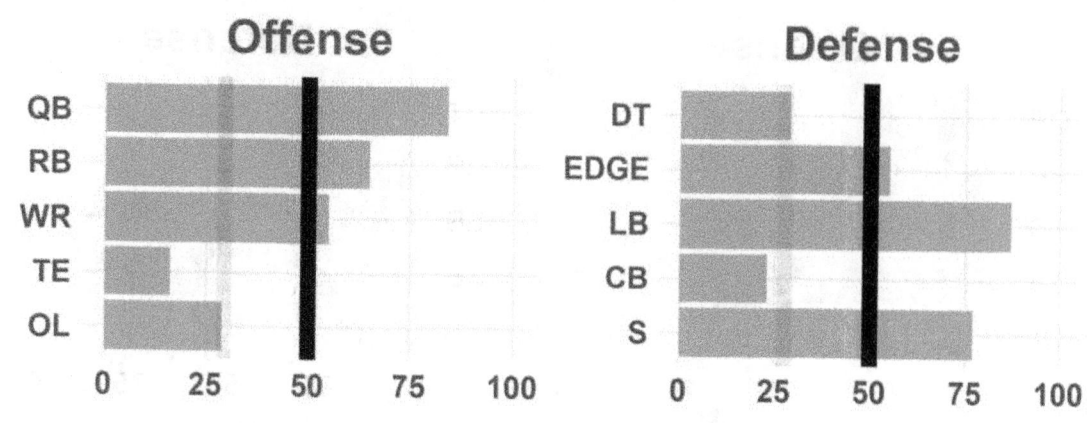

Percentile rank of Total Points for each team by position

Top Personnel Groupings

Group	Pct	Rank	EPA/P	Rank
11	64%	14	0.01	16
12	30%	4	0.14	2
10	2%	11	0.19	6

Key 2020 Rookies

Rd	Player	Pos	Total Points
1	J. Brooks	LB	27
3	D. Lewis	G	16
5	A. Robinson	DE	15

Offensive Identity

Split	Pct	Rank	EPA/P	Rank
Shotgun	69%	13	0.02	15
Under Center	31%	20	0.05	6
Motion	45%	15	0.05	8
No Motion	55%	18	0.01	13
Gap Run	21%	25	-0.05	17
Zone Run	79%	8	-0.06	10
Play Action	25%	18	0.12	16
Dropback	75%	15	0.08	12
vs. Man	30%	21	0.03	17
vs. Zone	61%	5	0.12	11
vs. Blitz	29%	8	0.07	14
Under Pres	33%	11	-0.31	11

Defensive Identity

Split	Pct	Rank	EPA/P	Rank
Base	38%	2	-0.12	9
Nickel	54%	20	0.06	22
Dime+	7%	20	0.10	23
Gap Run	24%	27	-0.01	14
Zone Run	76%	6	-0.17	2
Man	20%	31	0.12	24
Zone	68%	3	0.07	16
3 Rushers	9%	10	-0.03	11
4 Rushers	60%	25	0.08	22
5 Rushers	22%	12	-0.04	9
6+ Rushers	7%	9	0.32	28
Pressure	33%	15	-0.38	12

Tampa Bay Buccaneers

2nd NFC South

SIS-WAR xWins	Pythagorean Wins	Actual Wins	Decision Score Rank
14.6	11.6	11	30 / 32

Position Strengths

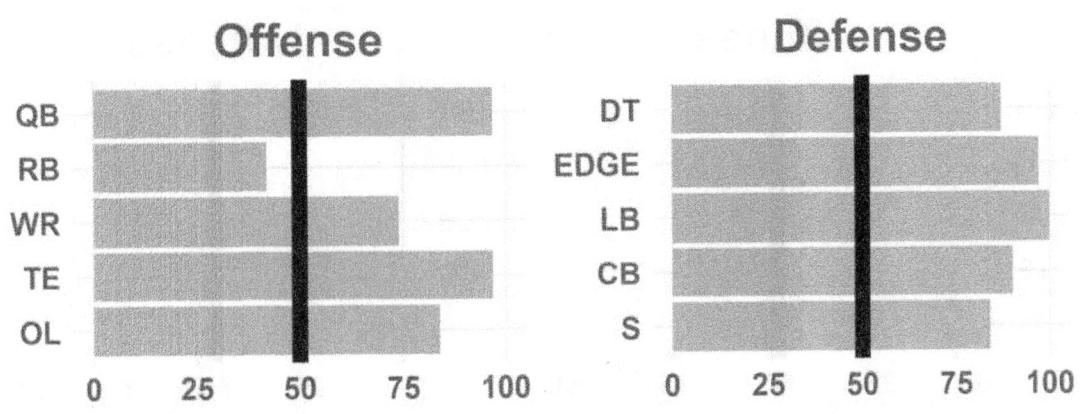

Percentile rank of Total Points for each team by position

Top Personnel Groupings

Group	Pct	Rank	EPA/P	Rank
11	61%	17	0.03	13
12	22%	12	0.10	7
10	6%	3	0.12	9

Key 2020 Rookies

Rd	Player	Pos	Total Points
1	T. Wirfs	T	36
2	A. Winfield Jr.	S	29
5	T. Johnson	WR	3

Offensive Identity

Split	Pct	Rank	EPA/P	Rank
Shotgun	56%	25	0.06	9
Under Center	44%	8	0.07	3
Motion	49%	9	0.19	1
No Motion	51%	24	-0.05	20
Gap Run	40%	7	0.11	5
Zone Run	60%	26	-0.13	24
Play Action	19%	30	0.32	2
Dropback	81%	3	0.08	11
vs. Man	35%	7	0.19	6
vs. Zone	52%	28	0.13	10
vs. Blitz	23%	24	-0.09	26
Under Pres	24%	29	-0.37	15

Defensive Identity

Split	Pct	Rank	EPA/P	Rank
Base	33%	7	0.00	25
Nickel	62%	12	-0.12	3
Dime+	1%	30	-0.64	2
Gap Run	30%	16	-0.31	1
Zone Run	70%	17	-0.14	10
Man	24%	24	-0.05	14
Zone	66%	7	0.02	10
3 Rushers	6%	16	-0.13	5
4 Rushers	56%	29	0.03	16
5 Rushers	29%	3	0.01	12
6+ Rushers	8%	6	-0.32	3
Pressure	39%	5	-0.35	15

Tennessee Titans

1st AFC South

SIS-WAR xWins	Pythagorean Wins	Actual Wins	Decision Score Rank
7.1	9.3	11	14 / 32

Position Strengths

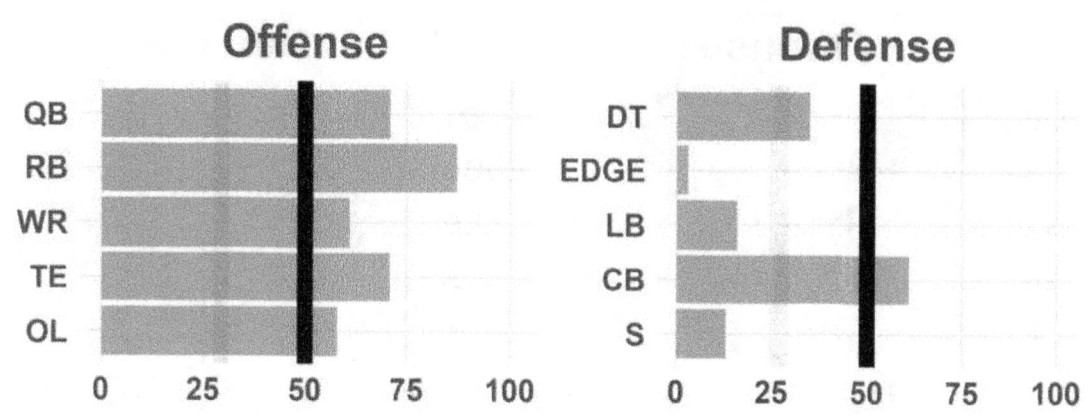

Percentile rank of Total Points for each team by position

Top Personnel Groupings

Group	Pct	Rank	EPA/P	Rank
11	40%	31	0.10	6
12	33%	2	0.13	4
21	10%	9	0.01	19

Key 2020 Rookies

Rd	Player	Pos	Total Points
2	K. Fulton	CB	7
UD	T. Tart	DT	3
1	I. Wilson	T	—

Offensive Identity

Split	Pct	Rank	EPA/P	Rank
Shotgun	42%	30	0.13	4
Under Center	58%	3	0.10	1
Motion	57%	4	0.13	3
No Motion	43%	29	0.08	4
Gap Run	16%	30	0.10	6
Zone Run	84%	3	0.02	1
Play Action	36%	1	0.21	7
Dropback	64%	32	0.16	6
vs. Man	37%	3	0.07	12
vs. Zone	55%	22	0.29	1
vs. Blitz	29%	7	0.20	3
Under Pres	30%	21	-0.38	17

Defensive Identity

Split	Pct	Rank	EPA/P	Rank
Base	21%	20	-0.01	21
Nickel	51%	26	0.11	28
Dime+	26%	6	0.09	22
Gap Run	33%	10	0.09	29
Zone Run	67%	23	-0.14	11
Man	36%	13	0.22	31
Zone	51%	21	0.18	27
3 Rushers	12%	6	0.32	25
4 Rushers	66%	16	0.12	27
5 Rushers	17%	22	0.14	25
6+ Rushers	3%	24	0.26	26
Pressure	27%	29	-0.21	27

Washington Football Team

1st NFC East

SIS-WAR xWins	Pythagorean Wins	Actual Wins	Decision Score Rank
8.4	8.2	7	31 / 32

Position Strengths

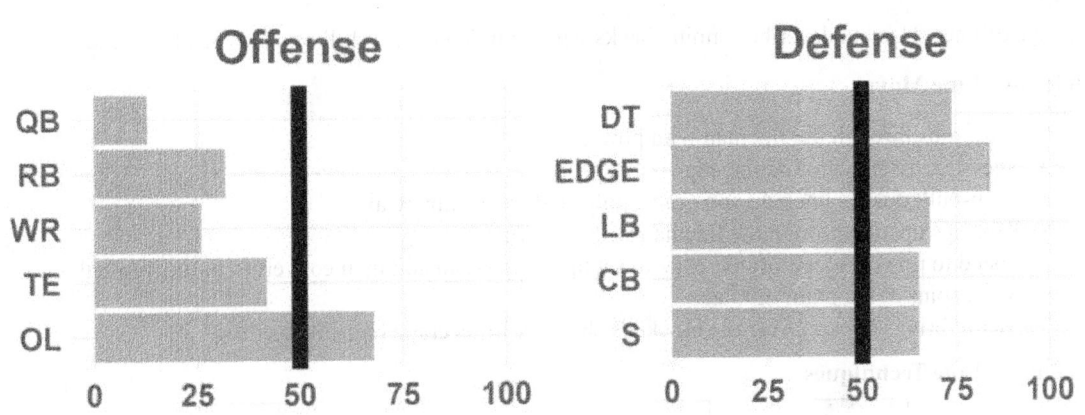

Percentile rank of Total Points for each team by position

Top Personnel Groupings

Group	Pct	Rank	EPA/P	Rank
11	68%	11	-0.10	29
12	15%	22	-0.14	31
21	12%	7	0.02	16

Key 2020 Rookies

Rd	Player	Pos	Total Points
1	C. Young	DE	38
7	K. Curl	S	36
3	A. Gibson	RB	11

Offensive Identity

Split	Pct	Rank	EPA/P	Rank
Shotgun	76%	8	-0.10	29
Under Center	24%	25	-0.17	30
Motion	53%	6	-0.09	27
No Motion	47%	27	-0.15	31
Gap Run	33%	10	-0.01	14
Zone Run	67%	23	-0.07	12
Play Action	27%	14	-0.08	28
Dropback	73%	19	-0.18	31
vs. Man	27%	29	-0.17	27
vs. Zone	61%	4	-0.14	32
vs. Blitz	21%	29	-0.04	21
Under Pres	29%	23	-0.65	31

Defensive Identity

Split	Pct	Rank	EPA/P	Rank
Base	26%	11	-0.11	10
Nickel	64%	11	-0.15	2
Dime+	2%	24	0.27	27
Gap Run	35%	6	-0.10	7
Zone Run	65%	27	-0.15	5
Man	24%	25	-0.26	3
Zone	63%	9	-0.10	4
3 Rushers	5%	21	-0.05	8
4 Rushers	67%	11	-0.09	4
5 Rushers	22%	13	-0.25	3
6+ Rushers	5%	19	-0.50	2
Pressure	35%	9	-0.68	1

Football Terminology

Ankle Flexion

The degree of ability for a player to bend at the ankles. Ankle flexibility is important for balance and leverage at many positions.

COD

Change of Direction.

COP

Change of Pace. Used to describe running backs with complementary skill sets to typical starters.

Defensive Line Moves

- Bull: runs through the lineman with power
- Speed: beats him around the edge with speed
- Push-pull: pushes lineman and grabs, pulls and sheds him away
- Rip: rips up and through the lineman with one arm
- Speed to power: speed off the edge to set up the lineman and then convert to power through him
- Spin: spins at the point of attack
- Swim: brings his arm over the blocker's shoulder to leverage himself past him

Defensive Line Techniques

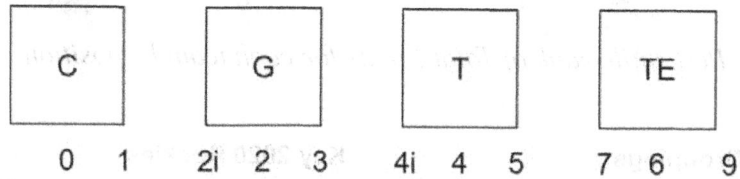

EPA (Expected Points Added)

The change in Expected Points for the offense on a play. Expected Points quantifies the value of any down, distance, and field position situation in terms of the average value of the next scoring event. The EPA of a play is the difference between the Expected Points before and after the play happened.

FBI

Football Intelligence.

Force Defender

The defender who is schematically responsible for leveraging the point of attack in a given situation. This is most commonly used to refer to an edge defender responsible for outside contain, tasked with forcing the run back to the inside.

Injury Designations

➕ *Currently injured* players have an injury which has affected their ability to participate in draft preparation and may affect their ability to participate in the combine, pro days, and/or OTAs, but they have limited long-term risk.

✳ *Long-term injury risk* players have had extensive injury histories, severe injuries, and/or injuries which historically have a high rate of aggravation or recurrence.

LOS
Line of Scrimmage.

Man/Gap Blocking
A run scheme which is designed to attack a specific gap, with each blocker being assigned to block a certain defensive player, depending on alignment and stunts.

Mesh Point
The exchange point, usually between the QB and RB, on a read-option play.

Navigating Trash
The ability for a defender to work through tight spaces amongst big bodies while visioning the ball carrier in order to arrive at the play.

Personnel Packages (11, 12, 21, etc.)
Two-digit codes that represent the number of RBs and TEs, respectively, the offense has on the field. For example, '21' personnel means there are 2 RBs and 1 TE on the field.

POA
Point of Attack.

Reducing Down
Moving the alignment of a defensive lineman towards the interior of the line. This is usually used to describe edge defenders with the ability to move inside in obvious passing situations.

Sam, Mike, and Will Linebackers
Strongside, Middle, and Weakside Linebackers.

Set the Edge
Prevent a ball carrier from running outside by controlling the outermost gap on the play.

Single High Coverage
Any coverage in which a defender is playing zone in the deep middle of the field (e.g., Cover 1, Cover 3). Also known as MOFC (Middle of the Field Closed).

Two High Coverage
Any coverage in which two secondary defenders are in split deep zones (e.g., Cover 2, Cover 4). Also known as MOFO (Middle of the Field Open).

Zone Blocking
A run scheme in which the offensive linemen move in the same direction as one another and each is assigned to block whatever defender enters their area of assignment, with the runner ultimately attacking a gap based on how the blocking influences the leverage of a keyed defender.

4-digit height code
Player heights are expressed in a 4-digit code, with the first digit representing their height in feet, the second and third digits combining to represent inches, and the fourth digit representing eighths of an inch (e.g., 6043 is 6-foot-4-and 3/8 inches; 5110 is 5-foot-11 even). An 'E' after the height (or weight) code indicates an estimated number, while a 'V' indicates a verified number (from either CGS or Senior Bowl weigh-ins).

Sports Info Solutions Grading Scale

Before we get into the reports, it's important that we explain how our grading scale works. As a scouting staff, we use a common terminology to grade every trait that we evaluate. We use a 1-9 scale with a 1 representing a "Reject" grade and a 9 meaning a "Rare" grade for whatever trait we are evaluating. We spend a lot of time in Scout School making sure that our scales are calibrated with one another, and this common scale and set of language is a key aspect to ensuring that our evaluations are consistent (that…and cross-checks).

As you look at the scale, note that there is a bold line separating Good (6) from Sufficient (5). Good signifies a trait that wins at the NFL level most of the time. It is the minimum target that needs to be met in order to build a Super Bowl-level roster.

Grade	Key Term	Definition
9	Rare	Performs this factor **with rare ease and consistency every time**. Shows absolutely no weakness. Can be expected to do the seemingly impossible on occasion, and it shows against all levels of competition. **Consistently dominates.**
8	Excellent	Performs this factor **with ease and consistency a high percentage of the time**. Shows no weakness. Makes difficult plays look routine, and it shows against all levels of competition. **Has the ability to do the unusual**. Can dominate.
7	Very Good	Performs this factor **effectively a high percentage of the time** and is **capable of flashes of brilliance**. Can't make all the great plays, but will make some of them, and it shows against all levels of competition.
6	Good	Performs this factor in an **effective manner most of the time or has a level of inconsistency**. He gives a solid performance and will contribute to a winning effort. He can hold his own against top competition. <u>**6 wins at the NFL level most of the time!**</u>
5	Sufficient	Performs this factor in an **adequate/sufficient manner most of the time but may have trouble against top competition**.
4	Mediocre	Performs this factor in an **adequate manner some of the time**, but he **will** have trouble against top competition. **His inconsistency to perform is obvious**, and it keeps him at a 4.
3	Poor	**Does not** perform this factor at an adequate level. Inconsistent and will probably hurt the team. If he does perform at an acceptable level, it is usually against weaker competition.
2	Terrible	Has a **major deficiency** in this particular factor, which he will not be able to overcome.
1	Reject	No redeemable qualities.

Additionally, as you get to the beginning of each position in the book, you will notice that there are positional grading scales. As opposed to grading traits, these scales apply to stacking the final grades for each prospect. For example, in a few pages you can find our Quarterback Grading Scale.

The final grades are listed in the left column (unlike trait grades, these have decimals), but you won't find traditional round-based grades here. Like certain teams, we organize our scale based on how the players project to contribute, not based on the traditional, "he looks like a third rounder," which we think can lead to confusion. For quarterbacks (and at every position), the top grade level is 9.0-7.0, which signifies a perennial Pro Bowl-level player (not an alternate!). The rest of our draftable grades flow down from there.

One final note: all of these grades and descriptions refer to where the player is projected to be by the first game of their second season in the NFL. Sound complicated? Like most things football, you'll see that it's actually quite simple.

Our 2020 Charting Process

John Todd

Sports Info Solutions was no stranger to the adversity of COVID-19. While Nathan Cooper and I run the scouting process for the *Football Rookie Handbook*, first and foremost our job—along with many others—is to work with Dan Foehrenbach to oversee the daily operation of our charting process. Quarantine hit a little over a month after last year's *Handbook* was completed as we were in the beginning stages of our offseason projects and preparing to begin interviewing for the fall class of Football Video Scouts. Unlike our baseball operation, which did a commendable job of adjusting on the fly in the middle of training for the 2020 season, we were able to transition into remote work and prepare our plan of attack. However, even that extra time didn't matter when we got to August.

Our first day of training was scheduled for mid-August, and the official news of Group of Five conferences like the Mountain West postponing their seasons finally came one week before that, with the Big Ten and Pac-12 soon to follow. As a result, we were left requiring a smaller Video Scout class than in years past, based on the significantly fewer games expected to be played. We carried out a socially-distanced, in-person two-week training period for the scouts, strictly adhering to protocols, and were off and running.

As conferences began announcing their returns to the fall season, we found ourselves in need of additional scouts in a short amount of time. In total, we conducted four different training sessions to get staggered newcomers up to speed and into the mix, all while continuing our usual day to day. We are very thankful for our entire 2020 Video Scout class for their supreme flexibility throughout our roller coaster of a year.

We have long felt conducting our charting operation in person is an important part of ensuring accuracy within our data collection processes. We are accustomed to constant, open communication, and nothing facilitates that like being in the same place as one another. However, naturally we needed to adapt to the times this fall and transitioned into a hybrid process that involved more remote work. Our IT department coordinated the remote accessibility we needed so scouts were able to work safely and efficiently. Shift times and deadlines were still strictly followed, and while we would have all preferred working together in person, we're very pleased with our data quality after the change.

From a new data perspective, the biggest 2020 addition was beginning to analyze games through Frame Timer Data. Scouts were tasked with timing different aspects of passing and kicking plays, resulting in a more complete picture of throwing, kicking, and pressure information. We also added specificity to the screen routes that we collect, added several data points related to special teams, added detail to broken and missed tackles to give these events more context, refined the way that we track motion, and made dozens of enhancements to continually improve the Football Operation. Our recruiting, training, and charting processes are incredibly thorough and in-depth in normal years, so successfully completing them all in 2020 was no small feat. Adding in the scouting aspect of our company to complete the other half of this *Handbook* was another story...

Our 2020 Scouting Process

Nathan Cooper

2020 was some kind of year. Normally our scouting season officially kicks off with visits to the College Gridiron Showcase down in Ft. Worth, TX, and then the Senior Bowl in Mobile, AL, but this year was different, as were most things. With the outbreak of COVID-19 and all of the quarantining regulations associated with travel, unfortunately, we felt it best to not make those trips this season and to do our scouting from afar. We commend everyone associated with CGS and the Senior Bowl for completing their weeks successfully, efficiently, and most important, safely.

A lot changed with our scouting process last season, and while we kept most of those same processes, we still had to make some on-the-fly adjustments. First, we got a head start with a number of full-time staff watching film and writing reports on prospects throughout the summer leading up to the 2020 season. Then, with the college football season drastically altered, we were only able to bring in about half as many Football Video Scouts as compared to usual. Suffice it to say that this led to some major changes in how we had to approach things.

One of the big wrenches thrown into the mix, along with the cancellation of so many college football games, was the fact that this year's eligibility essentially didn't count. Freshmen will once again return as freshmen next year, 4th-year seniors could return next year, and even players who had already played six seasons in college could return for a seventh in 2021. This made our scouting assignments challenging. While we mainly focus on seniors and the top underclassmen throughout the season, we were at risk of any seniors going back to school and having to mark them off our list. There were over 100 players for whom we had reports, including a few underclassmen, who ultimately decided to go back to school next season.

Something that we were able to keep consistent that worked well last season was John and I splitting our cross-checking responsibilities into regions. While both of us crossed into the other region to write up a few select players, the cross-checking responsibilities stayed the same as last year. I was the primary cross-checker for players in the SEC East, Big 12, American, Mountain West, MAC, and any small school east of the Mississippi. John was responsible for players in the SEC West, Big Ten, Pac-12, C-USA, Sun Belt, and any Independent or small school west of the Mississippi. This allowed us to hone in on specific conferences and teams to really get a sense of the draftable players in that area.

We had over 600 players in our database, with over 450 of those who ultimately decided to throw their name into the mix for this year's NFL Draft. Between the two of us, we looked at every report submitted, over 740, and edited and/or cross-checked all 318 players in this year's *Handbook*. The number of reports that made the book have gone from 254 to 284 to 318, and that's a testament to all the hard work of everyone associated with Sports Info Solutions. With all the adversity we were presented with, we feel great about how the year went and the overall processes that we continue to improve upon. With that, we hope you enjoy the third edition of *The SIS Football Rookie Handbook*.

Quarterbacks

Mark Simon

We measure many player skills with our charting, but one that's a little trickier to measure than others for quarterbacks is leadership.

We can measure pass accuracy with numbers. We can measure deep- and short-passing success and mobility with them too. But leadership is harder.

I asked Matt Manocherian, who used to work for the Saints and Browns, for his opinion. He explained leadership as the idea that your leader would be somebody who inspires others to work to achieve their best. It's particularly important at quarterback, where the player often is the face of the franchise and the best player on the team.

Matt tells the story of working in training camp on a day off for the players. As he went through the locker room to deliver some reports from the trainers to the front office, he saw Drew Brees sitting alone. Brees was doing visualization work, imagining all of the potential coverage permutations that he could see for a new offensive package that had just been installed. As Matt explained, Brees impacted the entire program by always being both their best player *and* their hardest-working player.

Looking for leadership on the field is hard. It's more subtle and our scouts do their best to pick up on the little things that players do. We look for players who pick their teammates up, take control of the huddle in times of adversity, have the respect of their teammates, and make big plays when their teams need them the most.

And then they put a number on it, as you'll see on these next few pages. Five quarterbacks scored a 7 in that trait, the highest grade we gave to any quarterback in this year's draft class. One of them is a superstar who is viewed as a franchise quarterback—Trevor Lawrence. But let's look at the other quarterbacks who scored a 7 because these strike us as players you'll want to know a little more about, even if their skills don't make them superstar players.

You would figure that a quarterback who won a national championship for Alabama would grade a 7 for leadership and Mac Jones does. Jones is just outside the elite class of quarterbacks after a season in which he beat out a 5-star recruit to win the starting job and had to deal with the pressure of replacing Tua Tagovailoa.

Jones also graded a 7 in accuracy and deep accuracy. He has great touch albeit with limited arm strength and a release that isn't quite up to top-quarterback status that prevents his ranking with the best-of-the-best.

Texas' Sam Ehlinger's best trait is his leadership. It's the only one in which he was graded a 7, He's the No. 10-ranked quarterback with a projection of being a circumstantial starter and needing the right system to thrive.

Notre Dame prides itself on building not just football players but leaders and Ian Book fits that description. Book has grades of 7 for leadership and mobility. The trouble spots for him are in his decision making and deep-ball accuracy. Can those be taught and picked up on by someone with Book's leadership ability? That's a question any team considering a flier on him might ponder.

Last among the top-graded leaders is Brady White of Memphis. White has a way to go, but there's upside in his footwork, smarts and toughness. White is 24 years old and has led by example off the field (he's currently pursuing his *doctorate* in liberal studies). It will be challenging for White to make an NFL roster. But a level of leadership that can't be taught might be the key factor that helps him find his way.

QUARTERBACK

Quarterback Grading Scale

GRADE	DESCRIPTION
9.0 – 7.0	Pro Bowl level player. Difference-maker.
6.9 – 6.7	Strong starter. One of the reasons you win.
6.6 – 6.5	Sufficient starter. You can win with him.
6.4 – 6.2	Circumstantial starter or high-quality backup.
6.1 – 6.0	Developmental. Top traits but needs time.
5.9	Career #2 backup.
5.8	Eventual #2 backup.
5.7	3rd-string or practice squad candidate.

Quarterback Rankings

Rank	Name	Grade	Page
1	Trevor Lawrence	7.2	110
2	Justin Fields	6.9	112
3	Zach Wilson	6.9	114
4	Trey Lance	6.6	116
5	Mac Jones	6.6	118
6	Kyle Trask	6.4	120
7	Davis Mills	6.4	122
8	Kellen Mond	6.3	124
9	Jamie Newman	6.3	126
10	Sam Ehlinger	6.2	128
11	Ian Book	5.9	130
12	Peyton Ramsey	5.9	131
13	Feleipe Franks	5.8	132
14	Brady White	5.8	133
15	Shane Buechele	5.8	134
16	Kevin Thomson	5.8	135

Glossary

ANY/A
Adjusted Net Yards Per Attempt, which is calculated as:
(Pass Yards - Sack Yards + (20 * Passing TDs) - (45 * INTs)) / (Pass Attempts + Sacks)

ADoC (Avg Depth of Completion)
Average yards downfield that the quarterback completed his passes, from the LOS to the catch point.

ADoT (Avg Depth of Target)
Average yards downfield that the quarterback attempted his passes, from the LOS to the intended catch point.

Cbl% (Catchable%)
The percentage of throws that conceivably could have been caught by the receiver. Excludes spikes, miscommunications, Hail Mary throws, and passes that were batted down.

IQR
Sports Info Solutions' proprietary quarterback metric that builds on the traditional Passer Rating formula by isolating competitive throws (e.g. by excluding throwaways and only including accurate completions) and eliminating the effects of results outside his control (e.g. dropped passes, dropped interceptions).

On-Trgt% (On-Target%)
The percentage of throws that did not require the receiver to unnecessarily adjust. Excludes spikes, miscommunications, Hail Mary throws, and passes that were batted down.

pComp%
Predicted Completion Percentage, which is based on Sports Info Solutions' Predicted Completions model that factors in route type, the defensive coverage, distance of throw, and whether or not the defensive line was able to generate pressure to determine how likely each pass was to be completed.

pComp +/-
Predicted Completion Percentage Plus/Minus, or how much better or worse a player's actual completion percentage was than what was predicted.

Rating
Traditional Passer Rating.

Total Points
Sports Info Solutions' proprietary player value metric that uses an Expected Points framework and distributes the value gained or lost on a play to the players involved based on their impact on the play.

Total Points Rating
Total Points per play compared to average, scaled so that 50 is poor and 99 is excellent.

Y/A (Passing split)
Yards per pass attempt.

Y/A (Rushing split)
Yards per rush attempt, not counting sacks.

Quarterback Leaderboards

	Total Points Per Game		
Rk	Player	School	Tot Pts / G
1	M. Jones	Alabama	14.9
2	J. Fields	Ohio State	13.4
3	K. Trask	Florida	13.3
4	Z. Wilson	BYU	11.6
5	S. Buechele	SMU	11.1
6	T. Lawrence	Clemson	10.3
7	I. Book	Notre Dame	9.9
8	D. Mills	Stanford	9.8
9	K. Mond	Texas A&M	9.0
10	P. Ramsey	Northwestern	7.9

	Total Points Rating Per Play		
Rk	Player	School	Rating
1	Z. Wilson	BYU	99
1	M. Jones	Alabama	99
3	J. Fields	Ohio State	98
4	K. Trask	Florida	97
5	K. Mond	Texas A&M	95
6	I. Book	Notre Dame	94
7	T. Lawrence	Clemson	92
8	S. Buechele	SMU	89
9	P. Ramsey	Northwestern	87
10	D. Mills	Stanford	86

	Passing Total Points Per Game		
Rk	Player	School	Tot Pts / G
1	M. Jones	Alabama	15.1
2	K. Trask	Florida	13.6
3	Z. Wilson	BYU	11.8
4	J. Fields	Ohio State	10.6
5	K. Mond	Texas A&M	9.7
6	I. Book	Notre Dame	9.3
7	T. Lawrence	Clemson	9.2
8	S. Buechele	SMU	9.1
9	D. Mills	Stanford	9.0
10	P. Ramsey	Northwestern	7.7

	Total Points Rating Per Pass		
Rk	Player	School	Rating
1	Z. Wilson	BYU	99
1	M. Jones	Alabama	99
3	K. Trask	Florida	98
4	J. Fields	Ohio State	97
5	K. Mond	Texas A&M	96
6	I. Book	Notre Dame	95
7	T. Lawrence	Clemson	92
8	P. Ramsey	Northwestern	88
8	S. Buechele	SMU	88
10	2 tied with		86

	Rushing Total Points Per Game		
Rk	Player	School	Tot Pts / G
1	J. Fields	Ohio State	2.8
2	S. Buechele	SMU	2.1
3	T. Lawrence	Clemson	1.1
4	D. Mills	Stanford	0.8
5	I. Book	Notre Dame	0.7
6	S. Ehlinger	Texas	0.4
7	P. Ramsey	Northwestern	0.2
7	B. White	Memphis	0.2
9	M. Jones	Alabama	-0.2
9	F. Franks	Arkansas	-0.2

	Total Points Rating Per Rush		
Rk	Player	School	Rating
1	J. Fields	Ohio State	99
1	S. Buechele	SMU	99
3	T. Lawrence	Clemson	96
3	D. Mills	Stanford	96
5	I. Book	Notre Dame	82
6	S. Ehlinger	Texas	73
6	P. Ramsey	Northwestern	73
6	B. White	Memphis	73
9	F. Franks	Arkansas	63
10	Z. Wilson	BYU	59

On-Target Percentage

Rk	Player	School	On-Trgt%
1	T. Lawrence	Clemson	85%
1	M. Jones	Alabama	85%
3	Z. Wilson	BYU	83%
4	F. Franks	Arkansas	82%
5	K. Trask	Florida	80%
6	I. Book	Notre Dame	78%
6	P. Ramsey	Northwestern	78%
6	S. Buechele	SMU	78%
9	D. Mills	Stanford	77%
10	S. Ehlinger	Texas	76%

Independent Quarterback Rating

Rk	Player	School	IQR
1	M. Jones	Alabama	145.2
2	Z. Wilson	BYU	138.6
3	K. Trask	Florida	129.0
4	T. Lawrence	Clemson	123.6
5	J. Fields	Ohio State	123.5
6	F. Franks	Arkansas	118.6
7	S. Buechele	SMU	117.2
8	S. Ehlinger	Texas	110.0
9	I. Book	Notre Dame	109.6
10	B. White	Memphis	102.0

Catchable Percentage

Rk	Player	School	Cbl%
1	M. Jones	Alabama	91%
2	Z. Wilson	BYU	90%
3	T. Lawrence	Clemson	89%
3	K. Trask	Florida	89%
5	J. Fields	Ohio State	87%
5	F. Franks	Arkansas	87%
7	D. Mills	Stanford	86%
8	K. Mond	Texas A&M	85%
8	P. Ramsey	Northwestern	85%
10	2 tied with		84%

IQR Under Pressure

Rk	Player	School	IQR
1	M. Jones	Alabama	136.5
2	I. Book	Notre Dame	114.2
3	Z. Wilson	BYU	111.2
4	K. Trask	Florida	107.2
5	S. Ehlinger	Texas	99.8
6	J. Fields	Ohio State	93.4
7	T. Lawrence	Clemson	92.3
8	F. Franks	Arkansas	86.1
9	B. White	Memphis	80.0
10	K. Mond	Texas A&M	77.0

Completion Percentage

Rk	Player	School	Comp%
1	M. Jones	Alabama	77%
2	Z. Wilson	BYU	74%
3	J. Fields	Ohio State	70%
4	T. Lawrence	Clemson	69%
4	K. Trask	Florida	69%
6	F. Franks	Arkansas	68%
7	D. Mills	Stanford	66%
8	I. Book	Notre Dame	65%
8	S. Buechele	SMU	65%
10	K. Mond	Texas A&M	63%

IQR Without Pressure

Rk	Player	School	IQR
1	Z. Wilson	BYU	136.7
2	M. Jones	Alabama	136.1
3	K. Trask	Florida	132.5
4	J. Fields	Ohio State	127.4
5	S. Buechele	SMU	124.5
6	T. Lawrence	Clemson	123.9
7	F. Franks	Arkansas	120.0
8	K. Mond	Texas A&M	110.1
9	I. Book	Notre Dame	106.2
10	2 tied with		104.9

Passing Yards Per Game

Rk	Player	School	Yds/G
1	K. Trask	Florida	357
2	M. Jones	Alabama	346
3	T. Lawrence	Clemson	315
4	S. Buechele	SMU	310
5	Z. Wilson	BYU	308
5	B. White	Memphis	308
7	D. Mills	Stanford	302
8	J. Fields	Ohio State	263
9	S. Ehlinger	Texas	257
10	I. Book	Notre Dame	236

Total Touchdowns Per Game

Rk	Player	School	TD/G
1	K. Trask	Florida	3.8
2	Z. Wilson	BYU	3.6
3	J. Fields	Ohio State	3.4
3	S. Ehlinger	Texas	3.4
5	T. Lawrence	Clemson	3.2
5	M. Jones	Alabama	3.2
7	B. White	Memphis	3.0
8	S. Buechele	SMU	2.5
9	K. Mond	Texas A&M	2.3
10	3 tied with		2.0

Yards Per Attempt

Rk	Player	School	Y/A
1	M. Jones	Alabama	11.2
2	Z. Wilson	BYU	11.0
3	K. Trask	Florida	9.8
4	T. Lawrence	Clemson	9.4
5	J. Fields	Ohio State	9.3
6	F. Franks	Arkansas	8.9
7	S. Buechele	SMU	8.4
8	B. White	Memphis	8.1
9	S. Ehlinger	Texas	8.0
9	I. Book	Notre Dame	8.0

Adjusted Net Yards Per Attempt

Rk	Player	School	ANY/A
1	M. Jones	Alabama	12.0
2	Z. Wilson	BYU	11.0
3	K. Trask	Florida	10.0
4	T. Lawrence	Clemson	9.0
5	J. Fields	Ohio State	8.0
5	K. Mond	Texas A&M	8.0
5	S. Buechele	SMU	8.0
8	D. Mills	Stanford	7.0
8	S. Ehlinger	Texas	7.0
8	3 tied with		7.0

Expected Points Added Per Dropback

Rk	Player	School	EPA/DB
1	M. Jones	Alabama	0.49
2	Z. Wilson	BYU	0.39
3	T. Lawrence	Clemson	0.25
3	K. Trask	Florida	0.25
5	J. Fields	Ohio State	0.24
6	K. Mond	Texas A&M	0.20
7	I. Book	Notre Dame	0.17
8	D. Mills	Stanford	0.16
9	S. Buechele	SMU	0.15
10	S. Ehlinger	Texas	0.10

Total Expected Points Added Per Game

Rk	Player	School	EPA/G
1	M. Jones	Alabama	16.7
2	Z. Wilson	BYU	13.0
3	J. Fields	Ohio State	11.9
4	T. Lawrence	Clemson	9.6
5	K. Trask	Florida	9.5
6	S. Buechele	SMU	7.7
7	I. Book	Notre Dame	7.6
8	D. Mills	Stanford	7.4
9	K. Mond	Texas A&M	6.1
10	S. Ehlinger	Texas	5.1

Trevor Lawrence

Final Grade: 7.2

Report by Jordan Edwards

School	Height	Weight	Year	Jersey #	Hometown
Clemson	6055 V	213 V	3JR	16	Cartersville, GA

One Liner
Lawrence has the potential to be a transcendent quarterback and leader with his exceptional combination of accuracy and arm strength.

Overall
Trevor Lawrence leads the spread RPO offense for the Clemson Tigers, operating exclusively out of shotgun. Clemson likes to get its athletes out in space with quick screens and create mismatches on the outside with its big wide receivers. Lawrence has competed in 40 career games and started in 36 of those games, including winning a National Championship as a true freshman. He will be getting labrum surgery on his non-throwing shoulder leading up to the draft. He has a tall and long-limbed frame with a big upper body, but has continued to fill out his frame throughout his collegiate career. He's a tough competitor who shows the ability to overcome adversity and stay poised in big games.

Pass Game
Lawrence is an accurate thrower at all levels. He is excellent in the short game, and his misses are few and far between. His ball placement in the intermediate area is exceptional as well. He shows good ball placement on deep throws, allowing his receivers to have a chance at making a catch. He has very good arm strength and delivers the ball with a good combination of velocity and touch. Lawrence is very fluid mechanically and has good footwork in the pocket. He throws with a consistent base, and rarely throws off platform when it isn't needed. Due to his big upper body, his release can seem elongated, but the ball still jumps out of his hand. He shows the ability to extend plays and escape the pocket to make on-target throws while on the move. He has the poise and toughness to complete throws under heavy pressure as well. His arm strength also allows him to make awkward throws on the run with ease. Lawrence works well in the Clemson offense that utilizes half-field reads and progressions, but as he enters the league, he needs to improve his ability to work the entire field. He has a tendency to lock onto targets and try to force throws into small windows. Ball security in the pocket is an area of concern as well. He's shown that he can be a clutch performer in critical points of games, as well as lead comebacks against top competition.

Run Game
Lawrence became an integral part of the running game over his career at Clemson. He isn't a dual-threat quarterback by definition, but he shows the ability to execute designed run plays, such as QB draws and option plays. He shows the ability to extend plays and run for big gains scrambling out of the pocket as well. His awareness and IQ as a runner are steadily improving, but he still needs to know when to slide or get out of bounds instead of taking big hits.

Last Word
Lawrence projects to become an elite quarterback at the next level and will be an immediate starter. He will need to keep developing his ability to read defenses and work through his progressions, but his combination of accuracy and arm strength will allow him to be the reason why his team will win at the next level.

Strengths

- Arm strength
- Leadership
- Accuracy & touch

Weaknesses

- Full-field progressions
- Ball security

Critical Factors

Accuracy	Decision Making / Mental	Clutch Performance
7	6	7

Positional Factors

Short Accuracy	Deep Accuracy	Pocket Awareness	Footwork
8	6	7	6
Under Pressure	**Mobility**	**Arm Strength**	**Release**
6	6	7	7
Awkward Throw	**Eye Discipline**	**Leadership**	**Body Comp**
6	6	7	7

Basic

				Passing						
Year	Att	Comp	Comp%	Yds	Y/A	TD / INT	Sacks	ANY/A	Rating	IQR
2018	397	259	65%	3280	8.3	30 / 4	12	8.0	111.9	122.2
2019	407	268	66%	3665	9.0	36 / 8	18	9.0	115.8	129.9
2020	334	231	69%	3153	9.4	24 / 5	15	9.0	116.8	123.6
	1138	758	67%	10098	8.9	90 / 17	45	9.0	114.7	125.4

Advanced

			Passing			Rushing (Excluding Sacks)					Dropbacks
Year	ADoT	ADoC	On-Trgt%	Cbl%	EPA	Att	Yards	Y/A	Scrmbl	EPA	EPA/DB
2018	8.7	6.0	79%	84%	86.8	48	252	5.3	10	-4.6	0.22
2019	9.6	6.3	75%	84%	75.9	85	695	8.2	26	44.8	0.20
2020	8.3	5.5	85%	89%	86.7	53	311	5.9	11	5.2	0.25
	8.9	6.0	79%	85%	249.4	186	1258	6.8	47	45.4	0.22

Deep Dive

	pComp		IQR Detail				Total Points			Total Points Rtg		
Year	%	+/-	Under Pres	No Pres	vs. Man	vs. Zone	Pass	Rush	Total	Per Pass	Per Rush	Per Play
2018	61%	+5%	129.0	116.7	139.3	113.7	146	-12	134	99	50	98
2019	61%	+5%	143.1	115.9	125.3	118.0	132	43	175	95	99	96
2020	65%	+4%	92.3	123.9	120.9	115.2	92	11	103	92	96	92
	62%	+5%	125.6	119.3	131.1	116.0	370	42	412	-	-	-

Justin Fields

Report by Matt Manocherian

School	Height	Weight	Year	Jersey #	Hometown
Ohio State	6025 E	228 E	3JR	1	Kennesaw, GA

One Liner

Fields has very good physical traits across the board with a history of high-level production, and if he can refine his decision-making and develop consistent accuracy, he will be a top-tier player in the NFL.

Overall

Justin Fields is the centerpiece of Ohio State's shotgun-heavy offense. The true junior spent his freshman year backing up Jake Fromm at Georgia and playing in 12 games before transferring to the Buckeyes, where he started each of their 22 games over the last two years. He has very good size for the position including a thick, sturdy frame, and he is an excellent athlete who jumps off the film in this regard, even relative to top competition. He has every physical tool required of a top-level NFL quarterback, and he shows good leadership and toughness on the field.

Pass Game

Fields is a very difficult player to defend in the pass game because he can hurt the defense in so many ways. He shows ample arm strength to stretch the field both vertically and horizontally, with the ability to make every throw. He flashes an elite deep ball, but he also shows some inconsistency, allowing some shots down the sideline to veer out of bounds. Because of his athleticism and coordination, he is at his best when mixing the quick game with designed bootlegs and sprint-outs. He shows excellent accuracy when throwing on the run to his right, and he also shows the ability to make throws while moving to his left. For a young quarterback, he shows great understanding of how to throw with touch and optimize ball placement for running after the catch, but he does show inconsistency at times. Pre-snap, he does a good job of finding and attacking matchups, but on deeper drops he relies on his arm strength to make throws rather than showing anticipation to throw receivers open. Indiana appeared to confuse him by disguising coverages. Because of his strength and athleticism, Fields frustrates pass rushers by being difficult to bring down, and he is very offensive line-friendly, erasing several mistakes made up front every game. He also shows great feel and movement in the pocket, keeping his eyes downfield as he navigates behind the line of scrimmage.

Run Game

Fields is a strong threat in the run game, both on designed runs and scrambles. He has the speed to break contain on read options and the strength to run QB power, which make him a tough matchup in the red zone. His speed is a bit deceptive, which causes many defenders to take bad angles in pursuit, and he can change direction quickly. Once pass plays go off schedule, he is likely to pull it down and is difficult to tackle in the open field.

Last Word

Fields has tantalizing upside based on his combination of youth and having all the physical tools. There is nothing keeping him from developing into a true dropback QB, but the best fit for him early in his career is a Shanahan-style bootleg play action scheme that gets him on the move and allows him to attack the defense from a variety of angles.

Strengths

- Athleticism
- Arm strength
- Playmaking ability

Weaknesses

- Anticipation/processing
- Accuracy is inconsistent at times
- Takes some unncessary risks

Critical Factors

Accuracy	Decision Making / Mental	Clutch Performance
6	6	7

Positional Factors

Short Accuracy	Deep Accuracy	Pocket Awareness	Footwork
6	7	7	6
Under Pressure	Mobility	Arm Strength	Release
6	7	7	6
Awkward Throw	Eye Discipline	Leadership	Body Comp
6	7	6	7

Basic

						Passing				
Year	Att	Comp	Comp%	Yds	Y/A	TD / INT	Sacks	ANY/A	Rating	IQR
2018	39	27	69%	328	8.4	4 / 0	5	8.0	129.0	134.8
2019	354	238	67%	3273	9.2	41 / 3	31	9.0	131.7	132.4
2020	225	158	70%	2100	9.3	22 / 6	21	8.0	121.0	123.5
	618	423	68%	5701	9.2	67 / 9	57	9.0	127.6	130.3

Advanced

			Passing					Rushing (Excluding Sacks)			Dropbacks
Year	ADoT	ADoC	On-Trgt%	Cbl%	EPA	Att	Yards	Y/A	Scrmbl	EPA	EPA/DB
2018	9.7	6.6	74%	79%	4.2	37	295	8.0	13	18.9	0.19
2019	11.7	9.2	73%	84%	123.3	106	689	6.5	41	15.6	0.32
2020	9.4	8.6	75%	87%	50.0	60	516	8.6	31	29.1	0.24
	10.7	8.8	74%	85%	177.5	203	1500	7.4	85	63.6	0.28

Deep Dive

	pComp		IQR Detail				Total Points			Total Points Rtg		
			Under	No	vs.	vs.				Per	Per	Per
Year	%	+/-	Pres	Pres	Man	Zone	Pass	Rush	Total	Pass	Rush	Play
2018	63%	+6%	78.6	148.2	139.0	113.5	12	22	34	96	99	99
2019	58%	+10%	115.5	136.1	126.8	131.2	158	29	187	99	99	99
2020	62%	+8%	93.4	127.4	129.6	112.3	85	22	107	97	99	98
	60%	+9%	104.3	135.7	128.8	125.7	255	73	328	-	-	-

Zach Wilson

Report by Alec Mallon

School	Height	Weight	Year	Jersey #	Hometown
BYU	6023 E	210 E	3JR	1	Draper, UT

One Liner
Wilson is an athletic quarterback who has the arm talent and off-script playmaking ability to become an instant-impact player in the NFL if he can limit the overzealous mistakes.

Overall
Zach Wilson is the quarterback for BYU's high-powered RPO spread offense, primarily operating out of shotgun but regularly taking under center snaps, as well. He has played in 30 games over the past 3 years with 28 starts. Wilson underwent off-season labrum surgery to fix a nagging tear in his throwing shoulder in 2019, and has also admitted to having unsolved labral issues in his non-throwing shoulder, but has not missed game time. He is an agile quarterback with a solid build. He is a natural leader with great instincts and will routinely put his body on the line for his team.

Pass Game
Wilson is electric inside and outside of the pocket. In the pocket, he plays on his toes, keeping his feet and shoulders moving simultaneously to reset his base as he works through reads. He will shuffle his feet on throws against pressure in his face, leading to occasional accuracy issues, but more often than not he's willing to stand tall and take a hit. Wilson does a good job of setting up zone defenders to create throwing windows for himself and is capable of full-field progressions, but can occasionally be caught staring down a read. He has great arm talent to all areas of the field, and while he holds the ball low and has a slight windup motion, he has a lightning quick release to get throws off in tight quarters. He is very accurate with a clean pocket. He prefers to put heat behind his intermediate throws instead of lofting over-under balls, but he does show good touch short and deep. On deep throws specifically, Wilson combines his arm strength to routinely display the ability to place balls in stride over the top of the last line of defense. Wilson is even better on the move and shows the ability to create big plays off-script. However, he also will put too much trust in his arm on occasion and force plays that aren't there as opposed to taking a checkdown. He keeps his eyes downfield on the move and looks to throw, not to run. His dominant offense and weaker schedule had him playing with leads often, but in infrequent comeback situations he showed he was capable.

Run Game
Whether by design or scrambling, Wilson is a threat on the ground. He has more than enough agility and speed to beat linebackers and defensive linemen in the open field. He is capable of turning the corner on outside runs and is not one to get down at the first sign of a defender in his path. He isn't afraid of contact and can be seen running through arm tackles and finishing runs with toughness if extra yards are needed.

Last Word
Wilson projects as a very solid starting QB with real flashes of "win because of" traits. He best fits in a zone offense that utilizes play action to get him on the move and take deep shots. His strong football IQ and arm talent will make him difficult to prepare for, but he will have to prove his breakout 2020 campaign wasn't a fluke.

Strengths

- Arm talent on the move
- Quick release
- Athleticism

Weaknesses

- Greedy decision making
- Overtrusting his arm

Critical Factors

Accuracy	Decision Making / Mental	Clutch Performance
7	6	6

Positional Factors

Short Accuracy	Deep Accuracy	Pocket Awareness	Footwork
6	7	7	7
Under Pressure	Mobility	Arm Strength	Release
6	7	7	6
Awkward Throw	Eye Discipline	Leadership	Body Comp
7	6	6	6

Basic

Year	Passing									
	Att	Comp	Comp%	Yds	Y/A	TD / INT	Sacks	ANY/A	Rating	IQR
2018	182	120	66%	1578	8.7	12 / 3	25	7.0	108.3	112.4
2019	317	197	62%	2372	7.5	11 / 9	19	6.0	84.8	78.2
2020	336	247	74%	3692	11.0	33 / 3	12	11.0	138.1	138.6
	835	564	68%	7642	9.2	56 / 15	56	8.0	111.4	110.3

Advanced

Year	Passing					Rushing (Excluding Sacks)					Dropbacks
	ADoT	ADoC	On-Trgt%	Cbl%	EPA	Att	Yards	Y/A	Scrmbl	EPA	EPA/DB
2018	9.2	7.9	77%	82%	11.4	50	372	7.4	24	17.3	0.10
2019	10.3	7.5	68%	81%	-27.6	48	303	6.3	19	3.3	-0.09
2020	10.4	8.9	83%	90%	136.6	58	362	6.2	16	13.5	0.39
	10.1	8.2	76%	85%	120.5	156	1037	6.6	59	34.1	0.14

Deep Dive

Year	pComp		IQR Detail				Total Points			Total Points Rtg		
	%	+/-	Under Pres	No Pres	vs. Man	vs. Zone	Pass	Rush	Total	Per Pass	Per Rush	Per Play
2018	60%	+5%	61.2	123.7	137.7	100.9	57	27	84	94	99	95
2019	59%	+3%	38.8	78.6	79.9	52.5	32	6	39	65	88	66
2020	62%	+12%	111.2	136.7	151.6	121.6	142	-3	139	99	59	99
	61%	+7%	69.9	113.5	123.8	93.0	231	30	262	-	-	-

Trey Lance

Report by Nathan Cooper

School	Height	Weight	Year	Jersey #	Hometown
North Dakota State	6030 E	226 E	3SO	5	Marshall, MN

One Liner

Lance has the raw tools, arm strength, and mobility both inside and outside the pocket to be a potential starter at the next level, however, inconsistency in his release, accuracy, and limited anticipation on his throws will make it a steeper learning curve early in his career.

Overall

Trey Lance leads North Dakota State's pro-style offense predicated on using play-action passes off the run game. He started 17 of 19 games during his career. Being a redshirt sophomore, Lance will still only be 20 years of age at the time of the NFL Draft. He's a very good athlete with the size and frame needed to withstand hits at the next level. He's a competitor and shows it both as a passer and runner.

Pass Game

Lance is very mechanical in his drops and exaggerates his steps away from center. His base gets a little wide when striding to throw. He gathers a little bit and rocks forward, which generates a lot of torque and velocity on the ball. His release is elongated, bringing the ball down near his hip at times. His follow-through goes more across his body rather than down, especially in the pocket. It'll come across his torso and then up parallel to his shoulder. This forces inconsistent release points, as well as accuracy. On the run, he does a good job of finishing down instead of across, though he rarely gets downhill, nearly always falling to the sideline. When everything goes right mechanically, Lance shows the spot-on accuracy to put the ball where it needs to be and give his receivers a chance to finish the play. He throws the deep ball well, putting air under it when needed and allowing his receiver the chance to go get it. He does a good job using his eyes to look off the safety. Many of his reads were pre-snap or half-field, however, he's able to quickly work back to the opposite side when initial reads aren't there. Overall, he makes good decisions and doesn't normally put the ball in harm's way, though he rarely throws with any anticipation. The receiver needs to be open or coming open for him to pull the trigger. With an elongated release and limited anticipation, he'll have a tougher time fitting balls into smaller windows at the next level. He shows good poise, manipulating the pocket well and working away from pressure, rarely letting it affect him. When needing to throw under duress, he stays calm and can deliver an accurate ball. If he scrambles, it's nearly always because no one is open. He does a great job of keeping his eyes downfield and only running if required. Most of their games were blowouts, but when throws and plays were needed, Lance seemed to come through.

Run Game

Lance is very mobile and moves well as a runner. He's built like a back and can run like it. He ran a lot of veers and QB powers where he showcased his running ability. As a scrambler, he can get outside the pocket and make plays with his feet. At the end of runs, he lowers his shoulder for extra yards.

Last Word

Lance projects as a sufficient win-with starting quarterback in the NFL who can thrive in a system that focuses on the run and play-action pass. He has the tools, but his inconsistency and limited experience likely make it more than 2 years until he reaches his full potential.

Strengths
- Throws deep ball well
- Generates a lot of torque
- Threat as a runner

Weaknesses
- Lacks anticipation
- Inconsistent release & follow-through
- On-the-spot short accuracy

Critical Factors

Accuracy	Decision Making / Mental	Clutch Performance
5	5	6

Positional Factors

Short Accuracy	Deep Accuracy	Pocket Awareness	Footwork
5	6	6	5
Under Pressure	Mobility	Arm Strength	Release
6	7	6	5
Awkward Throw	Eye Discipline	Leadership	Body Comp
5	6	6	7

Basic

	Passing									
Year	Att	Comp	Comp%	Yds	Y/A	TD / INT	Sacks	ANY/A	Rating	IQR
2019	287	192	67%	2786	9.7	28 / 0	13	10.0	130.8	133.7
2020	30	15	50%	149	5.0	2 / 1	2	3.0	72.8	99.2
	317	207	65%	2935	9.3	30 / 1	15	10.0	125.3	130.5

Advanced

	Passing					Rushing (Excluding Sacks)					Dropbacks
Year	ADoT	ADoC	On-Trgt%	Cbl%	EPA	Att	Yards	Y/A	Scrmbl	EPA	EPA/DB
2019	10.6	7.7	78%	85%	105.3	156	1159	7.4	33	63.9	0.40
2020	11.9	4.9	62%	69%	-14.3	13	164	12.6	2	10.7	-0.39
	10.7	7.5	77%	84%	91.0	169	1323	7.8	35	74.6	0.33

Deep Dive

	pComp		IQR Detail				Total Points			Total Points Rtg		
Year	%	+/-	Under Pres	No Pres	vs. Man	vs. Zone	Pass	Rush	Total	Per Pass	Per Rush	Per Play
2019	62%	+5%	123.8	132.5	107.0	130.8	94	53	147	95	99	96
2020	63%	-13%	54.5	86.6	75.5	81.0	-5	9	5	50	99	53
	62%	+3%	120.1	128.7	108.0	127.1	89	62	152	-	-	-

Career stats only include seasons since 2019

Mac Jones

Report by Jeff Dean & Danny Shirilla

School	Height	Weight	Year	Jersey #	Hometown
Alabama	6025 V	217 V	4JR	10	Jacksonville, FL

One Liner

Jones uses his sound decision making, deep-ball touch, and composed command of his offense to provide a steady hand at the helm, but his limited arm strength and improvisational skills may keep him from being an elite starter.

Overall

Mac Jones is the quarterback for Alabama's RPO-heavy record-breaking offense. He has played in 39 career games, but most of them came as a holder or in mop-up duty early in his career. He replaced the injured Tua Tagovailoa late in 2019 and went on to start 17 games and lead the Crimson Tide to the 2020 national title. Jones has a solid frame and enough agility to maneuver the pocket but lacks athleticism as a pocket-bound QB. He has a calm, composed demeanor about him and played his best football as the stage got larger.

Pass Game

Jones used his accuracy, decision making ability, and consistency to fuel the Alabama offense all season. He has clean footwork on his dropback, with or without play action. His footwork when throwing can be unsettled, especially under pressure. He doesn't always step into his throws and falling off in the face of pressure leaves balls floating on him. He does a good job overall of reading the defense and rarely puts the ball in harm's way. He can get stuck on his first read and didn't always have to play with much anticipation with how efficient his offense and route runners were. However, he's very comfortable checking down if the throw isn't there. Jones has a sufficient release, but has a slight hitch in his throwing motion that limits the velocity the ball comes out with. He has good pocket awareness and became more comfortable standing in the pocket as he gained experience. He does a fantastic job of subtly maneuvering the pocket to open space and cleaner throwing lanes while keeping his eyes downfield. He has good spot-on short accuracy to put the ball in front of his targets to maximize yards after the catch, something his offense greatly benefitted from. Jones has great deep accuracy and his touch is his best asset. He doesn't have the strongest arm to drive off his back foot and fit it into tight windows on a rope, but he can drop the ball in a bucket against tight coverage downfield beautifully. He was sufficient throwing on the move and made good decisions on extended plays, but he isn't much of an off-script playmaker.

Run Game

Jones is not a threat to run with the ball on designs, but he can pick up a few yards on scrambles, if necessary. He tucks and runs as a last resort and usually gets down before he even has the choice to make someone miss or fight for extra yardage. He understands his limitations in open space.

Last Word

Jones projects as a win-with starter who fits best in a West Coast offense that mixes in some deep shots. He rarely puts the ball in dangerous positions and has winning accuracy and touch to all levels. He doesn't have a flashy arm or perfect mechanics, and he certainly played with elite talent to support him, but Jones proved he is more than just a game manager with his performances down the stretch on his way to winning the championship.

Strengths

- Touch
- Accuracy
- Pocket mobility

Weaknesses

- Footwork under pressure
- Arm strength
- Throwing mechanics

Critical Factors

Accuracy	Decision Making / Mental	Clutch Performance
7	6	6

Positional Factors

Short Accuracy	Deep Accuracy	Pocket Awareness	Footwork
6	7	6	6
Under Pressure	Mobility	Arm Strength	Release
5	4	5	5
Awkward Throw	Eye Discipline	Leadership	Body Comp
6	6	7	6

Basic

Year	Att	Comp	Comp%	Yds	Y/A	TD / INT	Sacks	ANY/A	Rating	IQR
2018	13	5	38%	123	9.5	1 / 0	1	9.0	99.2	99.2
2019	141	97	69%	1503	10.7	14 / 3	2	11.0	128.1	134.7
2020	402	311	77%	4500	11.2	41 / 4	13	12.0	143.0	145.2
	556	413	74%	6126	11.0	56 / 7	16	11.0	138.2	142.7

(Passing)

Advanced

	Passing					Rushing (Excluding Sacks)					Dropbacks
Year	ADoT	ADoC	On-Trgt%	Cbl%	EPA	Att	Yards	Y/A	Scrmbl	EPA	EPA/DB
2018	6.6	6.6	69%	77%	-2.6	2	-1	-0.5	0	-3.1	-0.19
2019	8.3	5.8	75%	82%	33.5	14	54	3.9	12	5.3	0.24
2020	8.3	6.7	85%	91%	202.7	22	87	4.0	9	8.5	0.49
	8.3	6.5	82%	88%	233.7	38	140	3.7	21	10.7	0.41

Deep Dive

	pComp		IQR Detail				Total Points			Total Points Rtg		
Year	%	+/-	Under Pres	No Pres	vs. Man	vs. Zone	Pass	Rush	Total	Per Pass	Per Rush	Per Play
2018	64%	-26%	64.6	118.8	64.6	118.8	-1	0	-1	52	50	52
2019	65%	+4%	116.2	126.9	115.8	110.6	49	3	52	98	94	97
2020	66%	+12%	136.5	136.1	144.5	134.1	196	-2	194	99	57	99
	65%	+9%	131.3	134.2	136.1	129.0	244	1	245	-	-	-

Kyle Trask

Report by Joe McDonald & Luke DeCello

School	Height	Weight	Year	Jersey #	Hometown
Florida	6036 E	240 E	5SR	11	Manvel, TX

One Liner

Trask shows a quick release with good accuracy and an ability to read the defense, but lacks the decision making, poise, and overall mobility to make him a great starting quarterback at the next level.

Overall

Kyle Trask is the quarterback for Florida's pro-style, shotgun-heavy offense. He started 22 of 28 games for the Gators. He tore his meniscus which caused him to miss the 2017 season, missed 11 games after suffering a foot injury in 2018, and played through a sprained MCL in 2019. Trask is a tall, big-bodied quarterback, though he's not an incredible athlete. He's a competitor and shows it through his play style and leadership.

Pass Game

Trask is a little herky-jerky prior to taking the snap, but then looks comfortable setting up in the pocket. He shows good accuracy with adequate arm strength to make difficult throws in tight windows. He does a good job throwing with anticipation, putting the ball away from the defenders, and giving his receivers a chance to make plays after the catch. He is a smart quarterback who has shown the ability to make multiple reads and hit the open man. However, he will also occasionally stare down his targets or make an ill-advised throw to a covered receiver on his 2nd or 3rd read. He is very comfortable in the pocket and not afraid to take hits, frequently making accurate, smart throws while being hurried or hit. However, there are times where he struggles to sense pressure, especially from his back side. While he is not a very mobile quarterback, he is very adept at navigating the pocket and finding the space to plant and make a strong throw. When Trask has to leave the pocket and make a throw on the run, he is reliable doing so. He has improved his instincts and feel of the pocket since 2019, tucking the ball away or moving in the pocket to avoid the rush.

Run Game

In the run game, Trask is not a legitimate running threat to the defense. He doesn't have the speed to outrun defenders, but is able to lumber and pick up short yardage when he has to and lower his shoulder to gain the extra yard.

Last Word

Trask projects as a good quality backup or circumstantial starter in a run-first system where he can benefit from play action and short passes to take advantage of his quick release and short on-the-spot accuracy.

Strengths

- On-the-spot short accuracy
- Ability to read defenses
- Smooth release

Weaknesses

- Inconsistent decision making
- Poise to sense pressure
- Lacks overall mobility

Critical Factors

Accuracy	Decision Making / Mental	Clutch Performance
6	6	6

Positional Factors

Short Accuracy	Deep Accuracy	Pocket Awareness	Footwork
6	5	6	5
Under Pressure	Mobility	Arm Strength	Release
5	4	5	6
Awkward Throw	Eye Discipline	Leadership	Body Comp
6	6	6	6

Basic

Year	Passing									
	Att	Comp	Comp%	Yds	Y/A	TD / INT	Sacks	ANY/A	Rating	IQR
2018	22	14	64%	162	7.4	1 / 0	1	7.0	100.9	113.8
2019	354	237	67%	2941	8.3	25 / 7	21	7.0	107.8	109.1
2020	437	301	69%	4285	9.8	43 / 8	20	10.0	125.5	129.0
	813	552	68%	7388	9.1	69 / 15	42	9.0	117.1	120.0

Advanced

Year	Passing					Rushing (Excluding Sacks)					Dropbacks
	ADoT	ADoC	On-Trgt%	Cbl%	EPA	Att	Yards	Y/A	Scrmbl	EPA	EPA/DB
2018	9.9	6.3	65%	85%	3.0	4	9	2.3	0	-0.9	0.13
2019	8.3	6.0	79%	85%	39.5	42	175	4.2	12	0.1	0.11
2020	9.4	7.8	80%	89%	121.7	43	176	4.1	13	-2.6	0.25
	9.0	7.0	79%	87%	164.2	89	360	4.0	25	-3.4	0.19

Deep Dive

Year	pComp		IQR Detail				Total Points			Total Points Rtg		
	%	+/-	Under Pres	No Pres	vs. Man	vs. Zone	Pass	Rush	Total	Per Pass	Per Rush	Per Play
2018	60%	+3%	58.3	127.6	95.8	115.1	8	-2	6	98	50	97
2019	61%	+6%	88.6	115.7	121.1	89.3	100	-9	91	91	50	90
2020	61%	+8%	107.2	132.5	129.4	113.4	163	-5	159	98	54	97
	61%	+7%	97.2	125.4	124.8	104.0	271	-16	256	-	-	-

Davis Mills

Report by Ben Hrkach

School	Height	Weight	Year	Jersey #	Hometown
Stanford	6031 E	225 E	4SR	15	Duluth, GA

One Liner
Mills has the natural ability and demeanor of a capable starter, but he'll need to greatly improve his eye discipline and susceptibility to turnovers to consistently start and win games moving forward.

Overall
Davis Mills is the quarterback for Stanford's run-heavy power offense that features a vertical passing game. He regularly worked from under center as well as in shotgun. He has started 11 games in his career, appearing in 14. He has a history of knee injuries and missed 2 games in 2019 to a related issue. A former top-ranked recruit, he is a solid athlete for the position and can make plays with his legs when needed. He displays good toughness, competitiveness, and leadership as a captain.

Pass Game
In the pass game, Mills is a natural thrower. He throws a tight spiral and has good touch. He has the ability to make every level of throw. He does not have an explosive arm, but he has enough juice to get the ball down the field and squeeze it into small windows. He has good accuracy on underneath routes and consistently puts the ball on the correct shoulder. His deep accuracy is inconsistent and he will miss on some open shots downfield. His misses are often due to lapses in footwork and he occasionally opens his front hip and steps off throws. Mills' biggest issue is tunnel vision. He frequently stares down one man and does not recognize nearby defenders waiting to make a play on the ball. Mills does not show an ability to make more than two reads, and his issues in this area did not show improvement through his career. He displays good toughness in the pocket and will deliver the ball while taking a shot but struggles to do so accurately. He has sufficient pocket awareness and always has his eyes downfield, but does not do much to manipulate the pocket with his feet and can be a statue at times. Mills has the ability to extend plays and can make throws on the run. He is a solid improviser and keeps his receivers alive deep into plays.

Run Game
Mills is enough of a threat that the defense has to respect his ability to run. He has a good feel for when to pull the ball on reads and can sufficiently picks up critical yards. He is not a dynamic runner, but he takes what the defense gives him and he knows how to pick up the first when needed. Mills doesn't scramble often and prefers to use his feet to keep passes alive rather than taking off.

Last Word
Mills has the physical tools to be a successful QB at the next level, but inconsistent footwork, decision making, and eye discipline currently project him as more of a circumstantial starter than a player teams can win with week in and week out. His high school pedigree and natural talent will give him opportunities, but he showed minimal improvement in his weakest areas over his two years as a starter. With defenses only getting more complex moving forward, he'll need to take a big leap to see the field consistently and limit turnovers.

Strengths

- Natural talent
- Short accuracy
- Toughness under pressure

Weaknesses

- Decision making and turnovers
- Staring down receivers
- Pocket awareness

Critical Factors

Accuracy	Decision Making / Mental	Clutch Performance
6	5	6

Positional Factors

Short Accuracy	Deep Accuracy	Pocket Awareness	Footwork
6	5	5	5
Under Pressure	**Mobility**	**Arm Strength**	**Release**
5	5	5	6
Awkward Throw	**Eye Discipline**	**Leadership**	**Body Comp**
6	4	6	6

Basic

						Passing				
Year	Att	Comp	Comp%	Yds	Y/A	TD / INT	Sacks	ANY/A	Rating	IQR
2018	2	0	0%	0	0.0	0 / 0	0	-	39.6	39.6
2019	241	158	66%	1954	8.1	11 / 5	12	7.0	97.1	98.0
2020	195	129	66%	1508	7.7	7 / 3	10	7.0	95.0	94.3
	438	287	66%	3462	7.9	18 / 8	22	7.0	95.7	95.9

Advanced

			Passing			Rushing (Excluding Sacks)					Dropbacks
Year	ADoT	ADoC	On-Trgt%	Cbl%	EPA	Att	Yards	Y/A	Scrmbl	EPA	EPA/DB
2018	18.0	-	50%	50%	-2.0	1	5	5.0	1	-0.5	-0.83
2019	8.8	6.1	77%	85%	23.1	20	108	5.4	15	-5.0	0.09
2020	7.3	6.3	77%	86%	32.8	20	98	4.9	11	3.5	0.16
	8.2	6.2	77%	85%	54.0	41	211	5.1	27	-2.0	0.12

Deep Dive

	pComp		IQR Detail				Total Points			Total Points Rtg		
Year	%	+/-	Under Pres	No Pres	vs. Man	vs. Zone	Pass	Rush	Total	Per Pass	Per Rush	Per Play
2018	52%	-52%	-	39.6	39.6	-	-	-	0	-	-	-
2019	64%	+2%	72.6	101.9	96.3	80.0	53	1	54	83	73	83
2020	64%	+2%	44.9	104.9	77.9	101.9	45	4	49	86	96	86
	64%	+2%	61.3	102.7	86.5	90.3	98	5	103	-	-	-

Kellen Mond

Report by Chad Tedder

School	Height	Weight	Year	Jersey #	Hometown
Texas A&M	6024 V	205 V	4SR	11	San Antonio, TX

One Liner
Mond has the arm strength, mobility, and toughness to be an effective circumstantial starter at the next level, but his inconsistencies with the deep ball and throwing under pressure will keep him out of a consistent starting role.

Overall
Kellen Mond is the 3-year starter at quarterback in Texas A&M's spread offense. He played in 47 games, starting in 44 of them for the Aggies. He has a long, slender frame with good size for the position. He's a tough athlete with plenty of arm strength who plays with good competitiveness and leadership to try to lead his team to a win.

Pass Game
Mond shows good footwork both out of the shotgun and the occasional under center dropbacks. He holds the ball with a high elbow allowing him to keep it high and tight, and away from danger. This allows him to have a short and quick release, but also makes him more constricted when it comes to throwing on the move or under pressure. He often relies on his natural upper-body strength to get the ball downfield, struggling with timing and driving through his lower body on such a quick release. This leads to some of his intermediate and deep throws being off the back foot, and consequently leads to inaccuracies. Occasionally, he can get into a rhythm and show flashes of his mechanics working together to make a strong, accurate throw downfield into a tight window. However, his release point can be inconsistent, making it tough for him to show a consistent follow-through. He often makes good decisions in reading coverages and doesn't put the ball in danger too often, but there are a few instances where he misreads coverages, or open receivers, and forces the ball into dangerous areas. He shows good mobility in moving up in the pocket, feeling pressure, and rolling out when he needs to, and also understands the athleticism he possesses to pull the ball down and run the ball himself.

Run Game
In the run game, Mond shows the ability to hurt the defense on scrambles and designed runs out in space. He's effective as a zone-read rusher and shows he can gain valuable yards by pulling and running. He uses his length to eat up grass and accelerate downfield. He also has the savviness to slide and get out of bounds to avoid taking a big hit and risk injury.

Last Word
Mond best projects as a quality backup quarterback or circumstantial starter where he can show his natural talent as a thrower and a runner. He fits best in a scheme where he can utilize his short accuracy and designed running ability. His struggles with throwing under pressure, the deep ball, and lower-body mechanics will keep him from being a starter. He has plenty of talent and experience worth developing to grow into a low-end "win with" starter if he can put it all together.

Strengths

- Short, quick release
- Arm talent
- Running ability

Weaknesses

- Driving through his lower body
- Deep ball consistency
- Throwing under pressure

Critical Factors

Accuracy	Decision Making / Mental	Clutch Performance
6	6	5

Positional Factors

Short Accuracy	Deep Accuracy	Pocket Awareness	Footwork
7	5	5	5
Under Pressure	Mobility	Arm Strength	Release
5	6	7	6
Awkward Throw	Eye Discipline	Leadership	Body Comp
5	5	6	6

Basic

					Passing					
Year	Att	Comp	Comp%	Yds	Y/A	TD / INT	Sacks	ANY/A	Rating	IQR
2017	227	117	52%	1375	6.1	8 / 6	19	4.0	71.0	84.8
2018	415	238	57%	3107	7.5	24 / 9	33	6.0	91.3	95.6
2019	419	258	62%	2897	6.9	20 / 9	32	5.0	89.2	92.4
2020	297	188	63%	2282	7.7	19 / 3	8	8.0	104.0	101.3
	1358	801	59%	9661	7.1	71 / 27	92	6.0	90.0	94.1

Advanced

			Passing			Rushing (Excluding Sacks)					Dropbacks
Year	ADoT	ADoC	On-Trgt%	Cbl%	EPA	Att	Yards	Y/A	Scrmbl	EPA	EPA/DB
2017	9.7	5.1	-	76%	-45.1	71	480	6.8	20	11.2	-0.17
2018	9.5	6.6	72%	78%	24.4	116	679	5.9	25	-7.7	0.07
2019	8.7	6.1	74%	82%	0.2	95	705	7.4	30	20.7	0.03
2020	8.9	6.6	75%	85%	55.7	67	328	4.9	17	-3.0	0.20
	9.1	6.2	74%	80%	35.2	349	2192	6.3	92	21.1	0.04

Deep Dive

	pComp		IQR Detail				Total Points			Total Points Rtg		
Year	%	+/-	Under Pres	No Pres	vs. Man	vs. Zone	Pass	Rush	Total	Per Pass	Per Rush	Per Play
2017	58%	-7%	84.4	76.8	66.8	86.0	-	-	-	-	-	-
2018	57%	+1%	63.8	107.5	90.6	79.6	96	12	108	86	83	86
2019	59%	+2%	66.4	103.9	67.2	109.1	99	20	120	85	96	86
2020	61%	+2%	77.0	110.1	85.7	102.5	97	-7	90	96	54	95
	59%	0%	70.4	101.7	79.0	96.2	292	25	318	-	-	-

Jamie Newman

Report by Nathan Cooper

School	Height	Weight	Year	Jersey #	Hometown
Georgia	6027 V	235 V	5SR	9	Graham, NC

One Liner
Newman has the decision making and eye discipline to scan the field and move defenders with the arm strength to make all the throws, but he'll need to improve his on-the-spot accuracy at all levels of the field and poise in the pocket to find playing time at the next level.

Overall
Jamie Newman is a quarterback for Georgia, but never played for them after opting out and declaring for the Draft. He transferred to Georgia after spending 4 seasons at Wake Forest (2016-19) where he operated mostly out of shotgun in 11 personnel. He started 16 of 21 games while at Wake. Even though he has good size and body composition, durability has been an issue, as he's been knocked out of multiple games. He's a good athlete for the position, but isn't super twitchy. He plays hard and competes, also showing toughness in battling through some big hits.

Pass Game
One of the biggest questions for Newman is his accuracy. At times, he shows flashes of good on-the-spot accuracy all over the field, but misses his spot too often. Throwing the bubble or swing out to the flat has proven difficult for him as the majority of the time the ball sails high. On the intermediate-deep ball, he can hit receivers in stride, but will overthrow often and doesn't always use touch on his passes when needed. Newman possesses a compact, over-the-top release which allows him to get the ball out quickly with very good velocity, but can dip his shoulder and shot put the ball which forces it to sail. He is very mechanical with his footwork and exaggerates his drops to make sure his timing is correct. He'll overstride at times at the throw. He will sometimes simulate pressure which affects him following through on throws. When pressure is coming, he's able to recognize it and work the pocket to extend the play and keep his eyes downfield. He stands in the pocket and delivers an accurate ball knowing the hit is coming. As a decision maker, Newman normally makes good decisions, but will put the ball in harm's way at times. He shows good eye discipline and works the entire field to go through his progressions and rarely fixates onto a single target. He can make all the throws on the field possessing a very strong arm. He can throw from the pocket or on the move. In the clutch, he can put the ball where it needs to be in order to move the chains or get into the end zone.

Run Game
As a runner, Newman can be a threat to the defense. He doesn't have a ton of speed, but has the mobility to escape the pocket and gain yardage with his legs or even win with designed QB runs. He's a tough runner and tries for extra yardage, rarely sliding.

Last Word
Newman projects as circumstantial starting Quarterback at the next level, but would prove best as a quality backup. He'd succeed best in a pro-style offense that focuses on the run and short-to-intermediate passing game. He has traits to be effective at the next level, but needs more experience and learning to become a more efficient overall passer.

Strengths

- Arm strength
- Works the field
- Mobility

Weaknesses

- Inconsistent on-the-spot accuracy
- Simulates pressure
- Lacks touch on passes

Critical Factors

Accuracy	Decision Making / Mental	Clutch Performance
5	6	5

Positional Factors

Short Accuracy	Deep Accuracy	Pocket Awareness	Footwork
5	5	5	5
Under Pressure	Mobility	Arm Strength	Release
6	6	7	5
Awkward Throw	Eye Discipline	Leadership	Body Comp
5	6	6	6

Basic

Year	Passing									
	Att	Comp	Comp%	Yds	Y/A	TD / INT	Sacks	ANY/A	Rating	IQR
2017	4	2	50%	8	2.0	0 / 1	0	-	16.7	64.6
2018	141	84	60%	1083	7.7	9 / 4	11	6.0	93.2	90.5
2019	360	220	61%	2868	8.0	26 / 11	21	7.0	97.5	98.8
	505	306	61%	3959	7.8	35 / 16	32	6.0	95.1	95.6

Advanced

Year	Passing					Rushing (Excluding Sacks)					Dropbacks
	ADoT	ADoC	On-Trgt%	Cbl%	EPA	Att	Yards	Y/A	Scrmbl	EPA	EPA/DB
2017	15.5	-1.0	-	100%	-2.8	1	5	5.0	0	0.1	-0.70
2018	9.9	8.1	73%	77%	6.7	53	290	5.5	5	6.9	0.04
2019	10.6	8.6	66%	79%	26.3	159	716	4.5	35	-8.1	0.06
	10.5	8.4	68%	79%	30.2	213	1011	4.7	40	-1.1	0.05

Deep Dive

Year	pComp		IQR Detail				Total Points			Total Points Rtg		
	%	+/-	Under Pres	No Pres	vs. Man	vs. Zone	Pass	Rush	Total	Per Pass	Per Rush	Per Play
2017	58%	-8%	-	64.6	56.3	-	-	-	-	-	-	-
2018	59%	0%	90.1	80.8	82.7	75.7	23	8	31	76	91	77
2019	59%	+2%	87.4	96.8	95.7	95.0	55	1	56	73	66	72
	59%	+2%	88.7	91.0	89.2	92.0	78	9	87	-	-	-

Sam Ehlinger

Report by Lathon Lax & Evan Butler ✳

School	Height	Weight	Year	Jersey #	Hometown
Texas	6014 V	222 V	4SR	11	Austin, TX

One Liner

Ehlinger is a good athlete with the moxy and toughness to compete as a backup at the next level, but his gunslinger mentality and inconsistent decision making skills hurts his chances of becoming a starter.

Overall

Sam Ehlinger is a quarterback in the spread RPO-based offense at Texas, running primarily out of 11 personnel sets. He played in 46 games during his time with the Longhorns, starting in 43 of them. He had meniscal surgery on both knees and a fractured wrist in 2016 during high school and then suffered a right shoulder AC sprain and a concussion in 2018. His toughness and dependability make him a quality leader and someone teammates can rally around. He has a good, strong frame and is able to take the hits required at the quarterback position.

Pass Game

Ehlinger displays the ability to stand in the pocket and deliver an accurate football to his receivers, especially in the short area of the defense. He has a quick, natural throwing motion and an adequate level of arm strength. He can make all the throws needed, though he's best when getting the ball out of his hands quickly. His decision making has proven to be an issue at times, as he too often tries to fit the ball into tight coverage rather than taking what the defense gives him. That said, he recognizes matchups and attacks weaker defenders. He's accurate on uncovered targets, but doesn't show much anticipation to throw them open. He is not overly impressive in 3rd down situations, especially on 3rd and long. However, he consistently put the team on his shoulders and brought them back from deficits for huge comeback wins. Ehlinger possesses quality athleticism, which allows him to work the pocket and get out of trouble when things break down and he does a decent job of keeping his eyes downfield when doing so. His accuracy suffers a bit when under pressure, most often leading to high passes. At times, he does hold onto the ball too long, leading to more sacks than necessary.

Run Game

Ehlinger is impressive when escaping the pocket and running against the defense. He's not twitched up, but his speed allows him to hold his own against the majority of linebackers, while his strength allows him to absorb contact and gain some hard-earned yards. When the team was presented with critical short yardage situations, it would most often be Ehlinger that carried the football. He's a competitor with the football in his hands, and that's also apparent when he runs the ball. He does have the tendency to take unnecessary hits, rather than getting down or out of bounds.

Last Word

Ehlinger projects as a circumstantial starter, but better backup in a balanced RPO-based offense that utilizes timing routes and allows him to make quick decisions with the football. His inconsistent decision making and struggles on 3rd downs have proven to be the biggest hurdles that would prevent him reaching his full potential, though his leadership qualities and mobility give his coaches something to work with.

Strengths	Weaknesses
• Mobility	• Decision making
• Recognizes matchups	• Eye discipline
• Leadership	• Deep ball accuracy

Critical Factors

Accuracy	Decision Making / Mental	Clutch Performance
6	5	6

Positional Factors

Short Accuracy	Deep Accuracy	Pocket Awareness	Footwork
6	5	5	5
Under Pressure	Mobility	Arm Strength	Release
5	6	5	6
Awkward Throw	Eye Discipline	Leadership	Body Comp
4	5	7	6

Basic

	Passing									
Year	Att	Comp	Comp%	Yds	Y/A	TD / INT	Sacks	ANY/A	Rating	IQR
2017	275	158	57%	1915	7.0	11 / 7	11	6.0	81.7	94.1
2018	426	276	65%	3290	7.7	25 / 5	27	7.0	102.9	110.7
2019	454	296	65%	3663	8.1	32 / 10	34	7.0	104.4	109.0
2020	322	194	60%	2566	8.0	26 / 5	23	7.0	105.9	110.0
	1477	924	63%	11434	7.7	94 / 27	95	7.0	100.1	107.1

Advanced

	Passing					Rushing (Excluding Sacks)					Dropbacks
Year	ADoT	ADoC	On-Trgt%	Cbl%	EPA	Att	Yards	Y/A	Scrmbl	EPA	EPA/DB
2017	9.4	5.5	-	79%	-16.8	102	480	4.7	32	-5.3	0.00
2018	9.0	6.3	76%	83%	73.3	138	670	4.9	45	25.1	0.16
2019	9.9	6.9	73%	81%	61.1	129	847	6.6	62	25.7	0.16
2020	10.1	6.0	76%	80%	24.9	90	513	5.7	34	14.4	0.10
	9.6	6.3	75%	81%	142.5	459	2510	5.5	173	59.9	0.12

Deep Dive

	pComp		IQR Detail				Total Points			Total Points Rtg		
Year	%	+/-	Under Pres	No Pres	vs. Man	vs. Zone	Pass	Rush	Total	Per Pass	Per Rush	Per Play
2017	58%	0%	79.4	96.9	84.6	87.7	-	-	-	-	-	-
2018	59%	+5%	93.7	111.3	129.8	84.4	121	14	135	93	83	93
2019	63%	+2%	106.7	103.7	112.4	96.8	129	12	141	90	81	90
2020	63%	-2%	99.8	104.9	79.7	107.5	74	4	77	85	73	84
	61%	+2%	95.5	105.0	109.8	95.7	324	30	353	-	-	-

Ian Book

Report by Colin Schappert & Justin Serovich

School	Height	Weight	Year	Jersey #	Hometown
Notre Dame	6000 V	210 V	5SR	12	El Dorado Hills, CA

One Liner

Book has the leadership qualities and athleticism to create plays outside of the pocket to contribute at the next level, but a lack of anticipation, decisiveness, and deep ball accuracy will likely hold him back.

Strengths: Extending plays; Threat as a runner; Leadership & toughness
Weaknesses: Deep throw accuracy; Lacks anticipation & decisiveness; Tucks and runs too quickly

Ian Book is the starting quarterback in Notre Dame's pro-style offense. He started 35 of 47 games for the Irish. He's been a durable player and a great competitor. Although undersized with a sufficient frame, he makes up for it with his athleticism to create plays outside of the pocket.

Book's overall accuracy as a passer is sufficient, consistently overthrowing or underthrowing balls each game. Where he excels is on play actions, plays designed to get him outside the pocket on the run, or extending broken plays. His mobility is very good and his ability to extend plays keeps drives alive. With good pocket awareness, he can sense pressure and manipulates the pocket well. Book has the arm strength to deliver the football to his target and has displayed many times he's able to make opposite-hash throws with no issues. He struggles with his deep-ball accuracy, consistently failing to lead his receiver through the ball. He rarely puts the ball in harm's way, but tends to bail out of the pocket if his initial read isn't there instead of working through his progressions. He also lacks anticipation and decisiveness in his throws. He doesn't pull the trigger when he should and fails to throw receiver's open with consistency.

Book is a threat whether by designed runs or as a scrambler. He does tuck and run too quickly at times, failing to make the decision to deliver a ball into tight windows after a play has broken down. He has the agility to escape the pocket and make defensive linemen miss, and when he reaches the second level, he's not afraid to lower his shoulder for extra yardage.

Overall, Book projects as a backup quarterback due to his overall inaccuracy as a thrower, though his leadership and competitiveness will be great to have in the locker room. Given his athleticism, toughness, and his ability to create plays outside of the pocket, he does have a chance to become a circumstantial starter where using his mobility can extend plays and be an advantage against defenses.

				Passing						
Year	Att	Comp	Comp%	Yds	Y/A	TD / INT	Sacks	ANY/A	Rating	IQR
2017	75	46	61%	456	6.1	4 / 4	6	4.0	74.1	77.1
2018	314	214	68%	2628	8.4	19 / 7	20	7.0	104.6	107.9
2019	399	240	60%	3034	7.6	34 / 6	13	8.0	106.0	112.9
2020	353	228	65%	2835	8.0	15 / 3	25	7.0	100.0	109.6
	1141	728	64%	8953	7.8	72 / 20	64	7.0	101.7	108.1

	Passing					Rushing (Excluding Sacks)				Dropbacks
Year	ADoT	ADoC	On-Trgt%	Cbl%	EPA	Att	Yards	Y/A	Scrmbl	EPA	EPA/DB
2017	9.5	5.6	-	80%	-12.7	32	237	7.4	12	9.7	-0.10
2018	8.5	6.2	78%	84%	63.4	75	382	5.1	39	3.2	0.17
2019	8.4	6.8	71%	83%	63.1	100	616	6.2	48	19.2	0.16
2020	8.1	6.1	78%	84%	50.1	92	626	6.8	54	16.9	0.17
	8.4	6.3	76%	84%	163.9	299	1861	6.2	153	49.1	0.15

	pComp		IQR Detail				Total Points			Total Points Rtg		
Year	%	+/-	Under Pres	No Pres	vs. Man	vs. Zone	Pass	Rush	Total	Per Pass	Per Rush	Per Play
2017	61%	+1%	76.7	77.1	88.2	66.7	-	-	-	-	-	-
2018	61%	+7%	62.7	114.8	106.4	100.6	100	-3	97	96	62	95
2019	60%	0%	77.4	121.0	102.0	108.0	107	0	107	90	65	89
2020	60%	+4%	114.2	106.2	98.4	112.8	111	8	119	95	82	94
	60%	+3%	85.0	111.4	103.2	104.2	318	5	323	-	-	-

Critical Factors	
Accuracy	5
Decision Making / Mental	4
Clutch Performance	6

Positional Factors	
Short Accuracy	5
Deep Accuracy	4
Pocket Awareness	6
Footwork	5
Under Pressure	6
Mobility	7
Arm Strength	6
Release	6
Awkward Throw	5
Eye Discipline	5
Leadership	7
Body Comp.	5

QB Rank: 12 of 16 — **Peyton Ramsey** — Final Grade: 5.9

Report by Ronan Potts & DJ Marquardt

School	Height	Weight	Year	Jersey #	Hometown
Northwestern	6017 V	215 V	5SR	12	Cincinnati, OH

One Liner
Ramsey is a dual-threat quarterback with solid leadership and accuracy, but his size, arm strength, and turnover frequency will likely limit him to a backup role in the NFL.

Strengths: Throwing on the run; Athleticism; Short accuracy
Weaknesses: Arm strength; Turnover prone; Deep accuracy

Peyton Ramsey is a mobile quarterback who plays in Northwestern's spread offense. He has played in 41 games, starting 32. He spent 4 seasons at Indiana before grad transferring to Northwestern in 2020. Ramsey is athletic with good play speed, and although he is slightly undersized, he has a well-proportioned frame. He brings competitive toughness to the position and plays with good leadership qualities and a high motor.

As a passer, Ramsey runs hot-and-cold and lacks special arm talent to make every throw. He has good ball placement in short to intermediate areas, but he is forced to rely on touch due to his mediocre arm strength. Ramsey gets the ball out quickly, but he has a somewhat awkward release which could cause some of his velocity issues. He usually keeps things on schedule and usually throws the ball away instead of taking unnecessary sacks. Unfortunately, he can overlook open receivers or get overconfident forcing throws he doesn't have the arm for, often resulting in turnovers. He extends plays well and is at his best on the move, excelling on designed rollouts and improvising against pressure. He has had sufficient production in clutch moments, moving the chains well and sparking comebacks but also misfiring in some big moments when he needs to win with his arm.

Ramsey can keep defenses honest with his running ability. He isn't a burner, but he is a threat to keep the ball on zone reads and plenty capable of escaping the pocket and making plays with his legs. His ball security as a runner is a cause for concern, however.

Due to his limited arm strength and overall solid, yet unspectacular, skill set, Ramsey's best fit is as a backup at the NFL level. His mobility and accuracy will allow him to move an offense if necessary, but he doesn't have enough top traits to be a player teams win with long term. He best fits in a quick-passing scheme that utilizes play action to get its quarterbacks on the move.

Passing										
Year	Att	Comp	Comp%	Yds	Y/A	TD / INT	Sacks	ANY/A	Rating	IQR
2017	205	134	65%	1246	6.1	10 / 5	13	5.0	88.0	98.5
2018	446	295	66%	2875	6.4	19 / 13	28	5.0	86.1	91.2
2019	299	204	68%	2454	8.2	13 / 5	24	7.0	100.7	101.6
2020	282	172	61%	1733	6.1	12 / 8	13	5.0	80.9	88.8
	1232	805	65%	8308	6.7	54 / 31	78	5.0	88.8	94.4

	Passing					Rushing (Excluding Sacks)				Dropbacks
Year	ADoT	ADoC	On-Trgt%	Cbl%	EPA	Att	Yards	Y/A	Scrmbl	EPA	EPA/DB
2017	5.9	4.1	-	87%	-11.4	79	316	4.0	25	-9.6	-0.03
2018	8.0	6.1	80%	84%	-43.9	83	513	6.2	29	22.0	-0.05
2019	8.7	6.2	77%	86%	26.6	73	388	5.3	33	21.4	0.11
2020	8.4	6.2	78%	85%	3.3	70	349	5.0	35	-3.8	0.02
	7.9	5.8	79%	85%	-25.3	305	1566	5.1	122	30.1	0.01

	pComp		IQR Detail				Total Points			Total Points Rtg		
Year	%	+/-	Under Pres	No Pres	vs. Man	vs. Zone	Pass	Rush	Total	Per Pass	Per Rush	Per Play
2017	59%	+6%	62.7	99.0	65.4	102.8	-	-	-	-	-	-
2018	60%	+6%	61.9	97.7	80.9	93.3	87	11	99	82	88	82
2019	61%	+8%	46.7	118.8	95.3	101.4	91	13	104	93	93	93
2020	59%	+2%	56.5	91.4	72.9	79.7	69	2	71	88	73	87
	60%	+6%	57.1	102.0	78.7	93.3	247	26	274	-	-	-

Critical Factors	
Accuracy	6
Decision Making / Mental	5
Clutch Performance	5

Positional Factors	
Short Accuracy	6
Deep Accuracy	5
Pocket Awareness	5
Footwork	6
Under Pressure	5
Mobility	6
Arm Strength	4
Release	5
Awkward Throw	6
Eye Discipline	5
Leadership	6
Body Comp	5

131

Feleipe Franks

Report by Ty Dorner

School	Height	Weight	Year	Jersey #	Hometown
Arkansas	6063 V	234 V	5SR	13	Crawfordville, FL

One Liner

Franks has good size, athleticism, and mobility to battle for playing time at the next level, but inconsistent footwork, poise, and overall accuracy will ultimately limit him.

Strengths: Ability to extend plays; Earns respect of teammates; Strong build
Weaknesses: Deep accuracy; Poise in the pocket; Inconsistent footwork

Feleipe Franks is a quarterback in Arkansas' shotgun, RPO-heavy offensive attack running mainly 11 personnel looks. He started 24 of 27 games at Florida before finishing up with 9 starts at Arkansas in 2020. He missed 10 games in 2019 with a broken ankle. A high school baseball player, Franks was selected by the Red Sox in the 31st Round of the 2019 MLB Draft. Franks is a sufficiently athletic quarterback with a long frame and very good size. He earns the respect of his teammates through leadership and has shown to be a tough competitor.

With a combination of size and athleticism, Franks is also a sufficient passer. His greatest strength in the pass game is his ability to extend plays with good mobility. He usually makes good decisions though he struggles to throw with anticipation. On short-to-intermediate passes, he has moments where he can put the ball right on his receiver and others where he misses his spot. Usually, this results from inconsistent footwork. His build makes it tough for him to use consistent footwork getting away from center. If his first read isn't open, he gets antsy and begins to sense false pressure, scrambling or throwing from unorthodox positions to get rid of the ball. He shows an adequate, compact release with sufficient arm strength to make most throws required.

Franks poses a threat to take off and run both on designed runs or when scrambling. He has good mobility and shows he can sufficiently operate zone reads and gain yardage with his legs. He's not the best athlete in the world and won't wow as a runner, but the defense has to at least account for him.

Franks projects as an eventual backup quarterback at the next level in an RPO system where he can make easy progressions and that features the short-to-intermediate passing game. He has the size to take the shots needed at the next level, and his leadership skills and mobility can't be taught, but his deficiencies are too much to overcome to say he'll become a starting quarterback in the NFL.

Year	Att	Comp	Comp%	Yds	Y/A	TD / INT	Sacks	ANY/A	Rating	IQR
						Passing				
2017	229	125	55%	1438	6.3	9 / 8	29	4.0	72.3	80.1
2018	322	188	58%	2457	7.6	24 / 6	15	7.0	99.6	104.6
2019	71	54	76%	698	9.8	5 / 3	3	8.0	112.3	115.3
2020	238	163	68%	2107	8.9	17 / 4	30	7.0	112.9	118.6
	860	530	62%	6700	7.8	55 / 21	77	6.0	97.0	102.9

Year	ADoT	ADoC	On-Trgt%	Cbl%	EPA	Att	Yards	Y/A	Scrmbl	EPA	EPA/DB
		Passing					**Rushing (Excluding Sacks)**				**Dropbacks**
2017	10.2	5.1	-	78%	-66.3	29	212	7.3	22	0.7	-0.22
2018	9.6	6.1	75%	80%	17.3	95	441	4.6	21	-1.1	0.07
2019	7.3	5.5	81%	90%	15.7	18	80	4.4	8	-7.2	0.19
2020	6.9	5.9	82%	87%	0.7	75	371	4.9	33	-4.9	-0.01
	8.8	5.8	78%	82%	-32.7	217	1104	5.1	84	-12.6	-0.02

Year	%	+/-	Under Pres	No Pres	vs. Man	vs. Zone	Pass	Rush	Total	Per Pass	Per Rush	Per Play
	pComp		**IQR Detail**				**Total Points**			**Total Points Rtg**		
2017	57%	-3%	43.1	92.6	55.1	80.0	-	-	-	-	-	-
2018	59%	-1%	79.4	106.0	97.1	79.8	66	-9	57	84	56	82
2019	64%	+12%	73.1	116.8	92.4	93.9	32	-5	27	99	50	99
2020	64%	+5%	86.1	120.0	104.4	113.0	58	-2	56	86	63	84
	60%	+1%	65.3	108.2	86.7	89.4	156	-16	140	-	-	-

Critical Factors

Accuracy.	5
Decision Making / Mental	5
Clutch Performance.	6

Positional Factors

Short Accuracy	5
Deep Accuracy.	4
Pocket Awareness.	4
Footwork.	3
Under Pressure	4
Mobility	6
Arm Strength	5
Release.	5
Awkward Throw	4
Eye Discipline	5
Leadership	6
Body Comp.	7

Brady White

Report by Carter Hayden

School	Height	Weight	Year	Jersey #	Hometown
Memphis	6015 E	210 E	6SR	3	Santa Clarita, CA

One Liner

White's footwork, smarts, and leadership show some good upside as a signal caller at the next level, but he'll need to improve his anticipation and deep accuracy if he wants to make a team and see success.

Strengths: Understands DB leverage; Solid footwork; Short accuracy
Weaknesses: Deep accuracy; Anticipating throws; Long delivery

Brady White is a quarterback at Memphis who operated out of shotgun and utilized play-action rollouts and half-field reads. He missed 6 games in 2016 and all of 2017 due to a multiple-fracture Lisfranc injury. He started 1 of 3 games for Arizona State before transferring to Memphis where he started all 39 games. Even with a slight frame, White's toughness and competitiveness have brought him a lot of success as he's never afraid of a challenge.

White will try to make the difficult throw instead of taking what the defense gives him, while also staring down receivers too often. He has good pocket awareness, but gets a little panicky even if there is little to no pressure. However, he does manipulate the pocket well to avoid pressure. White has enough strength and velocity to make off platform throws when needed. His footwork and overall mechanics are solid, but has a long throwing motion, really extending the ball back behind his body. He shows good short accuracy, but his deep accuracy is inconsistent. He understands DB leverage well and knows where to put the ball away from defenders. However, he's shown limited ability to fit balls into tight windows and doesn't throw with much anticipation. With that said, he's able to make throws on the run and under pressure with accuracy. Even with getting a little antsy at times, White stays calm under pressure and keeps his eyes down field when scrambling. This demeanor also helps him convert on 3rd downs and elevate his game when trailing.

White can pick up yards with his legs. He won't run away from anyone, but is willing to tuck it and pick up yards. He needs to work on his ball security, however, as he fumbles too much when he gets hit, especially when he is in the pocket.

White projects best as an eventual backup QB in a run-heavy offense that has a lot of play action and quick, easy reads. White will need to improve his ability to anticipate throws if he wants to be able to complete passes on obvious passing downs.

Passing

Year	Att	Comp	Comp%	Yds	Y/A	TD / INT	Sacks	ANY/A	Rating	IQR
2016	49	25	51%	259	5.3	2 / 1	1	5.0	71.7	86.3
2018	392	246	63%	3299	8.4	26 / 9	26	7.0	102.0	113.6
2019	420	269	64%	4014	9.6	33 / 11	27	8.0	110.6	112.2
2020	421	255	61%	3390	8.1	31 / 10	22	7.0	100.8	102.0
	1282	795	62%	10962	8.6	92 / 31	76	8.0	103.2	108.3

Passing / Rushing (Excluding Sacks) / Dropbacks

	Passing					Rushing (Excluding Sacks)				Dropbacks
Year	ADoT	ADoC	On-Trgt%	Cbl%	EPA	Att	Yards	Y/A	Scrmbl	EPA	EPA/DB
2016	8.5	3.4	-	79%	-7.1	2	7	3.5	1	-0.7	-0.15
2018	8.4	6.1	77%	83%	64.6	27	107	4.0	18	0.1	0.16
2019	9.9	7.5	74%	81%	74.7	34	98	2.9	15	2.1	0.16
2020	9.5	7.3	71%	81%	26.7	41	207	5.0	25	11.5	0.08
	9.3	6.9	74%	82%	158.8	104	419	4.0	59	13.0	0.12

pComp / IQR Detail / Total Points / Total Points Rtg

	pComp		IQR Detail				Total Points			Total Points Rtg		
Year	%	+/-	Under Pres	No Pres	vs. Man	vs. Zone	Pass	Rush	Total	Per Pass	Per Rush	Per Play
2016	62%	-11%	7.0	114.0	76.5	90.2	-	-	-	-	-	-
2018	62%	+1%	85.3	113.3	95.4	109.9	106	-4	102	92	53	91
2019	62%	+2%	64.5	119.4	108.7	111.4	121	-3	117	91	54	90
2020	61%	-1%	80.0	100.4	99.2	90.9	68	2	69	76	73	76
	62%	0%	68.9	110.7	101.7	102.7	295	-5	288	-	-	-

Critical Factors

Accuracy	5
Decision Making / Mental	4
Clutch Performance	6

Positional Factors

Short Accuracy	6
Deep Accuracy	4
Pocket Awareness	6
Footwork	6
Under Pressure	6
Mobility	6
Arm Strength	5
Release	5
Awkward Throw	6
Eye Discipline	5
Leadership	7
Body Comp	5

Shane Buechele

Report by Noah Chang

School	Height	Weight	Year	Jersey #	Hometown
SMU	6010 E	207 E	5SR	7	Arlington, TX

One Liner

Buechele's short accuracy, ability to manipulate safeties with his eyes, and toughness give him the tools to be a backup quarterback, but his lack of mobility, arm strength, and long release will hold him back.

Strengths: Accurate short passer; Eye discipline; Toughness
Weaknesses: Mobility; Arm strength; Long release

Shane Buechele plays quarterback in SMU's air raid offense featuring an abundance of screens, RPOs, and play-action. He started 19 of 23 games for Texas before starting all 23 games while at SMU. He had sports hernia surgery in 2018. His father, Steve, played 11 years in MLB. He is on the shorter and lighter side as a quarterback with a slight frame. Additionally, he lacks some athleticism, but compensates with a competitive drive and toughness.

Buechele is a rhythm and timing passer who can make decisive half-field reads and quick throws in the flow of the offense. He has good spot-on short accuracy and puts balls on receivers so they can make plays. Buechele has adequate accuracy on deep balls, slightly underthrowing most opportunities. However, he shows touch and good ball placement from time to time, but his accuracy is limited by his arm strength. He's adequate under pressure and lacks some anticipation on his throws to fit tight windows. The low windup on his release limits his awkward throw ability both on the run and under pressure within the pocket. He shows good pocket awareness to escape the rush, but lacks the lateral quickness to consistently avoid athletic rushers and improvise. His sufficient mobility has forced him to take many hard hits both inside and outside of the pocket.

Buechele doesn't have the athleticism or mobility to make him a threat to run as a runner, though he can scramble and gain a few yards when needed. He gets trapped when the pocket collapses, and runs into sacks when trying to escape. Additionally, he's been caught behind the line multiple times when keeping the ball on zone reads. That said, he shows very good toughness to get up quickly after taking hits behind the line of scrimmage and when rolling out.

Buechele projects as an eventual No. 2 quarterback who can thrive in a run-heavy, RPO system. His team elected to run the ball on third down many times which speaks to his lack of clutch ability. He was a boom-or-bust player when he got the ball on third downs, either making deep throws or taking sacks.

					Passing					
Year	Att	Comp	Comp%	Yds	Y/A	TD / INT	Sacks	ANY/A	Rating	IQR
2016	391	236	60%	2958	7.6	21 / 11	30	6.0	90.1	98.3
2017	213	137	64%	1405	6.6	7 / 4	23	5.0	86.3	88.6
2019	491	308	63%	3950	8.0	34 / 10	17	8.0	102.5	117.2
2020	370	242	65%	3095	8.4	23 / 6	20	8.0	105.4	117.2
	1509	953	63%	11681	7.7	87 / 32	92	7.0	97.3	106.9

			Passing			Rushing (Excluding Sacks)				Dropbacks
Year	ADoT	ADoC	On-Trgt%	Cbl%	EPA	Att	Yards	Y/A	Scrmbl	EPA	EPA/DB
2016	10.1	6.2	-	84%	-22.3	66	320	4.8	24	4.3	-0.04
2017	8.0	4.5	-	83%	-37.2	39	221	5.7	17	7.5	-0.14
2019	9.5	6.7	75%	82%	78.9	47	213	4.5	19	1.5	0.15
2020	8.0	5.5	78%	84%	47.0	38	249	6.6	20	16.1	0.15
	9.0	5.9	75%	83%	66.0	198	1033	5.2	85	26.7	0.05

	pComp		IQR Detail				Total Points			Total Points Rtg		
Year	%	+/-	Under Pres	No Pres	vs. Man	vs. Zone	Pass	Rush	Total	Per Pass	Per Rush	Per Play
2016	58%	+2%	27.0	106.7	94.2	78.5	-	-	-	-	-	-
2017	62%	+2%	54.2	94.0	90.4	66.6	-	-	-	-	-	-
2019	60%	+3%	59.3	119.3	131.9	94.8	145	6	153	93	88	93
2020	64%	+2%	61.3	124.5	106.8	113.7	91	21	111	88	99	89
	61%	+2%	48.1	112.7	104.7	92.0	232	24	256	-	-	-

Redshirt season not shown but included in totals

Critical Factors	
Accuracy.	6
Decision Making / Mental	5
Clutch Performance.	5

Positional Factors	
Short Accuracy	6
Deep Accuracy.	5
Pocket Awareness.	6
Footwork.	5
Under Pressure	5
Mobility.	5
Arm Strength	5
Release.	5
Awkward Throw.	5
Eye Discipline	6
Leadership	6
Body Comp.	5

Kevin Thomson   Final Grade: 5.8

Report by Kyle Rodemann

School	Height	Weight	Year	Jersey #	Hometown
Washington	6004 V	206 V	6SR	7	Auburn, WA

One Liner

Thomson lacks the footwork, pocket awareness, and deep ball accuracy to contribute at the next level, but his short accuracy and mobility give him a chance to eventually become a quality backup.

Strengths: Short accuracy; Mobility
Weaknesses: Pocket awareness; Footwork; Release

Kevin Thomson is a quarterback for Washington who didn't see action after transferring over from Sacramento State's Air Raid offense. He transferred from UNLV after 2 seasons to Sacramento State where he started 27 of 28 games. The 25 year old missed the 2016 season after undergoing Tommy John surgery and struggled with injuries in 2020. He possesses above-average athletic ability with good toughness and competitive drive.

Thomson has mediocre pocket awareness. He often doesn't feel pressure and has been hit from behind or allows his arm to get hit by a defender. He shows the ability to step up in the pocket, but only when the pass rush is obvious. His footwork is marginal, taking the snap and playing flat-footed, without staying on the balls of his feet ready to throw. He tends to throw all arm, barely stepping into the throw and finishing his follow-through. This leads to some inaccuracy down the field. His overall accuracy is sufficient as he can hit open receivers, though he tends to struggle leading receivers on deep balls.

This limits the upside of those explosive plays, as the receiver's momentum is stopped and thus the receiver can't do much after the catch. He does a decent job at throwing from awkward angles, but his release causes him to be inaccurate on some of these throws. Due to his good mobility, he can avoid pressure, but he tucks and runs too often not keeping his eyes downfield.

In the run game, Thomson can be somewhat of a threat. He routinely runs away from defenders and is successful on QB sneaks. While he won't amaze with his rushing ability, defenses will have to account for him running the ball.

Thomson projects to be an eventual career backup in the NFL. He fits best in a pass-first system in which he can get the ball out quickly or use his legs to pick up first downs. His lack of fundamentals and footwork will limit his upside at the next level, but should be able to fix those issues with good coaching.

Kevin Thomson's path to NFL Draft consideration has been long and winding with an elbow injury that required Tommy John Surgery and cost him 18 months. Thomson persevered through an arduous rehab and upon returning was the Big Sky Offensive Player of the Year in his junior year at Sacramento State.

"It was a really long rehab process," Thomson said on an episode of the *That's How You Feel* podcast. "You question it a little bit. Am I good enough? Do I have what it takes? But then I got out there, started practicing, and maybe a week in, I thought, 'I'm the best guy [here].'"

Thomson turned out to be right. He also thinks he has what it takes to play in the NFL. We'll see if that turns out to be true, too.

Critical Factors	
Accuracy	5
Decision Making / Mental	5
Clutch Performance	5

Positional Factors	
Short Accuracy	6
Deep Accuracy	5
Pocket Awareness	4
Footwork	3
Under Pressure	4
Mobility	6
Arm Strength	5
Release	5
Awkward Throw	5
Eye Discipline	6
Leadership	5
Body Comp	6

Running Backs

Sarah Thompson

While there's some debate about the value of running backs in today's NFL, the 2021 draft class is rife with talent that can immediately contribute upon arrival to the professional level. Before we dive deep, let's briefly review the position and the stats important to evaluating the players coming out of college.

The most important qualities to consider when projecting running back performance from college to the NFL are a player's vision, contact balance, and passing game impact.

A running back relies on his vision to quickly make his read and enter the second level. Furthermore, he also has to work in concert with his OL to help blocks properly develop.

A back's ability to stay upright upon contact is essential to success at the position. Shorter running backs often benefit from a lower center of gravity and naturally can stay more balanced than their taller, more upright counterparts, though that is not always the case. A superb player at this position can break tackles and fight for as many yards as possible after first contact, all while keeping the ball secure.

Yards after contact (YAContact) and yards after contact per attempt (YAC/A) are useful for getting a sense of how well a running back evades and breaks tackles while keeping the run alive. YAContact is the amount of additional yards the ballcarrier gains after first contact is made by a defender, and YAC/A tells us how many yards after contact the ballcarrier averages on a single rushing attempt. Broken Tackle %, the ballcarrier's broken and missed tackles per carry, tells a similar story of elusiveness.

The Tar Heels' Javonte Williams led FBS rushers in Broken Tackle % (46.5%) and Broken Tackles (50) in 157 carries this year. His 6.9 final grade projects him to be a strong starter who plays on all 3 downs. Meanwhile, Buffalo's Jaret Patterson averages the most yards gained after first contact by the defense (4.9 YAC/Att) on rushing plays among RBs with at least 100 carries in 2020. Our scouts expect him to be a backup who can play all 3 downs (6.2 final grade).

While the running back is often the main character of rushing plays, he plays an important part in the passing game as well. A running back's ability to help their quarterback complete clean throws and move downfield by protecting against the pass rush is just as important as his ability to gain yards himself. A running back who can run receiver routes and threaten the defense vertically is a dangerous weapon.

For this reason, receiving statistics such as targets, receptions, yards, yards per target, routes run, and yards per route run are considered in addition to rushing stats. Blocking statistics like Blown Blocks and Blown Block % (the percentage of blocking snaps that the player had a blown block) also illustrate how the running back impacts the passing game. It can sometimes be a challenge to quantify a running back's pass protection ability in a single number, but it is something Total Points takes into account, in addition to rushing and receiving plays. Javonte Williams leads 2020 running backs in Pass Block Points Earned with 5 on the year and earned a 7 pass protection grade from our scouts, indicating that this projects to be a "very good" trait for him at the NFL level.

Among running backs in 2020, Clemson's Travis Etienne (6.6 final grade) was tops in receiving yards (588) and receiving yards after catch (650) while accruing the third-most targets. Demetric Felton's 6.3 final grade reflects his value as a receiving weapon for UCLA—in fact, he began his career at WR and was converted to a RB in 2019, but went to the Senior Bowl as a WR. In 2020, he averaged 26.5 Receiving Yards per Game and 111.3 Rushing Yards per Game. In 2019, his rushing and receiving yards were flipped, with 49.5 Receiving Yards per Game and 27.6 Rushing Yards per Game.

There are more than a few metrics used to evaluate the following running backs that will be touched on here. Yards per Attempt (Y/A) is the familiar rate stat that conveys how many yards a running back is gaining on average. North Carolina's Michael Carter led FBS backs with at least 100 carries in rushing yards per attempt (8.0). He also scored 9 touchdowns. His 6.5 final grade projects him to be a lower-end starter. Virginia Tech's Khalil Herbert (6.2 final grade) is right behind him at 7.7 Y/A on 154 carries, and he also averaged 4.3 yards after contact per carry.

Total Points is a player value metric that uses an Expected Points framework and distributes the value gained or lost on a play to the different players involved based on their impact on the play. For rushers, this includes accounting for offensive line play, run direction, broken tackles, and fumbles during rushing, receiving, and pass protection plays.

Javonte Williams sits on top of the Total Points leaderboard for 2020 FBS running backs with 74 Total Points. This is accounted for by approximately 68 Rushing Points, 1 Receiving Point, and 5 Pass Block Points. Not far behind him is Alabama's Najee Harris (7.0 final grade) with 69. There's a gap of 13 Points Earned that separates them from the rest of the pack—Michael Carter finished the year with 56.

Since Total Points is a counting stat, we can't neglect sample size when discussing it, especially because some schools played fewer games than others. Total Points Rating allows us to compare players across different conferences and accounts for differences in schedules and quality of competition and operates on a 50-99 scale, with 99 being the best. North Carolina's Javonte Williams is the sole RB with significant playing time to earn a Total Points Rating per Play of 99 in 2020. North Carolina's Michael Carter and Louisville's Javian Hawkins are not far behind him, each with a 97 and 96 rating, respectively. On a Per Play basis, Total Points Rating goes deeper than just rushing and route running by incorporating blocking performance. For example, Najee Harris has excellent per Rush and per Route ratings (96 each), but a solid-if-unspectacular Total Points per Play rating (89) because of some blown blocks.

Clearly, this class has plenty of talent and tons of players who can start contributing at the professional level right away.

RUNNING BACK

Running Back Grading Scale

GRADE	DESCRIPTION
9.0 – 7.0	High-end 3 down starter. Pro Bowl level.
6.9 – 6.7	Strong starter who plays on all 3 downs.
6.6 – 6.5	Lower-end starter. Starting player on early downs.
6.3	Role playing starter. 3rd down difference maker.
6.2	Backup who can play on all 3 downs.
6.1 – 6.0	Developmental. Top traits but needs time.
5.6 – 5.5	Backup. Either base or 3rd down role.

Running Back Rankings

Rank	Name	Grade	Page	Rank	Name	Grade	Page
1	Najee Harris	7.0	144	14	Khalil Herbert	6.2	165
2	Javonte Williams	6.9	146	15	Jaret Patterson	6.2	166
3	Travis Etienne	6.6	148	16	Javian Hawkins	6.2	167
4	Kylin Hill	6.6	150	17	Elijah Mitchell	6.2	168
5	Michael Carter	6.5	152	18	CJ Marable	6.2	169
6	Chuba Hubbard	6.5	154	19	Chris Evans	6.2	170
7	Kenneth Gainwell	6.5	156	20	Brenden Knox	6.2	171
8	Larry Rountree III	6.5	158	21	Spencer Brown	6.2	172
9	Demetric Felton	6.3	160	22	Shane Simpson	6.2	173
10	Rhamondre Stevenson	6.3	161	23	Otis Anderson	6.2	174
11	Trey Sermon	6.3	162	24	Rakeem Boyd	6.2	175
12	Jermar Jefferson	6.3	163	25	Josh Johnson	6.2	176
13	Pooka Williams Jr.	6.3	164				

Glossary

Broken Tackles
Times where a defender was in position to make a tackle but failed to bring down the ballcarrier. Counts both broken tackles (physical) and missed tackles (elusive).

Heavy Box%
Percentage of a running back's carries that came against a heavy box (eight or more defenders at or near the line of scrimmage).

Inside (Positive% split)
Runs with a designed gap between the tackles.

Outside (Positive% split)
Runs with a designed gap outside of the tackles.

Positive%
Percentage of carries by the running back with a positive Expected Points Added.

Split Out%
Percentage of plays on which the running back was not lined up in the backfield at the snap.

Total Points
Sports Info Solutions' proprietary player value metric that uses an Expected Points framework and distributes the value gained or lost on a play to the players involved based on their impact on the play.

Total Points Rating
Total Points per play compared to average, scaled so that 50 is poor and 99 is excellent.

YAC/A
The amount of additional yards the ballcarrier achieves after first contact is made by a defender per rush attempt.

Y/A
Yards per rush attempt.

Y/RR
Receiving yards per route run.

Y/Trgt
Receiving yards per pass attempt in which the receiver is targeted, including incompletions.

Running Back Leaderboards

	Total Points Per Game		
Rk	Player	School	Tot Pts / G
1	J. Hawkins	Louisville	6.9
2	J. Patterson	Buffalo	6.8
3	J. Williams	North Carolina	6.7
4	N. Harris	Alabama	5.3
5	M. Carter	North Carolina	5.2
6	K. Herbert	Virginia Tech	5.1
7	T. Sermon	Ohio State	4.3
8	T. Etienne	Clemson	3.2
9	E. Mitchell	UL-Lafayette	2.7
10	D. Felton	UCLA	2.2

	Total Points Rating Per Play		
Rk	Player	School	Rating
1	J. Williams	North Carolina	99
2	M. Carter	North Carolina	97
3	J. Hawkins	Louisville	96
4	K. Herbert	Virginia Tech	93
4	J. Patterson	Buffalo	93
6	T. Sermon	Ohio State	92
7	T. Etienne	Clemson	90
8	N. Harris	Alabama	89
9	E. Mitchell	UL-Lafayette	83
10	L. Rountree III	Missouri	76

	Rushing Total Points Per Game		
Rk	Player	School	Tot Pts / G
1	J. Patterson	Buffalo	6.8
2	J. Williams	North Carolina	6.2
3	J. Hawkins	Louisville	6.0
4	K. Herbert	Virginia Tech	4.9
5	M. Carter	North Carolina	4.5
6	N. Harris	Alabama	4.1
7	T. Sermon	Ohio State	3.8
8	E. Mitchell	UL-Lafayette	2.4
9	T. Etienne	Clemson	2.0
9	D. Felton	UCLA	2.0

	Total Points Rating Per Rush		
Rk	Player	School	Rating
1	J. Williams	North Carolina	99
1	M. Carter	North Carolina	99
1	K. Herbert	Virginia Tech	99
1	J. Patterson	Buffalo	99
1	J. Hawkins	Louisville	99
6	T. Sermon	Ohio State	98
7	N. Harris	Alabama	96
8	E. Mitchell	UL-Lafayette	93
9	T. Etienne	Clemson	90
10	D. Felton	UCLA	82

	Receiving Total Points Per Game		
Rk	Player	School	Tot Pts / G
1	N. Harris	Alabama	1.4
2	T. Etienne	Clemson	0.9
3	M. Carter	North Carolina	0.6
4	C. Marable	Coastal Carolina	0.5
5	D. Felton	UCLA	0.3
5	T. Sermon	Ohio State	0.3
5	J. Hawkins	Louisville	0.3
5	E. Mitchell	UL-Lafayette	0.3
9	J. Williams	North Carolina	0.1
9	B. Knox	Marshall	0.1

	Total Points Rating Per Route		
Rk	Player	School	Rating
1	N. Harris	Alabama	96
2	T. Etienne	Clemson	92
3	M. Carter	North Carolina	91
4	C. Marable	Coastal Carolina	76
5	J. Hawkins	Louisville	75
6	E. Mitchell	UL-Lafayette	74
7	T. Sermon	Ohio State	72
8	D. Felton	UCLA	69
8	B. Knox	Marshall	69
10	J. Williams	North Carolina	65

Rushing Yards Per Game

Rk	Player	School	Yds/G
1	J. Patterson	Buffalo	178.7
2	J. Jefferson	Oregon State	143.0
3	K. Herbert	Virginia Tech	118.3
4	J. Hawkins	Louisville	116.4
5	M. Carter	North Carolina	113.2
6	N. Harris	Alabama	112.8
7	D. Felton	UCLA	111.3
8	S. Brown	UAB	110.9
9	T. Sermon	Ohio State	108.8
10	J. Williams	North Carolina	103.6

Yards Per Attempt

Rk	Player	School	Y/A
1	M. Carter	North Carolina	8.0
2	K. Herbert	Virginia Tech	7.7
3	J. Patterson	Buffalo	7.6
4	T. Sermon	Ohio State	7.5
5	J. Williams	North Carolina	7.3
6	J. Jefferson	Oregon State	6.5
7	J. Hawkins	Louisville	6.2
7	E. Mitchell	UL-Lafayette	6.2
9	N. Harris	Alabama	5.8
10	T. Etienne	Clemson	5.4

Yards After Contact Per Game

Rk	Player	School	YAC/G
1	J. Patterson	Buffalo	115.2
2	D. Felton	UCLA	74.3
3	J. Jefferson	Oregon State	71.3
4	J. Hawkins	Louisville	70.9
5	K. Herbert	Virginia Tech	66.9
6	J. Williams	North Carolina	65.7
7	S. Brown	UAB	63.9
8	N. Harris	Alabama	54.7
9	T. Sermon	Ohio State	52.8
10	E. Mitchell	UL-Lafayette	51.1

Yards After Contact Per Attempt

Rk	Player	School	YAC/A
1	J. Patterson	Buffalo	4.9
2	J. Williams	North Carolina	4.6
3	K. Herbert	Virginia Tech	4.3
4	J. Hawkins	Louisville	3.8
5	M. Carter	North Carolina	3.6
5	T. Sermon	Ohio State	3.6
5	E. Mitchell	UL-Lafayette	3.6
8	T. Etienne	Clemson	3.4
8	D. Felton	UCLA	3.4
10	J. Jefferson	Oregon State	3.2

Broken Tackles Per Game

Rk	Player	School	BT/G
1	N. Harris	Alabama	7.7
1	D. Felton	UCLA	7.7
3	J. Williams	North Carolina	7.2
4	J. Patterson	Buffalo	6.5
5	T. Sermon	Ohio State	4.8
6	T. Etienne	Clemson	4.6
7	M. Carter	North Carolina	4.5
8	J. Hawkins	Louisville	4.4
9	K. Herbert	Virginia Tech	4.3
10	2 tied with		3.6

Broken Tackles Per 100 Touches

Rk	Player	School	BT/100
1	J. Williams	North Carolina	43
2	N. Harris	Alabama	34
3	D. Felton	UCLA	30
3	T. Sermon	Ohio State	30
5	M. Carter	North Carolina	28
5	J. Patterson	Buffalo	28
7	K. Herbert	Virginia Tech	26
8	T. Etienne	Clemson	25
9	E. Mitchell	UL-Lafayette	23
9	J. Johnson	Louisiana-Monroe	23

Receptions Per Game

Rk	Player	School	Rec/G
1	T. Etienne	Clemson	4.0
2	D. Felton	UCLA	3.7
3	N. Harris	Alabama	3.3
4	C. Marable	Coastal Carolina	2.6
5	J. Williams	North Carolina	2.3
5	M. Carter	North Carolina	2.3
5	J. Hawkins	Louisville	2.3
8	J. Johnson	Louisiana-Monroe	2.1
9	E. Mitchell	UL-Lafayette	1.6
10	3 tied with		1.5

Split Out Percentage

Rk	Player	School	Split Out %
1	C. Marable	Coastal Carolina	12%
2	E. Mitchell	UL-Lafayette	9%
3	D. Felton	UCLA	6%
4	N. Harris	Alabama	4%
4	T. Etienne	Clemson	4%
6	L. Rountree III	Missouri	3%
6	T. Sermon	Ohio State	3%
6	K. Herbert	Virginia Tech	3%
9	J. Hawkins	Louisville	2%
10	2 tied with		1%

Receiving Yards Per Game

Rk	Player	School	Yds/G
1	T. Etienne	Clemson	49.0
2	N. Harris	Alabama	32.7
3	J. Williams	North Carolina	27.7
4	D. Felton	UCLA	26.5
5	M. Carter	North Carolina	24.3
6	C. Marable	Coastal Carolina	19.0
7	J. Hawkins	Louisville	18.1
8	K. Herbert	Virginia Tech	17.9
9	E. Mitchell	UL-Lafayette	15.3
10	T. Sermon	Ohio State	11.9

Yards Per Route Run

Rk	Player	School	Y/RR
1	T. Etienne	Clemson	1.6
2	M. Carter	North Carolina	1.2
3	J. Williams	North Carolina	1.1
4	N. Harris	Alabama	0.9
5	E. Mitchell	UL-Lafayette	0.7
6	D. Felton	UCLA	0.6
6	K. Herbert	Virginia Tech	0.6
6	J. Hawkins	Louisville	0.6
9	T. Sermon	Ohio State	0.5
10	2 tied with		0.4

Total Touchdowns Per Game

Rk	Player	School	TD/G
1	J. Patterson	Buffalo	3.2
2	N. Harris	Alabama	2.3
3	J. Williams	North Carolina	2.0
4	C. Marable	Coastal Carolina	1.6
5	L. Rountree III	Missouri	1.4
6	T. Etienne	Clemson	1.3
6	D. Felton	UCLA	1.3
6	S. Brown	UAB	1.3
9	J. Jefferson	Oregon State	1.2
10	2 tied with		1.1

Total Expected Points Added Per Game

Rk	Player	School	EPA/G
1	J. Patterson	Buffalo	8.3
2	J. Williams	North Carolina	5.3
3	M. Carter	North Carolina	5.2
4	K. Herbert	Virginia Tech	4.3
5	N. Harris	Alabama	4.0
6	E. Mitchell	UL-Lafayette	2.9
7	T. Etienne	Clemson	2.7
8	T. Sermon	Ohio State	2.4
9	J. Hawkins	Louisville	2.2
10	J. Jefferson	Oregon State	1.6

Najee Harris

Report by Ronan Potts & Kyle Rodemann

School	Height	Weight	Year	Jersey #	Hometown
Alabama	6017 V	230 V	4SR	22	Antioch, CA

One Liner

Harris is more than just a product of his offense; he's a chunk-yardage creator who can make defenders miss in a variety of ways to highly impact games on all three downs.

Overall

Najee Harris is a running back in Alabama's RPO-heavy offense, which runs a balance of zone and gap blocking. He played in 55 career games with 25 starts coming his final 2 years. He underwent meniscus surgery before enrolling in 2017. He is a tall back with thick thighs and good lower body strength. He displays technically sound footwork along with impressive acceleration and initial burst, though he lacks elite breakaway speed. He's extremely tough and has been an every-down workhorse for the Crimson Tide.

Run Game

Harris shows good patience behind his blockers and very impressive decision making. He's a one-cut downhill runner capable of lowering his pads and driving through contact, as well as seeking out cutbacks and dancing for plays on his own. He jump cuts with square shoulders into open space and is proficient between and outside the tackles. Harris isn't the type to seek out contact, but he is able to absorb inordinate amounts of contact and bounce off of would-be tacklers with fantastic contact balance. He has an impressive stiff arm and surprising elusiveness for his size. He shows the ability to slalom through run lanes and wiggle around tacklers in tight spaces, even hurdling players cleanly on occasion. He doesn't have breakaway speed in the open field, but he wears down defenses with chunk yardage and consistent first downs. He runs

with technical ball security and is rarely stood up, routinely falling forward to finish runs.

Pass Game

Harris is a quality difference maker on passing downs. He has soft hands and very good natural catching skills to snatch the ball away from his body in most instances. He runs crisp routes and has been used as more than just a checkdown option. He is intelligent on check and releases to not leave before he's sure the rush has been picked up. He's alert to blitzes in pass protection and squares to contact with a sound base and positioning. However, he lacks the stoutness at contact his size would indicate and doesn't consistently sustain on extended plays. He shows good technique for his limited usage, as he's often carrying out run fakes on RPOs, and his frame and physicality in the run game project well to pass protection with more reps.

Last Word

Harris projects as a high-end starting running back from Day 1 in the NFL. He's scheme-versatile and battle tested at the highest level of college football, rarely leaving the field for a team with a bevy of top recruits behind him waiting for snaps. He may not hit many home runs, but he hits plenty of doubles, and his ability to grind down defenses and keep the chains moving is a highly-valued asset in its own right. He doesn't have special teams experience as a returner or otherwise, but he could fill various roles if necessary.

Strengths

- Contact balance
- Passing game impact
- All-around skill set

Weaknesses

- Stoutness in pass protection
- Home run speed

Critical Factors

Vision	Contact Balance	Passing Game Impact
7	7	7

Positional Factors

Play Speed	Elusiveness	Power
6	6	6
Playmaker	Catching Skill	Pass Pro
6	7	6
Ball Security	Toughness	ST Value
7	8	6

Basic

Year	Rushing					Receiving				
	Att	Yds	Y/A	YAC/A	TD	Targets	Rec	Yds	Y/Trgt	TD
2017	61	370	6.1	4.5	3	11	6	45	4.1	0
2018	117	783	6.7	4.1	4	5	4	7	1.4	0
2019	209	1224	5.9	3.0	13	35	27	304	8.7	7
2020	251	1466	5.8	2.8	26	53	43	425	8.0	4
	638	3843	6.0	3.3	46	104	80	781	7.5	11

Advanced

Year	Positive %				Per 100 Touches		EPA			
	Inside	Outside	Zone	Gap	Fumbles	Brk Tkl	Rush	Per Att	Rec	Per Trgt
2017	60%	50%	46%	58%	0.0	36	9	0.15	-2	-0.16
2018	69%	58%	58%	78%	0.0	31	24	0.21	-2	-0.47
2019	51%	69%	49%	60%	0.4	28	36	0.17	4	0.12
2020	52%	53%	64%	47%	0.3	34	40	0.16	12	0.23
	56%	58%	57%	57%	0.3	32	109	0.17	12	0.12

Deep Dive

Year	Usage		Receiving		Total Points			Total Points Rtg		
	Split Out %	Heavy Box %	Routes Run	Y/RR	Rush	Rec	Total	Per Rush	Per Route	Per Play
2018	2%	6%	58	0.1	47	0	50	99	60	98
2019	4%	13%	148	2.1	49	13	61	97	93	86
2020	4%	25%	476	0.9	53	18	69	96	96	89
	4%	17%	682	1.1	149	31	180	-	-	-

Javonte Williams

Report by John Todd

School	Height	Weight	Year	Jersey #	Hometown
North Carolina	5096 E	220 E	3JR	25	Wallace, NC

One Liner
Williams' size doesn't suggest it, but he breaks tackles at a truly elite rate and his individual pass protection abilities will make for a three-down stalwart at the next level.

Overall
Javonte Williams is a running back in UNC's high-powered offense and balanced rushing attack, operating almost exclusively out of shotgun. He played 35 career games but only started twice, splitting time with fellow prospect Michael Carter. A former high school linebacker, he has explosive strength within his standard frame. He's a good athlete and flashes quickness in tight quarters, but most notably, he has a workhorse mentality and packs a serious punch at contact to wear down opponents for four quarters.

Run Game
Williams is a downhill, north-south thumper and breaks tackles at a ridiculous clip. He has good vision to the front side behind the line of scrimmage and even better vision in the open field to sense tackling angles. He does an excellent job of pressing holes and forcing defenders to show their hand before bursting the other direction. He shows great patience to let blocks develop. He is a better playmaker working between the tackles and getting upfield quickly; he'll bust a D-gap run on occasion but struggles to find success stretching wide zones laterally. The best chance defenses have of bottling him up is behind the line, because Williams is a tank in the open field with momentum behind him. He runs behind his pads and prefers delivering blows to absorbing them, although he does both very well. He actually has decent agility and elusiveness to juke and spin around tacklers expecting his physicality, but his calling card is his power. Despite not having typical "big back" size, he explodes through contact and easily bounces off attempts of defenders not bringing their best. He consistently drops the first player to the ball and requires team efforts downfield. On limited opportunities, he's naturally shown to be a devastating lead blocker, too.

Pass Game
Williams has comfortable hands and will make most of the plays he's expected to at the catch point. He counters his share of body and double catches with off-frame plucks and the occasional contested opportunity. Typically only used on flares and screens, he's also shown the quickness to break down and separate from linebackers on choice routes up the middle. His best trait, however, is his one-on-one pass protection. While he can be a bit tepid looking for work and chipping, Williams does a phenomenal job of squaring up to blitzers on the balls of his feet and delivering blows. He stands up to all comers and holds his own despite any size disadvantages.

Last Word
Williams projects as a very strong starting running back in the league, whose skill set fits best in an inside power scheme. However, his violence as a ballcarrier and pass protection skills will play in any offense. His lack of top-tier open-field electricity could hinder him at the next level if his playing style at his size doesn't hold up against professionals, but his dominant production in merely a rotational role implies great potential given a full complement of carries. He has minimal special teams experience but could be a great personal protector or lead back on returns.

Strengths

- Explosive power
- One-on-one pass protection
- Interior playmaking

Weaknesses

- Stretching outside runs
- Breakaway speed

Critical Factors

Vision	Contact Balance	Passing Game Impact
7	7	6

Positional Factors

Play Speed	Elusiveness	Power
6	6	8
Playmaker	Catching Skill	Pass Pro
7	6	7
Ball Security	Toughness	ST Value
6	7	7

Basic

Year	Rushing					Receiving				
	Att	Yds	Y/A	YAC/A	TD	Targets	Rec	Yds	Y/Trgt	TD
2018	43	224	5.2	3.2	5	11	8	58	5.3	0
2019	167	933	5.6	3.9	5	18	17	176	9.8	1
2020	157	1140	7.3	4.6	19	31	25	305	9.8	3
	367	2297	6.3	4.1	29	60	50	539	9.0	4

Advanced

Year	Positive %				Per 100 Touches		EPA			
	Inside	Outside	Zone	Gap	Fumbles	Brk Tkl	Rush	Per Att	Rec	Per Trgt
2018	50%	60%	56%	68%	0.0	22	9	0.21	-4	-0.37
2019	44%	68%	49%	54%	1.6	28	7	0.04	7	0.37
2020	57%	62%	53%	69%	0.5	43	49	0.31	9	0.30
	52%	64%	52%	61%	1.0	34	65	0.18	12	0.20

Deep Dive

Year	Usage		Receiving		Total Points			Total Points Rtg		
	Split Out %	Heavy Box %	Routes Run	Y/RR	Rush	Rec	Total	Per Rush	Per Route	Per Play
2018	1%	5%	31	1.9	10	1	11	96	87	71
2019	1%	10%	68	2.6	31	0	33	94	62	82
2020	0%	20%	266	1.1	68	1	74	99	65	99
	1%	14%	365	1.5	109	2	118	-	-	-

Travis Etienne

Report by Bryce Rossler

School	Height	Weight	Year	Jersey #	Hometown
Clemson	5095 E	205 E	4SR	9	Jennings, LA

One Liner
Etienne is a fast and explosive, slight-of-frame back whose finesse running style and timid pass protection may prevent him from becoming a team's primary option at the NFL level.

Overall
Travis Etienne is a running back at Clemson. He played in a shotgun-heavy offense that primarily ran inside zone, power, and counter schemes which were often tagged with RPO and/or option elements. Clemson backs were incorporated in the passing game via a diverse screen package. He played in 55 games during his career, starting in 42 of them for the Tigers. He is a very good athlete with excellent quickness and explosiveness, very good agility, and good balance. He has a slight frame and below-average size for the position.

Run Game
Within zone concepts, Etienne has the ability to press gaps and process blocking development, and has excellent burst and good footwork to make one cut and transition upfield quickly. Within moving parts and gap concepts, he displays mediocre timing/discipline and inefficient footwork, and has a tendency to outpace pullers to the POA or abort the design of the play to cut into flashes of space that quickly fill. When confronted with immediate backfield penetration, he struggles to mitigate lost yardage or create for himself. He is hesitant to stick his nose into a pile and take tough yards. His mediocre power results in struggles to fall forward and generate YAC in face-up situations. He has excellent burst to challenge pursuit angles and outrun second- and third-level defenders. He wins by creating unfavorable tackling positions for defenders at the 2nd-level and in space and has good contact balance to bounce off resulting arm tackle attempts. He demonstrates sufficient ball security and can be loose with the ball when attempting to evade tackles.

Pass Game
Etienne demonstrates sufficient mental processing to identify threats in pass protection. His lack of willingness to square up blitzers results in suboptimal body positioning, which is compounded by his less than desirable stoutness to anchor and sustain. He has the requisite athletic traits to function as a matchup problem out of the backfield and from the slot, although he was not often asked to do so at Clemson. He has sufficient hands and does not track or adjust to the ball naturally and has difficulty addressing off-target throws.

Last Word
Etienne projects best as a lower-end starter in an inside zone/duo-heavy scheme with minimal power-scheme run types. His play speed, playmaking ability, and vision within zone schemes will allow him to contribute as a runner early, but he will need to be utilized on screens and as part of 5-man route concepts in order to mitigate his liability in pass protection. He has kick return experience and could contribute in that area at the next level, but likely won't contribute much elsewhere.

Strengths

- Play speed
- Elusiveness
- Zone vision

Weaknesses

- Pass pro
- Scheme discipline in gap runs
- Power

Critical Factors

Vision	Contact Balance	Passing Game Impact
6	6	5

Positional Factors

Play Speed	Elusiveness	Power
8	7	4
Playmaker	Catching Skill	Pass Pro
7	5	4
Ball Security	Toughness	ST Value
5	4	5

Basic

Year	Rushing					Receiving				
	Att	Yds	Y/A	YAC/A	TD	Targets	Rec	Yds	Y/Trgt	TD
2017	107	766	7.2	4.7	13	7	5	57	8.1	0
2018	204	1658	8.1	4.0	24	18	12	78	4.3	2
2019	207	1614	7.8	5.0	19	42	37	432	10.3	4
2020	168	914	5.4	3.4	14	61	48	588	9.6	2
	686	4952	7.2	4.3	70	128	102	1155	9.0	8

Advanced

Year	Positive %				Per 100 Touches		EPA			
	Inside	Outside	Zone	Gap	Fumbles	Brk Tkl	Rush	Per Att	Rec	Per Trgt
2017	63%	58%	64%	45%	0.9	27	30	0.28	1	0.12
2018	53%	54%	55%	56%	0.5	26	65	0.32	-1	-0.07
2019	63%	51%	59%	51%	0.8	42	55	0.27	21	0.50
2020	57%	41%	56%	36%	1.9	25	1	0.01	31	0.51
	58%	50%	58%	48%	1.0	31	152	0.22	51	0.40

Deep Dive

Year	Usage		Receiving		Total Points			Total Points Rtg		
	Split Out %	Heavy Box %	Routes Run	Y/RR	Rush	Rec	Total	Per Rush	Per Route	Per Play
2018	4%	11%	97	0.8	75	0	79	99	59	94
2019	4%	10%	127	3.4	86	7	96	99	84	96
2020	4%	17%	379	1.6	24	11	38	90	92	90
	4%	13%	603	1.8	185	18	213	-	-	-

Kylin Hill

Report by DJ Marquardt & Jeremy Percy

School	Height	Weight	Year	Jersey #	Hometown
Mississippi State	5103 V	214 V	4SR	8	Columbus, MS

One Liner

Hill is a physical, explosive playmaker who can beat a defense in multiple ways, but he'll need to continue proving his passing game reliability to become a true three-down workhorse at the next level.

Overall

Kylin Hill is a running back for Mississippi State, briefly in their Air Raid offense in 2020 and formerly in a more ground-based attack in which he led the SEC in rushing yards per game. He played in 40 career games and was a 27-game starter before opting out early in the 2020 season, partially due to differences with the new coaching staff. He has a cut but slightly narrow frame yet plays much bigger than his size. He has good lateral agility and a very explosive lower half. He runs with a chip on his shoulder and brings a very physical mentality to the position.

Run Game

Behind the line, Hill shows sufficient vision to follow his blocks and burst upfield, but he has a tendency to bounce runs more than he needs to and can get impatient behind pullers. His ball-carrier vision in the open field is very good, however, sensing tackling angles and finding cutbacks downfield. He plays with superb short-area wiggle in tight spaces to diminish his strike zone and receive glancing blows instead of square contact. Once through the hole, Hill displays great acceleration and excellent explosion into contact, regularly seeking out defenders to hit before stepping out of bounds. He can be caught from behind against speedy secondary players, but he plays faster and harder than he'll time. He mostly wins at the point of attack with his impressive contact balance and good power for his size. He delivers and absorbs contact very well for his frame and takes advantage of defenders gearing up for his physicality by hurdling often. He pops at contact but doesn't have the true bulk to leg-drive through bigger defenders for extra yards to finish. He can run loosely with the ball in open space but has not had an issue with fumbles, tucking it soundly in traffic.

Pass Game

Hill was sparingly used in the passing game until 2020, yet in his brief season in the Air Raid showed he can be a capable receiver. He has had a few drops on limited targets overall and seems to fight the ball in at times, but he's generally a sufficient hands catcher. He hasn't been asked to be an overly impressive route runner but has the movement skills to cut sharply on angle routes and do more than swings and wheels. He has been a good pass protector on limited reps but needs more experience to prove consistency. He is very willing and will strike at the point of attack but needs to improve his fundamentals to sustain beyond first contact.

Last Word

Hill projects as a top-tier early-down starter in the NFL and with further development in the passing game has a high ceiling for all three downs. He has the versatility to play in multiple schemes but prefers to get downhill quickly rather than drift laterally in wide zones. His physical mentality and play style can be further supported with additional bulk to his frame, as long as he doesn't lose his explosiveness.

Strengths

- Burst and explosion
- Contact balance
- Short-area wiggle

Weaknesses

- Natural receiving skills
- Pass pro fundamentals
- Inconsistent patience and vision

Critical Factors

Vision	Contact Balance	Passing Game Impact
5	7	5

Positional Factors

Play Speed	Elusiveness	Power
6	6	6
Playmaker	Catching Skill	Pass Pro
6	5	5
Ball Security	Toughness	ST Value
6	7	5

Basic

	Rushing					Receiving				
Year	Att	Yds	Y/A	YAC/A	TD	Targets	Rec	Yds	Y/Trgt	TD
2017	78	393	5.0	3.4	2	5	4	38	7.6	0
2018	118	733	6.2	3.7	4	28	21	177	6.3	4
2019	243	1349	5.6	2.9	10	23	18	180	7.8	1
2020	15	58	3.9	2.3	0	28	23	237	8.5	1
	454	2533	5.6	3.2	16	84	66	632	7.5	6

Advanced

	Positive %				Per 100 Touches		EPA			
Year	Inside	Outside	Zone	Gap	Fumbles	Brk Tkl	Rush	Per Att	Rec	Per Trgt
2017	57%	44%	48%	53%	1.2	27	8	0.10	0	0.08
2018	51%	55%	51%	56%	0.0	32	19	0.16	3	0.12
2019	46%	43%	46%	48%	0.0	26	16	0.07	-5	-0.23
2020	42%	-	55%	0%	0.0	32	-2	-0.13	7	0.24
	48%	47%	48%	50%	0.2	28	41	0.09	5	0.06

Deep Dive

	Usage		Receiving		Total Points			Total Points Rtg		
Year	Split Out %	Heavy Box %	Routes Run	Y/RR	Rush	Rec	Total	Per Rush	Per Route	Per Play
2018	4%	5%	78	2.3	34	5	38	99	94	74
2019	1%	7%	110	1.6	47	4	54	94	76	86
2020	8%	0%	107	2.2	-1	6	6	58	94	90
	3%	6%	295	2.0	80	15	98	-	-	-

Michael Carter

Report by Alec Mallon & David Simmons

School	Height	Weight	Year	Jersey #	Hometown
North Carolina	5077 V	202 V	4SR	8	Navarre, FL

One Liner
Carter is a twitchy back whose combination of elusiveness and body control make him very difficult to bring down in the open field, but he lacks the size and workhorse traits to be a true every-down player at the next level.

Overall
Michael Carter is a running back for North Carolina in their RPO-heavy offense, lining up exclusively in shotgun and working behind both zone and man blocking schemes. He has appeared in 44 games with 28 starts. He tore his PCL in high school in 2015. He is a really good athlete with great burst and elusiveness but lacks sufficient size. However, he plays tougher than he looks and brings physicality with him every play.

Run Game
Carter shows strong vision and patience behind the line. He does a nice job of letting his blocks develop in front of him and explodes when he finds a hole. Between the tackles, Carter lacks the true power to run through and over defenders, largely due to his stature in the box. However, his quick feet, acceleration, and speed allow him to get to the second level extremely quickly. Carter shows great stop-and-start skills to avoid tackles but also displays very good contact balance when engaging with defenders to absorb hits. He does a good job of keeping his legs churning through arm tackles and accelerating through them. He has a low center of gravity to quickly regain his balance and get his feet back under him. In the open field, Carter routinely creates missed tackles because of his change-of-direction skills. He can plant and go to cleanly get around defenders, but even if they do make contact he has the balance to stay upright. His combination of these traits makes him a big play waiting to happen.

Pass Game
In the passing game, Carter is best utilized in space. His hands are solid on quick hitters designed to get him the ball with room to run. He bursts upfield and has good speed to turn the corner. In pass protection, Carter may lack size, but he's willing and aggressive enough to pick up blitzers and attacks with sound technique. His strength causes issues against stout linebackers or when chipping linemen.

Last Word
Carter projects as a lower-end starter in the NFL. He can be a weapon in space on early downs with sufficient third-down traits to be used situationally there, as well. He fits best in a zone scheme where he can patiently pick and hole and one-cut downhill out to the perimeter. Combining him with a short yardage thumper will make for a complete backfield. He has been the Tarheels' primary kick returner throughout his career and has had moderate success. Outside of this, however, his special teams flexibility is somewhat limited.

Strengths

- Elusiveness
- Acceleration and body control
- Playmaking ability

Weaknesses

- Delivering blows
- Pass protection strength
- Small stature

Critical Factors

Vision	Contact Balance	Passing Game Impact
6	7	5

Positional Factors

Play Speed	Elusiveness	Power
6	7	4
Playmaker	Catching Skill	Pass Pro
7	6	5
Ball Security	Toughness	ST Value
6	6	5

Basic

	Rushing					Receiving				
Year	Att	Yds	Y/A	YAC/A	TD	Targets	Rec	Yds	Y/Trgt	TD
2017	97	559	5.8	3.0	8	17	11	100	5.9	1
2018	84	597	7.1	4.0	2	30	25	135	4.5	1
2019	177	1003	5.7	3.4	3	24	21	154	6.4	2
2020	156	1245	8.0	3.6	9	30	25	267	8.9	2
	514	3404	6.6	3.5	22	101	82	656	6.5	6

Advanced

	Positive %				Per 100 Touches		EPA			
Year	Inside	Outside	Zone	Gap	Fumbles	Brk Tkl	Rush	Per Att	Rec	Per Trgt
2017	46%	41%	44%	41%	0.0	33	5	0.05	3	0.18
2018	57%	38%	45%	42%	1.8	37	11	0.13	-6	-0.20
2019	40%	41%	42%	41%	0.5	22	2	0.01	3	0.14
2020	59%	53%	57%	47%	0.0	28	47	0.30	11	0.35
	51%	43%	48%	43%	0.5	28	65	0.13	11	0.11

Deep Dive

	Usage		Receiving		Total Points			Total Points Rtg		
Year	Split Out %	Heavy Box %	Routes Run	Y/RR	Rush	Rec	Total	Per Rush	Per Route	Per Play
2018	2%	2%	77	1.8	19	2	23	97	77	89
2019	3%	3%	90	1.7	23	-1	26	87	58	77
2020	0%	1%	232	1.2	49	7	57	99	91	97
	2%	2%	399	1.4	91	8	106	-	-	-

Chuba Hubbard

Report by Jordan Edwards & Dan Foehrenbach

School	Height	Weight	Year	Jersey #	Hometown
Oklahoma State	6002 E	208 E	4JR	30	Sherwood Park, AB, CAN

One Liner
Hubbard shows the vision, explosion, elusiveness, and big-play ability to make an impact at the next level, but his minimal pass-catching prowess and inability to pass protect will need to improve before he can contribute as a consistent 3-down back.

Overall
Chuba Hubbard is the feature back for Oklahoma State's RPO based zone running attack. He played in 33 games and started in 24 of those games in his career at Oklahoma State. He competed for the Youth Canadian National Track Team, and also competed as a sprinter for the Oklahoma State track team. He's a fluid, long-strider with fast feet and good body control. Hubbard has a good motor and is a tough runner who has shown the ability to handle a heavy workload.

Run Game
Hubbard excels in Oklahoma State's zone blocking scheme. He is a patient, one-cut runner that allows his blockers to create run lanes for him and has good body control to maneuver through bodies and fight for extra yards. He's an elusive runner and has very good short-area agility and quickness. He has a knack to consistently make the first man miss and get vertical for more yards. He sees cutback lanes very well, and his eyes and feet work in unison. He displays good burst and acceleration that helps him get to the 2nd level of the defense and show off his track speed downfield. Hubbard has good contact balance and runs low to the ground. He shows that he can carry a heavy workload and get the tough yards when needed; however, he doesn't show much power. He shows some inconsistency controlling the ball at the mesh point with the QB and has had some costly fumbles in his career as well.

Pass Game
Hubbard's impact in the passing game has some room for improvement. He was sparingly used as a receiver in Oklahoma State's offense. He ran a limited route tree mostly running swings and flats out of the backfield. He does show some good flashes in the screen game utilizing his elusiveness and speed out in the open field. He has sufficient catching skills and his agility and acceleration allow him to gain yards after the catch. Pass protection is an area that needs to improve drastically for Hubbard. He'll cut block incoming blitzers rather than square up and take them on. His physical ability to pass block isn't the question, but his willingness and effort is a major concern in this area.

Last Word
Hubbard projects as a low-end starting running back in a zone blocking run scheme. His ability to stay patient, plant his foot in the ground and get vertical would be an asset for teams with this run scheme. He's limited in a 3rd down role, but has sufficient ability to eventually be a threat as a receiver out of the backfield. Hubbard's ability to pass protect will need to improve drastically to prove he's a 3-down back. Hubbard does have experience and production as a returner in college, but likely won't contribute much elsewhere.

Strengths

- Vision
- Contact balance
- Elusiveness

Weaknesses

- Receiving ability
- Pass pro
- Power

Critical Factors

Vision	Contact Balance	Passing Game Impact
7	6	4

Positional Factors

Play Speed	Elusiveness	Power
6	7	5
Playmaker	Catching Skill	Pass Pro
6	5	4
Ball Security	Toughness	ST Value
5	5	6

Basic

Year	Rushing					Receiving				
	Att	Yds	Y/A	YAC/A	TD	Targets	Rec	Yds	Y/Trgt	TD
2018	124	740	6.0	2.9	7	28	22	229	8.2	2
2019	327	2090	6.4	3.7	21	30	24	197	6.6	0
2020	133	625	4.7	2.2	5	10	8	52	5.2	1
	584	3455	5.9	3.2	33	68	54	478	7.0	3

Advanced

Year	Positive %				Per 100 Touches		EPA			
	Inside	Outside	Zone	Gap	Fumbles	Brk Tkl	Rush	Per Att	Rec	Per Trgt
2018	57%	41%	54%	50%	2.7	23	14	0.12	13	0.47
2019	53%	51%	50%	51%	1.4	21	42	0.13	-1	-0.02
2020	38%	20%	40%	47%	0.7	19	-4	-0.03	-1	-0.11
	51%	44%	49%	50%	1.6	21	53	0.09	11	0.17

Deep Dive

Year	Usage		Receiving		Total Points			Total Points Rtg		
	Split Out %	Heavy Box %	Routes Run	Y/RR	Rush	Rec	Total	Per Rush	Per Route	Per Play
2018	5%	4%	130	1.8	19	6	28	91	86	89
2019	2%	8%	104	1.9	38	1	43	85	63	74
2020	3%	5%	208	0.3	6	0	8	74	60	71
	3%	6%	442	1.1	63	7	79	-	-	-

Kenneth Gainwell

Report by Jacob Halleen & Lathon Lax

School	Height	Weight	Year	Jersey #	Hometown
Memphis	5106 E	195 E	3SO	19	Yazoo City, MS

One Liner
Gainwell lacks experience, strength, and is limited in pass protection, but his versatility, playmaking abilities, and receiving impact should allow him to see the field as a low-end starter at the next level.

Overall
Kenneth Gainwell is a running back in Memphis' RPO-heavy, spread offense, although he did often line up out wide or in the slot. He only played in 18 career games, starting 13 of them for the Tigers. He opted out of the entire 2020 season. He is slightly undersized and has only one full season of reps, so filling out his frame will be important for him to stay durable. He's a good athlete which is on display as he lines up all over the field. He is tough with the ball in his hands and does not shy away from contact, competing for every yard.

Run Game
Gainwell uses his burst and acceleration through the hole to get vertical. He's a one-cut runner who has good vision, and when he sees a hole, he attacks it with some wiggle between the tackles. His elusiveness allows him to make defenders miss, as he uses jump cuts and an occasional spin move to change directions. For his size, he has good contact balance and is difficult to bring down, rarely losing yards. He maintains forward progress and lowers his pads when needed, though he's not an incredibly powerful runner. While he shows burst at the LOS and into the 2nd level, he lacks some breakaway speed. Ball security is not an issue as he holds the ball high and tight to his chest.

Pass Game
In the pass game, Gainwell is versatile enough to line up anywhere on the field. While he runs a lot of shorter routes and the core running back route tree, he also runs the occasional wheel or seam and does a good job adjusting to the ball in the air. Due to his small frame, he has a small catch radius and struggles to make difficult catches. He doesn't always look natural as a receiver, but easily makes most catches on his frame. Once he catches the ball, he looks upfield and uses his playmaking abilities to make defenders miss in open space. In pass pro, he shows a willingness to block, but his small stature and lack of strength makes it tough for him to sustain. He'll attempt to just throw a shoulder instead of square up and often gets driven back into the quarterback.

Last Word
Gainwell projects as a low-end starter in a zone-run scheme based on his acceleration, elusiveness, and versatility. His 3rd down ability is somewhat limited early on due to inconsistencies as a pass protector, but he can be an effective receiver that lines up anywhere on the field. On special teams, he has the skill set to return kicks, though he doesn't have that experience in college, and could help out in some other areas even though his size may limit him until he gets into an NFL weight room.

Strengths	Weaknesses
• Elusiveness	• Size/strength combo
• Receiving skills	• Pass pro
• Versatility	• Experience

Critical Factors

Vision	Contact Balance	Passing Game Impact
6	6	6

Positional Factors

Play Speed	Elusiveness	Power
6	7	5
Playmaker	Catching Skill	Pass Pro
6	6	5
Ball Security	Toughness	ST Value
6	6	5

Basic

	Rushing					Receiving				
Year	Att	Yds	Y/A	YAC/A	TD	Targets	Rec	Yds	Y/Trgt	TD
2018	4	91	22.8	20.0	1	7	6	52	7.4	0
2019	230	1459	6.3	3.3	13	61	51	610	10.0	3
	234	1550	6.6	3.6	14	68	57	662	9.7	3

Advanced

	Positive %				Per 100 Touches		EPA			
Year	Inside	Outside	Zone	Gap	Fumbles	Brk Tkl	Rush	Per Att	Rec	Per Trgt
2018	-	50%	50%	100%	0.0	10	5	1.23	5	0.67
2019	49%	66%	52%	49%	1.1	25	13	0.06	18	0.29
	49%	65%	52%	50%	1.0	25	18	0.08	22	0.33

Deep Dive

	Usage		Receiving		Total Points			Total Points Rtg		
Year	Split Out %	Heavy Box %	Routes Run	Y/RR	Rush	Rec	Total	Per Rush	Per Route	Per Play
2018	67%	0%	14	3.7	5	2	7	99	99	99
2019	15%	17%	189	3.2	32	7	47	89	80	93
	17%	17%	203	3.3	37	9	54	-	-	-

Larry Rountree III

Report by Ben Hrkach, DJ Marquardt, & Noah Chang

School	Height	Weight	Year	Jersey #	Hometown
Missouri	5106 V	216 V	4SR	34	Raleigh, NC

One Liner
Rountree has the size, vision, and contact balance to be a starting back at the next level, but a lack of top-end speed and passing game impact likely limits how much time he sees on 3rd downs early in his career.

Overall
Larry Rountree III plays running back in Missouri's RPO-heavy scheme out of shotgun and pistol formations. The offense utilized both zone- and power-blocking concepts. He played in 48 games during his career at Mizzou, starting 29 of them. Rountree is an explosive athlete with tremendous balance and body control. He demonstrates good toughness by finishing runs, as well as punishing defenders in pass pro and with the ball in his hands.

Run Game
In the run game, Rountree works best as a one-cut runner in a zone scheme. He has good vision, patience, and burst, as well as the ability to make a man miss in the hole. He gets upfield quickly and can run through arm tackles as well as make people miss. He runs with a good lean and nearly always falls forward. He displays very good contact balance by bouncing off defenders and maintaining speed through his moves. In the open field, he can use a jump cut and has a devastating spin move. He also packs a punch with his stiff arm. Rountree runs with a desired mentality and always keeps his legs churning. His contact balance and determination have helped him pick up many first downs that other running backs would not have. He has been chased down on some long runs, lacking the elite speed and second gear to consistently outrun defenders, but it's not a glaring issue. He has had fumble issues and his ability to work the mesh point is not always as clean as desired.

Pass Game
In the pass game, Rountree shows reliable hands and always catches the ball away from his body. At times, he doesn't look incredibly natural as a receiver as he tends to hop as he catches passes instead of keeping his feet planted on the ground. He has shown the ability to run all traditional backfield routes, though he's not a back that can line up consistently out wide or in the slot and run true receiver routes. When he gets the ball in his hands, he quickly converts to a runner and easily makes people miss in the open field. Rountree has shown he can hold up against linebackers and has even stoned defensive linemen in pass pro, but most of the time he comes in a little out of control and can get pushed off his base and back into his quarterback. He's smart and has a good feel for blitzers and works well with the offensive line.

Last Word
Rountree is a well-rounded player who projects as a low-end starter that can be a workhorse running back in a zone blocking scheme with a limited 3rd down role early in his career until he improves in that area. When on the field for 3rd down, he'd be best used as a check-down receiver or running routes to the flats. He provides special teams value due to his skill set.

Strengths
- Contact balance
- Vision
- Yards after contact

Weaknesses
- Passing game impact
- Long speed
- Ball security

Critical Factors

Vision	Contact Balance	Passing Game Impact
6	7	5

Positional Factors

Play Speed	Elusiveness	Power
5	6	6
Playmaker	Catching Skill	Pass Pro
5	5	5
Ball Security	Toughness	ST Value
5	6	6

Basic

	Rushing					Receiving				
Year	Att	Yds	Y/A	YAC/A	TD	Targets	Rec	Yds	Y/Trgt	TD
2017	126	703	5.6	2.7	6	8	5	57	7.1	0
2018	225	1216	5.4	3.0	11	16	14	62	3.9	0
2019	187	835	4.5	2.7	9	16	13	70	4.4	0
2020	210	985	4.7	2.3	14	20	15	100	5.0	0
	748	3739	5.0	2.7	40	60	47	289	4.8	0

Advanced

	Positive %				Per 100 Touches		EPA			
Year	Inside	Outside	Zone	Gap	Fumbles	Brk Tkl	Rush	Per Att	Rec	Per Trgt
2017	46%	38%	48%	42%	0.0	12	8	0.07	1	0.14
2018	54%	48%	54%	38%	0.4	18	23	0.10	-3	-0.17
2019	44%	28%	47%	38%	1.5	15	-17	-0.09	-3	-0.20
2020	43%	52%	43%	52%	0.4	16	-8	-0.04	-9	-0.43
	47%	43%	48%	42%	0.6	16	6	0.01	-13	-0.22

Deep Dive

	Usage		Receiving		Total Points			Total Points Rtg		
Year	Split Out %	Heavy Box %	Routes Run	Y/RR	Rush	Rec	Total	Per Rush	Per Route	Per Play
2018	1%	12%	81	0.8	20	1	25	82	66	81
2019	2%	11%	93	0.8	-6	-5	-9	60	51	59
2020	3%	13%	344	0.3	11	-1	14	75	59	76
	2%	12%	518	0.4	25	-5	30	-	-	-

Demetric Felton

Report by Ben Hrkach

School	Height	Weight	Year	Jersey #	Hometown
UCLA	5085 V	189 V	5SR	10	Temecula, CA

One Liner

Felton lacks the size and strength to be an every-down back, but his speed, quickness, route running and toughness will make for a strong chance-of-pace weapon.

Strengths: Natural receiving ability; Elusiveness; Balance and toughness for size
Weaknesses: Power; Backfield patience; Pass pro technique

Demetric Felton played both WR and RB in UCLA's spread read-option offense that utilized zone and gap blocking. He converted to RB in 2019 after starting 8 games at WR the year before. In total, he played in 42 games, starting 16. He's well cut but undersized at either position. He is an explosive, twitchy athlete with good balance and body control. He's tough and willing to run between the tackles and take on defenders of all sizes.

Felton is a slashing, one-cut back. He can turn any daylight into a huge gain and has enough long speed to run away from defenders. He displays sufficient vision, but his patience is an issue and he will often try to hit holes too quickly. He has the ability to make a man miss in tight, but he lacks power and frequently gets swallowed up in the backfield. Once in the open field, his contact balance to bounce off of tacklers and elusive jump cuts and spins make him very difficult to take down. He has been handed the ball in a variety of ways as a gadget weapon.

Felton is a natural mismatch as a receiving back. He easily beats LB's with his speed and route running ability out of the backfield and can even beat nickel corners from the slot. He has a good feel for finding soft spots in zones and helping his QB on broken plays. His hands are good but he has too many cradles and body catches for a converted receiver. He quickly transitions into a runner and doesn't often get taken down by the first man to the ball. In pass protection, he is surprisingly stout and doesn't shy from contact. He does lack technique however, and his size will often be a detriment.

Overall, Felton combines his route running and WR skills with viable vision, contact balance and toughness to project as a change-of-pace zone runner. Further developed feel behind the line will raise his ceiling, but he'll get early playing time as a receiving mismatch. He has also been a productive KR and could return punts, too.

Year	Att	Yds	Y/A	YAC/A	TD	Targets	Rec	Yds	Y/Trgt	TD
2017	10	75	7.5	4.8	1	4	2	-2	-0.5	0
2018	5	27	5.4	1.0	0	40	20	207	5.2	1
2019	86	331	3.8	3.0	1	70	55	594	8.5	4
2020	132	668	5.1	3.4	5	26	22	159	6.1	3
	233	1101	4.7	3.2	7	140	99	958	6.8	8

Rushing / Receiving

Year	Inside	Outside	Zone	Gap	Fumbles	Brk Tkl	Rush	Per Att	Rec	Per Trgt
2017	-	67%	50%	100%	0.0	50	6	0.58	-5	-1.30
2018	-	60%	60%	-	0.0	20	1	0.11	-12	-0.31
2019	40%	29%	34%	47%	0.7	28	-29	-0.34	17	0.24
2020	45%	50%	49%	38%	0.6	30	-4	-0.03	3	0.12
	43%	47%	44%	43%	0.6	29	-27	-0.11	2	0.02

Positive % / Per 100 Touches / EPA

Year	Split Out %	Heavy Box %	Routes Run	Y/RR	Rush	Rec	Total	Per Rush	Per Route	Per Play
2018	98%	0%	236	0.9	-1	-1	-1	50	58	64
2019	13%	6%	234	2.5	-6	2	-5	56	63	58
2020	6%	17%	263	0.6	12	2	13	82	69	71
	42%	12%	733	1.3	5	3	7	-	-	-

Usage / Receiving / Total Points / Total Points Rtg

Critical Factors

Vision	5
Contact Balance.	6
Passing Game Impact	7

Positional Factors

Play Speed	6
Elusiveness	6
Power	4
Playmaker.	6
Catching Skill.	6
Pass Pro	4
Ball Security	6
Toughness	6
ST Value	6

Rhamondre Stevenson

Report by John Todd

School	Height	Weight	Year	Jersey #	Hometown
Oklahoma	5115 V	227 V	4SR	29	Las Vegas, NV

One Liner

Stevenson is a big back with the passing down reliability and interior vision to contribute, but his lack of electricity in the open field to create chunk plays on his own may limit his role.

Strengths: Navigating traffic; Reliable on passing downs; Toughness
Weaknesses: Manufacturing his own yards; Open-field speed and elusiveness; Consistent utilization of his size

Rhamondre Stevenson is a running back in Oklahoma's spread RPO offense, receiving exclusively gun runs. He has started 5 of his 19 career D-I games played. He broke his foot his senior year of high school and took a year off before going to JUCO and ultimately winding up at Oklahoma, where he was suspended by the NCAA for 6 games over a failed drug test. He has good size as a high-cut big back with a thick lower half. He isn't twitchy or explosive in space and lacks breakaway speed, but he's a solid athlete for his size. He's a tough finisher and has been a good, four-down effort player.

Stevenson is a downhill ballcarrier who runs with a forward lean. He knows how to patiently let reaches and pulls develop and leverage defenders into them before slipping behind. Stevenson does not create for himself well, as a vast majority of his big plays came as a result of great blocking and strictly following his play design. He shows good ball security through tight spaces. In the open field, he lacks the long speed to pull away and needs shuffle steps in order to change direction with a head of steam. He prefers to stiff-arm rather than lower his shoulder and drive, and he has a smooth agility that won't shake many top defenders.

Stevenson offers a very reliable, but not threatening, passing down skill set. He's a comfortable hands catcher and lets his blocks develop on screens before attacking open space. In pass protection, he plays with great positioning and willingness. He strafes and mirrors well to and through contact, but needs to utilize his strength to pop at the point of attack more consistently.

Stevenson projects as a role-playing change of pace option to complement a more agile big-play starter in the NFL. He best fits an inside power scheme where he can limit the need to manufacture his own yardage. He should work short yardages, spell on early downs, and rotate on third downs as a protection replacement. He was a productive special teams member and offers the toughness and effort to contribute on multiple units.

Year	Rushing					Receiving				
	Att	Yds	Y/A	YAC/A	TD	Targets	Rec	Yds	Y/Trgt	TD
2019	64	515	8.0	6.2	6	10	10	87	8.7	0
2020	101	665	6.6	3.9	7	24	18	211	8.8	0
	165	1180	7.2	4.8	13	34	28	298	8.8	0

Year	Positive %				Per 100 Touches		EPA			
	Inside	Outside	Zone	Gap	Fumbles	Brk Tkl	Rush	Per Att	Rec	Per Trgt
2019	47%	47%	45%	50%	2.7	30	10	0.16	4	0.37
2020	58%	45%	57%	52%	0.8	37	17	0.17	3	0.12
	53%	46%	52%	51%	1.6	34	27	0.16	7	0.19

Year	Usage		Receiving		Total Points			Total Points Rtg		
	Split Out %	Heavy Box %	Routes Run	Y/RR	Rush	Rec	Total	Per Rush	Per Route	Per Play
2019	4%	9%	30	2.9	13	2	17	95	93	95
2020	1%	11%	177	1.2	27	-2	27	99	52	90
	2%	10%	207	1.4	40	0	44	-	-	-

Critical Factors	
Vision	6
Contact Balance	5
Passing Game Impact	6

Positional Factors	
Play Speed	5
Elusiveness	4
Power	5
Playmaker	4
Catching Skill	6
Pass Pro	6
Ball Security	6
Toughness	6
ST Value	7

Trey Sermon

Report by Jordan Edwards

School	Height	Weight	Year	Jersey #	Hometown
Ohio State	6002 V	213 V	4SR	8	Marietta, GA

One Liner

Sermon's combination of contact balance and power will allow him to be a contributor in the run game, but his lack of elusiveness and top-end speed can keep him from being a consistent starter at the next level.

Strengths: Contact balance; Power; Toughness
Weaknesses: Elusiveness; Play speed; Catching skills

Trey Sermon lines up at RB in the outside zone-heavy run scheme for the Buckeyes. Sermon graduate transferred from Oklahoma before the 2020 season. He played in 45 total games and started 21 of them. He missed his final 5 games at Oklahoma with a knee injury and left the National Championship this year with a shoulder injury on the first play. Sermon has a solid build with a thick lower half. He has active feet and is a sneaky good athlete at his size. He's a tough and physical runner who can carry a heavy workload.

Sermon shows off good vision in zone. He's patient to wait for cutback lanes and has the ability to get upfield quickly. He shows good initial burst but doesn't possess the top-end speed or elusiveness to break away in the open field consistently. Sermon has good contact balance and core strength to bounce off tacklers and fight for extra yards. He isn't a playmaker by definition, but he shows the ability to wear a defense down through a game and consistently gain chunk yardage on early downs.

Sermon takes care of the football as well and hasn't lost a fumble since his freshman season. He runs behind his pads and gains yards after contact regularly.

Sermon isn't as good a pass catcher as he is as a runner, but he can play a role in the pass game at the next level. He is a better pass protector than receiver, stout enough to take on rushers in the pocket and showing flashes of finishing weaker rushers to the ground. Sermon isn't a true difference maker out of the backfield, but he has sufficient hands and can be a reliable checkdown option.

Sermon can serve as a role-playing starter at the next level, with his tough running demeanor and combination of contact balance and power. He can have a low-end early down role in the run game and his pass protection abilities can get him time in passing situations. Sermon doesn't project to be a return threat, but his toughness indicates he'd be a sufficient special teams contributor elsewhere.

	Rushing					Receiving				
Year	Att	Yds	Y/A	YAC/A	TD	Targets	Rec	Yds	Y/Trgt	TD
2017	121	744	6.1	4.4	5	21	16	139	6.6	2
2018	164	947	5.8	3.4	13	15	12	181	11.8	0
2019	54	385	7.1	3.7	4	11	8	71	6.5	1
2020	116	870	7.5	3.6	4	17	12	95	5.6	0
	455	2946	6.5	3.8	26	64	48	486	7.5	3

	Positive %				Per 100 Touches		EPA			
Year	Inside	Outside	Zone	Gap	Fumbles	Brk Tkl	Rush	Per Att	Rec	Per Trgt
2017	51%	60%	46%	58%	0.7	33	16	0.14	2	0.10
2018	43%	71%	42%	60%	0.6	36	13	0.08	8	0.51
2019	55%	67%	55%	50%	0.0	19	10	0.18	-1	-0.07
2020	52%	40%	52%	50%	0.0	30	21	0.18	-2	-0.10
	49%	58%	48%	57%	0.4	31	60	0.13	7	0.11

	Usage		Receiving		Total Points			Total Points Rtg		
Year	Split Out %	Heavy Box %	Routes Run	Y/RR	Rush	Rec	Total	Per Rush	Per Route	Per Play
2018	3%	7%	101	1.8	39	0	45	97	62	87
2019	5%	17%	56	1.3	17	2	22	99	74	96
2020	3%	9%	204	0.5	30	2	34	98	72	92
	4%	9%	361	1.0	86	4	101	-	-	-

Critical Factors

Vision	6
Contact Balance	6
Passing Game Impact	5

Positional Factors

Play Speed	5
Elusiveness	4
Power	6
Playmaker	5
Catching Skill	5
Pass Pro	6
Ball Security	7
Toughness	6
ST Value	5

Jermar Jefferson

Report by Nathan Cooper

School	Height	Weight	Year	Jersey #	Hometown
Oregon State	5091 E	217 E	3JR	6	Harbor City, CA

One Liner
Jefferson shows the burst, acceleration, and receiving ability to be a rotational back, but his upright running style with limited power and ball security issues need to get cleaned up if he wants to see the field consistently.

Strengths: Burst through the hole; Start-stop ability; Soft hands
Weaknesses: Upright runner; Limited power; Some ball security issues

Jermar Jefferson is a running back in Oregon State's pro-style offense running mainly zone and duo run schemes. He started 21 of 27 games played in his career. He missed 3 games due to a lingering ankle injury during the 2019 season. He has good size and a strong frame with just adequate lower-leg build for the position. He's a good athlete who runs hard and competes, playing tough on every down.

Jefferson is a downhill, one-cut runner. He likes to get north and south, only getting east and west when needed. He has the vision to find the holes and cutback lanes. When he finds it, he shows good burst and acceleration to get vertical into the 2nd and 3rd levels of the defense. Though he's not tall, he runs a bit upright, making it tough for him to consistently stay balanced. He can stay on his feet when contacted, but struggles to run through arm tackles consistently. He isn't incredibly elusive, but slippery, starting and stopping quickly and changing directions to elude defenders. He lacks power and usually doesn't deliver a blow at the end of runs.

He's had some fumbling issues that stems from holding the ball a little low and loose on most runs.

Jefferson wasn't used a ton in the passing game, but made plays when he was. He was mainly used as a check & release, swing, and curl player out of the backfield, occasionally lining up out wide. Even with seeing limited targets, he shows strong, soft hands to catch balls all around his frame. In pass pro, he's smart and normally knows where the blitzes are coming from and who to block. While he isn't big or strong enough to consistently neutralize rushers, he can get in their way and uses his hands and footwork to sustain long enough.

Jefferson projects as a role-playing starter at the next level where he can come in on 3rd downs early on in his career. He can give the starter a rest, and then use his ability in pass pro and as a receiver to find time on 3rd/passing downs. With his play speed and toughness, he should contribute on most special teams units.

Year	Rushing					Receiving				
	Att	Yds	Y/A	YAC/A	TD	Targets	Rec	Yds	Y/Trgt	TD
2018	239	1380	5.8	3.1	12	32	25	147	4.6	0
2019	142	685	4.8	2.4	8	11	9	85	7.7	2
2020	133	858	6.5	3.2	7	11	9	67	6.1	0
	514	2923	5.7	2.9	27	54	43	299	5.5	2

Year	Positive %				Per 100 Touches		EPA			
	Inside	Outside	Zone	Gap	Fumbles	Brk Tkl	Rush	Per Att	Rec	Per Trgt
2018	47%	42%	45%	41%	1.1	21	13	0.05	-5	-0.15
2019	54%	63%	45%	65%	1.3	18	4	0.03	-2	-0.16
2020	50%	72%	50%	56%	2.1	11	8	0.06	1	0.11
	50%	58%	47%	49%	1.4	18	25	0.05	-5	-0.10

Year	Usage		Receiving		Total Points			Total Points Rtg		
	Split Out %	Heavy Box %	Routes Run	Y/RR	Rush	Rec	Total	Per Rush	Per Route	Per Play
2018	3%	16%	120	1.2	16	4	26	78	79	83
2019	2%	11%	64	1.3	1	1	1	66	63	61
2020	1%	14%	238	0.3	-8	-1	-8	58	56	60
	2%	14%	422	0.7	9	4	19	-	-	-

Critical Factors	
Vision	6
Contact Balance	5
Passing Game Impact	6

Positional Factors	
Play Speed	6
Elusiveness	5
Power	4
Playmaker	5
Catching Skill	6
Pass Pro	5
Ball Security	5
Toughness	6
ST Value	6

Pooka Williams Jr.

Report by Jeff Dean & Drew Barmore

School	Height	Weight	Year	Jersey #	Hometown
Kansas	5090 E	170 E	3JR	1	New Orleans, LA

One Liner

Williams has the elusiveness, speed, and receiving ability to be a true difference maker on 3rd down, but his size and strength bring limitations to being an every-down running back at the next level.

Strengths: Elusiveness; COD & acceleration; Big-play ability
Weaknesses: Power; Pass pro; Size limitations

Pooka Williams Jr. is a running back for Kansas' shotgun zone running scheme. He started 24 of 26 career games. He's a very good athlete who is undersized and needs to add significant weight. He has very good speed with an explosive burst and is a fierce competitor who is always running hard, even in blowouts.

Williams is a dynamic playmaker with the ball in his hands. He is difficult to tackle and routinely makes defenders look foolish one-on-one. He is a dancer who waits for a crease. This style results in a lot of negative plays, but also creates something out of nothing on numerous accounts. He has good vision and can find the smallest creases anywhere along the line with the wiggle to get through them. Though undersized, Williams isn't afraid of contact and will attack defenders head-on. He is extremely agile, changing directions on a dime to go along with impressive stop-and-start ability. He breaks arm tackles often and shows good contact balance due to a low center of gravity. Once in the open field, he has a deep bag of tricks to get past defenders and can execute these maneuvers at top speed.

Williams has diverse experience as a receiver who has natural hands and is comfortable working out in space. His fluid hips and quick feet project an ability to create separation once his route tree develops further. What makes him special in the open field is on display after the catch as he makes defenders miss one-on-one and is always a threat to take it to the house. Williams struggles with pass protection due to his size and lack of strength, but shows an acceptable ability to read blitzes and throws his body at incoming blitzers when needed.

Williams projects as a difference-making 3rd down back at the next level. He shows a natural ability out in space and could see most of his snaps in the slot or on passing downs. His versatility on offense makes him an ideal 3rd down candidate, but will need to add strength to improve in pass pro. He has experience in the return game, but has limited use on other special team units.

Year	Rushing Att	Yds	Y/A	YAC/A	TD	Receiving Targets	Rec	Yds	Y/Trgt	TD
2018	161	1144	7.1	4.4	7	40	33	289	7.2	2
2019	203	1041	5.1	2.6	3	31	27	215	6.8	2
2020	50	202	4.0	2.5	2	9	6	31	3.4	0
	414	2387	5.8	3.3	12	80	66	535	6.7	4

Year	Positive % Inside	Outside	Zone	Gap	Per 100 Touches Fumbles	Brk Tkl	EPA Rush	Per Att	Rec	Per Trgt
2018	51%	39%	33%	54%	1.5	29	9	0.06	10	0.26
2019	41%	40%	42%	43%	0.0	36	-11	-0.05	-4	-0.13
2020	35%	43%	40%	25%	0.0	29	-6	-0.12	-3	-0.37
	44%	40%	39%	46%	0.6	32	-8	-0.02	3	0.04

Year	Usage Split Out %	Heavy Box %	Receiving Routes Run	Y/RR	Total Points Rush	Rec	Total	Total Points Rtg Per Rush	Per Route	Per Play
2018	5%	3%	138	2.1	27	8	39	92	92	90
2019	5%	11%	126	1.7	24	8	35	86	88	84
2020	14%	10%	117	0.3	1	-2	1	71	52	71
	6%	8%	381	1.4	52	14	75	-	-	-

Critical Factors

Vision	6
Contact Balance	6
Passing Game Impact	6

Positional Factors

Play Speed	7
Elusiveness	7
Power	4
Playmaker	7
Catching Skill	6
Pass Pro	4
Ball Security	6
Toughness	6
ST Value	4

Khalil Herbert

Report by Jeff Dean & Christian Vega

School	Height	Weight	Year	Jersey #	Hometown
Virginia Tech	5087 V	204 V	5SR	21	Fort Lauderdale, FL

One Liner

Herbert does a little bit of everything in the run game with the vision and patience to provide value as a backup, but his lack of elite traits and experience as a receiver will limit his upside.

Strengths: Ball security; Vision/patience; Shiftiness in the hole
Weaknesses: True playmaking ability; Size/speed combo; Experience as a receiver

Khalil Herbert is a running back in Virginia Tech's play-action heavy, zone scheme. He started 22 of 46 career games. He began his career at Kansas before transferring to Virginia Tech for 2020. He missed 5 games between 2016-17 for undisclosed reasons. He's undersized, but has a compact frame with good muscle tone. He's a sufficient athlete with a calm demeanor, but runs hard and competes.

Herbert is a patient runner who uses good vision to read the line before making a move. However, he's sometimes too patient, resulting in some negative plays. He doesn't attack the hole, but has some wiggle to make defenders miss. His low center of gravity and stiff-arm allow him to break tackles, though he won't run defenders over and his legs can stop moving when contacted. Herbert can make defenders miss with jump cuts, but isn't overly elusive in the open field. He lacks the burst to gain the edge or the deep speed to make big plays. Most of his big plays come from multiple cuts or getting east-west. While he lacks an elite trait, he's consistent and provides a little bit of everything. He consistently braces for impact whether going through the hole or meeting defenders downfield.

Herbert doesn't seem incredibly comfortable in the passing game. He doesn't drop many passes, but he seems to fight the ball in and looks unnatural as a receiver. He has value as a checkdown option, but ran a limited RB route tree. His lack of explosiveness after the catch limits his appeal. Herbert has sufficient pass pro ability, though can seem unenthusiastic at times and miss blocks. He can get overmatched some by bigger defenders, but his stout frame and base allow him to take on most blitzers.

Herbert projects as a backup COP back in a zone scheme. His reliability should allow him to see carries on early downs and has enough pass pro ability and checkdown appeal to contribute on 3rd downs. He has some kick return experience and could contribute sufficiently on other units.

	Rushing					Receiving				
Year	Att	Yds	Y/A	YAC/A	TD	Targets	Rec	Yds	Y/Trgt	TD
2016	44	189	4.3	2.3	3	7	6	42	6.0	0
2017	120	663	5.5	3.5	4	14	8	38	2.7	0
2018	113	494	4.4	3.2	5	13	9	39	3.0	0
2020	154	1183	7.7	4.3	8	14	10	179	12.8	1
	474	2913	6.1	3.7	22	49	34	297	6.1	1

	Positive %				Per 100 Touches		EPA			
Year	Inside	Outside	Zone	Gap	Fumbles	Brk Tkl	Rush	Per Att	Rec	Per Trgt
2016	30%	50%	38%	20%	0.0	8	-1	-0.02	-6	-0.80
2017	29%	40%	32%	33%	0.0	20	-9	-0.08	-8	-0.60
2018	40%	40%	28%	46%	0.8	20	-17	-0.15	-5	-0.38
2020	65%	51%	52%	53%	0.0	26	40	0.26	3	0.24
	41%	49%	41%	41%	0.4	22	23	0.05	-17	-0.34

	Usage		Receiving		Total Points			Total Points Rtg		
Year	Split Out %	Heavy Box %	Routes Run	Y/RR	Rush	Rec	Total	Per Rush	Per Route	Per Play
2018	2%	5%	42	0.9	0	4	7	67	98	83
2020	3%	14%	284	0.6	49	-1	51	99	54	93
	2%	11%	350	0.6	61	3	71	-	-	-

Redshirt season not shown but included in totals

Critical Factors	
Vision	6
Contact Balance	5
Passing Game Impact	5

Positional Factors	
Play Speed	5
Elusiveness	5
Power	5
Playmaker	5
Catching Skill	5
Pass Pro	5
Ball Security	7
Toughness	5
ST Value	5

Jaret Patterson

Report by Nathan Cooper

School	Height	Weight	Year	Jersey #	Hometown
Buffalo	5085 E	195 E	3JR	26	Glenn Dale, MD

One Liner

Patterson has the patience, vision, and elusiveness to be an effective back, though he'll need to show he can contribute consistently in the passing game to be more than just a change-of-pace player.

Strengths: Patient runner; Leg drive; Shifty & elusive
Weaknesses: Tight hips when up to speed; Strength in pass pro; Not much of a receiver

Jaret Patterson is a running back operating out of shotgun and pistol formations in Buffalo's primary zone-run scheme. He started 25 of 33 games for the Bulls. He has a short, compact frame with a thick lower body. He's a good athlete that shows some twitch, competing as a tough runner.

Patterson is a patient and elusive one-cut runner who runs with a low center of gravity. He'll dance at times between the tackles, but shows patience finding the hole and elusiveness to make defenders miss, nearly always running through arm tackles. When getting outside, he shows the burst to break angles and gain the edge. He has the vision to find the open holes and does a solid job of following his blockers. His strong lower half makes him tough to bring down as he keeps his legs churning when tacklers are latched on. With the ball in his hands, he shows that he can squeak through piles and turn a loss into a gain, though he doesn't have the overall speed to be a consistent playmaker. He's elusive and moves well laterally to force misses near the LOS, but when he's up to speed, he has a tough time breaking down and changing directions due to tight hips.

Patterson isn't used much in Buffalo's passing game. He's an effective receiver with solid hands when given the opportunity, looking the ball all the way in. With that said, he likely can't be lined up consistently outside of the backfield. He makes plays out of the backfield on swings, flats, and check & releases. With the ball in his hands, he shows his ability as a runner and can gain good YAC. In pass pro, he's inconsistent, but does just enough most of the time. He's smart, but lacks overall strength and body control at the POA to sustain most blocks.

Patterson projects as a backup COP back in either a zone or gap scheme. He hasn't been used much in the passing game, but shows the traits to be sufficient in that aspect, especially on 3rd downs. His toughness and play speed should translate to most special teams units with the skill set to also be used as a kick returner.

	Rushing					Receiving				
Year	Att	Yds	Y/A	YAC/A	TD	Targets	Rec	Yds	Y/Trgt	TD
2018	183	1013	5.5	3.6	14	8	7	62	7.8	0
2019	313	1804	5.8	3.1	19	16	12	204	12.8	1
2020	141	1072	7.6	4.9	19	0	0	0	-	0
	637	3889	6.1	3.6	52	24	19	266	11.1	1

	Positive %				Per 100 Touches		EPA			
Year	Inside	Outside	Zone	Gap	Fumbles	Brk Tkl	Rush	Per Att	Rec	Per Trgt
2018	36%	59%	47%	49%	2.1	35	14	0.07	3	0.39
2019	53%	58%	55%	52%	0.3	31	64	0.21	11	0.71
2020	61%	53%	59%	53%	0.7	28	50	0.35	0	-
	51%	57%	54%	51%	0.9	32	128	0.20	14	0.60

	Usage		Receiving		Total Points			Total Points Rtg		
Year	Split Out %	Heavy Box %	Routes Run	Y/RR	Rush	Rec	Total	Per Rush	Per Route	Per Play
2018	5%	9%	82	0.8	37	3	42	95	80	88
2019	5%	27%	134	1.5	58	6	66	93	82	92
2020	0%	32%	199	0.0	41	-1	41	99	55	93
	4%	23%	415	0.6	136	8	149	-	-	-

Critical Factors	
Vision	6
Contact Balance	6
Passing Game Impact	5

Positional Factors	
Play Speed	6
Elusiveness	6
Power	5
Playmaker	5
Catching Skill	6
Pass Pro	4
Ball Security	6
Toughness	6
ST Value	6

Javian Hawkins

Report by Griffin Sullivan & Nathan Cooper

School	Height	Weight	Year	Jersey #	Hometown
Louisville	5085 E	196 E	3SO	10	Titusville, FL

One Liner

Hawkins' speed, elusiveness, and overall vision likely allow him to contribute at the next level, though he must improve his strength and pass-blocking skills to hit his full potential.

Strengths: Top-end speed; Elusive playmaker; Good vision
Weaknesses: Limited pass pro ability; Wears down in physical games; Lacks power

Javian Hawkins is a running back in Louisville's spread offense which is exclusively run out of shotgun and features zone run schemes. He started 19 of 24 career games and opted out of the final 4 games in 2020. Although small, Hawkins is quick, fast, and adds athleticism to his game. He's tough and competitive for his size, never backing down.

Hawkins uses multiple running styles, showing the ability to move east/west, make one cut, and be a little bit of a dancer. He uses good vision to find the open hole and slither through the line, as his size helps to disguise him. He's uncanny at finding the cutback lanes, using his playmaking ability to reverse field with regular success. His elusiveness in the open field makes him tough to bring down. He uses a combination of spins, jukes, and stiff-arms to make defenders miss. In addition to his elusiveness, Hawkins has the play speed and second gear to consistently run away from defenders. He has good contact balance for his size, running through arm tackles and bouncing off would-be tacklers. He

carries the ball a little too loose and puts the ball on the ground too often. In addition, his size causes him to wear down late in games, as he's not a powerful back who can take on a full workload.

Hawkins mainly runs the primary RB route tree and is used as a check-down receiver. In limited targets, he shows the ability to catch the football cleanly and make electric runs after. In pass pro, he shows minimal anchor ability and technique, mainly due to his frame. He seems to know where to pick up blitzers, but lacks the strength at the POA to sustain. He attempts cut blocks often, but they rarely hold up rushers.

Hawkins projects as a COP back in a zone-run scheme at the next level where he can use his vision, speed, and elusiveness as a runner. On 3rd downs, he'd likely be a short-route or check-down back out of the backfield and shouldn't be called upon to pass protect. He has a little experience as a kick returner and could help out there, but his size likely limits his overall special teams impact.

	Rushing					Receiving				
Year	Att	Yds	Y/A	YAC/A	TD	Targets	Rec	Yds	Y/Trgt	TD
2018	2	8	4.0	2.5	0	1	1	4	4.0	0
2019	264	1525	5.8	3.3	9	7	4	58	8.3	0
2020	131	815	6.2	3.8	7	19	16	127	6.7	1
	397	2348	5.9	3.4	16	27	21	189	7.0	1

	Positive %				Per 100 Touches		EPA			
Year	Inside	Outside	Zone	Gap	Fumbles	Brk Tkl	Rush	Per Att	Rec	Per Trgt
2018	50%	-	50%	-	33.3	0	-5	-2.42	0	-0.14
2019	42%	39%	40%	67%	0.7	28	1	0.00	3	0.38
2020	46%	39%	40%	25%	2.0	21	9	0.07	6	0.32
	44%	39%	40%	50%	1.4	25	5	0.01	9	0.32

	Usage		Receiving		Total Points			Total Points Rtg		
Year	Split Out %	Heavy Box %	Routes Run	Y/RR	Rush	Rec	Total	Per Rush	Per Route	Per Play
2018	9%	0%	4	1.0	-2	0	-3	50	57	50
2019	2%	19%	56	1.0	51	0	55	94	59	83
2020	2%	27%	214	0.6	42	2	48	99	75	96
	2%	21%	274	0.7	91	2	100	-	-	-

Critical Factors	
Vision	6
Contact Balance	6
Passing Game Impact	4

Positional Factors	
Play Speed	7
Elusiveness	7
Power	4
Playmaker	6
Catching Skill	6
Pass Pro	3
Ball Security	5
Toughness	6
ST Value	4

Elijah Mitchell

Report by Daniel Jankuloski

School	Height	Weight	Year	Jersey #	Hometown
Louisiana Lafayette	5102 V	215 V	4SR	15	Erath, LA

One Liner

Mitchell is tough to bring down with his low center of gravity and strength through contact, but his athleticism limits his playmaking in space, and he'll need to improve his technique in passing situations.

Strengths: Contact balance; Running behind his pads; Backfield vision
Weaknesses: Pass pro technique; Elusiveness; Speed

Elijah Mitchell is a running back in Louisiana's zone running scheme. He played in 42 career games with 12 starts as he split time in a heavy committee. He missed most of his 2017 freshman season after undergoing 2 foot surgeries. He has sufficient size and solid lower-half thickness. He is athletic in tight spaces but is not an open-field athlete. Rather, he plays with motor and toughness between the tackles and is physical at the point of attack.

Mitchell has good vision behind the line in zone to cut and get downhill, as well as seek out cutback lanes. He runs behind his pads and is able to push forward to get whatever he can even if nothing opens up. He can create some yardage for himself with his leg drive through contact. He does not have much horizontal quickness in the open field, but he can wiggle in tight quarters to lessen the quality of contact he faces. He also doesn't possess breakaway speed. Mitchell runs with great pad level and a low center of gravity, and his power and contact balance to absorb and deliver blows at all levels is very

impressive. He finishes runs and fights for extra yardage while keeping good protection of the ball.

Mitchell is capable in the passing game, but his experience there is limited. His hands are sufficient but he doesn't make every play cleanly, even as he is typically only a checkdown option. In pass protection, he has the thump to throw a shoulder at heavy rushers, but he often relies on the big hit and doesn't stay in front of his man on extended plays well.

Mitchell projects as a capable backup on all three downs, especially with some improved passing game technique. He has the size and willingness to pass protect, and his strength can be an asset in the open field, but he more easily profiles as an early down between-the-tackles thumper and short-yardage back. He has worked well in a committee and can complement a quicker space player well. His speed isn't ideal, but he has all the other tools to be a solid special teamer.

Year	Rushing					Receiving				
	Att	Yds	Y/A	YAC/A	TD	Targets	Rec	Yds	Y/Trgt	TD
2017	42	257	6.1	3.9	4	5	3	25	5.0	1
2018	145	977	6.7	4.6	13	23	20	349	15.2	3
2019	198	1147	5.8	3.3	16	13	10	70	5.4	1
2020	141	878	6.2	3.6	8	19	16	153	8.1	0
	526	3259	6.2	3.8	41	60	49	597	10.0	5

Year	Positive %				Per 100 Touches		EPA			
	Inside	Outside	Zone	Gap	Fumbles	Brk Tkl	Rush	Per Att	Rec	Per Trgt
2017	53%	70%	58%	50%	2.2	47	7	0.17	-7	-1.39
2018	49%	44%	50%	44%	1.2	34	31	0.21	26	1.15
2019	59%	50%	57%	63%	0.0	29	39	0.20	4	0.27
2020	50%	53%	56%	17%	1.3	23	25	0.18	4	0.22
	53%	52%	55%	46%	0.9	30	103	0.20	27	0.45

Year	Usage		Receiving		Total Points			Total Points Rtg		
	Split Out %	Heavy Box %	Routes Run	Y/RR	Rush	Rec	Total	Per Rush	Per Route	Per Play
2018	5%	14%	61	5.7	30	7	40	95	99	96
2019	7%	24%	79	0.9	37	2	39	94	71	82
2020	9%	13%	234	0.7	24	3	27	93	74	83
	7%	18%	374	1.5	91	12	106	-	-	-

Critical Factors	
Vision	6
Contact Balance	7
Passing Game Impact	4

Positional Factors	
Play Speed	5
Elusiveness	5
Power	7
Playmaker	5
Catching Skill	5
Pass Pro	4
Ball Security	6
Toughness	7
ST Value	5

CJ Marable

Report by Jake Johnson

School	Height	Weight	Year	Jersey #	Hometown
Coastal Carolina	5093 E	200 E	4SR	1	Decatur, GA

One Liner

Marable is undersized, but he plays with great toughness and strength for his frame and offers natural receiving skills out of the backfield to be a nice complementary player off the bench.

Strengths: Balance and toughness through contact; Receiving skills; Special teams value
Weaknesses: Undersized; Extra gear of twitch and speed; Pass protection

CJ Marable is a running back in Coastal Carolina's triple-option hybrid scheme that uses a combination of zone and gap out of shotgun. He started 32 of 36 career games in his 3 years for the Chants after transferring from Presbyterian, where he was an 11-game starter as a true freshman. His size and athletic profile don't jump off the screen, but he's a fiery competitor who plays with the grit of a much larger back.

As an innately north-south runner, as well as a frequent pitch man, Marable doesn't have much room to get creative with his vision. He works downhill quickly and shows good burst to accelerate to top speed. He has the ability to break big runs, but he lacks an extra gear to turn the corner or truly separate downfield. He has sufficient lateral agility to make defenders miss on occasion and wiggle through tight spaces, but he mostly plays behind his pads. He has good power and contact balance for his size, but at the next level his raw strength in comparison may hinder these traits. He does a good job of reducing his strike zone and flashes impressive tackle-breaking ability with his compacted toughness.

Marable has proven, natural hands that are put on display as a frequent passing target and as an option-pitch receiver. He was occasionally used in jet actions from the slot but more commonly on backfield swings. He is very comfortable in space and his tough running style is an asset on the perimeter. However, his pass protection abilities are a question mark. He was not given many reps based on his volume as a receiver, and his size is a cause for concern, but his toughness and power project well and could make him sparingly viable.

Marable projects as a three-down backup as a good change-of-pace option on early downs and a comfortable receiver in passing situations. His size will always be a detriment, but his toughness is a great counter asset. Those traits could make him a good coverage player on special teams, and he offers additional versatility as a kickoff returner.

Year	Rushing					Receiving				
	Att	Yds	Y/A	YAC/A	TD	Targets	Rec	Yds	Y/Trgt	TD
2017	16	162	10.1	4.1	0	0	0	0	-	0
2018	119	733	6.2	3.0	6	21	15	175	8.3	2
2019	204	1085	5.3	2.4	11	43	38	295	6.9	3
2020	169	894	5.3	2.5	12	41	31	228	5.6	7
	508	2874	5.7	2.6	29	105	84	698	6.6	12

Year	Positive %				Per 100 Touches		EPA			
	Inside	Outside	Zone	Gap	Fumbles	Brk Tkl	Rush	Per Att	Rec	Per Trgt
2017	38%	100%	40%	67%	6.3	19	7	0.46	0	-
2018	46%	54%	49%	54%	1.5	17	18	0.15	0	-0.01
2019	44%	66%	45%	56%	0.4	17	25	0.12	11	0.25
2020	38%	54%	45%	43%	1.5	16	6	0.03	3	0.08
	42%	58%	46%	52%	1.2	17	56	0.11	14	0.13

Year	Usage		Receiving		Total Points			Total Points Rtg		
	Split Out %	Heavy Box %	Routes Run	Y/RR	Rush	Rec	Total	Per Rush	Per Route	Per Play
2018	5%	8%	96	1.8	7	3	11	76	77	76
2019	7%	19%	187	1.6	-6	4	2	61	70	70
2020	12%	12%	507	0.4	-1	6	6	65	76	69
	8%	14%	790	0.9	0	13	19	-	-	-

Critical Factors	
Vision	5
Contact Balance	5
Passing Game Impact	6

Positional Factors	
Play Speed	5
Elusiveness	5
Power	5
Playmaker	6
Catching Skill	7
Pass Pro	4
Ball Security	6
Toughness	7
ST Value	6

Stats only include games that featured at least one FBS team

Chris Evans

Report by Carter Hayden & Michael Bonneville

School	Height	Weight	Year	Jersey #	Hometown
Michigan	5107 V	219 V	5SR	9	Indianapolis, IN

One Liner
Evans has the elusiveness and catching ability to be a solid COP back at the next level, but his lack of contact balance, a second gear, or much strength in pass pro may limit him.

Strengths: Elusiveness; Pass catching; Versatility
Weaknesses: Breaking tackles; Lacks a 2nd gear; Pass pro strength

Chris Evans is a back in Michigan's pro-style offense, mainly running zone concepts. He also saw time in the slot and out wide. He started only 6 of 42 career games, however, he missed the entire 2019 season due to academic suspension. A former track star, he has some unique athletic abilities. He's a team-first player who is willing to battle against anyone.

Even at his smaller stature, Evans is a willing runner between the tackles. He hasn't shown the ability to run through arm tackles consistently, but his vision helps him find open holes. What Evans lacks in power he makes up for with elusiveness and lateral quickness. His ability to elude defenders and make them miss is his biggest strength in the run game. He can cut on a dime and avoid defenders with regularity. He plays with good speed, but lacks a true second gear. Evans has always split time with other running backs at Michigan. While he doesn't have the tread on his tires that most backs do, he hasn't

shown he can be a bell cow in an offense.

In the pass game, Evans has very soft hands and shows the ability to catch the ball in traffic. He has good route running ability and his lateral quickness helps him create space against linebackers. He's mainly run curls, flats, and swings out of the backfield, but his ability to run routes from the receiver position as well make him a versatile threat in an offense. He is most dangerous with the ball in space, creating and gaining extra yards. In pass pro, he's willing, but lacks the strength at the POA to consistently sustain oncoming rushers.

Evans projects as a backup COP back where he can utilize his pass catching ability and mix in some rushes due to his vision and quickness. On 3rd downs, he'll be effective as a pass-catching back. He has little return experience, but his skill set suggests he could assist on special teams in that fashion or help in other ways on most units.

Year	Rushing					Receiving				
	Att	Yds	Y/A	YAC/A	TD	Targets	Rec	Yds	Y/Trgt	TD
2016	88	614	7.0	3.6	4	8	6	87	10.9	0
2017	135	685	5.1	3.7	6	20	16	157	7.9	1
2018	81	423	5.2	3.0	4	20	18	148	7.4	1
2020	16	73	4.6	2.2	1	11	9	87	7.9	0
	320	1795	5.6	3.4	15	59	49	479	8.1	2

Year	Positive %				Per 100 Touches		EPA			
	Inside	Outside	Zone	Gap	Fumbles	Brk Tkl	Rush	Per Att	Rec	Per Trgt
2016	51%	28%	47%	41%	2.1	32	11	0.12	1	0.18
2017	39%	42%	39%	32%	0.7	32	-11	-0.08	11	0.53
2018	43%	20%	38%	42%	1.0	27	0	0.00	7	0.33
2020	50%	0%	33%	100%	0.0	36	2	0.11	6	0.54
	44%	33%	41%	39%	1.1	31	2	0.01	25	0.42

Year	Usage		Receiving		Total Points			Total Points Rtg		
	Split Out %	Heavy Box %	Routes Run	Y/RR	Rush	Rec	Total	Per Rush	Per Route	Per Play
2018	15%	6%	76	1.9	9	7	18	84	99	93
2020	21%	38%	74	1.2	2	7	10	88	99	99
	16%	11%	150	1.6	11	14	28	-	-	-

Critical Factors	
Vision	6
Contact Balance	4
Passing Game Impact	6

Positional Factors	
Play Speed	6
Elusiveness	7
Power	4
Playmaker	5
Catching Skill	7
Pass Pro	4
Ball Security	6
Toughness	6
ST Value	6

Brenden Knox

Report by Stephen Marciello

School	Height	Weight	Year	Jersey #	Hometown
Marshall	5112 E	223 E	4JR	20	Columbus, OH

One Liner
Knox is a durable, downhill workhorse with very good vision and a physical running style at contact, but his lack of burst and receiving usage could limit his ceiling.

Strengths: Vision and patience; Balance; Workhorse reliability
Weaknesses: Route-running experience; Pass pro aggression and awareness; Burst

Brenden Knox is a running back in Marshall's inside zone rushing attack, operating out of shotgun. He played in 35 games with 24 starts after earning the job late in his redshirt freshman season. He is a thick, durable back with enough athleticism to surprise defenders bracing for his strength. He is a tough competitor with the ball in his hands and finishes runs with physicality between the tackles.

Knox has great vision and patience behind the line. He does a good job of waiting for his zone blocks to settle and works upfield quickly, while also showing the ability to locate cutback lanes to the back side. He doesn't have great explosiveness into the open field and lacks long speed to break big runs, but he gains chunk yardage with his vision, physicality, and sneaky elusiveness. He delivers and absorbs contact to his lower half well while keeping his balance. Secondary defenders often glance off of him and he runs with an innate toughness that's difficult to handle at the POA. He can sufficiently jump cut and change direction when defenders are expecting contact, but he isn't a truly shifty player. He has been a very reliable workhorse in his career with no fumble concerns despite his high volume.

Knox was scarcely used as a receiver, capably catching check-and-release dump offs, but essentially having no experience running actual routes beyond that. He was kept in to pass protect often and proved he has the strength to anchor but needs to work on his aggression and awareness. He tends to let rushers get into him instead of delivering contact himself, and he will leave early without scanning the whole box for unassigned rushers at times.

Knox projects as a strong early-down backup, especially in short yardages, and while his receiver skills are a question mark, his pass protection potential and sufficient hands are developmental assets. He would fit best as a physical change-of-pace complement in a downhill interior system. He has experience on special teams and should be a sufficient blocker on some units.

Year		Rushing					Receiving			
	Att	Yds	Y/A	YAC/A	TD	Targets	Rec	Yds	Y/Trgt	TD
2018	95	578	6.1	3.6	4	8	6	24	3.0	0
2019	270	1385	5.1	3.2	11	19	14	129	6.8	0
2020	185	887	4.8	2.4	9	11	7	86	7.8	1
	550	2850	5.2	3.0	24	38	27	239	6.3	1

Year	Positive %				Per 100 Touches		EPA			
	Inside	Outside	Zone	Gap	Fumbles	Brk Tkl	Rush	Per Att	Rec	Per Trgt
2018	47%	25%	49%	22%	0.0	21	5	0.06	-1	-0.16
2019	52%	36%	46%	52%	0.4	21	5	0.02	-1	-0.06
2020	47%	60%	48%	78%	0.0	14	11	0.06	0	-0.03
	50%	40%	47%	46%	0.2	19	22	0.04	-3	-0.07

Year	Usage		Receiving		Total Points			Total Points Rtg		
	Split Out %	Heavy Box %	Routes Run	Y/RR	Rush	Rec	Total	Per Rush	Per Route	Per Play
2018	0%	6%	41	0.6	5	1	8	76	75	78
2019	1%	10%	87	1.5	21	3	29	79	74	75
2020	0%	11%	221	0.4	5	1	10	71	69	71
	0%	10%	349	0.7	31	5	47	-	-	-

Critical Factors	
Vision	7
Contact Balance	6
Passing Game Impact	5

Positional Factors	
Play Speed	5
Elusiveness	5
Power	6
Playmaker	5
Catching Skill	5
Pass Pro	5
Ball Security	7
Toughness	6
ST Value	5

Spencer Brown

Report by Christian Vega & DJ Marquardt

School	Height	Weight	Year	Jersey #	Hometown
UAB	5105 E	208 E	4SR	4	Warrior, AL

One Liner

Brown's power and contact balance as a runner will help with his transition to the next level, but his limited speed, elusiveness, and catching ability likely limit how much he contributes.

Strengths: Power; Contact balance; Ball security
Weaknesses: Speed; Elusiveness; Pad level

Spencer Brown is a running back in UAB's shotgun, primary zone-run scheme. He started 34 of 46 games. He missed 4 games in 2019 due to an ankle injury. Brown is a big back with a thick lower body, who lost 20 pounds from 2019 to 2020, improving his athleticism. He has sufficient acceleration and speed, but runs hard and competes for extra yards.

Brown displays adequate vision and shows he can make the first person miss with his one cut, downhill running style. When he runs behind his pads, he shows he can punish defenders downfield. He shows he can run with a low center of gravity, but too often runs with a high pad level and gets brought down too easily. That said, his balance allows him to absorb contact and bounce off defenders who don't fully wrap up. He displays some shiftiness, but is a bit stiff overall. Brown isn't the fastest, though has enough speed to get vertical quickly and into the secondary. He hasn't had any ball-security issues over the years and is fundamentally sound carrying the football.

Brown was occasionally featured in the backfield on passing downs, but rarely contributed much as a receiver, being called upon to pass protect most of the time. He struggles at times identifying blitzers, but shows the physicality and willingness to keep his quarterback clean using his size and power. He was mainly used as a check down option, running flats or swings from the backfield. He didn't see many balls come his way, showing adequate hands and not looking incredibly natural as a catcher.

Brown projects as a change-of-pace back at the next level in any scheme where he can use his powerful running style to gain yards on the ground on early downs. On 3rd downs, he'll have a limited role until he can improve and become more experienced in the passing game. He has the toughness and power to possibly contribute on minimal special teams units, but a lack of overall speed likely limits his appeal.

	Rushing					Receiving				
Year	Att	Yds	Y/A	YAC/A	TD	Targets	Rec	Yds	Y/Trgt	TD
2017	250	1329	5.3	3.3	10	4	4	42	10.5	0
2018	272	1222	4.5	2.5	16	12	8	20	1.7	1
2019	150	564	3.8	2.3	5	3	3	16	5.3	0
2020	185	887	4.8	2.8	10	6	5	35	5.8	0
	857	4002	4.7	2.8	41	25	20	113	4.5	1

	Positive %				Per 100 Touches		EPA			
Year	Inside	Outside	Zone	Gap	Fumbles	Brk Tkl	Rush	Per Att	Rec	Per Trgt
2017	49%	55%	49%	33%	0.8	26	17	0.07	-6	-1.39
2018	48%	39%	46%	38%	0.4	16	1	0.00	-6	-0.50
2019	46%	19%	39%	31%	0.7	20	-20	-0.13	0	0.10
2020	54%	48%	48%	0%	0.5	12	-2	-0.01	0	-0.01
	49%	41%	47%	35%	0.6	19	-4	0.00	-11	-0.45

	Usage		Receiving		Total Points			Total Points Rtg		
Year	Split Out %	Heavy Box %	Routes Run	Y/RR	Rush	Rec	Total	Per Rush	Per Route	Per Play
2018	0%	12%	58	0.3	8	-1	11	72	55	70
2019	0%	15%	28	0.6	-7	-1	-4	59	55	73
2020	0%	18%	223	0.2	5	-1	6	71	58	71
	0%	14%	309	0.2	6	-3	13	-	-	-

Critical Factors	
Vision	5
Contact Balance	6
Passing Game Impact	5

Positional Factors	
Play Speed	5
Elusiveness	4
Power	6
Playmaker	5
Catching Skill	5
Pass Pro	5
Ball Security	6
Toughness	6
ST Value	4

Shane Simpson

Report by Max Nuscher

School	Height	Weight	Year	Jersey #	Hometown
Virginia	5083 V	199 V	6SR	31	Easton, PA

One Liner
Simpson has the vision and elusiveness to be a quality backup running back and return man at the next level, but his struggles in pass protection and contact balance likely keep him from being a consistent starter.

Strengths: Elusiveness; Vision; Hands as a receiver
Weaknesses: Contact balance; Pass pro strength; Lacks a true 2nd gear

Shane Simpson plays running back in Virginia's RPO, zone-run offense. He started 1 of 10 games for Virginia after spending 2015-2019 at Towson where he started 22 of 35 games. He missed 9 games in 2019 with a torn ACL and also suffered injuries in 2015 and 2017 that caused him to miss 13 additional games. He has a short, but strong frame and is a very good athlete with some quick-twitch ability. He plays with a high motor and competes on every play.

Simpson possesses good vision and patience to find holes. If a hole doesn't open initially, he has the patience to wait behind his offensive line until one opens up. As soon as he sees the hole, he shows good burst and acceleration to get vertical with his shoulders over his feet, always falling forward when he is tackled. He has enough power to run through arm tackles and it takes more than one defender to bring him down, though he'll get knocked off balance a little too easily at times. In the open field, he shows some slippery athleticism and possesses

quick feet to elude defenders with relative ease. He has the speed to outrun some defenders, but lacks a true 2nd gear in the open field. He has the intelligence to take what the defense gives him and avoid taking the big losses.

Simpson is a good receiver who excels on flats, swings, and wheels out of the backfield. He has soft hands and tracks the ball well on throws downfield, showing he can make catches off his frame. In the open field, he shows his running style to create YAC. In pass pro, he has the intelligence to pick up late blitzers and knows who to block, but is hesitant taking them head on, and doesn't have the size or strength to sustain for long.

Simpson projects as a backup COP back in a zone scheme. On 3rd down, he will best be utilized as a pass-catching back, not as a pass protector. Due to his skill set and both kick and punt return experience, he should return kicks at the next level.

	Rushing					Receiving						Critical Factors	
Year	Att	Yds	Y/A	YAC/A	TD	Targets	Rec	Yds	Y/Trgt	TD		Vision	6
2016	5	2	0.4	0.4	0	2	0	0	-	0		Contact Balance	5
2017	12	25	2.1	1.7	0	8	7	53	6.6	0		Passing Game Impact	5
2018	8	18	2.3	1.9	0	3	2	18	6.0	1			
2020	53	281	5.3	2.0	2	19	14	130	6.8	1			
	78	326	4.2	1.9	2	32	23	201	6.3	2			

	Positive %				Per 100 Touches		EPA					Positional Factors	
						Brk		Per		Per		Play Speed	6
Year	Inside	Outside	Zone	Gap	Fumbles	Tkl	Rush	Att	Rec	Trgt		Elusiveness	6
2016	0%	-	0%	0%	20.0	0	-5	-1.04	-2	-0.82		Power	5
2017	14%	33%	0%	40%	5.3	5	-4	-0.34	4	0.53		Playmaker	5
2018	17%	0%	13%	-	0.0	40	-5	-0.59	2	0.80		Catching Skill	6
2020	50%	25%	50%	14%	1.5	13	-3	-0.06	-2	-0.09		Pass Pro	4
	39%	25%	38%	19%	3.0	14	-17	-0.22	3	0.10		Ball Security	5

	Usage		Receiving		Total Points			Total Points Rtg				Toughness	6
	Split	Heavy	Routes					Per	Per	Per		ST Value	6
Year	Out %	Box %	Run	Y/RR	Rush	Rec	Total	Rush	Route	Play			
2018	0%	0%	13	1.4	-4	2	-2	50	99	81			
2020	7%	9%	158	0.8	-1	4	4	64	81	78			
	6%	8%	171	0.9	-5	6	2	-	-	-			

Stats only include games that featured at least one FBS team

Otis Anderson

Report by Danny Shirilla & Jake Johnson

School	Height	Weight	Year	Jersey #	Hometown
UCF	5112 E	174 E	4SR	2	Jacksonville, FL

One Liner

Anderson is a versatile playmaker who has the speed and acceleration to make plays as a runner or receiver, though his size limits his power, contact balance, and contributions as a pass protector.

Strengths: Versatility; Home run speed; Acceleration to gain the edge
Weaknesses: Physicality; Pass pro; Contact balance

Otis Anderson is a running back in UCF's up-tempo, zone and RPO-heavy offense who also takes a significant number of snaps in the slot. He started 26 of 46 games for the Knights. He has a slight frame lacking some muscle definition, but is a very good athlete. Anderson has a high motor and has been praised by coaches as being the best all-around football player on the team at times due to his contributions on offense and special teams.

Anderson is a one-cut runner who likes getting north/south, but will get east/west when needed and has the speed to gain the edge. He shows good patience, sometimes too much, when running the ball, though it leads to him being able to find the open hole. He'll take his time dancing in the backfield to choose the right path in which he can make someone miss. Anderson is electric in the open field as a runner and is a true home run threat if given space, but struggles to make tacklers miss or run through arm tackles near the LOS. He runs with a decent base, but is often knocked off-balance by arm and ankle tackles a little too often.

Anderson excels as a route runner whether it's from the backfield or the slot. Many of his routes are check & releases, curls, outs, and swings, routes designed to get him the ball quickly so he can get out in space and run after the catch. Catching the ball seems to come naturally to him, as he shows soft, natural hands. He's a willing participant in pass pro, but lacks strength due to his size. He lunges and cut blocks a lot since he can't take on most defenders.

Anderson projects as a 3-down COP back in a zone scheme where he can use his ability in space as a runner or receiver. On 3rd down, he's best utilized as a receiver and shouldn't be looked at to help in pass pro. He's a proven punt returner and shows the toughness and speed necessary for most units, though size concerns may factor in.

Year	Rushing					Receiving				
	Att	Yds	Y/A	YAC/A	TD	Targets	Rec	Yds	Y/Trgt	TD
2017	69	494	7.2	3.1	4	40	30	351	8.8	3
2018	51	273	5.4	2.2	4	35	16	230	6.6	3
2019	112	720	6.4	2.4	5	44	31	365	8.3	3
2020	125	687	5.5	2.9	4	18	14	79	4.4	0
	357	2174	6.1	2.7	17	137	91	1025	7.5	9

Year	Positive %				Per 100 Touches		EPA			
	Inside	Outside	Zone	Gap	Fumbles	Brk Tkl	Rush	Per Att	Rec	Per Trgt
2017	37%	50%	38%	46%	1.0	15	14	0.20	10	0.24
2018	52%	64%	54%	48%	0.0	18	7	0.13	-8	-0.22
2019	46%	54%	47%	48%	0.0	17	13	0.11	9	0.21
2020	54%	38%	49%	45%	0.7	19	7	0.05	-1	-0.04
	48%	51%	47%	47%	0.4	17	40	0.11	11	0.08

Year	Usage		Receiving		Total Points			Total Points Rtg		
	Split Out %	Heavy Box %	Routes Run	Y/RR	Rush	Rec	Total	Per Rush	Per Route	Per Play
2018	69%	0%	147	1.6	9	6	17	91	86	88
2019	45%	4%	132	2.8	5	-7	1	73	50	60
2020	4%	12%	171	0.5	13	2	16	85	71	76
	41%	7%	450	1.5	27	1	34	-	-	-

Critical Factors	
Vision	6
Contact Balance	4
Passing Game Impact	6

Positional Factors	
Play Speed	6
Elusiveness	6
Power	3
Playmaker	5
Catching Skill	7
Pass Pro	4
Ball Security	6
Toughness	5
ST Value	6

Rakeem Boyd

Report by Spencer Schultz & Steven Penn

School	Height	Weight	Year	Jersey #	Hometown
Arkansas	5115 E	206 E	4SR	5	Houston, TX

One Liner

Boyd has good speed and natural talent, but he needs to improve his effort in the technical aspects of the game to see regular playing time moving forward.

Strengths: Linear speed; Contact balance; Ball security
Weaknesses: Making the first player miss; Finishing runs and effort; Pass protection

Rakeem Boyd is a running back in Arkansas' mostly zone running scheme. He began his career with Texas A&M before transferring to Independence CC due to academic issues. There, he starred on the Netflix series "Last Chance U." He then joined the Razorbacks where he started 26 of 30 career games. He had multiple shoulder surgeries in 2018 and played with an ankle sprain sustained midseason in 2020, limiting his explosiveness. He's a fairly big back and an upright runner with good straight line speed but limited lateral agility. He doesn't finish plays consistently strong and is not a high-effort player without the ball.

Boyd strictly follows his run play design, which can be to his detriment as he misses opportunities to bounce runs out of congested boxes. He's patient to let blocks develop but he does not consistently create yardage for himself if his blocking doesn't open run lanes. He has good long speed to pull away from defenders downfield. He's a long strider, but lacks the foot frequency to cut on a dime and make most

defenders miss. He's a big body who will fall forward, but he doesn't drive his feet at contact or deliver blows. He does possess good body control to keep moving through arm tackles and soft contact in traffic, and always has the ball tucked high and tight.

Boyd is a solid hands catcher, who was often used in the screen game to get him the ball in space. He wasn't a high-volume receiver overall, but he showed he was capable of being a checkdown option. He's shown improvement with his pass protection, but his technique is still very much a work in progress. Too often he relies on low-effort cut blocks to merely get in the way.

Boyd projects as a sufficient three-down backup at the next level, ideally in a power blocking scheme where he can work downhill and hit holes hard. He'll be a solid complementary player who is capable of big plays if he can regain his explosiveness. He'll need to improve his pass protection to see regular time on third downs and offers sufficient special teams versatility.

	Rushing					Receiving				
Year	Att	Yds	Y/A	YAC/A	TD	Targets	Rec	Yds	Y/Trgt	TD
2018	123	732	6.0	2.6	2	26	23	166	6.4	0
2019	183	1127	6.2	3.0	8	27	19	160	5.9	0
2020	82	309	3.8	2.1	3	13	10	33	2.5	0
	388	2168	5.6	2.7	13	66	52	359	5.4	0

	Positive %				Per 100 Touches		EPA			
Year	Inside	Outside	Zone	Gap	Fumbles	Brk Tkl	Rush	Per Att	Rec	Per Trgt
2018	31%	50%	30%	46%	2.1	13	-5	-0.04	-1	-0.05
2019	41%	38%	43%	46%	0.5	14	0	0.00	-4	-0.15
2020	63%	29%	54%	31%	1.1	8	-8	-0.09	-10	-0.75
	44%	41%	43%	44%	1.1	13	-13	-0.03	-15	-0.23

	Usage		Receiving		Total Points			Total Points Rtg		
Year	Split Out %	Heavy Box %	Routes Run	Y/RR	Rush	Rec	Total	Per Rush	Per Route	Per Play
2018	3%	4%	83	2.0	7	4	13	77	90	78
2019	2%	15%	117	1.4	1	-2	2	66	56	66
2020	4%	1%	119	0.3	-3	1	-3	61	71	56
	3%	9%	319	1.1	5	3	12	-	-	-

Critical Factors	
Vision	5
Contact Balance	6
Passing Game Impact	5

Positional Factors	
Play Speed	6
Elusiveness	5
Power	5
Playmaker	5
Catching Skill	6
Pass Pro	4
Ball Security	6
Toughness	5
ST Value	5

Josh Johnson

Report by Jeff Dean, Tobin Sharp, & Luke DeCello

School	Height	Weight	Year	Jersey #	Hometown
Louisiana-Monroe	5085 V	210 V	5SR	8	Hurtsboro, AL

One Liner

Johnson's ability to pass protect is a coveted trait, and his effort and toughness as a ballcarrier are useful, but his inability to threaten defenses in space will likely limit him to a backup role.

Strengths: Pass protection; Strong lower body; Effort and toughness
Weaknesses: Big-play generation; Comfort as a receiver; Consistent impact

Josh Johnson is a running back in Louisiana-Monroe's zone blocking scheme. He played in 28 career games with 19 starts. He bounced around between community colleges to begin his career, then transferred to Louisiana-Monroe in 2018. He is well-built with a thick lower body but a little undersized. He lacks the twitch or acceleration to break away from defenders. He is a solid competitor who fights hard for four quarters and puts in the work to execute the small details of winning football.

Johnson is a patient downhill runner who relies on his power to pick up extra yards. His patience can become noncommittal, failing to take advantage of sufficient enough creases, resulting in TFLs. He doesn't bounce many runs outside and trusts his blockers to create run lanes. He does a good job of breaking through arm tackles but won't run over defenders, rather consistently falling forward for extra yardage. In doing so, he can become lax with his ball security. He lacks the burst to hit holes hard and the top-end speed to burn defenses in the open field. He doesn't create for himself well and is not a big-play threat.

Johnson is a little raw as a receiver, but his pass protection abilities allow him to see the field on third downs. He has a sturdy frame and squares his body up to step to incoming defenders and stonewall at the POA. He reads well and scarcely misses assignments. He has a tendency to put his head down, limiting his effectiveness, but he's shown improvement there. His route tree is confined to checkdowns and he doesn't have natural hands, but he sufficiently operates as a bailout option.

Johnson projects as an adequate three-down backup who fits best in a zone scheme. He lacks home run explosive traits, but he is a solid between-the-tackles runner whose pass protection could be his quickest way to playing time. He should be a contributing special teams player due to his toughness and willingness to do the little things.

	Rushing					Receiving				
Year	Att	Yds	Y/A	YAC/A	TD	Targets	Rec	Yds	Y/Trgt	TD
2018	19	69	3.6	2.8	1	1	1	-1	-1.0	0
2019	200	1298	6.5	3.9	11	19	14	133	7.0	0
2020	88	321	3.6	2.3	4	20	17	54	2.7	1
	307	1688	5.5	3.4	16	40	32	186	4.7	1

	Positive %				Per 100 Touches		EPA			
Year	Inside	Outside	Zone	Gap	Fumbles	Brk Tkl	Rush	Per Att	Rec	Per Trgt
2018	47%	-	44%	0%	0.0	20	0	0.00	-1	-1.10
2019	46%	67%	48%	50%	1.4	27	11	0.06	1	0.06
2020	36%	0%	32%	45%	2.9	23	-30	-0.35	-10	-0.49
	43%	40%	43%	48%	1.8	25	-19	-0.06	-10	-0.24

	Usage		Receiving		Total Points			Total Points Rtg		
Year	Split Out %	Heavy Box %	Routes Run	Y/RR	Rush	Rec	Total	Per Rush	Per Route	Per Play
2018	1%	5%	12	-0.1	1	-1	1	74	51	74
2019	0%	9%	98	1.4	26	-1	27	87	58	69
2020	1%	14%	204	0.3	-21	-2	-20	50	55	59
	1%	10%	314	0.6	6	-4	8	-	-	-

Critical Factors	
Vision	5
Contact Balance	5
Passing Game Impact	6

Positional Factors	
Play Speed	5
Elusiveness	5
Power	5
Playmaker	4
Catching Skill	5
Pass Pro	7
Ball Security	5
Toughness	6
ST Value	6

Wide Receivers

Sarah Thompson

The 2021 wide receiver draft class is looking pretty deep, even when compared to last year's class. Our scouts evaluated this class to have two All-Pro level receivers (7.0 final grade or above), a true No. 1 (6.9 final grade), three true No. 2s (6.7 final grade), and double-digit players projected to contribute as No. 3 or No. 4 receivers by their second seasons in the league. Before we dive in, let's briefly review the position and the stats important to evaluating the players coming out of college.

Wide receivers can generally be split into groups based on their skill sets, as some receivers specialize in the slot and others are better suited on the outside. A wide receiver need not occupy the same role all the time—Ja'Marr Chase, for example, showed the ability to line up in multiple spots for LSU. Chase opted out of the 2020 season, but he dominated in 2019. Most of Chase's best work is done after the catch. In 2019, he led FBS wide receivers in Yards per Target (14.4) and averaged 8.3 yards gained after catching a pass. He has the physicality to fight through coverage and the elusiveness to make defenders miss—in 2019, he averaged 4.9 Yards After Contact per Reception and broke 23 tackles on the year in 84 receptions. He earned an 8 grade in the evaluation of run after catch from our scouts, which projects this to be an "excellent" trait for him at the NFL level. His 7.0 final grade suggests exceptional talent.

Two other guys to keep an eye on are Alabama's DeVonta Smith and Jaylen Waddle. Smith, who is expected to be a true No. 1 WR with a 6.9 final grade, is a successful X and Z receiver and won the Heisman Trophy in 2020. Jaylen Waddle, whose 7.0 final grade projects Pro Bowl level performance in the NFL, is a slot receiver for the Crimson Tide who made the most of his 29 Catchable Targets in 2020 by catching 28 passes and averaging more than 21 Yards per Reception. Not only can he catch, but he can run—he earned a 9 grade from our scouts in play speed, indicating that he shows absolutely no weakness in this trait.

There are a few FBS wideouts who we project to only play the slot, and for that reason are graded 6.4 overall but stand out among the rest of the role-playing receivers who earned 6.4 final grades. Western Michigan's D'Wayne Eskridge played only six games in 2020 but still made headlines— he returned a kickoff 100 yards for a touchdown versus Northern Illinois and racked up 212 receiving yards on only 4 catches during a game versus Central Michigan. Rondale Moore (Purdue) misses out on our stat leaderboards due to injury-missed games, but he had one of the greatest statistical freshman seasons ever and projects to succeed in the slot at the NFL level due to his speed and elusiveness. Kadarius Toney and Elijah Moore are also in this group of high-end 6.4 graded receivers.

It's always important to look for good hands in a receiver. A wideout with strong, reliable hands will be able to snatch passes out of the air and make plays on the ball outside their frame. It's preferable to make a catch with hands rather than body to maximize catch radius, and a receiver with great hands benefits from fewer drops and more contested catches. Among wide receivers with at least 70 Catchable Targets, Ole Miss' Elijah Moore and Oklahoma State's Tylan Wallace are the only 2021 draft eligible wideouts with only 1 drop. They both earned 7 grades for their hands, indicating that this projects to be a "very good" trait for them in the NFL. Wallace is projected to be a strong starter with a final grade of 6.7 from our scouts.

A wide receiver needs to be able to run well after he makes the catch. Maximizing yards after catch is not only done by leveraging speed and acceleration, but also by shaking off defenders and missing tackles. Florida's Kadarius Toney stands out in these areas—in the 2020 season, he accumulated 508 yards after catch and broke 12 tackles on his 70 receptions. UCF's Marlon Williams has displayed similar success, accumulating 457 yards after the catch and 13 broken tackles in 71 receptions on the year.

Total Points allows us to wrap up all of the good and the bad of a player's value into one number. Total Points Rating is an even better way to evaluate different players between schools with different schedules, playing time, and quality of competition. There were more than a few WRs whose excellence is captured in their Total Points Rating per Route Run of 99. This group includes, but is not limited to, DeVonta Smith, Jaylen Waddle, and Ja'Marr Chase (2019), but also guys who didn't benefit from a full schedule or playing in the most competitive conference—D'Wayne Eskridge, Dax Milne, and Jaelon Darden, to name a few.

WIDE RECEIVER

Wide Receiver Grading Scale

GRADE	DESCRIPTION
9.0 – 7.0	High-end 3 down starter. Pro Bowl level.
6.9 – 6.7	Strong starter who plays on all 3 downs.
6.4	3rd receiver. Role player.
6.1 – 6.0	Developmental. Top traits but needs time.
5.9	4th receiver (with special teams ability).
5.8	5th receiver (with special teams ability).
5.6	4th receiver (no special teams ability).
5.5	5th receiver (no special teams ability).

Wide Receiver Rankings

Rank	Name	Grade	Page	Rank	Name	Grade	Page
1	Jaylen Waddle	7.1	184	25	Dez Fitzpatrick	5.9	226
2	Ja'Marr Chase	7.0	186	26	Damonte Coxie	5.9	227
3	DeVonta Smith	6.9	188	27	Frank Darby	5.9	228
4	Rashod Bateman	6.7	190	28	Cade Johnson	5.9	229
5	Tylan Wallace	6.7	192	29	Josh Imatorbhebhe	5.9	230
6	Sage Surratt	6.7	194	30	Dax Milne	5.9	231
7	Kadarius Toney	6.4	196	31	Dazz Newsome	5.9	232
8	D'Wayne Eskridge	6.4	198	32	Tyler Vaughns	5.9	233
9	Elijah Moore	6.4	200	33	Tamorrion Terry	5.9	234
10	Rondale Moore	6.4	202	34	Trevon Grimes	5.9	235
11	Amon-Ra St. Brown	6.4	204	35	Warren Jackson	5.9	236
12	Amari Rodgers	6.4	206	36	Anthony Schwartz	5.9	237
13	Terrace Marshall Jr.	6.4	208	37	Isaiah McKoy	5.9	238
14	Tutu Atwell	6.4	210	38	Jonathan Adams Jr.	5.9	239
15	Dyami Brown	6.4	212	39	Javon McKinley	5.9	240
16	Jaelon Darden	6.4	214	40	Blake Proehl	5.9	241
17	Marquez Stevenson	6.4	216	41	Ben Skowronek	5.8	242
18	Austin Watkins Jr.	6.4	218	42	Brandon Smith	5.8	243
19	Nico Collins	6.4	220	43	Khalil McClain	5.8	244
20	Shi Smith	6.4	221	44	Tre Walker	5.8	245
21	Seth Williams	6.4	222	45	Simi Fehoko	5.8	246
22	Josh Palmer	5.9	223	46	Bailey Gaither	5.8	247
23	Cornell Powell	5.9	224	47	Marlon Williams	5.8	248
24	Ihmir Smith-Marsette	5.9	225	48	Whop Philyor	5.8	249

Glossary

ADoT (Avg Depth of Target)
Average yards downfield at which the player was targeted, from the LOS to the intended catch point.

Air Yards
The total number of yards the ball traveled downfield from the line of scrimmage on receptions.

Catchable Catch%
The percentage of receptions on catchable targets. Excludes spikes, miscommunications, Hail Mary throws, and passes that were batted down.

Deep% (Route Running Split)
Percentage of routes run by a receiver that have an average target depth of at least 15 yards.

On-Trgt Catch% (On-Target Catch%)
The percentage of receptions on targets that did not require the receiver to unnecessarily adjust. Excludes spikes, miscommunications, Hail Mary throws, and passes that were batted down.

Positive%
Percentage of targets to the receiver with a positive Expected Points Added on the play.

Receiver Rating
Traditional Passer Rating on throws when this receiver is targeted.

Slot%
Percentage of plays on which the receiver lined up in the slot or in a reduced (nasty) split.

TAE (Targets Above Expectation)
The number of times per 100 routes a receiver is targeted above the number of times that he would be expected to be targeted based on a number of contextual factors.

Trgt Share (Target Share)
Percentage of a team's targets that went to a receiver.

Total Points
Sports Info Solutions' proprietary player value metric that uses an Expected Points framework and distributes the value gained or lost on a play to the players involved based on their impact on the play.

Total Points Rating
Total Points per play compared to average, scaled so that 50 is poor and 99 is excellent.

Unique Routes
Number of distinct routes that a receiver ran at least once in a season.

YAC
Yards after catch, the amount of additional yards the receiver gains after catching the ball.

Y/RR
Receiving yards per route run.

Yds/Trgt
Receiving yards per pass attempt in which the receiver is targeted, including incompletions.

Wide Receiver Leaderboards

Total Points Per Game

Rk	Player	School	Tot Pts / G
1	E. Moore	Ole Miss	5.5
2	D. Smith	Alabama	4.7
3	D. Eskridge	Western Michigan	4.0
4	M. Williams	UCF	3.9
5	J. Darden	North Texas	3.4
6	T. Wallace	Oklahoma State	3.2
7	K. Toney	Florida	3.1
7	D. Milne	BYU	3.1
9	R. Bateman	Minnesota	3.0
10	3 tied with		2.7

Receiving Total Points Per Game: Slot

Rk	Player	School	Tot Pts / G
1	E. Moore	Ole Miss	4.5
2	M. Williams	UCF	3.5
3	J. Darden	North Texas	2.9
4	D. Smith	Alabama	2.6
5	K. Toney	Florida	2.2
6	R. Bateman	Minnesota	2.0
7	T. Atwell	Louisville	1.8
8	A. Rodgers	Clemson	1.5
9	S. Smith	South Carolina	1.4
9	D. Newsome	North Carolina	1.4

Receiving Total Points Per Game

Rk	Player	School	Tot Pts / G
1	E. Moore	Ole Miss	5.4
2	D. Smith	Alabama	4.4
3	D. Eskridge	Western Michigan	3.8
3	M. Williams	UCF	3.8
5	J. Darden	North Texas	3.6
6	T. Wallace	Oklahoma State	3.2
7	R. Bateman	Minnesota	2.8
7	D. Milne	BYU	2.8
9	A. Watkins Jr.	UAB	2.6
10	3 tied with		2.5

Receiving Total Points Per Game: Wide

Rk	Player	School	Tot Pts / G
1	D. Eskridge	Western Michigan	3.1
2	I. McKoy	Kent State	2.8
3	T. Wallace	Oklahoma State	2.6
4	C. Powell	Clemson	2.4
5	D. Brown	North Carolina	2.2
6	A. Watkins Jr.	UAB	2.1
6	D. Milne	BYU	2.1
8	D. Smith	Alabama	1.8
8	A. St. Brown	USC	1.8
10	J. Adams Jr.	Arkansas State	1.7

Total Points Rating Per Route

Rk	Player	School	Rating
1	D. Smith	Alabama	99
1	R. Bateman	Minnesota	99
1	T. Wallace	Oklahoma State	99
1	D. Eskridge	Western Michigan	99
1	E. Moore	Ole Miss	99
1	J. Darden	North Texas	99
1	A. Watkins Jr.	UAB	99
1	D. Milne	BYU	99
1	M. Williams	UCF	99
10	4 tied with		98

Targets Above Expectation Per 100 Routes

Rk	Player	School	TAE
1	R. Bateman	Minnesota	15.1
2	T. Wallace	Oklahoma State	12.0
3	J. Darden	North Texas	11.5
4	S. Williams	Auburn	11.1
5	S. Smith	South Carolina	9.6
6	J. Adams Jr.	Arkansas State	7.4
7	D. Milne	BYU	7.3
8	S. Fehoko	Stanford	7.1
9	D. Smith	Alabama	6.9
9	E. Moore	Ole Miss	6.9

Wide Receiver Leaderboards

Receptions Per Game

Rk	Player	School	Rec/G
1	E. Moore	Ole Miss	10.8
2	D. Smith	Alabama	9.0
3	M. Williams	UCF	8.9
4	J. Darden	North Texas	8.2
5	J. Adams Jr.	Arkansas State	7.9
6	R. Bateman	Minnesota	7.2
7	T. Marshall Jr.	LSU	6.9
8	A. St. Brown	USC	6.8
8	W. Philyor	Indiana	6.8
10	T. Wallace	Oklahoma State	6.6

Yards Per Route Run

Rk	Player	School	Y/RR
1	D. Smith	Alabama	2.8
2	D. Milne	BYU	2.4
3	D. Eskridge	Western Michigan	2.3
3	J. Darden	North Texas	2.3
3	S. Fehoko	Stanford	2.3
6	E. Moore	Ole Miss	2.1
6	B. Gaither	San Jose State	2.1
8	I. McKoy	Kent State	2.0
9	K. Toney	Florida	1.9
9	2 tied with		1.9

Receiving Yards Per Game

Rk	Player	School	Yds/G
1	E. Moore	Ole Miss	149.1
2	D. Smith	Alabama	142.8
3	J. Darden	North Texas	132.2
4	D. Eskridge	Western Michigan	130.7
5	M. Williams	UCF	129.9
6	I. McKoy	Kent State	113.8
7	J. Adams Jr.	Arkansas State	111.1
8	T. Marshall Jr.	LSU	104.4
9	B. Gaither	San Jose State	103.6
10	T. Wallace	Oklahoma State	102.4

Yards Per Target

Rk	Player	School	Yds/Trgt
1	D. Eskridge	Western Michigan	14.8
2	D. Brown	North Carolina	13.1
3	D. Milne	BYU	12.6
4	D. Smith	Alabama	12.5
5	J. McKinley	Notre Dame	12.2
6	B. Gaither	San Jose State	12.1
7	E. Moore	Ole Miss	11.8
8	D. Fitzpatrick	Louisville	11.4
8	I. McKoy	Kent State	11.4
10	K. Toney	Florida	11.3

Yards After Catch Per Game

Rk	Player	School	YAC/G
1	D. Eskridge	Western Michigan	81.3
2	D. Smith	Alabama	72.8
3	E. Moore	Ole Miss	64.1
4	J. Darden	North Texas	64.0
5	M. Williams	UCF	57.1
6	A. Rodgers	Clemson	51.3
7	A. Schwartz	Auburn	49.0
8	K. Toney	Florida	44.6
9	T. Marshall Jr.	LSU	43.7
10	R. Bateman	Minnesota	40.0

Yards After Catch Per Reception

Rk	Player	School	YAC/Rec
1	D. Eskridge	Western Michigan	14.4
2	A. Schwartz	Auburn	9.1
3	D. Fitzpatrick	Louisville	8.7
4	D. Smith	Alabama	8.1
5	A. Rodgers	Clemson	8.0
6	J. Darden	North Texas	7.8
7	K. Toney	Florida	7.3
8	D. Newsome	North Carolina	6.7
9	B. Skowronek	Notre Dame	6.6
10	2 tied with		6.5

Target Share

Rk	Player	School	Trgt Share
1	D. Smith	Alabama	36%
2	D. Eskridge	Western Michigan	35%
2	J. Darden	North Texas	35%
4	I. McKoy	Kent State	32%
4	W. Philyor	Indiana	32%
6	R. Bateman	Minnesota	31%
6	E. Moore	Ole Miss	31%
8	T. Wallace	Oklahoma State	29%
8	S. Smith	South Carolina	29%
8	S. Williams	Auburn	29%

Catchable Catch Percentage

Rk	Player	School	Catch%
1	E. Moore	Ole Miss	98%
1	T. Atwell	Louisville	98%
3	B. Skowronek	Notre Dame	97%
4	I. Smith-Marsette	Iowa	96%
5	D. Newsome	North Carolina	95%
5	J. McKinley	Notre Dame	95%
7	D. Smith	Alabama	93%
7	K. Toney	Florida	93%
7	C. Powell	Clemson	93%
10	3 tied with		92%

Deep Percentage

Rk	Player	School	Deep Pct
1	S. Fehoko	Stanford	34%
2	K. McClain	Troy	32%
3	C. Powell	Clemson	30%
4	J. Palmer	Tennessee	29%
4	J. Adams Jr.	Arkansas State	29%
6	D. Fitzpatrick	Louisville	28%
7	J. McKinley	Notre Dame	27%
8	T. Atwell	Louisville	26%
8	B. Proehl	East Carolina	26%
10	2 tied with		25%

Unique Routes

Rk	Player	School	Unique Rts
1	A. Rodgers	Clemson	19
2	K. Toney	Florida	17
2	E. Moore	Ole Miss	17
2	T. Atwell	Louisville	17
5	D. Smith	Alabama	16
5	D. Milne	BYU	16
7	S. Smith	South Carolina	15
7	D. Newsome	North Carolina	15
9	T. Marshall Jr.	LSU	14
9	5 tied with		14

Total Touchdowns Per Game

Rk	Player	School	TD/G
1	J. Darden	North Texas	2.1
2	D. Smith	Alabama	1.8
3	T. Marshall Jr.	LSU	1.4
4	D. Eskridge	Western Michigan	1.3
4	I. McKoy	Kent State	1.3
4	M. Williams	UCF	1.3
7	A. St. Brown	USC	1.2
7	J. Adams Jr.	Arkansas State	1.2
9	K. Toney	Florida	1.0
9	E. Moore	Ole Miss	1.0

Total Expected Points Added Per Game

Rk	Player	School	EPA/G
1	D. Smith	Alabama	9.4
2	E. Moore	Ole Miss	8.7
3	D. Eskridge	Western Michigan	6.6
4	M. Williams	UCF	6.2
5	D. Milne	BYU	5.8
6	J. Adams Jr.	Arkansas State	5.7
7	J. Darden	North Texas	5.5
8	B. Gaither	San Jose State	4.7
9	A. St. Brown	USC	4.4
9	D. Brown	North Carolina	4.4

Jaylen Waddle

Final Grade: 7.1

Report by Nathan Cooper

School	Height	Weight	Year	Jersey #	Hometown
Alabama	5096 E	182 E	3JR	17	Houston, TX

One Liner
Waddle is a dynamic playmaker in all facets of the game who has the speed, savvy, and route running ability to consistently separate and then win with the ball in his hands.

Overall
Jaylen Waddle is primarily a slot receiver for Alabama's pro-style, RPO offense, but moved outside more in 2020. He started 9 of the 34 games he played for the Crimson Tide. He suffered a fractured ankle in the middle of 2020 which forced him to miss 7 games. He has an average frame, but is a quick-twitch athlete who has rare speed to compensate. He plays hard and competes, also showing toughness in his game, as evidenced by attempting to play in the National Championship.

Pass Game
Off the line, Waddle shows his speed and quickness. He gets into his route very quickly. Due to his size, he can have a little trouble against bigger defenders when they get hands on, though his foot quickness is enough to avoid them most plays. He ran a diverse route tree, but digs, slants, outs, and crossers were his most prevalent. He does an excellent job of varying his speed mid-route. Instead of just running full speed all the time, he throttles down before showing incredible burst and acceleration. He can obviously win with his speed and quickness, but his route running and savvy allow him to consistently win at the top of routes. He has good hands, but sometimes seems to not know whether to put thumbs together or thumbs away when reaching out for balls off his frame. Waddle shows good body control and tracking ability to find the ball downfield. He's also able to make catches in traffic, holding onto passes with defenders bearing down or attached to his hip. When he gets the ball in his hands, he has a chance to take it the distance. His speed allows him to easily break angles of defenders and leave them chasing. He also has the speed and elusiveness to make moves on defenders and make them miss to gain the extra yards. He's a player that not only can run by guys down the field, but can be used as a screen player or on routes near the LOS to allow him to create yardage on his own.

Run Game
As a blocker, Waddle shows the willingness to get in front of defenders and get his hands on, but doesn't have the strength to sustain or move them off their spot. In the run game, he can be a recipient of jet sweep and end around runs to get him the ball at full speed and use his ability to make plays.

Last Word
Waddle projects as a future No. 1 receiver at the next level who can work on the outside or inside. His speed, quickness, and route running ability will allow him to be a featured receiver. On 3rd downs, he fits best in the slot where he can use his speed on screens, run away from defenders on crossers, or win over the top with verticals. He also possesses dynamic return ability in both the kick and punt games.

Strengths

- Home run speed
- Savvy route runner
- Wins at the top of routes

Weaknesses

- Inconsistent hand placement
- Lacks block strength

Critical Factors

Hands	Separation	Run After Catch
6	8	8

Positional Factors

Release	Route Running	Route Savvy	Play Speed
6	7	8	9
Contested Catch	Playmaker	Tracking	Body Control
6	8	7	6
Clutch Performance		Blocking	Toughness
7		4	7

Basic

				Receiving						
Year	Trgt	Rec	Comp%	Yds	Air Yds	YAC	TD	ADoT	Yds/Trgt	Drops
2018	59	45	76%	848	486	362	7	11.0	14.4	3
2019	40	33	83%	552	156	396	6	5.7	13.8	3
2020	32	28	88%	591	304	287	4	11.3	18.5	1
	131	106	81%	1991	946	1045	17	9.4	15.2	7

Advanced

	Advanced Receiving						EPA		Positive %	
Year	On-Trgt Catch %	Catchable Catch %	YAC/ Rec	Trgt Share	TAE	Rec Rating	Total	Per Trgt	vs. Man	vs. Zone
2018	94%	94%	8.0	14%	1.9	143.1	51.3	0.87	70%	76%
2019	91%	86%	12.2	10%	-5.1	158.3	35.3	0.88	62%	85%
2020	96%	96%	10.3	8%	-1.1	158.3	38.6	1.21	80%	80%
	94%	92%	9.9	11%	-1.4	152.0	125.2	0.96	70%	79%

Deep Dive

	Route Running					Total Points				Total Points Rtg	
Year	Routes Run	Y/RR	Deep Pct	Unique Routes	Slot%	Slot	Wide	Rec Total	Total	Per Route	Per Play
2018	213	4.0	28%	13	72%	20	6	27	30	99	99
2019	198	2.8	22%	12	80%	8	0	9	11	90	88
2020	200	3.0	24%	11	48%	12	7	19	19	99	99
	611	3.3	25%	15	68%	40	13	55	60	-	-

Ja'Marr Chase

Report by John Todd

School	Height	Weight	Year	Jersey #	Hometown
LSU	6002 E	208 E	3JR	1	Harvey, LA

One Liner

Chase is a dominant hands catcher and a headache for defenses as a ballcarrier, whose ridiculous production against the nation's best in 2019 suggests he'll do the same at the next level.

Overall

Ja'Marr Chase was a receiver for LSU's record-breaking offense, splitting time in X, Z and slot alignments on both sides of the formation. He played in 27 career games with 21 starts his freshman and sophomore years until opting out before the 2020 season. He will turn 21 the month before the draft, playing his two years at LSU as only a teenager. A partially torn PCL ended his high school career early. He has standard height and an average frame for the position but explosive athleticism and breakaway speed as a former state-champion long jumper. His effort through his route running can be sporadic, but he competes at the catch point and finishes plays.

Pass Game

Chase has multiple elite traits, but he isn't a spotless prospect. His releases against soft coverage show some short-area quickness and ingenuity to feign and burst into his route. However, he struggles fighting through physicality to not get rerouted and stay on his line. He competes and has won his share against press, but he doesn't have the frame to avoid getting knocked off consistently. He sinks his hips into full change-of-direction cuts well and accelerates through 90-degree breakers efficiently, but he's not an inventive or high-energy route runner. Outside of any initial wiggle off free releases, Chase doesn't vary speeds or body fake his way through routes to separate consistently before the ball is out. He doesn't always play as fast as he could or use savvy to get away from defenders underneath, but his late acceleration through the catch point is outstanding. Chase has natural hands and makes a concerted effort to pluck the ball away from his frame on all targets. He has the strength in his hands to fight through tight coverage and does a great job of immediately tucking it away and absorbing contact in traffic. He knows how to subtly work his off hand to clear space on curls and back-shoulders late, and he's explosive to attack jump balls. While he may not always win before the ball is out, Chase's abilities at the catch point and after are exceptional. He's extremely slippery with the ball in his hands, regularly making the first defender miss or slithering out of arm tackles to convert unexpected first downs and bust chunk plays. He has the ability to upshift an extra few gears to pull away from a crowd.

Run Game

When Chase isn't occupying corners on the back side of RPOs, he's generally an uninterested blocker. He has enough size and football IQ to execute the bare minimum, but he largely isn't a factor in the ground game.

Last Word

Chase projects as an immediate high-level receiving option in the NFL, capable of operating out of multiple alignments but offering the most impact as an X attracting secondary attention downfield. While there's no doubt he benefited from playing with a quarterback who was spot-on with his accuracy at a ridiculously high clip, he certainly often made his quarterback look right as well, leading the nation in receiving yards after contact and broken tackles and skewing the odds of 50/50 balls in his favor. He faced a bevy of first round corners in 2019 and managed to come away with the Biletnikoff.

Strengths
- Slipping tackles and YAC
- Consistent hands off of frame
- Catch point savvy

Weaknesses
- Physicality through reroutes
- Creativity as a route runner
- Separation before the throw

Critical Factors

Hands	Separation	Run After Catch
7	6	8

Positional Factors

Release	Route Running	Route Savvy	Play Speed
5	6	6	7
Contested Catch	Playmaker	Tracking	Body Control
8	7	7	6
Clutch Performance	Blocking		Toughness
7	4		5

Basic

	Receiving									
Year	Trgt	Rec	Comp%	Yds	Air Yds	YAC	TD	ADoT	Yds/Trgt	Drops
2018	39	23	59%	313	260	53	3	10.2	8.0	4
2019	124	84	68%	1780	1081	699	20	13.3	14.4	6
	163	107	66%	2093	1341	752	23	12.6	12.8	10

Advanced

	Advanced Receiving						EPA		Positive %	
Year	On-Trgt Catch %	Catchable Catch %	YAC/ Rec	Trgt Share	TAE	Rec Rating	Total	Per Trgt	vs. Man	vs. Zone
2018	81%	81%	2.3	10%	-5.7	110.3	9.5	0.24	52%	56%
2019	85%	84%	8.4	22%	2.1	139.8	84.7	0.69	60%	67%
	84%	83%	7.1	18%	0.3	140.6	94.2	0.58	58%	65%

Deep Dive

	Route Running					Total Points				Total Points Rtg	
Year	Routes Run	Y/RR	Deep Pct	Unique Routes	Slot%	Slot	Wide	Rec Total	Total	Per Route	Per Play
2018	157	2.0	40%	7	8%	-1	5	4	5	75	71
2019	547	3.3	36%	15	40%	31	30	61	62	99	99
	704	3.0	37%	15	30%	30	35	65	67	-	-

DeVonta Smith

Report by Jordan Edwards

School	Height	Weight	Year	Jersey #	Hometown
Alabama	6005 E	175 E	4SR	6	Amite City, LA

One Liner

Smith is a graceful route runner who makes up for his slender stature with exceptional hands and body control.

Overall

DeVonta Smith is a versatile receiver for the Crimson Tide who played as a traditional X and Z receiver, but also showed the ability to play in the slot to create mismatches against opposing defenses. He played 54 games in his illustrious career and started 34 of them. He has a wiry frame with long arms and skinny legs. Smith isn't a twitchy or explosive athlete, but he has fluid and graceful body control with good long speed. Despite his slight stature, he is a tough competitor who isn't afraid to get physical.

Pass Game

Smith releases from the LOS with ease and quickness, but may struggle at the next level getting off physical press-man corners. He creates separation with quickness and route running. He is a detail-oriented route runner who uses his body control and quickness to attack the leverage of defenders in coverage before breaking at the stem of his routes. He has exceptional stop and start ability when setting up double moves and running for yards after the catch. He's a long strider with good burst and acceleration. He can run every route on the route tree and swiftly transitions into a ballcarrier after the catch point. Smith is able to maintain his speed to not slow down when tracking deep balls. He has very good body control along the sideline and in the air. However, he struggles staying on course when coming across the field, navigating bumps and reroutes by safeties and linebackers. Smith has strong and dependable hands at the catch point and plucks balls out of the air. He rarely uses his body to catch and shows the ability to flash late hands on deep routes. He won't overpower secondary defenders, but he will make them miss in the open field. He has demonstrated the ability to be a clutch performer on multiple occasions in his career, in the red zone and in crucial situations.

Run Game

Smith is a willing blocker out on the edge and executes sufficiently, but he won't drive off defenders physically. His speed and run-after-the-catch ability have been and should continue to be utilized in the jet sweep and screen games.

Last Word

Smith can be utilized at any of the receiver positions at the next level and can be a No. 1 or a top tier No. 2 WR. On third downs he will be best utilized as an outside receiver making plays down the field. Smith continued to play gunner as his stardom rose, which speaks to his toughness and winning mentality, but he does not project well to special teams roles outside of punt returns in the NFL. He took over punt return duties at Alabama after injuries mounted and became a dynamic threat. Early in his career he was sparingly used within a loaded WR group for the Crimson Tide, but capped off his Alabama career as a two-time National Champion and Heisman Trophy winner.

<table>
<tr><td colspan="2">Strengths</td><td colspan="2">Weaknesses</td></tr>
<tr><td colspan="2">

- Hands
- Route running
- Body control
</td><td colspan="2">

- Body composition
- Releases against press
</td></tr>
</table>

Critical Factors

Hands	Separation	Run After Catch
7	6	6

Positional Factors

Release	Route Running	Route Savvy	Play Speed
6	7	7	6
Contested Catch	**Playmaker**	**Tracking**	**Body Control**
6	6	6	7
Clutch Performance		**Blocking**	**Toughness**
6		5	6

Basic

				Receiving						
Year	Trgt	Rec	Comp%	Yds	Air Yds	YAC	TD	ADoT	Yds/Trgt	Drops
2017	17	8	47%	160	113	47	3	14.6	9.4	1
2018	60	42	70%	693	373	320	6	11.0	11.6	1
2019	89	67	75%	1259	504	755	14	8.9	14.1	2
2020	148	117	79%	1856	909	947	23	9.9	12.5	3
	314	234	75%	3968	1899	2069	46	10.1	12.6	7

Advanced

	Advanced Receiving						EPA		Positive %	
Year	On-Trgt Catch %	Catchable Catch %	YAC/ Rec	Trgt Share	TAE	Rec Rating	Total	Per Trgt	vs. Man	vs. Zone
2017	-	67%	5.9	5%	-21.3	120.1	4.8	0.28	42%	50%
2018	87%	85%	7.6	14%	-6.0	141.9	33.7	0.56	47%	67%
2019	91%	90%	11.7	23%	0.5	151.8	74.9	0.84	60%	76%
2020	93%	93%	8.1	36%	6.9	155.5	122.0	0.82	73%	74%
	91%	89%	9.0	20%	-0.5	153.2	235.5	0.75	59%	73%

Deep Dive

	Route Running					Total Points				Total Points Rtg	
Year	Routes Run	Y/RR	Deep Pct	Unique Routes	Slot%	Slot	Wide	Rec Total	Total	Per Route	Per Play
2018	306	2.3	31%	10	22%	8	10	18	21	93	92
2019	364	3.5	35%	14	28%	7	32	39	43	99	99
2020	672	2.8	22%	16	38%	34	23	57	61	99	99
	1342	2.8	27%	18	30%	49	65	114	125	-	-

Rashod Bateman

Report by Jeff Dean

School	Height	Weight	Year	Jersey #	Hometown
Minnesota	6010 E	210 E	3JR	0	Tifton, GA

One Liner
Bateman has the size, speed, and natural feel for the receiver position to be a very solid starter, and if he can polish up a few technical aspects, he could be a star.

Overall
Rashod Bateman's primary position is the X receiver in Minnesota's RPO-heavy offense, although he lined up in the slot for the majority of his 2020 snaps. He has started all 31 of his career games. He has a chiseled frame with long limbs and good acceleration and speed control to sink his hips and change directions. He plays with a visible competitive fire and is always looking to make an impact in the biggest games.

Pass Game
Bateman earned a starting role from Day 1 due to his ability to dominate the passing game. He has only a sufficient release due to some false steps, but he has quick feet and can shake a defender off the line of scrimmage. He has a limited route tree but has shown very good footwork on double moves. He gets solid separation at the top of his routes using savvy jab steps to misdirect and break in the opposite direction, as opposed to true short-area quickness. When downfield, he uses his off hand well to win the positioning battle at the catch point. Bateman wins more than his fair share of 50/50 balls due to his strong hands and very good body control. He has an impressive catch radius and makes circus catches look routine. He extends from his body while showing an innate ability to keep his feet inbounds down the sideline to secure the catch. Cornerbacks with length that can compete above the rim and stay connected through physicality can cause him issues, however. He can be a force after he catches the ball and difficult to bring down in the open field. He doesn't have elite burst, but he sees the field well and is able to get upfield quickly. He is a tough runner in space who isn't afraid to go across the middle and break tackles.

Run Game
Bateman is a good blocker who has the frame and positioning to win the majority of battles. While he doesn't block with great enthusiasm, he makes a solid effort each play and doesn't require runs to go away from him. He hasn't been used as a ballcarrier but has the skill set to do so.

Last Word
Bateman projects as a solid starter in the NFL who can work in almost any offensive scheme. While he is best suited for the outside, he can be used inside occasionally due to his route savvy and after catch skills. He lacks the top-end speed or elite separation ability to be a sure-fire No. 1 target, but he will thrive in a Z-receiving role as a number two.

Strengths

- Strong hands
- Body control
- Sideline awareness

Weaknesses

- Footwork at LOS
- Limited route tree
- Handling lengthy defenders

Critical Factors

Hands	Separation	Run After Catch
7	6	6

Positional Factors

Release	Route Running	Route Savvy	Play Speed
5	6	6	6
Contested Catch	Playmaker	Tracking	Body Control
7	6	6	7
Clutch Performance	Blocking		Toughness
6	6		6

Basic

				Receiving						
Year	Trgt	Rec	Comp%	Yds	Air Yds	YAC	TD	ADoT	Yds/Trgt	Drops
2018	100	51	51%	704	380	324	6	12.3	7.0	6
2019	98	60	61%	1219	860	359	11	15.8	12.4	5
2020	56	36	64%	472	272	200	2	9.8	8.4	3
	254	147	58%	2395	1512	883	19	13.1	9.4	14

Advanced

	Advanced Receiving						EPA		Positive %	
Year	On-Trgt Catch %	Catchable Catch %	YAC/ Rec	Trgt Share	TAE	Rec Rating	Total	Per Trgt	vs. Man	vs. Zone
2018	85%	86%	6.4	29%	-1.3	73.1	-6.4	-0.06	30%	48%
2019	96%	91%	6.0	31%	1.2	121.1	53.9	0.55	53%	61%
2020	84%	82%	5.6	31%	15.1	80.4	6.5	0.12	53%	55%
	89%	87%	6.0	30%	2.7	93.2	53.9	0.21	42%	56%

Deep Dive

	Route Running					Total Points				Total Points Rtg	
Year	Routes Run	Y/RR	Deep Pct	Unique Routes	Slot%	Slot	Wide	Rec Total	Total	Per Route	Per Play
2018	353	2.0	40%	12	9%	8	17	25	25	97	93
2019	468	2.6	35%	16	15%	12	33	45	45	99	99
2020	297	1.6	15%	10	67%	10	4	14	15	99	99
	1118	2.1	31%	20	22%	30	55	84	85	-	-

Tylan Wallace

Report by Chad Tedder

School	Height	Weight	Year	Jersey #	Hometown
Oklahoma State	5110 V	193 V	4SR	2	Fort Worth, TX

One Liner
Wallace has the hands, body control, and catch radius to be a solid No. 2 at the next level, but his inability to create consistent separation and yards after the catch may hold him back.

Overall
Tylan Wallace is the X receiver in Oklahoma States' spread RPO offense and would move to the slot in trips sets. He played in 44 games, starting in 28 of them. He suffered a major ACL tear in practice in the middle of the 2019 season that forced him to miss 5 games. He's a fast and sudden athlete that possesses immense body awareness and control. He plays with a hot and competitive edge to make big plays and compete on every play.

Pass Game
Wallace is an over-the-top, big play threat down the field. He uses his quick feet to accelerate off the snap and get by his defender. When pressed, he shows good hand usage in swimming over the top of the defender or pushing them out of his way to release to the boundary. He predominantly utilizes go, fade, and the occasional hitch & go routes to get over the top. He attacks these routes fast and gets defenders on his inside hip to allow enough room for his QB to drop it in between him and the sideline where he can turn, extend, and lay out for catches. He shows great athleticism in jumping over defenders and twisting in the air to adjust to passes and make great hands-catches. In contested situations, he has the ability to turn a 50/50 ball into 75/25. When defenders play off him, he attacks upfield off the snap identically to his deep routes, breaking their cushion, and getting them to flip their hips before he plants his foot in the ground to break inside or underneath on digs, outs, slants, posts, or curls. However, he doesn't show much explosion in short-to-intermediate routes and allows defenders to stay on his hip too often. Once he brings in the ball, he turns upfield and fights hard for every yard he can get; he's not afraid to lower his shoulder to fight for extra yards. He doesn't break a ton of tackles, but can use his power to bounce off of a weak tackle or deliver a stiff arm in space.

Run Game
On run plays, Wallace shows a willingness to block downfield and set an edge for his rushers out wide. He can lock up a corner and anchor himself to create running lanes and is also willing to throw his body around and make a hit on a defender out in space.

Last Word
Wallace projects as a starting No. 2 receiver, playing mostly on the outside with the ability to play down in the slot. On 3rd downs, he can play outside and use his jump-ball ability over-the-top or inside where he can get a clean release to win over the middle. His speed, toughness, and motor could make him a useful member on special teams units and a returner as well.

Strengths

- Jump ball ability
- Body control & adjust
- Catch radius

Weaknesses

- Route explosion
- YAC consistency

Critical Factors

Hands	Separation	Run After Catch
7	5	5

Positional Factors

Release	Route Running	Route Savvy	Play Speed
6	6	6	6
Contested Catch	**Playmaker**	**Tracking**	**Body Control**
7	6	7	7
Clutch Performance	**Blocking**		**Toughness**
6	6		6

Basic

	Receiving									
Year	Trgt	Rec	Comp%	Yds	Air Yds	YAC	TD	ADoT	Yds/Trgt	Drops
2017	12	7	58%	118	82	36	0	13.6	9.8	1
2018	150	86	57%	1491	1192	299	12	16.7	9.9	9
2019	85	53	62%	895	357	538	8	10.3	10.5	2
2020	93	59	63%	922	611	311	6	13.4	9.9	1
	340	205	60%	3426	2242	1184	26	14.1	10.1	13

Advanced

	Advanced Receiving						EPA		Positive %	
Year	On-Trgt Catch %	Catchable Catch %	YAC/ Rec	Trgt Share	TAE	Rec Rating	Total	Per Trgt	vs. Man	vs. Zone
2017	-	70%	5.1	2%	-	91.7	7.7	0.64	75%	43%
2018	81%	81%	3.5	31%	14.5	101.0	48.9	0.33	48%	55%
2019	88%	87%	9.9	24%	1.8	128.5	39.1	0.46	40%	50%
2020	94%	92%	5.3	29%	12.0	95.4	21.2	0.23	44%	60%
	86%	85%	5.7	21%	10.3	106.0	116.9	0.34	47%	55%

Deep Dive

	Route Running					Total Points				Total Points Rtg	
Year	Routes Run	Y/RR	Deep Pct	Unique Routes	Slot%	Slot	Wide	Rec Total	Total	Per Route	Per Play
2018	471	3.2	41%	12	6%	5	37	41	42	98	95
2019	261	3.4	40%	10	13%	7	6	13	16	91	93
2020	537	1.7	21%	10	11%	5	23	29	29	99	99
	1269	2.6	32%	15	9%	17	66	83	87	-	-

Sage Surratt

Report by Nathan Cooper

School	Height	Weight	Year	Jersey #	Hometown
Wake Forest	6025 V	215 V	4JR	14	Lincolnton, NC

One Liner
Surratt has incredibly strong, natural hands, is a precise route runner, and even positively assists as a blocker in the run game, though struggles against physical defenders and lacking a 2nd gear may occasionally prove troublesome.

Overall
Sage Surratt mainly plays the X receiver in Wake Forest's RPO offense, occasionally lining up at Z and in the slot. He started 18 of 22 games before shoulder surgery caused him to miss the final 4 games of 2019. He then opted out of the 2020 season. A former All-State basketball star in high school, Surratt is an excellent athlete with a good frame and size for the position. He plays hard and competes as a receiver.

Pass Game
Off the line, Surrat uses quick feet to defeat press coverage, though he will get held up by physical defenders. Once he gets into his route, he lacks a little savvy and seems to get contacted and rerouted too much against those physical DBs. He ran a very limited route tree in college with his main routes being curls, slants, and verticals, of which he ran more than 60% of the time. If he stays clean and uses his strength, he runs precise routes and wins with his breaks at the top. He mainly separates from defenders with his route running and off hand ability. He also shows late hands which allows him to get them up to the ball before the defender can react. Surratt has very strong hands with a wide catch radius. He can also make catches in traffic and is able to hold onto the ball even with the defender's hands swiping at his. He'll show a little hesitancy coming across the middle from time to time, but makes most grabs when the ball comes his way. He tracks the ball well down the field and adjusts well to the ball in the air, though there are more than an average amount of passes that go off of his fingertips. With the ball in his hands, he runs hard and is always competing for extra yards, occasionally making defenders miss. While he has good play speed, he doesn't possess a 2nd gear to run away from many defenders.

Run Game
Surratt is a good blocker and competes against the defender across from him. He takes good angles to get in front of defenders and moves his feet to stay between man and ball. He's strong at the POA and is able to drive defenders back off the ball and down the field.

Last Word
Surratt projects as a No. 2 receiver in any scheme at the next level. He can play outside or in the slot using route running, play speed, quick feet, and strong hands to beat defenders. On 3rd downs, he fits best in the slot where he can stay cleaner off the line and make catches to move the chains. He could use his play speed, toughness, and strength to contribute on special teams.

Strengths

- Strong hands
- Off-hand separation
- POA blocker

Weaknesses

- Struggles against physical defenders
- Lacks a 2nd gear
- Limited route tree

Critical Factors

Hands	Separation	Run After Catch
7	5	5

Positional Factors

Release	Route Running	Route Savvy	Play Speed
5	6	5	6
Contested Catch	Playmaker	Tracking	Body Control
6	6	6	6
Clutch Performance		Blocking	Toughness
6		6	6

Basic

				Receiving						
Year	Trgt	Rec	Comp%	Yds	Air Yds	YAC	TD	ADoT	Yds/Trgt	Drops
2018	84	41	49%	581	422	159	4	13.0	6.9	4
2019	103	66	64%	1001	689	312	11	12.4	9.7	3
	187	107	57%	1582	1111	471	15	12.7	8.5	7

Advanced

	Advanced Receiving						EPA		Positive %	
Year	On-Trgt Catch %	Catchable Catch %	YAC/ Rec	Trgt Share	TAE	Rec Rating	Total	Per Trgt	vs. Man	vs. Zone
2018	84%	82%	3.9	19%	-0.6	77.5	7.7	0.09	44%	41%
2019	91%	90%	4.7	22%	0.8	127.5	40.3	0.39	50%	62%
	88%	86%	4.4	21%	0.2	105.1	48.1	0.26	47%	55%

Deep Dive

	Route Running					Total Points				Total Points Rtg	
Year	Routes Run	Y/RR	Deep Pct	Unique Routes	Slot%	Slot	Wide	Rec Total	Total	Per Route	Per Play
2018	391	1.5	37%	11	13%	3	11	14	13	84	72
2019	433	2.3	26%	14	24%	4	22	25	25	94	90
	824	1.9	31%	15	18%	7	33	39	38	-	-

Kadarius Toney

Report by John Todd

School	Height	Weight	Year	Jersey #	Hometown
Florida	5111 V	189 V	4SR	1	Mobile, AL

One Liner
Toney is a dangerous weapon out of the slot and backfield with flashes of uncanny separation skills and acceleration, but doing so on a consistent snap-to-snap basis will take his game to the next level.

Overall
Kadarius Toney is a slot receiver in Florida's spread RPO offense, also seeing time outside, at running back, and as a wildcat quarterback after spending his high school career there. He played in 38 career games with 11 of his 13 starts coming his senior year. He suffered significant shoulder injuries his freshman and junior seasons that resulted in multiple missed games. He's slightly undersized but has enough bulk to his frame to absorb and deliver some contact. He's a dynamic athlete with the long strides and speed to win over the top, as well as the phone booth twitch underneath. He does not run every rep full speed and his feisty toughness is come and go.

Pass Game
Often put in motion, Toney was a chess piece for the Gators whose combination of alignment variation and his own separation abilities made him a difficult matchup for most opponents. He was often given free releases out of the slot, but working the middle of the field gives him two-way go's and open field through which to operate. He has an incredible knack for finding a way to cross the face and open up the hips of heavily inside-leveraged defenders whose assignment is to deny him of just that. When Toney turns it on, he's an elite separator using body-fakes, double-moves, and acceleration out of the top of his routes. However, it's evident when he's an early progression option or just a decoy, as he doesn't run every route with the same voracity. Top competition has proven that staying patient through his extra actions at the stem can hinder his separation ability. He struggles to sit in open zones and wasn't on the same page with his quarterback on some option routes. He also has issues playing under control. He's often too quick for his own good and will slip into and out of sharp cuts. Toney has soft hands when uncovered and will make plays on the ball outside his frame, but he relies on route separation for clean catch points, as he doesn't have the strength to fight through contested situations. He's a true threat with the ball, showing breakaway explosion, elusiveness, and some physicality to finish.

Run Game
Toney can be a pest as a blocker and will throw his body around, but he lacks the strength to sustain. More notably, however, he is very comfortable receiving not just jets and reverses, but also standard singleback handoffs. He has impressive vision and patience to set up blocks like a back and burst through running lanes.

Last Word
Toney projects as a high-caliber No. 3 receiver, with dynamic flexibility to the backfield and elite weapon potential for a forward-thinking coaching staff. He'll struggle on the perimeter with less space to work against the NFL's lengthy elite, but his ability to threaten all levels of a defense from the slot will make an immediate impact, and he offers gadget versatility as a legitimate ballcarrier and even passer. He'll be a reliable third-down target and an explosive return specialist, as well.

Strengths

- Setting up and manipulating leverage
- Playmaking
- Vision and patience as a ballcarrier

Weaknesses

- Consistent-effort route running
- Contested situations
- Staying under control

Critical Factors

Hands	Separation	Run After Catch
6	7	7

Positional Factors

Release	Route Running	Route Savvy	Play Speed
6	6	6	7
Contested Catch	Playmaker	Tracking	Body Control
5	7	6	5
Clutch Performance	Blocking		Toughness
6	4		5

Basic

				Receiving						
Year	Trgt	Rec	Comp%	Yds	Air Yds	YAC	TD	ADoT	Yds/Trgt	Drops
2017	19	15	79%	152	7	145	0	3.8	8.0	0
2018	36	25	69%	260	59	201	1	6.5	7.2	2
2019	12	10	83%	194	-2	196	1	1.3	16.2	1
2020	87	70	80%	984	493	491	10	7.4	11.3	4
	154	120	78%	1590	557	1033	12	6.3	10.3	7

Advanced

	Advanced Receiving						EPA		Positive %	
Year	On-Trgt Catch %	Catchable Catch %	YAC/ Rec	Trgt Share	TAE	Rec Rating	Total	Per Trgt	vs. Man	vs. Zone
2017	-	88%	9.7	6%	3.4	100.0	5.3	0.28	75%	43%
2018	89%	89%	8.0	10%	-3.8	99.3	3.3	0.09	25%	55%
2019	91%	91%	19.6	3%	1.0	146.5	7.1	0.59	0%	33%
2020	94%	93%	7.3	19%	-0.1	133.0	38.4	0.44	58%	85%
	93%	91%	8.8	10%	-0.5	124.8	54.1	0.35	52%	69%

Deep Dive

	Route Running					Total Points				Total Points Rtg	
Year	Routes Run	Y/RR	Deep Pct	Unique Routes	Slot%	Slot	Wide	Rec Total	Total	Per Route	Per Play
2018	122	2.1	27%	10	44%	0	3	2	23	72	93
2019	53	3.7	20%	2	69%	0	0	1	12	67	97
2020	528	1.9	17%	17	70%	25	-1	26	34	96	95
	703	2.0	19%	20	63%	24	2	29	69	-	-

D'Wayne Eskridge

Report by Nathan Cooper

School	Height	Weight	Year	Jersey #	Hometown
Western Michigan	5091 V	188 V	5SR	1	Bluffton, IN

One Liner
Eskridge is a dynamic playmaker whose release, play speed, and run-after-catch ability make him a home run threat each time he touches the ball, however, he needs to eliminate the easy drops, get stronger, and learn an NFL route tree to be a consistent contributor at the next level.

Overall
D'Wayne Eskridge primarily plays the X receiver in Western Michigan's RPO spread offense and occasionally works into the slot as well. In 2019, he spent time as both a receiver and cornerback, before switching back to receiver for 2020. He played in 45 games, starting 27 at WR and 4 at CB. He missed 9 games in 2019 due to a broken right clavicle. He'll turn 24 years old not long before the NFL Draft. He's got a small frame, but has quick-twitch athleticism that is apparent on offense, defense, and special teams. He plays fast with good toughness and competitiveness.

Pass Game
Eskridge has the speed and quickness to win off the line. He faced a good amount of press coverage and shows refined release skills to avoid the jam and win against press. He also uses his hands well to swipe away the defender's hands to stay clean into his route. His route tree is mainly limited to curls, slants, and vertical routes. He takes too many steps getting out of the top of his route on curls and comebacks, but shows fluid and smooth route running ability elsewhere. He's also shows savvy as a route runner by stemming his routes and staying away from contact mid-route. Eskridge mainly creates separation using his speed and quickness at the top of routes, though he does show the ability to use his off hand to create late separation. He battles with physical defenders, but likely won't win many routes with power. He shows the ability to pluck the ball out of the air when it comes his way. Though he doesn't have a huge catch radius due to his size, he can still go and get it when it's outside his frame. He shows good body control and tracks the ball well, but struggles to consistently come down with contested opportunities. His best traits come after the ball is in his hands and is a threat to score every time he touches it. He has the speed and elusiveness to make defenders miss and create extra yardage. He consistently takes 10-yard slants the distance. His burst and 2nd gear breaks the angles of defenders and allows him to gain YAC in chunks.

Run Game
In the run game, Eskridge can be used as a jet sweep and end around ballcarrier, and shows he can gain large chunks of yardage on those plays. As a blocker, he's mostly willing and really competes, but lacks the overall strength to stay latched onto defenders for the entirety of plays.

Last Word
Eskridge projects as a No. 3 receiver at the next level who profiles best as a slot receiver, and could slide outside in some formations, though long corners could hinder him. On 3rd downs, he fits best in the slot where he can use his speed and quickness. He has the speed, elusiveness, and vision to be a dynamic kick returner at the next level. Also, he could fill in at jammer or gunner with the traits he showed as a corner.

Strengths
- Play speed
- Wins off the line
- Dynamic RAC & return ability

Weaknesses
- Will drop some easy passes
- Play strength
- Limited route tree

Critical Factors

Hands	Separation	Run After Catch
6	6	7

Positional Factors

Release	Route Running	Route Savvy	Play Speed
6	6	6	8
Contested Catch	Playmaker	Tracking	Body Control
5	7	6	6
Clutch Performance	Blocking		Toughness
6	4		6

Basic

				Receiving						
Year	Trgt	Rec	Comp%	Yds	Air Yds	YAC	TD	ADoT	Yds/Trgt	Drops
2016	19	17	89%	121	-38	159	1	-0.7	6.4	1
2017	67	31	46%	518	237	281	3	13.6	7.7	8
2018	72	37	51%	767	562	205	3	19.9	10.7	3
2019	4	3	75%	73	52	21	0	14.8	18.3	0
2020	53	34	64%	784	296	488	8	11.0	14.8	3
	215	122	57%	2263	1109	1154	15	13.8	10.5	15

Advanced

	Advanced Receiving						EPA		Positive %	
Year	On-Trgt Catch %	Catchable Catch %	YAC/ Rec	Trgt Share	TAE	Rec Rating	Total	Per Trgt	vs. Man	vs. Zone
2016	-	94%	9.4	5%	-	110.7	4.4	0.23	0%	67%
2017	-	74%	9.6	23%	-	75.3	1.5	0.02	21%	41%
2018	80%	77%	5.5	18%	12.3	91.6	15.7	0.22	33%	55%
2019	75%	75%	7.0	1%	49.6	116.7	4.3	1.07	50%	100%
2020	87%	85%	14.4	35%	-1.9	147.2	38.5	0.73	47%	54%
	83%	80%	9.6	13%	6.7	108.7	64.3	0.30	33%	53%

Deep Dive

	Route Running					Total Points				Total Points Rtg	
Year	Routes Run	Y/RR	Deep Pct	Unique Routes	Slot%	Slot	Wide	Rec Total	Total	Per Route	Per Play
2018	257	3.0	43%	8	1%	0	18	18	19	95	88
2019	8	9.1	25%	0	13%	2	1	2	7	99	81
2020	334	2.3	19%	13	30%	4	19	23	24	99	99
	599	2.7	28%	15	12%	6	38	43	50	-	-

Elijah Moore

Report by Alec Mallon

School	Height	Weight	Year	Jersey #	Hometown
Ole Miss	5085 E	185 E	3JR	8	Fort Lauderdale, FL

One Liner
Moore is undersized, but his speed, quickness, and reliable hands will make him a difference maker on all four downs.

Overall
Elijah Moore is a wide receiver in Ole Miss's RPO-heavy spread offense, primarily operating out of the slot. He played in 32 games in his 3 years in Oxford, while starting the final 24. While undersized, he has some stockiness to his lower half. He's a tremendous athlete, with the lateral agility and straight-line speed to win at all levels of the field. He's a four-quarter competitor, but he will naturally take some plays off, given his high volume of production.

Pass Game
Moore's athletic ability can create mismatches at the next level. He was usually given free releases out of the slot, but when faced with true press coverage he showed he was able to get rerouted. His distinguished speed is always a threat to take the top off and must be respected by secondaries. He shows the body control to throttle back and accelerate through stems on standard routes well, but especially on double moves. However, he's at his best in the middle of the field, where he can use his quickness to create space and receive the ball in yards-after-catch situations. Moore is great at selling short routes and then breaking upfield, or leveraging his deep threat to sit underneath. He has soft and natural hands to pluck away from his body and hauls in most targets within his radius. He tracks the ball in the air well to adjust his routes and position himself to make a play on the ball. He isn't afraid of contact at the catch point and knows how to high-point and protect, but his height limits his ability to truly play above the rim. In the open field, Moore is difficult to bring down. He uses his elite change-of-direction skills to shake oncoming defenders and then pull away, but he can be corralled when contacted. He's more of a playmaker before the catch than after.

Run Game
Moore's size affects his ability as a blocker. When he isn't running routes on the back side of RPOs, he can be overpowered by linebackers and bigger corners. He's willing to compete, but lacks the strength to make a difference. However, he did often receive carries to get him the ball in space, even as a true running back. He follows his blocks and hits holes hard, but his traits are best served on the perimeter.

Last Word
Moore projects as a high-end third receiver at the NFL level. He's ideally suited to work out of the slot, where he has more space through which to work and can stay clean from lengthy press corners. His ridiculous level of production made him a First-Team All-American, but he did not need to be forced the ball to produce. Moore has significant experience returning both kickoffs and punts in college and should certainly be given a chance to do so in the NFL. His speed and elusiveness make him difficult to keep up with in open spaces.

Strengths
- Steady hands
- Elusiveness
- Home run speed

Weaknesses
- Run blocking
- Release vs press

Critical Factors

Hands	Separation	Run After Catch
7	6	6

Positional Factors

Release	Route Running	Route Savvy	Play Speed
5	7	6	7
Contested Catch	Playmaker	Tracking	Body Control
6	6	6	6
Clutch Performance	Blocking		Toughness
6	4		5

Basic

				Receiving						
Year	Trgt	Rec	Comp%	Yds	Air Yds	YAC	TD	ADoT	Yds/Trgt	Drops
2018	50	36	72%	398	195	203	2	8.5	8.0	2
2019	119	67	56%	850	520	330	6	10.7	7.1	10
2020	101	86	85%	1193	680	513	8	10.1	11.8	1
	270	189	70%	2441	1395	1046	16	10.0	9.0	13

Advanced

	Advanced Receiving						EPA		Positive %	
Year	On-Trgt Catch %	Catchable Catch %	YAC/ Rec	Trgt Share	TAE	Rec Rating	Total	Per Trgt	vs. Man	vs. Zone
2018	90%	90%	5.6	12%	-8.5	91.9	5.2	0.10	35%	56%
2019	88%	87%	4.9	37%	12.1	88.6	-1.9	-0.02	44%	41%
2020	99%	98%	6.1	31%	6.9	125.8	68.1	0.67	78%	75%
	93%	92%	5.6	25%	5.4	105.5	71.3	0.26	50%	58%

Deep Dive

	Route Running					Total Points				Total Points Rtg	
Year	Routes Run	Y/RR	Deep Pct	Unique Routes	Slot%	Slot	Wide	Rec Total	Total	Per Route	Per Play
2018	207	1.9	23%	13	94%	7	0	7	8	79	81
2019	404	2.1	25%	16	94%	24	1	23	27	94	92
2020	578	2.1	15%	17	78%	36	4	43	44	99	99
	1189	2.1	20%	23	88%	67	5	73	79	-	-

Rondale Moore

Report by Jeff Dean

School	Height	Weight	Year	Jersey #	Hometown
Purdue	5090 E	180 E	3SO	4	New Albany, IN

One Liner
Moore is a true playmaker who has the speed and separation ability to become a dangerous receiver, but his size and overall skill set likely limit him to the slot.

Overall
Rondale Moore's primary position is slot receiver in Purdue's RPO-heavy offense. He played in 20 career games with 17 starts. He missed 8 games during the 2019 season with a hamstring injury and 3 more games in 2020 with an undisclosed lower body injury. Moore is a very good athlete who has good top-end speed and very good acceleration. He is undersized, but has a solid frame that should help ease some concerns. He has extremely quick feet and can change directions on a dime. He was a marvel in 2018 before injuries took over, but he has fought back and always seemed to come up big when his team needs a play.

Pass Game
Moore excels as a slot receiver due to his burst and ability to set up his routes. He has a good release but can be prone to too many false steps as he tries to create immediate separation. He uses hard plants and quick jabs to get defenders off-balance before he takes off. He has clean breaks on his routes and uses his entire body to sell fakes and create very good separation. His double-moves are devastating and he uses his speed control to make defenders look foolish. Moore's route savvy is better against man coverage than zone as he is only sufficient at finding open holes and doesn't look to help out his quarterback if his initial route is smothered. His effort can wane on plays where he doesn't expect to get the ball. His size causes issues outside the numbers as he can struggle with contested catches or clearing from longer cornerbacks down the sideline. He has room to improve at the catch point as he has too many drops and body catches instead of plucking the ball from the air. Before the catch and after the catch is where he really shines. Once he has the ball in his hands, he is electric and can turn any short gain into a touchdown. He is elusive in the open-field and is a tough handle one-on-one.

Run Game
Moore is willing to get in the way of a defender and blocks with some enthusiasm, but his size limits his ability as a blocker. He sets up his blocks well, but can be a little hesitant to take on bigger defenders. As a runner, Moore is always a threat and must be accounted for. He was given many chances to get the ball quickly as either a runner or on screens and jet sweeps because of his ball-carrying prowess and often rewarded his team for the opportunity.

Last Word
Moore projects as a top-end third receiver who can work in any scheme. His size and lack of ability outside limit him to a slot role, but he is an explosive playmaker that should see the field often. He should become a fixture on third and fourth downs with his reliable separation quickness and open-field ball skills.

Strengths

- Footwork to set up routes
- Explosive burst
- Open-field ability

Weaknesses

- Ability outside the numbers
- Size
- Consistent hands

Critical Factors

Hands	Separation	Run After Catch
5	7	7

Positional Factors

Release	Route Running	Route Savvy	Play Speed
6	7	6	7
Contested Catch	Playmaker	Tracking	Body Control
5	7	5	6
Clutch Performance	Blocking		Toughness
6	5		5

Basic

Year	Trgt	Rec	Comp%	Yds	Air Yds	YAC	TD	ADoT	Yds/Trgt	Drops
2018	159	114	72%	1257	351	906	12	5.2	7.9	9
2019	42	29	69%	387	179	208	2	7.9	9.2	4
2020	44	35	80%	270	30	240	0	2.6	6.1	1
	245	178	73%	1914	560	1354	14	5.2	7.8	14

Advanced

Year	On-Trgt Catch %	Catchable Catch %	YAC/ Rec	Trgt Share	TAE	Rec Rating	EPA Total	Per Trgt	vs. Man	vs. Zone
2018	92%	92%	7.9	32%	1.4	109.4	28.6	0.18	58%	43%
2019	90%	90%	7.2	8%	5.8	104.0	13.3	0.32	60%	45%
2020	97%	97%	7.1	17%	13.2	82.8	0.8	0.02	50%	41%
	93%	93%	7.7	20%	4.1	104.0	42.7	0.17	58%	43%

Deep Dive

Year	Routes Run	Y/RR	Deep Pct	Unique Routes	Slot%	Slot	Wide	Rec Total	Total	Per Route	Per Play
2018	475	2.6	26%	17	85%	30	1	29	37	95	91
2019	133	2.9	37%	10	73%	4	6	9	8	95	93
2020	145	1.9	19%	9	81%	4	1	4	6	85	85
	753	2.5	27%	20	82%	37	8	42	51	-	-

Amon-Ra St. Brown

Report by Noah Chang & Jake Johnson

School	Height	Weight	Year	Jersey #	Hometown
USC	6006 E	195 E	3JR	8	Anaheim Hills, CA

One Liner
St. Brown lacks explosive athleticism, but he's a well-rounded receiver who can create separation with intelligent route savvy, ball tracking, and reliable hands.

Overall
Amon-Ra St. Brown is a wide receiver in USC's Air Raid offense, where he split time between slot and outside alignments in its three- and four-wide sets. He has started 23 of his 31 career games played. He has standard size and a lean, muscular frame with smooth athleticism and body control to maintain his speed through cuts. He left the final game of his career with an AC sprain but has otherwise fought through injury with a fierce competitiveness and desire to never leave the field.

Pass Game
St. Brown lacks explosive traits to play high above the rim or pull away from defenders with bursts of acceleration but he's a steady, reliable target at all levels of the field. He's shown he's struggled to cleanly release against press or physical flat zone corners and avoid getting rerouted, but usually comes off and gets to top speed quickly. He's a sound route runner who utilizes quick jab steps and sudden, subtle body fakes to get defenders off-balance and create separation. He isn't an elite, quick-footed athlete, but he has enough twitch and route intelligence to get open. He mostly ran curls and outs through his career, but had a varied route tree beyond that, including shallow crossers, double moves and fades, which he excelled on. St. Brown has very reliable hands that are best proven within his ability to track deep balls and adjust with the ball in the air. He's very comfortable catching over his shoulder, in contested situations, along the sideline, and high-pointing. After the catch, he turns into a physical runner and fights for extra yards, but he won't run over or around most defenders. He isn't considered a burner or an agile playmaking threat, but he has a well-rounded skillset that allows him to move the chains underneath, on intermediate crossers, and over the top.

Run Game
St. Brown is a willing, yet inconsistent blocker. He has the toughness and effort level to work hard on run plays, but he will counter physical reps and good seals with some poor angles and timing that lead to whiffs. He is also an effective threat on jet motion to take occasional handoffs and find yardage.

Last Word
St. Brown projects as a well-balanced No. 3 option in the NFL, who can operate in the slot or as a Z receiver. His three-level route running ability is scheme-diverse, but he best profiles as a motionable third-down option with his savvy footwork and strong hands. He has experience as a kick and punt returner and would be a safe but less dynamic option, but he also has the speed and toughness to be a core special teams member on coverage units.

Strengths	Weaknesses
• Reliable hands	• Explosive traits
• Deep ball tracking	• Releases against press
• Detailed footwork	• Blocking inconsistencies

Critical Factors

Hands	Separation	Run After Catch
7	6	5

Positional Factors

Release	Route Running	Route Savvy	Play Speed
5	6	6	5
Contested Catch	Playmaker	Tracking	Body Control
6	5	7	6
Clutch Performance		Blocking	Toughness
6		5	6

Basic

				Receiving						
Year	Trgt	Rec	Comp%	Yds	Air Yds	YAC	TD	ADoT	Yds/Trgt	Drops
2018	90	60	67%	750	527	223	3	11.1	8.3	3
2019	106	77	73%	1042	618	424	6	8.9	9.8	5
2020	58	41	71%	478	315	163	7	10.4	8.2	2
	254	178	70%	2270	1460	810	16	10.0	8.9	10

Advanced

	Advanced Receiving						EPA		Positive %	
Year	On-Trgt Catch %	Catchable Catch %	YAC/ Rec	Trgt Share	TAE	Rec Rating	Total	Per Trgt	vs. Man	vs. Zone
2018	92%	89%	3.7	23%	8.9	75.7	1.8	0.02	45%	64%
2019	91%	91%	5.5	21%	-2.5	114.6	42.9	0.40	55%	62%
2020	89%	89%	4.0	23%	1.6	120.5	26.2	0.45	75%	56%
	91%	90%	4.6	22%	1.9	102.3	70.8	0.28	51%	60%

Deep Dive

	Route Running					Total Points				Total Points Rtg	
Year	Routes Run	Y/RR	Deep Pct	Unique Routes	Slot%	Slot	Wide	Rec Total	Total	Per Route	Per Play
2018	273	2.7	34%	16	54%	7	9	16	18	90	88
2019	517	2.0	20%	16	85%	22	3	26	33	88	84
2020	352	1.4	14%	11	31%	0	11	12	13	88	84
	1142	2.0	21%	19	64%	30	23	54	64	-	-

Amari Rodgers

Report by Ronan Potts

School	Height	Weight	Year	Jersey #	Hometown
Clemson	5094 V	211 V	4SR	3	Knoxville, TN

One Liner
Rodgers is a tough slot receiver who excels at making plays with the ball in his hands, but his size and inconsistent ability to create separation will likely limit his role at the next level.

Overall
Amari Rodgers is a wide receiver in Clemson's RPO-heavy offense primarily lining up in the slot with occasional snaps out wide. He started 37 of 55 career games for the Tigers. In 2016, he suffered a shoulder labrum injury and then in 2018 he tore his ACL. His father, Tee Martin, was a former NFL player and current Wide Receivers Coach for the Baltimore Ravens. Rodgers is built more like a running back than a wide receiver, short and stocky with good lower body strength. He's a solid athlete with good play speed and impressive burst.

Pass Game
Rodgers is at his best once he has the ball in his hands. He excels at getting yardage after the catch, and he plays with toughness and power that allows him to get extra yardage after contact as well. Due to Clemson's offense, Rodgers is often schemed open or moving horizontally at the snap on bubble screens and jet sweeps. When he's asked to run more traditional routes, he can get off the line with his quick feet, though jammed up against physical defenders in press coverage at times due to his size. This can also affect his ability to generate consistent separation when asked to run downfield routes. He often uses stutter steps before breaking into his routes to try to help him create separation. As the slot receiver in Clemson's RPO-based scheme, Rodgers' route tree will need to be developed at the next level, as he was mainly asked to run bubble screens, jet sweeps, curls, and outs. He needs to work on his footwork as well, as he tends to round out his breaks when running routes and will stumble at times when trying to turn upfield and create extra yardage. He somewhat makes up for his lack of crisp route running with his route savvy, as he is good at finding openings in zone and getting to spots where he knows his quarterback will be able to find him. Rodgers has soft hands and is good at tracking and adjusting to the ball in the air, making him a reliable target.

Run Game
In the run game, Rodgers is a willing blocker. He needs to work on sustaining his blocks, but has sufficient toughness and power behind his blocks for a receiver and can generally be relied on to handle his assignments.

Last Word
Rodgers projects as a quality No. 3 receiver at the next level fitting best for a role in the slot in a scheme that relies on the short passing game. Rodgers should be a reliable target out of the slot on 3rd downs, as he has good hands and a tendency to make big plays with the ball in his hands. He has shown the ability to serve as a reliable punt returner, although he is not a gamebreaker in this aspect. His play speed and toughness should allow him to contribute elsewhere on other units as well.

Strengths
- Run after catch
- Playmaking ability
- Hands

Weaknesses
- Inconsistent separation
- Underdeveloped route tree

Critical Factors

Hands	Separation	Run After Catch
6	5	7

Positional Factors

Release	Route Running	Route Savvy	Play Speed
6	5	6	6
Contested Catch	Playmaker	Tracking	Body Control
5	7	6	5
Clutch Performance	Blocking		Toughness
6	5		6

Basic

					Receiving					
Year	Trgt	Rec	Comp%	Yds	Air Yds	YAC	TD	ADoT	Yds/Trgt	Drops
2017	22	19	86%	123	45	78	0	2.7	5.6	2
2018	72	55	76%	575	165	410	4	5.9	8.0	4
2019	41	30	73%	426	88	338	4	5.7	10.4	0
2020	100	77	77%	1020	405	615	7	7.0	10.2	5
	235	181	77%	2144	703	1441	15	6.1	9.1	11

Advanced

	Advanced Receiving						EPA		Positive %	
Year	On-Trgt Catch %	Catchable Catch %	YAC/ Rec	Trgt Share	TAE	Rec Rating	Total	Per Trgt	vs. Man	vs. Zone
2017	-	90%	4.1	5%	37.7	90.0	1.2	0.06	50%	50%
2018	90%	89%	7.5	14%	-0.2	111.7	20.0	0.28	50%	54%
2019	97%	97%	11.3	8%	-7.6	128.7	10.9	0.27	40%	58%
2020	89%	89%	8.0	21%	1.4	123.8	35.0	0.35	62%	57%
	91%	90%	8.0	12%	-1.2	118.5	67.1	0.29	52%	56%

Deep Dive

	Route Running					Total Points				Total Points Rtg	
Year	Routes Run	Y/RR	Deep Pct	Unique Routes	Slot%	Slot	Wide	Rec Total	Total	Per Route	Per Play
2018	277	2.1	33%	10	15%	2	9	10	11	83	75
2019	284	1.5	27%	15	83%	6	0	6	12	74	70
2020	568	1.8	17%	19	83%	19	0	18	18	90	85
	1129	1.8	23%	24	60%	27	9	34	41	-	-

Terrace Marshall Jr. Final Grade: 6.4

Report by Nathan Cooper

School	Height	Weight	Year	Jersey #	Hometown
LSU	6031 E	200 E	3JR	6	Bossier City, LA

One Liner

Marshall was mainly schemed open and lacks some suddenness to his route running, but his size/speed combination, catch radius, and ability to snatch the ball out of the air should allow him to see the field and contribute as a No. 3 wide receiver.

Overall

Terrace Marshall Jr. is primarily a slot receiver who motions a lot in LSU's up-tempo, RPO offense, though he played more of the X and Z prior to 2020. He started 20 of 32 games for the Tigers. He suffered a fibula fracture in 2017 and missed 3 games in 2019 due to a foot fracture that required surgery. He has a big frame with good size for the position, but his hips are a little tight and he lacks some overall flexibility. He possesses good speed and plays with a high toughness level and competitiveness.

Pass Game

Marshall isn't incredibly explosive off the line, but has speed and power in his release. When pressed, he struggles to consistently avoid contact and will have a tough time getting into his route. As a route runner, he isn't very sudden and has a tough time creating for himself. Most of his receptions are due to his speed or being schemed open by way of picks, clearouts, or misdirection. He ran slant routes the most of any route and can separate with speed at the top of the route. He also ran a lot of verticals where he was able to use speed to outrun defenders over the top. Other common routes were outs, curls, and digs. His sticky hips are apparent when running routes like curls and outs. He lacks a little route savvy and seems to run to defenders and gets contacted too much mid-route. He has strong hands and has the ability to snatch the ball out of the air. He has a wide catch radius to make grabs outside of his frame, especially over his head and below his waist. His hands are strong enough to make the contested catches with defenders close by. After the catch, Marshall shows off his speed. He can make defenders miss occasionally, but has the speed to break angles and take short passes for long gains.

Run Game

As a blocker, Marshall competes. He's willing and shows enough strength at the POA to deliver a blow and drive defenders, a reason why he was sometimes used in the short slot or tight in the run game. He also moves his feet to be able to stay between man and ball. Additionally, there are times he brings a little nastiness and attitude to his blocking.

Last Word

Marshall projects as a No. 3 receiver who fits best as a big slot, but can also line up on the outside. On 3rd downs, and in general, he fits best inside where he can win with speed on crossers or take the top off the defense with verticals. Due to high play speed and toughness, he's someone that can be looked at to contribute on most special teams units.

Strengths

- Play speed
- Catch radius
- Snatch ability

Weaknesses

- Schemed open
- Lacks suddenness
- Contacted too much mid-route

Critical Factors

Hands	Separation	Run After Catch
7	5	6

Positional Factors

Release	Route Running	Route Savvy	Play Speed
5	5	5	6
Contested Catch	Playmaker	Tracking	Body Control
6	5	6	6
Clutch Performance		Blocking	Toughness
6		6	6

Basic

	Receiving									
Year	Trgt	Rec	Comp%	Yds	Air Yds	YAC	TD	ADoT	Yds/Trgt	Drops
2018	23	12	52%	192	119	73	0	11.0	8.3	1
2019	67	46	69%	671	503	168	13	14.2	10.0	2
2020	72	48	67%	731	425	306	10	8.9	10.2	5
	162	106	65%	1594	1047	547	23	11.4	9.8	8

Advanced

	Advanced Receiving						EPA		Positive %	
Year	On-Trgt Catch %	Catchable Catch %	YAC/ Rec	Trgt Share	TAE	Rec Rating	Total	Per Trgt	vs. Man	vs. Zone
2018	86%	80%	6.1	6%	-6.3	80.3	6.0	0.26	47%	50%
2019	84%	82%	3.7	12%	-4.4	140.6	39.2	0.58	69%	66%
2020	91%	91%	6.4	18%	5.8	133.7	10.0	0.14	64%	46%
	87%	86%	5.2	12%	-1.0	134.6	55.2	0.34	63%	55%

Deep Dive

	Route Running					Total Points				Total Points Rtg	
Year	Routes Run	Y/RR	Deep Pct	Unique Routes	Slot%	Slot	Wide	Rec Total	Total	Per Route	Per Play
2018	122	1.6	41%	8	18%	1	4	5	5	82	79
2019	414	1.6	44%	12	41%	8	5	17	20	81	82
2020	391	1.9	18%	14	72%	8	5	13	14	89	87
	927	1.7	33%	14	46%	16	14	35	39	-	-

Tutu Atwell

Report by Jarrett Rodgers

School	Height	Weight	Year	Jersey #	Hometown
Louisville	5091 E	165 E	3JR	1	Miami, FL

One Liner
Atwell is a dynamic slot receiver and return man whose electric speed and quickness is most limited by size, strength, and post-catch abilities.

Overall
Chatarius "Tutu" Atwell is a wide receiver in Louisville's spread pistol offensive scheme. He played in 34 games and started 18 of those in his 3-year career for the Cardinals. He came to Louisville after competing as a dual-threat quarterback in high school before converting to receiver and working primarily out of the slot. He is a quick, twitchy athlete with explosive speed in the open field, though he lacks ideal size and has a light frame. He plays with a near-constant motor and has been a willing competitor throughout his time in Louisville.

Pass Game
In the pass game, Atwell always plays with a strong release off the line of scrimmage. He has quick feet and can set up a press defender at the snap or use his powerful strides to quickly reach full speed. He seems to struggle to get off the line with physicality, but rarely finds himself in those situations due to superior quickness. A common fixture in jet and bubble motions, he traditionally lines up off the line of scrimmage. Atwell creates separation mostly with blazing speed and promising footwork. He is gifted at opening seams in the middle of the field, stemming routes away from defenders and finding gaps against zone coverage. Despite having game-changing speed, he has struggled against stronger man coverage defenders. He needs to uses his strength, though limited, and superior route running to separate from those types of defenders. He plays with a burst to the catch point and good tracking skills on deep balls, allowing him to be a playmaker on passing downs. Playing with good hands and having the control to finish tough catches are strong points, but Atwell rarely is able to create yardage after initial contact aside from using his speed to run away from defenders.

Run Game
In the run game, Atwell is a willing blocker, but undersized when matched up against most defenders. He doesn't exhibit much in the way of block strength and will be a liability if counted on. He is regularly used in pre-snap motions to supplement the run game and has proven that he has the patience and vision to read the blockers in front of him. While not a dynamic runner, he has the speed to play sideline to sideline and win on jet sweeps and end arounds.

Last Word
Atwell projects a No. 3 receiver at the next level where he'd be best suited working out of the slot using his explosive quickness and mid-field playmaking ability to an offense's advantage. He can contribute to the passing game on 3rd downs either through creative gadget plays or creating a mismatch downfield. An experienced returner on special teams, Atwell deserves a look in kick and punt return situations, though his size likely limits him from contributor much elsewhere.

Strengths

- Open-field speed & quickness
- Route-running awareness
- Tracking acumen

Weaknesses

- Jump-ball ability
- Evading defenders after the catch
- Undersized run blocker

Critical Factors

Hands	Separation	Run After Catch
6	5	5

Positional Factors

Release	Route Running	Route Savvy	Play Speed
6	6	6	7
Contested Catch	**Playmaker**	**Tracking**	**Body Control**
5	6	6	6
Clutch Performance	**Blocking**		**Toughness**
5	3		5

Basic

	Receiving									
Year	Trgt	Rec	Comp%	Yds	Air Yds	YAC	TD	ADoT	Yds/Trgt	Drops
2018	52	24	46%	406	293	113	2	15.5	7.8	5
2019	106	70	66%	1276	531	745	12	10.6	12.0	7
2020	71	46	65%	625	341	284	7	11.3	8.8	3
	229	140	61%	2307	1165	1142	21	11.9	10.1	15

Advanced

	Advanced Receiving						EPA		Positive %	
Year	On-Trgt Catch %	Catchable Catch %	YAC/ Rec	Trgt Share	TAE	Rec Rating	Total	Per Trgt	vs. Man	vs. Zone
2018	79%	79%	5.3	14%	-6.0	46.3	-8.6	-0.17	38%	41%
2019	88%	88%	10.6	37%	0.8	125.4	57.8	0.55	63%	48%
2020	98%	98%	6.2	24%	0.9	102.1	15.9	0.22	53%	44%
	89%	89%	8.3	24%	-1.8	100.1	65.1	0.28	54%	45%

Deep Dive

	Route Running					Total Points				Total Points Rtg	
Year	Routes Run	Y/RR	Deep Pct	Unique Routes	Slot%	Slot	Wide	Rec Total	Total	Per Route	Per Play
2018	330	1.2	37%	16	98%	8	0	8	8	73	72
2019	293	4.4	33%	15	83%	27	0	27	43	99	98
2020	380	1.6	26%	17	88%	17	1	18	19	96	95
	1003	2.3	32%	24	89%	52	1	53	70	-	-

Dyami Brown

Report by Nathan Cooper

School	Height	Weight	Year	Jersey #	Hometown
North Carolina	6006 E	185 E	3JR	2	Charlotte, NC

One Liner

Brown has the precise route running skill, speed to win off the line, and tracking ability down the field to make plays at the next level, though he needs to get stronger, improve his route savvy, and limit the concentration drops to become a more reliable target.

Overall

Dyami Brown is an outside wide receiver who primarily lines up to the left of the formation in North Carolina's up-tempo, RPO-heavy offense. He played in 34 games, starting 30 of them for the Tar Heels. He's a good athlete with some wiggle and possesses a solid, but somewhat slight frame. He competes in his route running, but shows just adequate toughness when the ball isn't coming his way.

Pass Game

Brown shows the foot quickness and speed to get clean releases off the line and get into his route. He also shows good hand use to help get by press coverage. He's a very good, precise route runner despite running four routes (curls, verticals, slants, and outs) nearly 80% of the time. He is able to drop his weight at the top of the route and break quickly. He lacks a little bit of route savvy as he seems to get contacted too much mid-route, whether it's simply knocking him off his plane or completely rerouting him. In terms of gaining separation, he does it with his precise route running and speed. However, he isn't able to consistently separate against more physical corners. When the ball comes his way, he shows good, strong hands the majority of the time. He'll drop some easy passes, but those seem to be concentration drops more than anything. He has a solid catch radius and is able to make receptions outside of his frame. Brown also shows the ability to track the ball down the field and adjust to make a play on it. He can make contested catches by way of going up over the top of defenders to make the catch. With the ball in his hands, he has enough speed to break angles and work through arm tackles.

Run Game

Brown shows a willingness to get in front of defenders in the run game. He won't always go out of his way to make the block unless he needs to and lacks strength to sustain at the POA, but when latched, he can run his feet and stay between man and ball.

Last Word

Brown projects as a No. 3 receiver at the next level who can play outside or inside. He has the speed and enough size to win with his route running on the outside and also has the quickness to win off the line and get into his route from the slot. On 3rd downs, he fits best on the outside where he can use his route running to win at the top of the route and keep drives alive. His skill set suggests he could contribute as a gunner or similar role on special teams, but likely won't be a core guy. Although he doesn't have college return experience, with his tracking ability, he likely could contribute in that aspect as well.

Strengths

- Precise route runner
- Speed off the line
- Downfield tracking

Weaknesses

- Contacted too often
- Drops some easy passes
- Lacks some strength

Critical Factors

Hands	Separation	Run After Catch
6	5	6

Positional Factors

Release	Route Running	Route Savvy	Play Speed
6	7	5	6
Contested Catch	Playmaker	Tracking	Body Control
6	6	6	6
Clutch Performance		Blocking	Toughness
5		5	5

Basic

				Receiving						
Year	Trgt	Rec	Comp%	Yds	Air Yds	YAC	TD	ADoT	Yds/Trgt	Drops
2018	35	17	49%	173	90	83	1	11.1	4.9	2
2019	86	51	59%	1034	732	302	12	16.8	12.0	10
2020	84	55	65%	1099	813	286	8	17.6	13.1	5
	205	123	60%	2306	1635	671	21	16.2	11.2	17

Advanced

	Advanced Receiving						EPA		Positive %	
Year	On-Trgt Catch %	Catchable Catch %	YAC/ Rec	Trgt Share	TAE	Rec Rating	Total	Per Trgt	vs. Man	vs. Zone
2018	89%	89%	6.5	9%	-1.6	60.8	-8.0	-0.23	14%	44%
2019	84%	84%	5.9	21%	-5.6	136.3	47.9	0.56	60%	55%
2020	80%	80%	5.2	24%	-0.3	125.6	48.5	0.58	52%	65%
	83%	83%	5.7	18%	-2.9	122.9	88.4	0.43	47%	58%

Deep Dive

	Route Running					Total Points				Total Points Rtg	
Year	Routes Run	Y/RR	Deep Pct	Unique Routes	Slot%	Slot	Wide	Rec Total	Total	Per Route	Per Play
2018	147	1.2	36%	6	11%	2	1	3	6	72	74
2019	520	2.0	46%	13	3%	2	13	15	17	80	77
2020	601	1.8	25%	9	5%	1	24	25	26	96	93
	1268	1.8	35%	13	5%	5	38	43	49	-	-

Jaelon Darden

Report by Nathan Cooper

School	Height	Weight	Year	Jersey #	Hometown
North Texas	5076 E	174 E	4SR	1	Houston, TX

One Liner
Darden is a gadget-type playmaker whose quickness and elusiveness allow him to thrive with the ball in his hands, though his size is a concern, and inconsistent contested-catch ability could limit how much he sees the field at the next level.

Overall
Jaelon Darden mainly lines up as a slot receiver in the RPO-based offense of North Texas, but will occasionally slide outside as well. A high school quarterback, Darden started 24 of 38 games at receiver for the Mean Green. He has a small frame, but possesses excellent quick-twitch athleticism and suddenness. He shows adequate toughness overall, but competes in his play and will get visibly upset when he's open and the ball doesn't come his way.

Pass Game
Darden possesses excellent quickness and elusiveness and that allows him to cleanly release off the line on most plays. His quick feet and hand use allow him to beat press, though bigger defenders will give him a tough time every once in a while. As a route runner, he's run a good variety of routes having played both outside and in the slot, though the main routes he runs are curls, screens, outs, and slants. He's a very savvy route runner, knowing how to stem his routes and stay away from defenders, but some of his routes lack crispness. His separation comes in the form of speed and quickness at the top of routes or to run away from defenders. When running deep, he shows good off hand ability to gain some extra separation. When defenders get hands on, he has a tough time getting into his route, so his success comes from not being contacted. He has good hands overall, but has some concentration drops on occasion. In addition, his size limits his ability to come down with contested catches. He tracks the ball well down the field and shows late hands. After the catch is where Darden is at his best. He has excellent playmaking ability and is very good with the ball in his hands. He has the quickness, elusiveness, and athleticism to stop on a dime to make defenders miss and then immediately accelerate and burst to get back up to speed. There are times where he doesn't step upfield after the catch and dances too much after the catch, but with his ability, he rarely loses out on extra yardage. When the ball gets into his hands, he's a threat to take it the distance every time.

Run Game
Darden shows willingness as a blocker some of the time, but doesn't have the size or strength to sustain many blocks. He wasn't used much as a rusher, though his ability suggests he'd contribute on end arounds and jet sweeps.

Last Word
Darden projects as a No. 3 receiver at the NFL level who mainly operates out of the slot, but could also run some routes out wide if needed. On 3rd downs, he fits best in the slot where he can run away from defenders and win with the ball in his hands. He does have kick and punt return ability, and while he'd be a solid asset in that facet, that'd likely be the only way he could contribute on special teams.

Strengths

- Playmaking ability
- Savvy route runner
- Quick & elusive

Weaknesses

- Can struggle vs. larger defenders
- Size limits contested-catch ability
- Dances after the catch

Critical Factors

Hands	Separation	Run After Catch
6	6	7

Positional Factors

Release	Route Running	Route Savvy	Play Speed
6	5	7	7
Contested Catch	Playmaker	Tracking	Body Control
4	8	6	6
Clutch Performance	Blocking		Toughness
6	3		5

Basic

				Receiving						
Year	Trgt	Rec	Comp%	Yds	Air Yds	YAC	TD	ADoT	Yds/Trgt	Drops
2017	49	32	65%	281	104	177	3	6.8	5.7	4
2018	63	48	76%	575	245	330	4	6.2	9.1	2
2019	112	76	68%	736	253	483	12	6.3	6.6	8
2020	113	74	65%	1190	614	576	19	11.8	10.5	7
	337	230	68%	2782	1216	1566	38	8.2	8.3	21

Advanced

	Advanced Receiving						EPA		Positive %	
Year	On-Trgt Catch %	Catchable Catch %	YAC/ Rec	Trgt Share	TAE	Rec Rating	Total	Per Trgt	vs. Man	vs. Zone
2017	-	80%	5.5	10%	-	92.3	-2.0	-0.04	50%	33%
2018	96%	96%	6.9	13%	1.6	118.2	21.0	0.33	68%	40%
2019	91%	91%	6.4	26%	6.6	110.6	5.2	0.05	48%	50%
2020	90%	89%	7.8	35%	11.5	129.1	50.3	0.45	59%	47%
	92%	90%	6.8	19%	6.8	121.0	74.5	0.22	55%	45%

Deep Dive

	Route Running					Total Points				Total Points Rtg	
Year	Routes Run	Y/RR	Deep Pct	Unique Routes	Slot%	Slot	Wide	Rec Total	Total	Per Route	Per Play
2018	268	2.1	23%	15	94%	14	0	13	18	88	87
2019	377	2.0	25%	14	86%	5	-1	7	4	71	64
2020	520	2.3	22%	14	76%	26	6	32	31	99	99
	1165	2.1	23%	20	84%	44	5	52	53	-	-

Marquez Stevenson

Report by Jeff Dean

School	Height	Weight	Year	Jersey #	Hometown
Houston	5100 V	182 V	5SR	5	Shreveport, LA

One Liner
Stevenson has the speed, acceleration, and open-field ability to become a solid No. 3 receiver at the NFL level if he can eliminate his mental lapses, get stronger, and show more consistent effort.

Overall
Marquez Stevenson primarily plays slot receiver in Houston's up-tempo, RPO-heavy offense. He started 29 of 32 games for the Cougars. He missed the first 7 games in 2016 with a broken collarbone then played the next game and a half before another injury caused him to miss the final 4 games. In 2017, he tore his left ACL in spring practice forcing him to miss the entire season and missed 4 games during 2020 with an ankle injury. He's a very good athlete with the acceleration and top-end speed to leave defenders in the dust. His competitive fire comes into question as he will take plays off, especially if he knows the ball isn't coming to him. That being said, he has come back very strong from numerous injuries to reclaim the starting job.

Pass Game
Stevenson's release gets a step on the defender right from the start. He has a fairly undeveloped route tree, but has good footwork and runs the more technical routes with clean breaks. His quick feet and acceleration create separation at the top of his route. He has limited experience dealing with press and lacks the physicality to handle bigger corners on the outside, but his release and footwork allow him to beat most press slot defenders. He can lose focus and take his eye off too many simple throws, though he catches the ball with his hands and extends out from his frame well. He shows the ability to make difficult catches, but needs to improve the consistency of his hands.

His route savvy is sufficient, but he will give up on a play when the play starts to break down. He shows better route savvy on double-moves and feels defenders, using good body control and tracking ability to high point the ball. Stevenson finds the ball well, but struggles with outmuscling defenders and consistently coming down with 50/50 balls. After the catch, his speed breaks pursuit angles and his elusiveness in the open-field makes him a threat to take it to the house every time he touches the ball. He lacks the physicality to break many tackles if a defender gets their arms on him, but that's hard to do.

Run Game
Stevenson shows sufficient effort when blocking, but will give up on a play if beaten early. He doesn't actively seek out blocks and lacks the muscle to drive defenders away, but will at least get between them and the ball. However, he's a threat as a runner, whether by receiving a handoff, or on a screen, to break off huge gains on the ground.

Last Word
Stevenson projects as a No. 3 wide receiver who should become a team's primary slot receiver by his 2nd season. He will see the field on 3rd downs to take advantage of his speed to win over the top or across the field. He has experience returning kicks and has the speed and open-field vision to excel in that role at the next level.

Strengths

- Play speed
- Open-field ability
- Body control

Weaknesses

- Mental lapses
- Physicality
- Consistent effort

Critical Factors

Hands	Separation	Run After Catch
5	6	7

Positional Factors

Release	Route Running	Route Savvy	Play Speed
6	6	5	7
Contested Catch	Playmaker	Tracking	Body Control
5	6	6	6
Clutch Performance	Blocking		Toughness
6	5		5

Basic

	Receiving									
Year	Trgt	Rec	Comp%	Yds	Air Yds	YAC	TD	ADoT	Yds/Trgt	Drops
2016	0	0	-	34	0	0	0	-	-	0
2018	116	75	65%	1019	458	561	9	9.2	8.8	11
2019	91	52	57%	907	351	556	9	11.2	10.0	5
2020	28	20	71%	307	172	135	4	10.8	11.0	0
	235	147	63%	2267	981	1286	22	10.2	9.6	16

Advanced

	Advanced Receiving						EPA		Positive %	
Year	On-Trgt Catch %	Catchable Catch %	YAC/ Rec	Trgt Share	TAE	Rec Rating	Total	Per Trgt	vs. Man	vs. Zone
2018	83%	83%	7.5	25%	4.5	114.8	43.1	0.37	36%	56%
2019	87%	85%	10.7	30%	1.7	105.9	15.8	0.17	30%	54%
2020	95%	95%	6.8	10%	1.7	146.9	13.6	0.49	50%	46%
	86%	85%	8.5	22%	2.8	116.1	72.5	0.31	36%	54%

Deep Dive

	Route Running					Total Points				Total Points Rtg	
Year	Routes Run	Y/RR	Deep Pct	Unique Routes	Slot%	Slot	Wide	Rec Total	Total	Per Route	Per Play
2018	377	2.7	28%	15	78%	21	-3	17	21	88	85
2019	307	3.0	35%	15	84%	17	10	27	37	99	97
2020	184	1.7	22%	11	80%	6	1	6	9	88	91
	868	2.6	29%	19	81%	43	7	50	67	-	-

Austin Watkins Jr.

Report by Carter Hayden & Griffin Sullivan

School	Height	Weight	Year	Jersey #	Hometown
UAB	6014 V	207 V	5SR	6	Fort Myers, FL

One Liner
Watkins has the speed, hands, and RAC ability to be a very reliable and consistent receiver at the next level, though he'll need to improve his savviness as a route runner and learn a NFL route tree to hit his full potential.

Overall
Austin Watkins Jr. is a wide receiver for UAB where he played mostly X and Z while occasionally sliding into the slot for their shotgun, run-first offense. He started his career at Dodge City CC before transferring to UAB and starting 19 of 25 games played the past 3 seasons. He's cousins with current Kansas City Chiefs wide receiver Sammy Watkins. He's a big-body receiver who is a good athlete and competes by running every route with a purpose.

Pass Game
Watkins shows good burst off the line and uses quick feet and hands to avoid contact against press coverage. He runs crisp and clean routes, however, UAB mainly used him as a vertical route runner with a lot of curls and digs. His route running is a little raw with having run a minimal route tree, but the routes he does run are run with precision. Watkins can create separation with both strength and very good speed, and also shows the ability to use his off hand to help him create separation from defenders at the top of routes. He has good hands and is able to pluck the ball out of the air with ease while showing a fairly large catch radius. He doesn't always show late hands and puts them up a little early which allows the defender to get his up in time to make a play on the ball. However, he tracks and adjusts to the football in the air to make consistent grabs down the field. There are times where he fails to tuck the ball away quickly after making the grab, as defenders often knock the ball out of his hands when in traffic. After the catch, Watkins rarely goes down on first contact. He isn't the most elusive player and isn't going to make a lot of athletes miss, but he does a good job of getting north and south on his runs and fighting for extra yards.

Run Game
In the run game, Watkins shows the willingness to block downfield when needed. He has good technique and strength on his blocks to create running lanes and drive defenders off the ball, though he doesn't always do it with consistency.

Last Word
Watkins projects to be a No. 3 receiver at the next level where he can thrive out of the slot, but also line up outside. His speed, route running, and hands make him a solid target in any NFL offense. On 3rd down, his speed and strong hands make him a very reliable target for quarterbacks looking to move the chains. He also has the speed, blocking ability, and toughness to be a solid contributor on most special teams units.

Strengths	Weaknesses
• Strong hands	• Route savvy
• Speed & quickness	• Consistent contested-catch ability
• Precise route runner	• Limited route tree

Critical Factors

Hands	Separation	Run After Catch
6	6	5

Positional Factors

Release	Route Running	Route Savvy	Play Speed
6	6	5	7
Contested Catch	Playmaker	Tracking	Body Control
5	6	6	6
Clutch Performance		Blocking	Toughness
6		5	6

Basic

				Receiving						
Year	Trgt	Rec	Comp%	Yds	Air Yds	YAC	TD	ADoT	Yds/Trgt	Drops
2018	8	7	88%	82	67	15	0	10.9	10.3	0
2019	95	57	60%	1092	793	299	6	19.0	11.5	2
2020	55	34	62%	468	373	95	3	15.7	8.5	0
	158	98	62%	1642	1233	409	9	17.5	10.4	2

Advanced

	Advanced Receiving						EPA		Positive %	
Year	On-Trgt Catch %	Catchable Catch %	YAC/ Rec	Trgt Share	TAE	Rec Rating	Total	Per Trgt	vs. Man	vs. Zone
2018	100%	100%	2.1	2%	-9.8	109.4	10.0	1.25	0%	86%
2019	93%	91%	5.2	29%	3.4	99.1	28.4	0.30	45%	53%
2020	89%	89%	3.1	23%	2.7	92.1	21.1	0.38	40%	56%
	92%	91%	4.3	18%	2.2	97.6	59.6	0.38	42%	56%

Deep Dive

	Route Running					Total Points				Total Points Rtg	
Year	Routes Run	Y/RR	Deep Pct	Unique Routes	Slot%	Slot	Wide	Rec Total	Total	Per Route	Per Play
2018	73	1.1	35%	2	5%	0	3	4	4	91	85
2019	334	3.3	42%	11	6%	0	24	24	26	94	91
2020	357	1.3	19%	10	13%	3	15	18	19	99	98
	764	2.1	29%	12	8%	3	42	46	49	-	-

Nico Collins

Report by Theo Fornaciari & DJ Marquardt

School	Height	Weight	Year	Jersey #	Hometown
Michigan	6042 V	215 V	4SR	1	Birmingham, AL

One Liner

Collins is a big-bodied deep threat with raw athleticism and very good playmaking ability to tip 50/50 balls in his favor, who could become a high-end starter with refined technique as a route runner.

Strengths: Athleticism at his size; Deep ball tracking; Contested-catch playmaker
Weaknesses: Route separation; Staying alive off-script; Route tree versatility

Nico Collins played the X receiver in Michigan's spread RPO offense. He played in 29 games with 22 starts for the Wolverines before opting out of the 2020 season. He underwent foot surgery in 2019. Collins is a superb athlete with great height and overall size for a big receiver. He has good physical toughness and is a very good competitor with the ball in the ball, but a slightly inconsistent motor.

Collins has a good stutter-step release to win leverage then utilize his speed to stack defenders on vertical routes. He could improve his hand use at the LOS to win versus physical corners. He has a slightly-limited route tree as primarily a vertical deep threat. He is a sufficient route runner despite underutilizing his size during the stem phase. He has subtle footwork to quickly get in and out of breaks and the athleticism to sink his hips and move fluidly, but he isn't a sharp route runner at this stage. He has sufficient route savvy and struggles to make himself available on off-script plays. Collins has had some easy drops, but overall shows strong hands and is a

very good playmaker at the catch point. He's a natural ball tracker on deep throws and has the explosiveness and timing to extend and high point over most secondary defenders. He is very good on contested passes and consistently delivered on 50/50 balls and in the red zone. After the catch he is a powerful finisher but won't make good athletes miss in space.

In the run game, Collins is a good, willing blocker who uses his big body and athleticism to stalk and drive. He has the requisite toughness to stick his nose in and sustain or crack down.

Collins projects as an outside No. 3 receiver in a vertical passing scheme. He will be a good red zone target and downfield threat in a Z receiver role where his sufficient releases and route running won't hinder him as much. He doesn't have much fourth down experience but his size and blocking strength could be an asset if he buys in.

Receiving

Year	Trgt	Rec	Comp%	Yds	Air Yds	YAC	TD	ADoT	Yds/Trgt	Drops
2017	7	3	43%	27	18	9	0	8.4	3.9	0
2018	56	38	68%	632	496	136	6	15.5	11.3	1
2019	67	37	55%	729	501	228	7	13.8	10.9	6
	130	78	60%	1388	1015	373	13	14.3	10.7	7

Advanced Receiving

Year	On-Trgt Catch %	Catchable Catch %	YAC/ Rec	Trgt Share	TAE	Rec Rating	EPA Total	Per Trgt	vs. Man	vs. Zone
2017	-	75%	3.0	2%	-	53.9	-2.7	-0.39	50%	0%
2018	85%	85%	3.6	17%	-6.1	126.5	21.7	0.39	65%	57%
2019	78%	77%	6.2	17%	-2.9	115.8	29.2	0.44	50%	60%
	82%	80%	4.8	12%	-4.3	117.1	48.2	0.37	56%	56%

Positive % columns: vs. Man, vs. Zone

Route Running / Total Points

Year	Routes Run	Y/RR	Deep Pct	Unique Routes	Slot%	Slot	Wide	Rec Total	Total	Per Route	Per Play
2018	281	2.2	41%	11	15%	2	7	10	11	81	79
2019	319	2.3	31%	10	14%	6	12	18	22	91	92
	600	2.3	36%	12	15%	8	20	28	33	-	-

Critical Factors

Hands	6
Separation	5
Run After Catch	5

Positional Factors

Release	6
Route Running	5
Route Savvy	5
Play Speed	6
Contested Catch	7
Playmaker	7
Tracking	7
Body Control	6
Clutch Performance	6
Blocking	6
Toughness	6

Shi Smith

Report by Jeff Dean

School	Height	Weight	Year	Jersey #	Hometown
South Carolina	5100 V	186 V	4SR	13	Union, SC

One Liner
Smith uses his burst, separation at the top of the route, and RAC ability to find value as a receiver, but his lack of downfield ability and effort on 50/50 balls will limit his role.

Strengths: Burst; Plucks balls; Open-field ability
Weaknesses: Route tree; 50/50 ball aggression; Lack of downfield plays

Shi Smith is primarily a slot receiver in South Carolina's up-tempo, spread, RPO-offense. He started 35 of 43 career games. He missed 1 game in 2017 with an undisclosed injury, 1 game in 2018 with back spasms, 2 games in 2019 with a hamstring injury, and 1 in 2020 with a concussion. Smith is a good athlete who is slightly undersized, but has a chiseled, filled-out frame. He plays tough, but lacks some aggression without the ball.

Smith uses quick feet and burst at the top of his route to create separation. His route tree is limited to mostly short, quick breaks as he struggles to find holes on deeper routes or when the play breaks down. Despite his quick feet, he can have issues breaking free from press. Smith does a good job plucking passes away from his body. On contested catches, he puts himself in position to have a chance, but rarely in a position to win. He seems complacent being close to the ball and doesn't fight at the catch point. He shows strong hands to hang onto the ball through contact, but loses the majority of 50/50 balls.

After the catch, he shows a good burst and can hit top speed in minimal steps. Spin moves, cut backs, and hesitation moves are all in his bag of tricks and have been consistently effective. Smith doesn't make many plays down the field, but he can turn a short gain into a first down play with his RAC ability.

Smith is a sufficient blocker who shows good enthusiasm despite not having the biggest frame. He won't drive many defenders off of the line, but knows his assignment. While rarely used as a runner, he looks comfortable with the ball in his hands and has the open field ability to make him a credible threat.

Smith projects as a No. 3 receiver who only has a role in the slot. His lack of size, aggression at the catch point, and struggles with physical defenders will keep him inside, but should be a safety valve on 3rd downs. He has experience returning kickoffs in college and should be in contention for that role at the next level.

Receiving

Year	Trgt	Rec	Comp%	Yds	Air Yds	YAC	TD	ADoT	Yds/Trgt	Drops
2017	44	29	66%	409	245	164	3	10.5	9.3	0
2018	65	45	69%	673	376	297	4	10.5	10.4	3
2019	78	43	55%	489	247	242	2	11.1	6.3	3
2020	84	57	68%	633	278	355	4	6.9	7.5	5
	271	174	64%	2204	1146	1058	13	9.5	8.1	11

Advanced Receiving

Year	On-Trgt Catch %	Catchable Catch %	YAC/ Rec	Trgt Share	TAE	Rec Rating	EPA Total	EPA Per Trgt	Positive % vs. Man	Positive % vs. Zone
2017	-	94%	5.7	11%	-10.1	109.0	16.4	0.37	48%	60%
2018	91%	89%	6.6	15%	-4.3	117.0	36.4	0.56	53%	59%
2019	96%	91%	5.6	17%	4.7	72.0	-15.4	-0.20	35%	44%
2020	93%	89%	6.4	29%	9.6	100.9	23.4	0.28	50%	59%
	93%	90%	6.1	17%	1.5	97.8	60.8	0.22	47%	54%

Route Running / Total Points

Year	Routes Run	Y/RR	Deep Pct	Unique Routes	Slot%	Slot	Wide	Rec Total	Total	Per Route	Per Play
2018	351	1.9	24%	14	88%	22	-1	20	22	91	89
2019	327	1.5	39%	14	78%	16	1	18	21	92	90
2020	448	1.4	16%	15	70%	12	2	18	17	98	94
	1126	1.6	25%	18	80%	50	1	56	60	-	-

Critical Factors

Hands	6
Separation	6
Run After Catch	6

Positional Factors

Release	6
Route Running	6
Route Savvy	5
Play Speed	6
Contested Catch	4
Playmaker	5
Tracking	6
Body Control	5
Clutch Performance	4
Blocking	5
Toughness	5

Seth Williams

Report by Dan Foehrenbach

School	Height	Weight	Year	Jersey #	Hometown
Auburn	6016 E	211 E	3JR	18	Cottondale, AL

One Liner

Williams is a contested-catch fiend who wins with body control and the ability to run routes effectively, though inconsistent playmaking ability and dependability limits him to a role-playing receiver.

Strengths: Body control; Route running; Ability to make catches in traffic
Weaknesses: Uncontested drops; Playmaking ability; Clutch performance

Seth Williams is a wide receiver who primarily lines up outside in Auburn's diverse RPO offense, with occasional snaps in the slot. He played in 36 career games with 27 starts. He was an all-state honoree in basketball and a state medalist in the long and high jump, so he's a great athlete, but lacks some foot quickness. He has a big, strong frame with prototypical size and drive for the position.

Williams is physical and works through jams well. He does a good job obtaining inside leverage and stacking on vertical routes. He may not be the most dynamic, crisp route runner, but he's efficient and usually puts himself in positions to make plays. He separates from defenders using strength, instincts and leaping ability. Williams is primarily a hands catcher and doesn't often use his body, but he had way too many easy drops throughout his career. However, he is strong in traffic and fearless over the middle. He has very good body control to high point jump balls and shows great awareness near the sidelines. He tracks deep balls well and helps his quarterback on inaccurate throws downfield. He has the desire after the catch but lacks true one-on-one tackle evasion skills. Williams was underwhelming in critical situations beyond the red zone and his hands aren't the most dependable on third downs.

In the run game, Williams was used as an effective blocker. He is not afraid of contact and is strong at the POA. He is willing to block, shows the ability to drive defenders back, and has the functional strength to contribute in the run game.

Williams projects as a role-playing receiver with some inside-out flexibility depending on his offense. He profiles best as a big-bodied receiver who can thrive in the red zone and on vertical routes, 50/50 balls, and back-shoulders. He frustratingly will make many difficult plays but struggle with the easy ones and needs to improve his consistency and reliability. While he does not have great speed, his strength will allow him to contribute on special teams.

					Receiving					
Year	Trgt	Rec	Comp%	Yds	Air Yds	YAC	TD	ADoT	Yds/Trgt	Drops
2018	46	26	57%	534	404	130	5	14.0	11.6	3
2019	110	58	53%	821	573	248	8	12.8	7.5	5
2020	101	47	47%	760	489	271	4	12.6	7.5	10
	257	131	51%	2115	1466	649	17	12.9	8.2	18

	Advanced Receiving						EPA		Positive %	
Year	On-Trgt Catch %	Catchable Catch %	YAC/ Rec	Trgt Share	TAE	Rec Rating	Total	Per Trgt	vs. Man	vs. Zone
2018	76%	74%	5.0	13%	4.3	133.8	26.3	0.57	43%	67%
2019	87%	86%	4.3	30%	15.0	93.8	15.6	0.14	41%	49%
2020	76%	76%	6.5	29%	11.1	77.2	10.7	0.11	32%	45%
	81%	79%	5.2	24%	10.9	94.4	52.6	0.20	38%	50%

	Route Running					Total Points			Total Points Rtg	
Year	Routes Run	Y/RR	Deep Pct	Unique Routes	Slot%	Slot	Wide	Rec Total	Total	Per Route	Per Play
2018	249	2.1	37%	10	58%	12	6	17	20	95	93
2019	322	2.5	47%	14	15%	5	21	26	28	99	95
2020	545	1.4	23%	14	27%	13	13	28	30	98	96
	1116	1.9	33%	17	32%	29	40	71	78	-	-

Critical Factors	
Hands	5
Separation	6
Run After Catch	5

Positional Factors	
Release	6
Route Running	6
Route Savvy	6
Play Speed	5
Contested Catch	6
Playmaker	5
Tracking	6
Body Control	7
Clutch Performance	5
Blocking	6
Toughness	6

Josh Palmer

Report by Evan Butler

School	Height	Weight	Year	Jersey #	Hometown
Tennessee	6012 V	210 V	4SR	5	Brampton, ON, CAN

One Liner

Palmer has the athleticism, body control, and ball skills to be a contributor, but his inconsistent route running with a limited route tree may see him as a more of a depth-level player.

Strengths: Body control; Ball skills; Toughness
Weaknesses: Route savvy; Limited route tree; Separation

Josh Palmer is an outside receiver in Tennessee's RPO-heavy offense. He started 36 of 47 games for the Vols. Palmer is a good athlete with a solid, thick frame. He shows good competitiveness and toughness in all areas.

Palmer shows body control and hands to high point passes and comes down with the ball. He's a good hands catcher and plucks the ball while rarely letting the ball get to his body. He lacks some key attributes with his route running. Palmer struggles with his release off the line, especially against physical defenders, and needs to mix up his releases by improving his hand usage. In short routes, he struggles to get constant separation with sloppy footwork. He shows no fluidity in his breaks as he takes too many short and choppy steps which telegraphs the move he is going to make. That said, he does show some wiggle in his route stems. It just lacks consistency. He does get behind defenders on deep routes with his speed and ability to use his body to create space. On deep balls, Palmer's body control

and athleticism shine. He can high point the ball and make contested catches over top of or through defenders. In an RPO-heavy offense, his route tree was limited to a large number of curls, verticals, and digs. After the catch, his size and toughness make him tough to bring down.

In the run game, Palmer shows his toughness and competitiveness with his willingness to block. He doesn't shy away from contact and likes to mix it up with DBs even after the whistle. He's strong at the point of attack and uses his feet to mirror his defenders.

Palmer projects as a No. 4 receiver at the next level. He fits best outside, but can play inside on occasion. His athleticism and ball skills will allow him to contribute and, with some improvements to his route running, can increase his impact. On 3rd down, he's a threat to take the top off of the defense or use speed to run away from man coverage. He has the speed and toughness to contribute on special teams.

					Receiving					
Year	Trgt	Rec	Comp%	Yds	Air Yds	YAC	TD	ADoT	Yds/Trgt	Drops
2017	31	9	29%	98	85	13	0	17.5	3.2	2
2018	45	23	51%	484	379	105	2	18.4	10.8	1
2019	58	34	59%	457	361	96	1	14.5	7.9	3
2020	61	33	54%	475	402	73	4	15.5	7.8	0
	195	99	51%	1514	1227	287	7	16.2	7.8	6

	Advanced Receiving						EPA		Positive %	
Year	On-Trgt Catch %	Catchable Catch %	YAC/ Rec	Trgt Share	TAE	Rec Rating	Total	Per Trgt	vs. Man	vs. Zone
2017	-	53%	1.4	10%	-6.4	13.4	-17.2	-0.55	20%	45%
2018	79%	73%	4.6	15%	0.6	104.3	18.4	0.41	45%	39%
2019	94%	94%	2.8	17%	-8.6	68.0	14.2	0.24	41%	56%
2020	86%	86%	2.2	22%	3.2	81.0	0.2	0.00	48%	41%
	87%	80%	2.9	16%	-3.0	71.6	15.6	0.08	40%	47%

	Route Running					Total Points			Total Points Rtg	
Year	Routes Run	Y/RR	Deep Pct	Unique Routes	Slot%	Slot	Wide	Rec Total	Total	Per Route	Per Play
2018	205	2.4	42%	9	20%	8	9	17	19	98	96
2019	344	1.3	49%	13	24%	5	7	13	11	80	76
2020	443	1.1	29%	11	28%	4	12	16	18	92	91
	992	1.4	38%	13	24%	17	28	46	48	-	-

Critical Factors

Hands	6
Separation	5
Run After Catch	6

Positional Factors

Release	5
Route Running	5
Route Savvy	5
Play Speed	6
Contested Catch	6
Playmaker	5
Tracking	6
Body Control	7
Clutch Performance	6
Blocking	6
Toughness	6

Cornell Powell

Report by Daniel Jankuloski

School	Height	Weight	Year	Jersey #	Hometown
Clemson	6001 V	205 V	5SR	17	Greenville, NC

One Liner

Powell's release, route running, and ability after the catch should allow him to contribute at the next level, though he needs to improve his tracking ability and eliminate the body catches to reach his full potential.

Strengths: Release; RAC; Route running
Weaknesses: Tracking; Body catches; Block strength

Cornell Powell is an outside receiver in Clemson's RPO offense, though he slides into the slot occasionally. As a Tiger, he played in 54 games in his career, starting in 12 of them, all coming during his senior year. Clemson has had a crowded receiving room during Powell's time at the school and he was finally able to get significant playing time in 2020. Powell has an average frame for the receiver position while showing good toughness and athletic ability.

Powell shows consistency in his release off the line of scrimmage. He consistently uses quick feet with no wasted movement or false steps to get off the line on nearly every play. This allows him to defeat press coverage and quickly get into his routes. He's a good route runner overall, especially showing precision on curls and in-cutting routes, though some routes will get rounded cuts when they shouldn't. Once the ball comes his way, he uses his body way too often to make catches. Instead of extending his arms and plucking the ball out of the air, he lets it into his body, making him susceptible to occasional drops.

When he uses his hands, he can bring in passes, but also sees a fair number of balls go through his hands. Powell also has a difficult time making contested catches on a consistent basis due to his size and lack of hand use. When he gets the ball in his hands it is difficult to bring him down, as he uses speed and quickness to make defenders miss.

Powell gives sufficient effort on his blocking in the run and screen game. He drops his hips very well and drives through the defender, though he'll occasionally get overpowered.

Powell projects as a No. 4 receiver who has the skills to play both inside and outside in the pros. On 3rd downs, he fits best in the slot where he can use his release and route running or speed over the top to move the sticks. As a former kick returner, Powell should be able to contribute on most special teams, whether as a return man or as a gunner on coverage teams.

					Receiving					
Year	Trgt	Rec	Comp%	Yds	Air Yds	YAC	TD	ADoT	Yds/Trgt	Drops
2016	15	12	80%	87	11	76	0	2.5	5.8	0
2017	11	8	73%	57	16	41	1	8.3	5.2	0
2019	25	15	60%	122	67	55	2	10.5	4.9	2
2020	80	53	66%	882	577	305	7	12.9	11.0	3
	139	93	67%	1211	701	510	10	10.6	8.7	6

		Advanced Receiving					EPA		Positive %	
Year	On-Trgt Catch %	Catchable Catch %	YAC/ Rec	Trgt Share	TAE	Rec Rating	Total	Per Trgt	vs. Man	vs. Zone
2016	-	100%	6.3	2%	-	90.8	3.8	0.26	67%	43%
2017	-	80%	5.1	2%	61.4	114.6	2.3	0.21	50%	25%
2019	83%	83%	3.7	5%	11.1	65.8	-14.8	-0.59	50%	42%
2020	93%	93%	5.8	17%	0.5	122.0	41.2	0.51	63%	57%
	89%	89%	5.5	5%	3.2	106.1	32.0	0.23	58%	51%

		Route Running				Total Points			Total Points Rtg	
Year	Routes Run	Y/RR	Deep Pct	Unique Routes	Slot%	Slot	Wide	Rec Total	Total	Per Route	Per Play
2019	105	1.2	37%	9	48%	-2	-1	-3	-2	52	52
2020	489	1.8	30%	12	11%	1	29	30	32	98	96
	626	1.7	32%	15	19%	-1	27	26	29	-	-

Redshirt season not shown but included in totals

Critical Factors	
Hands	5
Separation	6
Run After Catch	6

Positional Factors	
Release	6
Route Running	6
Route Savvy	6
Play Speed	6
Contested Catch	5
Playmaker	6
Tracking	5
Body Control	5
Clutch Performance	6
Blocking	5
Toughness	6

Ihmir Smith-Marsette

Final Grade: 5.9

Report by Ben Hrkach

School	Height	Weight	Year	Jersey #	Hometown
Iowa	5116 E	179 E	4SR	6	Newark, NJ

One Liner

Smith-Marsette is a good athlete and route runner that can make people miss with the ball in his hands, but his struggles at the catch point and effort inconsistencies may keep him from a starting role.

Strengths: Speed; Separation; Route running
Weaknesses: Playing through contact; Natural hands; Consistent effort and toughness

Ihmir Smith-Marsette played WR for Iowa's power offense, lining up primarily outside with regular slot snaps, as well. He played in 44 career games with 20 starts. He was suspended for a game in 2020 for an OWI charge and left the final game of his career with a leg injury after flipping into the end zone in celebration. He has solid length and a narrow frame. He's a smooth athlete with a high school track background. His motor is hot and cold, showing flashes of both feistiness and disinterest.

Smith-Marsette displays good athleticism, agility, and route running. He struggles when being jammed but can slip by poor technique with his foot quickness. He naturally stems his routes to set up defenders and has the burst to leave them. At the top of his route, Smith-Marsette gets separation with sharpness and is fluid in and out of his breaks. He has plenty of long speed to pull away from defenders and uses this threat well to sell deep routes and break off underneath. He isn't comfortable going across the middle. He has sufficient ball tracking skills and good leaping ability and body control. Combined with his long arms, he has a large catch radius. However, he has issues with body catches, concentration drops, and really struggles fighting through contact. He's a natural runner with the ball in his hands and has good vision. He can make defenders miss and slips off arm tackles, but needs to be careful with his ball security.

In the run game, Smith-Marsette shows little ability or willingness to block. He will fight once engaged, but would prefer to be an observer. He was often used as a runner at Iowa on jet sweeps and out of the backfield because of his ball-carrying vision and running skills.

Smith-Marsette projects as a reserve outside receiver, potential gadget weapon, and kick returner at the next level. He returned kickoffs all four years of his college career with some great success and should continue to do so. He has the speed and quickness to get open, but lacks the all-around game to be a consistent starter in the league.

					Receiving					
Year	Trgt	Rec	Comp%	Yds	Air Yds	YAC	TD	ADoT	Yds/Trgt	Drops
2017	38	18	47%	187	124	63	2	13.4	4.9	6
2018	54	23	43%	370	246	124	3	12.3	6.9	4
2019	74	44	59%	722	497	225	5	11.5	9.8	5
2020	41	25	61%	345	217	128	4	13.0	8.4	2
	207	110	53%	1624	1084	540	14	12.4	7.8	17

		Advanced Receiving					EPA		Positive %	
Year	On-Trgt Catch %	Catchable Catch %	YAC/ Rec	Trgt Share	TAE	Rec Rating	Total	Per Trgt	vs. Man	vs. Zone
2017	-	69%	3.5	11%	-	57.7	-4.8	-0.13	43%	27%
2018	79%	73%	3.8	14%	5.6	66.4	-9.9	-0.18	35%	40%
2019	90%	91%	5.1	19%	-2.3	109.2	25.2	0.34	46%	60%
2020	96%	96%	5.1	17%	3.7	110.3	12.0	0.29	38%	67%
	88%	83%	4.6	15%	1.3	88.8	22.5	0.11	42%	53%

		Route Running					Total Points			Total Points Rtg	
Year	Routes Run	Y/RR	Deep Pct	Unique Routes	Slot%	Slot	Wide	Rec Total	Total	Per Route	Per Play
2018	210	1.8	35%	9	29%	-1	7	7	11	78	77
2019	323	2.2	45%	12	25%	1	17	18	25	89	88
2020	300	1.2	20%	10	39%	6	2	9	10	87	87
	833	1.7	34%	13	30%	6	26	34	46	-	-

Critical Factors

Hands	5
Separation	6
Run After Catch	6

Positional Factors

Release	5
Route Running	6
Route Savvy	5
Play Speed	6
Contested Catch	4
Playmaker	6
Tracking	5
Body Control	6
Clutch Performance	6
Blocking	4
Toughness	4

Dez Fitzpatrick

Report by Nathan Cooper

School	Height	Weight	Year	Jersey #	Hometown
Louisville	6021 V	202 V	5SR	7	Farmington Hills, MI

One Liner

Fitzpatrick has the hands, play speed, and toughness to contribute as a depth receiver at the next level, but limited hip fluidity and inconsistent separation could likely hold him back.

Strengths: Good hands; Solid route runner; Competes
Weaknesses: Tight hips; Struggles to consistently separate; Rerouted too often

Dez Fitzpatrick mainly plays the X receiver while also occasionally sliding into the slot in Louisville's up-tempo, spread offense. He started 34 of 49 games during his career. He has a good frame for the position and is a solid athlete, yet he's not super twitchy and possesses more straight-line speed than COD ability. He plays tough and competes in all aspects of his game.

Fitzpatrick shows good explosion and release off the line. Against press, he's able to get around the defender most times, but will occasionally get stunned or rerouted. He gets into his route quickly, but his tight hips make it tough for him to change directions, especially on curl routes, though he shows that he can transition smoothly out of the top of other routes. With that said, he does a good job working back to the football. As an overall route runner, he runs good routes, running nearly all routes in the route tree. He shows some savvy to set up routes and work away from defenders, but it's inconsistent, getting contacted and rerouted too often mid-route.

He is able to separate with route running or off-hand, but doesn't do so with regularity. He snatches passes away from his body and shows a solid catch radius. He's able to make catches in traffic and has adequate tracking skills to find the ball in the air and go get it. He doesn't show outstanding playmaking ability, but when he gets the ball in his hands, he can make defenders miss.

Fitzpatrick is a willing blocker in the run game and competes with defenders across from him. He moves his feet to get into position and shows good strength at the POA, but doesn't always take the best angles causing him to miss some blocks.

Fitzpatrick projects as a No. 4 receiver at the next level who fits best in the slot, but can also play on the outside. On 3rd downs, operating out of the slot will allow him to use his quickness off the line and even use speed to win over the top. He could be a solid contributor on special teams due to willingness as a blocker, play speed, and competitiveness.

Receiving

Year	Trgt	Rec	Comp%	Yds	Air Yds	YAC	TD	ADoT	Yds/Trgt	Drops
2017	78	45	58%	699	531	168	9	15.1	9.0	8
2018	60	31	52%	422	249	173	3	12.0	7.0	5
2019	64	35	55%	635	458	177	6	13.5	9.9	4
2020	73	43	59%	833	459	374	3	14.2	11.4	4
	275	154	56%	2589	1697	892	21	13.8	9.4	21

Advanced Receiving

Year	On-Trgt Catch %	Catchable Catch %	YAC/ Rec	Trgt Share	TAE	Rec Rating	EPA Total	Per Trgt	Positive % vs. Man	vs. Zone
2017	-	76%	3.7	17%	-	115.3	31.9	0.41	53%	56%
2018	83%	83%	5.6	16%	-0.3	91.1	6.9	0.11	43%	44%
2019	83%	83%	5.1	22%	-7.0	120.2	30.4	0.48	47%	51%
2020	91%	87%	8.7	25%	-3.9	95.3	17.6	0.24	59%	50%
	86%	82%	5.8	19%	-3.8	105.9	86.8	0.32	51%	51%

Route Running / Total Points

Year	Routes Run	Y/RR	Deep Pct	Unique Routes	Slot%	Slot	Wide	Rec Total	Total	Per Route	Per Play
2018	285	1.5	44%	11	66%	-1	4	3	5	66	71
2019	278	2.3	38%	11	28%	5	11	16	21	89	89
2020	497	1.7	28%	12	23%	2	17	19	19	92	87
	1060	1.8	34%	14	36%	6	32	38	45	-	-

Critical Factors

Hands	6
Separation	5
Run After Catch	6

Positional Factors

Release	5
Route Running	6
Route Savvy	5
Play Speed	6
Contested Catch	6
Playmaker	5
Tracking	5
Body Control	5
Clutch Performance	6
Blocking	6
Toughness	6

Damonte Coxie

Report by Danny Shirilla

School	Height	Weight	Year	Jersey #	Hometown
Memphis	6021 E	200 E	5SR	10	Reserve, LA

One Liner

Coxie is a long, athletic receiver with reliable hands who can have an impact on the outside, but may be limited due to a lack of burst, quickness, and wiggle.

Strengths: Size/speed combo; Reliable hands; Tracking ability
Weaknesses: Burst; RAC ability; Contested-catch consistency

Damonte Coxie is a wide receiver in Memphis' RPO-based offensive scheme lining up the majority of his snaps on the outside at either the X or Z position. He started 30 of 43 games, opting out after 2 games in 2020. He had meniscus surgery in 2015 and 2016. Coxie is long and athletic with good speed to go with his size, which is evident by his track background. He is a durable and tough competitor who plays hard each play.

Off the line, Coxie uses his size, strength and footwork to get off press. He does a good job of setting the defender up with his footwork and then using his hands and strength to beat the defender, though he'll get driven off his route occasionally. Once in his route, he's not the most savvy route runner, but does an adequate job of stemming and cleanly breaking out of his routes. For a big guy he sinks his hips well at the top of his routes to get in and out of breaks and create separation, but he lacks the quickness and twitch to consistently separate. His body control shows on deep balls as he can track and adjust to the ball, especially in the red zone. He's a hands catcher with reliable hands and shows the ability to make difficult, contested catches, but isn't consistent enough with it. After the catch, he can gain yards, but isn't going to make many defenders miss in the open field.

Coxie is a willing blocker and definitely isn't scared to get in the mix. His length and strength allow him to latch on, but will fall off too many blocks to be considered good.

Coxie projects as a solid No. 4 receiver who has the potential to become a starter-level player on the outside. He fits best on the outside as an X or Z due to his long frame, big-receiver play style, and good speed, which is where he should line up on 3rd downs. He could use his route running from the slot, but not consistently. Coxie's speed and willingness to block paired with his solid release shows that he can potentially contribute as a gunner and some other areas of special teams.

Receiving

Year	Trgt	Rec	Comp%	Yds	Air Yds	YAC	TD	ADoT	Yds/Trgt	Drops
2017	28	21	75%	323	270	53	3	14.1	11.5	2
2018	119	72	61%	1174	711	463	7	12.4	9.9	9
2019	128	76	59%	1276	855	421	9	13.6	10.0	6
2020	25	16	64%	186	155	31	1	10.4	7.4	0
	300	185	62%	2959	1991	968	20	12.9	9.9	17

Advanced Receiving / EPA / Positive %

Year	On-Trgt Catch %	Catchable Catch %	YAC/Rec	Trgt Share	TAE	Rec Rating	Total	Per Trgt	vs. Man	vs. Zone
2017	-	88%	2.5	6%	-	148.4	28.5	1.02	71%	77%
2018	82%	81%	6.4	29%	9.0	106.2	63.4	0.53	55%	52%
2019	85%	83%	5.8	30%	4.3	100.8	44.2	0.35	42%	64%
2020	87%	82%	2.0	6%	5.0	99.9	11.0	0.44	57%	75%
	84%	83%	5.3	17%	6.0	107.3	147.1	0.49	52%	63%

Route Running / Total Points / Total Points Rtg

Year	Routes Run	Y/RR	Deep Pct	Unique Routes	Slot%	Slot	Wide	Rec Total	Total	Per Route	Per Play
2018	353	3.3	40%	13	6%	1	40	41	44	99	99
2019	412	3.1	47%	14	11%	3	30	33	34	97	89
2020	115	1.6	31%	6	5%	0	5	6	6	93	92
	880	3.0	42%	15	8%	4	75	80	84	-	-

Critical Factors

Hands	6
Separation	5
Run After Catch	5

Positional Factors

Release	6
Route Running	6
Route Savvy	5
Play Speed	6
Contested Catch	5
Playmaker	6
Tracking	6
Body Control	6
Clutch Performance	5
Blocking	5
Toughness	6

Frank Darby

Report by Alec Mallon

School	Height	Weight	Year	Jersey #	Hometown
Arizona State	6001 V	194 V	5SR	84	Jersey City, NJ

One Liner

Darby has the speed to take the top off of defenses but needs to refine some of the fundamental aspects of his game before he can see the field in a larger capacity.

Strengths: Downfield playmaking; Top-of-route suddenness; Releases against press
Weaknesses: Concentration drops; Manufacturing YAC; Boxing out at the catch point

Frank Darby is a wide receiver for Arizona State who rotates playing its X and Z roles. Over his five years in college, he appeared in 39 games, starting 28 after redshirting his first season. Darby is a long strider with a standard but strong frame. His toughness and competitiveness is apparent as he will lay his body on the line to make plays downfield.

Darby excels at being a deep threat. He has good speed and the ability to track and create big plays when the ball comes his way. He uses his quickness and physicality to get off the line, doing his best to avoid getting jammed and rerouted. Darby shows good technique at the top of his routes, offering little to no wasted movements when creating separation. However, he ran a limited route tree of mostly deep shots and quick-hitting curls. At the catch point, he can get sloppy at times with easy drops, but usually has shown to be a sufficient hands catcher. Darby shows his toughness in jump-ball situations and isn't afraid of contact deep down the field or over the middle, bouncing back up quickly from big hits. He

has struggled to wall off defenders with his size and prevent pass breakups. After the catch, Darby has the speed to pull away from a crowd but can get too cute relying on east-west athleticism instead of gaining positive yardage.

Darby is a willing participant in the run game. He shows good aggression and strength to body up secondary defenders and dominate smaller players. However, he lacks the technique and size to consistently handle box defenders when cracking down inside.

Darby projects as a No. 4 backup receiver in the NFL, who will also have a significant role on special teams. His downfield ability alone will allow him to see the field on obvious passing downs, but he has enough route-running ability to be used underneath, as well. As a special teamer, Darby briefly was a punt returner in 2019 and his quickness and change-of-direction skills could fulfill that same role for a team, as well as on both kickoff units.

					Receiving					
Year	Trgt	Rec	Comp%	Yds	Air Yds	YAC	TD	ADoT	Yds/Trgt	Drops
2017	17	9	53%	234	201	33	2	22.8	13.8	1
2018	50	21	42%	421	347	74	2	21.2	8.4	6
2019	57	31	54%	616	479	137	8	16.8	10.8	4
2020	12	6	50%	46	31	15	1	11.5	3.8	1
	136	67	49%	1317	1058	259	13	18.7	9.7	12

		Advanced Receiving						EPA		Positive %	
Year	On-Trgt Catch %	Catchable Catch %	YAC/ Rec	Trgt Share	TAE	Rec Rating	Total	Per Trgt	vs. Man	vs. Zone
2017	-	82%	3.7	4%	-	113.0	8.6	0.51	40%	63%
2018	65%	65%	3.5	13%	-1.6	77.2	4.2	0.08	42%	37%
2019	85%	83%	5.2	15%	-7.1	132.0	32.7	0.57	50%	46%
2020	83%	83%	2.5	14%	-5.1	87.5	-2.4	-0.20	0%	43%
	76%	76%	4.2	11%	-5.0	109.2	43.1	0.32	41%	45%

		Route Running				Total Points				Total Points Rtg	
Year	Routes Run	Y/RR	Deep Pct	Unique Routes	Slot%	Slot	Wide	Rec Total	Total	Per Route	Per Play
2018	264	1.6	57%	9	12%	2	-3	-1	0	59	58
2019	330	1.9	50%	12	22%	-1	14	13	16	80	80
2020	90	0.5	29%	5	14%	-1	2	2	2	77	77
	684	1.6	50%	13	18%	0	14	14	18	-	-

Critical Factors	
Hands	5
Separation	6
Run After Catch	5

Positional Factors	
Release	6
Route Running	6
Route Savvy	6
Play Speed	6
Contested Catch	5
Playmaker	6
Tracking	6
Body Control	5
Clutch Performance	5
Blocking	5
Toughness	6

Cade Johnson

Report by Nathan Cooper

School	Height	Weight	Year	Jersey #	Hometown
South Dakota State	5103 V	186 V	5SR	15	Papillion, NE

One Liner
Johnson is an explosive playmaker with speed and RAC ability, though he'll need to become a better route runner and get stronger if he wants to be more than a depth-level rotational receiver.

Strengths: Explosion off the line; Play speed; Playmaking ability
Weaknesses: Not crisp route runner; Bullied by physical DBs; Lacks some savvy

Cade Johnson primarily plays slot receiver, but will occasionally slide out to the X or Z in South Dakota State's balanced spread offense. He appeared in 40 games, starting 27 of them. He's got a small frame, but he's an exceptional, quick-twitch athlete who plays extremely fast. Despite his size, he shows good toughness and competitiveness in all levels of his game.

Johnson is quick and explosive off the line with good burst and acceleration to quickly get into his routes. He didn't go up against press much, but did struggle in other areas against physical defenders. He ran a lot of crossing routes with the occasional curl or vertical route. His speed allows him to round a lot of cuts at the top of routes, but he isn't an extremely crisp route runner. He shows some savvy, but doesn't always avoid contact with defenders. To separate, Johnson wins with speed and quickness and he's mostly running away from defenders instead of having to win at the top of routes. He has good hands to haul in passes. He will occasionally let the ball into his body, but rarely drops any balls. For a smaller player, he's able to consistently make contested catches across the middle with strong hands. Johnson's speed, quickness, and elusiveness allow him to force missed tackles in the open field. He's not going to run through anyone, but has the playmaking ability to make guys miss and gain extra yardage.

Johnson has the speed and quickness to be used and effective on jet sweeps and end arounds. He's a willing blocker and battles, but doesn't have the size or strength at the POA to be effective. He'll also take some bad angles down the field.

Johnson projects as a No. 4 receiver at the next level operating exclusively out of the slot. His speed and quickness should allow him to win off the line. He's the type of player that needs the ball in his hands in the open field to make plays. On 3rd downs, he fits best in the slot running away from defenders on crossers. He shows good vision, speed, and playmaking ability to be a successful returner at the next level.

South Dakota State has had a toehold in the NFL since 1996 when kicker Adam Vinatieri signed with the Patriots.

Cade Johnson, a former walk-on at the school, is looking to solidify the school's firm footing. His football pedigree is strong. His father was a wingback who won two national championships at Nebraska in the 1990s. Johnson solidified the family name by earning first-team All-American honors in 2019. He holds school records both for touchdown receptions and kickoff return yards in a season.

Johnson could be the third South Dakota State player selected in the last four seasons. Tight end Dallas Goedert went to the Eagles in the second round in 2018 and cornerback Jordan Brown was selected by the Bengals in the seventh round in 2019.

Critical Factors	
Hands	6
Separation	5
Run After Catch	6

Positional Factors	
Release	6
Route Running	5
Route Savvy	5
Play Speed	7
Contested Catch	6
Playmaker	7
Tracking	6
Body Control	6
Clutch Performance	6
Blocking	4
Toughness	6

Josh Imatorbhebhe

Report by Evan Butler & David Simmons

School	Height	Weight	Year	Jersey #	Hometown
Illinois	6010 E	220 E	5SR	9	Suwanee, GA

One Liner

Imatorbhebhe has the physical tools and mid-air ball skills to excel at the next level, but he needs to create more separation in his route running and improve his consistency to earn regular snaps.

Strengths: Length and leaping ability; Catch radius and body control; Physicality
Weaknesses: Route running sharpness; Limited route tree; Consistency

Josh Imatorbhebhe is an outside receiver in Illinois' RPO-heavy scheme. He played and started in 18 games for the Illini after playing in 7 games for USC and transferring. Imatorbhebhe has a strong frame and good length, with sufficient speed and lateral agility. Additionally, he's an extremely explosive leaper, as viral videos confirm. He is physical in necessary situations to block or fight for extra yards.

Imatorbhebhe has a collection of tools that can't be taught, but he has room to develop his technique. He is big and physical enough to work through press and has enough wiggle to open defenders' hips. He does not generate much separation in his route running, showing stiffness in and out of breaks and little lateral suddenness. He ran a limited route tree of curls, verticals, and the occasional slant, working to open space when available. He is a hands catcher and counters his share of easy concentration drops with exceptional efforts above the rim to high point. Imatorbhebhe has very good body control and is an elite vertical leaper above the secondary, allowing him to make unusual catches outside of his frame. Any lack of separation he earns through his routes can be wiped away with a well-placed jump ball. After the catch, he runs well and grinds his way for extra yards but is not overly elusive or fast in the open field.

Imatorbhebhe is a willing blocker who likes to use his physicality in the run game. He doesn't sustain as well as he should but he shows the motor to find work downfield, and his overall strength and size let him overpower defensive backs and even some linebackers.

Imatorbhebhe projects as a reserve X receiver with a skill set worth further development. In a vertical offense he will be a threat using his explosiveness and ball skills to succeed downfield and in the red zone. With refined technique and exposure to a larger route tree, he could grow into a starter. He has the toughness and physicality to be a contributor on special teams.

					Receiving					
Year	Trgt	Rec	Comp%	Yds	Air Yds	YAC	TD	ADoT	Yds/Trgt	Drops
2017	5	2	40%	11	7	4	0	9.0	2.2	0
2019	63	33	52%	634	411	223	9	13.5	10.1	5
2020	46	22	48%	297	158	139	3	11.3	6.5	4
	114	57	50%	942	576	366	12	12.4	8.3	9

	Advanced Receiving						EPA		Positive %	
Year	On-Trgt Catch %	Catchable Catch %	YAC/ Rec	Trgt Share	TAE	Rec Rating	Total	Per Trgt	vs. Man	vs. Zone
2017	-	100%	2.0	1%	-	8.3	-5.6	-1.11	0%	-
2019	81%	81%	6.8	18%	-4.1	107.4	15.7	0.25	46%	44%
2020	86%	87%	6.3	24%	4.1	90.6	0.4	0.01	31%	46%
	83%	84%	6.4	11%	-1.3	98.6	10.5	0.09	37%	45%

	Route Running					Total Points			Total Points Rtg	
Year	Routes Run	Y/RR	Deep Pct	Unique Routes	Slot%	Slot	Wide	Rec Total	Total	Per Route	Per Play
2019	377	1.7	43%	9	4%	1	17	18	19	90	85
2020	359	0.8	24%	9	8%	2	0	2	3	67	70
	737	1.3	34%	11	6%	4	16	20	22	-	-

Critical Factors	
Hands	6
Separation	5
Run After Catch	5

Positional Factors	
Release	5
Route Running	4
Route Savvy	5
Play Speed	6
Contested Catch	6
Playmaker	6
Tracking	6
Body Control	7
Clutch Performance	5
Blocking	6
Toughness	6

Dax Milne

Report by John Todd

School	Height	Weight	Year	Jersey #	Hometown
BYU	5116 E	190 E	3JR	5	South Jordan, UT

One Liner

Milne is a detailed route runner and a tireless worker who won't let his size and athletic limitations hold him back from carving a reserve role in the NFL.

Strengths: Detailed footwork; Route and speed control; Effort and winning plays
Weaknesses: Dynamism; Breakaway speed; Play strength

Dax Milne is a wide receiver in BYU's high-powered spread offense, rotating through each of their receiver roles but most often as an X. A preferred walk-on turned go-to target, he earned immediate playing time and has logged 35 career games played with 12 starts. Milne has slightly below-average measurables and quicker-than-fast athleticism, but he lacks an extra gear of dynamism to his game. However, he is a max effort teammate who does all the little things and makes winning plays.

Milne will struggle against longer press corners, but his refined footwork begins off the line with his release. He's a short-strider, and his quick-footed nature simulates an enhanced shiftiness. That and his detailed, subtle technique at the stem buoy his true route-running ability. Hesitations, head-nods, body fakes, and great speed control to sell deep routes before sinking his hips are Milne's tools of separation, because he doesn't have the long speed, innate suddenness, or leaping ability to win otherwise consistently. He runs every route hard and

sharp, no matter the progression. He has strong hands to fight through traffic underneath, but he doesn't play above the rim and often settles for body catches when left open. After the catch, his choppy feet can make an initial defender miss, but he won't pull away from a crowd or finish with physicality.

Despite Milne's size and strength, he's proven to be a good asset as a blocker with superior positioning and desire. He's sprung numerous extended plays for larger gains by hustling from distant areas of the field to get involved. BYU also regularly utilized him on jet sweeps and reverses to modest success.

Milne projects as a reserve receiver at the next level, whose collegiate usage on the perimeter should be eschewed in favor of his better fit in the slot. He plays the position with a walk-on's mentality, and his detail-oriented execution and high motor will give him a chance at a long career. He has kick and punt return experience and profiles as a reliable but unspectacular option.

Receiving

Year	Trgt	Rec	Comp%	Yds	Air Yds	YAC	TD	ADoT	Yds/Trgt	Drops
2018	18	10	56%	69	60	9	1	9.8	3.8	3
2019	43	21	49%	285	248	37	2	13.0	6.6	1
2020	94	70	74%	1188	775	413	8	12.8	12.6	3
	155	101	65%	1542	1083	459	11	12.5	9.9	7

Advanced Receiving

Year	On-Trgt Catch %	Catchable Catch %	YAC/Rec	Trgt Share	TAE	Rec Rating	EPA Total	EPA Per Trgt	Positive % vs. Man	Positive % vs. Zone
2018	77%	77%	0.9	5%	1.3	82.9	-1.8	-0.10	33%	83%
2019	95%	90%	1.8	10%	-0.8	85.9	-7.6	-0.18	35%	42%
2020	92%	92%	5.9	26%	7.3	140.2	66.2	0.70	59%	69%
	90%	90%	4.5	13%	3.3	118.8	56.8	0.37	44%	63%

Route Running

Year	Routes Run	Y/RR	Deep Pct	Unique Routes	Slot%	Total Points Slot	Total Points Wide	Rec Total	Total	Total Points Rtg Per Route	Total Points Rtg Per Play
2018	69	1.0	29%	5	47%	-1	1	0	-3	59	63
2019	199	1.4	40%	11	51%	1	-1	0	-1	60	57
2020	505	2.4	15%	16	23%	8	26	34	37	99	99
	773	2.0	23%	19	36%	8	26	34	33	-	-

Critical Factors

Hands	5
Separation	5
Run After Catch	5

Positional Factors

Release	6
Route Running	6
Route Savvy	7
Play Speed	5
Contested Catch	5
Playmaker	5
Tracking	5
Body Control	7
Clutch Performance	7
Blocking	6
Toughness	5

Dazz Newsome

Report by Ben Hrkach & Griffin Sullivan

School	Height	Weight	Year	Jersey #	Hometown
North Carolina	5106 E	190 E	4SR	5	Hampton, VA

One Liner

Newsome has the speed, burst, and big-play ability to make an impact as a depth receiver at the next level, but he'll need to improve his route savvy and limit the focus drops to be a consistent contributor.

Strengths: Speed & burst; RAC ability; Big plays
Weaknesses: Route savvy; Release; Focus drops

Dazz Newsome played wide receiver in North Carolina's spread, RPO system lining up almost exclusively in the slot. He started 32 of 44 games for the Tar Heels, though he missed 3 games in 2017 with an undisclosed injury and 1 in 2019 as a result of missing practice during the week. Newsome is a twitched-up, sudden athlete. He shows average toughness and high level of competitiveness.

Newsome does most of his damage with the ball in his hands. He's dangerous on bubbles and jet sweeps. He has natural vision and an ability to make people miss, though he doesn't gain many yards after contact. His release off the line is inconsistent, and he frequently looks unprepared for the snap. He tends to hop off the LOS to set up the defender and will struggle gaining a free release against press coverage. He gets low in and out of breaks and gains separation with his quickness. He's a precise route runner, though he can be overly mechanical. Newsome lacks some route savvy and runs routes nearly the same exact way regardless of his opponent. He also lacks some zone awareness and feel to find holes in zones and occasionally runs his route into defenders. On broken plays, he does a good job of working back to his quarterback. Newsome cradles or body catches a lot of passes and will have some focus drops on occasion. This makes him struggle fighting through contact to make contested catches. After the catch, he quickly converts into a runner. He has a competitive spirit and makes big plays when his team needs him to.

Newsome shows some interest in blocking, but lacks strength and technique. He is productive in the jet sweep game and is clearly a natural runner.

Newsome projects as a No. 4 receiver who can be a gadget player out of the slot. On 3rd downs, he has the speed, quickness, and vision to make plays and move the chains. He has proven to be a quality punt returner and returned some kicks as well, though his value on teams is limited outside of that.

Receiving

Year	Trgt	Rec	Comp%	Yds	Air Yds	YAC	TD	ADoT	Yds/Trgt	Drops
2017	29	18	62%	227	83	144	0	9.1	7.8	2
2018	70	44	63%	506	165	341	2	7.5	7.2	5
2019	104	72	69%	1018	609	409	10	10.2	9.8	6
2020	70	54	77%	684	322	362	6	8.2	9.8	4
	273	188	69%	2435	1179	1256	18	8.9	8.9	17

Advanced Receiving

Year	On-Trgt Catch %	Catchable Catch %	YAC/ Rec	Trgt Share	TAE	Rec Rating	EPA Total	EPA Per Trgt	Positive % vs. Man	Positive % vs. Zone
2017	-	82%	8.0	7%	-	86.4	6.6	0.23	50%	67%
2018	91%	90%	7.8	17%	0.2	82.2	-1.3	-0.02	39%	40%
2019	90%	91%	5.7	25%	4.0	124.6	51.2	0.49	55%	61%
2020	95%	95%	6.7	20%	-6.9	135.7	33.5	0.48	52%	64%
	92%	91%	6.7	18%	-1.0	112.5	90.1	0.33	50%	59%

Route Running

Year	Routes Run	Y/RR	Deep Pct	Unique Routes	Slot%	Slot	Wide	Rec Total	Total	Per Route	Per Play
2018	239	2.1	39%	14	92%	4	0	3	15	69	72
2019	474	2.1	24%	15	91%	34	1	36	39	99	97
2020	625	1.1	18%	15	99%	17	0	17	18	87	85
	1338	1.7	24%	19	94%	55	1	56	72	-	-

(Route Running table also spans: Total Points — Slot, Wide, Rec Total; Total Points Rtg — Per Route, Per Play)

Critical Factors

Hands	5
Separation	5
Run After Catch	6

Positional Factors

Release	5
Route Running	6
Route Savvy	5
Play Speed	6
Contested Catch	4
Playmaker	6
Tracking	5
Body Control	5
Clutch Performance	6
Blocking	4
Toughness	5

Tyler Vaughns

Report by Justin Serovich & Christian Vega

School	Height	Weight	Year	Jersey #	Hometown
USC	6010 E	190 E	5SR	21	Pasadena, CA

One Liner

Vaughns is an intelligent receiver with a reliable skillset to work different levels of the field, but his lack of play strength and top traits should keep him from becoming a top NFL target.

Strengths: Extended play savviness; Length and speed; Downfield playmaking
Weaknesses: Play strength; Hands through contact; Top traits

Tyler Vaughns is an outside receiver in USC's Air Raid offense. He played in 45 career games and started 37 of them dating back to his freshman season. He has a lean, long-limbed frame with good length, but lacks the strength to fight for extra yards. He's a long strider with good speed and sufficient change-of-direction quickness.

Vaughns had occasional struggles against reroutes, but when given free releases he accelerates smoothly and eats up ground. He ran a varied route tree, but had a high volume of curls, outs, digs and slants. He does a good job of throttling back and sinking his hips into sharp cuts. He has good footwork and gets defenders to commit before breaking. His short routes keep defenders honest, which lead to success on double moves. Vaughns excels at helping his quarterback on extended plays, staying active to work back to the ball and finding open space as a big target. He has good hands and has shown he can make big plays downfield along the sideline and at awkward angles. Vaughns has a good catch radius and can high point, but he struggles fighting through contested situations in traffic. He's a sufficient ballcarrier after the catch, doing a solid job of understanding tackling angles and finding creases to slip through. He's not a physical tackle-breaker though and he occasionally dances laterally too much instead of getting upfield.

Vaughns has the length and willingness to contribute as a run blocker and make the necessary blocks, but his play strength needs to improve to sustain longer and more consistently. When bunched in tight in short-yardage situations he showed solid effort to do just enough, but his narrow frame really holds him back against aggressive or bigger defenders.

Vaughns projects as a solid fourth receiving option who has some inside-out versatility. He has a solid overall skill set and the length and speed to contribute in a limited role. He was a multi-unit special teams contributor, including as a return man, and should be sufficient there moving forward with improved play strength.

Receiving

Year	Trgt	Rec	Comp%	Yds	Air Yds	YAC	TD	ADoT	Yds/Trgt	Drops
2017	75	57	76%	809	567	242	5	12.2	10.8	1
2018	99	58	59%	674	500	174	6	11.4	6.8	6
2019	111	74	67%	913	710	203	6	11.3	8.2	5
2020	50	33	66%	406	266	140	3	11.0	8.1	3
	335	222	66%	2802	2043	759	20	11.5	8.4	15

Advanced Receiving

Year	On-Trgt Catch %	Catchable Catch %	YAC/ Rec	Trgt Share	TAE	Rec Rating	EPA Total	Per Trgt	Positive % vs. Man	vs. Zone
2017	-	92%	4.2	16%	-	121.5	43.6	0.58	63%	69%
2018	81%	80%	3.0	26%	4.4	99.5	20.8	0.21	47%	47%
2019	89%	88%	2.7	22%	3.5	98.7	16.5	0.15	58%	56%
2020	89%	89%	4.2	20%	3.8	85.9	3.3	0.07	42%	61%
	86%	87%	3.4	21%	3.9	102.1	84.3	0.25	54%	57%

Route Running

Year	Routes Run	Y/RR	Deep Pct	Unique Routes	Slot%	Slot	Wide	Rec Total	Total	Per Route	Per Play
2018	366	1.8	33%	13	16%	4	9	13	18	79	79
2019	502	1.8	24%	10	4%	0	15	15	17	76	75
2020	325	1.2	14%	8	6%	2	9	11	12	86	84
	1193	1.7	24%	15	9%	6	33	39	47	-	-

(Columns under "Total Points" = Slot, Wide, Rec Total; under "Total Points Rtg" = Total, Per Route, Per Play)

Critical Factors

Hands	6
Separation	5
Run After Catch	5

Positional Factors

Release	5
Route Running	6
Route Savvy	6
Play Speed	6
Contested Catch	5
Playmaker	6
Tracking	6
Body Control	6
Clutch Performance	6
Blocking	4
Toughness	5

Tamorrion Terry

Report by Nathan Cooper

School	Height	Weight	Year	Jersey #	Hometown
Florida State	6031 E	203 E	4JR	5	Ashburn, GA

One Liner

Terry has the strength, explosiveness, and tracking ability to be a solid receiver, though inconsistent hands, route savvy, and an unsettling regression from 2019 to 2020 could affect his overall contribution.

Strengths: Play strength; Explosive off the line; High point ability
Weaknesses: Too many body catches; Can get rerouted vs. press; 2019 to 2020 regression

Tamorrion Terry mainly plays the X in Florida State's RPO-heavy offense. He started 28 of 30 games for the Seminoles, but left the team after Week 10 in 2020. He's undergone meniscal surgery on both knees. He's a good athlete with a big frame for the position. He's competitive and plays tough with the man across from him, although his motor will cool down from time to time in the run game.

Terry shows explosiveness out of his stance and gets into his route quickly. Going up against press, he'll struggle to get off the line and get rerouted, but has shown he can win with quick feet and strength. Even though he ran a lot of curls and vertical routes, he knows how to run most routes on the route tree with precision. He's a good route runner that shows quickness at the top of routes. He has some savvy to his route running with stems, but runs into contact too often. His separation mainly comes in the form of speed or box-out ability. He shows strong hands to bring in the football, but catches too many passes

with his body. He has the tracking ability to find the ball in the air and adjust to make the catch whether he's wide open or contested. Once the ball gets into his hands, he can run through arm tackles or make defenders miss to gain extra yards.

As a blocker, most times Terry will come off the line and approach the defender, but nothing more. When it's vital for him to block with the play coming his way, he doesn't mind latching with good strength at the POA, occasionally showing some competitiveness depending on the defender.

Terry projects as a No. 4 depth receiver at the next level. He fits best as an outside receiver, but can also slide inside and be used as a big slot to create mismatches against smaller defenders. On 3rd downs, he's best on the outside where he can use his route running and post-up ability. He likely isn't a core contributor on special teams, but his speed and toughness should allow him to assist on some units.

					Receiving				
Year	Trgt	Rec	Comp%	Yds	Air Yds	YAC	TD	ADoT	Yds/Trgt	Drops
2018	72	35	49%	744	548	196	8	16.9	10.3	5
2019	105	60	57%	1191	576	615	9	13.3	11.3	7
2020	40	23	58%	289	203	86	1	13.0	7.2	1
	217	118	54%	2224	1327	897	18	14.4	10.2	13

	Advanced Receiving						EPA		Positive %	
Year	On-Trgt Catch %	Catchable Catch %	YAC/ Rec	Trgt Share	TAE	Rec Rating	Total	Per Trgt	vs. Man	vs. Zone
2018	72%	71%	5.6	16%	-1.6	111.1	18.2	0.25	49%	33%
2019	86%	86%	10.2	25%	-0.3	113.6	33.7	0.32	61%	41%
2020	88%	88%	3.7	15%	1.2	78.0	5.0	0.13	58%	43%
	82%	81%	7.6	19%	-0.6	106.2	56.9	0.26	55%	40%

	Route Running					Total Points				Total Points Rtg	
Year	Routes Run	Y/RR	Deep Pct	Unique Routes	Slot%	Slot	Wide	Rec Total	Total	Per Route	Per Play
2018	422	1.8	53%	10	12%	0	16	17	18	84	77
2019	447	2.7	35%	12	9%	3	22	25	24	93	88
2020	203	1.4	22%	10	6%	1	8	10	9	96	92
	1072	2.1	38%	15	10%	4	46	52	51	-	-

Critical Factors	
Hands	5
Separation	5
Run After Catch	6

Positional Factors	
Release	5
Route Running	6
Route Savvy	5
Play Speed	6
Contested Catch	6
Playmaker	5
Tracking	6
Body Control	6
Clutch Performance	6
Blocking	5
Toughness	5

Trevon Grimes

Report by Theo Fornaciari & DJ Marquardt

School	Height	Weight	Year	Jersey #	Hometown
Florida	6037 V	217 V	4SR	8	Fort Lauderdale, FL

One Liner

Grimes is an athletic, downfield playmaker with good speed and hands who needs significant refinement as a route runner to sustain an NFL career.

Strengths: Natural hands catcher; Tracking/adjust; RAC ability
Weaknesses: Route savvy; Explosiveness out of breaks; Concentration over the middle

Trevon Grimes is the X/Z receiver in Florida's RPO-based offense who also aligns in the slot in tight formations. He started 23 of 37 games for Florida after playing 2 games at Ohio State in 2017. He suffered a torn ACL in 2016. A high school track hurdler, he's a very good athlete with the frame and size desired. He has good physical toughness, though has lapses in mental toughness/focus.

Grimes has a sufficient release, showing good speed and an effective stutter release, yet he lacks the repertoire and nuance necessary to win consistently against good press corners. With a free release, Grimes has good speed to stretch the field vertically and horizontally. He's an adequate route runner with sufficient separation ability who struggles to sink his hips at the top of routes and lacks explosiveness out of his breaks. He has mediocre route savvy, lacking the zone-processing skills to be effective with his stems and struggling to find vacant space. Grimes is a good, natural hands catcher with good tracking ability and a wide catch radius. He consistently adjusts to off-target throws and has the hand dexterity and body control to pluck passes from all around his frame. Outside the hashes/downfield, he can win contested catches against defensive backs, though he shows lapses in concentration in traffic over the middle. After the catch, he has the toughness and athletic ability to make defenders miss.

Grimes is a very good run blocker. He has the physical toughness to mix it up with bigger players while also maintaining a good blocking base with proper pad level and hand placement to neutralize DBs on the perimeter, however, he struggles to get his hands on some quicker corners.

Grimes projects as a No. 4 X/Z receiver in a run-first offense with an emphasis on the vertical passing game. He has reliable hands and downfield playmaking ability to be a complementary and/or decoy player on 3rd downs. His speed and toughness suggest he can be a good special teams contributor.

Receiving

Year	Trgt	Rec	Comp%	Yds	Air Yds	YAC	TD	ADoT	Yds/Trgt	Drops
2017	3	3	100%	20	19	1	0	6.3	6.7	0
2018	42	26	62%	364	161	203	2	10.7	8.7	1
2019	46	33	72%	491	226	265	3	10.7	10.7	2
2020	60	38	63%	589	384	205	9	13.1	9.8	2
	151	100	66%	1464	790	674	14	11.5	9.7	5

Advanced Receiving

Year	On-Trgt Catch %	Catchable Catch %	YAC/ Rec	Trgt Share	TAE	Rec Rating	EPA Total	Per Trgt	Positive % vs. Man	Positive % vs. Zone
2017	-	100%	0.3	1%	-	94.4	1.4	0.47	-	100%
2018	89%	89%	7.8	12%	0.6	105.7	16.2	0.39	46%	44%
2019	94%	94%	8.0	10%	-7.4	110.0	26.1	0.57	64%	60%
2020	80%	76%	5.4	13%	0.9	135.3	30.0	0.50	43%	64%
	87%	85%	6.7	9%	-2.5	123.1	73.8	0.49	49%	59%

Route Running

Year	Routes Run	Y/RR	Deep Pct	Unique Routes	Slot%	Total Points Slot	Wide	Rec Total	Total	Per Route	Per Play
2018	146	2.5	35%	7	28%	2	11	13	14	98	91
2019	267	1.8	38%	9	33%	1	8	9	12	80	79
2020	405	1.5	25%	14	22%	3	13	15	17	88	87
	818	1.8	31%	15	28%	6	32	37	43	-	-

Critical Factors

Hands	6
Separation	5
Run After Catch	6

Positional Factors

Release	5
Route Running	5
Route Savvy	4
Play Speed	6
Contested Catch	5
Playmaker	5
Tracking	6
Body Control	6
Clutch Performance	5
Blocking	7
Toughness	6

Warren Jackson

Report by Alec Mallon & Jarrett Rodgers

School	Height	Weight	Year	Jersey #	Hometown
Colorado State	6055 E	215 E	4SR	9	Mission Hills, CA

One Liner

Jackson is a big body who uses his size and body control to win on the outside, but a lack of deep speed and overall separation skills will likely limit his potential.

Strengths: Short-area burst; Body control; High-point ability
Weaknesses: Long speed; Downfield separation; Release vs. press

Warren Jackson mainly plays outside receiver for Colorado State's pro-style offense, but saw a significant amount of time in the slot in 2018. He started 13 of 33 games before opting out of the entire 2020 season. He doesn't have great straight-line speed, but has a big frame and long arms to compete. Jackson is tough for a receiver and shows off his competitive nature going up against edge defenders routinely in the run.

Jackson can get jammed and forced to reroute at the line. He can be slow off the ball because of his size, but does a good job pushing downfield once clean. He has good short-area quickness skills, creating small windows for his quarterback. He lacks the deep speed to create separation and defenders can stay in his hip pocket through his breaks. Jackson does a good job of using his body to his advantage. He can wall off defenders and simply box them out, but can also out jump nearly anyone to get the ball. He's a natural hands catcher and displays good body control on inaccurate throws as well as back shoulder

throws. He can flip his hips to get himself in the proper position to adjust to the ball. After the catch, he's a strong runner and isn't afraid of contact. He's a long strider to get upfield, but doesn't have the natural elusiveness to make defenders miss in the open field.

As a run blocker, Jackson has the determination and strength to handle defensive backs on the outside, but doesn't have the pure power to move defenders in the box. He doesn't deliver the strongest blow, but when he has position, he uses his long arms to keep smaller defenders away from the ball.

Jackson best fits as a No. 4 backup receiver working best out on the outside, but does have experience playing out of the slot. Because of his build, Jackson is a viable option in the red zone, on 3rd downs, or in situations where he can use his body to win. Jackson didn't have a special teams impact in college, but figures to have a strong role on punt and kickoff units.

					Receiving					
Year	Trgt	Rec	Comp%	Yds	Air Yds	YAC	TD	ADoT	Yds/Trgt	Drops
2017	24	15	63%	265	184	81	2	15.0	11.0	1
2018	51	32	63%	405	317	88	4	11.4	7.9	3
2019	124	77	62%	1119	772	347	8	11.8	9.0	5
	199	124	62%	1789	1273	516	14	12.1	9.0	9

	Advanced Receiving						EPA		Positive %	
Year	On-Trgt Catch %	Catchable Catch %	YAC/ Rec	Trgt Share	TAE	Rec Rating	Total	Per Trgt	vs. Man	vs. Zone
2017	-	88%	5.4	5%	47.8	88.4	4.8	0.20	45%	64%
2018	94%	94%	2.8	10%	-6.5	97.3	14.7	0.29	55%	63%
2019	89%	89%	4.5	29%	8.1	106.2	53.6	0.43	59%	55%
	91%	90%	4.2	15%	2.4	98.2	73.1	0.37	56%	58%

	Route Running					Total Points				Total Points Rtg	
Year	Routes Run	Y/RR	Deep Pct	Unique Routes	Slot%	Slot	Wide	Rec Total	Total	Per Route	Per Play
2018	306	1.3	37%	12	78%	5	3	8	9	73	71
2019	341	3.3	39%	14	30%	14	25	40	44	99	99
	647	2.4	38%	15	51%	19	28	48	53	-	-

Critical Factors	
Hands	6
Separation	5
Run After Catch	5

Positional Factors	
Release	5
Route Running	6
Route Savvy	5
Play Speed	5
Contested Catch	6
Playmaker	6
Tracking	5
Body Control	6
Clutch Performance	6
Blocking	5
Toughness	6

Anthony Schwartz

Report by Stephen Marciello

School	Height	Weight	Year	Jersey #	Hometown
Auburn	5116 E	179 E	3JR	1	Pembroke Pines, FL

One Liner
Schwartz's world-record speed is an impactful trait moving to the next level, but he needs to continue improving his technical receiver skills to be used as more than just a gadget weapon.

Strengths: Elite track speed; Gadget versatility; Playmaking
Weaknesses: Play strength; Lateral quickness; Route tree and technique

Anthony Schwartz is an offensive weapon in Auburn's complex offense that often put him in jet motion. He played in 36 career games with 19 starts. He has solid height and a narrow but athletic frame. A world record-holding sprinter, Schwartz has blazing straight-line speed but merely sufficient lateral quickness. He has enough toughness to finish runs on occasion, but he is not a physical player and will find the sideline when available.

Schwartz ran a limited route tree consisting of screens, vertical routes, and simple curls or outs. His speed creates panic and heightens his route running at times as defenders are on their heels for his breaks. He shows sufficient route running technique but he doesn't have the full route tree experience of most receivers. He is able to sink his hips into cuts and control his speed, but he's at his best when he's turned loose in a straight line. He lacks the strength to fight through contact when pressed or at the catch point and won't win many jump balls. He often only gets separation with his speed or the threat of it. He does show strong hands in uncovered situations, however. After the catch, he's a playmaker. He regularly creates huge plays with the ball in his hands and explodes into open space. He isn't necessarily shifty or powerful, but he destroys tackling angles.

Schwartz shows some willingness but is not an asset as a run blocker at his play strength. However, he is a constant threat when put in jet motion and forces defenses to react to the idea of him receiving a handoff. He follows his blocks well and can turn the corner for big gains, but he doesn't manufacture yardage for himself if the defense contains the play.

Schwartz projects as a reserve slot receiver in the NFL who should see ample playing time as a gadget player for a creative offense. He'll need to refine his true receiving skills, but he can be used in a variety of ways while he develops. He has not been used as a returner but has high potential there if he becomes comfortable receiving kicks.

Receiving
Year	Trgt	Rec	Comp%	Yds	Air Yds	YAC	TD	ADoT	Yds/Trgt	Drops
2018	35	22	63%	357	91	266	2	7.9	10.2	3
2019	52	41	79%	440	181	259	1	8.6	8.5	3
2020	87	54	62%	636	146	490	3	7.6	7.3	8
	174	117	67%	1433	418	1015	6	7.9	8.2	14

Advanced Receiving
Year	On-Trgt Catch %	Catchable Catch %	YAC/ Rec	Trgt Share	TAE	Rec Rating	EPA Total	Per Trgt	Positive % vs. Man	Positive % vs. Zone
2018	81%	81%	12.1	10%	-0.6	104.1	5.5	0.16	22%	56%
2019	93%	93%	6.3	14%	-0.6	108.3	20.4	0.39	45%	55%
2020	88%	88%	9.1	25%	-0.4	81.4	9.2	0.11	32%	48%
	88%	88%	8.7	16%	-0.5	94.3	35.1	0.20	33%	52%

Route Running / Total Points / Total Points Rtg
Year	Routes Run	Y/RR	Deep Pct	Unique Routes	Slot%	Slot	Wide	Rec Total	Total	Per Route	Per Play
2018	162	2.2	23%	9	38%	5	-2	3	13	70	84
2019	180	2.4	30%	11	39%	1	2	3	10	70	78
2020	442	1.4	17%	13	49%	9	3	13	11	89	85
	784	1.8	22%	17	43%	15	3	19	34	-	-

Critical Factors
Hands	6
Separation	5
Run After Catch	7

Positional Factors
Release	5
Route Running	5
Route Savvy	5
Play Speed	8
Contested Catch	4
Playmaker	7
Tracking	5
Body Control	6
Clutch Performance	6
Blocking	4
Toughness	4

Isaiah McKoy

Report by Ben Hrkach & Joe McDonald

School	Height	Weight	Year	Jersey #	Hometown
Kent State	6021 E	200 E	3JR	23	Brooklyn, NY

One Liner

McKoy's natural athleticism to create separation can be used all over the field, though inconsistent hands and inability to play the ball likely keep him from being a reliable starter at the next level.

Strengths: Separation; Release; Route savvy
Weaknesses: Hands; Tracking; Contested catch

Isaiah McKoy plays outside receiver in Kent State's RPO-heavy offense, but also played a decent amount in the slot. He started 22 of 27 games in his career. He's a live athlete with wiry strength and shows fluidity in his movements. He is highly competitive and always down to scrap with anyone.

McKoy frequently wins at the LOS by varying his release techniques to gain an advantage off the line. Against press, he utilizes a jab step and swipes the hands of the defender, then can use a deke or stutter step to burst as soon as the defender is off balance. Against off coverage, he will use a long stride to close the gap while attacking the toes of the defender. McKoy shows a natural savvy for route running and can adapt his route for different types of coverage. He's good at stemming his route and breaking it off as soon as the defender commits. He's also adept at gaining body position against man and gets separation at the catch point with physicality and adjusting in air. He sets up defenders for later in the game as well. He gives a lot of upper-body movement and forces his defender to respect every action. He's not the most refined route runner, but shows all of the innate skills and athleticism to improve. At the catch point, McKoy isn't a natural hands catcher and will allow it into his body, double catch, and drop easy balls. He's sufficient at tracking and will occasionally not pick up the flight path of the ball. Once in his hands, he's a tough runner with good vision.

McKoy shows strength and feistiness as a run blocker, though he lacks some technique. He has enough speed and running ability to be used on jet sweeps and end arounds.

McKoy's athleticism and innate feel for gaining separation should allow him to be a No. 4 receiver at the next level who can play inside or outside and should be able to contribute from either on 3rd downs with his release and route savvy. He'll also be a contributing member on special teams with additional kick return upside.

Receiving

Year	Trgt	Rec	Comp%	Yds	Air Yds	YAC	TD	ADoT	Yds/Trgt	Drops
2018	81	42	52%	423	222	201	3	10.4	5.2	7
2019	79	57	72%	877	617	260	8	12.8	11.1	3
2020	40	25	63%	455	320	135	5	15.5	11.4	5
	200	124	62%	1755	1159	596	16	12.3	8.8	15

Advanced Receiving

Year	On-Trgt Catch %	Catchable Catch %	YAC/ Rec	Trgt Share	TAE	Rec Rating	EPA Total	EPA Per Trgt	Positive % vs. Man	Positive % vs. Zone
2018	79%	79%	4.8	20%	-2.5	74.3	-8.4	-0.10	38%	30%
2019	95%	95%	4.6	23%	-5.4	142.2	41.6	0.53	45%	61%
2020	85%	85%	5.4	32%	5.6	130.7	12.6	0.32	36%	65%
	87%	87%	4.8	23%	-2.6	112.8	45.8	0.23	40%	54%

Route Running / Total Points

Year	Routes Run	Y/RR	Deep Pct	Unique Routes	Slot%	Slot	Wide	Rec Total	Total	Per Route	Per Play
2018	320	1.3	27%	9	12%	-4	-3	-7	-5	54	54
2019	398	2.2	30%	7	11%	6	11	17	17	88	79
2020	222	2.0	20%	7	10%	-1	11	10	10	98	96
	940	1.9	27%	11	11%	1	19	20	22	-	-

Critical Factors

Hands	5
Separation	6
Run After Catch	5

Positional Factors

Release	6
Route Running	5
Route Savvy	6
Play Speed	5
Contested Catch	5
Playmaker	6
Tracking	5
Body Control	5
Clutch Performance	5
Blocking	5
Toughness	6

Jonathan Adams Jr.

Report by Nathan Cooper

School	Height	Weight	Year	Jersey #	Hometown
Arkansas State	6026 E	220 E	4SR	9	Jonesboro, AR

One Liner

Adams is a highlight reel player who wins with tracking ability and body control, though inconsistent separation, limited RAC ability, and unrefined route running skills likely limits him to being a depth receiver.

Strengths: Makes highlight reel, contested catches; Body control; Tracking ability
Weaknesses: Gets contacted too much; Struggles to separate consistently; Limited RAC ability

Jonathan Adams Jr. normally lines up as a left side receiver in Arkansas State's up-tempo, RPO offense. A high school basketball and track standout, Adams started 24 of 47 games with the Red Wolves. In 2020, he suffered a partially torn MCL that he played through and a hairline fracture in his hip that caused him to miss the final game. He has a big, strong frame with very good size for the position. He's a good athlete and competes with toughness, though lacks some overall play speed.

Adams shows a good release off the LOS. He knows how to beat press at the line with his hands and footwork. He hasn't run much of a route tree, mainly running curls, crossers, and verticals. He runs sufficient routes overall and doesn't seem to be very crisp or sudden. In addition, he gets contacted too often mid-route. He lacks some flexibility which makes it tough for him to consistently win at the top of routes. His separation comes in the form of his size and post-up ability. Adams uses strong hands to catch the ball away from his body. He tracks the ball

well and has the body control to find the ball in the air and adjust to it. This also allows him to consistently make highlight reel and contested catches, making him a clutch performer, as he makes these catches to move the chains or score touchdowns with regularity. He's more of a possession receiver and doesn't have the ability to consistently make defenders miss and create YAC.

As a blocker, Adams is strong at the POA. He's willing to block and when he latches on, he can drive defenders back and stay between man and ball.

Adams projects as a No. 4 receiver mainly lining up on the outside. He profiles best as a big, possession receiver who can thrive in clutch situations and in the red zone. On 3rd downs, he should play on the outside where he can use his big frame to box out defenders and make contested catches. While he doesn't have great speed, he plays fast and hard with good toughness which should allow him to compete on some special teams units.

Receiving

Year	Trgt	Rec	Comp%	Yds	Air Yds	YAC	TD	ADoT	Yds/Trgt	Drops
2017	13	8	62%	77	45	32	1	7.5	5.9	0
2018	39	17	44%	267	184	83	3	13.8	6.8	8
2019	106	62	58%	851	603	248	5	13.9	8.0	2
2020	121	79	65%	1111	857	254	12	14.3	9.2	11
	279	166	59%	2306	1689	617	21	13.8	8.3	21

Advanced Receiving

Year	On-Trgt Catch %	Catchable Catch %	YAC/ Rec	Trgt Share	TAE	Rec Rating	EPA Total	Per Trgt	Positive % vs. Man	vs. Zone
2017	-	100%	4.0	3%	-	103.7	-1.0	-0.08	20%	71%
2018	62%	63%	4.9	8%	3.6	71.2	-3.9	-0.10	44%	25%
2019	94%	85%	4.0	23%	-2.4	88.2	6.3	0.06	39%	55%
2020	83%	83%	3.2	27%	7.4	127.8	56.5	0.47	53%	63%
	83%	82%	3.7	15%	2.7	103.7	57.9	0.21	45%	56%

Route Running / Total Points / Total Points Rtg

Year	Routes Run	Y/RR	Deep Pct	Unique Routes	Slot%	Slot	Wide	Rec Total	Total	Per Route	Per Play
2018	151	1.8	47%	9	18%	-3	-1	-4	-4	52	53
2019	525	1.6	37%	13	8%	0	16	16	18	78	75
2020	623	1.8	29%	14	13%	-3	17	15	15	80	78
	1299	1.7	35%	18	11%	-6	32	27	29	-	-

Critical Factors

Hands	6
Separation	4
Run After Catch	5

Positional Factors

Release	6
Route Running	5
Route Savvy	5
Play Speed	5
Contested Catch	7
Playmaker	6
Tracking	6
Body Control	7
Clutch Performance	7
Blocking	6
Toughness	6

Javon McKinley

Report by Blake Moore

School	Height	Weight	Year	Jersey #	Hometown
Notre Dame	6016 E	215 E	5SR	88	Corona, CA

One Liner

McKinley is a deep-threat receiver who can excel as a run blocker but will need to vastly improve his route-running suddenness before he can be a consistent starter in the NFL.

Strengths: Run blocking; Toughness; Size/speed combo
Weaknesses: Route running ability; After-catch dynamism; Production

Javon McKinley is an outside receiver in Notre Dame's pro-style offense, who also saw snaps out of the slot. He played in 31 games, starting 14 of them. He missed the entire 2017 season recovering from a season-ending foot injury halfway through the previous campaign. He is a big, athletic receiver who has good deep speed to go along with very good toughness but lacks suddenness and agility.

McKinley has good speed and acceleration for a receiver of his size. His route tree was limited at Notre Dame, primarily running verticals, hitches, and shallow crossers. He frequently ran very rounded routes, limiting his ability to separate against tight coverage. When he was able to create separation, he did so with his speed or his physicality with the ball in the air. He's had a few bad drops but was also able to consistently make quality catches in traffic and off his frame. He showed the ability to get downfield, high point, and outmuscle his man to come down with 50/50 chances. After the catch, McKinley was infrequently able to make people miss or break

tackles. He has the speed and toughness to pull away and finish, but doesn't create for himself as a ballcarrier.

McKinley excels as a run blocker with his size, strength, and enthusiasm. In Notre Dame's run-heavy offense, he played a pivotal role in their success on the ground, often knifing inside from wider alignments and cracking corners and linebackers within the box to spring big runs. He regularly finished disinterested run defenders, as well.

McKinley projects best as an outside backup receiver in the pros with his size and speed. His lack of quickness and agility will limit his slot versatility, but he can see the field as a deep ball threat and very strong run blocker to close out games. Injuries and receiver depth limited his college production but he may have his best football ahead of him. His toughness and blocking efforts will immediately project well to special teams duties as he works on the technical aspects of his receiving skills.

				Receiving						
Year	Trgt	Rec	Comp%	Yds	Air Yds	YAC	TD	ADoT	Yds/Trgt	Drops
2016	1	0	0%	0	0	0	0	26.0	0.0	0
2019	20	11	55%	268	152	116	4	12.4	13.4	1
2020	59	42	71%	717	497	220	3	12.4	12.2	3
	80	53	66%	985	649	336	7	12.6	12.3	4

	Advanced Receiving						EPA		Positive %	
Year	On-Trgt Catch %	Catchable Catch %	YAC/ Rec	Trgt Share	TAE	Rec Rating	Total	Per Trgt	vs. Man	vs. Zone
2016	-	-	-	0%	-	39.6	-1.2	-1.21	0%	-
2019	85%	85%	10.5	5%	-9.3	118.8	9.9	0.50	50%	60%
2020	95%	95%	5.2	17%	-7.9	129.0	37.8	0.64	67%	65%
	93%	93%	6.3	7%	-8.4	132.6	46.5	0.58	59%	64%

	Route Running					Total Points			Total Points Rtg	
Year	Routes Run	Y/RR	Deep Pct	Unique Routes	Slot%	Slot	Wide	Rec Total	Total	Per Route	Per Play
2019	138	1.9	47%	6	25%	0	3	3	3	71	64
2020	616	1.2	27%	13	30%	3	12	15	16	83	82
	756	1.3	31%	13	29%	4	14	18	19	-	-

Critical Factors	
Hands	6
Separation	5
Run After Catch	4

Positional Factors	
Release	5
Route Running	4
Route Savvy	4
Play Speed	6
Contested Catch	6
Playmaker	6
Tracking	6
Body Control	6
Clutch Performance	5
Blocking	7
Toughness	7

Blake Proehl

Report by Joe McDonald

School	Height	Weight	Year	Jersey #	Hometown
East Carolina	6002 E	186 E	4JR	11	Charlotte, NC

One Liner
Proehl is a twitchy route runner with good hands and footwork, but needs to improve his release, separation, and run-after-catch abilities to be a starting receiver at the NFL level.

Strengths: Hands; Quick feet; Route running
Weaknesses: Release vs. press; Run after catch; Playmaking ability

Blake Proehl is a wide receiver for East Carolina's spread, RPO-heavy offense typically lining up outside, but occasionally sliding into the slot. He started 22 of 31 career games. He missed all of 2017 after tearing his ACL in fall camp and also missed the final 2 games of 2018 with shoulder surgery. His father, Ricky, played 17 seasons in the NFL. He is a well-built receiver despite his size with long arms and a frame that should support him adding more weight. He has a high motor and gives a good level of effort on a consistent basis.

In the pass game, Proehl uses quickness off the line of scrimmage to get a clean release from defenders. However, when releasing against press, he struggles with the hand fighting aspect and gets jammed up at times, struggling to gain separation. He uses his quick feet in his routes as well, stemming defenders away from where his route is heading or making sharp cuts at the top of routes to get enough separation. He shows some twitch at the top of routes and mixes up speed well to create separation. He is typically a hand catcher who can pluck the ball away from his body and has the ability to make catches with defenders contesting him. He's not much of a playmaker with the ball in his hands and isn't going to consistently make defenders miss or break many tackles, but shows some skills with finesse moves, such as jukes to create some occasional additional yardage.

In the run game, Proehl is a willing blocker with good aggression. However, he lacks some strength at the POA in order to consistently sustain blocks on the edge.

Proehl projects as a No. 4 wide receiver where his speed and quickness allow him to work best inside, though he could see the occasional wide rep. He has the athleticism and technical skills to contribute on all three downs out of the slot. His toughness and speed should allow him to see reps as a contributor on special teams units as well as bringing return ability.

Receiving

Year	Trgt	Rec	Comp%	Yds	Air Yds	YAC	TD	ADoT	Yds/Trgt	Drops
2018	46	29	63%	329	218	111	1	8.8	7.2	1
2019	85	53	62%	658	533	125	4	12.6	7.7	1
2020	66	47	71%	577	414	163	4	10.8	8.7	2
	197	129	65%	1564	1165	399	9	11.1	7.9	4

Advanced Receiving

Year	On-Trgt Catch %	Catchable Catch %	YAC/ Rec	Trgt Share	TAE	Rec Rating	EPA Total	Per Trgt	Positive % vs. Man	vs. Zone
2018	85%	83%	3.8	9%	-8.0	91.7	12.6	0.27	42%	68%
2019	94%	92%	2.4	19%	-1.5	97.1	21.1	0.25	39%	63%
2020	92%	92%	3.5	23%	5.8	105.4	16.2	0.25	59%	58%
	91%	90%	3.1	16%	-1.9	98.6	50.0	0.25	47%	62%

Route Running / Total Points / Total Points Rtg

Year	Routes Run	Y/RR	Deep Pct	Unique Routes	Slot%	Slot	Wide	Rec Total	Total	Per Route	Per Play
2018	294	1.1	40%	12	78%	4	0	4	4	67	62
2019	435	1.5	49%	13	8%	5	19	24	24	90	80
2020	387	1.5	26%	10	7%	3	10	13	13	87	83
	1116	1.4	39%	15	25%	12	29	41	41	-	-

Critical Factors

Hands	6
Separation	5
Run After Catch	4

Positional Factors

Release	5
Route Running	6
Route Savvy	6
Play Speed	6
Contested Catch	6
Playmaker	4
Tracking	6
Body Control	6
Clutch Performance	6
Blocking	5
Toughness	6

Ben Skowronek

Report by Noah Chang

School	Height	Weight	Year	Jersey #	Hometown
Notre Dame	6027 V	211 V	5SR	11	Fort Wayne, IN

One Liner

Skowronek is a physical receiver with contested-catch ability and tough blocking, but without better agility and route separation he'll struggle to impact regular passing downs.

Strengths: Contested catches; Catch radius; Run blocking
Weaknesses: Route separation; Play speed; Footwork and agility

Ben Skowronek is a wideout in Notre Dame's pro-style offense. He played 4 years at Northwestern before suffering a season-ending ankle injury and then grad transferring in 2020. He then missed 2 games due to a hamstring injury and had his Senior Bowl week cut short with a potentially serious foot injury. Overall, he played in 53 games and started 40 of them. Skowronek is a stoutly-built big receiver who lacks agility. Skowronek is competitive and displays a workman-like toughness at the catch point and as a blocker.

Skowronek has a sufficient release off the line. He is a long strider with sufficient speed but isn't a burner downfield. On shorter routes he rounds his cuts and isn't able to make sudden moves without extra steps. Skowronek also has issues decelerating into his breaks. Despite his size, he can be thrown off his route against length and physicality. He doesn't consistently find holes in zones and will take himself into traffic. Despite all of that, Skowronek is comfortable operating without space and making tough hands catches in traffic short and deep. He tracks the ball well and is a good post-up target. He has good control of his body in the air and a wide catch radius. He is a physical runner who doesn't shy away from contact but won't make people miss downfield.

Skowronek is more than a willing blocker. He mirrors defensive backs and fits in space very well, with a good understanding of how to shield himself between them and the ball. He also cracks down on linebackers well and showed versatility to seal run lanes in the box and on the perimeter.

Skowronek projects as a backup receiver who brings value to a team with his size and physicality in the red zone and as a blocker. He'll need to improve the sharpness in his route running to see regular playing time, but he's proven to be a player who doesn't need much separation to still make an impact. He should be a very good special teams player with his competitive toughness.

Receiving										
Year	Trgt	Rec	Comp%	Yds	Air Yds	YAC	TD	ADoT	Yds/Trgt	Drops
2016	29	8	28%	70	67	3	0	12.4	2.4	4
2017	78	45	58%	644	516	128	5	12.5	8.3	6
2018	77	45	58%	562	423	139	3	11.6	7.3	1
2020	45	29	64%	444	252	192	5	11.0	9.9	2
	246	139	57%	1861	1362	499	13	11.6	7.6	14

Advanced Receiving							EPA		Positive %	
Year	On-Trgt Catch %	Catchable Catch %	YAC/ Rec	Trgt Share	TAE	Rec Rating	Total	Per Trgt	vs. Man	vs. Zone
2016	-	62%	0.4	6%	-	25.2	-9.6	-0.33	31%	27%
2017	-	83%	2.8	17%	-	100.6	17.0	0.22	43%	58%
2018	83%	80%	3.1	15%	-2.7	67.1	1.6	0.02	47%	58%
2020	97%	97%	6.6	13%	-5.1	133.9	22.6	0.50	50%	54%
	89%	84%	3.6	12%	-3.2	84.8	34.8	0.14	47%	53%

Route Running					Total Points				Total Points Rtg	
Year	Routes Run	Y/RR	Deep Pct	Unique Routes	Slot%	Slot	Wide	Rec Total	Total	Per Route	Per Play
2018	428	1.3	33%	9	25%	0	1	1	1	61	58
2020	476	0.9	22%	9	18%	4	7	11	13	80	80
	984	1.2	26%	10	24%	5	10	15	17	-	-

Redshirt season not shown but included in totals

Critical Factors	
Hands	6
Separation	4
Run After Catch	5

Positional Factors	
Release	5
Route Running	4
Route Savvy	5
Play Speed	5
Contested Catch	6
Playmaker	5
Tracking	6
Body Control	5
Clutch Performance	5
Blocking	7
Toughness	6

Brandon Smith

Final Grade: 5.8

Report by Jeff Dean & Christian Vega

School	Height	Weight	Year	Jersey #	Hometown
Iowa	6010 E	215 E	4SR	12	Lake Cormorant, MS

One Liner

Smith has the measurables and footwork to make it as an NFL receiver, but he will need to show he can open up his route tree and make plays consistently to earn regular time.

Strengths: Release and acceleration; Footwork at top of routes; Physicality
Weaknesses: Route tree experience; Big play creation; Consistent hands

Brandon Smith is an X receiver in Iowa's run-heavy offense. He played in 39 career games with 27 starts. He missed a game in 2018 with a concussion and 4 games in 2019 with a right ankle bone bruise. Smith has good size and muscle definition throughout. He has a good burst and quick feet to get up to top speed quickly. He is an emotional player who plays with an attitude and can get chippy at times but does well to keep it in check.

Smith has multiple quick releases he uses off the line based on the leverage of the defender. He runs hard and breaks down at the top of his route to explode through the break. His route tree in Iowa's offense was limited, but he's capable of more. When running routes that don't utilize sharp cuts, he can struggle to get separation against man coverage. Smith uses his off hand well at the top of routes but has a tendency to get tied up with more physical cornerbacks. His hands are inconsistent, habitually body catching rather than snatching the ball from the air. His physicality through his route running doesn't translate to the catch point, as he is merely sufficient in contested situations and doesn't show up in the red zone often. Smith has enough burst and bulk to get a few extra yards after the catch, but he is more of a chain mover and struggled to manufacture big plays on his own.

Smith shows sufficient blocking ability with inconsistent effort. He has the frame and physicality to handle smaller defenders, but seems tentative at times and doesn't attack. He has the potential to be a good blocker if he brings the same energy in the run game that he does when running routes.

Smith projects as a reserve receiver in the NFL with slight inside-out flexibility but probably best fitting in the slot. He struggles to compete with length and superior vertical athletes on the perimeter. He has some potential to see the field in a more open, downfield passing offense. He has the size and strength to be a quality special teams player.

Receiving

Year	Trgt	Rec	Comp%	Yds	Air Yds	YAC	TD	ADoT	Yds/Trgt	Drops
2017	6	3	50%	15	-3	18	0	0.2	2.5	0
2018	51	28	55%	357	290	67	2	13.1	7.0	4
2019	53	37	70%	439	344	95	5	11.6	8.3	2
2020	41	23	56%	231	179	52	2	11.1	5.6	4
	151	91	60%	1042	810	232	9	11.5	6.9	10

Advanced Receiving

Year	On-Trgt Catch %	Catchable Catch %	YAC/Rec	Trgt Share	TAE	Rec Rating	EPA Total	Per Trgt	Positive % vs. Man	vs. Zone
2017	-	75%	6.0	2%	-	56.3	-8.0	-1.33	0%	0%
2018	90%	90%	2.4	13%	-4.6	74.0	8.8	0.17	52%	50%
2019	86%	86%	2.6	14%	-2.4	126.2	25.2	0.48	44%	66%
2020	85%	85%	2.3	17%	-4.6	88.6	3.6	0.09	75%	39%
	87%	86%	2.5	11%	-3.8	95.5	29.6	0.20	51%	52%

Route Running / Total Points

Year	Routes Run	Y/RR	Deep Pct	Unique Routes	Slot%	Slot	Wide	Rec Total	Total	Per Route	Per Play
2018	289	1.2	44%	10	19%	2	7	8	10	76	75
2019	231	1.9	45%	10	23%	0	11	10	11	83	81
2020	386	0.6	16%	12	22%	0	2	2	3	66	66
	906	1.1	32%	14	21%	1	20	20	24	-	-

Critical Factors

Hands	5
Separation	5
Run After Catch	5

Positional Factors

Release	6
Route Running	6
Route Savvy	5
Play Speed	6
Contested Catch	5
Playmaker	5
Tracking	5
Body Control	5
Clutch Performance	5
Blocking	5
Toughness	5

Khalil McClain

Report by Jacob Halleen & Spencer Schultz

School	Height	Weight	Year	Jersey #	Hometown
Troy	6030 V	217 V	4SR	6	Fairburn, GA

One Liner

McClain's big frame, body control, and catch-point athleticism can make him a jump-ball threat at the next level, but his lack of speed and elusiveness before and after the catch may limit his ceiling.

Strengths: Contested catch radius; Stacking and positioning; Tracking and body control
Weaknesses: Run-after-catch ability; Play speed; Route sharpness

Khalil McClain played primarily outside receiver in Troy's spread offense. He played in 23 games for Troy with 20 starts. He began his career as a quarterback at Tulane and played 2 games as a reserve before transferring to Hutchinson CC, moving to WR, and then ending up at Troy. He has a big frame and strong build. He's a sufficient athlete and lacks top-end speed, but has some suddenness for his size. He shows a consistent motor and can be a bully at the catch point.

McClain uses quick feet to vary his releases but has trouble against press coverage. He does a good job of stacking his man and using his big frame to win positioning, despite not running the most crisp routes. While not fast, he has good speed control to change gears through vertical routes. He makes up for inconsistently sharp route running with good route savvy with his off hand, subtle head fakes, and having great control of his body to adjust to off-target throws. He separates mostly with his size, sufficient route suddenness, and catch radius. He tracks the ball well and can go up over a defense to make catches. He is a good competitor in contested situations and plucks the ball off his frame with strong hands, but he's prone to body catches when uncovered. After the catch, McClain's big body can be tough to bring down, but he doesn't show any elusiveness or breakaway speed and has limited production creating yards for himself.

McClain shows a willingness and aggression to block and does so effectively. He uses his strength and strong hands to sustain blocks and drive defenders back. He needs to take better angles to better position himself and refine his technique, but his physicality is a positive trait in the running game.

McClain projects as a potential fifth receiver at the next level who best fits on the outside and as a strong red zone threat. His size, catch radius and savvy are ready-made while he develops his route technique. His lack of dynamism after the catch doesn't project well as a returner, but he should be a good blocker on return units.

				Receiving						
Year	Trgt	Rec	Comp%	Yds	Air Yds	YAC	TD	ADoT	Yds/Trgt	Drops
2019	69	45	65%	562	470	92	7	12.0	8.1	1
2020	53	32	60%	383	271	112	6	12.1	7.2	3
	122	77	63%	945	741	204	13	12.0	7.7	4

	Advanced Receiving						EPA		Positive %	
Year	On-Trgt Catch %	Catchable Catch %	YAC/Rec	Trgt Share	TAE	Rec Rating	Total	Per Trgt	vs. Man	vs. Zone
2019	96%	96%	2.0	14%	-5.7	100.0	21.4	0.31	61%	58%
2020	84%	84%	3.5	12%	-4.2	112.4	13.1	0.25	47%	46%
	90%	90%	2.6	13%	-5.0	105.4	34.5	0.28	54%	54%

	Route Running					Total Points				Total Points Rtg	
Year	Routes Run	Y/RR	Deep Pct	Unique Routes	Slot%	Slot	Wide	Rec Total	Total	Per Route	Per Play
2019	396	1.4	44%	13	7%	1	12	13	15	78	76
2020	440	0.9	32%	11	10%	0	3	3	3	65	64
	836	1.1	38%	15	8%	1	14	16	18	-	-

Critical Factors	
Hands	6
Separation	6
Run After Catch	4

Positional Factors	
Release	5
Route Running	5
Route Savvy	6
Play Speed	5
Contested Catch	6
Playmaker	5
Tracking	6
Body Control	7
Clutch Performance	6
Blocking	6
Toughness	6

Tre Walker

Report by Joe McDonald & Ryan Newman

School	Height	Weight	Year	Jersey #	Hometown
San Jose State	5110 E	175 E	4SR	10	Inglewood, CA

One Liner

Walker has the hands to make contested grabs with consistency and the RAC ability to make plays, but lacks the precise route-running ability and separation skills needed to be more than just a depth receiver.

Strengths: Catch in traffic; RAC playmaking ability
Weaknesses: Separation; Precise route running; Raw speed

Tre Walker is a left wide receiver in San Jose State's spread, pass-heavy offense, and occasionally slides into the slot in certain formations. He started 25 of 39 games for the Spartans. He tore his ACL in 2017. He has a shorter, slight frame, but plays bigger than listed. He's a good athlete who plays with a high motor and tough competitive spirit.

Walker has solid hands, but has shown enough drops of simple passes to cause concern. He consistently struggles to get separation due to his routes not being disguised well and his lack of precise cuts in and out of routes, but is occasionally able to get separation using his quickness and acceleration. For his size, he shows an advanced ability to make difficult catches through traffic with strong hands and good body control to adjust to the pass. He also shows good sideline awareness, being able to make contested grabs while keeping his feet in bounds. Walker consistently catches using his hands rather than his body, but will use his body on routes across the middle to brace for any potential hits. Although not fast, he has enough wiggle and slipperiness to typically make the first defender miss, and tends to finish his runs, putting his shoulder down and gaining hard yards.

In the run game, Walker is a tough, willing, and capable blocker. He typically shows consistency, but lacks some strength at the POA. Although he's only received a single rushing attempt in college, he has the elusiveness and run-after-catch ability to be a viable threat for end arounds and jet sweeps.

Walker projects as a No. 5 receiver at the NFL level, fitting best in the slot, though he could play on the outside in certain formations. On 3rd downs, he fits best in the slot where he can make catches across the middle and use his RAC ability to move the chains. His athleticism and enough speed and toughness should allow him to be a minimal contributor on special teams; however, his tracking ability could make him a punt return option at the next level.

Receiving

Year	Trgt	Rec	Comp%	Yds	Air Yds	YAC	TD	ADoT	Yds/Trgt	Drops
2017	38	26	68%	288	170	118	1	9.2	7.6	2
2018	59	39	66%	714	595	119	5	15.6	12.1	2
2019	118	79	67%	1161	756	405	2	10.3	9.8	7
2020	73	45	62%	625	335	290	4	9.2	8.6	6
	288	189	66%	2788	1856	932	12	10.9	9.7	17

Advanced Receiving

Year	On-Trgt Catch %	Catchable Catch %	YAC/Rec	Trgt Share	TAE	Rec Rating	EPA Total	EPA Per Trgt	Positive % vs. Man	Positive % vs. Zone
2017	-	90%	4.3	9%	-	98.8	3.5	0.09	71%	56%
2018	95%	93%	3.1	13%	-3.4	121.6	28.4	0.48	62%	50%
2019	87%	86%	5.1	24%	4.0	101.0	53.0	0.45	51%	69%
2020	88%	86%	6.4	26%	1.6	107.4	14.3	0.20	50%	52%
	89%	88%	4.9	18%	1.3	106.5	99.2	0.34	54%	58%

Route Running / Total Points

Year	Routes Run	Y/RR	Deep Pct	Unique Routes	Slot%	Slot	Wide	Rec Total	Total	Per Route	Per Play
2018	244	2.9	38%	10	19%	5	11	16	16	93	90
2019	435	2.7	33%	17	16%	0	26	25	26	91	89
2020	402	1.6	18%	12	22%	1	11	12	12	84	79
	1081	2.3	28%	19	19%	6	48	53	54	-	-

Critical Factors

Hands	5
Separation	5
Run After Catch	6

Positional Factors

Release	5
Route Running	5
Route Savvy	5
Play Speed	5
Contested Catch	6
Playmaker	6
Tracking	6
Body Control	6
Clutch Performance	6
Blocking	5
Toughness	5

Simi Fehoko

Report by Ben Hrkach

School	Height	Weight	Year	Jersey #	Hometown
Stanford	6032 E	227 E	3SO	13	Sandy, UT

One Liner

Fehoko is a big-play threat that can play as a big-body receiver, but his inability to consistently separate before the catch point will limit his playing time.

Strengths: Big plays; Downfield speed; Winning at the catch point
Weaknesses: Separation; Release; Route running

Simi Fehoko plays WR in Stanford's vertical passing offense, mostly lining up out wide but also seeing regular time in the slot. He started 5 of 22 games played. The top recruit in the state of Utah, Fehoko completed a two-year LDS mission before arriving at Stanford. He comes from a long family of D-I athletes and has a tall, strong frame. He is a smooth athlete with easy speed and good body control, as well as requisite competitive toughness.

Fehoko is a constant threat to take the top off of the defense and uses his size well. He runs primarily vertical routes with a few slants, drags, and screens. He struggles against physicality off the snap. He shows some suddenness in his route running, but does not maintain speed in and out of cuts. Fehoko wins at the catch point consistently. He has good tracking skills, high points the ball, and can snatch it out of the defender's hands. He is also adept at using late hands on go balls and back shoulders to keep tight coverage unaware. Fehoko is a natural hands catcher that can make spectacular catches as well as contested ones. He will have some concentration drops and is clearly hesitant when going across the middle. Fehoko does show sufficient savvy against the zone and more often than not will find a soft spot. Once the ball is in his hands, he has speed to run away from players and the power to run through arm tackles but is not very shifty.

Fehoko was not asked to participate much in the run game. Stanford had a separate package for run situations and he was not on the field for it. When he did attempt to block, he showed sufficient physicality and tenacity.

Fehoko projects as a reserve receiver with some inside-out flexibility in a vertical offense at the next level. His lack of separation skills with his route running will limit him, but he has a knack for big plays with his combination of size and speed. He has the size, strength, athleticism, and mindset to contribute on all four special teams units.

				Receiving						
Year	Trgt	Rec	Comp%	Yds	Air Yds	YAC	TD	ADoT	Yds/Trgt	Drops
2018	3	1	33%	6	6	0	0	7.0	2.0	0
2019	54	24	44%	566	401	165	6	20.9	10.5	3
2020	59	37	63%	574	368	206	3	11.8	9.7	5
	116	62	53%	1146	775	371	9	15.9	9.9	8

	Advanced Receiving						EPA		Positive %	
Year	On-Trgt Catch %	Catchable Catch %	YAC/ Rec	Trgt Share	TAE	Rec Rating	Total	Per Trgt	vs. Man	vs. Zone
2018	100%	100%	0.0	1%	-19.4	42.4	-1.9	-0.65	0%	0%
2019	77%	77%	6.9	12%	-4.7	112.1	16.4	0.30	45%	39%
2020	86%	86%	5.6	27%	7.1	104.8	23.3	0.39	58%	57%
	83%	83%	6.0	11%	-1.0	106.5	37.7	0.33	50%	47%

	Route Running					Total Points			Total Points Rtg	
Year	Routes Run	Y/RR	Deep Pct	Unique Routes	Slot%	Slot	Wide	Rec Total	Total	Per Route	Per Play
2018	28	0.2	74%	2	18%	0	-1	-1	0	52	78
2019	264	2.1	66%	11	42%	8	4	12	12	83	83
2020	250	2.3	34%	8	29%	6	8	14	14	95	94
	542	2.1	53%	11	36%	14	11	25	26	-	-

Critical Factors	
Hands	6
Separation	4
Run After Catch	5

Positional Factors	
Release	4
Route Running	5
Route Savvy	5
Play Speed	6
Contested Catch	6
Playmaker	7
Tracking	6
Body Control	6
Clutch Performance	5
Blocking	5
Toughness	6

Bailey Gaither

Report by Nathan Cooper

School	Height	Weight	Year	Jersey #	Hometown
San Jose State	6000 E	182 E	6SR	84	Paso Robles, CA

One Liner

Gaither has the speed, quick release against press, and natural hands to produce out of the slot at the next level, but a lack of strength, overall savvy, and separation just make him a depth receiver.

Strengths: Play speed; Release off the line; Natural hands
Weaknesses: Rerouted against physical defenders; Lacks some savvy; Weak blocker

Bailey Gaither plays the X and Z receiver in San Jose State's spread offense, occasionally sliding into the slot as well. The 24-year old played in 44 games with 26 starts for the Spartans. In 2018, he ruptured his Achilles and missed 8 games. He has a lanky frame that lacks bulk, though it should allow him to add some weight and muscle. He's a quick-twitch athlete who plays fast and competes as a route runner.

Gaither shows speed and quickness in his releases off the line. When up against press, he uses good technique and quick feet to avoid contact. When not pressed, he's fluid off the line using speed to get into his route quickly. He's a precise route runner and ran a good majority of the route tree, with his main routes being screens, curls/comebacks, digs, and posts. He mainly wins with his speed and route running. When up against physical defenders, he can get rerouted and taken out of the play fairly often and easily. Due to his frame, he needs to be better with his savvy in order to set up his routes and steer clear of contact from defenders. Gaither possesses strong hands and does a good job of catching the ball away from his body. He has a good catch radius, making receptions outside his frame. He easily tracks the ball down the field and can stretch the defense. After the catch, he uses his speed to run away from defenders and make some occasionally miss, but won't break many tackles.

Gaither's block willingness is hot and cold, and most of the time he just hopes being in the way is enough. When he does latch on, he doesn't possess the play strength to sustain the block for very long.

Gaither projects as a No. 5 receiver working out of the slot where he can use his speed and release off the line and either work across the field or stretch the defense vertically, especially on 3rd downs. He has the skill set to occasionally work on the outside, but will need to get stronger before he can consistently. His play speed and toughness should play on special teams, but he likely won't be a core contributor.

Receiving

Year	Trgt	Rec	Comp%	Yds	Air Yds	YAC	TD	ADoT	Yds/Trgt	Drops
2017	39	21	54%	318	221	97	4	17.4	8.2	1
2018	35	16	46%	327	241	86	3	14.8	9.3	2
2019	100	52	52%	812	588	224	6	16.6	8.1	7
2020	60	41	68%	725	458	267	4	13.0	12.1	3
	240	133	55%	2224	1538	686	18	15.6	9.3	14

Advanced Receiving

Year	On-Trgt Catch %	Catchable Catch %	YAC/Rec	Trgt Share	TAE	Rec Rating	EPA Total	EPA Per Trgt	Positive % vs. Man	Positive % vs. Zone
2017	-	84%	4.6	10%	-	104.4	6.7	0.17	45%	57%
2018	84%	80%	5.4	8%	15.8	83.9	-1.1	-0.03	47%	33%
2019	80%	78%	4.3	21%	9.5	90.9	10.4	0.10	46%	50%
2020	84%	84%	6.5	21%	3.3	124.7	32.9	0.55	72%	60%
	82%	81%	5.2	12%	8.5	101.5	52.3	0.22	50%	50%

Route Running / Total Points / Total Points Rtg

Year	Routes Run	Y/RR	Deep Pct	Unique Routes	Slot%	Slot	Wide	Rec Total	Total	Per Route	Per Play
2018	92	3.6	33%	7	74%	4	5	8	9	98	97
2019	391	2.1	37%	12	5%	3	15	19	19	87	84
2020	340	2.1	21%	10	9%	4	6	12	11	88	85
	823	2.3	29%	14	15%	11	26	39	39	-	-

Critical Factors

Hands	6
Separation	5
Run After Catch	5

Positional Factors

Release	6
Route Running	6
Route Savvy	5
Play Speed	6
Contested Catch	5
Playmaker	5
Tracking	6
Body Control	6
Clutch Performance	6
Blocking	3
Toughness	5

Redshirt season not shown but included in totals

Marlon Williams

Report by Jordan Edwards

School	Height	Weight	Year	Jersey #	Hometown
UCF	5116 E	215 E	4SR	6	Mobile, AL

One Liner
Williams' unique body type and RAC ability can help him carve out a backup role, but his lack of separation and limited route tree can hinder his ability to see the field on a consistent level.

Strengths: RAC ability; Hands; Body control
Weaknesses: Separation; Release; Limited route tree

Marlon Williams mainly lines up as a slot receiver in UCF's RPO offense. He started 16 of 46 career games. He has a unique body type for a slot player and looks more like a running back rather than receiver. He lacks length, but has good body control and short-area quickness. Williams shows toughness as a ballcarrier and has made some tough acrobatic catches while absorbing contact as well.

Williams shows good hands keeping the ball away from his body and rarely double catching passes. He shows some fearlessness coming across the middle absorbing big hits at the catch point. He does have a few drops in traffic, but they are few and far between. He fails to create separation on a consistent level downfield and lacks desired long speed. Due to UCF's scheme, he ran a limited route tree, mostly running quick screens, slants, and curls, but he does show good awareness as a route runner finding soft areas in zones and working back to his quarterback when plays break down. Williams doesn't show a variety of releases off the line, though has the

physicality to work through defenders in press. He shows good tracking ability and has the body control to adjust to off-target throws. However, due to his smaller frame and lack of length, he struggles in contested-catch situations down the field. He shows toughness as a runner after the catch and, while not shifty, he can break tackles and has the physicality to fight for extra yards.

Williams has the toughness and physicality to be a good blocker in the run game, but fails to show the willingness and desire on a consistent level. He was used in a variety of roles as a blocker at the collegiate level, even being a lead back in some run schemes.

Williams can serve as a backup big slot receiver at the next level in a pass-heavy offense where he can work as a short and intermediate receiving threat. He does have special teams experience as a returner, and his physicality and toughness can translate into becoming a part of a core special teams unit.

Receiving

Year	Trgt	Rec	Comp%	Yds	Air Yds	YAC	TD	ADoT	Yds/Trgt	Drops
2017	25	17	68%	270	146	124	2	10.6	10.8	1
2018	25	18	72%	234	141	93	1	8.7	9.4	2
2019	69	51	74%	717	273	444	6	7.7	10.4	4
2020	104	71	68%	1039	582	457	10	9.8	10.0	5
	223	157	70%	2260	1142	1118	19	9.1	10.1	12

Advanced Receiving

Year	On-Trgt Catch %	Catchable Catch %	YAC/Rec	Trgt Share	TAE	Rec Rating	EPA Total	Per Trgt	Positive % vs. Man	vs. Zone
2017	-	94%	7.3	6%	-	97.1	8.1	0.32	67%	60%
2018	90%	90%	5.2	7%	-1.5	97.8	6.4	0.26	62%	67%
2019	92%	92%	8.7	15%	-7.1	136.0	33.0	0.48	52%	56%
2020	86%	85%	6.4	26%	6.5	128.6	49.7	0.48	46%	70%
	89%	89%	7.1	14%	-0.8	123.9	97.2	0.44	52%	64%

Route Running / Total Points

Year	Routes Run	Y/RR	Deep Pct	Unique Routes	Slot%	Slot	Wide	Rec Total	Total	Per Route	Per Play
2018	91	2.6	31%	6	38%	3	0	3	6	75	81
2019	343	2.1	19%	14	87%	11	2	13	15	84	75
2020	548	1.9	11%	10	83%	28	2	30	31	99	98
	982	2.0	16%	16	77%	42	3	46	52	-	-

Critical Factors

Hands	6
Separation	4
Run After Catch	6

Positional Factors

Release	5
Route Running	5
Route Savvy	6
Play Speed	5
Contested Catch	5
Playmaker	5
Tracking	6
Body Control	6
Clutch Performance	5
Blocking	5
Toughness	6

Whop Philyor

Report by Michael Churchward & Ryan Rubinstein

School	Height	Weight	Year	Jersey #	Hometown
Indiana	5096 E	180 E	4SR	1	Tampa, FL

One Liner
Philyor has good speed, hands, and route savviness to find ways to get open and produce, but he lacks electric playmaking skills to become more than a reliable reserve out of the slot.

Strengths: Natural hands; Ability to find holes in zone
Weaknesses: Separation against man coverage; Playmaking ability; Size and strength

Whop Philyor is a slot receiver in Indiana's spread RPO offense. He played 38 career games and started 21. He was limited to only 7 games in 2018 due to a high-ankle sprain and tore his LCL in 2019. He's a smaller wide receiver with a narrow frame. He has good speed and quick feet in small spaces. He doesn't show much aggression at contact to finish runs.

Philyor does a good job as a reliable underneath option to move the chains. He's usually schemed for free releases but has been decent at maneuvering around press when faced with it. He has short-area quickness but isn't a refined route runner and struggles to separate against tight man coverage. What he does do consistently well is work to open areas of the field and adjust his routes to find creases within zone coverage, then making himself available to his quarterback. He does a good job of finding seams downfield and can make the occasional big play with his speed. He has natural hands to catch the ball off his body but lacks much of a catch radius.

After the catch, he's a sufficient ballcarrier who can gain yards straight-line but lacks the toughness to fight through contact or special elusiveness to consistently make defenders miss.

Philyor wasn't asked to block much at all, usually running screens behind RPO runs or being removed in heavier personnels. When he did need to block, he did not show a strong willingness to mix it up physically, and his size would suggest he'd struggle to do so even with improved effort. He did play some running back in high school and has shown the flexibility to receive jet sweeps.

Philyor best projects as a backup slot receiver in a spread offense in the NFL. He should work well on crossers and as a solid checkdown option and chain mover on third downs, but he won't threaten defenses with his elusiveness before or after the catch much. He has solid hands and could continue to be a safe but unspectacular punt return option.

Receiving

Year	Trgt	Rec	Comp%	Yds	Air Yds	YAC	TD	ADoT	Yds/Trgt	Drops
2017	46	33	72%	335	132	203	3	4.9	7.3	4
2018	30	23	77%	235	73	162	1	4.1	7.8	2
2019	102	70	69%	987	495	492	5	10.4	9.7	7
2020	91	54	59%	495	257	238	3	8.2	5.4	3
	269	180	67%	2052	957	1095	12	8.0	7.6	16

Advanced Receiving

Year	On-Trgt Catch %	Catchable Catch %	YAC/ Rec	Trgt Share	TAE	Rec Rating	EPA Total	Per Trgt	Positive % vs. Man	vs. Zone
2017	-	86%	6.2	9%	-	104.3	14.5	0.32	57%	69%
2018	88%	88%	7.0	7%	0.1	109.7	10.2	0.34	71%	53%
2019	89%	89%	7.0	23%	3.3	110.7	30.4	0.30	46%	51%
2020	93%	91%	4.6	32%	5.1	80.6	-4.6	-0.05	39%	42%
	90%	89%	6.1	16%	3.5	99.3	50.5	0.19	48%	51%

Route Running / Total Points

Year	Routes Run	Y/RR	Deep Pct	Unique Routes	Slot%	Slot	Wide	Rec Total	Total	Per Route	Per Play
2018	113	2.1	19%	8	84%	4	0	-1	2	59	61
2019	365	2.7	29%	16	91%	17	1	18	18	89	86
2020	452	1.1	20%	14	76%	10	8	19	19	93	93
	930	1.8	24%	19	84%	31	10	36	39	-	-

Critical Factors

Hands	6
Separation	5
Run After Catch	5

Positional Factors

Release	5
Route Running	5
Route Savvy	6
Play Speed	6
Contested Catch	4
Playmaker	5
Tracking	5
Body Control	6
Clutch Performance	5
Blocking	3
Toughness	4

Tight Ends

Alex Vigderman

Tight ends are arguably the most trying position to evaluate because, at the peak of the position, the skills required are quite varied. A true every-down tight end has to be able to move defenders off the ball in the run game, handle the agility and power of increasingly specialized edge rushers, and get open and make plays as a receiver.

In this section, we give you the tools to evaluate the position in every relevant dimension.

Given recent trends in the NFL and at the position, the receiver traits are most important. We offer a full complement of advanced metrics that we use to evaluate receivers.

"How are his hands?"

We have two different Catch Rates, one for catchable throws and one for on-target throws. Think of these as catch rate on throws that are plausible to catch and on throws that are right on the money, respectively. After all, we want to measure catching ability and it's not fair to punish a player for an inaccurate quarterback.

"Can he threaten the defense at the second level?"

Average Depth of Target (ADoT) is the most projectable stat for receivers as they enter the NFL, so if you can stretch the field in college, you're probably going to do so as a professional. Of course, it helps to be able to make plays after the catch, and we have Yards After Catch per Reception to illustrate that. If you can be above average at both, now you're really a threat.

"Can he get open?"

On average, NFL tight ends are spending more than a quarter of their time split out from the formation, so they need to get open against defensive backs and not just linebackers. You can see in the Deep Dive for each player how often he is split out, and additionally can see how he fared against both man and zone coverages. Man coverage at the NFL level is a whole different ball game than at the college level, so watch out for stragglers in that regard.

This season there's one top-of-the-first-round talent at the position in Kyle Pitts, and he checks those boxes with aplomb. He led the position in yards and touchdowns and didn't drop a pass in his final season in Gainesville, and he offers an athletic profile that will make your mouth water.

In the same mold but perhaps not as likely to overcome limitations as a blocker is Brevin Jordan, He pops athletically and statistically (check out that 99 Total Points Rating as a receiver) but grades both on film and statistically as an inferior blocker to Pitts.

Blocking is not only a less crucial skill set for a tight end, but it's also harder to evaluate, especially statistically. Blocking involves so much interaction between players that we focus on identifiable events like blown blocks and runs directly behind a player to determine how effective he is.

Among the top players at the position, the most productive blocker (according to our Total Points calculation) has been Pat Freiermuth, despite a 2020 season in which he was both less effective and less frequent a blocker than he had been prior. It's a testament to his effectiveness that he still easily paced Pitts and Jordan in terms of Blocking Total Points over their careers.

From a scouting perspective, Luke Farrell and Tony Poljan show very good traits in the blocking game, and unsurprisingly were split out from the formation as little as anyone at the position. They also have shown similar statistical profiles overall, both in terms of solid blocking and less exciting receiving exploits.

The tight end section benefits as much as any from the addition of a dozen new leaderboards, although it might feel like a lot of ways to reaffirm Pitts', Jordan's, and Freiermuth's production. We can now give context for a bevy of familiar and new statistics, from receptions to yards after the catch to Expected Points Added to Total Points just from tight alignments. It's a wide world of stats out there, and we're here to guide you through it.

TIGHT END

Tight End Grading Scale

GRADE	DESCRIPTION
9.0 – 7.0	High-end 3 down starter. Pro Bowl level.
6.9 – 6.7	3 down starter with Y and H ability.
6.6 – 6.5	Lower-end starter with Y or H ability.
6.1 – 6.0	Developmental. Top traits but needs time.
5.9	Backup with Y and H ability.
5.8	Backup with Y or H ability.
5.7	3rd TE (special teams ability desired).

Tight End Rankings

Rank	Name	Grade	Page
1	Kyle Pitts	7.1	258
2	Pat Freiermuth	6.7	260
3	Brevin Jordan	6.6	262
4	Tre' McKitty	6.6	264
5	Tommy Tremble	6.5	266
6	Hunter Long	6.5	268
7	Tony Poljan	6.5	270
8	Kenny Yeboah	5.9	272
9	John Bates	5.9	273
10	Quintin Morris	5.8	274
11	Noah Gray	5.8	275
12	Kylen Granson	5.8	276
13	Luke Farrell	5.8	277
14	Pro Wells	5.8	278
15	Miller Forristall	5.8	279
16	Cary Angeline	5.8	280
17	Briley Moore	5.8	281
18	Dylan Soehner	5.8	282
19	Nick Eubanks	5.8	283
20	Shaun Beyer	5.8	284
21	Jack Stoll	5.8	285
22	Matt Bushman	5.8	286

Glossary

ADoT (Avg Depth of Target)
Average yards downfield at which the player was targeted, from the LOS to the intended catch point.

Air Yards
The total number of yards the ball traveled downfield from the line of scrimmage on receptions.

Blown Blk% (Blown Block%)
The percentage of blocking snaps that the player had a blown block.

Catchable Catch%
The percentage of receptions on catchable targets. Excludes spikes, miscommunications, Hail Mary throws, and passes that were batted down.

Comp%
Percentage of targets to a receiver that resulted in completions.

On-Trgt Catch% (On-Target Catch%)
The percentage of receptions on targets that did not require the receiver to unnecessarily adjust. Excludes spikes, miscommunications, Hail Mary throws, and passes that were batted down.

Positive%
Percentage of targets to the receiver with a positive Expected Points Added on the play.

Rec Rating (Receiver Rating)
The traditional Passer Rating on throws when this receiver is targeted.

Split Out%
Percentage of plays on which the player lined up as a wide receiver.

Trgt Share (Target Share)
Percentage of a team's targets that went to a receiver.

Total Points
Sports Info Solutions' proprietary player value metric that uses an Expected Points framework and distributes the value gained or lost on a play to the players involved based on their impact on the play.

Total Points Rating
Total Points per play compared to average, scaled so that 50 is poor and 99 is excellent.

YAC
Yards after catch, the amount of additional yards the receiver gains after catching the ball.

Y/RR
Receiving yards per route run.

Yds/Trgt
Receiving yards per pass attempt in which the receiver is targeted, including incompletions.

Tight End Leaderboards

Total Points Per Game

Rk	Player	School	Tot Pts / G
1	K. Pitts	Florida	4.5
2	B. Jordan	Miami FL	3.0
3	H. Long	Boston College	2.2
4	K. Yeboah	Ole Miss	2.1
5	K. Granson	SMU	1.8
5	C. Angeline	NC State	1.8
7	N. Gray	Duke	1.5
8	B. Moore	Kansas State	1.2
9	N. Eubanks	Michigan	1.0
10	2 tied with		0.8

Total Points Rating Per Play

Rk	Player	School	Rating
1	K. Pitts	Florida	99
2	B. Jordan	Miami FL	94
3	K. Granson	SMU	90
4	N. Gray	Duke	89
4	S. Beyer	Iowa	89
6	H. Long	Boston College	88
6	C. Angeline	NC State	88
6	B. Moore	Kansas State	88
9	K. Yeboah	Ole Miss	85
9	N. Eubanks	Michigan	85

Receiving Total Points Per Game

Rk	Player	School	Tot Pts / G
1	K. Pitts	Florida	4.1
2	B. Jordan	Miami FL	2.8
3	K. Yeboah	Ole Miss	1.9
4	H. Long	Boston College	1.8
4	K. Granson	SMU	1.8
6	N. Gray	Duke	1.3
6	C. Angeline	NC State	1.3
8	B. Moore	Kansas State	1.0
9	M. Forristall	Alabama	0.6
9	N. Eubanks	Michigan	0.6

Total Points Rating Per Route

Rk	Player	School	Rating
1	K. Pitts	Florida	99
1	B. Jordan	Miami FL	99
3	K. Yeboah	Ole Miss	95
4	N. Gray	Duke	94
4	K. Granson	SMU	94
6	C. Angeline	NC State	91
7	H. Long	Boston College	88
8	B. Moore	Kansas State	86
9	S. Beyer	Iowa	85
10	2 tied with		79

Blocking Total Points Per Game

Rk	Player	School	Tot Pts / G
1	K. Granson	SMU	0.5
2	K. Pitts	Florida	0.4
2	H. Long	Boston College	0.4
2	K. Yeboah	Ole Miss	0.4
2	C. Angeline	NC State	0.4
2	N. Eubanks	Michigan	0.4
7	T. Poljan	Virginia	0.3
7	L. Farrell	Ohio State	0.3
7	M. Forristall	Alabama	0.3
10	3 tied with		0.2

Total Points Rating Per Block

Rk	Player	School	Rating
1	N. Eubanks	Michigan	97
2	B. Moore	Kansas State	95
3	K. Pitts	Florida	90
3	S. Beyer	Iowa	90
5	H. Long	Boston College	89
5	K. Granson	SMU	89
7	L. Farrell	Ohio State	82
8	C. Angeline	NC State	78
9	T. Poljan	Virginia	76
10	D. Soehner	Iowa State	69

Rk	Player	School	Tot Pts / G
	Receiving Total Points Per Game: Tight		
1	K. Pitts	Florida	2.5
2	H. Long	Boston College	1.0
2	B. Moore	Kansas State	1.0
4	K. Yeboah	Ole Miss	0.8
5	K. Granson	SMU	0.7
5	S. Beyer	Iowa	0.7
7	T. Poljan	Virginia	0.6
7	M. Forristall	Alabama	0.6
9	C. Angeline	NC State	0.5
9	N. Eubanks	Michigan	0.5

Rk	Player	School	Tot Pts / G
	Receiving Total Points Per Game: Split		
1	B. Jordan	Miami FL	1.9
2	K. Pitts	Florida	1.6
3	K. Granson	SMU	1.2
4	K. Yeboah	Ole Miss	1.0
4	N. Gray	Duke	1.0
6	H. Long	Boston College	0.8
6	C. Angeline	NC State	0.8
8	D. Soehner	Iowa State	0.4
9	Q. Morris	Bowling Green	0.3
10	4 tied with		0.1

Rk	Player	School	Trgt Share
	Target Share		
1	Q. Morris	Bowling Green	36%
2	H. Long	Boston College	24%
3	T. Poljan	Virginia	16%
4	K. Granson	SMU	15%
5	K. Pitts	Florida	14%
5	B. Jordan	Miami FL	14%
5	B. Moore	Kansas State	14%
8	P. Freiermuth	Penn State	13%
9	N. Gray	Duke	12%
10	2 tied with		10%

Rk	Player	School	Catch%
	Catchable Catch Percentage		
1	N. Gray	Duke	97%
2	M. Forristall	Alabama	96%
3	K. Pitts	Florida	95%
4	K. Yeboah	Ole Miss	91%
4	N. Eubanks	Michigan	91%
6	S. Beyer	Iowa	90%
7	C. Angeline	NC State	89%
8	B. Jordan	Miami FL	88%
8	B. Moore	Kansas State	88%
10	2 tied with		86%

Rk	Player	School	Y/RR
	Yards Per Route Run		
1	K. Pitts	Florida	2.5
2	B. Jordan	Miami FL	1.8
3	K. Granson	SMU	1.2
4	H. Long	Boston College	1.1
4	K. Yeboah	Ole Miss	1.1
4	C. Angeline	NC State	1.1
7	T. Poljan	Virginia	1.0
7	B. Moore	Kansas State	1.0
9	Q. Morris	Bowling Green	0.9
10	2 tied with		0.7

Rk	Player	School	Yds/Trgt
	Yards Per Target		
1	K. Yeboah	Ole Miss	15.4
2	K. Pitts	Florida	11.7
3	B. Jordan	Miami FL	10.9
4	C. Angeline	NC State	10.6
5	B. Moore	Kansas State	9.7
6	K. Granson	SMU	9.6
7	D. Soehner	Iowa State	9.3
8	M. Forristall	Alabama	9.0
9	N. Eubanks	Michigan	8.4
10	3 tied with		7.5

Receptions Per Game

Rk	Player	School	Rec/G
1	K. Pitts	Florida	5.4
2	H. Long	Boston College	5.2
3	B. Jordan	Miami FL	4.8
4	Q. Morris	Bowling Green	4.2
5	T. Poljan	Virginia	3.8
6	K. Granson	SMU	3.5
7	K. Yeboah	Ole Miss	3.4
8	N. Gray	Duke	2.9
9	B. Moore	Kansas State	2.4
10	C. Angeline	NC State	2.3

Total Touchdowns Per Game

Rk	Player	School	TD/G
1	K. Pitts	Florida	1.5
2	B. Jordan	Miami FL	0.9
3	K. Yeboah	Ole Miss	0.8
4	T. Poljan	Virginia	0.6
5	H. Long	Boston College	0.5
5	K. Granson	SMU	0.5
5	C. Angeline	NC State	0.5
8	B. Moore	Kansas State	0.3
9	N. Gray	Duke	0.2
9	2 tied with		0.2

Yards After Catch Per Game

Rk	Player	School	YAC/G
1	B. Jordan	Miami FL	45.6
2	K. Pitts	Florida	34.6
3	Q. Morris	Bowling Green	34.4
4	K. Yeboah	Ole Miss	32.5
5	K. Granson	SMU	22.4
6	H. Long	Boston College	17.6
7	B. Moore	Kansas State	16.9
8	D. Soehner	Iowa State	14.1
9	N. Gray	Duke	13.3
10	M. Forristall	Alabama	12.2

Yards After Catch Per Reception

Rk	Player	School	YAC/Rec
1	K. Yeboah	Ole Miss	10.0
2	B. Jordan	Miami FL	9.6
3	Q. Morris	Bowling Green	8.2
4	K. Granson	SMU	7.7
5	D. Soehner	Iowa State	7.1
6	B. Moore	Kansas State	6.9
7	K. Pitts	Florida	6.4
8	M. Forristall	Alabama	5.8
9	S. Beyer	Iowa	5.5
10	N. Gray	Duke	4.6

Receiving Yards Per Game

Rk	Player	School	Yds/G
1	K. Pitts	Florida	96.3
2	B. Jordan	Miami FL	72.0
3	K. Yeboah	Ole Miss	65.5
4	H. Long	Boston College	62.3
5	K. Granson	SMU	53.6
6	Q. Morris	Bowling Green	50.4
7	T. Poljan	Virginia	41.1
8	B. Moore	Kansas State	37.6
9	C. Angeline	NC State	32.8
10	N. Gray	Duke	28.5

Total Expected Points Added Per Game

Rk	Player	School	EPA/G
1	K. Pitts	Florida	6.2
2	K. Yeboah	Ole Miss	4.3
3	B. Jordan	Miami FL	4.2
4	C. Angeline	NC State	2.3
5	K. Granson	SMU	1.8
6	M. Forristall	Alabama	1.3
7	H. Long	Boston College	1.2
8	N. Eubanks	Michigan	0.9
9	N. Gray	Duke	0.8
10	T. Poljan	Virginia	0.5

Kyle Pitts

Report by John Todd

School	Height	Weight	Year	Jersey #	Hometown
Florida	6052 E	240 E	3JR	84	Philadelphia, PA

One Liner
Pitts could almost be considered a wide receiver with his fluidity and dominance with the ball in the air, but adding in his size and sufficient blocking efforts makes him a matchup nightmare in the NFL.

Overall
Kyle Pitts is a tight end in Florida's spread RPO offense, also lining up as an X receiver and slot. He played in 32 career games, starting 20 of them. He won't turn 21 until October of his upcoming rookie season. He suffered a concussion and received surgery on his nose following a brutal hit in 2020, missing 2 games. Pitts has great length but very thin limbs and a narrow waist. He's a smooth glider in space and an exceptionally flexible athlete with the ball in the air. He makes it look easy in the passing game, but he's a grinder in the trenches to accommodate for his lack of strength.

Pass Game
Pitts is a truly unique mismatch threat for a tight end, who forces defenses to deploy lighter personnels and looks genuinely comfortable operating as a lone receiver against No. 1 cornerbacks. Whether in tight or out wide, he struggles against physical press defenders. He likes to slow play his releases and clear out from the box to space, but his narrow frame is easy to reroute in traffic. He is an elite separator against linebackers with crisp, efficient route running and acceleration. He isn't sudden, but he glides through his stems and sinks his hips like a receiver. He was more often blanketed through his routes against defensive backs, but still impressively won his share of battles. Pitts does lack route savvy, and he can run his routes through defenders instead of around them, diminishing his athleticism and route separation. However, with his ability to adjust to off-target throws, track the ball on back-shoulders, and out jump defenders no matter how tight the coverage, his catch point separation makes up for any missteps through his routes. He's dominant in the red zone with hands that engulf the ball through contact. After the catch, his speed and burst are special, but he doesn't finish with authority or make you miss. He's shown surprising technique in pass protection to keep his elbows tight and feet mirroring through contact, but keeping him in on passing downs is a waste of his talents.

Run Game
Pitts is a very willing blocker who will mix it up in the box, but his strength and anchor let him get tossed around a bit. He usually addresses defenders with good technique to stay square up to contact, and he'll latch on and fight while engaged, but doesn't have the bulk to sustain or drive off the ball. He does a good job of executing his assignments, however, and has proven to not be a negative number in the run game.

Last Word
Pitts projects as a Day 1 difference maker for an NFL offense. While his listed position is tight end, he has legitimate X receiver skills and alignment flexibility. He had some astounding reps as a wideout against top SEC defensive backs, let alone what he did to linebackers at his size. Given his passing game prowess, his efforts as an H-TE in the run game should be plenty sufficient, especially with added bulk to his frame. He will be a critical-situation playmaker and touchdown magnet in the league.

Strengths

- Elite mismatch
- Catch point separation
- Flexible movement skills

Weaknesses

- Play strength
- Releases against physicality
- Route savvy

Critical Factors

Blocking Ability	Receiving Ability	FBI
5	8	6

Positional Factors

Run Block	Pass Block	Play Strength	Play Speed
5	5	4	7
Mismatch	Release	Catching Skills	Separation
8	5	7	7
Run After Catch	Clutch Performance	Toughness	ST Value
6	7	6	5

Basic

Year					Receiving					
	Trgt	Rec	Comp%	Yds	Air Yds	YAC	TD		Yds/Trgt	Drops
2018	10	3	30%	73	22	51	1		7.3	3
2019	80	54	68%	649	420	229	5		8.1	6
2020	66	43	65%	770	493	277	12		11.7	0
	156	100	64%	1492	935	557	18		9.6	9

Advanced

Year	Advanced Receiving						EPA		Positive %	
	On-Trgt Catch %	Catchable Catch %	YAC Per Rec	Trgt Share	ADoT	Rec Rating	Total	Per Trgt	vs. Man	vs. Zone
2018	60%	60%	17.0	3%	12.9	90.8	-0.9	-0.09	29%	33%
2019	87%	85%	4.2	18%	9.3	102.6	15.4	0.19	64%	47%
2020	95%	95%	6.4	14%	12.8	144.6	49.7	0.75	79%	53%
	89%	88%	5.6	12%	11.0	128.5	64.2	0.41	67%	49%

Deep Dive

Year	Route Running		Split Out %	Blown Blk %		Total Points					Total Points Rtg		
	Rtes Run	Y/RR		Run	Pass	Tight	Split	Rec Total	Blk	Total	Per Rte	Per Blk	Per Play
2018	33	2.2	92%	0.0%	0.0%	0	0	0	1	1	59	93	73
2019	283	2.3	36%	2.5%	2.8%	14	3	17	13	29	90	80	83
2020	306	2.5	35%	0.0%	2.2%	20	13	33	3	36	99	90	99
	622	2.4	41%	1.4%	2.5%	34	16	50	17	66	-	-	-

Pat Freiermuth

Report by Matt Manocherian

School	Height	Weight	Year	Jersey #	Hometown
Penn State	6046 E	258 E	3JR	87	Merrimac, MA

One Liner
Freiermuth lacks top-end athleticism, but his value lies in his versatility and football intelligence, putting the defense in a bind with his ability to play in both phases.

Overall
Pat Freiermuth plays tight end in Penn State's shotgun-heavy offense, splitting his time between lining up in line, as a wing, and in the slot. He is a rare two-time team captain as a true junior, and he started 26 of the 30 games that he participated in before shoulder surgery ended his 2020 season in November. He has good size with an even build throughout, and he is a bit of a throwback in that he has a traditional tight end skill set. He shows good but not special athleticism, and he consistently plays under control with strong football intelligence. He shows good effort and toughness, and he can contribute in both phases.

Pass Game
In the pass game, Freiermuth uses his hands well and shows good route refinement to get off the line. He doesn't show top-end juice, but he has very good route savvy with a quarterback-level understanding of how to play leverages. He is a very good route runner with excellent route precision. He does a great job of using body positioning to create a passing window, especially in the red zone. He also works well in the scramble drill to make himself available to the QB. All that said, he lacks the speed and athleticism to consistently pose a threat one-on-one against good NFL coverage defenders. He is a strong hands catcher, especially in contested catch situations

and through contact but has had a few drops from time to time. He is a threat to break tackles after the catch, but he doesn't show breakaway speed. He is a good pass blocker for the position who can handle blitzers and low-end pass rushers one-on-one.

Run Game
In the run game, Freiermuth can fulfill all the duties required of an in-line tight end. He is more of a stalemate and mirror guy rather than a true road grader, but he does a good job of neutralizing defenders and turning his rear end towards the hole. He functions very well in combination blocks, with good redirect ability and a good feel for when to move to the second level. He shows good balance, playing on his feet and under control. He is a very good stalk blocker when lined up on the outside, as well.

Last Word
Freiermuth is a true Y-tight end with the versatility to also play H. He can put the defense in a bind because he can exploit poor linebackers in coverage but will make the defense pay in the run game if they try to counter him with an extra defensive back. He is not a high-end game-changer, but his value is that he will exploit defenses that have linebackers who are merely sufficient in coverage.

Strengths

- Versatility
- Football intelligence
- Body control

Weaknesses

- Top-end speed
- Elusiveness
- Neutralized by top defenders

Critical Factors

Blocking Ability	Receiving Ability	FBI
6	6	7

Positional Factors

Run Block	Pass Block	Play Strength	Play Speed
6	6	6	5
Mismatch	Release	Catching Skills	Separation
6	7	6	6
Run After Catch	Clutch Performance	Toughness	ST Value
5	6	6	6

Basic

	Receiving								
Year	Trgt	Rec	Comp%	Yds	Air Yds	YAC	TD	Yds/Trgt	Drops
2018	46	26	57%	368	267	101	8	8.0	3
2019	61	43	70%	507	235	272	7	8.3	2
2020	38	23	61%	310	176	134	1	8.2	1
	145	92	63%	1185	678	507	16	8.2	6

Advanced

	Advanced Receiving						EPA		Positive %	
Year	On-Trgt Catch %	Catchable Catch %	YAC Per Rec	Trgt Share	ADoT	Rec Rating	Total	Per Trgt	vs. Man	vs. Zone
2018	87%	84%	3.9	13%	10.1	122.1	8.5	0.18	60%	50%
2019	95%	93%	6.3	17%	7.6	126.9	31.9	0.52	60%	57%
2020	95%	95%	5.8	13%	9.0	73.4	8.9	0.23	58%	50%
	93%	91%	5.5	14%	8.7	117.2	49.2	0.34	59%	54%

Deep Dive

	Route Running			Blown Blk %		Total Points					Total Points Rtg		
Year	Rtes Run	Y/RR	Split Out %	Run	Pass	Tight	Split	Rec Total	Blk	Total	Per Rte	Per Blk	Per Play
2018	249	1.5	34%	0.0%	0.0%	8	4	12	15	28	87	99	95
2019	292	1.7	34%	0.3%	2.1%	7	14	21	16	37	96	92	92
2020	215	1.4	54%	2.7%	3.3%	8	3	11	0	12	98	53	94
	756	1.6	37%	0.5%	1.6%	23	22	44	31	77	-	-	-

Brevin Jordan

Report by Alec Mallon & Jake Johnson

School	Height	Weight	Year	Jersey #	Hometown
Miami FL	6026 E	245 E	3JR	9	Las Vegas, NV

One Liner
Jordan is an athletic pass catcher who can win all over the field and create valuable yardage after the catch, but must improve as a blocker before he can be counted upon on every down.

Overall
Brevin Jordan is a tight end for Miami's up-tempo, RPO offense. After spending most of his first 2 seasons in tight, he saw more time in the slot in 2020. He appeared in 30 games over his career, starting 29 of them for the Hurricanes. Jordan will still only be 20 years old at the time of the NFL Draft. missed 1 game in 2018, 3 games in 2019 with an ankle injury, and 3 games in 2020 with a shoulder injury. He's an exceptional athlete with a big body whose physical traits pop up all over the field. In addition, he's a high-effort player on most downs and plays with good toughness and competitive spirit.

Pass Game
Jordan is a playmaker as a receiver. He wasn't pressed much at the line, but his combination of power and speed will allow for him to sufficiently get off the line at the next level. As a receiver, his speed isn't matched by linebackers and he can be a nightmare against zone coverage. He shows good route-running skills and can separate easily from linebackers because of his quickness. He's a savvy route runner and consistently knows how to set up his routes and create separation at the top of his breaks. Against defensive backs, he uses his size and body control to box out while making sure he can still make a play on the ball. Jordan doesn't have drop issues, but constantly uses his body to make catches, sometimes impeding his momentum and limiting his RAC potential. With the ball in his hands, his speed makes him a threat to take any pass the distance, but he also displays the agility to make defenders miss. Jordan struggles in pass protection. He can be successful when given help, such as a back to help double an edge defender, but 1-on-1 on the edge, he lacks the technique and footwork to be a sound blocker. On an island, he lunges often, putting himself off balance and out of position.

Run Game
In the run game, Jordan is willing and loves initiating contact to deliver a strong blow to edge defenders and linebackers. He shows good technique most of the time, keeping himself square and under control. He excels when he is asked to get to the second level. His quickness and speed allow for him to cut off linebackers before they can read their keys, and he has the strength to wall them off. Jordan struggles most against edge defenders. He gets caught lunging and dropping his head, making him susceptible to blown blocks.

Last Word
Jordan best projects as a lower-end starter as an H-tight end in a system where he can be split out in the slot and use his ability as a receiver to create big plays or off the ball to be a split-zone or 2nd-level blocker. On 3rd down, he should line up in the slot to utilize his receiving skills against linebackers and slot corners. Jordan's athletic ability, speed, and toughness make a strong candidate for special teams.

Strengths

- Separation skills
- RAC ability
- Speed & quickness

Weaknesses

- Body catcher
- Pass pro
- Run block fundamentals

Critical Factors

Blocking Ability	Receiving Ability	FBI
5	7	6

Positional Factors

Run Block	Pass Block	Play Strength	Play Speed
5	4	5	7
Mismatch	Release	Catching Skills	Separation
7	5	5	6
Run After Catch	Clutch Performance	Toughness	ST Value
7	6	6	6

Basic

	Receiving								
Year	Trgt	Rec	Comp%	Yds	Air Yds	YAC	TD	Yds/Trgt	Drops
2018	49	32	65%	287	98	189	4	5.9	3
2019	49	35	71%	495	190	305	2	10.1	2
2020	53	38	72%	576	211	365	7	10.9	2
	151	105	70%	1358	499	859	13	9.0	7

Advanced

	Advanced Receiving						EPA		Positive %	
Year	On-Trgt Catch %	Catchable Catch %	YAC Per Rec	Trgt Share	ADoT	Rec Rating	Total	Per Trgt	vs. Man	vs. Zone
2018	86%	84%	5.9	14%	6.3	91.1	-1.5	-0.03	45%	23%
2019	94%	94%	8.7	12%	7.7	117.3	19.1	0.39	42%	66%
2020	90%	88%	9.6	14%	7.6	146.7	34.7	0.65	50%	58%
	90%	89%	8.2	13%	7.2	120.7	52.3	0.35	46%	55%

Deep Dive

	Route Running			Blown Blk %		Total Points					Total Points Rtg		
Year	Rtes Run	Y/RR	Split Out %	Run	Pass	Tight	Split	Rec Total	Blk	Total	Per Rte	Per Blk	Per Play
2018	270	1.1	26%	0.4%	0.0%	0	2	2	12	14	65	87	75
2019	203	2.4	21%	1.8%	1.1%	7	4	11	8	20	90	74	82
2020	315	1.8	61%	0.0%	2.2%	2	15	22	0	24	99	50	94
	788	1.7	35%	0.6%	1.2%	9	21	35	20	58	-	-	-

Tre' McKitty

Report by Ronan Potts

School	Height	Weight	Year	Jersey #	Hometown
Georgia	6041 V	247 V	4SR	87	Wesley Chapel, FL

One Liner
McKitty has the temperament, athleticism, and blocking ability to be a starting Y-tight end at the next level, but needs to develop more as a receiver and in his ability to create consistent separation in order to become a complete three-down player.

Overall
Tre' McKitty is a tight end in Georgia's pro-style offense. He lined up as both a Y and H, inline and in the slot, though he was primarily used as an extra blocker. He started 19 of 35 games for Florida State before starting all 7 he played in at Georgia in 2020. He missed the first 2 games of the 2020 season after having arthroscopic meniscus surgery. McKitty is a good athlete with a solid frame for the position. He's an intelligent, aggressive player and a fierce competitor.

Pass Game
In the passing game, McKitty is sufficient as a receiving threat. He has a quick release and adequate long speed that can lead to him getting open against zone, but when he is forced to rely on his technique as a route runner against man coverage, he can struggle to create consistent separation. With that said, he shows the ability to win at the top of routes with good off-hand separation. He has good ball skills, excelling at adjusting to the ball while it is in the air and putting himself in position to make the catch. He isn't the most natural hands catcher, often relying on his body to help him secure the ball, though he has the ability to show sticky hands with a wide catch radius. He is a threat as a runner after the catch, with impressive power and contact balance to break tackles and gain valuable YAC. In pass pro, he shows good feet to mirror rushers and when he latches on, he's able to sustain his block until the quarterback has released the ball.

Run Game
In the running game, McKitty shines as a blocker. He is very effective as both an inline blocker and as a split zone blocker with an aggressive temperament and the athletic ability to consistently hold off edge defenders. He uses his power and leverage very well in the run game, which has led to him being as productive of a blocker against SEC defenders as he was against ACC competition. He uses strong hands and overall strength to win at the POA against edge defenders. He is an intense player who always knows his assignment and doesn't take any plays off.

Last Word
McKitty projects as a starting Y-tight end who is a real asset as a blocker and a sufficient receiving threat. On third downs, he would be best utilized as an inline blocker for third-and-short running plays. On longer third downs, he can stay inline as an extra blocker for his quarterback or utilize his route running ability and hands from the tight position on short-to-intermediate route concepts. Due to his temperament, speed, and toughness, McKitty should be able to serve as a core special teams player who can contribute on all units.

Strengths
- Overall blocking ability
- High FBI
- Toughness

Weaknesses
- Inconsistent at creating separation
- Lacks some speed

Critical Factors

Blocking Ability	Receiving Ability	FBI
6	5	7

Positional Factors

Run Block	Pass Block	Play Strength	Play Speed
6	6	6	5
Mismatch	Release	Catching Skills	Separation
5	6	6	5
Run After Catch	Clutch Performance	Toughness	ST Value
6	6	7	6

Basic

Year	Trgt	Rec	Comp%	Yds	Air Yds	YAC	TD	Yds/Trgt	Drops
2017	1	1	100%	23	13	10	0	23.0	0
2018	49	26	53%	256	121	135	2	5.2	5
2019	29	23	79%	241	85	156	0	8.3	1
2020	10	6	60%	108	50	58	1	10.8	1
	89	56	63%	628	269	359	3	7.1	7

Advanced

Year	On-Trgt Catch %	Catchable Catch %	YAC Per Rec	Trgt Share	ADoT	Rec Rating	EPA Total	EPA Per Trgt	Positive % vs. Man	Positive % vs. Zone
2017	-	100%	10.0	0%	13.0	118.8	1.7	1.67	100%	-
2018	76%	76%	5.2	11%	6.9	56.2	-16.5	-0.34	42%	37%
2019	95%	95%	6.8	7%	4.2	86.9	6.5	0.22	55%	67%
2020	86%	86%	9.7	3%	8.8	130.4	5.3	0.53	100%	43%
	84%	84%	6.4	6%	6.3	76.4	-3.1	-0.04	54%	46%

Deep Dive

Year	Route Running Rtes Run	Route Running Y/RR	Route Running Split Out %	Blown Blk % Run	Blown Blk % Pass	Total Points Tight	Total Points Split	Total Points Rec Total	Total Points Blk	Total Points Total	Total Points Rtg Per Rte	Total Points Rtg Per Blk	Total Points Rtg Per Play
2018	274	0.9	39%	0.0%	2.7%	3	-3	-1	8	7	59	69	63
2019	129	1.9	22%	0.5%	2.4%	4	1	6	6	12	85	59	67
2020	204	0.5	26%	1.4%	0.0%	4	0	4	1	5	88	72	86
	607	1.0	31%	0.5%	2.3%	10	-3	9	15	24	-	-	-

Tommy Tremble

Report by Nathan Cooper

School	Height	Weight	Year	Jersey #	Hometown
Notre Dame	6031 E	248 E	3JR	24	Johns Creek, GA

One Liner
Tremble has the competitive run blocking and route-running ability to make an impact in multiple ways at the next level, though he'll need to get stronger and become more savvy mid-route in order to maximize his full potential.

Overall
Tommy Tremble is primarily the H-tight end in Notre Dame's pro-style offense, lining up off-ball, inline, fullback, slot, and wide. He started 17 of 25 games played with the Irish. He suffered a fractured fibula in 2017. He has a long frame with good speed and athletic ability. His competitive motor runs hot all the time, and he plays hard and tough throughout each rep. He's only 20 years old and still learning but he's a smart player who does his job.

Pass Game
In the pass game, Tremble shows the ability to release cleanly off the line and avoid contact. He shows good footwork off the line and knows how to use his hands to get by defenders. He runs a lot of the main tight end routes, including crossers, curls, flats/outs, and seams. He's fluid in and out of cuts and is mostly able to win with his route running and speed. He was able to win and was open much more than his limited receiving stats suggested, though his route savvy is something that can be improved. Even though he's able to avoid contact off the line, there are too many times he gets contacted mid-route or settles down next to a defender instead of finding an opening. He has strong, natural hands to haul in passes. He doesn't show a large catch radius, but nearly always pulls down passes on his frame. After the catch, he fights for extra yards, but isn't going to make many defenders

miss. In pass pro, he stops his feet at the POA and struggles to stay with good edge rushers, though most of the time he's able to sustain long enough.

Run Game
Tremble competes in the run game. He doesn't have the most strength or keep his feet moving at the POA, but he goes hard and is willing to block to the whistle. On many run blocks, he seems to block like a fullback, whether he's coming from the backfield or not. He comes with a full head of steam and delivers a blow. His ability to sustain is inconsistent, though there are times he's able to ride defenders well off the ball and into the ground. He'll occasionally dip his head at the POA, but never does it two plays in a row. He was used as a lead back, to set the edge, or kick out on split zones, and while he won't always overwhelm, he's usually effective.

Last Word
Tremble projects as a starting H-tight end at the next level where he can be moved around the formation and use his traits as both a receiver and run blocker, as he doesn't have the build or strength to hold up as a Y consistently. On 3rd downs, he fits best as the move tight end or lined up in the slot to enhance his mismatch ability. With his play speed and competitive playing style, he could turn into a core special teams player.

Strengths

- Competitive blocker
- Route running
- Release

Weaknesses

- Block strength
- Route savvy

Critical Factors

Blocking Ability	Receiving Ability	FBI
5	6	5

Positional Factors

Run Block	Pass Block	Play Strength	Play Speed
6	5	5	6
Mismatch	**Release**	**Catching Skills**	**Separation**
6	6	6	6
Run After Catch	**Clutch Performance**	**Toughness**	**ST Value**
5	6	7	7

Basic

	Receiving								
Year	Trgt	Rec	Comp%	Yds	Air Yds	YAC	TD	Yds/Trgt	Drops
2019	24	16	67%	183	100	83	4	7.6	3
2020	29	19	66%	218	153	65	0	7.5	3
	53	35	66%	401	253	148	4	7.6	6

Advanced

	Advanced Receiving						EPA		Positive %	
Year	On-Trgt Catch %	Catchable Catch %	YAC Per Rec	Trgt Share	ADoT	Rec Rating	Total	Per Trgt	vs. Man	vs. Zone
2019	83%	75%	5.2	6%	7.3	129.0	10.3	0.43	60%	61%
2020	86%	86%	3.4	9%	8.2	73.6	-1.9	-0.07	57%	50%
	85%	80%	4.2	7%	7.8	105.9	8.4	0.16	58%	55%

Deep Dive

	Route Running		Blown Blk %			Total Points				Total Points Rtg		
	Rtes		Split					Rec			Per	Per	Per
Year	Run	Y/RR	Out %	Run	Pass	Tight	Split	Total	Blk	Total	Rte	Blk	Play
2019	127	1.4	30%	0.0%	0.0%	2	-2	1	6	7	62	88	73
2020	411	0.5	21%	1.5%	0.0%	-1	1	0	1	0	60	53	60
	538	0.7	24%	1.0%	0.0%	1	-1	1	7	7	-	-	-

Hunter Long

Report by Jeff Dean, Sales Pinckney, & Danny Shirilla

School	Height	Weight	Year	Jersey #	Hometown
Boston College	6051 V	254 V	4JR	80	Exeter, NH

One Liner
Long has the versatility, blocking ability, and route savvy to be an effective NFL tight end, but will need to improve his hands in traffic and his production in the red zone to reach his true potential.

Overall
Hunter Long plays tight end in Boston College's 11/12 personnel, up-tempo, RPO offense. He started 14 of 36 games in his career. He's a good athlete with requisite size who moves well in space. He is well-built and has enough strength in his lower body to hold up at the line. He plays with an even-keel mindset and doesn't show much emotion, but is nearly always on the field playing hard and competing.

Pass Game
Long looks comfortable in space and when lined up all over the field. He looks as comfortable in the slot as he does in tight. His release is sufficient as he doesn't have a great burst, but limits the false steps to minimize the impact. While he mainly ran out routes and deep crosses, he did show the ability to run more routes. He doesn't break down well at the top of his routes and his breaks aren't always smooth. He has good route savvy against zone coverage and finds the hole in the defense. He's willing to go over the middle of the field and take shots, but doesn't offer much after the catch. He lacks the speed to burn by defenders and doesn't break many tackles, but can stretch the field vertically. He catches the ball away from his body, though he lacks strong hands and struggles to make the catch through contact. When given space, he doesn't drop many passes, but with tight coverage, he doesn't come down with many 50/50 balls. Long had limited targets in the red zone and had minimal production down there as well. This was partly due to his limited ability to separate against man coverage, as well as the lack of holes in the middle of the field. In pass pro, he shows he can square up rushers and neutralize them at the POA.

Run Game
Long uses his big frame and strength to seal off defenders as a blocker. He has a firm grasp on blocking technique and has the strength to handle defensive ends at the line and beat linebackers on the edge. He keeps his feet under him and squares up before making contact which limits the amount of ground given up. He attacks under control to the 2nd level and rarely misses his block. He lacks some aggression and tenacity, but his recognition, strength, and effort make him a good all-around blocker.

Last Word
Long projects as a starting H-tight end at the next level who could turn into a complete tight end with a little more time. His ability to find holes in the zone and consistent effort to catch the ball away from the body make him a great safety blanket on 3rd down. He has the size, strength, and mindset to be a contributing special teams player from the start.

Strengths	Weaknesses
• Route savvy	• Hand strength
• Blocking ability	• RAC ability
• Alignment versatility	• Red-zone production

Critical Factors

Blocking Ability	Receiving Ability	FBI
6	6	6

Positional Factors

Run Block	Pass Block	Play Strength	Play Speed
6	6	6	5
Mismatch	Release	Catching Skills	Separation
5	5	5	5
Run After Catch	Clutch Performance	Toughness	ST Value
5	5	5	6

Basic

	Receiving								
Year	Trgt	Rec	Comp%	Yds	Air Yds	YAC	TD	Yds/Trgt	Drops
2018	4	4	100%	103	44	59	2	25.8	0
2019	40	28	70%	509	206	303	2	12.7	1
2020	91	57	63%	685	491	194	5	7.5	4
	135	89	66%	1297	741	556	9	9.6	5

Advanced

	Advanced Receiving						EPA		Positive %	
Year	On-Trgt Catch %	Catchable Catch %	YAC Per Rec	Trgt Share	ADoT	Rec Rating	Total	Per Trgt	vs. Man	vs. Zone
2018	100%	100%	14.8	1%	11.0	158.3	11.1	2.77	100%	-
2019	88%	88%	10.8	14%	8.2	108.3	21.6	0.54	40%	65%
2020	85%	85%	3.4	24%	9.4	90.2	12.8	0.14	53%	56%
	86%	86%	6.2	13%	9.1	103.8	45.4	0.34	54%	58%

Deep Dive

	Route Running			Blown Blk %		Total Points					Total Points Rtg		
Year	Rtes Run	Y/RR	Split Out %	Run	Pass	Tight	Split	Rec Total	Blk	Total	Per Rte	Per Blk	Per Play
2018	27	3.8	7%	0.0%	0.0%	4	2	5	3	8	99	84	94
2019	143	3.6	16%	0.3%	0.0%	9	-1	8	16	24	90	95	90
2020	650	1.1	25%	1.0%	0.0%	12	9	20	4	24	88	89	88
	820	1.6	20%	0.6%	0.0%	24	10	33	23	56	-	-	-

Tony Poljan

Report by Jeff Dean, Steven Penn, & DJ Marquardt

School	Height	Weight	Year	Jersey #	Hometown
Virginia	6065 E	265 E	4SR	87	Lansing, MI

One Liner

Poljan shows the hand use and blocking ability to contribute as a starter, but he'll need to continue to show steady improvement with more experience as a receiver to stand out in the NFL.

Overall

Tony Poljan is a tight end in Virginia's motion-heavy, zone blocking offense. He played in 46 career games with 25 starts, 20 at tight end and 5 at quarterback. He began his career at Central Michigan as a quarterback and earned a few starts while splitting time at the tight end position before moving there full time. He transferred to Virginia in 2020 to finish his college career. Poljan has a very good frame that is packed with muscle throughout. He has very good strength and base to withstand constant hits. He's a sufficient athlete who has sufficient speed, but doesn't explode off of the line or out of breaks. He is a tough competitor who takes pride in his blocking and is willing to take defenders head-on at the line.

Pass Game

Poljan is still a little raw as a receiver and shows a sufficient release off the line, but lacks a developed route tree to sell other routes. He's best on in-breaking routes, as he can sell an out-breaking route better. He tends to round his cuts and looks more comfortable in the short game than in the long. He has a very good catch radius between his size and leaping ability, but has inconsistent hands and loses more 50/50 balls than he should due to struggling with body control in the air. Poljan struggles with positioning and sacrifices his advantage to smaller defensive backs occasionally. He is able to create some separation using his off-hand or initiating some contact at the top of the route, but lacks the burst to maximize the gap. He has enough speed to warrant downfield consideration, though he isn't a consistent threat. He's limited after the catch and won't break many tackles. While he won't take over many games as a receiver, he is comfortable as a safety blanket and is a red zone threat due to his size. As a blocker, he shows sound pass blocking footwork and recognition. He has the strength to knock defenders off the ball and the awareness to recognize blitzes and stunts to make the right read.

Run Game

Poljan is a dominant blocker who can be a force as a run blocker, just as he is in pass pro. He squares his shoulders up and does a good job of staying balanced through contact. He sustains blocks very well and can consistently neutralize defensive ends. He rarely looks lost when blocking and gives good effort to handle his assignment. His strength, size, and effort make him a valuable addition on run plays.

Last Word

Poljan projects as a low-end starter at Y-tight end who fits best in a run-heavy offense at the next level. He should see the field early due to his blocking ability and shows enough receiving ability to be a 3-down player, but shouldn't be looked at as a move tight end. He should be a contributing special teams member on most units with his size and skill set.

Strengths

- Blocking
- Hand use
- Frame

Weaknesses

- Inconsistent hands
- Underdeveloped route tree
- Lacks open-field ability

Critical Factors

Blocking Ability	Receiving Ability	FBI
7	5	6

Positional Factors

Run Block	Pass Block	Play Strength	Play Speed
7	7	7	5
Mismatch	**Release**	**Catching Skills**	**Separation**
6	5	5	5
Run After Catch	**Clutch Performance**	**Toughness**	**ST Value**
4	6	6	6

Basic

Year					Receiving					
Year	Trgt	Rec	Comp%	Yds	Air Yds	YAC	TD	Yds/Trgt	Drops
2017	6	5	83%	97	81	16	0	16.2	1
2018	13	7	54%	125	102	23	2	9.6	0
2019	52	33	63%	496	255	241	4	9.5	2
2020	60	38	63%	411	291	120	6	6.9	3
	131	83	63%	1129	729	400	12	8.6	6

Advanced

Year	Advanced Receiving						EPA		Positive %	
Year	On-Trgt Catch %	Catchable Catch %	YAC Per Rec	Trgt Share	ADoT	Rec Rating	Total	Per Trgt	vs. Man	vs. Zone
2017	-	83%	3.2	1%	14.3	118.8	6.0	1.00	100%	33%
2018	100%	88%	3.3	4%	18.6	126.6	7.9	0.61	50%	63%
2019	88%	85%	7.3	11%	8.2	112.3	23.4	0.45	62%	48%
2020	88%	85%	3.2	16%	9.4	116.7	5.2	0.09	59%	47%
	89%	85%	4.8	8%	10.1	118.1	42.5	0.32	62%	49%

Deep Dive

Year	Route Running			Blown Blk %		Total Points					Total Points Rtg		
Year	Rtes Run	Y/RR	Split Out %	Run	Pass	Tight	Split	Rec Total	Blk	Total	Per Rte	Per Blk	Per Play
2018	21	6.0	15%	0.0%	0.0%	2	3	5	0	-12	99	50	51
2019	269	1.8	21%	0.6%	1.1%	11	1	11	14	25	82	80	78
2020	424	1.0	6%	1.2%	1.4%	6	-1	4	3	8	69	76	71
	714	1.4	15%	0.6%	0.6%	19	2	20	17	21	-	-	-

Kenny Yeboah

Report by Alec Mallon, Ryan Newman, & David Simmons

School	Height	Weight	Year	Jersey #	Hometown
Ole Miss	6037 V	247 V	5SR	84	Allentown, PA

One Liner

Yeboah understands his assignments in the run and pass games, and is capable of making big plays as a receiver, but must become a better separator and more technical blocker to be a true difference maker.

Strengths: Contested catches; Release; Mismatch potential
Weaknesses: Separation suddenness; Leg drive; Blocking technique

Kenny Yeboah is a tight end in Ole Miss' hurry-up spread offense, often splitting out to the slot. He has appeared in 45 career games with 19 starts, spending his first 4 years at Temple before transferring. Yeboah has a good frame and ideal size for the position. He is a very good athlete with speed and competitiveness downfield and between the tackles alike.

Yeboah gets clean releases from the slot against press with his strength and speed. However, he struggles to create separation against man coverage. He can pull away from linebackers after his initial break but must use his frame to box out smaller defenders to create space when blanketed. He shows great tracking skills to locate and outjump defenders to high point. Yeboah doesn't have any mental lapses with drops but can be a body catcher at times. After the catch, he has enough speed and agility to outrun LBs but not DBs. He can hold his own as a pass protector with good strength and agility, but he lacks the technique to control one-on-one edge rushers consistently.

When attached to the line, Yeboah fires off and can strike defenders at contact, but he doesn't shock with his punch. He doesn't have the strongest lower half to drive off the line but displays good athleticism and footwork to stay square and sustain long enough to allow plays to develop. Yeboah acts as a fullback often to insert and lead up through to the second level. He usually attacks with his shoulders to deliver his strongest contact, but linebackers can take advantage with superior hand use to slip off his blocks.

Yeboah is a backup H-tight end at the next level, but he can fill a Y role, too. Although not his natural position, he can be a front-side blocker for wide zones and kick out defenders in power schemes as a capable OL extension. However, Yeboah best profiles as a receiver split out or off the line and should see ample usage in the passing game. Yeboah has been a special teams player at both programs and should be a core member moving forward.

Receiving

Year	Trgt	Rec	Comp%	Yds	Air Yds	YAC	TD	Yds/Trgt	Drops
2017	23	14	61%	136	52	84	0	5.9	5
2018	24	13	54%	154	80	74	1	6.4	1
2019	28	19	68%	233	121	112	5	8.3	4
2020	34	27	79%	524	264	260	6	15.4	2
	110	74	67%	1062	521	541	12	9.7	12

Advanced Receiving

Year	On-Trgt Catch %	Catchable Catch %	YAC Per Rec	Trgt Share	ADoT	Rec Rating	EPA Total	EPA Per Trgt	Positive % vs. Man	Positive % vs. Zone
2017	-	70%	6.0	5%	6.3	41.2	-3.5	-0.15	83%	38%
2018	75%	75%	5.7	5%	7.0	87.8	3.0	0.12	40%	25%
2019	78%	78%	5.9	6%	7.1	132.9	9.1	0.33	80%	36%
2020	91%	91%	10.0	10%	10.1	158.3	34.5	1.01	75%	75%
	82%	80%	7.4	5%	7.8	127.2	45.3	0.41	68%	49%

Route Running / Blown Blk % / Total Points / Total Points Rtg

Year	Rtes Run	Y/RR	Split Out %	Run	Pass	Tight	Split	Rec Total	Blk	Total	Per Rte	Per Blk	Per Play
2018	144	1.1	27%	0.5%	0.0%	-2	2	-1	7	6	58	69	62
2019	100	2.3	12%	0.4%	0.0%	5	0	4	13	17	79	86	82
2020	481	1.1	39%	1.1%	0.9%	6	8	15	3	17	95	56	85
	725	1.3	27%	0.7%	0.4%	9	9	18	23	40	-	-	-

Redshirt season not shown but included in totals

Critical Factors

Blocking Ability	5
Receiving Ability	6
FBI	6

Positional Factors

Run Block	5
Pass Block	5
Play Strength	5
Play Speed	6
Mismatch	6
Release	6
Catching Skills	6
Separation	5
Run After Catch	6
Clutch Performance	6
Toughness	5
ST Value	7

John Bates

Report by Evan Butler

School	Height	Weight	Year	Jersey #	Hometown
Boise State	6055 V	259 V	5SR	85	Lebanon, OR

One Liner

Bates' size, athleticism, and receiving upside should allow him time to evolve into a consistent contributor at the next level, though he needs to improve his strength and overall blocking ability to hit his potential.

Strengths: Athleticism; Body control; Hands
Weaknesses: POA strength; Sustaining blocks; Separation

John Bates is a tight end for Boise State's pro-style offense and will occasionally slide out into the slot. He started 27 of 46 games played for the Broncos. He dealt with a hamstring injury for much of the 2020 season. He has a big frame with good athletic movement and fluidity in space, evidenced by the fact he was a high school basketball and track & field standout. He's a good competitor and shows his toughness in all areas of the game.

Bates is a capable option with his good size and athleticism. Against linebackers, he can create enough of a mismatch to make plays. He's fluid in and out of breaks and runs a full route tree. His athleticism shines after the catch in gaining extra yards and doesn't shy away from contact. He shows good hands making catches in all areas of the field. He uses his size and speed to create separation, showing a little wiggle at the top of routes, though he struggles to do so consistently. He finds gaps in zone coverage and works well to get open in scramble situations.

Bates is a willing blocker, but lacks some strength to handle defensive linemen. He struggles to sustain blocks with wide hand usage. His successes come from his reactive athleticism and body control. Bates has the anchor and flexion at the POA, but gets overpowered too often. He has the FBI to get in position, though has limitations in moving defenders out of their gaps and shouldn't be counted on as a lead blocker between the tackles, however, he seeks out contact. On the 2nd level, he works well against smaller linebackers and defensive backs and approaches balanced and under control.

Bates projects as a backup tight end serving primarily as an H due to his athletic ability as a receiver to line up all over the field, but also has the size to line up inline. On 3rd downs, he fits best as a move tight end where he can use his athleticism and receiving ability to move the sticks. Bates possesses the physical tools and skill set to make an impact on special teams.

Receiving

Year	Trgt	Rec	Comp%	Yds	Air Yds	YAC	TD	Yds/Trgt	Drops
2017	6	3	50%	34	18	16	0	5.7	0
2018	14	10	71%	155	101	54	1	11.1	2
2019	34	22	65%	273	155	118	1	8.0	1
2020	15	12	80%	117	75	42	0	7.8	0
	69	47	68%	579	349	230	2	8.4	3

Advanced Receiving

Year	On-Trgt Catch %	Catchable Catch %	YAC Per Rec	Trgt Share	ADoT	Rec Rating	EPA Total	Per Trgt	Positive % vs. Man	Positive % vs. Zone
2017	-	100%	5.3	1%	7.8	27.8	-3.4	-0.57	33%	67%
2018	91%	91%	5.4	3%	10.8	141.5	9.8	0.75	50%	67%
2019	84%	84%	5.4	7%	8.1	102.2	11.6	0.35	0%	64%
2020	100%	100%	3.5	7%	8.1	99.2	5.3	0.35	33%	83%
	90%	90%	4.9	4%	8.6	100.3	23.2	0.35	29%	69%

Route Running / Blown Blk % / Total Points / Total Points Rtg

Year	Rtes Run	Y/RR	Split Out %	Run	Pass	Tight	Split	Rec Total	Blk	Total	Per Rte	Per Blk	Per Play
2018	129	1.2	9%	0.6%	0.0%	2	0	3	19	22	72	94	88
2019	202	1.4	11%	1.4%	3.0%	5	2	8	22	29	79	87	80
2020	130	0.9	20%	1.2%	4.2%	3	2	5	1	6	98	78	92
	461	1.2	11%	1.1%	1.9%	11	4	16	42	57	-	-	-

Critical Factors

Blocking Ability	5
Receiving Ability	6
FBI	6

Positional Factors

Run Block	5
Pass Block	5
Play Strength	5
Play Speed	6
Mismatch	5
Release	6
Catching Skills	6
Separation	5
Run After Catch	6
Clutch Performance	5
Toughness	6
ST Value	6

Quintin Morris

Report by Daniel Jankuloski & Theo Fornaciari

School	Height	Weight	Year	Jersey #	Hometown
Bowling Green	6022 V	251 E	4SR	80	Richmond, TX

One Liner

Morris has receiver tools with mismatch ability across the middle to contribute in the NFL, though he'll need to improve his strength and blocking ability to see the field for more than just passing situations.

Strengths: Clutch factor; Concentration; Break point separation
Weaknesses: Inline POA blocking; Play strength; Release vs. length

Quintin Morris is an H-tight end who was deployed primarily in wing and slot alignment in Bowling Green's heavy play action and misdirection offense. Beginning his career as a wide receiver, Morris started 28 of 40 games for the Falcons. He is a very good athlete with a well-built frame. He's a competitor and very clutch player who consistently made the big catches in critical situations with his best games against top competition.

Morris wins leverage off the line from slot/tight alignment with quickness and agility. He will struggle against top-end cornerbacks with length in press-engage due to sufficient strength. He shows savviness as a route runner to find soft spots in zone coverage and create leverage in his route stems. Morris has good separation ability and utilizes body lean and off-hand ability to set up breaks at the top of routes. His advanced footwork and frame allow him to box out smaller corners at the catch point. He has good catching skills with the concentration to make catches through contact. He also has good body control to track and adjust to off-target passes. Morris has very good speed and the toughness to finish runs after the catch, though he probably won't make many athletes miss in space. He's a mediocre pass blocker with the athletic ability and speed to make rim blocks and protect the pocket, but he bends too much at the waist and won't win many heads-up matchups against linebackers or defensive linemen.

Morris is a sufficient blocker who has the play speed and footwork to hold his own in space or on split-zones. He has good FBI to locate moving targets along with toughness and body control to sustain blocks at the 2nd level, however, he lacks the strength and hand placement to anchor at the POA.

Morris projects as a starting H who best fits a scheme that will utilize him from off-ball or slot alignment and away from the POA. His clutch factor along with his receiving ability make him an ideal 3rd-down tight end from the slot. He has the athletic ability and toughness to be a solid special teams player.

				Receiving					
Year	Trgt	Rec	Comp%	Yds	Air Yds	YAC	TD	Yds/Trgt	Drops
2017	13	8	62%	116	48	68	2	8.9	1
2018	67	42	63%	516	410	106	7	7.7	2
2019	94	54	57%	639	251	388	4	6.8	7
2020	44	21	48%	252	80	172	0	5.7	5
	218	125	57%	1523	789	734	13	7.0	15

	Advanced Receiving						EPA		Positive %	
Year	On-Trgt Catch %	Catchable Catch %	YAC Per Rec	Trgt Share	ADoT	Rec Rating	Total	Per Trgt	vs. Man	vs. Zone
2017	-	73%	8.5	3%	8.3	130.1	11.1	0.85	33%	80%
2018	91%	89%	2.5	17%	10.5	102.6	19.6	0.29	43%	81%
2019	87%	83%	7.2	30%	7.0	70.3	0.0	0.00	50%	44%
2020	80%	80%	8.2	36%	7.4	37.3	-19.9	-0.45	13%	38%
	87%	84%	5.9	18%	8.2	77.8	10.8	0.05	41%	51%

	Route Running		Blown Blk %		Total Points					Total Points Rtg		
Year	Rtes Run	Y/RR	Split Out %	Run	Pass	Tight	Split	Rec Total	Blk	Total	Per Rte	Per Blk	Per Play
2018	413	1.2	99%	0.0%	0.0%	0	11	11	1	13	76	54	72
2019	294	2.2	42%	0.9%	3.6%	6	3	11	15	26	80	97	86
2020	267	0.9	33%	2.3%	0.0%	-5	2	-4	0	-3	53	60	54
	974	1.4	65%	0.8%	1.3%	0	16	18	16	36	-	-	-

Critical Factors	
Blocking Ability	5
Receiving Ability	6
FBI.	6

Positional Factors	
Run Block.	5
Pass Block	4
Play Strength	5
Play Speed	7
Mismatch	6
Release	6
Catching Skills	6
Separation	6
Run After Catch	5
Clutch Performance.	6
Toughness	6
ST Value	6

Noah Gray

Report by DJ Marquardt & James Ashley

School	Height	Weight	Year	Jersey #	Hometown
Duke	6035 V	240 V	4SR	87	Leominster, MA

One Liner

Gray has the short-area quickness and potential mismatch ability to be a threat at the next level, but needs to get stronger and improve his blocking ability to be more than just a backup-level player.

Strengths: Short-area quickness; Hands; Competitiveness
Weaknesses: Strength at the POA; Pass pro; Body control

Noah Gray played in a variety of alignments in Duke's pistol offense which utilized a good amount of play action and triple option looks. He lined up anywhere from the slot to lead back in pistol 2-back sets. He started 21 of 46 games for the Blue Devils. He's a thin, but athletic player with good speed who moves around well. He is a competitively tough kid as he's always willing to perform his assignment to the best of his ability.

Gray has enticing attributes to become a mismatch in the passing game. While not often being challenged at the release point, he shows no signs of an inadequate release. He has some quick-twitch ability out of his release that enables good separation on his short routes. He plays with good speed, partly due to a smaller build, but when lined up in the slot can certainly become an easy mismatch on a linebacker. Gray struggles setting up his routes downfield which leads to less separation on longer developing routes. He lacks some route savvy as well, as he is often rugged sitting in zones. He shows natural pass-catching ability and can snatch the ball from different angles, but lacks the catch radius plus clutch factor to consistently make big, contested catches. In pass pro, he lacks POA strength and struggles to consistently sustain blocks.

Gray blocked out of a lot of different alignments at Duke and showed outstanding effort with each block. He is a very willing blocker and is always making good contact with defenders. He does a nice job of getting to the contact point and creating the collision, but lacks the strength and frame to be powerful at the POA and consistently sustain through the play.

Gray projects best as a backup H-tight end who fits well in split-zone schemes, as he is very capable of making split-zone blocks if lined up in tight. On 3rd downs, he would be best used in the slot against linebackers or smaller safeties to create separation off the line. He also has the toughness, speed, and competitiveness to play on special teams units.

	Receiving							
Year	Trgt	Rec	Comp%	Yds	Air Yds	YAC	TD	Yds/Trgt	Drops
2017	5	5	100%	37	17	20	2	7.4	0
2018	25	20	80%	234	162	72	1	9.4	1
2019	75	50	67%	388	255	133	3	5.2	1
2020	46	29	63%	285	152	133	2	6.2	1
	151	104	69%	944	586	358	8	6.3	3

	Advanced Receiving						EPA		Positive %	
Year	On-Trgt Catch %	Catchable Catch %	YAC Per Rec	Trgt Share	ADoT	Rec Rating	Total	Per Trgt	vs. Man	vs. Zone
2017	-	100%	4.0	1%	3.4	137.1	4.6	0.92	100%	50%
2018	95%	95%	3.6	5%	7.9	119.0	21.8	0.87	69%	90%
2019	96%	94%	2.7	21%	6.8	81.4	-1.7	-0.02	29%	58%
2020	97%	97%	4.6	12%	8.9	76.8	5.0	0.11	46%	44%
	96%	95%	3.4	9%	7.5	92.1	29.6	0.20	42%	56%

	Route Running		Blown Blk %		Total Points					Total Points Rtg		
Year	Rtes Run	Y/RR	Split Out %	Run	Pass	Tight	Split	Rec Total	Blk	Total	Per Rte	Per Blk	Per Play
2018	136	1.7	61%	0.0%	0.0%	0	6	8	3	12	91	73	83
2019	263	1.5	57%	0.0%	2.7%	1	14	16	5	21	90	54	69
2020	402	0.7	47%	1.8%	1.2%	1	10	13	2	15	94	68	89
	801	1.1	54%	0.7%	1.7%	3	30	37	10	48	-	-	-

Critical Factors	
Blocking Ability	5
Receiving Ability	6
FBI	6

Positional Factors	
Run Block	5
Pass Block	4
Play Strength	5
Play Speed	6
Mismatch	6
Release	6
Catching Skills	6
Separation	5
Run After Catch	6
Clutch Performance	5
Toughness	6
ST Value	5

Kylen Granson

Report by Joe McDonald, Carter Hayden, & Griffin Sullivan

School	Height	Weight	Year	Jersey #	Hometown
SMU	6021 V	242 V	5SR	83	Austin, TX

One Liner

Granson has the athleticism, hands, and overall receiving ability to make him a good No. 2 tight end, but his lack of strength and overall blocking ability may limit how much playing time he sees.

Strengths: Sure hands; Block intensity; Athleticism & versatility
Weaknesses: POA strength; Sustaining blocks; Press release

Kylen Granson is the starting tight end in SMU's Air Raid offense, lining almost a 50/50 split between tight and slot with occasional fullback and wide snaps as well. He started his career at Rice where he played in 18 games before transferring to SMU and starting all 23 games the last 2 seasons. He suffered an ankle injury in high school that resulted in him missing 7 games. A high school track & field athlete, Granson has a slight frame for the position, but has a strong build and good speed. He plays with competitiveness and a high motor on every play.

Granson's versatility to line up anywhere on the field amplifies his ability to be a threat to defenses. He has good catching ability, attacking the ball with quick hands to pluck away from his frame. He can struggle with consistently getting off press, but does a good job of using his hands to swipe defenders away from landing a clean punch. He separates by utilizing stems and his refined route running ability. He also utilizes his hands and positions his body to box out defenders. His speed and receiving ability make him a mismatch for linebackers. He uses contact balance and speed after the catch, making it tough for defenders to bring him down. He also uses a powerful stiff-arm and elusive jump cut to find space. In pass pro, he's too lungy and struggles at the POA to be a consistent contributor.

Granson is a willing run blocker and does so with intensity and high effort. He's a smart player, using his speed and angles to wall off defenders from the runner. He shows sufficient strength, but his smaller stature can make it difficult to move larger defenders with consistency. He's good at chipping defensive linemen as he works up to the 2nd level with tenacity and drive.

Granson's skills as a receiver and tenacity as a blocker project him to be a solid backup H-tight end. His mismatch ability and play speed should allow him to defeat linebackers, especially out of the slot on 3rd downs. He can contribute on special teams due to his play speed, toughness, and athleticism.

	Receiving								
Year	Trgt	Rec	Comp%	Yds	Air Yds	YAC	TD	Yds/Trgt	Drops
2016	48	29	60%	306	168	138	1	6.4	6
2017	33	17	52%	239	191	48	0	7.2	3
2019	64	43	67%	721	425	296	9	11.3	4
2020	56	35	63%	536	312	224	5	9.6	5
	201	124	62%	1802	1096	706	15	9.0	18

	Advanced Receiving						EPA		Positive %	
Year	On-Trgt Catch %	Catchable Catch %	YAC Per Rec	Trgt Share	ADoT	Rec Rating	Total	Per Trgt	vs. Man	vs. Zone
2016	-	80%	4.9	13%	6.5	76.3	-3.1	-0.07	36%	13%
2017	-	81%	2.8	15%	13.5	35.6	-25.2	-0.76	45%	37%
2019	91%	89%	6.9	13%	12.1	138.1	39.3	0.61	50%	64%
2020	85%	85%	7.7	15%	10.2	108.9	21.8	0.39	35%	65%
	88%	85%	6.1	14%	10.5	94.9	32.8	0.16	41%	55%

	Route Running		Blown Blk %		Total Points					Total Points Rtg		
Year	Rtes Run	Y/RR	Split Out %	Run	Pass	Tight	Split	Rec Total	Blk	Total	Per Rte	Per Blk	Per Play
2019	334	2.2	57%	0.8%	1.0%	5	13	19	14	34	90	79	83
2020	441	1.2	48%	0.4%	1.1%	7	12	18	5	18	94	89	90
	775	1.6	53%	0.6%	1.1%	12	25	37	19	52	-	-	-

Critical Factors	
Blocking Ability	5
Receiving Ability	6
FBI	6

Positional Factors	
Run Block	5
Pass Block	4
Play Strength	5
Play Speed	6
Mismatch	6
Release	5
Catching Skills	6
Separation	5
Run After Catch	6
Clutch Performance	6
Toughness	6
ST Value	6

Incomplete data for 2016, 2017 seasons due to limited available video

Luke Farrell

Report by Luke DeCello & Lathon Lax

School	Height	Weight	Year	Jersey #	Hometown
Ohio State	6046 E	258 E	5SR	89	Perry, OH

One Liner

Farrell has the toughness and run-blocking strength to see the field in early downs, but his lack of explosive receiving traits could limit his playing time in today's NFL.

Strengths: Strength and physicality; Block sustain; Box out ability
Weaknesses: Quickness and elusiveness; Route running and a varied route tree; Releases off the line

Luke Farrell is primarily an in-line tight end at Ohio State. He played in 36 games with 32 starts. He has a great frame for the tight end position and a strong build. He isn't quick or elusive, but he's a fluid mover with some build-up speed. He's a tough player in his blocking and ball carrying and does the little things that don't show up in the stat sheet to help his team win.

Farrell did not have a heavy workload in the receiving game. He struggles to get off the line and into his routes when pressed. He is not a good separator with his route-running ability, as he does not run crisp routes or a varied route tree and will not run past most defenders with his speed. However, he uses his size well to box out defenders. He has the awareness to sit in available holes and present a big target. He tends to double or body catch, even when wide open. Farrell won't make players miss after the catch but he does a great job of turning upfield, putting his head down, and falling forward for extra yards. He will struggle with change of direction in pass protection but he mostly does a solid job when asked to stay in.

Farrell is a very strong frontside lead anchor in the run game. He blocks down hard and generates movement off the ball. He has enough athleticism to work along the perimeter and good, quick hands to latch and sustain. He can struggle to get his head across and seal the back side in zone. His timing on combination blocks has caused issues, either leaving his initial chip too early or not getting to the second level quick enough.

Farrell projects as a nice No. 2 blocking tight end to complement a more athletic receiving option. He will seal the edge in 12 personnel and has enough receiving ability to be a reliable underneath safety blanket. He should be a good special teams member on every unit.

	Receiving								
Year	Trgt	Rec	Comp%	Yds	Air Yds	YAC	TD	Yds/Trgt	Drops
2017	7	2	29%	19	0	19	0	2.7	1
2018	26	20	77%	205	100	105	1	7.9	2
2019	12	7	58%	119	94	25	2	9.9	1
2020	9	5	56%	37	22	15	1	4.1	0
	54	34	63%	380	216	164	4	7.0	4

	Advanced Receiving						EPA		Positive %	
Year	On-Trgt Catch %	Catchable Catch %	YAC Per Rec	Trgt Share	ADoT	Rec Rating	Total	Per Trgt	vs. Man	vs. Zone
2017	-	67%	9.5	2%	3.1	0.0	-9.6	-1.36	33%	0%
2018	95%	95%	5.3	5%	7.2	111.9	12.5	0.48	67%	69%
2019	88%	88%	3.6	3%	12.8	131.6	9.3	0.78	33%	63%
2020	100%	83%	3.0	4%	5.1	102.5	-1.4	-0.15	-	50%
	94%	89%	4.8	3%	7.6	100.8	10.9	0.20	50%	58%

	Route Running			Blown Blk %		Total Points					Total Points Rtg		
Year	Rtes Run	Y/RR	Split Out %	Run	Pass	Tight	Split	Rec Total	Blk	Total	Per Rte	Per Blk	Per Play
2018	202	1.0	21%	2.5%	0.0%	5	-1	4	11	16	72	69	67
2019	117	1.0	21%	0.0%	1.9%	1	3	3	15	18	72	95	88
2020	284	0.1	23%	1.1%	0.0%	-1	1	0	2	2	60	82	71
	603	0.6	22%	1.3%	0.7%	5	2	7	28	36	-	-	-

Critical Factors	
Blocking Ability	7
Receiving Ability	5
FBI	5

Positional Factors	
Run Block	7
Pass Block	6
Play Strength	6
Play Speed	5
Mismatch	5
Release	4
Catching Skills	5
Separation	4
Run After Catch	5
Clutch Performance	5
Toughness	6
ST Value	6

Pro Wells

Report by Jacob Halleen, Jarrett Rodgers, & Griffin Sullivan

School	Height	Weight	Year	Jersey #	Hometown
TCU	6025 E	250 E	4JR	81	St. Petersburg, FL

One Liner
Wells has the athletic ability and hands to be a mismatch in the passing game, but his inconsistencies as a blocker and lack of functional strength will likely prevent him from becoming a starter.

Strengths: Mismatch ability; Contested catches; Play speed
Weaknesses: Inline block strength; Man-coverage separation; Release vs. press

Pro Wells is an H-tight end who plays in TCU's spread offense lining up tight, slot, and out wide. He started 6 of 26 games for the Horned Frogs after spending his freshman year at Northwest Mississippi CC. He has a solid build with good size and is a former high school basketball player which is brought out in his athletic abilities. He's a tough competitor who plays with a high motor and competes.

Wells has a sufficient release off the LOS that lacks quickness. He mainly ran curl, deep cross, and seam routes for TCU. He understands leverage and is able to properly identify and take advantage of holes in zones despite not being the most dynamic route runner. He has strong hands and can make contested catches in traffic with regularity. Wells shows good concentration and tracking ability down the field. His combination of size and speed with solid hands creates a mismatch for defenders. After the catch, he turns his eyes downfield and shows good speed and awareness to gain extra yards.

In the running game, Wells shows a willingness to block. He doesn't have great technique or power, but he understands his assignments. He moves his feet well and is able to make an impact as a blocker out on the edge or at the 2nd level. He holds his own against defensive ends and edge players, though he struggles to consistently drive defenders back and seems to do just enough to help make a lane for the ballcarrier to go through.

Wells projects to be a backup H-tight end at the next level who has the athleticism and hands to make an impact in the passing game. However, he needs to get stronger and refine his blocking technique to become an every-down player. On 3rd downs, he can use his mismatch abilities to gain much-needed yards in high-pressure situations. His speed, toughness, and athleticism will allow him to contribute on most special team units.

	Receiving								
Year	Trgt	Rec	Comp%	Yds	Air Yds	YAC	TD	Yds/Trgt	Drops
2018	2	2	100%	12	3	9	0	6.0	0
2019	31	17	55%	196	175	21	5	6.3	4
2020	22	13	59%	195	124	71	3	8.9	0
	55	32	58%	403	302	101	8	7.3	4

	Advanced Receiving						EPA		Positive %	
Year	On-Trgt Catch %	Catchable Catch %	YAC Per Rec	Trgt Share	ADoT	Rec Rating	Total	Per Trgt	vs. Man	vs. Zone
2018	100%	100%	4.5	0%	1.5	91.7	0.7	0.36	-	100%
2019	81%	77%	1.2	8%	11.0	100.3	8.3	0.27	50%	50%
2020	93%	93%	5.5	8%	12.0	108.9	6.7	0.31	50%	46%
	86%	84%	3.2	5%	11.1	105.5	15.7	0.29	50%	50%

	Route Running		Blown Blk %			Total Points				Total Points Rtg		
Year	Rtes Run	Y/RR	Split Out %	Run	Pass	Tight	Split	Rec Total	Blk	Total	Per Rte	Per Blk	Per Play
2018	12	1.0	48%	0.0%	0.0%	0	-1	-1	1	-1	50	89	53
2019	186	1.1	89%	0.0%	0.0%	-1	1	0	1	2	60	79	63
2020	223	0.9	74%	0.0%	0.0%	3	5	8	1	9	96	75	94
	421	1.0	80%	0.0%	0.0%	1	4	7	3	10	-	-	-

Critical Factors	
Blocking Ability	5
Receiving Ability	6
FBI	5

Positional Factors	
Run Block	5
Pass Block	4
Play Strength	5
Play Speed	6
Mismatch	6
Release	5
Catching Skills	6
Separation	5
Run After Catch	6
Clutch Performance	5
Toughness	5
ST Value	6

Miller Forristall

Report by Noah Chang & Michael Churchward

School	Height	Weight	Year	Jersey #	Hometown
Alabama	6045 E	244 E	5SR	87	Cartersville, GA

One Liner

Forristall lacks ideal athleticism and strength to be a starting-caliber two-way tight end, but his football intelligence and efforts in all phases will make him a sufficient backup.

Strengths: Reliable hands; Football intelligence; Body control
Weaknesses: Twitchy athleticism; Mismatch potential; Blocking strength

Miller Forristall is a tight end in Alabama's RPO spread offense. He played in 54 career games, starting 21 of them. He suffered a season-ending knee injury 3 games into his sophomore year and has also missed time due to throat, shoulder and ankle injuries. He has a top-heavy cut and merely sufficient athleticism in space. He plays with good intelligence and toughness to compete within his role.

Forristall has a sufficient release off the line. His adequate speed and acceleration make it difficult to separate, but he's a sufficient underneath route runner and plays with a sense of urgency. He understands the depths of his routes in relation to the sticks and plays with savvy to square himself to the quarterback in coverage openings. He flashes a bit of off-hand separation and is capable of boxing out defenders. He has proven to be a sure-handed safety valve at the catch point, although he lacks the athleticism to expand his catch radius on off-target throws. After the catch he's a no-nonsense runner who lowers his shoulder for extra yardage but won't offer much else. As a pass blocker, he does a good job of fitting well and sustaining with good effort and technique, even if his anchor strength is a bit lacking.

Forristall has good football intelligence as a run blocker to position himself well, but his play strength holds him back in some matchups. He has experience as a playside kickout, a backside seal, a split-zoner, and as a lead blocker from the backfield. He attacks with aggression, willingness, and a square base, but he can get thrown around by stronger defenders. He isn't a true drive blocker but executes soundly.

Forristall projects as a sufficient, athletically-limited number two tight end in the NFL. He is a passable receiver and blocker, but he'll mostly be limited to Y-TE roles in and around the box. He has the football smarts to be an assignment-sound backup and a good checkdown option on passing downs. He has special teams experience as a punt and kickoff return up-man and will be a reliable contributor there moving forward.

Receiving

Year	Trgt	Rec	Comp%	Yds	Air Yds	YAC	TD	Yds/Trgt	Drops
2016	8	5	63%	73	52	21	0	9.1	1
2017	1	1	100%	12	0	12	0	12.0	0
2019	18	15	83%	167	92	75	4	9.3	1
2020	28	23	82%	253	119	134	1	9.0	0
	56	44	79%	505	263	242	5	9.0	2

Advanced Receiving

Year	On-Trgt Catch %	Catchable Catch %	YAC Per Rec	Trgt Share	ADoT	Rec Rating	EPA Total	Per Trgt	Positive % vs. Man	Positive % vs. Zone
2016	-	83%	4.2	2%	7.8	92.2	2.3	0.29	50%	50%
2017	-	100%	12.0	0%	0.0	116.7	0.5	0.53	100%	-
2019	94%	94%	5.0	5%	6.1	144.9	9.3	0.52	0%	86%
2020	96%	96%	5.8	7%	6.1	101.3	13.1	0.47	67%	76%
	95%	93%	5.5	3%	6.2	126.6	24.0	0.43	46%	78%

Route Running / Blown Blk % / Total Points / Total Points Rtg

Year	Rtes Run	Y/RR	Split Out %	Blown Blk % Run	Blown Blk % Pass	Total Points Tight	Total Points Split	Total Points Rec Total	Blk	Total	Per Rte	Per Blk	Per Play
2019	138	1.2	14%	2.0%	5.1%	4	0	4	9	13	73	72	69
2020	472	0.5	20%	0.4%	2.4%	7	1	7	3	10	79	60	73
	630	0.7	16%	0.9%	3.4%	10	0	10	15	26	-	-	-

Redshirt season not shown but included in totals

Critical Factors

Blocking Ability	5
Receiving Ability	5
FBI	6

Positional Factors

Run Block	5
Pass Block	6
Play Strength	5
Play Speed	5
Mismatch	4
Release	5
Catching Skills	6
Separation	5
Run After Catch	4
Clutch Performance	5
Toughness	6
ST Value	6

Cary Angeline

Report by Chad Tedder

School	Height	Weight	Year	Jersey #	Hometown
NC State	6055 E	250 E	5SR	6	Chester Springs, PA

One Liner

Angeline has the length, hands, and catch radius to be a quality backup, but his inconsistencies as a blocker and lack of explosiveness off the ball may keep him from seeing the field consistently at the next level.

Strengths: Reliable hands; Attacks holes in zones; Length
Weaknesses: Explosion; Top-end speed; Diverse route tree

Cary Angeline plays tight end in North Carolina State's spread RPO offense, where he was used evenly in tight and the slot. He played in 35 games at NC State with 16 starts for the Wolfpack after transferring from USC. He is a long, big-bodied, sure-handed athlete that plays hard and competes, showing toughness on each play.

Angeline plays predominantly out of the slot, and presents himself as a sure-handed target where he can be a threat in short-yardage situations. He does not have the quick-twitch ability to get a fast release off the line and beat defenders with an expanded route tree; he creates his separation by finding soft spots in zones through seams, outs, digs, and deep crosses. He hasn't had many chances to show contested catches, as he has predominantly been targeted in open holes in zone coverage, but he has shown that he possesses a good catch radius. In these targets, he goes up and makes a strong-handed catch to bring the ball in and brace for a hit, if necessary. After the catch, Angeline doesn't flash a ton of speed, but he uses his length to eat up yardage in space. He shows enough strength and mirror ability to sustain in pass pro long enough for the pass to be thrown.

In the run game, Angeline is a move piece where he can play on the line, in the backfield and in the slot. He uses his size and power to get some movement on his zone, or split zone, blocks. In the screen game that NC State uses, he is more than willing to lock up a defensive back or linebacker in space and allow for his receivers to make the catch and get upfield. Though he is willing to block, he lacks the physical presence to dominate at the line of scrimmage.

Angeline best projects as a backup H-TE in a spread offense with a zone running scheme. His size and soft hands make him a quarterback-friendly target in 3rd-down situations. His motor and willingness to block makes him a viable member for all special team units.

Receiving

Year	Trgt	Rec	Comp%	Yds	Air Yds	YAC	TD	Yds/Trgt	Drops
2017	1	0	0%	0	0	0	0	0.0	1
2018	12	9	75%	169	113	56	1	14.1	1
2019	44	25	57%	379	272	107	5	8.6	2
2020	37	27	73%	393	282	111	6	10.6	1
	94	61	65%	941	667	274	12	10.0	5

Advanced Receiving

Year	On-Trgt Catch %	Catchable Catch %	YAC Per Rec	Trgt Share	ADoT	Rec Rating	EPA Total	EPA Per Trgt	Positive % vs. Man	Positive % vs. Zone
2017	-	0%	-	0%	1.0	39.6	-0.7	-0.68	-	0%
2018	82%	82%	6.2	2%	12.1	144.4	9.2	0.77	60%	80%
2019	93%	93%	4.3	10%	11.6	104.3	11.5	0.26	20%	63%
2020	89%	89%	4.1	10%	9.8	135.5	27.4	0.74	62%	70%
	89%	88%	4.5	5%	10.8	124.2	47.3	0.50	46%	66%

Route Running / Blown Blk % / Total Points / Total Points Rtg

Year	Rtes Run	Y/RR	Split Out %	Blown Blk % Run	Blown Blk % Pass	Tight	Split	Rec Total	Blk	Total	Per Rte	Per Blk	Per Play
2018	70	2.4	22%	2.3%	0.0%	1	2	5	6	10	91	71	74
2019	260	1.5	45%	0.0%	0.0%	0	8	8	11	19	75	92	84
2020	363	1.1	52%	0.0%	0.0%	6	10	16	5	21	91	78	88
	693	1.4	43%	0.7%	0.0%	7	20	29	22	50	-	-	-

Critical Factors

Blocking Ability	5
Receiving Ability	5
FBI	5

Positional Factors

Run Block	5
Pass Block	6
Play Strength	6
Play Speed	5
Mismatch	5
Release	5
Catching Skills	6
Separation	4
Run After Catch	5
Clutch Performance	6
Toughness	6
ST Value	6

Briley Moore

Report by James Ashley & Michael Bonneville

School	Height	Weight	Year	Jersey #	Hometown
Kansas State	6043 V	251 V	5SR	0	Blue Springs, MO

One Liner
Moore's route savvy in zone paired with his smarts as a run blocker should allow him to contribute at the next level, but a lack of speed, strength, and pass-blocking ability will likely hold him back.

Strengths: Run game FBI; Catch radius; Route savvy
Weaknesses: Body or double catches; Speed & quickness; Strength at the POA

Briley Moore is an H- and Y-tight end for Kansas State's run-heavy offense, occasionally lining up in the slot. He started 21 of 36 games for Northern Iowa before starting 7 of 9 for K-State in 2020. He suffered broken ankles and underwent multiple serious knee surgeries in high school. In 2018, he suffered a spinal cord stinger with short-term paralysis, but luckily only missed 1 game. He then fractured his coracoid and scapula in his shoulder in the 2019 season opener and missed the whole season. His athleticism really shows up in RAC situations where he displays acrobatic potential. He competes and never shies away from contact.

Moore shows consistent hands, but is prone to double- or body-catches too often. He uses his hands and strength well against DBs to create separation at the top of his routes. His main route types were curls, crossers, outs, and seams. Although not an incredible route runner, he uses savvy to find open space. Moore's release off the line isn't special, but he doesn't get easily contacted by edge defenders. He's not fast, but has the ability to shed defenders and fight for extra yards after the catch. He does struggle in 1-on-1 pass pro battles and just lacks the overall strength to sustain at the POA.

Moore uses his awareness of assignments and athleticism to create and seal run lanes. He rarely wins with pure power and is more of a finesse blocker who can wall off defenders. His hand accuracy is too high which results in linebackers sliding past him. He does well in slant and zone blocks where he can chip defenders or get to linebackers at the 2nd level.

Moore projects best as an H-tight end in a scheme where he can be utilized as a zone and split-zone blocker and run short-to-intermediate routes to take advantage of zone defenses. On 3rd downs, he fits best as a move tight end where he can run curls or crossers to help move the chains. His combination of toughness and athleticism with enough play speed should allow him to sufficiently contribute on special teams.

				Receiving					
Year	Trgt	Rec	Comp%	Yds	Air Yds	YAC	TD	Yds/Trgt	Drops
2016	1	1	100%	19	10	9	0	19.0	0
2017	4	4	100%	28	14	14	0	7.0	0
2018	8	6	75%	40	23	17	1	5.0	0
2020	35	22	63%	338	186	152	3	9.7	2
	54	37	69%	451	243	208	4	8.4	2

	Advanced Receiving						EPA		Positive %	
Year	On-Trgt Catch %	Catchable Catch %	YAC Per Rec	Trgt Share	ADoT	Rec Rating	Total	Per Trgt	vs. Man	vs. Zone
2016	-	100%	9.0	4%	10.0	118.8	1.0	1.01	100%	-
2017	-	100%	3.5	11%	3.5	95.8	0.7	0.17	100%	100%
2018	100%	100%	2.8	22%	3.9	125.0	1.6	0.20	100%	50%
2020	91%	88%	6.9	14%	9.6	87.6	3.9	0.11	20%	60%
	94%	90%	5.6	13%	7.5	95.5	7.6	0.14	38%	59%

	Route Running			Blown Blk %		Total Points					Total Points Rtg		
Year	Rtes Run	Y/RR	Split Out %	Run	Pass	Tight	Split	Rec Total	Blk	Total	Per Rte	Per Blk	Per Play
2018	32	1.3	50%	0.0%	-	1	0	1	1	2	76	99	86
2020	332	1.0	23%	1.8%	4.2%	9	0	9	2	11	86	95	88
	382	1.1	27%	1.5%	3.2%	10	0	10	3	12	-	-	-

Critical Factors	
Blocking Ability	5
Receiving Ability	5
FBI	6

Positional Factors	
Run Block	5
Pass Block	4
Play Strength	5
Play Speed	5
Mismatch	5
Release	5
Catching Skills	5
Separation	5
Run After Catch	5
Clutch Performance	6
Toughness	6
ST Value	5

Stats only include games that featured at least one FBS team; Redshirt season not shown but included in totals

Dylan Soehner

Report by Max Nuscher ✳

School	Height	Weight	Year	Jersey #	Hometown
Iowa State	6061 E	272 E	5SR	89	Prairie Grove, AR

One Liner

Soehner has the run-blocking ability and toughness to be a solid run game tight end, but his struggles in pass pro and as a receiver will keep him from consistently seeing the field as a three-down player.

Strengths: Run blocking; Hands; Toughness
Weaknesses: Pass pro; RAC ability; Precise route running

Dylan Soehner plays tight end in Iowa State's tight-end heavy, spread offense utilizing a high amount of zone runs and play action passes. He usually lines up inline or in the backfield with the occasional slot rep. He played in 49 games, starting in 15 of them. He had 2016 shoulder labrum surgery and had his 2019 season cut short with a fractured left fibula. His history as a high school football, basketball, baseball, and track athlete points to his solid athleticism. He is a tough competitor who plays with a high motor on every play.

In the passing game, Soehner has a slow release off the line due to a lack of initial burst and quickness. He isn't a receiving threat and gets open by finding the soft spots in the zone or using his leaping ability and tall frame. He has soft hands and is consistent when targeted. He doesn't possess much ability to run after the catch, as he'll attempt to run through defenders for extra yards. He struggles against edge defenders in pass pro and constantly needs chip help or he'll get pushed back into the quarterback in 1-on-1 situations, though his size allows him to sustain for long enough at times.

Soehner is the main blocking tight end in Iowa State's crowded tight end room, mainly being utilized as a blocker in running situations or RPOs. He's a successful split-zone blocker and also when used to chip defensive ends before moving to the 2nd level. He is very productive at the second level, using his big frame to drive linebackers and defensive backs off their mark and occasionally to the ground. When he lines up in the backfield as a sniffer, he acts as a lead blocker for the running back helping lead the way through the line.

Soehner projects as a backup tight end that will fit best as the Y where he can utilize his blocking ability at the POA and occasional route running. On 3rd downs, he fits best as the Y to block on short yardage or take advantage of his hands in zone to move the chains. On special teams, he should at least contribute as a personal protector or upback.

				Receiving					
Year	Trgt	Rec	Comp%	Yds	Air Yds	YAC	TD	Yds/Trgt	Drops
2018	1	1	100%	0	-2	2	0	0.0	0
2019	13	7	54%	107	75	32	1	8.2	1
2020	22	18	82%	205	78	127	0	9.3	2
	36	26	72%	312	151	161	1	8.7	3

	Advanced Receiving						EPA		Positive %	
Year	On-Trgt Catch %	Catchable Catch %	YAC Per Rec	Trgt Share	ADoT	Rec Rating	Total	Per Trgt	vs. Man	vs. Zone
2018	100%	100%	2.0	0%	-2.0	79.2	-0.3	-0.28	0%	-
2019	88%	88%	4.6	3%	8.3	74.8	-0.3	-0.02	75%	57%
2020	86%	86%	7.1	6%	4.9	105.5	2.2	0.10	50%	67%
	87%	87%	6.2	3%	5.9	96.1	1.6	0.04	55%	64%

	Route Running			Blown Blk %		Total Points				Total Points Rtg		
Year	Rtes Run	Y/RR	Split Out %	Run	Pass	Tight	Split	Rec Total	Blk	Total	Per Rte	Per Blk	Per Play
2018	24	0.0	7%	0.7%	0.0%	-1	0	-1	9	8	51	99	95
2019	56	1.9	9%	0.6%	0.0%	4	-1	3	9	11	85	96	91
2020	379	0.5	18%	0.7%	1.2%	-2	4	4	2	7	79	69	80
	459	0.7	13%	0.7%	0.7%	2	3	6	20	26	-	-	-

Critical Factors	
Blocking Ability	6
Receiving Ability	5
FBI	5

Positional Factors	
Run Block	6
Pass Block	5
Play Strength	5
Play Speed	4
Mismatch	4
Release	4
Catching Skills	6
Separation	4
Run After Catch	4
Clutch Performance	4
Toughness	6
ST Value	5

Nick Eubanks

Report by Ben Hrkach

School	Height	Weight	Year	Jersey #	Hometown
Michigan	6041 E	256 E	5SR	82	Plantation, FL

One Liner

Eubanks is an old school Y-tight end with the size and toughness to succeed on run downs and as a safety blanket receiver, but his overall passing game versatility hinders his ceiling.

Strengths: Blocking ability; Strong hands in traffic; Play strength
Weaknesses: Route-running separation; After-catch athleticism; Receiving production

Nick Eubanks is a tight end in Michigan's power RPO offense. He lined up primarily in-line but also took snaps in the slot. He started 19 of 36 career games and will be 24 when the 2021 season starts. In 2017, an elbow injury limited him to 4 games but otherwise he has been healthy and reliable. Eubanks lacks quickness but is a strong athlete with a big frame. A team captain and fifth-year senior, he is tough and battles well in the trenches.

Eubanks was infrequently used as a receiver but, when called upon, proved to be a reliable target for his QB. He does not get much separation through quickness or route running, rather getting open due to his size and boxing out smaller secondary defenders. He gains good depth in his routes and navigates through traffic on crossing routes well. He did a sufficient job of opening up late on broken plays and displayed capability of working into soft spots in underneath zones. He is a hands catcher that can secure the ball through contact and extend off his big frame but has had a few easy drops. Eubanks has little run-after-catch ability and usually just puts his head down and falls forward after securing the ball. In pass protection, Eubanks showed good footwork, hand use, and toughness to anchor and sustain.

Eubanks is a reliable blocker in the run game. It was clear that he was often the best blocking tight end on Michigan's roster and was typically utilized as a front-side lead anchor. He displays the ability to wall off defensive linemen of all sizes and can generate movement against less run-savvy edge defenders and linebackers. He does a good job of latching, sustaining, and finishing his blocks.

Overall, Eubanks is a classic in-line Y-tight end who fits well as a power scheme blocking substitute. He will be a good blocker in heavy personnels and can offer sufficient underneath reliability as a receiver with his size and strong hands in traffic. He does not make splash plays, but he has the football intelligence to execute within his role. He has a strong skill set for blocking duties on special teams.

Receiving

Year	Trgt	Rec	Comp%	Yds	Air Yds	YAC	TD	Yds/Trgt	Drops
2017	2	2	100%	61	47	14	0	30.5	0
2018	13	8	62%	157	105	52	1	12.1	0
2019	42	26	62%	254	140	114	4	6.0	4
2020	14	10	71%	117	83	34	1	8.4	0
	71	46	65%	589	375	214	6	8.3	4

Advanced Receiving

Year	On-Trgt Catch %	Catchable Catch %	YAC Per Rec	Trgt Share	ADoT	Rec Rating	EPA Total	EPA Per Trgt	Positive % vs. Man	Positive % vs. Zone
2017	-	100%	7.0	1%	23.5	118.8	3.5	1.74	100%	100%
2018	100%	100%	6.5	4%	11.7	129.3	5.0	0.38	50%	50%
2019	88%	88%	4.4	11%	8.5	90.8	0.7	0.02	42%	56%
2020	91%	91%	3.4	7%	8.6	90.5	4.6	0.33	67%	57%
	91%	91%	4.7	6%	9.5	101.2	13.7	0.19	52%	56%

Route Running / Blown Blk % / Total Points / Total Points Rtg

Year	Rtes Run	Y/RR	Split Out %	Run	Pass	Tight	Split	Rec Total	Blk	Total	Per Rte	Per Blk	Per Play
2018	63	2.5	6%	1.0%	0.0%	6	0	5	4	10	98	90	91
2019	207	1.2	19%	2.9%	3.0%	0	0	-1	13	12	59	86	70
2020	177	0.7	17%	3.8%	0.0%	2	0	3	2	5	75	97	85
	447	1.2	16%	2.6%	1.7%	8	0	7	19	27	-	-	-

Critical Factors

Blocking Ability	6
Receiving Ability	4
FBI	5

Positional Factors

Run Block	6
Pass Block	6
Play Strength	6
Play Speed	5
Mismatch	4
Release	5
Catching Skills	5
Separation	4
Run After Catch	4
Clutch Performance	5
Toughness	6
ST Value	5

Shaun Beyer

Report by Jeff Dean & Ryan Rubinstein

School	Height	Weight	Year	Jersey #	Hometown
Iowa	6050 V	249 V	5SR	42	Shellsburg, IA

One Liner

Beyer is an NFL-caliber blocker and his toughness and technique will give him opportunities, but he will need to improve as a receiver to see more varied playing time.

Strengths: Sustaining and controlling blocks; Consistent technique; Toughness
Weaknesses: Separation; Route running; Receiving production

Shaun Beyer is a Y-TE in Iowa's heavy personnel pro-style offense. He played in 29 career games with 14 starts. He missed the end of the 2018 season after suffering a meniscus tear in practice. The 24-year old was a multi-skill position athlete and even a high jumper in high school before adding weight at Iowa. He now is a sufficient athlete who lacks top speed and foot quickness. He has great size and plays with tremendous toughness.

Beyer has a sufficient release and shows solid acceleration to weave through traffic. His route running is shaky, as he uses rounded cuts and extra steps at the top of his breaks. He does show route savvy to find holes in zone, particularly on extended plays. He lacks the elusiveness needed to create effective separation from man coverage. In his infrequent receiving opportunities, he's shown sufficient hands but is prone to body catches. He was often removed in obvious passing situations entirely, but he has enough size, speed, and football intelligence to move the chains if called upon. He is a

sufficient pass blocker but is better attacking defenders downhill than sitting passively.

Beyer earned his playing time due to his blocking ability in the run game. His play strength is sufficient, but he consistently shows good technique to square up and keep his feet under him. He generates power from his lower half with momentum behind him. He holds his own against down linemen and sustains blocks well at all levels with great hand placement. He has good instincts to seek work in space and was consistently counted on as a key blocker in their offense.

Beyer projects as a backup Y-TE who could develop a higher ceiling with added polish to his receiving skills. He has some flexibility to play fullback and move around, but at least initially he will be an early-down in-line blocker and likely removed in passing situations. He has experience on special teams and the requisite size and toughness to be a core contributor moving forward.

Receiving									
Year	Trgt	Rec	Comp%	Yds	Air Yds	YAC	TD	Yds/Trgt	Drops
2017	1	0	0%	0	0	0	0	0.0	0
2018	1	0	0%	0	0	0	0	0.0	0
2019	18	7	39%	117	66	51	0	6.5	2
2020	21	11	52%	158	98	60	1	7.5	1
	41	18	44%	275	164	111	1	6.7	3

Critical Factors	
Blocking Ability	6
Receiving Ability	4
FBI	6

Advanced Receiving						EPA		Positive %	
Year	On-Trgt Catch %	Catchable Catch %	YAC Per Rec	Trgt Share	ADoT	Rec Rating	Total	Per Trgt	vs. Man	vs. Zone
2017	-	-	-	0%	6.0	39.6	-0.7	-0.70	0%	-
2018	-	-	-	0%	12.0	39.6	-2.9	-2.85	0%	-
2019	64%	64%	7.3	5%	11.8	61.6	1.0	0.06	38%	30%
2020	90%	90%	5.5	9%	8.8	73.1	-4.9	-0.23	60%	40%
	76%	76%	6.2	3%	10.1	64.6	-7.5	-0.18	40%	36%

Positional Factors	
Run Block	6
Pass Block	5
Play Strength	5
Play Speed	5
Mismatch	4
Release	5
Catching Skills	5
Separation	4
Run After Catch	4
Clutch Performance	4
Toughness	7
ST Value	6

Route Running			Blown Blk %		Total Points					Total Points Rtg		
Year	Rtes Run	Y/RR	Split Out %	Run	Pass	Tight	Split	Rec Total	Blk	Total	Per Rte	Per Blk	Per Play
2018	6	-	4%	0.0%	0.0%	0	0	0	0	0	58	50	50
2019	120	1.0	15%	0.9%	0.0%	6	-3	2	10	12	69	87	77
2020	271	0.6	8%	1.1%	0.0%	5	-1	4	1	5	85	90	89
	397	0.7	12%	0.9%	0.0%	11	-5	6	11	17	-	-	-

Jack Stoll

Report by Ben Hrkach & Steven Penn

School	Height	Weight	Year	Jersey #	Hometown
Nebraska	6037 V	247 V	5SR	86	Lone Tree, CO

One Liner

Stoll is a big-bodied tight end with enough blocking and receiving skills to be a reliable, yet unspectacular reserve.

Strengths: Size and strength; Route savvy; Hands
Weaknesses: Explosiveness; After-catch skills; Blocking consistency

Jack Stoll played TE in Nebraska's heavy personnel diverse run scheme. He lined up primarily as a Y-TE but often split out to the slot. Stoll played in 43 games and started 26. He tore his MCL in the 2020 opener against Ohio State and was limited for most of the remaining season. He is a hulking presence and a decent athlete with a surprising amount of wiggle in his routes. He displays good toughness by shocking defenders with his hands when blocking and occasionally bowling over would-be tacklers.

Stoll was mostly used as an underneath security blanket in the passing game. He is sufficient at getting off of the LOS and can beat a physical press with his hands. He did not run many sharp-breaking routes but when necessary flashed some suddenness and hand use at the top of routes against leaning defenders. He does a sufficient job at finding the soft spots in zones and sitting down. Stoll has reliable hands and usually catches the ball away from his body. He does not make exceptional catches but he's capable of boxing out in traffic. He does not provide much RAC ability and has some ball security issues, but he is a load to take down. When pass blocking, Stoll has a strong latch and finish but has poor footwork and reactive athleticism due to playing too upright.

In the run game, Stoll wipes defenders out when he latches on. He wins first contact with a strong punch and finishes when available. He works best in a phone booth and shows the strength to hold up in the trenches. He does have inconsistent footwork and pad level, causing issues at the point of attack to square-up cleanly, especially at the second level and in open space.

Overall, Stoll is an old school Y-TE and projects to be a 12 personnel power scheme substitute with finite responsibilities. He needs to improve his footwork and overall consistency when blocking, but he has prototypical size, strength, and toughness to work in-line. He has reliable hands and has the savvy to separate enough when called upon.

Receiving

Year	Trgt	Rec	Comp%	Yds	Air Yds	YAC	TD	Yds/Trgt	Drops
2017	11	8	73%	89	58	31	2	8.1	0
2018	34	21	62%	245	109	136	3	7.2	1
2019	38	25	66%	234	64	170	1	6.2	1
2020	8	7	88%	89	50	39	0	11.1	1
	91	61	67%	657	281	376	6	7.2	3

Advanced Receiving

Year	On-Trgt Catch %	Catchable Catch %	YAC Per Rec	Trgt Share	ADoT	Rec Rating	EPA Total	Per Trgt	vs. Man	vs. Zone
2017	-	89%	3.9	2%	7.5	136.0	4.9	0.44	0%	63%
2018	91%	91%	6.5	9%	6.5	113.0	6.7	0.20	33%	67%
2019	92%	92%	6.8	12%	4.6	69.4	-7.8	-0.21	33%	44%
2020	88%	88%	5.6	4%	6.3	113.0	5.3	0.66	100%	86%
	91%	91%	6.2	7%	5.8	100.8	9.1	0.10	33%	58%

Route Running / Blown Blk % / Total Points / Total Points Rtg

Year	Rtes Run	Y/RR	Split Out %	Run	Pass	Tight	Split	Rec Total	Blk	Total	Per Rte	Per Blk	Per Play
2018	253	1.0	43%	1.0%	0.8%	7	0	7	14	22	76	93	85
2019	251	0.9	44%	1.1%	1.0%	1	0	2	14	16	63	89	75
2020	78	1.1	41%	0.0%	0.0%	1	1	2	0	3	94	74	89
	582	1.0	43%	1.0%	0.9%	8	1	11	28	41	-	-	-

Critical Factors

Blocking Ability	5
Receiving Ability	5
FBI	5

Positional Factors

Run Block	5
Pass Block	5
Play Strength	6
Play Speed	5
Mismatch	4
Release	5
Catching Skills	5
Separation	5
Run After Catch	4
Clutch Performance	5
Toughness	6
ST Value	5

Matt Bushman

Report by Jordan Edwards

School	Height	Weight	Year	Jersey #	Hometown
BYU	6042 E	240 E	4SR	89	Tucson, AZ

One Liner

Bushman is a solid pass catcher with good hands and mismatch potential in the secondary, but he needs to improve his blocking technique and utilization of his size to see the field regularly.

Strengths: Hands; Size mismatch; Production and experience
Weaknesses: Blocking toughness; Natural athleticism; Strength in-line

Matt Bushman is a tight end in BYU's spread offense, lining up in-line, off the ball, and to the slot. He played in 39 career games with 29 starts. Bushman is an older prospect compared to others in this class due to going on a 2-year mission trip before enrolling as a football and baseball player at BYU. He suffered a season-ending torn Achilles in practice leading up to his senior year. Bushman has a tall frame and is stiff in the hips, lacking fluid athletic ability even before the injury. He doesn't show a competitive spirit as an in-line blocker but will fight for extra yards as a receiver.

Bushman displays soft hands and transitions well from pass catcher to ballcarrier. He has the ability to make tough catches using his size and frame to box out defenders. He has build-up speed down the field, but does not separate well with quickness in and out of breaks. He was often given opportunities to leak downfield for big plays or thrown jump balls and back-shoulder fades to win with his size. He isn't a savvy route runner and does not find the opening in zones well. He shows good body control and the ability to stay on his feet and create yards after the catch.

Bushman has prototypical size, but he needs a good amount of development as blocker to become an impact player in the run game. He can seal off second- and third-level players sufficiently, but he doesn't generate a push off the line and gives ground against stronger, more aggressive defenders. He attacks with his shoulder and doesn't square to contact well.

Despite his blocking inconsistencies, Bushman best projects as a Y-tight end at the next level. He doesn't profile as an athletic threat, but with improved technique and toughness at the point of attack, he could be a sufficient in-line player off the bench. His big hands are his best asset and he can be a good red zone threat and slot mismatch with his frame and catch point skills. He should be a capable special teams contributor.

Receiving

Year	Trgt	Rec	Comp%	Yds	Air Yds	YAC	TD	Yds/Trgt	Drops
2017	83	49	59%	520	325	195	3	6.3	2
2018	48	29	60%	511	325	186	2	10.6	1
2019	76	47	62%	688	458	230	4	9.1	1
	207	125	60%	1719	1108	611	9	8.3	4

Advanced Receiving

Year	On-Trgt Catch %	Catchable Catch %	YAC Per Rec	Trgt Share	ADoT	Rec Rating	EPA Total	EPA Per Trgt	Positive % vs. Man	Positive % vs. Zone
2017	-	84%	4.0	20%	8.8	64.3	-11.1	-0.13	48%	44%
2018	90%	90%	6.4	13%	11.9	102.0	7.7	0.16	56%	57%
2019	90%	90%	4.9	17%	10.9	92.4	10.6	0.14	39%	64%
	90%	88%	4.9	17%	10.3	83.4	7.2	0.03	47%	55%

Route Running / Total Points

Year	Rtes Run	Y/RR	Split Out %	Blown Blk % Run	Blown Blk % Pass	Total Points Tight	Total Points Split	Total Points Rec Total	Total Points Blk	Total Points Total	Total Points Rtg Per Rte	Total Points Rtg Per Blk	Total Points Rtg Per Play
2018	237	2.2	30%	1.7%	4.5%	6	7	14	7	21	87	61	70
2019	348	2.0	40%	1.0%	1.0%	8	16	24	10	34	93	66	80
	585	2.0	36%	1.3%	2.4%	13	23	38	17	55	-	-	-

Critical Factors

Blocking Ability	4
Receiving Ability	6
FBI	5

Positional Factors

Run Block	5
Pass Block	4
Play Strength	5
Play Speed	5
Mismatch	6
Release	5
Catching Skills	6
Separation	5
Run After Catch	5
Clutch Performance	5
Toughness	4
ST Value	5

Offensive Tackles

John Shirley

The 2020 NFL season seemed to confirm the notion that quarterback is the most important position on the field. The last four teams standing were all led by elite quarterback play, as Patrick Mahomes (2nd), Tom Brady (3rd), Aaron Rodgers (4th), and Josh Allen (5th) all ranked in the top five in Total Points at the position. The contribution of these players is undeniable, but while quarterback is the single most important position, the players who block for them should get their credit as well. If you don't believe us, turn on a replay of the Super Bowl and see for yourself how important a solid offensive line can be.

In Super Bowl LV, we saw an extreme dichotomy between the Chiefs' banged up offensive line whose starting tackles were playing out of position and the Buccaneers offensive line that played up to its reputation. The lack of protection up-front slowed the high-powered Chiefs offense despite Patrick Mahomes' best efforts. On the other side, Tom Brady enjoyed clean pockets most of the game thanks to his offensive line, which included 2020 *Football Rookie Handbook* alum Tristan Wirfs at right tackle.

After being graded as the third-best offensive tackle in last year's *Handbook*, Wirfs performed as the best of an all-around solid rookie class over the course of 2020. He ranked first among rookie offensive linemen and sixth overall among offensive tackles with 36 Total Points. This was 15 Total Points higher than the next best rookie offensive tackle, which was a three-way tie between the Browns' Jedrick Wills, the Jets' Mekhi Becton, and the Dolphins' Robert Hunt.

Overall, of the 19 offensive tackles who appeared in this book last year, 12 appeared in at least 10 games as rookies, six started at least 10 games, and 11 started at least one game.

After such a solid class that saw six offensive tackles taken in the first round a year ago, it's a little surprising to see that the 2021 class potentially has more upside. This year's class is led by Oregon's Penei Sewell and Northwestern's Rashawn Slater.

Sewell ranks as not only the top offensive tackle among the 2021 class, but is also tied for the top-graded *prospect* regardless of position, with QB Trevor Lawrence. His overall grade of 7.2 is tied for the third-highest ever given out by SIS, behind only Quinnen Williams in 2019 and Chase Young in 2020. This is extremely impressive considering he hasn't played a snap in over a year—he opted out of the 2020 season—and the fact that he will still be 20 years old when the 2021 NFL season starts. The last time we saw Sewell play, he won the 2019 Outland Trophy and was a unanimous All-American.

Rashawn Slater might not be graded as high, but he is still a top-tier prospect. In fact, his overall grade of 6.9 is tied for the second-highest offensive tackle grade SIS has given out in the past three years. Similar to Sewell, Slater also decided to opt out of the 2020 season. The last time we saw him play, he ranked 9th in Pass Blocking Total Points per Snap among tackles and was honorable mention All-Big Ten.

The 2021 tackle class also has depth beyond Sewell and Slater. Virginia Tech's Christian Darrisaw, Notre Dame's Liam Eichenberg, Texas's Samuel Cosmi, and Michigan's Jalen Mayfield all have overall grades of 6.7, which is considered strong starter potential. And right behind them, with a grade of 6.6, is this year's top FCS lineman, Dillon Radunz of North Dakota State.

This year's class also has a few analytics standouts whose production in college doesn't line up with how our scouting staff views their potential. Nebraska's Brenden Jaimes and Kentucky's Landon Young ranked highly by Total Points per Play in both 2019 and 2020. Jaimes ranked as the 4th-best tackle in the country in 2019 and the 8th best in 2020, while Young ranked 3rd in 2019 and 7th in 2020. Our scouting staff, on the other hand, views both as potential backup swing tackles in the NFL. It is important to note that college production does not directly translate to the next level, so it will be interesting to see how their careers play out.

As with most positions this year, opt-outs present some questions among the offensive tackle class. But as a whole, the 2021 class has elite talent at the top, solid depth, and a few players whose production is intriguing despite lesser traits.

OFFENSIVE TACKLE

Offensive Tackle Grading Scale

GRADE	DESCRIPTION
9.0 – 7.0	High-end starter. Pro Bowl level.
6.9 – 6.7	Strong starter with 2 position flexibility.
6.6 – 6.5	Lower end starter who plays only 1 position.
6.3	3rd OT. Swing OT that plays RT and LT.
6.2	Multi-positional backup.
6.1 – 6.0	Developmental. Top traits but needs time.
5.9	Backup LT. 1 position player.
5.8	Backup RT. 1 position player.
5.7	4th OT. Functional depth level player.

Offensive Tackle Rankings

Rank	Name	Grade	Page
1	Penei Sewell	7.2	294
2	Rashawn Slater	6.9	296
3	Christian Darrisaw	6.7	298
4	Liam Eichenberg	6.7	300
5	Samuel Cosmi	6.7	302
6	Jalen Mayfield	6.7	304
7	Dillon Radunz	6.6	306
8	James Hudson	6.5	308
9	Walker Little	6.5	310
10	Adrian Ealy	6.3	312
11	Robert Hainsey	6.3	313
12	Foster Sarell	6.3	314
13	Kayode Awosika	6.3	315
14	Brenden Jaimes	6.3	316
15	Brady Christensen	6.3	317
16	Landon Young	6.3	318
17	Royce Newman	6.2	319
18	Jake Curhan	6.2	320
19	Jaylon Moore	6.2	321
20	Josh Ball	5.9	322
21	Spencer Brown	5.8	323

Glossary

Blown Block%
The percentage of blocking snaps that the player had a blown block.

EPA/A (Runs to Gap Split)
Expected Points Added per rush attempt

Pos% (Runs To Gap split)
Positive Percentage, percentage of carries with a positive Expected Points Added.

Pressure% (Team Stat)
Percentage of total team plays where any defensive player recorded a quarterback hurry, hit, knockdown or sack.

Total Points
Sports Info Solutions' proprietary player value metric that uses an Expected Points framework and distributes the value gained or lost on a play to the players involved based on their impact on the play.

Total Points Rating
Total Points per play compared to average, scaled so that 50 is poor and 99 is excellent.

Y/A (Runs To Gap split)
Yards per rush attempt.

YBC/A (Runs To Gap split)
Yards before contact per rush attempt.

Offensive Tackle Leaderboards

Total Points Per Game

Rk	Player	School	Tot Pts / G
1	J. Moore	Western Michigan	3.8
2	B. Jaimes	Nebraska	3.6
3	L. Young	Kentucky	3.4
4	C. Darrisaw	Virginia Tech	2.9
4	A. Ealy	Oklahoma	2.9
6	L. Eichenberg	Notre Dame	2.8
6	F. Sarell	Stanford	2.8
6	R. Newman	Ole Miss	2.8
9	S. Cosmi	Texas	2.6
9	2 tied with		2.6

Total Points Rating Per Play

Rk	Player	School	Rating
1	J. Moore	Western Michigan	99
2	L. Young	Kentucky	97
3	B. Jaimes	Nebraska	96
4	A. Ealy	Oklahoma	92
4	B. Christensen	BYU	92
6	C. Darrisaw	Virginia Tech	91
7	J. Hudson	Cincinnati	90
8	L. Eichenberg	Notre Dame	89
8	F. Sarell	Stanford	89
8	J. Ball	Marshall	89

Pass Blocking Total Points Per Game

Rk	Player	School	Tot Pts / G
1	B. Christensen	BYU	1.6
2	S. Cosmi	Texas	1.5
2	A. Ealy	Oklahoma	1.5
4	L. Eichenberg	Notre Dame	1.3
4	J. Hudson	Cincinnati	1.3
4	R. Hainsey	Notre Dame	1.3
4	F. Sarell	Stanford	1.3
8	R. Newman	Ole Miss	1.2
9	C. Darrisaw	Virginia Tech	1.1
9	2 tied with		1.1

Total Points Rating Per Pass Block

Rk	Player	School	Rating
1	B. Christensen	BYU	98
2	J. Hudson	Cincinnati	97
3	L. Young	Kentucky	96
4	C. Darrisaw	Virginia Tech	95
4	A. Ealy	Oklahoma	95
6	R. Hainsey	Notre Dame	92
6	J. Moore	Western Michigan	92
6	J. Ball	Marshall	92
9	L. Eichenberg	Notre Dame	91
10	2 tied with		89

Run Blocking Total Points Per Game

Rk	Player	School	Tot Pts / G
1	J. Moore	Western Michigan	2.7
2	B. Jaimes	Nebraska	2.3
2	L. Young	Kentucky	2.3
4	C. Darrisaw	Virginia Tech	1.7
4	K. Awosika	Buffalo	1.7
6	R. Newman	Ole Miss	1.6
7	L. Eichenberg	Notre Dame	1.5
7	A. Ealy	Oklahoma	1.5
7	F. Sarell	Stanford	1.5
10	2 tied with		1.3

Total Points Rating Per Run Block

Rk	Player	School	Rating
1	B. Jaimes	Nebraska	99
1	J. Moore	Western Michigan	99
3	L. Young	Kentucky	97
4	F. Sarell	Stanford	95
5	A. Ealy	Oklahoma	89
6	L. Eichenberg	Notre Dame	88
7	C. Darrisaw	Virginia Tech	86
8	J. Ball	Marshall	85
9	K. Awosika	Buffalo	79
9	R. Newman	Ole Miss	79

	Total Blown Blocks Per Game		
Rk	Player	School	BB/G
1	B. Christensen	BYU	0.2
2	J. Hudson	Cincinnati	0.4
3	A. Ealy	Oklahoma	0.5
4	L. Young	Kentucky	0.6
5	C. Darrisaw	Virginia Tech	0.7
5	K. Awosika	Buffalo	0.7
5	J. Moore	Western Michigan	0.7
8	R. Hainsey	Notre Dame	0.8
9	L. Eichenberg	Notre Dame	0.9
9	3 tied with		0.9

	Overall Blown Block Percentage		
Rk	Player	School	BB%
1	B. Christensen	BYU	0.3%
2	J. Hudson	Cincinnati	0.7%
3	A. Ealy	Oklahoma	0.8%
4	L. Young	Kentucky	1.0%
5	C. Darrisaw	Virginia Tech	1.1%
5	K. Awosika	Buffalo	1.1%
5	J. Moore	Western Michigan	1.1%
8	S. Cosmi	Texas	1.2%
8	R. Hainsey	Notre Dame	1.2%
10	B. Jaimes	Nebraska	1.3%

	Pass Blown Blocks Per Game		
Rk	Player	School	BB/G
1	J. Hudson	Cincinnati	0.2
1	B. Christensen	BYU	0.2
3	C. Darrisaw	Virginia Tech	0.3
4	L. Eichenberg	Notre Dame	0.4
4	R. Hainsey	Notre Dame	0.4
4	B. Jaimes	Nebraska	0.4
4	J. Ball	Marshall	0.4
8	A. Ealy	Oklahoma	0.5
8	L. Young	Kentucky	0.5
8	J. Moore	Western Michigan	0.5

	Pass Blown Block Percentage		
Rk	Player	School	BB%
1	B. Christensen	BYU	0.5%
2	J. Hudson	Cincinnati	0.7%
3	C. Darrisaw	Virginia Tech	1.1%
4	L. Eichenberg	Notre Dame	1.2%
4	R. Hainsey	Notre Dame	1.2%
6	A. Ealy	Oklahoma	1.3%
6	B. Jaimes	Nebraska	1.3%
8	J. Ball	Marshall	1.4%
9	S. Cosmi	Texas	1.5%
10	J. Moore	Western Michigan	1.7%

	Rush Blown Blocks Per Game		
Rk	Player	School	BB/G
1	B. Christensen	BYU	0.0
2	A. Ealy	Oklahoma	0.1
2	K. Awosika	Buffalo	0.1
4	J. Hudson	Cincinnati	0.2
4	L. Young	Kentucky	0.2
4	J. Moore	Western Michigan	0.2
7	S. Cosmi	Texas	0.3
8	C. Darrisaw	Virginia Tech	0.4
8	R. Hainsey	Notre Dame	0.4
8	B. Jaimes	Nebraska	0.4

	Rush Blown Block Percentage		
Rk	Player	School	BB%
1	B. Christensen	BYU	0.0%
2	A. Ealy	Oklahoma	0.3%
3	K. Awosika	Buffalo	0.4%
4	L. Young	Kentucky	0.5%
4	J. Moore	Western Michigan	0.5%
6	J. Hudson	Cincinnati	0.7%
7	S. Cosmi	Texas	0.9%
8	C. Darrisaw	Virginia Tech	1.1%
9	R. Hainsey	Notre Dame	1.3%
9	B. Jaimes	Nebraska	1.3%

Career Games Started

Rk	Player	School	GS
1	B. Jaimes	Nebraska	40
1	J. Curhan	California	40
3	L. Eichenberg	Notre Dame	38
3	B. Christensen	BYU	38
5	R. Slater	Northwestern	37
6	C. Darrisaw	Virginia Tech	35
7	S. Cosmi	Texas	34
7	R. Hainsey	Notre Dame	34
9	L. Young	Kentucky	33
10	2 tied with		32

Yards Before Contact To Their Gap Per Attempt

Rk	Player	School	YBC/A
1	J. Hudson	Cincinnati	5.1
2	K. Awosika	Buffalo	4.3
3	L. Young	Kentucky	3.6
4	A. Ealy	Oklahoma	3.3
5	C. Darrisaw	Virginia Tech	3.2
5	B. Jaimes	Nebraska	3.2
7	L. Eichenberg	Notre Dame	3.1
8	J. Ball	Marshall	2.9
9	J. Moore	Western Michigan	2.7
10	F. Sarell	Stanford	2.6

Holding Penalties

Rk	Player	School	Holds
1	L. Eichenberg	Notre Dame	0
1	S. Cosmi	Texas	0
1	R. Hainsey	Notre Dame	0
1	F. Sarell	Stanford	0
1	K. Awosika	Buffalo	0
1	J. Ball	Marshall	0
7	C. Darrisaw	Virginia Tech	1
7	B. Jaimes	Nebraska	1
7	R. Newman	Ole Miss	1
7	J. Moore	Western Michigan	1

Yards Before Contact To Their Gap Per Game

Rk	Player	School	YBC/G
1	K. Awosika	Buffalo	55.9
2	C. Darrisaw	Virginia Tech	46.2
3	J. Hudson	Cincinnati	33.0
4	B. Jaimes	Nebraska	32.1
5	A. Ealy	Oklahoma	30.2
6	L. Eichenberg	Notre Dame	28.7
7	L. Young	Kentucky	28.1
8	B. Christensen	BYU	25.7
9	F. Sarell	Stanford	25.2
10	J. Moore	Western Michigan	22.8

Positive Percentage When Run Behind

Rk	Player	School	Pos%
1	L. Young	Kentucky	58%
2	F. Sarell	Stanford	57%
3	A. Ealy	Oklahoma	56%
3	J. Moore	Western Michigan	56%
5	C. Darrisaw	Virginia Tech	54%
5	J. Ball	Marshall	54%
7	J. Hudson	Cincinnati	52%
8	L. Eichenberg	Notre Dame	51%
8	B. Jaimes	Nebraska	51%
8	B. Christensen	BYU	51%

Yards When Run Behind Per Game

Rk	Player	School	Yds/G
1	C. Darrisaw	Virginia Tech	110.9
2	K. Awosika	Buffalo	105.7
3	A. Ealy	Oklahoma	63.4
4	B. Jaimes	Nebraska	59.9
5	B. Christensen	BYU	59.7
6	L. Eichenberg	Notre Dame	55.8
7	J. Hudson	Cincinnati	54.2
8	L. Young	Kentucky	53.9
9	R. Newman	Ole Miss	47.8
10	J. Moore	Western Michigan	47.7

Penei Sewell

Report by John Todd

School	Height	Weight	Year	Jersey #	Hometown
Oregon	6051 E	330 E	3JR	58	Malaeimi, Am. Samoa

One Liner
Sewell will immediately upgrade an NFL team's running game with his strength and fundamentals at all levels, and with minor upper-body refinements as a pass protector will be a more than reliable blind-side protector for years to come.

Overall
Penei Sewell was the left tackle for Oregon's zone offense for 2 years before opting out of the 2020 season. He had shoulder labrum surgery in 2017 before enrolling but then started as a true freshman from Day 1 for 20 of 21 career games. He missed 6 games his first year due to a high ankle sprain that needed surgery, but returned for his bowl game. He was a teenager for every collegiate game he played. He's high-waisted with ideal size for the position. He's a very fluid athlete for his size and is abnormally comfortable in space. He's a physical presence up front who sets a tone and will finish opponents at all levels of the field.

Pass Game
As a pass protector, Sewell is difficult to work past, but he isn't without his faults. He kicks off the ball with fundamentally sound short steps and square footwork to all set levels. He tends to bend at the waist slightly but he sits with good knee flexion and strafes to and through contact beautifully. He seeks work and senses moving parts up front well. He's not a quick-twitch athlete and has shown to be a bit rigid in pass pro with the occasional issue changing direction in tight quarters. Sewell's biggest issue is his wide hands in his initial punch. He consistently attacks rushers' shoulder pads instead of keeping his elbows tight and latching onto their chest plate. He can extend early and leave himself open to finesse moves inside. However, his anchor strength, sound, quick base, and body control at awkward angles keep him from losing most battles. Additionally, he's an exceptional blocker ahead of screen passes, stalking and swallowing up smaller defenders in space with ease.

Run Game
The most notable facet of Sewell's game, however, is his dominance in the run game. He was the anchor of Oregon's ground attack and a force in any scheme to any run direction. He fires off with good pad level for his size and his core strength and wide base and feet regularly walk defenders off the ball and reset the line of scrimmage. On the front side of wide zones he excels at exploding his hips through a straight arm and locking out after contact to clear running lanes. He skip-pulls inside fluidly and arrives with force, and pulls outside into space like a freight train. He sustains well with great grip strength and heavy feet, but he's at his best combination blocking up to the second level. Sewell's ability to knock off a lineman in a double team, then advance up to and engulf linebackers is phenomenal and was the staple concept of much of Oregon's inside run game. He still attacks with wide hands too often and can get caught hugging, but the rest of his elements in the run game add up to an ideal road grader.

Last Word
Sewell projects as an elite NFL tackle in any offensive scheme. There's no reason to move him from the blind side, but he'd make for a dominant right tackle or guard if necessary. Sewell can stand to refine his upper-body technique in pass protection with more patience and a tighter punch, but he's an immediate game-changer in the run and screen games.

Strengths
- Dominant run blocker
- 2nd-level and space blocking
- Core strength

Weaknesses
- Wide hands
- Slight rigidity in pass pro

Critical Factors

Reactive Athleticism	Anchor / Play Strength	Body Control
6	8	7

Positional Factors

Run Block	Pass Block	Awareness	Footwork
8	7	6	7
2nd Level	Range	Hand Use	Power
8	7	5	7
Sustain	Finish	Flexibility	Toughness
7	7	6	6

Basic

Year	G	GS	Penalties Holding	False Start	Blown Block Splits Run	Pressure	Sack	Total
2018	7	7	0	0	0	1	0	1
2019	14	13	2	0	8	7	2	17
	21	20	2	0	8	8	2	18

Team Stats

Year	Zone Run Blocking % of Runs	Y/A	Pos%	Gap Run Blocking % of Runs	Y/A	Pos%	Pass Block Pressure%
2018	81%	4.5	47%	18%	5.6	42%	30%
2019	77%	5.6	46%	22%	5.3	51%	27%
	79%	5.1	47%	20%	5.4	47%	29%

Deep Dive

Year	Blown Block % Run	Pass	When Running to their Gap Y/A	YBC/A	Pos%	EPA/A	Total Points Run	Pass	Total	Total Points Rtg Per Run	Per Pass	Per Play
2018	0.0%	0.5%	5.4	2.5	50%	-0.03	10	9	18	82	97	91
2019	1.8%	1.9%	5.5	2.5	49%	0.01	16	21	36	71	97	88
	1.2%	1.5%	5.5	2.5	49%	0.00	26	30	54	-	-	-

Rashawn Slater

Report by Ben Hrkach

School	Height	Weight	Year	Jersey #	Hometown
Northwestern	6041 E	314 E	4SR	70	Sugar Land, TX

One Liner
Slater is an athletic technician of a blocker, with the hands, feet, savvy, and body control to play right tackle at a high level.

Overall
Rashawn Slater played right and left tackle for Northwestern's balanced rushing attack and quick passing game. He started all 37 career games dating back to his true freshman season before opting out of his senior year. He started his first two years at right tackle before moving to LT in 2019. Slater is a nimble athlete that is very flexible and well proportioned, but he doesn't have the longest arms for a tackle.

Pass Game
In the pass game, Slater excels as a hand fighter. He lacks ideal size and length on the perimeter, so he makes up for it with savvy and hand strength. He uses a staggered punch and is adept at flashing hands and repositioning when needed. He has the ability to initiate the battle with a one handed shot to the chest and follow up by controlling with his off hand. He is also good at baiting the defender into committing, disarming their hands, and stonewalling their pass rush. No matter his tactic, Slater has a very good latch and sustain, along with a good finish. On occasion, he will get grabby outside of the frame of the defender against length and strength, which are his greatest vulnerabilities. He does show a good anchor and great body control to sit down and catch himself when being bull rushed at awkward angles. His reactive athleticism and feet are good and he primarily takes quick, low steps. He can get sloppy and will click his heels in his vertical sets, as well as crossing his feet against inside moves. Slater saves himself with his balance and very good ankle flexion. He shows a lack of awareness on stunts and crossers at times, tracking the initial movement too far making it difficult to recover for the loop behind, but again his recovery quickness is a strong counter skill.

Run Game
Slater is a very good run blocker, winning with quick, low feet, a square base, and very good hand strength. Once he latches, he almost never comes disengaged. He has sufficient power, but flashes nastiness to put a defender into the ground at multiple levels. He is adept at gaining body position and swiftly seals off defenders to open run lanes. He is not a body mover but has enough power to stalemate most interior players one-on-one. Slater shows good range on pulls and is very good at the second level. He arrives quickly with heavy hands and is under control enough to match quicker defenders. Slater does show a lack of awareness on some pulls and combo blocks to space. He is not a great multitasker and tends to complete his job before evaluating his next move.

Last Word
Overall, Slater projects best as a right tackle in a run-heavy power offense. He has all of the tools to be a great run blocker, should he develop some more power, and is a good pass protector. He could project to start at guard as a rookie if that's the easiest place to win a job. He also projects as a starting-level left tackle, but his skill set is ideally suited to the right side.

Strengths
- Hand fighting and grip strength
- Ankle flexion
- Run blocking

Weaknesses
- Arm length
- Power
- Awareness

Critical Factors

Reactive Athleticism	Anchor / Play Strength	Body Control
6	6	7

Positional Factors

Run Block	Pass Block	Awareness	Footwork
7	6	5	6
2nd Level	Range	Hand Use	Power
7	6	7	5
Sustain	Finish	Flexibility	Toughness
7	6	7	6

Basic

Year	G	GS	Penalties		Blown Block Splits			
			Holding	False Start	Run	Pressure	Sack	Total
2017	12	12	1	0	7	15	2	24
2018	14	14	0	0	1	7	3	11
2019	11	11	4	0	5	1	1	7
	37	37	5	0	13	23	6	42

Team Stats

Year	Zone Run Blocking			Gap Run Blocking			Pass Block
	% of Runs	Y/A	Pos%	% of Runs	Y/A	Pos%	Pressure%
2017	57%	4.8	43%	43%	5.0	47%	33%
2018	59%	4.0	39%	41%	4.2	44%	35%
2019	65%	5.0	43%	33%	3.8	34%	32%
	60%	4.6	42%	39%	4.4	42%	33%

Deep Dive

Year	Blown Block %		When Running to their Gap				Total Points			Total Points Rtg		
	Run	Pass	Y/A	YBC/A	Pos%	EPA/A	Run	Pass	Total	Per Run	Per Pass	Per Play
2018	0.2%	1.7%	4.5	1.4	41%	-0.04	14	16	30	64	77	71
2019	1.2%	0.6%	3.5	1.5	35%	-0.19	15	16	30	68	98	86
	0.7%	1.3%	4.0	1.4	38%	-0.12	29	32	60	-	-	-

Christian Darrisaw

Report by John Todd

School	Height	Weight	Year	Jersey #	Hometown
Virginia Tech	6045 E	314 E	3JR	77	Upper Marlboro, MD

One Liner
Darrisaw is a smooth operator with impressive anchor strength and body control, but improved urgency and explosion at the point of attack will help him reach a higher ceiling.

Overall
Christian Darrisaw is the left tackle in Virginia Tech's diverse but primarily zone blocking scheme. He played and started in all 35 career games. He missed the 2019 offseason after undergoing surgery for an ankle injury but has otherwise played through his ailments. He has a strong and stocky build, yet an athletic frame with little bad weight. He's a smooth mover with the good and bad that come with it. He's patient and fluid in space but lacks quick-twitch explosive traits and a sense of urgency. He's tough and will throw defenders around but doesn't attack or finish with tenacity consistently.

Pass Game
While Darrisaw isn't the quickest off the line into his pass sets, he's isn't often caught out of position. He kick-slides vertically with good footwork, a strong, sound base, and sits with proper form. He can reach the top of the rush arc without crossing over, but superior speed rushers will test him. He's patient to attack and does not get caught lunging. His awareness is adequate, but he has struggled adjusting to interior stunts and with looking for work. At the point of attack, Darrisaw does a great job of bracing for contact and absorbing with superior lower-body strength and upper-body form to anchor. Wide hands and inconsistent pop get him in trouble, especially against finesse rushers. He doesn't have refined counter skills in his hands and often relies on his anchor strength to compensate for losing the battle at initial contact. Still, he does not often lose one-on-ones and has a strong foundational skill set for pass protection.

Run Game
Darrisaw excels as a scheme-versatile run anchor for the Hokies. He has fluid hips to reach and seal interior defensive linemen from the back side and also pull inside and out. He is more of a catcher and pusher at the point of attack, but his wide base, leg drive, and raw power allow him to square up and move defenders off the ball. Darrisaw could become a force in the run game with more quickness off the snap, explosion to contact, and better pad level. He again relies on his raw strength to move defenders rather than putting together a package of techniques and tenacity to physically dominate and consistently finish. He moves very well in space and is an impressive second-level blocker, getting to his spots with ease.

Last Word
Darrisaw projects as a starting caliber tackle at the NFL level, ideally on the right side. He could protect the blind side if necessary, but his strength and projectable struggles against finesse and speed should prefer him to right tackle. He is scheme-diverse, with the power and pulling skills for man and the hip fluidity and second-level range for zone. If he can better utilize his raw strength at the point of attack and improve his technical hand use, he has the potential for a bright future.

Strengths	Weaknesses
• Raw strength	• Overall quickness and urgency
• Smooth mobility	• Hand technique
• Body control and positioning	• Explosion to contact

Critical Factors

Reactive Athleticism	Anchor / Play Strength	Body Control
5	7	7

Positional Factors

Run Block	Pass Block	Awareness	Footwork
6	6	5	6
2nd Level	Range	Hand Use	Power
7	6	5	6
Sustain	Finish	Flexibility	Toughness
6	5	6	6

Basic

Year	G	GS	Penalties		Blown Block Splits			
			Holding	False Start	Run	Pressure	Sack	Total
2018	12	12	2	0	1	4	5	10
2019	13	13	0	0	1	4	2	7
2020	10	10	1	0	4	2	1	7
	35	35	3	0	6	10	8	24

Team Stats

Year	Zone Run Blocking			Gap Run Blocking			Pass Block
	% of Runs	Y/A	Pos%	% of Runs	Y/A	Pos%	Pressure%
2018	64%	4.6	43%	34%	5.5	48%	33%
2019	42%	4.6	37%	54%	4.8	46%	35%
2020	67%	6.3	53%	31%	6.4	50%	29%
	57%	5.2	45%	40%	5.3	48%	32%

Deep Dive

Year	Blown Block %		When Running to their Gap				Total Points			Total Points Rtg		
	Run	Pass	Y/A	YBC/A	Pos%	EPA/A	Run	Pass	Total	Per Run	Per Pass	Per Play
2018	0.3%	2.1%	6.4	4.0	47%	0.12	18	11	29	92	73	83
2019	0.2%	1.6%	5.4	2.2	40%	-0.03	16	16	33	69	96	83
2020	1.1%	1.1%	7.7	3.2	54%	0.24	17	11	29	86	95	91
	0.5%	1.7%	6.5	3.0	47%	0.11	51	38	91	-	-	-

Liam Eichenberg

Report by Alec Mallon ✳

School	Height	Weight	Year	Jersey #	Hometown
Notre Dame	6051 E	302 E	5SR	74	Cleveland, OH

One Liner
Eichenberg's agility in pass protection and anchor strength project well to the left side, and if he can improve his movement in the run game, should be a solid starter on the perimeter.

Overall
Liam Eichenberg is the left tackle for Notre Dame in their zone-heavy run scheme. He has appeared in 43 games over his 5 years in college and started 38, all on the blind side. He underwent meniscus surgery on both knees in high school. Eichenberg has a powerful upper body along with a strong frame for the position. He's light on his feet but struggles redirecting against superior athletes. For a smart and intelligent player, he loves to throw his body around to display his toughness and nasty side.

Pass Game
In the pass game, Eichenberg gets into his sets quickly and fluidly. He has quick feet to get to his spots with urgency. Facing speed rushers, Eichenberg wins with his hands. He delivers a powerful punch and does a good job of winning initial contact. He shows great body control and footwork to keep a consistently square base, helping him maintain strong positioning. At times, Eichenberg can be caught lunging and miss with his hands, but he has enough athleticism and flexibility to reset. Eichenberg has a strong lower half, allowing him to handle power rushers well and drive smaller rushers around the pocket. He can sometimes catch instead of attack, but he absorbs well and uses his lower half to set a strong anchor to limit penetration. He has good awareness with stunts and is quick to recognize rushers crossing his face. He is most susceptible to counter rush moves inside as he can be too protective of the edge. Defenders can use spin and swim moves against him, but he shows enough second-effort recovery skills to usually give his quarterback time to evade.

Run Game
Eichenberg shows he can be effective in the run game, but there is room for improvement. He displays the athleticism to reach block and wall-off defenders up to the second level quickly, but he can come in a little out of control and struggles executing against quickness in space. He does not display the aggression and power at the point of attack to move the line of scrimmage, and his feet tend to slow at contact, but he sufficiently turns defenders away from the ball. His footwork when engaged leads to occasional issues to sustain, but when available, he's shown to be a nasty finisher. He is most effective on zone runs where he can double team with the guard to help move the LOS and flow laterally. He was not asked to pull much, but he does so sufficiently and can get out ahead of screens, although his effectiveness at the third level is inconsistent.

Last Word
Eichenberg projects as a starting left tackle at the NFL level with some flexibility to the right side if needed. However, his pass protection comfortability and limitations as a lead anchor in the run profile better to the left. He can play in both zone and gap schemes but will have more success in a zone offense where he can rely more on his athleticism rather than raw power.

Strengths	Weaknesses
• Pass set	• Effectiveness in open space
• Punch	• Generating movement off the line
• Anchor ability	• Counter rushes

Critical Factors

Reactive Athleticism	Anchor / Play Strength	Body Control
6	7	6

Positional Factors

Run Block	Pass Block	Awareness	Footwork
5	7	6	6
2nd Level	Range	Hand Use	Power
5	5	6	5
Sustain	Finish	Flexibility	Toughness
5	6	6	6

Basic

Year	G	GS	Penalties Holding	False Start	Blown Block Splits Run	Pressure	Sack	Total
2017	5	0	0	0	0	0	0	0
2018	13	13	0	0	4	8	3	15
2019	13	13	0	0	3	4	1	8
2020	12	12	0	0	6	5	0	11
	43	38	0	0	13	17	4	34

Team Stats

Year	Zone Run Blocking % of Runs	Y/A	Pos%	Gap Run Blocking % of Runs	Y/A	Pos%	Pass Block Pressure%
2017	52%	7.3	48%	45%	5.9	46%	40%
2018	56%	5.3	50%	39%	5.0	38%	39%
2019	48%	4.9	44%	48%	5.3	48%	32%
2020	74%	5.2	46%	23%	6.2	54%	36%
	57%	5.7	47%	39%	5.6	46%	36%

Deep Dive

Year	Blown Block % Run	Pass	When Running to their Gap Y/A	YBC/A	Pos%	EPA/A	Total Points Run	Pass	Total	Total Points Rtg Per Run	Per Pass	Per Play
2018	0.9%	2.2%	5.7	2.9	39%	-0.04	15	12	27	74	68	71
2019	0.9%	1.1%	7.2	2.5	46%	0.24	13	19	32	71	94	86
2020	1.6%	1.2%	6.1	3.1	51%	0.00	18	16	34	88	91	89
	1.1%	1.5%	6.3	2.8	45%	0.06	46	47	93	-	-	-

Samuel Cosmi

Report by Chad Tedder

School	Height	Weight	Year	Jersey #	Hometown
Texas	6061 E	309 E	4JR	52	Humble, TX

One Liner
Cosmi has the strength, athleticism, and football IQ to be a solid starter at the next level, but with some refinement in his lower half and technical ability he can reach a very high ceiling.

Overall
Samuel Cosmi is the starting left tackle for the Texas Longhorns' spread, zone running offense. He has started 34 of his 35 career games played, first at right tackle in 2018 before moving full-time to the blindside the final 2 years of his career. Cosmi is big and long, but has room to fill out his frame further. He's extremely athletic, as seen on his 2019 trick play touchdown. He's a tough player with his strength and athleticism but lacks a strong finish on most blocks.

Pass Game
In the pass game, Cosmi pops up out of his stance giving him a narrow base which results in tight hips and sufficient footwork. At the point of attack, he's able to sit back down and shows consistency in stifling rush attempts by setting a good anchor and communicating with his teammates. He shows good play strength and power in handling edge rushers, using his length and size to get his hands inside a defender's pads and bring their rush to a halt. His long-limbed athleticism wards off speed and rip techniques from edge defenders by controlling them and washing them out. Comsi does a good job of not showing his hands early, rather keeping them low and waiting for the rusher to get into range before attacking, although his initial punch could shock more consistently. He communicates well with his guard in trading off stunts up front and shows good quickness in strafing back into advantageous positions on tradeoffs. Cosmi does struggle with quick inside-rush maneuvers mainly due to his inability to stay square in his kick-slide off the line. His preference to work blockers out wide leaves him susceptible to opening his hips and struggling to redirect and mirror.

Run Game
In the run game, Cosmi uses his agility to seal off defenders and get across the face of interior linemen in zone. He is predominantly a shield blocker where he gets into position to anchor down and wall off defenders. He has solid power at the point of attack but impressive leg drive allows him to move defenders off the line and occasionally get to the second level, but he lacks the snap-to-snap nastiness needed to finish consistently. He is most effective on the boundaries in space where he can show off his athleticism and speed downfield.

Last Word
Cosmi best projects as a starting right tackle in a zone run scheme. With some development with his technique and lower-body work, he could eventually move over and start on the left side, but he's a safe bet on the right. He has the athleticism to work very well in space on wide zones and screen plays.

Strengths

- Agility
- Passing game awareness
- Anchor ability & leg drive

Weaknesses

- Inside rush maneuvers
- Lower-body technique
- Consistent nastiness

Critical Factors

Reactive Athleticism	Anchor / Play Strength	Body Control
6	7	7

Positional Factors

Run Block	Pass Block	Awareness	Footwork
6	6	7	5
2nd Level	Range	Hand Use	Power
5	6	6	6
Sustain	Finish	Flexibility	Toughness
6	5	6	6

Basic

Year	G	GS	Penalties		Blown Block Splits			
			Holding	False Start	Run	Pressure	Sack	Total
2018	14	13	1	0	2	6	3	12
2019	13	13	6	0	4	6	3	14
2020	8	8	0	0	2	3	2	7
	35	34	7	0	8	15	8	33

Team Stats

Year	Zone Run Blocking			Gap Run Blocking			Pass Block
	% of Runs	Y/A	Pos%	% of Runs	Y/A	Pos%	Pressure%
2018	71%	4.4	48%	26%	4.4	49%	34%
2019	74%	5.6	51%	24%	4.8	46%	28%
2020	85%	6.1	45%	10%	6.6	50%	31%
	75%	5.3	48%	21%	4.8	48%	31%

Deep Dive

Year	Blown Block %		When Running to their Gap				Total Points			Total Points Rtg		
	Run	Pass	Y/A	YBC/A	Pos%	EPA/A	Run	Pass	Total	Per Run	Per Pass	Per Play
2018	0.4%	1.9%	4.3	2.0	52%	0.06	19	13	32	83	71	77
2019	1.1%	1.8%	5.7	2.5	57%	0.15	20	22	43	95	92	94
2020	0.9%	1.5%	4.3	1.7	42%	-0.02	9	12	21	75	89	84
	0.8%	1.8%	4.8	2.1	52%	0.07	48	47	96	-	-	-

Jalen Mayfield

Report by Matt Manocherian

School	Height	Weight	Year	Jersey #	Hometown
Michigan	6052 E	320 E	3JR	73	Grand Rapids, MI

One Liner

Mayfield is a very young prospect who is just sufficient as a reactive athlete, but he shows the awareness, upper body strength, run blocking ability, and nastiness to develop into a strong starter on the right side of an NFL offensive line.

Overall

Jalen Mayfield lined up at right tackle for Michigan in each of his 15 starts over the last two years after subbing at left tackle for three games during his redshirt freshman season. He is a young player who will be drafted before he turns 21 and has excellent growth potential. He showed impressive strength improvements as a redshirt sophomore in limited exposures in 2020, but the combination of the shortened season and an ankle injury led to him playing in just two games. He possesses good size and strength to play tackle or guard at the NFL level, showing impressive upper body strength with a violent punch. He is not a top reactive athlete, but he plays on his feet with intelligence and a nasty streak.

Pass Game

In the pass game, Mayfield's size and strength project for him to be able to play at right tackle or either guard position, but he doesn't have the athleticism to be an ideal left tackle. At RT, he narrows his stance in obvious passing situations to help him get into his kick-step more quickly, and he might require help against top Edge athletes. He will open the door in pass protection at times and subsequently give ground, but he shows good balance to reestablish his anchor. He shows good awareness to handle stunts and blitzes, and he plays under control. He doesn't have the quickest hands, but he works to get inside hand placement and does a solid job of mirroring.

Run Game

Mayfield is powerful in the run game with the ability to move people off the ball and create running lanes. He shows a good ability to redirect on combos and finish at the second level. He sustains and finishes blocks with aggression and seems to toss somebody out of the club about once per game. He is a powerful down blocker who also functions well in the zone game, and he shows good ability to pull and play under control while in space. He projects to be a plus player in the run game from Day 1, and he fits well in both gap and zone schemes.

Last Word

Based on his length and strength, Mayfield's most likely fit is as a right tackle, but he could easily end up as a starter at either guard position. He is scheme and position flexible, and he has excellent upside for continued development as such a young prospect.

Strengths

- Run blocking
- Upper body strength
- Football intelligence

Weaknesses

- Athletic ability
- Gives ground in pass pro
- Limited experience

Critical Factors

Reactive Athleticism	Anchor / Play Strength	Body Control
5	6	6

Positional Factors

Run Block	Pass Block	Awareness	Footwork
7	6	7	5
2nd Level	Range	Hand Use	Power
7	6	6	7
Sustain	Finish	Flexibility	Toughness
7	7	5	6

Basic

Year	G	GS	Penalties Holding	False Start	Blown Block Splits Run	Pressure	Sack	Total
2018	3	0	0	0	0	0	0	0
2019	13	13	0	0	9	11	3	24
2020	2	2	0	0	0	0	0	0
	18	15	0	0	9	11	3	24

Team Stats

Year	Zone Run Blocking % of Runs	Y/A	Pos%	Gap Run Blocking % of Runs	Y/A	Pos%	Pass Block Pressure%
2018	59%	5.3	52%	40%	5.7	44%	33%
2019	67%	4.5	46%	32%	5.1	49%	33%
2020	51%	3.7	42%	49%	6.7	51%	28%
	61%	4.8	48%	38%	5.7	47%	32%

Deep Dive

Year	Blown Block % Run	Pass	When Running to their Gap Y/A	YBC/A	Pos%	EPA/A	Total Points Run	Pass	Total	Total Points Rtg Per Run	Per Pass	Per Play
2018	0.0%	0.0%	6.8	3.5	70%	0.19	1	0	2	97	91	95
2019	2.3%	3.5%	4.8	2.4	46%	-0.04	17	18	35	81	94	89
2020	0.0%	0.0%	9.7	6.7	65%	0.44	5	4	9	99	98	99
	1.9%	2.9%	5.5	3.0	50%	0.03	23	22	46	-	-	-

Dillon Radunz

Report by Nathan Cooper

School	Height	Weight	Year	Jersey #	Hometown
North Dakota State	6055 V	304 V	5SR	75	Becker, MN

One Liner
Radunz shows the finishing ability, 2nd-level control, and overall strength and power in the run game to be an effective lineman at the next level, though he'll need to improve his pad level, balance, and footwork to be a more consistent player.

Overall
Dillon Radunz is a left tackle in North Dakota State's pro-style offense that uses a balanced mix of zone, duo, and gap schemes. He played in 33 games at LT for the Bison, starting 32 of them. He only played a handful of snaps in the 2017 opener before suffering an ACL injury that cost him the rest of the season. He has a long frame and is a solid athlete with good ankle flexion, but only shows sufficient overall flexibility. He plays hard and competes with toughness on every snap.

Pass Game
In the passing game, Radunz uses more of a short-set off the line rather than a true kick-slide from the tackle position. At times, this will result in him over-setting and allowing rushers back inside of him. He has good length and uses his hands well, but doesn't always use his length and allows defenders to get into his chest. When he does use his length, his strong hands and latch ability are able to neutralize rushers. Even if he gets contacted first, he does show the ability to recover and anchor quickly, though there are times he'll be driven back into his quarterback. He'll struggle against speed around the edge at times as he starts to bend at the waist and fall off balance. He does a good job recognizing and taking on cross-face rushers and stunts. Due to limited flexibility, he will over-extend at times and bend too much at the waist instead of the knees.

Run Game
In the run game, Radunz shows good power and leg drive. He fires off the ball and delivers a blow at the POA. He's able to latch on with good hand placement and then drives his legs to move the defender off the ball with solid vertical push. He also does a good job comboing and redirects quickly to multiple defenders. When getting to the 2nd level, he's balanced and under control at the POA and is able to get a win a high majority of the time. In space, he shows good range to get outside of the tackle box and is able to get into position to latch onto smaller, quicker defenders. One of his best traits is his ability to finish. He's able to sustain blocks throughout the entirety of the play and finishes his blocks through the whistle. It's routine to see him planting a defender into the ground or blocking a defender 5-10 yards down the field.

Last Word
The skill set Radunz possesses makes him a better fit on the right side as a starting right tackle. However, he'll likely get a shot to play the left side and could succeed with his overall athleticism, but will need to improve his footwork, quickness, and overall consistency. He also could slide in and back up at one of the guard spots to use his push in the run game and short-set ability.

Strengths

- Finishing ability
- Combo blocking
- Control to 2nd level

Weaknesses

- Pad level too high at times
- A little too bendy at the waist
- Over-sets

Critical Factors

Reactive Athleticism	Anchor / Play Strength	Body Control
6	6	5

Positional Factors

Run Block	Pass Block	Awareness	Footwork
6	5	6	6
2nd Level	Range	Hand Use	Power
6	6	6	6
Sustain	Finish	Flexibility	Toughness
6	7	5	7

Basic

			Penalties		Blown Block Splits			
Year	G	GS	Holding	False Start	Run	Pressure	Sack	Total
2019	16	16	1	0	3	5	1	9
2020	1	1	0	0	0	0	0	0
	17	17	1	0	3	5	1	9

Team Stats

	Zone Run Blocking			Gap Run Blocking			Pass Block
Year	% of Runs	Y/A	Pos%	% of Runs	Y/A	Pos%	Pressure%
2019	40%	6.2	47%	59%	6.8	49%	25%
2020	30%	5.8	50%	68%	6.7	48%	32%
	39%	6.2	47%	59%	6.8	49%	26%

Deep Dive

	Blown Block %		When Running to their Gap				Total Points			Total Points Rtg		
										Per	Per	Per
Year	Run	Pass	Y/A	YBC/A	Pos%	EPA/A	Run	Pass	Total	Run	Pass	Play
2019	0.5%	1.8%	7.6	3.5	52%	0.31	32	13	45	95	93	95
2020	0.0%	0.0%	7.4	4.9	64%	0.39	3	1	5	99	96	99
	0.5%	1.6%	7.6	3.6	53%	0.32	35	14	50	-	-	-

Career stats only include seasons since 2019

James Hudson

Report by John Todd

School	Height	Weight	Year	Jersey #	Hometown
Cincinnati	6043 V	302 V	4JR	55	Toledo, OH

One Liner

Hudson has the natural athleticism and aggression at the point of attack of a former defender, but his impressive understanding of offensive line play will speed his development as he grows his body and gains further experience.

Overall

James Hudson is the left tackle in Cincinnati's zone offense. He played in only 14 career games and started 11, 10 coming in 2020. After signing with Michigan as a defensive end, redshirting during his position change, and then appearing in 3 games, he transferred to Cincinnati, where he sat out most of the 2019 season due to a denied hardship waiver. He's long-limbed and has room to add bulk to his athletic frame. Hudson is a fantastic athlete for the position whose open-field speed in front of screens and outside pulls is noteworthy. He plays with intensity and a defender's mentality to attack, finish, and let his opponent hear about it.

Pass Game

For only having one year of starting experience on offense, Hudson seems to be a quick learner and has flashed numerous advanced techniques in pass protection. He is quick off the snap and his foot speed and form into his vertical kick-slide is impressive. He stays connected with his interior and passes off and receives twists up front smoothly. At contact, Hudson is a bit of a waist bender, despite his athletic makeup, and he loses structure in his footwork while engaged. His upper and lower halves can lose congruity, which leads to lunging and erratic punch accuracy. This all stems from a current lack in anchor strength, and the waist bending is his way of compensating. However, Hudson understands high-level details of blocking. He will short-set wide-9s to take away their runway to attack his anchor limitations, he uses chops, yanks and counters to win hand fights, and his athleticism and aggression will often make up for shortcomings elsewhere. He knows how to play the position, and his physical execution will only continue to improve.

Run Game

In the run game, Hudson is an explosive attacker and tenacious finisher. He fires off the ball and delivers a solid punch, but his frame and overall strength limit his ability to square up and drive one-on-one if his initial contact doesn't generate movement. He works well within duo schemes to combo and kick out, and his hip fluidity is adequate to reach and seal in zone, but he's at his best moving in space. Hudson's speed is excellent for the position and he can be a unique factor outside the tackle box, although his ability to break down and negate second- and third-level defenders at the point of attack is inconsistent. When squared up inside, Hudson is aggressive and takes advantage of compromised defenders by driving them to the ground or riding them offscreen through the whistle.

Last Word

Hudson projects as a potential low-end starting left tackle in the NFL with a very high ceiling based on his level of development through one year of starting experience. He plays the position with the tenacity, enthusiasm, and swagger of a former defensive player, but mentally he's shown an impressive understanding of offensive line play. He has an intriguing skill set to bet on while he grows his body and earns more physical reps to tie together the sum of his parts.

<table>
<tr><td>

Strengths
- Athleticism
- High-level technique given experience
- Tenacity and aggression

</td><td>

Weaknesses
- Anchor and drive strength
- Footwork through contact
- Waist-bending tendencies

</td></tr>
</table>

Critical Factors

Reactive Athleticism	Anchor / Play Strength	Body Control
6	5	6

Positional Factors

Run Block	Pass Block	Awareness	Footwork
5	6	6	5
2nd Level	**Range**	**Hand Use**	**Power**
6	7	6	6
Sustain	**Finish**	**Flexibility**	**Toughness**
5	7	6	6

Basic

Year	G	GS	Penalties Holding	False Start	Blown Block Splits Run	Pressure	Sack	Total
2018	3	0	0	0	0	0	0	0
2019	1	1	0	0	0	0	0	0
2020	10	10	2	0	2	2	0	4
	14	11	2	0	2	2	0	4

Team Stats

Year	Zone Run Blocking % of Runs	Y/A	Pos%	Gap Run Blocking % of Runs	Y/A	Pos%	Pass Block Pressure%
2018	59%	5.3	52%	40%	5.7	44%	33%
2019	70%	5.2	47%	27%	5.2	48%	33%
2020	73%	6.2	40%	21%	4.7	51%	28%
	67%	5.5	47%	30%	5.4	47%	32%

Deep Dive

Year	Blown Block % Run	Pass	When Running to their Gap Y/A	YBC/A	Pos%	EPA/A	Total Points Run	Pass	Total	Total Points Rtg Per Run	Per Pass	Per Play
2018	0.0%	0.0%	2.0	0.5	0%	-0.42	1	0	1	77	90	82
2019	0.0%	0.0%	11.6	8.1	82%	0.79	5	2	7	99	97	99
2020	0.7%	0.7%	8.3	5.1	52%	0.13	12	13	25	77	97	90
	0.5%	0.6%	8.6	5.4	55%	0.21	18	15	33	-	-	-

Walker Little

Report by Ben Hrkach

School	Height	Weight	Year	Jersey #	Hometown
Stanford	6062 E	313 E	4SR	72	Houston, TX

One Liner
Little projects to be a serviceable left tackle with his pass protection skills and frame, but he'll need to continue improving his technique to reach his high ceiling.

Overall
Walker Little played left tackle in Stanford's run-heavy balanced offense. He started 19 of 22 games played and made his first start in his third game as a freshman. Little dislocated his knee in the season opener of 2019 and opted for season-ending surgery. He then opted out of the 2020 season. The former No. 1 high school recruit in the nation, Little is long with a big frame that shows some stiffness athletically. He shows sufficient toughness and his significant time off recently makes for an interesting evaluation.

Pass Game
Little shows a natural kick step on his vertical sets in pass protection. He likes to allow the defender to get upfield and use his length to lock them out or to ride them around the arc. He uses a straight two-handed punch which is inconsistently placed and he hasn't shown the ability to quickly reposition. He keeps his elbows tight and wants to punch and latch. He is sufficient at timing his punch but telegraphs his attack on occasion. When he does gain inside placement, he eliminates defenders with his length. He does leave his chest open and is vulnerable to push-pull moves. When everything works in unison he has solid anchor strength. Little's shown lumbering, incongruous footwork early in his career. He needs to continue to work on keeping his feet low and add quickness, two things that were noticeably improved in his short 2019 appearance. Little does show a natural feel for passing off stunts and is generally very aware in pass protection.

Run Game
In the run game, Little wins by gaining body positioning and walling off. He shows mediocre power once engaged, but can stalemate defensive ends and does a sufficient job at gaining the edge. His hand placement is an issue and can get outside the frame often. He did show improved foot quickness in 2019, but his 2018 tape left a lot to be desired. Ultimately, Little is a big body that does just enough to open up run lanes, but can be handled by powerful linemen with good hand strength. His strength is better anchoring against contact rather than delivering it and driving. He shows sufficient range and ability to work at the second level. He moves well for his size and more often than not will make good contact to take second-level defenders out of the play.

Last Word
Little has good size and length, as well as the feel and natural tools to be a low-end left tackle at the next level. He is a high-upside player based on his pedigree. but he'll need to improve his technique, quickness and explosion. He doesn't have the power to project to the right side well. His recent years off from playing may mean he'll require extra time to develop those weaknesses.

Strengths	Weaknesses
• Size and length	• Drive strength and power
• Pass protection	• Hand technique
• Awareness	• Foot quickness

Critical Factors

Reactive Athleticism	Anchor / Play Strength	Body Control
5	6	5

Positional Factors

Run Block	Pass Block	Awareness	Footwork
5	6	6	5
2nd Level	Range	Hand Use	Power
5	5	5	4
Sustain	Finish	Flexibility	Toughness
6	5	5	5

Basic

Year	G	GS	Penalties		Blown Block Splits			
			Holding	False Start	Run	Pressure	Sack	Total
2017	9	6	0	0	2	1	1	4
2018	12	12	2	0	6	8	4	18
2019	1	1	0	0	2	0	0	2
	22	19	2	0	10	9	5	24

Team Stats

Year	Zone Run Blocking			Gap Run Blocking			Pass Block
	% of Runs	Y/A	Pos%	% of Runs	Y/A	Pos%	Pressure%
2017	48%	6.2	45%	51%	7.0	37%	31%
2018	54%	4.4	38%	46%	4.3	38%	31%
2019	64%	4.2	37%	35%	4.5	40%	31%
	54%	5.0	40%	45%	5.6	38%	31%

Deep Dive

Year	Blown Block %		When Running to their Gap				Total Points			Total Points Rtg		
	Run	Pass	Y/A	YBC/A	Pos%	EPA/A	Run	Pass	Total	Per Run	Per Pass	Per Play
2018	1.9%	2.8%	5.3	2.1	42%	-0.06	11	14	25	71	86	80
2019	7.4%	0.0%	3.0	0.0	0%	-0.45	0	2	3	51	99	89
	2.4%	2.6%	5.3	2.1	41%	-0.06	11	16	28	-	-	-

Adrian Ealy

Report by Jeff Dean

School	Height	Weight	Year	Jersey #	Hometown
Oklahoma	6056 E	326 E	4JR	59	Gonzales, LA

One Liner

Ealy is an athletic tackle with a good anchor who flashes the violent initial punch teams look for, but he will need to improve his technique and consistency to earn his spot as a swing tackle.

Strengths: Anchor; Explosive punch; Movement in space
Weaknesses: Hand placement; Exposes his chest; Handling counter moves

Adrian Ealy plays right tackle for Oklahoma's up-tempo, RPO-heavy, spread offense. He played in 29 games, making 23 starts. He started 22 games at RT and 1 game at LT. He missed 2 games in 2019 with a right knee injury. Ealy's a good athlete with a big frame and good movement ability in space. He has good strength throughout his body, but very good strength in his upper body. He can play a little overzealous at times and miss a block, but his competitive fire should be sufficient at the next level.

Ealy has a quick short step and good strength to hold off defensive rushers. He tries to guess his opponent's move and is prone to false steps. His athleticism allows him to recover most of the time, though can get out of position and lose balance with a solid counter move. He shows adequate foot quickness and sets a wide base to rarely be driven back. Ealy has an explosive punch that quickly stuns defenders, but doesn't utilize it at the correct time and exposes his chest too often. He fires his hands late and too frequently gets them in a bad position because of it. When he does fire his hands early, he hits with very good force and creates noticeable separation. He will violently swat away the defender's hands, but not often enough.

Ealy tends to play too high and not extend his arms, but his anchor is good enough to create running lanes. He doesn't drive defenders off the ball as often as desired, but also is rarely driven back. He locks up defenders at the line and can work to the 2nd level. He moves well in space, though can seem a little too focused on one guy. Ealy sustains blocks well and doesn't let go once he latches on. He can turn his hips over and move the defender at will, though doesn't finish blocks with authority and seems content making the first block.

Ealy projects as a backup right tackle who can play left tackle as well. His athleticism and size provide optimism as does his violent punch if he can improve his technique and use his hands more efficiently.

			Penalties		Blown Block Splits			
Year	G	GS	Holding	False Start	Run	Pressure	Sack	Total
2018	6	0	0	0	1	0	0	1
2019	12	12	2	0	7	7	2	16
2020	11	11	3	0	1	2	3	6
	29	23	5	0	9	9	5	23

Team	Team Zone Run Blocking			Team Gap Run Blocking			Team Pass Block
Year	% of Runs	Y/A	Pos%	% of Runs	Y/A	Pos%	Pressure%
2018	48%	6.0	49%	49%	8.2	59%	26%
2019	47%	5.6	55%	49%	6.6	50%	39%
2020	51%	5.4	53%	46%	5.7	47%	30%
	49%	5.7	52%	48%	6.9	52%	32%

	Blown Block %		When Running to their Gap				Total Points			Total Points Rtg		
Year	Run	Pass	Y/A	YBC/A	Pos%	EPA/A	Run	Pass	Total	Per Run	Per Pass	Per Play
2018	3.2%	0.0%	1.3	1.0	0%	-0.52	1	0	1	75	97	85
2019	1.9%	2.5%	7.5	3.6	59%	0.24	18	12	30	90	84	87
2020	0.3%	1.3%	6.8	3.3	56%	0.11	16	16	32	89	95	92
	1.2%	1.9%	7.2	3.4	57%	0.18	35	28	63	-	-	-

Critical Factors	
Reactive Athleticism	5
Anchor / Play Strength	6
Body Control	5

Positional Factors	
Run Block	6
Pass Block	6
Awareness	5
Footwork	5
2nd Level	5
Range	6
Hand Use	5
Power	6
Sustain	6
Finish	5
Flexibility	5
Toughness	6

Robert Hainsey

Report by Joe McDonald & Nathan Cooper

School	Height	Weight	Year	Jersey #	Hometown
Notre Dame	6044 V	302 V	4SR	72	Pittsburgh, PA

One Liner
Hainsey's pass blocking ability, footwork, and reactive athleticism will allow him to be a serviceable player all over the line at the next level, though his lack of tenacity and finishing ability need improvement.

Strengths: Football IQ & stunt pick up; Pass pro; Quick feet
Weaknesses: Leg drive; Finish; Lack of intensity

Robert Hainsey is the starting right tackle for Notre Dame's pro-style offense where he blocked in a primarily zone run scheme with a lot of passes from shotgun. He started 34 of 46 games for the Irish, all coming at right tackle, only missing 5 games due to a broken ankle in 2019. He has a tall, wide frame that carries his weight well and is a tough competitor who plays with passion, but lacks some intensity.

In pass protection, Hainsey is a very fundamental blocker. He has quick feet and can use different sets to position himself in front of defenders with consistency. He's patient and has the quickness to react and position himself accordingly to different defenders and their moves. He has a high IQ and picks up on stunts and blitzes very well. However, he plays a little high and will occasionally stop his feet in his pass set leaving him vulnerable to a good speed rush. His punch is strong, but inaccurate, hurting his ability to latch onto defenders. He tends to catch rushers rather than attack them, but has the strength to set himself and anchor down quickly after impact.

In the run game, Hainsey doesn't have much tenacity nor does he create much movement outside of doubles. He tends to stop running his feet on impact and doesn't use much leg drive. He has the quickness to get to the 2nd level, but seems happy to just get in the way and not impose himself on the defender. He doesn't generate a lot of vertical push and has trouble sealing the edge on outside runs, tending to push defenders out to the sideline instead of getting his head across their body to wall them off. On pulls or out in space, he understands his assignment and is under control, but has trouble executing quickly and effectively.

Hainsey can play any position on the line, though he projects best at right tackle. He shows the pass blocking ability, footwork, and athleticism needed along the offensive line. He needs to improve his leg drive and finishing ability in the run game, but if he can, he could turn into a very valuable asset.

			Penalties		Blown Block Splits			
Year	G	GS	Holding	False Start	Run	Pressure	Sack	Total
2017	13	1	0	0	6	9	2	17
2018	13	13	1	0	1	11	2	14
2019	8	8	1	0	2	1	0	3
2020	12	12	0	0	5	2	2	10
	46	34	2	0	14	23	6	44

Team	Team Zone Run Blocking			Team Gap Run Blocking			Team Pass Block
Year	% of Runs	Y/A	Pos%	% of Runs	Y/A	Pos%	Pressure%
2017	52%	7.3	48%	45%	5.9	46%	40%
2018	56%	5.3	50%	39%	5.0	38%	39%
2019	48%	4.9	44%	48%	5.3	48%	32%
2020	74%	5.2	46%	23%	6.2	54%	36%
	57%	5.7	47%	39%	5.6	46%	36%

	Blown Block %		When Running to their Gap				Total Points			Total Points Rtg		
										Per	Per	Per
Year	Run	Pass	Y/A	YBC/A	Pos%	EPA/A	Run	Pass	Total	Run	Pass	Play
2018	0.2%	2.7%	4.1	2.1	46%	-0.04	17	11	28	84	66	74
2019	1.2%	0.4%	5.3	1.8	47%	-0.04	8	11	20	88	98	95
2020	1.3%	1.2%	5.0	2.1	41%	-0.11	15	16	31	78	92	86
	0.8%	1.6%	4.7	2.1	44%	-0.07	40	38	79	-	-	-

Critical Factors

Reactive Athleticism	6
Anchor / Play Strength	5
Body Control	5

Positional Factors

Run Block	4
Pass Block	6
Awareness	6
Footwork	6
2nd Level	5
Range	4
Hand Use	5
Power	5
Sustain	5
Finish	4
Flexibility	5
Toughness	6

Foster Sarell

Report by Max Nuscher

School	Height	Weight	Year	Jersey #	Hometown
Stanford	6061 E	315 E	4SR	79	Graham, WA

One Liner

Sarell is a good pass blocker who possesses quick footwork for his lengthy size, but his lack of agility and awareness could limit him from being a consistent starter.

Strengths: Pass blocking; Footwork; Length and strength
Weaknesses: Awareness; Range; Getting to the second level

Foster Sarell is the right tackle in Stanford's pro-style offense that uses gap and zone runs. He played in 34 games, starting 17 of them all on the right side. He suffered a knee injury in 2018 that forced him to miss 10 games in the middle of the season. A former top high school recruit, he is very tall with good length and quick footwork, especially for his size. He is an aggressive and tough player with a high motor.

In the passing game, Sarell is an anchor on the right side of the line who handles the speed rush well, thanks to impressive foot quickness. He gets his second step down quickly which allows him to keep defenders from getting around the edge. He will struggle with counter moves inside and superior hand usage. Sarell does not play with ideal awareness to identify outside blitzes or quickly react to twisting rushers up front. He packs a strong punch with great length that can stop defenders in their tracks if timed correctly.

Sarell is a strong and technically sound blocker but struggles winning the leverage battle. He uses short, choppy steps despite his long limbs and keeps his pads over his toes. He has good hands in the run game to square up and sustain with his natural strength. He doesn't allow himself to be pushed back and has a strong core to flip defenders with good hip explosion. However, he does not generate a lot of vertical push in the running game. He handles edge defenders well and can counter their length well. Sarell is not fluid in space and struggles to get up to and find work at the second level. He moves fairly well ahead of screens but is not fleet of foot to track down smaller secondary players.

Sarell projects as a solid swing tackle in the NFL. He is better suited at right tackle but has the pass protection skills and footwork to flex to left tackle, as well. He has sufficient run blocking traits to suit multiple schemes.

Year	G	GS	Penalties Holding	Penalties False Start	Blown Block Splits Run	Blown Block Splits Pressure	Blown Block Splits Sack	Blown Block Splits Total
2017	14	0	0	0	0	1	0	1
2018	3	0	1	0	0	0	0	0
2019	11	11	1	0	2	3	1	6
2020	6	6	0	0	3	3	2	8
	34	17	2	0	5	7	3	15

Team Year	Team Zone Run Blocking % of Runs	Team Zone Run Blocking Y/A	Team Zone Run Blocking Pos%	Team Gap Run Blocking % of Runs	Team Gap Run Blocking Y/A	Team Gap Run Blocking Pos%	Team Pass Block Pressure%
2017	48%	6.2	45%	51%	7.0	37%	31%
2018	54%	4.4	38%	46%	4.3	38%	31%
2019	64%	4.2	37%	35%	4.5	40%	31%
2020	60%	5.1	49%	34%	3.5	47%	23%
	55%	5.0	42%	44%	5.4	39%	30%

Year	Blown Block % Run	Blown Block % Pass	When Running to their Gap Y/A	When Running to their Gap YBC/A	When Running to their Gap Pos%	When Running to their Gap EPA/A	Total Points Run	Total Points Pass	Total Points Total	Total Points Rtg Per Run	Total Points Rtg Per Pass	Total Points Rtg Per Play
2018	0.0%	0.0%	1.3	0.3	0%	-0.70	0	0	1	61	87	71
2019	0.7%	0.9%	4.7	1.9	36%	-0.18	10	21	31	71	98	93
2020	1.7%	2.1%	4.7	2.6	57%	0.18	9	8	17	95	85	89
	1.1%	1.3%	4.6	2.2	45%	-0.02	19	29	49	-	-	-

Critical Factors

Reactive Athleticism	5
Anchor / Play Strength	6
Body Control	5

Positional Factors

Run Block	5
Pass Block	6
Awareness	5
Footwork	7
2nd Level	5
Range	5
Hand Use	6
Power	6
Sustain	6
Finish	5
Flexibility	6
Toughness	6

Kayode Awosika

Report by DJ Marquardt & Steven Penn

School	Height	Weight	Year	Jersey #	Hometown
Buffalo	6050 E	315 E	5SR	73	Plymouth, MN

One Liner

Awosika is athletic and versatile with a good foundation of skills to be an NFL tackle, but will need significant repetitions against superior competition to refine his skill set.

Strengths: Down blocks in zone; Athletic; Versatile
Weaknesses: 2nd-level engagement; Inconsistent leverage; Initial punch

Kayode Awosika is a left tackle in Buffalo's shotgun, play action offense. He started 32 of 37 games with 25 starts at RT before starting all 7 at LT in 2020. He's a good-sized tackle with a long frame who is a very fluid mover on the field and stands out athletically for his size. Awosika didn't show any signs of laziness or disinterest on the field, but could improve his overall desire to make plays happen when he has no immediate assignment on hand.

Awosika is a very composed pass blocker. His initial punch is inconsistent at times, but he's very aggressive with combating edge rushers' hand use with his own. His length and athleticism help him to mirror defenders while also staying engaged against any sort of counter attack. At times he can become over-leveraged while pass blocking and forgo his composure. Awosika showed enough flexibility with a more consistent amount of ankle flexion rather than knee bend. He can generate a lot of power via the flex in his ankles and proved that by handling his matchups well, despite not facing a premier edge defender during his time at Buffalo.

Awosika does a superb job of moving defenders out of gaps at the POA in the run game. He especially stands out at down blocking on zone runs. He generates good power from his big frame and uses his lower half and length to get defenders out of their gap responsibilities. He does a good job when reach-blocking due to his ability to move and seal defenders with his long arms. Awosika needs to improve his 2nd-level blocking, oftentimes struggling to engage with or relentlessly look for defenders.

Awosika projects as a versatile swing tackle in the NFL and has the traits to build upon in order to find the field at either tackle position. He poses all essential skills required by both positions. His versatility makes him a fit for any scheme, but his athleticism and ability to wash interior defenders out on down blocks best suits him for a zone-run offense.

			Penalties		Blown Block Splits			
Year	G	GS	Holding	False Start	Run	Pressure	Sack	Total
2017	5	0	0	0	0	0	0	0
2018	14	14	0	0	2	7	2	11
2019	11	11	1	0	7	3	4	16
2020	7	7	0	0	1	3	1	5
	37	32	1	0	10	13	7	32

Team	Team Zone Run Blocking			Team Gap Run Blocking			Team Pass Block
Year	% of Runs	Y/A	Pos%	% of Runs	Y/A	Pos%	Pressure%
2017	75%	4.3	43%	22%	4.2	30%	29%
2018	81%	4.7	46%	19%	5.5	48%	26%
2019	72%	5.2	49%	25%	5.4	48%	27%
2020	81%	7.0	51%	18%	6.6	50%	14%
	77%	5.2	47%	21%	5.3	45%	26%

	Blown Block %		When Running to their Gap				Total Points			Total Points Rtg		
Year	Run	Pass	Y/A	YBC/A	Pos%	EPA/A	Run	Pass	Total	Per Run	Per Pass	Per Play
2018	0.4%	2.0%	4.8	2.1	50%	-0.01	23	14	36	89	80	85
2019	1.3%	3.6%	4.8	2.0	50%	0.05	28	6	34	94	65	87
2020	0.4%	2.6%	8.1	4.3	49%	0.25	12	5	17	79	82	80
	0.8%	2.6%	5.6	2.6	50%	0.07	63	25	87	-	-	-

Critical Factors	
Reactive Athleticism	6
Anchor / Play Strength	6
Body Control	5

Positional Factors	
Run Block	6
Pass Block	6
Awareness	5
Footwork	5
2nd Level	5
Range	5
Hand Use	6
Power	6
Sustain	5
Finish	5
Flexibility	5
Toughness	5

Brenden Jaimes Final Grade: 6.3

Report by Jacob Halleen & Michael Bonneville

School	Height	Weight	Year	Jersey #	Hometown
Nebraska	6054 V	300 V	4SR	76	Austin, TX

One Liner
Jaimes has the athleticism, range, and grip strength to play at the next level, but his lack of power and reactive quickness may limit him to a backup swing role.

Strengths: Range and movement skills; Upper-body strength; Sustain
Weaknesses: Vertical drive; Inconsistent hand use; Sluggish vertical pass set

Brenden Jaimes is an offensive lineman in Nebraska's shotgun spread offense. He played and started in 40 career games. He played right tackle his freshman year before moving to left tackle for his final 3 seasons. He has good height but could add strength in his lower half. He's athletic and moves well in space with good flexibility, but struggles changing directions in short areas. He shows some toughness but lacks a tenacious mentality.

Jaimes displays sufficient footwork in pass pro but can be late getting to the top of the arc. He will lunge in some situations and lose balance but overall, he has a strong base and good bend in his knees and ankles. He uses his hands well, but he's occasionally late with his initial punch which hinders his anchor strength. When he does work a well-timed attack, he is able to latch on and sustain. He has issues reacting quickly enough to twitchy edge rushers and struggles adjusting to inside moves. He shows good awareness and understands his assignments in the pass game.

In the running game, Jaimes sustains blocks well and keeps his feet moving but has trouble with vertical push. His strength is good enough for holding off defenders but he needs to use his lower half more to drive defenders back. He moves with ease in space and pulls well to all directions. Once getting to the second level, he can look lost at times and does not have an aggressive mentality. He needs to be more consistent on his aiming points and play more physically. While he can sustain blocks in the trenches, he does not aggressively finish.

Jaimes projects best as a swing tackle in multiple blocking schemes, but most comfortably at right tackle in zone. He isn't quick enough to consistently handle premier talents as a starter at left tackle like he was in college. His natural athleticism to move in space projects well but he needs to become more balanced in pass protection and to add strength and power to his run game.

Year	G	GS	Penalties Holding	False Start	Run	Blown Block Splits Pressure	Sack	Total
2017	9	9	0	0	6	15	4	25
2018	12	12	1	0	3	3	5	11
2019	12	12	2	0	6	2	2	10
2020	7	7	1	0	3	3	0	6
	40	40	4	0	18	23	11	52

Team Year	Team Zone Run Blocking % of Runs	Y/A	Pos%	Team Gap Run Blocking % of Runs	Y/A	Pos%	Team Pass Block Pressure%
2017	79%	4.0	40%	20%	4.5	37%	39%
2018	66%	5.1	50%	33%	8.0	51%	30%
2019	64%	5.2	46%	35%	4.6	44%	36%
2020	61%	4.8	46%	28%	5.1	58%	29%
	67%	4.8	45%	30%	5.7	47%	34%

Year	Blown Block % Run	Pass	When Running to their Gap Y/A	YBC/A	Pos%	EPA/A	Total Points Run	Pass	Total	Total Points Rtg Per Run	Per Pass	Per Play
2018	0.8%	1.8%	7.5	2.9	53%	0.18	16	14	30	84	82	83
2019	1.4%	1.0%	6.1	4.2	49%	0.08	29	17	46	99	96	98
2020	1.3%	1.3%	5.9	3.2	51%	0.17	16	8	25	99	89	96
	1.2%	1.4%	6.4	3.6	51%	0.13	61	39	101	-	-	-

Critical Factors	
Reactive Athleticism	5
Anchor / Play Strength	6
Body Control	5

Positional Factors	
Run Block	6
Pass Block	5
Awareness	6
Footwork	5
2nd Level	6
Range	6
Hand Use	5
Power	5
Sustain	6
Finish	5
Flexibility	6
Toughness	5

Brady Christensen

Report by Jordan Edwards

School	Height	Weight	Year	Jersey #	Hometown
BYU	6052 E	300 E	4JR	67	Bountiful, UT

One Liner

Christensen has the football IQ, awareness, and play strength to be a solid swing tackle, but his athletic limitations may hinder his ability to become a consistent starter at the next level.

Strengths: Awareness; Anchor/play strength; Sustain
Weaknesses: Natural athleticism; Flexibility; Hand use

Brady Christensen is the left tackle for the Cougars' zone running spread offense. He played and started all 38 games in his career. He has a solid and lean frame with a big upper body and adequate arm length. He's limited in his lower-body movements and lacks flexibility there. He's a tough player who has logged nearly every available snap over his career.

Christensen plays with good play strength and anchors well as a pass protector. His awareness as a pass protector is his best attribute as a prospect, as he diagnoses twists, stunts, and incoming rush moves very well. He has the hand strength to latch onto defenders, sustain, and keep them at bay. His hand placement can be high and he can leave his chest open more often than desired. His footwork in his pass sets is adequate and he can reach his landmarks with a good base, but he lacks the natural athleticism that is desired in a true blindside protector. He struggles with twitchy, lengthier pass rushers and can struggle to react and recover after initially losing at the POA, due to a tendency to waist bend.

Christensen plays with good leverage and a solid base as a run blocker. He displays good power and toughness to generate push at the POA. He has good short-area footwork to help get him in positions to reach defenders and can wall off the back side of runs adequately. He generates good power in double teams and has the hand strength to latch and keep defenders in close. He has adequate range, but his lack of reactive athleticism and flexibility hinder his ability to seal run lanes in open space.

Christensen has spent his collegiate career at LT, but his athletic limitations may best suit him at RT. His football IQ and awareness will allow him to be a high-quality backup at both tackle positions, and in the right scheme he could even be a guard for some teams. He doesn't possess the mentality of a mauler, but he best fits in a power scheme, where his functional strength and power can shine.

Year	G	GS	Penalties		Blown Block Splits			
			Holding	False Start	Run	Pressure	Sack	Total
2018	13	13	4	0	2	5	1	8
2019	13	13	2	0	1	4	1	6
2020	12	12	2	0	0	1	1	2
	38	38	8	0	3	10	3	16

Team	Team Zone Run Blocking			Team Gap Run Blocking			Team Pass Block
Year	% of Runs	Y/A	Pos%	% of Runs	Y/A	Pos%	Pressure%
2018	67%	4.6	47%	30%	5.8	48%	37%
2019	75%	5.7	53%	23%	4.8	43%	29%
2020	88%	6.0	52%	9%	5.8	68%	22%
	76%	5.5	51%	21%	5.4	49%	30%

	Blown Block %		When Running to their Gap				Total Points			Total Points Rtg		
Year	Run	Pass	Y/A	YBC/A	Pos%	EPA/A	Run	Pass	Total	Per Run	Per Pass	Per Play
2018	0.5%	1.4%	6.5	2.8	49%	0.01	16	15	31	82	89	86
2019	0.3%	1.0%	6.1	3.6	52%	0.13	25	24	49	99	98	98
2020	0.0%	0.5%	5.7	2.4	51%	0.11	12	19	31	73	98	92
	0.3%	1.0%	6.1	2.9	51%	0.09	53	58	111	-	-	-

Critical Factors	
Reactive Athleticism	5
Anchor / Play Strength	6
Body Control	5

Positional Factors	
Run Block	5
Pass Block	6
Awareness	7
Footwork	5
2nd Level	5
Range	5
Hand Use	5
Power	6
Sustain	6
Finish	5
Flexibility	5
Toughness	6

Landon Young

Report by Theo Fornaciari

School	Height	Weight	Year	Jersey #	Hometown
Kentucky	6062 E	321 E	5SR	67	Lexington, KY

One Liner
Young is a good run and pass blocker who wins with strength and toughness, but the lack of explosiveness in his lower body and hands is preventing him from being a starting NFL tackle.

Strengths: Grip strength; Drive/base blocking; Competitive toughness
Weaknesses: Range; Explosiveness; 2nd-level ability

Landon Young is a left tackle in Kentucky's spread, RPO-heavy, zone running scheme. He started 33 of 49 games with all starts coming at LT. He suffered a right knee injury late in 2018 fall camp that forced him to miss the entire season. A high school discus and wrestling competitor, Young is a good athlete with a solid, but not bulky frame. He is a smart, disciplined player with good leadership qualities and very good physical and mental toughness.

Young has good pre-snap awareness, recognizes pressure/blitzes and anticipates pass-rush moves from edge players across from him. He uses good footwork to maintain a proper base. However, he lacks explosiveness out of his stance, thus will shrink his base and cause his pad level to rise when protecting his outside edge against very good speed rushers. He has good anchor/play strength along with enough flexibility to quickly gather and maintain pocket integrity. His reactive athleticism and body control allow him to mirror enough to stay square against inside/outside moves and recover against good speed rushers. Young lacks pop in his punch, particularly against power moves, though he shows good grip strength when latching on. He has adequate hand use overall and shows the accuracy and discipline to stay inside the defender's frame and recognize when to release.

Young has sufficient, but not explosive power. He has good anchor ability at the POA by utilizing hand strength, footwork, and body control to latch and steer defenders and create running lanes in either scheme. He's a good run blocker who consistently executes and sustains base, combo, down, and scoop blocks. Young has mediocre range and labors across the formation as a puller. He is sufficient at the 2nd level and struggles to maintain good balance in space with a tendency to reach and grab moving targets. He is a good finisher at least to the whistle.

Young projects as a swing tackle in a primarily zone-run scheme. He's a better fit at left tackle due to his hand use and emphasis on strength over power.

			Penalties		Blown Block Splits			
Year	G	GS	Holding	False Start	Run	Pressure	Sack	Total
2016	12	3	0	0	3	5	4	12
2017	13	6	1	1	0	6	4	12
2019	13	13	2	0	3	3	1	7
2020	11	11	3	0	2	4	1	7
	49	33	6	1	8	18	10	38

Team	Team Zone Run Blocking			Team Gap Run Blocking			Team Pass Block
Year	% of Runs	Y/A	Pos%	% of Runs	Y/A	Pos%	Pressure%
2016	66%	6.0	47%	34%	6.3	46%	35%
2017	63%	5.0	42%	36%	4.2	40%	35%
2019	65%	6.8	50%	33%	6.4	46%	28%
2020	70%	5.5	52%	27%	5.8	51%	29%
	66%	5.9	48%	33%	5.7	45%	32%

	Blown Block %		When Running to their Gap				Total Points			Total Points Rtg		
Year	Run	Pass	Y/A	YBC/A	Pos%	EPA/A	Run	Pass	Total	Per Run	Per Pass	Per Play
2019	0.7%	1.5%	5.8	3.9	46%	0.05	32	12	44	99	97	99
2020	0.5%	1.8%	6.9	3.6	58%	0.20	25	12	37	97	96	97
	0.6%	1.6%	6.2	3.8	51%	0.11	57	24	81	-	-	-

Critical Factors
Reactive Athleticism	5
Anchor / Play Strength	6
Body Control	6

Positional Factors
Run Block	5
Pass Block	6
Awareness	6
Footwork	6
2nd Level	5
Range	4
Hand Use	5
Power	5
Sustain	6
Finish	6
Flexibility	5
Toughness	7

Royce Newman

Report by Joe McDonald & Luke DeCello

School	Height	Weight	Year	Jersey #	Hometown
Ole Miss	6051 V	306 V	5SR	72	Nashville, IL

One Liner

Newman has the frame, athleticism, and position versatility of an NFL lineman, but improvements in his technical hand accuracy and drive strength will heighten his overall game.

Strengths: 1st step quickness and positioning; Athleticism; Punch strength
Weaknesses: Punch accuracy; Grip strength to sustain; Balance and body control

Royce Newman is an offensive lineman in Ole Miss' hurry-up spread offense, where he operates out of a two-point stance. He played in 43 games with 12 starts at left guard in 2019 and 10 starts at right tackle in 2020. He is a tall, athletic lineman with shorter arms and a good frame that could support added bulk. He is a strong, tough competitor and has taken to his position change well.

Newman's initial foot quickness off the snap is very good, stepping to his spots with precision and a wide base. He works best in a short set to shuffle up to wide techniques and cut off their runway. His footwork on deeper drops can be choppy, but he stays connected with good form to contact. His punch is strong but his accuracy is erratic, which is the cause of many of his issues. He loses the battle at initial contact and doesn't have the body control or flexibility to recover consistently. He has the length to lock out and stalemate, but his grip can be disarmed. He has good anchor strength to handle most power rushes, and enough athleticism to handle speed, although his footwork can break down to reach the top of the arc. He plays with good awareness to feel loops and stunts coming.

Newman doesn't drive defenders off the ball consistently, but he does wall off his run lanes sufficiently. He is a quick and effective puller and has the athleticism, 1st step quickness, and hip fluidity to reach and seal from the back side before defenders can react. He works up to the second level well on combinations, but again, his hand placement is often inaccurate and hinders his overall ability at the point of attack. He lacks the grip strength and balance to sustain, resulting in being cast aside by superior upper-body strength.

Newman projects best as a versatile backup at right tackle or either guard spot in the league. Without added bulk and power to move inside, he best fits at right tackle for a zone offense. He doesn't have the innate blindside reliability to be a swing tackle at this stage.

Year	G	GS	Penalties		Blown Block Splits			
			Holding	False Start	Run	Pressure	Sack	Total
2017	9	0	0	0	0	0	0	0
2018	12	0	0	0	2	0	0	2
2019	12	12	1	0	14	1	2	18
2020	10	10	1	0	7	7	2	16
	43	22	2	0	23	8	4	36

Team	Team Zone Run Blocking			Team Gap Run Blocking			Team Pass Block
Year	% of Runs	Y/A	Pos%	% of Runs	Y/A	Pos%	Pressure%
2017	46%	3.9	45%	51%	6.7	49%	32%
2018	36%	5.5	48%	53%	5.6	47%	29%
2019	74%	5.7	42%	23%	6.6	40%	32%
2020	69%	4.8	51%	27%	4.7	47%	30%
	59%	5.1	46%	36%	5.9	46%	31%

	Blown Block %		When Running to their Gap				Total Points			Total Points Rtg		
										Per	Per	Per
Year	Run	Pass	Y/A	YBC/A	Pos%	EPA/A	Run	Pass	Total	Run	Pass	Play
2018	5.0%	0.0%	6.5	3.8	31%	-0.08	1	1	2	63	98	81
2019	2.9%	1.0%	5.5	2.4	40%	-0.06	11	15	26	56	90	70
2020	1.8%	2.2%	4.8	1.5	48%	0.06	16	12	28	79	79	79
	2.5%	1.6%	5.3	2.2	42%	-0.02	28	28	56	-	-	-

Critical Factors	
Reactive Athleticism	6
Anchor / Play Strength	5
Body Control	5

Positional Factors	
Run Block	5
Pass Block	5
Awareness	6
Footwork	6
2nd Level	6
Range	6
Hand Use	5
Power	5
Sustain	4
Finish	5
Flexibility	5
Toughness	6

Jake Curhan

Report by Nathan Cooper

School	Height	Weight	Year	Jersey #	Hometown
California	6056 V	323 V	5SR	71	Larkspur, CA

One Liner

Curhan has the raw strength and anchoring ability to be an effective depth-level player at the next level, though his balance issues and struggles sustaining blocks will challenge him early on in his career.

Strengths: Anchor in pass pro; Raw strength; Handles games & stunts
Weaknesses: Upright out of stance; Balance issues; Struggles to sustain in run game

Jake Curhan is a right tackle in California's West Coast offense. Curhan only started playing football as a sophomore in high school. He started all 40 games he played in at right tackle for Cal, although he missed 2 games in 2020 due to COVID-19 contact tracing. Curhan has a big frame with good size. He's got some athleticism, but isn't a great overall athlete and lacks some flexibility with loose joints. He plays hard and shows toughness and competitiveness in his play.

Curhan stands straight up out of his stance before working back down. Occasionally, rushers will get into him before he sits back down and that's when he gets pushed back. When in position, which is often, he shows strong anchoring ability. Even if a little off-balance, he re-adjusts and rarely gets pushed into the pocket. He handles speed or bull rushes effectively, but struggles when rushers counter with spins, swims, or push-pulls. His lack of balance makes it tough for him to sustain when rushers counter. He has enough reactive athleticism to handle games and stunts, but has trouble staying in front of rushers using inside moves. He uses good length to quickly deliver a strong, heavy initial punch.

Curhan fires out of his stance and can get an initial push on defenders, but isn't able to consistently keep hands on and sustain throughout the play. He gets a little too bendy in his waist and doesn't have great balance, so he gets thrown aside too easily too often. He has a difficult time reaching 2- and 3-techniques to wall them off. When he can latch onto defenders, he keeps his feet moving with good leg drive and can gain vertical push to drive them off the ball. He shows he can get to the 2nd level under control, but with limited balance and COD ability, he usually isn't able to sustain.

Curhan projects as a backup right tackle who could also slide inside at guard. With his anchoring ability and strength, he should be a solid player on the right side. He's a durable player who has enough traits that coaches can mold at the next level.

			Penalties			Blown Block Splits		
Year	G	GS	Holding	False Start	Run	Pressure	Sack	Total
2017	12	12	3	0	5	13	4	23
2018	13	13	2	0	2	5	5	13
2019	13	13	1	0	6	6	6	18
2020	2	2	0	0	1	0	0	2
	40	40	6	0	14	24	15	56

Team	Team Zone Run Blocking			Team Gap Run Blocking			Team Pass Block
Year	% of Runs	Y/A	Pos%	% of Runs	Y/A	Pos%	Pressure%
2017	72%	4.2	46%	27%	5.7	37%	34%
2018	71%	4.4	41%	24%	5.1	44%	31%
2019	75%	3.8	40%	23%	6.3	53%	34%
2020	60%	4.1	43%	39%	4.5	33%	31%
	72%	4.2	42%	26%	5.5	42%	33%

	Blown Block %		When Running to their Gap				Total Points			Total Points Rtg		
Year	Run	Pass	Y/A	YBC/A	Pos%	EPA/A	Run	Pass	Total	Per Run	Per Pass	Per Play
2018	0.5%	2.2%	4.7	1.9	42%	-0.03	15	12	27	80	69	73
2019	1.7%	2.5%	5.7	2.1	42%	0.08	10	17	27	63	86	76
2020	1.9%	1.2%	0.9	-1.0	11%	-0.51	0	3	2	50	85	61
	1.1%	2.3%	5.0	1.8	41%	0.00	25	32	56	-	-	-

Critical Factors	
Reactive Athleticism	5
Anchor / Play Strength	7
Body Control	4

Positional Factors	
Run Block	5
Pass Block	6
Awareness	6
Footwork	5
2nd Level	5
Range	5
Hand Use	6
Power	6
Sustain	5
Finish	5
Flexibility	4
Toughness	6

Jaylon Moore

Report by Ryan Rubinstein

School	Height	Weight	Year	Jersey #	Hometown
Western Michigan	6041 V	311 V	5SR	76	Detroit, MI

One Liner

Moore is a strong, stout blocker at the POA to be an effective lineman at the next level, but his lack of knee bend and ability to handle speed around the edge likely limits him to the right side.

Strengths: Anchor ability; Fast hands; Leg drive
Weaknesses: Lacks knee bend; Speed rushers; Body control

Jaylon Moore plays left tackle in Western Michigan's offense which is run mainly out of shotgun using a high amount of play action passes off their primary zone run scheme. He started 32 of 37 career games, all at left tackle. Moore has a big frame, but is a little top-heavy which can affect his ability to move swiftly. He plays physically in the trenches with a strong motor and a willingness to finish every play.

In the pass game, he's more of a short-setter, but does show that he can kick-slide. The short set paired with a slight lack of knee bend and ankle flexion hinder Moore's ability to effectively set the width of the pocket and beat edge rushers to their spot. He is often placed in awkward positions and, while he can recover a sufficient amount of the time, it sometimes seems as if the game is too quick for him on the left side. He can hold his ground against bull rushes, showing a very good anchor and rarely getting pushed back into the backfield. He uses quick hands to combat against pass rushers' hand-fighting techniques. He shows patience when dealing with cross face rushes that are thrown at him.

In the run game, Moore is a force that moves bodies off and away from the line of scrimmage while keeping them in front of him. He shows good range when blocking on outside runs and was able to quickly and effectively move to the 2nd level to land blocks. He's sometimes put in awkward body positions, but is able to recover and sustain the blocks before finishing with strength and inside hand placement. He's a smart lineman who understands his job on run plays and who he needs to block.

Moore best projects as a right tackle in a zone running scheme who could also kick down to right guard. His powerful blocking style and stoutness at the POA suits him better on the right side. That paired with his ability to anchor quickly allow him to be a versatile player that can be used at tackle and guard.

Year	G	GS	Penalties		Blown Block Splits			
			Holding	False Start	Run	Pressure	Sack	Total
2017	5	0	0	0	2	0	0	2
2018	13	13	0	0	3	3	2	8
2019	13	13	3	0	3	4	4	11
2020	6	6	1	0	1	2	1	4
	37	32	4	0	9	9	7	25

Team Year	Team Zone Run Blocking			Team Gap Run Blocking			Team Pass Block
	% of Runs	Y/A	Pos%	% of Runs	Y/A	Pos%	Pressure%
2017	81%	5.1	44%	14%	5.8	44%	25%
2018	88%	4.9	49%	11%	5.8	42%	24%
2019	84%	6.0	47%	15%	5.4	38%	25%
2020	91%	5.4	59%	8%	5.4	59%	18%
	85%	5.3	48%	12%	5.6	43%	24%

Year	Blown Block %		When Running to their Gap				Total Points			Total Points Rtg		
	Run	Pass	Y/A	YBC/A	Pos%	EPA/A	Run	Pass	Total	Per Run	Per Pass	Per Play
2018	0.6%	1.2%	6.0	3.3	53%	0.10	21	15	35	83	87	85
2019	0.7%	1.8%	5.4	3.1	38%	-0.07	22	19	40	91	95	93
2020	0.5%	1.7%	5.7	2.7	56%	0.11	16	6	23	99	92	99
	0.6%	1.5%	5.7	3.1	48%	0.04	59	40	98	-	-	-

Critical Factors	
Reactive Athleticism	5
Anchor / Play Strength	6
Body Control	4

Positional Factors	
Run Block	6
Pass Block	5
Awareness	5
Footwork	5
2nd Level	5
Range	6
Hand Use	5
Power	6
Sustain	5
Finish	6
Flexibility	4
Toughness	6

Josh Ball

Report by Jeff Dean

School	Height	Weight	Year	Jersey #	Hometown
Marshall	6076 E	309 E	5SR	79	Fredericksburg, VA

One Liner

Ball has the athleticism, size, and comfortability in pass protection teams look for in a left tackle, but his issues with balance, drive, and lateral footwork will likely limit him to a backup role.

Strengths: Athleticism for his height; Anchor; Kick-slide footwork
Weaknesses: Balance; Lateral footwork; Reacting to counter moves

Josh Ball is the left tackle in Marshall's zone offense. He played in 30 career games with 18 starts, all at LT. He began his career at Florida State where he started as a redshirt freshman before being suspended due to a domestic situation, transferred to Butler CC, and ended up at Marshall for his final two years. He has a huge frame with thick thighs, long arms and minimal bad weight. He has quick feet and is fluid in open space. He typically plays with a reserved attitude, but can let his emotions boil over at times.

Ball has a very fluid vertical drop in pass protection. Slide protections show his lateral foot quickness needs work, however. He is susceptible to quicker edge rushers and counter moves, showing some balance issues in reactive situations. His great length, lower-body strength, and wide base make it difficult to push him backwards on bull rushes. Ball shows sufficient hand strength and wins initial contact often with his long arms, but he doesn't sustain well against superior hand fighters. He has the physical tools to be a good professional pass protector.

Ball uses his frame, a good first step, and anchor strength to stalemate defenders in the run game. He doesn't drive defenders off the ball vertically despite his lower-body strength, but he will wash lines out on down blocks and kicks out the play side with better hand placement than as a pass protector. He shows issues on wide reach blocks when moving laterally and has a tendency to bend at the waist to close space. He wasn't asked to pull much, but his movement skills are great for his size and he can locate blocks outside the box. He can get hung up at the line on combinations, but he's adept when getting to the second level.

Ball projects as a backup left tackle in a zone scheme. He will need to improve his upper-body strength and tenacity in the run game to become a true swing tackle. He had a nonlinear college career, but it speaks to his ability that he started at LT for each school at which he played.

			Penalties			Blown Block Splits			
Year	G	GS	Holding	False Start	Run	Pressure	Sack		Total
2017	9	9	1	0	12	9	3		24
2019	13	1	1	0	2	2	3		7
2020	8	8	0	0	4	1	0		7
	30	18	2	0	18	12	6		38

Team	Team Zone Run Blocking			Team Gap Run Blocking			Team Pass Block
Year	% of Runs	Y/A	Pos%	% of Runs	Y/A	Pos%	Pressure%
2017	79%	5.4	49%	20%	5.1	38%	40%
2019	87%	5.4	50%	10%	5.2	43%	38%
2020	95%	4.9	48%	5%	5.9	53%	27%
	87%	5.2	49%	12%	5.2	41%	36%

	Blown Block %		When Running to their Gap				Total Points			Total Points Rtg		
Year	Run	Pass	Y/A	YBC/A	Pos%	EPA/A	Run	Pass	Total	Per Run	Per Pass	Per Play
2019	0.7%	2.4%	7.0	4.2	47%	0.13	10	7	17	71	83	76
2020	1.8%	1.4%	5.4	2.9	54%	0.07	10	8	18	85	92	89
	1.2%	1.9%	6.4	3.7	50%	0.11	20	15	35	-	-	-

Critical Factors	
Reactive Athleticism	5
Anchor / Play Strength	6
Body Control	4

Positional Factors	
Run Block	5
Pass Block	6
Awareness	6
Footwork	5
2nd Level	5
Range	6
Hand Use	5
Power	5
Sustain	5
Finish	5
Flexibility	5
Toughness	5

Spencer Brown

Report by Jeff Dean & Lathon Lax

School	Height	Weight	Year	Jersey #	Hometown
Northern Iowa	6084 V	314 V	5SR	76	Lenox, IA

One Liner

Brown has an ideal frame, and his athleticism and tenacity stand out as an FCS lineman, but he needs much improved hand use, reactive footwork, and lower-body strength to maximize his potential.

Strengths: Finishing ability; Kick-slide in pass pro; Sealing run lanes
Weaknesses: Reactive footwork; Handling rush moves; Blocking in space

Spencer Brown is the right tackle in Northern Iowa's zone blocking scheme. He played in 33 career games with 32 starts, all at right tackle. He missed the final 8 games of the 2017 season with a knee injury. Brown has a massive frame that can still be filled out, especially in his lower half. He is a fluid athlete who moves well for his size but struggles with his reactive quickness. Brown is a fierce competitor who routinely throws FCS defenders on the ground and jumps on top for good measure.

Brown has a smooth kick-slide and gets great depth in his vertical sets, making it difficult to beat him with speed. His steps are clean, controlled, and natural before contact. He reads and passes off incoming defenders well and does not miss assignments often. His hand-fighting skills need work as he can inexplicably let defenders into his chest at his length, resulting in balance issues and an exposure to push-pull moves. Brown struggles with pass rushers who have a plan of attack. His reactive footwork leaves much to be desired when handling outside-in moves. He has a sufficient anchor to handle bull rushes but needs to bulk up for NFL competition.

Brown uses his massive frame and a good first step to seal run lanes. He doesn't generate much vertical drive for his level of competition, but he washes lines down well and can pin defenders inside. He is a nasty finisher who plays with good leverage for his height and explosive hips to roll through contact and bury. He plays with an edge in the run game. He struggles out in space to locate and execute. He looks lost as a puller and doesn't work up to the second level with precision.

Brown projects as a backup right tackle who fits best in a zone blocking scheme. He's still learning the position after playing tight end in high school, but his size and raw athleticism give hope for a future as a swing tackle, albeit not without significant work. He needs refined footwork and hand technique, as well as time in an NFL weight room.

Spencer Brown comes at you big. At 6-foot-8 1/2, 314 pounds, he lives up to his bulk by bench-pressing 500 pounds, double what he benched when he entered the school as a freshman, and up from 420 pounds a year earlier.

"This kid's work ethic and drive is what made him," said Northern Iowa strength and conditioning coach Jed Smith.

UNI has had a good draft showing recently, with a player selected in 2015 (the most notable, David Johnson), 2016 (cornerback Deiondre' Hall) and 2018 (wide receiver Daurice Fountain) after not having anyone selected from 2009 to 2014.

Critical Factors	
Reactive Athleticism	5
Anchor / Play Strength	5
Body Control	5

Positional Factors	
Run Block	6
Pass Block	5
Awareness	6
Footwork	5
2nd Level	5
Range	6
Hand Use	5
Power	5
Sustain	6
Finish	7
Flexibility	7
Toughness	6

Offensive Guards

Bryce Rossler

Offensive guard is by no means a glorious position, but somebody's gotta do it. If we're being honest, it's not the most exciting position group to watch, either. Nevertheless, we at SIS are up to the task and have done the work so that you don't have to. This year, 22 guards made the cut and we have scouting reports and data on all of them, as always.

As you might have imagined, 2020 has us doing some things differently. This year, we made some significant changes to the leaderboard page. This was partially done to account for the disparity in games played across FBS conferences, but we're also rolling out our Total Points Rating. It is our hope that this new, more intuitive version of our flagship metric will help you more readily interpret performance and compare players. This will of course be accompanied by the familiar Blown Block rates and gap-specific yards before contact stats from editions past.

Those who bought last year's Handbook may recall that we were bearish on the 2020 crop of guards. We only gave one strong starting (6.7+) grade last year—to Michigan's Ben Bredeson, who was taken in the fourth round by the Baltimore Ravens. We'd like to think the NFL agreed with us about the 2020 batch of guards. When the dust settled last April, no guards had been taken through the first two rounds and only three were selected in the third round.

Rookies have been getting more and more playing time on the offensive interior since 2017; drafted rookie guards played in 18% of the possible offensive snaps in 2020, the highest rate since SIS began charting football data. We believe that trend will continue and that this year's class will have an opportunity to make an even bigger impact, as we've awarded five strong starting grades.

In our estimation, this class will be more appealing to teams looking for a road grader in the run game than those looking to safeguard their quarterback. Seventeen players received a grade of 6 or better in run blocking, whereas only 12 received a grade of 6 or better for pass protection. This is likely somewhat attributable to the relative lack of athletic ability in the class as a whole; only six players were deemed to have good or better reactive athleticism. Power (18) is more readily available for teams who want it.

On a micro level, this class is headlined by Ohio State's Wyatt Davis, USC's Alijah Vera-Tucker, and two projected tackle-to-guard converts—Oklahoma State's Teven Jenkins and Alabama's Alex Leatherwood. In fact, seven of our top eight guards either started games at tackle and/or are true guard projections from tackle.

Other names that will likely be of interest are Leatherwood's teammate, Deonte Brown, and Tennessee's Trey Smith. Leatherwood, Brown, and Smith were all first-team All-SEC selections in 2020, as was Georgia's Ben Cleveland. As an aside, 8 of the 22 guards featured in this book played their high school ball in the south.

As has been previously alluded to, this is a much better year to need a guard than last year. However, no combine testing is especially interesting for this class of players because of the relative lack of athleticism observed on film. Of course, teams talk themselves into athletic underperformers at the combine every year, but it's still important to have measurements to see who meets thresholds. Relying on Pro Day data is suboptimal, and teams will have to rely on their background and film work more than they have in years past. These players impressed on film, but overall concerns about athleticism can't be addressed by the spandex Olympics. For these reasons, this guard class will be interesting to observe moving forward.

OFFENSIVE GUARD

Offensive Guard Grading Scale

GRADE	DESCRIPTION
9.0 – 7.0	High-end starter. Pro Bowl level.
6.9 – 6.7	Strong starter with 2 position flexibility.
6.6 – 6.5	Lower end starter. Backup flexibility at OT or OC.
6.4	Starter with no position flexibility.
6.2	Multi-positional backup.
6.1 – 6.0	Developmental. Top traits but needs time.
5.7	Backup with no position flexibility. #4 OG

Offensive Guard Rankings

Rank	Name	Grade	Page
1	Alijah Vera-Tucker	6.8	332
2	Alex Leatherwood	6.7	334
3	Wyatt Davis	6.7	336
4	Teven Jenkins	6.7	338
5	Cole Van Lanen	6.7	340
6	Jackson Carman	6.6	342
7	Trey Smith	6.6	344
8	Sadarius Hutcherson	6.5	346
9	Kendrick Green	6.5	348
10	Tommy Kraemer	6.5	350
11	Aaron Banks	6.4	352
12	Deonte Brown	6.4	354
13	Ben Cleveland	6.4	356
14	William Sherman	6.2	358
15	Alaric Jackson	6.2	359
16	D'Ante Smith	6.2	360
17	Robert Jones	6.2	361
18	Larry Borom	6.2	362
19	Joe Sculthorpe	6.2	363
20	Jake Burton	6.2	364
21	Quinn Meinerz	6.2	365
22	Donavaughn Campbell	6.2	366

Glossary

Blown Block%
The percentage of blocking snaps that the player had a blown block.

EPA/A (Runs to Gap Split)
Expected Points Added per rush attempt

Pos% (Runs To Gap split)
Positive Percentage, percentage of carries with a positive Expected Points Added.

Pressure% (Team Stat)
Percentage of total team plays where any defensive player recorded a quarterback hurry, hit, knockdown or sack.

Total Points
Sports Info Solutions' proprietary player value metric that uses an Expected Points framework and distributes the value gained or lost on a play to the players involved based on their impact on the play.

Total Points Rating
Total Points per play compared to average, scaled so that 50 is poor and 99 is excellent.

Y/A (Runs To Gap split)
Yards per rush attempt.

YBC/A (Runs To Gap split)
Yards before contact per rush attempt.

Offensive Guard Leaderboards

Total Points Per Game

Rk	Player	School	Tot Pts / G
1	C. Van Lanen	Wisconsin	4.0
2	L. Borom	Missouri	3.0
3	W. Davis	Ohio State	2.9
3	K. Green	Illinois	2.9
5	A. Vera-Tucker	USC	2.8
5	A. Leatherwood	Alabama	2.8
5	T. Smith	Tennessee	2.8
8	T. Jenkins	Oklahoma State	2.7
8	A. Banks	Notre Dame	2.7
10	3 tied with		2.5

Total Points Rating Per Play

Rk	Player	School	Rating
1	C. Van Lanen	Wisconsin	98
2	T. Jenkins	Oklahoma State	92
2	L. Borom	Missouri	92
4	T. Smith	Tennessee	91
5	A. Leatherwood	Alabama	89
5	K. Green	Illinois	89
7	W. Davis	Ohio State	88
8	A. Vera-Tucker	USC	87
8	J. Carman	Clemson	87
8	B. Cleveland	Georgia	87

Pass Blocking Total Points Per Game

Rk	Player	School	Tot Pts / G
1	L. Borom	Missouri	1.9
2	A. Vera-Tucker	USC	1.8
3	C. Van Lanen	Wisconsin	1.6
4	R. Jones	Middle Tennessee	1.5
5	J. Carman	Clemson	1.4
5	T. Smith	Tennessee	1.4
5	J. Burton	Baylor	1.4
8	D. Brown	Alabama	1.2
9	T. Jenkins	Oklahoma State	1.1
9	2 tied with		1.1

Total Points Rating Per Pass Block

Rk	Player	School	Rating
1	L. Borom	Missouri	99
2	C. Van Lanen	Wisconsin	98
3	T. Jenkins	Oklahoma State	96
4	T. Smith	Tennessee	94
5	J. Carman	Clemson	92
6	R. Jones	Middle Tennessee	91
7	A. Vera-Tucker	USC	90
8	D. Brown	Alabama	87
9	B. Cleveland	Georgia	86
10	K. Green	Illinois	85

Run Blocking Total Points Per Game

Rk	Player	School	Tot Pts / G
1	C. Van Lanen	Wisconsin	2.4
2	W. Davis	Ohio State	1.9
2	K. Green	Illinois	1.9
4	A. Leatherwood	Alabama	1.8
5	T. Jenkins	Oklahoma State	1.6
5	A. Banks	Notre Dame	1.6
7	T. Smith	Tennessee	1.5
7	T. Kraemer	Notre Dame	1.5
7	W. Sherman	Colorado	1.5
10	A. Jackson	Iowa	1.4

Total Points Rating Per Run Block

Rk	Player	School	Rating
1	C. Van Lanen	Wisconsin	98
2	A. Leatherwood	Alabama	96
3	W. Davis	Ohio State	94
4	K. Green	Illinois	92
5	B. Cleveland	Georgia	89
6	T. Jenkins	Oklahoma State	88
6	T. Smith	Tennessee	88
8	T. Kraemer	Notre Dame	87
8	A. Banks	Notre Dame	87
10	D. Brown	Alabama	84

Total Blown Blocks Per Game			
Rk	Player	School	BB/G
1	T. Jenkins	Oklahoma State	0.4
1	T. Smith	Tennessee	0.4
1	B. Cleveland	Georgia	0.4
4	R. Jones	Middle Tennessee	0.5
5	C. Van Lanen	Wisconsin	0.6
5	K. Green	Illinois	0.6
5	L. Borom	Missouri	0.6
8	A. Vera-Tucker	USC	0.7
8	S. Hutcherson	South Carolina	0.7
8	A. Banks	Notre Dame	0.7

Overall Blown Block Percentage			
Rk	Player	School	BB%
1	T. Smith	Tennessee	0.6%
2	T. Jenkins	Oklahoma State	0.7%
3	C. Van Lanen	Wisconsin	0.8%
3	B. Cleveland	Georgia	0.8%
3	R. Jones	Middle Tennessee	0.8%
6	A. Vera-Tucker	USC	0.9%
6	L. Borom	Missouri	0.9%
8	K. Green	Illinois	1.0%
8	A. Banks	Notre Dame	1.0%
10	S. Hutcherson	South Carolina	1.1%

Pass Blown Blocks Per Game			
Rk	Player	School	BB/G
1	L. Borom	Missouri	0.1
2	T. Smith	Tennessee	0.2
2	B. Cleveland	Georgia	0.2
4	T. Jenkins	Oklahoma State	0.3
4	A. Banks	Notre Dame	0.3
6	C. Van Lanen	Wisconsin	0.4
6	S. Hutcherson	South Carolina	0.4
6	K. Green	Illinois	0.4
6	D. Brown	Alabama	0.4
6	R. Jones	Middle Tennessee	0.4

Pass Blown Block Percentage			
Rk	Player	School	BB%
1	L. Borom	Missouri	0.3%
2	T. Smith	Tennessee	0.6%
3	B. Cleveland	Georgia	0.7%
4	A. Banks	Notre Dame	0.9%
4	R. Jones	Middle Tennessee	0.9%
6	A. Vera-Tucker	USC	1.0%
6	T. Jenkins	Oklahoma State	1.0%
8	C. Van Lanen	Wisconsin	1.1%
9	S. Hutcherson	South Carolina	1.2%
9	D. Brown	Alabama	1.2%

Rush Blown Blocks Per Game			
Rk	Player	School	BB/G
1	T. Jenkins	Oklahoma State	0.1
1	R. Jones	Middle Tennessee	0.1
3	A. Vera-Tucker	USC	0.2
3	C. Van Lanen	Wisconsin	0.2
3	T. Smith	Tennessee	0.2
3	B. Cleveland	Georgia	0.2
7	J. Carman	Clemson	0.3
7	S. Hutcherson	South Carolina	0.3
7	K. Green	Illinois	0.3
7	4 tied with		0.3

Rush Blown Block Percentage			
Rk	Player	School	BB%
1	T. Jenkins	Oklahoma State	0.4%
2	R. Jones	Middle Tennessee	0.5%
3	A. Vera-Tucker	USC	0.6%
3	C. Van Lanen	Wisconsin	0.6%
5	T. Smith	Tennessee	0.7%
5	K. Green	Illinois	0.7%
7	B. Cleveland	Georgia	0.8%
7	W. Sherman	Colorado	0.8%
7	J. Sculthorpe	NC State	0.8%
10	3 tied with		1.0%

Career Games Started			
Rk	Player	School	GS
1	A. Jackson	Iowa	42
2	A. Leatherwood	Alabama	41
2	T. Smith	Tennessee	41
4	S. Hutcherson	South Carolina	39
4	T. Kraemer	Notre Dame	39
6	T. Jenkins	Oklahoma State	35
7	K. Green	Illinois	33
8	A. Banks	Notre Dame	31
8	J. Burton	Baylor	31
10	D. Smith	East Carolina	30

Yards Before Contact To Their Gap Per Attempt			
Rk	Player	School	YBC/A
1	K. Green	Illinois	3.6
2	A. Banks	Notre Dame	3.5
2	W. Sherman	Colorado	3.5
4	A. Leatherwood	Alabama	3.4
5	B. Cleveland	Georgia	3.3
6	C. Van Lanen	Wisconsin	2.9
7	T. Kraemer	Notre Dame	2.8
7	D. Brown	Alabama	2.8
9	L. Borom	Missouri	2.7
10	3 tied with		2.6

Holding Penalties			
Rk	Player	School	Holds
1	S. Hutcherson	South Carolina	0
1	B. Cleveland	Georgia	0
1	R. Jones	Middle Tennessee	0
4	W. Davis	Ohio State	1
4	T. Jenkins	Oklahoma State	1
4	T. Kraemer	Notre Dame	1
4	A. Banks	Notre Dame	1
4	D. Brown	Alabama	1
4	W. Sherman	Colorado	1
4	3 tied with		1

Yards Before Contact To Their Gap Per Game			
Rk	Player	School	YBC/G
1	K. Green	Illinois	39.5
2	L. Borom	Missouri	37.5
3	B. Cleveland	Georgia	37.1
4	W. Sherman	Colorado	36.8
5	D. Brown	Alabama	35.0
5	A. Jackson	Iowa	35.0
7	A. Banks	Notre Dame	34.3
8	A. Leatherwood	Alabama	33.9
9	T. Smith	Tennessee	33.2
10	C. Van Lanen	Wisconsin	29.8

Positive Percentage When Run Behind			
Rk	Player	School	Pos%
1	A. Leatherwood	Alabama	61%
2	T. Smith	Tennessee	57%
2	D. Brown	Alabama	57%
4	C. Van Lanen	Wisconsin	56%
5	T. Kraemer	Notre Dame	55%
5	B. Cleveland	Georgia	55%
7	A. Banks	Notre Dame	53%
8	R. Jones	Middle Tennessee	50%
8	L. Borom	Missouri	50%
10	J. Carman	Clemson	49%

Yards When Run Behind Per Game			
Rk	Player	School	Yds/G
1	S. Hutcherson	South Carolina	77.2
2	K. Green	Illinois	76.8
3	D. Brown	Alabama	71.2
4	L. Borom	Missouri	67.6
5	B. Cleveland	Georgia	67.2
6	A. Leatherwood	Alabama	66.8
7	A. Banks	Notre Dame	64.3
8	W. Sherman	Colorado	63.2
9	T. Smith	Tennessee	62.6
10	A. Jackson	Iowa	62.5

Alijah Vera-Tucker Final Grade: 6.8

Report by Noah Chang & Christian Vega

School	Height	Weight	Year	Jersey #	Hometown
USC	6032 E	315 E	4JR	75	Oakland, CA

One Liner
Vera-Tucker possesses ideal versatility for the NFL to consider, but his football awareness and technical lower half make for a dominant guard candidate.

Overall
Alijah Vera-Tucker is an offensive lineman in USC's Air Raid offense and primarily zone blocking scheme. He played in 31 games with 19 starts, 13 at left guard in 2019 and 6 at left tackle in 2020. He's thickly built with good movement skills in space and great flexibility for his size. He's a tough competitor and a team captain, but doesn't play with an overly physical mindset.

Pass Game
Vera-Tucker has some difficulties getting out of his stance vertically, especially against speed on the perimeter, but otherwise is a very impressive pass protector. Once off the ball he has very quick and technically sound footwork to mirror pass rushers. His best trait may be his awareness. He senses moving parts up front very well, always working inside out and keeping his head on a swivel to identify late movement. He is able to kick-slide as a left tackle with good depth to his drops and sits with flexible bend in his lower half. Vera-Tucker occasionally attacks with wide hands, and he anchors better with his lower body than with shock in his punch, but he does a good job of recovering and replacing his hands through contact to work through rush moves. He plays with great balance when engaged and reacts quickly in short areas. He was a shutdown pass protector inside, but it says a lot about his athleticism and technical ability that he held up so well at left tackle, as well.

Run Game
Vera-Tucker positions himself very well in the run game, especially within zone blocking schemes. He has good lateral strength and great flexibility to flip his hips and seal run lanes horizontally. He has the awareness and athleticism to work multiple defenders downfield and find success at the second level. He's quick in tight spaces to redirect against slanting fronts and still find ways to execute. His hands don't always connect accurately, but his footwork and positioning usually allow him to avoid whiffs and penalties. Where he struggles is with his power at the point of attack. Vera-Tucker has the leg drive to move defenders off the ball but he doesn't consistently pack a punch at contact or explode through defenders to wash them out. He plays with intelligence and toughness in the trenches and executes his assignments fluidly.

Last Word
Vera-Tucker is an impressive blocker whose best position will be viewed differently by many. He put impressive tape on display at left tackle and could certainly be a starting-caliber player there. However, his highest ceiling is at guard, ideally in a zone blocking scheme. His high-end pass protection skills have fewer weaknesses inside, and his awareness is better displayed along the interior when working together with his linemates. He'll need to become a more physical presence to handle the NFL's strongest players, but his reactive quickness is a strong asset inside.

Strengths	Weaknesses
• Awareness	• Quickness off the snap
• Lower-body technique	• Power at the point of attack
• Versatility	• Nasty disposition

Critical Factors

Reactive Athleticism	Anchor / Play Strength	Body Control
7	6	7

Positional Factors

Run Block	Pass Block	Awareness	Footwork
6	7	7	7
2nd Level	Range	Hand Use	Power
6	6	6	5
Sustain	Finish	Flexibility	Toughness
6	5	7	6

Basic

Year	G	GS	Penalties		Blown Block Splits			
			Holding	False Start	Run	Pressure	Sack	Total
2018	12	0	0	0	0	0	0	0
2019	13	13	0	0	4	1	0	5
2020	6	6	2	0	1	1	2	4
	31	19	2	0	5	2	2	9

Team Stats

Year	Zone Run Blocking			Gap Run Blocking			Pass Block
	% of Runs	Y/A	Pos%	% of Runs	Y/A	Pos%	Pressure%
2018	67%	4.8	42%	32%	6.0	49%	27%
2019	79%	5.2	48%	20%	5.1	42%	30%
2020	65%	3.8	46%	28%	4.2	38%	32%
	71%	4.8	45%	27%	5.3	45%	29%

Deep Dive

Year	Blown Block %		When Running to their Gap				Total Points			Total Points Rtg		
	Run	Pass	Y/A	YBC/A	Pos%	EPA/A	Run	Pass	Total	Per Run	Per Pass	Per Play
2018	0.0%	0.0%	3.6	1.4	29%	-0.16	3	3	5	98	96	97
2019	1.2%	0.2%	4.3	1.6	55%	0.02	16	26	42	89	98	96
2020	0.6%	1.0%	4.6	1.5	47%	0.03	7	11	17	80	90	87
	0.9%	0.4%	4.3	1.6	49%	0.00	26	40	64	-	-	-

Alex Leatherwood

Report by Alec Mallon & Tobin Sharp

School	Height	Weight	Year	Jersey #	Hometown
Alabama	6051 V	312 V	4SR	70	Pensacola, FL

One Liner

Leatherwood is a powerful and lengthy lineman who has the versatile, all-around skill set to be an impactful guard at the next level.

Overall

Alex Leatherwood is an offensive lineman for Alabama in their RPO-heavy offense. He saw action in 7 games in 2017 but then started all 15 at right guard the following year. Since then, he moved to left tackle and started all 26 games over the last 2 seasons. Leatherwood has great length and sufficient athleticism, both of which are heightened along the interior. A consistent anchor for Alabama's offensive line, Leatherwood is an energetic leader on the field.

Pass Game

Leatherwood's strong lower half allows for him to be successful in pass protection. In his sets, he shows good footwork to keep his shoulders square and stay balanced. At tackle, he lacks the foot quickness to reach the vertical depth to meet top speed rushers, but at guard in short sets he's sound. He shows the ability to throw a punch with strong hands and stalemate and negate opposing rush moves at the line of scrimmage. Leatherwood will occasionally overextend and get caught lunging, putting him in compromised situations. He keeps his hands low and will misfire or mistime his punch against premier edge talents. Inside, Leatherwood shows good eye discipline, always looking for work when he is left available. His athletic ability is a plus there, as he is fluid with his movements and recovery flexibility up and down the pocket for his quarterback.

Run Game

While he can be slow off the line, at the point of attack in the run game, Leatherwood has the strength to not only jolt defenders back but move them off of the line. Leatherwood has heavy hands and powerful legs to drive. If he wins hand positioning at the snap, it is extremely difficult for the defender to get back into a winning situation. On the move, Leatherwood has the quickness to reach and wall off defenders on the back side, as well as the fluid hips to pull and clear out run lanes. He shows good technique and strong footwork when climbing to the second level, often cutting off linebackers before they can get to their run fits, creating open lanes for the backs. He can occasionally get caught being too aggressive and will again overextend after taking a bad angle. Leatherwood eats up explosive contact inside while not giving ground and will wash lines out on down blocks, but his finishing tenacity is inconsistent. He has the power and athleticism to recover in awkward positions and make enough of a block to usually execute.

Last Word

Leatherwood has multi-position experience, but his best position in the NFL will be as a guard. He best fits in a gap scheme with his strength, aggression and pulling fluidity, but he has the movement skills to work laterally in zone, as well. He could be a low-end starting tackle on either side, but a move inside masks some of his weaknesses to perimeter athletes.

Strengths
- Leg drive and anchor
- Impactful puller
- Interior hand use

Weaknesses
- Overextension on the perimeter
- Vertical foot quickness
- Sluggish get-off

Critical Factors

Reactive Athleticism	Anchor / Play Strength	Body Control
6	7	6

Positional Factors

Run Block	Pass Block	Awareness	Footwork
6	6	6	6
2nd Level	**Range**	**Hand Use**	**Power**
6	6	6	6
Sustain	**Finish**	**Flexibility**	**Toughness**
6	5	6	6

Basic

Year	G	GS	Holding	False Start	Run	Pressure	Sack	Total
			Penalties		**Blown Block Splits**			
2017	7	0	0	0	2	1	1	4
2018	15	15	0	0	12	8	3	23
2019	13	13	1	0	5	6	0	12
2020	13	13	3	0	6	9	5	20
	48	41	4	0	25	24	9	59

Team Stats

Year	% of Runs	Y/A	Pos%	% of Runs	Y/A	Pos%	Pressure%
	Zone Run Blocking			**Gap Run Blocking**			**Pass Block**
2017	64%	5.9	51%	35%	6.8	52%	39%
2018	68%	5.2	54%	31%	6.0	55%	32%
2019	52%	5.4	48%	48%	5.8	59%	26%
2020	56%	5.8	62%	43%	5.3	46%	26%
	61%	5.5	54%	38%	6.0	53%	31%

Deep Dive

Year	Run	Pass	Y/A	YBC/A	Pos%	EPA/A	Run	Pass	Total	Per Run	Per Pass	Per Play
	Blown Block %		**When Running to their Gap**				**Total Points**			**Total Points Rtg**		
2018	2.7%	2.3%	6.1	2.5	56%	0.20	17	10	28	76	65	70
2019	1.6%	1.7%	5.0	2.2	49%	0.05	17	18	34	93	96	95
2020	1.5%	3.1%	6.7	3.4	61%	0.30	24	13	37	96	79	89
	2.0%	2.4%	6.0	2.8	56%	0.20	58	41	99	-	-	-

Wyatt Davis

Report by John Todd

School	Height	Weight	Year	Jersey #	Hometown
Ohio State	6026 E	315 E	4JR	52	Bellflower, CA

One Liner

Davis is a brick wall of a guard who relies on his anchor strength and vision to make up for some technical issues in his foot quickness and body control in order to be a reliable force inside.

Overall

Wyatt Davis is an offensive lineman in Ohio State's zone scheme. He has started 24 of 36 games, all at right guard. He exited both 2020 playoff games early with left knee injuries. He has a thick lower half and good bubble, but he's also well cut up-top with broad shoulders. He's a good athlete for his size and a decent mover, but he struggles to redirect in tight spaces at times. He's a mauler in close quarters and competes through the whistle.

Pass Game

While not fleet of foot, Davis is a solid pass protector. He pushes back off the line quickly and squares with a wide base. He does a great job of recognizing stunts and late blitzes even when engaged. He passes off moving pieces well and can work laterally when he sees it coming; but otherwise his heavy footwork gives him trouble adjusting in quick change-of-direction situations. He keeps his head on a swivel looking for work and packs a punch on exposed ribs. He tends to attack with a wide hand or two and will lose control of his chest against length. However, Davis possesses ridiculous anchor strength to absorb and sit against most defenders, even when compromised. He locks out well when his technique is right but can get overaggressive and play over his toes at the point of attack. His anchor abilities mask some occasional slips in technique.

Run Game

Davis is a physical presence inside in the run game. He sets himself off the snap with a quick synchronous shuffle of his feet and hands to get in rhythm and square to contact. He's a good driver off the line of scrimmage, but his most impressive trait is his ability to eat up massive collisions from run blitzers and explosive interior defenders at the point of attack while not losing ground. He's very difficult to overpower in a phone booth, even when he gets too high after contact. He is flexible enough to snatch on the move, but reaching and sealing in wide zones isn't his strong suit. He can smother when he gets there but doesn't execute at the second level consistently, struggles to find work as a skip-puller, and is a non-factor in space in the screen game. That said, Davis is dominant in head-up one-on-one situations and blows holes open on double teams. His attacking mindset will overextend him outside his immediate range, and he's had balance issues he needs to clean up. He plays with flashes of a mean streak and seems to enjoy ruffling feathers.

Last Word

Davis projects as a solid plug-and-play guard at the next level for power-based run-heavy teams looking to get tougher inside. He has played well in the Buckeye's zone scheme, but a downhill gap system suits him best in the future. He does not have the ability to flex out to tackle based on his limited foot quickness and lack of sudden reactive skills in space, but those concerns are mitigated at guard. He has the combination of size, smarts, and strength offensive line coaches will covet.

Strengths	Weaknesses
• Anchor strength	• Space blocking and range
• Phone-booth tenacity	• Body control
• Blitz and stunt awareness	• Losing chest and pad level

Critical Factors

Reactive Athleticism	Anchor / Play Strength	Body Control
5	8	5

Positional Factors

Run Block	Pass Block	Awareness	Footwork
7	6	7	5
2nd Level	Range	Hand Use	Power
5	4	5	6
Sustain	Finish	Flexibility	Toughness
6	6	5	7

Basic

Year	G	GS	Penalties		Blown Block Splits			
			Holding	False Start	Run	Pressure	Sack	Total
2018	14	2	0	0	2	0	1	3
2019	14	14	1	0	7	5	1	14
2020	8	8	1	0	6	3	1	10
	36	24	2	0	15	8	3	27

Team Stats

Year	Zone Run Blocking			Gap Run Blocking			Pass Block
	% of Runs	Y/A	Pos%	% of Runs	Y/A	Pos%	Pressure%
2018	74%	5.1	51%	24%	4.0	48%	26%
2019	83%	6.5	50%	17%	6.1	53%	35%
2020	89%	7.1	53%	10%	3.3	43%	36%
	81%	6.1	51%	18%	4.8	50%	31%

Deep Dive

Year	Blown Block %		When Running to their Gap				Total Points			Total Points Rtg		
	Run	Pass	Y/A	YBC/A	Pos%	EPA/A	Run	Pass	Total	Per Run	Per Pass	Per Play
2018	2.4%	1.0%	4.3	2.1	47%	0.01	1	2	5	51	68	60
2019	1.5%	1.6%	6.5	2.5	48%	0.15	23	14	37	90	80	86
2020	2.3%	1.6%	4.2	1.9	44%	-0.02	15	7	23	94	77	88
	1.9%	1.5%	5.5	2.2	46%	0.08	39	23	65	-	-	-

Teven Jenkins

Report by Jordan Edwards & Joe McDonald

School	Height	Weight	Year	Jersey #	Hometown
Oklahoma State	6052 E	320 E	5SR	73	Topeka, KS

One Liner
Jenkins is a functionally strong lineman with solid athleticism and an aggressive play style, but a lack of body control and footwork on the edge means a move to the interior of the offensive line may suit him best at the next level.

Overall
Teven Jenkins lines up at right tackle in Oklahoma State's zone-heavy running attack. He's competed in 44 games in his career at Oklahoma State, and has logged starts in 35 of those games, mostly coming at right tackle with a few starts at right guard and left tackle as well. He opted out after 7 games in 2020 due to some nagging lower-back injuries. Jenkins is a powerful athlete with strong hands, good length, and a sturdy lower half. He plays with an aggressive demeanor and plays to the echo of the whistle.

Pass Game
Jenkins is a solid pass blocker who displays good athleticism in pass pro. He has very good play strength and can control rushers with his strong hands. He can struggle to anchor against powerful pass rushers who get into his chest, but he plays with active and strong hands to disengage and recoil his hands back. Jenkins displays the intelligence and effectiveness to vary his pass sets to throw off the timing of opposing rushers. He's much more effective in his quick sets, when he can get his hands onto rushers and control their movements. He has average footwork in his vertical pass sets and struggles to reach his landmarks against speedy edge rushers. He does show the ability to lean on rushers and run the arc to let his quarterback step up into the pocket. Jenkins doesn't have poor body control or flexibility, but he does have the tendency to stop his feet and lunge at contact.

Run Game
Jenkins is a powerful run blocker who plays with an aggressive mindset at the LOS. He consistently finishes blocks into the ground and is always looking for extra work when unoccupied. He is functionally strong and displays good core strength to roll his hips on contact. He has the mobility and athleticism to reach blocks and display his range in a zone scheme. His natural power and mauling ability can fit in a gap run scheme as well. He can seal off and anchor on the back side of run plays. Additionally, he's effective in double team situations and can create and sustain contact at the 2nd level. He can wash down interior defenders to create run lanes and has the power and strength to push defenders back at the POA in 1-on-1 situations.

Last Word
Although Jenkins has spent the majority of his career as a right tackle, his play style and traits project best as a guard at the next level. His ability to generate power and sustain blocks at the POA translate with a move inside playing against interior defensive lineman. Jenkins can provide some versatility and could be a low-end starting right tackle at the next level, but he could thrive transitioning inside to either guard position.

Strengths	Weaknesses
• Functional strength	• Body control
• Aggressive demeanor	• Footwork
• Run blocking	• Flexibility

Critical Factors

Reactive Athleticism	Anchor / Play Strength	Body Control
6	7	5

Positional Factors

Run Block	Pass Block	Awareness	Footwork
7	6	6	5
2nd Level	Range	Hand Use	Power
6	6	6	7
Sustain	Finish	Flexibility	Toughness
7	7	5	6

Basic

			Penalties		Blown Block Splits			
Year	G	GS	Holding	False Start	Run	Pressure	Sack	Total
2017	12	3	0	0	1	5	1	7
2018	13	13	0	0	1	7	3	11
2019	12	12	1	0	3	1	2	6
2020	7	7	1	0	1	1	1	3
	44	35	2	0	6	14	7	27

Team Stats

	Zone Run Blocking			Gap Run Blocking			Pass Block
Year	% of Runs	Y/A	Pos%	% of Runs	Y/A	Pos%	Pressure%
2017	83%	5.4	46%	12%	4.9	41%	25%
2018	75%	5.7	49%	13%	4.6	51%	32%
2019	73%	6.0	48%	20%	5.3	50%	28%
2020	80%	4.9	38%	13%	4.1	40%	28%
	78%	5.5	45%	15%	4.8	46%	28%

Deep Dive

	Blown Block %		When Running to their Gap				Total Points			Total Points Rtg		
										Per	Per	Per
Year	Run	Pass	Y/A	YBC/A	Pos%	EPA/A	Run	Pass	Total	Run	Pass	Play
2018	0.2%	1.9%	5.3	3.2	54%	0.14	21	14	35	94	74	84
2019	0.7%	0.8%	5.7	2.2	46%	-0.03	17	17	34	70	97	86
2020	0.4%	1.0%	5.5	2.6	42%	0.11	11	8	19	88	96	92
	0.4%	1.3%	5.6	2.6	48%	0.06	49	39	88	-	-	-

Cole Van Lanen

Report by Ben Hrkach

School	Height	Weight	Year	Jersey #	Hometown
Wisconsin	6052 E	312 E	5SR	71	Green Bay, WI

One Liner
Van Lanen's size, footwork, and strength will fit well inside at guard, where his skill set is much more well-rounded and less volatile than at tackle.

Overall
Cole Van Lanen played left tackle in Wisconsin's balanced, run-first scheme, starting in 19 of his 45 games played all on the blind side. He is a powerful player who uses his hands and feet in synchrony. He lacks ideal length but otherwise has great size. Van Lanen missed a game in 2019 due to a head injury suffered in practice, as well as the final 2 games of his career with an undisclosed injury. He displays good toughness and always finishes blocks.

Pass Game
In the pass game, Van Lanen looked more comfortable in a short set. At tackle, he would allow speed rushers to gain the edge on him. To combat this, he would overstep and expose himself to counter steps and long arms. His hand placement was often wide and he would allow rushers to get a hand in his chest. These weaknesses converged in his 2019 matchup with Chase Young. However, he did show the strength to reset and recover positioning. When faced with power rushers, Van Lanen frequently won by beating his man off the ball, getting a strong punch and latch, and quickly anchoring. These skills will translate well to setting a shelf for the QB at the next level. He displayed good communication skills and was sound passing off stunts and slants. He easily moved from one rusher to the next and always had his feet in the proper position. On screens, Van Lanen was very good at getting to a defender in space, latching on, and finishing the block.

Run Game
In the run game, Van Lanen has everything you are looking for. He fires out of his stance, sticks to his man, and drives him out of the play. Van Lanen wins with his feet first and then displays a strong punch followed by very good hand strength to latch. His hand placement can be wide at times, but he has the strength and balance to reset. He has a square base and keeps his feet pumping. Although he doesn't get many pancakes, he does a great job of eliminating his man from the play. He can get lazy to play high and lunge at times, but these plays are few and far between when run blocking. On combo blocks, Van Lanen easily wipes his man out and smoothly transfers to the next defender. When getting to the second level, Van Lanen is quick, fluid, and under control. His feet get him where he needs to be and he sticks to his man. He shows good range as well and a natural deftness when attacking defenders in space.

Last Word
While Van Lanen has been a career left tackle, his best fit at the next level should be at guard. He doesn't have the foot speed and length to play tackle consistently, at least on the left, but his weaknesses will be mitigated with a move inside. He is an ideal gap-blocking scheme player to get off the ball, attack downhill, and work up to the second level.

Strengths

- Second level
- Grip strength to sustain
- Easy mover in space

Weaknesses

- Reactive athleticism on the perimeter
- Flexibility
- Hand placement

Critical Factors

Reactive Athleticism	Anchor / Play Strength	Body Control
6	6	6

Positional Factors

Run Block	Pass Block	Awareness	Footwork
6	6	6	6
2nd Level	Range	Hand Use	Power
7	6	6	6
Sustain	Finish	Flexibility	Toughness
7	6	5	6

Basic

Year	G	GS	Penalties		Blown Block Splits			
			Holding	False Start	Run	Pressure	Sack	Total
2017	14	0	0	0	0	0	0	0
2018	13	1	0	0	6	2	2	10
2019	13	13	1	0	5	6	2	13
2020	5	5	2	0	1	1	1	3
	45	19	3	0	12	9	5	26

Team Stats

Year	Zone Run Blocking			Gap Run Blocking			Pass Block
	% of Runs	Y/A	Pos%	% of Runs	Y/A	Pos%	Pressure%
2017	67%	5.5	44%	32%	5.5	48%	38%
2018	67%	6.6	59%	31%	7.2	55%	29%
2019	55%	5.7	51%	42%	6.0	51%	27%
2020	65%	4.7	48%	33%	3.9	47%	22%
	63%	5.7	51%	35%	5.9	50%	29%

Deep Dive

Year	Blown Block %		When Running to their Gap				Total Points			Total Points Rtg		
	Run	Pass	Y/A	YBC/A	Pos%	EPA/A	Run	Pass	Total	Per Run	Per Pass	Per Play
2018	1.8%	1.9%	7.9	4.2	57%	0.24	15	6	21	87	82	85
2019	1.0%	2.2%	6.2	3.1	45%	-0.03	28	15	43	96	95	95
2020	0.6%	1.1%	5.2	2.9	56%	0.11	12	8	20	98	98	98
	1.2%	1.9%	6.6	3.4	51%	0.09	55	29	84	-	-	-

Jackson Carman Final Grade: 6.6

Report by Nathan Cooper

School	Height	Weight	Year	Jersey #	Hometown
Clemson	6045 E	335 E	3JR	79	Fairfield, OH

One Liner
Carman has the overall strength, run-game power, and finishing ability to be a low-end starting guard at the next level with versatility, but he'll need to work on his pad level, balance, and body control if he wants to be a consistent contributor early on.

Overall
Jackson Carman is the left tackle in Clemson's RPO offense running mainly zone schemes. He started 27 of 40 games during his career with the Tigers. He's a solid athlete who has a good frame for the position and moves well, but he is a little top heavy and doesn't possess great overall flexibility or ankle flexion. He plays hard and competes with whomever is lined up over him.

Pass Game
Carman struggles to keep up when facing off against speed and finesse rushers. Even when going up against someone who doesn't possess great speed, he'll open his gate too early which leaves him susceptible to being beaten back to the inside, and he's not the most reactive athlete to be able to redirect and get back into position. When he's in awkward positions, he struggles to recover when a defender engages. His kick-slide also turns into a backpedal at times. Most of this stems from only sufficient flexibility and his pad level being a little too high, though that improved some in 2020. Once he gets his feet under himself, he can anchor down quickly. When he shows good footwork and can get latched on, his quick, heavy hands and initial punch give a jolt to the defender. He shows good awareness and communication taking on slant rushes and stunts. Once he gets his hands on defenders and remains balanced, it's tough for defenders to shed him due to his strong grip and overall strength. At times, he won't sustain his blocks and will just give a push, but when he latches on he finishes and makes it tough for defenders to do much after that.

Run Game
In the run game, Carman provides good strength, leg drive, and push to create a new line of scrimmage. He fires off the ball and gets hands up and on the defender quickly, giving a strong jolt to the defender. He's strong at the POA and plays with good power. His pad level will rise some, but it generally stays lower in the run game as compared to pass pro. When combo blocking, he's quick to scrape and redirect to pick up the second defender. Carman doesn't have much speed, but he shows good range laterally and to the 2nd level. He works up to the 2nd level balanced and under control and is able to get into good position to make the block. He rarely pulls and it's obvious he hasn't done it much, but he shows good athleticism in space. He knows how to finish his blocks in the run game, taking defenders to the ground with regularity.

Last Word
Carman projects best as a right guard in a zone scheme at the next level, though he could be effective in a gap scheme with more practice on pulls. He also has the versatility to kick out to right tackle and be effective given his strength, length, and power.

Strengths	Weaknesses
• Heavy hands	• Pad level can be too high
• Strength & power	• Struggles vs. speed
• Nasty finisher	• Lacks balance & body control

Critical Factors

Reactive Athleticism	Anchor / Play Strength	Body Control
5	6	5

Positional Factors

Run Block	Pass Block	Awareness	Footwork
6	5	6	5
2nd Level	Range	Hand Use	Power
6	6	6	7
Sustain	Finish	Flexibility	Toughness
5	7	5	7

Basic

Year	G	GS	Penalties		Blown Block Splits			
			Holding	False Start	Run	Pressure	Sack	Total
2018	13	0	0	0	3	2	0	5
2019	15	15	2	0	7	8	3	19
2020	12	12	4	0	4	6	4	14
	40	27	6	0	14	16	7	38

Team Stats

Year	Zone Run Blocking			Gap Run Blocking			Pass Block
	% of Runs	Y/A	Pos%	% of Runs	Y/A	Pos%	Pressure%
2018	64%	7.1	53%	34%	7.1	53%	23%
2019	63%	6.5	56%	32%	6.2	56%	31%
2020	60%	5.0	56%	34%	5.1	41%	26%
	63%	6.4	55%	33%	6.2	51%	27%

Deep Dive

Year	Blown Block %		When Running to their Gap				Total Points			Total Points Rtg		
	Run	Pass	Y/A	YBC/A	Pos%	EPA/A	Run	Pass	Total	Per Run	Per Pass	Per Play
2018	2.3%	2.5%	7.7	2.6	40%	0.30	5	2	7	74	76	75
2019	2.0%	2.8%	6.8	2.6	60%	0.31	18	12	31	93	75	84
2020	1.3%	2.2%	5.1	2.0	49%	0.11	13	17	30	79	92	87
	1.8%	2.5%	6.4	2.4	52%	0.24	36	31	68	-	-	-

Trey Smith

Report by Dan Foehrenbach

School	Height	Weight	Year	Jersey #	Hometown
Tennessee	6054 V	331 V	4SR	73	Jackson, TN

One Liner
Smith has the overall power, mauler's mentality and strong hands to be a starting guard at the next level, but he will need to work on his flexibility, range, and pass-blocking techniques if he wants to be an elite-level player.

Overall
Trey Smith is the left guard in Tennessee's RPO-heavy zone-run offense. He played in 42 games during his career, starting 41 of them for the Volunteers. After spending time at both guard and tackle positions in 2017, he started 7 games at LT in 2018 and started 22 games at LG over the past 2 seasons. In 2018, his season was cut short after experiencing blood clots, which may be career threatening. One of the nation's top high school recruits in 2017, Smith is an elite volunteer and vital member throughout the community. He's a solid athlete who has a large frame and moves well for the position, but he does not possess much quickness or great lateral movement. He is very dependable and plays with exceptional mental toughness and grit on each play.

Pass Game
In the pass game, Smith displays sufficient overall skills. He lacks some awareness and fails to pick up on defensive fronts and 2nd-level blitzes. However, he does keep his head on a swivel and looks for work when uncovered. He struggles against defenders that use finesse-rush techniques. He relies on his pure physicality and strength in order to block effectively. He focuses on a particular defender lined up opposite of him, and sometimes floats in an area. One area of concern is his flexibility. While in pass protection, he tends to be more upright which results in him being off balance at times. He does neutralize the power rush by defensive linemen with his strength and anchor ability, keeping the integrity of the pocket intact. At the POA, it's tough for defenders to shed him due to his quick, strong hands. He shows the ability to sustain and finish blocks once he's able to get latched onto defenders.

Run Game
In the run game, Smith can get movement by getting his mammoth body into the neutral zone while keeping his pads square to his target. He is effective in zone blocking schemes, opening big holes for the running back. His straight-line athleticism enables him to get to the 2nd level quickly and under control, creating mismatches against linebackers and defensive backs. He has very good willingness and aggressiveness to finish plays in the run game. He plays with a mauler's mentality and takes defenders to the ground with regularity. He does show some weakness in his lateral movement. Smith plays a little stiff and is slow to pull and get out on the perimeter. He can, at times, get a bit over-aggressive and find himself whiffing on a defender.

Last Word
Smith projects best as a left guard in a zone-run based offensive scheme. With his skill set and experience, he can also play right tackle. He needs to improve his overall pass pro techniques, but he will immediately help out with his power in the running game. His health history is obviously a concern, but his on-field plays speaks for itself.

Strengths
- Strength & power
- Finishing ability
- Hand use

Weaknesses
- Lower-half technique
- Range
- Flexibility

Critical Factors

Reactive Athleticism	Anchor / Play Strength	Body Control
6	6	6

Positional Factors

Run Block	Pass Block	Awareness	Footwork
6	5	5	5
2nd Level	Range	Hand Use	Power
6	4	6	7
Sustain	Finish	Flexibility	Toughness
6	7	5	7

Basic

Year	G	GS	Penalties Holding	Penalties False Start	Blown Block Splits Run	Blown Block Splits Pressure	Blown Block Splits Sack	Blown Block Splits Total
2017	12	12	0	0	9	5	4	18
2018	7	7	1	0	2	1	1	4
2019	13	12	0	0	12	3	1	16
2020	10	10	2	0	2	2	0	4
	42	41	3	0	25	11	6	42

Team Stats

Year	Zone Run Blocking % of Runs	Zone Run Blocking Y/A	Zone Run Blocking Pos%	Gap Run Blocking % of Runs	Gap Run Blocking Y/A	Gap Run Blocking Pos%	Pass Block Pressure%
2017	74%	4.2	39%	22%	4.6	45%	43%
2018	69%	4.3	36%	30%	5.1	45%	38%
2019	75%	4.9	43%	20%	3.2	31%	35%
2020	80%	4.4	48%	18%	5.0	47%	35%
	74%	4.5	42%	23%	4.5	42%	38%

Deep Dive

Year	Blown Block % Run	Blown Block % Pass	When Running to their Gap Y/A	When Running to their Gap YBC/A	When Running to their Gap Pos%	When Running to their Gap EPA/A	Total Points Run	Total Points Pass	Total Points Total	Total Points Rtg Per Run	Total Points Rtg Per Pass	Total Points Rtg Per Play
2018	0.8%	1.1%	5.0	2.4	33%	-0.21	8	8	16	69	97	84
2019	3.3%	1.1%	5.2	1.9	42%	-0.13	12	15	27	66	94	82
2020	0.7%	0.6%	4.9	2.6	57%	0.15	15	14	28	88	94	91
	1.8%	0.9%	5.0	2.3	46%	-0.03	35	37	71	-	-	-

Sadarius Hutcherson Final Grade: 6.5

Report by Chad Tedder & Jarrett Rodgers

School	Height	Weight	Year	Jersey #	Hometown
South Carolina	6026 E	320 E	5SR	50	Huntingdon, TN

One Liner
Hutcherson has the power, anchor, and positional experience to be a low-end starter at the next level, but his inconsistencies at the 2nd level and out in space will hold him back from being truly dominant.

Overall
Sadarius Hutcherson is an offensive lineman in South Carolina's pro-style offense that runs a decent amount of RPOs and play action in a primary zone-run scheme. He played in 45 games, starting in 39 of them. He made 4 starts at LG in 2017, 12 starts at RG and 1 at LG in 2018, 11 starts at LT and 1 at LG in 2019, and all 10 starts at LG in 2020. A high school basketball player, he's a big-bodied lineman with plenty of power and flexibility. He is a smart, aggressive player who looks for work and a finish on almost every play.

Pass Game
In the pass game, Hutcherson is a solid interior guy who communicates and reacts well to defensive stunts and slants. He can keep a solid base with adequate footwork to maximize his power and absorb oncoming rush attempts. He does a good job at hand fighting, and once he gets his hands inside the rusher's pads he can anchor himself down quickly without getting driven back too far. However, he does occasionally struggle with a powerful bull rush and can get driven into the backfield. He looks for work when he doesn't have a rusher to engage with and often delivers a big hit in assisting a fellow blocker. He can get moved off his spot on some quick inside moves. He lacks the length and top-end reactive athleticism to reach and re-direct inside so he opens up to chase the rusher away from his quarterback.

Run Game
In the run game, Hutcherson shows the ability to move and/or seal off interior defensive linemen by getting his head across and inside their pads and using his power to manipulate their weight. He can drive defenders to the ground and occasionally finish with a pancake block. On combo blocks, he works well in getting a good vertical push and getting up to the 2nd level, rarely not getting movement in these blocks. Once at the 2nd level, he looks for work and a LB/DB to hit, but he doesn't always have the speed or length to reach them, latch on, and make an effective block. He lacks the same effectiveness on wide blocks as well, as he shows he can move to get out there and get in the way but isn't always able to latch on and sustain.

Last Word
Hutcherson projects as a low-end starter at left guard in a zone-running offensive scheme, but he has the experience to play on either side of the line and can kick out to a tackle position in a backup role if needed.

Strengths	Weaknesses
• Locking up rushers	• 2nd-level effectiveness
• Moving bodies	• Comfort in space
• Looking for work	• Length

Critical Factors

Reactive Athleticism	Anchor / Play Strength	Body Control
5	6	6

Positional Factors

Run Block	Pass Block	Awareness	Footwork
6	6	6	5
2nd Level	Range	Hand Use	Power
5	5	6	7
Sustain	Finish	Flexibility	Toughness
7	6	6	7

Basic

Year	G	GS	Penalties		Blown Block Splits			
			Holding	False Start	Run	Pressure	Sack	Total
2017	10	4	0	0	8	1	0	9
2018	13	13	0	0	2	6	2	11
2019	12	12	3	0	3	10	0	13
2020	10	10	0	0	3	2	1	7
	45	39	3	0	16	19	3	40

Team Stats

Year	Zone Run Blocking			Gap Run Blocking			Pass Block
	% of Runs	Y/A	Pos%	% of Runs	Y/A	Pos%	Pressure%
2017	62%	4.3	46%	37%	5.6	46%	37%
2018	72%	5.1	42%	27%	5.4	49%	37%
2019	38%	4.1	42%	56%	5.9	44%	32%
2020	67%	5.4	45%	30%	5.7	42%	39%
	60%	4.8	44%	38%	5.7	45%	36%

Deep Dive

Year	Blown Block %		When Running to their Gap				Total Points			Total Points Rtg		
	Run	Pass	Y/A	YBC/A	Pos%	EPA/A	Run	Pass	Total	Per Run	Per Pass	Per Play
2018	0.5%	1.9%	5.6	2.3	49%	0.08	17	11	28	86	66	75
2019	0.9%	2.1%	4.8	1.8	40%	-0.07	14	19	32	78	92	87
2020	1.0%	1.2%	5.1	1.9	44%	0.09	13	11	24	81	83	82
	0.8%	1.8%	5.2	2.0	44%	0.04	44	41	84	-	-	-

Kendrick Green

Report by Chad Tedder & Joe McDonald

School	Height	Weight	Year	Jersey #	Hometown
Illinois	6026 E	315 E	4JR	53	Peoria, IL

One Liner

Green is a strong, athletic interior lineman who plays with tenacity, but he needs to further develop his footwork and hand usage as a pass protector to become a more well-rounded player.

Overall

Kendrick Green is an offensive lineman in Illinois' primarily zone offense. He has started all 33 games in his career, 29 at left guard and 4 at center. He began his career as a defensive tackle before transitioning his redshirt year and starting from Day 1 at guard after that. He is a quick and rangy athlete who still has room to fill out his frame while maintaining his movement skills. Green plays offensive line with a lot of speed and a willingness to dominate and finish his blocks.

Pass Game

In the pass game, Green does a decent job in setting a short anchor on a standard pass rush. He looks for work fairly well, but he lacks the anticipatory instincts to react to quick movements up front. His overall athleticism is good, but he doesn't react smoothly with his lower-half footwork to stay square, often opening up his hips to inside moves. If he can get his hands inside the pads quickly, he can stand up defensive tackles and maintain good pocket depth with a strong punch. However, Green struggles to recover with his hands to superior technique up top. When he isn't engaged with a defender, he breaks his stance and lays blows to exposed ribs for his teammates. His instincts, awareness, and mechanics in pass protection are just a tick behind, but his athleticism and power often get him by.

Run Game

Green is a very powerful run blocker who consistently gets a good amount of vertical push. On zone runs, he shows great quickness and range in reaching across the face of defensive linemen, anchoring, and walling them off. He can also drive linemen off the ball and combo up to the second level. However, his hands struggle to recover when inaccurate, limiting his ability to consistently sustain. He gets good movement with a shoulder charge and moves fluidly in space to find work. He occasionally misses blocks outside the trenches against quicker defenders. He pulls comfortably and with a high degree of consistency. He has great speed to range gap to gap and beyond the box. He has shown the ability to flip defenders with his core strength and hip explosion through contact. He is a powerful finisher and always looks for pancakes at every level of the field.

Last Word

Green best projects as a low-end starting left guard in the NFL. He has the versatility to play in both man- and zone-blocking schemes with his power and movement skills. He has experience at center and could potentially start there as well, but he needs to improve the consistency in his shotgun snaps. Green has a lot of physical tools, but he needs to refine his technique, especially in the passing game.

Strengths	Weaknesses
• Athleticism	• Instincts and anticipation
• Temperament to finish	• Hand usage
• Core strength	• Pass pro footwork

Critical Factors

Reactive Athleticism	Anchor / Play Strength	Body Control
5	6	6

Positional Factors

Run Block	Pass Block	Awareness	Footwork
7	5	5	5
2nd Level	Range	Hand Use	Power
6	7	5	7
Sustain	Finish	Flexibility	Toughness
5	7	6	6

Basic

Year	G	GS	Penalties Holding	False Start	Blown Block Splits Run	Pressure	Sack	Total
2018	12	12	2	0	5	1	2	8
2019	13	13	3	0	2	3	2	7
2020	8	8	2	0	2	3	0	5
	33	33	7	0	9	7	4	20

Team Stats

Year	Zone Run Blocking % of Runs	Y/A	Pos%	Gap Run Blocking % of Runs	Y/A	Pos%	Pass Block Pressure%
2018	75%	6.3	51%	23%	7.7	48%	37%
2019	77%	4.6	42%	21%	5.1	48%	36%
2020	69%	4.8	43%	26%	5.9	39%	32%
	74%	5.3	46%	23%	6.3	46%	35%

Deep Dive

Year	Blown Block % Run	Pass	When Running to their Gap Y/A	YBC/A	Pos%	EPA/A	Total Points Run	Pass	Total	Total Points Rtg Per Run	Per Pass	Per Play
2018	1.2%	0.8%	7.5	3.7	53%	0.16	24	11	37	99	80	92
2019	0.5%	1.2%	5.0	2.5	43%	0.02	19	16	34	87	87	87
2020	0.7%	1.3%	7.0	3.6	48%	0.19	15	8	23	92	85	89
	0.8%	1.1%	6.5	3.2	48%	0.11	58	35	94	-	-	-

Tommy Kraemer

Report by Evan Butler

School	Height	Weight	Year	Jersey #	Hometown
Notre Dame	6046 E	317 E	5SR	78	Cincinnati, OH

One Liner
Kraemer is a big-bodied guard who has the size, length and strength to be a successful, well-balanced starter at the next level despite his issues against interior quickness.

Overall
Tommy Kraemer played right guard and tackle for Notre Dame's uptempo pro-style mostly zone blocking scheme. He played in 43 career games, starting 27 at right guard the last 3 seasons and 12 at right tackle in 2017. An appendectomy forced him to miss a game in 2020, and a sprained MCL ended his 2019 season early. Kraemer is athletic for his size, shown through his ability to find defenders in space. He shows nastiness in finishing his blocks and looks for a defender on every play. He has the toughness teams look for to play through the whistle and finish.

Pass Game
In the pass game, Kraemer shows a very strong anchor and high football intelligence to pick up rushers. He also communicates very well with his linemates to pick up blitzes. He rarely gets pushed back with a bull rush to lose pocket depth. He tends to be stiff and a little slow off the ball, which is what troubles him most. His sluggish foot speed and merely sufficient reactive athleticism cause issues against shifty rushers inside. However, he's very good in a phone booth away from open spaces. He has solid ankle and knee flexion to supplement his anchor strength. His technical hand use has shown inconsistencies and he doesn't have the grip strength to lock out regularly.

Run Game
In the run game, Kraemer shows his strength in sustaining blocks and opening run lanes. He can struggle in space with his sufficient footwork and athleticism, especially off-tackle and outside. He loves finding defenders to hit on every play and finishing them to the ground. He will tend to play over his feet and can get caught reaching and lunging when overaggressive. But his heavy footwork and leg drive support his interior strength and nastiness to dominate when locked in.

Last Word
Kraemer projects as a strong guard candidate at the next level who can fit in any scheme but his strength and power fit best in a gap blocking scheme. He could be a fill-in at right tackle if necessary, but his lack of foot speed and vertical kick-slide quickness would limit his success on the perimeter. Improved hand usage, footwork, and overall athleticism would help him become a more complete player at the next level.

Strengths

- Size and length
- Adjustments to twists and stunts
- Toughness and finishing

Weaknesses

- Reactive athleticism
- Foot speed
- Hand usage

Critical Factors

Reactive Athleticism	Anchor / Play Strength	Body Control
5	7	5

Positional Factors

Run Block	Pass Block	Awareness	Footwork
7	6	7	5
2nd Level	Range	Hand Use	Power
5	5	5	6
Sustain	Finish	Flexibility	Toughness
6	7	5	7

Basic

Year	G	GS	Penalties		Blown Block Splits			
			Holding	False Start	Run	Pressure	Sack	Total
2017	13	12	0	0	9	5	1	15
2018	12	10	3	0	3	10	0	13
2019	7	7	1	0	6	2	0	8
2020	11	10	1	0	4	5	3	12
	43	39	5	0	22	22	4	48

Team Stats

Year	Zone Run Blocking			Gap Run Blocking			Pass Block
	% of Runs	Y/A	Pos%	% of Runs	Y/A	Pos%	Pressure%
2017	52%	7.3	48%	45%	5.9	46%	40%
2018	56%	5.3	50%	39%	5.0	38%	39%
2019	48%	4.9	44%	48%	5.3	48%	32%
2020	74%	5.2	46%	23%	6.2	54%	36%
	57%	5.7	47%	39%	5.6	46%	36%

Deep Dive

Year	Blown Block %		When Running to their Gap				Total Points			Total Points Rtg		
	Run	Pass	Y/A	YBC/A	Pos%	EPA/A	Run	Pass	Total	Per Run	Per Pass	Per Play
2018	0.8%	2.5%	6.4	3.2	45%	0.14	12	6	18	74	54	61
2019	3.8%	0.9%	6.1	2.2	50%	0.23	4	7	11	57	83	71
2020	1.2%	2.2%	4.9	2.8	55%	0.19	16	8	24	87	66	76
	1.6%	2.1%	5.9	2.9	49%	0.17	32	21	53	-	-	-

Aaron Banks

Report by Jordan Edwards

School	Height	Weight	Year	Jersey #	Hometown
Notre Dame	6053 V	338 V	4JR	69	Alameda, CA

One Liner
Banks can be a solid starting guard with his massive frame and strong anchor in pass pro but he lacks the natural athleticism and positional flexibility to be an elite starter.

Overall
Aaron Banks aligns at left guard in the Notre Dame pro-style zone-based run scheme. He played in 38 games and started 31 of them all at left guard. He has flexed out to tackle as a mid game injury replacement on occasion. Prior to the 2019 season, Banks underwent surgery on a broken foot, but it didn't cause him to miss any game action. He has a massive frame and is built like a rock. He has a wide chest with a long wingspan and strong hands. Banks doesn't display a killer's instinct at the POA, but he's a tough-minded competitor and plays with a solid motor.

Pass Game
Banks displays an exceptional anchor and rarely gets moved off his spot solely based on his massive frame. His play strength overall is solid but doesn't overpower defenders on a consistent basis. He has strong hands and is able to control rushers with ease. He's an intelligent pass blocker who identifies and picks up stunts and blitzes well and understands how to play with leverage. Banks is an adequate athlete for his size but can struggle to quickly react in space to quicker rushers. Banks has decent body control but has been caught lunging and doesn't possess the athleticism or flexibility to recover in certain situations consistently. Banks can sustain blocks in the pocket well, and once he gets his hands on, rushers have a tough time counteracting him.

Run Game
For the raw strength Banks possess, he still lacks the true power that is desired in a guard. He isn't often pushed off his spot, but Banks doesn't create much push himself at the POA in man blocking schemes. He can control his man at the LOS and can generate push in a double team, but his ability to dominate in one-on-one situations must improve. Banks is agile enough to reach block and has the strength to turn defenders and create run lanes in zone schemes. His hand strength and placement is consistent and can sustain and finish blocks on a regular basis. Banks also shows some effectiveness to create run lanes at the second level with his intelligence and ability to manipulate defenders with his size and strength.

Last Word
Banks projects to be a starting-caliber guard at the next level. His size and length may suggest that he could be an effective tackle, but his lack of natural athleticism will restrict him to strictly be an interior lineman. Even with some of his deficiencies to generate power in one-on-one situations, Banks is better off in a gap scheme, as it complements his natural size and strength.

Strengths

- Anchor
- Awareness
- Sustain

Weaknesses

- Reactive athleticism
- Power in the run game
- Range

Critical Factors

Reactive Athleticism	Anchor / Play Strength	Body Control
5	7	5

Positional Factors

Run Block	Pass Block	Awareness	Footwork
5	7	7	5
2nd Level	Range	Hand Use	Power
6	5	6	5
Sustain	Finish	Flexibility	Toughness
6	6	5	6

Basic

Year	G	GS	Penalties		Blown Block Splits			
			Holding	False Start	Run	Pressure	Sack	Total
2018	13	6	1	0	3	2	1	6
2019	13	13	1	0	5	0	3	8
2020	12	12	1	0	4	4	0	8
	38	31	3	0	12	6	4	22

Team Stats

Year	Zone Run Blocking			Gap Run Blocking			Pass Block
	% of Runs	Y/A	Pos%	% of Runs	Y/A	Pos%	Pressure%
2018	56%	5.3	50%	39%	5.0	38%	39%
2019	48%	4.9	44%	48%	5.3	48%	32%
2020	74%	5.2	46%	23%	6.2	54%	36%
	59%	5.1	47%	37%	5.4	46%	35%

Deep Dive

Year	Blown Block %		When Running to their Gap				Total Points			Total Points Rtg		
	Run	Pass	Y/A	YBC/A	Pos%	EPA/A	Run	Pass	Total	Per Run	Per Pass	Per Play
2018	1.3%	1.2%	4.8	2.4	42%	-0.04	8	7	15	78	75	76
2019	1.4%	0.6%	4.6	2.3	46%	-0.08	11	17	28	65	87	77
2020	1.0%	0.9%	6.6	3.5	53%	0.18	19	13	32	87	81	84
	1.3%	0.9%	5.3	2.7	47%	0.02	38	37	75	-	-	-

Deonte Brown

Report by Alec Mallon, Joe McDonald, & Michael Bonneville

School	Height	Weight	Year	Jersey #	Hometown
Alabama	6032 V	364 V	5SR	65	Decatur, AL

One Liner
Brown is a bulldozing interior lineman who has the experience and strength to be a starter, but his balance and weight control will be keys to his success in the league.

Overall
Deonte Brown is a guard in Alabama's RPO-heavy varied running scheme. He is a fifth-year senior who has appeared in 48 games and started 26 at guard, 8 on the right side and 18 on the left. He was suspended for 6 games between the 2018-19 seasons due to NCAA violations. He is a massively wide body who has had issues managing his weight. He plays with nastiness and a durable toughness as a key cog of the Crimson Tide's OL group.

Pass Game
Brown relies on a very good anchor and good strong punch to stop interior defenders from getting through him to collapse the pocket. He can be late with his hands but his natural strength allows him to absorb initial contact. He's surprisingly light on his feet and plays with decent reactive athleticism and short-area quickness. Brown's footwork is deliberate, sharp and active through contact, and he plays with a wide base. However, the way to beat him is with lateral agility. Despite his impressive athleticism at his size, more athletic rushers can work around him with finesse moves. When contacted at awkward or unsuspecting angles, he doesn't have the flexibility or body control to recover. He does show high rush intelligence to pick up stunts and blitzes, and he has a nasty disposition to attack in assistance when uncovered.

Run Game
Brown has a mean streak as a run blocker, and his massive frame makes him a load to handle downhill. He shows good burst off the line and generates good power to collide with and drive defenders off the ball and potentially into the ground. He plays with an attacking mentality, which can lead to the occasional lunge and whiff or falling off a block. Once he locks up a defender in his chest plate it's usually over, but a late or mistimed punch can make it difficult to get to that point. He moves well at his weight and is nimble and flexible enough to work down the line in wide zone runs. He shoots to the second level well, but can have difficulty securing blocks against smaller, quicker players. He pulls both directions well and is a powerful kick-out blocker on power runs.

Last Word
Brown projects as a strong, but positionally-limited starter at the next level. He can work at either guard position, ideally in a gap-blocking scheme. He doesn't have the vertical foot quickness or reactive skills to play tackle, nor does he have the change-of-direction flexibility or snapping experience for center. He will definitely need to have his weight monitored moving forward, as his weight at the Senior Bowl seems untenable, but he moves well and has flashed dominance in spite of that.

Strengths

- Finishing tenacity
- Raw power
- Light footwork for size

Weaknesses

- Recovery and body control
- Hand quickness
- Weight management

Critical Factors

Reactive Athleticism	Anchor / Play Strength	Body Control
5	7	5

Positional Factors

Run Block	Pass Block	Awareness	Footwork
6	6	6	6
2nd Level	Range	Hand Use	Power
5	5	5	6
Sustain	Finish	Flexibility	Toughness
5	7	5	7

Basic

Year	G	GS	Penalties		Blown Block Splits			
			Holding	False Start	Run	Pressure	Sack	Total
2017	14	0	0	0	0	0	0	0
2018	12	5	0	0	5	3	0	8
2019	9	8	0	0	13	7	0	20
2020	13	13	1	0	8	4	1	13
	48	26	1	0	26	14	1	41

Team Stats

Year	Zone Run Blocking			Gap Run Blocking			Pass Block
	% of Runs	Y/A	Pos%	% of Runs	Y/A	Pos%	Pressure%
2017	64%	5.9	51%	35%	6.8	52%	39%
2018	68%	5.2	54%	31%	6.0	55%	32%
2019	52%	5.4	48%	48%	5.8	59%	26%
2020	56%	5.8	62%	43%	5.3	46%	26%
	61%	5.5	54%	38%	6.0	53%	31%

Deep Dive

Year	Blown Block %		When Running to their Gap				Total Points			Total Points Rtg		
	Run	Pass	Y/A	YBC/A	Pos%	EPA/A	Run	Pass	Total	Per Run	Per Pass	Per Play
2018	2.5%	1.8%	6.3	2.6	58%	0.29	8	4	12	79	71	75
2019	5.6%	2.6%	5.2	2.5	53%	0.06	13	8	22	95	79	88
2020	2.1%	1.2%	5.8	2.8	57%	0.23	17	15	32	84	87	86
	3.2%	1.7%	5.7	2.7	56%	0.19	38	27	66	-	-	-

Ben Cleveland

Report by Sales Pinckney & Joe McDonald

School	Height	Weight	Year	Jersey #	Hometown
Georgia	6063 V	354 V	5SR	74	Toccoa, GA

One Liner
Cleveland is a tough and aggressive downhill blocker who generates push into the 2nd level, but lacks positional versatility and needs to improve his athleticism in space to become more than a low-end starting level player.

Overall
Ben Cleveland aligned nearly exclusively at right guard in Georgia's run-heavy, pro-style offense. He played in 44 career games, starting 25 of them. He missed 6 games in 2018 after suffering a fracture in his lower left leg. He has a tall, stout frame with a thick lower half and is a sufficient overall athlete, but lacks length for his size. He plays with a mauler's mentality and displays toughness in the trenches.

Pass Game
As a pass blocker, Cleveland is always looking for work. He occasionally pops up too high out of his stance and gives up leverage as a result. He flashes a strong initial punch that can be used to shock opposing linemen and can win against slanting defenders when he executes properly. He does a good job of staying under control and maintaining the pocket, leaving vertical space for the quarterback to step up. He's able to keep his hips square and not overcommit while engaged, though he can struggle to react in space against a straight speed rush or finesse moves from more athletic defensive linemen. He excels against power and bull rushes, showing the ability to drop the anchor and use his strength to stalemate rushers. He maintains his discipline against stunts and keeps the inside of the pocket clean.

Run Game
In the run game, Cleveland displays a violent mentality and a desire to finish his blocks. He uses his strength and size to open and maintain running lanes while also generating good vertical push as a solo blocker or part of a double team. He does a good job of working to the 2nd level, and while he is often outclassed athletically in space, he does a sufficient job of occupying defenders and forcing them to reroute when he cannot lock on. As a puller, he does a sufficient job of getting out of his stance and moving to his spot in order to kick out defenders, but his merely adequate footwork leaves him vulnerable in space. While his hand use is generally good, he is not immune to occasionally throwing a shoulder or forearm and relying upon his size rather than technique to win battles. His lower-body flexibility is sufficient, but he will occasionally bend at the waist rather than the knees.

Last Word
Cleveland projects as a limited starting guard at the next level. He lacks positional versatility and will be limited to guard only due to his lack of length, struggles against quicker defenders, and his limited contributions as a blocker in space. He has scheme versatility, but his best fit will be in a zone scheme where he won't be frequently blocking in space as a puller.

Strengths

- Leg drive to 2nd level
- Anchor strength
- Mauler's mentality

Weaknesses

- Blocking in space
- Overall athleticism
- Positional versatility

Critical Factors

Reactive Athleticism	Anchor / Play Strength	Body Control
4	7	5

Positional Factors

Run Block	Pass Block	Awareness	Footwork
6	5	5	5
2nd Level	Range	Hand Use	Power
5	5	6	6
Sustain	Finish	Flexibility	Toughness
5	5	5	6

Basic

Year	G	GS	Penalties Holding	False Start	Blown Block Splits Run	Pressure	Sack	Total
2017	15	5	0	0	4	4	1	9
2018	8	4	0	0	0	0	0	0
2019	13	7	2	0	3	2	0	5
2020	9	9	0	0	2	0	2	4
	45	25	2	0	9	6	3	18

Team Stats

Year	Zone Run Blocking % of Runs	Y/A	Pos%	Gap Run Blocking % of Runs	Y/A	Pos%	Pass Block Pressure%
2017	88%	6.6	50%	10%	4.7	38%	31%
2018	93%	6.4	49%	3%	5.4	50%	25%
2019	85%	5.3	51%	11%	6.0	45%	27%
2020	78%	5.2	52%	18%	6.3	53%	31%
	87%	6.0	50%	10%	5.6	46%	28%

Deep Dive

Year	Blown Block % Run	Pass	When Running to their Gap Y/A	YBC/A	Pos%	EPA/A	Total Points Run	Pass	Total	Total Points Rtg Per Run	Per Pass	Per Play
2018	0.0%	0.0%	5.1	2.0	53%	-0.02	5	5	10	72	99	89
2019	1.2%	1.0%	5.5	2.7	53%	0.03	9	8	17	71	92	82
2020	0.8%	0.7%	5.9	3.3	55%	0.02	12	9	21	89	86	87
	0.8%	0.7%	5.6	2.9	54%	0.02	26	22	48	-	-	-

William Sherman

Report by Jeff Dean

School	Height	Weight	Year	Jersey #	Hometown
Colorado	6036 E	310 E	4JR	78	Allen, TX

One Liner

Sherman has the anchor, athleticism, and football IQ to play multiple positions, but he will need to work on his hand technique and footwork if he wants to earn a starting job.

Strengths: Anchor; Athleticism; Handling rush moves
Weaknesses: Reactive footwork; 1st step balance; Initial punch

William Sherman is an offensive lineman in Colorado's zone blocking scheme. He has started 27 of his 30 career games, 4 at right guard, 11 at left tackle, and 12 at right tackle. He has a good frame that holds his weight extremely well. He is deceptively strong with broad shoulders and wide hips. He's fluid in space with quick feet, but can struggle in reactive situations. He isn't an outwardly emotional player, but he's been a team captain and taken to each of his new positions well.

Sherman drops back with ease and shows quick feet getting into his set. He has a very good anchor and is rarely driven backwards with his wide base and square shoulders. He passes off defenders on stunts and patiently handles pass-rushing moves very well. His initial punch lacks oomph and he can struggle to create separation from the defender. Sherman uses good hand placement to consistently sustain his blocks and neutralize. He has a tendency to drop his foot back, open up his hips, and expose his inside shoulder on quick inside slants, and he doesn't have the reactive footwork to redirect on an island.

Sherman has the strength and athletic ability to be a good run blocker, but he has a few technical issues he needs to clean up. He doesn't fire his hands out with force and relies more on brute strength and churning his feet to generate movement. He has a quick first step but can overstep and lose his balance against slants if he isn't square to contact. While he wasn't asked to pull often, he looks comfortable in space and has the speed and control in space to block downfield. He flashes an ability to finish blocks with authority but not consistently.

Sherman projects as a backup guard who can play either tackle position in a pinch and has even practiced taking snaps. He is a potential starter at guard with time to develop, as he excels in tighter spaces and has the anchor strength to hold up along the interior. His length and reactive quickness would cause issues as a full-time tackle.

Year	G	GS	Penalties Holding	False Start	Blown Block Splits Run	Pressure	Sack	Total
2018	12	9	3	0	2	5	6	13
2019	12	12	3	0	7	2	4	13
2020	6	6	1	0	2	3	1	6
	30	27	7	0	11	10	11	32

Team Year	Team Zone Run Blocking % of Runs	Y/A	Pos%	Team Gap Run Blocking % of Runs	Y/A	Pos%	Team Pass Block Pressure%
2018	50%	4.1	35%	49%	4.7	39%	28%
2019	82%	4.8	47%	16%	4.0	44%	33%
2020	67%	4.6	42%	31%	5.9	47%	32%
	66%	4.6	42%	32%	4.9	42%	31%

Year	Blown Block % Run	Pass	When Running to their Gap Y/A	YBC/A	Pos%	EPA/A	Total Points Run	Pass	Total	Total Points Rtg Per Run	Per Pass	Per Play
2018	0.9%	2.7%	4.1	1.5	36%	-0.12	8	8	16	55	63	58
2019	1.8%	1.3%	5.0	2.7	50%	0.04	19	18	38	89	94	92
2020	0.8%	2.0%	6.0	3.5	48%	0.10	9	6	15	74	78	76
	1.2%	2.0%	4.9	2.4	44%	-0.01	36	32	69	-	-	-

Critical Factors	
Reactive Athleticism	5
Anchor / Play Strength	7
Body Control	5

Positional Factors	
Run Block	5
Pass Block	6
Awareness	6
Footwork	5
2nd Level	5
Range	6
Hand Use	6
Power	6
Sustain	6
Finish	5
Flexibility	6
Toughness	6

Alaric Jackson

Report by DJ Marquardt & Ryan Newman

School	Height	Weight	Year	Jersey #	Hometown
Iowa	6055 V	318 V	5SR	77	Detroit, MI

One Liner
Jackson has the pedigree as a four-year blind-side starter for Iowa, but his limited quickness and length on an island, coupled with his sound short-area execution in all phases best projects to an NFL guard.

Strengths: Accurate hands; Phone booth quickness; Experience
Weaknesses: Blocking in space; Balance; Finishing tenacity

Alaric Jackson is the left tackle for Iowa's pro-style, run-heavy offense. He played and started 42 games at left tackle in his career, missing 3 games early in 2019 with a knee sprain. Jackson has a thick lower half and short arms. He's generally a sufficient athlete but isn't fluid in space. He plays with an adequate motor and toughness.

Jackson is a strong pass blocker, but he lacks elite traits to hold up on the perimeter against elite edge talent. He has a good short-set anchor against bull rushes but struggles to get deep in his vertical slide to meet speed at the arc. He possesses the awareness and short-area quickness to react to inside slants and late blitzes. He is accurate with his hands but tends to bend at the waist and lunge for contact to compensate for his inferior length outside. He sufficiently counters finesse rushes and can latch on when engaged.

Jackson is quick off the line and has a good first step to position himself in the run game and square to contact. He is able to reach from the back side off his first step alone. He has good lower-body strength to thump and drive vertically off the ball, especially within a double team. However, he has occasional body control issues at the point of attack and can be thrown aside when playing too far over his feet or attacking with a narrow base. He can move to the second level sufficiently and out into space on screens, but he can seem lost looking for work and when trying to keep up with smaller space players. He is stronger in a phone booth and locks into his assignments at the first level very well. He doesn't finish plays with nastiness, preferring to execute and move on.

Despite his collegiate career, Jackson best fits as a guard in a gap scheme moving forward. He would struggle with premier NFL speed as a starting left tackle, but his assignment execution and lower-body strength will play inside. He can certainly flex out to either tackle spot in a pinch as the first man off the bench.

Year	G	GS	Penalties		Blown Block Splits			
			Holding	False Start	Run	Pressure	Sack	Total
2017	12	12	1	0	7	6	3	17
2018	12	12	1	0	6	5	2	13
2019	10	10	1	0	7	7	1	15
2020	8	8	2	0	4	5	3	12
	42	42	5	0	24	23	9	57

Team	Team Zone Run Blocking			Team Gap Run Blocking			Team Pass Block
Year	% of Runs	Y/A	Pos%	% of Runs	Y/A	Pos%	Pressure%
2017	78%	4.5	39%	20%	4.5	43%	41%
2018	85%	4.3	44%	12%	4.2	27%	31%
2019	83%	4.7	48%	16%	5.5	48%	31%
2020	78%	4.9	49%	21%	6.8	49%	27%
	81%	4.6	45%	17%	5.2	42%	33%

	Blown Block %		When Running to their Gap				Total Points			Total Points Rtg		
										Per	Per	Per
Year	Run	Pass	Y/A	YBC/A	Pos%	EPA/A	Run	Pass	Total	Run	Pass	Play
2018	1.5%	1.7%	4.3	2.2	47%	-0.09	12	14	26	66	86	77
2019	2.6%	2.5%	4.3	1.5	40%	-0.19	11	14	25	78	96	90
2020	1.5%	3.0%	4.6	2.6	47%	-0.05	11	7	18	79	73	76
	1.9%	2.3%	4.4	2.1	45%	-0.10	34	35	69	-	-	-

Critical Factors	
Reactive Athleticism	5
Anchor / Play Strength	6
Body Control	5

Positional Factors	
Run Block	5
Pass Block	6
Awareness	6
Footwork	6
2nd Level	5
Range	5
Hand Use	5
Power	6
Sustain	5
Finish	4
Flexibility	5
Toughness	5

D'Ante Smith

Report by Theo Fornaciari & Griffin Sullivan

School	Height	Weight	Year	Jersey #	Hometown
East Carolina	6050 V	294 V	5SR	67	Augusta, GA

One Liner

Smith is a smart player with the footwork and hands to be a versatile lineman, but needs to get stronger, more physical, and control his weight in order to be effective at the next level.

Strengths: Awareness; Footwork; 2nd-level blocking
Weaknesses: Power; Explosiveness; Physicality

D'Ante Smith is a left tackle in East Carolina's shotgun, RPO, zone running scheme. He started 30 of 33 games, 29 of which were at LT and 1 at LG. He missed all but the opener in 2016 and 2020 with undisclosed injuries. Smith is a sufficient athlete with a good frame, but concerning weight. His posted weight has fluctuated up and down between 274 and 336 pounds during college. He possesses sufficient toughness overall, though shows flashes of a mean streak.

Smith shows quick feet and a much-improved kick-slide since his first season. He shows the ability to vertical set under control and protect his inside edge during his punch. He has very good awareness to identify and pick up twists/stunts and keep his head on a swivel to look for work. Sufficient reactive athleticism and a lack of lateral explosiveness causes him to struggle to get into position and pick up blitzers. He possesses sufficient anchor/play strength and will get knocked back from his initial setpoint by power rushes, though he remains square with good extension while using his hands to swipe defenders' hands off his breastplate. He has adequate body control and flexibility forcing him to struggle when recovering from awkward positions to sustain blocks while showing waist bend and a lack of ankle flexion that makes him vulnerable to counter moves.

Smith lacks some explosiveness out of his stance, but shows good range to execute reach blocks, scoop blocks, get out on screens, and climb to the 2nd level. His lack of power limits his vertical push, but works as a good zone blocker who utilizes good footwork and hand use to steer defenders out of running lanes. At the 2nd level, he shows an understanding of angles combined with good footwork to block moving targets. He's a sufficient finisher who doesn't always play through the whistle.

Smith projects as a backup guard who also has versatility to play right tackle in a zone-based scheme. He has the footwork and competitiveness, but needs to work on getting meaner.

			Penalties		Blown Block Splits			
Year	G	GS	Holding	False Start	Run	Pressure	Sack	Total
2016	1	0	0	0	0	0	0	0
2017	7	5	0	0	3	4	3	10
2018	12	12	0	0	1	11	4	16
2019	12	12	4	0	5	8	1	15
2020	1	1	0	0	0	0	0	0
	33	30	4	0	9	23	8	41

Team	Team Zone Run Blocking			Team Gap Run Blocking			Team Pass Block
Year	% of Runs	Y/A	Pos%	% of Runs	Y/A	Pos%	Pressure%
2016	77%	5.1	45%	16%	5.4	40%	24%
2017	88%	3.6	38%	11%	3.7	31%	32%
2018	90%	4.1	33%	6%	3.3	29%	40%
2019	59%	3.9	39%	37%	4.8	38%	42%
2020	70%	4.4	39%	27%	5.5	42%	35%
	76%	4.2	39%	19%	4.8	38%	34%

	Blown Block %		When Running to their Gap				Total Points			Total Points Rtg		
Year	Run	Pass	Y/A	YBC/A	Pos%	EPA/A	Run	Pass	Total	Per Run	Per Pass	Per Play
2018	0.3%	2.5%	5.3	2.1	34%	-0.16	9	10	19	58	57	57
2019	1.3%	2.2%	5.2	2.5	43%	-0.01	12	17	29	61	91	78
2020	0.0%	0.0%	3.8	2.1	39%	-0.10	2	1	3	73	94	84
	0.8%	2.3%	5.1	2.3	39%	-0.08	23	28	51	-	-	-

Critical Factors	
Reactive Athleticism	5
Anchor / Play Strength	5
Body Control	5

Positional Factors	
Run Block	6
Pass Block	5
Awareness	7
Footwork	6
2nd Level	6
Range	6
Hand Use	6
Power	4
Sustain	5
Finish	5
Flexibility	5
Toughness	5

Robert Jones

Report by Ben Hrkach & DJ Marquardt

School	Height	Weight	Year	Jersey #	Hometown
Middle Tennessee	6042 V	319 V	4SR	64	Rockford, IL

One Liner
Jones is a scheme-versatile heavy-handed mauler whose reactive quickness issues in space will greatly benefit from a move inside.

Strengths: Run blocking; Hand strength; Nasty demeanor
Weaknesses: Reactive quickness in space; Flexibility to recover balance; Punch timing and accuracy

Robert Jones played right tackle in MTSU's shotgun gap-scheme offense. He played in 20 games and started 18 there after transferring in from community college. Jones had shoulder surgery after the 2019 season and had his 2020 campaign end in concussion protocol, but he was able to compete at the Senior Bowl. Jones is an intimidating presence and a powerful, heavy-handed player. He lacks reactive quickness in space but can dominate in tight quarters and finish with tenacity.

Jones kicks off the line with surprisingly nimble and technical footwork and upper-body form into a deep vertical set. However, his ability to change directions on an island is very limited, and he struggles adjusting to finesse moves and counters on the perimeter. He has solid length and attacks with a powerful punch and grip strength to latch when accurate and timed. His form at contact can fall apart if he loses his chest due to flexibility issues. He has good anchor strength to eat up power rushes, but he can be seen chasing superior athleticism when it doesn't meet him squarely.

Jones frequently wins position with his first step and can reach on seal blocks. He has good lateral strength and moves defenders off the line. He's a force washing down and is very influential at contact. He works a wide base and keeps his feet driving through contact to smother and finish. Jones works up to the second level well and he has sufficient pulling skills, but he doesn't always execute against smaller defenders in space.

Jones most comfortably projects as a backup guard at the next level, but he can fill in at right tackle in a pinch. He can work within zone runs or as a puller and down blocker. His run-blocking traits will translate quickly, and his weaknesses in pass protection will be mitigated with a move inside. His reactive athleticism is mediocre at best outside, but he can operate in a phone booth well, and his quick kick-slide footwork before contact suggests there's upside athletically.

			Penalties		Blown Block Splits			
Year	G	GS	Holding	False Start	Run	Pressure	Sack	Total
2019	12	11	1	0	1	7	1	9
2020	8	7	0	0	1	3	0	4
	20	18	1	0	2	10	1	13

Team	Team Zone Run Blocking			Team Gap Run Blocking			Team Pass Block
Year	% of Runs	Y/A	Pos%	% of Runs	Y/A	Pos%	Pressure%
2019	34%	5.1	38%	64%	5.4	48%	30%
2020	41%	5.1	42%	57%	3.4	43%	33%
	37%	5.1	40%	61%	4.6	46%	31%

	Blown Block %		When Running to their Gap				Total Points			Total Points Rtg		
										Per	Per	Per
Year	Run	Pass	Y/A	YBC/A	Pos%	EPA/A	Run	Pass	Total	Run	Pass	Play
2019	0.4%	2.7%	7.6	3.4	53%	0.22	11	10	21	85	85	85
2020	0.5%	0.9%	4.0	2.0	50%	-0.10	7	12	19	75	91	86
	0.5%	1.8%	5.9	2.7	52%	0.07	18	22	40	-	-	-

Critical Factors	
Reactive Athleticism	5
Anchor / Play Strength	6
Body Control	5

Positional Factors	
Run Block	6
Pass Block	5
Awareness	5
Footwork	6
2nd Level	5
Range	5
Hand Use	5
Power	6
Sustain	6
Finish	6
Flexibility	5
Toughness	6

Larry Borom

Report by Nathan Cooper

School	Height	Weight	Year	Jersey #	Hometown
Missouri	6052 E	332 E	4JR	79	Detroit, MI

One Liner

Borom possesses the overall power, strength, and leg drive in the run game with anchor ability in pass protection to be a versatile depth blocker, though weight, balance, and body control issues may give him a tough time early on.

Strengths: Leg drive; Anchor strength
Weaknesses: Lacks some balance; 2nd-level control; Struggles with speed & length

Larry Borom is the right tackle in Missouri's spread offense. He started 19 of 33 career games, starting 16 at RT, 2 at LG, and 1 at LT. He's a big body and an adequate athlete. He looks to have some weight concerns that affect his stamina late in games. That said, he competes, plays tough, and shows a little nastiness at times.

Borom struggles against speed and length which make it tough for him to win consistently on the edge. His calling card is his strength. Defenders have a tough time going through him. He's able to get hands up with a powerful punch, latch on, and drop his anchor. He doesn't have the greatest balance, and even when he's a little off balance or beaten early, he has enough ability to recover and reset quickly. He isn't the most reactive athlete, though does a good job handling slants and rush games coming across his face. He shows fairly-good footwork, but later in games when he begins to lose stamina, his legs get heavy and his foot quickness suffers as a result.

Borom brings power and leg drive in the run. He's powerful with some explosion out of his stance, and when he latches on, he's able to keep his legs driving to move defenders off the ball. He's able to combo block sufficiently and gets to the 2nd level, though he lacks some control and comes in with inefficient angles. He struggles to handle quicker defenders and sustain throughout the play, but if he lands his block in space, he shows his power by finishing them to the ground. He normally plays to the whistle and shows some nasty finishing ability.

Borom projects as a backup right guard in a zone scheme with the versatility to also play LG or RT. His strength and power are better utilized on the right side. While his struggles against speed make him a better fit inside, if he loses some weight and improves his stamina, his skill set on the outside could improve.

Year	G	GS	Penalties		Blown Block Splits			
			Holding	False Start	Run	Pressure	Sack	Total
2018	13	0	0	0	0	0	0	0
2019	12	11	3	0	6	9	0	15
2020	8	8	1	0	4	1	0	5
	33	19	4	0	10	10	0	20

Team Year	Team Zone Run Blocking			Team Gap Run Blocking			Team Pass Block
	% of Runs	Y/A	Pos%	% of Runs	Y/A	Pos%	Pressure%
2018	69%	5.1	51%	30%	5.1	41%	24%
2019	67%	4.6	46%	30%	4.2	39%	32%
2020	73%	4.5	45%	27%	5.0	46%	29%
	69%	4.8	48%	29%	4.8	42%	28%

Year	Blown Block %		When Running to their Gap				Total Points			Total Points Rtg		
	Run	Pass	Y/A	YBC/A	Pos%	EPA/A	Run	Pass	Total	Per Run	Per Pass	Per Play
2018	0.0%	0.0%	9.1	5.1	71%	0.48	2	0	3	98	91	98
2019	1.8%	2.3%	4.2	2.1	37%	-0.10	7	13	21	55	83	69
2020	1.5%	0.3%	4.9	2.7	50%	0.06	9	15	24	71	99	92
	1.6%	1.4%	4.7	2.5	44%	-0.01	18	28	48	-	-	-

Critical Factors	
Reactive Athleticism	5
Anchor / Play Strength	6
Body Control	5

Positional Factors	
Run Block	6
Pass Block	5
Awareness	5
Footwork	5
2nd Level	5
Range	5
Hand Use	6
Power	6
Sustain	5
Finish	6
Flexibility	5
Toughness	6

    # Joe Sculthorpe   **Final Grade: 6.2**

Report by Ty Dorner

School	Height	Weight	Year	Jersey #	Hometown
NC State	6022 E	307 E	5SR	71	Hampstead, NC

One Liner

Sculthorpe has the strong hands, mirror ability, and power to be an effective blocker at the next level, though he needs to improve his flexibility and balance to become a better overall player.

Strengths: Strong hands; Mirror ability in pass pro; Leg drive & power
Weaknesses: Flexibility; Balance & body control; Reach blocking

Joe Sculthorpe is an offensive guard in NC State's balanced offense, run almost exclusively out of shotgun, with play action and RPOs off of primarily zone runs. He appeared in 49 games, starting in 26 of them, spending time at both guard positions and center. He's a sufficient athlete with limited flexibility who has an average, but solid build. He has displayed an ability to be available for his team and has no durability questions.

In the pass game, Sculthorpe thrives with his ability to communicate with teammates when multiple pass rushers are in his area. He shows good awareness to pass off or take on rushers when necessary. He displays good reactive athleticism and is able to mirror and match the movements of the defender. He has strong hands and when he latches on, it can be difficult for defenders to disengage. His limited flexibility results in the inability to consistently anchor in pass protection. There are times when he really digs in and doesn't give any ground, but others where he gets caught with his weight out in front of him and falls off-balance, resulting in rushers getting by.

In the run game, Sculthorpe plays with good power, often firing off the ball and generating good leg drive. Once he gets his man, he can sustain blocks with a sufficient ability to finish the play off. He struggles with balance, as there are too many times where he leans onto his man and stops his feet. This causes him to fall off the block and off balance when defenders shed him aside. Similarly, he doesn't display the necessary range and athleticism to reach blocks consistently on stretch plays and outside zone runs to the C or D gaps.

Sculthorpe projects best as a backup at the right guard position with the communication skills to also play center. He would fit best in an inside zone or gap scheme. He should thrive in an offense that features the run and uses the play action pass game.

Year	G	GS	Penalties Holding	False Start	Blown Block Splits Run	Pressure	Sack	Total
2017	13	1	0	0	3	0	1	6
2018	13	2	1	0	4	4	1	9
2019	11	11	3	0	1	4	1	7
2020	12	12	1	0	3	5	5	13
	49	26	5	0	11	13	8	35

Team Year	Team Zone Run Blocking % of Runs	Y/A	Pos%	Team Gap Run Blocking % of Runs	Y/A	Pos%	Team Pass Block Pressure%
2017	93%	5.1	45%	5%	5.4	41%	21%
2018	95%	4.2	44%	4%	3.5	44%	29%
2019	77%	5.0	48%	22%	4.6	41%	29%
2020	83%	4.7	46%	16%	3.9	41%	35%
	88%	4.7	45%	11%	4.4	41%	28%

Year	Blown Block % Run	Pass	When Running to their Gap Y/A	YBC/A	Pos%	EPA/A	Total Points Run	Pass	Total	Total Points Rtg Per Run	Per Pass	Per Play
2018	2.0%	2.1%	3.7	1.1	43%	-0.08	7	4	11	72	58	63
2019	0.3%	1.4%	4.3	1.6	39%	-0.08	11	13	24	68	78	74
2020	0.8%	2.2%	4.3	1.7	47%	-0.03	15	12	26	78	72	75
	0.9%	1.9%	4.2	1.6	44%	-0.05	33	29	61	-	-	-

Critical Factors

Reactive Athleticism	6
Anchor / Play Strength	6
Body Control	5

Positional Factors

Run Block	6
Pass Block	5
Awareness	6
Footwork	5
2nd Level	5
Range	5
Hand Use	6
Power	6
Sustain	5
Finish	5
Flexibility	4
Toughness	6

Jake Burton

Report by Max Nuscher

School	Height	Weight	Year	Jersey #	Hometown
Baylor	6051 E	312 E	5SR	73	Alpine, CA

One Liner
Burton has the footwork, range and 2nd-level ability to be a versatile backup at the next level, but his inability to anchor in the passing game will keep him from being a consistent starter.

Strengths: Footwork; Range; 2nd-level ability
Weaknesses: Anchor ability; Power at the POA; Overall awareness

Jake Burton plays right guard in Baylor's spread offense with primarily zone runs. He started all 8 games at RG for Baylor in 2020 after coming over from UCLA where he started 23 of 29 games, 21 at RT and 2 at LT. He's a good athlete that can move well laterally. He is incredibly physical and tough and will play to the whistle on every snap.

Burton struggles off the snap to anchor in pass protection. Most rushers can walk him back too easily. He has the awareness to recognize stunts along the defensive line, but when he's uncovered, he takes too long to look for work and help out. He has good reactive athleticism and moves well laterally so the slant rush move or inside games don't give him issues. In the screen game, he is good at getting into space in front of the receiver while maintaining good footwork. Even if he doesn't get a clean block on a 2nd level defender, he can get hands-on to get in the way and force inadequate angles.

In the running game, Burton can get some movement at the POA, but lacks consistent leg drive. When he gets his hands squarely on defender's pads, he has the grip strength to stay latched and hold his ground. He uses good hand placement, but struggles with his initial punch. He does his best as a zone blocker and moves laterally and is able to reach defenders relatively easily. In the power and trap games, he is a good puller who can hit the end man on the LOS or get out in space to the 2nd level. On combo blocks, he transitions fluidly and quickly from the first defender to the second without losing momentum or balance.

Burton projects as a backup offensive lineman that will mainly play right guard, but does possess the reactive athleticism, awareness and footwork to be a right tackle as well. He will best be utilized in a gap scheme where he can pull or get out in space to use his range and athleticism. He needs to improve his strength and anchor technique on the inside to become a better pass blocker.

Year	G	GS	Penalties		Blown Block Splits			
			Holding	False Start	Run	Pressure	Sack	Total
2017	5	0	0	0	0	0	0	0
2018	12	11	2	0	3	10	4	17
2019	12	12	1	0	4	8	3	15
2020	8	8	1	0	2	5	1	8
	37	31	4	0	9	23	8	40

Team Year	Team Zone Run Blocking			Team Gap Run Blocking			Team Pass Block
	% of Runs	Y/A	Pos%	% of Runs	Y/A	Pos%	Pressure%
2017	72%	4.5	47%	27%	5.5	42%	29%
2018	81%	4.6	44%	18%	7.0	44%	42%
2019	79%	4.5	43%	20%	3.8	45%	37%
2020	61%	3.1	32%	29%	4.3	40%	36%
	75%	4.3	43%	23%	5.2	43%	36%

Year	Blown Block %		When Running to their Gap				Total Points			Total Points Rtg		
	Run	Pass	Y/A	YBC/A	Pos%	EPA/A	Run	Pass	Total	Per Run	Per Pass	Per Play
2018	0.9%	3.5%	7.2	3.8	52%	0.22	16	5	21	91	53	66
2019	1.1%	2.3%	3.6	2.1	35%	-0.24	14	15	30	76	81	79
2020	1.0%	1.6%	2.8	0.5	35%	-0.26	1	11	12	51	79	65
	1.0%	2.5%	4.3	2.0	40%	-0.11	31	31	63	-	-	-

Critical Factors	
Reactive Athleticism	6
Anchor / Play Strength	4
Body Control	5

Positional Factors	
Run Block	5
Pass Block	5
Awareness	5
Footwork	6
2nd Level	6
Range	6
Hand Use	5
Power	4
Sustain	5
Finish	5
Flexibility	5
Toughness	6

Quinn Meinerz Final Grade: 6.2

Report by Joe McDonald & Ryan Newman

School	Height	Weight	Year	Jersey #	Hometown
Wisconsin-Whitewater	6032 V	320 V	4SR	77	Hartford, WI

One Liner
Meinerz will need technical development and his balance is a real concern, but he has the toughness, strength, and Senior Bowl success worth taking a chance on as a versatile reserve.

Strengths: Anchor strength; Toughness; Power and finish
Weaknesses: Balance and body control; Flexibility; Lateral footwork

Quinn Meinerz is the left guard for D-III UW-Whitewater. He played in 31 career games and was a two-year starter before his 2020 season was postponed. He's barrel chested with good length and big hands, but could add bulk to his lower half. He's light on his feet but rigid athletically. He's proven to be very tough and consistently makes extra-effort plays.

Meinerz sets with a wide base and low pad level in pass protection. He has heavy hands to stun linemen and sustains with his vertical anchor strength. When everything is square, he latches on with tight elbows and strafes through contact smoothly. However, while he has some quickness laterally to slide and mirror in short areas, he is inconsistent catching stunts and working against broad horizontal movement. Meinerz tends to play well over his toes and is susceptible to push-pull moves after losing his chest to an inaccurate punch. He can be dominant in a phone booth, but he'll need to improve against quickness and advanced rush games at the next level.

Meinerz is able to create solid vertical push with his explosiveness off the snap. He positions himself quickly with his first step in zone and is a capable skip-puller who flashes real force at contact. He works up to the second level well and can comically wash out smaller defenders and finish. However, his balance is a major concern. Meinerz is on the ground way too often for his level of competition and too frequently falls off blocks or trips over himself. He's inflexible when changing directions and struggles to roll his hips through contact to sustain consistently.

Meinerz didn't show the consistent D-III dominance expected from a player attempting to make the NFL leap, but despite having not played football for over a year until the 2021 Senior Bowl, he had an eye-opening performance against D-I competition. The potential he showed in Mobile at guard and snapping at center gives hope he can take to professional coaching, build his body, refine his technique, and in time grow into a viable interior backup.

Quinn Meinerz was a Division III All-American, but he was particularly proud of being a team MVP at UW-Whitewater in the 2019 season.

"It's not typically heard that an offensive lineman gets the team MVP," Meinerz said in an interview with Draft Diamonds on YouTube. "It really showed that my teammates believe in me being a leader on the field as well as off the field, because to be voted that, you have to be more than just a good player on the field."

Though UW-Whitewater has had considerable success in Division III, only one player from the school has been drafted since 1973, wide receiver Derek Stanley who was taken in the seventh round by the Rams. Stanley played three seasons in the NFL. The school did have one football alum playing in 2020. Wide receiver Jake Kumerow had one reception for the Bills after having 20 in 2018-2019 for the Packers.

Critical Factors	
Reactive Athleticism	5
Anchor / Play Strength	6
Body Control	4

Positional Factors	
Run Block	5
Pass Block	6
Awareness	5
Footwork	5
2nd Level	6
Range	6
Hand Use	5
Power	6
Sustain	5
Finish	6
Flexibility	4
Toughness	7

Donavaughn Campbell

Report by Christian Vega & John Todd

School	Height	Weight	Year	Jersey #	Hometown
Louisiana Tech	6036 V	353 V	5SR	77	Ponchatoula, LA

One Liner

Campbell has the size, physical tools, and limited experience worth trying to develop inside at guard, but balance and technique issues could keep him from a starting role.

Strengths: Initial punch; Carries his weight well; Awareness
Weaknesses: Reactive quickness in space; Wide hands; Balance and footwork

Donavaughn Campbell plays left tackle for Louisiana Tech, mostly as a zone blocker but also often pulling. He transferred from LSU after playing only 15 games due to foot and shoulder injuries, off-field issues, and OL depth before starting 6 games for the Bulldogs and opting out early. He's a massive body who's light on his feet, carrying his weight fairly well. He plays with some nastiness in the trenches but not a consistently high motor.

Campbell has good play strength and the ability to anchor, but it's hindered by inaccurate hands that allow pass rushers to get into his body. He's flashed the hand quickness to recover, but he needs to attack with tighter elbows to better utilize his punch power. He does not vertically kick-slide with good or fast footwork, but he short sets well and has shown the ability to mirror. He passes off rushers well and generally identifies blitzers quickly. He has solid flexibility for his size to sit with good form. Balance issues arise when he loses his chest. He mostly wins off size alone and needs to develop his technique.

Campbell has a solid get-off but can play too over his feet at the point of attack and lose his balance as a run blocker. He plays with a strong initial punch when squared up to knock defenders off. He shows some explosion on occasion and flexible hips to drive through contact. He has a nasty play style and gets it done with size and physicality in a phone booth rather than technique. He's a fluid mover for his size but isn't consistently quick enough to redirect against smaller defenders in space. There's high upside here as a guard with improved balance and footwork.

Campbell is inexperienced with tantalizing size and physical skills worth development. His traits project best to guard in a power scheme, where he can short set and get after defenders in tight quarters. His experience at left tackle in 2020 was valuable, but he doesn't have the foot quickness to excel against NFL speed there. He should be a sufficient guard at either spot or as a reserve right tackle in a pinch.

			Penalties		Blown Block Splits			
Year	G	GS	Holding	False Start	Run	Pressure	Sack	Total
2016	4	0	0	0	1	0	0	1
2018	3	1	0	0	1	1	0	2
2019	7	0	0	0	0	4	0	4
2020	6	6	2	0	3	7	4	14
	21	7	2	0	5	12	4	21

Team	Team Zone Run Blocking			Team Gap Run Blocking			Team Pass Block
Year	% of Runs	Y/A	Pos%	% of Runs	Y/A	Pos%	Pressure%
2016	57%	6.1	44%	38%	7.6	49%	36%
2018	72%	4.8	48%	26%	4.5	37%	36%
2019	75%	6.0	53%	21%	4.3	54%	36%
2020	72%	3.8	45%	24%	3.2	35%	33%
	68%	5.2	48%	29%	5.6	47%	36%

	Blown Block %		When Running to their Gap				Total Points			Total Points Rtg		
Year	Run	Pass	Y/A	YBC/A	Pos%	EPA/A	Run	Pass	Total	Per Run	Per Pass	Per Play
2018	2.2%	4.2%	5.8	2.3	56%	0.27	1	0	1	58	50	53
2019	0.0%	18.2%	6.6	0.8	40%	0.16	1	-2	-1	88	50	50
2020	2.0%	4.3%	3.2	1.2	28%	-0.25	6	5	11	76	62	67
	1.8%	5.3%	4.3	1.4	37%	-0.06	8	3	11	-	-	-

Critical Factors	
Reactive Athleticism	5
Anchor / Play Strength	6
Body Control	4

Positional Factors	
Run Block	6
Pass Block	5
Awareness	6
Footwork	5
2nd Level	5
Range	5
Hand Use	5
Power	6
Sustain	5
Finish	5
Flexibility	6
Toughness	5

Redshirt season not shown but included in totals

Centers

Mark Simon

What should you be looking for when assessing future NFL centers?

According to John Todd—who helps oversee our player rankings—awareness, communication, leadership, and toughness are high on the list of intangible traits. A center's responsibilities normally include getting the other four linemen organized and working with the quarterback to point out blitzes and decide on protections.

Awareness comes into play in pass protection to keep their head on a swivel and to look to both sides of the offensive line to see if a teammate needs help or a rusher is running free. If you're going to be a center, toughness is a necessity, because you're going to take a considerable pounding over the course of a game. It's not an easy position to play.

Last year, Cesar Ruiz was clearly the top center on our draft board. But upon entering the NFL, he moved to right guard because the Saints already had 2019 second-round pick Erik McCoy at center. Ruiz made nine starts for the Saints in the regular season and then made two more in the playoffs.

Lloyd Cushenberry III, our No. 5 center last year, was the only one to start at least 10 regular season games. He started all 16 for the Broncos, who selected him in the third round of the 2020 Draft. Cushenberry finished 31st in Total Points at the position, perhaps indicating that our projection of him as being a multi-position reserve at the time of the draft could be a better role.

Per John's assessment, the top three centers in this year's class are extremely close in ranking, with any of the three capable of taking the top spot.

Creed Humphrey of Oklahoma is the most physically talented of the three, with good hands and quick feet, finishing with our top rating. Just behind him is Josh Myers of Ohio State, who was the only center to grade a 7 for pass blocking and for flexibility. The No. 3 center, Landon Dickerson of Alabama, has battled a slew of knee injuries, including a torn ACL at the end of this season, but he was the only center to grade an 8 in toughness. In fact, he was the only center to be graded an 8 in any area. You might remember Dickerson from the end of the National Championship Game, when he came onto the field to take the final two snaps of the game.

The highest-ranked player beyond the top three is Trey Hill of Georgia. At 330 pounds, Hill is the second-heaviest center in this draft class. He's viewed favorably for his size, durability, dependability, and football intelligence.

By Total Points, the highest-ranked center among draft prospects is Drake Jackson of Kentucky. He came out just ahead of Dickerson and Humphrey in 2020. Jackson rates well in awareness, footwork, and hand use, but what keeps him from being higher on the overall draft ranking list are grades of 4 in sustain, power, finish, and range. As the last line of his scouting report notes, he "needs to improve his strength and nastiness to truly make an impact at the next level."

This year's draft class at center is deeper in starting talent than last year's. Six players graded as at least low-level starters, meaning a grade of 6.4 or higher. That's two more than in 2020, though two fewer than received that grade in 2019.

Here's one last item of intrigue pertaining to this year's draft board. There are two centers who are from teams outside of the FBS: David Moore of Grambling State and Sam Cooper of Merrimack. Both will face uphill battles just to make an NFL roster, but their skills are strong enough to warrant a look from NFL scouts.

CENTER

Center Grading Scale

GRADE	DESCRIPTION
9.0 – 7.0	High-end starter. Pro Bowl level.
6.9 – 6.7	Strong starter with 2 position flexibility.
6.6 – 6.5	Lower end starter. Backup flexibility at OT or OG.
6.4	Starter with no position flexibility.
6.2	Multi-positional backup.
6.1 – 6.0	Developmental. Top traits but needs time.
5.7	Backup with no position flexibility. #3 OC.

Center Rankings

Rank	Name	Grade	Page
1	Creed Humphrey	6.7	374
2	Josh Myers	6.7	376
3	Landon Dickerson	6.7	378
4	Trey Hill	6.5	380
5	Jimmy Morrissey	6.4	382
6	Drew Dalman	6.4	383
7	Drake Jackson	6.2	384
8	David Moore	6.2	385
9	Orlando Umana	6.2	386
10	Ryan McCollum	6.2	387
11	Sam Cooper	6.2	388

Glossary

Blown Block%
The percentage of blocking snaps that the player had a blown block.

EPA/A (Runs to Gap Split)
Expected Points Added per rush attempt

Pos% (Runs To Gap split)
Positive Percentage, percentage of carries with a positive Expected Points Added.

Pressure% (Team Stat)
Percentage of total team plays where any defensive player recorded a quarterback hurry, hit, knockdown or sack.

Total Points
Sports Info Solutions' proprietary player value metric that uses an Expected Points framework and distributes the value gained or lost on a play to the players involved based on their impact on the play.

Total Points Rating
Total Points per play compared to average, scaled so that 50 is poor and 99 is excellent.

Y/A (Runs To Gap split)
Yards per rush attempt.

YBC/A (Runs To Gap split)
Yards before contact per rush attempt.

Center Leaderboards

Total Points Per Game

Rk	Player	School	Tot Pts / G
1	T. Hill	Georgia	3.1
2	D. Dalman	Stanford	3.0
3	D. Jackson	Kentucky	2.8
4	J. Myers	Ohio State	2.6
5	C. Humphrey	Oklahoma	2.5
6	L. Dickerson	Alabama	2.4
7	R. McCollum	Texas A&M	2.0
8	J. Morrissey	Pittsburgh	1.9

Total Points Rating Per Play

Rk	Player	School	Rating
1	T. Hill	Georgia	94
2	D. Dalman	Stanford	93
3	D. Jackson	Kentucky	90
4	L. Dickerson	Alabama	88
5	C. Humphrey	Oklahoma	87
6	J. Myers	Ohio State	80
7	R. McCollum	Texas A&M	72
8	J. Morrissey	Pittsburgh	70

Pass Blocking Total Points Per Game

Rk	Player	School	Tot Pts / G
1	D. Dalman	Stanford	2.0
2	C. Humphrey	Oklahoma	1.3
3	J. Morrissey	Pittsburgh	1.2
4	T. Hill	Georgia	1.1
5	L. Dickerson	Alabama	1.0
5	D. Jackson	Kentucky	1.0
5	R. McCollum	Texas A&M	1.0
8	J. Myers	Ohio State	0.9

Total Points Rating Per Pass Block

Rk	Player	School	Rating
1	D. Dalman	Stanford	98
2	D. Jackson	Kentucky	93
3	C. Humphrey	Oklahoma	90
4	T. Hill	Georgia	88
5	L. Dickerson	Alabama	85
6	R. McCollum	Texas A&M	78
7	J. Morrissey	Pittsburgh	73
8	J. Myers	Ohio State	67

Run Blocking Total Points Per Game

Rk	Player	School	Tot Pts / G
1	T. Hill	Georgia	2.0
2	J. Myers	Ohio State	1.9
3	D. Jackson	Kentucky	1.8
4	L. Dickerson	Alabama	1.4
5	C. Humphrey	Oklahoma	1.3
6	D. Dalman	Stanford	1.2
7	R. McCollum	Texas A&M	1.1
8	J. Morrissey	Pittsburgh	0.8

Total Points Rating Per Run Block

Rk	Player	School	Rating
1	T. Hill	Georgia	97
2	J. Myers	Ohio State	91
2	L. Dickerson	Alabama	91
4	D. Jackson	Kentucky	89
5	C. Humphrey	Oklahoma	85
6	D. Dalman	Stanford	76
7	R. McCollum	Texas A&M	67
8	J. Morrissey	Pittsburgh	65

Total Blown Blocks Per Game

Rk	Player	School	BB/G
1	C. Humphrey	Oklahoma	0.3
1	L. Dickerson	Alabama	0.3
3	D. Dalman	Stanford	0.5
3	D. Jackson	Kentucky	0.5
5	J. Morrissey	Pittsburgh	0.8
6	T. Hill	Georgia	0.9
7	R. McCollum	Texas A&M	1.8
8	J. Myers	Ohio State	2.0

Overall Blown Block Percentage

Rk	Player	School	BB%
1	C. Humphrey	Oklahoma	0.4%
2	L. Dickerson	Alabama	0.6%
3	D. Dalman	Stanford	0.7%
3	D. Jackson	Kentucky	0.7%
5	J. Morrissey	Pittsburgh	1.2%
6	T. Hill	Georgia	1.4%
7	R. McCollum	Texas A&M	2.7%
8	J. Myers	Ohio State	2.9%

Pass Blown Blocks Per Game

Rk	Player	School	BB/G
1	C. Humphrey	Oklahoma	0.1
1	T. Hill	Georgia	0.1
3	D. Dalman	Stanford	0.2
3	D. Jackson	Kentucky	0.2
5	L. Dickerson	Alabama	0.3
6	J. Morrissey	Pittsburgh	0.5
6	R. McCollum	Texas A&M	0.5
8	J. Myers	Ohio State	0.7

Pass Blown Block Percentage

Rk	Player	School	BB%
1	C. Humphrey	Oklahoma	0.3%
2	T. Hill	Georgia	0.4%
2	D. Dalman	Stanford	0.4%
4	D. Jackson	Kentucky	0.7%
5	L. Dickerson	Alabama	1.1%
6	J. Morrissey	Pittsburgh	1.3%
7	R. McCollum	Texas A&M	1.5%
8	J. Myers	Ohio State	2.0%

Rush Blown Blocks Per Game

Rk	Player	School	BB/G
1	L. Dickerson	Alabama	0.0
2	C. Humphrey	Oklahoma	0.2
3	J. Morrissey	Pittsburgh	0.3
3	D. Dalman	Stanford	0.3
3	D. Jackson	Kentucky	0.3
6	T. Hill	Georgia	0.8
7	J. Myers	Ohio State	1.3
7	R. McCollum	Texas A&M	1.3

Rush Blown Block Percentage

Rk	Player	School	BB%
1	L. Dickerson	Alabama	0.0%
2	C. Humphrey	Oklahoma	0.6%
3	D. Jackson	Kentucky	0.8%
4	J. Morrissey	Pittsburgh	1.0%
5	D. Dalman	Stanford	1.1%
6	T. Hill	Georgia	2.3%
7	J. Myers	Ohio State	3.7%
8	R. McCollum	Texas A&M	3.8%

Career Games Started

Rk	Player	School	GS
1	J. Morrissey	Pittsburgh	47
2	D. Jackson	Kentucky	44
3	C. Humphrey	Oklahoma	37
3	L. Dickerson	Alabama	37
5	T. Hill	Georgia	26
5	O. Umana	Utah	26
7	D. Dalman	Stanford	22
8	J. Myers	Ohio State	21
9	R. McCollum	Texas A&M	17

Yards Before Contact To Their Gap Per Attempt

Rk	Player	School	YBC/A
1	J. Myers	Ohio State	3.4
2	T. Hill	Georgia	3.2
3	J. Morrissey	Pittsburgh	3.0
4	D. Jackson	Kentucky	2.9
5	R. McCollum	Texas A&M	2.0
6	C. Humphrey	Oklahoma	1.8
7	L. Dickerson	Alabama	1.7
8	D. Dalman	Stanford	1.6

Holding Penalties

Rk	Player	School	Holds
1	J. Myers	Ohio State	0
1	L. Dickerson	Alabama	0
1	T. Hill	Georgia	0
1	J. Morrissey	Pittsburgh	0
5	D. Dalman	Stanford	1
5	D. Jackson	Kentucky	1
5	R. McCollum	Texas A&M	1
8	C. Humphrey	Oklahoma	2

Yards Before Contact To Their Gap Per Game

Rk	Player	School	YBC/G
1	D. Jackson	Kentucky	57.8
2	T. Hill	Georgia	51.3
3	J. Myers	Ohio State	46.0
4	J. Morrissey	Pittsburgh	26.5
5	R. McCollum	Texas A&M	24.1
6	L. Dickerson	Alabama	16.4
7	D. Dalman	Stanford	14.3
8	C. Humphrey	Oklahoma	12.2

Positive Percentage When Run Behind

Rk	Player	School	Pos%
1	L. Dickerson	Alabama	62%
2	R. McCollum	Texas A&M	61%
3	T. Hill	Georgia	53%
4	J. Myers	Ohio State	52%
5	C. Humphrey	Oklahoma	51%
6	D. Jackson	Kentucky	50%
7	D. Dalman	Stanford	45%
8	J. Morrissey	Pittsburgh	44%

Yards When Run Behind Per Game

Rk	Player	School	Yds/G
1	D. Jackson	Kentucky	113.1
2	T. Hill	Georgia	88.1
3	J. Myers	Ohio State	75.6
4	R. McCollum	Texas A&M	59.3
5	J. Morrissey	Pittsburgh	44.5
6	L. Dickerson	Alabama	44.1
7	D. Dalman	Stanford	42.5
8	C. Humphrey	Oklahoma	29.7

Creed Humphrey

Report by Nathan Cooper

School	Height	Weight	Year	Jersey #	Hometown
Oklahoma	6045 V	312 V	4JR	56	Shawnee, OK

One Liner
Humphrey's foot quickness, hand use, and overall strength suggest he'll be a solid starter at the next level, but his lack of awareness and length could get him into trouble at times.

Overall
Creed Humphrey is a left-handed starting center in Oklahoma's RPO-based spread offense that operates nearly exclusively out of the shotgun. He played in 39 games, starting 37 of them for the Sooners. He missed spring practices in 2019 due to hand surgery. He's a good, strong athlete that competes and plays tough on every down, but lacks some overall length. His snapping as a whole is solid, but can get a bit erratic at times, with some leaking to the quarterback's right.

Pass Game
In the pass game, Humphrey has the short-set anchor ability and play strength to shut down interior defenders. He is strong at the POA and rarely gets pushed back into his quarterback. However, on some occasions he stands up too tall and stops his feet which forces him to lunge at times allowing rushers to slither by. If he's beaten early in the play, he does a good job recovering from awkward angles to latch back onto his man. When he doesn't have someone in front of him to block, he does a good job looking for work, but normally only looks to one side instead of keeping his head on a swivel and keeping aware of what's going on to both sides. Most of these occasions, someone will leak through on the side he's not looking. Against interior rush games, he is quick and reactive to what's happening. He's able to redirect quickly and with strength, even being able to block two defenders at once. He has good grip strength and is able to latch on and stay in front of his man with good mirror ability. Although he fires his hands a bit late at times, he's still very quick and strong with his punch. With that said, his right (non-dominant) hand gets outside the defender's frame, while his left (dominant) hand nearly always strikes the chest plate. He shows good communication skill with his teammates.

Run Game
In the run game, Humphrey shows some mauling ability and power to finish blocks. He gets good leg drive and is able to push back defenders off the line of scrimmage. He's strong on down blocks and is quick enough to reach and scoop 2i's with ease, giving a strong club to the defender's shoulder to help him gain leverage and positioning. When getting to the 2nd level, he comes in quickly and under control to latch onto smaller, quicker defenders to make his block. When he pulls and gets down the line, he shows good mobility and strength with good range and leverage. On some occasions after he snaps the ball, he fires out with his head down, not seeing what he's aiming at and missing his block.

Last Word
Humphrey projects as a starting center with all the desired traits to succeed in any scheme. His length issues are a little concerning, but he has the size, strength, and fundamentals that should make for a minimal learning curve at the next level.

Strengths

- Quick, smooth feet
- Works with his hands
- Recovers well after beaten early

Weaknesses

- Lacks some awareness in pass pro
- Length issues

Critical Factors

Reactive Athleticism	Anchor / Play Strength	Body Control
6	7	6

Positional Factors

Run Block	Pass Block	Awareness	Footwork
7	6	5	6
2nd Level	Range	Hand Use	Power
6	6	6	6
Sustain	Finish	Flexibility	Toughness
6	6	6	7

Basic

Year	G	GS	Penalties Holding	False Start	Blown Block Splits Run	Pressure	Sack	Total
2018	14	12	0	0	5	4	1	11
2019	14	14	3	0	8	0	1	9
2020	11	11	2	0	2	1	0	3
	39	37	5	0	15	5	2	23

Team Stats

Year	Zone Run Blocking % of Runs	Y/A	Pos%	Gap Run Blocking % of Runs	Y/A	Pos%	Pass Block Pressure%
2018	48%	6.0	49%	49%	8.2	59%	26%
2019	47%	5.6	55%	49%	6.6	50%	39%
2020	51%	5.4	53%	46%	5.7	47%	30%
	49%	5.7	52%	48%	6.9	52%	32%

Deep Dive

Year	Blown Block % Run	Pass	When Running to their Gap Y/A	YBC/A	Pos%	EPA/A	Total Points Run	Pass	Total	Total Points Rtg Per Run	Per Pass	Per Play
2018	1.3%	1.5%	6.9	3.8	52%	0.15	18	12	30	93	83	89
2019	1.9%	0.2%	4.6	2.0	52%	-0.04	19	16	35	86	90	88
2020	0.6%	0.3%	4.3	1.8	51%	0.08	14	14	28	85	90	87
	1.3%	0.7%	5.5	2.7	52%	0.07	51	42	93	-	-	-

Josh Myers

Report by Jarrett Rodgers & John Todd

School	Height	Weight	Year	Jersey #	Hometown
Ohio State	6042 E	312 E	4JR	71	Miamisburg, OH

One Liner
Myers plays with highly-impressive awareness and reactive quickness to make for a fluid, zone lineman, as power and leg drive in the run game aren't his strong suits.

Overall
Josh Myers is the center in Ohio State's zone-based run scheme, delivering exclusively shotgun snaps. He played in 35 career games, starting all 21 over the past 2 seasons. He had shoulder surgery following his freshman season, but he didn't miss any games. He has a very solid frame for the interior and moves very fluidly to all areas of the field, flashing high-quality short-area quickness. He has a strong motor and is clearly the captain of their offensive line, regularly directing assignments pre-snap.

Pass Game
In the pass game, Myers does a great job of maintaining pocket depth and stalemating against some serious competition. He plays with high football IQ and keeps his head on a swivel to identify moving parts before and after the snap. He predicts blitzes well and often has his linemates in the correct positions to pick up late movement. His ability to stay square and rely on flexible knee and ankle bend is very impressive. He wins his share of battles at the line of scrimmage due to his anchor strength and technique, as well as good hand use up top. He has generally proven to be very stout against the power rush, with most of his losses coming against finesse moves. He has shown good footwork and subtly high-quality reactive instincts to shuffle his wide base and match odd angles.

Run Game
In the run game, Myers is tough but is not necessarily a power blocker to drive and finish head-up linemen. He identifies the Mike and works well on double teams, down blocks, and pulls into space, but he isn't a true people mover. However, he excels in his zone scheme. He sustains well with great hand placement and technique. He has the instincts to reach and seal wide techniques and cut off second-level players with smart angles. Myers is very smooth moving laterally and has the foot speed to regularly beat defenders to their spots. He lacks a forceful punch at contact and has an inconsistent mean streak.

Last Word
Myers projects as a starting center at the next level who fits perfectly in a zone-based offense. He would be sufficient in a gap scheme but he'd need to improve his forward leg drive and attacking power. He can also play guard, but his ability to communicate pre-snap and look for work both ways is ideally suited for center. He has had no snapping issues out of shotgun. His intelligence, pass protection skills, and ability to work laterally and in space give him a high ceiling if drafted to the right system.

Strengths

- Rush awareness
- Knee and ankle flexion
- Zone-blocking skills

Weaknesses

- Punch power and leg drive
- Finishing tenacity

Critical Factors

Reactive Athleticism	Anchor / Play Strength	Body Control
7	6	6

Positional Factors

Run Block	Pass Block	Awareness	Footwork
6	7	7	6
2nd Level	Range	Hand Use	Power
7	6	6	5
Sustain	Finish	Flexibility	Toughness
6	5	7	6

Basic

Year	G	GS	Penalties Holding	False Start	Blown Block Splits Run	Pressure	Sack	Total
2018	14	0	0	0	1	1	0	2
2019	14	14	0	0	8	5	5	18
2020	7	7	0	0	9	2	3	14
	35	21	0	0	18	8	8	34

Team Stats

Year	Zone Run Blocking % of Runs	Y/A	Pos%	Gap Run Blocking % of Runs	Y/A	Pos%	Pass Block Pressure%
2018	74%	5.1	51%	24%	4.0	48%	26%
2019	83%	6.5	50%	17%	6.1	53%	35%
2020	89%	7.1	53%	10%	3.3	43%	36%
	81%	6.1	51%	18%	4.8	50%	31%

Deep Dive

Year	Blown Block % Run	Pass	When Running to their Gap Y/A	YBC/A	Pos%	EPA/A	Total Points Run	Pass	Total	Total Points Rtg Per Run	Per Pass	Per Play
2018	7.1%	7.7%	4.2	1.3	33%	-0.15	0	0	1	52	92	66
2019	1.7%	2.3%	5.7	2.7	47%	0.16	22	10	33	88	66	78
2020	3.7%	2.0%	5.6	3.4	52%	0.11	13	6	18	91	67	80
	2.5%	2.3%	5.7	2.9	49%	0.14	35	16	52	-	-	-

Landon Dickerson

Report by Jeff Dean

School	Height	Weight	Year	Jersey #	Hometown
Alabama	6060 V	326 V	5SR	69	Hickory, NC

One Liner
Dickerson has the size, anchor, and persistently tough mentality to play at the next level across the interior, but he will need to show teams that he can overcome his foot quickness and durability concerns to be an elite player.

Overall
Landon Dickerson is an offensive lineman for Alabama's RPO-heavy offensive scheme, operating mostly out of shotgun. He has started 37 of his 38 career games played, with 20 starts at center, 11 at right guard, 4 at left guard and 1 at each tackle spot. He began his career at Florida State where he tore his right ACL to end his 2016 season early, injured his right ankle twice that ended his 2017 and 2018 seasons early, transferred to Alabama in 2019, and had his final season cut short after suffering another torn ACL. Dickerson is a sufficient athlete who has great size and is tall for the interior. He has very good strength in both his lower body and upper body, but his slow feet can affect his leverage. He is an extremely tough competitor, who has fought back from essentially four season-ending injuries to become a fixture in Alabama's starting lineup, and a clearly beloved teammate. He somehow snapped the final two plays of the 2020 National Championship despite suffering the ligament damage only three weeks earlier.

Pass Game
Dickerson has sound form and a very good anchor to allow him to consistently stonewall defenders in pass protection. He shows some rigidity and stagnant feet at times that can cost him against quicker interior linemen, but his body control and effort help him recover. While his footwork is hindered by his foot quickness, he creates a wide base to force defenders to work around him. He works his length to keep defenders away and shows a good understanding of hand placement to lock up and sustain when engaged. Dickerson does a good job of recognizing stunts. He finishes blocks with authority and routinely looks for extra work to knock defenders to the ground. His consistency week to week is commendable.

Run Game
Dickerson can drive defenders off the ball or seal them with regularity to be a very effective run blocker. He has a good first step and the anchor and form to neutralize. He gets a solid vertical push and is a very effective combo blocker. He can lunge or misstep against hesitation and finesse moves, but his length and wide base still put him in a good position to make blocks. As a puller, he is able to find blocks in the open field and square defenders up. He looks comfortable in space and has the skill set to be used in a power scheme. Dickerson has a sound understanding of hand fighting. He's nasty and will bury defensive linemen using proper leverage and tenacity, especially through his final season.

Last Word
Dickerson projects as a solid starter at any interior position, but his limited foot quickness, ability to assist both directions, and leadership fit best as a center in a power scheme. Injuries have greatly limited his playing time and will be a cause for concern moving forward, but he has consistently dominated against top competition and his combination of size, experience, and finishing ability should translate well to the next level.

Strengths	Weaknesses
• Punch and finishing tenacity	• Slow footwork against quickness
• Anchor strength	• Flexibility
• Leadership and toughness	• Durability

Critical Factors

Reactive Athleticism	Anchor / Play Strength	Body Control
6	7	6

Positional Factors

Run Block	Pass Block	Awareness	Footwork
7	6	6	5
2nd Level	**Range**	**Hand Use**	**Power**
6	6	7	6
Sustain	**Finish**	**Flexibility**	**Toughness**
6	7	5	8

Basic

Year	G	GS	Penalties Holding	False Start	Blown Block Splits Run	Pressure	Sack	Total
2016	7	7	0	0	1	6	4	11
2017	4	4	0	0	5	5	3	14
2018	2	2	1	0	0	1	0	1
2019	13	13	1	0	6	4	0	10
2020	12	11	0	0	0	4	0	4
	38	37	2	0	12	20	7	40

Team Stats

Year	Zone Run Blocking % of Runs	Y/A	Pos%	Gap Run Blocking % of Runs	Y/A	Pos%	Pass Block Pressure%
2016	72%	5.8	47%	26%	7.5	54%	33%
2017	79%	5.4	49%	20%	5.1	38%	40%
2018	66%	4.4	36%	30%	2.1	27%	37%
2019	52%	5.4	48%	48%	5.8	59%	26%
2020	56%	5.8	62%	43%	5.3	46%	26%
	65%	5.4	49%	33%	5.3	47%	33%

Deep Dive

Year	Blown Block % Run	Pass	When Running to their Gap Y/A	YBC/A	Pos%	EPA/A	Total Points Run	Pass	Total	Total Points Rtg Per Run	Per Pass	Per Play
2018	0.0%	1.4%	0.4	-2.1	0%	-0.64	0	2	2	50	90	56
2019	2.0%	1.0%	4.4	2.2	55%	0.02	18	15	32	96	91	93
2020	0.0%	1.1%	4.5	1.7	62%	0.07	17	12	29	91	85	88
	0.9%	1.1%	4.3	1.8	56%	0.02	35	29	63	-	-	-

Trey Hill

Report by DJ Marquardt ⊕ ✳

School	Height	Weight	Year	Jersey #	Hometown
Georgia	6032 E	330 E	3JR	55	Warner Robins, GA

One Liner
Hill's durability and dependability along with his football intelligence and short-area quickness makes him a solid fit for the interior offensive line, though he will need to improve his leverage and play strength to hit his full potential.

Overall
Trey Hill is a starting center in Georgia's pro-style offense running mainly zone-run schemes, who has also rotated at times to play guard. Hill played in 36 career games while making starts in 26 of those games with 22 starts at OC and 4 starts at RG. He missed the last 3 games of 2020 after meniscus surgery on both knees. He has a massive lower half, and is thick throughout his frame which has helped him be so dependable and durable during his time at Georgia. Hill was a star shot putter in high school, but overall is athletically limited at his size. He is a very tough competitor who is constantly on the field looking to make a play with each rep.

Pass Game
In pass protection, Hill is a very aware center who is very good at identifying threats and looking for work when uncovered. He is also very good at picking up stunts and reacting to inside rushes whenever need be. Hill's sufficient play strength and average ankle flexion sometimes forces him to give up depth in the pocket because he loses power by anchoring through the balls of his feet. However, he is built solid enough to stand ground and anchor at the last possible point and recover if beaten or pushed back early. He needs to improve his leverage as he often dips his head and finds himself over leveraged on his defender and leaning a bit.

Run Game
Hill is an aggressor at the point of attack in the run game. He has good short-area quickness to snap the ball and immediately zone step to pick up his covered defender, or immediately double the nearest technique and work up to the 2nd level. He's very good at getting to the 2nd-level with quickness and control in a zone scheme and positioning his body to square up defenders. He gets his hips in front of defenders and seals them. Hill does a good job of finishing his double teams and solo run blocks. He is a sufficient sustainer because he gets turned too quickly by stronger defenders which leads to an inconsistent run lane anchor.

Last Word
Hill projects best as a starting center in a zone run scheme at the next level with position versatility to play guard. He has the football intelligence, instincts, and immediate quickness to work well in a zone scheme. He has good size and solid man-blocking ability for a gap scheme, but lacks the range to pull if needed and does not maul defenders out of gaps. He is best at working through doubles to the second level to square up a box defender.

Strengths

- Body position at 2nd level
- Short-area quickness
- Football intelligence

Weaknesses

- Leverage
- Play strength
- Ankle Flexion

Critical Factors

Reactive Athleticism	Anchor / Play Strength	Body Control
7	5	6

Positional Factors

Run Block	Pass Block	Awareness	Footwork
6	6	7	6
2nd Level	Range	Hand Use	Power
7	5	5	6
Sustain	Finish	Flexibility	Toughness
5	6	5	6

Basic

Year	G	GS	Penalties		Blown Block Splits			
			Holding	False Start	Run	Pressure	Sack	Total
2018	14	4	0	0	5	2	1	8
2019	14	14	3	0	9	1	1	11
2020	8	8	0	0	6	0	1	7
	36	26	3	0	20	3	3	26

Team Stats

Year	Zone Run Blocking			Gap Run Blocking			Pass Block
	% of Runs	Y/A	Pos%	% of Runs	Y/A	Pos%	Pressure%
2018	93%	6.4	49%	3%	5.4	50%	25%
2019	85%	5.3	51%	11%	6.0	45%	27%
2020	78%	5.2	52%	18%	6.3	53%	31%
	86%	5.8	50%	10%	6.1	50%	27%

Deep Dive

Year	Blown Block %		When Running to their Gap				Total Points			Total Points Rtg		
	Run	Pass	Y/A	YBC/A	Pos%	EPA/A	Run	Pass	Total	Per Run	Per Pass	Per Play
2018	2.1%	1.8%	5.0	1.6	51%	0.11	4	4	7	52	68	56
2019	2.1%	0.5%	4.9	2.3	50%	0.03	16	17	33	74	94	85
2020	2.3%	0.4%	5.6	3.2	53%	0.02	16	9	25	97	88	94
	2.2%	0.7%	5.1	2.4	51%	0.04	36	30	65	-	-	-

Jimmy Morrissey

Report by Jon Drillings

School	Height	Weight	Year	Jersey #	Hometown
Pittsburgh	6021 E	305 E	5SR	67	Huntingdon Valley, PA

One Liner

Morrissey has enough awareness pre-snap and body control post-snap to make up for his sufficient hand usage and become a nice starting option inside for a team.

Strengths: Awareness; Anchor the pocket; Shooting his hands off the snap
Weaknesses: Technical hand use; Finishing ability; Elite vertical power

Jimmy Morrissey is a center for Pittsburgh in its balanced blocking scheme. He has started all 47 of his career games played, only missing 3 due to a broken ankle near the end of his 2018 season. Morrissey is a good athlete but is going to win more often with his smarts than raw athleticism. He has a slightly narrow frame and solid length. Named the 2020 winner of the Burlsworth Award, given to the nation's top former walk-on, he is a strong competitor who uses toughness to his advantage in the trenches.

In pass protection, Morrissey sees the game at a high level and has very good awareness at the line of scrimmage. A two-time team captain, he communicates well pre- and post-snap, showing the ability to pass off rushers. He has a strong anchor for his lighter frame and isn't often driven back deep into the pocket. Morrissey has a good first step and is very quick to get his hands up against nose tackles. He has the athleticism after the snap to square his footwork and keep them moving through contact.

His hands when engaged are just sufficient though, and he may struggle against top competition as he can be susceptible to superior upper-body rush moves. He does have the ability to recover from awkward angles well and tie up defenders even after he's beaten.

In the run game, Morrissey is effective at the point of attack and is able to generate decent movement in some power situations. He has good reactive athleticism and can turn his hips to create running lanes. He also has good body control, using flexible knee bend to help with his balance. He sometimes struggles to finish off a combo block, but he is able to get to the second level and cut off the angles of linebackers efficiently.

Morrissey projects best as a gap-blocking scheme center, but he can also play in zone based on his quickness, effective strength at the point of attack, and ability to block in space. He could grow into a suitable backup guard, but he'll need to improve his bulk and drive strength.

Year	G	GS	Penalties Holding	False Start	Blown Block Splits Run	Pressure	Sack	Total
2017	12	12	2	0	8	2	1	12
2018	11	11	0	0	1	3	0	4
2019	13	13	1	0	2	3	0	5
2020	11	11	0	0	3	5	1	9
	47	47	3	0	14	13	2	30

Team Year	Team Zone Run Blocking % of Runs	Y/A	Pos%	Team Gap Run Blocking % of Runs	Y/A	Pos%	Team Pass Block Pressure%
2017	65%	5.1	45%	34%	3.8	40%	36%
2018	60%	5.7	48%	39%	7.5	48%	39%
2019	50%	4.0	43%	44%	4.3	38%	37%
2020	60%	4.0	44%	32%	4.2	40%	31%
	59%	4.8	45%	38%	5.2	42%	36%

Year	Blown Block % Run	Pass	When Running to their Gap Y/A	YBC/A	Pos%	EPA/A	Total Points Run	Pass	Total	Total Points Rtg Per Run	Per Pass	Per Play
2018	0.3%	1.0%	6.9	2.4	61%	0.34	24	13	37	99	98	99
2019	0.5%	0.5%	3.9	1.3	43%	-0.18	14	21	34	75	86	82
2020	1.0%	1.3%	5.1	3.0	44%	0.08	9	13	21	65	73	70
	0.6%	0.9%	5.3	2.4	49%	0.08	47	47	92	-	-	-

Critical Factors	
Reactive Athleticism	6
Anchor / Play Strength	6
Body Control	6

Positional Factors	
Run Block	6
Pass Block	6
Awareness	7
Footwork	6
2nd Level	6
Range	6
Hand Use	5
Power	5
Sustain	6
Finish	5
Flexibility	6
Toughness	6

Drew Dalman   Final Grade: 6.4

Report by Max Nuscher

School	Height	Weight	Year	Jersey #	Hometown
Stanford	6022 E	300 E	4SR	51	Salinas, CA

One Liner
Dalman is a consistent contributor in the run and pass game, and his football intelligence should allow him to become a sufficient starter with improved lower-body strength.

Strengths: Football intelligence; Pulling and range; Hand usage
Weaknesses: Blocking in awkward positions; Sustain and finishing tenacity; Lower-body strength;

Drew Dalman is a center in Stanford's pro-style offense, operating fairly equally out of shotgun and under center. Of his 28 career games played, he started 20 at center and 2 at right guard. His father is a former Stanford football player and Super Bowl champion with the 49ers. He's well proportioned and has good lateral quickness and movement skills in space. He is a team captain and plays with a high motor.

Dalman is the leader of the OL and signals moving parts up front to his linemates well. He has very good awareness to see delayed blitzes and stunts, and he doesn't hesitate to help his guards. He packs a punch in his hands and does a great job of bracing for contact with sound technique and a wide base, but he doesn't possess the strongest lower half to anchor with that alone. He struggles blocking in awkward positions and anchoring against lengthier, stronger interior linemen. He plays with good hand usage and tight elbows when square and is very effective ahead of screens.

Dalman does a great job of pulling from his center position and hitting defenders on the perimeter. He has a good, powerful punch at contact to generate initial movement but hasn't shown to be a forceful drive blocker off the line. He has some issues sustaining blocks against heavy two-gapping anchors. Dalman prefers to get to the second level and does so frequently. He could improve his ability to shock initial defenders on combos before releasing upfield. He doesn't show the desire to finish blocks through the whistle, often slowing his effort once the ball is past him. He has had issues clearing run lanes in short-yardage situations.

Dalman projects as a low-end starting center for zone blocking offenses, based on his lineage, movement skills, and intelligence. He would struggle to be a starting-level player in a heavy gap scheme, and would need to improve his lower-body strength to be more than an adequate backup at guard.

			Penalties		Blown Block Splits			
Year	G	GS	Holding	False Start	Run	Pressure	Sack	Total
2018	10	4	2	0	2	2	0	4
2019	12	12	2	0	4	3	1	8
2020	6	6	1	0	2	1	0	3
	28	22	5	0	8	6	1	15

Team	Team Zone Run Blocking			Team Gap Run Blocking			Team Pass Block
Year	% of Runs	Y/A	Pos%	% of Runs	Y/A	Pos%	Pressure%
2018	54%	4.4	38%	46%	4.3	38%	31%
2019	64%	4.2	37%	35%	4.5	40%	31%
2020	60%	5.1	49%	34%	3.5	47%	23%
	59%	4.5	40%	40%	4.2	40%	30%

	Blown Block %		When Running to their Gap				Total Points			Total Points Rtg		
Year	Run	Pass	Y/A	YBC/A	Pos%	EPA/A	Run	Pass	Total	Per Run	Per Pass	Per Play
2018	1.6%	1.7%	2.5	0.3	20%	-0.49	1	3	4	50	77	54
2019	1.4%	0.8%	4.2	1.8	36%	-0.09	5	18	23	53	89	73
2020	1.1%	0.4%	4.8	1.6	45%	0.03	7	12	18	76	98	93
	1.3%	0.8%	4.0	1.5	34%	-0.15	13	33	45	-	-	-

Critical Factors	
Reactive Athleticism	6
Anchor / Play Strength	5
Body Control	6

Positional Factors	
Run Block	6
Pass Block	6
Awareness	7
Footwork	5
2nd Level	6
Range	7
Hand Use	6
Power	6
Sustain	5
Finish	4
Flexibility	6
Toughness	5

Drake Jackson

Report by Michael Churchward

School	Height	Weight	Year	Jersey #	Hometown
Kentucky	6017 V	290 V	5SR	52	Versailles, KY

One Liner
Jackson has the tools in the run and pass game with good communication to contribute as a center, but needs to improve his strength and nastiness to truly make an impact at the next level.

Strengths: Intelligence; Hand placement; Footwork
Weaknesses: Aggressiveness/finish; Play strength; Range

Drake Jackson is the center for Kentucky's spread, RPO-heavy, zone-run scheme. He played in 47 games, finishing out his career by consecutively starting 44 of those games, even playing through a high-ankle sprain in 2019. He's a sufficient athlete with decent size for the position, though his frame allows for him to add more weight and muscle. He plays hard and tough, though lacks some nasty and aggressiveness in his game.

In the pass game, Jackson excels at line calls and adjusting the line to the right protection. He shows good recognition in picking up twists and stunts and shows strength at awkward angles with the ability to recover due to his sufficient body control. He does well in short-set anchoring due to proper hand use and footwork, but Jackson lacks the weight and sand in his pants to really sit down against bigger, stronger opponents. He'll occasionally stop his feet upon contact and tends to bend at the waist, forcing him to lunge a little and fall off his block. When he's in space, his lack of top-end athleticism hurts his range and overall effectiveness at the 2nd-level. He comes in under control, but will have a tough time locating and latching onto quicker mid-level defenders.

Jackson does well with his blocking IQ and technique. He uses his footwork and hand placement to wall off defenders to have a proficient run lane anchor, however, he can be stood up due to a lack of strength. He works well at double teams and help blocks, but tends to stop moving his feet which can lead to just leaning on the defender and falling off balance once they counter. He lacks the mean streak and aggressiveness to finish blocks into the ground. He does pull from the center position, but has some trouble getting to his block in space.

Jackson projects as a backup center in a zone-run scheme. He has the pass-blocking intelligence and technique to be able to slide over to the guard position, but needs to get bigger and stronger before he'll be able to hit his ceiling at that spot.

			Penalties		Blown Block Splits			
Year	G	GS	Holding	False Start	Run	Pressure	Sack	Total
2017	10	7	1	0	5	3	1	9
2018	13	13	3	0	12	2	1	15
2019	13	13	2	0	4	3	1	8
2020	11	11	1	0	3	0	1	5
	47	44	7	0	24	8	4	37

Team	Team Zone Run Blocking			Team Gap Run Blocking			Team Pass Block
Year	% of Runs	Y/A	Pos%	% of Runs	Y/A	Pos%	Pressure%
2017	63%	5.0	42%	36%	4.2	40%	35%
2018	68%	5.3	46%	31%	5.3	48%	36%
2019	65%	6.8	50%	33%	6.4	46%	28%
2020	70%	5.5	52%	27%	5.8	51%	29%
	67%	5.7	48%	32%	5.4	46%	33%

	Blown Block %		When Running to their Gap				Total Points			Total Points Rtg		
Year	Run	Pass	Y/A	YBC/A	Pos%	EPA/A	Run	Pass	Total	Per Run	Per Pass	Per Play
2018	2.6%	0.9%	5.7	2.1	49%	0.09	9	12	21	53	86	62
2019	0.8%	1.4%	7.5	3.5	53%	0.18	31	13	44	97	98	97
2020	0.8%	0.7%	5.7	2.9	50%	0.08	20	11	31	89	93	90
	1.4%	1.0%	6.3	2.8	51%	0.12	60	36	96	-	-	-

Critical Factors	
Reactive Athleticism	5
Anchor / Play Strength	5
Body Control	5

Positional Factors	
Run Block	5
Pass Block	5
Awareness	6
Footwork	6
2nd Level	5
Range	4
Hand Use	6
Power	4
Sustain	4
Finish	4
Flexibility	5
Toughness	5

David Moore

Report by Joe McDonald & Nathan Cooper

School	Height	Weight	Year	Jersey #	Hometown
Grambling State	6015 V	350 V	5SR	60	Little Rock, AR

One Liner

Moore shows flashes in pass protection and has the strength and anchor ability to be a capable backup interior lineman at the next level, but needs to put on better weight and improve his leg drive to maximize his potential.

Strengths: Pass pro; Strong punch; 2nd-level quickness & body control
Weaknesses: Leg drive; Handling pass-rush plans; Range

David Moore is the starting left guard for Grambling State who runs mostly zone and throws entirely out of shotgun. He played in 27 games, starting 17 of those for the Tigers. 16 of his starts came at left guard while a lone start came at right guard. He is a big body with a large frame that can support his weight, though he is a little top-heavy. He is a tough player with a motor that can run hot or cold depending on the play.

In the pass game, Moore is a good quarterback protector. He has a strong punch and solid latch when he is accurate with his hands, though he does not do this with enough consistency. He has some reactive athleticism in a phone booth, moving well horizontally. However, when a pass rusher is prepared with an attack plan, he has a tough time reacting. His big body and leg strength allows him to anchor down quickly against power. He uses good footwork to stay in front of defenders, but gets too bendy and over-extends at the POA. He shows good awareness and is always looking for work when uncovered and uses his strong upper body to pancake engaged defenders.

In the run game, Moore does not generate much vertical push unless involved in a double team, but has enough strength to anchor and open run lanes. He uses the aforementioned punch well, but tends to stop his feet on impact and settle for a stalemate. He can navigate zone blocking well, giving help and getting to the 2nd level balanced and under control. He struggles to get a reach block at times, because he will abandon his footwork and just try to wash the defender out.

Moore projects best as a backup center, something he did at the Senior Bowl, in a zone-run scheme with the flexibility to back up at guard as well. His strength and versatility will give him a shot, as he needs time in an NFL weight room to lose some bad weight and build up more muscle. That'll also allow him to move better in space.

Yes, David Moore is a small-school player who didn't play in 2020 due to the pandemic, but he stood out when he went up against a considerable number of standouts at the Senior Bowl. Moore was selected as the top offensive lineman on the American team roster in a vote by the team's defensive linemen.

"They're gonna get somebody who's going to go out and be a hard worker, determined, never try to lose a matchup on a play at all, no matter who's lined up in front of me," Moore said in an interview with the *Life and Football* podcast last December.

The last player drafted from Grambling State was Chad Williams by the Cardinals in the third round in 2017. The only offensive lineman to be drafted from Grambling since 1977 was Herman Arvie in the fifth round by the Browns in 1993. Arvie played four seasons in the NFL.

Critical Factors	
Reactive Athleticism	5
Anchor / Play Strength	6
Body Control	5

Positional Factors	
Run Block	5
Pass Block	5
Awareness	6
Footwork	5
2nd Level	5
Range	4
Hand Use	5
Power	5
Sustain	5
Finish	5
Flexibility	5
Toughness	6

Orlando Umana

Report by Jeff Dean & Christian Vega

School	Height	Weight	Year	Jersey #	Hometown
Utah	6032 E	311 E	4SR	50	Sacramento, CA

One Liner

Umana has the anchor in pass protection and position flexibility teams desire in interior linemen, but he will have to improve his footwork and overall effort to execute more consistently.

Strengths: Anchor strength; Sealing in the run game; Body composition
Weaknesses: Slow footwork; Pad level; Awareness and effort

Orlando Umana is an offensive lineman in Utah's zone running scheme. He played in 40 career games with 26 starts, 4 at left guard in 2018 before moving to center the rest of his career. He missed the majority of his senior season with an undisclosed injury. Umana is a sufficient athlete who lost nearly 30 pounds before his senior year and showed improved movement skills. He now has a well-proportioned body with thick thighs. He has good strength but slow feet and struggles to move out in space. He far too often will look lethargic and unenthusiastic on extended plays.

Umana has a good anchor in pass protection and infrequently gets driven back. He has strong hands and a wide base to keep power rushers in front of him with enough reactive athleticism to handle counters. He can struggle against speed rushes and stunts but keeps his hips over his ankles to stay in solid position. His lateral quickness isn't great, but his recent weight loss has given him extra mobility. Umana has a tendency to stop moving his feet on scrambles and can look disinterested seeking out work.

Umana doesn't drive defenders off the ball as often as one would suspect with his size. He plays too upright and will lose leverage battles. He seals his positioning with a strong first step and a wide base, then uses consistent hand placement, flexible hips, and leg strength to wall off run lanes. He doesn't have the hand quickness to recover through hand fights. He flashes the desire to drive defenders into the ground on occasion. Umana looks uncomfortable in space and has difficulties locating blocks outside the trenches. He also has shown some balance issues adjusting to moving targets.

Umana projects as a versatile backup lineman who fits best in a power blocking scheme. His experience across the interior is a valuable asset, and his recent efforts to get in better shape give reason for optimism moving forward if he can parlay that into quicker footwork and space mobility.

			Penalties		Blown Block Splits			
Year	G	GS	Holding	False Start	Run	Pressure	Sack	Total
2017	13	0	0	0	0	0	0	0
2018	14	13	2	0	2	3	1	6
2019	12	12	2	0	10	2	0	12
2020	1	1	1	0	0	0	0	0
	40	26	5	0	12	5	1	18

Team	Team Zone Run Blocking			Team Gap Run Blocking			Team Pass Block
Year	% of Runs	Y/A	Pos%	% of Runs	Y/A	Pos%	Pressure%
2017	57%	4.8	50%	41%	5.1	52%	40%
2018	66%	5.3	52%	33%	4.9	42%	28%
2019	75%	5.5	49%	25%	5.1	52%	40%
2020	83%	5.4	42%	16%	6.4	42%	41%
	68%	5.3	49%	31%	5.1	48%	36%

	Blown Block %		When Running to their Gap				Total Points			Total Points Rtg		
Year	Run	Pass	Y/A	YBC/A	Pos%	EPA/A	Run	Pass	Total	Per Run	Per Pass	Per Play
2018	0.4%	0.9%	5.3	2.8	52%	0.08	24	15	38	94	86	91
2019	2.7%	0.6%	4.8	1.7	49%	-0.01	11	11	23	63	85	73
2020	0.0%	0.0%	4.0	2.0	33%	-0.16	0	1	1	54	83	71
	1.4%	0.7%	5.1	2.4	50%	0.04	35	27	62	-	-	-

Critical Factors	
Reactive Athleticism	5
Anchor / Play Strength	6
Body Control	5

Positional Factors	
Run Block	5
Pass Block	5
Awareness	5
Footwork	5
2nd Level	5
Range	4
Hand Use	6
Power	6
Sustain	5
Finish	5
Flexibility	5
Toughness	5

Ryan McCollum

Report by Alec Mallon

School	Height	Weight	Year	Jersey #	Hometown
Texas A&M	6052 V	300 V	5SR	77	Spring, TX

One Liner

McCollum is an intelligent center with strong pass protecting traits, but must develop his traits in the run to win more consistently.

Strengths: Anchor ability; Awareness; Balance at the point of attack
Weaknesses: Power; Hand technique; Downfield blocking

Ryan McCollum is a center in Texas A&M's zone-heavy scheme. He played in 43 games while starting 17, spending most of his time at right guard in 2018 before moving to center in 2020. He had a lingering back injury that cost him playing time in 2019. McCollum is strong and versatile, using his frame to win at the POA. He displays enough intelligence, toughness, and nastiness to play at the next level.

McCollum demonstrates he can read defenses and make calls at the LOS, routinely putting his linemates in situations to win. He shows awareness off the snap, taking on the man in front of him, and if no one is there, finding work elsewhere quickly. At contact, McCollum is often late to punch and constantly shoots his hands low. Defenders can chop and swipe his hands down, but McCollum displays good balance and has the ability to reshoot and stay well positioned enough to hold the pocket. When square, McCollum has a strong anchor to negate his opponents movements at the line. His lower half and body control allow for him to sustain pocket depth for his QB to step up.

McCollum is strong at the POA in the run game. He can deliver a punch to stop defenders at the line but doesn't have the leg drive to reset the LOS. He is quick off the snap, getting to his reach blocks with good technique, and with the help of his guards, they can move defenders backwards. At the second level, McCollum lacks the quickness and reaction skills to mirror off-ball defenders. His hand usage combined with his slower feet in open space make it difficult for him to consistently execute.

McCollum projects best as a multi-positional backup in the NFL. His limited, but noteworthy production at guard will make him a candidate to play multiple positions at the next level. McCollum can play in both zone and gap schemes, but will be more efficient in a gap environment where he can use his frame and leg strength to open holes rather than his speed and athleticism.

			Penalties		Blown Block Splits			
Year	G	GS	Holding	False Start	Run	Pressure	Sack	Total
2017	13	0	1	0	3	6	3	12
2018	12	7	1	0	8	6	2	16
2019	8	0	0	0	0	2	3	5
2020	10	10	1	0	13	4	0	18
	43	17	3	0	24	18	8	51

Team	Team Zone Run Blocking			Team Gap Run Blocking			Team Pass Block
Year	% of Runs	Y/A	Pos%	% of Runs	Y/A	Pos%	Pressure%
2017	69%	3.8	36%	30%	6.5	36%	35%
2018	65%	6.0	51%	33%	6.4	49%	42%
2019	73%	6.2	52%	25%	4.4	44%	42%
2020	74%	5.7	58%	25%	6.2	49%	32%
	70%	5.4	49%	29%	6.0	44%	38%

	Blown Block %		When Running to their Gap				Total Points			Total Points Rtg		
Year	Run	Pass	Y/A	YBC/A	Pos%	EPA/A	Run	Pass	Total	Per Run	Per Pass	Per Play
2018	2.8%	2.8%	6.2	2.0	51%	0.04	7	3	10	61	52	55
2019	0.0%	5.7%	4.8	1.4	35%	0.05	1	0	1	54	50	51
2020	3.8%	1.5%	5.0	2.0	61%	0.13	11	10	20	67	78	72
	3.0%	2.6%	5.5	2.0	55%	0.09	19	13	31	-	-	-

Critical Factors	
Reactive Athleticism	5
Anchor / Play Strength	6
Body Control	6

Positional Factors	
Run Block	5
Pass Block	6
Awareness	6
Footwork	5
2nd Level	5
Range	6
Hand Use	5
Power	4
Sustain	6
Finish	5
Flexibility	5
Toughness	6

Sam Cooper

Report by Ben Hrkach

School	Height	Weight	Year	Jersey #	Hometown
Merrimack	6015 V	318 V	6SR	77	Bensalem, PA

One Liner

Cooper is a mauler with a mean streak who has the strength and awareness to hang in pass pro, but needs to improve his hand placement, quickness, and range in order to make a consistent impact.

Strengths: Footwork; Lower-body strength; Nasty
Weaknesses: Hand placement; Athleticism; Length

Sam Cooper plays left guard for Merrimack focusing mainly on the read-option run. He worked at center in spring of 2018 before injury. He played 4 games in 3 seasons at Maine before transferring and starting 10 of 16 games at Merrimack. He suffered a partially-torn patellar tendon and ankle injury that caused him to miss the first half of 2018. He's a heavy-handed, squatty blocker with sufficient agility who gives good effort and is non-stop nasty.

Cooper pops out of his stance, has a square base, and naturally anchors down, though his anchor is just adequate. He shows sufficient foot quickness and ability to slide. Occasionally, he hops and doesn't stay grounded, but is more often than not in good position. His upper body and feet move in unison, which leads to his balance and strength. He is sufficient at reading stunts and blitzers and swiftly moves from one man to another. When left in space, he can get exposed when he doesn't see his man early. He has enough flexibility and can reset his feet when he doesn't need to cover much ground. At the

POA, Cooper has a strong punch and heavy hands, though his placement can get wide and grabby. Sometimes he'll replace his hands, but often doesn't bother. He also struggles with longer defenders due to length issues.

Cooper's power, hand strength, and nastiness are on full display. He explodes out of his stance, delivers a blow, and finishes. His hand placement is masked by his body positioning and leg drive. He maintains a wide base and leg drive through contact. On combos, he eliminates defenders and promptly works upfield. He's gets to the 2nd-level under control, but gets beat with quickness and grabs too often. Cooper has mediocre lateral strength and range on pulls and doesn't look comfortable turning and running.

Cooper projects as a backup center in a run-heavy, zone scheme who has enough strength to work at guard too. He's a phone-booth player with foot quickness, balance, and looks the part, as he played at a level above his teammates and competition.

Sam Cooper is working towards a Master's degree in management. He's already more than earned his Master's in on- and off-field excellence.

"Sam had a tremendous playing career here at Merrimack, but his impact on our program was much greater than his production on gameday. He was an elite student, tremendous leader, fantastic teammate, and just a great ambassador for Merrimack football and the college," said head coach Dan Curran.

Cooper would be the first player from Merrimack selected in the NFL Draft. The most prominent Merrimack football alum to get a chance at playing in the NFL is linebacker Shawn Loiseau, who signed with the Texans in 2012 and Colts in 2013 but did not make either team.

Critical Factors	
Reactive Athleticism	5
Anchor / Play Strength	5
Body Control	5

Positional Factors	
Run Block	5
Pass Block	5
Awareness	5
Footwork	6
2nd Level	5
Range	4
Hand Use	5
Power	5
Sustain	5
Finish	6
Flexibility	6
Toughness	6

Nose Tackles

Alex Vigderman

The participants in this year's Super Bowl remind us of some great first round nose tackles of recent vintage. The Bucs' Vita Vea was taken in the top half of the first round in the 2018 draft, and the Chiefs took Glenn Dorsey and Dontari Poe in 2008 and 2012, respectively.

While the tendency towards pass-heavy offenses leaves two-gapping noses less valuable than they used to be, the relative lack of options each year in the draft means that those teams who are in the market have to choose wisely. In fact, you'll see in the Deep Dive section of each player's stat page that half of the players we have projected to play in the middle spent at least half their 2020 snaps elsewhere.

Conveniently enough, one of our two highest-graded players, Tommy Togiai, is among those who spent less than half their time in 2020 as a 0- or 1-technique. He showed the ability to flex out as far as a 5-tech at Ohio State, and was the most productive pass rusher of this group in terms of Pass Rush Total Points.

Of course, a nose tackle has to be stout in the run game, whether by making a tackle up front or forcing the play somewhere else. While Togiai is no slouch in this regard, our other top-graded nose tackle Alim McNeill has 20 pounds on him and is a better fit for teams looking to stuff inside runs.

The statistical argument for McNeill as a quality run-stuffer is rich. He's the best of the bunch in terms of Forced Bounce Rate, which tells you how often runs towards a defender were forced elsewhere. He also made 27 tackles without a broken tackle and made tackles significantly upfield of what you'd expect given his alignment, which we show using Adjusted Tackle Depth Plus.

McNeill and Togiai are the only nose tackle prospects who we project as three-down starters at the next level, so it's not surprising that we have an accord between the stats and the scouting reports. They don't always agree, though.

Besides Togiai, the other player with a good pass rush grade is Roy Lopez, who only became a dedicated nose this year after transferring from New Mexico State to Arizona before the season. Lopez flashed some pass rush ability but had limited production in terms of generating pressure on the quarterback in his short time as a Wildcat.

Because the responsibilities of different defensive line positions are so different, it's worth reiterating that you should keep an eye on the alignment data on the player pages. Sacks and tackles for loss are the best way to make a name for yourself, and the further inside you play the harder it is to accumulate those kinds of numbers. While we project these players to the same position at the next level, they didn't all have the same role in college.

Take Jack Heflin, who is at the back end of the group but was the most productive player in terms of Total Points over his career. He's another transfer player, in his case from Northern Illinois to Iowa. He had the most productive single season of any of these prospects in his last year at NIU, specifically in terms of generating pressure on the quarterback. However, that season he barely played at the nose, so you have to take his production in the appropriate context.

Another player with a less inspiring projection who you'll see high on the leaderboards (faint praise as it is, since everyone who played in 2020 fits on the leaderboard) is Bobby Brown III, who generated what we'd probably view as an unsustainable amount of production in his final year at Texas A&M. He was among the most successful noses in pressuring the quarterback, but he more than doubled the sack production (both in count and EPA saved) of his counterparts in 2020.

It's a small group that belongs to a fading population in general, but there's plenty of variety in how these projected nose tackles were deployed and what their production looked like in college that you just might spend more time than you think in the next bunch of pages.

NOSE TACKLE

Nose Tackle Grading Scale

GRADE	DESCRIPTION
9.0 – 7.0	High-end starter. Pro Bowl level.
6.9 – 6.7	Strong starter who plays on all 3 downs.
6.3	Solid 2 down starter. Run only player.
6.2	Versatile backup with positional flexibility.
6.1 – 6.0	Developmental. Top traits but needs time.
5.9	Top backup NT. Only 1 position player.
5.8	Average backup NT. Only 1 position player.
5.7	Low-end backup NT with growable upside.

Nose Tackle Rankings

Rank	Name	Grade	Page
1	Alim McNeill	6.8	396
2	Tommy Togiai	6.7	398
3	Tyler Shelvin	6.3	400
4	Khyiris Tonga	6.3	402
5	Roy Lopez	6.2	404
6	Tedarrell Slaton	5.9	405
7	Bobby Brown III	5.8	406
8	Quinton Bohanna	5.8	407
9	Jack Heflin	5.8	408

Glossary

ATD+ (Adjusted Tackle Depth Plus)
ATD+ compares actual tackle depth to the expected tackle depth based on personnel, intended run gap, and the defender's pre-snap alignment. This figure is then scaled so that 100 is average. A figure of 110 indicates a player who is 10% better than average; a figure of 90 indicates a player who is 10% worse than average.

Bnc% (Forced Bounce Rate) (When Run At split)
The percentage of runs that didn't go through the designed gap.

BT% (Broken Tackle%)
Percentage of tackle attempts where the defender in position to make a tackle failed to bring down the ballcarrier. Counts both broken tackles (physical) and missed tackles (elusive).

Deflected
Plays where the defender either knocked a pass down or deflected a pass at the line of scrimmage.

Hits
Plays with meaningful contact made by the defender on the quarterback before or as he releases the football.

Hurries
Plays where the defender forced the QB to alter his throwing motion, leave the pocket, or rush his throw.

Knockdowns
Plays where the quarterback gets knocked down to the ground by the defender after he releases the football.

Pos% (Positive Percentage) (When Run At split)
The percentage of plays that result in a positive EPA for the offense. Lower numbers are better for defenders.

Pres% (Pressure Rate)
The percentage of pass rushes that resulted in a quarterback hurry, hit, knockdown, or sack.

Pres Share (Pressure Share)
Percentage of a team's individual pressures made by the defender.

Run At%
Percentage of carries where the defender was positioned in the designed gap.

Sack%
Percentage of pass rushes that resulted in a sack.

Tackle Share
Percentage of a team's tackles made by the defender.

Total Points
Sports Info Solutions' proprietary player value metric that uses an Expected Points framework and distributes the value gained or lost on a play to the players involved based on their impact on the play.

Total Points Rating
Total Points per play compared to average, scaled so that 50 is poor and 99 is excellent.

True Pres% (True Pressure Rate)
Pressure rate that isolates straight dropbacks which are more likely to be similar across situations.

Nose Tackle Leaderboards

Total Points Per Game

Rk	Player	School	Tot Pts / G
1	T. Togiai	Ohio State	3.4
2	A. McNeill	NC State	2.3
3	B. Brown III	Texas A&M	2.2
4	K. Tonga	BYU	1.8
4	Q. Bohanna	Kentucky	1.8
6	T. Slaton	Florida	1.6
7	J. Heflin	Iowa	1.3
8	R. Lopez	Arizona	1.2

Total Points Rating Per Play

Rk	Player	School	Rating
1	T. Togiai	Ohio State	98
2	B. Brown III	Texas A&M	92
3	A. McNeill	NC State	82
3	Q. Bohanna	Kentucky	82
5	K. Tonga	BYU	79
6	T. Slaton	Florida	75
7	J. Heflin	Iowa	70
8	R. Lopez	Arizona	67

Pass Rush Total Points Per Game

Rk	Player	School	Tot Pts / G
1	T. Togiai	Ohio State	1.4
2	B. Brown III	Texas A&M	0.9
3	K. Tonga	BYU	0.7
4	Q. Bohanna	Kentucky	0.6
5	T. Slaton	Florida	0.5
6	J. Heflin	Iowa	0.4
7	R. Lopez	Arizona	0.0
8	A. McNeill	NC State	-0.2

Total Points Rating Per Pass Rush

Rk	Player	School	Rating
1	T. Togiai	Ohio State	93
2	B. Brown III	Texas A&M	86
3	K. Tonga	BYU	74
4	Q. Bohanna	Kentucky	71
5	T. Slaton	Florida	68
6	J. Heflin	Iowa	66
7	R. Lopez	Arizona	55
8	A. McNeill	NC State	53

Run Defense Total Points Per Game

Rk	Player	School	Tot Pts / G
1	A. McNeill	NC State	1.7
2	T. Togiai	Ohio State	1.6
3	R. Lopez	Arizona	1.4
4	B. Brown III	Texas A&M	1.3
5	T. Slaton	Florida	1.1
6	Q. Bohanna	Kentucky	0.9
6	J. Heflin	Iowa	0.9
8	K. Tonga	BYU	0.6

Total Points Rating Per Run Snap

Rk	Player	School	Rating
1	T. Togiai	Ohio State	99
2	A. McNeill	NC State	98
3	B. Brown III	Texas A&M	97
4	Q. Bohanna	Kentucky	89
5	R. Lopez	Arizona	81
5	T. Slaton	Florida	81
7	K. Tonga	BYU	73
7	J. Heflin	Iowa	73

Pressure Rate			
Rk	Player	School	Pres%
1	T. Togiai	Ohio State	11%
2	J. Heflin	Iowa	8%
3	B. Brown III	Texas A&M	7%
3	Q. Bohanna	Kentucky	7%
5	K. Tonga	BYU	6%
5	T. Slaton	Florida	6%
7	A. McNeill	NC State	4%
7	R. Lopez	Arizona	4%

True Pressure Rate			
Rk	Player	School	Pres%
1	T. Togiai	Ohio State	11%
2	B. Brown III	Texas A&M	9%
3	K. Tonga	BYU	8%
3	Q. Bohanna	Kentucky	8%
5	J. Heflin	Iowa	6%
6	R. Lopez	Arizona	5%
6	T. Slaton	Florida	5%
8	A. McNeill	NC State	4%

Pressures Per Game			
Rk	Player	School	Pres/G
1	T. Togiai	Ohio State	2.7
2	Q. Bohanna	Kentucky	1.6
3	J. Heflin	Iowa	1.5
4	K. Tonga	BYU	1.4
4	B. Brown III	Texas A&M	1.4
6	T. Slaton	Florida	1.3
7	A. McNeill	NC State	1.0
8	R. Lopez	Arizona	0.8

Pressure Share			
Rk	Player	School	Pres Share
1	R. Lopez	Arizona	15%
2	T. Togiai	Ohio State	10%
2	J. Heflin	Iowa	10%
4	K. Tonga	BYU	9%
4	Q. Bohanna	Kentucky	9%
6	B. Brown III	Texas A&M	8%
7	T. Slaton	Florida	7%
8	A. McNeill	NC State	6%

Passes Deflected Per Game			
Rk	Player	School	Defl/G
1	K. Tonga	BYU	0.4
2	T. Togiai	Ohio State	0.3
2	Q. Bohanna	Kentucky	0.3
4	A. McNeill	NC State	0.1
5	R. Lopez	Arizona	0.0
5	T. Slaton	Florida	0.0
5	B. Brown III	Texas A&M	0.0
5	J. Heflin	Iowa	0.0

Holds Drawn			
Rk	Player	School	Holds
1	B. Brown III	Texas A&M	4
2	A. McNeill	NC State	2
2	T. Slaton	Florida	2
4	R. Lopez	Arizona	1
5	T. Togiai	Ohio State	0
5	K. Tonga	BYU	0
5	Q. Bohanna	Kentucky	0
5	J. Heflin	Iowa	0

Sacks Per Game

Rk	Player	School	Sacks/G
1	B. Brown III	Texas A&M	0.6
2	T. Togiai	Ohio State	0.4
3	K. Tonga	BYU	0.2
3	R. Lopez	Arizona	0.2
5	A. McNeill	NC State	0.1
5	T. Slaton	Florida	0.1
5	J. Heflin	Iowa	0.1
8	Q. Bohanna	Kentucky	0.0

Sack Expected Points Added Per Game

Rk	Player	School	EPA/G
1	B. Brown III	Texas A&M	-1.0
2	T. Togiai	Ohio State	-0.6
3	K. Tonga	BYU	-0.4
4	R. Lopez	Arizona	-0.2
4	T. Slaton	Florida	-0.2
4	J. Heflin	Iowa	-0.2
7	A. McNeill	NC State	-0.1
8	Q. Bohanna	Kentucky	0.0

Tackles For Loss Per Game

Rk	Player	School	TFL/G
1	R. Lopez	Arizona	0.8
1	B. Brown III	Texas A&M	0.8
3	T. Togiai	Ohio State	0.6
4	A. McNeill	NC State	0.4
4	J. Heflin	Iowa	0.4
6	T. Slaton	Florida	0.3
6	Q. Bohanna	Kentucky	0.3
8	K. Tonga	BYU	0.2

Tackle For Loss EPA Per Game

Rk	Player	School	EPA/G
1	R. Lopez	Arizona	-1.2
2	A. McNeill	NC State	-1.0
2	T. Togiai	Ohio State	-1.0
4	T. Slaton	Florida	-0.5
5	Q. Bohanna	Kentucky	-0.4
6	B. Brown III	Texas A&M	-0.3
6	J. Heflin	Iowa	-0.3
8	K. Tonga	BYU	0.0

Forced Bounce Rate

Rk	Player	School	Bounce%
1	A. McNeill	NC State	49%
2	Q. Bohanna	Kentucky	45%
3	B. Brown III	Texas A&M	41%
4	T. Togiai	Ohio State	40%
5	K. Tonga	BYU	32%
6	T. Slaton	Florida	30%
7	R. Lopez	Arizona	21%
8	J. Heflin	Iowa	20%

Adjusted Tackle Depth Plus

Rk	Player	School	ATD+
1	Q. Bohanna	Kentucky	168
2	B. Brown III	Texas A&M	157
3	R. Lopez	Arizona	154
4	A. McNeill	NC State	138
5	J. Heflin	Iowa	115
6	T. Slaton	Florida	95
7	T. Togiai	Ohio State	89
8	K. Tonga	BYU	72

Alim McNeill

Report by John Todd

School	Height	Weight	Year	Jersey #	Hometown
NC State	6016 E	320 E	3JR	29	Raleigh, NC

One Liner
McNeill is a trench-bound nightmare for offensive centers, offering the lower-body strength to anchor and drive as well as fast hands off the snap that compromise blockers from the jump.

Overall
Alim McNeill played exclusively a 0-tech non-shaded nose tackle in NC State's 3-down front. He played in 36 career games with 19 starts. He's a wide body with a thick lower half ideally suited for his role. A former high school linebacker, short yardage running back, and even outfielder, he's solidly athletic for his size but is not fast or shifty by any means. He's a very difficult handle in the trenches and will give multiple efforts, but his range and motor beyond that is lacking.

Run Game
McNeill is a massive interior presence, but the combination of his hands and lower-body strength is what makes him so challenging to control. Immediately off the snap he's consistently the first to contact, shooting his hands into the center's chest and winning the leverage battle right away. From there, he does a great job of reading and feeling blocking schemes and angles and quickly adjusting his body to the flow. Against single coverage, he manipulates left and right before shedding at will. Against double teams, he possesses tremendous lower-body strength to seldom give ground, fully occupying the interior's attention. And as a one-gapper, he's flashed the ability to rip or swim and get skinny upfield. He has the leg drive to disrupt backfields and create chaos for his teammates to clean up. He's a sound tackler in close quarters but his tackling range is limited when backs have escape routes. McNeill is a fantastic physical mismatch who requires a quick-handed center and multiple bodies to contain. He can redirect some outside zone runs before they extend, but he doesn't offer much impact outside the tackles, conserving his energy for the trenches.

Pass Game
McNeill saw plenty of pass rush reps outside of two-minute situations and was not restricted to just early down duty. However, extended drives or third and longs after two run stops often resulted in passive rush reps. When his stamina was running, he showed valuable pocket-collapsing power and a decent repertoire of moves. He needs to refine the rush technique in his hands and lessen his number of finesse attempts, which saw occasional success surprising opponents bracing for his mass but didn't strike the same fear as his bull rush. He does do a good job of chopping his feet to the quarterback and keeping constant pressure on blockers when invested, but he needs to keep his stamina up to limit the line of scrimmage stalemate and spy reps.

Last Word
McNeill projects as a very solid starting three-down nose tackle at the next level. He's scheme-versatile, offering the anchor strength to dominate double teams and enough upfield disruptiveness to one-gap across the interior. However, his best position is head up over centers where he has immediate access to first contact and requires extra attention to handle, freeing up his teammates. His impact outside of that may be somewhat limited, and his snaps should be managed for maximum energy, but he excels at his role and should be a headache for opposing interiors in the league.

Strengths

- Hand-shooting off the snap
- Lower-body strength
- Blocking-scheme diagnosis

Weaknesses

- Stamina for passing downs
- Agility and range
- Rush plan

Critical Factors

Anchor / Play Strength	Mismatch	Body Control
7	7	6

Positional Factors

Pass Rush	On-Ball Impact	Disruption
5	5	7
Range	Hand Use	FBI
4	7	7
Tackling	Stamina	Toughness
5	5	6

Basic

Year	G	GS	Tackling			Pass Rush					
			Tackles	TFL	FF	Sacks	Hurries	Hits	KD	Pressures	Deflected
2018	13	1	22	6.5	1	3.5	9	6	2	13	3
2019	12	8	28	7.5	0	5.5	9	3	1	16	1
2020	11	10	27	4.0	1	1.0	8	6	1	11	1
	36	19	77	18.0	2	10.0	26	15	4	40	5

Advanced

Year	Tackling				Impact				
	Broken Tackles	BT%	Tackle Share	ATD+	Pres%	Pres Share	Holds Drawn	EPA on TFL	EPA on Sacks
2018	0	0%	3%	136	6%	6%	0	-9.5	-5.9
2019	6	18%	3%	121	6%	9%	1	-2.7	-9.1
2020	0	0%	3%	138	4%	6%	2	-10.9	-0.9
	6	7%	3%	132	6%	7%	3	-23.1	-16.0

Deep Dive

Year	Lined Up			Pass Rush		When Run At		Total Points			Total Points Rtg		
	NT%	DT%	DE%	Sack%	True Pres%	Bnc%	Pos%	Run Def	Pass Rush	Total	Per Run	Per PR	Per Play
2018	14%	75%	12%	1.5%	7%	19%	48%	9	6	19	97	73	89
2019	91%	7%	1%	2.2%	7%	33%	41%	11	3	14	85	63	72
2020	91%	7%	1%	0.4%	4%	49%	30%	19	-2	25	98	53	82
	68%	27%	4%	1.4%	6%	38%	37%	39	7	58	-	-	-

Tommy Togiai

Report by Nathan Cooper

School	Height	Weight	Year	Jersey #	Hometown
Ohio State	6016 E	300 E	3JR	72	Pocatello, ID

One Liner
Togiai has the overall strength, explosiveness, and disruptiveness to be a mismatch on the interior at the next level, though he'll need to get quicker laterally and improve his balance to maximize his full ability.

Overall
Tommy Togiai is a nose tackle with both one- and two-gapping responsibilities in Ohio State's base 4-3 defense. He played in 34 games for the Buckeyes, starting 7 of them, all of which came in 2020. He has a big frame with good size for the position. He's a good athlete for his size and plays hard with toughness and competitiveness.

Run Game
Against the run, Togiai is strong at the POA. He fires off the ball with good explosion, strength, and 1st step length to create a new line of scrimmage. He isn't extremely quick getting laterally down the line, but he shows good strength and mobility and rarely gets pushed well off his base. He doesn't have outstanding range, so he's more of a box player, though his pursuit and motor allows him to get to ballcarriers near the numbers. Against doubles, he will get pushed off his spot occasionally, but has the strength and power to hold his ground and at least create a stalemate. When runs come his way, he's willing to do the dirty work. He will stick his nose in and hold his ground to force cutback lanes or allow his teammates to swarm and make the play. He beats up interior offensive lineman with strong, heavy hands and overall power. He has the endurance to hold up for entire drives, putting his body on the line play after play. When he gets in on tackles, ballcarriers rarely are able to slip through his grasp and get away.

Pass Game
Togiai brings good pass rush ability from the interior defensive line position. He shows that he can use finesse moves by firing off the ball with quickness to rip through gaps to the backfield, but can also use power by using his strength to bull rush and walk blockers back into the lap of the quarterback. In addition, he shows counter moves, such as push-pulls, and was part of a variety of stunts and games to collapse the pocket from the outside. Quick and heavy hands allow him to get a good initial punch into the chest of blockers to give him the edge early on in the play. When stunting, he usually stands too upright and is too high at the POA, allowing blockers to easily neutralize him or knock him off balance. He's likely not someone that needs to be accounted for, but goes on streaks where he can consistently get into the backfield and pressure the passer with the occasional sack.

Last Word
Togiai projects best as a starting nose tackle in a 4-3 scheme where he's given both one- and two-gapping responsibilities. He also possesses the skill set to work in at 3-technique or as a 5-technique in a 3-4. On 3rd down, his explosiveness and strength will allow him to get a push from the interior against guards and centers.

Strengths

- Play strength
- Disruptive
- Mismatch ability

Weaknesses

- Some balance concerns
- Adequate range

Critical Factors

Anchor / Play Strength	Mismatch	Body Control
7	6	5

Positional Factors

Pass Rush	On-Ball Impact	Disruption
6	6	6
Range	Hand Use	FBI
5	6	6
Tackling	Stamina	Toughness
6	6	6

Basic

Year	G	GS	Tackling			Pass Rush					
			Tackles	TFL	FF	Sacks	Hurries	Hits	KD	Pressures	Deflected
2018	13	0	9	1.5	0	0.0	2	2	2	2	0
2019	14	0	17	1.0	0	0.0	3	2	1	4	1
2020	7	7	25	4.0	1	2.5	13	8	1	19	2
	34	7	51	6.5	1	2.5	18	12	4	25	3

Advanced

Year	Tackling				Impact				
	Broken Tackles	BT%	Tackle Share	ATD+	Pres%	Pres Share	Holds Drawn	EPA on TFL	EPA on Sacks
2018	0	0%	1%	156	3%	1%	0	-4.9	0.0
2019	1	6%	2%	135	4%	2%	0	-2.1	0.0
2020	1	4%	5%	89	11%	10%	0	-6.8	-4.3
	2	4%	2%	118	7%	4%	0	-13.8	-4.3

Deep Dive

Year	Lined Up			Pass Rush		When Run At		Total Points			Total Points Rtg		
	NT%	DT%	DE%	Sack%	True Pres%	Bnc%	Pos%	Run Def	Pass Rush	Total	Per Run	Per PR	Per Play
2018	74%	25%	0%	0.0%	3%	36%	27%	3	2	5	99	79	94
2019	63%	36%	1%	0.0%	4%	43%	26%	8	4	14	94	80	90
2020	47%	51%	3%	1.4%	11%	40%	30%	11	10	24	99	93	98
	58%	40%	2%	0.7%	8%	41%	28%	22	16	43	-	-	-

Tyler Shelvin

Report by Alec Mallon

School	Height	Weight	Year	Jersey #	Hometown
LSU	6016 E	346 E	4JR	72	Lafayette, LA

One Liner
Shelvin's sheer size and strength will get him on the field as a line-anchoring fire hydrant, but his inability to shed blockers and range or rush the passer will limit his usage.

Overall
Tyler Shelvin is a nose tackle for the LSU Tigers. He played in 21 games over his 2 year career in Baton Rouge, starting 14 during their National Championship run in 2019. He had ankle surgery prior to the 2018 season. Additionally, he opted out of the 2020 season to prepare for the NFL draft. A former five-star recruit, Shelvin has massive size but very limited athletic ability. He showed impressive stamina for a player his size and good toughness to battle in the trenches for four quarters, but he does not possess a motor outside of his immediate assignment.

Run Game
In the run game, Shelvin can be truly dominant at times. His biggest asset is his size and anchor strength, as he is not easily moved off the ball. He executes as a two-gapper from 0 and 1 techniques very well. He draws double teams consistently and does a great job of holding his ground and keeping the line of scrimmage. He sufficiently stacks centers and braces for contact well from other angles. He does not shed blocks well, nor does he show much vertical leg drive to attack. By holding onto double teams and eating interior attention, he allows his teammates around him to stay clean, fill gaps, and make plays. Shelvin does not have the lateral quickness to flow with stretch and outside runs, and he's fairly easily reached with limited snap explosion. He cannot be expected to make plays on the ball outside of the tackles. He's very strong and is very willing to take on blocks and create congestion in the middle, disrupting blocking schemes and hindering interior runs. However, he doesn't have the technique or burst to create negative plays on his own upfield.

Pass Game
Shelvin does not offer much in the passing game from his nose tackle role. His strength often requires help from guards to double team and keep him in check, but he isn't a consistent pocket pusher. He is freed up as a pass rusher more from a 3-technique role and flashes a powerful bull rush one-on-one, but he lacks any kind of rush repertoire or range to pursue.

Last Word
Shelvin projects as a scheme-specific very solid two-down starting nose tackle. For teams that deploy three-man fronts and are looking for true two-gapping space eaters, he'll be well regarded. However, he does not offer passing down or alignment versatility, and his range and athletic abilities limit his ceiling. Some teams won't have a use for his old-school skill set, but those that do, he'll execute his role soundly.

Strengths
- Anchor and lower-body strength
- Mass

Weaknesses
- Range beyond his gaps
- Block shedding
- Pass rush ability

Critical Factors

Anchor / Play Strength	Mismatch	Body Control
7	5	5

Positional Factors

Pass Rush	On-Ball Impact	Disruption
4	4	6
Range	Hand Use	FBI
3	5	5
Tackling	Stamina	Toughness
4	6	6

Basic

Year	G	GS	Tackles	TFL	FF	Sacks	Hurries	Hits	KD	Pressures	Deflected
2018	6	0	9	1.5	0	1.5	2	1	0	4	0
2019	15	14	37	2.5	0	0.0	7	3	0	7	1
	21	14	46	4.0	0	1.5	9	4	0	11	1

Advanced

Year	Broken Tackles	BT%	Tackle Share	ATD+	Pres%	Pres Share	Holds Drawn	EPA on TFL	EPA on Sacks
2018	1	10%	1%	50	6%	2%	0	0.0	-3.3
2019	3	8%	4%	93	2%	3%	0	-4.5	0.0
	4	8%	3%	88	3%	2%	0	-4.5	-3.3

Deep Dive

Year	NT%	DT%	DE%	Sack%	True Pres%	Bnc%	Pos%	Run Def	Pass Rush	Total	Per Run	Per PR	Per Play
2018	95%	5%	0%	2.3%	9%	40%	33%	2	3	5	66	82	74
2019	84%	16%	0%	0.0%	4%	45%	32%	19	1	21	98	58	81
	86%	14%	0%	0.4%	5%	44%	33%	21	4	26	-	-	-

Khyiris Tonga

Report by Blake Moore, Luke DeCello, & DJ Marquardt

School	Height	Weight	Year	Jersey #	Hometown
BYU	6032 E	321 E	4SR	95	West Valley, UT

One Liner
Tonga is a large, physical presence along the interior with impressive athletic ability relative to his size, but while he has skills that translate to multiple schemes, he isn't a perfect fit in any one system.

Overall
Khyiris Tonga is a nose tackle in BYU's three-man front. He played in 50 games through his collegiate career, starting in 32 of them. He has lined up anywhere from guard to guard across the interior in his career. He underwent back surgery prior to the 2018 season. He has broad shoulders and overall massive size but, as a former rugby player, impressive movement skills and pursuit ability. He's a very tough competitor who gives good effort to all areas, even if he isn't the most nimble athlete in space.

Run Game
Tonga is a strong interior run defender. He has good upper-body strength and length to create separation from blockers that allows him to read plays and shed in close. He can manipulate single blockers two ways easily. He needs to improve his anchor strength to more frequently anchor against double teams, however. He does a solid job of absorbing contact from different angles, but he can be driven and knocked off balance at times against two opponents. Tonga's height makes it difficult to play with consistent pad level. He is a physical mismatch when left alone against centers. He struggles to work through lateral run plays and hold the line of scrimmage horizontally. He's shown to be difficult to handle as an upfield one-gapping disruptor and can clog blocking schemes with his size and attacking nature. He gives good effort to pursue but while athletic for his size, still can't keep up with ballcarriers to range outside the tackles and make plays. He's a sufficient tackler inside and can swallow blocks and plug gaps with his length.

Pass Game
As a pass rusher, Tonga has shown solid get-off and can explode between gaps and through solo blockers. He mostly utilizes a bull rush with his massive momentum behind him, but he also has good hand strength to throw linemen around. His height again makes it difficult to brace against different angles and win the leverage battle, but it also allows him to get his hands into passing lanes very well. He works hard to give multiple efforts and chase, but without more refined rush techniques he's limited to physical rush attempts or sitting back to try to spy.

Last Word
Tonga projects well as either a true 3-4 nose tackle or a 1-technique in a 4-3 front, but he will have difficulties in both and should be kept over centers. He eats up space well and requires a lot of interior attention in a system that asks him to take on double teams, but he needs to improve his anchor strength and pad level. He also flashes some real chaos-producing explosion as an upfield penetrator, but his relative agility and quickness isn't special given his size. He'll need to improve as a technical pass rusher to see regular time on third downs, but he offers a versatile skill set as a big-bodied interior defender, and even special teams ability for forward-thinking coordinators.

Strengths
- Size mismatch
- Upfield disruption
- Movement skills for size

Weaknesses
- Pad level
- Consistent anchor strength
- Range

Critical Factors

Anchor / Play Strength	Mismatch	Body Control
6	6	5

Positional Factors

Pass Rush	On-Ball Impact	Disruption
5	6	6
Range	Hand Use	FBI
4	5	5
Tackling	Stamina	Toughness
5	6	6

Basic

Year	G	GS	Tackling			Pass Rush					
			Tackles	TFL	FF	Sacks	Hurries	Hits	KD	Pressures	Deflected
2017	13	2	19	4.0	1	2.0	3	2	2	6	2
2018	13	8	29	4.5	0	2.0	10	6	3	15	2
2019	13	11	50	4.0	0	1.0	9	4	1	10	3
2020	11	11	38	2.5	1	2.5	11	7	1	15	4
	50	32	136	15.0	2	7.5	33	19	7	46	11

Advanced

Year	Tackling				Impact				
	Broken Tackles	BT%	Tackle Share	ATD+	Pres%	Pres Share	Holds Drawn	EPA on TFL	EPA on Sacks
2017	3	14%	2%	-	-	5%	0	-5.7	-2.9
2018	0	0%	4%	113	7%	9%	1	-3.9	-4.8
2019	1	2%	6%	71	4%	7%	0	-4.8	-1.2
2020	2	5%	5%	72	6%	9%	0	0.0	-4.0
	6	4%	4%	81	6%	8%	1	-14.3	-12.9

Deep Dive

Year	Lined Up			Pass Rush		When Run At		Total Points			Total Points Rtg		
	NT%	DT%	DE%	Sack%	True Pres%	Bnc%	Pos%	Run Def	Pass Rush	Total	Per Run	Per PR	Per Play
2018	48%	50%	1%	0.9%	7%	39%	48%	8	5	16	78	68	75
2019	66%	29%	5%	0.4%	3%	33%	43%	9	3	16	77	62	72
2020	62%	36%	2%	1.0%	8%	32%	44%	7	8	20	73	74	79
	59%	37%	3%	0.8%	6%	34%	45%	24	16	52	-	-	-

Roy Lopez

Report by John Todd

School	Height	Weight	Year	Jersey #	Hometown
Arizona	6005 E	318 E	5SR	51	Tempe, AZ

One Liner

Lopez needs improved consistency against the run, but his combination of violent hands and flexible anchor strength should make for a versatile interior presence.

Strengths: Violent, powerful hands; Rush repertoire; Mobility and stamina
Weaknesses: Visioning ballcarriers when engaged; Run lane recovery; Consistent attacking mindset

Roy Lopez was a nose tackle for Arizona's 3-down base front in 2020, after playing mostly 3-technique in his 4 years at New Mexico State. He played in 45 games for the 2 programs with 40 starts. He suffered a lower-leg injury in the 2019 season opener and medically redshirted before transferring to Arizona for his final season. He's stout but not massive with good mobility and flexibility. He has a hot motor within the box and showed impressive stamina at NMST where he rarely ever left the field.

Lopez's lower-body strength to anchor was an issue early in his career but has become much improved. He's done a better job of sustaining against double teams and eating contact from different angles moving to nose. He plays with sound leverage and a flat back off the snap. He struggles to recover his run lanes after losing positioning and has issues finding the ball when engaged. However, as a former state champion wrestler, Lopez has great hand use and upper-body strength to manipulate and discard single blockers. He can get in a groove eating double teams and lose his upfield aggression and attacking mindset. His tackling range is inconsistent, but he has the pop at contact and athleticism to make plays on the ball.

When single covered, Lopez flashes dominance as a pass rusher, especially when bumped out over a guard. He works head slaps, swims, push-pulls, and swipe moves all based around the severe violence in his hands, occasionally embarrassing opponents. He didn't show this same proficiency at Arizona rushing from 0-tech with multiple pairs of eyes on him, but the flashes of grip strength and punch power were still there. He was more passive as a stunter at NMST, but when turned loose one-on-one he showed the hand quickness and agility to win.

Lopez projects as a scheme- and alignment-versatile reserve interior lineman in the NFL. He'll be energized working in a rotation with some variety in his roles, from space-eater to upfield disruptor to pass rusher, ideally in a shifting defensive front that lets him work from different angles.

Year	G	GS	Tackling			Pass Rush					
			Tackles	TFL	FF	Sacks	Hurries	Hits	KD	Pressures	Deflected
2016	11	7	21	0.5	0	0.0	2	1	0	2	0
2017	13	13	37	4.5	0	2.0	22	12	3	26	3
2018	12	12	60	12.0	1	4.0	15	5	2	20	1
2020	5	5	18	4.0	0	1.0	2	3	0	4	0
	45	40	147	23.5	1	9.0	50	23	5	63	4

Year	Tackling				Impact				
	Broken Tackles	BT%	Tackle Share	ATD+	Pres%	Pres Share	Holds Drawn	EPA on TFL	EPA on Sacks
2016	2	9%	2%	-	-	2%	0	-0.9	0.0
2017	5	12%	4%	-	-	12%	3	-3.9	-3.3
2018	8	12%	6%	116	6%	13%	7	-14.7	-8.3
2020	3	14%	5%	154	4%	15%	1	-6.2	-0.8
	19	11%	4%	124	10%	10%	11	-26.8	-15.6

Year	Lined Up			Pass Rush		When Run At		Total Points			Total Points Rtg		
	NT%	DT%	DE%	Sack%	True Pres%	Bnc%	Pos%	Run Def	Pass Rush	Total	Per Run	Per PR	Per Play
2018	16%	63%	21%	1.2%	7%	25%	47%	12	8	21	58	68	63
2020	90%	10%	0%	1.1%	5%	21%	56%	7	0	6	81	55	67
	30%	55%	15%	1.3%	8%	27%	52%	22	11	34	-	-	-

Critical Factors	
Anchor / Play Strength	6
Mismatch	5
Body Control	5

Positional Factors	
Pass Rush	6
On-Ball Impact	6
Disruption	5
Range	5
Hand Use	7
FBI	5
Tackling	5
Stamina	7
Toughness	6

Redshirt season not shown but included in totals

Tedarrell Slaton

Report by Carter Hayden

School	Height	Weight	Year	Jersey #	Hometown
Florida	6042 E	340 E	4SR	56	Fort Lauderdale, FL

One Liner

Slaton needs to become more of a consistent force up front by improving his block shedding and pad level, but his strength and high motor should put him in a position to be a rotational interior defensive lineman at the next level.

Strengths: Block eater; Play strength; High motor
Weaknesses: Block shedding; Range; Pass rush repertoire

Tedarrell Slaton plays nose tackle in Florida's 3-3-5 defense where he mainly 2-gaps and occasionally kicks out to 3-tech. He started 14 of 45 games for the Gators. He came to Florida as a highly recruited OL, but was quickly flipped to the DL. Slaton has a big body with very good size to eat up space and he's a tough competitor who plays with a high motor to the whistle.

In the run game, Slaton has shown flashes of excellence, though inconsistent. When he's able to create first contact and keep his pad level/leverage low, he wins most battles. He flashes a strong initial punch and can be a handful to move. When he's late with his hands or his pad level rises, it leaves him susceptible to being washed by double teams. He can eat up blocks and get to the right gap, but struggles to disengage. He has mediocre range, but he can get where he needs to be and will make the tackle more times than not if he can get his hands on the ballcarrier.

Although Slaton needs to improve his pass-rushing repertoire, he has shown the ability to be a disruptor in the backfield. He has a good swim/rip move that he wins with in 1-on-1 situations. He can also collapse the pocket with his strength using a bull rush. When he creates initial contact, he's able to win more battles than not. He has heavy hands, but again has difficulty shedding blockers. He usually doesn't win against doubles, but fights for stalemates. Though not incredibly productive on the stat sheet, he occasionally can get pressure on the quarterback and show some disruption.

Slaton projects as a nose tackle in any scheme who can 1-gap or 2-gap. Though best suited for 1st and 2nd down, if in on 3rd down, he should be able to use his strength and power against opposing centers to get a push into the pocket. He's shown tremendous flashes, but a lot of inconsistency.

			Tackling			Pass Rush					
Year	G	GS	Tackles	TFL	FF	Sacks	Hurries	Hits	KD	Pressures	Deflected
2017	11	0	11	1.5	0	0.0	2	1	0	3	0
2018	10	2	21	1.0	0	0.0	2	2	1	3	0
2019	12	0	29	4.0	0	2.0	8	6	3	11	1
2020	12	12	41	4.0	0	1.5	6	10	6	15	0
	45	14	102	10.5	0	3.5	18	19	10	32	1

	Tackling				Impact				
Year	Broken Tackles	BT%	Tackle Share	ATD+	Pres%	Pres Share	Holds Drawn	EPA on TFL	EPA on Sacks
2017	0	0%	2%	-	-	2%	0	-1.9	0.0
2018	1	5%	2%	85	4%	2%	0	-1.9	0.0
2019	1	3%	4%	148	9%	5%	1	-4.0	-4.5
2020	2	5%	5%	95	6%	7%	2	-5.6	-2.8
	4	4%	3%	108	7%	4%	3	-13.4	-7.2

	Lined Up			Pass Rush		When Run At		Total Points			Total Points Rtg		
Year	NT%	DT%	DE%	Sack%	True Pres%	Bnc%	Pos%	Run Def	Pass Rush	Total	Per Run	Per PR	Per Play
2018	7%	74%	19%	0.0%	4%	33%	52%	5	1	3	87	64	66
2019	48%	51%	0%	1.6%	10%	48%	33%	11	6	19	99	90	97
2020	48%	48%	5%	0.6%	5%	30%	53%	13	6	19	81	68	75
	39%	54%	6%	0.8%	6%	35%	48%	29	13	41	-	-	-

Critical Factors	
Anchor / Play Strength	6
Mismatch	5
Body Control	6

Positional Factors	
Pass Rush	5
On-Ball Impact	6
Disruption	5
Range	4
Hand Use	5
FBI	4
Tackling	6
Stamina	5
Toughness	7

Bobby Brown III

Report by Nathan Cooper

School	Height	Weight	Year	Jersey #	Hometown
Texas A&M	6032 E	325 E	3JR	5	Arlington, TX

One Liner

Brown has the strength and heavy hands to win with power as a rotational defensive lineman, but a high pad level, balance issues, and a lack of endurance will keep him from seeing the field on a consistent basis.

Strengths: Strong at the POA; Heavy hands
Weaknesses: Pad level too high; Struggles with balance; Lacks stamina

Bobby Brown III primarily plays nose tackle in Texas A&M's 3-3-5 defense lining up between 0- to 3-technique. He mainly one-gapped, but also two-gapped on occasion. He played in 35 career games, starting 18 of them for the Aggies. He missed a game in 2020 after injuring his knee celebrating a sack. He's a big body with very good size and build, but lacks some athleticism. He competes and plays with adequate toughness and a decent motor, but he lacks stamina late in games.

Against the run, Brown brings good strength to win at the POA. He isn't incredibly explosive out of his stance, but is powerful. His heavy hands shock offensive linemen and is able to use his strength and leg drive to get leverage and extension, though he doesn't consistently create a new LOS. He doesn't have great lateral strength, range, or balance to work down the line and make plays often, as he plays high and gets knocked off his base too easily. He uses his leg strength to anchor against doubles and neutralize them a majority of the time. He's willing to make plays against the run and has the strength to shed, he just doesn't have the intangibles to be a mismatch and consistently get to the ballcarrier.

Too often does Brown stand straight up out of his stance and try to use finesse moves to get into the backfield which results in him getting washed out of the play. When he uses power (bull rush, push-pull) as his primary move and then switches to finesse (swim, slither), he's much more effective. He has the strength and hand use to get into the chest of blockers and drive them back into the pocket. He produces by way of pressures more than sacks, though he improved that in 2020.

Brown projects as a backup nose tackle in a 3-4 scheme where he can play straight ahead and use his power mainly as a two-gapper. He has enough skill to work in a 4-3 as well, but doesn't warrant much of a look elsewhere. On 3rd downs, playing in a 0- or 1-technique should allow him to use his power and leverage to help collapse the pocket.

			Tackling			Pass Rush					
Year	G	GS	Tackles	TFL	FF	Sacks	Hurries	Hits	KD	Pressures	Deflected
2018	13	0	14	1.0	0	0.0	5	5	1	6	0
2019	13	10	21	2.5	0	1.5	6	6	1	11	2
2020	9	8	23	7.5	0	5.5	6	4	1	13	0
	35	18	58	11.0	0	7.0	17	15	3	30	2

	Tackling				Impact				
Year	Broken Tackles	BT%	Tackle Share	ATD+	Pres%	Pres Share	Holds Drawn	EPA on TFL	EPA on Sacks
2018	3	18%	2%	48	6%	3%	0	-1.0	0.0
2019	3	13%	3%	76	5%	5%	2	-1.2	-4.5
2020	3	12%	4%	157	7%	8%	4	-3.0	-8.9
	9	13%	3%	95	6%	5%	6	-5.2	-13.4

	Lined Up			Pass Rush		When Run At		Total Points			Total Points Rtg		
Year	NT%	DT%	DE%	Sack%	True Pres%	Bnc%	Pos%	Run Def	Pass Rush	Total	Per Run	Per PR	Per Play
2018	0%	4%	92%	0.0%	4%	35%	35%	5	5	10	86	89	87
2019	44%	53%	3%	0.7%	6%	37%	39%	10	6	18	81	76	80
2020	32%	66%	2%	3.2%	9%	41%	31%	12	8	20	97	86	92
	30%	46%	22%	1.4%	7%	38%	36%	27	19	48	-	-	-

Critical Factors	
Anchor / Play Strength	6
Mismatch	4
Body Control	4

Positional Factors	
Pass Rush	5
On-Ball Impact	5
Disruption	4
Range	5
Hand Use	6
FBI	6
Tackling	6
Stamina	4
Toughness	5

Quinton Bohanna

Report by Chad Tedder & Joe McDonald

School	Height	Weight	Year	Jersey #	Hometown
Kentucky	6032 E	357 E	4SR	95	Cordova, TN

One Liner

Bohanna is a big, explosive tackle who will see some snaps at the next level due to his size and strength, but his lack of speed and pass-rush consistency will keep him as a two-down rotational backup.

Strengths: Explosive off snap; Effective hands; Anchor
Weaknesses: Speed; Pass rush; 3rd-down ability

Quinton Bohanna is a nose tackle in Kentucky's 3-4/ 3-3-5 defense sometimes sliding to a 3-tech. He has been asked to play both 1-gap and 2-gap assignments and shown he can do both. He started 33 of 45 games for the Wildcats. He missed the first 3 games of 2020 with a knee injury. He is a massive, stout player, but shows quick bursts and powerful hands. He plays with power looking to cause disruption up the middle on every play.

Bohanna shows explosiveness off the snap and can occasionally shoot an inside gap or swim over the top of a lineman to get into the backfield. He uses his big frame to be a plug in the middle of the line. When asked to 1-gap, he shows the ability to flow with the play and maintain his gap, as well as to get across the face of the center to get into his gap first and drive into the backfield. He can also eat up some double teams and anchor down in his gap. Occasionally he can get driven off his gap relatively easily if he can't get there first. When asked to 2-gap, he shoots his

hands quickly to the center's pads, extends, and holds them at the LOS to read the rusher. He does a good job at keeping his arms outside to shed and make a tackle. Overall, he does lack the consistency to throw lineman around to present a mismatch at the POA.

Against the pass, Bohanna shows some of the same explosives, but lacks the speed to get around interior linemen. He can occasionally walk a center back into the quarterback, but not consistent enough. His rush attempts are often stifled by doubles, leading to low production numbers. He does do a good job at stacking and not allowing for the quarterback to escape through the middle.

Bohanna projects as a solid two-down backup nose tackle ideally playing in a 3-4 base defense, where he can 2-gap and anchor in the middle. With his lack of production in his pass rush, he will often be subbed out for a better pass rusher on 3rd-down packages.

			Tackling			Pass Rush					
Year	G	GS	Tackles	TFL	FF	Sacks	Hurries	Hits	KD	Pressures	Deflected
2017	12	5	14	0.0	0	0.0	4	2	2	4	0
2018	12	7	18	3.5	1	1.0	2	0	0	3	0
2019	13	13	18	3.0	0	1.0	4	0	0	5	1
2020	8	8	9	2.0	0	0.0	12	6	3	13	2
	45	33	59	8.5	1	2.0	22	8	5	25	3

	Tackling				Impact					
Year	Broken Tackles	BT%	Tackle Share	ATD+	Pres%	Pres Share	Holds Drawn	EPA on TFL	EPA on Sacks	
2017	0	0%	2%	-	-	2%	0	0.0	0.0	
2018	0	0%	2%	133	3%	1%	1	-7.7	-2.1	
2019	2	10%	3%	157	3%	3%	3	-2.1	-2.4	
2020	1	10%	1%	168	7%	9%	0	-2.9	0.0	
	3	5%	2%	150	5%	3%	4	-12.7	-4.4	

	Lined Up			Pass Rush		When Run At		Total Points			Total Points Rtg		
Year	NT%	DT%	DE%	Sack%	True Pres%	Bnc%	Pos%	Run Def	Pass Rush	Total	Per Run	Per PR	Per Play
2018	93%	6%	1%	1.1%	4%	48%	41%	11	2	13	99	64	98
2019	85%	13%	1%	0.6%	2%	38%	46%	12	4	16	90	63	79
2020	88%	12%	0%	0.0%	8%	45%	36%	7	5	14	89	71	82
	88%	11%	1%	0.4%	5%	44%	41%	30	9	43	-	-	-

Critical Factors	
Anchor / Play Strength	6
Mismatch	5
Body Control	5

Positional Factors	
Pass Rush	4
On-Ball Impact	5
Disruption	5
Range	5
Hand Use	6
FBI	6
Tackling	6
Stamina	5
Toughness	6

Jack Heflin

Report by Colin Schappert & Noah Chang

School	Height	Weight	Year	Jersey #	Hometown
Iowa	6034 V	306 V	5SR	96	Prophetstown, IL

One Liner

Heflin has good body control and hand usage to win some battles at the LOS, but lacks explosiveness and consistency as a pass rusher to be much more than a rotational defensive lineman at the next level.

Strengths: Body control; Hand use; Strength at the POA
Weaknesses: Pass rush repertoire; Explosiveness; Mismatch ability

Jack Heflin is a defensive tackle in Iowa's 3-3-5/4-2-5 defense spending most of his time between 1- and 3-technique. He started 36 of 46 games in his career. He began his career at Northern Illinois before finishing at Iowa in 2020. He redshirted in 2016 because shoulder labrum surgery. Heflin is a stout built player with a thick frame. Heflin is physical and powerful, but not the most agile or reactive athlete. He plays hard and shows toughness in his game.

In the run game, Heflin's a sufficient anchor and can eat up double teams most of the time. He doesn't have an explosive 1st step to push the interior and create a new LOS, but is able to hold his ground with good body control and strength. He uses strong hands and leverage to bench press the blocker off him and disrupt the play by forcing the ballcarrier to bounce. He isn't going to bring much mismatch ability as he can win his 1-on-1 battles against weak competition, but struggles to make an impact against top competition. He's a reliable wrap-up tackler and has the ability to strike violently and deliver a blow.

Against the pass, Heflin isn't a consistent contributor as a pass rusher. He can create pressure using mainly his power and body control, but won't need to be accounted for. He lacks an explosive 1st step and doesn't have much of a pass rush repertoire. If the power move doesn't work, he's usually contained. He shows good hand usage to stalemate with his blocker, spy the quarterback as he's stepping up in the pocket, and then react quickly to make a play if he decides to scramble. He's relentless and whether he's stopped or not, he's at least competing to get to the quarterback.

Heflin projects as a middle-of-the road depth-level nose tackle in a 4-3 scheme who will contribute most on early downs. He'd do his best as a two-gapper where he can use his strength and extension to stack and shed blockers. If in on 3rd down, he can play as a 1- or 3-tech and use his power to get into the backfield.

Year	G	GS	Tackling Tackles	TFL	FF	Pass Rush Sacks	Hurries	Hits	KD	Pressures	Deflected
2017	13	13	9	1.0	0	0.0	7	6	4	9	0
2018	14	5	35	7.5	0	6.0	10	9	2	19	1
2019	11	11	32	8.5	3	3.0	21	17	6	28	0
2020	8	7	22	3.5	0	1.0	6	8	2	12	0
	46	36	98	20.5	3	10.0	45	40	14	69	1

Year	Tackling Broken Tackles	BT%	Tackle Share	ATD+	Pres%	Impact Pres Share	Holds Drawn	EPA on TFL	EPA on Sacks
2017	4	31%	1%	-	-	3%	0	-1.6	0.0
2018	2	5%	4%	95	6%	9%	4	-4.1	-10.5
2019	11	26%	5%	168	13%	18%	5	-8.1	-5.1
2020	1	4%	4%	115	8%	10%	0	-2.7	-1.3
	18	16%	3%	126	10%	8%	9	-16.5	-16.9

Year	Lined Up NT%	DT%	DE%	Pass Rush Sack%	True Pres%	When Run At Bnc%	Pos%	Total Points Run Def	Pass Rush	Total	Total Points Rtg Per Run	Per PR	Per Play
2018	20%	77%	3%	2.0%	7%	39%	29%	11	9	22	85	74	80
2019	4%	88%	6%	1.3%	14%	24%	35%	16	14	30	92	94	93
2020	36%	61%	2%	0.6%	6%	20%	40%	7	3	10	73	66	70
	18%	77%	4%	1.5%	9%	28%	35%	34	26	62	-	-	-

Critical Factors	
Anchor / Play Strength	5
Mismatch	4
Body Control	6

Positional Factors	
Pass Rush	4
On-Ball Impact	5
Disruption	5
Range	5
Hand Use	6
FBI	5
Tackling	5
Stamina	5
Toughness	6

Redshirt season not shown but included in totals

Defensive Tackles

John Shirley

Defensive tackles in today's NFL need to be able to stop the run and generate interior pressure. Getting pressure up the middle is the quickest way to the quarterback and it takes away his ability to step up into the pocket and make a clean throw. Defensive tackles who can do this—while also being sufficient against the run—are rare.

During the 2020 NFL season, only nine defensive tackles ranked in the Top 15 in both Pass Rush Total Points and Run Defense Total Points. This list included a mix of veterans who are still elite and youth who are just now coming into their own. Among the veterans, we see that Akiem Hicks and Ndamukong Suh are still causing havoc eight and 10 years into their careers, respectively. On the youth side, second-year players Quinnen Williams and Ed Oliver started to realize their potential in 2020.

As good as those players were, there was still one name above the rest on the list. Aaron Donald has consistently been well above his peers when it comes to just about any metric, and Total Points is no different. In each of the five years Total Points has existed, Donald has ranked first among defensive tackles in both the counting version of the stat and on a per-play basis. During that time frame he has averaged 50 Total Points a season, with a low of 46 in 2019. The top Total Points season by a defensive tackle other than Donald? A two way tie between Fletcher Cox in 2018 and Akiem Hicks in 2016 with only 40.

Comparing any defensive tackle prospect to what Aaron Donald has accomplished is obviously unfair. A more reasonable comparison would be to more recent draft prospects, and not one of the best defensive linemen of all-time. When compared to the past two defensive tackle draft classes, the 2021 class probably falls somewhere well below the stacked 2019 class, which featured Williams and Oliver, and slightly above the 2020 class.

The 2019 draft class had nine defensive tackles graded at 6.7 or above, while the 2020 class had only two such players. The 2019 class also included the two highest rated prospects we've graded at the position, Williams (7.4) and Oliver (7.1). As mentioned above, this year's class falls somewhere in between the previous two, with five prospects graded at 6.7 or above, but only one prospect reaching a 6.8.

This year's class is the first in our three years of doing the *Handbook* to not have an elite prospect who graded at 7.0 or better. 2019 had the aforementioned Williams and Oliver, while 2020 had Derrick Brown (7.0). Similar to his 2019 counterparts, Brown was a Top-10 draft selection and has already flashed his potential in the NFL. During his rookie season, he ranked first among rookies and 18th among all defensive tackles with 21 Total Points. Fellow rookie and first-round pick Javon Kinlaw (6.8) also cracked the top 30 in Total Points among defensive tackles, ranking 26th with 16.

The 2021 class' top prospect is Christian Barmore from Alabama. His traits project him to be a strong starter in the NFL, and he also has the college production to back it up. In 2020, as a redshirt sophomore, he ranked first among all defensive tackles in Pass Rush Total Points Per Snap, Total Points Per Snap, and Total Points, with 15 more than second place. He also ranked first in Total Points Per Snap in 2019 as a redshirt freshman, though he was used sparingly and primarily as a pass rush specialist.

Of the four defensive tackles rated below Barmore with a grade of 6.7, only Iowa's Daviyon Nixon suited up in 2020. He had an impressive season for the Hawkeyes, as he showed solid traits and rated well by our metrics. He ranked 9th in Total Points among all defensive tackles, with 27.

The other three tackles who graded at 6.7, USC's Jay Tufele, Pittsburgh's Jaylen Twyman, and Washington's Levi Onwuzurike, all opted out of the 2020 season.

The 2021 defensive tackle class might not have the star power of previous years, but it offers some solid prospects and has decent depth. And at the top, Barmore has the tape, analytics, and the Alabama pedigree to back up his ranking as the best in the class.

DEFENSIVE TACKLE

Defensive Tackle Grading Scale

GRADE	DESCRIPTION
9.0 – 7.0	High-end 3 down starter. Pro Bowl level.
6.9 – 6.7	Strong starter who plays on all 3 downs.
6.6 – 6.5	Lower-end starter. 2 down player or plus pass rusher.
6.2	Versatile backup with positional flexibility.
6.1 – 6.0	Developmental. Top traits but needs time.
5.9	Top backup. 3 down, 1 position player.
5.8	Role playing backup. Base or 3rd down role.
5.7	Low-end backup.

Defensive Tackle Rankings

Rank	Name	Grade	Page
1	Christian Barmore	6.8	416
2	Daviyon Nixon	6.7	418
3	Levi Onwuzurike	6.7	420
4	Jay Tufele	6.7	422
5	Jaylen Twyman	6.7	424
6	Darius Stills	6.6	426
7	Dayo Odeyingbo	6.6	428
8	Osa Odighizuwa	6.5	430
9	Marvin Wilson	6.5	432
10	Marlon Tuipulotu	6.2	434
11	Malik Herring	6.2	435
12	Carlo Kemp	6.2	436
13	Isaiahh Loudermilk	5.9	437
14	Raymond Johnson III	5.9	438
15	Mustafa Johnson	5.9	439

Glossary

ATD+ (Adjusted Tackle Depth Plus)
ATD+ compares actual tackle depth to the expected tackle depth based on personnel, intended run gap, and the defender's pre-snap alignment. This figure is then scaled so that 100 is average. A figure of 110 indicates a player who is 10% better than average; a figure of 90 indicates a player who is 10% worse than average.

Bnc% (Forced Bounce Rate) (When Run At split)
The percentage of runs that didn't go through the designed gap.

BT% (Broken Tackle%)
Percentage of tackle attempts where the defender in position to make a tackle failed to bring down the ballcarrier. Counts both broken tackles (physical) and missed tackles (elusive).

Deflected
Plays where the defender either knocked a pass down or deflected a pass at the line of scrimmage.

Hits
Plays with meaningful contact made by the defender on the quarterback before or as he releases the football.

Hurries
Plays where the defender forced the QB to alter his throwing motion, leave the pocket, or rush his throw.

Knockdowns
Plays where the quarterback gets knocked down to the ground by the defender after he releases the football.

Pos% (Positive Percentage) (When Run At split)
The percentage of plays that result in a positive EPA for the offense. Lower numbers are better for defenders.

Pres% (Pressure Rate)
The percentage of pass rushes that resulted in a quarterback hurry, hit, knockdown, or sack.

Pres Share (Pressure Share)
Percentage of a team's individual pressures made by the defender.

Run At%
Percentage of carries where the defender was positioned in the designed gap.

Sack%
Percentage of pass rushes that resulted in a sack.

Tackle Share
Percentage of a team's tackles made by the defender.

Total Points
Sports Info Solutions' proprietary player value metric that uses an Expected Points framework and distributes the value gained or lost on a play to the players involved based on their impact on the play.

Total Points Rating
Total Points per play compared to average, scaled so that 50 is poor and 99 is excellent.

True Pres% (True Pressure Rate)
Pressure rate that isolates straight dropbacks which are more likely to be similar across situations.

Defensive Tackle Leaderboards

Total Points Per Game

Rk	Player	School	Tot Pts / G
1	C. Barmore	Alabama	3.8
1	I. Loudermilk	Wisconsin	3.8
3	D. Nixon	Iowa	3.4
4	D. Odeyingbo	Vanderbilt	3.1
4	O. Odighizuwa	UCLA	3.1
6	D. Stills	West Virginia	2.9
7	M. Herring	Georgia	2.8
8	M. Tuipulotu	USC	2.7
9	R. Johnson III	Georgia Southern	2.5
10	M. Johnson	Colorado	2.0

Total Points Rating Per Play

Rk	Player	School	Rating
1	C. Barmore	Alabama	99
2	M. Herring	Georgia	98
3	I. Loudermilk	Wisconsin	97
4	D. Odeyingbo	Vanderbilt	92
5	R. Johnson III	Georgia Southern	91
6	D. Nixon	Iowa	87
6	D. Stills	West Virginia	87
6	M. Tuipulotu	USC	87
9	O. Odighizuwa	UCLA	86
10	M. Wilson	Florida State	78

Pass Rush Total Points Per Game

Rk	Player	School	Tot Pts / G
1	C. Barmore	Alabama	2.1
2	D. Odeyingbo	Vanderbilt	1.8
3	M. Tuipulotu	USC	1.5
3	M. Herring	Georgia	1.5
5	O. Odighizuwa	UCLA	1.4
6	I. Loudermilk	Wisconsin	1.2
7	R. Johnson III	Georgia Southern	1.1
8	D. Nixon	Iowa	0.9
8	D. Stills	West Virginia	0.9
10	2 tied with		0.7

Total Points Rating Per Pass Rush

Rk	Player	School	Rating
1	C. Barmore	Alabama	99
2	M. Herring	Georgia	98
3	M. Tuipulotu	USC	95
4	D. Odeyingbo	Vanderbilt	94
5	R. Johnson III	Georgia Southern	87
6	I. Loudermilk	Wisconsin	84
7	O. Odighizuwa	UCLA	82
8	D. Stills	West Virginia	78
9	M. Wilson	Florida State	76
10	D. Nixon	Iowa	73

Run Defense Total Points Per Game

Rk	Player	School	Tot Pts / G
1	I. Loudermilk	Wisconsin	2.5
2	O. Odighizuwa	UCLA	1.7
3	D. Nixon	Iowa	1.6
3	D. Stills	West Virginia	1.6
5	R. Johnson III	Georgia Southern	1.5
6	C. Barmore	Alabama	1.3
6	D. Odeyingbo	Vanderbilt	1.3
8	M. Tuipulotu	USC	1.2
8	M. Johnson	Colorado	1.2
10	M. Herring	Georgia	1.1

Total Points Rating Per Run Snap

Rk	Player	School	Rating
1	C. Barmore	Alabama	99
1	I. Loudermilk	Wisconsin	99
3	M. Herring	Georgia	96
3	R. Johnson III	Georgia Southern	96
5	O. Odighizuwa	UCLA	94
6	D. Nixon	Iowa	91
7	D. Stills	West Virginia	90
8	M. Johnson	Colorado	89
9	D. Odeyingbo	Vanderbilt	88
10	M. Wilson	Florida State	82

Pressure Rate

Rk	Player	School	Pres%
1	R. Johnson III	Georgia Southern	13%
2	C. Barmore	Alabama	12%
2	D. Odeyingbo	Vanderbilt	12%
2	M. Herring	Georgia	12%
5	O. Odighizuwa	UCLA	8%
5	M. Tuipulotu	USC	8%
7	M. Wilson	Florida State	7%
7	C. Kemp	Michigan	7%
7	I. Loudermilk	Wisconsin	7%
10	M. Johnson	Colorado	6%

True Pressure Rate

Rk	Player	School	Pres%
1	R. Johnson III	Georgia Southern	16%
2	D. Odeyingbo	Vanderbilt	13%
2	M. Herring	Georgia	13%
4	C. Barmore	Alabama	12%
5	M. Tuipulotu	USC	11%
6	O. Odighizuwa	UCLA	8%
7	M. Wilson	Florida State	7%
7	I. Loudermilk	Wisconsin	7%
9	D. Nixon	Iowa	6%
9	2 tied with		6%

Pressures Per Game

Rk	Player	School	Pres/G
1	D. Odeyingbo	Vanderbilt	3.5
2	C. Barmore	Alabama	3.1
3	R. Johnson III	Georgia Southern	2.9
4	O. Odighizuwa	UCLA	2.7
5	M. Herring	Georgia	2.5
6	M. Johnson	Colorado	2.2
7	C. Kemp	Michigan	2.0
8	M. Tuipulotu	USC	1.8
8	I. Loudermilk	Wisconsin	1.8
10	D. Nixon	Iowa	1.6

Pressure Share

Rk	Player	School	Pres Share
1	D. Odeyingbo	Vanderbilt	27%
2	R. Johnson III	Georgia Southern	22%
3	O. Odighizuwa	UCLA	15%
4	C. Barmore	Alabama	14%
5	C. Kemp	Michigan	13%
5	M. Johnson	Colorado	13%
7	M. Herring	Georgia	12%
7	I. Loudermilk	Wisconsin	12%
9	D. Nixon	Iowa	11%
9	2 tied with		11%

Passes Deflected Per Game

Rk	Player	School	Defl/G
1	C. Barmore	Alabama	0.4
2	D. Nixon	Iowa	0.3
3	M. Herring	Georgia	0.2
3	I. Loudermilk	Wisconsin	0.2
5	D. Odeyingbo	Vanderbilt	0.1
5	R. Johnson III	Georgia Southern	0.1
7	D. Stills	West Virginia	0.0
7	O. Odighizuwa	UCLA	0.0
7	M. Wilson	Florida State	0.0
7	3 tied with		0.0

Holds Drawn

Rk	Player	School	Holds
1	D. Stills	West Virginia	6
2	O. Odighizuwa	UCLA	3
2	I. Loudermilk	Wisconsin	3
4	D. Nixon	Iowa	2
4	D. Odeyingbo	Vanderbilt	2
4	M. Tuipulotu	USC	2
4	M. Herring	Georgia	2
4	R. Johnson III	Georgia Southern	2
9	C. Barmore	Alabama	1
9	2 tied with		1

Sacks Per Game

Rk	Player	School	Sacks/G
1	C. Barmore	Alabama	0.7
1	D. Odeyingbo	Vanderbilt	0.7
3	D. Nixon	Iowa	0.6
3	O. Odighizuwa	UCLA	0.6
5	M. Johnson	Colorado	0.5
6	D. Stills	West Virginia	0.4
6	R. Johnson III	Georgia Southern	0.4
8	M. Tuipulotu	USC	0.3
8	C. Kemp	Michigan	0.3
8	I. Loudermilk	Wisconsin	0.3

Sack Expected Points Added Per Game

Rk	Player	School	EPA/G
1	M. Tuipulotu	USC	-1.4
2	D. Nixon	Iowa	-1.2
3	D. Odeyingbo	Vanderbilt	-1.1
3	O. Odighizuwa	UCLA	-1.1
5	C. Barmore	Alabama	-0.9
5	R. Johnson III	Georgia Southern	-0.9
7	M. Johnson	Colorado	-0.8
8	D. Stills	West Virginia	-0.6
9	C. Kemp	Michigan	-0.5
10	I. Loudermilk	Wisconsin	-0.4

Tackles For Loss Per Game

Rk	Player	School	TFL/G
1	D. Nixon	Iowa	1.3
2	D. Odeyingbo	Vanderbilt	1.2
3	R. Johnson III	Georgia Southern	1.1
4	O. Odighizuwa	UCLA	0.9
4	M. Johnson	Colorado	0.9
6	C. Barmore	Alabama	0.8
6	D. Stills	West Virginia	0.8
8	M. Tuipulotu	USC	0.6
9	M. Wilson	Florida State	0.5
10	2 tied with		0.4

Tackle For Loss EPA Per Game

Rk	Player	School	EPA/G
1	D. Nixon	Iowa	-1.4
2	R. Johnson III	Georgia Southern	-0.9
3	M. Johnson	Colorado	-0.8
4	D. Stills	West Virginia	-0.6
5	D. Odeyingbo	Vanderbilt	-0.4
5	O. Odighizuwa	UCLA	-0.4
5	M. Wilson	Florida State	-0.4
5	M. Tuipulotu	USC	-0.4
9	C. Barmore	Alabama	-0.3
9	2 tied with		-0.3

Forced Bounce Rate

Rk	Player	School	Bounce%
1	O. Odighizuwa	UCLA	45%
2	M. Tuipulotu	USC	42%
2	M. Herring	Georgia	42%
4	D. Stills	West Virginia	38%
5	M. Wilson	Florida State	36%
6	I. Loudermilk	Wisconsin	33%
7	R. Johnson III	Georgia Southern	31%
8	C. Kemp	Michigan	26%
9	D. Odeyingbo	Vanderbilt	25%
9	M. Johnson	Colorado	25%

Adjusted Tackle Depth Plus

Rk	Player	School	ATD+
1	M. Johnson	Colorado	186
2	R. Johnson III	Georgia Southern	184
3	D. Stills	West Virginia	158
4	D. Nixon	Iowa	157
5	M. Herring	Georgia	153
6	I. Loudermilk	Wisconsin	114
7	M. Tuipulotu	USC	106
8	D. Odeyingbo	Vanderbilt	101
9	C. Barmore	Alabama	96
10	O. Odighizuwa	UCLA	80

Christian Barmore

Report by John Todd

School	Height	Weight	Year	Jersey #	Hometown
Alabama	6046 E	310 E	3SO	58	Philadelphia, PA

One Liner
Barmore is a bowling ball with the short-area quickness and physicality to dominate in an attacking scheme, but he needs continued reps on early downs to become a more reliable, well-rounded lineman.

Overall
Christian Barmore is a defensive tackle in Alabama's versatile four-man front, primarily lining up as a 3-technique. He played in 23 career games with only 6 starts. He's played under 40 percent of potential snaps in his 2 seasons in Tuscaloosa, initially earning time as a sub package interior pass rusher before growing into a more regular three-down rotation member as 2020 progressed. He's built like a tank up top, with broad shoulders and a barrel chest. He has a strong lower half and is fairly athletically cut given his mass. Barmore is an impressive mover for his size with intimidating closing speed. He's a physical presence in the trenches and lets the opposition know about it.

Run Game
Barmore's lack of experience is most evident in the run game, as the Crimson Tide coaching staff clearly preferred him on passing downs. When given upfield rush responsibility, he fires off fast and explodes into contact. His run anchor is hit and miss, especially laterally. He has the strength and flexibility to hold his ground against double teams sufficiently, but he can get washed when out-leveraged in the horizontal running game. He prefers to swim around blocks or cut behind into gaps, which results in highlights and missed gap assignments alike. When engaged, Barmore does a great job of stacking and locking out then shedding in the hole one-on-one, but he prefers beating up his blocker rather than staying patient and reading with his eyes. He plays with a good motor and has surprising build-up speed in space. He'll smother runners in the box and leave his feet to make plays on the ball outside his immediate range.

Pass Game
Barmore's skill set translates much more comfortably to his pass rush. When he's turned loose in obvious passing situations he's a bulldozer. He's shot out of a cannon off the snap and is tough to anchor against head-up. He executes within Alabama's constantly twisting front schemes well, but he's often utilized as the first stunter to attract attention and free up his teammates. These have given him opportunities to rush the arc and flash some bend off the edge but limit more advantageous chances for him inside. He's flashed superb agility at the point of attack to leverage compromised linemen as they brace for a bull rush. The quickness and violence in his hands shocks blockers and leads to easy manipulation. He has terrifying speed to close to the quarterback but despite his athleticism, he does have balance issues when contacted from the side and can get knocked off in passive rushes.

Last Word
Barmore is football young and has room to develop, but he projects as an interior force in the NFL and an immediate contributor on passing downs. He should be deployed as a one-gapping 3-technique and schemed as many opportunities to attack upfield against a solo guard as possible. The athleticism he displays at his size is exceptional and he has a desirable skill set to build upon.

Strengths

- Body type and athleticism
- One-on-one pass rush
- Energy and violence

Weaknesses

- Interior contact balance
- Run lane discipline
- Experience

Critical Factors

1st Step Explosion	Play Strength	Pass Rush
7	6	7

Positional Factors

Shed Ability	Hand Use	Body Control
6	6	5
Agility	Tackling	FBI
7	7	5
Discipline	Motor	Toughness
5	6	7

Basic

Year	G	GS	Tackling			Pass Rush					
			Tackles	TFL	FF	Sacks	Hurries	Hits	KD	Pressures	Deflected
2019	11	1	27	7.0	0	2.0	18	8	6	23	1
2020	12	5	37	9.5	3	8.0	24	16	8	37	5
	23	6	64	16.5	3	10.0	42	24	14	60	6

Advanced

Year	Tackling				Impact				
	Broken Tackles	BT%	Tackle Share	ATD+	Pres%	Pres Share	Holds Drawn	EPA on TFL	EPA on Sacks
2019	2	7%	3%	171	15%	10%	0	-6.8	-4.9
2020	4	10%	5%	96	12%	14%	1	-4.2	-10.6
	6	9%	4%	130	13%	12%	1	-11.0	-15.5

Deep Dive

Year	Lined Up			Pass Rush		When Run At		Total Points			Total Points Rtg		
	NT%	DT%	DE%	Sack%	True Pres%	Bnc%	Pos%	Run Def	Pass Rush	Total	Per Run	Per PR	Per Play
2019	16%	61%	22%	1.3%	17%	26%	42%	12	10	23	99	96	99
2020	19%	56%	25%	2.6%	12%	18%	27%	15	25	46	99	99	99
	18%	58%	24%	2.2%	13%	22%	34%	27	35	69	-	-	-

Daviyon Nixon

Report by Nathan Cooper

School	Height	Weight	Year	Jersey #	Hometown
Iowa	6021 E	305 E	4JR	54	Kenosha, WI

One Liner
Nixon has the explosion, strength, and shed ability to be an effective three-down starter in the NFL, though his lack of COD ability, agility, and stamina may keep him from hitting his potential.

Overall
Daviyon Nixon primarily one-gaps in a 1- through 3-technique for Iowa's 3-3-5/4-2-5 defense. After playing his freshman season at Iowa Western CC, he started 9 of 21 games the past 2 seasons for the Hawkeyes. He has a big, strong frame with very good size for the position. He's athletic and competes with toughness nearly every down. Although he rarely exits the game and plays with a high motor, he does lack some stamina as the game goes on.

Run Game
Against the run, Nixon is strong and explosive. Off the line, he shows good first step explosion and length, something he visibly improved from 2019 to 2020. He plays with good strength at the POA and also possesses lateral strength and mobility to get down the line of scrimmage. He uses heavy hands to gain leverage and extension on blockers to stack before shedding to get to the ballcarrier. He also possesses a strong, quick punch into the chest of offensive linemen. He has the smarts and intelligence to read the offensive line and find where the ballcarrier is headed on most occasions. He then shows the quickness to knife through gaps to get into the backfield, but lacks some agility to change directions with ease. When up against doubles, Nixon has the strength to neutralize most of them and rarely gets pushed off the line. When he gets to the ballcarrier, he will slip off of some tackles and lose out on some opportunities. However, when he makes the tackle, he delivers a blow to the rusher.

Pass Game
In the pass game, Nixon shows good pass rush ability. His explosion off the line allows him to get a step on blockers. He mainly uses bull and rip moves to get into the backfield, but will also swim and push-pull. He tries to use finesse moves more than power, though he seems to be more effective when using his strength to battle blockers and get to the quarterback. When hit from all angles, he still has the strength and body control to keep his base and plane getting to the backfield. He's been productive getting to the quarterback and producing sacks, but also gets pressures by way of hurries, hits, and knockdowns. He shows flashes of mismatch ability and should be accounted for when he's on the field.

Last Word
Nixon projects as a starting 3-technique in a 4-3 base defense with mainly one-gap responsibilities. Though he has room for improvement in his game, he has the skill set against both the run and pass to play on all three downs at the next level. On 3rd down, he fits best as a one-gapper who can line up at either 3- or 1-tech where he can use his explosion and strength to get a push into the pocket.

Strengths
- Plays with good extension & leverage
- Strong at POA
- Ability to stack & shed

Weaknesses
- Can struggle to change directions
- Slips off some tackles
- Loses stamina as game progresses

Critical Factors

1st Step Explosion	Play Strength	Pass Rush
6	6	6

Positional Factors

Shed Ability	Hand Use	Body Control
6	6	6
Agility	Tackling	FBI
5	5	6
Discipline	Motor	Toughness
6	6	6

Basic

Year	G	GS	Tackling			Pass Rush					
			Tackles	TFL	FF	Sacks	Hurries	Hits	KD	Pressures	Deflected
2019	13	1	28	5.5	0	3.0	14	9	5	17	1
2020	8	8	45	10.0	1	5.0	6	4	0	13	2
	21	9	73	15.5	1	8.0	20	13	5	30	3

Advanced

Year	Tackling				Impact				
	Broken Tackles	BT%	Tackle Share	ATD+	Pres%	Pres Share	Holds Drawn	EPA on TFL	EPA on Sacks
2019	4	13%	4%	113	7%	9%	1	-3.3	-4.0
2020	1	2%	8%	157	5%	11%	2	-11.5	-10.0
	5	6%	6%	140	6%	10%	3	-14.8	-14.0

Deep Dive

Year	Lined Up			Pass Rush		When Run At		Total Points			Total Points Rtg		
	NT%	DT%	DE%	Sack%	True Pres%	Bnc%	Pos%	Run Def	Pass Rush	Total	Per Run	Per PR	Per Play
2019	11%	75%	8%	1.3%	7%	40%	45%	7	5	13	95	67	77
2020	45%	52%	1%	2.1%	6%	18%	26%	13	7	27	91	73	87
	30%	62%	4%	1.7%	6%	26%	33%	20	12	40	-	-	-

Levi Onwuzurike

Report by Bryce Rossler

School	Height	Weight	Year	Jersey #	Hometown
Washington	6027 V	290 V	5SR	95	Allen, TX

One Liner
Onwuzurike is an athletic, slightly undersized three-down interior penetrator who wins thanks to first-mover advantage and has untapped pass rush upside.

Overall
Levi Onwuzurike is a defensive tackle in Washington's multiple defense. He primarily aligned as a nose in odd space fronts and as a 2- and 3-tech in even space fronts. He has played in 39 career games, starting 16 of them. He last played as a redshirt junior in 2019, as he opted out of the 2020 season. He has solid size for the position with an athletic cut. He demonstrates very good athleticism, showing the ability to change directions laterally in space, finesse his way through the trenches with quickness, and explode off the ball. He has good balance and flexibility to recover at awkward angles but has some overly frenetic moments he'll need to keep under control.

Run Game
In the run game, Onwuzurike does a good job of keying the snap and engaging blockers with great explosiveness and pad level. He gets hands on quickly, powerfully, and very accurately to win early control and constrict gaps against base blocks. His high-end lateral quickness and burst make it difficult for opposing linemen to reach him. He flashes the play strength to anchor versus double teams but has an inconsistent feel for pressure, limiting his effectiveness to stalemate. Onwuzurike is a skilled block shedder to make plays on the ball in his gap. His athleticism allows him to mirror ballcarriers in tight spaces and provide good pursuit range. He takes correct angles to the ball and is a good tackler but only shows a sufficient motor.

Pass Game
In the pass game, Onwuzurike demonstrates the ability to key high hats and explode off the ball low. He jolts with his hands and creates torque with his upper body strength, timing his strikes sufficiently. As a finesse rusher, he possesses a good repertoire of initial pass rush moves combined with his innate athleticism to threaten guards in one-on-one situations. As a bull rusher, he demonstrates sufficient power and ability to refit his hands and releverage himself late in the rep. Most of Onwuzurike's wins come early in the down and he has not shown a consistent ability to counter and win. Occasional out of control movements result in top-heavy reps playing too far over his feet. He functions as a looper well with his movement skills and lateral burst. He does a good job of diagnosing and reacting to screens and gives consistent effort throughout the game.

Last Word
Onwuzurike projects best as a 3-tech in an even spacing front at the NFL level. He played out of position at Washington; an inordinate number of 3-man rushes and reps into the half-slide capped his college production, but he has the requisite traits to be a quality interior pass rusher moving forward. He will need to improve his pass rush plan as a pro in order to maximize his athleticism and quick hands.

Strengths	Weaknesses
• Athleticism	• Feel vs doubles
• Hand use	• Pass rush counters
• Shed ability	• Uncontrolled movements as a rusher

Critical Factors

1st Step Explosion	Play Strength	Pass Rush
7	5	6

Positional Factors

Shed Ability	Hand Use	Body Control
6	6	6
Agility	**Tackling**	**FBI**
7	6	5
Discipline	**Motor**	**Toughness**
6	5	6

Basic

			Tackling			Pass Rush					
Year	G	GS	Tackles	TFL	FF	Sacks	Hurries	Hits	KD	Pressures	Deflected
2017	12	0	18	3.0	0	2.0	5	4	2	8	0
2018	14	4	29	5.0	0	3.0	20	6	4	23	0
2019	13	12	45	5.5	0	2.0	17	11	4	23	1
	39	16	92	13.5	0	7.0	42	21	10	54	1

Advanced

	Tackling				Impact					
Year	Broken Tackles	BT%	Tackle Share	ATD+	Pres%	Pres Share	Holds Drawn	EPA on TFL	EPA on Sacks	
2017	0	0%	2%	-	-	4%	0	-2.3	-2.4	
2018	1	3%	3%	102	13%	10%	2	-5.3	-5.1	
2019	3	6%	6%	99	9%	11%	3	-5.7	-3.8	
	4	4%	4%	100	12%	9%	5	-13.3	-11.3	

Deep Dive

	Lined Up			Pass Rush		When Run At		Total Points			Total Points Rtg		
Year	NT%	DT%	DE%	Sack%	True Pres%	Bnc%	Pos%	Run Def	Pass Rush	Total	Per Run	Per PR	Per Play
2018	41%	47%	9%	1.7%	17%	29%	44%	9	11	20	90	95	92
2019	45%	48%	6%	0.8%	10%	43%	43%	14	12	27	95	85	90
	43%	48%	7%	1.1%	13%	35%	43%	23	23	47	-	-	-

Jay Tufele

Report by Evan Butler

School	Height	Weight	Year	Jersey #	Hometown
USC	6015 E	310 E	4JR	78	Salt Lake City, UT

One Liner

Tufele is an explosive and athletic interior lineman with a hot motor to match, who will be a successful one-gapping defender as he continues to improve his anchor strength and refine his pass-rush upside.

Overall

Jay Tufele is primarily a 3-tech in USC's nickel defense. In his 2 seasons playing with the Trojans he played in 25 games, starting 18. He opted out of the 2020 season to focus on the upcoming draft. Tufele has a well-cut frame and great thickness in his lower half, but lacks length to consistently reach out and win first contact. He's a fluid mover and very athletic along the interior. He plays with a hot motor to pursue the ball to all areas of the field.

Run Game

In the run game, Tufele's athleticism shines through. He has the lateral agility and motor within the box to make plays along the line. He's able to diagnose and track well, especially against zone run schemes. Against power schemes, he's at his best shooting gaps with his explosiveness and ability to get skinny to knife into the backfield early. Tufele doesn't have the arm length to straight-arm or true anchor stoutness to eat up double teams in heavy traffic, but he's flexible enough to maneuver out of awkward angles. His pad level gets too high at times, which can wash him out of run lanes when one-gapping, and he's better at beating blocks before contact than shedding to disengage. He has fast and athletic hands which help make up for his lack of length. His great lower body strength is at its best attacking vertically to overpower blockers. His tackling range is decent but benefits from his pursuit skills.

Pass Game

In the pass game, Tufele's success comes from his first step explosion off the snap, leg drive, and athleticism to pressure the QB. His motor shines through as his feet are constantly moving. Tufele uses a quick swim move to decent success but has a limited repertoire outside of that. He does not counter when beaten on an initial attempt and resorts to pushing or pursuit. He can win with speed to narrow his strike zone and rush upfield. He has a good ceiling as a pass rusher, but he needs to improve his technique to have success beyond his energy and explosion.

Last Word

Tufele projects as starting-caliber one-gapping 3-technique at the next level. His athleticism, motor, and first step explosion will allow him to make an impact in all facets of the game while he refines his technique and consistency. He's more of an upfield, agile disruptor than a stout space eater and should be put in advantageous situations to reflect those skills.

Strengths

- Athleticism
- Explosion off the snap
- Motor

Weaknesses

- Pass rush repertoire
- High pad level and anchor strength
- Length and shedding ability

Critical Factors

1st Step Explosion	Play Strength	Pass Rush
7	6	6

Positional Factors

Shed Ability	Hand Use	Body Control
5	5	6
Agility	Tackling	FBI
7	5	6
Discipline	Motor	Toughness
5	7	6

Basic

Year	G	GS	Tackling			Pass Rush					
			Tackles	TFL	FF	Sacks	Hurries	Hits	KD	Pressures	Deflected
2018	12	5	23	5.5	0	3.0	13	5	2	17	0
2019	13	13	41	6.0	0	4.5	19	8	2	26	1
	25	18	64	11.5	0	7.5	32	13	4	43	1

Advanced

Year	Tackling				Impact				
	Broken Tackles	BT%	Tackle Share	ATD+	Pres%	Pres Share	Holds Drawn	EPA on TFL	EPA on Sacks
2018	2	8%	3%	148	6%	9%	0	-3.1	-3.9
2019	3	7%	5%	81	8%	11%	4	-2.9	-8.2
	5	7%	4%	104	7%	10%	4	-6.0	-12.1

Deep Dive

Year	Lined Up			Pass Rush		When Run At		Total Points			Total Points Rtg		
	NT%	DT%	DE%	Sack%	True Pres%	Bnc%	Pos%	Run Def	Pass Rush	Total	Per Run	Per PR	Per Play
2018	16%	77%	5%	1.1%	8%	60%	40%	7	6	14	69	68	68
2019	3%	95%	2%	1.3%	8%	31%	36%	15	9	25	87	73	79
	9%	87%	3%	1.2%	8%	39%	37%	22	15	39	-	-	-

Jaylen Twyman

Report by Jeff Dean & DJ Marquardt

School	Height	Weight	Year	Jersey #	Hometown
Pittsburgh	6015 E	290 E	4JR	97	Washington, DC

One Liner

Twyman has the quickness, hands, and pass rushing ability teams desire in interior defensive linemen, but he will need to polish up some technical aspects to his game and show more consistent effort to continually see all three downs at the NFL level.

Overall

Jaylen Twyman primarily plays 3-tech in Pittsburgh's base 4-3 defense, though he also saw a lot of time over the center as well. He started 14 of 26 career games, opting out of the entire 2020 season. Twyman is a good athlete who moves fluidly in space. He shifts his weight well laterally and has a strong base to withstand initial contact. He played the majority of snaps each game, but lacked effort as the play went on and didn't hustle to chase down players after attempting to win his initial battle.

Run Game

Twyman is active in the run game and has the strength to hold his gap at the line. He is more strong than explosive and doesn't fire off the snap. He has a wide base and strong hands to battle offensive linemen, though doesn't keep his hands active throughout the play. When he decides to use his hands, he can discard offensive linemen efficiently, without losing gap integrity. He moves down the line very well and can play outside of his area. He struggles against double teams and rarely wins those battles. He doesn't play angry which hinders some of his quick-twitch ability, but flashes the ability to disrupt the run game. His ability to get skinny on slants causes problems for the offensive line and he's a consistent tackler who may need a little help bringing down the ballcarrier, but rarely fails to finish a play.

Pass Game

Twyman has the strong hands and lateral movement to be a consistent disruptive force on the interior. He seems more comfortable in the 3-tech role, but reduced down to play over the center on passing downs. He has a solid first step, but doesn't fire out with force and it leaves something to be desired. He has strong hands that can swat away the offensive lineman's hands and the violent finish to leave them off-balance or on the ground. While he has the strength to win, he doesn't keep his hands active and they can get locked up by better offensive linemen. Twyman has a very good swim move who understands how to keep his balance to not give up ground. He has a developing swipe move, but lacks any other rush moves. He struggles to win later in the play and looks a little lost if his initial attempt fails. His quickness allows him to be effective with stunts and schemed up to be a more effective pass rusher.

Last Word

Twyman projects as a solid 3-down defensive tackle that fits best as a 3-technique in a 4-3 scheme that utilizes stunts. He is a solid run defender who shouldn't be a liability on early downs and has the potential to be a difference maker as a pass rusher. He can move inside on 3rd downs, but works better when given a little space.

Strengths

- Swim move
- Strong hands
- Lateral movement

Weaknesses

- Pass rush repertoire
- Handling double teams
- Late play effort

Critical Factors

1st Step Explosion	Play Strength	Pass Rush
5	6	6

Positional Factors

Shed Ability	Hand Use	Body Control
6	6	5
Agility	**Tackling**	**FBI**
6	6	5
Discipline	**Motor**	**Toughness**
6	5	5

Basic

Year	G	GS	Tackling			Pass Rush					
			Tackles	TFL	FF	Sacks	Hurries	Hits	KD	Pressures	Deflected
2018	13	1	16	1.5	0	0.5	11	8	1	12	0
2019	13	13	43	12.0	0	10.5	23	16	3	38	1
	26	14	59	13.5	0	11.0	34	24	4	50	1

Advanced

Year	Tackling				Impact				
	Broken Tackles	BT%	Tackle Share	ATD+	Pres%	Pres Share	Holds Drawn	EPA on TFL	EPA on Sacks
2018	2	11%	2%	107	8%	6%	0	-1.7	-1.5
2019	2	4%	6%	114	9%	15%	2	-3.0	-19.6
	4	6%	4%	111	9%	11%	2	-4.6	-21.0

Deep Dive

Year	Lined Up			Pass Rush		When Run At		Total Points			Total Points Rtg		
	NT%	DT%	DE%	Sack%	True Pres%	Bnc%	Pos%	Run Def	Pass Rush	Total	Per Run	Per PR	Per Play
2018	26%	71%	3%	0.3%	7%	35%	58%	7	7	14	87	87	87
2019	25%	62%	13%	2.6%	12%	32%	48%	11	19	31	77	86	83
	25%	64%	10%	2.0%	11%	33%	51%	18	26	45	-	-	-

Darius Stills

Report by Nathan Cooper

School	Height	Weight	Year	Jersey #	Hometown
West Virginia	6005 E	285 E	4SR	56	Fairmont, WV

One Liner
Stills is an explosive one-gapper that possesses the strength, heavy hands, and range to be a solid contributor at the next level, though issues with balance, gap control, and stamina may factor into how much time he'll see on the field.

Overall
Darius Stills is a nose tackle in West Virginia's primary 3-3-5 defense that slants a lot up front. He mainly plays in a 0 through 2i, but will also bump out to 3-tech every so often. He plays mostly as a one-gapper, but will two-gap occasionally. He played 43 games for the Mountaineers, starting in 21 of them. His father, Gary, played at West Virginia and then 9 seasons in the NFL. Additionally, his brother, Dante, is also currently a defensive lineman at WVU. He's an adequate athlete, though he competes and plays tough. He plays fast with an extremely high motor at all times, though stamina will slow him down some.

Run Game
Against the run, Stills shows good strength and power at the POA. He's not only strong, but also explosive. He doesn't two-gap too much, but when he does, he shows heavy hands with good placement, a strong punch, and plays with good leverage. When he gets his hands in good position, he is able to shed the blocker the majority of the time. When stamina factors in, he will struggle to get off blocks. Gap control can be an issue for him at times, as he will get pushed out of his gap or anticipate and jump to other gaps which opens up running lanes. He's able to get down the line laterally, but doesn't have great body control. He seems to play with his body out over his toes, so he falls off-balance too often. This also turns into missed tackle opportunities. When he does convert on tackles, Stills delivers a blow and makes sure the ballcarrier goes down. He shows good range and pursuit ability to run down plays from behind or once they get extended.

Pass Game
As a pass rusher, Stills is productive in both getting sacks and pressures on the quarterback. He possesses a very explosive first step and nearly always gains ground. He doesn't have the biggest repertoire of moves as most of the time he just attempts to dip and rip through the blocker, but he will also mix in some swims, spins, and bull rushes. His quickness and relentless attitude forces offensive linemen to hold him at a higher rate than most interior rushers. His heavy hands are apparent when getting into blockers, giving a jolt to knock them off balance with regularity. He's able to collapse the pocket with power and also get into the backfield using finesse moves. In addition, his high motor and no-quit attitude allows him to clean up on coverage sacks.

Last Word
Stills projects as a one-gapping 3-technique in a 4-3 defense at the next level. He was extremely productive in the limited time he bumped out to 3-tech at WVU. He could fit in as a 5-tech in an odd-front as well with his strength and hand use. On 3rd downs, he should be given one-gapping responsibilities over guards or the center where he can use his get-off to get to the passer.

Strengths
- Heavy hands
- Explosive 1st step
- Good range & pursuit ability

Weaknesses
- Some balance issues
- Loses gap control at times
- Stamina concerns

Critical Factors

1st Step Explosion	Play Strength	Pass Rush
7	6	5

Positional Factors

Shed Ability	Hand Use	Body Control
6	6	5
Agility	Tackling	FBI
5	5	6
Discipline	Motor	Toughness
5	7	6

Basic

Year	G	GS	Tackling			Pass Rush					
			Tackles	TFL	FF	Sacks	Hurries	Hits	KD	Pressures	Deflected
2017	9	0	1	0.0	0	0.0	2	0	0	2	0
2018	12	0	12	3.5	0	1.0	8	4	2	10	0
2019	12	11	43	12.5	1	6.0	31	18	10	38	1
2020	10	10	26	7.5	0	3.5	7	2	2	12	0
	43	21	82	23.5	1	10.5	48	24	14	62	1

Advanced

Year	Tackling				Impact					
	Broken Tackles	BT%	Tackle Share	ATD+	Pres%	Pres Share	Holds Drawn	EPA on TFL	EPA on Sacks
2017	0	0%	0%	-	-	1%	0	0.0	0.0
2018	1	8%	2%	157	6%	6%	1	-3.1	-1.3
2019	7	14%	5%	147	12%	22%	3	-10.2	-9.1
2020	2	7%	4%	158	5%	11%	6	-5.9	-5.9
	10	11%	3%	152	8%	10%	10	-19.2	-16.3

Deep Dive

Year	Lined Up			Pass Rush		When Run At		Total Points			Total Points Rtg		
	NT%	DT%	DE%	Sack%	True Pres%	Bnc%	Pos%	Run Def	Pass Rush	Total	Per Run	Per PR	Per Play
2018	90%	3%	4%	0.6%	8%	33%	42%	5	3	8	79	63	69
2019	77%	22%	1%	1.9%	13%	36%	38%	23	15	40	98	86	94
2020	55%	39%	5%	1.4%	6%	38%	44%	16	9	29	90	78	87
	72%	24%	3%	1.4%	10%	36%	41%	44	27	77	-	-	-

Dayo Odeyingbo

Report by Alec Mallon & Ryan Rubinstein

School	Height	Weight	Year	Jersey #	Hometown
Vanderbilt	6051 E	276 E	4SR	10	Irving, TX

One Liner

Odeyingbo is a dynamic and quick interior tackle with good hands and leg drive who needs to improve his strength and power at the LOS before making an impact on all three downs.

Overall

Dayo Odeyingbo plays defensive tackle for Vanderbilt in their nickel defense. He primarily lines up at a five technique, but is extremely effective when kicked inside, playing 3-tech and 0-tech. During his Vanderbilt career, Odeyingbo appeared in 44 games and started 29 of them. Odeyingbo suffered a torn Achilles tendon in January 2021 during training, forcing him to miss the Senior Bowl. He possesses a long frame with quickness inside to be an impact. He has a strong motor and is competitive on every play through the whistle.

Run Game

Against the run, Odeyingbo shows very good hands. He delivers a strong punch and continuously works his hands until he gets into a winning position. His long arms allow him to stack and shed opponents while keeping his eyes on the ball. He shows good explosiveness through blocks and can impact plays behind the LOS. In between the tackles, Odeyingbo displays his quickness with his first step. He routinely beats guards off the ball with his burst and uses his leg drive to force his way into the backfield. He can hold his own against guards and tackles in 1-on-1 situations, but when doubles come his way, he struggles to hold his ground. He's late recognizing blockers, and doesn't brace. He can be knocked off balance and taken out of plays, but does a good job of keeping his eyes up to find the ball and make plays down the field.

Pass Game

Odeyingbo is more efficient as a rusher inside, playing in a 3- or 0-technique. Off the ball, he uses his quickness to immediately get into the faces of guards and centers and move them off the ball. He has quick and powerful hands, which allows him to easily shed linemen and get into the face of the quarterback. When he fails to win with his quickness, he relies on his legs. His strong lower half and powerful leg drive allows for him to push the pocket into the lap of the quarterback. On the edge, Odeyingbo's first step is slow, almost as if he isn't watching the ball. His late start allows for tackles to get into the pass sets and dictate where he goes. His powerful lower half can be used to push the pocked outside, but lacks the secondary rush moves and technique to consistently win on the edge. He also doesn't have the pure speed and bend to turn the corner and be a successful edge rusher.

Last Word

Odeyingbo projects as a lower-end starter at the next level, fitting best as a 3-technique in an even front where he can use his quickness and athleticism to win inside as a one-gapper. His ability to rush the passer from the inside will give him the chance to see the field in obvious passing situations, like 3rd downs. He also has the skill set and versatility to kick down to 0 or out to a 5 in certain situations.

Strengths	Weaknesses
• Hand technique	• Secondary pass rush moves
• Power/leg drive	• Bend
• Quickness	• Anchor ability vs. doubles

Critical Factors

1st Step Explosion	Play Strength	Pass Rush
6	5	6

Positional Factors

Shed Ability	Hand Use	Body Control
6	7	5
Agility	Tackling	FBI
7	6	5
Discipline	Motor	Toughness
6	6	7

Basic

Year	G	GS	Tackling			Pass Rush					
			Tackles	TFL	FF	Sacks	Hurries	Hits	KD	Pressures	Deflected
2017	12	0	14	3.5	0	2.5	7	4	1	11	1
2018	12	10	28	6.5	1	2.5	16	9	4	21	1
2019	12	11	47	12.0	0	1.5	25	18	11	31	0
2020	8	8	32	9.5	1	5.5	16	12	6	28	1
	44	29	121	31.5	2	12.0	64	43	22	91	3

Advanced

Year	Tackling				Impact					
	Broken Tackles	BT%	Tackle Share	ATD+	Pres%	Pres Share	Holds Drawn	EPA on TFL	EPA on Sacks	
2017	1	7%	2%	-	-	6%	0	-1.8	-4.0	
2018	4	13%	3%	140	9%	12%	1	-5.1	-4.4	
2019	6	11%	6%	118	11%	22%	4	-16.0	-3.8	
2020	5	14%	5%	101	12%	27%	2	-3.5	-8.8	
	16	12%	4%	118	11%	15%	7	-26.4	-21.0	

Deep Dive

Year	Lined Up			Pass Rush		When Run At		Total Points			Total Points Rtg		
	NT%	DT%	DE%	Sack%	True Pres%	Bnc%	Pos%	Run Def	Pass Rush	Total	Per Run	Per PR	Per Play
2018	3%	29%	67%	1.1%	8%	40%	48%	10	10	22	91	83	88
2019	5%	34%	57%	0.5%	13%	26%	46%	18	14	32	91	88	89
2020	7%	14%	78%	2.3%	13%	25%	54%	10	14	25	88	94	92
	5%	27%	66%	1.2%	11%	30%	49%	38	38	79	-	-	-

Osa Odighizuwa

Report by Jordan Edwards & Joe McDonald

School	Height	Weight	Year	Jersey #	Hometown
UCLA	6020 V	280 V	5SR	92	Portland, OR

One Liner
Odighizuwa has the heavy hands and movement skills to be an energetic interior role-playing starter at the next level, but improving his technique in run defense will make him a more consistent starter.

Overall
Osa Odighizuwa plays defensive tackle in the Bruins' multiple defensive front. He primarily lines up as a 3-tech, but has moved all over the interior and has some versatility to the nose and out on the edge. Odighizuwa played in 43 games in his collegiate career and has started in 27 of those games. He has a lean body with long arms and a thick lower half. He carries his weight well and displays very good short-area quickness and agility. A former high school state champion wrestler, he's flexible and shows good explosion out of his stance. He competes at a high level with an exceptional motor to the whistle.

Run Game
Odighizuwa shows solid play strength at the point of attack against the run. He has heavy hands and shows good flexibility to anchor and plug gaps. As a one gapper, his pad level can get high on occasion trying to shoot gaps quickly, resulting in washouts. His hand use is inconsistent and he tries to use his quickness to disrupt rather than stacking and shedding to blocks to make plays in the backfield. He has good body control and quickness to make plays laterally down the line. He can lose run lane discipline at times when he tries to knife upfield too quickly, which opens big holes behind him. He also struggles with his play diagnosis and can fall for misdirection. Despite these instances, Odighizuwa excels more as a one-gapping run defender, although he has displayed some decent reps as a two-gapping nose as well.

Pass Game
Odighizuwa is an active pass rusher and shows the versatility to rush from the edge as well as the interior. He's explosive out of his stance and has great agility and energy in pursuit to be a relentless pass rusher. He utilizes an array of hand moves like swims, rips and swipes. He mostly uses his speed and quickness to create pressure, but shows the ability to generate power in his lower half and collapse the pocket with a strong bull rush, too. Odighizuwa can rush too far upfield at times and lose his rush lanes, but his motor always keeps him alive on extra efforts. He doesn't play with a consistently low pad level, which allows blockers to get into his chest and control his movements, but he has the speed and agility through counter moves to keep working to the ball.

Last Word
Odighizuwa projects to be a one-gapping 3-technique in an even front. His pass-rush production will allow him to see the field quickly in sub packages, but while he has enough natural-movement skills to contribute on run downs, he needs to be a more consistently technical run defender to carve out a more expansive role. On third downs, Odighizuwa can use his agility and explosiveness to rush from the interior as a 3- or 1-tech.

Strengths
- Agility
- Motor and competitiveness
- 1st step explosion

Weaknesses
- Rush discipline
- Consistent pad level
- Awareness

Critical Factors

1st Step Explosion	Play Strength	Pass Rush
6	6	6

Positional Factors

Shed Ability	Hand Use	Body Control
5	5	6
Agility	**Tackling**	**FBI**
7	6	5
Discipline	**Motor**	**Toughness**
5	7	6

Basic

Year	G	GS	Tackling			Pass Rush					
			Tackles	TFL	FF	Sacks	Hurries	Hits	KD	Pressures	Deflected
2017	13	0	15	5.5	1	1.0	4	2	0	6	0
2018	11	8	28	5.0	1	3.0	10	7	2	15	2
2019	12	12	45	10.5	0	4.5	19	14	5	32	1
2020	7	7	30	6.0	0	4.0	10	8	4	19	0
	43	27	118	27.0	2	12.5	43	31	11	72	3

Advanced

Year	Tackling				Impact					
	Broken Tackles	BT%	Tackle Share	ATD+	Pres%	Pres Share	Holds Drawn	EPA on TFL	EPA on Sacks
2017	7	32%	2%	-	-	4%	0	-6.4	-1.3
2018	3	10%	4%	82	8%	14%	2	-4.7	-4.7
2019	4	8%	6%	140	9%	18%	3	-9.2	-7.6
2020	4	12%	6%	80	8%	15%	3	-2.5	-7.6
	18	13%	4%	107	9%	13%	8	-22.9	-21.2

Deep Dive

Year	Lined Up			Pass Rush		When Run At		Total Points			Total Points Rtg		
	NT%	DT%	DE%	Sack%	True Pres%	Bnc%	Pos%	Run Def	Pass Rush	Total	Per Run	Per PR	Per Play
2018	23%	67%	10%	1.6%	8%	21%	29%	5	10	18	62	91	81
2019	21%	62%	16%	1.3%	11%	36%	48%	19	12	33	97	78	89
2020	29%	54%	17%	1.7%	8%	45%	66%	12	10	22	94	82	86
	24%	61%	15%	1.5%	9%	38%	52%	36	32	73	-	-	-

Marvin Wilson

Report by Chad Tedder & Ben Hrkach

School	Height	Weight	Year	Jersey #	Hometown
Florida State	6034 V	319 V	4SR	21	Houston, TX

One Liner
Wilson uses strength, power, and some heavy hand techniques to be effective at the POA, though he needs to improve his quickness off the ball, pass-rush consistency, and discipline in order to maximize his full potential as a 3-down player at the next level.

Overall
Marvin Wilson is a defensive tackle in Florida State's 3-4 base defense. He plays predominantly at 3-technique with one-gap responsibility, but occasionally reduces down to a nose tackle on sub packages or out to 5-tech as well. He started in 19 of 39 games for the Seminoles. He missed the final 4 games of the 2019 season with a significant hand injury and then a leg injury sidelined him for the final 3 games of 2020. Wilson has a big frame and very good size for the position while also possessing good athleticism for his size. He competes and plays hard, though he shows some signs of losing stamina later in games.

Run Game
Against the run, Wilson does not seem to anticipate snaps, rather he reacts after the snap. He is a little slow to get out of his stance and establish a new line of scrimmage in the backfield, but what he lacks in quickness he brings in power and explosion. Once he gets out of his stance, he does a good job anchoring at the line, taking on double teams, moving laterally with the play, and trying to hold his gap. He occasionally plays a little high and gets moved off his base allowing a cut back lane for the rusher, however, he does a decent job at keeping one hand free while flowing with the play to allow for swims, push/pull, and swipe techniques in order to get off blocks and make tackles. Wilson is a big guy with great strength, power, and short space quickness to be a bully inside. He is a wrecking ball inside using his power and some technique to try to make a play on the ball.

Pass Game
Wilson is relentless in getting after the quarterback. In one-on-ones with a guard or tackle, he mixes up his hand techniques to ward off the linemen from getting to the inside of his pads. He utilizes hand chops, swipes, bull-rushes, swims, push/pulls, rips, and occasional stunts to get the offensive linemen off balance, and even drive them to the ground. With a variety of moves, his go-to is swim or bull rushes. He lacks some ability to consistently be effective with many speed or finesse moves. However, when he uses leverage and extension in his bull rush, he's able to walk blockers back into the lap of the quarterback. When getting to the QB, he not only produces by applying pressure, but is also able to finish with sacks.

Last Word
Wilson projects as a low-end starting 3-technique with 1-gap responsibilities in a 4-3 base defense. He has the heavy hands, power, and body control to be a force against the run and occasionally make his way back to the quarterback in passing situations. He fits best as a one-gapping 3-tech on 3rd downs where he can use his explosion and power to get into blockers and work them back to the quarterback.

Strengths

- Manipulating linemen
- Power
- Body control

Weaknesses

- Quickness off the snap
- Pass-rush consistency
- Gap control

Critical Factors

1st Step Explosion	Play Strength	Pass Rush
6	7	5

Positional Factors

Shed Ability	Hand Use	Body Control
5	6	7
Agility	Tackling	FBI
6	6	5
Discipline	Motor	Toughness
6	6	7

Basic

Year	G	GS	Tackles	TFL	FF	Sacks	Hurries	Hits	KD	Pressures	Deflected
2017	12	0	7	0.5	0	0.0	2	1	1	2	0
2018	12	5	40	4.5	1	3.5	16	11	6	22	2
2019	9	9	43	8.5	1	5.0	14	11	5	24	5
2020	6	5	17	3.0	0	1.0	5	6	3	8	0
	39	19	107	16.5	2	9.5	37	29	15	56	7

Advanced

Year	Broken Tackles	BT%	Tackle Share	ATD+	Pres%	Pres Share	Holds Drawn	EPA on TFL	EPA on Sacks
2017	0	0%	1%	-	-	1%	0	-1.6	0.0
2018	2	5%	5%	109	8%	10%	2	-2.0	-5.9
2019	5	10%	4%	92	9%	10%	0	-7.0	-17.2
2020	3	15%	3%	53	7%	8%	0	-2.5	-1.9
	10	9%	3%	92	8%	7%	2	-13.0	-25.0

Deep Dive

Year	NT%	DT%	DE%	Sack%	True Pres%	Bnc%	Pos%	Run Def	Pass Rush	Total	Per Run	Per PR	Per Play
2018	29%	70%	1%	1.2%	9%	33%	43%	12	9	24	95	75	87
2019	9%	67%	24%	1.8%	11%	19%	34%	14	12	33	96	86	94
2020	3%	83%	15%	0.8%	7%	36%	71%	5	4	9	82	76	78
	16%	71%	12%	1.4%	10%	29%	44%	31	25	66	-	-	-

Marlon Tuipulotu

Report by John Todd

School	Height	Weight	Year	Jersey #	Hometown
USC	6016 V	308 V	4JR	93	Independence, OR

One Liner

Tuipulotu plays with a consistent motor and his upside and versatility are intriguing, but he needs to improve the strength in his lower half to become a more reliable interior run defender.

Strengths: Upper-body and grip strength; Motor and stamina; Alignment versatility
Weaknesses: Anchor strength; Vertical disruption; Consistent leverage

Marlon Tuipulotu is a two-gapping defensive tackle for USC, lining up from guard to guard and often as a nose. He started 29 of his 33 career games. He medically redshirted his freshman year after undergoing lower back surgery. He's barrel-chested and very strongly built throughout, showing good athleticism to chase and change directions in space. His ruggedness to eat blocks inside can be touch and go, but he plays with a consistent motor and impressive stamina.

When Tuipulotu fires out with good leverage, he can dominate solo blockers with his initial punch and grip strength to latch on and manipulate two ways, then shed and make plays in the hole. However, if he loses the leverage battle or faces a double team, he doesn't have the ability to anchor and loses gap integrity. Against zone schemes, he does a great job of reading flow and covering his responsibilities, but power schemes give him trouble, especially as a nose. His leg drive and scheme haven't resulted in much of an upfield disruptor. Tuipulotu is always moving toward the ball and presents himself with opportune situations to clean up tackles. He's a good mover for his size and has had a few eye-opening reps in pursuit.

Tuipulotu struggled as a pass rushing nose in USC's three-man front, but when rushing over a guard or given a solo matchup he showed a variety of techniques to win. His grip strength results in violent push-pulls. He has active hands to work through his rush, and while not a twitchy athlete, he's shown surprising wiggle to cut inside. He has good hip explosion at contact and again shows the motor to give second efforts and pursue.

Tuipulotu projects best as a two-gapping versatile rotation piece in the NFL. He's a bit of a nose-DT tweener, but he's at his best head-up over guards or at an inside shade. He'll need to improve his anchor strength to fill a fire hydrant role on run downs, but he profiles well to a third-down sub package 1-tech.

			Tackling			Pass Rush					
Year	G	GS	Tackles	TFL	FF	Sacks	Hurries	Hits	KD	Pressures	Deflected
2017	3	1	2	0.0	0	0.0	0	0	0	0	0
2018	12	10	32	5.0	0	4.5	4	3	0	10	0
2019	12	12	46	5.0	1	2.0	10	7	2	16	3
2020	6	6	23	3.5	1	2.0	7	7	1	11	0
	33	29	103	13.5	2	8.5	21	17	3	37	3

	Tackling				Impact				
Year	Broken Tackles	BT%	Tackle Share	ATD+	Pres%	Pres Share	Holds Drawn	EPA on TFL	EPA on Sacks
2017	0	0%	0%	-	-	0%	0	0.0	0.0
2018	8	20%	4%	100	5%	5%	0	-0.9	-6.5
2019	6	12%	6%	78	6%	7%	4	-4.1	-5.3
2020	4	15%	6%	106	8%	11%	2	-2.3	-8.3
	18	15%	4%	91	6%	5%	6	-7.3	-20.1

	Lined Up			Pass Rush		When Run At		Total Points			Total Points Rtg		
Year	NT%	DT%	DE%	Sack%	True Pres%	Bnc%	Pos%	Run Def	Pass Rush	Total	Per Run	Per PR	Per Play
2018	39%	56%	5%	2.0%	4%	46%	33%	7	5	12	61	69	65
2019	17%	82%	0%	0.8%	8%	20%	50%	14	7	24	91	72	85
2020	68%	32%	1%	1.4%	11%	42%	47%	7	9	16	79	95	87
	37%	61%	2%	1.4%	7%	35%	43%	28	21	52	-	-	-

Critical Factors	
1st Step Explosion	5
Play Strength	6
Pass Rush	5

Positional Factors	
Shed Ability	6
Hand Use	6
Body Control	6
Agility	5
Tackling	6
FBI	6
Discipline	5
Motor	7
Toughness	5

Malik Herring

Report by Jordan Edwards

School	Height	Weight	Year	Jersey #	Hometown
Georgia	6032 V	283 V	4SR	10	Forsyth, GA

One Liner

Herring is a strong run defender with true position flexibility as an edge defender, but needs to improve his explosion and pass-rush consistency to hit his ceiling.

Strengths: FBI; Play strength; Discipline
Weaknesses: Pass rush ability; Explosiveness; Shed ability

Malik Herring is a strong-side defensive end for Georgia's base 4-2-5 defense. In base formations, he will line up as a 4i- or 5-tech and will occasionally bump down to a 1 or 3 in pass rush situations. He started 18 of 52 games played through his career. Herring suffered a torn right ACL during Senior Bowl practice, something he also did in high school. He has a solid frame with a strong lower body and good functional strength, however, he lacks the desired size at the position. He plays with a good motor and competes play in play out.

Herring has strong hands and plays with good leverage when setting the edge at the POA. He's intelligent and stays disciplined when initially unblocked. He has the strength to take on and engage pulling lineman and create congestion at the LOS. He has good hand strength, but his hand placement and speed needs improvement. He has good agility and body control at his size which allows him to play on the edge. He's a good tackler with decent production and good technique.

Herring has adequate initial explosion, but lacks the twitchiness and natural athleticism to be a consistent pass rusher off the edge. He plays with sufficient hand use and needs to improve his ability to disengage from blocks. Herring has experience rushing from the interior and can collapse the pocket. He has good body control and discipline to stay in his rush lanes while showing good awareness and intelligence to get his hands up in passing lanes with the occasional batted pass at the LOS. He wins with power and strength, and on occasion with speed and quickness when rushing from the interior.

Herring projects to be a versatile backup with inside/outside flexibility. He can be a 5-tech edge player in a 3-4 on early down situations, but will be best used as an interior pass rusher on third downs. His versatility will allow him to carve out a role for a team at the next level, and if he can become a more consistent pass rusher, he could become a low-end starter.

			Tackling			Pass Rush					
Year	G	GS	Tackles	TFL	FF	Sacks	Hurries	Hits	KD	Pressures	Deflected
2017	15	0	6	0.0	0	0.0	4	6	4	7	0
2018	14	1	24	3.5	1	1.5	13	6	2	17	0
2019	13	9	25	5.0	0	0.5	18	13	3	24	4
2020	10	8	18	3.5	0	2.0	18	16	4	25	2
	52	18	73	12.0	1	4.0	53	41	13	73	6

	Tackling				Impact				
Year	Broken Tackles	BT%	Tackle Share	ATD+	Pres%	Pres Share	Holds Drawn	EPA on TFL	EPA on Sacks
2017	0	0%	1%	-	-	3%	0	0.0	0.0
2018	3	11%	3%	114	14%	9%	0	-3.5	-4.8
2019	0	0%	3%	180	11%	9%	0	-6.7	-2.7
2020	4	18%	3%	153	12%	12%	2	-2.8	-3.3
	7	9%	2%	149	13%	8%	2	-13.0	-10.8

	Lined Up			Pass Rush		When Run At		Total Points			Total Points Rtg		
Year	NT%	DT%	DE%	Sack%	True Pres%	Bnc%	Pos%	Run Def	Pass Rush	Total	Per Run	Per PR	Per Play
2018	1%	25%	73%	1.2%	15%	38%	44%	7	11	18	98	99	99
2019	1%	13%	84%	0.2%	11%	38%	46%	14	10	27	99	87	97
2020	1%	8%	87%	1.0%	13%	42%	32%	11	15	28	96	98	98
	1%	14%	82%	0.7%	13%	40%	40%	32	36	73	-	-	-

Critical Factors	
1st Step Explosion	5
Play Strength	6
Pass Rush	4

Positional Factors	
Shed Ability	5
Hand Use	5
Body Control	5
Agility	5
Tackling	6
FBI	6
Discipline	6
Motor	6
Toughness	6

Carlo Kemp

Report by Sales Pinckney and Nathan Cooper

School	Height	Weight	Year	Jersey #	Hometown
Michigan	6021 E	286 E	5SR	2	Boulder, CO

One Liner

Kemp is a tough defensive lineman with explosive get-off and the ability to disrupt plays through penetration, but his inability to disengage from blockers and remain stout in the run game will limit his potential roles.

Strengths: Get-off; Initial punch; Stunts
Weaknesses: Disengaging blockers; Combatting doubles; Pass rush repertoire

Carlo Kemp is a defensive lineman in Michigan's 4-3 defense, utilized mainly as a one-gapper between 0-tech and 2i, though has played nearly every technique along the line. He started 29 of 45 career games for the Wolverines. Kemp's an explosive short-area athlete, but struggles with balance. He has a stout build with thick thighs and midsection, but lacks length. He's a high-motor player who exhibits toughness and grit on the interior.

Kemp displays good get-off and explosion at the snap. He has a strong initial punch, but displays merely sufficient overall hand usage. He possesses the short-area quickness to shoot gaps, though his lack of length often results in getting tangled up with opposing linemen after contact. He flashes, but shows inconsistency in his ability to disrupt the backfield. Kemp doesn't give up much ground vertically against lone blockers, however, he does tend to get washed laterally. Against doubles, he lacks the anchor strength required to hold ground and struggles to remain on his feet, often ending up on the ground as the play develops.

Kemp fails to make a consistent impact as a pass rusher despite his quick get-off. His inability to consistently disengage from blockers hinders his overall effectiveness, but he flashes the ability to generate pressure. His get-off and agility allow him to be effective when crossing the face of blockers. His speed rush can overwhelm interior linemen if they cannot get their hands on him quickly. He doesn't have a deep pass rush repertoire, but occasionally shows a good push-pull. Kemp often lacks a plan of attack and as a result, ends up entangled with blockers. He has experience and success running stunts as opposed to generating pressure on his own.

Kemp projects as a backup one-gapping 3-tech in a slant and stunt-heavy 4-3 scheme, though somewhat a tweener, he has the versatility to move around the line. He's not going to overwhelm 1-on-1, but his quickness should allow him to see production.

			Tackling			Pass Rush					
Year	G	GS	Tackles	TFL	FF	Sacks	Hurries	Hits	KD	Pressures	Deflected
2017	13	0	3	0.0	0	0.0	1	1	1	2	0
2018	13	12	19	3.5	0	1.0	8	6	2	9	0
2019	12	12	41	4.5	0	2.0	10	9	5	15	1
2020	6	5	20	2.0	0	2.0	6	8	3	12	0
	45	29	83	10.0	0	5.0	25	24	11	38	1

	Tackling				Impact				
Year	Broken Tackles	BT%	Tackle Share	ATD+	Pres%	Pres Share	Holds Drawn	EPA on TFL	EPA on Sacks
2017	1	25%	0%	-	-	1%	0	0.0	0.0
2018	3	14%	3%	134	5%	5%	1	-3.5	-1.8
2019	3	7%	5%	118	6%	6%	1	-2.6	-5.4
2020	2	9%	5%	52	7%	13%	1	0.0	-3.2
	9	10%	3%	106	6%	5%	3	-6.0	-10.4

	Lined Up			Pass Rush		When Run At		Total Points			Total Points Rtg		
Year	NT%	DT%	DE%	Sack%	True Pres%	Bnc%	Pos%	Run Def	Pass Rush	Total	Per Run	Per PR	Per Play
2018	13%	80%	6%	0.6%	4%	43%	48%	9	8	18	89	88	88
2019	38%	61%	1%	0.8%	8%	25%	49%	15	17	33	82	97	90
2020	6%	47%	47%	1.1%	5%	26%	39%	5	3	8	66	64	65
	22%	63%	15%	0.9%	6%	28%	47%	29	28	59	-	-	-

Redshirt season not shown but included in totals

Critical Factors

1st Step Explosion	6
Play Strength	5
Pass Rush	5

Positional Factors

Shed Ability	5
Hand Use	5
Body Control	4
Agility	5
Tackling	6
FBI	5
Discipline	5
Motor	6
Toughness	6

Isaiahh Loudermilk

Report by Christian Vega & DJ Marquardt

School	Height	Weight	Year	Jersey #	Hometown
Wisconsin	6062 E	293 E	5SR	97	Howard, KS

One Liner

Loudermilk has ideal length and strength to be a strong run stuffing 5- or 3-tech at the next level, but his lack of agility and pass-rushing skills greatly limit his versatility.

Strengths: Use of length to stack and read; Play strength; Run defense
Weaknesses: Agility; Pass-rushing ability; Hand fighting and shedding

Isaiahh Loudermilk is a two-gapping defensive lineman in Wisconsin's base 3-man front, typically lining up shaded in the B-gap. He played in 40 career games with 26 starts. He has missed games in previous seasons due to left leg and arm injuries. He has fantastic length and size with great upper- and lower-body strength to match. He was a four-sport star in high school, but despite that, he is not an agile football player. What he lacks in athleticism he makes up for with toughness in the trenches.

Loudermilk's two-gapping role restricts his upfield attacking nature. Off the snap he does a fantastic job to immediately feel blocking schemes and stack oncoming linemen with his elite length. His anchor strength combined with his long and powerful first punch often neutralize blockers instantly and let him keep great gap discipline. From there, he reads run flow well and can shed enough to make plays to either of his gaps while still engaged. However, Loudermilk does not shed cleanly with consistency and lacks quick hands to beat blocks with finesse. He

does not have the mobility to range beyond the box and his inconsistent motor is a reflection of that understanding.

Loudermilk comes off high and lacks a rush plan against pass protecting linemen. He most often resorts to a straight-arm bull rush to modest success, but his hands are sluggish when attempting rush moves. He has generated some production within twists up front, giving him the ability to attack unsuspecting or compromised linemen, but he is not a consistent threat one-on-one. However, he does a great job of getting his elite frame into passing lanes after unsuccessful rushes.

Loudermilk projects as a quality early-down reserve in a two-gapping system where he can focus his efforts on dominating against the run. He can play anywhere over tackles and guards and still usually find a length advantage. He does not offer much third-down versatility beyond batting passes, nor special teams beyond rushing and blocking for field goals.

			Tackling			Pass Rush					
Year	G	GS	Tackles	TFL	FF	Sacks	Hurries	Hits	KD	Pressures	Deflected
2017	11	0	11	1.5	0	1.5	4	3	1	7	1
2018	9	6	15	2.5	0	1.0	8	4	1	11	5
2019	14	14	27	6.0	2	3.0	14	6	2	19	5
2020	6	6	13	2.5	0	2.0	9	5	1	11	1
	40	26	66	12.5	2	7.5	35	18	5	48	12

	Tackling				Impact				
Year	Broken Tackles	BT%	Tackle Share	ATD+	Pres%	Pres Share	Holds Drawn	EPA on TFL	EPA on Sacks
2017	2	15%	2%	-	-	3%	1	0.0	-3.3
2018	2	12%	2%	120	6%	7%	1	-1.7	-0.8
2019	2	7%	4%	127	5%	8%	1	-4.9	-6.8
2020	0	0%	4%	114	7%	12%	3	-1.8	-2.5
	6	8%	3%	122	7%	6%	6	-8.4	-13.3

	Lined Up			Pass Rush		When Run At		Total Points			Total Points Rtg		
Year	NT%	DT%	DE%	Sack%	True Pres%	Bnc%	Pos%	Run Def	Pass Rush	Total	Per Run	Per PR	Per Play
2018	19%	66%	15%	0.5%	5%	43%	52%	7	5	18	79	72	83
2019	6%	76%	18%	0.8%	6%	24%	47%	16	12	32	93	77	87
2020	6%	63%	31%	1.2%	7%	33%	42%	15	7	23	99	84	97
	10%	70%	20%	0.8%	6%	31%	47%	38	24	73	-	-	-

Critical Factors	
1st Step Explosion	5
Play Strength	7
Pass Rush	4

Positional Factors	
Shed Ability	5
Hand Use	5
Body Control	6
Agility	4
Tackling	5
FBI	6
Discipline	7
Motor	5
Toughness	6

Raymond Johnson III

Report by Noah Chang & Ryan Newman

School	Height	Weight	Year	Jersey #	Hometown
Georgia Southern	6026 E	270 E	4SR	0	Sumter, SC

One Liner

Johnson is a disruptive gap penetrator with a great frame and quick hands, but he needs to improve his stoutness against the run and consistent explosion to reach his high ceiling.

Strengths: Quick hands; Motor and finish; Run discipline
Weaknesses: Anchor stoutness; Finding the ball when engaged; Range

Raymond Johnson III is a one-gapping defensive lineman in Georgia Southern's base 3-4 defensive front. He consistently aligned shaded to both sides or head-up over left tackles. He played in 50 career games and started all but 3 of them over his four-year career. He has a chiseled frame and solid strength throughout. He is a good athlete for his size but lacks twitchy COD skills and open-field speed. However, his limited range is not for lack of effort, as he consistently gives great pursuit.

Johnson's first step explosion and pad level are inconsistent but can beat linemen with those alone when both are in sync. He does a good job of getting skinny through gaps to diminish his strike zone for blockers. Johnson has very quick hands at the POA and does well to swipe away first contact. He can shed at times, but more often than not needs to win the initial battle to stay alive. He does not have much anchor stoutness, especially against double teams, and he struggles to locate ballcarriers when engaged. He forces gives as the read man and can still make plays on the handoff. He keeps solid contain on the back side, hustles sideline to sideline, and is a physical tackler in the box.

Johnson wins in the passing game with his quick hands and a bevy of solid hand-fighting techniques. He is not twitchy and doesn't threaten a speed rush around the edge, showing mediocre bend at the top. He is at his best cutting inside tackles or slanting onto guards, as he can get narrow to contact and slip through at awkward angles. He can convert speed to power and push the pocket. It doesn't always look pretty and he can lack a rush plan, but his motor on extended plays rewards him often.

Johnson projects best as a backup 5-technique, who can reduce to a one-gapping 3-tech situationally. His body composition, quick hands, and motor are good developmental assets, but he needs to improve his lower-body strength and pass-rushing prowess to see a bigger role. His consistency over four seasons is commendable.

Year	G	GS	Tackling			Pass Rush					
			Tackles	TFL	FF	Sacks	Hurries	Hits	KD	Pressures	Deflected
2017	12	9	36	6.5	0	4.0	23	16	2	30	1
2018	13	13	42	6.5	1	4.0	25	12	6	32	2
2019	12	12	33	7.0	0	3.0	29	16	6	36	2
2020	13	13	38	14.0	1	5.0	26	20	8	38	1
	50	47	149	34.0	2	16.0	103	64	22	136	6

Year	Tackling				Impact				
	Broken Tackles	BT%	Tackle Share	ATD+	Pres%	Pres Share	Holds Drawn	EPA on TFL	EPA on Sacks
2017	5	12%	6%	-	-	17%	0	-4.0	-9.4
2018	5	11%	5%	106	11%	19%	1	-2.6	-9.3
2019	7	18%	4%	157	14%	20%	4	-5.7	-4.1
2020	2	5%	5%	184	13%	22%	2	-11.6	-11.2
	19	11%	5%	147	16%	20%	7	-23.8	-34.0

Year	Lined Up			Pass Rush		When Run At		Total Points			Total Points Rtg		
	NT%	DT%	DE%	Sack%	True Pres%	Bnc%	Pos%	Run Def	Pass Rush	Total	Per Run	Per PR	Per Play
2018	1%	11%	88%	1.4%	11%	29%	58%	10	19	31	74	96	89
2019	0%	8%	86%	1.2%	19%	24%	45%	18	17	38	96	96	96
2020	0%	12%	83%	1.7%	16%	31%	50%	19	14	33	96	87	91
	0%	10%	86%	1.5%	15%	28%	51%	47	50	102	-	-	-

Critical Factors	
1st Step Explosion	5
Play Strength	5
Pass Rush	5

Positional Factors	
Shed Ability	5
Hand Use	6
Body Control	5
Agility	5
Tackling	6
FBI	5
Discipline	6
Motor	7
Toughness	6

Mustafa Johnson

Final Grade: 5.9

Report by Stephen Marciello

School	Height	Weight	Year	Jersey #	Hometown
Colorado	6005 V	292 V	4SR	34	Turlock, CA

One Liner

Johnson is a stocky and disciplined defensive tackle with a plus swim move and wiggle in tight spaces, but a lack of power and sheer pass-rush skills will likely make him a backup in the NFL.

Strengths: Swim move and short-area quickness; Discipline; Motor
Weaknesses: Elite strength; Athleticism; Consistent tackling

Mustafa Johnson is a versatile defensive tackle in Colorado's multiple defensive front. He has lined up at every technique possible on the defensive line from mainly out of a four-point stance, although he most often lines up at a 3-tech. He played and started 27 games in his 3 years at Colorado after starting his career in JUCO. He missed three games in 2019 because of an ankle injury. Johnson is a short and stocky interior player with average athleticism and a plus motor.

Johnson is disciplined against the run, whether his assignment is to slant, keep contain, or occupy. While he shows solid on-ball production, he is more often asked to eat blocks and force bounces. He uses a good initial punch and hand placement to stalemate but lacks elite strength to drive. Johnson's lateral quickness is a strength, as he can beat linemen to the spot trying to reach him. However, he can get washed out on the move with a limited anchor. He tends to tackle high and doesn't have the reactive quickness to contain shifty runners. His agility is more of an

asset in tight quarters against interior linemen, but that also is where his lower body strength is most vulnerable. He isn't fast, but he has a hot motor to pursue the ball.

Johnson utilizes a great swim move to either direction to juke linemen trying to meet his low pad level in pass protection. He also flashes a push-pull to shed blocks, but he isn't a dynamic one-on-one pass rusher overall. He is often used within stunts and moved around frequently, which varied his approaches and either had him occupy extra attention or often gave him free lanes to the QB. His sack production is misleading, as much of it came untouched or cleaning up other pressures in pursuit.

Johnson projects best as a 4-3 defensive tackle, which will play to his short-area quickness. He doesn't possess the strength to play nose and he doesn't have the length or pass-rush skills to bump over tackles. He can be utilized in situational passing downs with his ability to move around and flash his quickness.

			Tackling			Pass Rush					
Year	G	GS	Tackles	TFL	FF	Sacks	Hurries	Hits	KD	Pressures	Deflected
2018	12	12	48	15.5	0	8.5	34	19	6	44	2
2019	9	9	27	5.0	0	4.5	10	3	1	16	0
2020	6	6	19	5.5	0	3.0	9	3	1	13	0
	27	27	94	26.0	1	16.0	53	25	8	73	2

	Tackling				Impact				
Year	Broken Tackles	BT%	Tackle Share	ATD+	Pres%	Pres Share	Holds Drawn	EPA on TFL	EPA on Sacks
2018	5	9%	6%	131	12%	24%	2	-10.1	-12.4
2019	3	10%	4%	45	8%	11%	1	-1.0	-9.9
2020	3	14%	6%	186	6%	13%	1	-4.5	-4.5
	11	10%	5%	118	9%	17%	4	-15.7	-26.9

	Lined Up			Pass Rush		When Run At		Total Points			Total Points Rtg		
Year	NT%	DT%	DE%	Sack%	True Pres%	Bnc%	Pos%	Run Def	Pass Rush	Total	Per Run	Per PR	Per Play
2018	4%	61%	34%	2.4%	13%	46%	31%	13	18	33	90	89	89
2019	4%	55%	41%	2.2%	9%	44%	50%	6	10	16	70	87	79
2020	25%	54%	20%	1.3%	6%	25%	25%	7	4	12	89	65	73
	9%	58%	32%	2.0%	10%	42%	35%	26	32	61	-	-	-

Critical Factors	
1st Step Explosion	6
Play Strength	5
Pass Rush	5

Positional Factors	
Shed Ability	6
Hand Use	6
Body Control	5
Agility	5
Tackling	5
FBI	6
Discipline	6
Motor	7
Toughness	5

Edge Rushers

Sam Linker

In the NFL, the quarterback is king. To defeat their opponents, teams must have defenders who can pressure the opponent's king. NFL teams will look to the Edge players in this year's class to help them improve their pass rush. 4-3 defensive ends and on-the-ball linebackers make up the Edge position group.

Edge defenders occupy a unique responsibility on the defense as they have many different roles combined into one. Their main priority is to rush the passer and create havoc in the backfield, but they also must be prepared to stop the run and occasionally drop into coverage. With all these responsibilities, Edge becomes one of the most important positions on defense and requires a high level of athleticism above all else.

This year's draft class boasts starting-caliber talent that can help teams generate pressure on the opposing QB. Jaelan Phillips reigns supreme among the group as our highest-graded Edge. He excels in using his hand strength and motor to attack the quarterback which projects him as a starting-caliber Edge. If he can land with the right team to help him develop his skill set to pair with his already great athleticism and strength, Phillips has the potential to become a top pass rusher in the NFL.

After Phillips, six Edges stand out among the rest as they are also starting-caliber talents who grade just below Phillips. Those six are Georgia's Azeez Ojulari, Michigan's Kwity Paye, Pittsburgh's Rashad Weaver, Miami's Gregory Rousseau, Miami's Quincy Roche, and Penn State's Jayson Oweh.

What makes this group of defenders unique is that they all have separate strengths, so teams can target specific tools they wish to add to their defense. Ojulari and Roche each earned the top pass rush grade but have different methods for their success. Ojulari has a great first step and makes good use of his hands, while Roche wins with a variety of pass rush moves. Similarly to Ojulari, Weaver makes good use of his hands and his length along with his top graded FBI to attack the offensive line and pressure the quarterback.

Paye also possesses a very good first step that he pairs with a great motor to help him set the edge in run defense. His natural athleticism makes him a very versatile player to have at the defensive end position. Oweh may be the most interesting player of the bunch. His excellent range grade along with his other good grades across other areas offer tremendous potential to any team that could help develop his skill set.

Miami's Gregory Rousseau is by far the most intriguing Edge prospect in the class. As a redshirt freshman in 2019, Rousseau dominated the competition and earned Second Team All-American honors along with the ACC's Defensive Rookie of the Year. After an excellent 2019, Rousseau decided to opt-out of the 2020 season making him the true definition of a "one year wonder" as he only has one season worth of playing time to evaluate. Regardless, he will be a player to watch as his 2019 season has a lot of teams excited about him.

Besides some basic box score stats, we offer more advanced metrics such as Total Points to assist in evaluating these players' college production. The section includes an in-depth look at key areas such as how many broken tackles the defender had, how many holding penalties they have drawn, and the EPA that they created on tackles for loss and sacks.

We also show how often they rush the passer for an even deeper breakdown into how they were deployed. The Total Points for each Edge is made up of their pass rush, run defense, and pass coverage. We provide a pass rush/run defense split for Total Points that highlights the areas of importance for an Edge. This breakdown provides a look at where each player is excelling and how their pass rush and run defense compare to their contemporaries on a Total Points basis.

Overall, the 2021 NFL Draft class offers teams a good set of Edge prospects with 17 players having a score of at least 6.5 which represent at least a low-end starter. While thin at the top, the Edge positional class offers strong depth, including many players who can become contributors on NFL defenses.

EDGE RUSHER

Edge Rusher Grading Scale

GRADE	DESCRIPTION
9.0 – 7.0	High-end 3 down starter. Pro Bowl level.
6.9 – 6.7	Strong starter who plays on all 3 downs.
6.6 – 6.5	Lower-end starter. 2 down player or plus pass rusher.
6.2	Versatile backup with positional flexibility.
6.1 – 6.0	Developmental. Top traits but needs time.
5.9	Top backup. Quality special teamer.
5.8	Average backup. Quality special teamer.
5.7	Low-end backup Edge with growable upside.

Edge Rusher Rankings

Rank	Name	Grade	Page	Rank	Name	Grade	Page
1	Jaelan Phillips	6.8	448	17	Patrick Johnson	6.5	480
2	Azeez Ojulari	6.7	450	18	Cameron Sample	6.2	482
3	Kwity Paye	6.7	452	19	Tarron Jackson	6.2	483
4	Rashad Weaver	6.7	454	20	Wyatt Hubert	6.2	484
5	Gregory Rousseau	6.7	456	21	Payton Turner	6.2	485
6	Quincy Roche	6.7	458	22	Daelin Hayes	5.9	486
7	Jayson Oweh	6.7	460	23	Elerson Smith	5.9	487
8	Carlos Basham Jr.	6.6	462	24	Jonathon Cooper	5.9	488
9	Ronnie Perkins	6.5	464	25	William Bradley-King	5.9	489
10	Joe Tryon	6.5	466	26	Jordan Smith	5.9	490
11	Shaka Toney	6.5	468	27	Chauncey Golston	5.9	491
12	Patrick Jones II	6.5	470	28	Malcolm Koonce	5.9	492
13	Adetokunbo Ogundeji	6.5	472	29	Hamilcar Rashed Jr.	5.8	493
14	Joseph Ossai	6.5	474	30	Charles Snowden	5.8	494
15	Chris Rumph II	6.5	476	31	Joshua Kaindoh	5.8	495
16	Victor Dimukeje	6.5	478				

Glossary

3-Point Stance%
Percentage of plays where the defender was lined up with a hand on the ground (includes 4-point stances).

ATD+ (Adjusted Tackle Depth Plus)
ATD+ compares actual tackle depth to the expected tackle depth based on personnel, intended run gap, and the defender's pre-snap alignment. This figure is then scaled so that 100 is average. A figure of 110 indicates a player who is 10% better than average; a figure of 90 indicates a player who is 10% worse than average.

Bnc% (Forced Bounce Rate) (When Run At split)
The percentage of runs that didn't go through the designed gap.

BT% (Broken Tackle%)
Percentage of tackle attempts where the defender in position to make a tackle failed to bring down the ball carrier. Counts both broken tackles (physical) and missed tackles (elusive).

Deflected
Plays where the defender either knocked a pass down or deflected a pass at the line of scrimmage.

Hits
Plays with meaningful contact made by the defender on the quarterback before or as he releases the football.

Hurries
Plays where the defender forces the quarterback to rush a throw before he may have otherwise thrown it.

Knockdowns
Plays where the quarterback gets knocked down to the ground by the defender after he releases the football.

Pos% (Positive Percentage) (When Run At split)
The percentage of plays that result in a positive EPA for the offense. Lower numbers are better for defenders.

Pres% (Pressure Rate)
The percentage of pass rushes that resulted in a quarterback hurry, hit, knockdown, or sack.

Pres Share (Pressure Share)
Percentage of a team's individual pressures made by the defender.

Rush%
Percentage of quarterback dropbacks where the defender rushed the quarterback.

Sack%
Percentage of pass rushes that resulted in a sack.

Tackle Share
Percentage of a team's tackles made by the defender.

Total Points
Sports Info Solutions' proprietary player value metric that uses an Expected Points framework and distributes the value gained or lost on a play to the players involved based on their impact on the play.

Total Points Rating
Total Points per play compared to average, scaled so that 50 is poor and 99 is excellent.

True Pres% (True Pressure Rate)
Pressure rate that isolates straight dropbacks which are more likely to be similar across situations.

Edge Rusher Leaderboards

Total Points Per Game

Rk	Player	School	Tot Pts / G
1	R. Weaver	Pittsburgh	5.1
2	K. Paye	Michigan	4.8
3	J. Phillips	Miami FL	4.5
4	P. Turner	Houston	4.4
5	T. Jackson	Coastal Carolina	4.3
6	J. Ossai	Texas	4.1
7	A. Ojulari	Georgia	3.9
8	Q. Roche	Miami FL	3.8
8	P. Jones II	Pittsburgh	3.8
8	2 tied with		3.8

Total Points Rating Per Play

Rk	Player	School	Rating
1	A. Ojulari	Georgia	99
1	R. Weaver	Pittsburgh	99
1	P. Turner	Houston	99
4	J. Phillips	Miami FL	98
4	R. Perkins	Oklahoma	98
6	K. Paye	Michigan	97
7	P. Jones II	Pittsburgh	96
7	J. Smith	UAB	96
9	J. Oweh	Penn State	95
9	T. Jackson	Coastal Carolina	95

Pass Rush Total Points Per Game

Rk	Player	School	Tot Pts / G
1	R. Weaver	Pittsburgh	3.1
2	K. Paye	Michigan	3.0
3	A. Ojulari	Georgia	2.8
3	T. Jackson	Coastal Carolina	2.8
5	R. Perkins	Oklahoma	2.3
5	C. Golston	Iowa	2.3
7	W. Hubert	Kansas State	2.2
8	V. Dimukeje	Duke	2.1
8	J. Cooper	Ohio State	2.1
10	P. Turner	Houston	2.0

Total Points Rating Per Pass Rush

Rk	Player	School	Rating
1	A. Ojulari	Georgia	99
1	K. Paye	Michigan	99
1	R. Weaver	Pittsburgh	99
1	R. Perkins	Oklahoma	99
1	P. Johnson	Tulane	99
1	P. Turner	Houston	99
7	S. Toney	Penn State	98
7	V. Dimukeje	Duke	98
7	T. Jackson	Coastal Carolina	98
7	2 tied with		98

Run Defense Total Points Per Game

Rk	Player	School	Tot Pts / G
1	J. Phillips	Miami FL	2.1
1	J. Oweh	Penn State	2.1
1	J. Ossai	Texas	2.1
4	P. Turner	Houston	2.0
5	Q. Roche	Miami FL	1.8
6	R. Weaver	Pittsburgh	1.7
6	P. Jones II	Pittsburgh	1.7
8	C. Sample	Tulane	1.6
9	K. Paye	Michigan	1.5
9	T. Jackson	Coastal Carolina	1.5

Total Points Rating Per Run Snap

Rk	Player	School	Rating
1	J. Oweh	Penn State	99
1	P. Jones II	Pittsburgh	99
1	P. Turner	Houston	99
4	J. Phillips	Miami FL	98
4	R. Weaver	Pittsburgh	98
6	J. Ossai	Texas	96
7	Q. Roche	Miami FL	95
8	R. Perkins	Oklahoma	94
9	A. Ojulari	Georgia	90
9	J. Smith	UAB	90

Pressure Rate

Rk	Player	School	Pres%
1	K. Paye	Michigan	23%
2	A. Ojulari	Georgia	21%
2	J. Smith	UAB	21%
4	C. Rumph II	Duke	20%
5	R. Perkins	Oklahoma	18%
6	R. Weaver	Pittsburgh	16%
6	J. Cooper	Ohio State	16%
8	J. Oweh	Penn State	15%
8	A. Ogundeji	Notre Dame	15%
8	2 tied with		15%

True Pressure Rate

Rk	Player	School	Pres%
1	K. Paye	Michigan	29%
2	A. Ojulari	Georgia	25%
3	R. Perkins	Oklahoma	22%
3	J. Smith	UAB	22%
5	J. Oweh	Penn State	21%
5	C. Rumph II	Duke	21%
7	T. Jackson	Coastal Carolina	19%
8	R. Weaver	Pittsburgh	18%
8	C. Sample	Tulane	18%
8	2 tied with		18%

Pressures Per Game

Rk	Player	School	Pres/G
1	K. Paye	Michigan	7.3
2	R. Perkins	Oklahoma	5.2
2	J. Smith	UAB	5.2
4	R. Weaver	Pittsburgh	5.0
5	T. Jackson	Coastal Carolina	4.9
6	J. Cooper	Ohio State	4.3
7	C. Rumph II	Duke	4.1
8	C. Sample	Tulane	3.8
8	M. Koonce	Buffalo	3.8
10	J. Ossai	Texas	3.7

Pressure Share

Rk	Player	School	Pres Share
1	T. Jackson	Coastal Carolina	33%
2	J. Smith	UAB	32%
3	K. Paye	Michigan	31%
4	C. Rumph II	Duke	28%
5	V. Dimukeje	Duke	25%
6	W. Bradley-King	Baylor	24%
6	C. Golston	Iowa	24%
8	C. Basham Jr.	Wake Forest	22%
8	J. Ossai	Texas	22%
8	2 tied with		22%

Passes Deflected Per Game

Rk	Player	School	Defl/G
1	P. Turner	Houston	0.4
2	P. Jones II	Pittsburgh	0.3
2	P. Johnson	Tulane	0.3
2	C. Snowden	Virginia	0.3
5	J. Phillips	Miami FL	0.2
5	A. Ojulari	Georgia	0.2
5	R. Weaver	Pittsburgh	0.2
5	W. Bradley-King	Baylor	0.2
5	J. Smith	UAB	0.2
5	M. Koonce	Buffalo	0.2

Holds Drawn

Rk	Player	School	Holds
1	A. Ogundeji	Notre Dame	5
2	R. Weaver	Pittsburgh	4
2	P. Jones II	Pittsburgh	4
2	P. Johnson	Tulane	4
2	C. Sample	Tulane	4
2	T. Jackson	Coastal Carolina	4
2	W. Hubert	Kansas State	4
2	D. Hayes	Notre Dame	4
9	A. Ojulari	Georgia	3
9	5 tied with		3

Sacks Per Game

Rk	Player	School	Sacks/G
1	P. Turner	Houston	1.0
2	A. Ojulari	Georgia	0.9
2	R. Perkins	Oklahoma	0.9
2	P. Johnson	Tulane	0.9
2	W. Hubert	Kansas State	0.9
6	J. Phillips	Miami FL	0.8
6	R. Weaver	Pittsburgh	0.8
6	P. Jones II	Pittsburgh	0.8
6	C. Rumph II	Duke	0.8
6	2 tied with		0.8

Sack Expected Points Added Per Game

Rk	Player	School	EPA/G
1	P. Turner	Houston	-2.4
2	R. Weaver	Pittsburgh	-2.2
3	J. Ossai	Texas	-2.1
4	A. Ojulari	Georgia	-2.0
5	C. Golston	Iowa	-1.9
6	J. Phillips	Miami FL	-1.8
6	P. Jones II	Pittsburgh	-1.8
6	C. Snowden	Virginia	-1.8
9	Q. Roche	Miami FL	-1.6
9	P. Johnson	Tulane	-1.6

Tackles For Loss Per Game

Rk	Player	School	TFL/G
1	P. Turner	Houston	2.1
2	J. Ossai	Texas	1.9
3	R. Perkins	Oklahoma	1.8
4	Q. Roche	Miami FL	1.7
5	R. Weaver	Pittsburgh	1.6
6	J. Phillips	Miami FL	1.5
7	A. Ojulari	Georgia	1.3
7	P. Johnson	Tulane	1.3
7	W. Hubert	Kansas State	1.3
7	C. Snowden	Virginia	1.3

Tackle For Loss EPA Per Game

Rk	Player	School	EPA/G
1	J. Ossai	Texas	-1.9
2	Q. Roche	Miami FL	-1.6
3	J. Phillips	Miami FL	-1.3
4	P. Turner	Houston	-1.2
5	J. Oweh	Penn State	-1.1
5	R. Perkins	Oklahoma	-1.1
7	T. Jackson	Coastal Carolina	-1.0
8	C. Rumph II	Duke	-0.9
9	R. Weaver	Pittsburgh	-0.8
9	2 tied with		-0.8

Sack Rate

Rk	Player	School	Sack%
1	P. Turner	Houston	5.4%
2	C. Snowden	Virginia	5.3%
3	A. Ojulari	Georgia	4.9%
4	P. Johnson	Tulane	4.0%
5	C. Rumph II	Duke	3.7%
6	R. Perkins	Oklahoma	3.2%
6	M. Koonce	Buffalo	3.2%
8	J. Phillips	Miami FL	3.0%
9	W. Hubert	Kansas State	2.8%
10	P. Jones II	Pittsburgh	2.7%

Adjusted Tackle Depth Plus

Rk	Player	School	ATD+
1	J. Kaindoh	Florida State	224
2	A. Ojulari	Georgia	200
3	D. Hayes	Notre Dame	166
4	Q. Roche	Miami FL	160
5	J. Ossai	Texas	159
6	P. Turner	Houston	157
7	J. Phillips	Miami FL	153
7	R. Perkins	Oklahoma	153
9	A. Ogundeji	Notre Dame	148
10	T. Jackson	Coastal Carolina	142

Jaelan Phillips

Report by Ben Hrkach

School	Height	Weight	Year	Jersey #	Hometown
Miami FL	6042 E	266 E	4JR	15	Redlands, CA

One Liner
Phillips is the prototypical SDE, with good length, strength, and ability to rush the passer and has the upside to be a high-level pass rusher if he can add moves to his toolbox.

Overall
Jaelan Phillips played edge in Miami's nickel defense where he mainly lined up on the left side with his hand in the dirt and standing up. He began his career at UCLA, starting 6 of 11 games in 2 seasons. He then retired from football after the 2018 season due to severe injuries to his left wrist, both ankles, and multiple concussions. He then transferred to Miami, sat out the 2019 season, and started all 10 games he played in during 2020. He's a powerful player with very good bend and sufficient agility for his position. He consistently plays with a high motor and displays good toughness.

Pass Game
Phillips wins with his strength and ability to run the arc around the tackle from both the down and up position. He has very good ankle flexion and easily flattens at the apex of his rush. He has a good get-off at the snap and the hand strength to get clean. He does stall out occasionally and has a penchant for trying to scoop the inside arm of the tackle and toss them, though not effective enough to be a weapon. Phillips can win with a bull rush using good length to walk a lineman back into the quarterback when he wins the initial hand placement. He has sufficient torque in his lower body and very good hand strength. Outside of a speed and bull rush, Phillips doesn't have many moves in his toolbox. He attempts a counter spin that needs refinement and does not show a good feel for when to cross the face of a tackle who has overset. He's a raw pass rusher that's currently getting by with length, strength, and a natural ability to bend the corner. He can also reduce on 3rd down and beats interior blockers with agility and length. When covering the flat, it isn't natural for him to drop, but he can get to a spot and sufficiently read the quarterback.

Run Game
Phillips is very stout at the POA when squared up 1-on-1. He easily controls and tosses tight ends and doesn't often getting pushed off his spot by tackles. However, he does struggle at feeling doubles and cross blockers. He can occasionally get earholed and will lunge and whiff on blockers coming down the line. He also doesn't quickly diagnose the play and will allow the runner right by him even when he has won at the POA. He struggles with read options and is frequently flat-footed keying on the wrong guy. He's a sufficient tackler who sometimes struggles to bring guys down. When defending the run, Phillips is an ideal force defender, but has issues at the finer points that would allow him to be a high-level playmaker.

Last Word
Overall, Phillips projects as a high-end 4-3 strong-side defensive end, somewhere he'll thrive as a 3rd-down rusher, with ability to stand up as well. With his skill set and playing style, he should contribute on special teams.

Strengths

- Hand strength
- Hustle player
- Ankle flexion

Weaknesses

- Pass rush moves
- Awareness
- Tackling

Critical Factors

Pass Rush Ability	1st Step Explosion	POA / Set Edge
6	6	6

Positional Factors

Pass Rush Repertoire	Bend	Hand Use	Play Strength
5	7	7	6
Range	Flat Coverage	Motor	FBI
6	5	7	5
Discipline	Tackling	Toughness	ST Value
6	5	6	6

Basic

Year	G	GS	Tackling			Pass Rush					
			Tackles	TFL	FF	Sacks	Hurries	Hits	KD	Pressures	Deflected
2017	7	4	23	7.0	0	3.5	11	6	4	15	1
2018	4	2	20	1.0	0	1.0	3	5	0	6	0
2020	10	10	46	14.5	0	8.0	22	17	2	35	2
	21	16	89	22.5	0	12.5	36	28	6	56	3

Advanced

Year	Tackling				Impact					
	Broken Tackles	BT%	Tackle Share	ATD+	Pres%	Pres Share	Holds Drawn	EPA on TFL	EPA on Sacks
2017	1	4%	3%	-	-	10%	0	-4.0	-9.1
2018	3	13%	3%	96	12%	5%	1	0.0	-1.2
2020	7	13%	6%	153	13%	18%	1	-13.5	-17.7
	11	11%	4%	135	16%	12%	2	-17.5	-28.1

Deep Dive

Year	Stance	Pass Rush			When Run At		Total Points			Total Points Rtg		
	3-Point Stance%	Rush%	Sack%	True Pres%	Bnc%	Pos%	Run Def	Pass Rush	Total	Per Run	Per PR	Per Play
2018	1%	72%	1.9%	6%	29%	86%	2	2	5	62	81	70
2020	46%	94%	3.0%	13%	20%	40%	21	19	45	98	97	98
	36%	90%	2.8%	12%	22%	50%	23	21	50	-	-	-

Azeez Ojulari Final Grade: 6.7

Report by Nathan Cooper

School	Height	Weight	Year	Jersey #	Hometown
Georgia	6026 E	240 E	3SO	13	Marietta, GA

One Liner
Ojulari has the first step ability, hand use, and strength against both the run and pass to be a solid starter at the next level, though limited change-of-direction ability and an inability to keep blockers guessing may hold him back early on.

Overall
Azeez Ojulari primarily plays on the right side in Georgia's 4-2-5 defense lining up in 5- through 9-technique with his hand in the ground and also stands up on the edge a third of the time. He started 23 of 27 games for the Bulldogs and will be drafted before he turns 21 years old. He had surgery for a torn right ACL after his senior season of high school and also underwent another procedure on the same knee in the summer of 2018. Also a high school basketball player, Ojulari is a good athlete with a strong frame and build for the position. He plays with a high motor and toughness with a high competitive level.

Pass Game
Ojulari spent time coming off the edge in a 2- and 3-point stance with equal production from both. His first step quickness and length allow him to quickly reposition the line of scrimmage and get into the blocker. He shows very good hand use in terms of getting them up quickly with good strength and accuracy. He's able to grab or swipe the blocker's arm/hand away nearly every play. His pass rush repertoire consists mainly of speed rushes, swipes, and speed-to-power, but also throws in some bull rushes and push-pulls. Even with a large variety of moves, he will tend to use the same move over and over too often instead of mixing it up to get the blocker guessing. With that said, he's still relentless in trying to get to the passer. When getting around the edge, he shows good bend and incredible ankle flexion to dip under tackles and flatten to get to the quarterback. He's able to produce with a lot of sacks, but is also able to disrupt the quarterback's rhythm with pressure and even get hands up in passing lanes to knock balls away. In coverage, he's a smooth mover who shows good awareness and is able to disrupt receivers coming through his area.

Run Game
Against the run, Ojulari shows good strength to set the edge. He takes on pullers head on and rarely gets moved off his spot. He gets hands on against tackles and tight ends with good leverage and extension to dictate the POA. He will get overpowered on occasion by larger blockers, but fights to hold his ground. He has the lateral strength and mobility to get down the line and run down ballcarriers from behind. He has the numbers-to-numbers range and pursuit to make plays out of his immediate area. He does lack some change-of-direction ability and usually needs to take a gather step before redirecting, but he's a strong tackler and doesn't straight-up miss opportunities very often.

Last Word
Ojulari projects best as a stand up OLB in a 3-4 scheme at the next level. He has the pass rush ability and strength in the run game to play on all three downs. On 3rd downs, he should stand up on the edge and use his pass rush skill and athleticism to get to the quarterback, though he could put his hand down as well to mix it up. With his play speed, motor, and toughness, he could excel on most special teams units.

Strengths

- 1st step length
- Hand use
- Strength to set edge

Weaknesses

- Lacks some COD ability
- Uses same move too often

Critical Factors

Pass Rush Ability	1st Step Explosion	POA / Set Edge
7	7	6

Positional Factors

Pass Rush Repertoire	Bend	Hand Use	Play Strength
6	6	7	6
Range	Flat Coverage	Motor	FBI
7	6	6	5
Discipline	Tackling	Toughness	ST Value
6	6	6	6

Basic

Year	G	GS	Tackling Tackles	TFL	FF	Pass Rush Sacks	Hurries	Hits	KD	Pressures	Deflected
2018	3	0	3	0.0	0	0.0	1	1	0	1	0
2019	14	13	36	6.0	1	5.5	22	19	5	37	0
2020	10	10	31	12.5	4	8.5	19	17	8	36	2
	27	23	70	18.5	5	14.0	42	37	13	74	2

Advanced

Year	Tackling Broken Tackles	BT%	Tackle Share	ATD+	Pres%	Impact Pres Share	Holds Drawn	EPA on TFL	EPA on Sacks
2018	1	25%	0%	-20	6%	1%	1	0.0	0.0
2019	1	3%	4%	79	13%	14%	1	-1.3	-12.6
2020	5	14%	5%	200	21%	18%	3	-5.9	-20.0
	7	9%	3%	120	16%	12%	5	-7.2	-32.6

Deep Dive

Year	Stance 3-Point Stance%	Pass Rush Rush%	Sack%	True Pres%	When Run At Bnc%	Pos%	Total Points Run Def	Pass Rush	Total	Total Points Rtg Per Run	Per PR	Per Play
2018	66%	89%	0.0%	8%	-	-	1	0	1	77	56	64
2019	63%	90%	2.0%	13%	29%	38%	8	21	32	84	98	95
2020	58%	78%	4.9%	25%	18%	45%	8	28	39	90	99	99
	61%	85%	3.0%	17%	25%	41%	17	49	72	-	-	-

Kwity Paye

Report by Jordan Edwards

School	Height	Weight	Year	Jersey #	Hometown
Michigan	6026 E	272 E	4SR	19	Providence, RI

One Liner
Paye is a naturally explosive and powerful pass rusher, and if he can improve his pass rush repertoire he can be a dominant edge defender at the next level.

Overall
Kwity Paye lines up primarily as a weak-side defensive end in Michigan's base four-man front. He typically lines up as a 5- or 7-technique, but also stands up at times and has even shown the versatility to reduce down over guards and centers in certain passing situations. He played in 38 games and started in 20. He missed 2 games in the already shortened 2020 season with a groin injury. Paye has a thick, well-cut frame but lacks ideal length as an edge defender. He displays really good athleticism with the agility and burst to pair with his functional strength and power. Paye is a tough competitor who plays with a consistently high motor, rarely taking plays off.

Pass Game
Paye is a twitchy and explosive pass rusher off the edge, who also has the power and strength to collapse the pocket. He has good bend and hip mobility to dip and rip around the arc. Paye displays an effective bull rush as well, getting his hands inside the chest of blockers and generating power in his lower half to drive them into the backfield. He doesn't display a wide variety of pass rush moves, but his natural athleticism can mask some of these issues. He has strong, quick, and accurate hands to attack. He's disciplined as a pass rusher and stays in his rush lanes and soundly plays contain. Paye isn't utilized in coverage often, and when he does it's usually just as a QB spy at the line. His ability to read and react is adequate, but he has shown flashes of making good instinctive plays.

Run Game
Paye is a solid run defender who can set the edge and play with the good strength and power at the POA. He plays with good leverage and pad level when engaging blockers. He displays powerful hands to stack, but his ability to shed off of blocks can be refined. He's disciplined to his gap responsibilities, whether it be setting the edge or taking on blockers trying to wash him out inside. Paye is a solid tackler as well, displaying good technique and production. He has the motor and range to fly around to the ball at all areas of the field. Paye can improve his instincts and his ability to key and diagnose against the run. He's often a split-second late to read mesh points in the backfield or trigger to outside runs in his directions.

Last Word
Paye projects to be a three-down caliber player as an open side edge defender at the next level, with the ability to also rush the passer as a stand-up end. On third downs, his combination of power and quickness can be utilized from multiple alignments, as he reduces down well. If he can improve his instincts and rush repertoire up to his natural athleticism and power, his potential as a pass rusher can be special.

Strengths

- Natural athleticism
- POA/Set Edge
- Versatility

Weaknesses

- FBI/Instincts
- Pass rush repertoire
- Length

Critical Factors

Pass Rush Ability	1st Step Explosion	POA / Set Edge
6	7	6

Positional Factors

Pass Rush Repertoire	Bend	Hand Use	Play Strength
5	6	6	6
Range	**Flat Coverage**	**Motor**	**FBI**
6	4	7	5
Discipline	**Tackling**	**Toughness**	**ST Value**
6	6	6	5

Basic

| Year | G | GS | Tackling | | | Pass Rush | | | | | |
			Tackles	TFL	FF	Sacks	Hurries	Hits	KD	Pressures	Deflected
2017	9	0	5	2.0	0	1.0	1	0	0	2	0
2018	13	4	29	5.5	1	2.0	12	9	3	16	1
2019	12	12	49	11.0	0	6.5	20	15	4	33	0
2020	4	4	17	4.0	0	2.0	17	23	4	29	0
	38	20	100	22.5	1	11.5	50	47	11	80	1

Advanced

| Year | Tackling | | | | Impact | | | | |
	Broken Tackles	BT%	Tackle Share	ATD+	Pres%	Pres Share	Holds Drawn	EPA on TFL	EPA on Sacks
2017	0	0%	1%	-	-	1%	0	-2.2	-1.6
2018	3	9%	4%	104	8%	8%	1	-4.6	-3.5
2019	2	4%	6%	98	11%	14%	0	-5.8	-14.8
2020	2	11%	4%	113	23%	31%	0	-2.5	-2.9
	7	7%	4%	102	13%	10%	1	-15.1	-22.8

Deep Dive

| Year | Stance | Pass Rush | | | When Run At | | Total Points | | | Total Points Rtg | | |
	3-Point Stance%	Rush%	Sack%	True Pres%	Bnc%	Pos%	Run Def	Pass Rush	Total	Per Run	Per PR	Per Play
2018	98%	99%	1.0%	10%	25%	42%	9	11	22	99	92	97
2019	90%	99%	2.3%	12%	22%	33%	13	19	32	79	95	88
2020	91%	99%	1.6%	29%	40%	40%	6	12	19	83	99	97
	92%	99%	1.7%	14%	25%	36%	28	42	73	-	-	-

Rashad Weaver

Report by Matt Manocherian

School	Height	Weight	Year	Jersey #	Hometown
Pittsburgh	6043 V	265 V	5SR	17	Fort Lauderdale, FL

One Liner
Weaver lacks top explosiveness as a pass rusher but has a prototypical left defensive end skill set, winning in both the pass and run games with a combination of length, strength, and technique.

Overall
Rashad Weaver lines up at defensive end, usually on the left side, in Pitt's four-man front. He usually aligns in a three-point stance but will switch to a two- or four-point stance at times. He missed the entire 2019 season with a torn right ACL, but has started 28 of the 35 games that he has participated in for the Panthers. He has very good length and strength for the position, and he plays with great balance. He is more of a smooth athlete than dynamic, with just sufficient twitch and explosiveness. While he did rotate in and out of the game for Pitt, he showed good motor, working hard through the whistle.

Pass Game
In the pass game, Weaver lacks the burst off the line to be a top-end edge rusher, but he makes great use of his length to create space from those trying to block him. His best asset as a pass rusher is his hand use, effectively swiping blockers' hands away from his body. He shows a strong rip and dip move to try to get around the edge, and he also has an effective swim move that he uses to counter inside. He also has a spin move in his arsenal. He is not an elite bender and is more smooth than sudden as an athlete, so he will need to rely on variety and technique to win on the next level. He flashes power to complement his length, especially when working against tight ends. He does a good job of getting his hands up to disrupt passing lanes, but he is not well suited to consistently drop into coverage.

Run Game
In the run game, Weaver's calling card is the way he uses his length and strength very well to stack and shed, keeping offensive linemen away from his body. He shows the ability to dominate tight ends in the run game, and he does a very good job of setting the edge, keeping his outside arm free and working to hold his ground. He plays with very good discipline to stay home against the threat of a read option. He also displays a good motor and pursues plays from behind. He is a good tackler in general, but will let running backs squirm out of his arms from time to time.

Last Word
Weaver fits best as a left defensive end on the NFL level, where he can line up over tight ends and disrupt strongside run games. He is a very good 1st and 2nd down player who doesn't have top-end pass rush ability, but can win with hand use and variety. His skill set also might translate to the ability to reduce down and rush from the inside on 3rd downs. He can contribute on special teams, but doesn't project to be a core player.

Strengths
- Hand use
- Play strength
- Length

Weaknesses
- Lacks explosiveness
- Shows some stiffness
- Not a top-end pass rusher

Critical Factors

Pass Rush Ability	1st Step Explosion	POA / Set Edge
6	5	7

Positional Factors

Pass Rush Repertoire	Bend	Hand Use	Play Strength
6	5	7	7
Range	Flat Coverage	Motor	FBI
6	5	6	7
Discipline	Tackling	Toughness	ST Value
7	6	6	5

Basic

Year	G	GS	Tackling Tackles	TFL	FF	Pass Rush Sacks	Hurries	Hits	KD	Pressures	Deflected
2017	12	5	30	6.0	1	3.0	16	11	6	22	4
2018	14	14	47	14.0	2	7.0	30	22	10	45	5
2020	9	9	35	14.5	3	7.5	26	21	5	45	2
	35	28	112	34.5	6	17.5	72	54	21	112	11

Advanced

Year	Tackling Broken Tackles	BT%	Tackle Share	ATD+	Pres%	Impact Pres Share	Holds Drawn	EPA on TFL	EPA on Sacks
2017	4	12%	5%	-	-	13%	0	-4.2	-3.6
2018	6	11%	6%	144	14%	22%	2	-8.0	-11.8
2020	6	15%	5%	133	16%	19%	4	-7.2	-19.7
	16	13%	5%	140	18%	18%	6	-19.4	-35.1

Deep Dive

Year	Stance 3-Point Stance%	Pass Rush Rush%	Sack%	True Pres%	When Run At Bnc%	Pos%	Total Points Run Def	Pass Rush	Total	Total Points Rtg Per Run	Per PR	Per Play
2018	90%	98%	2.3%	13%	22%	33%	19	18	42	99	93	98
2020	97%	100%	2.6%	18%	50%	50%	15	28	46	98	99	99
	93%	99%	2.4%	16%	29%	37%	34	46	88	-	-	-

Gregory Rousseau

Report by Bryce Rossler

School	Height	Weight	Year	Jersey #	Hometown
Miami FL	6045 E	260 E	3SO	15	Hialeah, FL

One Liner
Rousseau is a young, length-and-strength projection whose physical profile and early production warrant confidence he'll develop into a quality NFL starter.

Overall
Greg Rousseau aligns as the left defensive end in Miami's even space fronts and has experience playing both standing up and with a hand in the ground. He opted out of the 2020 season and last played in 2019 as a 19-year-old redshirt freshman (13 games). He has excellent height/length and good weight with a wiry build that should be able to accommodate more weight. He is a good athlete with good quickness/agility/body control and sufficient explosiveness.

Pass Game
As a pass rusher, Rousseau has sufficient FBI to key high hats. He demonstrates adequate 1st step explosion due to long strides and an elevated pad level out of his stance. He shows good closing burst and wins primarily by utilizing his excellent length and good hand placement to soften the corner. He shows workable rip, push-pull, bull rush, and long-arm moves as a young and relatively inexperienced player. He projects to develop very good bull rush ability as he grows into his frame and adds strength. He may struggle to speed rush top competition at the NFL level. He flashes good bend to trim the corner. He has not consistently shown the ability to counter inside. Rousseau plays with a hot motor and has a lot of second-effort production. When asked to get out in the flats, he has mediocre coverage ability and appears uncomfortable dropping into fire zones.

Run Game
In the run game, Rousseau demonstrates sufficient ability to read his key, get off the ball, and engage the blocker. His excellent length and good play strength allow him to set the edge against base blocks. He has the ability to stack and shed blockers and is a consistently problematic assignment for tight ends. He shows good physicality and play strength to box pullers at the point of attack. His take-on technique against double teams is raw, but he has a natural anchor with which to hold ground and these blocks should not be a problem for him later in his development. He plays with good pursuit range and a high motor, and he can affect plays outside of his gap assignment late in downs. His athletic ability allows him to function well as a squeeze-and-pop defender against option runs. He plays with sufficient discipline on the edge. Natural issues with leverage and knee bend make him a sufficient overall tackler.

Last Word
Rousseau projects best as a strong-side defensive end in an even spacing front. His youth, relative inexperience, and time off legitimize concerns about the extent to which he'll have an impact as a rookie, but his physical profile is highly workable and sets his long-term floor as a three-down starter at the NFL level. He does not project as a core special teamer, but his length should allow him to contribute on kick and punt block units.

Strengths

- Hand use
- Length
- Play strength

Weaknesses

- 1st step explosion
- Pass rush repertoire
- Flat coverage

Critical Factors

Pass Rush Ability	1st Step Explosion	POA / Set Edge
6	5	6

Positional Factors

Pass Rush Repertoire	Bend	Hand Use	Play Strength
5	6	7	6
Range	Flat Coverage	Motor	FBI
6	4	6	5
Discipline	Tackling	Toughness	ST Value
5	5	6	5

Basic

Year	G	GS	Tackling			Pass Rush					
			Tackles	TFL	FF	Sacks	Hurries	Hits	KD	Pressures	Deflected
2018	2	0	5	0.0	0	0.0	0	0	0	0	0
2019	13	8	56	22.0	2	15.5	28	21	6	47	1
	15	8	61	22.0	2	15.5	28	21	6	47	1

Advanced

Year	Tackling				Impact					
	Broken Tackles	BT%	Tackle Share	ATD+	Pres%	Pres Share	Holds Drawn	EPA on TFL	EPA on Sacks	
2018	0	0%	1%	110	0%	0%	0	0.0	0.0	
2019	6	10%	8%	124	18%	20%	4	-8.7	-26.0	
	6	9%	4%	122	17%	11%	4	-8.7	-26.0	

Deep Dive

Year	Stance	Pass Rush			When Run At		Total Points			Total Points Rtg		
	3-Point Stance%	Rush%	Sack%	True Pres%	Bnc%	Pos%	Run Def	Pass Rush	Total	Per Run	Per PR	Per Play
2018	100%	100%	0.0%	0%	-	-	1	0	1	99	50	99
2019	87%	95%	5.8%	19%	28%	39%	17	26	47	97	99	99
	87%	95%	5.8%	19%	28%	39%	18	26	48	-	-	-

Quincy Roche

Report by Ronan Potts

School	Height	Weight	Year	Jersey #	Hometown
Miami FL	6027 V	243 V	5SR	2	Randallstown, MD

One Liner

Roche is a slithery, well-rounded edge rusher who projects as a three-down starter due to his advanced pass rush repertoire and explosiveness, though he needs to get stronger and improve his motor to reach his full potential.

Overall

Quincy Roche is an edge rusher in Miami's hybrid defense who predominantly lines up on the right side and splits time between putting his hand in the ground or standing up on the edge. He played in 49 career games, starting in 27, playing his first 3 seasons at Temple before joining Miami as a grad transfer in 2020. Roche is slightly undersized for an edge, but he is well proportioned, and he may still have room to bulk up, as he was able to do so after transferring to Miami. He is an explosive athlete with good play speed and very good pursuit ability. Roche's motor can run hot-and-cold at times, but when it's hot, he is a terrifying matchup for his opponent.

Pass Game

Roche is an impressive pass rusher with a diverse repertoire. His best move is his swipe, which he often uses to get inside of the tackle before transitioning to his speed rush to generate pressures and sacks. He also uses a pure speed rush, a rip move, an inside speed rush, and he has an impressive speed-to-power rush as well. He can generate pressure as both a stand-up and hand-down rusher. He is incredibly slithery as a pass rusher, with an impressive ability to make himself thinner and slither between the tackle and guard to generate pressure from the inside. When he's forced outside by the blocker, he shows good bend and ankle flexion. Roche is sufficient when asked to drop into coverage. He is best when asked to play the flat in zone coverage, but he has shown the ability to cover running backs man-to-man if needed.

Run Game

Roche is a solid defender against the run. As a tackler, he has good form and takes good angles, though he can struggle occasionally when his opponent forces him to quickly change direction. He can consistently produce tackles for loss due to his athleticism and ability to generate penetration, racking up over 50 throughout his career. He is sufficient at setting the edge, though he can get overpowered at times due to his size. That said, he competes and really attempts to stand his ground against doubles, occasionally forcing a stalemate at the POA. He has good discipline and uses his hands well against tackles and tight ends.

Last Word

Roche projects as a three-down starter, whose best fit is as a stand-up edge rusher due to his athleticism and being slightly undersized. He should shine on 3rd down, when he'll be able to pin his ears back and focus on rushing the passer. Roche profiles as a sufficient special teamer due to his play speed, toughness, and tackling ability.

Strengths
- Passrush ability
- Uses variety of rush moves
- 1st step explosion

Weaknesses
- Size/strength combo
- Hot-and-cold motor

Critical Factors

Pass Rush Ability	1st Step Explosion	POA / Set Edge
7	6	5

Positional Factors

Pass Rush Repertoire	Bend	Hand Use	Play Strength
7	6	6	5
Range	Flat Coverage	Motor	FBI
6	5	5	6
Discipline	Tackling	Toughness	ST Value
6	6	6	5

Basic

Year	G	GS	Tackling			Pass Rush					
			Tackles	TFL	FF	Sacks	Hurries	Hits	KD	Pressures	Deflected
2017	13	0	29	11.0	3	7.0	13	10	3	23	0
2018	13	5	56	9.0	2	6.0	24	10	6	31	3
2019	13	12	51	19.0	1	13.0	35	26	13	57	4
2020	10	10	49	16.5	2	4.5	17	22	7	34	1
	49	27	185	55.5	8	30.5	89	68	29	145	8

Advanced

Year	Tackling				Impact				
	Broken Tackles	BT%	Tackle Share	ATD+	Pres%	Pres Share	Holds Drawn	EPA on TFL	EPA on Sacks
2017	2	6%	3%	-	-	11%	1	-4.0	-12.7
2018	3	5%	6%	109	11%	16%	2	-4.5	-14.2
2019	8	14%	6%	132	16%	23%	3	-7.0	-25.0
2020	10	17%	6%	160	11%	18%	2	-15.8	-15.9
	23	11%	6%	133	15%	17%	8	-31.3	-67.8

Deep Dive

Year	Stance	Pass Rush			When Run At		Total Points			Total Points Rtg		
	3-Point Stance%	Rush%	Sack%	True Pres%	Bnc%	Pos%	Run Def	Pass Rush	Total	Per Run	Per PR	Per Play
2018	66%	84%	2.1%	13%	17%	48%	10	16	28	69	91	79
2019	59%	97%	3.6%	19%	36%	36%	15	27	45	87	98	94
2020	48%	97%	1.5%	13%	31%	54%	18	17	38	95	92	93
	58%	93%	2.4%	15%	28%	46%	43	60	111	-	-	-

Jayson Oweh

Final Grade: 6.7

Report by John Todd

School	Height	Weight	Year	Jersey #	Hometown
Penn State	6046 E	252 E	3SO	28	Howell, NJ

One Liner
Oweh is a raw specimen off the edge with rare straight-line speed for his size and impressive range in run defense, but he will need time to piece together his skill set to more consistently impact the passing game.

Overall
Jayson Oweh is an edge defender in Penn State's four-man base front, usually operating out of a three-point stance on the left side of his formation. He played in 24 career games with 8 starts. A natural basketball player, he didn't play organized football until his junior year of high school. He is a chiseled, athletic specimen with prototypical length for the modern edge defender. While not an exceptionally quick athlete laterally, his straight-line speed is jaw-dropping. He brings an impressive physicality and doesn't shy from contact.

Pass Game
Oweh has room to improve as a pass rusher, but his tools in this area are worth betting on. He has an explosive lower half but does not gain great depth in his first step or find himself first off the ball consistently. His play diagnosis is a weak point right now, as he too often bites on play action and hesitates when left uncovered to assess the situation. Oweh flashes mismatch potential, but his lack of a consistent rush plan hinders his win rate and results in wasted snaps with a sufficient motor to counter. His repertoire mostly consists of quick swipes inside and out and a straight arm bull rush using his long limbs to get the first punch. He has the ankle flexion to bend and shave the top of the arc. When he is able to find a window, he has great closing speed to finish hard and fast. He has minimal-coverage experience and would likely only be an asset in pursuit.

Run Game
Oweh has an impressive understanding of run defense given his brief playing experience. He fires into contact and does a good job of stalemating against most competition. His head-up run anchor doesn't hold up along the interior, but he sets a strong edge on the perimeter. He will lose the ball to misdirection, but otherwise does well to stack, read with his eyes, and make easy work of shedding in the hole with his length. He sticks to the hip of down blocks and wrong-arms split zones beautifully, physically dominating most tight ends. Oweh's technical skill set currently manifests itself better against the run than the pass; his hands are more active and he attacks with more conviction. However, his best traits are his excellent tackling range and pursuit. His length and closing speed allow him to force zone-read gives and still make the tackle, pinch run lanes and finish with an off hand, and most impressively chase down ballcarriers sideline to sideline and downfield.

Last Word
Oweh is still a bit of a projection, but he's a physical freak with the makings of an eventual high-end three-down starter. He is best suited as a wide-9 end, limiting his exposure to coverage responsibilities and interior-trench battles. He's made strides each year in college, and as he continues to better put his toolbox to use, his flashes of pass-rush prowess will become more consistent and his elite ceiling could be realized. Until then, he should be used in obvious game script situations as an exterior run defender and rotational pass rusher. His elite speed and size combo could be an asset on special teams if needed.

Strengths

- Range
- Perimeter run defense
- Freaky tools and potential

Weaknesses

- Play diagnosis
- Pass-rush plan and repertoire
- Change-of-direction skills

Critical Factors

Pass Rush Ability	1st Step Explosion	POA / Set Edge
6	6	6

Positional Factors

Pass Rush Repertoire	Bend	Hand Use	Play Strength
5	6	6	6
Range	Flat Coverage	Motor	FBI
8	3	5	4
Discipline	Tackling	Toughness	ST Value
5	6	6	6

Basic

Year	G	GS	Tackling			Pass Rush					
			Tackles	TFL	FF	Sacks	Hurries	Hits	KD	Pressures	Deflected
2018	4	0	3	2.0	0	2.0	1	0	0	3	1
2019	13	1	22	5.0	2	5.0	13	12	6	21	0
2020	7	7	38	5.5	0	0.0	14	17	7	24	1
	24	8	63	12.5	2	7.0	28	29	13	48	2

Advanced

Year	Tackling				Impact				
	Broken Tackles	BT%	Tackle Share	ATD+	Pres%	Pres Share	Holds Drawn	EPA on TFL	EPA on Sacks
2018	0	0%	0%	44	10%	1%	1	0.0	-2.0
2019	1	4%	2%	44	11%	8%	0	0.0	-9.7
2020	4	10%	7%	96	15%	18%	1	-8.0	0.0
	5	7%	3%	78	12%	8%	2	-8.0	-11.6

Deep Dive

Year	Stance	Pass Rush			When Run At		Total Points			Total Points Rtg		
	3-Point Stance%	Rush%	Sack%	True Pres%	Bnc%	Pos%	Run Def	Pass Rush	Total	Per Run	Per PR	Per Play
2018	97%	100%	6.7%	6%	0%	25%	0	1	2	51	67	60
2019	96%	98%	2.6%	10%	25%	58%	3	13	16	64	96	86
2020	92%	97%	0.0%	21%	40%	40%	15	8	23	99	88	95
	94%	98%	1.8%	14%	24%	48%	18	22	41	-	-	-

Carlos Basham Jr.

Report by Nathan Cooper

School	Height	Weight	Year	Jersey #	Hometown
Wake Forest	6033 V	281 V	5SR	9	Roanoke, VA

One Liner
Basham has the relentless pass rush ability, strength, and FBI to make a big impact at the next level, but his inconsistent motor, a high pad level, and lack of flexibility may hold him back.

Overall
Carlos Basham Jr. mainly lines up with his hand down as a defensive end to the field for Wake Forest in a hybrid even front. He mainly aligns in a 5-, 7-, or 9-technique, but sparingly stands up or reduces down. He started in 33 of 45 games during his career. He missed a game in 2020 after testing positive for COVID-19. He's a solid athlete, but doesn't possess great flexibility and is tight-hipped. He competes as a pass rusher, but his motor runs hot and cold, mostly in the run game.

Pass Game
Basham's production comes with his hand in the ground. He doesn't consistently have an explosive get-off, but is quick off the ball and relentless into the backfield. He uses speed rushes and swim moves way too frequently with a few rips and power moves sprinkled in, though he's a smart player and occasionally knows how to use the blocker's strengths against them and exploit their weaknesses. He uses good hand placement with good leverage. Basham's pad level will get too high at the POA allowing blockers to get into his chest and wash him out too easily. A lack of flexibility and tight hips also make it tough for him to bend effectively and efficiently around the edge. His lack of COD skills likely means he won't contribute much away from the line of scrimmage.

Run Game
Against the run, Basham is disciplined and does his job. However, he doesn't have the juice in the run game that he brings as a pass rusher. If he can't get into the backfield, he'll usually peel off and give up on the play, though he showed better pursuit in 2020 as compared to previous years. He also doesn't show the same strength in the run game as he brings as a rusher. He shows decent hand placement at times, but just doesn't seem to be strong enough to hold the edge, and gets washed out too often. Many times he'll try to get skinny and knife through holes completely running by the play instead of squaring up at the POA. Against tight ends, he shows good hands and that he can win those battles more times than not. He can deliver a blow as a tackler, though falls off too many opportunities. His tight hips make it tough for him to change directions quick enough against more elusive ballcarriers in the open field.

Last Word
Basham projects best as a low-end starting 4-3 defensive end with ability to reduce down as a rusher or use his strength as a 5-tech in an odd front. He possesses the skills to develop as a pass rusher and his deficiencies can be coached at the next level. On 3rd downs, he has the ability to come off the edge or reduce down. He could play on some select special teams units, but his inconsistent motor and tackling ability might hold him back from being a solid contributor.

Strengths
- Strong at POA
- Relentless pass rush
- High FBI

Weaknesses
- Pad level too high
- Tight hips
- Hot-and-cold motor

Critical Factors

Pass Rush Ability	1st Step Explosion	POA / Set Edge
6	6	5

Positional Factors

Pass Rush Repertoire	Bend	Hand Use	Play Strength
5	5	5	6
Range	Flat Coverage	Motor	FBI
5	5	5	6
Discipline	Tackling	Toughness	ST Value
6	5	6	5

Basic

Year	G	GS	Tackles	TFL	FF	Sacks	Hurries	Hits	KD	Pressures	Deflected
2017	13	1	25	2.0	0	0.0	12	8	4	15	3
2018	12	12	65	10.5	0	4.5	40	21	5	49	1
2019	13	13	57	18.0	3	11.0	39	27	10	61	4
2020	7	7	29	5.5	1	5.0	11	7	4	19	1
	45	33	176	36.0	4	20.5	102	63	23	144	9

Advanced

Year	Broken Tackles	BT%	Tackle Share	ATD+	Pres%	Pres Share	Holds Drawn	EPA on TFL	EPA on Sacks
2017	2	7%	3%	-	-	7%	1	-4.3	0.0
2018	9	12%	7%	115	13%	25%	7	-8.2	-8.5
2019	10	15%	7%	131	16%	32%	1	-9.3	-20.2
2020	5	15%	5%	7	10%	22%	1	-0.9	-8.7
	26	13%	5%	101	15%	21%	10	-22.8	-37.3

Deep Dive

	Stance	Pass Rush			When Run At		Total Points			Total Points Rtg		
Year	3-Point Stance%	Rush%	Sack%	True Pres%	Bnc%	Pos%	Run Def	Pass Rush	Total	Per Run	Per PR	Per Play
2018	97%	95%	1.2%	14%	35%	39%	10	22	34	64	92	81
2019	90%	96%	2.8%	18%	16%	47%	9	26	40	68	96	88
2020	83%	96%	2.5%	14%	21%	41%	5	11	18	68	92	83
	92%	96%	2.1%	15%	25%	42%	24	59	92	-	-	-

Ronnie Perkins

Report by DJ Marquardt

School	Height	Weight	Year	Jersey #	Hometown
Oklahoma	6026 E	247 E	3JR	7	St. Louis, MO

One Liner
Perkins has the athleticism, bend, and explosion teams covet in edge rushers, though he'll need to improve his repertoire and get stronger to hit his ceiling at the next level.

Overall
Ronnie Perkins is a weak-side defensive end in Oklahoma's base 3-3-5 defense. He started 25 of 33 career games for the Sooner. He served a 5-game suspension at the start of 2020 for a failed drug test prior to their 2019 bowl game. He is a very athletic player who moves around on the field at an exceptional level for his position. He is a competitively tough player with a very good motor. He consistently fires out of his stance and plays hard to the whistle on every snap.

Pass Game
Perkins is at his best when he utilizes his explosive burst to get off the line quicker than his opponent, where he then couples his rip move with very good bend to dip by tackles on the edge. He has active hands and is a polished hand fighter when rushing. He must improve upon his ways he beats blockers, as he has a limited arsenal of moves and relies on his rip move too often. He is a productive rusher who benefits more with a hand in the ground in order to stay low. He shows some athleticism when rushing from a 2-point stance, but he lacks the burst and repertoire to consistently be successful as a pass rusher on the next level. He rarely dropped into coverage at Oklahoma, though has the athletic ability and range to become a sufficient coverage player out in the flats if called upon to do so.

Run Game
Perkins is a tough run defender who does a good job setting the edge against pullers or tight ends, handling tight ends with ease. However, he struggles against double teams and lacks the ideal strength needed to eat up two defenders. When doubles come his way, he gets pushed off the ball too often and is rarely able to stand his ground and cause stalemates. He sometimes lacks gap integrity to cover his assignment, but overall, shows good discipline to play his gap when needed. He has the quickness and wiggle to slither through gaps and get into the backfield to make a play. He also shows burst on the edge to squeeze laterally down the line to make tackles and keep runs to short guns. He has quick hands, which allows him to shed blocks quickly to make up for his lack of length. That said, sometimes he'll try to shoulder off blockers instead of squaring up and using his hands.

Last Word
Perkins projects as a starting weak-side defensive end in a 4-3 scheme who could develop into a 3-4 OLB rusher, but would need some time and more polish before finding a starting role. He would be most comfortable in a 4-3 scheme, though he does need to add some weight to his frame. On 3rd downs, he should be coming off the edge with his hand in the ground, however, he could eventually reduce down with his skill set. He should provide value on special teams with his athleticism and play style.

Strengths

- Athleticism
- 1st step explosion
- Flexion/bend

Weaknesses

- Pass rush repertoire
- Double teams
- Play strength

Critical Factors

Pass Rush Ability	1st Step Explosion	POA / Set Edge
6	6	6

Positional Factors

Pass Rush Repertoire	Bend	Hand Use	Play Strength
5	7	5	5
Range	Flat Coverage	Motor	FBI
6	5	7	6
Discipline	Tackling	Toughness	ST Value
6	6	6	6

Basic

Year	G	GS	Tackling			Pass Rush					
			Tackles	TFL	FF	Sacks	Hurries	Hits	KD	Pressures	Deflected
2018	14	7	37	8.5	0	5.0	11	6	3	16	1
2019	13	13	37	13.0	1	6.0	25	13	3	32	0
2020	6	5	24	10.5	0	5.5	17	13	7	31	0
	33	25	98	32.0	1	16.5	53	32	13	79	1

Advanced

Year	Tackling				Impact				
	Broken Tackles	BT%	Tackle Share	ATD+	Pres%	Pres Share	Holds Drawn	EPA on TFL	EPA on Sacks
2018	4	10%	4%	125	7%	8%	0	-4.9	-4.9
2019	3	8%	5%	179	10%	14%	1	-7.1	-8.7
2020	3	11%	4%	153	18%	13%	1	-6.4	-9.2
	10	9%	4%	151	11%	12%	2	-18.4	-22.8

Deep Dive

Year	Stance	Pass Rush			When Run At		Total Points			Total Points Rtg		
	3-Point Stance%	Rush%	Sack%	True Pres%	Bnc%	Pos%	Run Def	Pass Rush	Total	Per Run	Per PR	Per Play
2018	64%	86%	2.2%	9%	19%	41%	8	10	18	68	83	74
2019	99%	100%	2.0%	12%	30%	45%	18	20	38	98	96	96
2020	91%	99%	3.2%	22%	44%	22%	6	14	20	94	99	98
	84%	95%	2.4%	13%	27%	39%	32	44	76	-	-	-

Joe Tryon

Report by Jeff Dean & Ty Dorner

School	Height	Weight	Year	Jersey #	Hometown
Washington	6045 E	262 E	4JR	9	Renton, WA

One Liner
Tryon has the physical gifts and motor to be an effective pass rusher, but his technique is raw and he will need to grow his rush plan and run defense to become a three-down player.

Overall
Joe Tryon is an edge defender in Washington's DB-heavy defense, evenly splitting his time between two- and three-point stances. He played in 25 career games with 14 starts, opting out of the 2020 season before it began. He has a long, athletic frame, that he's begun to add more muscle to, and fluid movement skills. He has burst out of the blocks and the speed to turn the corner. His motor runs very hot and he is active on every play, although his toughness in trench battles is inconsistent.

Pass Game
Tryon has a solidly explosive get-off that doesn't waste any steps. He fires out and has strong hands to drive into blockers. He attacks with an aggressive mindset and plays angry when rushing the passer. While his physical gifts are evident, he often lacks a plan to the QB, which results in wasted reps. He will show an occasional swim inside, but outside of a swipe and speed rush, lacks a high-level go-to move. Tryon doesn't consistently put pressure on the quarterback through his repertoire alone, which leads to a lot of production coming from opportunistic situations and extra efforts in pursuit. He shows a great deal of energy to continue working on extended plays and closes at the QB fast when he finds an opening. He showed an ability to cover the flat proficiently, but has minimal experience in man coverage. His hips are a little tight in space and can lock in on the QB instead of feeling routes, more often acting as a spy and downhill trigger player than a true underneath zone defender.

Run Game
Tryon can hold his own in the run game but will disappear for longer periods of time without making a play. His combination of length and strength allow him to hold the perimeter well enough, but he lacks discipline and will get fooled by play action, misdirection, and zone-read plays. He can be too preoccupied with trying to beat his block that he loses sight of the ballcarrier. He doesn't discard tight ends as consistently as he should, but he typically wins more battles than he loses. He will allow linemen to get into his pads and wall him off, and he hasn't shown a strong ability to shed in the trenches. He is at his best on the back side of run plays where he can use his motor to chase down ballcarriers from behind. He doesn't miss many tackles but needs extra help bringing down ballcarriers at times.

Last Word
Tryon projects as a pass rushing specialist who can work his way onto the field for all three downs with time. He fits best in a 4-3 scheme, as he's shown to be more explosive out of a three-point stance, but he'll need to continue improving his ability to set a strong edge. His natural pass rushing ability should allow him to see the field early on third downs, especially as he refines his rush plan and repertoire, and he should be a contributing member on special teams.

Strengths

- Get-off
- Motor and energy
- Attacking mindset

Weaknesses

- Rush plan and repertoire
- Run discipline
- Consistent block shedding inside

Critical Factors

Pass Rush Ability	1st Step Explosion	POA / Set Edge
6	6	5

Positional Factors

Pass Rush Repertoire	Bend	Hand Use	Play Strength
5	5	6	5
Range	Flat Coverage	Motor	FBI
6	4	7	5
Discipline	Tackling	Toughness	ST Value
4	5	5	5

Basic

Year	G	GS	Tackling			Pass Rush					
			Tackles	TFL	FF	Sacks	Hurries	Hits	KD	Pressures	Deflected
2018	12	2	19	2.0	0	1.0	8	5	3	10	2
2019	13	12	43	12.5	0	8.0	23	18	6	35	0
	25	14	62	14.5	0	9.0	31	23	9	45	2

Advanced

Year	Tackling				Impact				
	Broken Tackles	BT%	Tackle Share	ATD+	Pres%	Pres Share	Holds Drawn	EPA on TFL	EPA on Sacks
2018	1	5%	2%	119	11%	4%	2	-0.9	-1.5
2019	11	20%	5%	121	13%	16%	5	-7.3	-12.5
	12	16%	4%	121	12%	10%	7	-8.3	-14.0

Deep Dive

Year	Stance	Pass Rush			When Run At		Total Points			Total Points Rtg		
	3-Point Stance%	Rush%	Sack%	True Pres%	Bnc%	Pos%	Run Def	Pass Rush	Total	Per Run	Per PR	Per Play
2018	29%	70%	1.1%	11%	25%	50%	5	3	16	96	78	95
2019	52%	85%	2.9%	16%	25%	45%	1	20	32	55	97	86
	46%	81%	2.5%	14%	25%	47%	6	23	48	-	-	-

Shaka Toney   Final Grade: 6.5

Report by Ben Hrkach

School	Height	Weight	Year	Jersey #	Hometown
Penn State	6022 V	238 V	5SR	18	Philadelphia, PA

One Liner
Toney has innate pass-rush athleticism and burst that will allow him to get after quarterbacks early in his career, but he'll need to continue developing his run anchor and discipline will make him a three-down starter.

Overall
Shaka Toney played defensive end in Penn State's four-man base front, usually in a 3- or 4-point stance but standing up on occasion as well. He has started 22 of his 47 career games over his last 2 seasons. He's slightly undersized but has great length. He is an explosive athlete with good bend and agility. He displayed good toughness and had no issues sticking his face in the chest of blockers.

Pass Game
Toney does most of his damage against the pass. His go-to move is a speed rush out of a wide 9 in a 4-point stance, which is where his explosive get-off is the most impressive. His first step alone wins him many one-on-ones. He uses his burst and bend to beat tackles around the edge and shows good ankle flexion to flatten out and get to the quarterback. He shows a good rip move when tackles meet him at the top of his rush arc to get clean. He shows a sufficient spin move and general feel for when to jump inside blockers, but overall he'll need to improve these other rush techniques to become an elite rush specialist. On stunts, his agility helps him wrap tightly around the inside man, but he does not always finish and frequently stalls out. Toney excels in obvious passing situations when he can put two hands down and pin his ears back without having to consider runs or misdirection, but he's still a sufficient pass rusher on early downs. In 2020, he was asked to drop into the flat more and showed improvement. He has the raw athleticism to be sufficient in this area.

Run Game
Toney is a different player when asked to play the run, lacking the same explosion he shows on clear passing downs. He shows a sufficient ability to set the edge with a good straight arm and initial hand placement, but lacks the play strength to really anchor. He wins his battles by beating his man off the snap and shocking him with a one arm jab in the chest. When he wins first contact and keeps blockers extended, he does a good job of reading and reacting. Against larger, plodding linemen, Toney can use his agility to dip inside and rip through to the backfield, but this also washes him out of some runs and loses his gap discipline. Linemen with superior strength and footwork can swallow him up in the run game. He does have the strength and length to control tight ends, read, and shed. He is a sufficient tackler with the ability to wrap and roll.

Last Word
Toney projects as a passing-down rush specialist out of wide-9 alignments. He has improved his toolbox and three-down abilities through his career, but furthering to develop his play strength in run defense will get him more time on early downs. He was on both punt and punt return teams in college and shows the athleticism and toughness to play on NFL coverage units.

Strengths

- 1st step explosion
- Pass-rush athleticism
- Bend and flexibility

Weaknesses

- Edge setting and discipline
- Anchor strength
- Coverage technique

Critical Factors

Pass Rush Ability	1st Step Explosion	POA / Set Edge
6	7	5

Positional Factors

Pass Rush Repertoire	Bend	Hand Use	Play Strength
5	6	6	5
Range	Flat Coverage	Motor	FBI
5	5	6	5
Discipline	Tackling	Toughness	ST Value
5	5	6	6

Basic

			Tackling			Pass Rush					
Year	G	GS	Tackles	TFL	FF	Sacks	Hurries	Hits	KD	Pressures	Deflected
2017	12	0	20	6.5	2	3.5	22	20	7	31	0
2018	13	0	22	7.5	1	5.0	6	3	1	12	1
2019	13	13	41	8.0	0	6.5	28	17	1	39	1
2020	9	9	29	7.5	1	5.0	9	11	4	21	0
	47	22	112	29.5	4	20.0	65	51	13	103	2

Advanced

	Tackling				Impact				
Year	Broken Tackles	BT%	Tackle Share	ATD+	Pres%	Pres Share	Holds Drawn	EPA on TFL	EPA on Sacks
2017	1	5%	2%	-	-	11%	1	-4.2	-9.1
2018	2	8%	3%	68	7%	5%	4	-3.0	-8.1
2019	3	7%	4%	105	12%	15%	3	-3.0	-11.4
2020	3	9%	5%	88	11%	16%	1	-3.8	-7.2
	9	7%	4%	90	14%	12%	9	-14.1	-35.8

Deep Dive

	Stance	Pass Rush			When Run At		Total Points			Total Points Rtg		
Year	3-Point Stance%	Rush%	Sack%	True Pres%	Bnc%	Pos%	Run Def	Pass Rush	Total	Per Run	Per PR	Per Play
2018	91%	96%	2.8%	7%	40%	40%	4	6	11	65	77	74
2019	89%	94%	2.0%	13%	26%	32%	18	17	38	97	90	94
2020	80%	92%	2.5%	11%	20%	40%	7	15	22	72	98	88
	87%	94%	2.4%	11%	28%	37%	29	38	71	-	-	-

Patrick Jones II

Report by Nathan Cooper

School	Height	Weight	Year	Jersey #	Hometown
Pittsburgh	6044 V	264 V	5SR	91	Chesapeake, VA

One Liner
Jones possesses the explosion, heavy hands, and high motor to become a solid contributor at the next level, though a lack of flexibility and consistent finishing ability could hold him back initially.

Overall
Patrick Jones II primarily plays either left or right defensive end in a 5 through 9-technique depending on the game plan for Pittsburgh's 4-3 base defense after lining up at WDE in 2019. He started 24 of 48 career games for the Panthers. He's a solid athlete with a long and slender, but strong frame. He's a little stiff with tight hips, lacking some flexibility. He competes and plays tough with an extremely high motor.

Pass Game
Jones provides strong pass rush ability, primarily from a 3-point stance, though he has stood up at times. His first step and burst give him an advantage over bigger and/or slower blockers. Not only is he quick off the line, but he's explosive as well, often getting good first step length. He shows a decent repertoire which consists mostly of speed, bull, and rip moves, but lacks counter moves on a consistent basis. He can win with speed at times, but his stiff hips and lack of flexibility make it tough for him to efficiently bend around the edge. He will also jump at the POA when trying to gain the edge, often leaving himself vulnerable to getting knocked off his base. He performs best when he can use his strength. He has a long frame and uses very good extension and leverage at the POA. He's able to give a jolt to blockers with a strong initial punch and his strength and leverage allow for him to get under them. When he gets tired, there are times his pad level will rise, making it easier for blockers to neutralize him. He rarely drops into coverage, but his lack of flexibility and change-of-direction skills suggest he'd struggle in man coverage, though he could get by in zone coverage with his smarts and instincts.

Run Game
Jones is strong at the POA, showing explosion off the line and heavy hands which give him a leg up against blockers and allow him to dictate most of the movement at the line. Against tight ends, he's able to use his heavy hands and good extension to shock and shed them aside to get in on the tackle. He's disciplined and strong on the edge, showing good burst to squeeze down and close on ballcarriers once he reads run. He slips off of tackle attempts too often, especially when he has to change directions quickly, whether in the backfield or out in space, failing to finish the play.

Last Word
Jones projects as a low-end starting 4-3 defensive end at the next level. He has enough pass rush ability to be a contributor, but needs to become more consistent in the run game and convert on more of his tackle attempts. On 3rd downs, he could reduce down to use his power and leverage inside to rush the passer, something he did some in 2018. He could even provide some help on special teams due to a high motor and good play speed.

Strengths	Weaknesses
• Explosive off the line	• Rigid
• Heavy hands	• Lacks counter moves
• High motor	• Slips off some tackles

Critical Factors

Pass Rush Ability	1st Step Explosion	POA / Set Edge
6	7	5

Positional Factors

Pass Rush Repertoire	Bend	Hand Use	Play Strength
5	5	6	6
Range	Flat Coverage	Motor	FBI
5	4	7	6
Discipline	Tackling	Toughness	ST Value
6	5	6	5

Basic

			Tackling			Pass Rush					
Year	G	GS	Tackles	TFL	FF	Sacks	Hurries	Hits	KD	Pressures	Deflected
2017	10	0	6	1.0	0	0.5	2	0	0	3	0
2018	14	0	23	7.5	1	4.0	14	12	3	23	0
2019	13	13	42	11.5	4	8.5	38	30	9	54	1
2020	11	11	42	13.0	0	9.0	22	16	3	37	3
	48	24	113	33.0	5	22.0	76	58	15	117	4

Advanced

	Tackling				Impact				
Year	Broken Tackles	BT%	Tackle Share	ATD+	Pres%	Pres Share	Holds Drawn	EPA on TFL	EPA on Sacks
2017	0	0%	1%	-	-	2%	0	-1.4	-1.6
2018	0	0%	3%	107	10%	11%	0	-5.5	-7.4
2019	10	19%	5%	116	14%	21%	2	-4.4	-19.3
2020	2	5%	6%	131	11%	16%	4	-4.5	-20.0
	12	10%	4%	120	12%	14%	6	-15.8	-48.4

Deep Dive

	Stance	Pass Rush			When Run At		Total Points			Total Points Rtg		
Year	3-Point Stance%	Rush%	Sack%	True Pres%	Bnc%	Pos%	Run Def	Pass Rush	Total	Per Run	Per PR	Per Play
2018	93%	98%	1.7%	13%	50%	21%	8	11	19	87	87	86
2019	97%	99%	2.2%	18%	18%	18%	13	36	49	85	99	97
2020	95%	99%	2.7%	12%	40%	7%	19	20	42	99	94	96
	95%	99%	2.3%	15%	38%	15%	40	67	110	-	-	-

Adetokunbo Ogundeji

Report by Jordan Edwards

School	Height	Weight	Year	Jersey #	Hometown
Notre Dame	6043 V	256 V	5SR	91	West Bloomfield, MI

One Liner
Ogundeji has the ability to set the edge consistently with his length and attack power, but he needs to keep developing as a pure pass rusher to see the field on more critical downs at the next level.

Overall
Adetokunbo Ogundeji lines up primarily as a weak-side defensive end for the Fighting Irish. He has spent most of his career with his hand in the ground as a 5- or 7-tech, but also reduces inside as a 3-tech in sub package pass-rush situations. While Ogundeji has been overshadowed by a deep edge group in his career at Notre Dame, he played in 43 games with 12 of his 13 starts coming in the 2020 season. He has a towering frame with a wide wingspan and heavy hands. He's a high energy and high effort player, and a team captain, who doesn't take plays off.

Pass Game
Ogundeji is a heavy-handed pass rusher and shows good power at the POA. He shows good extension at the top of his rushes and the functional strength to collapse the pocket consistently. He has strong hands and his placement is consistent. He is still developing as a natural pass rusher, but his motor and competitiveness make up for his lack of pass-rush moves. Ogundeji isn't overly explosive off the edge, but he's sufficient with his first step quickness off the line. The biggest area of concern for Ogundeji is his lack of flexibility and bend around the corner. He seems to be aware of this deficiency, utilizing more bull rushes and long arm moves when rushing the passer. Ogundeji's power and length allows him to rush from the interior, as well. He's disciplined and stays in his rush lane, and his

FBI and awareness is steadily improving as he sees more reps. Ogundeji was sparingly used in coverage and his lack of range doesn't project well to do so at the next level either.

Run Game
Ogundeji can set the edge consistently and force runs back into the defense. He plays with heavy hands and can stack and stalemate blockers at the POA. He possesses a strong upper body and can extend well, but sometimes can be pushed back in double-team situations due to his less dominant anchor strength. His awareness and intelligence as a run defender are still works in progress, but his competitiveness and high motor will mask some of these issues in the interim. Ogundeji is a solid tackler and has good body control to make tough tackles at the LOS. His range and ability to gain ground quickly to recover against wide zone or misdirection plays is an area of concern.

Last Word
Ogundeji projects to be a solid starting first- and second-down edge defender at the next level with his hand in the ground in a four-man front. As he continues to develop his pass rush skill set, Ogundeji can still add versatility to reduce down and rush the pass from the interior on 3rd downs. His consistent motor will play in all situations while he develops his technique and football awareness.

Strengths
- Play strength
- Setting an edge
- Consistent motor

Weaknesses
- Bend off the edge
- Pass rush repertoire
- Range

Critical Factors

Pass Rush Ability	1st Step Explosion	POA / Set Edge
5	5	7

Positional Factors

Pass Rush Repertoire	Bend	Hand Use	Play Strength
5	4	6	7
Range	**Flat Coverage**	**Motor**	**FBI**
5	4	7	5
Discipline	**Tackling**	**Toughness**	**ST Value**
6	6	6	5

Basic

Year	G	GS	Tackling			Pass Rush					
			Tackles	TFL	FF	Sacks	Hurries	Hits	KD	Pressures	Deflected
2017	5	0	0	0.0	0	0.0	2	2	0	3	0
2018	13	0	24	3.0	2	1.5	9	5	3	12	2
2019	13	1	33	6.0	3	4.5	13	13	3	24	0
2020	12	12	22	7.0	1	7.0	27	23	8	43	0
	43	13	79	16.0	6	13.0	51	43	14	82	2

Advanced

Year	Tackling				Impact				
	Broken Tackles	BT%	Tackle Share	ATD+	Pres%	Pres Share	Holds Drawn	EPA on TFL	EPA on Sacks
2017	0	-	0%	-	-	1%	0	0.0	0.0
2018	1	4%	3%	73	9%	5%	1	-5.7	-3.0
2019	1	3%	4%	53	12%	12%	1	-2.7	-12.4
2020	6	21%	4%	148	15%	21%	5	0.0	-11.1
	8	9%	3%	83	13%	10%	7	-8.4	-26.5

Deep Dive

Year	Stance	Pass Rush			When Run At		Total Points			Total Points Rtg		
	3-Point Stance%	Rush%	Sack%	True Pres%	Bnc%	Pos%	Run Def	Pass Rush	Total	Per Run	Per PR	Per Play
2018	99%	99%	1.1%	8%	33%	50%	6	8	17	90	92	94
2019	96%	100%	2.3%	10%	19%	43%	11	15	26	97	97	97
2020	98%	99%	2.4%	15%	35%	38%	7	20	28	77	97	91
	98%	99%	2.1%	12%	29%	42%	24	43	71	-	-	-

Joseph Ossai

Report by Chad Tedder

School	Height	Weight	Year	Jersey #	Hometown
Texas	6031 E	253 E	3JR	46	Conroe, TX

One Liner
Ossai is an incredibly athletic and talented player, though raw, but with proper development on his pass rush technique, anticipation, and plan he could grow into a solid 3-down starter.

Overall
Joseph Ossai is an edge rusher in Texas' nickel defense, where he played as a Will LB, stand-up edge, and a wide-tech DE. In 2019, he was used mainly as a Will, lining up in the slot and covering the flats, rotating down to an edge on 3rd downs. In 2020, he was used exclusively as an edge rusher out of a 2- or 3-point stance. He started 24 of 36 games for the Longhorns. He's a long, sturdy athlete with quick acceleration and sideline-to-sideline speed, but has the room to put on some muscle. He plays with a hot motor and drives to be around the ball and make the extra-effort play.

Pass Game
Ossai uses his speed and athleticism with a little bend to beat the tackle around the outside. He is also utilized in twists to work inside. Occasionally he will use a quick inside rush to work a quicker line to the quarterback. He constantly works to get into the backfield, forcing tackles to chase him. Once he gets a clear line to the quarterback, Ossai shows good acceleration in closing to get pressure, or even a sack. However, he's limited in his hand techniques and lacks a plan of attack when rushing. Once he gets locked up inside on his bull and speed rushes, he is easy to stifle and run off the play. He is a straightforward rusher and relies on his athleticism to win, but with more development, he can mix his athleticism with technique, anticipation, and plan to become a well-rounded pass rusher. When asked to drop in coverage, he shows good athleticism in the flat or picking up a running back out of the backfield.

Run Game
Ossai is relatively slow off the snap and has a more reactionary approach. He shows some play strength to anchor down in his gap, hold a lineman up, and keep a hand free to make a tackle. He uses the same inside rush maneuver from before to meet the back in the backfield for TFLs. When the play is run away from him, he sprints down the line, searching for a path to the runner. His hand fighting struggles continue against the run, and he can get caught inside and easily driven off his gap. Sometimes, he gets caught up getting to the backfield too quickly that he doesn't notice the ballcarrier go by him.

Last Word
Ossai best projects as a low-end starter edge in a base 3-4 defense, where he can be utilized out of a two-point stance. He does need development in his hand usage, plan of attack, and expanding his repertoire on his pass rush. He has shown before that he can cover a zone out in the flat which, along with his pass rush, can make him a useful piece on 3rd down. His raw athleticism, physicality, and motor can make him a core member on all special teams units.

Strengths

- Hot motor & effort plays
- Speed rush
- Raw athleticism

Weaknesses

- Hand techniques
- Slow reaction to snap

Critical Factors

Pass Rush Ability	1st Step Explosion	POA / Set Edge
6	5	5

Positional Factors

Pass Rush Repertoire	Bend	Hand Use	Play Strength
5	5	4	5
Range	Flat Coverage	Motor	FBI
6	6	7	5
Discipline	Tackling	Toughness	ST Value
5	6	7	7

Basic

Year	G	GS	Tackling			Pass Rush					
			Tackles	TFL	FF	Sacks	Hurries	Hits	KD	Pressures	Deflected
2018	14	2	14	1.0	1	1.0	0	0	0	1	0
2019	13	13	89	14.5	1	4.0	35	30	13	44	2
2020	9	9	57	17.0	4	5.0	16	19	7	33	1
	36	24	160	32.5	6	10.0	51	49	20	78	3

Advanced

Year	Tackling				Impact				
	Broken Tackles	BT%	Tackle Share	ATD+	Pres%	Pres Share	Holds Drawn	EPA on TFL	EPA on Sacks
2018	2	13%	2%	32	3%	1%	1	0.0	-1.8
2019	23	21%	11%	124	20%	20%	2	-14.5	-7.2
2020	6	10%	8%	159	11%	22%	3	-16.8	-18.6
	31	16%	7%	126	14%	14%	6	-31.3	-27.6

Deep Dive

Year	Stance	Pass Rush			When Run At		Total Points			Total Points Rtg		
	3-Point Stance%	Rush%	Sack%	True Pres%	Bnc%	Pos%	Run Def	Pass Rush	Total	Per Run	Per PR	Per Play
2018	2%	70%	2.6%	4%	33%	33%	1	4	6	52	99	76
2019	1%	46%	1.9%	19%	8%	50%	23	15	61	95	93	95
2020	55%	90%	1.7%	11%	18%	41%	19	17	37	96	92	93
	22%	64%	1.8%	14%	16%	43%	43	36	104	-	-	-

Chris Rumph II

Report by Nathan Cooper

School	Height	Weight	Year	Jersey #	Hometown
Duke	6026 E	235 E	4JR	96	Gainesville, FL

One Liner
Rumph has the athleticism, bend, and range to be a high-end pass rusher at the next level, but his lack of strength, pass-rush moves, and ability to do much in the run game likely limits how much he can actually see the field.

Overall
Chris Rumph II lines up all over in Duke's base 4-2-5 defense, lining up mostly in a 5-through 9-technique with his hand in the ground, but also stands up on the edge and every other part of the line. He started 12 of 36 games for the Blue Devils. He has very good length with a lanky frame, but is an excellent athlete who is twitched up. He plays fast and competes with a high motor and toughness.

Pass Game
Rumph is an incredibly raw athlete. He has the length and twitch desired, but doesn't always know what he's doing. He played all over, so he rushed the passer from a 3-point stance on the edge and also standing up on the edge or over the interior. He isn't super explosive off the line but shows good first step quickness. He rarely uses any counter moves and mainly just tries to speed rush, swim, or slither between linemen to get into the backfield. On the edge, he shows very good bend and ankle flexion; he just lacks strength and gets pushed out of the play too easily. He produces more with pressures than sacks as he either narrowly skates by or slides off of sack opportunities. When he drops into coverage, he doesn't always know what's happening around him, but he's a smooth mover side to side, gaining depth in his drops and is able to stick with some backs and tight ends in man.

Run Game
Rumph lacks the strength at the POA to hold his ground and set the edge. He doesn't have the lateral strength to stay on track down the line, but has the speed and mobility to quickly burst down the line and make a play on the ballcarrier. He doesn't use his hands as much as he should at the POA, because when he does, he has the length and extension to get under linemen and better dictate the block. Even when he gets hands on linemen, he can struggle some due to his lack of strength, but on tight ends, he shows that he can gain control. He shows very good range to make plays outside the tackle box and pursue ballcarriers. As a tackler, he slips off some opportunities and doesn't always deliver a blow, but can sufficiently bring down runners.

Last Word
Rumph projects as a pass rusher that fits best as a 3-4 OLB. He has the athleticism and versatility to also fit as a 4-3 Sam or even a Will. He could also put his hand in the ground on occasion and rush the passer. Once he gets into an NFL weight room, he should add the desired muscle and strength to play these multiple positions without hindrance. On 3rd downs, he'd be best standing up and coming off the edge using his raw athleticism and skill set to get to the quarterback. That athleticism and competitiveness should allow him to play on most special teams units.

Strengths

- Incredible athleticism
- Bend around the edge
- Range & pursuit

Weaknesses

- Lacks strength
- Minimal counter moves
- Very raw

Critical Factors

Pass Rush Ability	1st Step Explosion	POA / Set Edge
6	6	4

Positional Factors

Pass Rush Repertoire	Bend	Hand Use	Play Strength
4	7	5	4
Range	Flat Coverage	Motor	FBI
7	6	6	5
Discipline	Tackling	Toughness	ST Value
5	5	6	6

Basic

Year	G	GS	Tackling			Pass Rush					
			Tackles	TFL	FF	Sacks	Hurries	Hits	KD	Pressures	Deflected
2018	13	1	23	7.5	0	3.0	7	6	1	13	1
2019	12	0	45	13.5	1	6.5	36	20	9	44	1
2020	11	11	53	13.0	1	8.5	26	24	8	45	1
	36	12	121	34.0	2	18.0	69	50	18	102	3

Advanced

Year	Tackling				Impact				
	Broken Tackles	BT%	Tackle Share	ATD+	Pres%	Pres Share	Holds Drawn	EPA on TFL	EPA on Sacks
2018	4	15%	3%	153	14%	7%	1	-5.5	-5.0
2019	3	6%	6%	115	23%	21%	3	-10.2	-10.3
2020	7	12%	8%	120	20%	28%	3	-10.2	-15.1
	14	10%	5%	124	20%	18%	7	-25.9	-30.4

Deep Dive

Year	Stance	Pass Rush			When Run At		Total Points			Total Points Rtg		
	3-Point Stance%	Rush%	Sack%	True Pres%	Bnc%	Pos%	Run Def	Pass Rush	Total	Per Run	Per PR	Per Play
2018	41%	83%	3.3%	13%	0%	44%	5	5	11	85	90	85
2019	57%	94%	3.4%	21%	30%	50%	17	21	41	99	99	99
2020	50%	85%	3.7%	21%	41%	53%	8	13	23	70	91	80
	51%	88%	3.5%	19%	28%	50%	30	39	75	-	-	-

Victor Dimukeje

Report by Sales Pinckney

School	Height	Weight	Year	Jersey #	Hometown
Duke	6022 E	265 E	4SR	51	Baltimore, MD

One Liner
Dimukeje is a tough player with a high motor on the edge who wins with speed around the corner and with pursuit skills, but would benefit from using more secondary moves and becoming more explosive to be a true all-around player.

Overall
Victor Dimukeje is an edge rusher in Duke's base 4-2-5 scheme, aligning primarily as a hand down 5- or 7-technique while also taking snaps as a stand-up backer on the edge. He started all 49 possible games for the Blue Devils in his career. He has a thick and muscular frame with good flexibility and athleticism, but only has average length. He plays with toughness and has a relentless motor in both pass rush and pursuit.

Pass Game
Dimukeje sports a sufficient get-off that doesn't have much true explosion at the snap, but makes up for it with good burst around the edge once he's into his pass rush. He tends to raise up out of his stance, sacrificing some of his natural leverage as a result. While he flashes a strong and accurate initial punch, he will often engage opposing linemen with wide hands out on the shoulder pads and can struggle to disengage if blockers get their hands on him early. He has a good single-arm chop to keep blockers from getting their hands on him, and combines it with good bend and rip to get around the corner. Despite lacking some long speed, his primary weapon is a good speed rush while flashing the ability to convert it into a power with a single-arm post using strong hands. His athleticism allows him to set up inside counter moves after pushing a hard speed rush, and while he doesn't utilize them often, he has shown he can do so effectively.

This also makes him effective when executing stunts as either the initial crosser or as the secondary looping rusher. He can disrupt and pressure the passer even when he can't get the sack, even causing the occasional fumble. He has minimal experience in coverage, and though he's a good overall athlete, he lacks the requisite range to project well as a flat or hook/curl defender.

Run Game
Dimukeje shows he can set the edge and prevent plays from getting to the outside and has the ability to consistently take on and beat tight ends. He displays good discipline against the read option and is a sound tackler both at the LOS and in the backfield. He struggles to disengage when blockers get their hands inside, but can cause stalemates instead of being driven back.

Last Word
Dimukeje projects as a low-end starter on the edge as a 4-3 defensive end who can contribute against both the run and pass. He can also stand up on the edge if needed. On passing downs, he can contribute on the edge or reduce down, though is better suited on the outside where he can use his speed. He has the requisite motor and toughness to play on special teams if needed, but his lack of long speed could hold him back on some units.

Strengths	Weaknesses
• Speed rush	• Consistency with secondary moves
• Setting the edge	• Initial punch
• Sound tackler	• Range

Critical Factors

Pass Rush Ability	1st Step Explosion	POA / Set Edge
6	5	6

Positional Factors

Pass Rush Repertoire	Bend	Hand Use	Play Strength
5	6	5	6
Range	Flat Coverage	Motor	FBI
5	4	7	6
Discipline	Tackling	Toughness	ST Value
6	7	6	5

Basic

Year	G	GS	Tackling			Pass Rush					
			Tackles	TFL	FF	Sacks	Hurries	Hits	KD	Pressures	Deflected
2017	13	13	42	8.0	0	2.5	19	12	4	24	1
2018	13	13	40	8.5	2	3.5	30	19	5	37	0
2019	12	12	38	10.0	1	9.0	25	22	9	38	2
2020	11	11	43	11.5	2	7.5	22	18	9	40	0
	49	49	163	38.0	5	22.5	96	71	27	139	3

Advanced

Year	Tackling				Impact				
	Broken Tackles	BT%	Tackle Share	ATD+	Pres%	Pres Share	Holds Drawn	EPA on TFL	EPA on Sacks
2017	4	9%	5%	-	-	12%	0	-4.7	-4.6
2018	7	15%	4%	94	10%	19%	3	-11.6	-6.4
2019	7	16%	5%	34	14%	18%	1	-2.2	-16.5
2020	2	4%	6%	81	13%	25%	3	-3.5	-15.1
	20	11%	5%	74	14%	18%	7	-22.0	-42.6

Deep Dive

Year	Stance	Pass Rush			When Run At		Total Points			Total Points Rtg		
	3-Point Stance%	Rush%	Sack%	True Pres%	Bnc%	Pos%	Run Def	Pass Rush	Total	Per Run	Per PR	Per Play
2018	99%	98%	1.0%	10%	14%	38%	13	13	26	75	79	76
2019	85%	98%	3.3%	16%	29%	55%	16	23	42	88	99	96
2020	76%	99%	2.4%	15%	32%	50%	12	23	36	73	98	88
	87%	98%	2.1%	13%	27%	49%	41	59	104	-	-	-

Patrick Johnson

Report by DJ Marquardt & Luke DeCello

School	Height	Weight	Year	Jersey #	Hometown
Tulane	6021 E	255 E	4SR	7	Chattanooga, TN

One Liner

Johnson's overall athleticism, physicality, and pass rush repertoire should allow him to experience success as a pass rusher off the edge until he gets stronger and can set the edge and shed blocks in the run game.

Overall

Patrick Johnson is a stand-up edge in Tulane's nickel defense, though has put his hand in the ground, played off-ball, and covered the slot. He played in 49 games, starting 37 of them for the Green Wave. He battled and played through several minor injuries, but didn't miss any games. Johnson is a very athletic football player who moves well at his size and plays fluidly throughout. He's a tough competitor who's always on the field trying to make plays happen for his team.

Pass Game

Johnson brings a solid set of skills and assets to the pass game. He attacks tackles from a stand-up edge position with a variety of different moves. He is more of a finesse and athletic rusher, but shows potential to improve as a power rusher as well. Johnson possesses good bend when beating defenders with speed on the edge, as he is able to get under the offensive tackle's hand usage and rip through. He also uses an athletic spin move to set up tackles on the outside and spin back inside. He struggles some with tackles who have a lot of length and strong hands to latch on, something he'll need to continue to improve upon, and mixing up moves even more should help. Johnson has the athletic ability and experience to zone cover properly and efficiently, showing fluidity and depth in his drops. While he didn't often play man coverage, he brings an aggressive and physical approach to running backs and tight ends that projects him as a capable man defender at the next level.

Run Game

Johnson dominates tight ends in the run game as he uses his strength to get them out of a gap and set the edge. However, he really struggles shedding blocks after setting the edge against tackles. He'll get turned inside too easily, allowing the edge to become an open running lane for ballcarriers. Against pullers, he shows inconsistency in taking them head-on to hold the edge. While being an aggressor and a fine tackler between the tackles, he struggles bringing players down in space and in the open field against outside runs or the screen game.

Last Word

Johnson best projects as low-end starting standup 3-4 OLB who can drop into coverage as well as get after the passer. He'll likely start out as a rotational pass rusher until he gets strong enough to hold the edge and make more consistent plays in the run game. Coming off the edge is likely what he'll be tasked to do 3rd downs. He is tough player with speed who can play on all special teams units if needed.

Strengths

- Athleticism
- Physicality/aggression
- Pass rush repertoire

Weaknesses

- Pass rushing vs. length
- Block shedding vs. the run
- Open-field tackling

Critical Factors

Pass Rush Ability	1st Step Explosion	POA / Set Edge
6	6	5

Positional Factors

Pass Rush Repertoire	Bend	Hand Use	Play Strength
6	6	6	5
Range	Flat Coverage	Motor	FBI
6	6	6	6
Discipline	Tackling	Toughness	ST Value
5	5	6	6

Basic

Year	G	GS	Tackling			Pass Rush					
			Tackles	TFL	FF	Sacks	Hurries	Hits	KD	Pressures	Deflected
2017	12	1	11	1.0	0	0.0	5	1	1	5	0
2018	13	12	50	17.0	4	10.0	32	22	9	47	1
2019	13	13	35	8.5	0	4.0	21	12	7	27	2
2020	11	11	38	14.5	2	10.0	19	15	5	32	3
	49	37	134	41.0	6	24.0	77	50	22	111	6

Advanced

Year	Tackling				Impact				
	Broken Tackles	BT%	Tackle Share	ATD+	Pres%	Pres Share	Holds Drawn	EPA on TFL	EPA on Sacks
2017	5	31%	2%	-	-	4%	1	-1.0	0.0
2018	5	9%	6%	155	19%	21%	4	-9.6	-15.0
2019	14	29%	5%	163	10%	15%	0	-6.5	-7.2
2020	7	16%	5%	94	13%	16%	4	-8.7	-18.0
	31	19%	4%	140	14%	15%	9	-25.8	-40.2

Deep Dive

Year	Stance	Pass Rush			When Run At		Total Points			Total Points Rtg		
	3-Point Stance%	Rush%	Sack%	True Pres%	Bnc%	Pos%	Run Def	Pass Rush	Total	Per Run	Per PR	Per Play
2018	3%	61%	4.2%	21%	56%	16%	12	18	38	71	97	86
2019	1%	68%	1.5%	12%	14%	38%	4	9	19	58	74	67
2020	8%	74%	4.0%	13%	15%	40%	8	21	31	64	99	82
	4%	67%	3.2%	15%	33%	29%	24	48	88	-	-	-

Cameron Sample

Report by Evan Butler

School	Height	Weight	Year	Jersey #	Hometown
Tulane	6026 V	274 V	4SR	5	Snellville, GA

One Liner

Sample has the athleticism, explosion off the snap, and versatility, even with some of his physical limitations to be a contributor at the next level.

Strengths: 1st step explosion; Strength; Versatility
Weaknesses: Range; Coverage skills; Length

Cameron Sample played primarily as a stand-up edge rusher in Tulane's nickel defense. He started in 38 of the 46 games he played over his 4 years for the Green Wave. What he may lack with some physical tools, Sample has the explosion and athleticism as an edge rusher to make a difference in both the passing and run games. He shows the toughness to compete on every down.

Sample is quick off the snap and shows his athleticism in getting to the quarterback. He doesn't possess great bend and sees success from inside swim and speed rushes. He has good strength which he uses in his bull rush. When his first move is unsuccessful, he reads the quarterback and tries to get his hands up in passing lanes. He has limited length, but makes up for it with good hand usage. In coverage, Sample has sufficient speed, which limits his range, but does possess short-area quickness. He's a good tackler even when in space.

In the run game, Sample shows his good strength and athleticism to engage at the POA and sufficiently set the edge. His 1st step explosion and get-off allows him to disrupt plays in the backfield. He shows good FBI as he's able to read and diagnose the play quickly while using his lateral quickness to make plays. Using his good grip strength and anchor, he can stack and shed blockers. Sample can be neutralized by linemen at times due to his lack of length. He doesn't possess top-end speed, which shows in his mediocre range to the D gap.

Sample projects as a reserve defensive lineman with the versatility to play multiple positions along the line, though fitting best as a defensive end in a 4-3. His strength and explosion give him the tools for success, but his limitations with length and speed make it difficult to be an every down starter. On 3rd downs or true passing situations, he can reduce down and rush from the interior. He projects well on special teams, but his lack of top-end speed could hinder him in space.

			Tackling			Pass Rush					
Year	G	GS	Tackles	TFL	FF	Sacks	Hurries	Hits	KD	Pressures	Deflected
2017	11	3	25	2.0	0	0.0	7	2	0	7	2
2018	11	11	40	6.0	0	4.0	8	5	2	12	1
2019	13	13	44	5.5	0	1.5	19	12	5	24	4
2020	11	11	53	8.5	2	6.0	31	16	4	42	1
	46	38	162	22.0	2	11.5	65	35	11	85	8

	Tackling				Impact				
Year	Broken Tackles	BT%	Tackle Share	ATD+	Pres%	Pres Share	Holds Drawn	EPA on TFL	EPA on Sacks
2017	2	7%	4%	-	-	5%	0	-2.9	0.0
2018	0	0%	5%	116	4%	5%	2	-4.0	-7.4
2019	3	6%	6%	91	6%	14%	0	-4.8	-1.6
2020	3	5%	7%	90	15%	22%	4	-4.2	-13.1
	8	5%	5%	98	9%	12%	6	-15.9	-22.1

	Stance	Pass Rush			When Run At		Total Points			Total Points Rtg		
Year	3-Point Stance%	Rush%	Sack%	True Pres%	Bnc%	Pos%	Run Def	Pass Rush	Total	Per Run	Per PR	Per Play
2018	100%	100%	1.4%	5%	26%	40%	13	6	20	90	68	80
2019	97%	99%	0.4%	7%	26%	47%	18	9	31	88	70	81
2020	36%	86%	2.1%	18%	9%	32%	18	20	38	86	96	90
	77%	95%	1.2%	10%	21%	41%	49	35	89	-	-	-

Critical Factors	
Pass Rush Ability	6
1st Step Explosion	6
POA / Set Edge	5

Positional Factors	
Pass Rush Repertoire	5
Bend	5
Hand Use	6
Play Strength	6
Range	4
Flat Coverage	5
Motor	6
FBI	6
Discipline	6
Tackling	6
Toughness	6
ST Value	6

Tarron Jackson

Report by Jeff Dean

School	Height	Weight	Year	Jersey #	Hometown
Coastal Carolina	6024 V	260 V	5SR	9	Aiken, SC

One Liner
Jackson uses his strong hands, football IQ, and diverse moves to creatively beat offensive lineman, but his lack of length and quickness may force him into a backup role at the next level.

Strengths: Strong hands; Pass-rushing diversity; Compact power
Weaknesses: Length; Tight hips; Lacks counter moves

Tarron Jackson plays strong-side defensive end in Coastal Carolina's base 3-4. He started 37 of 48 career games, 4 of which came when CCU was an FCS member in 2016. He missed 8 games in 2016 with a deep thigh contusion that formed a calcium deposit, 4 games with an undisclosed injury in 2017, and battled through a leg injury in 2018. While undersized, he's a sufficient athlete with a compact frame who possesses a solid initial burst and power using lower-body strength and leverage. He's a tough competitor who fights hard throughout the play.

Jackson is more successful as a pass rusher with his hand in the ground. He has a sufficient get-off, but places his feet well to create a low center of gravity with good balance. He has a diverse pass rush repertoire that includes developed swim, swat, and rip moves with a solid bull rush. When he can create pressure, he frquently finishes the play. His lack of length and inconsistent bend can hurt on the edge. Jackson has strong hands that allow him to swipe a lineman's hands off his chest or throw them past as he works around them. He lacks counter moves and can appear lost when his first move is thwarted. Without any real experience in coverage and tight hips, he likely won't be a consistent presence in coverage.

Jackson can sufficiently set the edge, but struggles against doubles. His FBI and understanding of placement put him in good position to hold the edge, though his lack of length and strength allows him to be swallowed up when more bodies are thrown at him. He's a sufficient tackler who wraps up well, but can be juked at the POA. When he wants to attack, he generates enough power to drive blockers back and be disruptive.

Jackson projects as a backup 4-3 DE utilized mainly as a pass rusher. Although he has limited experience reducing down, his stout frame, strong hands, and diverse repertoire could make him an interior presence on 3rd downs. He has limited special teams appeal and likely won't contribute much.

Year	G	GS	Tackling			Pass Rush					
			Tackles	TFL	FF	Sacks	Hurries	Hits	KD	Pressures	Deflected
2017	8	1	18	4.5	1	3.5	4	3	1	9	0
2018	12	12	57	11.0	0	3.0	16	11	4	22	0
2019	12	12	58	13.0	2	10.0	37	26	8	54	3
2020	12	12	52	13.0	3	8.5	37	31	11	59	0
	44	37	185	41.5	6	25.0	94	71	24	144	3

Year	Tackling				Impact				
	Broken Tackles	BT%	Tackle Share	ATD+	Pres%	Pres Share	Holds Drawn	EPA on TFL	EPA on Sacks
2017	3	14%	2%	-	-	6%	0	-4.8	-6.1
2018	4	7%	8%	117	7%	20%	4	-13.3	-2.9
2019	10	15%	8%	88	16%	36%	4	-4.4	-21.8
2020	11	17%	7%	142	14%	33%	4	-11.6	-18.1
	28	13%	6%	116	14%	24%	12	-34.1	-48.9

Year	Stance	Pass Rush			When Run At		Total Points			Total Points Rtg		
	3-Point Stance%	Rush%	Sack%	True Pres%	Bnc%	Pos%	Run Def	Pass Rush	Total	Per Run	Per PR	Per Play
2018	95%	99%	1.0%	8%	52%	42%	12	6	19	69	68	68
2019	79%	99%	3.0%	17%	27%	52%	8	32	43	65	99	92
2020	65%	99%	2.0%	19%	35%	56%	18	33	52	89	98	95
	79%	99%	2.1%	15%	37%	50%	38	71	114	-	-	-

Critical Factors	
Pass Rush Ability	6
1st Step Explosion	5
POA / Set Edge	5

Positional Factors	
Pass Rush Repertoire	6
Bend	5
Hand Use	7
Play Strength	5
Range	5
Flat Coverage	4
Motor	5
FBI	5
Discipline	6
Tackling	5
Toughness	6
ST Value	4

Wyatt Hubert

Report by Griffin Sullivan

School	Height	Weight	Year	Jersey #	Hometown
Kansas State	6026 V	265 V	4JR	56	Topeka, KS

One Liner

Hubert has enough pass rush skill, FBI, and a hot motor to be an effective rotational pass rusher, though a lack of strength and inconsistency in explosion and against the run likely limit him to a backup.

Strengths: Pass-rush skill; High FBI; Consistently hot motor
Weaknesses: Run-game effectiveness; Lacks some strength; Inconsistent explosion

Wyatt Hubert is a defensive end in Kansas State's nickel defense where he split time between having his hand in the ground or standing up on the edge. He started 29 of 34 games for the Wildcats. A high school wrestler, Hubert has a solid frame and shows good athleticism off the edge with a combination of speed and quickness. Hubert is a competitive, high-motor player who is always attacking and pursuing the ball.

Hubert can produce from both a 2- and 3-point stance with not only a high number of pressures, but also sacks, and even forcing his fair share of fumbles as well. He's quick off the ball, but lacks some explosion. He uses a variety of pass-rush moves that include spins, rips, swims, and bull rushes. He also makes the best of twists and stunts to work toward the interior of the line. He has a strong initial punch and uses good hand-fighting techniques to help him stay clean. He lacks some twitch and strength, and this limits his effectiveness against bigger, stronger offensive tackles. His motor is a lot of the reason why he makes as many plays as he does in the backfield. Hubert also shows smarts in that if he can't get to the quarterback, he gets his hands in passing lanes for deflections and batted passes. He didn't drop into coverage much, but has enough athleticism to at least be sufficient in that aspect.

Hubert gets overmatched by most offensive tackles and struggles to set the edge, getting sealed on most runs. He combats that with good play recognition to read blocking assignments and flow. He has enough burst to make plays from the back side, though he lacks the overall speed to do it consistently. He's a strong tackler who wraps up and brings ballcarriers down without issues the majority of the time.

Hubert projects as a 4-3 defensive end who has the versatility to stand up or even reduce down to 3-tech. On 3rd downs, 3-tech is his best fit to use his speed and pass-rush skill against interior rushers. His athleticism and high motor allow him to contribute on special teams.

Year	G	GS	Tackling Tackles	Tackling TFL	Tackling FF	Pass Rush Sacks	Pass Rush Hurries	Pass Rush Hits	Pass Rush KD	Pass Rush Pressures	Pass Rush Deflected
2018	12	7	34	8.5	0	4.5	23	15	9	28	2
2019	12	12	33	11.5	1	7.0	29	28	12	46	1
2020	10	10	28	13.0	2	8.5	15	10	2	30	1
	34	29	95	33.0	3	20.0	67	53	23	104	4

Year	Tackling Broken Tackles	Tackling BT%	Tackling Tackle Share	ATD+	Pres%	Impact Pres Share	Impact Holds Drawn	Impact EPA on TFL	Impact EPA on Sacks
2018	11	24%	5%	126	9%	16%	0	-7.1	-7.5
2019	8	20%	5%	115	19%	22%	3	-5.1	-13.8
2020	9	24%	4%	119	10%	19%	4	-7.3	-9.9
	28	23%	5%	120	12%	19%	7	-19.6	-31.2

Year	Stance 3-Point Stance%	Pass Rush Rush%	Pass Rush Sack%	Pass Rush True Pres%	When Run At Bnc%	When Run At Pos%	Total Points Run Def	Total Points Pass Rush	Total Points Total	Total Points Rtg Per Run	Total Points Rtg Per PR	Total Points Rtg Per Play
2018	92%	97%	1.5%	10%	21%	54%	8	12	27	76	82	85
2019	63%	95%	2.8%	20%	7%	38%	10	24	37	83	99	97
2020	55%	98%	2.8%	12%	24%	43%	7	22	30	70	97	89
	70%	97%	2.3%	13%	16%	45%	25	58	94	-	-	-

Critical Factors

Pass Rush Ability	6
1st Step Explosion	5
POA / Set Edge	4

Positional Factors

Pass Rush Repertoire	6
Bend	5
Hand Use	6
Play Strength	5
Range	6
Flat Coverage	5
Motor	7
FBI	6
Discipline	6
Tackling	6
Toughness	6
ST Value	6

Payton Turner

Report by Ben Hrkach

School	Height	Weight	Year	Jersey #	Hometown
Houston	6053 V	270 V	4SR	98	Houston, TX

One Liner

Turner is a versatile defender who has the length, ability, and explosiveness to be a rotational contributor, though he needs to get stronger, improve his pad level, and add to his repertoire before he'll hit his ceiling.

Strengths: Explosiveness; COD ability; Length
Weaknesses: Plays high; Pass-rush moves; Lower-body strength

Payton Turner is a defensive end in Houston's nickel defense. He played 3- & 5-tech in 2018-19 before moving to the edge in 2020. He started 27 of 39 games, and missed the final game of 2018 with a foot injury and missed time in 2020 with knee and hand injuries. He's a power forward on the field and blends agility, COD, and explosiveness with his size. He shows good toughness and plays with violent hands.

When lined up on the edge, Turner looks more explosive when standing up. He wins with length and get-off and has sufficient bend to flatten at the top of speed rushes. He has active, violent hands and can get clean from linemen as well as shock them. He doesn't display many moves and sticks with an outside dip & rip and bull rush, though he's begun to develop a push-pull as well. He currently beats interior blockers with his agility and length. He can jab-step and swim a lunging lineman, as well as stun them with his hands. Turner stalls out too frequently because he tends to play high, giving up his chest with mediocre leg drive. However, he does a good job of getting his hands in passing lanes. Turner rarely dropped into coverage, but has good COD skills and eye discipline.

Turner is better at penetrating than setting the edge. He plays too high and will get moved off of his spot by double teams or powerful linemen. He can split doubles and is a good back-side defender. He has good range, agility, and a feel for where the play is heading. He's a good tackler and has shown some attacking mentality. Using his COD, Turner can rapidly retrace and chase when a play gets outside of him. In 2020, he displayed an improved motor and was frequently making tackles down the field.

Turner projects as a versatile, reserve defensive end. He has very good length and agility, and has displayed a much improved feel for the game, though needs to continue to add strength. His skill set allows him to bring special teams value.

			Tackling			Pass Rush				
Year	G	GS	Tackles	TFL	FF	Sacks	Hurries	Hits	KD	Pressures	Deflected
2017	11	0	14	2.0	0	1.0	5	2	1	6	2
2018	11	11	40	5.5	0	0.0	7	5	3	7	5
2019	12	12	33	8.0	0	4.0	21	14	8	29	3
2020	5	4	25	10.5	1	5.0	4	6	2	13	2
	39	27	112	26.0	1	10.0	37	27	14	55	12

	Tackling				Impact				
Year	Broken Tackles	BT%	Tackle Share	ATD+	Pres%	Pres Share	Holds Drawn	EPA on TFL	EPA on Sacks
2017	3	18%	2%	-	-	4%	0	-1.1	-1.4
2018	5	11%	4%	130	2%	4%	1	-8.5	0.0
2019	3	8%	5%	147	10%	16%	3	-6.1	-8.9
2020	1	4%	5%	157	14%	10%	0	-6.0	-12.0
	12	10%	4%	142	8%	9%	4	-21.7	-22.3

	Stance	Pass Rush		When Run At		Total Points			Total Points Rtg		
Year	3-Point Stance%	Rush%	Sack%	True Pres%	Bnc%	Pos%	Run Def	Pass Rush	Total	Per Run	Per PR	Per Play
2018	98%	100%	0.0%	4%	11%	41%	10	6	16	63	56	63
2019	89%	98%	1.4%	11%	32%	50%	18	11	32	98	82	92
2020	67%	97%	5.4%	18%	6%	25%	10	10	22	99	99	99
	90%	99%	1.3%	9%	18%	41%	38	22	70	-	-	-

Critical Factors	
Pass Rush Ability	5
1st Step Explosion	6
POA / Set Edge	4

Positional Factors	
Pass Rush Repertoire	5
Bend	5
Hand Use	6
Play Strength	5
Range	6
Flat Coverage	5
Motor	6
FBI	5
Discipline	5
Tackling	6
Toughness	6
ST Value	6

Daelin Hayes

Report by Sales Pinckney & Max Nuscher

School	Height	Weight	Year	Jersey #	Hometown
Notre Dame	6036 V	261 V	5SR	9	Belleville, MI

One Liner
Hayes is a strong run defender on the edge with an ideal frame and growable traits as a pass rusher if he can refine his rush plan and repertoire on passing downs.

Strengths: 1st step and initial-punch power; Edge setting; Run discipline
Weaknesses: Block shedding; Rush plan and repertoire depth; Coverage and space comfortability

Daelin Hayes played as an outside linebacker in Notre Dame's 3-4 defense. He played in 53 career games, starting 25 of them. He missed the final 9 games of the 2019 season with a torn labrum, something he did in both shoulders during high school. He has a good frame for the position with good length and strong acceleration, but only sufficient overall athleticism. He plays with good toughness and a high motor on every play.

Hayes has a good, explosive first step and closes hard to the ball with strength and power. He has a strong initial punch that shocks linemen. He flashes a good speed-to-rip combo around the corner but isn't consistent with it and can run himself out of plays. He has a good feel for cross-face moves to get skinny to the inside when he can keep blockers away from his chest. He doesn't dominate with a bull rush beyond initial contact, and overall has limited depth to his repertoire and lacks a rush plan for counters. In coverage, he has good range in space but isn't natural moving backwards. He has enough athleticism to contribute to the flats but isn't effective covering backs and tight ends outside of that.

Hayes is stout at the point of attack and sets a strong edge. His heavy hands and strong initial punch allow him to shuck off tight ends and disrupt linemen. He plays with good pad level and leverage to hold his ground. However, while he has active hands, he struggles to disengage at the line, especially when blockers get into his chest. He shows good discipline against zone read plays and options and holds his gaps soundly to force runs inside. He's a solid tackler at the line of scrimmage but has had issues in the open field.

Hayes projects as a good rotational edge defender at the next level. He played a stand-up role in college but would best fit in a three-point stance moving forward with his edge strength and inconsistencies dropping in coverage. He will be a good early-down run defender while he refines his pass rush abilities, and should be a capable special teams contributor.

		Tackling			Pass Rush					
Year	G	GS	Tackles	TFL	FF	Sacks	Hurries	Hits	KD	Pressures	Deflected
2016	12	0	11	2.0	1	0.0	1	0	0	1	1
2017	13	12	31	6.5	0	3.0	17	12	3	22	0
2018	12	1	27	4.5	0	2.0	18	10	5	21	2
2020	12	12	18	6.0	2	3.0	14	18	6	26	1
	53	25	92	22.0	3	9.0	52	42	14	74	5

	Tackling				Impact				
Year	Broken Tackles	BT%	Tackle Share	ATD+	Pres%	Pres Share	Holds Drawn	EPA on TFL	EPA on Sacks
2016	0	0%	1%	-	-	1%	0	-6.4	0.0
2017	3	9%	4%	-	-	10%	2	-3.9	-4.4
2018	4	13%	3%	112	9%	9%	2	-2.4	-7.0
2020	5	22%	3%	166	12%	13%	4	-2.7	-7.1
	12	12%	2%	140	14%	8%	8	-17.7	-19.9

	Stance	Pass Rush			When Run At		Total Points			Total Points Rtg		
Year	3-Point Stance%	Rush%	Sack%	True Pres%	Bnc%	Pos%	Run Def	Pass Rush	Total	Per Run	Per PR	Per Play
2018	2%	83%	0.8%	11%	24%	24%	5	11	18	68	84	78
2020	3%	83%	1.4%	9%	10%	38%	5	17	30	73	97	93
	2%	83%	1.2%	10%	17%	31%	13	30	54	-	-	-

Redshirt season not shown but included in totals

Critical Factors	
Pass Rush Ability	5
1st Step Explosion	6
POA / Set Edge	6

Positional Factors	
Pass Rush Repertoire	5
Bend	5
Hand Use	5
Play Strength	6
Range	6
Flat Coverage	5
Motor	6
FBI	5
Discipline	6
Tackling	5
Toughness	6
ST Value	5

Elerson Smith

Report by Nathan Cooper

School	Height	Weight	Year	Jersey #	Hometown
Northern Iowa	6064 V	262 V	5SR	16	Minneapolis, MN

One Liner

Smith is a long, athletic edge that plays with good leverage and hand use, though a lack of play strength, flexibility, and ineffectiveness against double teams likely forces him into a backup role.

Strengths: Plays with leverage; Hand use/punch; Mixes up pass-rush moves
Weaknesses: Lacks play strength; Negated vs. doubles; Too stiff

Elerson Smith primarily plays right defensive end in Northern Iowa's hybrid 4-3/3-3-5 defense, but will also reduce to a 3- or 4-tech in odd-fronts and even stand up on occasion. He started 15 of 38 career games. A 4-sport athlete, he has good athleticism with a long frame that still has room for growth. He competes with toughness and a high motor out on the field.

Smith uses a wide variety of moves, of which his favorites seem to be speed rushes and swipes when getting around the edge, but will also mix in speed-to-power, swim, and push-pulls. He relies on counters on the majority of his speed rushes, because he lacks some flexibility and bend. His first step explosion is apparent when he can pin his ears back and get to the quarterback. Though he mainly put his hand in the ground, he can win standing up as well. His long frame allows him to play with good leverage and he also shows strong hands and initial punch, though his pad level will get high at times. He was rarely asked to cover, and while his skill set allows him to be effective in the flats, he'd have some trouble changing directions to stay with receivers.

Smith delivers a jolt and latches on with good hands at the POA and can work over tight ends when 1-on-1. However, he lacks the overall strength to consistently set the edge, especially against doubles. He lacks explosion on non-obvious passing situations. Smith shows discipline by squeezing down and making sure nothing comes around his way before closing on the ball. He's more of a wrap-up and drag-down tackler and rarely knocks ballcarriers back.

Smith projects as a 3-4 outside linebacker at the next level where he can primarily be used as a pass rusher. In a 4-3 scheme, he bulk up and add some weight to play with his hand in the ground. On 3rd downs, he's at his best on the edge and getting to the quarterback. He's not going to be a core special teamer, but he can be a quality guy on most units.

Elerson Smith was 6-foot-6, 205 pounds entering college but gained 50 pounds within his first two years in school. That helped make him into an impactful defensive lineman without hurting any important skills. Smith didn't play in 2020 but he was highly regarded last time he experienced game action. Phil Steele pegged him as the FCS Preseason Player of the Year before the season was halted.

"He brings speed," Northern Iowa defensive line coach Bryce Paup said in the fall of 2019. "He's a longer (former UNI standout and now CFL linebacker) Rickey Neal that is really quick off the ball. He's got long levers. He's really strong."

The last Northern Iowa defensive lineman to be drafted was James Jones by the Browns in the third round in 1991. As noted earlier in the book with Spencer Brown, UNI has had a good draft showing recently, with a player selected in 2015 (the most notable, David Johnson), 2016 (cornerback Deiondre' Hall) and 2018 (wide receiver Daurice Fountain) after not having anyone selected from 2009 to 2014.

Critical Factors	
Pass Rush Ability	6
1st Step Explosion	5
POA / Set Edge	5

Positional Factors	
Pass Rush Repertoire	7
Bend	5
Hand Use	6
Play Strength	5
Range	5
Flat Coverage	5
Motor	6
FBI	6
Discipline	6
Tackling	5
Toughness	6
ST Value	6

    # Jonathon Cooper   **Final Grade: 5.9**

Report by Stephen Marciello

School	Height	Weight	Year	Jersey #	Hometown
Ohio State	6026 V	254 V	5SR	0	Gahanna, OH

One Liner
Cooper is a solid overall edge defender with good leadership qualities, a strong first step and quick hands, but his limited anchor strength and raw rush technique need refinement.

Strengths: Discipline and intelligence; Initial-punch power; Get-off and play speed
Weaknesses: Anchor strength; Pass-rush plan; Length

Jonathon Cooper is a three-point defensive end for Ohio State, playing on both sides of their four-man front. He played in 45 career games with 25 starts. He was limited to only 4 games in 2019 due to an ankle injury. Cooper is a very good athlete with decent quickness and straight-line speed but lacks some length for his size. A team captain, he plays with a hot motor and commands the respect of his teammates.

Cooper has a strong get-off from his wide techniques and gains good depth with his initial step. He shows good, technical hand use to attack linemen and win in multiple ways. He loves to use an inside swipe move to plant outside and juke through the box, as well as the leg drive and strong hands at contact to shock linemen in a bull rush. He works a decent speed rush but lacks some bend and runs himself out of plays at times with wide angles. He generates solid pressure despite sufficient overall pass rush abilities, but he didn't convert sacks at a high clip and often lacks a counter plan. He has had minimal experience dropping into coverage, but his speed and flexible hips are sufficient traits in space.

Cooper thrives when slanting inside against the run, knifing through run lanes with his first step. Otherwise, while he sets a sufficient edge, he lacks the anchor strength to consistently stalemate at the line. He struggles to shed blocks after being engaged and is better making a move before contact. His quick initial punch makes up for his lack of length at times to keep outside contain. Cooper plays with good run discipline and football intelligence against zone reads, pulling linemen, and other misdirection. He is a sure tackler and shows strong motor and pursuit skills from the back side.

Cooper projects as a 4-3 wide edge at the next level where he can attack with a runway and stay out of true trench battles. He needs to improve his rush technique and his lower-body strength to become a more complete player. He would make for a sufficient special teamer but his abilities in space are questionable.

Year	G	GS	Tackling			Pass Rush					
			Tackles	TFL	FF	Sacks	Hurries	Hits	KD	Pressures	Deflected
2016	6	0	6	1.0	0	1.0	1	0	0	2	0
2017	14	0	14	3.0	0	2.0	5	2	0	7	0
2018	13	13	26	6.5	0	2.5	23	15	5	30	0
2020	8	8	26	4.0	2	4.0	20	17	7	34	1
	45	25	77	15.5	2	10.5	57	38	12	82	1

Year	Tackling				Impact				
	Broken Tackles	BT%	Tackle Share	ATD+	Pres%	Pres Share	Holds Drawn	EPA on TFL	EPA on Sacks
2016	0	0%	1%	-	-	1%	0	0.0	-0.4
2017	0	0%	2%	-	-	2%	0	-1.1	-3.0
2018	3	10%	3%	120	9%	11%	3	-6.2	-3.6
2020	2	7%	6%	77	16%	18%	0	0.0	-8.1
	6	7%	2%	76	13%	7%	3	-7.2	-16.6

Year	Stance	Pass Rush			When Run At		Total Points			Total Points Rtg		
	3-Point Stance%	Rush%	Sack%	True Pres%	Bnc%	Pos%	Run Def	Pass Rush	Total	Per Run	Per PR	Per Play
2018	98%	95%	0.8%	10%	19%	48%	16	11	32	99	77	94
2020	96%	97%	1.8%	18%	38%	62%	6	17	23	80	98	94
	97%	96%	1.2%	14%	25%	58%	22	33	59	-	-	-

Redshirt season not shown but included in totals

Critical Factors	
Pass Rush Ability	5
1st Step Explosion.	6
POA / Set Edge	5

Positional Factors	
Pass Rush Repertoire	5
Bend	5
Hand Use	6
Play Strength	5
Range	6
Flat Coverage	5
Motor	6
FBI	6
Discipline	6
Tackling	6
Toughness	5
ST Value	5

William Bradley-King

Final Grade: 5.9

Report by Jeff Dean & Jarrett Rodgers

School	Height	Weight	Year	Jersey #	Hometown
Baylor	6033 V	254 V	5SR	99	Kansas City, MO

One Liner

William Bradley-King has the football IQ, violent hands, and motor to make an NFL team, but his limited athletic profile as an edge rusher limits the appeal to a valuable backup role.

Strengths: Violent hands; Diverse pass rush repertoire; High motor
Weaknesses: Bend; COD ability; Limited upside

William Bradley-King plays edge in Baylor's 3-3-5 defense, mainly playing with his hand in the ground. He started 24 of 39 career games and began his career at Arkansas State before transferring to Baylor in 2020. A high school discus and wrestling competitor, Bradley-King is a sufficient athlete who lacks ideal COD skill. He has good strength throughout his frame and is fairly filled out. He plays with a high motor and his effort wears down blockers, winning late in games because of it.

Bradley-King wins battles with his pass-rushing technique. He has an explosive first step that fires out into the chest of the lineman. He has strong hands to knock away block attempts, using good leverage and extension. He keeps his outside arm free and pushes the pocket inwards instead of trying to run the arc. He lacks the ideal bend to get under the opposition and turn the corner. Bradley-King has a diverse set of pass-rushing moves. He has a developed speed-to-power, rip, bull rush, and swipe that all showcase his violent hands. He flashes an inside move and a push-

pull, but lacks comfortability with those. When he stalls, he gets his hands into passing lanes causing numerous deflections. He looks comfortable in coverage, but struggles to stick with shiftier backs because of his tight hips.

Bradley-King uses his strength and discipline to hold the edge in the run game, but lacks burst to squeeze down the line. He has good form against the run and will make a few plays in the backfield. He's a sufficient tackler when tracking down ballcarriers, but struggles a little to finish in the open-field. His football IQ and technique allow him to be a steady run defender even when he isn't making big plays.

Bradley-King projects as a backup 4-3 defensive end, but could play in a 3-4. He wins by understanding his strengths, but his lack of twitch and bend limit his pass-rush growth potential. He should be a quality special teams player with his athleticism and skill set.

			Tackling					Pass Rush				
Year	G	GS	Tackles	TFL	FF	Sacks	Hurries	Hits	KD	Pressures	Deflected
2017	5	0	6	1.0	0	1.0	1	1	1	3	1
2018	12	3	31	9.0	2	6.0	15	10	5	23	1
2019	13	13	50	13.0	2	8.5	48	20	11	61	0
2020	9	8	30	4.5	0	2.5	19	12	3	28	2
	39	24	117	27.5	4	18.0	83	43	20	115	4

	Tackling						Impact			
Year	Broken Tackles	BT%	Tackle Share	ATD+	Pres%	Pres Share	Holds Drawn	EPA on TFL	EPA on Sacks
2017	2	25%	1%	-	-	1%	0	0.0	-1.6
2018	1	3%	4%	124	12%	13%	3	-2.9	-13.6
2019	7	12%	5%	130	14%	31%	3	-4.8	-9.9
2020	4	12%	5%	110	12%	24%	2	-1.3	-6.0
	14	11%	4%	123	13%	17%	8	-9.0	-31.1

	Stance	Pass Rush		When Run At			Total Points			Total Points Rtg		
Year	3-Point Stance%	Rush%	Sack%	True Pres%	Bnc%	Pos%	Run Def	Pass Rush	Total	Per Run	Per PR	Per Play
2018	89%	97%	3.1%	14%	38%	38%	7	18	27	94	99	98
2019	90%	98%	2.0%	16%	16%	29%	20	25	46	86	94	89
2020	65%	92%	1.1%	14%	20%	40%	7	16	25	67	96	84
	82%	96%	2.0%	15%	21%	34%	34	59	98	-	-	-

Critical Factors	
Pass Rush Ability	5
1st Step Explosion	6
POA / Set Edge	5

Positional Factors	
Pass Rush Repertoire	6
Bend	4
Hand Use	6
Play Strength	6
Range	5
Flat Coverage	4
Motor	7
FBI	6
Discipline	6
Tackling	5
Toughness	6
ST Value	6

Jordan Smith

Report by John Todd

School	Height	Weight	Year	Jersey #	Hometown
UAB	6061 V	255 V	5SR	22	Lithonia, GA

One Liner

Smith profiles as an intriguing, lengthy mismatch off the edge, but his rigidity and lack of stoutness could keep him from reaching his potential.

Strengths: Length; Closing speed; Block shedding
Weaknesses: Bend and flexibility; Run anchor; Rush repertoire

Jordan Smith is a standup edge defender in UAB's base nickel defense. He has started 22 of 23 games for the Blazers after initially signing with Florida. Smith was suspended for the 2017 season for his involvement in a credit card scandal and left the program. He attended JUCO before ending up at UAB for the last 2 years of his career. He is extremely long and lanky and has been slowly adding bulk to his frame. He has good burst and closing speed but is a bit rigid laterally and lacks flexibility. He works hard to give multiple efforts in his rush, but his interior toughness wanes.

Smith often gets a good jump off the snap and uses his long strides to eat up ground upfield. He attacks with active but unrefined and inaccurate hands. His exceptional length is a great asset but he doesn't take advantage of it enough. Smith lacks the ankle flexion and leg drive to flatten down and straight-arm at the top of the arc. Smith often utilizes predetermined finesse rushes that show potential, but most of his success comes second-efforting his way into pressures. He finishes fast, and his length alone can often unsettle the pocket. He can reroute off the line and cover ground in pursuit, but otherwise is not much of an asset in coverage.

Smith will attack with violence on occasion but is not a consistent physical presence against the run. He lacks an anchor to stalemate inside against even tight ends. He doesn't make life difficult for most competition at the point of attack physically and will give ground at contact, but Smith is an adept block shedder and has good tackling range. He also plays zone-reads very well, staying disciplined to force decisions and make plays on the ball both ways.

Smith projects as a reserve edge defender with a compelling ceiling, ideally in a wide-9 or standup role. He lacks the versatility to bump inside in sub packages and would need additional development to play off-ball. You can't teach his length, but until he improves his play strength and raw technique as a pass rusher, he should be a sufficient special teams coverage unit addition.

			Tackling			Pass Rush					
Year	G	GS	Tackles	TFL	FF	Sacks	Hurries	Hits	KD	Pressures	Deflected
2016	0	0	1	0.0	0	0.0	1	1	1	1	0
2019	14	13	59	18.5	4	10.0	35	31	15	55	1
2020	9	9	42	9.5	0	4.5	33	26	15	47	2
	23	22	102	28.0	4	14.5	69	58	31	103	3

	Tackling				Impact				
Year	Broken Tackles	BT%	Tackle Share	ATD+	Pres%	Pres Share	Holds Drawn	EPA on TFL	EPA on Sacks
2016	0	0%	0%	-	-	0%	0	0.0	0.0
2019	6	9%	8%	135	19%	21%	3	-15.1	-16.2
2020	3	7%	8%	138	21%	32%	3	-5.8	-8.2
	9	8%	5%	136	20%	17%	6	-20.9	-24.4

	Stance	Pass Rush			When Run At		Total Points			Total Points Rtg		
Year	3-Point Stance%	Rush%	Sack%	True Pres%	Bnc%	Pos%	Run Def	Pass Rush	Total	Per Run	Per PR	Per Play
2019	11%	95%	3.5%	20%	25%	44%	12	33	46	90	99	99
2020	18%	88%	2.0%	22%	9%	18%	12	17	34	90	98	96
	14%	92%	2.9%	21%	19%	33%	24	50	80	-	-	-

Critical Factors

Pass Rush Ability	5
1st Step Explosion	6
POA / Set Edge	5

Positional Factors

Pass Rush Repertoire	4
Bend	4
Hand Use	5
Play Strength	4
Range	6
Flat Coverage	4
Motor	6
FBI	6
Discipline	6
Tackling	6
Toughness	5
ST Value	5

Chauncey Golston

Report by Griffin Sullivan & Michael Churchward

School	Height	Weight	Year	Jersey #	Hometown
Iowa	6046 V	268 V	5SR	57	Detroit, MI

One Liner
Golston has ideal measurables and is a proficient run stopper on the edge, but he'll need to improve his solo pass-rush abilities in order to see more playing time.

Strengths: Length and hand use; Edge discipline; Stack and shed
Weaknesses: Rush plan; Lower-half explosion and anchor; Motor

Chauncey Golston is an edge defender in Iowa's nickel-heavy defense, usually as a 5-tech but also comfortably reducing inside on some passing downs and even standing up. He played 43 career games with 21 starts the past 2 years. He has an athletic frame and a massive wingspan and hands. He moves well for his size but isn't a quick change-of-direction athlete. He rarely leaves the field, but his motor suffers on extended drives and late in games.

Golston doesn't consistently explode off the ball, but he plays with good pad level into contact. He does a great job of utilizing his immense length to win first contact on the perimeter. From there, however, Golston doesn't rush with a plan or show a bevy of moves to stack on top of one another. He shows a solid bull rush into a blocker's chest and will flash quick hands, but more often than not he lacks creativity once engaged to win one-on-one and can't tightly shave down the arc. He works well when reduced inside with more pronounced athletic and length advantages. He doesn't have the open-field range and flexibility to chase down flushed mobile quarterbacks or drop into coverage.

Golston sets a strong, technical edge with his long arms and stays disciplined to his gap assignments to contain and force. He does a great job of immediately getting his hands on blockers off the snap and stacking right away while he reads, then shedding in run lanes. He will work to the sideline if a run bounces outside, but he isn't rangy enough to make abnormal solo efforts. While he has flexed inside in passing situations, he is a liability there in run defense, as he lacks the anchor strength to hold up in his lower half. He's a solid tackler and packs a punch on ballcarriers between the tackles.

Golston projects as a backup edge defender on run downs, with the ability to reduce inside in pass-rushing sub packages. He'll need to improve his rush plan to more consistently take advantage of his length and work different alignments on third downs. He could have a role on certain special teams units.

			Tackling			Pass Rush					
Year	G	GS	Tackles	TFL	FF	Sacks	Hurries	Hits	KD	Pressures	Deflected
2017	12	0	2	0.0	0	0.0	0	0	0	0	0
2018	13	0	34	9.0	0	3.5	11	5	3	16	1
2019	13	13	49	9.5	0	3.0	28	14	6	35	5
2020	8	8	43	8.5	1	5.5	15	14	4	28	1
	46	21	128	27.0	1	12.0	54	33	13	79	7

	Tackling				Impact				
	Broken		Tackle			Pres	Holds	EPA on	EPA on
Year	Tackles	BT%	Share	ATD+	Pres%	Share	Drawn	TFL	Sacks
2017	0	0%	0%	-	-	0%	0	0.0	0.0
2018	2	6%	4%	100	7%	10%	4	-7.3	-5.3
2019	7	13%	6%	100	8%	20%	1	-11.5	-4.9
2020	4	9%	8%	104	11%	24%	2	-4.4	-15.3
	13	9%	4%	101	9%	12%	7	-23.3	-25.5

	Stance	Pass Rush			When Run At		Total Points			Total Points Rtg		
	3-Point			True			Run	Pass		Per	Per	Per
Year	Stance%	Rush%	Sack%	Pres%	Bnc%	Pos%	Def	Rush	Total	Run	PR	Play
2018	95%	98%	1.6%	8%	43%	48%	4	12	20	57	90	80
2019	87%	97%	0.7%	8%	41%	34%	15	11	34	90	71	83
2020	84%	97%	2.2%	12%	18%	47%	7	18	30	69	97	92
	88%	97%	1.3%	9%	36%	42%	26	41	84	-	-	-

Redshirt season not shown but included in totals

Critical Factors	
Pass Rush Ability	5
1st Step Explosion	5
POA / Set Edge	6

Positional Factors	
Pass Rush Repertoire	5
Bend	4
Hand Use	6
Play Strength	5
Range	5
Flat Coverage	4
Motor	4
FBI	6
Discipline	6
Tackling	6
Toughness	5
ST Value	5

Malcolm Koonce

Report by Jacob Halleen

School	Height	Weight	Year	Jersey #	Hometown
Buffalo	6030 E	250 E	4SR	50	Peekskill, NY

One Liner

Koonce is an athletic pass rusher who uses an explosive 1st step and speed to get the quarterback, but his inconsistencies in the run game and lack of counter moves likely limit him to a rotational pass rusher.

Strengths: 1st step explosion; Speed rush; Motor
Weaknesses: Setting the edge; Pass rush repertoire; Shedding blocks

Malcolm Koonce is an edge rusher in Buffalo's base 3-4 defense. He mostly stands up, but also aligned at 5- and 7-technique when his hand was in the dirt. He started 19 of 45 games at Buffalo. Koonce has a long frame with good size for the position and is a good athlete who shows quick initial burst at the snap. He shows competitiveness and displays a high motor as he rushes the passer.

Koonce uses his 1st step explosion to get to the quarterback. He played both standing up and with his hand down, but was a more explosive pass rusher standing up. He shows good bend and ankle flexion when turning the corner against offensive tackles. While he lacks consistent play strength, he uses his length and an arm bar to get into the lineman's chest before turning the corner. He doesn't show an array of pass-rush moves, but uses his speed and a rip move most frequently with an occasional spin. He's effective with his initial move, but lacks counters to consistently get to the passer. He'll take himself too deep and away from the pocket before attempting to

counter back into the play. He was rarely used in coverage, but has the athleticism and discipline to sufficiently drop into the flats.

Koonce does a sufficient job of setting the edge, but struggles to shed stronger blockers. He gets too upright and lacks lower body strength to consistently get free. He shows the ability to use his quick hands and feet to get around tight ends and offensive tackles to make plays in the backfield. He understands his run assignments and stays disciplined by not losing contain. He's an efficient tackler who shows good technique to wrap up the ballcarrier.

Koonce projects to be a backup, stand-up edge rusher in a 3-4 front at the next level. Due to his inconsistencies as a run defender and his strong ability to get to the quarterback, he will likely play mostly on 3rd downs initially. He has the speed and toughness to be a contributor on special teams units.

Year	G	GS	Tackling			Pass Rush					
			Tackles	TFL	FF	Sacks	Hurries	Hits	KD	Pressures	Deflected
2017	12	0	15	1.0	0	1.0	4	1	1	5	0
2018	14	0	28	4.0	1	3.0	19	12	3	24	1
2019	13	13	32	11.0	3	9.0	31	25	4	49	0
2020	6	6	29	6.5	0	5.0	11	10	3	23	1
	45	19	104	22.5	4	18.0	65	48	11	101	2

Year	Tackling				Impact				
	Broken Tackles	BT%	Tackle Share	ATD+	Pres%	Pres Share	Holds Drawn	EPA on TFL	EPA on Sacks
2017	4	21%	2%	-	-	4%	0	0.0	-1.2
2018	1	3%	3%	80	10%	13%	0	-1.6	-5.1
2019	3	9%	5%	78	18%	25%	3	-2.6	-24.8
2020	4	12%	6%	82	15%	22%	0	-2.9	-6.3
	12	10%	4%	80	15%	16%	3	-7.1	-37.4

Year	Stance	Pass Rush			When Run At		Total Points			Total Points Rtg		
	3-Point Stance%	Rush%	Sack%	True Pres%	Bnc%	Pos%	Run Def	Pass Rush	Total	Per Run	Per PR	Per Play
2018	43%	95%	1.3%	11%	16%	42%	7	12	20	72	88	82
2019	23%	94%	3.3%	20%	25%	50%	8	33	41	74	99	98
2020	14%	95%	3.2%	15%	33%	33%	2	6	11	60	80	72
	27%	94%	2.6%	15%	22%	44%	17	51	72	-	-	-

Critical Factors	
Pass Rush Ability	5
1st Step Explosion	6
POA / Set Edge	5

Positional Factors	
Pass Rush Repertoire	5
Bend	6
Hand Use	5
Play Strength	5
Range	5
Flat Coverage	5
Motor	6
FBI	5
Discipline	5
Tackling	6
Toughness	6
ST Value	5

Hamilcar Rashed Jr.

Report by John Todd

School	Height	Weight	Year	Jersey #	Hometown
Oregon State	6031 V	254 V	5SR	9	Phoenix, AZ

One Liner

Rashed Jr.'s statistical production is a bit misleading in the context of his true pass-rush abilities, but his quick hands and movement skills should make for a versatile rotational-edge defender at the next level.

Strengths: Quick hands; Comfortable mover in space
Weaknesses: Consistent burst; Play strength; Lane discipline

Hamilcar Rashed Jr. is an edge defender in Oregon State's base nickel defense, operating out of a two-point stance. He played in 43 career games with 28 starts, playing through a broken thumb in 2019 and lower-body injuries in 2020. He's athletically cut with good length but little bulk. He's a fluid, comfortable athlete in space but lacks explosion and a consistently hot motor to finish.

Off the snap, Rashed lacks a consistent burst upfield to speed rush and tighten down at the top. He is often used on end-tackle stunts but has shown some rush lane issues and struggles to avoid getting stunned by guards. Rashed's best quality is the quickness in his hands to swipe, swim, and counter at the point of attack, as well as strike into the chest and generate a bull rush. However, his overall strength, explosive, and bend limitations result in less-impactful pressure production than his 2019 numbers suggest, commonly tallying cleanup and coverage sacks. In coverage, he has proven to be comfortable in a backpedal, is capable of redirecting, and shows solid feel for routes around him.

Rashed isn't much of an anchor against the run, lacking the lower-body strength to stack and stalemate head up in the trenches. However, he does set a solid edge with his straight arm to flush runs inside and can swipe off blocks to make tackles in the hole. He handles most competition from tight ends and split zones well. Rashed's jump cutting to avoid blocks causes problems with his run lane discipline. He has good speed in pursuit but is missing the extra gear required to make abnormal plays outside his range. He is a solid tackler for an edge and will deliver the occasional blow.

Rashed projects as a backup edge defender in a two-point stance, where he can work within various blitz schemes on passing downs and occasionally bail into coverage. He lacks the ability to be a true one-on-one pass rusher at this stage, but his hands are worth developing. His movement skills in space project well to special teams duties.

			Tackling			Pass Rush					
Year	G	GS	Tackles	TFL	FF	Sacks	Hurries	Hits	KD	Pressures	Deflected
2017	12	0	0	0.0	0	0.0	0	0	0	0	0
2018	12	10	46	11.0	1	2.5	6	2	0	10	3
2019	12	11	61	20.5	2	13.0	22	8	2	38	3
2020	7	7	23	2.0	1	0.0	9	5	1	11	0
	43	28	130	33.5	4	15.5	37	15	3	59	6

	Tackling				Impact				
Year	Broken Tackles	BT%	Tackle Share	ATD+	Pres%	Pres Share	Holds Drawn	EPA on TFL	EPA on Sacks
2017	1	100%	0%	-	-	0%	0	0.0	0.0
2018	11	19%	6%	99	8%	9%	0	-12.8	-5.3
2019	11	15%	8%	135	14%	23%	4	-14.3	-24.6
2020	8	26%	5%	85	8%	13%	2	-1.9	0.0
	31	19%	5%	110	11%	13%	6	-29.0	-29.9

	Stance	Pass Rush		When Run At		Total Points			Total Points Rtg		
Year	3-Point Stance%	Rush%	Sack%	True Pres%	Bnc%	Pos%	Run Def	Pass Rush	Total	Per Run	Per PR	Per Play
2018	0%	62%	1.9%	8%	40%	55%	2	6	13	50	87	58
2019	0%	77%	4.9%	16%	5%	40%	14	16	36	86	92	89
2020	1%	75%	0.0%	9%	6%	63%	3	2	1	61	61	57
	0%	72%	2.9%	13%	18%	52%	19	24	50	-	-	-

Critical Factors	
Pass Rush Ability	5
1st Step Explosion	5
POA / Set Edge	5

Positional Factors	
Pass Rush Repertoire	5
Bend	5
Hand Use	7
Play Strength	4
Range	5
Flat Coverage	6
Motor	5
FBI	5
Discipline	4
Tackling	6
Toughness	5
ST Value	6

Charles Snowden

Report by Blake Moore, Daniel Jankuloski, & Joe McDonald ⊕

School	Height	Weight	Year	Jersey #	Hometown
Virginia	6062 E	232 E	4SR	11	Silver Spring, MD

One Liner

Snowden has most of the physical skills needed with solid range and tackling ability, but will need to develop some variety to his pass rush and improve his motor to become a consistent contributor.

Strengths: Tackling; Range; Length
Weaknesses: Pass rush repertoire; Play recognition; Inconsistent motor

Charles Snowden is stand-up edge rusher in Virginia's 3-4/2-4-5 defense playing to the short side of the field. He started 35 of 45 games for the Cavaliers, missing the final 2 games of 2020 with a broken ankle. Snowden has a long, but very skinny frame with merely sufficient athleticism. He plays hard, but shows an inconsistent motor, though some of it looks to stem from stamina issues.

Against the pass, Snowden shows good length on his 1st step, but lacks the explosiveness to make an impact off the snap. He plays with a high pad level and lacks ideal bend to get underneath offensive tackles. He shows flashes of good hand usage when speed rushing along the outside, but rarely shows any other moves. He has shown he can win if he sets up his moves, such as speed-to-power, to get blockers guessing or on their heels, but doesn't do it often enough. In coverage, he does a good job of using his length and size. He has enough long speed to stick down the field, but lacks the acceleration and COD ability to cover quicker receivers. In zone, though high in his back pedal, he gets depth and shows good range, but lacks some overall awareness.

Snowden is a very good tackler against the run. When the ball comes his way, he's able to force bounces or make plays, but when the ball doesn't, he lacks the fire and desire to pursue from the back side. Even though he can set the edge against college tackles, he currently lacks the overall strength to do it with consistency in the future. He showed decent hand usage when required, but would throw a shoulder in every once in a while instead of squaring up to pullers.

Snowden projects as a depth 3-4 OLB who can rush the passer or drop into coverage. He has some skill with enough athleticism to pair with his size which can't be taught, though he'll need to bulk up and get stronger. On 3rd downs, he can drop into flat coverage or rush the passer off the edge. He needs to improve his motor, but has enough speed and toughness to play some special teams.

			Tackling			Pass Rush					
Year	G	GS	Tackles	TFL	FF	Sacks	Hurries	Hits	KD	Pressures	Deflected
2017	10	0	9	2.0	1	1.5	2	1	1	4	0
2018	13	13	56	7.5	1	2.5	20	16	5	24	8
2019	14	14	70	10.5	0	5.0	34	17	12	43	4
2020	8	8	45	10.0	1	6.0	4	5	2	12	2
	45	35	180	30.0	3	15.0	60	39	20	83	14

	Tackling					Impact			
Year	Broken Tackles	BT%	Tackle Share	ATD+	Pres%	Pres Share	Holds Drawn	EPA on TFL	EPA on Sacks
2017	0	0%	1%	-	-	2%	0	-1.1	-3.7
2018	7	11%	7%	102	12%	16%	2	-8.3	-4.7
2019	10	13%	8%	54	19%	16%	4	-9.1	-9.4
2020	6	12%	7%	89	11%	7%	3	-6.2	-14.4
	23	11%	6%	78	15%	11%	9	-24.7	-32.2

	Stance	Pass Rush			When Run At		Total Points			Total Points Rtg		
Year	3-Point Stance%	Rush%	Sack%	True Pres%	Bnc%	Pos%	Run Def	Pass Rush	Total	Per Run	Per PR	Per Play
2018	1%	48%	1.3%	10%	38%	28%	11	7	37	62	74	77
2019	0%	54%	2.2%	24%	10%	38%	13	16	43	77	93	87
2020	0%	54%	5.3%	13%	11%	56%	5	7	16	68	92	78
	0%	52%	2.5%	16%	23%	37%	29	30	96	-	-	-

Critical Factors	
Pass Rush Ability	5
1st Step Explosion	5
POA / Set Edge	5

Positional Factors	
Pass Rush Repertoire	4
Bend	5
Hand Use	6
Play Strength	5
Range	6
Flat Coverage	5
Motor	5
FBI	5
Discipline	6
Tackling	7
Toughness	5
ST Value	5

Joshua Kaindoh Final Grade: 5.8

Report by Nathan Cooper

School	Height	Weight	Year	Jersey #	Hometown
Florida State	6056 E	265 E	4JR	13	Baltimore, MD

One Liner

Kaindoh is a very long player with the strength, leverage, and competitiveness to be a depth defender, though limited flexibility, struggles in change of direction, and bend force too many missed opportunities.

Strengths: Play strength; Length & leverage; Competitive
Weaknesses: Struggles to change directions; Limited bend & flexibility; Too many missed opportunities

Joshua Kaindoh mainly plays strong-side defensive end in Florida State's 3-4/3-3-5 defense lining up in 5- or 7-techniques and occasionally standing up. He started 10 of 39 career games. He missed all but 3 games in 2019 with an ankle injury and 1 game in 2020 with a left knee injury that visibly hampered him most of the season. He has a long frame with good size, but is rigid and doesn't have great flexibility, limiting his athleticism. However, he plays hard and competes.

Kaindoh has some explosiveness off the line, and once he gets hands-on, he's able to control the POA. His strength and leverage allow him to be effective with and counter off of bull rushes and speed-to-power. He'll try to use speed and rips on the edge, but mediocre bend and flexibility limits his consistency to win. He stood up occasionally, but is and would be more effective out of a 3-point stance. When getting into the backfield, he's able to force some pressure, but his sack production has declined in recent years, though mainly due to injury. He can get to the flat if needed, but likely isn't going to move well enough to stay with many receivers.

Against the run, Kaindoh uses heavy hands to bully tight ends. He lands his hands with good accuracy and uses his length and extension to get under blockers. When against tackles, he gets leverage to push them into the backfield and force the ballcarrier to bounce. He plays disciplined on the edge, showing burst and explosiveness when squeezing down the line to make a play. As an overall tackler, he slips off a few too many ballcarriers. He has good strength and can deliver a blow, but a lack of COD ability and overall speed force some missed tackles.

Kaindoh projects as a backup strong-side or left defensive end in a 4-3 at the next level. On 3rd downs, he has the length and power to reduce down and be a mismatch against interior linemen. Though he has toughness, his limited play speed and inconsistent tackling ability might make it difficult for him to contribute much on teams.

Year	G	GS	Tackling			Pass Rush					
			Tackles	TFL	FF	Sacks	Hurries	Hits	KD	Pressures	Deflected
2017	13	0	17	6.5	1	4.0	9	9	3	14	0
2018	12	1	18	4.0	0	3.0	17	16	3	23	2
2019	3	1	10	2.5	0	1.0	8	8	4	10	0
2020	8	8	13	3.0	0	0.0	14	7	1	15	0
	36	10	58	16.0	1	8.0	48	40	11	62	2

Year	Tackling		Tackle Share	ATD+	Pres%	Impact			EPA on TFL	EPA on Sacks
	Broken Tackles	BT%				Pres Share	Holds Drawn			
2017	1	6%	2%	-	-	7%	0		-10.0	-6.4
2018	3	14%	2%	85	11%	11%	2		-0.7	-4.0
2019	1	9%	1%	115	19%	4%	0		-1.8	-2.2
2020	3	19%	2%	224	8%	14%	1		-5.1	0.0
	8	12%	2%	147	13%	8%	3		-17.7	-12.5

Year	Stance	Pass Rush			When Run At		Total Points			Total Points Rtg		
	3-Point Stance%	Rush%	Sack%	True Pres%	Bnc%	Pos%	Run Def	Pass Rush	Total	Per Run	Per PR	Per Play
2018	93%	97%	1.5%	12%	20%	60%	8	8	19	91	83	88
2019	42%	82%	1.9%	13%	17%	67%	1	5	3	60	99	76
2020	79%	99%	0.0%	10%	25%	35%	8	2	15	84	59	76
	80%	96%	0.9%	11%	22%	47%	17	15	37	-	-	-

Critical Factors	
Pass Rush Ability	5
1st Step Explosion	5
POA / Set Edge	6

Positional Factors	
Pass Rush Repertoire	5
Bend	4
Hand Use	6
Play Strength	7
Range	5
Flat Coverage	4
Motor	6
FBI	6
Discipline	6
Tackling	5
Toughness	6
ST Value	5

Mike Linebackers

Bryce Rossler

Modern linebackers look a lot different than the two-down thumpers of yesteryear. In a run-heavier incarnation of the NFL, a premium was placed on bigger body types who could function at the point of attack first and foremost. Gone are the days of base defense being your base defense, though, and we should probably start calling the front seven the front six. Teams have swapped their strongside linebacker for a true nickel in order to combat 11 personnel and spread formations. Now more than ever, linebackers need to be able to cover in a pass-happy league. Athletic ability is at a premium and linebackers who can't hang in coverage become easy marks for quarterbacks.

An updated leaderboards page acknowledges this trend with an infusion of passing game-oriented metrics. Chief among these is our new Total Points Rating, a more intuitive expression of our staple player value stat. Linebacker is one of the more difficult positions to evaluate, but we've nevertheless compiled an assortment of advanced stats that we believe will help you better understand a player's ability to contribute to both passing and rushing defense.

That said, it can be hard to find linebackers who can run and cover and still bang inside. Players like Luke Kuechly and Bobby Wagner don't grow on trees and this class embodies just how difficult the position has become. Of the 13 Mikes who meet our cutoff for inclusion, just two have grades of 6 or better in 3-down ability. There are some appealing prospects who have the requisite strength and athletic ability to be plus defenders against both the pass and the run, but, in our estimation, said prospects will need to develop their games in order to do so. Other prospects represent tradeoffs between athletic ability and strength.

Grim as it may be, we aren't projecting any of the members of this year's class to be strong 3-down starters by Year 2 in the NFL. Furthermore, just four received low-end starter grades. That makes for slim pickings for Mike-needy teams. Therefore, it can be said that the 2021 Mikes will come to be defined by their development at the pro level. In our estimation, Missouri's Nick Bolton and Ohio State's Baron Browning are physically the best bets to do so, but both have technical weaknesses that dampen our confidence in them.

More common in this class are depth players and special teamers with athletic limitations that cap their upside and dim their prospects as NFL starters. Teams looking to shore up the back end of their depth charts may be content with this class, but franchises with immediate needs at the position will be hard-pressed to upgrade, especially with the talent scarcity in this class.

Teams looking for middle linebackers this year will need to decide which traits they wish to prioritize. Given the relative values of passing and running, we'd expect teams to opt for athletes and cover guys over thumpers, but it's obviously a case-by-case basis. And ultimately, this book is for you, the reader, and it is our hope that the analytics and scouting reports in this section will help you determine which middle linebackers will be the best of this year's class.

MIKE LINEBACKER

Mike Linebacker Grading Scale

GRADE	DESCRIPTION
9.0 – 7.0	High-end 3 down starter. Pro Bowl level.
6.9 – 6.7	Strong starter who plays on all 3 downs.
6.6 – 6.5	Low-end starter. 3rd down coverage LB.
6.2	Versatile backup with positional flexibility.
6.1 – 6.0	Developmental. Top traits but needs time.
5.9	Top backup. Quality special teamer.
5.8	Average backup. Quality special teamer.
5.7	Low-end backup LB with growable upside.

Mike Linebacker Rankings

Rank	Name	Grade	Page
1	Nick Bolton	6.6	504
2	Baron Browning	6.5	506
3	Cameron McGrone	6.5	508
4	Amen Ogbongbemiga	6.5	510
5	Derrick Barnes	6.2	512
6	Rashad Byrd	5.9	513
7	KJ Britt	5.9	514
8	Monty Rice	5.9	515
9	Jake Hansen	5.9	516
10	Paddy Fisher	5.9	517
11	Rayshard Ashby	5.8	518
12	Erroll Thompson	5.8	519
13	David Curry	5.8	520

Glossary

ATD+ (Adjusted Tackle Depth Plus)
ATD+ compares actual tackle depth to the expected tackle depth based on personnel, intended run gap, and the defender's pre-snap alignment. This figure is then scaled so that 100 is average. A figure of 110 indicates a player who is 10% better than average; a figure of 90 indicates a player who is 10% worse than average.

Blitz%
Percentage of quarterback dropbacks where the defender rushed the quarterback.

Broken Tackles
Tackle attempts where the defender in position to make a tackle failed to bring down the ballcarrier. Counts both broken tackles (physical) and missed tackles (elusive).

BT% (Broken Tackle%)
Percentage of tackle attempts where the defender in position to make a tackle failed to bring down the ball carrier. Counts both broken tackles (physical) and missed tackles (elusive).

Deserved Catch%
The percentage of targets as the primary defender that the receiver either caught or dropped the ball when the pass was catchable.

PBU (Pass Breakups)
The number of times the defender batted, deflected for an incompletion, or defensed a pass attempt.

Positive%
The percentage of plays where the defender was targeted that resulted in a positive EPA for the offense. Lower numbers are better for defenders.

Pres% (Pressure Rate)
The percentage of pass rushes that resulted in a quarterback hurry, hit, knockdown, or sack.

Sack%
Percentage of pass rushes that resulted in a sack.

Tackle Share
Percentage of a team's tackles made by the defender.

Total Points
Sports Info Solutions' proprietary player value metric that uses an Expected Points framework and distributes the value gained or lost on a play to the players involved based on their impact on the play.

Total Points Rating
Total Points per play compared to average, scaled so that 50 is poor and 99 is excellent.

Mike Linebacker Leaderboards

Total Points Per Game

Rk	Player	School	Tot Pts / G
1	D. Barnes	Purdue	5.2
2	P. Fisher	Northwestern	3.7
3	N. Bolton	Missouri	3.6
4	E. Thompson	Mississippi State	3.0
5	B. Browning	Ohio State	2.9
6	A. Ogbongbemiga	Oklahoma State	2.8
7	R. Byrd	Georgia Southern	2.4
8	J. Hansen	Illinois	2.0
9	R. Ashby	Virginia Tech	1.7
10	D. Curry	Georgia Tech	1.4

Total Points Rating Per Play

Rk	Player	School	Rating
1	D. Barnes	Purdue	96
2	N. Bolton	Missouri	89
2	B. Browning	Ohio State	89
4	R. Byrd	Georgia Southern	84
4	E. Thompson	Mississippi State	84
6	P. Fisher	Northwestern	83
7	A. Ogbongbemiga	Oklahoma State	81
8	J. Hansen	Illinois	72
9	M. Rice	Georgia	71
10	R. Ashby	Virginia Tech	68

Pass Coverage Total Points Per Game

Rk	Player	School	Tot Pts / G
1	D. Barnes	Purdue	3.2
2	P. Fisher	Northwestern	2.1
3	N. Bolton	Missouri	1.3
4	E. Thompson	Mississippi State	1.0
5	A. Ogbongbemiga	Oklahoma State	0.8
6	B. Browning	Ohio State	0.6
6	R. Byrd	Georgia Southern	0.6
8	J. Hansen	Illinois	0.5
8	R. Ashby	Virginia Tech	0.5
10	D. Curry	Georgia Tech	0.3

Total Points Rating Per Coverage Snap

Rk	Player	School	Rating
1	D. Barnes	Purdue	99
2	P. Fisher	Northwestern	86
3	N. Bolton	Missouri	82
4	E. Thompson	Mississippi State	78
5	A. Ogbongbemiga	Oklahoma State	73
5	R. Byrd	Georgia Southern	73
7	B. Browning	Ohio State	70
8	R. Ashby	Virginia Tech	68
9	J. Hansen	Illinois	67
10	C. McGrone	Michigan	64

Run Defense Total Points Per Game

Rk	Player	School	Tot Pts / G
1	D. Barnes	Purdue	1.8
2	N. Bolton	Missouri	1.6
3	A. Ogbongbemiga	Oklahoma State	1.4
3	R. Byrd	Georgia Southern	1.4
3	P. Fisher	Northwestern	1.4
3	E. Thompson	Mississippi State	1.4
7	B. Browning	Ohio State	1.1
7	J. Hansen	Illinois	1.1
9	M. Rice	Georgia	0.7
10	C. McGrone	Michigan	0.6

Total Points Rating Per Run Snap

Rk	Player	School	Rating
1	B. Browning	Ohio State	93
1	R. Byrd	Georgia Southern	93
3	N. Bolton	Missouri	92
4	D. Barnes	Purdue	90
5	M. Rice	Georgia	84
5	P. Fisher	Northwestern	84
5	E. Thompson	Mississippi State	84
8	A. Ogbongbemiga	Oklahoma State	82
9	J. Hansen	Illinois	71
10	C. McGrone	Michigan	63

Pass Rush Total Points Per Game

Rk	Player	School	Tot Pts / G
1	B. Browning	Ohio State	1.0
2	R. Ashby	Virginia Tech	0.8
3	E. Thompson	Mississippi State	0.7
4	N. Bolton	Missouri	0.6
4	A. Ogbongbemiga	Oklahoma State	0.6
6	R. Byrd	Georgia Southern	0.5
6	D. Curry	Georgia Tech	0.5
8	C. McGrone	Michigan	0.4
8	J. Hansen	Illinois	0.4
10	M. Rice	Georgia	0.3

Total Points Rating Per Pass Rush

Rk	Player	School	Rating
1	B. Browning	Ohio State	99
2	A. Ogbongbemiga	Oklahoma State	96
3	N. Bolton	Missouri	95
4	E. Thompson	Mississippi State	93
5	J. Hansen	Illinois	90
5	R. Ashby	Virginia Tech	90
7	M. Rice	Georgia	89
8	C. McGrone	Michigan	83
9	R. Byrd	Georgia Southern	82
10	D. Curry	Georgia Tech	79

Pressures Per Game

Rk	Player	School	Pres/G
1	R. Ashby	Virginia Tech	2.0
2	E. Thompson	Mississippi State	1.8
3	D. Curry	Georgia Tech	1.7
4	N. Bolton	Missouri	1.6
5	A. Ogbongbemiga	Oklahoma State	1.5
6	D. Barnes	Purdue	1.2
6	R. Byrd	Georgia Southern	1.2
8	B. Browning	Ohio State	1.0
9	J. Hansen	Illinois	0.8
10	M. Rice	Georgia	0.7

Pressure Rate

Rk	Player	School	Pres%
1	A. Ogbongbemiga	Oklahoma State	31%
2	N. Bolton	Missouri	30%
3	J. Hansen	Illinois	23%
4	B. Browning	Ohio State	22%
4	E. Thompson	Mississippi State	22%
6	M. Rice	Georgia	19%
7	D. Barnes	Purdue	18%
7	R. Ashby	Virginia Tech	18%
7	D. Curry	Georgia Tech	18%
10	R. Byrd	Georgia Southern	17%

Sacks Per Game

Rk	Player	School	Sacks/G
1	R. Ashby	Virginia Tech	0.4
2	J. Hansen	Illinois	0.3
2	E. Thompson	Mississippi State	0.3
4	N. Bolton	Missouri	0.2
4	A. Ogbongbemiga	Oklahoma State	0.2
4	R. Byrd	Georgia Southern	0.2
4	D. Curry	Georgia Tech	0.2
8	B. Browning	Ohio State	0.1
8	C. McGrone	Michigan	0.1
8	M. Rice	Georgia	0.1

Tackles For Loss Per Game

Rk	Player	School	TFL/G
1	J. Hansen	Illinois	1.3
2	D. Barnes	Purdue	0.9
2	D. Curry	Georgia Tech	0.9
4	N. Bolton	Missouri	0.8
5	R. Ashby	Virginia Tech	0.7
6	B. Browning	Ohio State	0.6
7	A. Ogbongbemiga	Oklahoma State	0.5
7	R. Byrd	Georgia Southern	0.5
9	C. McGrone	Michigan	0.4
9	2 tied with		0.4

Tackle Share

Rk	Player	School	Tkl Share
1	N. Bolton	Missouri	16%
1	P. Fisher	Northwestern	16%
3	D. Barnes	Purdue	14%
4	A. Ogbongbemiga	Oklahoma State	12%
4	J. Hansen	Illinois	12%
4	E. Thompson	Mississippi State	12%
7	D. Curry	Georgia Tech	11%
8	R. Byrd	Georgia Southern	10%
8	R. Ashby	Virginia Tech	10%
10	M. Rice	Georgia	8%

Adjusted Tackle Depth Plus

Rk	Player	School	ATD+
1	R. Byrd	Georgia Southern	136
2	E. Thompson	Mississippi State	115
3	R. Ashby	Virginia Tech	114
4	M. Rice	Georgia	111
5	D. Curry	Georgia Tech	106
6	B. Browning	Ohio State	103
7	C. McGrone	Michigan	102
7	D. Barnes	Purdue	102
9	A. Ogbongbemiga	Oklahoma State	97
10	N. Bolton	Missouri	95

Tackles Per Game

Rk	Player	School	Tackles/G
1	P. Fisher	Northwestern	9.6
2	N. Bolton	Missouri	9.4
3	D. Barnes	Purdue	9.0
4	J. Hansen	Illinois	8.5
5	E. Thompson	Mississippi State	8.4
6	D. Curry	Georgia Tech	7.9
7	A. Ogbongbemiga	Oklahoma State	7.6
8	R. Ashby	Virginia Tech	6.3
9	R. Byrd	Georgia Southern	5.7
10	M. Rice	Georgia	5.6

Broken Tackle Rate

Rk	Player	School	BT%
1	C. McGrone	Michigan	0%
2	M. Rice	Georgia	6%
2	J. Hansen	Illinois	6%
4	R. Ashby	Virginia Tech	9%
5	D. Barnes	Purdue	10%
5	R. Byrd	Georgia Southern	10%
7	A. Ogbongbemiga	Oklahoma State	11%
8	B. Browning	Ohio State	14%
8	P. Fisher	Northwestern	14%
10	E. Thompson	Mississippi State	15%

Yards Per Target

Rk	Player	School	Yds/Trgt
1	D. Barnes	Purdue	2.4
2	N. Bolton	Missouri	2.9
3	P. Fisher	Northwestern	3.5
4	R. Ashby	Virginia Tech	4.0
5	C. McGrone	Michigan	6.3
6	E. Thompson	Mississippi State	6.8
7	A. Ogbongbemiga	Oklahoma State	7.1
8	D. Curry	Georgia Tech	7.9
9	J. Hansen	Illinois	8.0
10	B. Browning	Ohio State	8.8

Passes Broken Up Per Game

Rk	Player	School	PBU/G
1	P. Fisher	Northwestern	0.7
2	D. Barnes	Purdue	0.5
2	J. Hansen	Illinois	0.5
4	N. Bolton	Missouri	0.4
4	R. Byrd	Georgia Southern	0.4
6	B. Browning	Ohio State	0.3
7	C. McGrone	Michigan	0.2
7	E. Thompson	Mississippi State	0.2
7	D. Curry	Georgia Tech	0.2
10	A. Ogbongbemiga	Oklahoma State	0.1

Nick Bolton

Report by John Todd

School	Height	Weight	Year	Jersey #	Hometown
Missouri	5116 E	232 E	3JR	32	Frisco, TX

One Liner
Bolton has off-ball tweener traits, but his rangy movement skills to all areas of the field will play at the next level while he better develops his feel for routes and take-on abilities.

Overall
Nick Bolton is primarily a Will linebacker in Missouri's base nickel defense. He played in 35 career games, starting 22 straight the past 2 seasons. He's slightly undersized inside but has a stocky build with a thick lower half. He has great lateral quickness and noteworthy straight-line speed for the position. While not the hottest, his motor is consistent to always get him around the ball. He attacks the ball with violence and a strong burst to close.

Pass Game
In coverage, Bolton has the movement skills and range to be an asset, but some technical shortcomings may hold him back. In zone, he does a great job dropping smoothly and efficiently. He has a natural flow to his backpedal and comfortably reaches all depths. He's extremely disciplined with his eyes to always key the quarterback, which has its positives and negatives. It allows him to constantly spy and range downhill on scrambles, as well as jump throws when the QB locks in heavily. However, not keeping his head on a swivel results in poor route awareness and feel for the moving parts around him. Bolton struggles to pass off routes and communicate mid-play. He's strong in man coverage to the flats when he can fly straight to the sidelines, but he's hesitant changing directions when picking up backs and tight ends in the middle of the field on breakers and option routes. He's a violent finisher when left untouched as a blitzer and has shown good timing on delays, but he is not a technical rusher with his hands to win one-on-one.

Run Game
As a run defender, Bolton is always near the ball and is a tackling machine, especially outside the box. He locks in on pulling guards, which again leads to good and bad plays. He keys quickly and jumps blocking schemes with early penetration to beat blockers to the spot, but his lack of peripheral feel will take him out of plays on false pulls and misdirection. Bolton is not a take-on thumper and prefers to avoid or outrun blockers rather than power through or anchor against. Between the tackles he navigates traffic well, sifting through bodies with his eyes in the backfield and triggering through creases. He breaks down and strikes with good technique and power in a phone booth and leaves his feet to extend for rangy arm tackles sideline to sideline.

Last Word
Bolton projects as a starting-caliber linebacker at the next level, but he's a unique fit. He plays the run better as a Will, where he can stay clean from second-level blocks and pursue with his great range. However, he'd be better in coverage as a Mike, where he can hook zone from the box and receive more standard man-coverage responsibilities. Ultimately, Bolton should fill a Mike role in the NFL, ideally behind a space-eating defensive line and next to a backer who counters his skill set. He'd be a forceful special teams contributor if necessary.

Strengths

- Tackling range
- Trigger and closing speed
- Zone depth and fluidity

Weaknesses

- Feel and eye discipline
- Take-on disposition vs blockers
- Change of direction in man coverage

Critical Factors

3-Down Ability	FBI / Instincts	Play Speed
5	6	7

Positional Factors

3-Level Impact	QB Defense	Stoutness	Shed Ability
6	5	5	5
Navigate Trash	Tackling	Man Coverage	Zone Coverage
6	7	5	6
Range	Blitz	Toughness	ST Value
7	5	6	7

Basic

	Tackling			Pass Rush		Coverage					
Year	Tackles	TFL	FF	Sacks	Pres	Trgt	Comp	Comp%	Yds	Yds/Trgt	Int
2018	16	1.0	0	1.0	5	1	0	0%	0	0.0	0
2019	105	7.5	0	1.0	10	20	8	40%	63	3.2	2
2020	94	7.5	0	2.0	16	19	10	53%	56	2.9	0
	215	16.0	0	4.0	31	40	18	45%	119	3.0	2

Advanced

	Tackling				Coverage				Positive%		
Year	Broken Tackles	BT%	Tackle Share	ATD+	PBU	Deserved Catch %	YAC	EPA	Man	Zone	Total
2018	3	16%	2%	83	0	-	0	-0.8	-	0%	0%
2019	9	8%	16%	116	10	63%	12	-13.7	13%	17%	15%
2020	18	16%	16%	95	4	88%	34	-8.8	27%	50%	37%
	30	12%	11%	105	14	76%	46	-23.3	21%	29%	25%

Deep Dive

	Pass Rush			Total Points				Total Points Rtg			
Year	Blitz%	Pres%	Sack%	Run Def	Pass Rush	Pass Cov	Total	Per Run	Per PR	Per Cov	Per Play
2018	13%	63%	28.6%	1	3	1	6	55	99	73	83
2019	9%	29%	3.2%	28	6	24	58	98	93	94	97
2020	16%	30%	3.9%	16	6	13	36	92	95	82	89
	12%	33%	5.6%	45	15	38	100	-	-	-	-

Baron Browning

Report by Blake Moore, Jake Johnson, & James Ashley

School	Height	Weight	Year	Jersey #	Hometown
Ohio State	6031 V	241 V	4SR	5	Fort Worth, TX

One Liner

Browning is more "athlete" than football player at times with inconsistent instincts, but he has an excellent blend of size, speed, physicality, and movement skills to deploy at the linebacker position.

Overall

Baron Browning is a versatile off-ball linebacker in Ohio State's 4-3 defense, as he has rotated through all 3 linebacker roles in his career. He played in 43 career games with 10 starts. He had surgery for a shoulder laburm injury prior to the 2017 season. He has great size and excellent length. He's a fantastic athlete for the position, with great speed and leaping ability at his size but lacks some lateral agility. He plays with a high motor and toughness to fight through injuries and still contribute.

Pass Game

Browning was not asked to be the signal caller at Ohio State, but he showed sufficient communication skills as he moved around to different alignments. He is a good coverage linebacker when matched up with backs and tight ends. He sticks in and out of cuts well and has impressive ball skills when put on an island to compete at the catch point. However, his man coverage success doesn't translate against slot receivers as well. He gets good depth to his zone drops and flows to his spots quickly and fluidly. He has good awareness to keep his head on a swivel and knock underneath receivers off their routes as they pass through, but his instincts and feel for space are inconsistent. He has great range in pursuit in the open field and drives downhill hard to the ball. As a blitzer, his speed and strength are great assets in the trenches. He lacks bend around the corner and shows sufficient hand technique to hand fight and cut inside.

Run Game

Browning has all the physical tools to be a strong run defender, but he doesn't put them all together and can be slow to process. He is very willing to engage with blockers, but his lower body stoutness doesn't match his attacking mindset, and he can struggle to anchor and shed in the box. He doesn't use his fantastic length to keep blockers at bay consistently. He has issues navigating traffic and finding holes to knife through, but when he does, he flies to the ball and makes good, strong tackles. He has shown mediocre balance when changing direction quickly in tight quarters. His range outside the box is very impressive, and when he diagnoses plays early, he uses his natural athleticism to make unexpected plays and big hits.

Last Word

Browning has played both Mike and Will linebacker in his career, but his combination of size and athleticism will give him a higher ceiling as a Mike. Playing inside a 3-4 defense will allow him to show his best traits in both areas. His playing time at Ohio State has been up and down due to his inconsistencies against the run, but he showed improvement as a true three-down player in 2020. His coverage abilities are better suited as a Mike, as the added responsibilities of playing as a space backer could expose some weaknesses. He has a great skill set and just needs to further develop his instincts to match his raw athleticism. Additionally, he should be a force on special teams.

Strengths

- Play speed and range
- Natural athleticism
- Size and length

Weaknesses

- Instincts and processing
- Short-area change of direction
- Stack and shed

Critical Factors

3-Down Ability	FBI / Instincts	Play Speed
6	5	7

Positional Factors

3-Level Impact	QB Defense	Stoutness	Shed Ability
7	5	5	5
Navigate Trash	Tackling	Man Coverage	Zone Coverage
5	6	6	6
Range	Blitz	Toughness	ST Value
7	6	7	7

Basic

Year	Tackling			Pass Rush		Coverage					
	Tackles	TFL	FF	Sacks	Pres	Trgt	Comp	Comp%	Yds	Yds/Trgt	Int
2017	13	1.5	0	0.0	1	0	0	-	0	-	0
2018	22	3.5	0	1.0	9	5	3	60%	33	6.6	0
2019	44	10.0	0	5.0	18	11	4	36%	76	6.9	0
2020	32	4.0	3	1.0	7	14	10	71%	123	8.8	0
	111	19.0	3	7.0	35	30	17	57%	232	7.7	0

Advanced

Year	Tackling				Coverage				Positive%		
	Broken Tackles	BT%	Tackle Share	ATD+	PBU	Deserved Catch %	YAC	EPA	Man	Zone	Total
2017	0	0%	2%	-	0	-	0	0.0	-	-	-
2018	3	12%	3%	129	0	60%	22	0.2	50%	0%	40%
2019	7	14%	6%	119	1	88%	40	0.2	20%	50%	36%
2020	5	14%	7%	103	2	83%	65	0.4	40%	44%	43%
	15	12%	4%	117	3	80%	127	0.8	36%	44%	40%

Deep Dive

Year	Pass Rush			Total Points				Total Points Rtg			
	Blitz%	Pres%	Sack%	Run Def	Pass Rush	Pass Cov	Total	Per Run	Per PR	Per Cov	Per Play
2018	35%	14%	1.6%	4	5	0	8	72	92	57	72
2019	19%	33%	13.0%	4	14	-3	16	73	99	55	85
2020	15%	22%	3.1%	8	7	4	20	93	99	70	89
	22%	22%	5.6%	16	26	1	44	-	-	-	-

Cameron McGrone Final Grade: 6.5

Report by Sales Pinckney

School	Height	Weight	Year	Jersey #	Hometown
Michigan	5116 E	236 E	3JR	44	Indianapolis, IN

One Liner
McGrone has the physical mentality and athleticism to be a solid contributor in the NFL for a long time, but he needs to improve his take-on abilities and take better advantage of his movement skills in coverage.

Overall
Cameron McGrone aligned as the Mike linebacker in Michigan's 4-3 defense. He played in 19 career games, starting 15 of them. He'll still just be 20 years old at the time of the NFL Draft. He has a muscular build with good athleticism and balance. He tore his ACL in 2017, played with a cast on his left hand for much of the 2020 season, and was carted off against Rutgers with a non-contact left knee injury. He was forced to miss the final game of the year with a lower body injury. He is a tough and competitive player and enjoys contact.

Pass Game
In coverage, McGrone has good overall range and gets sufficient depth in his zone drops. He displays the ability to read and recognize what is happening but occasionally plays flat-footed, resulting in being a step slow to react and trigger downhill. He shows discipline in zone and communicates well. He has the athleticism to match up with running backs to the flats, and his physicality allows him to cover tight ends crossing the middle of the field. However, he has not shown the overall pass-coverage ability that his athleticism would indicate. McGrone does not have a history of production in coverage and is not an impactful player in deeper intermediate areas. He's much better moving forward and has shown the ability to rush the passer. As a blitzer, he can generate pressure to disrupt the quarterback both from inside and off the edge and uses his speed and

quickness to win one-on-one battles at an efficient level.

Run Game
Against the run, McGrone displays an innate feel for developing plays. He can take control of a defense and is often communicating with his teammates to all levels before the snap to ensure everyone is on the same page. He stays on his feet and navigates trash around the line and scrapes over the top. He bursts through gaps quickly to disrupt in the backfield. He has the range to make plays on the perimeter and takes good pursuit angles. He is stout enough against tight ends and blocking backs, but against linemen he gives ground and is often outmatched. Fully disengaging from blockers can be a struggle for him but he works his off-hand well to still make plays in the hole. He is not afraid of contact and is a good overall tackler but does not generate much leg drive through contact and can give ground at the point of attack.

Last Word
McGrone projects as a low-end three-down starting Mike linebacker at the next level. His toughness and range will allow him to succeed in the run game, and his natural athleticism and blitzing abilities will allow him to stay on the field in passing situations. He will fit best in an aggressive, blitz-heavy system where he isn't a focal point in coverage. He has the gritty mentality and athleticism to be a high-quality special teams player.

Strengths
- Athleticism
- Physical mentality
- Blitz ability

Weaknesses
- Stoutness against linemen
- Ability to disengage
- Reactive quickness in coverage

Critical Factors

3-Down Ability	FBI / Instincts	Play Speed
6	6	6

Positional Factors

3-Level Impact	QB Defense	Stoutness	Shed Ability
5	6	4	5
Navigate Trash	Tackling	Man Coverage	Zone Coverage
6	6	5	5
Range	Blitz	Toughness	ST Value
6	6	6	7

Basic

Year	Tackles	TFL	FF	Sacks	Pres	Trgt	Comp	Comp%	Yds	Yds/Trgt	Int
2019	67	9.5	1	3.5	19	10	3	30%	76	7.6	0
2020	25	2.0	0	0.5	2	4	3	75%	25	6.3	0
	92	11.5	1	4.0	21	14	6	43%	101	7.2	0

Advanced

Year	Broken Tackles	BT%	Tackle Share	ATD+	PBU	Deserved Catch %	YAC	EPA	Man	Zone	Total
2019	9	12%	8%	130	1	83%	42	-0.1	38%	0%	30%
2020	0	0%	6%	102	1	75%	16	2.6	100%	0%	75%
	9	9%	8%	123	2	80%	58	2.5	55%	0%	43%

Deep Dive

Year	Blitz%	Pres%	Sack%	Run Def	Pass Rush	Pass Cov	Total	Per Run	Per PR	Per Cov	Per Play
2019	23%	24%	5.3%	12	13	-1	24	78	99	58	79
2020	18%	9%	4.3%	3	2	1	6	63	83	64	66
	22%	20%	5.1%	15	15	0	30	-	-	-	-

     Amen Ogbongbemiga   Final Grade: 6.5

Report by Nathan Cooper

School	Height	Weight	Year	Jersey #	Hometown
Oklahoma State	5116 E	235 E	5SR	7	Calgary, AB, CAN

One Liner
Ogbongbemiga is a disruptive zone defender who reads and reacts well to flow in the run game, but an inability to consistently shed with just adequate overall speed may prove troublesome at the next level.

Overall
Amen Ogbongbemiga mainly plays Mike, but rotates through all of the linebacker positions for Oklahoma State's 3-3-5 defense. He played 49 games for the Cowboys, starting 24 of them. He played through thumb and finger injuries in 2019 and tested positive for COVID-19 prior to the 2020 season. His build is good for the position and he plays fast, but lacks overall speed. He competes and shows toughness in his play. He moves fairly well, but is a little stiff when redirecting.

Pass Game
Ogbongbemiga shows good awareness and disruption in coverage. In zone, he sees receivers coming through his zone and nearly always gets hands on to slow them down or disrupt the timing of their route. He gets good depth on his zone drops, but works much better east to west and downhill. He also gets his hands up in throwing lanes to knock passes away or even convert them into interceptions. In man, he's able to stick with running backs out of the backfield and stay on them down the field, but isn't someone who has the athleticism to be a sticky cover defender on slot receivers or most tight ends. As a blitzer, Ogbongbemiga shows the ability to get to the quarterback, but mostly due to scheme. He can occasionally create on his own to get by blockers, but most of his pressures and sacks come off stunts and free rushes. He is a very good communicator and always seems to be pointing and talking to his teammates.

Run Game
In the run game, Ogbongbemiga does a good job at reading flow and reacting to what he sees, though this can get him out of position against misdirection. When coming downhill, he doesn't shy away from contact, but is more effective when sliding by defenders and navigating the trash. He shows some stoutness to meet fullbacks and tight ends in the hole, but struggles to stack and shed offensive linemen when head on. He's a strong tackler when given the opportunity, but will miss some every once in a while against shiftier backs. He tends to leave or stop his feet on contact which allows ballcarriers to gain extra yards unless teammates come in on gang tackles. With that said, he has the range and pursuit to make tackles at every level of the defense and even make them at or behind the LOS. With his communication ability, he shows that he can be the QB in the middle of the defense.

Last Word
Ogbongbemiga projects as a low-end starting Mike Linebacker in either a 3-4 or 4-3 scheme at the next level with enough coverage ability to shift out to Will if needed. His man coverage ability on backs and disruption in zone allows him to stay on the field on 3rd downs. His toughness and play speed suggests he should be a solid contributor on most special teams units.

Strengths

- Zone disruption
- Reads flow & reacts
- Communicates well

Weaknesses

- Struggles to shed consistently
- Lacks some speed
- A little stiff

Critical Factors

3-Down Ability	FBI / Instincts	Play Speed
5	6	5

Positional Factors

3-Level Impact	QB Defense	Stoutness	Shed Ability
5	7	6	5
Navigate Trash	Tackling	Man Coverage	Zone Coverage
6	6	5	6
Range	Blitz	Toughness	ST Value
6	5	7	6

Basic

Year	Tackling			Pass Rush		Coverage					
	Tackles	TFL	FF	Sacks	Pres	Trgt	Comp	Comp%	Yds	Yds/Trgt	Int
2017	16	1.5	0	0.0	6	2	2	100%	8	4.0	0
2018	7	3.0	0	1.5	3	0	0	-	0	-	0
2019	98	15.0	0	5.0	22	15	10	67%	93	6.2	1
2020	84	6.0	3	2.5	16	8	6	75%	57	7.1	0
	205	25.5	3	9.0	47	25	18	72%	158	6.3	1

Advanced

Year	Tackling				Coverage				Positive%		
	Broken Tackles	BT%	Tackle Share	ATD+	PBU	Deserved Catch %	YAC	EPA	Man	Zone	Total
2017	0	0%	2%	-	0	100%	1	-0.9	0%	-	0%
2018	1	13%	1%	137	0	-	0	0.0	-	-	-
2019	16	14%	12%	106	1	100%	48	4.1	50%	44%	47%
2020	10	11%	12%	97	1	100%	34	1.0	33%	60%	50%
	27	12%	7%	102	2	100%	83	4.2	36%	50%	44%

Deep Dive

Year	Pass Rush			Total Points				Total Points Rtg			
	Blitz%	Pres%	Sack%	Run Def	Pass Rush	Pass Cov	Total	Per Run	Per PR	Per Cov	Per Play
2018	36%	50%	40.0%	-1	2	1	2	50	99	91	62
2019	17%	29%	8.8%	11	9	11	31	72	98	76	80
2020	13%	31%	6.5%	15	7	9	31	82	96	73	81
	15%	31%	9.2%	25	18	21	64	-	-	-	-

Derrick Barnes

Report by Chad Tedder & Jon Drillings

School	Height	Weight	Year	Jersey #	Hometown
Purdue	6004 V	245 V	4SR	55	Covington, KY

One Liner

Barnes is a powerful, versatile linebacker that can see some situational snaps at the next level, but his lack of consistent motor, technique, and dominance at one position will keep him from a starting role.

Strengths: Tackling strength; Range against the run; Unique versatility
Weaknesses: Stack-and-shed consistency; Route recognition and disruption; Man coverage

Derrick Barnes is a versatile linebacker in Purdue's nickel defense. He played in 43 games with 31 starts. He was essentially a full-time off-ball player in 2020, full-time edge in '19, and played both in '18. He is a stout, powerful athlete that has some sideline-to-sideline speed. He's tough but his inconsistent motor can slow down his overall play.

Barnes mostly plays the Mike but will reduce down to a two- or three-point rusher in sub packages. As a Mike, he usually drops into shallow hook zones and spies the quarterback. He doesn't create much disruption to reroute crossers, but he plays with sufficient eye discipline. His infrequent man reps resulted in difficulties changing direction and easy separation. As an edge, Barnes predominantly uses a bull rush along with inside stunts. His pressure production is relatively low, but has shown that he can occasionally overpower linemen with thump to contact. He often lacks a rush plan and has an underdeveloped arsenal of hand techniques.

Barnes shows better sideline range against the run to find his way through traffic and close physically for tackles. He is a sufficient communicator from off the ball. He's disciplined to his gap assignments before attacking open holes but will commit too quickly at times and remove himself from plays. He has the stoutness to anchor at the second level, but he has occasional issues shedding from strong hands. Barnes has enough speed to beat runners to the perimeter and arrives with force but can seem disinterested in backside pursuit opportunities.

Barnes profiles as a uniquely versatile reserve linebacker at the next level. He best projects as a backup Mike linebacker with simple zone coverage responsibilities and a run-first mentality. However, on third downs, his flexibility as a standup or hand down power edge rusher allows him to stay on the field more than other non-space linebackers would. He will need development in his technique at both positions to become a true difference maker, but he could offer intriguing versatility.

	Tackling			Pass Rush		Coverage					
Year	Tackles	TFL	FF	Sacks	Pres	Trgt	Comp	Comp%	Yds	Yds/Trgt	Int
2017	12	0.5	1	0.0	1	2	1	50%	9	4.5	0
2018	93	8.0	0	3.0	22	16	11	69%	126	7.9	0
2019	66	11.5	1	7.5	36	6	5	83%	24	4.0	0
2020	54	5.5	0	0.0	7	10	5	50%	24	2.4	1
	225	25.5	2	10.5	66	34	22	65%	183	5.4	1

	Tackling				Coverage				Positive%		
Year	Broken Tackles	BT%	Tackle Share	ATD+	PBU	Deserved Catch %	YAC	EPA	Man	Zone	Total
2017	1	8%	1%	-	0	100%	6	0.0	-	50%	50%
2018	7	7%	11%	82	0	100%	71	6.2	25%	67%	56%
2019	4	6%	9%	37	2	100%	10	0.3	-	50%	50%
2020	6	10%	14%	102	3	75%	14	-8.4	0%	25%	20%
	18	7%	8%	78	5	92%	101	-2.0	17%	50%	44%

	Pass Rush			Total Points				Total Points Rtg			
Year	Blitz%	Pres%	Sack%	Run Def	Pass Rush	Pass Cov	Total	Per Run	Per PR	Per Cov	Per Play
2018	40%	11%	1.6%	14	8	7	29	70	76	70	72
2019	78%	12%	3.0%	15	17	8	41	80	91	94	87
2020	21%	18%	0.0%	11	1	19	31	90	68	99	96
	51%	12%	2.2%	40	26	34	101	-	-	-	-

Critical Factors

3-Down Ability	5
FBI / Instincts	5
Play Speed	6

Positional Factors

3-Level Impact	5
QB Defense	5
Stoutness	6
Shed Ability	5
Navigate Trash	5
Tackling	6
Man Coverage	4
Zone Coverage	5
Range	5
Blitz	6
Toughness	6
ST Value	6

Rashad Byrd

Report by Jeff Dean

School	Height	Weight	Year	Jersey #	Hometown
Georgia Southern	6003 V	236 V	5SR	45	North Augusta, SC

One Liner

Byrd has the stoutness, block shedding ability, and football IQ teams look for in a Mike linebacker, but he will have to raise his coverage ability to a similar level to see consistent time as a starter.

Strengths: Taking on blocks; Navigating trash; Instincts against the run
Weaknesses: Experience in man coverage; Top-end speed and range in pursuit; Finding receivers in space

Rashad Byrd is a Mike linebacker in Georgia Southern's base 3-4 zone defense. He played in 48 career games with 28 starts. Byrd has a good frame with clear muscle definition. He has good burst to close but lacks rangy speed. He plays with a controlled aggression that allows him to minimize his mistakes and strike in close quarters.

Byrd doesn't have great instincts in zone coverage, but uses his eyes and discipline to be a factor. He has sufficient hips in his drops and can struggle to find receivers in zone coverage, but makes plays on the ball when given the chance. He can be seen directing guys on the field pre-snap. Byrd has very limited experience in man coverage and would be mediocre doing so outside of tracking checkdowns. He lacks the deep speed or quickness to stay with faster targets and is better suited in zone. He is a good blitzer who excels at taking on blocks and getting pressure. He brings some thump behind him and closes hard.

Byrd reads offensive lines well and has natural instincts to find the ball against the run. He is good at shedding blocks and rarely gives up ground with great stoutness and power generation in small areas at the point of attack. He attacks the line and keeps an arm free to fill gaps. Byrd's controlled aggression is evident against the run as he makes few mistakes, but explodes to meet the ballcarrier at the line and minimize yards after contact. While his sideline range is only sufficient and he can be beaten to the perimeter, his box navigation and tackle-to-tackle instincts are sound.

Rashad Byrd projects as a top backup Mike linebacker who fits best in a zone-heavy team with flexibility to play in either a 4-3 or 3-4. His instincts and abilities against the run, as well as his blitzing strength, could allow him to see playing time, and if he develops more in coverage, he could end up being a three-down starter. He should be a solid special teams playmaker from Day 1.

Year	Tackling			Pass Rush		Coverage					
	Tackles	TFL	FF	Sacks	Pres	Trgt	Comp	Comp%	Yds	Yds/Trgt	Int
2017	42	1.5	0	0.0	13	13	8	62%	94	7.2	0
2018	54	5.0	0	0.0	4	9	6	67%	50	5.6	1
2019	82	9.0	2	2.0	9	11	6	55%	35	3.2	2
2020	74	6.0	1	2.0	15	11	8	73%	108	9.8	2
	252	21.5	3	4.0	41	44	28	64%	287	6.5	5

Year	Tackling				Coverage				Positive%		
	Broken Tackles	BT%	Tackle Share	ATD+	PBU	Deserved Catch %	YAC	EPA	Man	Zone	Total
2017	6	13%	7%	-	5	80%	56	-2.2	50%	67%	54%
2018	4	7%	7%	116	1	88%	11	1.2	100%	50%	56%
2019	10	11%	11%	124	3	80%	14	-3.5	100%	30%	36%
2020	8	10%	10%	136	5	82%	46	1.3	100%	50%	55%
	28	10%	8%	126	14	82%	127	-3.2	62%	45%	50%

Year	Pass Rush			Total Points				Total Points Rtg			
	Blitz%	Pres%	Sack%	Run Def	Pass Rush	Pass Cov	Total	Per Run	Per PR	Per Cov	Per Play
2018	12%	16%	0.0%	7	1	12	20	80	65	95	85
2019	11%	23%	5.1%	2	6	14	23	56	97	83	72
2020	25%	17%	2.3%	18	6	8	31	93	82	73	84
	17%	18%	2.7%	27	13	34	74	-	-	-	-

Critical Factors	
3-Down Ability	5
FBI / Instincts	6
Play Speed	5

Positional Factors	
3-Level Impact	5
QB Defense	6
Stoutness	7
Shed Ability	6
Navigate Trash	6
Tackling	6
Man Coverage	4
Zone Coverage	5
Range	5
Blitz	6
Toughness	6
ST Value	6

KJ Britt

Report by Chad Tedder

School	Height	Weight	Year	Jersey #	Hometown
Auburn	6001 V	239 V	4SR	33	Oxford, AL

One Liner

Britt is a powerful run-stopping linebacker with good speed and stoutness, but his athletic limitations in coverage and inconsistencies as a pass rusher will limit his passing-down usage.

Strengths: Power behind his pads; Downhill speed; Stacking and shedding blocks
Weaknesses: Coverage awareness; Quick-mirror skills; Pass-rush technique

KJ Britt is a Mike linebacker in Auburn's nickel and dime defensive personnels. He played in 42 games, starting in 14. Britt missed the majority of the 2020 season after undergoing surgery to repair a torn ligament in his thumb. He has a squatty build with a strong lower half. He plays with some power behind him but is limited athletically in space. He plays with good toughness in the middle of the box.

Against the pass, Britt was predominantly used in hook zone over the middle and occasionally tracking backs in man. In zone, he doesn't disrupt routes well and has shown to be slow reacting to receivers entering his area. He has good play speed to keep up with targets in a straight line, but he struggles at the top of routes to change directions on breakers. Although he didn't get a lot of production with the ball in the air, he would use his downhill speed to close fast and make good tackles in space. He wasn't asked to rush the passer often, but when he was, he had moderate success within loops or with his ability to take on blocks, but lacked hand technique to be a consistent threat.

Britt shows the ability to read, react, and get downhill to the ballcarrier in the run game. He doesn't have a large tackling radius and can be susceptible to misses against elusiveness, but when he squares up he's a powerful, wrap-up finisher. He is better at attacking between the tackles where he can stack, shed, and speed around blockers to make a tackle near the line of scrimmage, but he has enough natural speed at his size to meet some rushers at the edges of the field. He does communicate well as often the lone off-ball linebacker to get his DBs in place.

Britt best projects as a Mike backer in a 4-3 defensive scheme, but his lack of coverage skills will likely keep him in a backup role and out of 3rd-down scenarios. The power, speed, and motor he plays with can make him a core member of all special teams.

	Tackling			Pass Rush		Coverage						
Year	Tackles	TFL	FF	Sacks	Pres	Trgt	Comp	Comp%	Yds	Yds/Trgt	Int	
2017	1	0.0	0	0.0	1	1	1	100%	14	14.0	0	
2018	21	1.0	0	0.0	3	1	0	0%	0	0.0	0	
2019	72	10.0	1	2.5	11	11	7	64%	140	12.7	0	
2020	21	1.0	0	0.0	0	1	1	100%	3	3.0	0	
	115	12.0	1	2.5	15	14	9	64%	157	11.2	0	

	Tackling				Coverage				Positive%		
Year	Broken Tackles	BT%	Tackle Share	ATD+	PBU	Deserved Catch %	YAC	EPA	Man	Zone	Total
2017	1	50%	0%	-	0	100%	1	0.9	-	100%	100%
2018	2	9%	3%	131	1	0%	0	-0.8	0%	-	0%
2019	11	13%	9%	130	1	89%	110	1.4	25%	57%	45%
2020	3	13%	3%	81	0	100%	1	-0.3	-	0%	0%
	17	13%	4%	121	2	83%	112	1.2	20%	56%	43%

	Pass Rush			Total Points				Total Points Rtg			
Year	Blitz%	Pres%	Sack%	Run Def	Pass Rush	Pass Cov	Total	Per Run	Per PR	Per Cov	Per Play
2018	22%	20%	0.0%	2	-1	3	4	84	50	85	75
2019	10%	35%	11.1%	16	6	10	31	94	99	80	90
2020	9%	0%	0.0%	2	0	3	5	67	73	86	75
	12%	27%	6.5%	20	5	16	40	-	-	-	-

Critical Factors

3-Down Ability	5
FBI / Instincts	5
Play Speed	6

Positional Factors

3-Level Impact	5
QB Defense	6
Stoutness	6
Shed Ability	6
Navigate Trash	6
Tackling	6
Man Coverage	5
Zone Coverage	5
Range	5
Blitz	5
Toughness	6
ST Value	6

Monty Rice

Report by Ben Hrkach

School	Height	Weight	Year	Jersey #	Hometown
Georgia	6002 V	236 V	4SR	32	Huntsville, AL

One Liner
Rice has the shedding ability, stoutness, and leadership qualities of a defensive quarterback, but his inefficiencies in coverage and short-area quickness ultimately cap his overall potential.

Strengths: Block shedding; Stoutness; QB of the defense
Weaknesses: 3-down ability; Awareness in coverage; Change-of-direction skill

Monty Rice is the Mike linebacker in Georgia's hybrid 4-2-5 defense rarely staying on the field in sub packages or passing downs. He started 28 of 47 games. He battled a foot injury during 2020 that kept him from participating in the Senior Bowl. Rice is a powerful straight-line athlete. He's a good athlete who shows the toughness and competitive drive required at the position.

Rice is mediocre in zone and man coverage. He doesn't have a good feel for his zone and is often found covering air. He rarely recognizes receivers running in behind him, however, he does display good instincts. He is quick to identify screens and pulls the trigger immediately. He's sufficient at reading the quarterback's eyes and quickly closes to the ball. In man, he does an average job of staying with running backs on outs and flats. He struggles covering routes that extend up the field and mirroring tight ends. As a blitzer, Rice flashes good hand moves and wiggle to beat offensive linemen. He has average-to-good timing on his blitzes, though lacks

production behind the LOS. He's constantly communicating with all 10 players on the field.

Against the run, Rice has good stoutness. He shows the ability to stack and shed, rarely getting stuck on blockers, however, he can get caught in the trash at times, struggling to evade blockers. Rice plays best downhill and can wrap up while still punishing the ballcarrier. He has good instincts and usually meets the RB in the hole. When setting the edge, he's able to stalemate offensive linemen and force the ballcarrier to change course. He's clearly the QB of the defense and is looked at as the leader in the middle of the defense.

Overall, Rice projects as a classic B-gap-to-B-gap Mike. He plays downhill, takes on offensive linemen, and punishes ballcarriers. He doesn't have the instincts to be highly productive with this style of play or have the physical tools to develop much in coverage. However, he does have the physicality and mentality that is desired for special teams.

	Tackling			Pass Rush		Coverage					
Year	Tackles	TFL	FF	Sacks	Pres	Trgt	Comp	Comp%	Yds	Yds/Trgt	Int
2017	22	2.0	0	0.0	1	4	2	50%	13	3.3	0
2018	59	2.0	1	1.0	3	10	8	80%	67	6.7	0
2019	87	4.0	0	0.0	15	24	14	58%	99	4.1	0
2020	50	4.0	2	1.0	6	9	7	78%	136	15.1	0
	218	12.0	3	2.0	25	47	31	66%	315	6.7	0

	Tackling				Coverage				Positive%		
Year	Broken Tackles	BT%	Tackle Share	ATD+	PBU	Deserved Catch %	YAC	EPA	Man	Zone	Total
2017	0	0%	2%	-	0	100%	5	0.2	67%	0%	50%
2018	2	3%	7%	90	1	100%	26	1.5	50%	50%	50%
2019	17	16%	11%	111	3	80%	53	-6.0	22%	40%	33%
2020	3	6%	8%	111	0	89%	72	5.6	60%	75%	67%
	22	9%	7%	105	4	88%	156	1.3	42%	46%	45%

	Pass Rush			Total Points				Total Points Rtg			
Year	Blitz%	Pres%	Sack%	Run Def	Pass Rush	Pass Cov	Total	Per Run	Per PR	Per Cov	Per Play
2018	8%	27%	9.1%	6	1	6	13	87	77	81	83
2019	18%	23%	0.0%	17	6	18	41	98	92	91	95
2020	17%	19%	3.4%	6	3	-1	8	84	89	56	71
	15%	22%	2.0%	29	10	23	62	-	-	-	-

Critical Factors	
3-Down Ability	4
FBI / Instincts	6
Play Speed	5

Positional Factors	
3-Level Impact	5
QB Defense	6
Stoutness	6
Shed Ability	6
Navigate Trash	5
Tackling	6
Man Coverage	4
Zone Coverage	4
Range	5
Blitz	5
Toughness	6
ST Value	6

Jake Hansen Final Grade: 5.9

Report by Daniel Jankuloski

School	Height	Weight	Year	Jersey #	Hometown
Illinois	5116 E	230 E	5SR	35	Tarpon Springs, FL

One Liner
Hansen is a high-volume tackler with the requisite motor, leadership and toughness needed for a Mike linebacker, but his athletic limitations may keep him from a starting role.

Strengths: Effort, leadership and toughness; Hand usage; Tackling production
Weaknesses: Speed and range; Play action diagnosis; Coverage quickness

Jake Hansen is a fifth-year senior linebacker at Illinois as the signal caller of their base defense. He played in 41 games, starting in 30 of them. He tore his right ACL during 2017's preseason camp and missed the year, and also missed time due to a head injury. He's slightly undersized but has good upper-body strength. He does not have eye-popping athleticism, but he makes up for it with exceptional toughness and motor.

Hansen spent most passing downs in zone coverage or blitzing. He bites on play action often and struggles to recover and regain depth in his drops, resulting in passing success behind him. When keyed correctly, he's sufficient at opening his hips and working his eyes as he sinks into hook zones and even the occasional Tampa 2. He has shown decent ball production and will convert interceptions when available. He's an adequate rusher and uses his hands well to fight at contact, but hasn't logged many pressures that aren't schemed for him.

Hansen is a very sure tackler in the run game. He has a high level of on-ball production over his career and forces fumbles at a high rate, as well. He has an adequate first step and instincts to meet runners in holes. He excels at using his hands to engage and stay active through contact with blockers. He logs tackles at all areas of the field, for good and bad. His motor lets him pursue and make plays outside his immediate area, but he doesn't have the natural speed and range to beat many rushers to the perimeter, resulting in deeper tackles. He is a great communicator and clearly in charge of getting everyone lined up correctly.

Hansen projects as a top backup Mike linebacker at the next level. His motor and effort that he always shows will be his best chances at seeing the field. He's a very strong tackler and an energetic leader, but his athletic traits and coverage skills will hinder his playing time. He profiles as a solid contributor on all special teams units from Day 1.

	Tackling			Pass Rush		Coverage					
Year	Tackles	TFL	FF	Sacks	Pres	Trgt	Comp	Comp%	Yds	Yds/Trgt	Int
2016	6	0.0	0	0.0	1	1	1	100%	9	9.0	0
2018	102	8.0	1	1.0	6	35	23	66%	281	8.0	0
2019	71	7.5	7	3.5	8	14	7	50%	88	6.3	1
2020	68	10.0	2	2.5	6	16	12	75%	128	8.0	2
	247	25.5	10	7.0	21	66	43	65%	506	7.7	3

	Tackling				Coverage				Positive%		
Year	Broken Tackles	BT%	Tackle Share	ATD+	PBU	Deserved Catch %	YAC	EPA	Man	Zone	Total
2016	1	14%	1%	-	0	100%	0	-0.5	-	0%	0%
2018	6	6%	13%	96	2	89%	109	5.8	56%	59%	57%
2019	11	13%	8%	111	2	80%	40	-9.8	67%	27%	36%
2020	4	6%	12%	84	4	87%	40	5.9	0%	67%	63%
	22	8%	8%	98	8	87%	189	1.4	55%	52%	53%

	Pass Rush			Total Points				Total Points Rtg			
Year	Blitz%	Pres%	Sack%	Run Def	Pass Rush	Pass Cov	Total	Per Run	Per PR	Per Cov	Per Play
2018	8%	17%	3.1%	18	1	8	27	83	59	69	74
2019	8%	33%	17.4%	14	11	13	37	78	99	85	89
2020	10%	23%	12.0%	9	3	4	16	71	90	67	72
	9%	24%	10.0%	41	15	25	80	-	-	-	-

Critical Factors	
3-Down Ability	5
FBI / Instincts	5
Play Speed	5

Positional Factors	
3-Level Impact	5
QB Defense	7
Stoutness	5
Shed Ability	6
Navigate Trash	6
Tackling	7
Man Coverage	4
Zone Coverage	5
Range	5
Blitz	5
Toughness	7
ST Value	6

Paddy Fisher

Report by Jeff Dean

School	Height	Weight	Year	Jersey #	Hometown
Northwestern	6034 V	239 V	5SR	42	Katy, TX

One Liner

Fisher has the smarts, size, and base athleticism to lead a unit at middle linebacker at the next level, but his physical limitations against the run and pass limit his impact and may hinder his playing time.

Strengths: Flowing to the ball; Discipline; Instincts
Weaknesses: Block shedding; Lateral stoutness; Consistent impact near the line

Paddy Fisher is the Mike linebacker behind Northwestern's 4-down base front. He has started 47 of his 48 career games played. He's very tall and long for the position. His marginal hip fluidity makes him look stiff, but his sound footwork, instincts, and sufficient play speed allow for him to change directions fairly well. The former All-American is a two-time captain and always finds himself around the ball with infectious competitive fire.

Fisher understands the principles of coverage well. While he doesn't have the range or burst to play in the slot, he is a more than capable, midfield zone defender. He communicates well with his teammates and is rarely out of place intellectually. He drops with clean footwork and passes receivers off with eyes on the quarterback. Peeking in the backfield and lacking the quick cutting ability to stay close in man stem from limited reps and inflexibility. His ball skills are adequate, but he tends to play his man conservatively and not the ball. He was used minimally as a blitzer

and wasn't an factor, but there is some upside due to his size and instincts.

Fisher always seems to be around the ball and flows to it well. He is good at navigating trash but struggles with his stoutness on the move and ability to disengage, getting washed out by blockers and leaving open cutback lanes. Fisher's instincts help make up for his physical limitations and allow him to be a volume tackler, although he doesn't consistently impact run plays at or behind the line. He is a sufficient tackler but can have issues allowing extra yards after contact or breaking down against superior lateral agility.

Fisher projects as a top-end back up who fits best in a 4-3 scheme. He can make a sufficient impact on third downs in zone but is not a coverage specialist, and his run defense is buoyed by his football intelligence and tackling production. At the very least, he should become a core special teams player immediately.

	Tackling			Pass Rush		Coverage					
Year	Tackles	TFL	FF	Sacks	Pres	Trgt	Comp	Comp%	Yds	Yds/Trgt	Int
2017	122	9.0	4	0.0	10	28	18	64%	117	4.2	1
2018	118	5.0	4	1.0	6	28	22	79%	214	7.6	1
2019	92	6.0	2	1.0	6	16	8	50%	50	3.1	1
2020	86	3.5	1	0.0	4	22	10	45%	77	3.5	1
	418	23.5	11	2.0	26	94	58	62%	458	4.9	4

	Tackling				Coverage				Positive%		
Year	Broken Tackles	BT%	Tackle Share	ATD+	PBU	Deserved Catch %	YAC	EPA	Man	Zone	Total
2017	9	7%	15%	-	4	83%	64	-8.1	0%	33%	32%
2018	17	13%	14%	95	6	92%	93	4.2	50%	63%	61%
2019	18	16%	6%	107	5	71%	28	-6.0	0%	33%	31%
2020	14	14%	16%	93	6	75%	15	-15.3	33%	32%	32%
	58	12%	11%	98	21	82%	200	-25.2	33%	41%	40%

	Pass Rush			Total Points				Total Points Rtg			
Year	Blitz%	Pres%	Sack%	Run Def	Pass Rush	Pass Cov	Total	Per Run	Per PR	Per Cov	Per Play
2018	8%	13%	2.3%	16	4	17	37	77	70	75	75
2019	6%	23%	4.3%	12	2	14	29	74	67	79	75
2020	7%	16%	0.0%	13	2	19	33	84	67	86	83
	7%	17%	2.2%	41	8	50	99	-	-	-	-

Critical Factors	
3-Down Ability	5
FBI / Instincts	6
Play Speed	5

Positional Factors	
3-Level Impact	5
QB Defense	6
Stoutness	5
Shed Ability	4
Navigate Trash	6
Tackling	5
Man Coverage	4
Zone Coverage	6
Range	5
Blitz	4
Toughness	5
ST Value	7

Rayshard Ashby

Report by Jacob Halleen, Max Nuscher, & Noah Chang

School	Height	Weight	Year	Jersey #	Hometown
Virginia Tech	5096 E	245 E	4SR	23	Chesterfield, VA

One Liner
Ashby has the zone coverage skills, range, and tackling ability to be a quality backup, but his inability to produce in man coverage or as a blitzer likely keep him from being a three-down player.

Strengths: Zone defender; Instincts; Aggressiveness
Weaknesses: 3-down ability; Blitz production; Man-coverage skill

Rayshard Ashby is the Mike linebacker in Virginia Tech's primary 4-2-5 defense, occasionally lining up on the edge as well. He started 35 of 49 career games. He has a strong build, but lacks height and length for the position. He's a decent athlete who attacks the ball and is a tough competitor that displays a consistently high motor.

In the pass game, Ashby understands where he needs to be, though he will bite on play action too often. He doesn't cover a ton of ground, but plays smart and does a good job of covering his area with solid depth in his drops. At times, he gets stuck flat-footed and is slow to react to traffic around him. Although he didn't play much man coverage, he lacks flexibility and COD skills to be a consistent contributor when matched up against quicker receivers. As a blitzer, Ashby is most effective as a green dog or delayed blitzer. His production comes from looking for holes in the line. If he's met at the POA, he struggles to shed linemen, but shows he can beat running backs with quick swim moves to get to the backfield. As

the QB of the defense, his communication ability only seems to show up when the defense is on its heels.

Against the run, Ashby shows patience and reads flow well. He reads and reacts quickly to what gap the ballcarrier is running, though this can leave him susceptible to cutbacks. He's a stout defender and uses quick hands and strength to adequately shed blockers. He takes good angles on running plays to the outside, but lacks overall speed to make consistent plays out on the edge. He is a good tackler at all three levels and can make tackles near and behind the LOS, also showing good pursuit down the field.

Ashby projects to be a backup Mike linebacker on 1st and 2nd down at the next level. His lack of lateral agility and blitz production will make it difficult for him to be on the field on 3rd downs in obvious passing situations. He has the toughness, stoutness, and enough play speed to be a contributor on special teams.

Year	Tackling			Pass Rush		Coverage					
	Tackles	TFL	FF	Sacks	Pres	Trgt	Comp	Comp%	Yds	Yds/Trgt	Int
2018	103	9.0	2	1.0	17	13	8	62%	53	4.1	0
2019	119	17.5	2	5.0	25	28	20	71%	208	7.4	0
2020	69	7.5	0	4.0	22	4	3	75%	16	4.0	0
	291	34.0	4	10.0	64	45	31	69%	277	6.2	0

Year	Tackling				Coverage				Positive%		
	Broken Tackles	BT%	Tackle Share	ATD+	PBU	Deserved Catch %	YAC	EPA	Man	Zone	Total
2018	9	8%	13%	112	1	100%	22	-3.4	50%	55%	54%
2019	19	14%	15%	131	1	88%	72	12.3	60%	65%	64%
2020	7	9%	10%	114	0	100%	3	-0.8	0%	100%	75%
	35	11%	13%	119	2	91%	97	8.1	50%	65%	62%

Year	Pass Rush			Total Points				Total Points Rtg			
	Blitz%	Pres%	Sack%	Run Def	Pass Rush	Pass Cov	Total	Per Run	Per PR	Per Cov	Per Play
2018	19%	23%	1.5%	11	6	11	29	70	90	79	77
2019	17%	28%	8.4%	23	14	0	36	95	99	60	84
2020	29%	18%	3.3%	4	9	6	19	58	90	68	68
	21%	22%	4.4%	38	29	17	84	-	-	-	-

Critical Factors	
3-Down Ability	5
FBI / Instincts	6
Play Speed	5

Positional Factors	
3-Level Impact	5
QB Defense	5
Stoutness	6
Shed Ability	5
Navigate Trash	6
Tackling	6
Man Coverage	4
Zone Coverage	6
Range	6
Blitz	4
Toughness	6
ST Value	6

Erroll Thompson Final Grade: 5.8

Report by Ty Dorner

School	Height	Weight	Year	Jersey #	Hometown
Mississippi State	6006 E	250 E	5SR	40	Florence, AL

One Liner

Thompson is a gritty, run-stuffing linebacker who can provide stoutness, toughness and leadership to an organization, but his coverage limitations will make it hard for him to see the field.

Strengths: Physical against the run; Pursuit; Upper-body strength and power
Weaknesses: Hip fluidity; Man coverage; Athleticism in space

Erroll Thompson is a Mike linebacker in Mississippi State's base nickel defense. He has started 40 of his 50 career games played dating back to his redshirt freshman season. He has a solid build and a squatty, strong frame that has aided his durability. He has sufficient downhill speed but is not an athletic player in space. He is tough, aggressive, and the heartbeat of his defense as a captain and four-year starter.

Thompson is not great in coverage, and his best value on passing downs is as a blitzer. He has shown that he can sufficiently disrupt the quarterback by charging downhill and driving blocking backs and even some linemen further into the pocket with his upper-body strength and power. However, he relies on momentum and does not have technical hands to counter after being stalemated. In man coverage, he doesn't consistently stick with pass catchers regardless of position because he is usually the inferior athlete. He displays stiff hips to change directions quickly. In zone, he has the football intelligence to know where he needs to be, but is often a tick late getting there. He's a good communicator and directs traffic well.

Thompson is a tough, physical competitor in the run game and doesn't shy away from contact. He plays with very good stoutness to leverage blockers and sheds well with his upper-body strength. He has good vision to weave through traffic and position himself for tackles. Despite his limited athleticism, he ranges well sideline to sideline against the run because of his quick instincts and anticipation. He shocks blockers with his punch strength and strikes ballcarriers hard at the point of attack. He's a volume tackler and sparks his team when he makes stops.

Thompson projects as a sufficient backup Mike linebacker at the next level. He's a classic old-school run stuffer, whose coverage abilities will limit his ceiling in today's NFL. His sufficient speed isn't ideal, but he has every other mental and physical trait to be a core special teamer.

	Tackling			Pass Rush		Coverage						
Year	Tackles	TFL	FF	Sacks	Pres	Trgt	Comp	Comp%	Yds	Yds/Trgt	Int	
2017	50	5.5	1	2.5	5	14	5	36%	55	3.9	0	
2018	87	9.0	0	3.5	15	14	6	43%	48	3.4	2	
2019	82	3.5	1	0.5	17	9	7	78%	150	16.7	0	
2020	92	3.5	0	3.0	20	11	10	91%	75	6.8	1	
	311	21.5	2	9.5	57	48	28	58%	328	6.8	3	

	Tackling				Coverage				Positive%		
Year	Broken Tackles	BT%	Tackle Share	ATD+	PBU	Deserved Catch %	YAC	EPA	Man	Zone	Total
2017	7	12%	6%	-	2	60%	11	-2.3	0%	31%	29%
2018	10	10%	11%	137	3	80%	43	-16.1	33%	27%	29%
2019	16	16%	11%	119	1	88%	106	10.8	33%	100%	78%
2020	16	15%	12%	115	2	91%	16	-2.8	-	64%	64%
	49	14%	10%	123	8	79%	176	-10.4	29%	49%	46%

	Pass Rush			Total Points				Total Points Rtg			
Year	Blitz%	Pres%	Sack%	Run Def	Pass Rush	Pass Cov	Total	Per Run	Per PR	Per Cov	Per Play
2018	25%	15%	5.0%	16	11	27	53	92	96	97	95
2019	27%	19%	1.2%	17	5	-7	15	90	85	52	73
2020	25%	22%	3.4%	15	8	11	33	84	93	78	84
	25%	18%	3.3%	48	24	31	101	-	-	-	-

Critical Factors	
3-Down Ability	4
FBI / Instincts	6
Play Speed	5

Positional Factors	
3-Level Impact	5
QB Defense	6
Stoutness	7
Shed Ability	6
Navigate Trash	6
Tackling	6
Man Coverage	4
Zone Coverage	5
Range	6
Blitz	5
Toughness	7
ST Value	6

David Curry

Report by Ben Hrkach

School	Height	Weight	Year	Jersey #	Hometown
Georgia Tech	6011 V	230 V	6SR	6	Buford, GA

One Liner

Curry is a run-stopping Mike who shows good stoutness and shed ability, but his inefficiencies in coverage likely limits his 3rd-down ability and ultimately his overall potential.

Strengths: Stack-and-shed ability; Awareness; Special teams
Weaknesses: COD ability; Suddenness; 3rd-down contribution

David Curry plays Mike linebacker in Georgia Tech's nickel defense. He started 35 of 48 career games. He missed the 2017 season with a foot injury and played through a broken bone in his hand in 2020. Curry is one of the oldest prospects in this draft class at 25. His father, Buddy, is a former NFL player and the 1980 Defensive Rookie of the Year. A high school track athlete, Curry is a linear, downhill player. He has good strength and consistently shows a good motor, as well as toughness.

Curry is more comfortable in zone than he is in man. He has a good feel for the receivers around him and is good at reading the quarterback. He's able to keep his momentum in the right direction and that aids his break on the ball. In man, his lack of COD is exposed. He has enough long speed to stay with tight ends up the seam and can close on the flat after he's built up speed. When forced to mirror, he rarely stays with them. Curry is a sufficient blitzer. He times blitzes well and uses his natural shed moves to easily beat tight ends and backs.

Curry clearly has a natural ability to get off blocks. He has strong hands and can stack and shed blockers while keeping his head up and reading the play. He is also stout, being able to push a blocker back who is attempting to climb to the 2nd level. Sometimes he can get caught in the wrong hole, though he is frequently in the correct lane and makes the most of his contact at the LOS. He has good discipline and can set the edge when needed. He didn't make many calls at GT, but works well with his teammates when dropping into a zone, as well as attacking a read option. Curry is a reliable tackler, chopping his feet at the point of contact, staying low, and wrapping up.

Curry projects as a good backup Mike who is more effective on early downs. He can keep up with tight ends and backs, but can get exposed against sudden route runners in coverage. He will be a core special teams player and brings desired energy and toughness.

	Tackling			Pass Rush		Coverage					
Year	Tackles	TFL	FF	Sacks	Pres	Trgt	Comp	Comp%	Yds	Yds/Trgt	Int
2016	9	0.0	0	0.0	2	2	2	100%	37	18.5	0
2018	48	0.5	0	0.5	8	9	4	44%	23	2.6	1
2019	96	6.0	2	2.0	15	12	7	58%	90	7.5	1
2020	79	9.0	1	2.0	17	9	7	78%	71	7.9	0
	232	15.5	3	4.5	42	32	20	63%	221	6.9	2

	Tackling				Coverage			Positive%		
Year	Broken Tackles	BT%	Tackle Share	ATD+	PBU	Deserved Catch %	YAC	EPA	Man	Zone	Total
2016	4	31%	1%	-	0	100%	0	4.6	-	100%	100%
2018	12	20%	7%	91	1	83%	7	-7.0	-	33%	33%
2019	15	14%	12%	99	4	83%	56	-5.3	33%	44%	42%
2020	15	16%	11%	106	2	89%	21	0.5	67%	67%	67%
	46	17%	8%	100	7	86%	84	-7.3	56%	48%	50%

	Pass Rush			Total Points				Total Points Rtg			
Year	Blitz%	Pres%	Sack%	Run Def	Pass Rush	Pass Cov	Total	Per Run	Per PR	Per Cov	Per Play
2018	16%	16%	2.1%	2	4	15	21	50	80	87	62
2019	22%	20%	2.7%	4	4	10	18	58	80	79	66
2020	24%	18%	3.1%	5	5	3	14	60	79	63	64
	21%	18%	2.8%	11	13	28	53	-	-	-	-

Critical Factors

3-Down Ability	4
FBI / Instincts	5
Play Speed	5

Positional Factors

3-Level Impact	5
QB Defense	5
Stoutness	6
Shed Ability	6
Navigate Trash	5
Tackling	5
Man Coverage	4
Zone Coverage	5
Range	5
Blitz	5
Toughness	6
ST Value	6

Will Linebackers

Matt Manocherian

"Analytics people" are supposed to devalue off-ball linebackers. While we understand and try to participate in the positional value conversation, I struggle with the notion that any defensive position is inherently that much more or less valuable than another. Wouldn't it be preferable to have Lawrence Taylor over almost any defensive back and to have Deion Sanders over almost any pass rusher?

While these are admittedly fringe cases, there was nothing fringy about the way that Lavonte David and Devin White helped lead the Bucs defense that stifled Patrick Mahomes (he of the most valuable position) en route to a Lombardi Trophy. David is having a Hall of Fame-worthy career, and he is one of the best examples in the NFL of the skills that make a successful weakside linebacker with his combination of coverage ability, play speed, and football intelligence, our three critical factors.

Speaking of White, he was our top Mike linebacker in our inaugural Football Rookie Handbook, and he has lived up to his 7.0 final grade, especially during the Bucs' Super Bowl season. The top Will in the book that year was Devin Bush, who as a rookie in 2019 was already playing at a level that surpassed his 6.8 final grade before he had his sophomore campaign derailed by injury.

Last year, the Will position was highlighted by Clemson's Isaiah Simmons, who had the top grade in the entire linebacker class at 6.9. After being drafted in the top 10, he struggled to find a role with the Cardinals as one of many rookies who had difficulty finding their footing with no training camp in 2020. It will be interesting to see if he can live up to his final grade in the all-important Year 2.

This year, nobody quite reaches the heights of a 6.9 final grade, but two players slot in with 6.8s. One of our more experienced scouts, Jeff Dean, was effusive in his praise of our top ranked Will, Jeremiah Owusu-Koramoah of Notre Dame:

> *"He is the prototypical new school Will who could play every snap in the slot and be comfortable at the next level. He also started his career at Edge, so he can do some of that, too. Super fast, violent, doesn't have the bulk to really power his way through blocks, but he can shed and definitely range."*

Besides eliciting strong feelings from our scout who has studied him most closely, the computer also found one trait that it likes in particular about Owusu-Koramoah. He led all WLBs with an Adjusted Tackle Depth Plus (ATD+) of 135 during the 2020 season. ATD+ is one of my favorite metrics that we have to evaluate linebackers, but to better understand it let's deconstruct what it means.

At its core, ATD+ is about average tackle depth, or how far down the field you are making your tackles. Generally, players who line up in different alignments make tackles at different depths. Therefore, just looking at the average tackle depth for a player might tell us more about their usage than their talent. This is where the "Adjusted" comes into play. By understanding each tackle depth in relation to an expected tackle depth based on the player's pre-snap alignment, we can create a much more meaningful signal than we would by just looking at the unadjusted average.

Finally, if you aren't familiar with "Plus" stats, it's just a way to scale things so that they are more interpretable. In any given season, a 100 represents an average performance in ATD+, and any amount above or below 100 reflects the player's performance above or below an average player. So, Owusu-Koramoah's ATD+ of 135 in 2020 means that he made his tackles 35 percent closer to the line of scrimmage than the average player who shared the same alignments. His ATD+ of 84 indicates that he was 16 percent below average in 2019, so the computer is less excited now.

The player who the computer really has its eyes on is our fifth-ranked player in the class, LSU's Jabril Cox, who graded out at a 6.6. He led all WLBs with 5.4 Total Points per game, including a position-leading 3.8 Coverage Total Points per game. He was also No. 2 in Total Points Rating per play at 93 out of a maximum possible rating of 99. Total Points Rating is just like Total Points, except that it is a rate stat as opposed to a counting stat, and it is scaled in an intuitive way that is a little bit like either classroom or video game grades, depending on your preference: a 50 is very bad, a 75 is average, and a 99 is top notch.

WILL LINEBACKER

Will Linebacker Grading Scale

GRADE	DESCRIPTION
9.0 – 7.0	High-end 3 down starter. Pro Bowl level.
6.9 – 6.7	Strong starter who plays on all 3 downs.
6.6 – 6.5	Low-end starter. 3rd down coverage LB.
6.2	Versatile backup with positional flexibility.
6.1 – 6.0	Developmental. Top traits but needs time.
5.9	Top backup. Quality special teamer.
5.8	Average backup. Quality special teamer.
5.7	Low-end backup LB with growable upside.

Will Linebacker Rankings

Rank	Name	Grade	Page
1	Jeremiah Owusu-Koramoah	6.8	528
2	Dylan Moses	6.8	530
3	Zaven Collins	6.7	532
4	Micah Parsons	6.7	534
5	Jabril Cox	6.6	536
6	Chazz Surratt	6.5	538
7	Jamin Davis	6.5	540
8	Justin Hilliard	6.2	542
9	Pete Werner	6.2	543
10	Grant Stuard	6.2	544
11	Tony Fields II	5.9	545
12	Garret Wallow	5.9	546
13	Blake Gallagher	5.9	547
14	Max Richardson	5.9	548
15	Rodjay Burns	5.8	549
16	Isaiah McDuffie	5.8	550

Glossary

ATD+ (Adjusted Tackle Depth Plus)
ATD+ compares actual tackle depth to the expected tackle depth based on personnel, intended run gap, and the defender's pre-snap alignment. This figure is then scaled so that 100 is average. A figure of 110 indicates a player who is 10% better than average; a figure of 90 indicates a player who is 10% worse than average.

Blitz%
Percentage of quarterback dropbacks where the defender rushed the quarterback.

Broken Tackles
Tackle attempts where the defender in position to make a tackle failed to bring down the ballcarrier. Counts both broken tackles (physical) and missed tackles (elusive).

BT% (Broken Tackle%)
Percentage of tackle attempts where the defender in position to make a tackle failed to bring down the ball carrier. Counts both broken tackles (physical) and missed tackles (elusive).

Deserved Catch%
The percentage of targets as the primary defender that the receiver either caught or dropped the ball when the pass was catchable.

PBU (Pass Breakups)
The number of times the defender batted, deflected for an incompletion, or defensed a pass attempt.

Positive%
The percentage of plays where the defender was targeted that resulted in a positive EPA for the offense. Lower numbers are better for defenders.

Pres% (Pressure Rate)
The percentage of pass rushes that resulted in a quarterback hurry, hit, knockdown, or sack.

Sack%
Percentage of pass rushes that resulted in a sack.

Tackle Share
Percentage of a team's tackles made by the defender.

Total Points
Sports Info Solutions' proprietary player value metric that uses an Expected Points framework and distributes the value gained or lost on a play to the players involved based on their impact on the play.

Total Points Rating
Total Points per play compared to average, scaled so that 50 is poor and 99 is excellent.

Will Linebacker Leaderboards

Total Points Per Game

Rk	Player	School	Tot Pts / G
1	J. Cox	LSU	5.4
2	Z. Collins	Tulsa	4.3
3	J. Davis	Kentucky	3.9
4	B. Gallagher	Northwestern	3.7
5	J. Hilliard	Ohio State	3.5
6	C. Surratt	North Carolina	3.3
7	G. Wallow	TCU	3.2
8	J. Owusu-Koramoah	Notre Dame	3.1
9	D. Moses	Alabama	3.0
10	P. Werner	Ohio State	2.6

Total Points Rating Per Play

Rk	Player	School	Rating
1	J. Hilliard	Ohio State	97
2	J. Cox	LSU	93
3	Z. Collins	Tulsa	91
4	J. Davis	Kentucky	88
5	G. Wallow	TCU	87
6	B. Gallagher	Northwestern	86
7	J. Owusu-Koramoah	Notre Dame	83
8	C. Surratt	North Carolina	82
9	P. Werner	Ohio State	80
10	2 tied with		79

Pass Coverage Total Points Per Game

Rk	Player	School	Tot Pts / G
1	J. Cox	LSU	3.8
2	Z. Collins	Tulsa	2.4
3	J. Davis	Kentucky	2.3
4	J. Owusu-Koramoah	Notre Dame	1.8
4	D. Moses	Alabama	1.8
4	J. Hilliard	Ohio State	1.8
7	C. Surratt	North Carolina	1.5
8	B. Gallagher	Northwestern	1.4
9	P. Werner	Ohio State	0.8
10	3 tied with		0.6

Total Points Rating Per Coverage Snap

Rk	Player	School	Rating
1	J. Cox	LSU	99
2	Z. Collins	Tulsa	98
3	J. Hilliard	Ohio State	97
4	J. Davis	Kentucky	95
5	J. Owusu-Koramoah	Notre Dame	91
6	D. Moses	Alabama	86
7	C. Surratt	North Carolina	83
8	B. Gallagher	Northwestern	81
9	P. Werner	Ohio State	69
9	2 tied with		69

Run Defense Total Points Per Game

Rk	Player	School	Tot Pts / G
1	G. Wallow	TCU	2.0
2	G. Stuard	Houston	1.9
3	J. Hilliard	Ohio State	1.7
3	R. Burns	Louisville	1.7
5	B. Gallagher	Northwestern	1.4
6	J. Davis	Kentucky	1.3
6	P. Werner	Ohio State	1.3
8	J. Cox	LSU	1.2
9	Z. Collins	Tulsa	1.1
9	T. Fields II	West Virginia	1.1

Total Points Rating Per Run Snap

Rk	Player	School	Rating
1	J. Hilliard	Ohio State	99
2	G. Wallow	TCU	94
3	G. Stuard	Houston	92
4	P. Werner	Ohio State	88
4	R. Burns	Louisville	88
6	B. Gallagher	Northwestern	85
7	T. Fields II	West Virginia	83
8	J. Davis	Kentucky	81
9	J. Cox	LSU	78
10	Z. Collins	Tulsa	76

Pass Rush Total Points Per Game

Rk	Player	School	Tot Pts / G
1	C. Surratt	North Carolina	1.4
2	G. Wallow	TCU	1.3
3	Z. Collins	Tulsa	0.8
3	P. Werner	Ohio State	0.8
3	B. Gallagher	Northwestern	0.8
6	J. Owusu-Koramoah	Notre Dame	0.6
7	J. Cox	LSU	0.5
8	D. Moses	Alabama	0.4
8	T. Fields II	West Virginia	0.4
8	I. McDuffie	Boston College	0.4

Total Points Rating Per Pass Rush

Rk	Player	School	Rating
1	C. Surratt	North Carolina	99
1	G. Wallow	TCU	99
3	B. Gallagher	Northwestern	98
4	Z. Collins	Tulsa	95
5	P. Werner	Ohio State	94
6	T. Fields II	West Virginia	93
7	J. Cox	LSU	89
8	J. Owusu-Koramoah	Notre Dame	85
9	J. Davis	Kentucky	77
10	I. McDuffie	Boston College	76

Pressures Per Game

Rk	Player	School	Pres/G
1	C. Surratt	North Carolina	3.0
2	Z. Collins	Tulsa	1.8
2	G. Wallow	TCU	1.8
2	M. Richardson	Boston College	1.8
5	P. Werner	Ohio State	1.3
5	G. Stuard	Houston	1.3
7	T. Fields II	West Virginia	1.2
8	J. Owusu-Koramoah	Notre Dame	1.1
8	I. McDuffie	Boston College	1.1
10	2 tied with		0.9

Pressure Rate

Rk	Player	School	Pres%
1	G. Wallow	TCU	42%
2	J. Cox	LSU	41%
3	C. Surratt	North Carolina	35%
4	P. Werner	Ohio State	32%
5	T. Fields II	West Virginia	31%
6	J. Davis	Kentucky	28%
7	J. Hilliard	Ohio State	27%
8	M. Richardson	Boston College	26%
9	Z. Collins	Tulsa	25%
10	G. Stuard	Houston	21%

Sacks Per Game

Rk	Player	School	Sacks/G
1	Z. Collins	Tulsa	0.5
1	C. Surratt	North Carolina	0.5
3	G. Wallow	TCU	0.3
3	M. Richardson	Boston College	0.3
3	I. McDuffie	Boston College	0.3
6	J. Davis	Kentucky	0.2
6	T. Fields II	West Virginia	0.2
6	B. Gallagher	Northwestern	0.2
6	R. Burns	Louisville	0.2
10	5 tied with		0.1

Tackles For Loss Per Game

Rk	Player	School	TFL/G
1	Z. Collins	Tulsa	1.6
2	B. Gallagher	Northwestern	1.1
3	G. Wallow	TCU	1.0
4	J. Owusu-Koramoah	Notre Dame	0.9
5	J. Hilliard	Ohio State	0.8
6	J. Cox	LSU	0.7
6	C. Surratt	North Carolina	0.7
6	M. Richardson	Boston College	0.7
6	R. Burns	Louisville	0.7
10	2 tied with		0.6

Tackle Share

Rk	Player	School	Tkl Share
1	G. Wallow	TCU	16%
1	I. McDuffie	Boston College	16%
3	B. Gallagher	Northwestern	15%
4	J. Davis	Kentucky	14%
4	T. Fields II	West Virginia	14%
4	M. Richardson	Boston College	14%
7	C. Surratt	North Carolina	13%
8	G. Stuard	Houston	12%
9	P. Werner	Ohio State	11%
10	D. Moses	Alabama	10%

Adjusted Tackle Depth Plus

Rk	Player	School	ATD+
1	J. Owusu-Koramoah	Notre Dame	135
2	G. Wallow	TCU	133
3	G. Stuard	Houston	120
4	Z. Collins	Tulsa	116
5	B. Gallagher	Northwestern	110
6	J. Hilliard	Ohio State	107
7	J. Cox	LSU	104
7	P. Werner	Ohio State	104
7	R. Burns	Louisville	104
10	T. Fields II	West Virginia	92

Tackles Per Game

Rk	Player	School	Tackles/G
1	J. Davis	Kentucky	10.7
2	T. Fields II	West Virginia	9.8
2	I. McDuffie	Boston College	9.8
4	G. Wallow	TCU	9.3
4	B. Gallagher	Northwestern	9.3
6	G. Stuard	Houston	8.6
7	C. Surratt	North Carolina	8.5
7	M. Richardson	Boston College	8.5
9	Z. Collins	Tulsa	6.8
9	P. Werner	Ohio State	6.8

Broken Tackle Rate

Rk	Player	School	BT%
1	J. Davis	Kentucky	4%
2	T. Fields II	West Virginia	7%
3	D. Moses	Alabama	8%
4	C. Surratt	North Carolina	10%
5	J. Hilliard	Ohio State	11%
5	I. McDuffie	Boston College	11%
7	G. Stuard	Houston	13%
7	B. Gallagher	Northwestern	13%
9	P. Werner	Ohio State	14%
9	G. Wallow	TCU	14%

Yards Per Target

Rk	Player	School	Yds/Trgt
1	Z. Collins	Tulsa	3.4
1	J. Cox	LSU	3.4
1	B. Gallagher	Northwestern	3.4
4	P. Werner	Ohio State	3.9
5	D. Moses	Alabama	4.6
6	J. Hilliard	Ohio State	5.1
7	J. Owusu-Koramoah	Notre Dame	5.2
8	G. Stuard	Houston	7.6
9	C. Surratt	North Carolina	8.4
10	J. Davis	Kentucky	8.5

Passes Broken Up Per Game

Rk	Player	School	PBU/G
1	Z. Collins	Tulsa	0.8
1	J. Cox	LSU	0.8
3	C. Surratt	North Carolina	0.4
3	J. Davis	Kentucky	0.4
5	J. Owusu-Koramoah	Notre Dame	0.3
5	D. Moses	Alabama	0.3
5	J. Hilliard	Ohio State	0.3
5	B. Gallagher	Northwestern	0.3
9	T. Fields II	West Virginia	0.2
9	2 tied with		0.2

Jeremiah Owusu-Koramoah

Report by Jeff Dean

School	Height	Weight	Year	Jersey #	Hometown
Notre Dame	6006 E	215 E	4SR	6	Hampton, VA

One Liner
Owusu-Koramoah has the speed, coverage ability, and versatility teams crave in today's NFL, and he should be able to make an immediate impact as a space linebacker.

Overall
Jeremiah Owusu-Koramoah's primary position is Will linebacker in Notre Dame's base 3-4 defense. He played in 27 career games with 25 starts. He missed most of the 2018 season with a broken foot. He is a high-quality athlete who is a bit undersized for the linebacker position, but shows the top-end speed, acceleration, and quick twitch to play anywhere on the field. He has a chiseled frame that could stand to add more bulk if he retains his athleticism. He is a fierce competitor who shows up in big games and plays with a chip on his shoulder.

Pass Game
Owusu-Koramoah is very good in coverage and looks comfortable in either zone or man schemes. He has a quick and smooth drop back in zone and keeps his eyes on the quarterback while feeling routes around him. He passes off receivers well and has a firm understanding of route design. He can play shallow or deep and has the burst to close quickly after the catch, but he doesn't make many plays with the ball in the air. He has the hips and speed to keep up with receivers down the field and keeps his feet active to react to breaks. Owusu-Koramoah lines up all over the field and was asked to cover running backs, tight ends, and receivers due to his comfortability in space. He is also a good blitzer and can cause problems for blockers with his combination of speed, aggression, and deceptive strength.

Run Game
Owusu-Koramoah has good football IQ and discipline to consistently make plays in the run game and backfield. He diagnoses plays and reads blocking schemes well before exploding. Although he is a ferocious tackler and delivers numerous big hits, his tackling form lapses at times and he will miss on occasion while going for the highlight hit. Owusu-Koramoah's impact between the tackles is suspect at times as he works better out in space. He prefers to attack blockers rather than anchor against them. He sheds blocks well but can struggle to meet linemen at the line of scrimmage and hold the point of attack. He has very good range and can make plays sideline to sideline without sacrificing depth on his tackles.

Last Word
Owusu-Koramoah projects as an impressive Will linebacker who fits best in a 4-3 defense but could also work in a 3-4 if he adds weight to handle the box more adequately. He is a three-down linebacker whose range and explosion will serve him well on run downs before excelling in passing situations from all over the field. He often looks to be one of the fastest players on the field and has a ferocious playing style, which would project very highly to special teams duties if necessary.

Strengths

- Play speed and range
- Comfortability in coverage
- Alignment versatility

Weaknesses

- Handling linemen
- Impact in the box
- Slightly undersized

Critical Factors

Pass Coverage	Play Speed	FBI / Instincts
7	7	6

Positional Factors

3-Level Impact	QB Defense	Man Coverage	Zone Coverage
7	6	6	7
Range	Blitz	Stoutness	Shed Ability
7	6	5	6
Navigate Trash	Tackling	Toughness	ST Value
6	6	6	8

Basic

	Tackling			Pass Rush		Coverage					
Year	Tackles	TFL	FF	Sacks	Pres	Trgt	Comp	Comp%	Yds	Yds/Trgt	Int
2019	70	13.5	3	5.5	13	15	6	40%	62	4.1	0
2020	57	10.5	3	1.5	13	26	13	50%	135	5.2	1
	127	24.0	6	7.0	26	41	19	46%	197	4.8	1

Advanced

	Tackling				Coverage				Positive%		
Year	Broken Tackles	BT%	Tackle Share	ATD+	PBU	Deserved Catch %	YAC	EPA	Man	Zone	Total
2019	11	14%	9%	84	3	58%	23	-3.9	29%	38%	33%
2020	12	17%	9%	135	4	74%	94	-14.8	21%	42%	31%
	23	15%	9%	108	7	68%	117	-18.7	24%	40%	32%

Deep Dive

	Pass Rush			Total Points				Total Points Rtg			
Year	Blitz%	Pres%	Sack%	Run Def	Pass Rush	Pass Cov	Total	Per Run	Per PR	Per Cov	Per Play
2019	13%	27%	12.8%	14	10	15	39	80	99	86	88
2020	20%	16%	2.6%	8	7	22	37	70	85	91	83
	17%	20%	6.5%	22	17	37	76	-	-	-	-

Dylan Moses

Final Grade: 6.

Report by Matt Manocherian

School	Height	Weight	Year	Jersey #	Hometown
Alabama	6016 E	235 E	4SR	32	Alexandria, LA

One Liner
Moses is a scheme-versatile off-ball linebacker with good size and great speed to become a strong every down contributor on the NFL level, but to achieve his potential he will have to return to his pre-injury form.

Overall
Dylan Moses lines up as an off-ball linebacker in Alabama's multiple defensive fronts, playing to both the strong and weak side at various times, and also occasionally splitting out to match up with RBs. He has played in 39 games for the Tide with 31 starts dating back to his freshman year. He had right ACL surgery in 2019 that caused him to miss that entire season. While he has good but not great size, he is a twitchy athlete with excellent burst for the position. He plays fast but under control, showing a good ability to stay on his feet despite flying all over the field. He showed some hitches in his play in 2020 that appeared consistent with a player coming off an ACL injury, but his burst is still very present.

Pass Game
Moses gets depth quickly in his pass drops, shows loose hips to change direction well, and blankets opponents tightly when in man-to-man. He is an intelligent defender who shows good understanding and functions well in Alabama's zone-match concepts, but he covers grass far too often in spot drop zones. He has the ability to become a very good man coverage defender who can match up well against tight ends and especially running backs, including moving outside to neutralize backs that can present a threat when lined up out wide. However, as it stands he commits too many penalties in man coverage and will need to adjust to illegal contact enforcement on the NFL level. His best asset in coverage is his closing speed, which covers for some of his deficiencies. He is a bit slow to make his run/pass read at times, including a lack of quickness to initiate his rush when his man responsibility stays in pass protection. That said, he shows the ability to time his planned blitzes well and get into the backfield quickly.

Run Game
Moses is not a thumper in run defense and doesn't show the ability to consistently stack and shed NFL offensive linemen to be ideally suited as a Mike, but he is slippery to get clean shot on and does a good job to avoid rather than take on. When he shoots gaps he is often in the backfield before the offensive line can react. He has a nose for the ball and a knack for playmaking, but he does give up some leaky yardage at times. He usually shows good discipline in the run game, but he occasionally gets himself into trouble guessing on read-options.

Last Word
Moses is ideally suited as a chase linebacker on the next level, but he has the flexibility to play multiple off-ball linebacker positions. He is best in an active rather than reactive role with disruptive ability in both phases. He is scheme-versatile, Swiss army knife-type player who can play in the more positionless defensive roles that are becoming common in the NFL. If he is not playing as an every down defender, he shows the speed and toughness to be an excellent core special teams player. His ACL injury slowed him down a bit in 2020, but if he can return to his pre-injury form, he is the sort of player who can make your entire defense faster.

Strengths
- Dynamic athleticism
- Play speed
- Playmaking ability

Weaknesses
- Take-on ability
- Zone awareness consistency
- Too many penalties in man

Critical Factors

Pass Coverage	Play Speed	FBI / Instincts
6	7	6

Positional Factors

3-Level Impact	QB Defense	Man Coverage	Zone Coverage
7	6	6	6
Range	**Blitz**	**Stoutness**	**Shed Ability**
7	6	5	5
Navigate Trash	**Tackling**	**Toughness**	**ST Value**
7	6	6	8

Basic

Year	Tackling			Pass Rush		Coverage					
	Tackles	TFL	FF	Sacks	Pres	Trgt	Comp	Comp%	Yds	Yds/Trgt	Int
2017	26	5.5	0	1.5	6	2	1	50%	11	5.5	1
2018	86	10.0	1	3.5	16	19	12	63%	182	9.6	0
2020	84	6.0	1	1.5	11	28	16	57%	128	4.6	1
	196	21.5	2	6.5	33	49	29	59%	321	6.6	2

Advanced

Year	Tackling				Coverage				Positive%		
	Broken Tackles	BT%	Tackle Share	ATD+	PBU	Deserved Catch %	YAC	EPA	Man	Zone	Total
2017	3	10%	3%	-	1	50%	13	-4.6	-	50%	50%
2018	6	7%	10%	107	2	100%	117	-0.2	73%	38%	58%
2020	7	8%	10%	91	4	83%	67	-9.9	33%	37%	36%
	16	8%	8%	99	7	87%	197	-14.7	55%	38%	45%

Deep Dive

Year	Pass Rush			Total Points				Total Points Rtg			
	Blitz%	Pres%	Sack%	Run Def	Pass Rush	Pass Cov	Total	Per Run	Per PR	Per Cov	Per Play
2018	21%	21%	6.7%	14	11	1	25	79	98	59	77
2020	15%	15%	2.7%	11	5	23	39	71	75	86	79
	18%	18%	4.7%	25	16	24	64	-	-	-	-

Zaven Collins Final Grade: 6.

Report by Alec Mallon

School	Height	Weight	Year	Jersey #	Hometown
Tulsa	6032 E	260 E	4JR	23	Hominy, OK

One Liner
Collins is an athletic and intelligent linebacker who will have an immediate impact, but must ge tougher inside before he can be a truly elite playmaker.

Overall
Zaven Collins is a Will linebacker in Tulsa's 3-3 front. He appeared in 32 games and started the final 30. He's huge for the linebacker position with an athletic frame and an explosive lower half. A former high school dual-threat quarterback and state-title winner, Collins has great movement and play diagnosis skills as a defender. He has a strong motor and the energy to make plays at all levels of the field.

Pass Game
Collins is a strong coverage linebacker. He has the speed to hang with backs out of the backfield and the size to carry tight ends down the field. In zone, he shows great eye discipline and a feel for his area while also tracking the quarterback. He picks up and passes off receivers as they come and go, but also understands when to stick and stay on a hip. He's instinctual to anticipate and trigger downhill quickly to limit yards after the catch. Collins has solid ball skills to contest catches and make plays on the ball and convert. Collins can stand up and rush the passer off the edge, but he can be overmatched when facing tackles one-on-one. He lacks the natural bend and technique of a true pass rusher but is successful against most backs and tight ends that can't match his blend of speed and power.

Run Game
Collins is explosive as a run defender. Hi instincts are very evident, as he can diagnos and see plays before they happen by shootin gaps and getting into the backfield to creat negative plays. He shows good technique an discipline with his keys against zone and ga schemes and rarely finds himself out o position with his eyes. He displays th footwork to dodge traffic in front to stay i phase with the run flow. In the open field, h ranges sideline to sideline very well and is sound tackler when under control. His instinct can lead to overaggression to beat ballcarrier to the spot, and his overpursuit will give u open cutback lanes. When addressin offensive linemen, Collins can be passive t attack on occasion and allows blockers t move him off the ball. Despite his size, h doesn't stack and shed well at the line, mor relying on his athleticism to get off of an around blocks. He needs to better use hi combination of explosion and size to compet with more aggression within the box.

Last Word
Collins projects as a strong three-down starte at the next level. His special speed and athleti ability will allow for him to make plays on al downs across the field. He will fit best in scheme that allows him to stay clean fron blocks, key and flow, and explode to the ball He also profiles as a menace on coverage unit with his size and speed.

Strengths

- Football intelligence
- Coverage ability
- Speed and athleticism

Weaknesses

- Aggression at the LOS
- Shed ability
- Technical pass rush

Critical Factors

Pass Coverage	Play Speed	FBI / Instincts
6	7	7

Positional Factors

3-Level Impact	QB Defense	Man Coverage	Zone Coverage
7	5	6	7
Range	Blitz	Stoutness	Shed Ability
7	5	5	5
Navigate Trash	Tackling	Toughness	ST Value
6	6	6	7

Basic

	Tackling			Pass Rush		Coverage					
Year	Tackles	TFL	FF	Sacks	Pres	Trgt	Comp	Comp%	Yds	Yds/Trgt	Int
2018	82	9.5	1	2.0	10	17	11	65%	63	3.7	1
2019	88	9.0	0	2.0	13	6	4	67%	79	13.2	0
2020	54	13.0	2	4.0	14	7	3	43%	24	3.4	4
	224	31.5	3	8.0	37	30	18	60%	166	5.5	5

Advanced

	Tackling					Coverage			Positive%		
Year	Broken Tackles	BT%	Tackle Share	ATD+	PBU	Deserved Catch %	YAC	EPA	Man	Zone	Total
2018	14	15%	10%	121	5	87%	30	-7.0	0%	40%	35%
2019	16	15%	11%	121	3	100%	37	2.7	33%	67%	50%
2020	10	16%	9%	116	6	80%	6	-8.8	0%	40%	29%
	40	15%	10%	120	14	88%	73	-13.1	14%	43%	37%

Deep Dive

	Pass Rush			Total Points				Total Points Rtg			
Year	Blitz%	Pres%	Sack%	Run Def	Pass Rush	Pass Cov	Total	Per Run	Per PR	Per Cov	Per Play
2018	14%	24%	7.5%	14	5	6	25	66	91	71	71
2019	13%	25%	4.3%	12	5	2	18	69	86	62	68
2020	23%	25%	7.4%	9	6	19	34	76	95	98	91
	16%	25%	6.4%	35	16	27	77	-	-	-	-

Micah Parsons

Report by Bryce Rossler

School	Height	Weight	Year	Jersey #	Hometown
Penn State	6021 E	245 E	3JR	11	Harrisburg, PA

One Liner
Parsons is a strong and athletic converted edge rusher, whose run defense and movement skill currently outpace his coverage instincts.

Overall
Micah Parsons aligned as the Will in a Penn State defense that primarily used even-spacing fronts and utilized both one- and two-high structures. He appeared in 26 career games with 13 starts. He opted out of the 2020 season and last played in 2019 as a 20-year-old true sophomore. He transitioned to linebacker after playing defensive end in high school and only has two years of experience at the position. He has good height and weight for the position with a solid build and is a very good athlete, showing high-end quickness, body control, agility, and explosiveness.

Pass Game
In zone coverage, Parsons gains good initial depth in his drops and demonstrates very good change of direction and fluidity to robot effectively. He does not consistently stack or leverage routes with zone integrity and has a mediocre feel for holding windows when being stretched horizontally. He shows good processing to react and break on throws when visioning the quarterback in zone. He has the ability to redirect and run with crossers. Processing route distributions within zone-match coverages is likely to be an issue for Parsons early in his career. In man coverage, he has very good short-area quickness to mirror routes. He demonstrates very good play speed to run with verticals. He was not asked to play man often at Penn State and his projection is based on having the requisite athletic traits to play man in the NFL. He offers very good value as a blitzer and shows grea timing, burst, power, and repertoire from edge mug, and off-ball alignments.

Run Game
In the run game, Parsons demonstrates good ability to read his keys and fit his gap. He ha solid run stoutness to take on and anchor at the point of attack, getting his hands on quickl and shedding blocks effectively. He demonstrates very good play speed to bea scooping linemen to a spot. He plays with very good body control and quickness to slithe around bodies and does a good job of playing under blockers when necessary. He has very impressive range to combine his play speed body control, and intelligent pursuit angle together. He is a good, tough tackler wit striking ability.

Last Word
Parsons projects as a Will in an even- or odd spacing front with Mike flexibility. He is likely to experience growing pains in coverage earl in his career, but his athletic traits and instinctiveness in other facets of play portend the development to be an impactful three dow starter. He offers instant value as a rur defender, and his blitzing ability should tempe zone coverage woes in Year 1. Hi combination of movement traits and toughnes project well to special teams duties if calle upon.

Strengths
- Play speed and range
- Trash navigation
- Athleticism

Weaknesses
- Zone instincts
- Man coverage inexperience

Critical Factors

Pass Coverage	Play Speed	FBI / Instincts
5	7	6

Positional Factors

3-Level Impact	QB Defense	Man Coverage	Zone Coverage
5	5	6	5
Range	**Blitz**	**Stoutness**	**Shed Ability**
7	7	6	6
Navigate Trash	**Tackling**	**Toughness**	**ST Value**
7	6	6	7

Basic

| | Tackling | | | Pass Rush | | Coverage | | | | | |
Year	Tackles	TFL	FF	Sacks	Pres	Trgt	Comp	Comp%	Yds	Yds/Trgt	Int
2018	76	4.5	2	2.5	12	17	11	65%	135	7.9	0
2019	107	14.0	4	5.0	23	25	16	64%	136	5.4	0
	183	18.5	6	7.5	35	42	27	64%	271	6.5	0

Advanced

| | Tackling | | | | | Coverage | | | Positive% | | |
Year	Broken Tackles	BT%	Tackle Share	ATD+	PBU	Deserved Catch %	YAC	EPA	Man	Zone	Total
2018	8	10%	9%	106	0	100%	92	5.7	25%	54%	47%
2019	5	4%	12%	142	5	81%	47	-2.6	67%	50%	52%
	13	7%	10%	127	5	89%	139	3.1	43%	51%	50%

Deep Dive

| | Pass Rush | | | Total Points | | | | Total Points Rtg | | | |
Year	Blitz%	Pres%	Sack%	Run Def	Pass Rush	Pass Cov	Total	Per Run	Per PR	Per Cov	Per Play
2018	16%	28%	7.5%	7	7	-4	9	60	98	53	63
2019	21%	27%	6.0%	33	13	4	51	99	99	65	96
	19%	27%	6.5%	40	20	0	60	-	-	-	-

Jabril Cox

Report by Nathan Cooper

School	Height	Weight	Year	Jersey #	Hometown
LSU	6027 V	233 V	5SR	19	Kansas City, MO

One Liner

Cox is a rangy athlete who excels in both man and zone coverage which will allow him to see the field in clutch situations at the next level, but missed tackles and too many inconsistencies in the run game could be a problem for him.

Overall

Jabril Cox mainly lines up at Will linebacker in LSU's 4-2-5 defense. In addition to playing off-ball, he lines up a fair amount in the slot and on the edge. He started 38 of 45 games for North Dakota State before transferring to LSU and starting all 10 in 2020. He suffered a torn ACL his Junior year of high school and played part of the 2019 season with a torn labrum that forced him to miss a game. A high school quarterback, he also excelled as a basketball player. Cox is a very good athlete who plays fast and competes on each play.

Pass Game

Cox has very good coverage ability for a linebacker. He has the speed and athleticism to stay with backs, tight ends, and most receivers out of the slot in man coverage. He also possesses fluid hips which allows him to transition with receivers out of the top of routes. Not only can he stay with receivers in the short-to-intermediate levels, he shows that he can turn and run with them down the seam or sideline as well. In zone coverage, he shows good drop depth and awareness to make plays on receivers and passes coming his way. He has the range to defend at every level of the defense and then pursue receivers in other areas. Cox is able to play the ball in the air and track it to the catch point. He does a good job knocking passes away, but also has the ball skills to turn them into interceptions. As a blitzer, he is effective and shows that he can pressure the quarterback when a part of stunt or 1-on-1 with backs, but struggles to get through linemen head up. He doesn't show a ton of communication on the field, but is smart and seems to always be in the right place.

Run Game

Against the run, Cox struggles at the POA. He has a tough time shedding linemen in the box and getting to the ballcarrier, normally getting driven back. He can adequately slither by blockers and navigate through the trash to occasionally get in on plays. If up against tight ends, he shows strong hands and good extension to shed them aside and get himself in position to make a play. He's a sufficient tackler overall and has his fair share of misses. When meeting backs in the hole, he fails to bring them down too often. He has very good range and pursues ballcarriers well laterally down the line, but will overpursue at times and miss tackles when cutbacks are made.

Last Word

Cox projects as a starting Will linebacker in any scheme with the ability to also play as a 4-3 Sam. On 3rd downs, he'd be best utilized manning up tight ends or backs out of the backfield. His athleticism, play speed, and toughness suggest he'd be a core special teams player.

Strengths

- Coverage ability
- Rangy athlete
- Hand use vs. tight ends

Weaknesses

- Lacks stoutness in run game
- Misses tackles in the hole

Critical Factors

Pass Coverage	Play Speed	FBI / Instincts
7	6	5

Positional Factors

3-Level Impact	QB Defense	Man Coverage	Zone Coverage
5	5	7	6
Range	Blitz	Stoutness	Shed Ability
7	5	4	5
Navigate Trash	Tackling	Toughness	ST Value
5	5	6	7

Basic

Year	Tackling			Pass Rush		Coverage					
	Tackles	TFL	FF	Sacks	Pres	Trgt	Comp	Comp%	Yds	Yds/Trgt	Int
2019	93	10.0	0	5.5	19	31	21	68%	181	5.8	1
2020	55	6.5	0	1.0	9	26	12	46%	88	3.4	3
	148	16.5	0	6.5	28	57	33	58%	269	4.7	4

Advanced

Year	Tackling					Coverage			Positive%		
	Broken Tackles	BT%	Tackle Share	ATD+	PBU	Deserved Catch %	YAC	EPA	Man	Zone	Total
2019	14	13%	9%	85	7	78%	86	0.2	50%	47%	48%
2020	10	15%	9%	104	8	59%	51	-23.9	28%	25%	27%
	24	14%	9%	94	15	69%	137	-23.7	38%	40%	39%

Deep Dive

Year	Pass Rush			Total Points				Total Points Rtg			
	Blitz%	Pres%	Sack%	Run Def	Pass Rush	Pass Cov	Total	Per Run	Per PR	Per Cov	Per Play
2019	10%	44%	15.0%	18	9	15	42	83	96	82	85
2020	5%	41%	5.3%	12	5	38	54	78	89	99	93
	8%	43%	11.9%	30	14	53	96	-	-	-	-

*Career stats only include seasons since 2019

Chazz Surratt

Report by Jordan Edwards

School	Height	Weight	Year	Jersey #	Hometown
North Carolina	6014 V	227 V	5SR	21	Denver, NC

One Liner
Surratt is still developing as a true off-ball linebacker and lacks some stoutness and instincts in the run game, but his range, athleticism, and coverage ability will make it hard to keep him off the field.

Overall
Chazz Surratt lines up as the Will linebacker for North Carolina's 2-4-5 defense. He's a three-down player who plays in the box and out in the slot. After playing 10 games as a QB for UNC, he switched to linebacker in 2019 and started 21 of 24 games. He underwent meniscus and elbow (throwing arm) surgery in 2015 and then tore a wrist ligment in 2017. In 2018, Surratt was suspended for the first 4 games for selling team-issued shoes which violated NCAA rules. He then played only 1 game before missing the rest of the season after re-injuring the same wrist he hurt in 2017. Additionally, he'll be 24 years old at the time of the NFL Draft. He's an explosive and sudden athlete with a solid frame. He has a relentless motor and competes every single play.

Pass Game
Surratt shows the ability to defend the pass in zone and man coverage. He has good instincts and recognition in zone coverage and has good burst to close the gap and disrupt receivers at the catch point. He has very good range to drop and get to his landmarks. His athletic ability and quickness allow him to stay on the hip of receivers in man coverage as well. He has good COD skills and plays with a suddenness to his game. Surratt is utilized as a blitzer and rusher off the edge a heavy amount. He has the burst and speed to blitz effectively from depth and finishes tackles in the backfield. He can power through blocks from RBs in pass pro as well. He isn't the vocal leader of the defense, but with his QB background, he has the ability to accept a leadership role on the defensive side of the ball.

Run Game
Surratt has below-average instincts and FB against the run. He's consistently slow reacting to the ball and recognizing the flow of the offensive line. His overall play speed and athletic ability can mask these deficiencies at times, however, this is an area that should improve as he gains more reps at LB. He isn' afraid to take on blocks, but doesn't display the stoutness to stack and shed blocks of offensive linemen to make a play on the ball. He struggles finding the ball through trash at the LOS, but his athleticism allows him to navigate his way through blocks. He tackles well overall, but has the tendency to overrun ballcarriers and miss tackles in small spaces. Surratt has very good range and can fly from sideline to sideline. When he does key and diagnose plays, he reacts quickly and has the closing speed to take away angles and run lanes for ballcarriers.

Last Word
It may take some time for Surratt to improve a a run defender, but he projects to be a starting Will at the next level. He can be a valuable defender on 3rd downs with his coverage ability and range from sideline to sideline. He also has the experience, competitiveness, and athleticism that will allow him to be a core special teamer as well at the next level.

Strengths	Weaknesses
• Coverage ability	• Stoutness
• Range	• Instincts vs. the run
• Play speed	• Navigating the trash

Critical Factors

Pass Coverage	Play Speed	FBI / Instincts
6	7	5

Positional Factors

3-Level Impact	QB Defense	Man Coverage	Zone Coverage
6	5	6	6
Range	Blitz	Stoutness	Shed Ability
7	6	4	4
Navigate Trash	Tackling	Toughness	ST Value
5	5	6	7

Basic

	Tackling			Pass Rush		Coverage					
Year	Tackles	TFL	FF	Sacks	Pres	Trgt	Comp	Comp%	Yds	Yds/Trgt	Int
2019	114	15.0	1	6.5	31	17	10	59%	95	5.6	1
2020	94	8.0	1	6.0	33	17	11	65%	142	8.4	1
	208	23.0	2	12.5	64	34	21	62%	237	7.0	2

Advanced

	Tackling					Coverage			Positive%		
Year	Broken Tackles	BT%	Tackle Share	ATD+	PBU	Deserved Catch %	YAC	EPA	Man	Zone	Total
2019	23	17%	14%	100	5	73%	31	-2.5	33%	43%	41%
2020	10	10%	13%	68	4	87%	91	0.1	100%	47%	53%
	33	14%	14%	87	9	80%	122	-2.5	60%	45%	47%

Deep Dive

	Pass Rush			Total Points				Total Points Rtg			
Year	Blitz%	Pres%	Sack%	Run Def	Pass Rush	Pass Cov	Total	Per Run	Per PR	Per Cov	Per Play
2019	25%	30%	8.1%	15	11	19	45	85	98	90	91
2020	21%	35%	7.1%	5	15	16	36	60	99	83	82
	23%	33%	7.7%	20	26	35	83	-	-	-	-

Jamin Davis

Report by Nathan Cooper

School	Height	Weight	Year	Jersey #	Hometown
Kentucky	6025 E	234 E	4JR	44	Ludowici, GA

One Liner
Davis is a fast, rangy linebacker that can be a difference maker in coverage at the next level, though a lack of overall instincts and inconsistencies in the run game may give him some trouble early on in his career.

Overall
Jamin Davis plays both Mike and Will linebacker in Kentucky's 3-4/3-3-5 defense. He played in 36 games for the Wildcats, starting 11 of them. He has a long frame with good size for the position and is a very athletic player who plays fast, tough, and competes.

Pass Game
Davis is a smooth mover who is fluid in space and shows enough awareness to know when receivers are moving through his area. He gets good depth on his drops and has the range to get north and south or east and west in a hurry. He's disruptive, showing the burst and acceleration to break on throws in front of him and make plays at the catch point. He also has the hands to go up and convert turnovers instead of just pass breakups. While he didn't play a ton of man coverage, he shows that he can stay with most tight ends and backs out of the backfield. He didn't communicate too much, but was always where he needed to be. As a blitzer, he doesn't get into the backfield enough to be a threat. He needs a clear lane where he can use his speed, but isn't able to shed linemen consistently enough to get pressure on the quarterback.

Run Game
Against the run, Davis struggles to stack and shed consistently. He lacks some hand strength and pop, not using his length to keep blockers at arm's length, getting thrown aside too often. In addition, his instincts are lacking at times. He reads flow well, though he doesn't jus react to what's going on in front of him quick enough to make more plays near the line o scrimmage. His play speed and numbers-to-numbers range allow him to work east and west to stretch out ballcarriers. When it's jus him and the back in the hole, he has the strength to stand them up. He's able to navigate the trash and avoid blockers to slither through gaps and make tackles. When in position, he's a solid tackler, but will miss some against shiftier backs. His tackles come at all levels o the defense, though he's not going to make a ton of tackles behind the line. He shouldn't be relied upon as a QB of the defense, though he is a smart player.

Last Word
Davis projects as a scheme-versatile starting Will linebacker in the NFL. His ability in the passing game outweighs his deficiencies in the run game. He's not a take-on type and navigates trash to make plays in the run game but his speed and awareness will allow him to consistently help against the pass. On 3rd downs, he can line up in the slot or as an overhang defender to cover tight ends, backs or other receivers. His motor, play speed, and toughness should allow him to become a solid contributor on most special teams units.

Strengths

- Range
- Coverage ability
- Plays fast

Weaknesses

- Lacks some instincts
- Struggles to consistently shed
- Not very stout

Critical Factors

Pass Coverage	Play Speed	FBI / Instincts
6	6	5

Positional Factors

3-Level Impact	QB Defense	Man Coverage	Zone Coverage
5	5	6	6
Range	Blitz	Stoutness	Shed Ability
7	5	4	5
Navigate Trash	Tackling	Toughness	ST Value
6	6	6	7

Basic

	Tackling			Pass Rush		Coverage					
Year	Tackles	TFL	FF	Sacks	Pres	Trgt	Comp	Comp%	Yds	Yds/Trgt	Int
2018	5	0.0	0	0.0	0	1	0	0%	0	0.0	1
2019	29	1.0	0	1.0	7	8	2	25%	19	2.4	1
2020	107	4.0	1	1.5	7	22	14	64%	186	8.5	3
	141	5.0	1	2.5	14	31	16	52%	205	6.6	5

Advanced

	Tackling					Coverage			Positive%		
Year	Broken Tackles	BT%	Tackle Share	ATD+	PBU	Deserved Catch %	YAC	EPA	Man	Zone	Total
2018	0	0%	1%	67	1	0%	0	-5.6	-	0%	0%
2019	3	9%	4%	74	1	50%	8	-7.4	0%	29%	25%
2020	5	4%	14%	78	4	85%	80	-6.5	100%	48%	50%
	8	5%	6%	77	6	76%	88	-19.5	50%	41%	42%

Deep Dive

	Pass Rush			Total Points				Total Points Rtg			
Year	Blitz%	Pres%	Sack%	Run Def	Pass Rush	Pass Cov	Total	Per Run	Per PR	Per Cov	Per Play
2018	6%	0%	0.0%	0	0	6	6	93	58	99	99
2019	20%	29%	4.3%	4	2	12	18	82	99	99	97
2020	7%	28%	9.1%	13	3	23	39	81	77	95	88
	10%	28%	6.5%	17	5	41	63	-	-	-	-

Justin Hilliard

Report by Joe McDonald

✳

School	Height	Weight	Year	Jersey #	Hometown
Ohio State	6006 V	227 V	6SR	47	Cincinnati, OH

One Liner
Hilliard has a long history of injures some teams may not be able to get past, but he still has a solid skill set and high motor to be a versatile reserve.

Strengths: Motor and effort; Tackling ability; Man coverage
Weaknesses: Zone instincts; Shed strength; Injury history

Justin Hilliard is a Will linebacker in Ohio State's 4-3 defense, rotating through multiple roles and lining up in the slot and box. He played in 49 games with only 7 starts. Hilliard will be 24 years old at the time of the NFL Draft. The sixth-year senior's career has been marred by injury, tearing his meniscus, each bicep, and Achilles. The former five-star recruit is still athletic and plays with a high motor and effort level. He's slightly undersized but has broad shoulders and a good frame that supports his weight well.

Hilliard is a sufficient coverage linebacker, using his athleticism to stay with backs, tight ends, and even some receivers. He drops and communicates well in zone, but can be slow to react to moving parts around him. He loves to get his hands on receivers to disrupt their routes in either coverage. He often presses in man and can run with backs and tight ends with good speed and stay connected with contact. He attacks the ball at the catch point and shows good hands to get in passing lanes. He is a solid blitzer who shows decent rush technique to bend and hand fight, but his impact as a rusher is inconsistent.

Hilliard is a sure tackler using good leverage and wrapping technique, as well as a good communicator both pre- and post-snap against the run. He has a high football IQ to diagnose and relay plays early. He navigates through traffic smoothly with his fluid movement skills, and is capable of taking on linemen in stack-and-shed situations, although he could add more lower-body strength to anchor. His effort and high motor aid his production between and outside the tackles.

Hilliard projects as a backup linebacker in the NFL who could play as both a Will and Mike. His size and coverage comfortability profile better as a Will, however. He has struggled with injuries through his career but he still has the athletic skill set to make an impact on three downs if he stays healthy. His speed and toughness should be valued on kickoff and punt teams.

Year	Tackling			Pass Rush		Coverage					
	Tackles	TFL	FF	Sacks	Pres	Trgt	Comp	Comp%	Yds	Yds/Trgt	Int
2017	4	0.0	0	0.0	0	0	0	-	0	-	0
2018	12	1.0	0	0.0	0	2	1	50%	21	10.5	0
2019	10	3.0	0	0.0	0	4	2	50%	8	2.0	1
2020	33	5.0	1	0.0	3	7	5	71%	36	5.1	1
	63	9.0	1	0.0	4	15	10	67%	79	5.3	2

Year	Tackling				Coverage				Positive%		
	Broken Tackles	BT%	Tackle Share	ATD+	PBU	Deserved Catch %	YAC	EPA	Man	Zone	Total
2017	1	20%	0%	-	0	-	0	0.0	-	-	-
2018	2	14%	2%	136	2	100%	10	-3.8	0%	0%	0%
2019	1	9%	1%	195	1	75%	1	-5.8	0%	33%	25%
2020	4	11%	7%	107	2	83%	9	-7.2	0%	67%	57%
	8	11%	2%	130	5	85%	40	-16.0	40%	50%	47%

Year	Pass Rush			Total Points				Total Points Rtg			
	Blitz%	Pres%	Sack%	Run Def	Pass Rush	Pass Cov	Total	Per Run	Per PR	Per Cov	Per Play
2018	21%	0%	0.0%	3	1	2	6	85	94	88	88
2019	7%	0%	0.0%	6	0	8	14	99	55	99	99
2020	7%	27%	0.0%	10	1	11	21	99	66	97	97
	10%	13%	0.0%	19	2	21	41	-	-	-	-

Redshirt season not shown but included in totals

Critical Factors	
Pass Coverage	5
Play Speed	6
FBI / Instincts	6

Positional Factors	
3-Level Impact	6
QB Defense	6
Man Coverage	6
Zone Coverage	5
Range	6
Blitz	5
Stoutness	5
Shed Ability	5
Navigate Trash	6
Tackling	6
Toughness	6
ST Value	6

Pete Werner

Report by Chad Tedder

School	Height	Weight	Year	Jersey #	Hometown
Ohio State	6021 E	242 E	4SR	20	Indianapolis, IN

One Liner
Werner has the speed, pursuit, and coverage ability to be a sub package contributor at the next level, but his inconsistent play diagnosis and struggles to stack and shed could limit his early-down presence in the box.

Strengths: Sure tackling; Lateral pursuit; Coverage drops
Weaknesses: Stacking and shedding blocks; Play diagnosis and reaction time; On-ball production

Pete Werner is the Will linebacker in Ohio State's base 4-3 defensive scheme, but has rotated through all LB positions and even dropped into a deep safety role. He played in 47 games, starting in 35. He is a big, rangy athlete with a strong motor and toughness to compete sideline to sideline.

Against the pass, Werner shows great range in zone coverage to the flat, through the middle, and even dropping into a deep third. He uses his speed to play in space and give pursuit to make tackles. He communicates well with his other LBs to pass off receivers through underneath zones. Werner also shows comfortability in covering running backs, tight ends, and even some slot receivers in man coverage. He can match receivers' movements and stay with them across the field. He does have a lack of ball production at the catch point, but overall he's an impressive coverage player at multiple levels. When asked to blitz, he attacks with speed and some power to meet blockers in the hole. However, a majority of his pressures come on schemed rushes and open lanes.

Werner has the instincts to attack and plug a running lane when he sees one, but he does struggle with reading plays and reacting quickly. When met by linemen, he has problems with shedding blocks and can occasionally be washed out, but he has enough athleticism to slip around many second-level blocks. He shows much better skill getting sideline-to-sideline and making a play out in space, where he makes sure, hard tackles at a high frequency.

Werner best projects as a sub package Will linebacker at the next level based on his coverage abilities and pursuit in space. He also could flex down into a Sam role, where he has enough lower-body strength to set an edge against tight ends. His experience across multiple LB positions helps his versatility moving forward. He will be a solid third-down substitute in passing situations, and his vast special teams experience should continue on all units in the league.

	Tackling			Pass Rush		Coverage					
Year	Tackles	TFL	FF	Sacks	Pres	Trgt	Comp	Comp%	Yds	Yds/Trgt	Int
2017	4	0.5	0	0.0	0	2	1	50%	3	1.5	0
2018	61	7.5	2	3.0	9	25	12	48%	97	3.9	0
2019	65	5.5	0	0.0	3	27	16	59%	171	6.3	0
2020	54	2.5	1	1.0	10	16	8	50%	62	3.9	0
	184	16.0	3	4.0	22	70	37	53%	333	4.8	0

	Tackling				Coverage				Positive%		
Year	Broken Tackles	BT%	Tackle Share	ATD+	PBU	Deserved Catch %	YAC	EPA	Man	Zone	Total
2017	0	0%	0%	-	0	100%	1	-0.1	50%	-	50%
2018	9	13%	8%	80	4	60%	61	-8.3	38%	44%	40%
2019	9	12%	8%	111	3	90%	66	0.4	44%	45%	44%
2020	9	14%	11%	104	1	85%	21	-4.3	0%	50%	38%
	27	13%	6%	99	8	79%	149	-12.3	37%	47%	41%

	Pass Rush			Total Points				Total Points Rtg			
Year	Blitz%	Pres%	Sack%	Run Def	Pass Rush	Pass Cov	Total	Per Run	Per PR	Per Cov	Per Play
2018	22%	9%	3.1%	12	7	14	34	74	79	78	77
2019	3%	30%	0.0%	11	1	16	28	80	61	88	82
2020	10%	32%	3.4%	10	6	6	21	88	94	69	80
	13%	16%	2.9%	33	14	36	83	-	-	-	-

Critical Factors	
Pass Coverage.............	6
Play Speed................	6
FBI / Instincts..............	5

Positional Factors	
3-Level Impact.............	6
QB Defense	5
Man Coverage	6
Zone Coverage.............	6
Range	7
Blitz.....................	5
Stoutness	5
Shed Ability	4
Navigate Trash............	5
Tackling	6
Toughness	6
ST Value	6

Grant Stuard

Report by Jarrett Rodgers, Griffin Sullivan, & Jon Drillings

School	Height	Weight	Year	Jersey #	Hometown
Houston	5114 V	230 V	4SR	0	Conroe, TX

One Liner

Stuard is a rangy athlete and field general who plays with his hair on fire at all times, though a lack of shed ability, comfortability in zone, and discipline could ultimately limit his defensive production.

Strengths: Man-coverage ability; Rangy athlete; Active & obvious leadership
Weaknesses: Stack & shed ability; Comfortability in zone drops; Lacks discipline at times

Grant Stuard is a Will linebacker in Houston's 3-3-5 defense. He made the transition to LB in 2020 after spending time at safety and RB. He's lined up at LB, in the slot, or on the edge. He started in 20 (7 at LB) of 39 games for the Cougars. He missed 4 games in 2017 with a torn meniscus and had offseason surgery for a sport hernia after 2019. He's a twitchy athlete, demonstrated by quickness and explosion. He plays with a relentless motor and unteachable toughness.

Stuard gets good depth in his zone drops, but isn't comfortable relying on his instincts to read laterally, as sometimes it takes him out of position. In man, he's able to rely on his reactive athleticism and quickness, something that stems from his DB experience. Sometimes he sits and waits for RBs to come to him in man, but when out in space, he can easily run with them and stay in phase. He has flashed the hand technique and explosive burst to beat offensive tackles around the edge as a blitzer. Stuard showcases good communication ability and

leadership qualities, which is noticeable when he's on the field directing traffic.

In the run game, Stuard operates as the QB of the defense and can be relied upon to communicate well in the face of adversity. He lacks the anchor-and-shed ability to take blockers head on, but shows enough speed and athleticism to navigate through the trash. His lateral speed and relentless nature has resulted in high production on the ball, although there is a level of inconsistency in tackling angles and missing leg tackles in space. He's shown solid tackle production at all levels of the field, but is susceptible to play fakes or misdirection.

Stuard fits best as a Will at the next level, with the speed and range to also fill in at safety if needed. On 3rd downs, he has the skill set to man up backs or tight ends, using his speed in the open field. His speed, range, athleticism, and motor suggests he'll be an essential core special teamer on all units.

	Tackling			Pass Rush		Coverage					
Year	Tackles	TFL	FF	Sacks	Pres	Trgt	Comp	Comp%	Yds	Yds/Trgt	Int
2017	0	0.0	0	0.0	0	0	0	-	0	-	0
2018	17	2.5	0	0.0	0	1	0	0%	0	0.0	0
2019	92	10.0	1	1.0	11	37	22	59%	232	6.3	0
2020	60	4.5	0	1.0	9	9	8	89%	68	7.6	0
	169	17.0	1	2.0	20	47	30	64%	300	6.4	0

	Tackling				Coverage				Positive%		
Year	Broken Tackles	BT%	Tackle Share	ATD+	PBU	Deserved Catch %	YAC	EPA	Man	Zone	Total
2017	1	100%	0%	-	0	-	0	0.0	-	-	-
2018	5	23%	2%	121	0	-	0	-0.9	-	0%	0%
2019	16	15%	13%	123	4	86%	94	6.7	40%	45%	43%
2020	9	13%	12%	120	0	100%	44	2.6	80%	75%	78%
	31	16%	6%	121	4	89%	138	8.5	50%	48%	49%

	Pass Rush			Total Points				Total Points Rtg			
Year	Blitz%	Pres%	Sack%	Run Def	Pass Rush	Pass Cov	Total	Per Run	Per PR	Per Cov	Per Play
2018	1%	0%	0.0%	4	0	2	7	63	54	69	63
2019	7%	31%	3.1%	27	5	19	52	99	90	85	94
2020	16%	21%	2.6%	13	-1	4	17	92	52	68	75
	9%	25%	2.8%	44	4	25	76	-	-	-	-

Critical Factors	
Pass Coverage	6
Play Speed	6
FBI / Instincts	5

Positional Factors	
3-Level Impact	6
QB Defense	6
Man Coverage	6
Zone Coverage.	5
Range	7
Blitz.	6
Stoutness	4
Shed Ability	4
Navigate Trash	5
Tackling	6
Toughness	7
ST Value	7

Tony Fields II

Report by Joe McDonald & Christian Vega

School	Height	Weight	Year	Jersey #	Hometown
West Virginia	6010 V	222 V	4SR	1	Las Vegas, NV

One Liner
Fields has the athleticism and play speed to be a good cover defender at the next level, but a lack of stoutness, strength, and tackling ability will ultimately determine how much playing time he sees.

Strengths: Pass coverage; Play speed; Communication
Weaknesses: Play recognition; In-the-box play; Play strength

Tony Fields II is the starting Mike linebacker in West Virginia's 3-3-5 defense. He started all 37 games at Arizona before transferring to West Virginia and starting 8 of 9 in 2020. He has a smaller stature for the LB position, but he's a tough, competitive player who makes up for it with good speed and effort.

Fields has the coverage ability to succeed in man and zone. He has sufficient FBI, showing a good feel for flow and routes through his area, but tends to bite on run fakes too often. He is a physical player and enjoys disrupting routes coming across his zone in the middle. He has a firm grasp on his defense and does a good job communicating to other defenders what is happening on the field and what their responsibilities are. Fields has good speed and moves easily in space, getting good vertical and horizontal depth in his zone drops. His athleticism allows him to easily run with backs and tight ends with sticky coverage. Being undersized with an inability to shed hinders his effectiveness as a blitzer unless he has a clean lane.

In the run game, Fields struggles with instincts recognizing run or pass or to decipher exactly where the run is going. He has the closing speed to make up for it in college, but will likely struggle at the next level. His size and lack of play strength at the POA not only makes it difficult for him to shed blocks, but he's also shown inconsistency with tackling physical backs. His speed and athleticism allow him to adequately slither through the trash and find ballcarriers.

Fields projects as a top backup Will linebacker in either scheme at the NFL level. He'll contribute mostly as a coverage linebacker, but his athleticism will allow him to play on all 3 downs. That said, his struggles shedding blocks and making tackles will limit his playing time on 1st and 2nd down. However, his speed, competitiveness, and toughness will make him a valuable special teams asset.

	Tackling			Pass Rush		Coverage					
Year	Tackles	TFL	FF	Sacks	Pres	Trgt	Comp	Comp%	Yds	Yds/Trgt	Int
2017	106	6.5	0	5.0	20	17	14	82%	123	7.2	1
2018	87	4.0	0	2.0	15	14	12	86%	112	8.0	0
2019	92	5.0	1	1.5	17	13	5	38%	79	6.1	1
2020	88	4.0	0	2.0	11	13	12	92%	125	9.6	1
	373	19.5	1	10.5	63	57	43	75%	439	7.7	3

	Tackling				Coverage				Positive%		
Year	Broken Tackles	BT%	Tackle Share	ATD+	PBU	Deserved Catch %	YAC	EPA	Man	Zone	Total
2017	12	10%	12%	-	2	93%	57	1.2	50%	54%	53%
2018	11	11%	11%	62	0	100%	72	8.9	100%	64%	71%
2019	26	22%	12%	88	5	70%	37	-9.4	50%	36%	38%
2020	7	7%	14%	92	2	100%	60	10.1	100%	92%	92%
	56	13%	12%	81	9	92%	226	10.7	70%	62%	63%

	Pass Rush			Total Points				Total Points Rtg			
Year	Blitz%	Pres%	Sack%	Run Def	Pass Rush	Pass Cov	Total	Per Run	Per PR	Per Cov	Per Play
2018	18%	19%	2.7%	6	4	7	17	53	74	69	62
2019	23%	19%	2.3%	6	4	11	21	62	79	78	71
2020	13%	31%	5.9%	10	4	5	20	83	93	69	79
	19%	21%	3.1%	22	12	23	58	-	-	-	-

Critical Factors	
Pass Coverage	6
Play Speed	6
FBI / Instincts	5

Positional Factors	
3-Level Impact	5
QB Defense	6
Man Coverage	6
Zone Coverage	6
Range	6
Blitz	4
Stoutness	4
Shed Ability	4
Navigate Trash	5
Tackling	5
Toughness	6
ST Value	6

Garret Wallow   **Final Grade: 5.9**

Report by Danny Shirilla & Michael Churchward

School	Height	Weight	Year	Jersey #	Hometown
TCU	6010 E	230 E	4SR	30	New Orleans, LA

One Liner

Wallow is a rangy, athletic linebacker who uses his speed to produce as a tackler, but his struggles shedding blockers and navigating the trash force him into being a limited depth linebacker.

Strengths: Tackling ability; Range; Versatility
Weaknesses: Shed ability; Fighting through traffic; Zone awareness

Garret Wallow is the SLB in TCU's 2-4-5/3-3-5 defense playing a lot of zone coverage. He started 29 of 49 games in his career. Recruited to TCU as a safety, he played some SS before moving to LB. He's a solid athlete with good range and play speed. His long build makes his athleticism look smooth and natural. He also shows good toughness and competitiveness along with a fast, relentless play style.

Wallow was used in the middle as a spy on quarterbacks a decent amount, but he also showed the ability to get depth in his drops and cover backs and tight ends man to man if necessary. He shows good communication skills in zone coverage, constantly pointing people out to his teammates. He shows natural instincts in zone when not spying the quarterback, but gets too fixated on the quarterback rather than keeping his head on a swivel for receivers. In man, he holds his own against tight ends and backs, but struggles against actual receivers.

When blitzing, he uses athleticism and speed to get to the backfield, but can't shed bigger blockers.

In the run game, Wallow shows good smarts and athleticism, but struggles to stack and shed. He plays with a good base and pace rarely overrunning plays while flowing to the ball. He has the range to get lateral and shoot gaps rather than take on blocks. He has consistently shown his ability to tackle well and produces all over the field.

Wallow projects best as a backup 4-3 Will linebacker in the NFL, because of his athleticism, range, and enough cover ability to play with tight ends and backs. He has the communication skills and cover ability to slide over to Mike on occasion, but will struggle shedding blocks in the trenches. On 3rd downs, he should contribute best as a man defender on tight ends. Wallow should impact all core special teams units because of his combination of his size, speed, and toughness.

	Tackling			Pass Rush		Coverage					
Year	Tackles	TFL	FF	Sacks	Pres	Trgt	Comp	Comp%	Yds	Yds/Trgt	Int
2017	2	0.0	0	0.0	0	1	1	100%	5	5.0	0
2018	67	5.5	0	2.0	9	22	12	55%	66	3.0	0
2019	121	17.5	0	3.5	11	18	12	67%	69	3.8	1
2020	93	10.0	3	3.0	18	15	11	73%	170	11.3	0
	283	33.0	3	8.5	38	56	36	64%	310	5.5	1

	Tackling				Coverage				Positive%		
Year	Broken Tackles	BT%	Tackle Share	ATD+	PBU	Deserved Catch %	YAC	EPA	Man	Zone	Total
2017	0	0%	0%	-	0	100%	0	-0.2	0%	-	0%
2018	17	20%	9%	114	2	82%	38	-11.1	14%	20%	18%
2019	14	10%	19%	125	1	93%	25	-9.5	20%	62%	50%
2020	15	14%	16%	133	1	93%	110	6.9	50%	64%	60%
	46	14%	10%	125	4	89%	173	-13.9	24%	46%	39%

	Pass Rush			Total Points				Total Points Rtg			
Year	Blitz%	Pres%	Sack%	Run Def	Pass Rush	Pass Cov	Total	Per Run	Per PR	Per Cov	Per Play
2018	11%	24%	5.7%	4	6	15	25	51	98	84	69
2019	11%	22%	8.7%	25	6	22	53	98	93	89	94
2020	10%	42%	8.3%	20	13	0	32	94	99	59	87
	11%	29%	7.7%	49	25	37	110	-	-	-	-

Critical Factors	
Pass Coverage	5
Play Speed	6
FBI / Instincts	5

Positional Factors	
3-Level Impact	5
QB Defense	6
Man Coverage	5
Zone Coverage	5
Range	6
Blitz	5
Stoutness	5
Shed Ability	4
Navigate Trash	5
Tackling	6
Toughness	6
ST Value	7

Blake Gallagher

Report by Stephen Marciello & Steven Penn

School	Height	Weight	Year	Jersey #	Hometown
Northwestern	5116 E	228 E	4SR	51	Raynham, MA

One Liner

Gallagher is a fast, intelligent Will linebacker who plays downhill and is comfortable in zone, but his strength and block-shedding weaknesses may keep him to a backup role in the NFL.

Strengths: Zone coverage; Acceleration; Durability
Weaknesses: Breaking down at POA; Block-shedding technique; Reactive quickness

Blake Gallagher is the Will linebacker in Northwestern's base 4-3 defense. He also saw time in the slot. He played in 48 career games, starting 35 of them. He has not missed a game in his career. He is a fast straight-line runner but doesn't possess elite quickness and agility. He has above-average motor and competitiveness.

Gallagher is most often used in zone coverage. He has good instincts and stays disciplined to his assignment. His speed allows him to get to zones near the sideline from the box and keep up with backs to the flats. He has a great feel for pass catchers entering and leaving his zone with his head on a swivel and does a great job communicating this to his teammates. His ability to break at the time of the pass is only sufficient however, as his lack of reactive quickness results in being a step late to the catch point. He has sufficient agility and strength to man up with backs and tight ends, but he gets shaken and boxed out somewhat regularly. Gallagher has the closing speed and thump to contact to be an effective blitzer, but has missed sack opportunities by overpursuing.

Gallagher diagnoses run plays very well. He loves to accelerate at the snap and attack downhill. He can often beat linemen to the spot and has great tackling production. He stacks with physicality and effort against blockers, but he lacks the strength and hand technique to shed with much consistency. He navigates trash sufficiently but can get caught up and is at his best with free lanes to the ball. His ability to break down to ballcarriers needs improvement. He has a few too many fly-bys, but he's a strong tackler when he makes contact and has enough range to get to the perimeter.

Gallagher projects as a backup Will linebacker at the next level behind a 4-man front that can keep him clean from blockers. He has the speed and zone coverage comfortability to see time on 3rd downs. He profiles as a productive special teams member on any coverage unit.

Year	Tackles	TFL	FF	Sacks	Pres	Trgt	Comp	Comp%	Yds	Yds/Trgt	Int
	Tackling			Pass Rush		Coverage					
2017	24	1.0	0	0.0	3	4	3	75%	26	6.5	0
2018	119	7.5	0	0.0	8	17	12	71%	104	6.1	1
2019	88	4.5	0	0.0	11	16	11	69%	146	9.1	3
2020	84	9.5	1	2.0	8	8	4	50%	27	3.4	1
	315	22.5	1	2.0	30	45	30	67%	303	6.7	5

Year	Broken Tackles	BT%	Tackle Share	ATD+	PBU	Deserved Catch %	YAC	EPA	Man	Zone	Total
	Tackling				Coverage				Positive%		
2017	5	17%	3%	-	0	100%	14	1.3	0%	67%	50%
2018	14	11%	14%	90	1	93%	50	0.4	67%	43%	47%
2019	11	11%	6%	129	4	93%	110	5.7	50%	60%	56%
2020	13	13%	15%	110	3	71%	10	-2.2	50%	33%	38%
	43	12%	8%	108	8	90%	184	5.2	50%	48%	49%

Year	Blitz%	Pres%	Sack%	Run Def	Pass Rush	Pass Cov	Total	Per Run	Per PR	Per Cov	Per Play
	Pass Rush			Total Points				Total Points Rtg			
2018	10%	16%	0.0%	14	2	13	29	71	63	75	72
2019	9%	32%	0.0%	17	5	18	39	85	88	87	86
2020	12%	20%	5.0%	13	7	13	33	85	98	81	86
	10%	22%	1.7%	44	14	44	101	-	-	-	-

Critical Factors	
Pass Coverage	5
Play Speed	6
FBI / Instincts	6

Positional Factors	
3-Level Impact	5
QB Defense	6
Man Coverage	5
Zone Coverage	6
Range	5
Blitz	6
Stoutness	6
Shed Ability	4
Navigate Trash	5
Tackling	6
Toughness	5
ST Value	6

Max Richardson

Report by John Todd

School	Height	Weight	Year	Jersey #	Hometown
Boston College	5114 V	226 V	5SR	14	Duluth, GA

One Liner

Richardson needs to improve his stoutness and play strength, but he's a solid coverage linebacker with enough box and space awareness to make plays in a backup capacity.

Strengths: Drop fluidity and coverage awareness; Sifting gap to gap; Take-on willingness
Weaknesses: Take-on strength; Block shedding; Sideline-to-sideline range

Max Richardson is an off-ball linebacker in BC's base nickel defense, alternating Will and Mike responsibilities. He has started 38 of 50 career games. He suffered a knee injury 4 games into his sophomore year that forced him to redshirt and end his season. He has a slightly narrow frame with decent lower half bulk and cut up top. He's comfortable in space but a bit rigid athletically. Despite his role and size, he's aggressive between the tackles and willing to get physical with linemen.

Richardson is very comfortable in coverage and does a great job of getting to his spots quickly and fluidly. He strafes with technical form and good eyes, showing a solid feel for route combinations. He does a sufficient job communicating pre- and post-snap but isn't a boisterous conductor. Athletically he can be a tick late redirecting and he's conservative to jump routes. In man, he smothers checkdowns to the flat but just sufficiently limits separation on choice routes over the middle. He can get handsy at times, and shiftier route runners should give him trouble.

He closes hard as a blitzer but much of his impact has come when untouched.

Against the run, Richardson flows to the ball well and is quick to key and diagnose. He sifts through trash to mirror backs, and he's very willing to attack blockers. However, his take-on strength is insufficient to plug holes or anchor, and he struggles to disengage when latched onto. His speed is sufficient but top competition has regularly beaten him to the perimeter and he doesn't play with an overly hot motor. He's a volume tackler but shoulder-high arm tackle attempts and his anchor concerns give up leaky yardage.

Richardson projects as a solid backup Will linebacker, who can also execute as a Mike with his aggression within the box and ability to read blocking flow. He's more comfortable in space however, and should be a solid contributor on passing downs as a zone dropper to all areas of the field and on special teams coverage units.

Year	Tackling			Pass Rush		Coverage					
	Tackles	TFL	FF	Sacks	Pres	Trgt	Comp	Comp%	Yds	Yds/Trgt	Int
2016	4	0.5	0	0.0	0	0	0	-	0	-	0
2018	70	9.5	0	2.5	17	11	6	55%	53	4.8	0
2019	110	16.0	1	3.5	22	16	10	63%	170	10.6	0
2020	94	8.0	0	3.5	20	9	7	78%	94	10.4	0
	303	34.5	1	10.0	60	39	24	62%	321	8.2	0

Year	Tackling				Coverage				Positive%		
	Broken Tackles	BT%	Tackle Share	ATD+	PBU	Deserved Catch %	YAC	EPA	Man	Zone	Total
2016	0	0%	1%	-		-	0	0.0	-	-	-
2018	7	9%	8%	104	5	60%	32	-0.2	33%	50%	45%
2019	20	15%	12%	112	2	85%	133	3.7	67%	38%	44%
2020	17	15%	14%	89	1	100%	60	4.0	100%	67%	78%
	46	13%	8%	102	8	82%	226	6.6	55%	50%	51%

Year	Pass Rush			Total Points				Total Points Rtg			
	Blitz%	Pres%	Sack%	Run Def	Pass Rush	Pass Cov	Total	Per Run	Per PR	Per Cov	Per Play
2018	21%	24%	4.6%	9	5	10	24	70	82	80	76
2019	17%	28%	5.2%	20	6	8	33	91	84	69	81
2020	17%	26%	5.8%	9	3	1	13	66	68	61	64
	18%	26%	5.2%	38	14	19	70	-	-	-	-

Critical Factors	
Pass Coverage	6
Play Speed	5
FBI / Instincts	5

Positional Factors	
3-Level Impact	5
QB Defense	5
Man Coverage	5
Zone Coverage	6
Range	5
Blitz	5
Stoutness	5
Shed Ability	4
Navigate Trash	6
Tackling	5
Toughness	6
ST Value	5

Redshirt season not shown but included in totals

Rodjay Burns

Report by Daniel Jankuloski

School	Height	Weight	Year	Jersey #	Hometown
Louisville	5116 E	215 E	5SR	10	Louisville, KY

One Liner

Burns is a versatile defender with a high motor and good range to become a depth linebacker, but a lack of play recognition, stack-and-shed ability, and tweener size will likely limit his upside.

Strengths: Range; Motor; Versatility
Weaknesses: Play recognition; Shedding offensive linemen; Size limitations

Rodjay Burns plays Will linebacker to the field side in Louisville's 3-4 defense. The Cardinals ran zone coverage the majority of the time and Burns often lined up in the slot or on the edge. He started 32 of 41 games for Louisville after playing 7 games at corner for Ohio State in 2017. He has very good athleticism for a linebacker, and he adds to it with an exceptional toughness and motor.

Burns didn't play much man to man. With his CB experience, he has some athleticism to hang with receivers, but gets beaten too often. He is very comfortable playing zone and deciphering the play in front of him. At the snap, he opens up his hips fluidly and keeps his eyes in front of him while getting to his spot. He shows good range and depth in his zone drops. He has shown relatively good instincts with his blitz ability, but lacks the size to create through blockers.

Burns is typically a sure tackler, though runners can bounce off him on occasion. He has displayed a slow reaction time to decipher where a run is going at the snap and that sometimes puts him in a bad position. Most of the tackles he has are within 5 yards of the LOS. He has trouble getting through offensive linemen once they latch onto him because he lacks the size and strength to stack and shed with consistency.

Burns projects to be a top backup Will linebacker in a 4-3 scheme at the next level. Depending on how his body develops with NFL training, he could bulk up and become an athletic linebacker or get leaner and become a box safety. He has 3rd-down ability and fits best playing a hook-curl or in the flats as a zone defender. Burns was a punt returner the past 3 seasons at Louisville, which is a nod to his athleticism, though he likely won't return punts at the next level. He could return kicks, though, with the motor and tackling ability that Burns has, he should become a core contributor on most special teams units.

	Tackling			Pass Rush		Coverage					
Year	Tackles	TFL	FF	Sacks	Pres	Trgt	Comp	Comp%	Yds	Yds/Trgt	Int
2016	0	0.0	0	0.0	0	0	0	-	0	-	1
2018	33	1.5	0	0.0	0	17	12	71%	177	10.4	1
2019	81	11.0	1	2.0	16	20	13	65%	116	5.8	1
2020	57	8.0	0	2.0	6	12	6	50%	144	12.0	0
	171	20.5	1	4.0	22	49	31	63%	437	8.9	3

	Tackling				Coverage				Positive%		
Year	Broken Tackles	BT%	Tackle Share	ATD+	PBU	Deserved Catch %	YAC	EPA	Man	Zone	Total
2016	0	-	0%	-	1	-	0	0.0	-	-	-
2018	4	11%	4%	95	1	100%	29	2.1	55%	50%	53%
2019	13	14%	10%	99	2	93%	26	2.4	75%	38%	45%
2020	18	24%	9%	104	2	90%	40	-0.6	50%	25%	33%
	35	17%	6%	100	6	95%	95	3.9	58%	37%	45%

	Pass Rush			Total Points				Total Points Rtg			
Year	Blitz%	Pres%	Sack%	Run Def	Pass Rush	Pass Cov	Total	Per Run	Per PR	Per Cov	Per Play
2018	4%	0%	0.0%	17	0	5	22	98	53	72	90
2019	23%	20%	2.5%	16	8	5	29	83	95	69	81
2020	20%	10%	3.3%	19	2	-5	16	88	66	54	70
	17%	15%	2.7%	52	10	5	67	-	-	-	-

Critical Factors	
Pass Coverage	5
Play Speed	5
FBI / Instincts	5

Positional Factors	
3-Level Impact	5
QB Defense	4
Man Coverage	4
Zone Coverage	5
Range	5
Blitz	6
Stoutness	5
Shed Ability	4
Navigate Trash	6
Tackling	5
Toughness	6
ST Value	7

Isaiah McDuffie

Report by Jacob Halleen

School	Height	Weight	Year	Jersey #	Hometown
Boston College	6010 E	224 E	4JR	55	Buffalo, NY

One Liner

McDuffie has the play speed and range to be an effective coverage linebacker at the next level, but his lack of stoutness and shed ability in the run game will prevent him from starting.

Strengths: Range; Play speed; Athleticism in coverage
Weaknesses: Stoutness near the line; Shedding blocks; Pass rush ability

Isaiah McDuffie primarily plays Will linebacker in Boston College's 4-2-5 defense. He started 19 of 40 games. He missed 9 games in 2019 with a knee injury. McDuffie has a thick, but average frame for the position. He possesses good play speed and range, but lacks strength. He also plays with sufficient toughness and has a high motor.

McDuffie primarily dropped back in zone coverage in the middle of the field. He shows good zone awareness and can cover a large area. There are moments when he becomes too stationary and is slow to react due to being flat-footed, but his COD skills make up for it. He played some man coverage against running backs and tight ends. He shows the quickness and anticipation to be effective in coverage, but lacks ball skills and tracking ability at the catch point. He has sufficient awareness and FBI and will occasionally bite on play fakes and leave a hole open over the top. As a blitzer, he's only really productive as part of stunts or delayed blitzes. He lacks pass-rush moves and does not have the strength

to go through linemen. He was not the main vocal leader of the defense, but uses hand signals pre-snap and shows some ability of developing into the quarterback of the defense.

In the run game, McDuffie shows good range and makes tackles from sideline to sideline, showing constant pursuit to the ball. However, he's only a sufficient tackler overall. He lacks strength and stoutness in the box to shed blockers and instead uses his speed and quickness to avoid them and navigate the trash. Most of his tackles are made at the 2nd and 3rd level of the defense.

McDuffie projects to be a backup Will linebacker at the next level. He lacks the strength and block shedding ability to be a starter, but his play speed and range will allow him to see playing time in some passing situations. On 3rd down, he can be used as a man or zone coverage defender with limited use as a blitzer. He should be a solid special teams player due to his play speed and toughness.

Year	Tackling			Pass Rush		Coverage					
	Tackles	TFL	FF	Sacks	Pres	Trgt	Comp	Comp%	Yds	Yds/Trgt	Int
2017	4	0.0	0	0.0	0	1	0	0%	0	0.0	0
2018	73	5.0	1	3.5	7	15	8	53%	90	6.0	0
2019	29	3.5	0	2.0	6	7	5	71%	53	7.6	0
2020	108	6.5	0	3.0	12	15	13	87%	180	12.0	1
	214	15.0	1	8.5	25	38	26	68%	323	8.5	1

Year	Tackling				Coverage				Positive%		
	Broken Tackles	BT%	Tackle Share	ATD+	PBU	Deserved Catch %	YAC	EPA	Man	Zone	Total
2017	0	0%	0%	-	0	100%	0	-0.7	0%	-	0%
2018	11	13%	9%	102	4	82%	35	-4.0	57%	38%	47%
2019	1	3%	3%	99	0	100%	13	2.5	0%	83%	71%
2020	13	11%	16%	76	2	100%	114	14.5	71%	75%	73%
	25	10%	7%	88	6	94%	162	12.3	56%	64%	61%

Year	Pass Rush			Total Points				Total Points Rtg			
	Blitz%	Pres%	Sack%	Run Def	Pass Rush	Pass Cov	Total	Per Run	Per PR	Per Cov	Per Play
2018	35%	8%	4.8%	5	4	9	18	58	72	86	71
2019	44%	12%	3.8%	4	3	-2	5	89	90	52	74
2020	20%	16%	4.1%	6	4	7	16	61	76	69	66
	29%	12%	4.3%	15	11	14	39	-	-	-	-

Critical Factors	
Pass Coverage	5
Play Speed	6
FBI / Instincts	5

Positional Factors	
3-Level Impact	5
QB Defense	5
Man Coverage	5
Zone Coverage	5
Range	6
Blitz	5
Stoutness	4
Shed Ability	5
Navigate Trash	5
Tackling	5
Toughness	5
ST Value	6

Cornerbacks

Sam Linker

The NFL is increasingly becoming more of an offensive league with new rules that greatly favor the quarterback and wide receivers. Because of these changes, it is even more important to have defenders who can excel in the secondary and limit the opposing team's receivers. Cornerbacks have the difficult job of covering these fast and skilled receivers and must be able to react quickly or else their team will suffer. There is a special premium on man-to-man coverage ability in the modern NFL, as few traits are as valuable as the ability to negate top wideouts one-on-one.

One necessary tool to be a successful NFL cornerback is the ability to react quickly to any small moves wide receivers make. The cornerback has to constantly adjust their body positioning and footwork based on the route of the wide receiver. Along with the ability to adjust on the fly, they must find the perfect balance between being physical with the wide receiver to cause discomfort, but not too physical where they would draw a penalty flag. This skill has become even more important because of the previously mentioned rule changes that favor the offense. As a result, cornerback is one of the most valuable positions on the entire team, let alone the defense.

To find the corner who shined the most, it is appropriate to first look to the undefeated National Champion Alabama Crimson Tide. While the Tide's offense got most of the attention for its historic performance, their defense had a few players who deserved as much attention as their offensive stars. One of those defenders was unanimous First-Team All-American Patrick Surtain II, and he appropriately ranks as the top cornerback in this year's draft class. He grades at the top for both reactive athleticism and football intelligence, and he is one of two players with top grades for both press-man and zone coverage.

The other player who matches Surtain's rating in both press-man and zone coverage is South Carolina's Jaycee Horn. He ranks tied for second in the final scouting grade. Like Surtain, he has No. 1 corner potential, and he is especially proficient in slot coverage ability.

Maybe the most intriguing cornerback prospect is Virginia Tech's Caleb Farley. He is viewed similarly to Horn as a starting-caliber corner with No. 1 potential. What makes him so intriguing is that he opted out before the 2020 season began, so he has not been seen on the field in a competitive game since the 2019 college football season. He is a true press-man corner on the strength of the best combination of reactive athleticism, play speed, and transition ability in the draft class.

Outside of the top three, this is shaping up to be a very deep cornerback class with four more players rated with starting level grades by their second seasons: Northwestern's Greg Newsome II, Oklahoma State's Rodarius Williams, Florida State's Asante Samuel Jr., and Georgia's Eric Stokes.

To complement the basic box score metrics, the advanced metrics show a corner's usage and success with different coverages. Also, they show their value on a per target basis using EPA which represents the expected points allowed when they are targeted, along with how often they allow a receiver to make a deserved catch and the yards after catch they allow per completion. A deserved catch helps properly credit corners for their defense and not reward them in case a receiver drops a catchable pass or if the pass was uncatchable.

A corner's Total Points can be broken down into pass coverage and run defense, with any Total Points that they earn in the pass rush game included in their cumulative total. Their pass coverage Total Points are further broken down by whether they occurred in slot versus wide alignments.

This year's cornerback class is one of the most exciting groups among the positions because of the superior talent at the top. It has seven players who we project to become starting-caliber corners on Super Bowl-caliber teams. The depth at the corner position is even more impressive as it has 21 corners who have a final grade of at least 6.4 or higher which represents at minimum a low-end starting-caliber cornerback who can help a team win.

CORNERBACK

Cornerback Grading Scale

GRADE	DESCRIPTION
9.0 – 7.0	High-end 3 down starter. Pro Bowl level.
6.9 – 6.7	Strong starter who plays on all 3 downs.
6.6 – 6.5	3rd CB. Capable starter with inside/outside flexibility.
6.4	3rd CB. Role-player. Lacks inside/outside flexibility.
6.2	Versatile backup with CB/DS flexibility.
6.1 – 6.0	Developmental. Top traits but needs time.
5.9	Top backup. 4th CB. Quality special teamer.
5.8	4th CB w/o special teams ability. 5th CB w/ SPT.
5.7	Low-end backup CB with growable upside.

Cornerback Rankings

Rank	Name	Grade	Page	Rank	Name	Grade	Page
1	Patrick Surtain II	7.0	558	21	Shemar Jean-Charles	6.4	598
2	Jaycee Horn	6.8	560	22	Benjamin St-Juste	6.2	600
3	Caleb Farley	6.8	562	23	Trill Williams	6.2	601
4	Greg Newsome II	6.7	564	24	Michael Carter II	6.2	602
5	Rodarius Williams	6.7	566	25	Tre Norwood	6.2	603
6	Asante Samuel Jr.	6.7	568	26	DJ Daniel	5.9	604
7	Eric Stokes	6.7	570	27	Kelvin Joseph	5.9	605
8	Ifeatu Melifonwu	6.6	572	28	Brandin Echols	5.9	606
9	Marco Wilson	6.5	574	29	Thomas Graham Jr.	5.9	607
10	Aaron Robinson	6.5	576	30	Deommodore Lenoir	5.9	608
11	Darren Hall	6.5	578	31	Nate Hobbs	5.9	609
12	Tyson Campbell	6.5	580	32	Shakur Brown	5.9	610
13	Tre Brown	6.5	582	33	Olaijah Griffin	5.9	611
14	Elijah Molden	6.4	584	34	Robert Rochell	5.9	612
15	Paulson Adebo	6.4	586	35	Camryn Bynum	5.8	613
16	Shaun Wade	6.4	588	36	Rachad Wildgoose II	5.8	614
17	Bryce Thompson	6.4	590	37	Bryan Mills	5.8	615
18	Ambry Thomas	6.4	592	38	Jerry Jacobs	5.8	616
19	Avery Williams	6.4	594	39	Tay Gowan	5.8	617
20	Keith Taylor	6.4	596				

Glossary

Brk Tkl (Broken Tackles)
Tackle attempts where the defender in position to make a tackle failed to bring down the ballcarrier. Counts both broken tackles (physical) and missed tackles (elusive).

BT% (Broken Tackle%)
Percentage of tackle attempts where the defender in position to make a tackle failed to bring down the ballcarrier. Counts both broken tackles (physical) and missed tackles (elusive).

Deserved Catch%
The percentage of targets as the primary defender that the receiver either caught or dropped the ball when the pass was catchable.

PBU (Pass Breakups)
The number of times the defender batted, deflected for an incompletion, or defensed a pass attempt.

Pos% (Coverage split)
The percentage of plays where the defender was targeted that resulted in a positive EPA for the offense. Lower numbers are better for defenders.

Press Cov%
The percentage of coverage snaps the defender was in press coverage.

Rating (Coverage split)
Traditional Passer Rating on passes where the defender was targeted.

Slot%
Percentage of plays the defender lined up across from a slot receiver.

Total Points
Sports Info Solutions' proprietary player value metric that uses an Expected Points framework and distributes the value gained or lost on a play to the players involved based on their impact on the play.

Total Points Rating
Total Points per play compared to average, scaled so that 50 is poor and 99 is excellent.

Cornerback Leaderboards

Total Points Per Game

Rk	Player	School	Tot Pts / G
1	G. Newsome II	Northwestern	5.9
2	A. Samuel Jr.	Florida State	5.3
3	J. Horn	South Carolina	5.1
4	S. Brown	Michigan State	4.7
5	D. Lenoir	Oregon	4.4
6	D. Hall	San Diego State	4.3
6	C. Bynum	California	4.3
8	S. Jean-Charles	Appalachian State	4.1
9	E. Stokes	Georgia	3.9
10	E. Molden	Washington	3.8

Total Points Rating Per Play

Rk	Player	School	Rating
1	G. Newsome II	Northwestern	97
2	A. Samuel Jr.	Florida State	95
3	J. Horn	South Carolina	94
4	C. Bynum	California	92
5	S. Brown	Michigan State	90
6	E. Stokes	Georgia	89
6	D. Hall	San Diego State	89
8	S. Jean-Charles	Appalachian State	88
9	R. Williams	Oklahoma State	87
10	3 tied with		86

Pass Coverage Total Points Per Game

Rk	Player	School	Tot Pts / G
1	G. Newsome II	Northwestern	5.0
2	J. Horn	South Carolina	3.7
3	A. Samuel Jr.	Florida State	3.4
4	D. Lenoir	Oregon	3.1
5	S. Brown	Michigan State	3.0
6	E. Stokes	Georgia	2.6
6	S. Jean-Charles	Appalachian State	2.6
8	D. Hall	San Diego State	2.5
8	E. Molden	Washington	2.5
10	M. Carter II	Duke	2.3

Total Points Rating Per Coverage Snap

Rk	Player	School	Rating
1	J. Horn	South Carolina	99
1	G. Newsome II	Northwestern	99
3	A. Samuel Jr.	Florida State	98
4	D. Lenoir	Oregon	97
5	E. Molden	Washington	96
5	S. Jean-Charles	Appalachian State	96
7	E. Stokes	Georgia	95
7	M. Carter II	Duke	95
7	S. Brown	Michigan State	95
10	R. Williams	Oklahoma State	93

Run Defense Total Points Per Game

Rk	Player	School	Tot Pts / G
1	C. Bynum	California	3.0
2	A. Samuel Jr.	Florida State	1.9
2	S. Brown	Michigan State	1.9
4	I. Melifonwu	Syracuse	1.8
4	D. Hall	San Diego State	1.8
6	K. Joseph	Kentucky	1.7
6	O. Griffin	USC	1.7
8	N. Hobbs	Illinois	1.6
9	B. Echols	Kentucky	1.5
10	4 tied with		1.4

Expected Points Added Per Target

Rk	Player	School	EPA/Trgt
1	T. Norwood	Oklahoma	-0.90
2	G. Newsome II	Northwestern	-0.69
3	E. Stokes	Georgia	-0.62
4	O. Griffin	USC	-0.36
5	P. Surtain II	Alabama	-0.32
6	B. St-Juste	Minnesota	-0.31
7	D. Lenoir	Oregon	-0.30
8	I. Melifonwu	Syracuse	-0.26
9	A. Samuel Jr.	Florida State	-0.25
10	E. Molden	Washington	-0.24

Coverage Total Points Per Game: Press			
Rk	Player	School	Tot Pts / G
1	J. Horn	South Carolina	1.9
1	G. Newsome II	Northwestern	1.9
3	D. Lenoir	Oregon	1.7
4	R. Williams	Oklahoma State	1.6
5	E. Molden	Washington	1.5
6	P. Surtain II	Alabama	1.2
7	A. Samuel Jr.	Florida State	1.1
8	E. Stokes	Georgia	1.0
8	T. Brown	Oklahoma	1.0
10	2 tied with		0.8

Press Percentage			
Rk	Player	School	Press%
1	P. Surtain II	Alabama	59%
2	J. Horn	South Carolina	50%
2	K. Taylor	Washington	50%
4	R. Williams	Oklahoma State	46%
5	D. Lenoir	Oregon	42%
6	T. Campbell	Georgia	40%
7	T. Brown	Oklahoma	39%
8	O. Griffin	USC	38%
9	E. Stokes	Georgia	35%
10	A. Williams	Boise State	34%

Coverage Total Points Per Game: Slot			
Rk	Player	School	Tot Pts / G
1	E. Molden	Washington	1.8
2	M. Carter II	Duke	1.6
2	S. Brown	Michigan State	1.6
4	A. Robinson	UCF	1.2
5	D. Lenoir	Oregon	1.1
6	A. Samuel Jr.	Florida State	0.8
6	B. St-Juste	Minnesota	0.8
8	E. Stokes	Georgia	0.6
9	O. Griffin	USC	0.5
10	3 tied with		0.4

Lined Up in Slot Percentage			
Rk	Player	School	Slot%
1	A. Robinson	UCF	82%
2	E. Molden	Washington	70%
3	M. Carter II	Duke	57%
4	S. Brown	Michigan State	39%
5	M. Wilson	Florida	36%
6	D. Lenoir	Oregon	35%
7	J. Horn	South Carolina	34%
8	C. Bynum	California	29%
9	T. Norwood	Oklahoma	28%
10	K. Taylor	Washington	27%

Coverage Total Points Per Game: Wide			
Rk	Player	School	Tot Pts / G
1	G. Newsome II	Northwestern	4.9
2	J. Horn	South Carolina	3.4
3	S. Jean-Charles	Appalachian State	2.8
4	A. Samuel Jr.	Florida State	2.6
5	D. Hall	San Diego State	2.4
6	T. Brown	Oklahoma	2.3
7	P. Surtain II	Alabama	2.2
8	E. Stokes	Georgia	2.0
9	R. Williams	Oklahoma State	1.9
9	D. Lenoir	Oregon	1.9

Lined Up Outside Percentage			
Rk	Player	School	Outside%
1	D. Hall	San Diego State	88%
2	A. Samuel Jr.	Florida State	85%
2	T. Brown	Oklahoma	85%
2	N. Hobbs	Illinois	85%
5	R. Williams	Oklahoma State	84%
6	S. Jean-Charles	Appalachian State	81%
6	O. Griffin	USC	81%
8	P. Surtain II	Alabama	80%
8	T. Campbell	Georgia	80%
8	B. St-Juste	Minnesota	80%

Man Coverage Yards Per Snap

Rk	Player	School	Yds/Snap
1	E. Molden	Washington	0.7
2	G. Newsome II	Northwestern	0.9
3	J. Horn	South Carolina	1.5
4	D. Lenoir	Oregon	3.2
5	T. Norwood	Oklahoma	3.9
6	S. Brown	Michigan State	4.3
7	S. Jean-Charles	Appalachian State	4.6
8	E. Stokes	Georgia	4.7
9	M. Carter II	Duke	4.9
9	O. Griffin	USC	4.9

Zone Coverage Yards Per Snap

Rk	Player	School	Yds/Snap
1	D. Lenoir	Oregon	1.6
2	T. Norwood	Oklahoma	1.8
3	M. Carter II	Duke	2.8
4	A. Samuel Jr.	Florida State	2.9
4	E. Stokes	Georgia	2.9
6	E. Molden	Washington	3.0
7	G. Newsome II	Northwestern	3.1
8	T. Brown	Oklahoma	3.3
9	P. Surtain II	Alabama	3.9
10	O. Griffin	USC	4.5

Receptions Allowed Per Game

Rk	Player	School	Rec/G
1	T. Norwood	Oklahoma	0.8
2	R. Williams	Oklahoma State	1.0
3	E. Stokes	Georgia	1.1
4	B. St-Juste	Minnesota	1.2
5	J. Horn	South Carolina	1.3
5	K. Taylor	Washington	1.3
5	O. Griffin	USC	1.3
5	C. Bynum	California	1.3
9	G. Newsome II	Northwestern	1.4
9	A. Williams	Boise State	1.4

Yards Allowed Per Game

Rk	Player	School	Yds/G
1	G. Newsome II	Northwestern	11.9
2	E. Stokes	Georgia	12.1
3	T. Norwood	Oklahoma	12.6
4	E. Molden	Washington	13.8
5	D. Lenoir	Oregon	14.9
6	O. Griffin	USC	15.0
7	C. Bynum	California	15.3
8	R. Williams	Oklahoma State	17.6
9	J. Horn	South Carolina	18.6
10	P. Surtain II	Alabama	19.3

Passes Broken Up Per Game

Rk	Player	School	PBU/G
1	G. Newsome II	Northwestern	1.4
1	S. Jean-Charles	Appalachian State	1.4
3	S. Brown	Michigan State	1.3
4	P. Surtain II	Alabama	1.1
4	J. Horn	South Carolina	1.1
6	A. Samuel Jr.	Florida State	1.0
6	A. Robinson	UCF	1.0
6	M. Carter II	Duke	1.0
9	D. Hall	San Diego State	0.9
10	7 tied with		0.8

Deserved Catch Rate

Rk	Player	School	D Catch%
1	G. Newsome II	Northwestern	43%
2	J. Horn	South Carolina	50%
3	S. Jean-Charles	Appalachian State	53%
4	P. Surtain II	Alabama	57%
5	R. Williams	Oklahoma State	60%
5	M. Carter II	Duke	60%
7	B. St-Juste	Minnesota	64%
7	O. Griffin	USC	64%
9	T. Norwood	Oklahoma	65%
10	E. Stokes	Georgia	67%

Patrick Surtain II

Report by Jordan Edwards

School	Height	Weight	Year	Jersey #	Hometown
Alabama	6010 E	202 E	3JR	2	Plantation, FL

One Liner
Surtain has ideal size, coverage ability, and football intelligence to be one of the top cornerbacks in the league for years to come.

Overall
Patrick Surtain II lines up at left cornerback to both the field and boundary for Alabama's base nickel defense. Surtain played in all 41 games in his collegiate career and has started in 38 of those games. Surtain has ideal size, arm length and fluid hip mobility desired at the cornerback position. A unanimous First-Team All-American, he plays with a good motor and mental toughness, and his willingness to be a special teamer while being an elite starter speaks to his competitiveness. He has also been coached and developed by his former Pro Bowler father.

Pass Game
Surtain plays with a confidence and comfortability that is hard to find in college corners. His ability to mirror and match receivers' movements and routes is exceptional. He is quick to react and recover when receivers get to the top of their routes. Surtain has the intelligence and awareness to run routes step-for-step in coverage. He trusts his ability to match movements in press-man coverage and hardly ever lets receivers get a clean release off the line of scrimmage. He has the hip mobility to turn and run down the field and has a clean transition, as well. Surtain has good overall in-game play speed, but doesn't possess elite top-end speed. However, his coverage ability and football intelligence mask this slight deficiency. Surtain really excels in zone coverage with his awareness and overall feel for the game. His footwork and play recognition are very impressive, and he goes long periods in games locking down one side of the field. He doesn't have a lot of on-ball production but has shown good ball skills when presented the opportunity. He knows when to play his man and when to play the ball to avoid penalties. Surtain will move into the slot on occasion and he can hold his own, but his lack of top-end speed may limit his ability to carry routes against speedy receivers across the field at the next level.

Run Game
Surtain is a capable and willing defender against the run. He has the play strength and recognition to force ballcarriers back inside. He is not overly aggressive against the run, but will still get physical and make tough tackles. He keys and diagnoses screens to the outside well and has blown up blockers to create negative plays. He's a good open-field tackler with solid production and good technique.

Last Word
Surtain projects to be an elite cornerback at the next level. He will best fit as a boundary cornerback where he can cover the short side of the field and take away an offense's primary receiver. Surtain can be a scheme-versatile cornerback with his combination of press-man and zone coverage ability, but he may be best utilized in a Cover 3 scheme where he can read the field. He has experience as a jammer and on kickoff coverage and could continue to do so if necessary.

Strengths	Weaknesses
• Reactive athleticism	• Top-end long speed
• Intelligence and awareness	• Slot coverage
• Scheme versatility	

Critical Factors

Reactive Athleticism	Play Speed	Ball Skills
7	6	6

Positional Factors

Off-Man	Press-Man	Zone Coverage	Slot Coverage
6	7	7	5
Transition	Closing Speed	FBI	Mental Toughness
6	6	7	6
Open-Field Tackling	Play Strength	Run Support	ST Value
6	6	5	6

Basic

				Coverage						Tackling			
Year	Trgt	Comp	Comp%	Yds	Yds/Trgt	Int	Int Drops	TD Alwd	Tkls	TFL	Brk Tkl	BT%
2018	55	20	36%	285	5.2	1	0	1	40	1.5	3	7%
2019	38	20	53%	248	6.5	2	0	1	41	1.0	8	16%
2020	48	19	40%	251	5.2	1	1	2	37	3.5	3	8%
	141	59	42%	784	5.6	4	1	4	118	6.0	14	11%

Advanced

		Coverage						Man		Zone	
Year	PBU	Deserved Catch %	YAC/ Comp	Rating	EPA	EPA/ Trgt	Pos%	Yds/ Snap	Pos%	Yds/ Snap	Pos%
2018	9	74%	2.4	52.5	4.4	0.08	36%	5.2	38%	4.1	37%
2019	9	69%	3.5	60.0	-1.3	-0.03	42%	4.4	32%	5.3	42%
2020	14	57%	4.3	62.1	-15.6	-0.32	33%	5.3	38%	3.9	32%
	32	67%	3.3	57.8	-12.4	-0.09	37%	5.0	36%	4.3	37%

Deep Dive

	Usage				Total Points					Total Points Rtg		
Year	Man%	Slot%	Press Cov%	Press	Slot	Wide	Cov Total	Run Def	Total	Per Cov	Per Run	Per Play
2018	65%	21%	-	-	0	9	8	20	30	66	94	78
2019	45%	30%	50%	12	11	16	29	14	45	92	78	84
2020	34%	19%	59%	16	1	28	29	18	48	86	84	82
	47%	23%	55%	28	12	53	66	52	123	-	-	-

Jaycee Horn

Report by Alec Mallon

School	Height	Weight	Year	Jersey #	Hometown
South Carolina	6002 E	205 E	3JR	1	Alpharetta, GA

One Liner
Horn is a physical and athletic corner with excellent ball skills and should have no issues transitioning into a true No. 1 corner in the NFL once he cleans up the penalties and improves his off-man coverage.

Overall
Jaycee Horn is a cornerback for the University of South Carolina who primarily plays out wide on both sides of the field, but does play in the slot with success. Horn played in 30 games over his career. starting 29, including the first 7 games of 2020 before opting out of the final 3. He has great athletic traits, having the speed and quickness to run with anyone. He is a bigger corner with excellent strength which he uses to his advantage. It doesn't get displayed much, but Horn enjoys showing his tougher side to create negative plays at the line of scrimmage.

Pass Game
Horn uses his physicality to his advantage and is very successful rerouting opposing receivers. He displays strong mirror-match skills, and doesn't often get beaten off the line. Horn has fluid hips and transitions very quickly. He can turn and run with ease, staying in the hip of his man. When asked to play off the line, Horn is a little uncomfortable. He can be beaten on quick hitting routes where he must rely solely on his speed, but he shows good quickness and closing ability, limiting yards after the catch as well as creating pass breakups. In zone, Horn excels at reading the quarterback's eyes. He has a good understanding of route concepts and timing and can follow both the quarterback's eyes as well as his man. His quick reaction and range allow him to make throws difficult, creating turnover opportunities for his defense. With the ball in the air, Horn shows superb ball skills. He is able to locate balls while simultaneously feeling for his man. He has very good body control and consistently puts himself in position to make plays on the ball. Occasionally, Horn can be a little too physical down the field, resulting in penalties here and there, but never puts his team in difficult situations by giving up the big play.

Run Game
In the run game, Horn is sufficient in all facets. In the open field, Horn does a good job of breaking down and limiting plays getting behind or around him. He shows he can lower his shoulder and deliver a blow to backs while showing solid technique to wrap up. On the edge, Horn shows he can be aggressive on opposing receivers, having the ability to stack and shed to limit plays on the outside. As a box defender, he doesn't show much aggression to be an impact in short-yardage situations.

Last Word
Horn projects as a very strong starting cornerback in the NFL. Horn can play both sides of the field, but is most effective on the outside where his physicality can be utilized. He can move into the slot on occasion, but he hasn't played there much. Because of his physicality and speed, Horn could be a key piece on special teams, being a part of all core units.

Strengths

- Press-man coverage
- Ball skills
- Transition ability

Weaknesses

- Off-man coverage
- Handsy down the field

Critical Factors

Reactive Athleticism	Play Speed	Ball Skills
7	7	7

Positional Factors

Off-Man	Press-Man	Zone Coverage	Slot Coverage
5	7	7	6
Transition	Closing Speed	FBI	Mental Toughness
7	6	7	6
Open-Field Tackling	Play Strength	Run Support	ST Value
5	6	5	6

Basic

	Coverage								Tackling			
Year	Trgt	Comp	Comp%	Yds	Yds/Trgt	Int	Int Drops	TD Alwd	Tkls	TFL	Brk Tkl	BT%
2018	38	19	50%	273	7.2	0	1	0	44	4.0	7	14%
2019	49	26	53%	352	7.2	0	2	2	39	2.0	7	15%
2020	29	9	31%	130	4.5	2	1	4	14	1.0	3	18%
	116	54	47%	755	6.5	2	4	6	97	7.0	17	15%

Advanced

	Coverage							Man		Zone	
Year	PBU	Deserved Catch %	YAC/ Comp	Rating	EPA	EPA/ Trgt	Pos%	Yds/ Snap	Pos%	Yds/ Snap	Pos%
2018	9	71%	4.6	73.7	3.9	0.10	42%	5.7	46%	3.0	25%
2019	9	75%	3.3	89.8	8.1	0.16	53%	6.1	41%	5.8	60%
2020	8	50%	2.7	46.6	-6.7	-0.23	31%	1.5	27%	7.1	36%
	26	68%	3.7	74.5	5.2	0.04	44%	4.8	39%	5.3	42%

Deep Dive

	Usage			Total Points						Total Points Rtg		
Year	Man%	Slot%	Press Cov%	Press	Slot	Wide	Cov Total	Run Def	Total	Per Cov	Per Run	Per Play
2018	56%	67%	-	-	0	7	8	14	23	71	94	81
2019	44%	23%	45%	10	1	13	15	19	38	79	87	83
2020	54%	34%	50%	13	0	24	26	10	36	99	83	94
	50%	39%	47%	23	1	44	49	43	97	-	-	-

Caleb Farley

Report by Nathan Cooper

School	Height	Weight	Year	Jersey #	Hometown
Virginia Tech	6010 E	207 E	4JR	3	Hickory, NC

One Liner

Farley has the reactive athleticism, fluid hips, transition ability, and man coverage skills that teams covet at the cornerback position, though he'll need to improve his eye discipline and fundamentals down the field to take his game to the next level.

Overall

Caleb Farley primarily plays left cornerback in Virginia Tech's defense that ran a balanced mix of coverages out of both 1- and 2-high looks. He opted out of the 2020 season, though he started 23 of his 24 games played over the previous 2 seasons. Farley redshirted in 2017 because of a torn ACL and missed the final 2 games of 2019 due to back surgery. A high school QB turned WR recruit, he transitioned to corner in 2018. He possesses a good frame and size for the position. He plays very fast and shows toughness and competes every play.

Pass Game

Farley has excellent hip fluidity and a smooth backpedal which allows him to react and transition quickly and cleanly to receivers at the top of their breaks. This effectiveness comes from his ability to change directions and get out of his backpedal. At times, it seems his hips are too quick for his feet as he'll stumble out of his backpedal, but those are fairly rare. He seems most confident and effective in man coverage, specifically press. He's inconsistent getting hands on at the LOS, but when he does, he's able to reroute receivers off the line. His reaction quickness allows him to stay in-phase for the entirety of routes in press. In off-man, his transition ability allows him to react to what he sees and break on routes that are in front of him. His quick feet and fluid hips give him the ability to mirror and match receivers' routes. He's a sufficient defender in zone coverage, however, he gets caught being too aggressive and with his eyes in the backfield too often. There are times he gets turned around downfield, but gets flipped back quickly and into the play. He shows very good ball skills with the ball in the air to break up passes and force turnovers. Even when receivers show late hands, he still has the reactionary skills to get his hands up and knock the ball away. Nearly anytime Farley's beat, he's able to catch up due to excellent acceleration. In addition, he shows good mental toughness following allowing a big play. He didn't play much in the slot, but his quickness and athleticism allows him to stick with receivers most of the time when asked.

Run Game

Farley's willingness to help out in run support is very hot and cold. As a tackler in the open-field, it's much of the same. He misses too many tackle attempts and just seems like he doesn't want to try tackling the ballcarrier.

Last Word

Farley projects as a potential No. 1 cornerback at the next level fitting best in a press-man scheme using his reactive athleticism and transition ability to become a solid cover corner. On 3rd downs, he'll fit best on the outside in man. Due to high-end play speed, but a lack of willingness as a tackler and in run support, he could bring adequate value to some special teams units.

Strengths

- Reactive athleticism
- Fluid hips & transition ability
- Man coverage skills

Weaknesses

- Gets turned around too much
- Eyes caught in the backfield
- Inconsistent tackler

Critical Factors

Reactive Athleticism	Play Speed	Ball Skills
7	7	6

Positional Factors

Off-Man	Press-Man	Zone Coverage	Slot Coverage
6	7	5	6
Transition	**Closing Speed**	**FBI**	**Mental Toughness**
7	7	6	6
Open-Field Tackling	**Play Strength**	**Run Support**	**ST Value**
4	5	4	5

Basic

Year				Coverage						Tackling			
	Trgt	Comp	Comp%	Yds	Yds/Trgt	Int	Int Drops	TD Alwd		Tkls	TFL	Brk Tkl	BT%
2018	47	25	53%	359	7.6	2	1	3		39	1.0	13	25%
2019	48	12	25%	206	4.3	4	0	1		19	0.0	6	24%
	95	37	39%	565	5.9	6	1	4		58	1.0	19	25%

Advanced

Year	PBU	Deserved Catch %	YAC/ Comp	Rating	EPA	EPA/ Trgt	Pos%	Man Yds/ Snap	Pos%	Zone Yds/ Snap	Pos%
2018	10	68%	4.6	90.6	10.2	0.22	49%	8.5	63%	4.6	32%
2019	18	47%	3.4	17.2	-26.4	-0.55	19%	3.5	19%	4.1	15%
	28	59%	4.2	51.4	-16.2	-0.17	34%	6.3	42%	4.3	23%

Deep Dive

Year	Usage Man%	Slot%	Press Cov%	Press	Slot	Wide	Cov Total	Run Def	Total	Per Cov	Per Run	Per Play
2018	44%	19%	-	-	-1	4	6	13	21	67	74	69
2019	35%	22%	16%	8	-1	35	33	8	41	97	71	88
	39%	20%	16%	8	-1	39	39	21	62	-	-	-

Greg Newsome II

Report by John Todd & Joe McDonald

School	Height	Weight	Year	Jersey #	Hometown
Northwestern	6002 E	190 E	3JR	2	Chicago, IL

One Liner
Newsome's balanced coverage skills and instincts for the ball make him a formidable cornerback, but cutting down on the penalties and improving his play strength and durability will take his game to an even higher level.

Overall
Greg Newsome II is a cornerback in Northwestern's base 4-3 zone defense, who typically plays to the boundary. He has started 17 of his 20 career games played, dating back to his true freshman season. He has missed games each year due to ankle, groin, and other undisclosed injuries and seems to often get nicked up. He has good length and a narrow frame. He is athletic, twitchy, and plays with supreme confidence and energy.

Pass Game
Newsome is a lockdown corner who is good in all aspects of man and zone, press and off. He has good mirror quickness in press to stick on his receiver's hip. He has long speed and shows no issues keeping up with the deep ball. In zone, he plays with opened hips on the balls of his feet to diagnose routes entering and leaving his area, as well as the quarterback's eyes and potential load to throw. Newsome is a very active corner who bounces between responsibilities well and prefers man and underneath zones to bailing deep. He does a great job of tying his feet to his eyes. He plays his man with quick peeks to the backfield while still in phase to better anticipate throws. He transitions from press to zone, off-man to turn and run, and triggering downhill to checkdowns all very well with minimal wasted movements. Despite his lack of turnover production, he has fantastic ball skills and shows a knack for breaking up passes. He's very aggressive to undercut routes and has an extra gear to the catch point when targeted. Newsome is very physical downfield and is often rightfully called for interference penalties when playing through receivers to the ball or refusing to disconnect his hands. But apart from those, he's shown the length, closing speed, and anticipation to regularly get his hands on the ball.

Run Game
In the run game, Newsome is a sufficient tackler for his position but lacks the play strength to typically keep ballcarriers from extra yards after contact. He struggles to shed blocks from invested receivers on the perimeter. He will occasionally duck his head from contact but more often than not is a willing participant in the run game when it comes his way.

Last Word
Newsome projects as a solid starter at the next level in a variety of defensive schemes, but ideally in an active role playing bump-and-run or shallow zones. His proclivity for penalties is an area of concern, but he has a well-rounded skill set, and his energy and nose for the ball will make more plays than not. He toes the line of competitive toughness very well. He would be a great jammer if necessary but doesn't have the play strength or strong tackling desire to make much of an impact on coverage units.

Strengths

- Ball skills
- Anticipatory instincts
- Mirror quickness

Weaknesses

- Overly physical downfield
- Play strength
- Durability

Critical Factors

Reactive Athleticism	Play Speed	Ball Skills
6	6	7

Positional Factors

Off-Man	Press-Man	Zone Coverage	Slot Coverage
6	6	6	5
Transition	Closing Speed	FBI	Mental Toughness
7	7	6	6
Open-Field Tackling	Play Strength	Run Support	ST Value
5	4	5	5

Basic

	Coverage								Tackling			
Year	Trgt	Comp	Comp%	Yds	Yds/Trgt	Int	Int Drops	TD Alwd	Tkls	TFL	Brk Tkl	BT%
2018	25	18	72%	271	10.8	0	0	3	23	0.0	3	12%
2019	46	27	59%	323	7.0	0	0	1	33	0.5	4	11%
2020	35	10	29%	83	2.4	1	0	0	13	0.0	2	13%
	106	55	52%	677	6.4	1	0	4	69	0.5	9	12%

Advanced

		Coverage						Man		Zone	
Year	PBU	Deserved Catch %	YAC/ Comp	Rating	EPA	EPA/ Trgt	Pos%	Yds/ Snap	Pos%	Yds/ Snap	Pos%
2018	4	87%	2.0	146.8	12.4	0.50	64%	9.3	22%	6.3	71%
2019	9	82%	2.7	87.5	10.2	0.22	50%	5.2	63%	8.3	57%
2020	10	43%	3.3	15.8	-24.3	-0.69	17%	0.9	9%	3.1	20%
	23	73%	2.6	76.7	-1.7	-0.02	42%	4.9	29%	6.4	52%

Deep Dive

	Usage			Total Points						Total Points Rtg		
Year	Man%	Slot%	Press Cov%	Press	Slot	Wide	Cov Total	Run Def	Total	Per Cov	Per Run	Per Play
2018	28%	15%	-	-	1	2	2	6	9	63	81	68
2019	21%	17%	17%	7	3	8	11	13	24	83	91	85
2020	22%	23%	29%	13	2	34	35	6	41	99	72	97
	23%	18%	22%	19	6	43	48	25	74	-	-	-

Rodarius Williams

Report by Jeff Dean, Noah Chang, & Blake Moore

School	Height	Weight	Year	Jersey #	Hometown
Oklahoma State	6001 V	193 V	5SR	8	Shreveport, LA

One Liner

Williams has the hips, speed, and instincts at the catch point teams covet in an NFL cornerback, and if he can improve against the run, he could have a long NFL career.

Overall

Rodarius Williams' primary position is outside cornerback in Oklahoma State's base 3-3-5, man-heavy defense. He started all 48 games he played in for the Cowboys. He missed the final regular season game of 2020 with a foot injury before opting out of the bowl game. He'll be 24 years old at the time of the NFL Draft, though he'll turn 25 right around time the 2021 season starts. Williams is a very good athlete with sufficient size for the position, although he could add some strength to his defined frame. He plays with a visible fire when he feels challenged and can be seen expressing his emotions after the play.

Pass Game

Williams uses fluid hips, clean footwork, and short-area quickness to stay with receivers down the field. He has extensive experience in press coverage and prefers to use his footwork to disrupt routes rather than his hands. Because of his ability to transition cleanly and quickly, he stays aggressive in the first few yards and doesn't allow easy releases. He can flip his hips and run downfield stride-for-stride and uses the sideline to his advantage. He flashes lockdown potential in man coverage and does a great job of getting in the way without drawing penalties. Williams saw significantly fewer targets in 2020, but has good ball skills when targeted. He is aggressive at the catch point and rarely allows an easy catch when in position. He turns his head and finds the ball, and the only real knock at the catch point is that he doesn't turn disruptions into interceptions. When playing zone, he's disciplined and isn't fooled by play design, finding shallow or deep receivers without losing focus of the quarterback. Williams plays with confidence and doesn't try to overplay his role which limits the mistakes in zone, although his effort wanes when not targeted. He has the athleticism to slide into the slot, but could have a learning curve without the sideline as a weapon.

Run Game

Williams appears very reserved in the run game and doesn't attack the line the same way he does the catch point. He doesn't go out of his way to get to the ballcarrier and seems content to let the ballcarrier come to him. He struggles to fight off blocks and is content to be taken out of the play, and too often he looks uninterested unless he is directly in the way. Williams is a good tackler who loves to try and knock the ball out. While he only has one forced fumble, his form and powerful punch at the ball should result in more forced fumbles in the future.

Last Word

Williams projects as a solid starting cornerback who can play in any system due to his experience in both zone and man coverage. He is best suited on the outside, but can kick inside if needed. There is no reason to take him off the field on 3rd down, but he will need to improve his effort in the run game to limit concerns on early downs. His speed and tackling ability will allow him to be a solid special teams player.

Strengths
- Press coverage
- Transition footwork
- Aggression at catch point

Weaknesses
- Run support
- Fighting off blocks
- Effort when not targeted

Critical Factors

Reactive Athleticism	Play Speed	Ball Skills
6	6	6

Positional Factors

Off-Man	Press-Man	Zone Coverage	Slot Coverage
6	7	6	5
Transition	Closing Speed	FBI	Mental Toughness
6	6	6	7
Open-Field Tackling	Play Strength	Run Support	ST Value
6	5	4	6

Basic

		Coverage								Tackling			
Year	Trgt	Comp	Comp%	Yds	Yds/Trgt	Int	Int Drops	TD Alwd	Tkls	TFL	Brk Tkl	BT%
2017	55	25	45%	612	11.1	0	2	5	44	0.0	0	0%
2018	51	24	47%	323	6.3	2	1	3	48	2.0	10	17%
2019	56	27	48%	402	7.2	0	0	2	55	1.5	10	15%
2020	22	9	41%	158	7.2	0	1	0	21	1.0	1	5%
	184	85	46%	1495	8.1	2	4	10	168	4.5	21	11%

Advanced

		Coverage						Man		Zone	
Year	PBU	Deserved Catch %	YAC/ Comp	Rating	EPA	EPA/ Trgt	Pos%	Yds/ Snap	Pos%	Yds/ Snap	Pos%
2017	10	73%	8.8	116.6	11.7	0.21	44%	-	-	-	-
2018	8	71%	2.3	71.0	1.8	0.04	41%	6.5	44%	5.1	42%
2019	7	79%	4.1	69.2	4.2	0.07	43%	4.9	42%	5.6	42%
2020	7	60%	3.6	47.2	-2.0	-0.09	36%	5.6	45%	10.7	33%
	32	73%	4.9	81.2	15.8	0.09	42%	5.8	44%	6.1	41%

Deep Dive

	Usage			Total Points						Total Points Rtg		
Year	Man%	Slot%	Press Cov%	Press	Slot	Wide	Cov Total	Run Def	Total	Per Cov	Per Run	Per Play
2018	61%	15%	-	-	8	16	24	16	40	87	88	84
2019	42%	13%	18%	4	-6	21	16	19	35	76	88	79
2020	58%	16%	46%	14	1	17	18	12	29	93	86	87
	52%	14%	26%	18	3	53	58	47	104	-	-	-

Asante Samuel Jr.

Report by Jarrett Rodgers & Luke DeCello

School	Height	Weight	Year	Jersey #	Hometown
Florida State	5095 E	184 E	3JR	26	Sunrise, FL

One Liner
Samuel has the mirror-match, transition ability, and man coverage skills to be a starter at the nex level, but his struggles against larger targets could hold him back and limit his overall ceiling.

Overall
Asante Samuel Jr. plays outside cornerback for Florida State's 3-4 defense while also spending some time in the slot and at safety. He played in 32 career games, starting 23 of them for the Seminoles before opting out of the final game of 2020. His father played 11 seasons in the NFL during the early 2000s. He is an electric athlete with very good instincts, speed, and agility. He's a competitor who has repeatedly faced team adversity in his college career and responds to failure with toughness.

Pass Game
In the pass game, Samuel thrives as an off-man and press-man defender. He has the reactive athletic ability to mirror and match body movements of receivers across from him, though his hip fluidity to turn and run has been an issue at times. He plays with good speed and transitions to close on the ball in front of him exceptionally well. He's comfortable working on smaller, quicker receivers in addition to bigger receivers on the outside, though the larger receivers can give him fits at the catch point. In zone coverage, he looks a little uncomfortable and lacks some lateral movement in space, but achieves depth in his drops quickly and can quickly close on the ball when it comes his way. Overall, he plays with good instincts and can control his body to make a play on the ball. However, he will struggle some to decelerate quickly from top speed to stay with back-shoulder throws or lat adjustments down the field.

Run Game
In the run game, Samuel has had good efficiency tackling in the open field, but a lack of upper-body strength and relentless moto prevents him from being able to consistently shed blocks effectively. He has good football intelligence overall and reads the play in from of him well. He's not very aggressive in pursuing tackles nor does he always showcase great technique, though he is willing to engage with blockers and work to make a play. He uses good speed and quickness to win on the edge as a force defender and turn ballcarriers back inside toward his teammates.

Last Word
At the next level, Samuel projects best as an outside No. 2 corner where he can work primarily in man coverage. He has the reactive athleticism and quickness to be trusted to handle smaller slot receivers on the inside, but will likely struggle some if paired across from most tight ends. On 3rd downs, he fits best on the outside in press-man where he can use his physicality and mirror abilities with more athletic receivers. Samuel has the speed and toughness to contribute in a limited capacity on special teams and won't likely be a core player

Strengths

- Reactive athleticism
- Man coverage ability
- Transition skills

Weaknesses

- Inconsistent vs. bigger targets
- Lacks zone-coverage technique
- Shedding blocks

Critical Factors

Reactive Athleticism	Play Speed	Ball Skills
7	6	6

Positional Factors

Off-Man	Press-Man	Zone Coverage	Slot Coverage
7	6	5	5
Transition	**Closing Speed**	**FBI**	**Mental Toughness**
7	7	6	6
Open-Field Tackling	**Play Strength**	**Run Support**	**ST Value**
6	4	4	5

Basic

Year	Trgt	Comp	Comp%	Yds	Yds/Trgt	Int	Int Drops	TD Alwd	Tkls	TFL	Brk Tkl	BT%
2018	37	15	41%	236	6.4	0	0	6	15	1.0	5	25%
2019	54	23	43%	299	5.5	1	3	1	52	2.0	7	12%
2020	31	16	52%	198	6.4	3	0	1	33	1.0	5	13%
	122	54	44%	733	6.0	4	3	8	100	4.0	17	15%

Advanced

Year	PBU	Deserved Catch %	YAC/ Comp	Rating	EPA	EPA/ Trgt	Pos%	Man Yds/ Snap	Man Pos%	Zone Yds/ Snap	Zone Pos%
2018	10	63%	7.7	79.5	2.5	0.07	38%	3.3	31%	9.0	33%
2019	12	69%	3.0	59.1	-12.6	-0.23	28%	3.2	23%	5.2	30%
2020	8	68%	2.5	55.6	-7.9	-0.25	48%	7.8	58%	2.9	25%
	30	67%	4.1	68.8	-18.0	-0.15	36%	4.6	37%	5.6	30%

Deep Dive

Year	Man%	Slot%	Press Cov%	Press	Slot	Wide	Cov Total	Run Def	Total	Per Cov	Per Run	Per Play
2018	48%	29%	-	-	-4	-2	-6	10	4	52	89	64
2019	20%	32%	17%	16	-1	28	28	13	41	92	77	82
2020	37%	13%	30%	9	6	21	27	15	42	98	93	95
	31%	26%	22%	25	1	47	49	38	87	-	-	-

Eric Stokes

Report by Alec Mallon

School	Height	Weight	Year	Jersey #	Hometown
Georgia	5116 E	185 E	3JR	27	Covington, GA

One Liner
Stokes is a physical corner with strong ball skills and mirror-match ability, but needs to improve his off-man ability and refine his techniques defending the run before he can be a real difference maker.

Overall
Eric Stokes is a cornerback in Georgia's 4-2-5 defense lining up on the outside on both sides of the field, but does have some snaps out of the slot. Over his career, he appeared in 36 games, starting 26 of them for the Bulldogs. Stokes is a strong athlete who is long and can be physically demanding at the line of scrimmage. He needs to get a little tougher inside, but is a good competitor with a high motor, never taking plays off.

Pass Game
Stokes possesses natural feet and fluid hips allowing him to compete against multiple body types on the outside. When matched up against speed receivers in off-man, he can be beaten to the inside with slants and digs, but does have the quickness and closing speed to make plays on the ball and limit run after the catch. When pressing on the outside, Stokes does a very good job with jamming receivers at the line, putting himself in situations to easily mirror and match his man at the line offering little-to-no separation. He shows strong footwork and route recognition skills as he's rarely seen out of position. Down the field, he has the speed and acceleration to turn and run with receivers while also understanding route concepts, putting himself in position to win at the catch point. In zone coverage, Stokes often occupies a deep third of the field. He has good eye discipline and FBI, as he can watch the quarterback as well as occupy his zone. He shows smooth hip fluidity going from his backpedal into a sprint and shows great ball skills. He does a good job of following the receiver's eyes and is quick to react at the catch point. He shows good body control, turning around to find the ball while also feeling for his man, resulting in plenty of pass breakups.

Run Game
In the run game, Stokes leaves much to be desired. On the outside, he hesitates when filling run fits. He's often soft with blockers and can be easily moved off of his spot. When engaged, he lacks the technique to shed blocks and make impact plays on the edge. In the open field, Stokes does a good job of breaking down and ensuring big plays don't occur because of his tackling. He doesn't attack ballcarriers with force as he can be seen catching backs and receivers, seeming content with just dragging ballcarriers to the ground.

Last Word
Stokes projects as a solid starting cornerback at the next level where he fits best outside and control a deep third of the field in zone, while also using the sideline as another defender in man coverage, something he should be asked to do on 3rd downs. Stokes was rarely a special teams contributor at late in his career, but should have the ability to be a key member of both punt and kickoff units.

Strengths
- In-air ball skills
- Press coverage
- Mirror-match at the LOS

Weaknesses
- Off-man coverage
- Run support/tackle aggression

Critical Factors

Reactive Athleticism	Play Speed	Ball Skills
6	6	7

Positional Factors

Off-Man	Press-Man	Zone Coverage	Slot Coverage
5	7	6	5
Transition	Closing Speed	FBI	Mental Toughness
6	6	6	5
Open-Field Tackling	Play Strength	Run Support	ST Value
4	6	4	6

Basic

Year	Trgt	Comp	Comp%	Yds	Yds/Trgt	Int	Int Drops	TD Alwd	Tkls	TFL	Brk Tkl	BT%
2018	27	9	33%	120	4.4	0	0	0	19	1.0	1	5%
2019	57	27	47%	273	4.8	0	2	2	36	1.0	4	10%
2020	26	10	38%	109	4.2	4	0	1	23	0.0	1	4%
	110	46	42%	502	4.6	4	2	3	78	2.0	6	7%

Advanced

Year	PBU	Deserved Catch %	YAC/ Comp	Rating	EPA	EPA/ Trgt	Pos%	Man Yds/ Snap	Man Pos%	Zone Yds/ Snap	Zone Pos%
2018	10	57%	1.8	48.4	-7.2	-0.27	30%	1.6	13%	5.3	33%
2019	10	71%	2.2	65.9	-10.9	-0.19	39%	5.9	46%	5.4	46%
2020	7	67%	2.2	24.8	-16.1	-0.62	31%	4.7	39%	2.9	20%
	27	66%	2.1	49.9	-34.2	-0.31	35%	4.4	36%	4.8	38%

Deep Dive

Year	Man%	Slot%	Press Cov%	Press	Slot	Wide	Cov Total	Run Def	Total	Per Cov	Per Run	Per Play
2018	61%	13%	-	-	-1	17	16	9	25	95	93	91
2019	51%	15%	48%	12	5	24	30	7	41	94	70	86
2020	41%	23%	35%	9	5	18	23	11	35	95	86	89
	50%	17%	42%	21	9	60	69	27	101	-	-	-

Ifeatu Melifonwu

Report by Nathan Cooper

School	Height	Weight	Year	Jersey #	Hometown
Syracuse	6025 V	212 V	4JR	2	South Grafton, MA

One Liner
Melifonwu is a smart, reactive athlete who possesses the transition ability and closing speed needed at the next level, though he'll need to get more physical at the line and convert on more of his opportunities if he wants to be a consistent contributor.

Overall
Ifeatu Melifonwu primarily plays right cornerback in Syracuse's 3-3-5 defense with a balanced approach of 1- and 2-high looks and man and zone coverages. He started 19 of 29 games for the Orange. He missed 7 games in 2018 and 2019 due to hamstring and lower leg injuries. His brother, Obi, currently plays in the NFL. A basketball, lacrosse, and track star in high school, Melifonwu is a good, reactive athlete with excellent size and length for the position. He plays tough and competes with the guy across from him.

Pass Game
Melifonwu has the skill set to be effective in any look or coverage. In press-man, he has the size and quickness to stay step for step with receivers off the line. However, he rarely jams at the line which allows receivers a clean release. In off-man, he has the reactive athleticism and transition ability with fluid hips to quickly get out of his backpedal and close on the receiver. His backpedal can be a little high at times, but that comes with his size. In zone coverage, he reads the quarterback's eyes well and has good awareness of where receivers are, but there are times where he'll try to bait the quarterback and rely on his speed and athleticism a little too much which makes him a hair late to making a play on the ball. He rarely played as a true slot corner, but has the size and quickness to stay with the quicker receivers or big tight ends to an adequate degree. His closing speed is his best trait. Whether when beat or just trailing, he has the burst to close quickly and get into position when the ball gets to the receiver. His on-ball production is sufficient but he's nearly always in position. Melifonwu seldom gets out of phase, but he's inconsistent locating the ball at the catch point and making a play. He was able to break up a lot of passes but missed on some opportunities and left some turnovers on the field.

Run Game
Melifonwu's run support is inconsistent and so is his tackling ability. As an overall tackler, he shows good strength to deliver a blow, but in the open field, he misses too many tackles. On receiver screens, he reads them quickly and explodes into the blocker to blow them up. He's a smart player and nearly always stays to the outside as the force defender.

Last Word
Melifonwu projects as a No. 3 cornerback fitting best on the outside in any scheme at the next level. He has the size and athleticism to slide into the slot if needed, but would be put to better use on the outside against bigger receivers. On 3rd downs, he'll do his best on the outside where he can use his athleticism against the bigger, more athletic receivers. His size, speed, and toughness suggest he'll be a solid contributor on special teams units.

Strengths

- Reactive athlete
- Closes quickly
- High FBI

Weaknesses

- Misses too many opportunities
- Inconsistent press fundamentals
- Slips off some tackles

Critical Factors

Reactive Athleticism	Play Speed	Ball Skills
6	6	5

Positional Factors

Off-Man	Press-Man	Zone Coverage	Slot Coverage
6	5	6	5
Transition	Closing Speed	FBI	Mental Toughness
6	7	6	6
Open-Field Tackling	Play Strength	Run Support	ST Value
4	6	5	6

Basic

	Coverage								Tackling			
Year	Trgt	Comp	Comp%	Yds	Yds/Trgt	Int	Int Drops	TD Alwd	Tkls	TFL	Brk Tkl	BT%
2018	25	12	48%	198	7.9	0	0	0	14	1.0	0	0%
2019	46	17	37%	306	6.7	2	1	1	19	1.0	3	14%
2020	43	25	58%	321	7.5	1	0	3	57	3.0	8	12%
	114	54	47%	825	7.2	3	1	4	90	5.0	11	11%

Advanced

	Coverage							Man		Zone	
Year	PBU	Deserved Catch %	YAC/ Comp	Rating	EPA	EPA/ Trgt	Pos%	Yds/ Snap	Pos%	Yds/ Snap	Pos%
2018	6	68%	5.3	75.1	4.1	0.16	48%	10.3	57%	6.0	44%
2019	12	61%	6.1	49.7	-12.0	-0.26	30%	6.7	25%	5.2	32%
2020	9	74%	2.4	65.3	-11.2	-0.26	53%	6.4	48%	6.9	58%
	27	68%	4.2	57.8	-19.1	-0.17	43%	7.3	40%	6.0	45%

Deep Dive

	Usage			Total Points						Total Points Rtg		
Year	Man%	Slot%	Press Cov%	Press	Slot	Wide	Cov Total	Run Def	Total	Per Cov	Per Run	Per Play
2018	51%	15%	-	-	3	5	8	4	12	93	89	85
2019	39%	13%	38%	11	1	22	22	10	31	96	79	86
2020	46%	20%	15%	-4	2	11	13	20	36	73	81	77
	44%	17%	24%	7	5	39	43	34	79	-	-	-

Marco Wilson

Report by Alec Mallon

School	Height	Weight	Year	Jersey #	Hometown
Florida	5116 E	191 E	4JR	3	Fort Lauderdale, FL

One Liner
Wilson is a fast and rangy corner who possesses very good transition ability to see the field in coverage situations, but needs to improve his tackling before he can become an every-down player

Overall
Marco Wilson plays cornerback for Florida's 3-3-5 defense running mainly zone coverages and spending the majority of his time playing out wide, but does have true experience in the slot. Over 4 years, Wilson appeared in 36 games, while starting 35 of them for the Gators. In the 2nd game of 2018, Wilson sustained a torn left ACL and missed the rest of the season, something he also did in 2015. He has a unique blend of speed and agility allowing him to play with anyone on the outside. He is a good competitor, but lacks toughness needed in the box.

Pass Game
Defending the pass, Wilson uses his speed to his advantage. At the LOS, he doesn't often jam his man, but relies on his mirror skills and quick feet to win. Wilson has fluid and fast hips, helping him transition out of his backpedal. He has strong change-of-direction skills, allowing him to stick with his man all over the field. Off ball, Wilson shows good acceleration and start/stop ability to close ground between his man and himself. When in zone, he displays good eye discipline, keeping track of both his zone and the quarterback's eyes. His speed allows for him to show off his range and cover lots of ground, creating tighter than expected throwing windows. When in the slot, Wilson is better in man coverage as he can use his agility to stay with receivers as they cross the field. At the catch point, Wilson needs to become more aware. He is a step slow with locating the ball down the field leading to completions that could be broken up, though he's good at limiting yards after the catch. His speed and closing ability keep him in phase and he wraps up well when trailing.

Run Game
Against the run, Wilson lacks the desire to fill in. He is hesitant at times and when blocked struggles to shed stalk blocks. In the open field, Wilson shows the desire to make tackles but can be extremely wild in his approach. He doesn't always break down and has a tendency to dive at ballcarriers making himself susceptible to broken and missed tackles.

Last Word
Wilson projects as a No. 3 cornerback at the next level. His ability to play both outside and in the slot will allow him to become a capable starter, but also used more as a depth player. Wilson should be able to see the field when the defense goes into nickel and/or dime package where he can be the 3rd cornerback on the field. Wilson could also be a key special teamer due to his speed and athleticism. With his ability to cover ground at a high rate, he could see time on both kickoff and punt units.

Strengths	Weaknesses
• Long speed & agility	• Open-field tackling
• Fluid transition	• Hesitancy in run game
• Press-man ability	• Ball skills

Critical Factors

Reactive Athleticism	Play Speed	Ball Skills
6	7	5

Positional Factors

Off-Man	Press-Man	Zone Coverage	Slot Coverage
5	7	6	6
Transition	Closing Speed	FBI	Mental Toughness
7	6	5	5
Open-Field Tackling	Play Strength	Run Support	ST Value
4	5	4	6

Basic

| | Coverage | | | | | | | | | Tackling | | | |
Year	Trgt	Comp	Comp%	Yds	Yds/Trgt	Int	Int Drops	TD Alwd		Tkls	TFL	Brk Tkl	BT%
2017	41	15	37%	294	7.2	0	1	3		32	0.0	8	20%
2018	2	0	0%	0	0.0	0	0	0		0	0.0	1	100%
2019	43	24	56%	306	7.1	3	1	4		38	2.5	10	21%
2020	40	24	60%	358	9.0	0	0	3		37	0.5	8	18%
	126	63	50%	958	7.6	3	2	10		107	3.0	27	20%

Advanced

| | Coverage | | | | | | | Man | | Zone | |
Year	PBU	Deserved Catch %	YAC/ Comp	Rating	EPA	EPA/ Trgt	Pos%	Yds/ Snap	Pos%	Yds/ Snap	Pos%
2017	12	57%	4.7	76.7	4.2	0.10	37%	-	-	-	-
2018	0	-	-	39.6	-1.9	-0.96	0%	0.0	0%	0.0	0%
2019	6	80%	3.0	80.2	5.3	0.12	49%	6.3	50%	6.1	50%
2020	3	90%	3.8	114.4	12.9	0.32	53%	7.3	67%	5.5	47%
	21	76%	3.7	88.7	20.4	0.16	45%	6.5	55%	5.7	48%

Deep Dive

| | Usage | | | Total Points | | | | | | Total Points Rtg | | |
Year	Man%	Slot%	Press Cov%	Press	Slot	Wide	Cov Total	Run Def	Total	Per Cov	Per Run	Per Play
2018	90%	28%	-	-	0	1	1	0	1	99	50	58
2019	27%	36%	28%	5	9	10	18	12	31	82	81	79
2020	33%	36%	23%	-4	1	4	4	11	15	64	77	68
	31%	36%	26%	1	10	15	23	23	47	-	-	-

Aaron Robinson

Report by Nathan Cooper

School	Height	Weight	Year	Jersey #	Hometown
UCF	5114 V	190 V	5SR	31	Deerfield Beach, FL

One Liner
Robinson is a strong, physical, versatile defender who can make plays on all three downs, thoug some tight hips, body control issues, and inconsistent fundamentals could hold him back from being a top-end corner.

Overall
Aaron Robinson is mainly a slot cornerback in UCF's 4-2-5 defense, running a balance of man and zone coverages, and will slide into the box against tight formations. He began his career at Alabama in 2016 where he appeared in 13 games, before starting 19 of 29 for UCF the last 3 seasons. He missed 6 games after suffering a serious concussion on the opening kickoff of the 2018 season. He has a good frame and size for the position. He's a solid athlete and plays fast, but lacks a little body control. However, he competes and plays tough and physical at nearly all times throughout the game.

Pass Game
Robinson shows some inconsistent fundamentals in his game. He turns his back to the ball at the top of routes and tight hips make it difficult for him to transition cleanly at times. However, his speed and burst give him the ability to make up deficits and close. In off-man, sticky hips make it tough to transition, but his closing speed gets him to the ball quickly. In press, where he's most comfortable, he's physical with receivers at the line and makes it hard for them to get into their route. When he isn't able to get hands on at the line, especially in the slot, quicker receivers can gain separation at the snap, forcing Robinson to have to close and make up ground right away. In zone, he turns his back to the ball a little too often, but nearly always looks to ge hands on and disrupt routes. In the slot, wher he played most, he has enough speed and quickness to stay with receivers. Howeve receivers break his cushion and he tends to catch them while flat-footed. He could use hi strength and physicality to battle tight ends i needed. Robinson shows good ball skills to find it and make a play at the catch point. He' able to break up a lot of passes and also show the ability to make the interception as well. He brings some ability to blitz from the slot or of the edge, and can dip under tackles or ru through backs to get to the quarterback.

Run Game
Against the run, Robinson's willingness can be hot and cold, but when it's hot, he fight through stalk blocks and comes in looking to deliver a blow. He's a strong tackler, but wil just throw a shoulder every once in a while forcing an occasional miss. However, this i something he cleaned up in 2020.

Last Word
Robinson projects as a No. 3 cornerback who can play outside or inside in a press-man o zone scheme who has the size, strength, and speed to also line up as a strong safety. On 3rd downs, he fits best in press-man on the LOS o as an extra blitzer. His skill set should allow him to be a core contributor on special teams.

Strengths
- Plays strong & physical
- Closing burst
- Versatility

Weaknesses
- Lacks body control
- Tight hips
- Inconsistent fundamentals

Critical Factors

Reactive Athleticism	Play Speed	Ball Skills
5	6	6

Positional Factors

Off-Man	Press-Man	Zone Coverage	Slot Coverage
5	6	5	6
Transition	Closing Speed	FBI	Mental Toughness
5	6	5	6
Open-Field Tackling	Play Strength	Run Support	ST Value
6	7	5	7

Basic

Year	Trgt	Comp	Comp%	Yds	Yds/Trgt	Int	Int Drops	TD Alwd	Tkls	TFL	Brk Tkl	BT%
2016	1	1	100%	6	6.0	0	0	0	4	1.0	0	0%
2018	8	4	50%	79	9.9	0	0	0	7	0.0	1	13%
2019	30	14	47%	187	6.2	3	0	1	48	6.5	11	19%
2020	38	19	50%	238	6.3	0	1	4	42	1.0	0	0%
	77	38	49%	510	6.6	3	1	5	101	8.5	12	11%

Advanced

Year	PBU	Deserved Catch %	YAC/ Comp	Rating	EPA	EPA/ Trgt	Pos%	Man Yds/ Snap	Man Pos%	Zone Yds/ Snap	Zone Pos%
2016	0	100%	9.0	91.7	0.9	0.91	100%	-	-	-	-
2018	1	80%	6.3	84.9	2.7	0.34	50%	8.4	50%	3.3	33%
2019	12	65%	4.6	64.2	-2.7	-0.09	33%	8.9	46%	3.2	27%
2020	9	68%	3.5	104.9	5.6	0.15	47%	5.0	48%	7.7	60%
	22	68%	4.3	87.0	6.6	0.09	43%	6.8	47%	5.1	42%

Deep Dive

Year	Usage Man%	Usage Slot%	Usage Press Cov%	Total Points Press	Total Points Slot	Total Points Wide	Total Points Cov Total	Total Points Run Def	Total Points Total	Total Points Rtg Per Cov	Total Points Rtg Per Run	Total Points Rtg Per Play
2018	70%	20%	-	-	-1	1	0	4	4	59	98	80
2019	35%	64%	14%	5	11	14	24	13	37	88	73	79
2020	53%	82%	17%	7	11	1	13	12	25	78	79	75
	45%	67%	15%	12	21	17	37	29	66	-	-	-

Darren Hall

Report by Chad Tedder

School	Height	Weight	Year	Jersey #	Hometown
San Diego State	5113 V	189 V	4JR	23	Pasadena, CA

One Liner

Hall has the speed, IQ, and overall coverage ability to see plenty of snaps at the next level, but with some development of consistent ball skills and press-man ability, he could become a solid 3-down starter.

Overall

Darren Hall is a cornerback in San Diego State's 3-3-5 zone-coverage scheme, where he played predominantly outside. Starting his career as a safety before switching to corner his 2nd season, he played in 34 games, starting in 22. He missed 7 games as a freshman in 2017 with a hamstring injury. Hall is a fast, reactive athlete that can make quick transitions and accelerate quickly. He plays with a high IQ and a willingness to play physical.

Pass Game

Against the pass, Hall spent most of his time playing outside to the boundary. He shows good reactive athleticism with his read-react ability to stick with receivers. He usually doesn't press and jam at the line of scrimmage, playing off the ball where he can diagnose routes, maintain good eye discipline, and get himself into position on receivers. In zone coverage, he shows good footwork, hip fluidity, and acceleration to close gaps on receivers in space. He can carry receivers and stay in their pocket on deep routes, either on the boundary or through the middle of the field. When asked to release and cover the flat, he is often unsuccessful in disrupting the receiver's routes before they release over the top, but he shows an overall good transition in attacking the underneath routes, and occasionally jumping them for an interception or pass breakup. While mostly playing zone, he also shows the ability to play off-man with success and stay in-phase with receivers. He

does a good job at hand fighting and getting his body into an advantageous position on the receiver. Once the ball is in the air, he has some inconsistencies in getting his head around to search for the ball, occasionally drawing a pass interference or allowing a good catch over him or to the back shoulder. When asked to play press, he uses athleticism to mirror-match the best that he can, but since he doesn't often jam at the line, he can get beaten on a quick move to get over the top or inside of him to create separation. However, he does have the acceleration to recover and get back into position or close the gap to make a tackle.

Run Game

Against the run, Hall plays with a swarm mentality, trying to shed stalk blocks and get to the ballcarrier. When in position, he usually makes a good, strong tackle, while occasionally getting downhill quickly and delivering a big hit on the runner.

Last Word

Hall best projects as a No. 3 cornerback in a predominant zone coverage scheme, where he can use his skills to play inside and out. On 3rd downs, his speed and willingness to play physical makes him a movable piece to play over TEs in the slot, pick up receivers out wide, rotate deep, or occasionally blitz. Hall can also be a core member of coverage units on special teams.

Strengths

- Read and react
- Hips to turn and run
- Closing speed

Weaknesses

- Ball-skill consistency
- Route disruption

Critical Factors

Reactive Athleticism	Play Speed	Ball Skills
6	6	5

Positional Factors

Off-Man	Press-Man	Zone Coverage	Slot Coverage
6	5	6	6
Transition	Closing Speed	FBI	Mental Toughness
6	7	6	6
Open-Field Tackling	Play Strength	Run Support	ST Value
6	5	6	6

Basic

	Coverage								Tackling			
Year	Trgt	Comp	Comp%	Yds	Yds/Trgt	Int	Int Drops	TD Alwd	Tkls	TFL	Brk Tkl	BT%
2017	1	1	100%	20	20.0	0	0	0	2	0.0	0	0%
2018	50	30	60%	315	6.3	2	1	3	42	2.0	5	11%
2019	62	30	48%	443	7.1	1	1	2	49	4.5	2	4%
2020	44	25	57%	334	7.6	3	0	2	38	2.0	2	5%
	157	86	55%	1112	7.1	6	2	7	131	8.5	9	6%

Advanced

	Coverage							Man		Zone	
Year	PBU	Deserved Catch %	YAC/ Comp	Rating	EPA	EPA/ Trgt	Pos%	Yds/ Snap	Pos%	Yds/ Snap	Pos%
2017	0	100%	7.0	118.8	1.1	1.10	100%	-	-	-	-
2018	6	78%	2.7	65.0	-4.3	-0.09	52%	4.9	52%	8.0	50%
2019	15	71%	2.8	82.9	-3.0	-0.05	44%	9.0	59%	0.8	13%
2020	7	80%	2.5	77.3	-8.0	-0.18	41%	7.9	39%	8.1	56%
	28	76%	2.7	76.2	-14.2	-0.09	46%	7.4	52%	5.6	42%

Deep Dive

	Usage			Total Points						Total Points Rtg		
Year	Man%	Slot%	Press Cov%	Press	Slot	Wide	Cov Total	Run Def	Total	Per Cov	Per Run	Per Play
2018	32%	13%	-	-	4	8	14	9	27	84	69	80
2019	31%	14%	10%	-4	10	11	20	13	37	85	87	85
2020	33%	12%	9%	-1	2	19	20	14	34	90	95	89
	32%	13%	9%	-5	15	38	54	36	98	-	-	-

Tyson Campbell

Report by Nathan Cooper

School	Height	Weight	Year	Jersey #	Hometown
Georgia	6012 E	185 E	3JR	3	Plantation, FL

One Liner

Campbell has the smarts, speed, and physicality to play multiple coverages in a variety of ways at the next level, though inconsistent zone awareness, change-of-direction ability, and tight hips may limit his starting ability.

Overall

Tyson Campbell is a cornerback who plays either on the left or right side depending on the drive and even slides into the slot given Georgia's rotation in their 4-2-5 defense playing a balanced mix of man and zone coverages. He started 24 of 33 games for the Bulldogs. In 2019, he missed 5 games due to a turf toe injury. He has a good frame with requisite size for the position. He's a good athlete who plays hard and competes in all facets of the game.

Pass Game

Campbell gets a little high when flipping his hips to turn and run, though he has the speed to compensate. In press-man, he is physical at the line and mid-route to throw off timing. When turning and running off the line, his tight hips don't affect him much. In off-man, he has the transition ability to quickly break downhill on routes in front of him. Where he gets in trouble is changing directions at the top of routes. He reacts quickly to route breaks, but just lacks some hip fluidity and COD ability to stay attached to receivers out of the top of their routes. He plays a fair share of bail technique and that exacerbates his change-of-direction struggles. In zone coverage, he shows good eye discipline to read the quarterback's eyes and break on passes, but lacks some awareness of receivers coming through his area. In the slot, he has the speed and strength to cover receivers or tight ends that line up across from him. He rarely gets beaten badly and seems to always be in phase. When beaten early, he has the speed to close on the receiver and get back in phase to make a play. At the catch point, he does a good job of being in position and getting his hands up, but seems to just miss too many opportunities and allow too many receptions.

Run Game

Campbell shows some willingness in run support and does a good job as a force defender. He doesn't always fight to get off stalk blocks, but if he's around the box or the play comes his way, he doesn't mind sticking his nose in. He's a good enough tackler to bring down ballcarriers the majority of the time, but will slip off some opportunities on occasion.

Last Word

Campbell projects as a No. 3 cornerback who can play any corner position in any scheme. His speed and strength allows him to play either outside or inside, though he fits better on the outside. On 3rd downs, he'd be best as a press-man defender on the outside where he can use his speed and physicality at the line. He's used to playing on special teams and should contribute on some units at the next level.

Strengths

- Speed to close
- Plays physical
- High FBI

Weaknesses

- Lacks some zone awareness
- Struggles to change directions
- High in hip turns

Critical Factors

Reactive Athleticism	Play Speed	Ball Skills
5	6	5

Positional Factors

Off-Man	Press-Man	Zone Coverage	Slot Coverage
5	6	5	6
Transition	Closing Speed	FBI	Mental Toughness
5	6	6	6
Open-Field Tackling	Play Strength	Run Support	ST Value
5	6	5	6

Basic

Year	Trgt	Comp	Comp%	Yds	Yds/Trgt	Int	Int Drops	TD Alwd	Tkls	TFL	Brk Tkl	BT%
2018	45	20	44%	284	6.3	0	0	2	45	0.5	3	6%
2019	17	6	35%	91	5.4	0	0	0	18	0.5	2	10%
2020	32	19	59%	302	9.4	1	1	5	30	2.5	3	9%
	94	45	48%	677	7.2	1	1	7	93	3.5	8	8%

Advanced

Year	PBU	Deserved Catch %	YAC/ Comp	Rating	EPA	EPA/ Trgt	Pos%	Yds/ Snap	Pos%	Yds/ Snap	Pos%
2018	2	85%	2.7	71.0	-3.9	-0.09	42%	7.3	48%	4.6	38%
2019	5	54%	2.7	53.8	-3.2	-0.19	29%	5.0	18%	3.1	43%
2020	6	77%	4.1	117.4	8.6	0.27	53%	8.2	53%	11.0	69%
	13	75%	3.2	87.9	1.4	0.02	44%	7.1	44%	6.3	49%

Deep Dive

Year	Man%	Slot%	Press Cov%	Press	Slot	Wide	Cov Total	Run Def	Total	Per Cov	Per Run	Per Play
2018	57%	14%	-	-	3	17	21	13	34	92	94	90
2019	50%	10%	45%	7	0	11	12	2	14	92	65	83
2020	40%	19%	40%	7	4	10	14	14	29	79	91	80
	48%	15%	42%	14	7	38	47	29	77	-	-	-

Tre Brown

Report by Danny Shirilla & Nathan Cooper

School	Height	Weight	Year	Jersey #	Hometown
Oklahoma	5096 V	188 V	4SR	6	Tulsa, OK

One Liner
Brown is a fast, quick defender who has fluid hips that allow him to mirror well in press coverage, though a lack of high-end instincts, off-man consistency, and willingness to support the run may factor in his ability to reach his full potential.

Overall
Tre Brown is an outside cornerback in Oklahoma's 3-3-5 defense running mainly zone coverage looks, but also mixing in man as well. He played a lot of press-engage near the line. He played in 51 games for the Sooners, starting 33 of them. Brown is a good athlete despite his shorter, more compact frame. He plays with very good speed, explosiveness, and quickness. His constant involvement on special teams shows that he is a tough competitor.

Pass Game
Brown shows the speed and quickness to stay with receivers. At the line, he's effective in press by mirroring receivers off the line, though doesn't get hands on right away. He uses his quick feet to mirror off the line immediately and then gets hands-on once receivers get in their route. In zone coverage, what he lacks in reactive athleticism he makes up for with speed and quickness. He'll rely on his athleticism over instincts and fundamentals at times, which will get him in trouble, especially in off-man. He has the transition ability to break quickly with receivers at the top of routes and make plays at the catch point. Brown has good ball skills and can come away with the ball if he is in good position. What he lacks in size and strength somewhat influences his ability to break up passes against larger targets, but when presented with opportunities he can make plays.

Run Game
In the run game, Brown is a sufficient tackler but isn't a guy who is overly willing to stick his nose in and assist in the run game. He'll make some tackles in the open field and when it comes his way, but doesn't always seek out the opportunity to take on ballcarriers and get into piles.

Last Word
Brown projects as a No. 3 cornerback due to his athleticism and solid coverage skills, fitting best in a press-man scheme. He has the quickness to be a versatile cover corner who can play inside or outside. On 3rd downs, he fits best on the inside where he can use his physicality in press against speedier receivers and deny them the ability to get into their route. He has kick return and special team experience, so his skill set should allow him to contribute on a variety of units whether it's as a returner, gunner, jammer, or in other areas.

Strengths

- Plays very fast
- Ability to mirror in press
- Fluid hips

Weaknesses

- Play strength
- Off-man consistency
- Willingness in run support

Critical Factors

Reactive Athleticism	Play Speed	Ball Skills
5	7	6

Positional Factors

Off-Man	Press-Man	Zone Coverage	Slot Coverage
5	6	5	6
Transition	**Closing Speed**	**FBI**	**Mental Toughness**
6	6	5	6
Open-Field Tackling	**Play Strength**	**Run Support**	**ST Value**
5	5	4	7

Basic

										Coverage				Tackling		
Year	Trgt	Comp	Comp%	Yds	Yds/Trgt	Int	Int Drops	TD Alwd	Tkls	TFL	Brk Tkl	BT%
2017	9	2	22%	67	7.4	0	0	0	7	0.5	0	0%
2018	66	34	52%	540	8.2	0	1	4	56	6.0	6	10%
2019	57	22	39%	344	6.0	1	1	4	40	1.0	5	11%
2020	41	18	44%	235	5.7	3	1	2	26	1.0	3	10%
	173	76	44%	1186	6.9	4	3	10	129	8.5	14	10%

Advanced

				Coverage				Man		Zone	
Year	PBU	Deserved Catch %	YAC/ Comp	Rating	EPA	EPA/ Trgt	Pos%	Yds/ Snap	Pos%	Yds/ Snap	Pos%
2017	2	43%	2.0	58.1	-0.5	-0.05	22%	-	-	-	-
2018	11	78%	3.4	99.3	18.0	0.27	45%	5.4	32%	8.5	50%
2019	14	60%	6.3	75.5	-1.2	-0.02	35%	5.0	42%	6.2	32%
2020	8	68%	3.2	48.3	-3.9	-0.09	34%	7.9	46%	3.3	26%
	35	68%	4.1	76.9	12.5	0.07	38%	5.8	39%	6.4	39%

Deep Dive

	Usage			Total Points						Total Points Rtg		
Year	Man%	Slot%	Press Cov%	Press	Slot	Wide	Cov Total	Run Def	Total	Per Cov	Per Run	Per Play
2018	40%	9%	-	-	-2	8	7	11	19	67	87	72
2019	37%	7%	54%	18	-4	27	25	16	41	93	94	90
2020	31%	14%	39%	10	-4	23	20	7	27	89	79	82
	36%	10%	47%	28	-10	58	52	34	87	-	-	-

Elijah Molden

Report by Nathan Cooper

School	Height	Weight	Year	Jersey #	Hometown
Washington	5095 E	190 E	4SR	3	West Linn, OR

One Liner
Molden is a slot defender that has the athleticism, ball skills, and cover ability to be a soli contributor at the NFL level, but will need to get stronger, work on his press fundamentals, an become a better tackler to be a consistent playmaker.

Overall
Elijah Molden is a slot cornerback in Washington's defense that mainly plays with 5 or 6 DBs and primarily shows a 1-high look with a balanced split of man and zone coverages. He'll also shift back to be that 1-high safety in certain looks. He's started 20 of 44 games he's played in for the Huskies. His father, Alex, played in the NFL for 8 seasons. He's a twitchy athlete that shows very good reactive athleticism. He competes and plays with toughness and aggression on nearly every down.

Pass Game
Molden excels in both man and zone coverages. As an off-man defender, he has the reactive athleticism and transition skills to stay with receivers. There will be times he'll lose out to very quick receivers at the top of their route, especially on double moves, but it's not enough to be a concern. Molden shows some inconsistency in press, showing physicality and a good initial punch some of the time and then giving up free releases at other times. In zone coverage, he plays smart and quickly diagnoses what's going on to read and react. He gets good depth on zone drops and plays the quarterback's eyes. When the ball comes to his zone, he's disruptive, using good ball skills to routinely and consistently break up passes. He has good play speed, but lacks the elite speed to consistently catch up to faster receivers once beaten. However, when he plays physical, he's able to turn and run and stay in-phase with receivers the majority of the time He also has enough strength to rerout receivers mid-route. After giving up a big pla or being beaten, he shows strong menta toughness to forget about it and move on to th next play. When asked to blitz from the slot, h is athletic and quick enough to find a lane int the backfield.

Run Game
Despite his size, Molden shows adequat aggression coming up in the run game. Thoug he's a fairly strong tackler and delivers a blo to ballcarriers, he misses quite a few tackl attempts. If he's the only one in the area t make the play, he does a good job breakin down and making a good form tackle. If he's i a crowd or up against bigger ballcarriers, he' lean toward diving at their legs to take then down, resulting in a high percentage of misse tackles.

Last Word
Molden projects as a starting slot corner at th next level where he can play a good mix o man and zone coverages. He doesn't have th size or speed to play outside, but has enoug quickness and reactive athleticism to defen the slot or even rotate back as a free safety. O 3rd downs, he fits best in the slot in ma coverage. He could produce some on specia teams due to play speed and toughness, bu may be limited some due to his size.

Strengths
- Disruptive cover defender
- Reactive athlete
- High FBI

Weaknesses
- Inconsistent press fundamentals
- Misses too many tackles
- Lacks overall closing speed

Critical Factors

Reactive Athleticism	Play Speed	Ball Skills
7	6	6

Positional Factors

Off-Man	Press-Man	Zone Coverage	Slot Coverage
6	5	6	7
Transition	Closing Speed	FBI	Mental Toughness
6	5	7	6
Open-Field Tackling	Play Strength	Run Support	ST Value
5	5	5	5

Basic

		Coverage							Tackling			
Year	Trgt	Comp	Comp%	Yds	Yds/Trgt	Int	Int Drops	TD Alwd	Tkls	TFL	Brk Tkl	BT%
2017	8	5	63%	44	5.5	0	0	0	18	0.5	2	10%
2018	29	16	55%	203	7.0	0	0	0	20	0.0	7	26%
2019	65	34	52%	410	6.3	4	1	2	80	5.5	13	14%
2020	12	6	50%	55	4.6	1	0	0	24	1.0	5	17%
	114	61	54%	712	6.2	5	1	2	142	7.0	27	16%

Advanced

		Coverage						Man		Zone	
Year	PBU	Deserved Catch %	YAC/ Comp	Rating	EPA	EPA/ Trgt	Pos%	Yds/ Snap	Pos%	Yds/ Snap	Pos%
2017	1	83%	1.4	77.1	-1.6	-0.19	38%	-	-	-	-
2018	5	76%	5.5	77.2	0.4	0.01	48%	9.6	54%	4.0	44%
2019	17	70%	4.1	63.0	-8.9	-0.14	34%	6.8	39%	4.5	33%
2020	3	73%	3.2	28.1	-2.9	-0.24	42%	0.7	20%	3.0	50%
	26	73%	4.2	63.9	-13.0	-0.11	39%	6.7	41%	4.1	38%

Deep Dive

	Usage			Total Points						Total Points Rtg		
Year	Man%	Slot%	Press Cov%	Press	Slot	Wide	Cov Total	Run Def	Total	Per Cov	Per Run	Per Play
2018	38%	92%	-	-	12	1	13	5	18	93	98	92
2019	39%	96%	10%	5	53	-2	53	21	74	99	92	96
2020	44%	70%	8%	6	7	2	10	4	15	96	71	86
	39%	91%	9%	12	73	1	76	30	107	-	-	-

Paulson Adebo

Report by Sales Pinckney & John Todd

School	Height	Weight	Year	Jersey #	Hometown
Stanford	6005 E	192 E	4SR	11	Mansfield, TX

One Liner
Adebo is a smart and competitive corner with high-quality ball skills, but his lack of scheme and slot versatility based on his inconsistent reactive footwork in man could limit him.

Overall
Paulson Adebo played primarily wide cornerback in Stanford's hybrid defense, although he has shown he will follow top receivers to all alignments circumstantially. He was an elite two-way high school recruit before focusing solely on corner at Stanford. He started 21 of his 22 career games until suffering an undisclosed injury after 9 games in 2019 that ended his year. He then opted out of 2020. He has a very long frame and great overall size, but his short-area quickness and change-of-direction skills are merely sufficient. He's active, tough, and competitive, especially at the catch point.

Pass Game
Adebo often lines up in a soft press but in a very upright stance and rarely engages receivers to jam with his length. He has to jump into a ready stance off the snap which puts him a step behind to start. He has fairly fluid hips and a smooth backpedal to stay in phase and turn and run with receivers. In man coverage, Adebo's ability to transition without taking false steps is inconsistent. His reactive quickness is hit and miss and he can be hesitant to break until he confirms the throw with his eyes. He has long strides and enough speed to keep up with most vertical routes, and his length is a great equalizer against any route separation. He doesn't reroute with his long arms, but he does a good job of using them to help stay connected. In zone, he shows good route recognition and plays with great eyes to vision the entire field and flow to critical areas. He can play flat-footed at times, but once he is able to change directions he closes quickly.

Adebo displays great ball skills and tracking ability, attacking the ball like the natural receiver he once was. He has a history of elite ball production that is a result of his impressive length, timing, and aggression at the catch point. At times his tendency to play the ball and not his man has gotten him in trouble, but his long arms and innate ball skills have resulted in turnovers and pass breakups at a high clip, despite any hiccups in route coverage.

Run Game
Adebo is quick to come downhill when uncovered in run support, but he doesn't show the willingness to fight through blocks from interested receivers, preferring to let the ball come to him on the front side. He has mediocre tackling form but displays sufficient aggression to throw his body around and close hard, yet somewhat out of control, on run blitzes. His size suggests better play strength but he often gives ground to blockers and ballcarriers.

Last Word
Adebo profiles as a role playing third cornerback in the NFL. His ceiling and projection will be viewed differently based on each team's defensive scheme, and primarily zone-based organizations may highly covet his skill set. He lacks the short-area quickness and reactive athleticism to slide into the slot although he could be a strong candidate to flex back to safety. His play speed and general toughness will allow him to contribute on coverage and return units.

Strengths

- Ball skills
- Eye discipline and intelligence in zone
- Closing speed

Weaknesses

- Foot quickness in man
- Press technique
- Breaking down to form tackles

Critical Factors

Reactive Athleticism	Play Speed	Ball Skills
5	6	7

Positional Factors

Off-Man	Press-Man	Zone Coverage	Slot Coverage
5	5	6	4
Transition	Closing Speed	FBI	Mental Toughness
5	6	6	5
Open-Field Tackling	Play Strength	Run Support	ST Value
4	4	5	6

Basic

	Coverage								Tackling			
Year	Trgt	Comp	Comp%	Yds	Yds/Trgt	Int	Int Drops	TD Alwd	Tkls	TFL	Brk Tkl	BT%
2018	71	34	48%	379	5.3	4	2	1	68	6.0	14	17%
2019	43	23	53%	382	8.9	4	2	3	37	0.0	9	20%
	114	57	50%	761	6.7	8	4	4	105	6.0	23	18%

Advanced

	Coverage							Man		Zone	
Year	PBU	Deserved Catch %	YAC/ Comp	Rating	EPA	EPA/ Trgt	Pos%	Yds/ Snap	Pos%	Yds/ Snap	Pos%
2018	23	62%	3.6	45.5	-13.0	-0.18	46%	3.7	44%	4.0	44%
2019	10	63%	3.5	68.2	-2.9	-0.07	49%	8.6	60%	6.5	45%
	33	63%	3.6	54.0	-16.0	-0.14	47%	4.9	48%	5.1	45%

Deep Dive

	Usage			Total Points						Total Points Rtg		
Year	Man%	Slot%	Press Cov%	Press	Slot	Wide	Cov Total	Run Def	Total	Per Cov	Per Run	Per Play
2018	57%	14%	-	-	-1	50	49	14	64	98	79	91
2019	33%	13%	3%	-2	3	12	15	12	26	83	86	81
	48%	14%	3%	-2	2	61	64	26	90	-	-	-

Shaun Wade

Report by Jordan Edwards

School	Height	Weight	Year	Jersey #	Hometown
Ohio State	6002 E	195 E	5SR	24	Jacksonville, FL

One Liner
Wade has had his struggles on the perimeter playing off, but he is an outstanding slot corner with very good athleticism, solid play speed, and coverage versatility in man or zone.

Overall
Shaun Wade lined up primarily as a slot corner and strong safety early in his career for Ohio State, before returning in 2020 with the opportunity to play as a boundary corner in the Buckeyes' base defense. He played in 35 games and started 19 of them. He has a wiry frame but has good length. Wade is a quick-twitch athlete with good burst and acceleration. He would have bad stretches in some games where he would give up back-to-back big plays but was always competing and showed good mental toughness while continuing to grow at a new position.

Pass Game
Wade excels playing in the slot in man-coverage. He is a very active corner and has good mirror-match abilities at the line of scrimmage to stay attached to the hip of receivers running across the field. His press-man skills are solid, but he needs to use his hands more consistently when engaging receivers at the line. In his first season playing as an outside corner, Wade struggled to develop as a more passive cover cornerback. He struggled to diagnose and react to certain concepts and routes in off-man and bail coverage. He had difficulties reacting to receivers who are more route savvy and technical, which caught him in some unfavorable situations in coverage. Wade is adequate in his transition, but he shows good burst and acceleration to close ground quickly. He does struggle at the catch point against more physical pass catchers who can high point the ball well. He also shows instances of an inability to locate the ball in the air when a play on it is available to be made.

Run Game
Wade shows willingness but lacks aggression in run support. He stays disciplined forcing ballcarriers back to the middle of the field. He doesn't shed blocks well and his play strength may be the weakest part of his game. He is a sufficient open-field tackler but needs improvement when attacking ballcarriers. He will occasionally lunge for tackles and show a lack of aggression at the point of attack.

Last Word
Wade tried to bet on himself and gain more experience as a traditional outside corner in 2020, but that bet didn't come to fruition. However, he still has the coverage skills and athleticism to be a solid third starter in the slot where he is easily most comfortable, and he can thrive in press-man or as an underneath zone defender. His reactive quickness in the slot will be an asset on passing downs. His size and run support don't project well to most special teams units, but he could fill a role sufficiently.

Strengths
- Slot coverage
- Reactive athleticism
- Press coverage

Weaknesses
- Play strength
- Ball skills
- Off-man coverage

Critical Factors

Reactive Athleticism	Play Speed	Ball Skills
6	6	5

Positional Factors

Off-Man	Press-Man	Zone Coverage	Slot Coverage
5	6	5	7
Transition	Closing Speed	FBI	Mental Toughness
5	6	5	6
Open-Field Tackling	Play Strength	Run Support	ST Value
5	4	5	5

Basic

| | Coverage | | | | | | | | Tackling | | | |
Year	Trgt	Comp	Comp%	Yds	Yds/Trgt	Int	Int Drops	TD Alwd	Tkls	TFL	Brk Tkl	BT%
2018	56	24	43%	395	7.1	3	0	1	33	0.0	2	6%
2019	39	18	46%	209	5.4	1	2	1	28	4.0	5	15%
2020	53	31	58%	500	9.4	2	2	6	35	1.0	6	15%
	148	73	49%	1104	7.5	6	4	8	96	5.0	13	12%

Advanced

| | Coverage | | | | | | | Man | | Zone | |
Year	PBU	Deserved Catch %	YAC/ Comp	Rating	EPA	EPA/ Trgt	Pos%	Yds/ Snap	Pos%	Yds/ Snap	Pos%
2018	9	69%	6.0	50.8	-8.8	-0.16	32%	7.5	35%	2.8	24%
2019	9	72%	3.9	50.1	-11.0	-0.28	38%	6.2	41%	4.6	39%
2020	6	80%	4.5	112.1	18.8	0.35	55%	10.5	48%	5.8	59%
	24	74%	4.8	72.6	-1.1	-0.01	42%	8.1	40%	4.7	44%

Deep Dive

| | Usage | | | | Total Points | | | | | Total Points Rtg | | |
Year	Man%	Slot%	Press Cov%	Press	Slot	Wide	Cov Total	Run Def	Total	Per Cov	Per Run	Per Play
2018	72%	67%	-	-	24	9	35	9	44	99	96	96
2019	55%	93%	25%	3	9	0	11	7	24	80	74	81
2020	33%	21%	23%	-9	-2	2	-1	10	9	58	85	66
	53%	60%	24%	-6	31	12	45	26	77	-	-	-

Bryce Thompson

Report by Ben Hrkach & Max Nuscher

School	Height	Weight	Year	Jersey #	Hometown
Tennessee	5112 E	190 E	3JR	0	Irmo, SC

One Liner
Thompson has the athletic ability, closing speed, and ball skills to be an effective cover corner a the next level, though a lack of instincts, technique, and zone awareness may hold him back.

Overall
Bryce Thompson plays outside cornerback for Tennessee's nickel defense that utilized mainly 2-high looks on the back end. He played in 32 games, starting 27 for the Vols. He played through a torn pec suffered in Week 2 of the 2020 season, as well as a right knee injury in 2019. He was also suspended 2 games to start the 2019 season after being arrested and charged with misdemeanor domestic assault. Thompson is a twitchy athlete with good closing speed and leaping ability. He lacks strength, but his frame allows for more room to fill out. He is a high confidence player that is constantly talking and does not shy away from contact.

Pass Game
In the pass game, Thompson is best in press-man coverage. He has the foot quickness to mirror players, as well as the speed and length to get in a receiver's hip and eradicate him from the play. Thompson's main move is to jab with his inside hip and force the receiver to release outside. He has good length and a sufficient punch. Once he has inside leverage, he can easily ride the receiver. He has the ability to locate the ball once it's in the air and naturally high points it. When he doesn't gain inside leverage, he is vulnerable to slants and in-breaking routes, but he uses his very good closing speed to close the gap and limit the damage. When lined up in the slot, Thompson has the agility and quickness to mirror some slot receivers, but lacks the overall reactive athleticism to hang there consistently. He wil overcommit on occasion and in doing so, wa: left behind by Kadarius Toney when Tennesse played Florida in 2020. When playing off-mar and bailing at the snap, Thompson will be late on in-breaking routes, though his closing spee helps mitigate the gap. He shows just adequat zone ability and can be a half-step late when he pulls the trigger or lose a man coming i behind him. His closing speed and sufficien tackling allow him to stop receivers near the catch point.

Run Game
Thompson is willing to get his hands or blockers and has long arms to keep them a distance. He is able to hold the edge and turn ballcarriers back inside as the force defender in the flat. He's also a sufficient tackler and though it's not always the prettiest form tackle he does get guys to the ground.

Last Word
Overall, Thompson projects as a backup cornerback that will thrive in a press-man defense at the next level. He lacks inside outside flexibility due to limited reactive athleticism to stay up with some of the speedier slot receivers, though he could guard some tight ends if tasked. On 3rd downs, he should man up on the outside where he can use his length and speed to win battles. His skill se allows for him to be a solid special team player at the next level.

Strengths
- Closing speed
- Ball tracking
- Suddenness

Weaknesses
- Zone awareness
- Instincts
- Technique

Critical Factors

Reactive Athleticism	Play Speed	Ball Skills
5	6	6

Positional Factors

Off-Man	Press-Man	Zone Coverage	Slot Coverage
5	6	5	5
Transition	Closing Speed	FBI	Mental Toughness
5	7	5	6
Open-Field Tackling	Play Strength	Run Support	ST Value
5	5	5	6

Basic

	Coverage								Tackling			
Year	Trgt	Comp	Comp%	Yds	Yds/Trgt	Int	Int Drops	TD Alwd	Tkls	TFL	Brk Tkl	BT%
2018	36	18	50%	267	7.4	3	1	3	34	4.0	10	23%
2019	34	20	59%	249	7.3	3	1	1	32	2.0	6	16%
2020	30	18	60%	199	6.6	2	0	2	40	3.5	6	13%
	100	56	56%	715	7.2	8	2	6	106	9.5	22	17%

Advanced

	Coverage							Man		Zone	
Year	PBU	Deserved Catch %	YAC/ Comp	Rating	EPA	EPA/ Trgt	Pos%	Yds/ Snap	Pos%	Yds/ Snap	Pos%
2018	9	69%	6.0	79.3	-1.5	-0.04	39%	8.7	41%	3.7	35%
2019	5	81%	1.8	66.9	-1.2	-0.03	50%	4.0	46%	6.7	47%
2020	5	78%	1.7	74.2	0.1	0.00	50%	5.1	56%	6.0	47%
	19	76%	3.1	73.5	-2.5	-0.03	46%	6.1	48%	5.4	43%

Deep Dive

	Usage			Total Points						Total Points Rtg		
Year	Man%	Slot%	Press Cov%	Press	Slot	Wide	Cov Total	Run Def	Total	Per Cov	Per Run	Per Play
2018	51%	17%	-	-	2	11	13	15	31	81	93	87
2019	27%	14%	5%	1	9	15	27	12	42	97	88	94
2020	41%	25%	18%	6	3	6	13	10	26	82	81	83
	39%	18%	12%	7	14	32	53	37	99	-	-	-

Ambry Thomas

Report by Ben Hrkach

School	Height	Weight	Year	Jersey #	Hometown
Michigan	5117 V	189 V	4SR	1	Detroit, MI

One Liner
Thomas is an outside corner that can excel in bump and run, take away the deep ball, and create turnovers, but he needs to improve his football instincts and technique to reach a higher ceiling.

Overall
Ambry Thomas played cornerback in Michigan's attacking man-to-man defense before opting out of the 2020 season. He lined up primarily outside on the right, but played some snaps in the slot, as well as a little on offense early in his career. Before this year he never missed a game, playing in 39 and starting all 13 his junior season. He is a sudden athlete that plays with good fluidity. He has decent size and length but small hands. He shows some toughness, but he would rather fight with someone after he's won and frequently gets bullied.

Pass Game
Against the pass, Thomas uses his natural athleticism and speed to stick with his man, excelling in bump and run and using the boundary well. He has sufficient strength and hand placement in his punch. He has the closing speed to recover against receivers that do beat him to the outside. He is high cut and his sloppy footwork takes him out of position on occasion and leaves him vulnerable to inside breaking routes. His closing speed is impressive and he reattaches to slants and drags quickly. When the ball is in the air, he utilizes his receiver ability and has impressive ball skills. When lined up inside, Thomas looks uncomfortable. He doesn't trust his feet and can get caught jumping by receivers that can set up their break well. He does have good athleticism and burst and could improve his slot ability with better technique. In zone coverage, Thomas' lack of instincts are apparent. He plays defense like a WR and can frequently be found covering no one and drifting into his teammates' zones looking to ball hawk. He often shirks his responsibility and Michigan was beaten on back-side plays because he overflowed. He does not project to have any safety flexion because of his lack of instincts.

Run Game
Against the run, Thomas provides little support. He rarely sheds blocks and frequently gets washed out by receivers. He is a hit-or-miss tackler and throws his body at the ballcarrier. He does not project to be a viable force defender in the flat.

Last Word
Thomas projects best as an outside corner in a man-to-man defense. He has good length, high points the ball, and does a sufficient job of getting his hands on receivers. His speed, ball skills, and man coverage strengths will be coveted by teams that want to eliminate the deep ball. He has the athleticism to play inside but his sloppy technique, lack of instincts, and limited run support limit him to the outside. Thomas' toughness and tackling would hinder him on coverage units, but he profiles as a good jammer on punt return and has been a dangerous kickoff returner through his career.

Strengths

- Speed
- Reactive athleticism in press
- Ball skills

Weaknesses

- Instincts
- Zone coverage
- Run support

Critical Factors

Reactive Athleticism	Play Speed	Ball Skills
6	6	6

Positional Factors

Off-Man	Press-Man	Zone Coverage	Slot Coverage
5	6	4	5
Transition	Closing Speed	FBI	Mental Toughness
5	6	4	5
Open-Field Tackling	Play Strength	Run Support	ST Value
5	4	4	6

Basic

| | Coverage | | | | | | | | Tackling | | | |
Year	Trgt	Comp	Comp%	Yds	Yds/Trgt	Int	Int Drops	TD Alwd	Tkls	TFL	Brk Tkl	BT%
2017	3	2	67%	13	4.3	0	0	0	4	0.5	0	0%
2018	5	0	0%	0	0.0	1	0	0	6	0.0	0	0%
2019	41	20	49%	315	7.7	3	1	1	39	3.0	8	17%
	49	22	45%	328	6.7	4	1	1	49	3.5	8	14%

Advanced

| | Coverage | | | | | | | Man | | Zone | |
Year	PBU	Deserved Catch %	YAC/ Comp	Rating	EPA	EPA/ Trgt	Pos%	Yds/ Snap	Pos%	Yds/ Snap	Pos%
2017	0	100%	4.5	75.7	0.3	0.12	67%	-	-	-	-
2018	1	0%	-	0.0	-5.9	-1.19	0%	0.0	0%	0.0	0%
2019	7	75%	5.5	43.3	-4.9	-0.12	32%	7.2	33%	4.5	29%
	8	70%	5.4	34.6	-10.5	-0.21	31%	6.1	28%	4.3	27%

Deep Dive

| | Usage | | | | Total Points | | | | | Total Points Rtg | | |
Year	Man%	Slot%	Press Cov%	Press	Slot	Wide	Cov Total	Run Def	Total	Per Cov	Per Run	Per Play
2018	91%	19%	-	-	2	5	6	3	10	99	95	98
2019	51%	19%	59%	12	-8	24	16	15	32	86	84	82
	56%	19%	59%	12	-7	29	22	18	42	-	-	-

Avery Williams

Report by Joe McDonald & Ryan Rubinstein

School	Height	Weight	Year	Jersey #	Hometown
Boise State	5085 E	188 E	5SR	26	Pasadena, CA

One Liner
Williams' speed and ability to mirror receivers combined with his impact on special teams make him a valuable asset at the next level, though a lack of ball skills and inconsistent tackling may affect how much time he sees on defense.

Overall
Avery Williams is the starting cornerback in Boise State's 3-3-5 defense, where he typically lines up to the field side. He also has experience playing free safety during the 2020 season. He played in 48 games during his career, starting in 44 of those for the Broncos. Williams is a former high school running back and his athleticism reflects that. He has good speed with quick-twitch ability. He plays with a high motor and a good degree of toughness, giving high effort on every play.

Pass Game
In the pass game, Williams uses his speed to stay step-for-step with receivers down the field. He's very twitchy and able to mirror and match the quick movements receivers put in front of him. He has a high FBI and can diagnose routes and jump passes as the receiver makes his break. His fluid hips and quick transition ability also allow him to quickly get out of his backpedal and burst on routes that are cut off in front of him. Although a smaller corner, he uses his hands well in press, holding his own and staying in stride with the receiver off the line, though he could stand to be more physical. In zone, he has good vision and can read the ball flight and adjust accordingly. If beaten, he has the closing speed to rally and catch up to his receiver, getting back in phase with a chance to make a play at the catch point. He tends to attack the receiver to break up the pass rather than attack the ball which somewhat limits his overall ball skills.

Run Game
In the run game, Williams shows some willingness to get in on tackles, but normally needs assistance. He uses good pursuit to rally to the ball, but lacks power behind his pads. In the open field, he can make tackles, but is more of a drag-down tackler rather than being able to stun ballcarriers and limit yards after contact.

Last Word
Williams projects to be a solid No. 3 cornerback who fits best in the slot. Although he has the speed and coverage ability to run with quicker receivers in the slot, his size will limit him frequently lining up against tight ends. He could also kick back to free safety where he can use his speed, eyes, and athleticism on the back end. On 3rd downs, he fits best in the slot manned up against the offense's quicker slot receivers. On special teams, he should be looked at as a core contributor. A 2-time Mountain West Special Teams Player of the Year, he has 9 total return touchdowns and shows the vision and speed to win as a punt or kick returner. He's also blocked 5 kicks and can come off the edge on field goal or punt blocks. He lacks some size to be on coverage units, but has the speed and toughness to contribute if his frame can hold up.

Strengths

- Play speed
- Mirror-match ability
- Stat-sheet stuffer

Weaknesses

- Ball skills
- Run support
- Size limitations

Critical Factors

Reactive Athleticism	Play Speed	Ball Skills
6	6	5

Positional Factors

Off-Man	Press-Man	Zone Coverage	Slot Coverage
6	6	6	5
Transition	Closing Speed	FBI	Mental Toughness
6	6	6	6
Open-Field Tackling	Play Strength	Run Support	ST Value
6	5	4	7

Basic

	Coverage									Tackling			
Year	Trgt	Comp	Comp%	Yds	Yds/Trgt	Int	Int Drops	TD Alwd	Tkls	TFL	Brk Tkl	BT%
2017	51	27	53%	386	7.6	2	0	4	43	0.0	6	12%
2018	68	40	59%	567	8.3	2	0	4	47	1.0	10	18%
2019	55	31	56%	518	9.4	0	0	3	40	1.5	11	22%
2020	13	10	77%	155	11.9	0	0	0	22	2.0	5	19%
	187	108	58%	1626	8.7	4	0	11	152	4.5	32	17%

Advanced

	Coverage							Man		Zone	
Year	PBU	Deserved Catch %	YAC/ Comp	Rating	EPA	EPA/ Trgt	Pos%	Yds/ Snap	Pos%	Yds/ Snap	Pos%
2017	12	65%	3.1	87.5	2.9	0.06	47%	-	-	-	-
2018	11	81%	4.4	99.3	10.4	0.15	53%	7.9	50%	5.3	41%
2019	7	83%	3.3	106.5	15.3	0.28	47%	5.1	33%	8.5	44%
2020	1	92%	1.9	115.9	10.1	0.77	62%	7.0	33%	14.4	63%
	31	78%	3.5	99.4	38.7	0.21	50%	6.9	44%	7.7	45%

Deep Dive

	Usage			Total Points						Total Points Rtg		
Year	Man%	Slot%	Press Cov%	Press	Slot	Wide	Cov Total	Run Def	Total	Per Cov	Per Run	Per Play
2018	43%	14%	-	-	0	16	16	16	32	79	94	83
2019	32%	12%	16%	-1	3	8	11	11	23	72	74	71
2020	30%	21%	34%	5	-4	7	3	4	7	69	65	65
	36%	14%	21%	4	-1	31	30	31	62	-	-	-

Keith Taylor

Report by Jordan Edwards

School	Height	Weight	Year	Jersey #	Hometown
Washington	6023 V	191 V	4SR	8	Long Beach, CA

One Liner
Taylor is a tall outside cover corner with good athleticism and press coverage ability, but he has some issues in run support and lacks production as a playmaker.

Overall
Keith Taylor lines up primarily on the right side of Washington's nickel defense, rotating boundary and field responsibilities. Washington is diverse in its coverages but likes to press and disrupt releases at the LOS. Taylor played in 43 games in his collegiate career and has started 19 of them. For a taller corner, surprisingly, Taylor doesn't possess a long wingspan, but he has a wiry frame and is a long strider. He is a tough competitor in coverage, but his lack of aggression and willingness to support the run is a bit worrisome.

Pass Game
Taylor is a sticky corner in man coverage and is comfortable living on an island. He's a natural athlete and shows the ability to mirror and match receivers' routes down the field. He plays with a wide base at the LOS in press coverage but is technically sound without being overly aggressive with his hands. He has good feet and good hip mobility to transition or turn and run down the field. His long strides gain ground quickly when bailing and playing zone coverage. Taylor plays with good overall play speed when he can stay in phase but doesn't possess the elite play speed that's desired in outside corners. Taylor's lack of interceptions is an area of concern, but he plays the ball well in the air and has the physicality and production to be disruptive at the catch point. He does have some experience playing in the slot, but his short-area quickness and closing speed are better suited outside.

Run Game
Against the run, Taylor has some weaknesses that can be improved upon. His play strength and open-field tackling ability are sufficient at best. He would rather lunge at ballcarriers than wrap up and make form tackles. His willingness and aggression to support the run are areas of concern, as well. However, it seems that he's coachable and shows the intelligence to know when to be a force player and turn ballcarriers back to the defense.

Last Word
Taylor projects to be a limited starter at the next level, primarily as a boundary corner. His athleticism and comfortability in press coverage allow him to control receivers early off the LOS, and he has the play speed to cover downfield. On 3rd downs, Taylor can play on the outside and allow other corners on his team to move into the slot, if needed. Even with some of his concerns as a tackler, Taylor can provide some value as a special teamer at the next level with his athleticism and solid play speed.

Strengths

- Reactive athleticism
- Press coverage
- Technically sound

Weaknesses

- Play strength
- Lack of on-ball production
- Run support aggression

Critical Factors

Reactive Athleticism	Play Speed	Ball Skills
6	6	5

Positional Factors

Off-Man	Press-Man	Zone Coverage	Slot Coverage
5	7	6	5
Transition	**Closing Speed**	**FBI**	**Mental Toughness**
6	5	6	5
Open-Field Tackling	**Play Strength**	**Run Support**	**ST Value**
5	5	4	6

Basic

Year	Trgt	Comp	Comp%	Yds	Yds/Trgt	Int	Int Drops	TD Alwd	Tkls	TFL	Brk Tkl	BT%
2017	15	8	53%	106	7.1	0	1	2	5	0.0	2	29%
2018	16	7	44%	50	3.1	0	1	0	13	1.5	3	19%
2019	48	25	52%	336	7.0	0	1	2	61	2.0	10	14%
2020	11	5	45%	82	7.5	0	0	0	10	0.0	3	23%
	90	45	50%	574	6.4	0	3	4	89	3.5	18	17%

Advanced

Year	PBU	Deserved Catch %	YAC/ Comp	Rating	EPA	EPA/ Trgt	Pos%	Man Yds/ Snap	Man Pos%	Zone Yds/ Snap	Zone Pos%
2017	0	90%	2.6	115.6	5.0	0.33	40%	-	-	-	-
2018	2	78%	1.9	51.6	-7.6	-0.48	31%	3.1	25%	2.4	43%
2019	8	76%	5.7	88.5	3.8	0.08	42%	4.2	30%	5.1	39%
2020	2	75%	3.0	71.0	1.1	0.10	36%	10.0	50%	4.7	29%
	12	78%	4.3	85.1	2.3	0.03	39%	4.6	31%	4.5	38%

Deep Dive

Year	Usage Man%	Usage Slot%	Usage Press Cov%	Total Points Press	Total Points Slot	Total Points Wide	Total Points Cov Total	Total Points Run Def	Total Points Total	Total Points Rtg Per Cov	Total Points Rtg Per Run	Total Points Rtg Per Play
2018	40%	20%	-	-	8	6	14	8	23	92	93	89
2019	39%	33%	36%	10	7	5	17	21	38	77	92	81
2020	43%	27%	50%	1	-1	4	3	2	5	72	62	66
	40%	28%	39%	12	14	15	34	31	66	-	-	-

Shemar Jean-Charles

Final Grade: 6.

Report by Jeff Dean & Jake Johnson

School	Height	Weight	Year	Jersey #	Hometown
Appalachian State	5100 V	184 V	5SR	8	Miramar, FL

One Liner

Jean-Charles has the athleticism, ball skills, and mindset to potentially earn a role in the slot at the next level, but his size limitations and hiccups in awareness could hold him back.

Overall

Shemar Jean-Charles is an outside cornerback in Appalachian State's base defense. He played in 50 career games with 25 starts. He is a good athlete with fluid hips, good speed, and quick feet. He accelerates quickly and chops his feet well to break down and change directions. He has sufficient size with a chiseled, narrow frame that could add bulk. He is a feisty competitor who plays with passion. He wears his emotions on his sleeve and can be seen directing his teammates when he sees a potential problem.

Pass Game

Jean-Charles uses his light footwork and good reactive athleticism to stick with receivers in man coverage. He has experience in press but lacks the length or strength to cause a huge disruption to releases, especially against bigger targets. His feet and aggressive mindset allow him to stick with receivers in press, but he looks more comfortable when given breathing room to read and react. He plays with good instincts to anticipate routes and reacts quickly out of breaks. He is physical throughout the route but typically does a good job keeping his contact inside and subtle to avoid calls. He has lots of experience playing both shallow and deep zone, but can struggle with route recognition. He has a tendency to stick to his zone and pass off receivers early even when there isn't another threat coming in. Jean-Charles communicates well to mitigate some of his issues, but his overall zone discipline is rigid and he doesn't adjust well to route concepts. He is aggressive at the catch point and forces numerous pass break ups due to his very good timing and pestering nature. He hasn't converted many into interceptions with his unexceptional length, but he also hasn't dropped opportunities. His fluid hips, quick feet, and good closing speed provide the framework for a transition inside to slot.

Run Game

Jean-Charles will help in run support but isn't actively looking to make a play. His primary concern is his receiver and he can become too focused on him and lose awareness of what else is happening on the play. This results in some late reads to runs, and while he shows an ability to shed blocks from receivers, he doesn't attack the line. Jean-Charles has good tackling form and keeps his head up when taking on bigger targets. He plays with sufficient strength and can deliver big hits but usually goes for the sure tackle.

Last Word

Shemar Jean-Charles projects as a potential third cornerback at the next level if he successfully transitions into the slot. He doesn't have the size to match up with outside receivers in the NFL consistently, but his short area quickness, feisty attitude and physicality through routes project well inside with time to develop. He fits best in a predominantly man scheme, and his speed and tackling abilities should allow him to contribute on special teams.

Strengths

- Fluid hips
- Reactive footwork
- Aggression at the catch point

Weaknesses

- Rigid zone discipline
- Awareness outside of assignment
- Aggression in run support

Critical Factors

Reactive Athleticism	Play Speed	Ball Skills
6	6	6

Positional Factors

Off-Man	Press-Man	Zone Coverage	Slot Coverage
6	5	5	6
Transition	Closing Speed	FBI	Mental Toughness
7	6	5	6
Open-Field Tackling	Play Strength	Run Support	ST Value
6	5	4	6

Basic

				Coverage						Tackling			
Year	Trgt	Comp	Comp%	Yds	Yds/Trgt	Int	Int Drops	TD Alwd	Tkls	TFL	Brk Tkl	BT%
2017	10	4	40%	53	5.3	0	0	0	7	0.0	1	13%
2018	7	1	14%	14	2.0	0	0	0	4	0.0	0	0%
2019	62	29	47%	397	6.4	1	1	3	44	0.0	7	14%
2020	54	19	35%	311	5.8	1	0	2	35	1.0	2	5%
	133	53	40%	775	5.8	2	1	5	90	1.0	10	10%

Advanced

			Coverage					Man		Zone	
Year	PBU	Deserved Catch %	YAC/ Comp	Rating	EPA	EPA/ Trgt	Pos%	Yds/ Snap	Pos%	Yds/ Snap	Pos%
2017	1	83%	5.0	57.5	-0.4	-0.04	40%	-	-	-	-
2018	2	25%	11.0	39.6	-4.7	-0.67	14%	3.5	25%	0.0	0%
2019	10	76%	3.3	70.4	-3.9	-0.06	35%	2.7	25%	6.7	37%
2020	17	53%	6.0	67.7	-12.2	-0.23	28%	4.6	30%	6.2	20%
	30	64%	4.5	65.8	-21.2	-0.16	32%	3.9	28%	6.1	29%

Deep Dive

	Usage			Total Points						Total Points Rtg		
Year	Man%	Slot%	Press Cov%	Press	Slot	Wide	Cov Total	Run Def	Total	Per Cov	Per Run	Per Play
2018	42%	10%	-	-	0	7	9	2	11	99	90	99
2019	18%	13%	15%	10	4	23	27	11	39	90	71	79
2020	29%	18%	23%	8	1	33	31	17	49	96	85	88
	24%	15%	19%	18	5	63	67	30	99	-	-	-

Benjamin St-Juste Final Grade: 6.2

Report by Jeff Dean & Michael Churchward

School	Height	Weight	Year	Jersey #	Hometown
Minnesota	6033 V	200 V	5SR	25	Montreal, QUE, CAN

One Liner

St-Juste has the length, press ability, and ball skills teams look for in an outside cornerback, but without improved footwork at the top of routes and effort against the run, he may be limited to reserve duties.

Strengths: Length; Hand use in press; Catch point disruption
Weaknesses: Slot-coverage flexibility; Reactive footwork; Tunnel vision

Benjamin St-Juste is an outside cornerback in Minnesota's balanced coverage scheme. He played in 30 career games with 14 starts. He missed the entire 2018 season with a hamstring injury. He began his career at Michigan but was nearly forced to medically retire before grad-transferring to Minnesota in 2019. St-Juste has very good size with long limbs and solid muscle on his frame. He has sufficient deep speed but lacks acceleration and some reactive quickness. He is a hot-and-cold competitor who looks dejected when beaten and would be taken off the field after multiple bad plays.

St-Juste uses his long arms and strength to disrupt receivers in press-coverage. He struggles to match his footwork with his jam and can lose his advantage due to stagnant feet at the line. His length and sufficient reactive athleticism allow him to stick with receivers in press, aids he doesn't have when playing off. His hips are a little stiff laterally, but he flips well enough to turn and run deep. St-Juste has issues keeping up with speed downfield. He has a good understanding of zone coverage, but he can occupy his area too rigidly, not carrying exiting routes even without another threat and lacking the peripheral vision to sense other assignments. While he lacks turnover production, his length is a plus at the catch point to disrupt receivers and throwing lanes.

St-Juste is passive in the run game and is often late to reacting to the play, but he has the tackling ability and physicality to bring down ballcarriers when he attacks. His play diagnosis fluctuates and he doesn't work through blocks well, despite his size. He is able to wrap up efficiently but can sacrifice yards by sitting back for the ball.

St-Juste projects as a reserve versatile defensive back who fits as an outside press cornerback, but he could flex to safety with developed zone feel in the back end. He does not project well to the slot and is merely passable against the run, but his length and strength will allow him to see defensive and special teams snaps.

			Coverage							Tackling			
Year	Trgt	Comp	Comp%	Yds	Yds/Trgt	Int	Int Drops	TD Alwd	Tkls	TFL	Brk Tkl	BT%	
2017	0	0	-	0	-	0	0	0	1	0.0	0	0%	
2019	41	23	56%	310	7.6	0	1	2	37	1.5	1	3%	
2020	17	6	35%	112	6.6	0	1	1	15	0.0	2	12%	
	58	29	50%	422	7.3	0	2	3	53	1.5	3	5%	

		Coverage						Man		Zone		
Year	PBU	Deserved Catch %	YAC/Comp	Rating	EPA	EPA/Trgt	Pos%	Yds/Snap	Pos%	Yds/Snap	Pos%	
2017	0	-	-	0.0	0.0	-	-	-	-	-	-	
2019	12	67%	3.4	96.6	2.7	0.07	41%	7.4	35%	4.6	46%	
2020	3	64%	12.0	78.6	-5.3	-0.31	29%	14.2	33%	9.4	44%	
	15	66%	5.2	91.3	-2.6	-0.04	38%	8.9	35%	6.4	45%	

	Usage			Total Points						Total Points Rtg		
Year	Man%	Slot%	Press Cov%	Press	Slot	Wide	Cov Total	Run Def	Total	Per Cov	Per Run	Per Play
2019	34%	17%	23%	2	0	10	10	13	23	79	89	82
2020	43%	20%	21%	3	4	4	9	6	15	91	78	83
	37%	18%	22%	5	5	14	19	19	38	-	-	-

Critical Factors	
Reactive Athleticism	5
Play Speed	5
Ball Skills	6

Positional Factors	
Off-Man	6
Press-Man	7
Zone Coverage	5
Slot Coverage	3
Transition	5
Closing Speed	6
FBI	5
Mental Toughness	4
Open-Field Tackling	5
Play Strength	6
Run Support	4
ST Value	6

Trill Williams

Report by Stephen Marciello

School	Height	Weight	Year	Jersey #	Hometown
Syracuse	6006 E	198 E	3JR	6	Yonkers, NY

One Liner

Williams is a tough defender who excels in man-coverage and on-ball production, but aggressive eye discipline in zone and a lack of impact against the run will result in a backup role at the NFL level.

Strengths: Man coverage; On-ball production; Toughness
Weaknesses: Eye discipline; Tackling ability; Elite athleticism

Trill Williams is a tough, big-framed defensive back for the Syracuse's base 3-3-5. He mainly plays in the slot, but has also seen time outside and at safety. He started 15 of 28 career games for the Orange, opting out of the final 4 games after missing 2 with ankle and hamstring injuries. Williams has sneaky athleticism, though he possesses an average motor and sufficient competitiveness.

Williams surprises pass catchers with his reaction to shorter routes with good footwork and transition from the slot and to stay locked onto his man. When he presses from the slot, he shows physicality at the LOS. He can successfully reroute receivers of equal size and stay locked through an arm bar. Although he's more athletic than he appears, he struggles with smaller, quicker receivers. In zone, Williams tends to peek into the backfield and loses receivers in his area. Too many passes have been completed in or near his zone due to a lack of awareness. His closing speed is sufficient, but could improve if he can get his eyes out of the backfield. At safety, he does a better job holding his ground in his zone as opposed to cheating, as he understands that he's the last line of defense. Although he tends to ball watch, this has led to interceptions and pass breakups. He's dangerous with the ball in his hands with 3 defensive returns for touchdowns in his career.

Williams is sufficient in run support. While he has good toughness and play strength, he doesn't show much aggressiveness when attacking a ballcarrier. He appears content with keeping contain and forcing him back inside. His tackling technique has room to grow as he too often dives at the legs of the ballcarrier instead of attacking with fundamentals.

Williams projects best as a slot cornerback in a man coverage scheme who can excel in passing situations. He also has the versatility to be used as a free safety on the back end with his athleticism and instincts. He will be used most often on 3rd down out of the slot and will also see the field on special teams, especially on coverage units, due to his toughness.

	Coverage								Tackling			
Year	Trgt	Comp	Comp%	Yds	Yds/Trgt	Int	Int Drops	TD Alwd	Tkls	TFL	Brk Tkl	BT%
2018	24	11	46%	196	8.2	2	0	1	31	2.5	1	3%
2019	32	17	53%	223	7.0	1	0	0	35	0.0	6	15%
2020	14	8	57%	71	5.1	1	1	1	25	1.0	6	19%
	70	36	51%	490	7.0	4	1	2	91	3.5	13	13%

	Coverage							Man		Zone	
Year	PBU	Deserved Catch%	YAC/Comp	Rating	EPA	EPA/Trgt	Pos%	Yds/Snap	Pos%	Yds/Snap	Pos%
2018	2	83%	7.5	53.5	-1.2	-0.05	42%	7.4	46%	6.3	40%
2019	3	87%	4.5	62.4	4.8	0.15	50%	4.8	42%	5.8	58%
2020	4	75%	3.5	94.6	0.0	0.00	36%	4.5	33%	2.2	40%
	9	83%	5.2	65.8	3.6	0.05	44%	5.7	41%	5.1	50%

	Usage			Total Points						Total Points Rtg		
Year	Man%	Slot%	Press Cov%	Press	Slot	Wide	Cov Total	Run Def	Total	Per Cov	Per Run	Per Play
2018	44%	38%	-	-	2	4	7	8	16	75	85	76
2019	44%	70%	16%	-3	14	-4	9	10	20	74	80	76
2020	44%	81%	5%	2	2	0	3	2	6	68	58	62
	44%	63%	12%	0	19	1	19	20	42	-	-	-

Critical Factors

Reactive Athleticism	6
Play Speed	5
Ball Skills	6

Positional Factors

Off-Man	6
Press-Man	6
Zone Coverage	5
Slot Coverage	6
Transition	6
Closing Speed	5
FBI	5
Mental Toughness	5
Open-Field Tackling	5
Play Strength	6
Run Support	5
ST Value	6

Michael Carter II

Report by Evan Butler

School	Height	Weight	Year	Jersey #	Hometown
Duke	5095 E	190 E	4SR	26	Douglasville, GA

One Liner

Carter is a tough, versatile defensive back with good ball skills, but his lack of size and top-end speed limit his overall ability to contribute at the next level.

Strengths: Lateral agility; Ball skills; Tackling
Weaknesses: Top-end speed; Range; Size limitations

Michael Carter II is a slot cornerback in Duke's 4-2-5 Nickel scheme where he also saw time playing safety and occasionally slid outside as well. He played in 46 games in his career for the Blue Devils with starts in 36 of those games. Carter is a smart and instinctive player even for his smaller stature. He shows his toughness with his willingness to stick his nose in plays.

In the passing game, Carter is a good athlete with man skills. He is able to use his athleticism to mirror-match slot receivers. He has good length which he uses to press receivers at the line of scrimmage. He struggles covering physical receivers who can overpower him or receivers with elite speed, but can hold his own the majority of the time. However, Carter shows good lateral quickness and reactive athleticism to cover faster receivers in short areas. All his movements are very smooth, including his hip fluidity. In zone coverage, he very rarely guesses on routes and instead uses his instincts in reading the play. He doesn't allow traffic in front of him to distract him and stays disciplined in his coverage. He displays good reaction skills and a smooth transition to stick his foot in the ground, burst, and accelerate to make plays on the ball. His on-ball production mainly consists of pass breakups, but he can create the occasional turnover.

In the run game, Carter shows his physicality and toughness by sticking his nose in the play whenever possible. He is a good tackler, but his smaller frame can be a struggle to bring down bigger backs and receivers. He is good at navigating traffic to make plays. His good transition skills and experience at safety allow him to make plays in space.

Carter projects best as a slot corner in a press-man scheme who adds quality, depth, and versatility with his ability to also play as a safety. His best fit is playing press in the slot or covering the flats on 3rd downs. He has good tackling traits and even returned kickoffs which will allow him to be a contributor on most special teams units.

Year	Trgt	Comp	Comp%	Yds	Yds/Trgt	Int	Int Drops	TD Alwd	Tkls	TFL	Brk Tkl	BT%
				Coverage						**Tackling**		
2017	13	6	46%	127	9.8	0	0	2	10	2.5	2	17%
2018	35	13	37%	128	3.7	1	0	0	21	0.0	1	5%
2019	52	26	50%	253	4.9	1	0	2	52	2.0	9	15%
2020	41	17	41%	258	6.3	2	0	2	39	2.0	8	17%
	141	62	44%	766	5.4	4	0	6	122	6.5	20	14%

Year	PBU	Deserved Catch %	YAC/Comp	Rating	EPA	EPA/Trgt	Pos%	Yds/Snap	Pos%	Yds/Snap	Pos%
			Coverage					**Man**		**Zone**	
2017	2	70%	6.2	120.8	3.9	0.30	38%	-	-	-	-
2018	5	73%	3.2	36.4	-13.5	-0.39	31%	2.1	20%	3.9	41%
2019	9	81%	3.8	68.8	-4.3	-0.08	42%	4.2	34%	3.3	50%
2020	11	60%	4.4	69.0	1.2	0.03	37%	4.9	30%	2.8	44%
	27	71%	4.0	66.7	-12.7	-0.09	38%	4.0	29%	3.3	45%

Year	Man%	Slot%	Press Cov%	Press	Slot	Wide	Cov Total	Run Def	Total	Per Cov	Per Run	Per Play
	Usage				**Total Points**					**Total Points Rtg**		
2018	65%	29%	-	-	10	14	25	15	40	99	98	97
2019	61%	80%	17%	4	19	5	27	16	44	92	81	85
2020	63%	57%	25%	0	18	9	25	11	36	95	73	83
	63%	59%	20%	3	47	28	77	42	120	-	-	-

Critical Factors	
Reactive Athleticism	6
Play Speed	5
Ball Skills	6

Positional Factors	
Off-Man	5
Press-Man	6
Zone Coverage	5
Slot Coverage	6
Transition	6
Closing Speed	5
FBI	5
Mental Toughness	6
Open-Field Tackling	6
Play Strength	5
Run Support	5
ST Value	6

Tre Norwood

Report by John Todd

School	Height	Weight	Year	Jersey #	Hometown
Oklahoma	5117 V	192 V	4JR	13	Fort Smith, AR

One Liner

Norwood doesn't have the same high-level trigger quickness he showed before his knee injury, but his football intelligence and communication abilities will get him by while he further rebuilds his health and confidence.

Strengths: Awareness and communication; Ball skills; Ceiling when healthy

Weaknesses: Play strength; Reactive and transition quickness post-injury; Single-high range

Tre Norwood is a DB in Oklahoma's nickel defense. He started 24 of his 39 career games. Before tearing his ACL in 2019's preseason, he was a twitchy shutdown wide corner. He returned in 2020 to a safety/ slot corner role and slowly worked back into the lineup. He has standard size but short arms and a narrow frame. He lost the elite reactive quickness he once had but is still a sufficient change-of-direction athlete with passable long speed.

Norwood counters his lessened COD skills with very impressive FBI, route awareness, and communication skills. His downhill trigger from off-coverages is a tick later than before, but he still shows enough man-coverage ability to limit drastic separation against slot WRs. He is most comfortable out of a quarter turn. In zone, he does a great job of playing with his eyes to sense and anticipate. He has aggressive ball skills but his body frequently let down his FBI in 2020, leaving him a step slow to more production. He drops into the deep third smoothly, but he does not have his former extra gear to close to the sideline from single high.

Norwood is quick to key and break downhill against the run, often neglecting occasional last man of defense responsibilities. However, he's a very inconsistent tackler, largely due to his marginal play strength. He will throw a shoulder in at times or square up with decent form, but he lacks the strength and interest to fight through blocks or bring down larger ballcarriers.

Norwood most comfortably profiles to the slot and can to roll to two-high. His physicality, strength, and range will be a disqualifier for some at safety, and his current reactive quickness will give caution to playing him in man against the league's elite slots. However, his zone awareness and anticipatory ball skills will play as a versatile reserve while he hopefully regains some of his athleticism further removed from the injury. His speed and physicality don't project well to most ST units.

			Coverage							Tackling			
Year	Trgt	Comp	Comp%	Yds	Yds/ Trgt	Int	Int Drops	TD Alwd		Tkls	TFL	Brk Tkl	BT%
2017	42	24	57%	293	7.0	0	2	3		29	0.0	4	12%
2018	57	35	61%	498	8.7	1	0	1		45	2.0	16	26%
2020	24	9	38%	139	5.8	5	0	2		23	0.0	6	21%
	123	68	55%	930	7.6	6	2	6		97	2.0	26	21%

			Coverage						Man		Zone	
Year	PBU	Deserved Catch %	YAC/ Comp	Rating	EPA	EPA/ Trgt	Pos%		Yds/ Snap	Pos%	Yds/ Snap	Pos%
2017	9	74%	2.4	92.7	11.5	0.27	50%		-	-	-	-
2018	6	86%	2.9	88.2	19.8	0.35	51%		7.9	50%	6.8	58%
2020	9	65%	8.6	45.7	-21.6	-0.90	33%		3.9	40%	1.8	33%
	24	77%	3.5	75.6	9.8	0.08	47%		7.1	48%	4.9	50%

	Usage			Total Points						Total Points Rtg		
Year	Man%	Slot%	Press Cov%	Press	Slot	Wide	Cov Total	Run Def	Total	Per Cov	Per Run	Per Play
2018	40%	22%	-	-	8	7	15	20	38	76	93	84
2020	28%	28%	11%	-5	4	2	19	2	21	88	59	75
	34%	24%	11%	-5	13	9	34	22	59	-	-	-

Critical Factors	
Reactive Athleticism	5
Play Speed	5
Ball Skills	6

Positional Factors	
Off-Man	5
Press-Man	5
Zone Coverage	6
Slot Coverage	5
Transition	5
Closing Speed	5
FBI	7
Mental Toughness	6
Open-Field Tackling	4
Play Strength	3
Run Support	5
ST Value	4

DJ Daniel

Report by Chad Tedder

School	Height	Weight	Year	Jersey #	Hometown
Georgia	5115 V	183 V	4SR	14	Griffin, GA

One Liner

Daniel has the instincts and zone coverage ability to see snaps situationally, but his lack of versatility and consistent ball skills will keep him in a backup role.

Strengths: Smart with good instincts; Zone discipline; Sure tackling
Weaknesses: Top-end speed; Ball skills; Grabby

DJ Daniel is a corner in Georgia's nickel defense, where he played predominantly out on the boundary to the left or right side depending upon the drive and rotation of its corners. He played in 21 games, starting 11 for the Bulldogs over the previous 2 seasons after spending his first 2 seasons at Georgia Military College. He has decent length and good physicality combined with his athleticism to be a cornerback. However, his toughness and competitiveness leave something to be desired.

Against the pass, Daniel starts plays with patient and controlled footwork and does a good job at reading routes, especially in zone coverage. He shows good spatial awareness to feel the routes around him and not getting caught with his eyes in the backfield. He doesn't possess great speed which leaves him vulnerable when a receiver gets over the top of him. He can stay close when beat, but lacks the ball skills to make a play at the catch point. He uses good footwork to read the receiver's underneath routes and use some hand fighting to redirect, and interrupt, their routes. In man, he shows decent athleticism in jamming, turning, and staying in-phase off the snap. However, he often gets handsy when trying to stay with receivers which could leave him open to getting penalized against top competition.

Against the run, Daniel does a decent job at working off stalk blocks to get his body into position to wrap up ballcarriers out on the edge. However, there are instances where he lacks the aggression to shed and allows for rushers to get to him up the field before trying to make a tackle. He doesn't miss many tackles, but doesn't have a ton of power behind his pads to make a solid hit.

Daniel best projects as a No. 4 corner at the next level, playing predominantly outside in a zone-heavy scheme. On 3rd downs, he can be a plus player in dime packages where he can read and react to make a solid tackle in space. He has a good mix of length, speed, and physicality to be a solid option as a jammer or in coverage on special teams.

Year			Coverage							Tackling			
	Trgt	Comp	Comp%	Yds	Yds/Trgt	Int	Int Drops	TD Alwd		Tkls	TFL	Brk Tkl	BT%
2019	52	26	50%	385	7.4	0	1	3		42	2.0	2	5%
2020	9	3	33%	46	5.1	0	0	1		8	1.0	0	0%
	61	29	48%	431	7.1	0	1	4		50	3.0	2	4%

Year		Coverage							Man		Zone	
	PBU	Deserved Catch %	YAC/Comp	Rating	EPA	EPA/Trgt	Pos%	Yds/Snap	Pos%	Yds/Snap	Pos%
2019	8	68%	3.7	93.8	5.7	0.11	44%	7.5	44%	7.0	44%
2020	1	67%	2.7	88.2	-0.3	-0.04	33%	9.0	25%	1.1	40%
	9	67%	3.6	93.0	5.4	0.09	43%	7.7	41%	5.6	44%

Year		Usage			Total Points					Total Points Rtg		
	Man%	Slot%	Press Cov%	Press	Slot	Wide	Cov Total	Run Def	Total	Per Cov	Per Run	Per Play
2019	49%	12%	42%	4	1	18	19	12	32	84	88	81
2020	34%	10%	41%	1	0	2	2	4	6	69	98	79
	46%	12%	42%	5	1	20	21	16	38	-	-	-

Critical Factors	
Reactive Athleticism	6
Play Speed	5
Ball Skills	5

Positional Factors	
Off-Man	6
Press-Man	5
Zone Coverage	6
Slot Coverage	5
Transition	5
Closing Speed	5
FBI	6
Mental Toughness	5
Open-Field Tackling	6
Play Strength	5
Run Support	5
ST Value	6

Kelvin Joseph

Report by Stephen Marciello

School	Height	Weight	Year	Jersey #	Hometown
Kentucky	6006 E	192 E	3SO	1	Baton Rouge, LA

One Liner
Joseph is a confident, tough, and physical defender who should make an impact as a press-man corner, but a lack of speed and awareness in zone coverage will likely lead him to filling a backup role.

Strengths: Physicality; Press coverage; Tackling
Weaknesses: Top-end speed; Zone awareness; Susceptible to double moves

Kelvin Joseph primarily lines up at outside corner in Kentucky's 3-4/3-3-5 hybrid defense playing a balance of zone and man coverage while also lining up in the slot and some at safety. He played 11 games for LSU in 2018 before transferring to Kentucky and starting all 9 games in 2020, opting out of their final 2 games. Joseph is a solid athlete with good COD ability and reactive athleticism. He plays bigger than his frame with a high motor and competitiveness.

Joseph has an impactful punch in press that he times well right at the snap and does a good job knocking the receiver off his intended route stem. Although he doesn't have elite speed, he understands his strengths and uses his body and strength to stay with bigger receivers. In off-man, he transitions well to break on routes as well as to turn and run down the field. He is prone to double moves in off-man and bites on most breaks. He shows good ball skills at the catch point to create turnovers. In zone, Joseph's biggest tendency is peeking into the backfield instead of feeling what's going on around him. He also fails to communicate when receivers leave his zone. Most commonly in Cover 2, he stays with receivers too long before passing off which allows another receiver underneath to come open. Overall, Joseph always shows confidence and loves to get in the ear of the receiver, however this has led to unfortunate penalties.

Against the run, Joseph is a willing and aggressive tackler. He loves to hit from the corner position and let the ballcarrier know about it afterwards. He understands tackling angles well and, while he looks to deliver a big hit, he also shows good form. He can consistently shed stalk blocks and never gives in.

Joseph projects as a No. 4 cornerback at the next level who has the flex to play outside or in the slot in a primary man coverage scheme. On 3rd downs, he fits best outside in press where he can use his size and physicality. With his plus toughness and tackling ability in space, he should be an asset on special teams coverage units.

			Coverage						Tackling			
Year	Trgt	Comp	Comp%	Yds	Yds/Trgt	Int	Int Drops	TD Alwd	Tkls	TFL	Brk Tkl	BT%
2018	15	8	53%	119	7.9	0	1	1	13	0.0	4	24%
2020	32	15	47%	243	7.6	4	0	3	32	0.5	4	11%
	47	23	49%	362	7.7	4	1	4	45	0.5	8	15%

		Coverage						Man		Zone	
Year	PBU	Deserved Catch %	YAC/Comp	Rating	EPA	EPA/Trgt	Pos%	Yds/Snap	Pos%	Yds/Snap	Pos%
2018	0	89%	1.9	74.0	5.2	0.35	53%	7.9	57%	11.0	50%
2020	5	73%	6.8	65.0	-1.1	-0.03	47%	10.5	55%	6.1	50%
	5	77%	5.1	67.9	4.1	0.09	49%	9.0	56%	6.7	50%

	Usage			Total Points					Total Points Rtg		
Year	Man%	Slot%	Press Cov%	Press	Slot	Wide	Cov Total	Run Def	Total	Per Cov	Per Run	Per Play
2018	61%	18%	-	-	-1	-1	-1	4	3	56	88	68
2020	21%	23%	10%	0	1	15	16	15	32	89	89	86
	33%	21%	10%	0	0	15	15	19	35	-	-	-

Critical Factors	
Reactive Athleticism	6
Play Speed	5
Ball Skills	6

Positional Factors	
Off-Man	5
Press-Man	6
Zone Coverage	4
Slot Coverage	5
Transition	6
Closing Speed	5
FBI	5
Mental Toughness	6
Open-Field Tackling	7
Play Strength	6
Run Support	6
ST Value	6

Brandin Echols

Report by Carter Hayden & Nathan Cooper

School	Height	Weight	Year	Jersey #	Hometown
Kentucky	5106 E	178 E	4SR	26	Southaven, MS

One Liner
Echols has the speed, press ability, and zone coverage skills to make an impact at the next level, though his read-react ability and sufficient transition skills are likely what will hold him back.

Strengths: Closing speed; Hand use; Zone coverage
Weaknesses: Pursuit angles; Reaction time; Diagnosing plays

Brandin Echols is the field cornerback in Kentucky's 3-4/3-3-5 defense, which plays a lot of zone coverage, but also took snaps in the slot. He started 22 of 24 games for the Wildcats after playing his first 2 seasons at Northwest Mississippi CC. Echols has a slight frame with long arms. He possesses good speed and plays more physical than his size might indicate.

In press, Echols understands good leverage points and does a good job of being physical at the line, though he tends to grab and push more than he needs to at times. He shows good technique and can flip his hips and break with receivers possessing the speed to stick with most of them. In off-man, he's a little slow to react to and transition against in-breaking routes to make plays at the catch point. However, his closing speed or 2nd gear is one of his best traits when he gets beaten. He can track the ball and affect it at the catch point, but can get boxed out by bigger targets. In zone, he shows the ability to read the quarterback's

eyes. He knows where he has help and does a good job of jumping routes that are near his area in which he can force pass breakups or interceptions.

Echols shows no fear in taking on blocks and can be a very hard hitter. However, he doesn't always show the willingness to stick his nose in near the trenches or large piles. His ability to make tackles in open space is merely sufficient as he likes to dive at the legs of ballcarriers too often instead of wrap up.

Echols projects as a No. 4 cornerback who fits best on the outside in a zone-heavy defensive scheme with some press-man mixed in. He can also slide into the slot on occasion to press and/or use his speed to stay with slot receivers. On 3rd downs, he fits best on the outside in a Cover 2 or Cover 3 look where he can use his zone instincts and eye discipline to jump routes. His skill set with the speed he has should allow him to play on special teams.

Coverage / Tackling

Year	Trgt	Comp	Comp%	Yds	Yds/Trgt	Int	Int Drops	TD Alwd	Tkls	TFL	Brk Tkl	BT%
2019	60	24	40%	246	4.1	0	1	3	56	3.5	8	13%
2020	32	22	69%	268	8.4	1	1	3	53	2.0	9	15%
	92	46	50%	514	5.6	1	2	6	109	5.5	17	13%

Coverage / Man / Zone

Year	PBU	Deserved Catch %	YAC/Comp	Rating	EPA	EPA/Trgt	Pos%	Yds/Snap	Pos%	Yds/Snap	Pos%
2019	11	76%	1.4	55.3	-12.6	-0.21	35%	1.6	22%	5.2	43%
2020	2	89%	3.0	112.5	10.3	0.32	56%	10.7	71%	5.5	59%
	13	82%	2.2	75.2	-2.3	-0.03	42%	4.5	36%	5.3	48%

Usage / Total Points / Total Points Rtg

Year	Man%	Slot%	Press Cov%	Press	Slot	Wide	Cov Total	Run Def	Total	Per Cov	Per Run	Per Play
2019	21%	23%	24%	6	4	27	31	17	51	97	88	94
2020	18%	26%	8%	-1	4	6	11	16	27	74	85	77
	19%	25%	16%	5	8	34	42	33	78	-	-	-

Critical Factors
Reactive Athleticism	5
Play Speed	6
Ball Skills	6

Positional Factors
Off-Man	5
Press-Man	6
Zone Coverage	6
Slot Coverage	6
Transition	5
Closing Speed	6
FBI	5
Mental Toughness	6
Open-Field Tackling	5
Play Strength	5
Run Support	5
ST Value	7

Thomas Graham Jr.

Report by Nathan Cooper

School	Height	Weight	Year	Jersey #	Hometown
Oregon	5104 V	193 V	4SR	4	Rancho Cucamonga, CA

One Liner
Graham has the patience, ball skills, and zone coverage ability to see playing time at the next level, but his tight hips, lack of consistent transition ability, and tackling woes likely force him to be a backup.

Strengths: Zone disruption; Ball skills; Doesn't get flustered
Weaknesses: Tight hips; Struggles to transition cleanly; Lacks twitch

Thomas Graham Jr. is a field cornerback for Oregon's primary 3-3-5 defense mainly playing zone coverage. He started 39 of 40 games for the Ducks, though he opted out of the entire 2020 season. He's a solid athlete who has good straight-line speed, but lacks burst and isn't super twitchy. He plays hard and competes with toughness throughout his play, though it's questionable in the run game.

In zone, Graham shows good eye discipline to read the quarterback and break on receivers in his area. He has good awareness and gets physical with receivers running through his zone. As a man defender, he lacks the reactive athleticism and transition ability to consistently stay with receivers out of the top of their routes. He shows a fairly quick backpedal, but is a little high at times. Tight hips make it tough for him to transition, especially once he's already flipped them. He shows patience, but will bail too early at times to compensate for his lack of speed. In press, he gives up too many free releases at the line. If beaten, he shows sufficient closing speed, and if he's in phase when the ball comes, he has a good chance to make a play on it.

Graham doesn't show great aggression toward the LOS and mainly only helps out when necessary. If the play comes his way, he does a good job as a force defender to turn ballcarriers back toward his teammates and will get in on the tackle if needed. As a tackler, too many times he dips his head and dives at the feet of the ballcarrier causing him to miss on too many opportunities.

Graham projects as a No. 4 outside cornerback at the next level in a primary zone scheme, though could slide into the slot to guard tight ends. On 3rd downs, he fits best outside in zone coverage where he can sit and read the eyes of the quarterback and use his ball skills to disrupt routes. He could contribute some on special teams, but likely won't be a core contributor due to inconsistent tackling ability and willingness in the run game.

			Coverage							Tackling			
Year	Trgt	Comp	Comp%	Yds	Yds/Trgt	Int	Int Drops	TD Alwd	Tkls	TFL	Brk Tkl	BT%
2017	79	40	51%	715	9.1	3	1	4	60	1.0	7	10%
2018	74	32	43%	552	7.5	3	1	5	54	4.0	4	7%
2019	62	33	53%	361	5.8	2	2	2	65	5.0	12	16%
	215	105	49%	1628	7.6	8	4	11	179	10.0	23	11%

		Coverage						Man		Zone	
Year	PBU	Deserved Catch %	YAC/Comp	Rating	EPA	EPA/Trgt	Pos%	Yds/Snap	Pos%	Yds/Snap	Pos%
2017	8	80%	4.7	83.0	10.9	0.14	41%	-	-	-	-
2018	19	64%	2.5	74.8	-13.7	-0.18	42%	6.3	32%	7.4	55%
2019	9	76%	2.0	68.0	-14.7	-0.24	39%	4.1	30%	5.1	38%
	36	73%	3.2	75.9	-17.4	-0.08	40%	5.4	31%	6.2	47%

	Usage				Total Points					Total Points Rtg		
Year	Man%	Slot%	Press Cov%	Press	Slot	Wide	Cov Total	Run Def	Total	Per Cov	Per Run	Per Play
2018	54%	13%	-	-	3	25	28	19	47	87	91	85
2019	38%	13%	28%	21	1	47	48	16	65	99	86	93
	46%	13%	28%	21	4	72	76	35	112	-	-	-

Critical Factors	
Reactive Athleticism	5
Play Speed	5
Ball Skills	6

Positional Factors	
Off-Man	5
Press-Man	5
Zone Coverage	6
Slot Coverage	5
Transition	5
Closing Speed	5
FBI	6
Mental Toughness	6
Open-Field Tackling	5
Play Strength	5
Run Support	5
ST Value	5

Deommodore Lenoir

Report by Jeremy Percy

School	Height	Weight	Year	Jersey #	Hometown
Oregon	5106 E	195 E	4SR	0	Los Angeles, CA

One Liner
Lenoir's football intelligence and toughness for his size are commendable traits, as well as his starting experience at a top program, but his lack of twitchy athleticism may keep him as a reserve.

Strengths: Press-man; Football intelligence; Staying in phase on deep routes
Weaknesses: Transition to mirror deep breaks; Closing speed; Reactive athleticism

Deommodore Lenoir is a boundary cornerback in Oregon's diverse coverage defense. He played in 47 career games and started all 34 the past 3 seasons. He has a smaller frame but plays and moves bigger than his size, with good toughness and physicality as well as limited reactive agility to change directions. He is a smart and vocal leader in the back end.

Lenoir is best when playing press-man coverage. He likes to get into the chest of the receiver and keep contact for as long as possible. Lenoir is sufficient at playing off coverages but often allows too much separation when doing so and lacks the closing speed to make up the ground lost. He is good in zone coverage and usually positions himself correctly to the flats in Cover 2 and deep third in Cover 3. He bumped to the slot somewhat regularly at Oregon but his difficulty matching receivers' quickness at the top of routes makes him an uncomfortable fit inside. Lenoir does well to flip his hips out of a backpedal deep, but his stiff lower half makes it difficult for him to transitionally recover after already

committing his hips. He takes false steps to break downhill and is a tick slow in his closing speed to recover separation. He shows decent ball skills attacking the catch point with aggression, and shows natural hands after an elite two-way prep career.

Lenoir does his job in the run game but doesn't go out of his way to make plays. He showed a bit more hesitancy to play the run his senior year than in previous campaigns. He does a good job of keeping his outside hand free and playing contain and is usually a good open-field tackler to strike for his size. He stays engaged mentally and doesn't back down from a physical challenge in either phase.

Lenoir projects as a good depth outside cornerback in any scheme, but ideally playing mostly zone. He is experienced, tough, and smart, but he hasn't shown to be sudden enough to consistently see the field and match up with top receivers. He can be a very serviceable special teams player with his long speed and physicality.

Year			Coverage						Tackling			
				Yds/		Int	TD				Brk	
Year	Trgt	Comp	Comp%	Yds	Trgt	Int	Drops	Alwd	Tkls	TFL	Tkl	BT%
2017	37	21	57%	326	8.8	1	1	4	22	1.5	0	0%
2018	70	36	51%	466	6.7	3	1	5	53	0.0	7	12%
2019	67	35	52%	488	7.3	1	0	3	50	2.5	6	11%
2020	26	13	50%	104	4.0	1	0	1	32	0.0	2	6%
	200	105	53%	1384	6.9	6	2	13	157	4.0	15	9%

Year		Coverage						Man		Zone	
		Deserved	YAC/			EPA/		Yds/		Yds/	
Year	PBU	Catch %	Comp	Rating	EPA	Trgt	Pos%	Snap	Pos%	Snap	Pos%
2017	7	79%	5.6	99.6	15.5	0.42	54%	-	-	-	-
2018	11	77%	2.4	72.7	2.0	0.03	47%	5.7	42%	4.5	48%
2019	7	86%	4.4	84.7	12.4	0.18	42%	7.3	53%	6.3	33%
2020	1	88%	1.0	57.2	-7.9	-0.30	38%	3.2	33%	1.6	25%
	26	82%	3.5	79.7	22.0	0.11	46%	5.8	44%	5.2	38%

Year	Usage			Total Points					Total Points Rtg		
			Press				Cov	Run		Per	Per	Per
Year	Man%	Slot%	Cov%	Press	Slot	Wide	Total	Def	Total	Cov	Run	Play
2018	52%	24%	-	-	6	17	24	18	42	84	88	81
2019	39%	23%	38%	14	0	15	16	16	34	78	89	80
2020	39%	35%	42%	12	8	13	22	9	31	97	77	86
	44%	26%	40%	26	14	46	62	43	107	-	-	-

Critical Factors	
Reactive Athleticism	5
Play Speed	6
Ball Skills	5

Positional Factors	
Off-Man	5
Press-Man	6
Zone Coverage	6
Slot Coverage	5
Transition	4
Closing Speed	5
FBI	6
Mental Toughness	6
Open-Field Tackling	6
Play Strength	5
Run Support	5
ST Value	6

Nate Hobbs

Report by Max Nuscher

School	Height	Weight	Year	Jersey #	Hometown
Illinois	5114 V	189 V	4SR	8	Louisville, KY

One Liner
Hobbs has a well-rounded skill set to succeed at the next level, but he lacks elite traits and needs to improve his ball skills to make an impact.

Strengths: Transition quickness; Zone coverage; Run support aggression
Weaknesses: Press technique; Locating the ball in the air; Consistent tackling form

Nate Hobbs typically plays outside cornerback in Illinois' base defense frequently playing zone coverage. He played in 39 games, starting 35 of them. He was suspended for 3 games his sophomore year due to violations of team rules and missed a game with a shoulder injury in 2020. He has a long and narrow frame. He was a high jumper and long jumper in high school and shows good athleticism with some quick-twitch ability. He plays with aggression when the ball enters his area.

In the passing game, Hobbs plays mainly off-man and zone coverage. He has the length to disrupt receivers in press but struggles with his punch timing and accuracy. He is good at matching the movements of receivers and has the speed to stay in phase deep. When receivers do get past him, he has good flexibility to transition and recover. In zone coverage, he is good at feeling where players are and doesn't cover grass. He plays on his toes and is twitchy to hop between assignments. His route recognition and closing speed allow him to read underneath routes, and he has good eye discipline to not fall for pump fakes. He showed decent ball skills to break up passes in previous seasons but struggled to get his head around and locate the ball to compete at the catch point in 2020.

In the run game, Hobbs possesses a strong willingness and aggression to attack the LOS in the run game. He has no fear in working against tight ends and pulling linemen. His length and strength allow him to stack a bit but he isn't always able to shed. His aggression has led to a high volume of tackles, but his form can be inconsistent.

Hobbs projects as a No. 4 corner on the outside, but he has some flexibility to the slot with his quick footwork. He is a strong zone corner but has the traits to develop his man skills and is not scheme specific. He will be a very strong special teams member based on his aggressive run support and play speed. He also was a kick and punt returner early in his career to modest success.

						Coverage							Tackling			
Year	Trgt	Comp	Comp%	Yds	Yds/Trgt	Int	Int Drops	TD Alwd	Tkls	TFL	Brk Tkl	BT%				
2017	45	27	60%	342	7.6	0	0	2	44	3.0	2	4%				
2018	15	9	60%	115	7.7	1	1	1	23	3.5	7	23%				
2019	60	28	47%	373	6.2	1	1	3	66	5.5	5	7%				
2020	24	21	88%	285	11.9	1	0	2	33	2.0	3	8%				
	144	85	59%	1115	7.7	3	2	8	166	14.0	17	9%				

		Coverage						Man		Zone	
Year	PBU	Deserved Catch %	YAC/Comp	Rating	EPA	EPA/Trgt	Pos%	Yds/Snap	Pos%	Yds/Snap	Pos%
2017	7	82%	4.3	80.0	4.6	0.10	51%	-	-	-	-
2018	1	83%	8.4	106.3	2.1	0.14	47%	7.5	54%	1.0	0%
2019	13	70%	2.2	62.7	-10.9	-0.18	42%	4.6	31%	4.2	39%
2020	3	91%	2.2	126.6	14.3	0.59	79%	17.4	88%	7.9	73%
	24	79%	3.5	84.7	10.0	0.07	51%	8.3	51%	5.0	46%

	Usage			Total Points						Total Points Rtg		
Year	Man%	Slot%	Press Cov%	Press	Slot	Wide	Cov Total	Run Def	Total	Per Cov	Per Run	Per Play
2018	54%	23%	-	-	5	8	13	12	25	89	88	86
2019	26%	21%	30%	3	4	8	12	32	44	76	94	86
2020	19%	13%	18%	-5	-5	6	1	8	10	63	90	75
	32%	20%	26%	-2	4	21	26	52	79	-	-	

Critical Factors	
Reactive Athleticism	5
Play Speed	6
Ball Skills	5

Positional Factors	
Off-Man	6
Press-Man	5
Zone Coverage	6
Slot Coverage	5
Transition	6
Closing Speed	6
FBI	5
Mental Toughness	6
Open-Field Tackling	5
Play Strength	5
Run Support	6
ST Value	7

Shakur Brown

Report by John Todd

School	Height	Weight	Year	Jersey #	Hometown
Michigan State	5106 E	190 E	4JR	29	Stockbridge, GA

One Liner

Brown is a feisty, physical zone corner with ball skills and a tenacity to play the run, but limited reactive athleticism and lapses in awareness and judgement could keep him from seeing the field consistently.

Strengths: Anticipation in zone; Closing speed and physicality; Ball skills
Weaknesses: Assignment lapses; Reactive athleticism; Keeping his emotions in check

Shakur Brown is a cornerback in Michigan State's balanced nickel defense, with experience in the slot and out wide on both sides. He played in 26 games with 12 starts. He missed 6 games in 2019 due to undisclosed injuries. Brown had a good frame with solid bulk and athleticism. He's extremely physical and tough for the position, occasionally to a fault.

In press-man coverage, missing with his jam or falling for a good release against quickness plagued Brown at times. He's better in press than off though, where he can be active and use his physicality to help stay connected. He has good enough speed to stay step-for-step with most receivers and fluid hips to turn and run, but his spotty reactive quickness and physical nature leads to getting handsy in desperate situations. In zone, Brown plays with great eye discipline to key the QB's load and jump routes. He does a good job of sinking from the flats and covering space, while also having very impressive closing speed to check downs or through the catch point, showing off natural ball skills. His instincts are usually solid, but he's had pre- and post-snap communication issues, flipped his hips the wrong way, and quizzically lost track of receivers in his area.

Brown overpowers stalk blockers to the play side and forces well but prefers to stick his nose in and make hits himself. He counters his share of poor technique lunges with massive hits. He often let negative plays in coverage carry over to the next rep, where he'd focus only on beating up his blocker and lose sight of the ball as it went right past him. He is a pest whose chippiness is an asset when he can toe the line of his emotions.

Brown projects as a reserve zone corner at the next level, whose tenacity in run defense and underneath coverage skill set could fit best in the slot despite his struggles against quickness. If he focuses on flat and hook zone responsibilities where he can key the backfield and make physical plays in front of him, he can be an impactful backup. His toughness projects well to special teams coverage units.

Year	Coverage									Tackling			
	Trgt	Comp	Comp%	Yds	Yds/Trgt	Int	Int Drops	TD Alwd		Tkls	TFL	Brk Tkl	BT%
2018	5	0	0%	0	0.0	1	0	0		1	0.0	0	0%
2019	32	14	44%	231	7.2	1	1	2		19	2.0	2	10%
2020	35	19	54%	272	7.8	5	0	1		24	0.0	5	17%
	72	33	46%	503	7.0	7	1	3		44	2.0	7	14%

Year	Coverage							Man		Zone	
	PBU	Deserved Catch %	YAC/Comp	Rating	EPA	EPA/Trgt	Pos%	Yds/Snap	Pos%	Yds/Snap	Pos%
2018	1	0%	-	0.0	-13.4	-2.69	0%	-	-	0.0	0%
2019	5	80%	1.7	63.4	-5.4	-0.17	34%	4.9	29%	7.0	42%
2020	9	76%	5.8	49.6	-1.1	-0.03	46%	4.3	33%	6.9	48%
	15	76%	4.1	43.7	-19.9	-0.28	38%	4.6	31%	6.4	41%

Year	Usage			Total Points						Total Points Rtg		
	Man%	Slot%	Press Cov%	Press	Slot	Wide	Cov Total	Run Def	Total	Per Cov	Per Run	Per Play
2018	23%	23%	-	-	4	5	9	1	10	99	90	99
2019	27%	19%	42%	6	2	1	3	5	12	67	80	75
2020	32%	39%	21%	2	11	9	21	13	33	95	90	90
	30%	30%	31%	7	17	15	33	19	55	-	-	-

Critical Factors	
Reactive Athleticism	5
Play Speed	5
Ball Skills	6

Positional Factors	
Off-Man	4
Press-Man	5
Zone Coverage	6
Slot Coverage	5
Transition	5
Closing Speed	7
FBI	5
Mental Toughness	4
Open-Field Tackling	6
Play Strength	6
Run Support	7
ST Value	6

Olaijah Griffin

Final Grade: 5.9

Report by Jeff Dean & Jarrett Rodgers

✳

School	Height	Weight	Year	Jersey #	Hometown
USC	6002 E	175 E	3JR	2	Long Beach, CA

One Liner

Griffin has the athleticism and coverage understanding to compete for time on the perimeter, but he will need to improve his technique and physicality to make an impact.

Strengths: Breaking downhill; Vertical transition and speed; Zone awareness

Weaknesses: Physicality at the line; Containing when leveraged; Producing impactful plays

Olaijah Griffin is an outside cornerback in USC's base nickel defense. He played in 25 career games with 15 starts. He missed 4 games in 2018 with labrum injuries to both shoulders and missed 2 in 2019 with back spasms. Griffin is a good straight-line athlete with fluid hips. He has sufficient size but will need to continue adding muscle throughout his frame. He is a tough competitor who has fought back from multiple injuries to earn a starting role.

Griffin doesn't have the play strength to control receivers through a jam. He is a good reactive athlete and transitions well vertically, but horizontal breaking routes give him issues. He often fails to contain against crossers when leveraged to the inside himself and can lose a step mirroring to sharp cuts. Griffin has the speed to stick with receivers downfield and looks more relaxed when playing off-man. He shows quick feet and sound technique at the top of routes to break on the ball with force. Griffin quickly diagnoses plays and has good zone awareness to recognize route concepts while still keeping his eyes on the quarterback. He tends to get a little handsy and is vulnerable to penalties but typically minimizes separation with a good burst. He has enough ball skills to pester through the catch point and force incompletions, but he struggles to convert deflections into interceptions. He has issues competing against above-the-rim targets.

Griffin isn't active in run support and will let bigger receivers bully him. He plays with discipline and keeps contain but doesn't often take initiative upfield. Griffin is a sufficient tackler but struggles bringing down bigger targets by himself and flashes inconsistent technique.

Olaijah Griffin projects as a top reserve CB who can play in either a man or zone scheme. While he isn't a major liability to play in the slot, he fits best outside where he can use his deep speed and reactive quickness most comfortably. He has good fourth-down experience and should be a sufficient special teams player on certain units.

Coverage / Tackling

Year	Trgt	Comp	Comp%	Yds	Yds/Trgt	Int	Int Drops	TD Alwd	Tkls	TFL	Brk Tkl	BT%
2018	9	5	56%	80	8.9	0	1	2	7	1.0	1	13%
2019	44	17	39%	200	4.5	0	1	1	38	0.5	3	7%
2020	18	8	44%	90	5.0	1	1	0	22	1.0	4	15%
	71	30	42%	370	5.2	1	3	3	67	2.5	8	11%

Coverage / Man / Zone

Year	PBU	Deserved Catch%	YAC/Comp	Rating	EPA	EPA/Trgt	Pos%	Man Yds/Snap	Man Pos%	Zone Yds/Snap	Zone Pos%
2018	1	86%	0.6	125.0	2.0	0.22	33%	10.0	38%	0.0	0%
2019	8	59%	1.0	60.8	-8.6	-0.20	32%	3.5	32%	3.1	29%
2020	4	64%	3.8	36.8	-6.6	-0.36	33%	4.9	25%	4.5	50%
	13	64%	1.7	67.2	-13.2	-0.19	32%	5.3	31%	3.2	32%

Usage / Total Points / Total Points Rtg

Year	Man%	Slot%	Press Cov%	Press	Slot	Wide	Cov Total	Run Def	Total	Per Cov	Per Run	Per Play
2018	71%	8%	-	-	-3	-4	-7	1	-6	50	55	50
2019	33%	19%	28%	8	1	25	26	11	38	93	82	86
2020	39%	18%	38%	5	3	9	12	10	22	86	88	82
	37%	18%	32%	13	1	30	31	22	54	-	-	-

Critical Factors	
Reactive Athleticism	5
Play Speed	6
Ball Skills	5

Positional Factors	
Off-Man	6
Press-Man	5
Zone Coverage	6
Slot Coverage	5
Transition	5
Closing Speed	6
FBI	6
Mental Toughness	5
Open-Field Tackling	5
Play Strength	4
Run Support	4
ST Value	5

Robert Rochell

Report by Evan Butler

School	Height	Weight	Year	Jersey #	Hometown
Central Arkansas	5117 V	195 V	5SR	9	Shreveport, LA

One Liner

Rochell has all the physical tools and traits, but has limitations with his technique which will need refinemen and development before he can have a consistent impact.

Strengths: Size/speed combo; Length; Tackling
Weaknesses: Zone coverage; FBI; Technique

Robert Rochell is an outside cornerback in the nickel defense of Central Arkansas playing primarily press-man coverage. He has started in 31 of the 42 games played in his 4 seasons for the Bears. Rochell has good size and is a very good athlete with raw talent. He plays fast, tough, and physical, though at times his motor is less than desired.

In the passing game, Rochell's athleticism shines. He has the length and physicality to jam receivers at the LOS and the speed to play sticky downfield. If he fails to jam off the line, he can struggle to recover and make up ground. His short-area quickness and ball skills allow him to make plays on the ball consistently. Out of his backpedal, he has an easier transition and fluid hips. He shows a tougher time transitioning at the top of routes with his back to the LOS as receivers are effective in any direction they choose. When playing zone, he can struggle reading space and the play overall, playing too hesitant. He has sufficient FBI, but relies more on athleticism for his success than his instincts.

In the run game, he has willingness to take o blockers, but struggles to shed in attempting to mak plays. His pad level can get high to the point he lose leverages and gets completely washed out. He's good tackler in space. Rochell shows physicalit when called upon and will stick his nose in the play though his back-side pursuit and motor is low especially when the play isn't near him. Additionally he doesn't always take a great angle at the ballcarrie leaving outside gaps open for big plays.

Rochell projects as a No. 4 cornerback at the nex level who has the versatility to play inside or out in mainly press-man scheme. His physicality at th LOS and his limitations in zone would see a ma scheme suit him best. On 3rd downs, he can use hi length, toughness, and athleticism to press at the lin either in the slot or out wide. All of his physical trai will allow him to compete on every special team unit.

Robert Rochell garnered some attention for a video he posted on social media of him utilizing his skill as a track athlete and jumping flat-footed onto the top of a pickup truck. That's one way to get noticed when you come from a small school. Another is to be a first-team All-American cornerback with high-end speed.

Rochell could be the sixth player selected from Central Arkansas since 2010, the most recent of those being Chiefs wide receiver Tremon Smith who was selected in the sixth round in 2018. Every Bears player is chasing the success of football alumni Monte Coleman, who spent 16 seasons in the NFL as a linebacker, and Willie Davis, an eight-year wide receiver.

Critical Factors	
Reactive Athleticism	5
Play Speed	6
Ball Skills	6

Positional Factors	
Off-Man	4
Press-Man	6
Zone Coverage	5
Slot Coverage	6
Transition	5
Closing Speed	5
FBI	5
Mental Toughness	6
Open-Field Tackling	6
Play Strength	5
Run Support	4
ST Value	6

Camryn Bynum

Report by Ty Dorner

School	Height	Weight	Year	Jersey #	Hometown
California	6003 V	198 V	5SR	24	Corona, CA

One Liner

Bynum is a tough competitor who possesses good speed, toughness, and zone coverage ability, but a lack of man coverage efficiency and transition ability likely affect how much defensive field time he sees.

Strengths: Zone coverage; Run support; Special teams ability
Weaknesses: Hip mobility; Double move susceptibility; Smooth backpedal

Camryn Bynum is a cornerback in California's nickel defense that mainly runs zone coverage looks, lining up on the opponent's boundary. He started all 42 games with the Golden Bears, never missing a game. He has a good frame with a solid build for the position. He plays with toughness, a high motor, and with confidence, all of which will lead him to being a strong competitor.

In the pass game, Bynum mainly uses a bail technique and doesn't backpedal much off the line. His strongest attribute is his play in zone coverage. He does a good job gaining depth in his drops and not allowing receivers to break his cushion. He plays with good range and recognizes route concepts. Likewise, he displays sufficient technique in off-man. His inability to quickly flip his hips, change direction, and transition to mirror a receiver's routes forces him to lose out at the top of the route and get beaten too often. He plays with adequate ability in press-man. While in press, he often lunges toward the receiver and gets caught on his heels trying to catch up off the line. However, he shows physicality and if he can get hands-on, he can reroute receivers and make it tough for them to get into their route.

When he's not in coverage, Bynum has shown he can support the run. He is a solid, willing tackler who doesn't shy away from contact. He rarely misses tackles when he breaks down and is in position, but in the open field, he can take inefficient pursuit angles and allow cutbacks.

Bynum projects as a backup No. 5 cornerback working outside primarily in a zone scheme. On 3rd downs, he fits best in zone coverage on the outside where he can gain depth in his drops and use his eyes to read the quarterback and find receivers coming through his area. Bynum's value will come from his ability to play on special teams. He's a tough competitor that possesses good mental toughness and play speed, both of which should allow him to be a core special teams player on all units at the next level.

				Coverage							Tackling			
Year	Trgt	Comp	Comp%	Yds	Yds/Trgt	Int	Int Drops	TD Alwd			Tkls	TFL	Brk Tkl	BT%
2017	59	28	47%	543	9.2	2	1	4			60	1.0	4	6%
2018	56	26	46%	375	6.7	2	0	3			50	3.0	6	11%
2019	53	28	53%	433	8.2	1	0	3			58	2.5	5	8%
2020	7	5	71%	61	8.7	1	1	1			18	2.0	4	18%
	175	87	50%	1412	8.1	6	2	11			186	8.5	19	9%

		Coverage						Man		Zone	
Year	PBU	Deserved Catch %	YAC/Comp	Rating	EPA	EPA/Trgt	Pos%	Yds/Snap	Pos%	Yds/Snap	Pos%
2017	10	73%	4.5	88.5	12.1	0.21	46%	-	-	-	-
2018	11	70%	3.0	79.1	1.9	0.03	39%	8.4	50%	2.5	25%
2019	10	72%	2.9	75.4	7.9	0.15	51%	8.8	56%	4.1	45%
2020	2	83%	1.4	137.5	4.3	0.62	71%	9.3	100%	5.5	100%
	33	72%	3.4	83.8	26.2	0.15	46%	8.6	54%	3.5	38%

	Usage			Total Points					Total Points Rtg		
Year	Man%	Slot%	Press Cov%	Press	Slot	Wide	Cov Total	Run Def	Total	Per Cov	Per Run	Per Play
2018	46%	14%	-	-	2	31	32	18	51	96	88	90
2019	28%	13%	32%	6	-1	13	12	18	31	71	88	76
2020	14%	29%	14%	0	1	5	5	12	17	80	99	92
	33%	16%	28%	5	1	48	49	48	99	-	-	

Critical Factors
Reactive Athleticism 5
Play Speed 6
Ball Skills 5

Positional Factors
Off-Man 5
Press-Man 5
Zone Coverage 6
Slot Coverage 5
Transition 4
Closing Speed 5
FBI 5
Mental Toughness 6
Open-Field Tackling 5
Play Strength 5
Run Support 6
ST Value 7

Rachad Wildgoose II

Report by Ronan Potts

School	Height	Weight	Year	Jersey #	Hometown
Wisconsin	5112 E	197 E	3JR	5	Miami, FL

One Liner

Wildgoose is an explosive, aggressive athlete with high upside, but his raw technique in coverage will need development before he can be a reliable cover corner.

Strengths: Explosive athleticism; Aggression; Recovery speed
Weaknesses: Raw coverage technique; FBI; Play strength

Rachad Wildgoose II is a cornerback in Wisconsin's nickel defense, playing both wide and slot corner in his career. He played in 25 career games with 17 starts dating back to his true freshman year. He was limited to 2 games in his final season after suffering a shoulder injury, then opted out early. Wildgoose has a well-proportioned frame, and he is an explosive athlete with very good play and closing speed.

Wildgoose relies more on his athleticism than technique. His technique in man coverage is very raw, and he relies mostly on his ability to run with his matchups in coverage rather than using leverage and knowing where the ball is going to be. He is a competitor in press but will take false steps and lose positioning. He's naturally very quick but his ability to mirror movements through routes is inconsistent. However, his speed is a great equalizer to close quickly even when giving up separation. He does a good job of reliably alternating assignments from wide to the slot as his defense sees fit. Wildgoose is generally sufficient in zone coverage, especially in the flats where he is able to rely on his aggression. He has good ball skills to get in passing lanes for breakups and disrupts receivers at the catch point but has only one career interception.

Wildgoose shows a lot of aggression in run support and the screen game, using his impressive closing speed to always put himself in position to make a play. He lacks the play strength to work through blockers but is often quick enough to work around them. He loves to get a head of steam and deliver big hits, and he is sufficient as both an open-field and clean-up tackler.

Due to his explosive athleticism and raw technique, Wildgoose projects as a fifth corner and special teamer as he begins his NFL career. On third down he can be utilized in dime packages, and his versatility in college should translate to the next level. Wildgoose has the play speed, aggressive mentality, and tackling desire to be a core special teams contributor.

			Coverage						Tackling			
Year	Trgt	Comp	Comp%	Yds	Yds/Trgt	Int	Int Drops	TD Alwd	Tkls	TFL	Brk Tkl	BT%
2018	39	18	46%	267	6.8	0	1	1	28	0.0	9	24%
2019	47	18	38%	228	4.9	1	1	3	22	3.0	4	15%
2020	10	5	50%	78	7.8	0	0	0	6	2.0	0	0%
	96	41	43%	573	6.0	1	2	4	56	5.0	13	19%

		Coverage						Man		Zone	
Year	PBU	Deserved Catch %	YAC/Comp	Rating	EPA	EPA/Trgt	Pos%	Yds/Snap	Pos%	Yds/Snap	Pos%
2018	6	73%	5.4	77.6	6.4	0.16	44%	7.0	33%	4.1	55%
2019	6	72%	3.2	57.8	-14.6	-0.31	30%	5.6	31%	2.5	18%
2020	1	63%	1.0	76.3	-3.3	-0.33	50%	7.1	38%	10.5	100%
	13	71%	3.9	67.8	-11.5	-0.12	38%	6.6	33%	3.6	37%

	Usage				Total Points					Total Points Rtg		
Year	Man%	Slot%	Press Cov%	Press	Slot	Wide	Cov Total	Run Def	Total	Per Cov	Per Run	Per Play
2018	50%	48%	-	-	1	4	6	11	18	70	94	81
2019	24%	67%	13%	6	17	8	23	5	28	94	68	83
2020	68%	10%	40%	9	0	6	6	2	8	99	98	99
	37%	55%	15%	14	17	18	35	18	54	-	-	-

Critical Factors	
Reactive Athleticism	5
Play Speed	7
Ball Skills	6

Positional Factors	
Off-Man	5
Press-Man	5
Zone Coverage	5
Slot Coverage	5
Transition	5
Closing Speed	7
FBI	4
Mental Toughness	6
Open-Field Tackling	5
Play Strength	4
Run Support	6
ST Value	7

Bryan Mills

Report by Joe McDonald & Ryan Newman

School	Height	Weight	Year	Jersey #	Hometown
North Carolina Central	6006 V	180 V	4SR	22	Palmdale, CA

One Liner

Mills has the length and coverage ability to be a solid depth corner, but his lack of reactive athleticism and transition ability will likely limit his playing time in the NFL.

Strengths: Mirror-match in man coverage; FBI; Play speed
Weaknesses: Transition ability; Body control; Run support

Bryan Mills is a starting cornerback in North Carolina Central's 4-3 defense, typically lining up on the outside, but is comfortable lining up in the slot as well. He spent his first 2 seasons at Antelope Valley College and College of the Canyons before transferring to NCCU and starting 10 of 12 games in 2019. Mills is a tall, skinny corner with very good length. He possesses good athleticism moving horizontally and vertically. He is a physical corner who plays with a chip on his shoulder, but lacks effort in the run game.

In the pass game, Mills is good in both man and zone coverages. He typically presses while in man and is able to mirror his receiver off the line, flip his hips, and run step-for-step with them on deep routes. However, when he gives his initial punch at the line in press, he will occasionally have it swiped away, allowing the receiver to gain a step on him. He has a high FBI and consistently recognizes double moves to make sure and not get beaten deep. However, on quick routes underneath, he struggles to react and

transition quick enough to meet the ball at the catch point and break up passes. He struggles to stay with receivers at the top of routes and that's usually where receivers can gain separation on him. His FBI transfers over in his zone coverage as well, as he's able to diagnose routes combinations and see where the ball is heading. He is athletic and able to high point passes, playing through the ball, but his lack of tracking and timing can hurt his effectiveness to break up many passes. With that said, he does show the ability to create turnovers by way of interceptions.

In the run game, Mills does not show much desire to participate. He is not an effective tackler, as he attempts to tackle high using only his arms.

Mills projects as a No. 5 backup cornerback with the ability to play inside and outside at the NFL level. He has the coverage ability to play on all three downs, and is fast and tough enough to be a solid contributor on special teams coverage units.

Length makes might for North Carolina Central cornerback Bryan Mills. At 6-feet, Mills described himself to the Music City Miracles blog last summer as "a very physical and long-armed corner. My length gives me a huge advantage over the opposition."

Mills' selection to the Senior Bowl marked the first time in 32 years that a North Carolina Central player had earned that honor. The last was Robert Massey in 1989.

North Carolina Central has a long history of NFL draftees, but has had only one since 2008 - Ryan Smith in the fourth round by the Buccaneers in 2016. The school's most prominent NFL player is Doug Wilkerson, who played guard for 15 seasons in the 1970s and 1980s.

Critical Factors	
Reactive Athleticism	5
Play Speed	6
Ball Skills	5

Positional Factors	
Off-Man	6
Press-Man	5
Zone Coverage	6
Slot Coverage	5
Transition	5
Closing Speed	6
FBI	6
Mental Toughness	6
Open-Field Tackling	5
Play Strength	5
Run Support	3
ST Value	6

Jerry Jacobs

Final Grade: 5.

Report by Kyle Rodemann & DJ Marquardt

School	Height	Weight	Year	Jersey #	Hometown
Arkansas	5101 V	209 V	5SR	0	Atlanta, GA

One Liner

Jacobs needs to improve his ability to transition without hesitation and trust his football smarts, but he has goo zone traits and potential inside-out versatility to contribute off the bench.

Strengths: Zone coverage; Football intelligence; Sound tackling form
Weaknesses: Slot experience; Vertical transitions; Instincts and closing speed

Jerry Jacobs is an outside cornerback in Arkansas' DB-heavy zone defense. He went from community college to Arkansas State to the Razorbacks after suffering a torn ACL in 2019, then opted out early in 2020. Overall, he played in 22 D-I games with 16 starts. He has standard size for the position with unspectacular length. He is a solid athlete with a bit of twitch and good speed. He isn't afraid to get physical in the ground game.

Jacobs does a decent job of staying in phase when pressed but doesn't use a jam and can be overpowered by larger receivers. His reactive quickness is often undone by hesitating with his eyes. In zone he's used to playing with his eyes in the backfield first and peripherally to receivers in his area, but when asked to play man coverage, he has trouble not peeking to the QB on breaks, making him a step late at times. He plays with good positioning in zone and is quick to jump between receivers passing through. He runs with deep routes well but lacks true explosion and closing speed to finish. He mirrors on lateral breaks with sufficient footwork but struggle to transition on full backward-to-forward cut without shuffling. He plays with good intelligence t read screens and other route concepts, but hi instincts are inconsistent in man and at the catc point. He has issues getting his head around whil keeping pace downfield, but usually competes wel to disrupt.

Jacobs lacks the play strength to be a true forc player and work through blocks in the run game, bu he is a willing contributor when it comes his way. H is a sound form tackler in the open field but can giv up extra yards after contact to bigger ballcarriers.

Jacobs projects as a depth cornerback in a zon system, whose usability would expand if he ca prove himself in the slot. He doesn't have th experience, and he'll need to improve his eyes an foot quickness in man, but his FBI and size projec decently inside. He should be a sufficient specia teamer with his speed and tackling ability.

Year		Coverage								Tackling			
	Trgt	Comp	Comp%	Yds	Yds/Trgt	Int	Int Drops	TD Alwd		Tkls	TFL	Brk Tkl	BT%
2018	36	15	42%	170	4.7	4	0	3		32	3.0	6	16%
2019	20	10	50%	174	8.7	0	0	0		20	1.0	1	5%
2020	17	9	53%	97	5.7	0	0	1		18	1.0	3	14%
	73	34	47%	441	6.0	4	0	4		70	5.0	10	13%

Year		Coverage						Man		Zone	
	PBU	Deserved Catch %	YAC/Comp	Rating	EPA	EPA/Trgt	Pos%	Yds/Snap	Pos%	Yds/Snap	Pos%
2018	13	54%	1.9	44.7	-15.5	-0.43	31%	5.1	35%	4.5	31%
2019	3	77%	4.6	80.0	3.9	0.19	50%	10.3	67%	6.1	50%
2020	0	90%	1.4	65.1	-0.9	-0.05	47%	10.1	86%	2.6	33%
	16	67%	2.6	55.8	-12.5	-0.17	40%	7.0	52%	4.6	39%

Year		Usage		Total Points						Total Points Rtg		
	Man%	Slot%	Press Cov%	Press	Slot	Wide	Cov Total	Run Def	Total	Per Cov	Per Run	Per Play
2018	62%	10%	-	-	1	29	29	20	50	97	96	94
2019	20%	7%	20%	2	1	0	2	4	5	70	86	76
2020	16%	7%	4%	-2	3	5	8	5	13	85	87	83
	44%	9%	9%	1	5	34	39	29	68	-	-	-

Critical Factors	
Reactive Athleticism	5
Play Speed	6
Ball Skills	5

Positional Factors	
Off-Man	5
Press-Man	5
Zone Coverage	6
Slot Coverage	5
Transition	4
Closing Speed	5
FBI	6
Mental Toughness	5
Open-Field Tackling	6
Play Strength	4
Run Support	5
ST Value	5

Tay Gowan

Report by Steven Penn & Justin Serovich

School	Height	Weight	Year	Jersey #	Hometown
UCF	6010 E	185 E	5SR	23	Covington, GA

One Liner

Gowan is a solid press corner with good ball skills, but a lack of speed and transition ability without many top-end traits may hold him back.

Strengths: Press coverage; Ball skills
Weaknesses: Closing speed; Transition; Run support

Tay Gowan is an outside cornerback in UCF's 4-2-5 defense running a lot of man coverage with a mix of zone. He played 3 games across 2016-17 at Miami OH before transferring to Butler CC in 2018 and finally UCF in 2019. He opted out of 2020 after testing positive for COVID-19. Gowan has a long, but slight frame. He plays hard, showing he's a tough competitor in coverage. He's a good athlete, though lacks some long speed.

Gowan primarily played press coverage and switched between bailing and engaging his receiver at the line. While mostly successful in press, he's not always physical at the line. When he gets beat, he lacks some closing speed to make up ground. In off-man, he has sufficient transition skill to break up on routes in front of him, but is a little late too often. In zone, he has decent zone awareness and is able to read the eyes of the quarterback. He rarely played in the slot, but has the length and reactive athleticism to at least be sufficient. He's physical with the receiver down the field, sometimes too physical, especially

for the next level. He has the ball skills to make plays on the ball, whether it be a pass breakup or interception. He was able to convert a couple interceptions in his lone season at UCF, but also had plenty in JUCO.

Gowan didn't present much help in the run game. He lacks aggression in the run game and if teammates were around the tackle, he stayed away, only helping out when needed. Though, when asked to tackle, he showed sufficient tackling ability in the open field. He also showed some speed and pursuit to run down ballcarriers down the field.

Gowan projects as a depth corner who fits best in a press-man scheme where he can use his length and reactive athleticism. He could play the slot, but fits better on the outside. On 3rd downs, he should play outside in press to make it tough for receivers to get off the line. His sufficient speed and lack of interest may limit his ability to contribute on some special teams units.

			Coverage						Tackling			
Year	Trgt	Comp	Comp%	Yds	Yds/Trgt	Int	Int Drops	TD Alwd	Tkls	TFL	Brk Tkl	BT%
2017	0	0	-	0	-	0	0	0	1	0.0	1	50%
2019	47	17	36%	281	6.0	2	0	2	31	1.0	4	11%
	47	17	36%	281	6.0	2	0	2	32	1.0	5	14%

		Coverage						Man		Zone	
Year	PBU	Deserved Catch %	YAC/Comp	Rating	EPA	EPA/Trgt	Pos%	Yds/Snap	Pos%	Yds/Snap	Pos%
2017	0	-	-	0.0	0.0	-	-	-	-	-	-
2019	9	64%	3.8	44.7	-8.3	-0.18	34%	9.6	47%	3.6	33%
	9	64%	3.8	44.7	-8.3	-0.18	34%	9.6	47%	3.6	33%

	Usage			Total Points					Total Points Rtg		
Year	Man%	Slot%	Press Cov%	Press	Slot	Wide	Cov Total	Run Def	Total	Per Cov	Per Run	Per Play
2019	36%	9%	33%	0	2	26	29	17	46	94	84	87

Critical Factors	
Reactive Athleticism	6
Play Speed	5
Ball Skills	6

Positional Factors	
Off-Man	5
Press-Man	6
Zone Coverage	5
Slot Coverage	5
Transition	5
Closing Speed	5
FBI	5
Mental Toughness	6
Open-Field Tackling	5
Play Strength	5
Run Support	4
ST Value	5

Safeties

Mark Simon

used to do play-by-play for football games at the United States Coast Guard Academy, a Division II school that placed height and weight limitations on its students, and thus provided significant challenges for the football team in trying to fill its roster.

remember instances of the offensive line going up against players considerably heavier and cornerbacks routinely giving up 4-to-5 inches to opposing wide receivers (a 5-foot-7 Coast Guard cornerback once had to play future NFL standout Pierre Garçon). Watching this happen week after week, I developed an affinity for the little guy and what he had to overcome on a football field.

Transitioning from what I like to how we rate players, I asked Nathan Cooper, who helps oversee scouting report content for the *Handbook*, how size comes into play when evaluating safeties. Here's what he said.

'When watching undersized guys, especially on defense, you want to see if they play bigger than they are. That means playing physical, being able to battle with bigger receivers across from them. Some matchups he'll have against receivers and tight ends that might have six to eight inches on him, but can he still be effective in covering those guys and winning his share of 50/50 balls? And is he willing to fill running lanes and come down full speed toward the line of scrimmage and not shy away from contact to shed blockers or attack bigger ball carriers?"

You need to overcome a lot if you're a small safety. All-Pro Tyrann Mathieu does it about as well as it can be done. But he and Pro Bowl selection Quandre Diggs are the exception more than the rule.

Sixty-two NFL safeties started at least eight games in 2020. Of those, 41 were listed at 6-feet or taller. Only nine were either 5-foot-9 (the shortest height) or 5-foot-10.

There are a couple of 'little guys' who are among the top draft prospects at this position. Let's look at them a little more closely.

Ar'Darius Washington of TCU is the smallest safety among our draft prospects at a little under 5-foot-8, but he earned a 6.7 scouting grade from Nathan, who wrote Washington's report. There weren't any safeties that small who played in the NFL last season (caveats about NFL-listed player heights notwithstanding).

Washington's scouting report details how he overcame that height, with Nathan pointing out how actively Washington communicates, how he has good instincts, eye discipline, and awareness in the passing game, along with aggression, physicality, surprising strength, and toughness that belie his size limitations. If the list of his positives weren't that long, he probably wouldn't rate as well as he does.

The other prominent 'little guy' (relative to others) among this group of draft prospects is Richard LeCounte of Georgia, who checks in at a little under 5-foot-10. He's another one who makes up what he lacks in size with good instincts and toughness.

LeCounte was the only safety to get a 7 grade for 3-Level Impact and didn't have any grade below a 5. To quote from his report "His FBI (football intelligence) shines through in diagnosing plays pre- and post-snap." Evan Butler, who wrote LeCounte's report, said "His impact was bigger than his size."

Washington and LeCounte are in the group of players ranked just behind the No. 1 safety, 6-foot-1 Trevon Moehrig. As you'll read, Moehrig separates himself with excellent instincts and outstanding ball skills and tracking. That he's 6-foot-1 allows him to disrupt passes at the catch point.

Last year in this book, we rated Minnesota's Antoine Winfield Jr. as the No. 2 safety among draft prospects with a 6.8 grade. Winfield measured a little under 5-foot-10 but was valued for his toughness and elite ball skills. Winfield isn't where Mathieu or Diggs are just yet, but he might very well be on his way. He was a 16-game starter for a Buccaneers team that won the Super Bowl

Something for Washington and LeCounte, and the other players listed in this chapter, to aspire to.

SAFETY

Safety Grading Scale

GRADE	DESCRIPTION
9.0 – 7.0	High-end 3 down starter. Pro Bowl level.
6.9 – 6.7	Strong starter who plays on all 3 downs.
6.4	3rd safety. Low-end starter.
6.2	Versatile backup with CB/DS flexibility.
6.1 – 6.0	Developmental. Top traits but needs time.
5.9	Top backup. Box safety type.
5.8	Average backup. 4th DS. Quality special teamer.
5.7	Low-end backup DS with growable upside.

Safety Rankings

Rank	Name	Grade	Page	Rank	Name	Grade	Page
1	Trevon Moehrig	6.9	626	16	Joshuah Bledsoe	6.2	655
2	Ar'Darius Washington	6.7	628	17	Israel Mukuamu	6.2	656
3	Jevon Holland	6.7	630	18	Richie Grant	6.2	657
4	Paris Ford	6.7	632	19	Mark Webb	6.2	658
5	Andre Cisco	6.7	634	20	Lawrence White IV	6.2	659
6	Richard LeCounte	6.7	636	21	Nahshon Wright	6.2	660
7	Damar Hamlin	6.4	638	22	Jacoby Stevens	5.9	661
8	Hamsah Nasirildeen	6.4	640	23	Divine Deablo	5.9	662
9	Talanoa Hufanga	6.4	642	24	Christian Uphoff	5.9	663
10	Tyree Gillespie	6.4	644	25	Brad Stewart Jr.	5.9	664
11	Aashari Crosswell	6.4	646	26	Dicaprio Bootle	5.9	665
12	Caden Sterns	6.4	648	27	Shawn Davis	5.8	666
13	Brady Breeze	6.4	650	28	JR Pace	5.8	667
14	Jamar Johnson	6.4	652	29	James Wiggins	5.8	668
15	Kary Vincent Jr.	6.2	654	30	Tariq Thompson	5.8	669

Glossary

ATD+ (Adjusted Tackle Depth Plus)
ATD+ compares actual tackle depth to the expected tackle depth based on personnel, intended run gap, and the defender's pre-snap alignment. This figure is then scaled so that 100 is average. A figure of 110 indicates a player who is 10% better than average; a figure of 90 indicates a player who is 10% worse than average.

Blitz%
Percentage of quarterback dropbacks where the defender rushed the quarterback.

Box%
Percentage of plays the defender lined up inside the box (within the extended tackle box at no more than eight yards depth).

Brk Tkl (Broken Tackles)
Tackle attempts where the defender in position to make a tackle failed to bring down the ballcarrier. Counts both broken tackles (physical) and missed tackles (elusive).

BT% (Broken Tackle%)
Percentage of tackle attempts where the defender in position to make a tackle failed to bring down the ballcarrier. Counts both broken tackles (physical) and missed tackles (elusive).

Deserved Catch%
The percentage of targets as the primary defender that the receiver either caught or dropped the ball when the pass was catchable.

PBU (Pass Breakups)
The number of times the defender batted, deflected for an incompletion, or defensed a pass attempt.

Pos% (Positive%) (Coverage split)
The percentage of plays where the defender was targeted that resulted in a positive EPA for the offense. Lower numbers are better for defenders.

Pres% (Pressure Rate)
The percentage of pass rushes that resulted in a quarterback hurry, hit, knockdown, or sack.

Sack%
Percentage of pass rushes that resulted in a sack.

Slot%
Percentage of plays the defender lined up across from a slot receiver.

Tackle Share
Percentage of a team's tackles made by the defender.

Total Points
Sports Info Solutions' proprietary player value metric that uses an Expected Points framework and distributes the value gained or lost on a play to the players involved based on their impact on the play.

Total Points Rating
Total Points per play compared to average, scaled so that 50 is poor and 99 is excellent.

Safety Leaderboards

Total Points Per Game

Rk	Player	School	Tot Pts / G
1	R. Grant	UCF	5.2
2	J. Johnson	Indiana	5.0
3	T. Hufanga	USC	4.7
4	D. Deablo	Virginia Tech	4.2
4	J. Wiggins	Cincinnati	4.2
6	R. LeCounte	Georgia	3.5
7	D. Hamlin	Pittsburgh	3.4
8	T. Moehrig	TCU	3.3
8	J. Stevens	LSU	3.3
8	T. Thompson	San Diego State	3.3

Total Points Rating Per Play

Rk	Player	School	Rating
1	J. Johnson	Indiana	95
2	R. Grant	UCF	93
3	J. Wiggins	Cincinnati	92
4	T. Hufanga	USC	91
5	R. LeCounte	Georgia	89
6	J. Stevens	LSU	86
7	D. Deablo	Virginia Tech	85
8	D. Hamlin	Pittsburgh	83
9	S. Davis	Florida	81
10	I. Mukuamu	South Carolina	80

Pass Coverage Total Points Per Game

Rk	Player	School	Tot Pts / G
1	J. Wiggins	Cincinnati	3.8
2	T. Hufanga	USC	3.2
3	T. Moehrig	TCU	3.1
4	J. Johnson	Indiana	3.0
5	R. Grant	UCF	2.8
5	D. Deablo	Virginia Tech	2.8
7	R. LeCounte	Georgia	2.7
8	T. Thompson	San Diego State	2.6
9	P. Ford	Pittsburgh	1.9
10	3 tied with		1.6

Total Points Rating Per Coverage Snap

Rk	Player	School	Rating
1	T. Hufanga	USC	99
1	J. Wiggins	Cincinnati	99
3	R. LeCounte	Georgia	98
3	J. Johnson	Indiana	98
5	T. Moehrig	TCU	96
6	R. Grant	UCF	95
7	I. Mukuamu	South Carolina	94
8	D. Deablo	Virginia Tech	91
8	T. Thompson	San Diego State	91
10	A. Washington	TCU	86

Run Defense Total Points Per Game

Rk	Player	School	Tot Pts / G
1	R. Grant	UCF	2.2
2	D. Hamlin	Pittsburgh	1.8
2	J. Stevens	LSU	1.8
4	N. Wright	Oregon State	1.7
4	S. Davis	Florida	1.7
6	J. Johnson	Indiana	1.6
6	D. Deablo	Virginia Tech	1.6
8	D. Bootle	Nebraska	1.1
9	T. Hufanga	USC	1.0
9	L. White IV	Iowa State	1.0

Total Points Rating Per Run Snap

Rk	Player	School	Rating
1	S. Davis	Florida	97
2	R. Grant	UCF	96
3	D. Hamlin	Pittsburgh	95
3	J. Stevens	LSU	95
5	J. Johnson	Indiana	93
6	N. Wright	Oregon State	88
7	D. Deablo	Virginia Tech	85
8	R. LeCounte	Georgia	81
9	L. White IV	Iowa State	79
10	T. Hufanga	USC	75

Lined Up in Slot Percentage

Rk	Player	School	Slot%
1	M. Webb	Georgia	82%
2	J. Bledsoe	Missouri	58%
3	B. Stewart Jr.	Florida	57%
3	T. Thompson	San Diego State	57%
5	L. White IV	Iowa State	43%
6	J. Wiggins	Cincinnati	33%
7	R. Grant	UCF	29%
8	D. Deablo	Virginia Tech	25%
9	J. Johnson	Indiana	22%
10	D. Hamlin	Pittsburgh	20%

Lined Up in Box Percentage

Rk	Player	School	Box%
1	T. Hufanga	USC	39%
2	J. Stevens	LSU	34%
3	J. Bledsoe	Missouri	32%
4	D. Deablo	Virginia Tech	28%
5	R. Grant	UCF	15%
6	T. Gillespie	Missouri	14%
7	B. Stewart Jr.	Florida	11%
8	J. Johnson	Indiana	9%
9	M. Webb	Georgia	8%
9	J. Pace	Northwestern	8%

Tackles For Loss Per Game

Rk	Player	School	TFL/G
1	T. Hufanga	USC	0.9
2	J. Stevens	LSU	0.6
3	P. Ford	Pittsburgh	0.4
3	D. Hamlin	Pittsburgh	0.4
3	J. Johnson	Indiana	0.4
3	R. Grant	UCF	0.4
7	J. Bledsoe	Missouri	0.3
7	B. Stewart Jr.	Florida	0.3
7	S. Davis	Florida	0.3
7	T. Thompson	San Diego State	0.3

Broken Tackle Rate

Rk	Player	School	BT%
1	N. Wright	Oregon State	7%
2	R. Grant	UCF	8%
2	D. Deablo	Virginia Tech	8%
4	M. Webb	Georgia	9%
5	C. Sterns	Texas	11%
5	J. Stevens	LSU	11%
7	T. Moehrig	TCU	13%
7	D. Bootle	Nebraska	13%
9	P. Ford	Pittsburgh	14%
10	4 tied with		15%

Tackle Share

Rk	Player	School	Tkl Share
1	T. Hufanga	USC	15%
2	J. Stevens	LSU	11%
3	D. Hamlin	Pittsburgh	10%
3	R. Grant	UCF	10%
5	J. Johnson	Indiana	9%
5	T. Thompson	San Diego State	9%
7	T. Moehrig	TCU	8%
7	T. Gillespie	Missouri	8%
7	C. Sterns	Texas	8%
7	3 tied with		8%

Adjusted Tackle Depth Plus

Rk	Player	School	ATD+
1	D. Bootle	Nebraska	142
2	P. Ford	Pittsburgh	130
3	J. Johnson	Indiana	122
4	D. Hamlin	Pittsburgh	113
5	R. LeCounte	Georgia	110
6	A. Washington	TCU	109
6	L. White IV	Iowa State	109
8	J. Bledsoe	Missouri	107
9	S. Davis	Florida	104
10	C. Sterns	Texas	101

Pressure Rate

Rk	Player	School	Pres%
1	J. Johnson	Indiana	43%
2	B. Stewart Jr.	Florida	42%
3	J. Stevens	LSU	41%
4	R. Grant	UCF	30%
5	M. Webb	Georgia	29%
5	L. White IV	Iowa State	29%
7	S. Davis	Florida	25%
8	T. Hufanga	USC	18%
9	T. Gillespie	Missouri	14%
9	J. Pace	Northwestern	14%

Yards Per Target

Rk	Player	School	Yds/Trgt
1	A. Washington	TCU	2.6
1	J. Wiggins	Cincinnati	2.6
3	D. Deablo	Virginia Tech	4.4
4	J. Pace	Northwestern	5.0
5	T. Thompson	San Diego State	5.3
6	R. Grant	UCF	5.4
7	D. Hamlin	Pittsburgh	5.9
8	T. Gillespie	Missouri	6.1
9	T. Moehrig	TCU	6.3
10	T. Hufanga	USC	6.6

Pressures Per Game

Rk	Player	School	Pres/G
1	T. Hufanga	USC	1.3
1	J. Stevens	LSU	1.3
3	J. Johnson	Indiana	0.8
3	R. Grant	UCF	0.8
5	B. Stewart Jr.	Florida	0.5
6	M. Webb	Georgia	0.3
7	R. LeCounte	Georgia	0.2
7	L. White IV	Iowa State	0.2
7	N. Wright	Oregon State	0.2
10	7 tied with		0.1

Passes Broken Up Per Game

Rk	Player	School	PBU/G
1	J. Johnson	Indiana	1.3
2	T. Moehrig	TCU	1.1
2	R. Grant	UCF	1.1
4	R. LeCounte	Georgia	1.0
5	D. Hamlin	Pittsburgh	0.9
5	D. Deablo	Virginia Tech	0.9
5	J. Wiggins	Cincinnati	0.9
8	T. Hufanga	USC	0.8
8	D. Bootle	Nebraska	0.8
10	3 tied with		0.7

Sacks Per Game

Rk	Player	School	Sacks/G
1	T. Hufanga	USC	0.5
2	J. Stevens	LSU	0.3
3	N. Wright	Oregon State	0.2
4	J. Johnson	Indiana	0.1
4	R. Grant	UCF	0.1
4	B. Stewart Jr.	Florida	0.1
4	J. Wiggins	Cincinnati	0.1
8	T. Moehrig	TCU	0.0
8	A. Washington	TCU	0.0
8	14 tied with		0.0

Interceptions Per Game

Rk	Player	School	INT/G
1	T. Hufanga	USC	0.7
2	R. LeCounte	Georgia	0.5
2	J. Johnson	Indiana	0.5
4	P. Ford	Pittsburgh	0.4
4	D. Deablo	Virginia Tech	0.4
6	I. Mukuamu	South Carolina	0.3
6	R. Grant	UCF	0.3
6	N. Wright	Oregon State	0.3
6	S. Davis	Florida	0.3
10	2 tied with		0.2

Trevon Moehrig

Final Grade: 6.9

Report by Jordan Edwards

School	Height	Weight	Year	Jersey #	Hometown
TCU	6010 E	202 E	3JR	7	Spring Branch, TX

One Liner
Moehrig has the instincts, coverage versatility, and ball skills to be a high-end starter at the next level, though he'll need to clean up some communication miscues and become more aggressive in the run game to ultimately hit his ceiling.

Overall
Trevon Moehrig lines up at free safety for TCU's primary 2-high zone defense. He primarily plays as a deep post defender, but rolled to the slot as well. The 2020 Thorpe Award winner, Moehrig started 24 of 35 games in his career. He's a solid and easy moving athlete with good size, length and quickness. He's a good competitor who can be physical against the run and at the catch point as well. As a true freshman in 2018, Moehrig was recognized as the Special Teams Player of the Year by his teammates, which speaks to his leadership and toughness.

Pass Game
Moehrig is a solid three-level defender, but excels most in the back end as a deep coverage safety. His natural feel for the position and comfortability in coverage stands out on every play. He has good eyes and trusts his keys when reading the QB and watching route concepts play out in front of him. He processes well and can transition quickly to find and make a play on the football at the catch point. He has the quickness and athleticism to stay attached to quicker receivers, and the strength to engage and reroute bigger receiving threats down field as well. Moehrig plays with good tempo and overall play speed, rarely letting receivers get on top of him to stretch the field vertically. As a deep safety, he can read and react to the quarterback's eyes quickly and has the tracking ability and range to make a play on the ball. He's comfortable in man coverage and has the ability to stay in phase vertically and also the play speed to run laterally. Moehrig has very good ball skills and shows the ability to get his hands on the ball to disrupt plays at the catch point. TCU hardly ever used him as a blitzer, which would take him away from his skills in coverage. There were a few communication miscues that led to some explosive plays in his area, but they were few and far between.

Run Game
Moehrig is an adequate and willing run defender, but will have his issues finding the ball from time to time. He is a productive tackler, who is physical at the POA, though looks hesitant at times running downhill. He takes good angles and doesn't over pursue, but he can lose track of the flow of the play causing him to react too slow. He is a good open-field tackler overall, and hardly lets ballcarrier get past him once he made contact.

Last Word
Moehrig projects to be a high-level starter at the free safety position. He can be scheme diverse with his ability to play as a lone deep safety and as a slot defender in man coverage. On 3rd downs, Moehrig can be used in a variety of different ways which can be valuable to defensive coordinators at the next level. He has the experience and skill set to be a special teams contributor as well.

Strengths

- Instincts
- Versatility
- Ball skills & tracking

Weaknesses

- Run support
- Communication miscues

Critical Factors

3-Level Impact	FBI / Instincts	Play Speed
6	7	6

Positional Factors

Man Coverage	Zone Coverage	Range
6	6	6
Ball Skills / Tracking	Tackling	Blitz
7	6	4
Physicality	Communication	ST Value
6	5	6

Basic

Year	Trgt	Comp	Comp%	Yards	Yds/Trgt	Int	Int Drops	TD Alwd	Tkls	TFL	Brk Tkl	BT%
2018	10	5	50%	100	10.0	1	0	1	11	1.0	7	39%
2019	31	12	39%	176	5.7	4	1	1	60	1.5	9	13%
2020	32	16	50%	200	6.3	2	0	1	48	2.0	7	13%
	73	33	45%	476	6.5	7	1	3	119	4.5	23	16%

Advanced

Year	PBU	Pos%	Deserved Catch %	EPA	EPA/Trgt	Tgt	Yds/Tgt	Pos%	Tackle Share	ATD+
2018	2	50%	71%	3.8	0.38	7	10.4	57%	1%	72
2019	15	29%	65%	-14.6	-0.47	12	7.9	42%	9%	84
2020	11	47%	65%	-5.5	-0.17	12	6.9	50%	8%	96
	28	40%	66%	-16.3	-0.22	31	8.1	48%	6%	87

Deep Dive

Year	Slot%	Box%	Blitz%	Pres%	Sack%	Pass Cov	Run Def	Total	Per Cov	Per Run	Per Play
2018	23%	2%	1%	0%	0.0%	8	6	13	92	92	89
2019	13%	2%	0%	-	-	25	12	37	90	76	81
2020	11%	2%	0%	-	-	31	2	33	96	56	77
	14%	2%	0%	0%	0.0%	64	20	83	-	-	-

Ar'Darius Washington

Report by Nathan Cooper

School	Height	Weight	Year	Jersey #	Hometown
TCU	5075 E	175 E	3SO	24	Shreveport, LA

One Liner

Washington has the speed and range to be a starting 3-level player on the back end at the next level, but size limitations and some inconsistent tackling ability may force him in and out of certain situations.

Overall

Ar'Darius Washington is a strong safety playing to the boundary in TCU's 2-4-5/3-3-5 defense which runs mainly 2-high zone coverage looks. He started 15 of the 27 games he played in for the Horned Frogs. He has a slight frame with average build to possibly put on a little more muscle/weight. He's a very twitchy athlete who flies around with good speed. His toughness and competitiveness really stands out for his size.

Pass Game

Washington's range stands out in the pass game. He flies around and shows good instincts in reading the quarterback and route concepts to get where he needs to and quickly. Even though he mainly played as a 2-high defender, he has the range of a 1-high safety who can make plays near the sidelines. In zone coverage, he has good eye discipline and awareness to know what's going on around him and where to be. He breaks quickly on receivers coming to his area and is able to meet the ball at the catch point. In off-man from the safety position, he shows good foot quickness and transition to break on routes in front of him. When he slides into the slot in man coverage, he has the speed and hip fluidity to turn and run and stay with receivers down the field. Washington also has the ball skills to make plays at the catch point. Though most of his on-ball production comes by way of pass breakups, he does have the burst to jump routes to force the occasional turnover. On the back end, he's always visibly communicating with his teammates. As a blitzer, he has the speed and twitch to navigate his way into the backfield, but isn't a reliable pass rusher.

Run Game

Against the run, Washington shows some aggression, physicality, and toughness despite his size. He isn't afraid to fill run lanes and put his body on the line to make tackles. While he is able to make tackles at all levels of the defense, his size limits his ability to consistently be effective. He's forced to throw a shoulder into ballcarriers or drag them down because he doesn't have the girth most of them do. However, he has surprising strength and is able to stand up some ballcarriers when filling run lanes and limit yards after contact.

Last Word

Washington projects as a starting free safety in any scheme. He can play 1-high, 2-high, or even slide into the slot. Though he has the skill set to interchangeably play SS as well, his size will likely limit him from consistently taking on linemen and ballcarriers around the box at the next level. His speed, toughness, and aggression allows him to contribute some on special teams, but his size is a concern.

Strengths
- Range
- 3-Level player
- Always communicating

Weaknesses
- Inconsistent tackling ability
- Size limitations

Critical Factors

3-Level Impact	FBI / Instincts	Play Speed
6	6	6

Positional Factors

Man Coverage	Zone Coverage	Range
6	6	7
Ball Skills / Tracking	Tackling	Blitz
6	5	5
Physicality	Communication	ST Value
5	6	5

Basic

Year	Trgt	Comp	Comp%	Yards	Yds/Trgt	Int	Int Drops	TD Alwd	Tkls	TFL	Brk Tkl	BT%
2018	1	0	0%	0	0.0	0	1	0	1	0.0	0	0%
2019	15	5	33%	88	5.9	5	0	0	44	0.5	9	17%
2020	23	9	39%	59	2.6	0	0	3	38	1.0	9	19%
	39	14	36%	147	3.8	5	1	3	83	1.5	18	18%

Advanced

Year	PBU	Pos%	Deserved Catch %	EPA	EPA/Trgt	Tgt	Yds/Tgt	Pos%	Tackle Share	ATD+
2018	0	0%	100%	-1.2	-1.21	0	-	-	0%	-
2019	8	27%	67%	-6.6	-0.44	5	5.8	20%	7%	111
2020	5	26%	59%	-9.8	-0.43	12	2.1	17%	7%	109
	13	26%	63%	-17.6	-0.45	17	3.2	18%	4%	110

Deep Dive

Year	Slot%	Box%	Blitz%	Pres%	Sack%	Pass Cov	Run Def	Total	Per Cov	Per Run	Per Play
2018	29%	0%	8%	0%	0.0%	-1	0	-1	50	74	50
2019	23%	4%	1%	33%	0.0%	27	7	34	99	75	93
2020	9%	2%	0%	-	-	16	5	21	86	64	74
	16%	3%	1%	25%	0.0%	42	12	54	-	-	-

Jevon Holland

Report by Matt Manocherian

School	Height	Weight	Year	Jersey #	Hometown
Oregon	6006 E	200 E	3JR	8	Coquitlam, BC, CAN

One Liner
Holland is ideally suited to enter the league as a nickel safety who should ascend to solid starter level by Year 2, but he is a very young player who has potential to grow into even more based on his enticing combination of instincts, ball skills, play speed, and physicality.

Overall
Jevon Holland usually lines up over the slot or as an overhang to the wide side of the field in Oregon's five defensive back system, where they play mostly single-high with a mix of man and zone. He only played in 2 seasons before opting out of 2020 and declaring for the NFL Draft, starting 16 of the 27 games that he played over that time. He has good length with just sufficient size overall for a strong safety, but he shows good play strength and physicality. He is also a very young prospect, so he has some growth potential. He is an active communicator with his teammates pre-snap, showing very good effort, intelligence, and instincts.

Pass Game
Holland matches up best with tight ends in man coverage, showing the ability to mirror them effectively in man, but he will struggle to blanket quicker slots and can get turned around by better route runners. He drives downhill very quickly out of his break, showing strong top-end speed, but he plays a bit over-aggressively at times, leaving him flat-footed and susceptible to double-moves and the deep ball going over his head. He will also have to learn to adjust illegal contact enforcement on the next level. He shows good awareness in underneath zones, but he was rarely asked to defend more than a deep third on the backend for the Ducks. That said, on the occasions where he had deep responsibilities, he showed good speed and range to defend up to the deep half. He has been a ball-hawk over his short college career with nine interceptions over his two seasons. He shows good ball skills, locating and adjusting to the trajectory of the ball very quickly, and his return ability shows once he has the ball in his hands. He seldom blitzed, but he has the skills necessary to beat backs in pass protection.

Run Game
While Holland doesn't have ideal size for a strong safety, he has good strength and toughness to contribute in the box. He is quick to fill from the overhang position when the tight end vacates on a down block, showing toughness. He has good length and hand use to shed stalk blocks effectively. He makes some good form-tackles showing explosiveness through contact, and he has the ability to knock running backs backwards, but he doesn't always wrap up, leading to broken tackles. He shows good range and open field tackling ability, but he does have some whiffs in this area, too.

Last Word
Holland projects as a hybrid safety who fits slightly better on the strong side based on him matching up better against tight ends than slot receivers in coverage and limited experience in deep zones. His best role is as he was used at Oregon, as an overhang defender and slot safety in the mold of many of the recent safeties who have entered the league. As a punt returner, he shows his great burst and instincts, and his floor is to become a very good special teams player at the next level.

Strengths

- Interception production
- Intelligence and communication
- Upside

Weaknesses

- Inconsistent in man coverage
- Lacks ideal size for a box safety
- Raw and inexperienced

Critical Factors

3-Level Impact	FBI / Instincts	Play Speed
5	7	6

Positional Factors

Man Coverage	Zone Coverage	Range
5	6	6
Ball Skills / Tracking	Tackling	Blitz
7	6	6
Physicality	Communication	ST Value
6	7	7

Basic

Year	Trgt	Comp	Comp%	Yards	Yds/Trgt	Int	Int Drops	TD Alwd	Tkls	TFL	Brk Tkl	BT%
2018	31	18	58%	203	6.5	5	0	2	37	0.0	7	16%
2019	53	29	55%	372	7.0	4	0	2	64	5.0	11	15%
	84	47	56%	575	6.8	9	0	4	101	5.0	18	15%

Advanced

Year	PBU	Pos%	Deserved Catch %	EPA	EPA/Trgt	Tgt	Yds/Tgt	Pos%	Tackle Share	ATD+
2018	10	55%	72%	1.8	0.06	26	5.5	58%	4%	75
2019	10	43%	79%	-3.7	-0.07	26	5.9	46%	7%	116
	20	48%	77%	-1.9	-0.02	52	5.7	52%	6%	105

Deep Dive

Year	Slot%	Box%	Blitz%	Pres%	Sack%	Pass Cov	Run Def	Total	Per Cov	Per Run	Per Play
2018	31%	6%	2%	11%	0.0%	31	8	39	96	76	85
2019	80%	11%	3%	25%	0.0%	17	11	30	77	74	74
	60%	9%	3%	20%	0.0%	48	19	69	-	-	-

Paris Ford

Report by Nathan Cooper

School	Height	Weight	Year	Jersey #	Hometown
Pittsburgh	5116 E	190 E	4JR	12	Pittsburgh, PA

One Liner
Ford has the ball skills, reactive athleticism, and physicality to be a standout starting safety and special teamer in the NFL, but he'll need to improve his man coverage skills and limit the over-aggression at times to make sure he reaches his full potential.

Overall
Paris Ford primarily plays strong safety for Pitt's defense that deploys a lot of 2-high looks and zone coverage, though he'll also rotate as the 1-high on occasion. He started 18 of 29 games he played in for the Panthers, opting out and declaring after 7 games in 2020. His cousin, Treyvon Hester, currently plays defensive line in the NFL. He has good size for the position with an average frame and strong build. He's a very fluid and reactive athlete who plays fast and competes on every play with toughness and physicality.

Pass Game
One of Ford's best traits is his ability to find the ball. His ball skills are very good and he nearly always seems to make a play at the catch point. He also has an uncanny ability to turn the ball over off of deflections. At times, he stands flat-footed waiting to see what's going to happen. Some of it stems from him waiting on play fakes, but other times it seems like he can be a tick slow in his processing. In zone coverage, he does a good job reading the eyes of the quarterback and knowing where to break, showing quick-twitch reactionary skills. He's a disruptive cover defender, making plays as the ball comes his way. He shows more 2-high range than he does 1-high, but plays fast with good pursuit to still make plays. When the ball is thrown underneath, he shows the aggressiveness to see it and break on it quickly. However, he does play a little too aggressive at times, taking very aggressive angles and undercutting routes, leaving him beaten over the top. In man coverage, he has the ability to cover tight ends and big targets, but will have a tough time sticking with faster receivers. He shows good communication ability with his teammates and rarely blows a coverage, aside from the over-aggression.

Run Game
Ford shows a lot of aggression and physicality against the run. He's not afraid to take running backs or even offensive linemen head-on. While he is more of a hard-hitter than a form-tackler, Ford will throw a shoulder and occasionally miss a tackle. He's able to make tackles at every level of the defense, even around and behind the LOS. He shows consistent pursuit to the ballcarrier regardless if the ball is coming his direction or not.

Last Word
Ford projects as a starting strong safety at the next level in a scheme that runs primarily 2-high shells. His skill set allows for him to be an interchangeable safety, being able to play either safety position. On 3rd downs, he fits best as a zone defender on the back end who can crash in the run game. His physical style, toughness, and play speed suggests he can be an excellent contributor on all special teams units.

Strengths

- Physicality
- Always find the ball
- Reactive athleticism

Weaknesses

- Too aggressive at times
- Processing can be a little slow
- Fast receivers in man

Critical Factors

3-Level Impact	FBI / Instincts	Play Speed
6	6	6

Positional Factors

Man Coverage	Zone Coverage	Range
5	6	6
Ball Skills / Tracking	Tackling	Blitz
7	6	5
Physicality	Communication	ST Value
7	6	8

Basic

Year	Trgt	Comp	Comp%	Yards	Yds/Trgt	Int	Int Drops	TD Alwd	Tkls	TFL	Brk Tkl	BT%
2018	8	5	63%	46	5.8	0	0	1	4	0.0	2	33%
2019	34	17	50%	209	6.1	3	1	1	97	3.0	21	18%
2020	19	11	58%	127	6.7	3	1	2	44	3.0	7	14%
	61	33	54%	382	6.3	6	2	4	145	6.0	30	17%

Advanced

		All Coverage				Man Coverage			Tackling	
Year	PBU	Pos%	Deserved Catch %	EPA	EPA/Trgt	Tgt	Yds/Tgt	Pos%	Tackle Share	ATD+
2018	0	50%	100%	1.2	0.15	5	3.2	40%	0%	109
2019	12	35%	81%	-4.7	-0.14	10	4.1	40%	12%	121
2020	5	53%	80%	4.6	0.24	8	4.6	38%	7%	130
	17	43%	83%	1.1	0.02	23	4.1	39%	6%	123

Deep Dive

	Lined Up		Blitz			Total Points			Total Points Rtg		
Year	Slot%	Box%	Blitz%	Pres%	Sack%	Pass Cov	Run Def	Total	Per Cov	Per Run	Per Play
2018	12%	0%	5%	0%	0.0%	1	3	3	70	90	80
2019	4%	5%	3%	33%	0.0%	30	21	53	94	97	93
2020	4%	4%	0%	50%	0.0%	13	5	18	84	69	76
	4%	4%	2%	31%	0.0%	44	29	74	-	-	-

Andre Cisco

Report by Stephen Marciello & Noah Chang

School	Height	Weight	Year	Jersey #	Hometown
Syracuse	5116 E	209 E	3JR	7	Valley Stream, NY

One Liner
Cisco's potential as a physical and rangy ball hawking safety who has the versatility to line up nearly anywhere on the defense makes him a valuable asset, though he'll need to limit his overaggressiveness to avoid getting beaten too often at the next level.

Overall
Andre Cisco is an interchangeable safety in Syracuse's 3-3-5 defense lining up deep middle, in the slot, or in the box. He started 21 of 24 games for the Orange. Cisco missed 3 games with a lower body injury in 2019 and 11 games in 2020 with a torn ACL after colliding with a teammate during pregame warmups. He is an exceptional athlete with the ideal frame and size for the position. He has adequate burst and agility, but plays hard with very good competitiveness and toughness.

Pass Game
Against the pass, Cisco shows consistent and advanced ball skills and anticipation. From the safety position, he's almost exclusively used in zone coverage as the 1-high defender in Cover 1 or Cover 3. His ability to react to the quarterback and explode to close space towards the intended receiver creates many opportunities for pass breakups and interceptions, opportunities Cisco consistently cashes in on with his outstanding ball skills. He can get a hand in the passing lane, deliver a big hit to create an incompletion, or jump the route to intercept the pass. He shows good range as a deep safety to get to balls from numbers to numbers. When lining up in the box or in the slot in man coverage, his athleticism allows him to stay in phase with most receivers and tight ends. He's at his best in slot man coverage against bigger receivers and tight ends where he can use his strength and win with his athleticism. However, he tends to peek in the backfield or jump routes, which causes him to lose his man at times. While this can lead to interceptions, it also leads to big plays that should be prevented. In zone coverage from the slot, Cisco can quickly diagnose the play and break on quicker, shorter routes. Cisco also shows good communication skills from all areas of the field by constantly talking to his teammates.

Run Game
When playing in the box, Cisco does a good job navigating through trash. While he doesn't show an advanced ability to shed the blocks of linemen, his athleticism allows him to maneuver around block attempts and get to the ballcarrier. He's a sure, physical tackler that loves to hit and let the ballcarrier know about it. When he lines up at safety, he attacks downhill and shows discipline to not over pursue, though he does take some inefficient angles when approaching ballcarriers near the sideline.

Last Word
Cisco projects as a free safety, but has the skill set to be interchangeable and play in the box or in the slot as well. His ability to roam center field makes him an asset for teams that primarily run 1-high schemes, and that's where he'd fit best on 3rd downs, so he can use his range and athleticism on the back-end. He has gunner and special teams coverage experience which project to him being an important piece on special teams at the next level.

Strengths
- Ball skills
- Back-end instincts
- Range

Weaknesses
- Overaggressiveness
- Inefficient tackling angles

Critical Factors

3-Level Impact	FBI / Instincts	Play Speed
6	7	6

Positional Factors

Man Coverage	Zone Coverage	Range
5	6	6
Ball Skills / Tracking	Tackling	Blitz
7	6	5
Physicality	Communication	ST Value
6	6	6

Basic

Year				Coverage						Tackling		
	Trgt	Comp	Comp%	Yards	Yds/Trgt	Int	Int Drops	TD Alwd	Tkls	TFL	Brk Tkl	BT%
2018	39	17	44%	341	8.7	7	0	2	59	2.0	14	19%
2019	38	26	68%	400	10.5	5	1	7	63	0.5	15	19%
2020	2	2	100%	20	10.0	1	0	0	10	0.5	3	23%
	79	45	57%	761	9.6	13	1	9	132	3.0	32	20%

Advanced

Year		All Coverage					Man Coverage		Tackling	
	PBU	Pos%	Deserved Catch %	EPA	EPA/Trgt	Tgt	Yds/Tgt	Pos%	Tackle Share	ATD+
2018	16	36%	74%	-3.8	-0.10	23	3.4	30%	8%	89
2019	11	55%	87%	6.9	0.18	13	7.5	62%	8%	88
2020	1	100%	100%	3.7	1.83	2	10.0	100%	1%	119
	28	47%	82%	6.7	0.09	38	5.2	45%	6%	91

Deep Dive

Year	Lined Up		Blitz			Total Points			Total Points Rtg		
	Slot%	Box%	Blitz%	Pres%	Sack%	Pass Cov	Run Def	Total	Per Cov	Per Run	Per Play
2018	13%	5%	0%	100%	-	34	9	44	94	58	76
2019	14%	4%	0%	-	-	13	9	22	82	71	73
2020	12%	30%	3%	0%	0.0%	5	1	5	86	58	71
	13%	7%	0%	33%	0.0%	52	19	71	-	-	-

Richard LeCounte

Report by Evan Butler

School	Height	Weight	Year	Jersey #	Hometown
Georgia	5096 E	190 E	4SR	2	Riceboro, GA

One Liner
LeCounte has the athleticism, play speed, and instincts to make plays all over the field which should see him make an impact as a starter at the next level, though a tendancy toward over aggressiveness and a lack of top-speed could hold him back.

Overall
Richard LeCounte aligned as the strong safety for Georgia while also covering the slot at times. They run a balanced mix of man and zone coverage and primarily show 2-high looks. He played in 44 games, starting 33 of them for the Bulldogs. LeCounte missed 4 games in 2020 after suffering a concussion, broken ribs, and a shoulder injury from a motorbike accident. A former high school basketball and track competitor, he is a very good athlete who shows the ability to make plays in every area of the field with his intelligence and physical play.

Pass Game
In the pass game, LeCounte makes plays all over the field with his very good athletic ability and play speed. His instincts can be seen at all three levels when diagnosing and disrupting plays. His eyes can get caught in the backfield causing him to lose space in zone coverage and become flat-footed with tight hips. He'll also get caught peeking in the backfield in man coverage as well, as he's vulnerable to double moves. Otherwise, he shows sufficient deep zone range. LeCounte has the range to play as a single-high safety due to his instincts and speed, but when he reacts late, it's clear his range fits better when in a 2-high shell. While he doesn't have top-end speed, he does show quick acceleration and burst to close and make plays. He can cover tight ends and running backs well, allowing little separation. He'll struggle to stay up with receivers who have good speed and agility. Along with his ability to read and diagnose plays quickly, he's shown the burst to blow up screens on numerous occasions. He's the communicator on the back end, making most of the defensive calls. He seldom blitzes and struggles to get much pressure on the quarterback when he does.

Run Game
In the run game, LeCounte shows his aggressiveness and willingness to make plays at the LOS. He likes to stick his nose in plays and has the physicality to do it. He is a good tackler in traffic and in space, though his smaller frame is a worry for tackling bigger players and fending off blockers. He's aggressive in support, as he puts his foot in the ground and explodes downhill. This leaves him prone to overpursuit at times. His FBI shines through in diagnosing plays pre- and post snap.

Last Word
LeCounte projects as 3-down, interchangeable safety at the next level with his ability to make plays as a 2-deep safety and near the box against the run. On 3rd downs, he fits best in the slot or near the box up against tight ends. His physicality and toughness along with adequate play speed should allow him to be a core contributor on all special teams units.

Strengths

- FBI/Instincts
- Run support
- Toughness

Weaknesses

- Top-end speed
- Overpursuit
- Blitz

Critical Factors

3-Level Impact	FBI / Instincts	Play Speed
7	6	5

Positional Factors

Man Coverage	Zone Coverage	Range
6	6	5
Ball Skills / Tracking	Tackling	Blitz
6	6	5
Physicality	Communication	ST Value
6	6	7

Basic

				Coverage						Tackling		
Year	Trgt	Comp	Comp%	Yards	Yds/Trgt	Int	Int Drops	TD Alwd	Tkls	TFL	Brk Tkl	BT%
2017	6	3	50%	48	8.0	0	0	0	14	0.0	2	13%
2018	23	20	87%	178	7.7	1	0	0	74	1.0	24	24%
2019	26	18	69%	267	10.3	4	1	0	60	4.5	11	15%
2020	9	4	44%	83	9.2	3	1	1	27	1.0	6	18%
	64	45	70%	576	9.0	8	2	1	175	6.5	43	20%

Advanced

			All Coverage				Man Coverage			Tackling	
Year	PBU	Pos%	Deserved Catch %	EPA	EPA/Trgt	Tgt	Yds/Tgt	Pos%	Tackle Share	ATD+
2017	1	50%	75%	1.6	0.27	1	17.0	100%	2%	-
2018	3	70%	100%	13.8	0.60	8	8.8	88%	8%	104
2019	10	54%	86%	5.7	0.22	18	6.9	50%	7%	124
2020	6	44%	67%	3.4	0.38	2	7.0	100%	4%	110
	20	58%	89%	24.6	0.38	29	7.8	66%	5%	111

Deep Dive

	Lined Up		Blitz			Total Points			Total Points Rtg		
Year	Slot%	Box%	Blitz%	Pres%	Sack%	Pass Cov	Run Def	Total	Per Cov	Per Run	Per Play
2018	11%	4%	0%	50%	0.0%	15	14	29	76	84	76
2019	11%	6%	2%	40%	10.0%	32	9	45	91	73	84
2020	13%	2%	1%	33%	0.0%	16	5	21	98	81	89
	11%	5%	1%	40%	7.1%	63	28	95	-	-	-

Damar Hamlin

Final Grade: 6.

Report by Joe McDonald & Nathan Cooper

School	Height	Weight	Year	Jersey #	Hometown
Pittsburgh	6005 V	201 V	5SR	3	McKees Rocks, PA

One Liner

Hamlin has a very high football IQ with the ball skills and coverage ability to be a solid coverag safety at the next level, but his fundamentals and inability to shed blocks in the run game likel hold him back.

Overall

Damar Hamlin is a starting safety for Pittsburgh's 4-3 defense running a mix of zone and man coverage. He played in 49 games for the Panthers, starting 40 of those games. He suffered a sports hernia his senior year of high school that he played through, but required 3 surgeries that forced missing 10 games in 2016 and 3 in 2017. A high school basketball and track athlete, his athleticism is on full display on the football field. He has a tall frame that and could benefit from filling out a little more. He is a tough player with a high motor and a confident competitive attitude.

Pass Game

In the pass game, Hamlin is a sufficient defender in zone coverage. He tends to catch receivers and wait until they have eaten up his cushion to turn to get deep and lacks the speed to catch up once beat. What he lacks in speed he makes up for with a high football IQ in zone as he diagnoses plays and breaks on underneath routes quickly. He uses this high IQ with good burst to bait quarterbacks and jump passes for interceptions or pass breakups. In man coverage, he can struggle a little against speedy receivers, but plays physical against backs and tight ends, and shows sticky coverage to negate them from being an option for the quarterback. He breaks up passes by both playing through the ball or bringing a high-impact hit on the receiver at the catch

point. He is highly aware of the play happening around him and is good a communicating with the rest of his secondary directing them where to go as plays develop.

Run Game

In the run game, Hamlin is a good, soli tackler who can wrap up or bring the boom b lowering his shoulder. He is highly effectiv making open-field tackles by breaking dow and attacking the runner low, though he'll mis a few too many. He's also able to diagnose th run and fills the run lane quickly. He i aggressive in the run game, occasionally to fault as he can bite on play action. Whe getting blocked, his light frame makes it toug to shed blocks, even against receivers However, he plays physical and still compete to get to the ballcarrier.

Last Word

Hamlin projects as a solid No. 3 free safety He's an interchangeable safety who has th range and ball skills on the back end to play a part of a 2-high set or can use his ma coverage and tackling ability to line up in th box or across from tight ends in the slot. O 3rd down, he would be best served in the slo manning up tight ends or in zone on the bac end in half-field coverage. He shows enoug play speed with the competitiveness an toughness to play on most special teams units.

Strengths
- Play diagnosis
- Playing through the ball
- Open-field tackling

Weaknesses
- Play speed
- Coverage funadmentals
- Block shedding

Critical Factors

3-Level Impact	FBI / Instincts	Play Speed
6	7	5

Positional Factors

Man Coverage	Zone Coverage	Range
6	5	5
Ball Skills / Tracking	Tackling	Blitz
6	6	4
Physicality	Communication	ST Value
6	6	6

Basic

	Coverage								Tackling			
Year	Trgt	Comp	Comp%	Yards	Yds/Trgt	Int	Int Drops	TD Alwd	Tkls	TFL	Brk Tkl	BT%
2016	14	10	71%	146	10.4	0	0	3	7	0.0	1	13%
2017	21	11	52%	208	9.9	1	1	3	40	1.0	6	13%
2018	48	24	50%	241	5.0	2	0	5	90	3.0	11	11%
2019	52	25	48%	346	6.7	1	0	1	82	2.5	10	11%
2020	34	13	38%	202	5.9	2	2	1	65	3.5	13	17%
	169	83	49%	1143	6.8	6	3	13	284	10.0	41	13%

Advanced

	All Coverage					Man Coverage			Tackling	
Year	PBU	Pos%	Deserved Catch %	EPA	EPA/Trgt	Tgt	Yds/Tgt	Pos%	Tackle Share	ATD+
2016	0	71%	77%	10.9	0.78	9	11.4	78%	1%	-
2017	2	48%	80%	1.6	0.08	12	13.2	50%	6%	-
2018	4	46%	94%	-6.9	-0.14	30	4.0	43%	11%	105
2019	12	44%	71%	-3.9	-0.08	17	4.8	35%	11%	114
2020	9	35%	77%	-9.6	-0.28	11	9.1	73%	10%	113
	27	46%	80%	-7.8	-0.05	79	7.1	51%	8%	110

Deep Dive

	Lined Up		Blitz			Total Points			Total Points Rtg		
Year	Slot%	Box%	Blitz%	Pres%	Sack%	Pass Cov	Run Def	Total	Per Cov	Per Run	Per Play
2018	23%	1%	0%	100%	-	20	11	31	86	72	78
2019	11%	2%	0%	33%	0.0%	19	10	30	82	72	75
2020	20%	2%	1%	0%	0.0%	16	18	34	79	95	83
	18%	1%	0%	29%	0.0%	55	39	95	-	-	-

Hamsah Nasirildeen

Report by Jordan Edwards

School	Height	Weight	Year	Jersey #	Hometown
Florida State	6031 V	213 V	4SR	5	Concord, NC

One Liner
Nasirildeen has the versatility, athleticism, and tackling ability to be a three-down player, bu needs to improve his overall instincts and tracking ability to hit his full potential.

Overall
Hamsah Nasirildeen lines up at strong safety in Florida State's 3-4 scheme running a balanced mix of man and zone coverage. He has experience as a post defender, box safety, and slot corner throughout his career. He started 19 of 39 games for the Seminoles. He played only 2 games in 2020 while recovering from a torn ACL that he suffered late in 2019. He has good athleticism with long arms and a wiry frame. Pre-knee injury, he was a smooth and fluid mover out in space. In his limited snaps in 2020, some of his movement and reaction ability looked restricted. His competitiveness and aggression as a defender stand out well as a run defender.

Pass Game
Nasirildeen's athleticism immediately stands out, showing flashes of very good play speed. He has good range and shows good burst to the ball. His footwork on his zone drops is erratic and his stance is too high in his backpedals, which slows up his transition reacting to the football. His ability to process plays developing is underwhelming. He will overreact to play action and misdirection from the offense. His range and athleticism allow his coverage ability as a deep safety to be sufficient. He doesn't react well to plays developing in front of him and fails to impact pass plays as a secondary defender over the top. He uses his length well in man coverage and stays attached to receivers out in space. As a former high school wide receiver, he displays good ball skills, but his tracking skills when the ball is in the air are sufficient. Hi athleticism also shows when rushing the passe and being used as a QB spy. He didn' communicate much pre-snap, however, ther was minimal communication as a whole from the Florida State defense.

Run Game
Nasirildeen is an aggressive and productiv tackler. He takes good angles filling the alle and shows good technique at the POA. He's playmaker as a tackler and has forced handful of fumbles. Because of his role as deep safety in 2019, he displayed the ability t tackle well in the open field, however, in hi return from injury in 2020, his open-fiel tackling ability was a little underwhelming His willingness to take on blocks is a goo sign, but due to his slight frame he can ge overpowered on occasion. In short-yardag and goal-line situations, he maneuvers throug trash well and makes plays on ballcarriers.

Last Word
Nasirildeen's versatility and athleticism allow him to play all over the field, and at the nex level, he's best suited as a strong safety. Hi ability to be a chess piece for defensiv coordinators can be valuable as well. Hi talents on 3rd down are best suited near th LOS in man coverage or even as an underneat zone defender. He has experience being a ke special teams player at FSU and should be core special teams player at the next level.

Strengths

- Tackling ability
- Versatility
- Athleticism

Weaknesses

- Tracking
- FBI/Instincts
- Communication

Critical Factors

3-Level Impact	FBI / Instincts	Play Speed
6	5	6

Positional Factors

Man Coverage	Zone Coverage	Range
6	5	6
Ball Skills / Tracking	**Tackling**	**Blitz**
5	7	5
Physicality	**Communication**	**ST Value**
6	5	7

Basic

Year	Trgt	Comp	Comp%	Yards	Yds/Trgt	Int	Int Drops	TD Alwd	Tkls	TFL	Brk Tkl	BT%
2017	16	8	50%	110	6.9	0	0	0	24	0.0	3	11%
2018	30	22	73%	293	9.8	1	0	4	89	0.5	9	9%
2019	21	10	48%	105	5.0	2	0	0	103	3.0	11	10%
2020	3	2	67%	25	8.3	1	0	0	12	1.5	2	14%
	70	42	60%	533	7.6	4	0	4	228	5.0	25	10%

Advanced

Year	PBU	Pos%	Deserved Catch %	EPA	EPA/Trgt	Tgt	Yds/Tgt	Pos%	Tackle Share	ATD+
2017	4	50%	75%	2.3	0.14	12	7.3	50%	3%	-
2018	3	73%	88%	14.4	0.48	12	8.0	83%	11%	111
2019	5	38%	92%	-8.5	-0.40	5	2.2	40%	11%	103
2020	2	67%	67%	0.6	0.19	3	8.3	67%	2%	148
	14	57%	85%	8.8	0.13	32	6.9	63%	7%	110

Deep Dive

Year	Slot%	Box%	Blitz%	Pres%	Sack%	Pass Cov	Run Def	Total	Per Cov	Per Run	Per Play
2018	25%	17%	8%	0%	0.0%	0	9	8	59	73	62
2019	5%	16%	11%	17%	2.4%	19	21	42	89	95	89
2020	20%	20%	5%	0%	0.0%	7	2	9	99	92	99
	14%	16%	10%	10%	1.5%	26	32	59	-	-	-

Talanoa Hufanga

Report by John Todd

School	Height	Weight	Year	Jersey #	Hometown
USC	6006 E	215 E	3JR	15	Corvallis, OR

One Liner

Hufanga plays with a frenzied motor, tone-setting physicality, and an alpha-dog mentality, but hi lapses in coverage and as a reliable tackler may keep him from an every-down role.

Overall

Talanoa Hufanga is a strong safety in USC's defense, playing more frequently in the box in 2020 and even starting an entire game at linebacker when depth was thin. He played in 24 career games, starting 21 of them. He broke his collarbone in 2018 then refractured it the following spring. After coming back, he then suffered a shoulder sprain and concussion. He has solid size and a strong frame for the position. He's not a twitchy athlete but plays faster than he'll time with an extremely hot motor and build-up speed to close.

Pass Game

Hufanga's presence is regularly felt in short to intermediate areas of the field, but he isn't a consistent playmaking threat from the deep third. He plays man coverage like a safety, in that he constantly peeks back to the quarterback instead of playing his receiver. This leads to the occasionally-jumped route but more commonly lost coverages. He's handsy over slots and tight ends and should have more penalties than he received. In zone, he's a solid hook defender and robber with his eyes in the backfield but has a lack of feel for routes around him and doesn't pass off well. He's shown major lapses in attention and awareness as a deep defender. Hufanga lacks over-the-top range to read, react, flip his hips, accelerate, and play the ball. He's a good athlete and drives well from the back side of Cover 4, even showing some comfortability from two-high, but the majority of his impactful production and ball skills have been displayed underneath. He has a knack for

finding the ball and shows natural hands to ge in passing lanes in such areas. Additionally he's a maniac as a blitzer in pursuit, but whil he's flashed quick hands, his punishing natur doesn't consistently show up when stepped u to by blockers.

Run Game

Hufanga's range and physicality shine in th run game. He naturally plays the run before th pass, which makes him late to coverag responsibilities but often the first to handoffs He's a comfortable off-ball linebacker, but h doesn't have the stoutness or take-on ability t do so full-time. His lateral and vertical moto are commendable and lead to a high volume o tackling opportunities. Despite his production however, Hufanga is not an efficient tackle Aggressive angles, leaving his feet, an wrapping up high have all led to way too man missed tackles. He's a violent finisher an plays with an infectious swagger that hi teammates feed off of, but he really needs t improve his tackling form.

Last Word

Hufanga has a three-down three-level ceiling but his best projection is as a role-playing thir safety-linebacker hybrid. He does not play th last line of defense role well in coverage or as tackler. If used in attacking, downhil situations where his assignment is to be first t the ball and not last, he has a bright future. H has the experience and perfect skill set to be a ace on special teams.

Strengths	Weaknesses
• Motor and pursuit	• Form tackling
• Short-to-intermediate playmaking	• Impact at the third level
• Tone-setting swagger	• Coverage awareness

Critical Factors

3-Level Impact	FBI / Instincts	Play Speed
5	6	7

Positional Factors

Man Coverage	Zone Coverage	Range
4	5	6
Ball Skills / Tracking	Tackling	Blitz
6	5	6
Physicality	Communication	ST Value
7	6	8

Basic

			Coverage						Tackling			
Year	Trgt	Comp	Comp%	Yards	Yds/Trgt	Int	Int Drops	TD Alwd	Tkls	TFL	Brk Tkl	BT%
2018	23	14	61%	140	6.1	0	0	1	51	2.5	11	18%
2019	18	12	67%	155	8.6	0	0	1	88	7.5	9	9%
2020	20	15	75%	131	6.6	4	1	1	63	5.5	12	16%
	61	41	67%	426	7.0	4	1	3	202	15.5	32	14%

Advanced

	All Coverage					Man Coverage			Tackling	
Year	PBU	Pos%	Deserved Catch %	EPA	EPA/Trgt	Tgt	Yds/Tgt	Pos%	Tackle Share	ATD+
2018	5	48%	74%	0.6	0.02	14	4.8	43%	7%	91
2019	3	67%	93%	10.9	0.60	8	9.5	88%	11%	96
2020	5	55%	94%	0.2	0.01	10	5.5	40%	15%	74
	13	56%	86%	11.6	0.19	32	6.2	53%	10%	89

Deep Dive

	Lined Up		Blitz			Total Points			Total Points Rtg		
Year	Slot%	Box%	Blitz%	Pres%	Sack%	Pass Cov	Run Def	Total	Per Cov	Per Run	Per Play
2018	19%	20%	4%	11%	0.0%	23	6	29	99	70	90
2019	16%	22%	9%	42%	10.6%	5	19	32	67	97	87
2020	15%	39%	23%	18%	6.8%	19	6	28	99	75	91
	17%	26%	11%	27%	7.6%	47	31	89	-	-	-

Tyree Gillespie

Report by Stephen Marciello & Blake Moore

School	Height	Weight	Year	Jersey #	Hometown
Missouri	5117 V	207 V	4SR	9	Ocala, FL

One Liner
Gillespie's discipline, versatility and 3-level impact will allow him to see the field, but a lack of on-ball production and communication will limit him to a rotational defensive back role at th NFL level.

Overall
Tyree Gillespie is a versatile safety in the Missouri Tigers base 3-3-5 defense seeing most of his time as the deep middle safety in zone, but also time in the slot and in the box in short yardage situations. He started 27 of 41 career games for the Tigers and only missed 1 game due to injury. He's a good athlete with better straight-line speed than quickness. Overall, he is a very quiet and reserved player, never jaws with the opponent, or celebrates a big play, and this approach carries over to his teammates.

Pass Game
Gillespie understands his role as the last line of defense. He's very disciplined and doesn't take many chances from his center field position. He rarely cheats to either side of the field and tends to only react to the quarterback after the ball is released. While this technique rarely gets him out of position, he's sometimes late to the catch point, especially on throws outside the numbers. With zero collegiate interceptions, taking a few more chances would improve his on-ball production. When not being used as a deep safety, Gillespie also sees time lined up over pass-catching tight ends. Most often in off-man coverage, he'll line up in the slot or in the box to shadow these types of players. He shows good reactive athleticism at the top of the routes to stay locked onto his man. While he tends to look flat-footed as a deep safety, he shows good footwork from the slot. He often matches or wins with his athleticism even though he' rarely aggressive with his upper half. Whe asked to blitz, though rare, he's a plus blitze with his straight-line speed and downhil attacking mentality.

Run Game
Against the run, Gillespie doesn't show muc aggression attacking the ballcarrier downhil but always stays disciplined in taking th proper angle. Most of his tackles in the ru game are at the 3rd-level with some coming a the 2nd-level. He has inconsistent tacklin technique and is most prone to missed tackle on jump cuts and juke moves from th ballcarrier, though he makes most tackles h has a chance on. In short-yardage situations Gillespie often lines up in the box and show much better aggressiveness and physicalit towards the ballcarrier, as he knows he doesn have to be relied on as the last line of defense.

Last Word
Gillespie projects best as a No. 3 free safety a the next level with the ability to play in the slo against tight ends and less athletic receiver: While taking some chances from the dee safety position would benefit him, he will b able to see the field on all three downs with hi discipline. He also projects to be a qualit special teams player with his straight-lin speed and ability to track down ballcarrier across the field.

Strengths
- Discipline
- Off-man coverage
- Versatility

Weaknesses
- Aggressiveness
- Communication
- Playmaking

Critical Factors

3-Level Impact	FBI / Instincts	Play Speed
6	5	6

Positional Factors

Man Coverage	Zone Coverage	Range
6	5	5
Ball Skills / Tracking	Tackling	Blitz
5	6	6
Physicality	Communication	ST Value
5	5	6

Basic

Year	Trgt	Comp	Comp%	Yards	Yds/Trgt	Int	Int Drops	TD Alwd	Tkls	TFL	Brk Tkl	BT%
2018	17	13	76%	211	12.4	0	0	4	42	1.5	6	13%
2019	13	4	31%	59	4.5	0	1	0	54	3.0	7	11%
2020	14	6	43%	86	6.1	0	1	0	49	0.5	10	17%
	44	23	52%	356	8.1	0	2	4	145	5.0	23	14%

Advanced

Year	PBU	Pos%	Deserved Catch %	EPA	EPA/Trgt	Tgt	Yds/Tgt	Pos%	Tackle Share	ATD+
2018	1	71%	88%	13.8	0.81	9	11.8	67%	6%	88
2019	7	31%	63%	-7.2	-0.55	7	0.7	14%	8%	95
2020	3	43%	78%	2.8	0.20	3	13.0	100%	8%	86
	11	50%	79%	9.5	0.21	19	7.9	53%	7%	90

Deep Dive

Year	Slot%	Box%	Blitz%	Pres%	Sack%	Pass Cov	Run Def	Total	Per Cov	Per Run	Per Play
2018	20%	15%	10%	14%	4.5%	-11	10	1	50	99	67
2019	10%	16%	2%	44%	12.5%	11	12	24	76	79	76
2020	3%	14%	3%	14%	0.0%	3	5	9	64	61	62
	10%	15%	4%	21%	5.4%	3	27	34	-	-	-

Aashari Crosswell

Report by Jeff Dean

School	Height	Weight	Year	Jersey #	Hometown
Arizona State	6002 E	205 E	3JR	16	Watts, CA

One Liner

Crosswell is a proven playmaker who can impact both the running and passing game, but he will need to clean up his technique out of breaks and at the catch point to become a reliable, every-down starter.

Overall

Aashari Crosswell is a slot cornerback and strong safety in Arizona State's base nickel defense. He played in 27 career games with 21 starts. In 2020, he was relegated to special teams duties Week 1 and suspended for violations of team rules before opting out of the rest of the year. Crosswell has a solid frame, but could add muscle particularly in his upper half. He has good deep speed but shows some stiffness in his hips when moving laterally. He is a tough competitor who plays with an aggressive mindset against both the run and the pass. He earned a starting spot as a true freshman and became an impact player very early on but may need to answer for his troubles in 2020.

Pass Game

Crosswell has experience playing both deep safety and in the slot and looks comfortable in each role. He has the football IQ and discipline to be an effective defensive back in either zone or man coverage. He understands zone coverage responsibilities but will have breakdowns in communication to leave receivers open. He covers receivers instead of grass when matched one-on-one without losing focus of the quarterback. Crosswell has the instincts to feel routes and the quick burst to break on the ball. When asked to cover deep, he stays disciplined and has the range to cover a large area. In man coverage, he has the speed and awareness to stick with receivers across the field or vertically. He can have some issues with his reactive footwork against quicker receivers moving laterally. He works better from off than in press as he is still learning how to use his hands. Crosswell is physical at the catch point and knocks away contested catches while also having the hands to secure interceptions. However, he can fail to get his head around and is prone to playing through his man and receiving penalties for arriving early. He was rarely asked to blitz, but with proper coverage technique, he can be very disruptive in the back end.

Run Game

Crosswell is a willing, consistent presence in run support and fights off blocks to make plays near the line. While he doesn't have many tackles broken, he comes in high and allows the ballcarrier to gain several extra yards after contact while focusing on turnovers instead of wrapping up. Crosswell tracks down ballcarriers all over the field and doesn't often lose contain responsibility when the ball comes to his side.

Last Word

Crosswell projects as a No. 3 safety who can play in any scheme. His comfortability and discipline allow him to play in either safety role or in the slot, especially if he has inside help with quicker receivers. He could see the field early on third downs and has the speed, physicality, and mindset to be a core special teams player.

Strengths

- Aggressive mindset
- Run support
- Instincts

Weaknesses

- Lateral agility
- Discipline at the catch point
- Tackling form

Critical Factors

3-Level Impact	FBI / Instincts	Play Speed
6	6	6

Positional Factors

Man Coverage	Zone Coverage	Range
5	6	6
Ball Skills / Tracking	Tackling	Blitz
6	5	4
Physicality	Communication	ST Value
6	5	6

Basic

	Coverage								Tackling			
Year	Trgt	Comp	Comp%	Yards	Yds/Trgt	Int	Int Drops	TD Alwd	Tkls	TFL	Brk Tkl	BT%
2018	39	18	46%	239	6.1	4	2	2	43	1.0	6	12%
2019	43	20	47%	346	8.0	2	1	5	47	2.0	5	10%
	82	38	46%	585	7.1	6	3	7	90	3.0	11	11%

Advanced

	All Coverage					Man Coverage			Tackling	
Year	PBU	Pos%	Deserved Catch %	EPA	EPA/Trgt	Tgt	Yds/Tgt	Pos%	Tackle Share	ATD+
2018	13	44%	69%	-10.6	-0.27	23	4.7	39%	5%	63
2019	11	44%	67%	1.3	0.03	28	5.8	43%	5%	86
	24	44%	68%	-9.3	-0.11	51	5.3	41%	5%	74

Deep Dive

	Lined Up		Blitz			Total Points			Total Points Rtg		
Year	Slot%	Box%	Blitz%	Pres%	Sack%	Pass Cov	Run Def	Total	Per Cov	Per Run	Per Play
2018	81%	1%	0%	0%	0.0%	16	19	34	80	92	84
2019	54%	3%	0%	0%	0.0%	34	8	42	95	68	83
	67%	2%	0%	0%	0.0%	50	27	76	-	-	-

Caden Sterns

Report by Ronan Potts

School	Height	Weight	Year	Jersey #	Hometown
Texas	6002 E	207 E	3JR	7	Cibolo, TX

One Liner
Sterns is a rangy, athletic safety with the versatility and coverage skills to be a depth safety at the NFL level, though he needs to work on taking more efficient tackling angles and become a more aggressive run support player to maximize his overall ability.

Overall
Caden Sterns is a free safety in Texas' nickel defense. He is primarily used as a deep safety, but he is also asked to cover receivers in the slot or play as a box safety on occasion. Sterns played in 29 career games, starting 28 of them for the Longhorns. He missed 4 games in 2019 with patellar tendonitis and missed a game in 2020 with a turf toe injury before opting out of the team's final 2 games to declare for the NFL Draft. He has a well-proportioned frame, and is an incredibly fluid athlete with very good play speed who competes and plays hard on every rep.

Pass Game
In pass defense, Sterns is a versatile chess piece with the ability to line up all over the defensive backfield. He has a smooth backpedal and is fluid and aggressive in transitioning to break downhill. He is good in zone coverage, especially as a single-high safety, where he is most able to showcase his range and speed in order to make plays. He is sufficient in man coverage with the ability to mirror and match his opponents well, but does have a bit of a matchup disadvantage against more physical receivers. He has good ball skills and tracking ability in both man and zone and has shown the ability to put himself in position to make a play when the ball comes his way. As a blitzer, he doesn't show much ability to create and disengage bigger blockers to get into the backfield and create pressure on the quarterback. Sterns is a very talkative player, constantly communicating with the sideline and his teammates to make sure everyone is in position and knows their assignments.

Run Game
Sterns is sufficient as an overall run support player. He is aggressive coming downhill as a tackler, and can deliver big, legal hits when he has a good head of steam, though he's best as a cleanup tackler in the short and intermediate areas of the field. He is prone to taking the occasional bad angle, which can result in missed tackles and big plays when he is the last line of defense.

Last Word
Sterns projects as a No. 3 safety who primarily plays free, but has the ability to move into the slot or even outside when matchups necessitate it. On 3rd downs, he can best be utilized as a single-high safety in order to maximize his range and proficency in zone coverage or move up and cover slot receivers or running backs. Due to his play speed, intelligence, and aggression, he has the ability to become a core special teams contributor on all units.

Strengths
- Play speed
- Range
- Versatility

Weaknesses
- Inefficient tackling angles
- Inconsistent run support aggression

Critical Factors

3-Level Impact	FBI / Instincts	Play Speed
6	5	7

Positional Factors

Man Coverage	Zone Coverage	Range
5	6	7
Ball Skills / Tracking	**Tackling**	**Blitz**
6	5	4
Physicality	**Communication**	**ST Value**
5	6	6

Basic

	Coverage								Tackling			
Year	Trgt	Comp	Comp%	Yards	Yds/Trgt	Int	Int Drops	TD Alwd	Tkls	TFL	Brk Tkl	BT%
2018	29	15	52%	249	8.6	4	0	3	62	3.0	12	16%
2019	26	16	62%	289	11.1	0	0	1	56	4.0	8	13%
2020	18	9	50%	144	8.0	1	0	1	54	1.0	7	11%
	73	40	55%	682	9.3	5	0	5	172	8.0	27	14%

Advanced

	All Coverage					Man Coverage			Tackling	
Year	PBU	Pos%	Deserved Catch %	EPA	EPA/Trgt	Tgt	Yds/Tgt	Pos%	Tackle Share	ATD+
2018	8	52%	76%	3.6	0.12	10	8.5	60%	8%	110
2019	1	54%	100%	2.6	0.10	8	15.3	38%	7%	106
2020	4	50%	73%	5.1	0.29	9	10.6	56%	8%	101
	13	52%	83%	11.3	0.16	27	11.2	52%	8%	107

Deep Dive

	Lined Up		Blitz			Total Points			Total Points Rtg		
Year	Slot%	Box%	Blitz%	Pres%	Sack%	Pass Cov	Run Def	Total	Per Cov	Per Run	Per Play
2018	13%	4%	3%	17%	8.3%	17	11	29	77	66	70
2019	16%	9%	6%	17%	5.6%	1	7	9	61	78	66
2020	8%	5%	0%	0%	0.0%	3	5	8	64	67	64
	13%	5%	3%	16%	6.5%	21	23	46	-	-	-

Brady Breeze

Report by Chad Tedder

School	Height	Weight	Year	Jersey #	Hometown
Oregon	5115 V	204 V	5SR	25	Lake Oswego, OR

One Liner
Breeze has the physicality, range, and motor to be a contributor at the next level, but his lack of on ball production and route anticipation limits his effectiveness in pass coverage.

Overall
Brady Breeze is a safety for Oregon's nickel defense where he appeared in 38 games, starting in only 4 of his last 5 games. He was used as both a free and strong safety, where he would play close to the line of scrimmage on run downs and rotate to the deep middle or half in passing situations. He opted out of the abbreviated 2020 season. He is a physically tough athlete that plays with a hot motor and plenty of speed any time he is in the game.

Pass Game
Against the pass, Breeze uses his speed to show good range and closing ability in zone coverages. He does a decent job at watching the quarterback's eyes, reading the play, and gauging his pursuit angles when playing deep coverage. When playing as a box safety, he does a good job at disrupting routes through the middle zone and can keep up with receivers as they exit. He does struggle with his mirror/match technique and route recognition in man coverage which opens him up to getting mismatched and singled out by offenses, limiting his pass defense production. He is fast enough to recover and make solid tackles on receivers if the ball is caught around him. When he does stick with a receiver he can get his head around and sufficiently break up passes. Overall, he communicates well with his other defensive backs in navigating motions and adjusting assignments. He has not bee asked to blitz nearly at all and wouldn't projec to be impactful as such beyond schemed fre rushes from the slot.

Run Game
Against the run, Breeze does a good job o playing downhill in pursuit of the ball. He ca sort his way through traffic and sideline-to sideline to meet the ballcarrier at the line o scrimmage and make a hard, strong tackle. H evades over and underneath blocks in pursuit rather than playing through them. He is no afraid to throw his body weight around i hitting runners. His hot motor does lead t overpursuit at times and results in misse tackles on shiftier runners.

Last Word
Breeze projects as a better depth strong safet that can become a capable starter by the start o his second season in the right role. He woul fit well as a nickel package substitute, wher he could rotate between deep half safet responsibilities or drop closer to the box an cover intermediate hook zones. He ma struggle in man coverage on the perimeter, bu he can smother checkdowns and play the flat and short areas of the field well. His hig motor, physicality, and speed will make him a ideal member of all special teams units.

Strengths

- Run game physicality
- Pursuit speed
- High energy and motor

Weaknesses

- Mirror/match ability
- Ball production in the air
- Route recognition

Critical Factors

3-Level Impact	FBI / Instincts	Play Speed
6	5	6

Positional Factors

Man Coverage	Zone Coverage	Range
5	6	6
Ball Skills / Tracking	**Tackling**	**Blitz**
5	6	4
Physicality	**Communication**	**ST Value**
7	5	7

Basic

Year	Trgt	Comp	Comp%	Yards	Yds/Trgt	Int	Int Drops	TD Alwd	Tkls	TFL	Brk Tkl	BT%
2016	0	0	-	0	-	0	0	0	2	0.0	0	0%
2017	3	1	33%	8	2.7	1	0	0	12	0.0	1	8%
2018	1	1	100%	71	71.0	0	0	1	3	0.0	2	40%
2019	20	9	45%	80	4.0	2	0	0	52	0.0	8	13%
	24	11	46%	159	6.6	3	0	1	69	0.0	11	14%

Advanced

Year	PBU	Pos%	Deserved Catch %	EPA	EPA/Trgt	Tgt	Yds/Tgt	Pos%	Tackle Share	ATD+
2016	0	-	-	0.0	-	0	-	-	0%	-
2017	3	33%	50%	-4.0	-1.32	0	-	-	1%	-
2018	0	100%	100%	6.4	6.36	0	-	-	0%	157
2019	5	40%	67%	-13.9	-0.69	8	3.9	38%	6%	109
	8	42%	67%	-11.5	-0.48	8	3.9	38%	2%	113

Deep Dive

Year	Slot%	Box%	Blitz%	Pres%	Sack%	Pass Cov	Run Def	Total	Per Cov	Per Run	Per Play
2018	17%	15%	9%	50%	0.0%	-6	1	-5	50	68	50
2019	23%	5%	0%	0%	0.0%	18	8	26	93	78	84
	22%	6%	1%	33%	0.0%	12	9	21	-	-	-

Jamar Johnson

Report by Jordan Edwards

School	Height	Weight	Year	Jersey #	Hometown
Indiana	6002 E	197 E	3JR	22	Sarasota, FL

One Liner
Johnson's exceptional ball skills and playmaking ability will add value to a secondary at the nex level, but his inconsistencies defending the run may hinder his ability to be an every-down contributor.

Overall
Jamar Johnson is a defensive back in the Hoosiers' base nickel defense. He primarily plays in the post as a deep safety after playing exclusively slot cornerback in 2019. He has competed in 31 games in his collegiate career and has started in 9, including all 8 in 2020. He doesn't have a big frame, but he's a fluid athlete with good hips, quick feet, and solid length. Johnson plays with good tempo and a solid motor but has some concerns with his willingness to defend against the run.

Pass Game
Johnson is a flat-out playmaker, displaying exceptional ball skills and tracking ability downfield as proven by his ball production through his career. He plays off the QB's eyes well and has the athleticism to transition and make plays at the catch point. He has good play speed and can close ground quickly. He can be diverse in both man and zone coverages. In the slot, Johnson displays good foot quickness and athleticism to carry receivers to all areas of the field. Johnson also displays the ability to blitz from different alignments, with enough physicality to collapse the pocket and finish behind the line.

Run Game
Johnson shows the physicality to be a solid run defender, but lacks the consistent willingness to do so. His instincts against the run are inconsistent, and he has some trouble locating ballcarriers through trash at the LOS. Johnson has solid production, but he's an ankle biter as a tackler. He likes to launch his shoulder into tackle attempts rather than keep his head up to strike and wrap up. He always tries to make a play on the ball and will force fumbles when possible. Johnson works poor pursuit angles at times and has had some bad misses on ballcarriers in the open field.

Last Word
Johnson projects to be a solid contributor to a defense as a versatile sub package starter. His best fit is at safety based on his ability to track and ball hawk at the third level. On third downs, he can either play deep on the back end or comfortably roll into the slot in man coverage. Johnson also has the experience and athleticism to be a core special teams contributor.

Strengths
- Ball skills and tracking
- Slot coverage
- Playmaking

Weaknesses
- Range and pursuit angles
- Open-field tackling
- Instincts against the run

Critical Factors

3-Level Impact	FBI / Instincts	Play Speed
5	5	6

Positional Factors

Man Coverage	Zone Coverage	Range
6	6	5
Ball Skills / Tracking	**Tackling**	**Blitz**
7	5	6
Physicality	**Communication**	**ST Value**
5	5	6

Basic

Year	Coverage								Tackling			
	Trgt	Comp	Comp%	Yards	Yds/Trgt	Int	Int Drops	TD Alwd	Tkls	TFL	Brk Tkl	BT%
2018	3	1	33%	58	19.3	1	0	0	1	0.0	0	0%
2019	6	3	50%	13	2.2	2	0	0	30	5.5	5	14%
2020	18	9	50%	140	7.8	4	0	0	42	3.5	12	22%
	27	13	48%	211	7.8	7	0	0	73	9.0	17	19%

Advanced

Year	All Coverage					Man Coverage			Tackling	
	PBU	Pos%	Deserved Catch %	EPA	EPA/Trgt	Tgt	Yds/Tgt	Pos%	Tackle Share	ATD+
2018	2	33%	50%	0.1	0.02	3	19.3	33%	0%	-
2019	4	33%	75%	-3.9	-0.64	3	0.0	0%	4%	120
2020	10	50%	69%	1.6	0.09	9	3.8	44%	9%	122
	16	44%	68%	-2.2	-0.08	15	6.1	33%	4%	122

Deep Dive

Year	Lined Up		Blitz			Total Points			Total Points Rtg		
	Slot%	Box%	Blitz%	Pres%	Sack%	Pass Cov	Run Def	Total	Per Cov	Per Run	Per Play
2018	57%	0%	0%	-	-	0	1	0	51	99	85
2019	89%	8%	14%	29%	14.3%	13	11	29	99	96	99
2020	22%	9%	5%	43%	8.3%	24	13	40	98	93	95
	48%	8%	8%	34%	12.1%	37	25	69	-	-	-

Kary Vincent Jr.

Report by Jeff Dean & Theo Fornaciari

School	Height	Weight	Year	Jersey #	Hometown
LSU	5096 E	189 E	4SR	5	Houston, TX

One Liner

Vincent has the track speed, alignment versatility, and ultra-fluid transition skills to be a contributing player a the next level, but his lateral agility and instincts haven't caught up yet.

Strengths: Straight-line speed; Transition fluidity; Communication
Weaknesses: Lateral footwork to mirror; Ball tracking; Instincts

Kary Vincent Jr. is primarily the nickel in LSU's base five-DB defense, rolling to safety often. He played in 38 career games with 18 starts. A member of the LSU track team, he has very good straight-line speed, but does struggle with lateral mobility. He is slightly undersized and lacks play strength. He communicates well across the back end and plays with energy and leadership.

Vincent is comfortable in man, but his feet slow at the top of routes when mirroring. He lacks the length to disrupt routes in press. He is able to make up for route separation with good burst to close gaps. He has fantastic transition fluidity in his hips to flip, accelerate, and range to deep routes and the sidelines. Vincent prefers to patiently sit and read from off coverages before breaking. His instincts have improved but he doesn't play to his true speed yet. He has good range to multiple levels and sufficient enough hands to convert at the catch point, although he struggles to get his head around and track consistently. He is not a competitor on jump balls

and plays through his man for penalties when h can't locate passes.

Vincent struggles to key and diagnose run plays fron off alignments. He lacks the play strength to worl through blocks and doesn't actively seek out run game involvement unless the ball enters his range He has sufficient physicality for his size and hi speed allows him to pursue the ball very well, but h can struggle to downshift and square up to shiftie players in the open field. Despite his size an strength, however, he does wrap with good form.

Vincent projects as a versatile reserve DB. He fit best mostly playing deep zones where he ca communicate, read the field, and range for long ball: His lateral quickness and play-strength deficiencie may hinder him as a true nickel corner, but he i comfortable in both areas, especially in a limite role. His speed and tackling should make him contributing special teamer, and returning kicks i high school suggests he could be a speedy optio there, as well.

	Coverage							Tackling			
Year	Trgt	Comp	Comp%	Yards	Yds/Trgt	Int	Int Drops	TD Alwd	Tkls	TFL	Brk Tkl	BT%
2017	17	6	35%	66	3.9	1	0	1	9	0.0	1	10%
2018	47	20	43%	315	6.7	1	0	2	31	1.5	3	9%
2019	72	34	47%	472	6.6	4	0	2	42	2.0	11	21%
	136	60	44%	853	6.3	6	0	5	82	3.5	15	15%

	All Coverage					Man Coverage			Tackling	
Year	PBU	Pos%	Deserved Catch %	EPA	EPA/Trgt	Tgt	Yds/Tgt	Pos%	Tackle Share	ATD+
2017	2	29%	70%	-4.0	-0.24	15	4.4	33%	1%	-
2018	8	36%	70%	-7.9	-0.17	31	4.6	29%	4%	47
2019	11	38%	76%	-9.2	-0.13	41	5.5	29%	5%	90
	21	36%	73%	-21.1	-0.16	87	5.0	30%	3%	72

	Lined Up		Blitz			Total Points			Total Points Rtg		
Year	Slot%	Box%	Blitz%	Pres%	Sack%	Pass Cov	Run Def	Total	Per Cov	Per Run	Per Play
2018	66%	1%	2%	29%	14.3%	21	12	35	89	95	89
2019	74%	1%	0%	-	-	40	3	42	97	57	82
	70%	1%	1%	29%	14.3%	61	15	77	-	-	-

Critical Factors	
3-Level Impact	5
FBI / Instincts	5
Play Speed	7

Positional Factors	
Man Coverage	5
Zone Coverage	6
Range	6
Ball Skills / Tracking	5
Tackling	5
Blitz	4
Physicality	5
Communication	6
ST Value	6

Joshuah Bledsoe

Report by Chad Tedder & Jon Drillings

School	Height	Weight	Year	Jersey #	Hometown
Missouri	5113 V	201 V	4SR	1	Houston, TX

One Liner

Bledsoe is a versatile, physical defensive back with burst to make an impact at the next level, but his lack of instincts and production at the catch point likely keep him from starting.

Strengths: Closing speed; Strong tackler; Positional versatility
Weaknesses: Route anticipation in man coverage; On-ball production; Anchoring the edge

Joshuah Bledsoe is a strong safety in Missouri's 3-3-5 defensive scheme spending most of his time in the slot or the box in 2020. He started 22 of 46 games for the Tigers. He is a quick, powerful athlete that plays with plenty of range and physicality, but has some room to fill out his frame. He is a tough competitor that seeks to make a play whenever he can.

Bledsoe shows his versatility in coverage. In man on slot receivers, he shows the ability to stay in phase and not allow a throwing window. When targeted, he gets his head around or fights for positioning to make a play on the ball. He uses his hands well to disrupt routes at the stem, using his strength to stay with receivers across the field. However, he can get caught a little flat-footed when not fully anticipating routes. He can get turned around in these situations, but has the acceleration to close when beat. While he can play nearly anywhere in zone, he has good spatial awareness to find receivers moving through his zone and is quick to close once the ball's thrown.

When he rotates to a single side, he shows decent range to get deep, but lacks tracking ability to make plays at the catch point. He communicates well, both pre-snap and in tradeoffs with his teammates.

Bledsoe shows sideline-to-sideline range to make a tackle out on the edge. He can weave his way through linemen, shoot gaps, and potentially make plays behind the line. He wraps up to make a sure tackle when given the chance and can attack the legs of bigger runners. When lined up in the box, he can get pushed around a bit and struggle to anchor out in the D-gap, getting driven further outside or pushed back inside.

Bledsoe projects as a backup strong safety with the versatility to be used as a slot corner as well. On 3rd down, he can be a moveable piece to rotate to the deep middle on blitzes, man up in the slot, or cover the flat in zone situations. His physicality, speed, and toughness make him a special teams contributor.

			Coverage						Tackling			
Year	Trgt	Comp	Comp%	Yards	Yds/Trgt	Int	Int Drops	TD Alwd	Tkls	TFL	Brk Tkl	BT%
2017	15	7	47%	142	9.5	0	0	2	12	1.0	1	8%
2018	19	7	37%	148	7.8	0	0	2	29	0.0	2	6%
2019	44	21	48%	387	8.8	0	1	3	49	3.5	12	20%
2020	40	20	50%	378	9.5	1	0	3	46	2.5	10	18%
	118	55	47%	1055	8.9	1	1	10	136	7.0	25	16%

		All Coverage				Man Coverage			Tackling	
Year	PBU	Pos%	Deserved Catch %	EPA	EPA/Trgt	Tgt	Yds/Tgt	Pos%	Tackle Share	ATD+
2017	0	33%	82%	3.8	0.25	10	9.2	30%	1%	-
2018	3	37%	62%	2.9	0.15	13	10.3	46%	4%	105
2019	8	48%	80%	9.9	0.22	33	9.3	52%	7%	62
2020	7	43%	78%	-5.6	-0.14	31	7.0	39%	8%	107
	18	42%	77%	10.9	0.09	87	8.6	44%	5%	85

	Lined Up		Blitz			Total Points			Total Points Rtg		
Year	Slot%	Box%	Blitz%	Pres%	Sack%	Pass Cov	Run Def	Total	Per Cov	Per Run	Per Play
2018	44%	4%	2%	33%	0.0%	8	7	15	74	67	69
2019	49%	26%	2%	50%	0.0%	6	9	16	67	66	66
2020	58%	32%	1%	25%	0.0%	15	9	24	80	68	72
	51%	22%	2%	39%	0.0%	29	25	55	-	-	-

Critical Factors	
3-Level Impact	6
FBI / Instincts	5
Play Speed	6

Positional Factors	
Man Coverage	5
Zone Coverage	6
Range	6
Ball Skills / Tracking	5
Tackling	6
Blitz	4
Physicality	6
Communication	6
ST Value	6

Israel Mukuamu

Report by Ronan Potts

School	Height	Weight	Year	Jersey #	Hometown
South Carolina	6026 E	205 E	3JR	24	Bossier City, LA

One Liner

Mukuamu is a versatile, ball-hawking defensive back whose limitations in outside man coverage an inconsistency as a tackler will likely lead to him being a role-playing safety at the NFL level.

Strengths: Ball skills; Range; Versatility
Weaknesses: Inconsistent in outside man coverage; Inefficient tackler; Limited physicality

Israel Mukuamu is a cornerback in South Carolina's base 3-3-5 defense where he primarily lines up as an outside corner, though he's used as a safety and slot corner as well. He started 19 of 31 career games with 15 starts at corner and 4 at safety. Mukuamu is tall, lanky, and high-waisted, with room to bulk up a little bit. He's a smart, aggressive player with good burst and sufficient long speed.

Mukuamu shows impressive ball skills when in coverage. He has a knack for undercutting routes and making plays, showing his on-ball production consists of pass breakups and interceptions. In zone, he shows good range and instincts with good burst and aggression when moving downhill. In man, because he's so high-waisted, he struggles to smoothly flip his hips and his somewhat deficient long speed makes him a liability against vertical routes when he is asked to cover on the outside. He performs better when asked to move inside and cover tight ends or slots, as he can keep the game in front of him and rely on his ball skills and instincts. He

shows the ability to communicate coverages an switches from both the corner and safety positions.

Mukuamu is good at sticking to his run fits and is a aggressive player who isn't afraid to come up and hi someone, but needs to work on his technique and hi inconsistent play strength, which can lead to hir giving up ground to stronger opponents. Mainl playing corner, the majority of his tackles come o the outside near the 2nd level, but from the safet position, he can and should be able to make som more plays near the line of scrimmage.

Because of his physical limitations that could hampe his effectiveness as a corner at the next level Mukuamu projects as a versatile backup safety wh can be moved around as a coverage specialist. O 3rd downs, he can play both deep safety and com down into the slot to cover TEs or bigger/slower slo receivers. Mukuamu's aggressive mentality an intelligence should be a fit for special teams, but hi lacking long speed and tackling ability will likel limit him.

			Coverage						Tackling			
Year	Trgt	Comp	Comp%	Yards	Yds/ Trgt	Int	Int Drops	TD Alwd	Tkls	TFL	Brk Tkl	BT%
2018	26	11	42%	141	5.4	1	0	1	16	2.0	3	16%
2019	56	25	45%	463	8.3	4	1	2	57	2.0	2	3%
2020	12	9	75%	162	13.5	2	0	3	10	0.0	3	23%
	94	45	48%	766	8.1	7	1	6	83	4.0	8	9%

	All Coverage					Man Coverage			Tackling	
Year	PBU	Pos%	Deserved Catch %	EPA	EPA/Trgt	Tgt	Yds/Tgt	Pos%	Tackle Share	ATD+
2018	2	31%	86%	-8.9	-0.34	17	3.1	18%	2%	93
2019	10	45%	82%	3.1	0.06	24	3.5	29%	8%	72
2020	2	75%	100%	4.2	0.35	5	17.6	80%	2%	79
	14	45%	86%	-1.7	-0.02	46	4.9	30%	4%	77

	Lined Up		Blitz			Total Points			Total Points Rtg		
Year	Slot%	Box%	Blitz%	Pres%	Sack%	Pass Cov	Run Def	Total	Per Cov	Per Run	Per Play
2018	19%	2%	1%	0%	0.0%	15	7	22	98	86	91
2019	14%	3%	0%	0%	0.0%	21	18	39	85	85	82
2020	19%	3%	0%	-	-	8	4	12	94	68	80
	16%	3%	0%	0%	0.0%	44	29	73	-	-	-

Critical Factors	
3-Level Impact	6
FBI / Instincts	6
Play Speed	6

Positional Factors	
Man Coverage	5
Zone Coverage	6
Range	6
Ball Skills / Tracking	7
Tackling	4
Blitz	5
Physicality	5
Communication	6
ST Value	5

Richie Grant

Report by Jeff Dean

School	Height	Weight	Year	Jersey #	Hometown
UCF	5115 V	200 V	5SR	27	Fort Walton Beach, FL

One Liner

Grant has the communication ability, physicality, and ball skills teams look for in a safety, but his issues in zone, lack of deep speed, and tackling form likely limit him to a versatile reserve player.

Strengths: Ball skills; Physicality; Communication skills
Weaknesses: FBI in zone coverage; Tackling form; Deep speed

Richie Grant rotated at both safety positions in UCF's 4-2-5 defense. He started 34 of 48 career games. Grant is a sufficient athlete who has solid burst, but lacks deep speed. He's slightly undersized with sticky hips and adequate strength, but could support more muscle on his frame. He is a fierce competitor who wants to make plays all over the field and steps up in clutch situations.

Grant isn't overly twitchy in man coverage which can lead to separation out of breaks, but has enough instincts and reactive ability to stay with receivers. He lacks deep speed to keep up, but is physical in the slot at the line. When up against bunch in zone, he's often late reacting to crossing routes and picks up the wrong man too often. He lacks some zone discipline and will get caught peeking in the backfield too much. When he plays farther back from the LOS, he does a better job of scanning the field. He tracks the ball well and frequently makes plays on the ball. His soft hands turn deflections into turnovers. He has sufficient range, but delayed play recognition and lack of deep speed can make him a liability when a play breaks into the open field. He shows very good communication skills and is seen lining his players up before the snap.

Grant is aggressive and frequently supports the run. Despite his size, he's willing to deliver big hits and sacrifice his body. However, this attitude can result in him not breaking down and missing too many tackles. He struggles to shed blocks, but shows solid effort continuously throughout a play. His knack for creating turnovers shows up in the run game as well with numerous forced fumbles credited to his hard hits. When patient and reading the play correctly, he consistently makes plays in the run game.

Richie Grant projects as a versatile backup strong safety who would best be utilized around the line of scrimmage in run support, but can also guard targets out of the slot as a nickel CB. His history of creating turnovers shows he can be a slot defender on 3rd downs. His playing style suggests he'd be a contributing special teams player.

			Coverage						Tackling			
Year	Trgt	Comp	Comp%	Yards	Yds/Trgt	Int	Int Drops	TD Alwd	Tkls	TFL	Brk Tkl	BT%
2017	16	9	56%	178	11.1	0	0	1	21	1.0	4	16%
2018	28	16	57%	248	8.9	6	0	2	106	2.5	21	17%
2019	30	13	43%	183	6.1	1	2	2	81	4.0	18	18%
2020	27	10	37%	145	5.4	3	1	1	74	4.0	6	8%
	101	48	48%	754	7.5	10	3	6	282	11.5	49	15%

	All Coverage					Man Coverage			Tackling	
Year	PBU	Pos%	Deserved Catch %	EPA	EPA/Trgt	Tgt	Yds/Tgt	Pos%	Tackle Share	ATD+
2017	4	44%	71%	1.8	0.11	10	10.2	50%	2%	-
2018	9	46%	83%	5.6	0.20	11	6.2	45%	11%	73
2019	7	33%	67%	-0.5	-0.02	12	4.4	33%	9%	96
2020	10	30%	61%	-11.2	-0.41	11	5.3	27%	10%	100
	30	38%	70%	-4.2	-0.04	44	6.4	39%	8%	87

	Lined Up		Blitz			Total Points			Total Points Rtg		
Year	Slot%	Box%	Blitz%	Pres%	Sack%	Pass Cov	Run Def	Total	Per Cov	Per Run	Per Play
2018	20%	13%	2%	0%	0.0%	15	16	30	76	65	67
2019	24%	4%	1%	25%	0.0%	11	10	21	71	66	67
2020	29%	15%	7%	30%	4.5%	25	20	47	95	96	93
	24%	10%	3%	23%	2.7%	51	46	98	-	-	-

Critical Factors	
3-Level Impact	5
FBI / Instincts	5
Play Speed	5

Positional Factors	
Man Coverage	6
Zone Coverage	5
Range	5
Ball Skills / Tracking	6
Tackling	5
Blitz	5
Physicality	6
Communication	7
ST Value	6

Mark Webb

Report by Sales Pinckney & Max Nuscher

School	Height	Weight	Year	Jersey #	Hometown
Georgia	6013 V	210 V	4SR	23	Philadelphia, PA

One Liner

Webb is a physical defensive back with good size and zone coverage skills, but needs to improve his change of direction and short-area quickness to become more than just a versatile backup at the next level.

Strengths: Long speed; Physicality; Form tackling
Weaknesses: Man coverage; Ball skills; Transition/COD ability

Mark Webb aligns as the STAR or slot cornerback in Georgia's nickel defense, but has lined up everywhere except on the line. He started 13 of 50 career games and was recruited as a wide receiver, but switched to defensive back early his freshman season. He has a lean, muscular frame and is a good overall athlete. He is a high-motor player with a tough and competitive mentality.

In coverage, Webb displays good route recognition and eye discipline while patrolling his zone, maintaining depth in his drops. He shows good pre-snap communication skills, but is often on the receiving end verifying calls. He can see and understand what is happening in front of him, but can be slow to react once he's diagnosed the play. His footwork and transition are sufficient, though hamper his ability to quickly change direction and close due to too many steps at the top of his drop. Occasionally he'll get flat-footed in coverage on long-developing plays, which can lead to a lack of burst when the time comes to react and make a play. When the ball's in

the air, he shows sufficient ball tracking ability, bu when he's in position, his ball skills leave somethin, to be desired. As a result, he doesn't have an extensive history of on-ball production, mainl stemming from poorly-thrown or ill-advised passes In man, he uses his long speed to remain wit receivers, but his merely sufficient short-are quickness can lead to gaps early in the route. He ha adequate blitz production when asked to do so though it's rare that he is.

Webb shows good tackling ability and aggression with good pursuit angles. Most of his production comes at the 2nd level and does a good job being th force defender to turn ballcarriers back inside.

Webb projects as a versatile backup strong safety in zone-heavy defense due to his range and tackling ability. He also has the skill set to back up as a slo corner where he can use his physicality against tight ends, especially on 3rd downs. He has the speed and toughness to be a valuable special teams player.

Year	\multicolumn{7}{Coverage}								\multicolumn{5}{Tackling}				

					Coverage								Tackling			
Year	Trgt	Comp	Comp%	Yards	Yds/Trgt	Int	Int Drops	TD Alwd		Tkls	TFL	Brk Tkl	BT%			
2017	0	0	-	0	-	0	0	0		0	0.0	0	-			
2018	17	13	76%	138	8.1	0	0	1		14	0.0	2	13%			
2019	38	25	66%	302	7.9	0	0	3		47	3.0	3	6%			
2020	25	12	48%	173	6.9	1	2	1		21	0.0	2	9%			
	80	50	63%	613	7.7	1	2	5		82	3.0	7	8%			

			All Coverage				Man Coverage			Tackling	
Year	PBU	Pos%	Deserved Catch %	EPA	EPA/Trgt	Tgt	Yds/Tgt	Pos%	Tackle Share	ATD+
2017	0	-		0.0	-	0	-	-	0%	-
2018	4	47%	76%	-2.1	-0.12	11	6.9	45%	2%	68
2019	3	55%	91%	7.6	0.20	23	9.0	57%	6%	117
2020	3	44%	94%	-7.9	-0.32	13	6.2	23%	3%	92
	10	50%	88%	-2.4	-0.03	47	7.7	45%	3%	101

	Lined Up		Blitz			Total Points			Total Points Rtg		
Year	Slot%	Box%	Blitz%	Pres%	Sack%	Pass Cov	Run Def	Total	Per Cov	Per Run	Per Play
2018	41%	28%	1%	50%	0.0%	6	5	11	83	99	92
2019	81%	15%	8%	10%	0.0%	7	6	14	69	77	70
2020	82%	8%	4%	29%	0.0%	2	2	5	62	70	65
	73%	16%	5%	16%	0.0%	15	13	30	-	-	-

Critical Factors	
3-Level Impact	5
FBI / Instincts	5
Play Speed	6

Positional Factors	
Man Coverage	5
Zone Coverage	6
Range	6
Ball Skills / Tracking	5
Tackling	6
Blitz	5
Physicality	6
Communication	5
ST Value	6

Lawrence White IV

Report by Nathan Cooper

School	Height	Weight	Year	Jersey #	Hometown
Iowa State	5117 V	195 V	5SR	11	Bakersfield, CA

One Liner

White can wear a lot of hats for a defense and plays fast and with the aggression to contribute at the next level, though he'll need to get stronger and improve his overall zone coverage and tackling ability to maximize his potential.

Strengths: Plays fast; Aggressive run support; Versatility
Weaknesses: Lacks zone awareness; Can take bad angles; Slips off some tackles

Lawrence White IV plays strong safety to the boundary in Iowa State's 3-3-5 defense. He wears a lot of hats, rotating as a single-high, half-field, flat, and slot defender. He started 31 of 49 games for the Cyclones. He's a twitchy athlete that plays with good speed. Despite a slight frame, he plays hard, physical, and competes with toughness.

White is a versatile defender that can play all over the field. He's a smooth mover and transitions easily which allows him to stay with most slot receivers, tight ends, and running backs. In zone, he's disruptive and breaks well on passes in front of him, but lacks a little awareness when receivers are running behind him. He has the speed to stay with crossers and the range to be a half-field defender. He shows that he can get up and make a play on the ball at the catch point. Some bigger receivers are able to post him up, but he knocks the majority of passes away. He didn't visibly show much as a communicator, but it's easy to see his FBI in ISU's complex defense. He can blitz and get into the backfield if given a lane, but isn't able to create much.

White is an aggressive run supporter, flying downhill and filling run lanes. Once he notices run, he breaks quickly and works to get off any blocks to get to the ballcarrier. His speed allows him to pursue from behind, but there are times he relies on that speed too much by taking bad angles. He mostly makes good tackles at every level of the defense, including near or behind the LOS, but will slip off some bigger backs. He's also more of a drag-down defender and isn't stout enough to deliver a true blow.

White projects as a scheme-versatile free safety at the next level, who can play interchangeably at strong safety and as a slot cornerback. On 3rd downs, he fits best rolling into the slot to man-up receivers and tight ends. Due to his aggressiveness and play speed, he has the ability to be a core special teams player.

			Coverage						Tackling			
Year	Trgt	Comp	Comp%	Yards	Yds/Trgt	Int	Int Drops	TD Alwd	Tkls	TFL	Brk Tkl	BT%
2017	4	3	75%	30	7.5	0	0	1	16	0.0	1	6%
2018	12	10	83%	169	14.1	0	0	1	46	2.5	8	15%
2019	23	9	39%	134	5.8	2	3	0	81	4.0	12	13%
2020	34	21	62%	342	10.1	1	0	4	56	1.5	10	15%
	73	43	59%	675	9.2	3	3	6	199	8.0	31	13%

	All Coverage					Man Coverage			Tackling	
Year	PBU	Pos%	Deserved Catch %	EPA	EPA/Trgt	Tgt	Yds/Tgt	Pos%	Tackle Share	ATD+
2017	1	75%	75%	3.2	0.79	1	9.0	100%	2%	-
2018	1	67%	92%	8.5	0.71	3	4.0	67%	6%	121
2019	6	26%	77%	-5.2	-0.23	4	6.5	25%	10%	115
2020	4	47%	84%	17.4	0.51	9	17.1	67%	8%	109
	12	45%	83%	23.9	0.33	17	11.8	59%	6%	116

	Lined Up		Blitz			Total Points			Total Points Rtg		
Year	Slot%	Box%	Blitz%	Pres%	Sack%	Pass Cov	Run Def	Total	Per Cov	Per Run	Per Play
2018	17%	2%	3%	25%	12.5%	-1	8	7	57	76	64
2019	45%	10%	6%	24%	4.0%	21	15	38	85	83	82
2020	43%	5%	2%	29%	0.0%	1	12	14	60	79	67
	38%	6%	4%	25%	5.0%	21	35	59	-	-	-

Critical Factors	
3-Level Impact	5
FBI / Instincts	5
Play Speed	6

Positional Factors	
Man Coverage	6
Zone Coverage	5
Range	6
Ball Skills / Tracking	6
Tackling	5
Blitz	5
Physicality	6
Communication	6
ST Value	7

Nahshon Wright

Report by Joe McDonald

School	Height	Weight	Year	Jersey #	Hometown
Oregon State	6031 E	188 E	3JR	2	East Palo Alto, CA

One Liner

Wright has exceptional length for the secondary, but while he has the cornerback experience, his skill set for safety will make for a solid versatile backup at the next level.

Strengths: Instincts in zone; Run-support aggression; Natural ball skills
Weaknesses: Reactive quickness in man; Body control; Consistent form tackling

Nahshon Wright is a cornerback in Oregon State's defense. He attended Laney Junior College before transferring to Oregon State in 2019. He has started 13 of 18 games played since arriving in Corvallis. He is a wide corner who typically lines up near his own sideline. A former wide receiver, Nahshon is extremely tall, long, and lanky. He plays with a high degree of confidence and intensity and has a short memory for negative plays.

In the pass game, Wright shows good instincts in zone but struggles to react quickly to receivers in man. His length is an asset in press but he doesn't have the quick foot speed to stay close against quality route runners, often getting desperate with his size and physicality to stay connected. His long strides eat up ground in straight-line situations and he shows solid closing speed. He consistently keeps his eyes on the quarterback in zone while feeling the routes around him. He has a good feel for the ball and uses his athleticism and natural ball skills to high point. He is a good communicator in the secondary,

consistently pointing and shouting to fellow defensive backs their assignments. He hasn't been asked to blitz much at all, but his size, speed and aggression could be decent qualities if asked.

In the run game, Wright is very aggressive in support. He is usually a good form tackler to wrap up, but his size hinders his pad level and leverage at the point of attack. He isn't afraid to mix it up in crowd or take on a player in the open field. He would benefit greatly from gaining weight to make him more formidable defender.

Wright has played corner through his collegiate career, but may best project as a free or strong safety in the NFL. His zone awareness, length and physicality would be good traits in the back end while also restricting his struggles with reactive quickness up close. He has fluid hips to flip, turn and run, and the range and ball skills to be playmaker. He should also be a good coverage unit member on special teams.

			Coverage							Tackling			
Year	Trgt	Comp	Comp%	Yards	Yds/Trgt	Int	Int Drops	TD Alwd	Tkls	TFL	Brk Tkl	BT%	
2019	48	28	58%	394	8.2	3	0	5	31	0.5	7	18%	
2020	26	12	46%	182	7.0	2	3	1	28	1.0	2	7%	
	74	40	54%	576	7.8	5	3	6	59	1.5	9	13%	

	All Coverage					Man Coverage			Tackling	
Year	PBU	Pos%	Deserved Catch %	EPA	EPA/Trgt	Tgt	Yds/Tgt	Pos%	Tackle Share	ATD+
2019	5	56%	89%	22.3	0.46	19	10.4	68%	4%	90
2020	4	31%	87%	-11.4	-0.44	10	8.4	30%	6%	55
	9	47%	88%	10.9	0.15	29	9.7	55%	5%	69

	Lined Up		Blitz			Total Points			Total Points Rtg		
Year	Slot%	Box%	Blitz%	Pres%	Sack%	Pass Cov	Run Def	Total	Per Cov	Per Run	Per Play
2019	13%	1%	1%	50%	0.0%	19	9	28	89	85	86
2020	19%	6%	1%	50%	50.0%	-1	10	12	57	88	75
	16%	3%	1%	50%	16.7%	18	19	40	-	-	-

Critical Factors	
3-Level Impact	5
FBI / Instincts	6
Play Speed	6

Positional Factors	
Man Coverage	5
Zone Coverage	6
Range	6
Ball Skills / Tracking	6
Tackling	5
Blitz	5
Physicality	6
Communication	6
ST Value	6

Jacoby Stevens

Report by Ty Dorner, Christian Vega, & Steven Penn

School	Height	Weight	Year	Jersey #	Hometown
LSU	6012 V	216 V	4SR	7	Murfreesboro, TN

One Liner

Stevens is a strong run defender and blitzer from his safety/ box hybrid position, but his inconsistencies in coverage may hinder his role and ceiling.

Strengths: Line-of-scrimmage run defense; Blitz timing and pursuit; Nose for the ball
Weaknesses: Deep coverage; Reactive quickness in man; Long speed

Jacoby Stevens is a strong safety in LSU's base nickel defense. He has played deep safety, slot corner, and on- and off-ball linebacker, even seeing time at wide receiver his freshman year. He played in 50 games, starting 29 of them for the Tigers' defense. Stevens is a big-bodied DB with a strong frame. He doesn't possess the speed or reactive quickness to match up well on the perimeter but plays with physicality and energy near the line of scrimmage.

Stevens can blitz, take on blockers, and shed with superior athleticism in the box, and he really excels with his timing and tempo on delays. He does a great job of getting his hands up when pursuing the quarterback. He is a mediocre cover corner on receivers in the slot, but he does a sufficient job smothering backs and tight ends from the box. He struggles with quick change-of-direction athletes. He is a solid intermediate-zone defender who plays with good instincts to sense routes and get his hands into passing lanes. He's shown flashes of deep range and he tracks the ball well to disrupt the catch point, but he shouldn't be relied upon as a true centerfielder.

Stevens is a high-volume tackler in the run game and provides great value as an extra box defender. He plays with good physicality and is able to read blocks and fill gaps much like a linebacker. Any hiccups in range in the passing game he makes up for against the run. He flows across the field and has good instincts to sniff out and strike ballcarriers. He does have some issues consistently wrapping up and plays better as a first player to the ball rather than a last line of defense.

Stevens projects as a top reserve strong safety at the next level. He should be treated similar to a Will linebacker and some teams may even want to bulk him up and move him there full time. His LOS run defense stacks up with many LBs, and he adds enough athleticism to present solid underneath versatility. He should be a valuable contributor on special teams.

			Coverage						Tackling			
Year	Trgt	Comp	Comp %	Yards	Yds/ Trgt	Int	Int Drops	TD Alwd	Tkls	TFL	Brk Tkl	BT%
2017	1	1	100%	9	9.0	0	0	0	0	0.0	1	100%
2018	12	4	33%	47	3.9	1	1	2	34	6.5	6	15%
2019	31	18	58%	206	6.6	3	0	0	93	9.5	11	11%
2020	11	3	27%	87	7.9	0	1	2	64	5.5	8	11%
	55	26	47%	349	6.3	4	2	4	191	21.5	26	12%

	All Coverage					Man Coverage			Tackling	
Year	PBU	Pos%	Deserved Catch %	EPA	EPA/Trgt	Tgt	Yds/Tgt	Pos%	Tackle Share	ATD+
2017	0	100%	100%	1.1	1.11	1	9.0	100%	0%	-
2018	7	33%	67%	1.2	0.10	10	3.6	20%	4%	91
2019	9	42%	88%	1.8	0.06	13	4.0	46%	11%	104
2020	3	27%	63%	-2.3	-0.21	7	11.3	29%	11%	97
	19	38%	79%	1.8	0.03	31	5.7	35%	6%	99

	Lined Up		Blitz			Total Points			Total Points Rtg		
Year	Slot%	Box%	Blitz%	Pres%	Sack%	Pass Cov	Run Def	Total	Per Cov	Per Run	Per Play
2018	51%	27%	14%	43%	10.0%	0	8	15	59	97	92
2019	35%	30%	11%	26%	7.7%	15	23	43	74	93	82
2020	9%	34%	8%	41%	11.1%	10	18	33	73	95	86
	29%	31%	10%	33%	8.9%	25	49	91	-	-	-

Critical Factors	
3-Level Impact	5
FBI / Instincts	6
Play Speed	5

Positional Factors	
Man Coverage	5
Zone Coverage	5
Range	6
Ball Skills / Tracking	6
Tackling	6
Blitz	7
Physicality	6
Communication	5
ST Value	6

Divine Deablo

Report by Justin Serovich & Michael Churchward

School	Height	Weight	Year	Jersey #	Hometown
Virginia Tech	6033 V	226 V	5SR	17	Winston-Salem, NC

One Liner

Deablo is a big, strong safety who has all the physical tools to compete at the next level, but needs to improv on his instincts and reaction time to see consistent playing time.

Strengths: Fundamental tackling; Long strider to cover ground; Size/frame
Weaknesses: Instincts/reaction time; Struggles to shed blocks; Limited man coverage ability

Divine Deablo is a safety in Virginia Tech's 4-2-5 defense who primarily plays in the deep middle of the field, but will also rotate into the slot and box. He started 22 of 51 games in his career. He missed 9 games in 2017 with a fractured left foot and 2 games in 2018 with an ankle injury. He has the frame of a linebacker and the range of a safety. He plays hard and shows toughness through physicality.

Deablo rarely allows defenders to get behind him when playing a deep zone and understands he's the last line of defense. He covers space well, using his long stride to make up ground. When playing underneath zone, Deablo tends to cover grass instead of receivers. He can close gaps, but he reacts slightly too late to make a play. In man, he has the speed and physicality to cover tight ends. Against faster receivers, he struggles to react and mirror their movements. He blitzed occasionally and had success getting pressure, but failed to secure sacks, mainly due to his depth at the snap.

Deablo has not shown a consistent presence in th run game. When playing in the box, he often make incorrect reads, or bites on the wrong choice on rea options. He is slow to read and react, which ha caused him to lag behind on plays. He doesn't attac the ball, and instead waits for the play to come t him. This hesitation leads to him getting easil blocked and taken out of plays. His biggest strengt in the run game is his consistent tackling. While h may miss a tackle occasionally, he's improved b limiting broken tackle attempts. Deablo has all of th physical tools to be successful in the run game, bu struggles to put it all together.

Deablo projects as a backup box safety at the nex level where he can use his athleticism and physicalit around the LOS while also showing enough range t play deep as well. On 3rd down, he should man-u tight ends in the slot. His size, athleticism, an physicality should allow him to contribute on mos special teams units.

			Coverage						Tackling			
Year	Trgt	Comp	Comp%	Yards	Yds/ Trgt	Int	Int Drops	TD Alwd	Tkls	TFL	Brk Tkl	BT%
2017	7	1	14%	11	1.6	1	0	0	7	1.5	0	0%
2018	28	12	43%	266	9.5	0	0	1	50	4.5	14	22%
2019	31	22	71%	318	10.3	1	2	2	77	5.0	11	13%
2020	14	6	43%	62	4.4	4	1	1	57	2.0	5	8%
	80	41	51%	657	8.2	6	3	4	191	13.0	30	14%

	All Coverage					Man Coverage			Tackling	
Year	PBU	Pos%	Deserved Catch %	EPA	EPA/Trgt	Tgt	Yds/Tgt	Pos%	Tackle Share	ATD+
2017	4	14%	25%	-3.7	-0.52	3	0.0	0%	1%	-
2018	2	32%	87%	2.7	0.10	12	7.7	25%	6%	119
2019	3	55%	96%	11.5	0.37	13	7.5	46%	10%	108
2020	8	36%	80%	-9.6	-0.69	5	7.0	60%	8%	77
	17	40%	85%	0.9	0.01	33	6.8	36%	6%	101

	Lined Up		Blitz			Total Points			Total Points Rtg		
Year	Slot%	Box%	Blitz%	Pres%	Sack%	Pass Cov	Run Def	Total	Per Cov	Per Run	Per Play
2018	44%	11%	2%	25%	0.0%	15	14	28	84	77	77
2019	33%	20%	2%	22%	0.0%	5	21	27	64	93	75
2020	25%	28%	4%	0%	0.0%	25	14	38	91	85	85
	34%	20%	3%	13%	0.0%	45	49	93	-	-	-

Critical Factors	
3-Level Impact	5
FBI / Instincts	5
Play Speed	5

Positional Factors	
Man Coverage	4
Zone Coverage	5
Range	6
Ball Skills / Tracking	4
Tackling	6
Blitz	5
Physicality	6
Communication	5
ST Value	6

Redshirt season not shown but included in totals

Christian Uphoff

Report by Nathan Cooper

School	Height	Weight	Year	Jersey #	Hometown
Illinois State	6024 V	213 V	5SR	24	Washington, IL

One Liner

Uphoff is a leader on the back end and excels best around the box whose indecisiveness, open-field tackling woes, and limited range ultimately force him into being a backup-level defender and special teams player at the next level.

Strengths: Runs the alley well; Zone defender; Leader & communicator
Weaknesses: Indecisive at times; Misses too many open-field tackles; Lacks range on the back end

Christian Uphoff mainly lines up to the field and plays both safety positions, but also comes in the box and off the edge in Illinois State's 3-4 defense which runs a lot of 2-high zone coverage looks. He started 15 of 37 career games for the Redbirds. Uphoff has a big frame with very good size for the position. He's a solid athlete who plays fast, hard, and competes with toughness.

Uphoff shows that he can be a good intermediate-level player. He lacks some overall range and instincts to be a single-high player, but has enough to be a solid 2-high defender. In man coverage, he has the size and play speed to line up with tight ends and stick to their hips, but isn't the reactive athlete that can stay with many quicker slot receivers. In zone, he has good eye discipline to read the quarterback and get to where the ball is going. He can make plays at the catch point and even create turnovers, but seems a tick late the majority of the time. As a blitzer, he shows good speed and relentlessness to find his way to the backfield. He struggles to get through linemen, but can usually win battles against backs. Uphoff is a leader on the field and communicates well with his teammates.

Uphoff runs the alleys well from the back end and can meet ballcarriers on the edge. As an open-field tackler, he isn't always in control and misses too many of those opportunities. When he's in the box, he's a much better tackler and seems to be more physical and under control when meeting ballcarriers. When he's making the tackle, it can come at all levels of the defense, as well as in the backfield when pursuing from behind.

Uphoff fits best as a strong safety in a scheme that mainly runs 2-high looks. He has the range to be a 2-high defender, can man up tight ends, or shift down and work off the edge. On 3rd downs, he fits best in a soft zone or as a 2-high safety. His toughness and speed should allow him to become a solid special teams contributor.

When ChicagoNow.com asked Christian Uphoff what he likes most about playing free safety, Uphoff said "I like having that range and being able to run all the way across the field. I like the freedom of it."

Football watchers thought Uphoff made the most of his freedom. He was a preseason third-team All-American selection for 2020 prior to his declaring for the draft.

Uphoff is trying to become the second Illinois State player to be drafted in the last four years, the most recent being Davontae Harris, who went to the Bengals in the fifth round in 2018. There were five Redbirds football alumni on NFL rosters in 2020, the most prominent of which were running back James Robinson and tight end James O'Shaughnessy, both of the Jaguars.

Critical Factors	
3-Level Impact	5
FBI / Instincts	5
Play Speed	6

Positional Factors	
Man Coverage	5
Zone Coverage	6
Range	5
Ball Skills / Tracking	5
Tackling	5
Blitz	6
Physicality	5
Communication	7
ST Value	6

Brad Stewart Jr.

Report by Ben Hrkach & Jordan Edwards

School	Height	Weight	Year	Jersey #	Hometown
Florida	5116 E	195 E	4SR	2	New Orleans, LA

One Liner

Stewart has the physical tools and zone coverage skills to be a productive player, but his instincts and ineffectiveness in man coverage will prevent him from being a consistent difference maker.

Strengths: Burst & speed; Zone coverage; Attacks the ball
Weaknesses: Instincts; Man coverage; Production

Brad Stewart Jr. plays safety in Florida's nickel defense that utilizes mainly Cover 3/4 looks. He primarily lined up in the slot in 2020, but also played as the boundary side safety or in the slot or down in the box. He started 20 of 41 games for the Gators in his career. He's an easy mover with good explosion and a solid frame. He displays sufficient toughness and is willing to take on blocks.

Stewart has the versatility to play as the single-high and eliminate the middle third, as well as hang underneath and disrupt the short and intermediate game. He's at his best in zone when he can see everything in front of him and pull the trigger. When taking the deep middle, Stewart gains ground in his backpedal, can fire to either sideline, and has loose hips when he needs to redirect. He lacks on-ball production, but has shown the ability to track the ball and high point. When playing underneath, he has a sufficient feel for his zone and shows good explosion when he breaks on a throw. He is a sufficient communicator and works well when passing off

receivers. Stewart will struggle in the play action and RPO game with his lack of instincts being exposed. In man, he can stay with tight ends and running backs and is sufficient against slots. He has some blitz ability and shows he can evade blockers that try to get their hands on him.

Stewart is sufficient at taking on blocks and bringing the ballcarrier down. He shows some physicality, though his willingness to mix it up varies from game to game. He's not a wrap up tackler and attempts to chop the runner down most of the time. His lack of instincts is apparent against the run, as he's frequently found in the wrong hole and there are multiple plays where the ballcarrier blows right past him without him knowing.

Stewart projects as a backup safety where he can play zone coverage near the short or intermediate levels of the secondary, but could also play deep in a 2-high set, but not consistently due to a lack of instincts. He has the play speed and toughness to play on special teams.

		Coverage								Tackling			
Year	Trgt	Comp	Comp%	Yards	Yds/Trgt	Int	Int Drops	TD Alwd	Tkls	TFL	Brk Tkl	BT%	
2017	0	0	-	0	-	1	1	0	9	0.0	1	10%	
2018	15	6	40%	119	7.9	2	1	2	38	0.0	6	14%	
2019	14	8	57%	113	8.1	0	0	1	28	2.0	3	10%	
2020	31	17	55%	231	7.5	0	0	0	45	2.5	8	15%	
	60	31	52%	463	7.7	3	2	3	120	4.5	18	13%	

	All Coverage					Man Coverage			Tackling		
Year	PBU	Pos%	Deserved Catch %	EPA	EPA/Trgt	Tgt	Yds/Tgt	Pos%	Tackle Share	ATD+	
2017	1	-		0.0	-	0		-	1%		
2018	3	33%	78%	-2.6	-0.17	4	6.5	50%	4%	99	
2019	1	50%	100%	6.1	0.44	4	5.5	25%	3%	113	
2020	3	48%	76%	4.7	0.15	13	9.8	46%	5%	92	
	8	45%	81%	8.3	0.14	21	8.3	43%	4%	100	

	Lined Up		Blitz			Total Points			Total Points Rtg		
Year	Slot%	Box%	Blitz%	Pres%	Sack%	Pass Cov	Run Def	Total	Per Cov	Per Run	Per Play
2018	9%	9%	4%	57%	0.0%	0	5	7	59	67	65
2019	7%	6%	2%	25%	12.5%	4	5	9	71	81	73
2020	57%	11%	4%	42%	8.3%	7	5	12	71	63	66
	30%	9%	4%	43%	6.8%	11	15	28	-	-	-

Critical Factors	
3-Level Impact	5
FBI / Instincts	4
Play Speed	6

Positional Factors	
Man Coverage	5
Zone Coverage	6
Range	6
Ball Skills / Tracking	6
Tackling	5
Blitz	5
Physicality	5
Communication	5
ST Value	6

Dicaprio Bootle

Report by Kyle Rodemann

School	Height	Weight	Year	Jersey #	Hometown
Nebraska	5096 E	195 E	5SR	7	Miami, FL

One Liner

Bootle is position flexible and has solid range and three-level playmaking, but he needs to improve his instincts to make a true impact as a starting-caliber player.

Strengths: Three-level impact; Range; Zone coverage

Weaknesses: Instincts; Top play speed and reactive quickness; Communication

Dicaprio Bootle is a defensive back in Nebraska's balanced coverage scheme. While he mainly played outside cornerback, he was in the slot often and was asked to play safety regularly in 2019. He played 44 games and finished his career with 32 consecutive starts. He has above-average athletic ability and shows good toughness, often playing bigger than he measures.

Bootle has experience playing at both CB and safety. He has good play recognition while playing in intermediate zones and is good at picking up receivers as they come through his area. He lacks the instincts to play as a single high safety but has but has the range and coverage skills to successfully play in a two-high scheme. In man coverage, he lacks the play speed and reactive quickness to keep up with real speed at receiver but has shown the ability to cover backs and TEs. He has a nose for the ball and does a good job of getting to the catch point for pass breakups but often fails to convert these opportunities into turnovers. Despite his often changing alignments, he has shown to be a strong communicator in the secondary.

In the run game, Bootle plays bigger than his size. He's shown improvement on run downs and does a good job playing the line of scrimmage. He misses more tackles than he should, as he tends to lower his head and fails to wrap up consistently, but he has the willingness and improved physicality to be a factor in run defense.

Bootle projects to be a backup safety in the NFL, who also has the natural position flex to play CB, having done so for much of his career. He's best suited as a strong safety who can pick up backs and tight ends and drop down in run defense. He's able to make an impact at all three levels of the field and has a lot of experience across the back end of a defense. He should be a sufficient but unspectacular special teams contributor.

			Coverage							Tackling			
Year	Trgt	Comp	Comp%	Yards	Yds/Trgt	Int	Int Drops	TD Alwd	Tkls	TFL	Brk Tkl	BT%	
2017	19	11	58%	200	10.5	0	0	2	15	1.0	2	12%	
2018	63	27	43%	374	5.9	0	1	2	40	0.0	8	17%	
2019	33	20	61%	217	6.6	0	0	5	31	0.0	11	26%	
2020	30	14	47%	211	7.0	1	1	2	26	0.0	4	13%	
	145	72	50%	1002	6.9	1	2	11	112	1.0	25	18%	

	All Coverage					Man Coverage			Tackling		
Year	PBU	Pos%	Deserved Catch %	EPA	EPA/Trgt	Tgt	Yds/Tgt	Pos%	Tackle Share	ATD+	
2017	1	53%	93%	12.0	0.63	11	11.4	45%	2%	-	
2018	15	33%	63%	-8.9	-0.14	51	6.3	35%	5%	91	
2019	5	58%	85%	10.3	0.31	19	4.4	53%	4%	93	
2020	6	43%	74%	-0.4	-0.01	11	5.6	36%	5%	142	
	27	43%	74%	13.0	0.09	92	6.4	40%	4%	99	

	Lined Up		Blitz			Total Points			Total Points Rtg		
Year	Slot%	Box%	Blitz%	Pres%	Sack%	Pass Cov	Run Def	Total	Per Cov	Per Run	Per Play
2018	16%	3%	1%	29%	0.0%	26	21	47	88	94	89
2019	15%	4%	1%	40%	0.0%	8	17	26	69	82	74
2020	14%	4%	1%	25%	0.0%	13	9	23	83	73	76
	15%	4%	1%	31%	0.0%	47	47	96	-	-	-

Critical Factors	
3-Level Impact	6
FBI / Instincts	5
Play Speed	5

Positional Factors	
Man Coverage	5
Zone Coverage	6
Range	6
Ball Skills / Tracking	6
Tackling	5
Blitz	4
Physicality	5
Communication	4
ST Value	5

Shawn Davis

Report by Jordan Edwards & Daniel Jankuloski

School	Height	Weight	Year	Jersey #	Hometown
Florida	5105 V	199 V	4SR	6	Miami, FL

One Liner

Davis has good range and tracking ability as a deep safety, but his small frame and lack of man coverage ability may hinder his ability to contribute on an every-down basis at the next level.

Strengths: Tracking ability; Range; Enforcer's mentality
Weaknesses: Finishing at the catch point; Man coverage; Stoutness vs. the run

Shawn Davis lines up at free safety in Florida's nickel defense. He can play both in single and two-high sets, and has limited experience playing in the slot. He started 16 of 38 games for the Gators. He missed 3 games early in 2018 with a knee injury and also a handful of games in 2020 due to undisclosed reasons. He has a short and squatty frame with decent twitch, but lacks some length. Davis plays with a feisty demeanor, and tries to play with an enforcers mentality.

Overall, Davis is a solid coverage safety along the back end of the defense. He's comfortable playing deep in a single-high role as the last line of defense. He displays good range and can track the ball to challenge receivers at the catch point, though he struggles to consistently finish at the catch point and rarely turns breakups into interceptions. He has sufficient instincts, though seems to be a bit slow to process and break on receivers' routes downhill. Davis has adequate play speed, but his lack of top-end speed may hinder his ability to keep a lid on elite vertical threats. His lack of length and true physical presence restrict his ability to play in the slot and cover tight ends in man coverage.

Davis shows the ability to play fast and physical running the alley against the run. He's a solid overall tackler and tries to enforce his will engaging ballcarriers. He's a kamikaze type of tackler, which can cause him to miss on occasion, however, it has been more effective than not. Due to Davis' smaller frame, he won't be a valuable contributor to play as a stout box safety, but his willingness and effort to stop the run should not be questioned.

Davis projects to be a depth free safety at the next level. He can play in multiple schemes and is comfortable playing in single and two-high safety defenses. On 3rd downs and in sub packages, he can play on the back end and allow other players to move into other roles in the secondary. Davis could be a valuable special teams contributor at the next level with his play demeanor and willingness to be physical.

Year	Trgt	Comp	Comp%	Yards	Yds/Trgt	Int	Int Drops	TD Alwd	Tkls	TFL	Brk Tkl	BT%
				Coverage						Tackling		
2017	3	2	67%	69	23.0	0	0	1	10	0.5	1	9%
2018	11	4	36%	58	5.3	0	1	0	20	2.0	1	5%
2019	24	14	58%	130	5.4	3	1	0	55	1.0	10	15%
2020	9	6	67%	126	14.0	2	0	3	39	2.0	7	15%
	47	26	55%	383	8.1	5	2	4	124	5.5	19	13%

Year	PBU	Pos%	Deserved Catch %	EPA	EPA/Trgt	Tgt	Yds/Tgt	Pos%	Tackle Share	ATD+
		All Coverage				Man Coverage			Tackling	
2017	1	67%	67%	5.6	1.86	1	21.0	100%	2%	-
2018	4	36%	56%	-1.4	-0.13	5	5.8	40%	2%	106
2019	6	42%	94%	-7.6	-0.32	12	6.8	50%	7%	118
2020	3	44%	75%	8.2	0.91	3	4.7	0%	5%	104
	14	43%	78%	4.7	0.10	21	7.0	43%	4%	110

Year	Slot%	Box%	Blitz%	Pres%	Sack%	Pass Cov	Run Def	Total	Per Cov	Per Run	Per Play
	Lined Up		Blitz			Total Points			Total Points Rtg		
2018	11%	3%	4%	0%	0.0%	0	5	6	60	98	78
2019	15%	4%	2%	50%	0.0%	17	6	24	91	70	82
2020	12%	6%	2%	25%	0.0%	3	12	15	67	97	81
	13%	4%	3%	27%	0.0%	20	23	45	-	-	-

Critical Factors

3-Level Impact 5
FBI / Instincts 5
Play Speed 5

Positional Factors

Man Coverage 4
Zone Coverage 6
Range 6
Ball Skills / Tracking 5
Tackling 6
Blitz 5
Physicality 6
Communication 5
ST Value 7

JR Pace

Report by Alec Mallon

School	Height	Weight	Year	Jersey #	Hometown
Northwestern	6006 E	210 E	4SR	5	College Park, GA

One Liner

Pace is a speedy safety with good eye discipline, but his physicality and impact at all three levels will prevent him from seeing the field in an expanded role.

Strengths: Eye discipline; Playing downhill; Ball skills
Weaknesses: Physicality near the line; Open-field tackling; Locating the ball in man

JR Pace is a safety from Northwestern in their base 4-3 defense, primarily lining up as the lone safety in the middle of the field. He played 47 games while starting the last 35. Pace is a quick thinker with good reaction skills who doesn't hesitate to break on the ball. He isn't the most physical player, but with a strong build, he shows toughness with the ability to lower his shoulder and deliver big hits.

Pace is most natural when playing deep in the secondary. In zone, he has good eyes and understands how to play both the quarterback and his area. He has good start and stop skills to transition downhill and drive in pursuit. His range is sufficient as a half-field player. Pace shows good ball skills when he can get his head around. He takes good angles to the ball and high points passes to break them up. However, especially in man coverage, he struggles to find the ball in the air and doesn't mirror his targets' movements when face guarding to make a play. He has the ability to drop down and cover tight ends in man to moderate success based on his superior athleticism and inferior strength. His lateral quickness has been an asset in infrequent man reps.

Pace acts as the final line of defense on run plays sufficiently. As an open-field tackler, he has issues reacting in close quarters and leaving his feet unnecessarily. Pace was useful slipping into the box as a run blitzer to shoot gaps, but he lacks the power and technique to take on blockers in the trenches. He can be a sound tackler working aggressively down to the ball wrapping up to limit yards after contact.

Pace projects as versatile safety at the next level. Based on his ability to read the QB's eyes and make plays on the ball with everything in front of him, he will work well in two-high looks. Additionally, his experience in the slot gives him some flexibility moving forward. He has enough reactive quickness to cover backs and tight ends from different alignments. He'll be a sufficient contributor on certain special teams units.

		Coverage							Tackling			
Year	Trgt	Comp	Comp%	Yards	Yds/Trgt	Int	Int Drops	TD Alwd	Tkls	TFL	Brk Tkl	BT%
2017	4	2	50%	30	7.5	2	1	1	3	0.0	2	40%
2018	35	16	46%	268	7.7	4	2	2	80	5.0	18	18%
2019	20	4	20%	78	3.9	1	0	1	42	0.0	9	18%
2020	11	4	36%	55	5.0	1	2	0	41	1.5	13	24%
	70	26	37%	431	6.2	8	5	4	166	6.5	42	20%

	All Coverage					Man Coverage			Tackling	
Year	PBU	Pos%	Deserved Catch %	EPA	EPA/Trgt	Tgt	Yds/Tgt	Pos%	Tackle Share	ATD+
2017	4	50%	75%	2.2	0.55	2	6.0	50%	0%	-
2018	11	31%	65%	-11.6	-0.33	10	0.8	0%	9%	100
2019	2	20%	86%	-10.3	-0.52	8	0.9	13%	3%	91
2020	3	36%	67%	-3.4	-0.31	3	3.0	33%	7%	94
	20	30%	70%	-23.1	-0.33	23	1.6	13%	4%	95

	Lined Up		Blitz			Total Points			Total Points Rtg		
Year	Slot%	Box%	Blitz%	Pres%	Sack%	Pass Cov	Run Def	Total	Per Cov	Per Run	Per Play
2018	14%	2%	1%	0%	0.0%	31	12	43	87	62	74
2019	16%	3%	0%	0%	0.0%	23	11	34	89	71	78
2020	9%	8%	2%	14%	0.0%	11	2	14	75	57	65
	14%	4%	1%	9%	0.0%	65	25	91	-	-	-

Critical Factors	
3-Level Impact	5
FBI / Instincts	6
Play Speed	6

Positional Factors	
Man Coverage	5
Zone Coverage	6
Range	5
Ball Skills / Tracking	5
Tackling	5
Blitz	5
Physicality	4
Communication	5
ST Value	5

James Wiggins

Report by Nathan Cooper, Michael Bonneville, & Spencer Schultz

School	Height	Weight	Year	Jersey #	Hometown
Cincinnati	5116 E	205 E	5SR	1	Miami, FL

One Liner
Wiggins has the athleticism, play speed, and zone-coverage ability to be a solid 2-high defender, but a lack of physicality and limited range likely force him into being only a backup contributor at the next level.

Strengths: Zone coverage; Plays fast
Weaknesses: Lacks physicality; Limited range; Won't take on blockers

James Wiggins plays safety in Cincinnati's 3-3-5 defense, running a balanced mix of man and zone coverages. He started 21 of 32 games for the Bearcats. He missed the entire 2019 season due to a torn ACL. He has a relatively small frame, but plays slightly bigger than his size. He's a good athlete who plays hard and competes, though lacks some physicality that's desired from the safety position.

Wiggins lacks some overall range on the back end. He has enough range to be a 2-high player, but doesn't show the consistent instincts or top-end speed to be an effective single-high player out near the numbers. He has the ability to stay with receivers in man coverage and shows enough athleticism to keep in-phase, especially against tight ends. In zone coverage, he shows sufficient eye discipline to read and react to the quarterback, but lacks some awareness to know exactly what's going on at all times around him. Although he plays fast, he doesn't possess the top-end speed or acceleration to consistently catch up to receivers and close the gap

once beaten. He tracks the ball fairly well and can make a play at the catch point if in position. Wiggins isn't much of a communicator and seems to get lost at times in coverage. He shows the ability to blitz a little bit with his speed and athleticism to come around the edge, but can't take on many blockers to get to the backfield.

Wiggins doesn't take on many blockers head on. He lacks some physicality and doesn't always want to mix it up or get in the scrums to make a play. When he gets a tackle opportunity, he can deliver a blow and lay a decent hit on the ballcarrier, but is mostly a drag-down tackler.

Wiggins projects as a backup free safety in a 2-high zone scheme where he can use his speed and athleticism on the back end, something he'd fit best at doing on passing downs. He has the speed and athleticism to play on special teams, though his lack of physicality may hinder how much he contributes.

		Coverage								Tackling			
Year	Trgt	Comp	Comp%	Yards	Yds/Trgt	Int	Int Drops	TD Alwd	Tkls	TFL	Brk Tkl	BT%
2018	50	22	44%	326	6.5	4	1	2	53	2.0	5	9%
2020	32	11	34%	84	2.6	1	0	1	34	1.0	6	15%
	82	33	40%	410	5.0	5	1	3	87	3.0	11	11%

	All Coverage					Man Coverage			Tackling	
Year	PBU	Pos%	Deserved Catch %	EPA	EPA/Trgt	Tgt	Yds/Tgt	Pos%	Tackle Share	ATD+
2018	9	40%	82%	-17.7	-0.35	38	5.8	37%	7%	100
2020	8	22%	61%	-16.0	-0.50	20	2.9	25%	5%	86
	17	33%	73%	-33.7	-0.41	58	4.8	33%	6%	94

	Lined Up		Blitz			Total Points			Total Points Rtg		
Year	Slot%	Box%	Blitz%	Pres%	Sack%	Pass Cov	Run Def	Total	Per Cov	Per Run	Per Play
2018	31%	3%	1%	33%	0.0%	24	15	40	91	91	87
2020	33%	6%	3%	11%	11.1%	34	-1	38	99	53	92
	32%	4%	2%	17%	9.1%	58	14	78	-	-	-

Critical Factors	
3-Level Impact	5
FBI / Instincts	5
Play Speed	6

Positional Factors	
Man Coverage	5
Zone Coverage.	5
Range	5
Ball Skills / Tracking	5
Tackling	5
Blitz	5
Physicality	5
Communication	5
ST Value	5

Tariq Thompson

Report by Nathan Cooper

School	Height	Weight	Year	Jersey #	Hometown
San Diego State	5116 E	210 E	4SR	14	San Diego, CA

One Liner

Thompson is a smart safety that plays fast and shows enough cover ability on the back end, but a lack of instincts, physicality, and consistent tackling ability will likely keep him from starting at the next level.

Strengths: Plays fast; High motor

Weaknesses: Not extremely instinctual; Lacks some physicality; Takes bad angles

Tariq Thompson plays field warrior in San Diego State's 3-3-5 scheme primarily aligning in the slot to the field side, but will also play as a deep safety. He started all 47 games he played in for the Aztecs. He's a fluid athlete that plays hard and competes, though he doesn't bring a ton of physicality to the safety position.

Thompson shows more of a 2-high type of range than the range of a single-high player. He plays best in off-man where he can read and react to the receiver. Even if beat, he has enough speed to close. When he presses, he isn't physical enough to stun the receiver at the line and will get beat with quickness. In zone, his instincts are just sufficient and he's more of a reactionary player with sufficient awareness, though he has a solid football IQ and does a good job of reading route combinations. In the slot, he jumps out routes before the receiver even breaks. He's a fluid athlete and can break and transition out of his back pedal quickly, but will overcommit and get beaten on double moves too frequently. He has some ball skills to make a play most times at the catch point. He doesn't talk much pre-snap, but communicates with his teammates a lot mid-play.

Thompson doesn't mind coming down to the box and helping out and pursuing the ballcarrier, but doesn't deliver a blow. He does a good job staying disciplined and forcing ballcarriers to cut back to the middle of the field, but takes bad angles allowing for extra yards. He leaves his feet too often and slides off or misses tackles completely, and in 1-on-1 situations, he struggles to bring down bigger ballcarriers by himself.

Thompson projects as a No. 4 depth safety at the next level and fits best as a FS in a 2-high scheme where he can also slide down into the slot. On 3rd downs, he should play as a 2-high deep defender to take advantage of his range and ball skills. He has special teams value, but will need to become more physical and clean up missed tackles to be a core contributor.

			Coverage						Tackling			
Year	Trgt	Comp	Comp%	Yards	Yds/Trgt	Int	Int Drops	TD Alwd	Tkls	TFL	Brk Tkl	BT%
2017	42	19	45%	335	8.0	5	1	0	67	4.0	11	14%
2018	44	23	52%	295	6.7	2	1	3	60	6.0	9	13%
2019	60	34	57%	355	5.9	4	2	2	52	3.0	22	30%
2020	30	14	47%	159	5.3	1	0	2	40	2.0	9	18%
	176	90	51%	1144	6.5	12	4	7	219	15.0	51	19%

	All Coverage					Man Coverage			Tackling	
Year	PBU	Pos%	Deserved Catch %	EPA	EPA/Trgt	Tgt	Yds/Tgt	Pos%	Tackle Share	ATD+
2017	8	31%	88%	-18.3	-0.44	12	6.1	50%	9%	-
2018	9	39%	76%	5.4	0.12	19	7.0	47%	8%	125
2019	11	43%	82%	-5.3	-0.09	25	6.0	40%	7%	87
2020	4	40%	90%	-3.9	-0.13	16	5.5	38%	9%	81
	32	39%	83%	-22.2	-0.13	72	6.2	43%	8%	108

	Lined Up		Blitz			Total Points			Total Points Rtg		
Year	Slot%	Box%	Blitz%	Pres%	Sack%	Pass Cov	Run Def	Total	Per Cov	Per Run	Per Play
2018	64%	4%	2%	14%	0.0%	23	14	37	86	72	76
2019	61%	5%	1%	25%	14.3%	27	6	38	87	63	80
2020	57%	3%	2%	0%	0.0%	21	5	26	91	65	78
	61%	4%	2%	15%	5.3%	71	25	101	-	-	-

Critical Factors	
3-Level Impact	5
FBI / Instincts	5
Play Speed	6

Positional Factors	
Man Coverage	5
Zone Coverage	5
Range	5
Ball Skills / Tracking	5
Tackling	5
Blitz	5
Physicality	5
Communication	6
ST Value	5

2020 NCAA Special Teams Leaders

John Shirley

In last year's *Football Rookie Handbook*, SIS introduced the special teams addition to the Total Points player value system, including a look at some of the top performing seniors of 2019. Both the top kicker and punter made their mark as rookies in the NFL. Rodrigo Blankenship was drafted by the Colts and went 32-for-37 on field goals, while punter Joseph Charlton signed with the Panthers and finished the season tied for 6th in Punting Total Points.

Before we get into the Special Teams Total Points leaderboards for the 2021 draft class, we want to provide any new readers with an overview of how these metrics work:

Special Teams Total Points Overview

The Total Points System combines the Expected Points Added (EPA) framework and SIS's charting data to break down how well players perform on every play depending on scheme and assignment factors. For special teams this is done by creating an initial expected points expectation for every kick, punt, and kickoff and then comparing it to what actually occurs. The difference in EPA between the expectation and the actual play is then distributed among players on the field based on their assignments and performance.

The expectation used for Punting Total Points is based on the swing in field position resulting from an average punt from each location of the field. There are then adjustments made to account for punts out of bounds, touchbacks, fair catches, downed punts, and the average return yards before contact. These adjustments allow us to distribute credit between the punter, coverage team, and return team. The final expectation is then compared to each punt's outcome, and the difference in Expected Points minus the adjustments becomes the punter's Points Above Average, which is then scaled to the national scoring average.

For field goals and extra points, Total Points is based on a distance-adjusted expected field goals model. This model provides the expected success rate of each kick, which can then be compared to actual outcomes. There is a small division of credit taken out to account for the possibility of a blocked kick and also for other players on the field including the snapper and holder. The final expected success rate of each kick is then multiplied by the number of possible points on the play, three for a field goal or one for an extra point, to get the kick's Expected Points. Each kick's Expected Points is then subtracted from its actual outcome to create Kicking Points Above Average. Points Above Average is then scaled by the national scoring average, resulting in a final Total Points Earned number.

Within the Total Points System, punts and kickoffs are evaluated in a similar fashion, with a few extra adjustments. Kickoff Points Above Average are calculated using an initial field position expectation and the actual result. One of the extra adjustments for kickoffs factors in mortar kickoffs, which are designed as short kicks that force a return compared to normal deep kickoffs. Different types of kickoffs are compared separately to their own expected field position. Kickers also get a credit for an onside kick recovery and receive a proportionally smaller debit for a failed onside kick.

Special Teams Leaderboards

Now that we have covered how Special Teams Points are calculated and without any further ado, let's get to the 2020 leaderboards for draft-eligible kickers and punters.

Kickers

Kicking Total Points Leaders (2020) Among Draft-Eligible Kickers

Player	Team	FG Points Earned	Extra Point Points Earned	Kickoff Points Earned	All Kicking Points Earned / Game	FG Points Earned / Attempt
Jose Borregales	Miami FL	19	3	3	2.3	0.9
Brian Johnson	Virginia Tech	15	3	0	1.7	0.6
Evan McPherson	Florida	13	4	1	1.6	0.6
Alex Kessman	Pittsburgh	13	2	3	1.6	0.5
Chris Naggar	SMU	11	0	2	1.3	0.5
Riley Patterson	Memphis	10	2	3	1.3	0.4
Keith Duncan	Iowa	8	2	--	1.2	0.4
Blake Lynch	Kansas State	6	3	0	1.0	0.4

Basic Kicking Stats (2020) For Draft-Eligible Kickers

Player	Team	FGM / FGA	FGM / FGA (40+)	Avg FG Dist	Touchbacks / Kickoffs
Jose Borregales	Miami FL	20 / 22	9 / 11	36.8	51 / 72
Brian Johnson	Virginia Tech	20 / 26	11 / 16	40.8	7 / 12
Evan McPherson	Florida	17 / 22	6 / 11	39.4	40 / 80
Alex Kessman	Pittsburgh	23 / 29	9 / 14	37.2	44 / 69
Chris Naggar	SMU	17 / 21	6 / 10	37.8	46 / 69
Riley Patterson	Memphis	15 / 22	8 / 15	42.7	38 / 63
Keith Duncan	Iowa	14 / 18	5 / 8	37.4	-- / --
Blake Lynch	Kansas State	12 / 17	3 / 8	37.2	0 / 6

Three of the top four draft-eligible kickers hail from the ACC, with Miami kicker and Lou Groza Award winner Jose Borregales topping the list. Borregales went 20/22 on field goals last year and was in a class by himself with 25 Points Earned from field goals, extra points, and kickoffs. He was perfect from under 40 yards, making 11/11 field goals and going 33/33 on extra points, while also making 9/11 from 40+. His 2020 was a marked improvement from 2019, when he went 21/29 on field goals and averaged only 0.6 Total Points Per Game, which ranked 57th among all kickers who appeared in at least five games.

While Borregales showed drastic improvement in 2020, Memphis' Riley Patterson (1st), Iowa's Keith Duncan (4th), and Florida's Evan McPherson (9th) were all in the top 10 among all kickers in Kicking Total Points Per Game in both 2019 and 2020.

Punters

Punting Total Points Per Punt Leaders (2020) Among Draft-Eligible Punters

Player	Team	Punting Points Earned	Punting Points Earned / Game	Punting Points Earned / Punt
Pressley Harvin III	Georgia Tech	19	2.1	0.4
Max Duffy	Kentucky	17	1.9	0.4
Drue Chrisman	Ohio State	10	1.5	0.4
James Smith	Cincinnati	14	1.4	0.4
Oscar Draguicevich III	Washington State	6	1.4	0.3
Zach Von Rosenberg	LSU	17	1.8	0.3
Nolan Cooney	Syracuse	18	1.7	0.2

Basic Punting Stats (2020) For Draft-Eligible Punters

Player	Team	Punts	Gross Avg	Net Avg	Inside 20%	Touchback%
Pressley Harvin III	Georgia Tech	45	48.0	44.8	40%	7%
Max Duffy	Kentucky	42	45.1	42.1	38%	2%
Drue Chrisman	Ohio State	27	45.0	39.9	41%	7%
James Smith	Cincinnati	40	43.9	41.2	45%	3%
Oscar Draguicevich III	Washington State	19	46.7	41.6	42%	16%
Zach Von Rosenberg	LSU	59	43.9	41.5	46%	3%
Nolan Cooney	Syracuse	74	44.8	42.6	32%	4%

The ACC had a strong showing on special teams in 2020, as the conference claims both the top kicker and punter by Total Points in the 2021 draft class. Ray Guy Award winner Pressley Harvin III from Georgia Tech averaged an impressive 48 yards per punt and 2.1 Punting Points per Game in 2020. Kentucky's Max Duffy also had an impressive senior season a year after winning the 2019 Ray Guy Award and ranking 3rd in the nation in Punting Points Earned.

Special Teams Timing Data

During the 2020 season, SIS added timing data for passing plays and special teams plays. For special teams this means we now have hang times, snap times, and operation times (which include the time between when the punter/holder touches the ball and when it is kicked). We are currently in the process of applying these new data points into our proprietary metrics such as the Total Points System, but would like to offer a first glimpse at the raw times here in the *Football Rookie Handbook*.

Punt Hang Times

Hang times for punts are relatively straightforward and should not be a new concept for most readers. But for any who are unfamiliar, hang time is the time a punt is in the air from the punter's foot until it is caught by the returner or hits the ground. Generally a higher hang time is preferred, as this gives the coverage team more time to get down the field.

As mentioned above, we will be showing raw times within these leaderboards, however, we will be making one important adjustment among hang times. The leaderboard below will only be showing hang times on punts that were not rugby style or directionally angled to pin the opponent or prevent a return. This should provide a more accurate representation of each punter's actual ability when it comes to hang time.

Normal Punt Hang Time Leaders (2020) Among Draft-Eligible Punters

Player	Team	Timed* Punts	Hang Time (Seconds)	National Rank (Out of 119)
Nolan Cooney	Syracuse	51	4.22	4
James Smith	Cincinnati	13	4.07	24
Pressley Harvin III	Georgia Tech	31	4.00	28
Oscar Draguicevich III	Washington State	14	3.93	40
Drue Chrisman	Ohio State	14	3.86	54
Max Duffy	Kentucky	13	3.85	55
Zach Von Rosenberg	LSU	24	3.83	63

Due to insufficient camera angles, punts that are unable to be timed accurately are omitted

Nolan Cooney from Syracuse ranks highest among the top punters in the 2021 draft class and is the only one to rank in the top 10 nationally. Drue Chrisman, Max Duffy, and Zach Von Rosenberg ranked relatively low compared to their counterparts, though it is important to remember these are still raw numbers. We accounted for punt type, but there are still other contextual factors such as field position that have not been accounted for in this chart.

Long Snap Times

Along with hang time, SIS also now times the snap on punts and field goals. This, for the first time, allows us to provide a metric for long snappers. Snap times are most likely not something many are familiar with, so for reference the NFL average snap time for field goals in 2020 was

.58 seconds and the average snap time for punts was 0.89 seconds. In the table below you can see how some of the top senior long snappers performed and where they ranked nationally.

Snap Time Leaders (2020) Among Draft-Eligible Long Snappers

Player	Team	Timed* FG Snaps	Avg FG Snap Time (National Rank)	Timed* Punt Snaps	Avg Punt Snap Time (National Rank)
Thomas Fletcher	Alabama	13	0.52 (2)	25	0.88 (14)
Kyle Poland	West Virginia	18	0.54 (10)	41	0.88 (17)
Ryan Langan	Georgia Southern	20	0.54 (9)	43	0.90 (29)

When compared to NFL numbers, these seniors performed very well, as they were all near or below the NFL average in both field goal snap times and punt snap times. Alabama's Thomas Fletcher ranks as the top draft-eligible long snapper when factoring in both types of snaps, and was rewarded for his performance with an invite to the 2021 Senior Bowl.

During the upcoming offseason, SIS will be hard at work incorporating these new timing data points into our proprietary metrics such as the Total Points system. We look forward to sharing our efforts with readers in next year's *Football Rookie Handbook*.

2022 Draft Lookahead

Bryce Rossler

Last year, we used advanced metrics in an attempt to identify returning skill position players who could be top draft prospects the following year. One may or may not be able to predict who the big names will be, but we'd like to think we fared well enough. Of course, some of the players highlighted were gimmes. It wasn't exactly Galilean to claim that Travis Etienne, Ja'Marr Chase, and Greg Rousseau would be big names, so it would be disingenuous to plant our flag on them. But, if you're reading this book, you likely already know most of the marquee names for next year. The point of this exercise is to identify players who are flying under the radar so as to keep tabs on them moving forward.

Last offseason, we highlighted linebackers Nick Bolton and Garrett Wallow as two linebackers to watch for. The former was relatively unknown at this point a year ago, but is now being projected as a first-round selection by ESPN's Todd McShay; the latter was a Senior Bowl attendee. UAB edge Jordan Smith was pinpointed as a pass rusher whose sack production belied his ability to generate pressure. While that trend continued in 2021 (22% pressure rate, 4.5 sacks), the personnel community still managed to take notice of the Blazer defender, as evidenced by his presence at the Senior Bowl. Furthermore, three of the six corners we identified also attended the Mobile showcase. While participation in the Senior Bowl is not a guarantee that a player will be a good pro or even drafted, it's a decent indicator that players are on the NFL radar.

What we couldn't have predicted, though, was the COVID-19 pandemic. While you're likely tired of writers musing ad nauseam about how unprecedented the 2020 season was, it is important to note how it affected the NCAA's eligibility rules. Because all college players have been afforded an extra year of eligibility, seniors now have until March 1st to decide whether or not they will make themselves eligible for selection in the 2021 NFL Draft. There will certainly be some surprise returns, but it's a fool's errand to guess who. Therefore, we will focus on underclassmen and seniors who have already announced their intent to return to school.

The leaderboards are composed using a tandem of Total Points—our proprietary player value metric which apportions EPA-based credit using charting data—and another positionally-relevant advanced stat.

Running Backs

Whereas last year's running backs watch list was headlined by some big names, the players on this leaderboard are relatively anonymous. Similarly, the 2022 leaderboard is not as impressive statistically as the 2021 leaderboard was—twelve of the thirteen Total Rushing Points/Carry leaders are either draft-bound or were true freshmen in 2020. Last year, all five players previewed ranked in the top ten of this metric.

The lone exception is Chris Rodriguez, Jr. The Kentucky running back didn't qualify for the carries threshold to be mentioned last year, but was efficient as a redshirt freshman when he averaged 0.33

Rushing Total Points per Carry and 34 Broken + Missed Tackles per 100 Carries. He ranked just sixth in rushing yardage in the SEC, but has been highly efficient whenever he's touched the ball.

The biggest curiosity on this list is Calvin Turner, who transferred to Hawaii from FCS Jacksonville University, where he played cornerback as a freshman before serving as an option quarterback his sophomore and junior seasons. Sample size is certainly a concern here, but Turner will have an opportunity to showcase his dynamic skill set in a full season, especially with starting running back Miles Reed intending to transfer. Eleven all-purpose scores (4 rushing, 6 receiving, 1 returning) on 105 total touches and 16.5 yards per catch may not be sustainable, but Turner is nevertheless intriguing.

2020 Total Points Per Carry Leaders, 2022 Eligible RBs (min. 50 attempts)

Player	College	Eligibility	Rushing Total Points / Carry (Rank)	Broken + Missed Tackles / 100 (Rank)
Chris Rodriguez, Jr.	Kentucky	4JR	0.30 (7th)	24 (44th)
Tyler Allgier	BYU	4JR	0.24 (14th)	21 (79th)
Jerrion Ealy	Ole Miss	3JR	0.24 (19th)	24 (50th)
Zonovan Knight	NC State	3JR	0.20 (23rd)	29 (20th)
Calvin Turner	Hawaii	5SR	0.20 (25th)	32 (8th)

Wide Receivers

This position group likewise lacks some of the no-brainer picks that were afforded to us last year. No reigning Biletnikoff winner and none of the heads of the Alabama hydra makes for less name brand recognition, but that's part of the fun.

Purdue's Rondale Moore garnered national attention when he filled up the box score against Ohio State as a true freshman, but he's only played seven games in the past two seasons due to injury. David Bell has been productive in his stead, posting over 1,600 receiving yards in 18 games during that span. Although Ohio State's Chris Olave is likely regarded as the best returning receiver in the Big Ten, Bell's efficiency metrics blew Olave's out of the water in 2020.

In fact, Olave might not even be the best returning receiver on his team. Garrett Wilson was comparable from a yards per route run standpoint (1.7 vs. 1.6, respectively), but was three times more efficient on a Total Points basis. We expect both to be good prospects when it's all said and done—we highlighted Olave in last year's lookahead—but Wilson might have more upside at this point.

2020 Total Points Per Route Run Leaders, 2022 Eligible WRs (min. 200 routes)

Name	School	Eligibility	Receiving Total Points / Route Run (Rank)	Yards / Route Run (Rank)
Khalil Shakir	Boise State	4SR	0.09 (2nd)	2.1 (15th)
David Bell	Purdue	3JR	0.08 (4th)	1.7 (34th)
Jaquarii Roberson	Wake Forest	5SR	0.07 (6th)	2.3 (4th)
Garrett Wilson	Ohio State	3JR	0.06 (11th)	1.6 (45th)
Erik Ezukanma	Texas Tech	4JR	0.06 (15th)	1.6 (37th)

Tight Ends

This year's rendition of the tight ends group features a leftover from last year's preview—Colorado State's Trey McBride. The Rams tight end's efficiency metrics are down from 2019, but he still performed well enough in 2020 to be included once again. Other names to watch include Oklahoma's Austin Stogner and UCLA's Greg Dulcich, a former walk-on who broke out and made All Pac-12 in an abbreviated 2020 season.

2020 Total Points Per Route Run Leaders, 2022 Eligible TEs (min. 200 routes)

Player	College	Eligibility	Receiving Points / Route (Rank)	Yards / Route Run (Rank)
Josh Whyle	Cincinnati	4JR	0.05 (4th)	1.4 (11th)
Austin Stogner	Oklahoma	3JR	0.05 (7th)	1.4 (4th)
Greg Dulcich	UCLA	4JR	0.05 (10th)	1.2 (8th)
Trey McBride	Colorado State	4SR	0.04 (11th)	1.2 (10th)

Edges

Perhaps unsurprisingly, there's a lot of SEC talent featured on this leaderboard, but looks can be deceiving. South Carolina's Jordan Strachan is a grad transfer from Georgia State who played in the Sun Belt in 2020. Strachan tied for the most sacks in college football in 2020, but it will be interesting to see if his relatively middling pressure rate and size (6'4", 225 lbs.) are harbingers of doom for his transition to SEC ball. The defender who tied with him for the sacks crown is none other than Iowa State's Will McDonald IV, who ranked in the top ten in both Total Points per Pass Rush and Pressure Rate while playing at the Power 5 level.

2020 Total Points Per Pass Rush Leaders, 2022 Eligible Edges (min. 100 pass rushes)

Player	College	Eligibility	Total Points / Pass Rush (Rank)	Pressure Rate (Rank)
Jordan Strachan	South Carolina	5SR	0.21 (2nd)	14% (39th)
Tyree Johnson	Texas A&M	4JR	0.18 (3rd)	18% (13th)
Will McDonald IV	Iowa State	4JR	0.15 (7th)	20% (8th)
Derick Hall	Auburn	3JR	0.14 (11th)	19% (12th)

Off-Ball Linebackers

Christian Harris is the big name to know here. Harris played WR and safety in high school at 6'2", 230 lbs., enrolled late at Alabama, and still managed to start for them at Will linebacker as a true freshman. His recruiting pedigree, athletic profile, and production, as well as Nick Saban's propensity for developing NFL defenders, are all strong indicators that Harris will play on Sundays.

2020 Coverage and Run Defense Standouts, 2022 Eligible LBs (min. 200 snaps)

Player	College	Eligibility	Coverage Total Points / Snap (Rank)	Run Def Total Points / Snap (Rank)
D'Marco Jackson	Appalachian State	5SR	0.08 (3rd)	0.03 (34th)
De'Marvion Overshown	Texas	4SR	0.05 (16th)	0.05 (19th)
Christian Harris	Alabama	3JR	0.04 (26th)	0.05 (17th)

Cornerbacks

Minnesota Vikings head coach Mike Zimmer once said, "I can find a Cover 2 corner anywhere—I can go down to the 7-Eleven in Bloomington and get one." Funnily enough, the Vikings led the NFL in Cover 2 usage in 2020 at 22%, just as the Hoosiers led the FBS at 29%. As a result, some trepidation about this list featuring two Indiana corners is understandable, but Total Points is mindful of coverages and attempts to account for the schemes players play in.

More recognizable names include TCU's Tre'vius Hodges-Tomlinson, the nephew of NFL Hall of Famer LaDainian Tomlinson, and LSU's Derek Stingley, Jr., who has been billed as a future first-round pick since he was a freshman.

2020 Coverage Total Points Per Snap Leaders, 2022 Eligible CBs (min. 200 snaps)

Player	College	Eligibility	Coverage Points / Snap (Rank)	Yards / Cover Snap (Rank)
Jaylin Williams	Indiana	4SR	0.16 (2nd)	0.69 (46th)
Tre'vius Hodges-Tomlinson	TCU	3JR	0.11 (8th)	0.60 (32nd)
Dreshun Miller	West Virginia	5SR	0.11 (9th)	0.51 (18th)
Tiawan Mullen	Indiana	3JR	0.10 (11th)	0.36 (5th)
Derek Stingley, Jr.	LSU	3JR	0.10 (15th)	0.93 (100th)
Montaric Brown	Arkansas	5SR	0.10 (16th)	0.59 (31st)

Of course, it seems unlikely that all these players will become NFL starters. Size, physical ability, and quality of competition are just a few of the many factors which may preclude a successful college player from making it at the next level. While we certainly wouldn't recommend these prospects based off of statistics alone, they're players we would recommend doing due diligence on. We'll continue to monitor them through next season and, with any luck, you'll be seeing a few of them in the *2022 SIS Football Rookie Handbook.*

Sports Info Solutions

Sports Info Solutions, originally founded as Baseball Info Solutions, has been delivering baseball data and analysis with the highest level of accuracy, detail, and timeliness for nearly two decades. We added football tracking in 2015, empowering us to dissect the many intricacies presented each week across the NFL and NCAA FBS, and basketball tracking in 2020, allowing us to study the NBA, NCAA, and international basketball competition.

The company provides the most accurate data in a timely manner using state-of-the-art technology. The commitment to service, customization, and customer support has allowed SIS to remain at the forefront of the sports data industry. We service teams, agents, companies, and fans.

SIS captures statistical snapshots of every on-field event. This produces an exhaustive database that includes traditional statistics and advanced analysis. SIS has leveraged this database to produce ground-breaking metrics such as Defensive Runs Saved (DRS) and Total Points.

John Dewan, the principal owner of SIS, has been a leader in sports analysis for more than 30 years. His experience dates to his time as Executive Director of Project Scoresheet, the Bill James-led effort that pioneered the new wave of baseball statistics that have become common in today's vernacular. This led to the incorporation and development of STATS Inc. from a bedroom office to its sale to News Corp in 2000. Without those efforts, many of the statistics and analytics that we all take for granted may not even be available at all.

The remainder of the Sports Info Solutions team includes former professional & collegiate players, coaches, and scouts, as well as research, programming, and database management experts. If you would like to contact Sports Info Solutions for data inquiries, potential job openings, or other information you can reach us at:

Sports Info Solutions
41 S. 2nd Street
Coplay, PA 18037
610-261-2370
www.sportsinfosolutions.com

Acknowledgments

Hi and thank you for reading. We hope you're safe, healthy, and doing well. This section is meant to salute the people who worked on *The SIS Football Rookie Handbook*.

This is our third edition of the book and we're very happy to continue bringing it to you. This past year presented many previously unexperienced challenges, but we were determined to get this book in your hands. If you've bought either of the previous editions (or both), thank you. If this was your first one, we hope you'll be coming back for more.

John and Sue Dewan are the principal owners of Sports Info Solutions. They founded the company in 2002 with Steve Moyer as Baseball Info Solutions, then changed the company's name to Sports Info Solutions when we began covering football in 2015. John brings a wealth of knowledge and experience to overseeing the *Handbook* process for this book, *The Bill James Baseball Handbook*, and *The Fielding Bible* series. Sue is the logistical mastermind that ensures the company can continue operating while we undertake this enormous effort.

Rob Dougherty is the President of Sports Info Solutions, leading our ever-expanding endeavors in baseball, football, and now basketball. Rob has many years of experience working in the sports data and media industries and has seamlessly stepped in to coordinate our efforts with the publisher and other fiduciary duties that often go unappreciated.

Our football work continues to be a success under the leadership of our Vice President of Football and Research, Matt Manocherian, and the guidance of our Football Operations Coordinator, Dan Foehrenbach. Matt and Dan have kept our football operation running smoothly, moving things forward and adding clients, which helps widen our reach in the industry.

Operations Associates Nathan Cooper and John Todd have been Matt's right-hand lieutenants throughout the production of this book, ensuring both its completion and its high quality. Brian Reiff and Ronan Potts in the IT Department also deserve special acknowledgment for their incredible work formatting and compiling the book.

Tim Kwilos is our Executive Consultant, advising on all aspects of our baseball, football, and basketball operations. His counsel helps ensure that our decisions on products like this book are sound and smart.

This book wouldn't be possible without the data and reports in it, and we have the Football Operations Department to thank for all that they do to collect all of the information and make sure that it is the most accurate source available. The work of Operations Associates Justin Stine, Mike Churchward, Segev Goldberg, and Evan Butler has been invaluable and is greatly appreciated, along with Senior Video Scouts Jeff Dean, Ben Hrkach, Alec Mallon, Jordan Edwards, Chad Tedder, and Stephen Marciello. Our Injury Coordinator, John Verros, has done a great job of researching and verifying every piece of injury information reported by our Video Scouts.

Matt Manocherian also leads our R&D department, which takes our collected data and analyzes it from a broad range of statistical perspectives. Joe Rosales leads our research efforts in baseball, Alex Vigderman leads it in football, and Stephen Pelkofer leads it in basketball. They are helped by John Shirley, Bryce Rossler, Lindsay Zeck, Sarah Thompson, and Sam Linker. Mark Simon leads our effort to communicate this research to both our private and public audiences.

In Business Development, Senior Business Development Analyst Corey March is responsible for coordinating the communication of our data, research, and analysis to the public and fostering our relationships with clients. He's assisted by Marketing and Website Coordinator Noah Gatsik and Business Development Associate Kyle Rodemann.

Providing the technical expertise that powers the company's engine is the IT Department. Led by Director of IT Patrick Coyle, the rest of the department features Analysts Brian Reiff, Tim Paul, Ruben Agosto, Megan McGrail, Will Creager, along with IT Associates Ronan Potts and Zachary Smith, and Intern Stephen Polacheck.

Our Baseball Operations department keeps our business in that area running smoothly, with a staff led by Director of Operations Jon Vrecsics and MLB Coordinator Dan Casey, along with Nathan Phares, Jason Paff, Josh Hofer, Ted Baarda, Todd Radcliffe, Ken Gaffney, and David Salway.

Our new Basketball department is just a few months old and we have high expectations for how that business will grow. It is led by Director of Basketball, Jake Loos. He's assisted by Senior Operations Analysts Spencer Pearlman and Derek Murray, Operations Analyst Brooks Bellman, Operations Associate Baxter Price, Senior Video Scout Grant Aqui, and part-time Operations Analysts Connor Ayubi and Max Carlin.

Carol Olsen, our office manager and social event planner, along with Melanie Pries and Richard Lively, have made sure that all of our operation runs smoothly from a human resources perspective. The accounting department, led by Kelly Pohl and the occasional assist from Jason Trifilo, plays an instrumental role in keeping the business finances in order.

We are especially grateful for all our outstanding Video Scouts. Their dedication and attention to detail provide the foundation of our business. Our full-time Senior Video Scouts include Dan Wallie, Nick Rabasco and Glen Mueller. Our Video Scout Associates include Jeremy Percy, Nick Giella, Daniel Jankuloski, Kenny Kirkpatrick, Sales Pinckney, Tim Nase, Trey Lake, Joey Mahon, and Christian Beyer.

Our Football Video Scout team consists of James Ashley, Andrew Barmore, Noah Chang, Ty Dorner, Jon Drillings, Theo Fornaciari, Jacob Halleen, Carter Hayden, Chris Heilman, Brendan Kennedy, Lathon Lax, DJ Marquardt, Joe McDonald, Blake Moore, Ryan Newman, Andrew Principe, Jarrett Rodgers, Ryan Rubinstein, Colin Schappert, Spencer Schultz, Justin Serovich, Tobin Sharp, Danny Shirilla, David Simmons, Kendall Stewart, Jordan Taylor, and Max Nuscher. Also, a special thanks to Christian Vega, Griffin Sullivan, Jake Johnson, Luke DeCello, Michael Bonneville, Steven Penn, and Jacob Devinney.

Our partners at ACTA Publications, Publisher Greg Pierce, Tom Wright, Patricia Lynch, Mary Rickey, and Isz. Thank you to all our friends in the football industry who have embraced our work over the last few years, spread the word about our work, and helped to make this book possible. And finally, thank you again for reading!

Index by Player

Index by School

Northern Iowa

Northwestern

Notre Dame

Ohio State

Oklahoma

Oklahoma State

Ole Miss

Oregon

Oregon State

Penn State

Pittsburgh

Purdue

San Diego State

San Jose State

NOTES

NOTES

NOTES

NOTES

NOTES

NOTES

NOTES

MORE FROM

Like what you read?   There are plenty of ways to get more of our content.

BLOG:
SPORTSINFOSOLUTIONSBLOG.COM

OFF THE CHARTS PODCAST
APPLE PODCASTS, SPOTIFY, ANCHOR, AND MORE

TWITTER:
@SPORTSINFO_SIS

SISDATAHUB.COM
ADVANCED NFL STATS AND LEADERBOARDS

NEWSLETTER:
SPORTSINFOSOLUTIONS.COM

SIS FOOTBALL ANALYTICS CHALLENGE
2ND ANNUAL CHARITY RESEARCH CONTEST – COMING IN 2021